The Professional Practice of Architectural Working Drawings

The Professional Practice of Architectural Working Drawings

SIXTH EDITION

Nagy R. Bakhoum

Osamu A. Wakita

WILEY

Copyright © 2024 by John Wiley & Sons, Inc. All rights reserved.

Published by John Wiley & Sons, Inc., Hoboken, New Jersey.
Published simultaneously in Canada.

No part of this publication may be reproduced, stored in a retrieval system, or transmitted in any form or by any means, electronic, mechanical, photocopying, recording, scanning, or otherwise, except as permitted under Section 107 or 108 of the 1976 United States Copyright Act, without either the prior written permission of the Publisher, or authorization through payment of the appropriate per-copy fee to the Copyright Clearance Center, Inc., 222 Rosewood Drive, Danvers, MA 01923, (978) 750-8400, fax (978) 750-4470, or on the web at www.copyright.com. Requests to the Publisher for permission should be addressed to the Permissions Department, John Wiley & Sons, Inc., 111 River Street, Hoboken, NJ 07030, (201) 748-6011, fax (201) 748-6008, or online at http://www.wiley.com/go/permission.

Trademarks: Wiley and the Wiley logo are trademarks or registered trademarks of John Wiley & Sons, Inc. and/or its affiliates in the United States and other countries and may not be used without written permission. All other trademarks are the property of their respective owners. John Wiley & Sons, Inc. is not associated with any product or vendor mentioned in this book.

Limit of Liability/Disclaimer of Warranty: While the publisher and author have used their best efforts in preparing this book, they make no representations or warranties with respect to the accuracy or completeness of the contents of this book and specifically disclaim any implied warranties of merchantability or fitness for a particular purpose. No warranty may be created or extended by sales representatives or written sales materials. The advice and strategies contained herein may not be suitable for your situation. You should consult with a professional where appropriate. Further, readers should be aware that websites listed in this work may have changed or disappeared between when this work was written and when it is read. Neither the publisher nor authors shall be liable for any loss of profit or any other commercial damages, including but not limited to special, incidental, consequential, or other damages.

For general information on our other products and services or for technical support, please contact our Customer Care Department within the United States at (800) 762-2974, outside the United States at (317) 572-3993 or fax (317) 572-4002.

Wiley also publishes its books in a variety of electronic formats. Some content that appears in print may not be available in electronic formats. For more information about Wiley products, visit our web site at www.wiley.com.

Library of Congress Cataloging-in-Publication Data:

Names: Wakita, Osamu A., author. | Bakhoum, Nagy R., author.
Title: The professional practice of architectural working drawings / Osamu A. Wakita, Nagy R. Bakhoum.
Description: Sixth edition. | Hoboken : Wiley, 2017. | Includes index.
Identifiers: LCCN 2016058964 (print) | LCCN 2016059766 (ebook) | ISBN 9781119875338 (paperback) | ISBN 9781119875352 (pdf) | ISBN 9781119875345 (epub)
Subjects: LCSH: Architecture—Designs and plans—Working drawings. |
BISAC: ARCHITECTURE / Design, Drafting, Drawing & Presentation.
Classification: LCC NA2713 .W34 2017 (print) | LCC NA2713 (ebook) |
DDC 720.28/4—dc23
LC record available at https://lccn.loc.gov/2016058964

Cover Design: Wiley
Cover Image: Courtesy of Clay Bakhoum

SKY10057302_101023

This book is dedicated to Art Wakita and the ten thousand plus students that were directly educated by him in his classroom. To all of the students that share the sleepless nights in preparation for their design presentations in order to achieve that amazing presentation for the love of architecture.

Art, you will be missed!

CONTENTS

PART III APPLICATION OF WORKING DRAWINGS IN PRACTICE 473

PREFACE

The purpose of this sixth edition of *The Professional Practice of Working Drawings* is to introduce and refine the knowledge of the student or young professional in the field of Architecture – specifically, the understanding of the schematic design, design development, and construction document phases that an architect produces for a client. This set of phases transforms the idea of architecture, into the contract that a client and contractor enter, such that the product of that design can become the built environment. This process is oversimplified into these three stages when in reality it can include many other phases with many more supporting documents to establish a more detailed built environment. But if we can just get a handle on these three, we are off to a great start.

The method of delivery is expanded upon in this text. If you are hand drafting, utilizing AutoCAD, BIM, or Revit drawing, the project goals are the same. These are just the tools of the trade that allow us to quickly document the ideas and produce a set of deliverables to the city that must review them for minimum life safety, to put them out to bid and for actual construction. The methods of communication used are just the tool; as a skill set is improved upon, the speed, clarity, and accuracy also improve. *The Professional Practice of Working Drawings* is a dialog of how to communicate more quickly, with the skill set you already have and with practice expand that into other methods of communication. This is not a text book on how to become a great Revit user; there are already great texts for that. This is a text that helps you communicate your ideas more quickly so that you can spend more time designing solutions and less time drafting them. With clarity of drawings and text comes great communication. Architecture is about communicating ideas and bringing them to life. Moreover, if the ideas are clearly drawn and written in a set of plans, the accuracy of the finished product will be what you were expecting it to be and what your client paid you a great deal of money for. In my practice of architecture, I say to my clients, the only surprise I want for you to experience is the surprise of how great the building turned out, even better than the plans prepared you for. There is something rewarding about being able to communicate an idea in any method of delivery and being able to achieve the desired goal.

Every chapter in the text has been reworked. More specifically you will note the order of operations has significantly changed. A set of drawings is a process that begins with understanding the task at hand, learning about the site, coming up with schematic ideas, refining them, and producing a contract. The process does not stop there; it continues to the bidding process and the construction administration of the actual project. These phases are very important to become familiar with and when each phase begins and ends. The text takes these concepts into this sixth edition and reworks the book to be driven by the process.

The first four chapters establish the Professional Foundations of architecture. It is a consolidation of the edition five's first six chapters – condensing the text into understanding the profession and what must be done to get the job completed. Items include understanding code and local and regional municipalities and how they impact the proposed project. Included in these chapters are discussion about Americans with Disabilities Act (ADA), office standards, specifications, sustainable architecture, and the program – all foundations that must be second hand to the student.

Chapters 5–12 will concentrate on the deliverables for the process of architecture and specifically the document evolution – beginning with the site analysis and quickly moving to the schematic layout of the architectural floor plan, and then proceeding to the roof, roof structure, and the foundation, and how the water flows off the roof and away from the building foundation. A study of the section of the building and the volume of space that is created as a result of the cut through a building and evolving that document into the exterior elevations and into the interior of the building with interior elevations. No text would be complete without schedules and ending with details.

The application of working drawings in practice is the title for Chapters 13–16 and will be a series of images and a dialog to help understand what a set of drawings looks like for a specific scope of work. For instance, we will show additions and remodels as a scope, new construction of residential and commercial types of work, including two-story and one-story buildings. All of these images and text will act as images that the individual can emulate to better express and communicate their design ideas.

As professionals in the field of architecture, there is an expectation of some knowledge when you begin your career in the field of architecture. An office only has so much time to expand that knowledge in a new employee before their value is diminished. This text is the key to help increase the value of an employee or a student in an educational setting. Having the opportunity to wear both hats, the professor's and architect's, this text is a dialog with the student or designer that wants to better communicate, more quickly and more accurately, and in a variety of possible delivery methods.

ACKNOWLEDGMENTS

Natalie K. Bakhoum, for lending an ear and allowing me to bounce ideas off of her for this sixth edition and providing the underpinning needed in this new venture.

Mercy Girala-Tye, a coworker, a friend, and my longest employee. For supporting my desire to create more beautiful architecture and architectural communication drawings.

Michael Villegas, a peer, a friend, and extremely qualified BIM expert having taught computer technology and Revit for nearly 30 years combined.

Todd Green, the sixth edition Executive Editor, for his help and guidance through another new and improved edition with Wiley.

Amy Odum, the sixth edition Managing Editor, for providing technical information and reviewing text for Wiley.

Kelly Gomez, the sixth edition Editorial Assistant, for providing technical information and responses from Wiley.

ABOUT THE COMPANION WEBSITE

This book is accompanied by a companion website:

www.wiley.com\go\bakhoum\theprofessionalpracticeofarchitecturalworkingdrawings

From the website, you can find the following online materials:

- Appendices A-C
- Lecture slides

PART

I

Professional Foundations

The information contained in Chapters 1–4 is intended to establish the fundamentals for those practicing in the field of architecture. These chapters will shape your understanding of an office, the practice, the stages, and the drawings of architecture.

chapter

1

PROFESSIONAL FOUNDATIONS

The Professional Practice of Architectural Working Drawings, Sixth Edition. Nagy R. Bakhoum and Osamu A. Wakita.
© 2024 John Wiley & Sons Inc. Published 2024 by John Wiley & Sons Inc.
Companion website: www.wiley.com\go\bakhoum\theprofessionalpracticeofarchitecturalworkingdrawings

INTRODUCTION

Working drawings is the collection of **schematic design (SD), design development (DD),** and **construction documents (CDs)** that an architect produces for a client. The purpose of the working drawings is to establish a contract between the client and the builder of the said project. This process has evolved over the years and the development of comprehensive drawings is the new norm. Where a single-family home took eight pages of drawings in the 1970s, the new base line is more near to one hundred pages. The profession relies on the ability of the architect to communicate with great clarity and accuracy, the ideas that are desired in the incorporation of the building. The speed in which the architect can achieve this process is instrumental in the profit of the service; after all architecture is not just about drawing great buildings, it's about getting paid for those great buildings. The process and procedures of developing working drawings are broken down in this text to better organize and educate the individuals in establishing this collection of drawings. Understanding the scope, defining the role, and developing the practices of the architect will aid in the education of what an architect does. Developing the fundamental of the practice of architecture will educate the individual on how to do it better and thus generate a more professional set of working drawings.

The expectation for the reader of this text is based on learning what an architect is, what an architect does, and how an architect does it. Once the stages of the work are understood the reader can better determine what type of drawings are required to be delivered to the client. Deliverables in the field of architecture is the basis of payment for services rendered. The ability to produce proper working drawings is based on the knowledge of what an architect does, how the architect does it, and what the drawing looks like in production. In the case of the student reader, the professor is the client, and the knowledge and understanding of what working drawings are substantially improve the delivered production drawings.

Let's expand on this idea for a moment. If you are student taking a class in college, the professor is like the client and the student is similar to the architect. In any architect and client relationship, it is expected to have a contract. Some jurisdictions don't require it, but a good contract is invaluable to disagreements, so let's say it is a must. The class is acting as a contract, it has a beginning date and an ending date, there is a form of payment agreement, in this case a grade, and there is a list of expectations from both the professor, to teach a skill set, and the student, to perform certain work to receive the payment of a grade. The professor establishes the program of the class describing what is needed and what is expected, and in return for this execution of the program, a fee will be paid. There are periodic delivery expectations from the professor; such as the student will submit work progress for review and critique. There are subsequent forms of review along the way, and this is to make sure that the program that was created by the client has been fulfilled. This progression will lead to a final exam that will establish the completion of the contract, and payment will be made for services rendered. Not unlike a class situation, there may be extra services that are needed along the progress of the job, let's call this extra credit. If this extra work is done, knowing that it was out of the original contract scope, an added payment will be made for this work. Upon completion of work the program will be reviewed, and if the work is exceptional an exceptional grade will be given.

The client has a need for an architect. Specifically, the need to have an individual creatively design a solution for a project that has a comprehensive list of objectives and desires of the client, we call that the **program**. An architect and client engage into a contract for this specific project, it may be a standard form of agreement outlined by the **American Institute of Architects (AIA),** or it can be a drafted contract by either party. This contract will typically outline several specific terms of the contract but not limited to these here: client name, job address, architect name, date of commencement and substantial completion, the program, progress payments, document deliverables, termination or suspension, contract sum, scope of work, miscellaneous provisions, establishment of consultants, ownership of drawings, labor and materials, schedule of values, mediation, and failure of payment. This service that the architect provides is typically broken down into three phases. Note that it can include more phases and will expand on these later in the text.

The first phase of architectural service is typically the SD documents. The AIA defines SD as the initial conceptual design drawings and diagrams that establish the general layout and appearance of the project. Within this phase, various levels of refinement exist, from simple line drawings, mass models, or to even elaborate Revit drawings and renderings to aid in the communication of ideas to the client. SD is a progression of reviews with the client in order to fine tune the project and align it with the client's needs. The more complex the project, the longer the process takes. The AIA does give architects a guideline for how much time to allow to this specific scope 15%. This is established by the recommendation for the fee structure. If your method of SD is done with **building information modeling (BIM)** or Revit, the suggested fee and time would be closer to 20%. The ability to work in BIM is amazing but it is front loaded meaning a significant amount of work is done in the SD phase of the project. Many of the DD decisions are ideally made early in the process and as a result, your contract may want to reflect that in its fee structure.

The second phase of architectural service is DD documents. DD documents described by the AIA as the various drawings and outline specifications provided by the architect. Another way to describe DD is to specify material selections, textures, colors, and finishes that the building will have and outline the manufacturers of the specific parts of the building including the interiors of the building: everything you wanted to know about the building, where to buy it, and what it's made of in an extremely simplified description. The AIA does give architects a guideline for how much time to allow to this specific scope 20%. This is established by the recommendation for the fee structure. If your method of DD is done with BIM or Revit, the fee and time would be closer to 25%. If this data is integrated into BIM, the next phase of drawing time is significantly reduced.

The third phase of architectural service is CD. The CDs are the completion of the prior two services including all material selections, manufactures, details, and specifications needed to construct the clients building. The AIA give architects a guideline for how much time to allow to this specific scope but based on the prior two phases, the balance of the fee is 55%. BIM demands a level of detail that can be specified early in the phases and when the time comes to complete the task drawing time is significantly reduced as compared to AutoCAD. There are additional services that an architect can provide and that will be expanded on in future chapters.

THE PHYSICAL OFFICE

The physical plant of the architectural office has begun to take on a new look. The firm that once worked only in a local community now has a global reach. Where proximity once limited the opportunity for a client to access global talent, the computer, transportation, and communications technology allow for interviews based on architectural ability rather than proximity. It is no longer necessary to select an architect in one's immediate community because technology allows for virtual meetings around the globe.

It is not one firm but many that may construct drawings in a collaborative effort based on the ebb and flow of the size of the project. The result is that any firm of any size can join another to achieve an assigned task. Today, network does more than just describe a system of communication; it also describes the architect's role. An individual may work on a drawing halfway around the world, while at the project location it is the middle of the night. **Redlines**, or corrected drawings, can be marked up electronically and dropped in cloud servers for the next work shift, resulting in two times the production in the normal time. An architecture firm that specializes in design can partner with another firm that specializes in CDs and utilize the strengths of each firm.

Architecture is a small crafts industry in which most offices employ one to four people. A home office may also be part of the office structure. A single drafter may be hired by two or more firms, in which case the office becomes a docking station for electronic project information, such as CDs. Because digital images can be rapidly moved electronically, one can send documents across the world instantly. In the traditional architectural firm, an architect in a firm leads the project and distributes the work among the staff within the firm. When a workload jam arises, the architect may hire a subcontractor to aid in development of the required drawings.

OFFICE STRUCTURE

The way in which an architectural firm is structured and the office practices it employs depend on the magnitude and type of its projects, the number of personnel, and the philosophies the architects hold with regard to office practice procedures. Normally, the architect/s are the owners and/or principals of the practice.

The architectural firm can be established as a sole proprietorship, partnership, or several options of corporations. When first establishing a firm, the principal of the firm must determine how to operate the business of architecture. The simplest of these is a **sole proprietorship**. This is not an ideal system for a large firm, but it may be ideal for a small firm that has a single owner that will file the income as part of the personal income tax. This does not preclude the firm from hiring employees but it does limit the ability to have partners and does not easily separate personal assets from company assets. A down side to this option is the expanded exposure to liability. If something goes wrong and there is litigation, personal assets can be attacked in this option of practice. A **partnership** is where two or more people share the ownership of the company. These partners do not have to own equal shares of the company, and they share the profits based on the percentage of the ownership in the firm. Liability is similar to that of the sole proprietor but you must choose your partner well, as their good or bad decisions will directly affect your bottom line. **Corporations** require at least two stockholders but could have hundreds of stockholders. While a corporation is the most complex system to establish due to laws that govern corporations, it's ideal for separation of personal/ corporate assets. Within the laws that govern corporations, there are a variety of corporation types to choose from: S corporation, C corporation, limited liability partnership (LLP), and limited liability corporation (LLC).

Although a small firm will differ from a medium, large, or extra-large firm, many of the functions will be the same. In all firms, a licensed architect will oversee staff as a direct supervisor. In each firm, services such as **programming** (determining the objectives of the project), **space planning** (the layout of the furnishings and fixtures), feasibility studies, site analysis, coordination, scheduling, and architectural design will be provided according to the firm's contract with the client. As a firm's size increases, one major factor does change: that of documentation of directives and communications. Of course, it is imperative for a firm of any size to track its work and communications with clients. However, as the firm size increases, the documentation becomes critical; as larger project teams mobilize to perform tasks, any lack of documentation can result in reworking projects and significant loss of revenue.

In general, an architectural office can be separated into three main departments: the business development, the design department, and the production department. The principal or partners oversee all three departments in addition to their other duties or it can be managed individually.

Business Development

The administration department handles all communications between the architectural firm and its clients on items such as contracts, fee schedules, billing for services, and similar matters. This department handles all secretarial duties, including all written correspondence, payment of operating costs, accounting procedures, paying salaries, marketing, and maintaining project records relating to individual project costs and procedures. This department may also handle **human resources (HR)** functions, including management of the firm's staff.

Under the purview of administration, many firms also include a marketing department. Tasks for this department might include development and maintenance of a web site, creation and dissemination of publication materials, assembly of competition entries, and development of promotional materials. Marketing is used to focus a firm on a particular area of work and take advantage of opportunities that may arise for a specific project type that the firm prefers or in which it specializes.

Design Department

The design department is normally headed by a principal architect, an associate architect, or partner. This person (or persons) meets with the client to determine the requirements of a project, the economics of the project, and the anticipated time frame for completing the CDs. These initial concerns determine the program for the project. The head (or heads) of this department delegates various work phases of a project to other staff members. The number of staff members depends on the size of the practice and the magnitude of the projects. Staff members may be assigned to teams or groups in their area of expertise for specific projects. A team takes a project from the initial SD concept, through DD, to the completed construction drawings and specifications. These stages may include model building, renderings, coordination among all consulting engineers to meet their individual job requirements, job billing, and reproduction responsibilities. The leader of a project and of the design team staff is designated the **project architect**. A project architect's responsibilities are to develop a "game plan" for a specific project, which will include the following:

1. Design studies, philosophy, and concept
2. Initial structural considerations
3. Exterior and interior materials
4. Municipality and building code requirements
5. Architectural committee reviews
6. Building equipment requirements, **Leadership in Energy and Environmental Design (LEED)**
7. Manufacturing resources
8. Selection of required consultants (soils/geology, structural, mechanical, etc.)
9. Planned man-hours, time sheets, and billing dates
10. Office standards, such as symbols, wall delineations, and other graphic depictions

Production Department

The production department, under the supervision of a project architect, prepares all the phases for a set of completed construction drawings. Working drawings may be produced by a senior drafter, intermediate drafter, or junior drafter under the supervision of a licensed architect. These staff members and the project architect or job captain work as a team to make the transition from the approved preliminary drawings to the completion and implementation of the working drawings. The transition from the approved preliminary drawings to the development of the working drawings is elaborated in Part II of this book. Other chapters provide step-by-step procedures on how different sections of the construction drawings are developed: the site and grading plans, foundation plans, floor plans, building sections, exterior elevations, roof and framing plans, interior elevations, architectural details, and schedules. During the process and completion of the various sections, the project architect and/or job captain repeatedly reviews the drawings for clarity, accuracy, and craftsmanship of detailing, and ensures that the drawings reflect all required revisions. Drawings are either created with the use of a **computer-aided drafting (CAD)** system, BIM, or drawn manually using conventional instruments. In larger offices a fourth department construction administration (CA) can also exist in order to oversee construction items.

The Architect

Architects are licensed by individual states in the United States or by provinces when in regions like Canada or Australia. The most common method of licensing is achieved by university education, **internship**, and examination. In the United States the formal education process is typical four to fiveyears long and is followed by threeyears minimum of internship. Exams can be started immediately upon graduation. A lesser utilized option is a minimum 8-year internship under a licensed architect. Working for engineers or contractors is also an option for the internship but are limited to just a portion of the eight years. Working for a licensed contractor counts as half time so two years is equal to one year of internship. An undergraduate four- or five-year degree or a six- to seven-year graduate program at an accredited university results in years counted towards experience. For a university to become accredited, the **National Architectural Accrediting Board (NAAB)** must certify that university for its merit in education. The **Architecture Registration Examination (ARE)**—testing that rivals the bar exam for lawyers in difficulty—must be taken after completion of one's education. The ARE is administered by the **National Council of Architectural Registration Boards (NCARB).** Programs such as the **Intern Development Program (IDP)** are instrumental in aiding candidates for licensing, because they allow candidates to obtain experience in the diverse areas that are required to run and supervise an architectural firm when they have been licensed. Once a license is obtained, the holder is required to pursue continuing education yearly for the AIA and every other year for architectural licensing.

While it is possible to receive an architectural license without a formal education, it is very difficult and requires eight years of direct supervision from a licensed architect or a combination of architect, engineer, and contractor. On-the-job training is an important aspect of education, and in conjunction with the IDP program and passing the ARE, one can be a licensed architect. There is an expectation that when an architect is licensed, they will have interns to pay the opportunity forward to the next generation of graduates.

■ RESOURCE LIBRARY

To find and detail all the equipment that is required for a structure (plumbing, hardware, finishes, etc.), it is necessary to have access to the various manufacturing resources for specific products. The most widely used organization format in our industry is the **MasterFormat.**

Electronic access allows architects and engineers to survey the resources available and select the equipment that will best enable the function of a building. Such equipment may be available from a myriad of different manufacturers, and range from conveying systems to windows, doors, and the like. Samples can be included in a firm's in-house library. Most of the literature found in electronic form is based on the **MasterFormat**, an organizational system widely used in the construction industry. These particular systems use the major divisions shown in Figure 1.1.

A wealth of product information is available directly from manufacturers, in the form of brochures, pamphlets, catalogs, manuals, and hardbound books. Actual samples of their products may also be obtained. The information available may include the following:

1. Advantages of a particular product over others
2. How the system works or is assembled
3. Necessary engineering/local approval numbers
4. Detailed drawings/CAD file/BIM/Revit file
5. Special design features/Sustainability
6. Colors, textures, and patterns
7. Safety tests/ICC or UL numbers
8. Dimensioning
9. Installation procedures

Adapt this information to your particular needs in your geographic location. Also, understand that a manufacturer's goal is to sell product, so verify from neutral sources that it will do what it states. In some jurisdictions you are required to include testing reports for specific items. Often elements like roofing, waterproofing, premanufactured railings, and skylights are required to be imported onto the CDs as a part of the details or other specification sheets.

You are limited only by your ability to navigate through the vast sea of information available through the Internet and your ability to retrieve the information necessary to satisfy and enhance completion of the working drawings. Digital drawings can also be obtained, making it unnecessary to draw configurations for products such as window profiles, stair rails, and so on. As the process of BIM becomes more mainstream, perhaps one of the greatest advantages is the family of information provided by the manufacturer to promote its product. Always verify the accuracy and appropriateness of a detail before you adopt it as your own.

Retail sources such as major book publishers produce architectural reference books. Many art supply and drafting supply stores also carry reference materials. Public libraries may have a variety of professional reference materials, including books, journals, and

MasterFormat Groups, Subgroups, and Divisions

PROCUREMENT AND CONTRACTING REQUIREMENTS GROUP

Division 00 – Procurement and Contracting Requirements
Introductory Information
Procurement Requirements
Contracting Requirements

SPECIFICATIONS GROUP

GENERAL REQUIREMENTS SUBGROUP

Division 01 – General Requirements

FACILITY CONSTRUCTION SUBGROUP

Division 02 – Existing Conditions
Division 03 – Concrete
Division 04 – Masonry
Division 05 – Metals
Division 06 – Wood, Plastics, and Composites
Division 07 – Thermal and Moisture Protection
Division 08 – Openings
Division 09 – Finishes
Division 10 – Specialties
Division 11 – Equipment
Division 12 – Furnishings
Division 13 – Special Construction
Division 14 – Conveying Equipment
Division 15 – Reserved for Future Expansion
Division 16 – Reserved for Future Expansion
Division 17 – Reserved for Future Expansion
Division 18 – Reserved for Future Expansion
Division 19 – Reserved for Future Expansion

FACILITY SERVICES SUBGROUP

Division 20 – Reserved for Future Expansion
Division 21 – Fire Suppression

Division 22 – Plumbing
Division 23 – Heating, Ventilating, and Air-Conditioning (HVAC)
Division 24 – Reserved for Future Expansion
Division 25 – Integrated Automation
Division 26 – Electrical
Division 27 – Communications
Division 28 – Electronic Safety and Security
Division 29 – Reserved for Future Expansion

SITE AND INFRASTRUCTURE SUBGROUP

Division 30 – Reserved for Future Expansion
Division 31 – Earthwork
Division 32 – Exterior Improvements
Division 33 – Utilities
Division 34 – Transportation
Division 35 – Waterway and Marine Construction
Division 36 – Reserved for Future Expansion
Division 37 – Reserved for Future Expansion
Division 38 – Reserved for Future Expansion
Division 39 – Reserved for Future Expansion

PROCESS EQUIPMENT SUBGROUP

Division 40 – Process Integration
Division 41 – Material Processing and Handling Equipment
Division 42 – Process Heating, Cooling, and Drying Equipment
Division 43 – Process Gas and Liquid Handling, Purification, and Storage Equipment
Division 44 – Pollution and Waste Control Equipment
Division 45 – Industry-Specific Manufacturing Equipment
Division 46 – Water and Wastewater Equipment
Division 47 – Reserved for Future Expansion
Division 48 – Electrical Power Generation
Division 49 – Reserved for Future Expansion

Figure 1.1 *MasterFormat* division numbers and titles. (The aforementioned excerpt is from *MasterFormat*™ 2016 Update, © 2016 The Construction Specifications Institute, Inc. (CSI) and is used under license from CSI. For more information, visit http://www.csinet.org, or contact CSI at 110 South Union Street, Suite 100, Alexandria, VA 22314.)

trade magazines. Colleges and universities offering architecture courses usually have a wealth of architectural resource materials. An example of a highly technical resource is the *AIA Architectural Graphics Standards* published by John Wiley & Sons. This book is found in almost all architectural offices. In addition, the AIA publishes standards and guidelines for architects to utilize as well. Reaching out to distribution centers that represent many products and showing interest in them will often land you a visit from the sales team and perhaps even a "lunch and learn." The distributer will buy and deliver lunch to your location to give you an hour of information while you and the appropriate office staff eat lunch.

Professional Organizations

Professional organizations can be an asset to the business performance and office functions of an architectural firm. The AIA is an example of a professional organization that will provide members with recommended documents, including client/architect contractual agreements, client/contractor agreements, standard forms, and many others. The AIA also provides recommended guidelines relative to fee schedules and disbursements, CDs, building specifications, and CA procedures and documentation.

Ethical procedures and office practice methods are recommended and defined as part of the many documents available from the AIA. It is recommended that associate architects and employees at the various technical levels become involved with a professional organization for a number of reasons, but primarily to stay aware of current technical information and activities within the architectural profession. The AIA also offers programs and directions for those in an internship phase of their careers. Student associate member programs available through the AIA provide an overall view of the architectural profession and often places students in direct contact with architects who may provide opportunities for internships or even job opportunities. Other professional organizations for students of architecture can be found through students' colleges and universities.

DESIGN PROCESS INTRODUCTION

Schematic Design

Meeting with a client during the SD phase, there is a level of expectation of drawing detail that is required in order to best communicate the ideas and concepts during the architect's presentation of the SD for the project. In this phase, an architect consults with the client to determine the project goals and requirements, often called the program. The program, or architectural program, is used to establish the required functions of the project. You typically include an estimated square footage of all the areas required in the project goals. In the SD phase, an architect develops study drawings, images, and documents that demonstrate the concepts of the design in scale that can best demonstrate the spatial relationships. It is not unusual for these early developed plans to be modified and reworked. That is the purpose of the SD phase. Typically, significant changes to design are included in the fees; however, significant changes to the size or square footage in the project would be considered a contractual change and charged additional for this scope of service. Often, a conceptual site plan and floor plan of the building areas are reviewed for the building orientation and the preservation of existing landscaping elements such as trees, topography, and other site conditions. Figure 1.2 shows an example of a conceptual site and building plan. The client for this project desires to build a three-bedroom residence. The site, which is located in a beach community, is a small property. The lot is located on a corner where side and front-yard setbacks use most of the lot area, and the garage must be additionally set back to allow for a driveway with visibility.

SD also is the phase where research is done with respect to the jurisdictional departments. After the client's initial review of the planning and design for the project, some revisions and alterations may be made to the design. In this case, the drawings are revised and presented again to the client for their approval. After the client approves the SD, the architect consults with and presents the schematic drawings to the various governing agencies, such as the planning department, for their review and comments. Any revisions and alterations that may be required by any of the agencies are executed and again reviewed by the client and approved. The schematic drawings are often used to estimate the initial construction costs, which are also submitted for client review and approval. Using BIM, it is possible to provide the client with a more accurate estimate of cost, because these programs incorporate the materials and methods of construction in the drafting process.

Wind direction, sun orientation, rainfall, flow of water on the site, and the most feasible automobile access to the site are considered (among other factors), and a schematic study is presented. From this initial schematic study, a preliminary floor plan is established, which shows the room orientations and their relationships to one another. Such a preliminary drawing is depicted in Figure 1.3. A second-floor-level preliminary plan is studied as it relates to the first-floor plan and the room orientation, as shown in Figure 1.4. Finally, a roof plan is designed to facilitate the use of a roof deck and roof garden; this preliminary study is illustrated in Figure 1.5. The studies of the exterior elevations evolved utilizing an asphalt shingle roof material, with a shallow pitched roof, and exterior walls of wood siding. After the client has approved the preliminary floor plans, the exterior elevations are presented to the client in preliminary form for approval and to the governmental agencies for their preliminary approvals. The north and west elevations are depicted in Figures 1.6 and 1.7. These preliminary drawings and designs are examples of the architect's studies that may be presented to a client for approval prior to implementation of the DD and construction drawings.

Within the SD process there is expected to be significant changes from the beginning of the process to the end of the process. Ideas are fast and furious at this stage and brainstorming ideas and options is the best way to generate great idea. Limit your filters in this stage to allow the most creativity and rely on the system of design to refine the ideas into a stronger architecture. Figure 1.8 demonstrates such an example. Utilizing BIM for the SD process generates great communication drawings very quickly. These typically need hours of refinement but for this stage of the design it is an effective tool for the job. To better understand the program provided, a church requested a small chapel that could house thirty four to fifty people and wanted it to have the ability to see outside from within and inside when you were outside. Figure 1.9 shows early concept drawings that could meet this goal.

BIM allowed us to generate quick renderings to help the client visualize the space. See Figures 1.10 for the

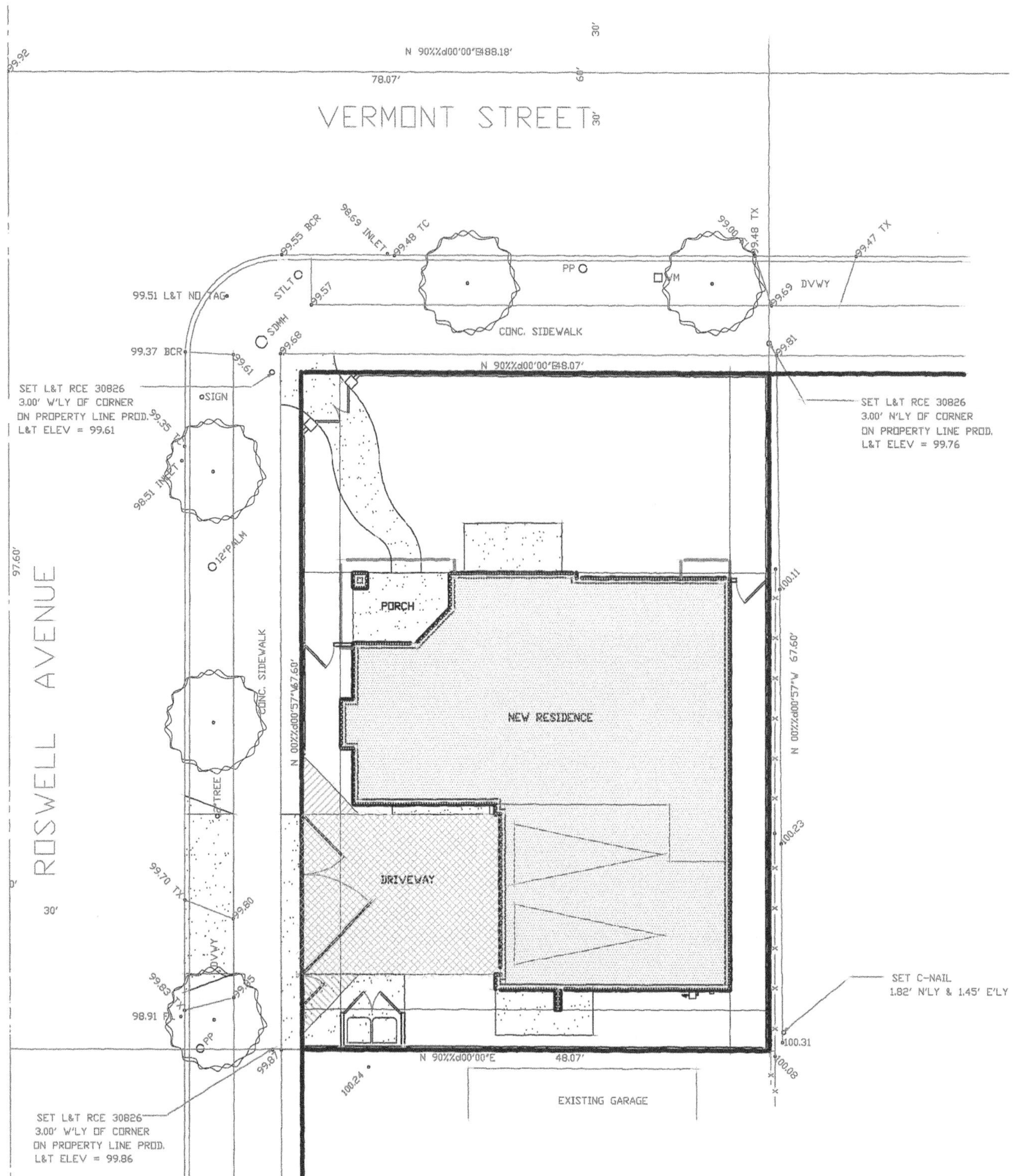

Figure 1.2 Schematic site design drawing.

complete first presentation to the board of the church for schematic review and comments. BIM allowed us to provide an added image which was a color 3-D image (in black and white here). This allowed us to learn about the color pallet that the board had in mind as well. See Figure 1.11. The concept used for this building was that of a dove symbolizing the symbol of peace. We called this presentation the Dove Chapel.

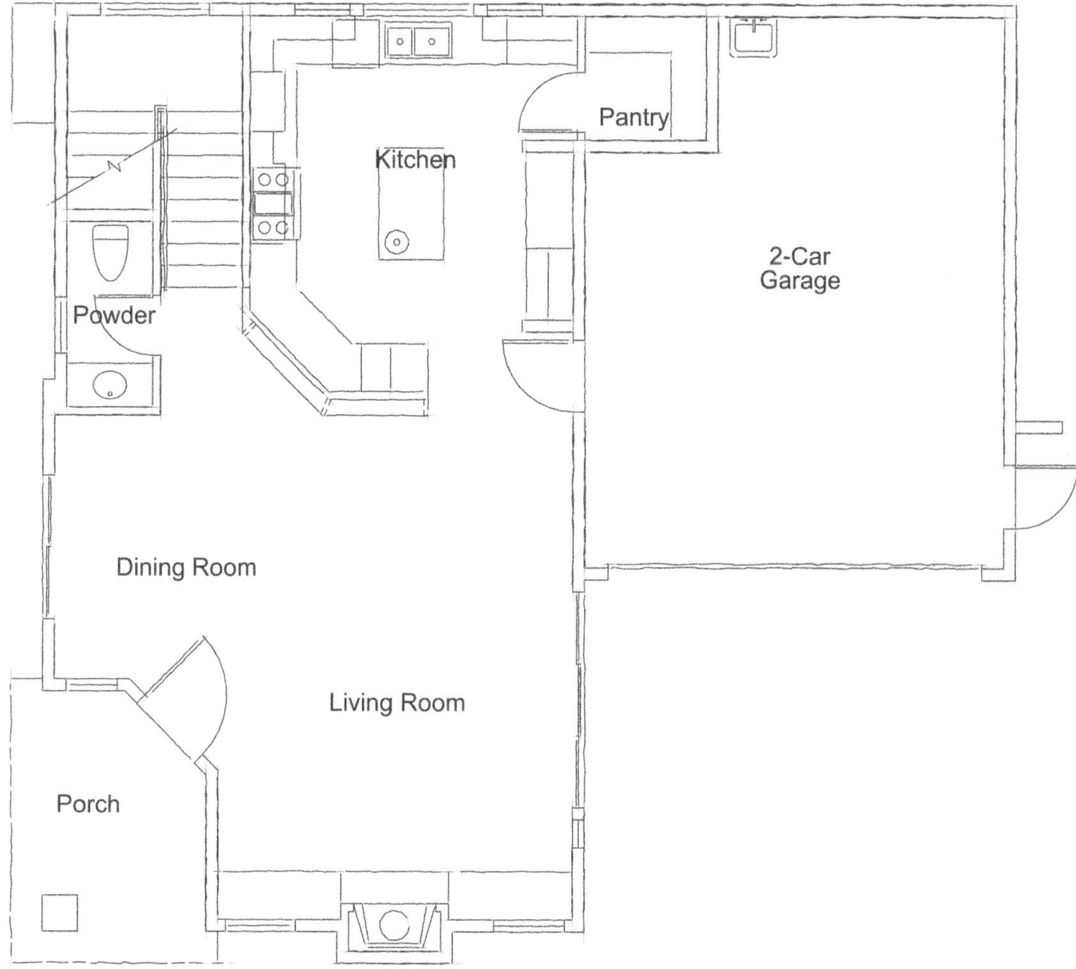

Figure 1.3 First-floor plan schematic design.

As mentioned earlier, after the first meeting, plans need to be revised and as is the process of SD, we modified the plans and provided new conceptual drawings. Comments from the first presentation used adjectives like sharp, harsh, and pointed. Could we soften the architecture and salvage or concept for the Dove Chapel? Back to the drawing board, a new layout of the building was proposed and we generated new drawings with a significant change, softened lines for the building. See Figures 1.12–1.17 and note the outside in and inside out. Client approved this plan and we moved forward to DD.

Design Development

With a BIM program it is often difficult to determine when SD ends and the next DD phase begins, because BIM includes so much specific data (such as material type, size, frequency, and construction methods) that is front-loaded into the computer. In BIM, even at SD a 3-D drawing of the design has already been developed and can be viewed after a limited amount of data is entered. Material texture color and finish are demonstrated in early phases such as SD and DD.

There will be many conferences between the architect and the client during the DD phase to select and determine items such as exterior and interior wall finishes, ceiling finishes, flooring, plumbing fixtures, hardware design, type of masonry, roofing materials, and so on. During these conferences, the selections of building equipment and systems are also determined and reviewed. The equipment selection may include such items as types of windows and doors and the manufacturer, elevator type and manufacturer, mechanical system, electrical fixtures, and so on. In this specific example was for a residence, but the process is not significantly different from one project type to another. Similar to the SD process, conceptual design drawings and diagrams get further refined and the general layout and appearance of the project is significantly refined and improved. Within this phase, various levels of refinement exist, such as more complex line drawings, mass models,

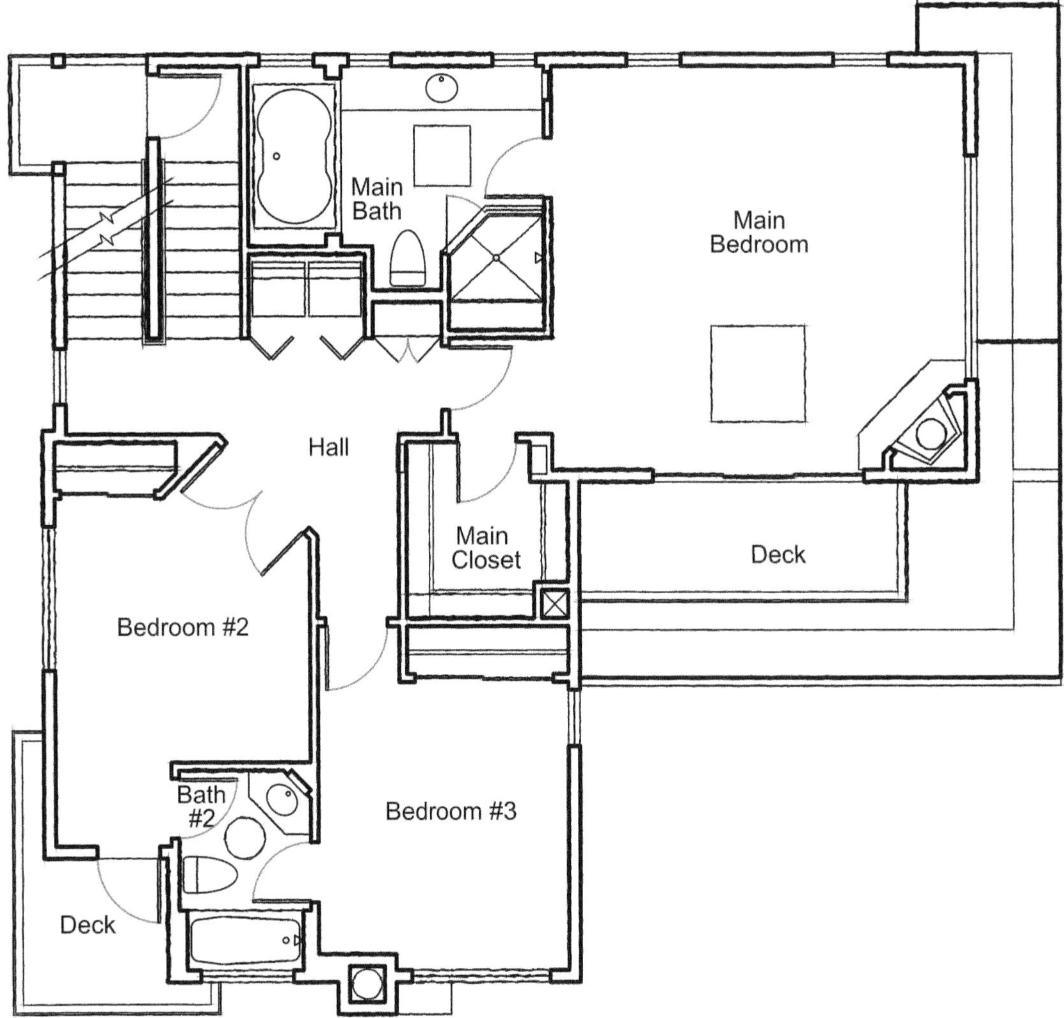

Figure 1.4 Second-floor plan schematic design.

or even elaborate Revit drawings and renderings to aid in the communication of ideas to the client at a much more elaborate level, often describing each and every room with more detail and specific recommendations for **finishes, furnishings, and equipment (FFE).** DD is also a progression of reviews with the client in order to further tune the project and align it with the client's needs. The more complex the project, the longer the process takes. Changes in this phase should be smaller in scale and less significant than the SD phase. If the client desires significant changes, the architect needs to charge the client for these changes. Like SD, if the program size and scope is significantly modified, fees must be modified to reflect the change, this is true if the scope is reduced, similarly fees would be reduced.

Construction Documents

After the client and the various governing agencies involved approve the SD and DD for a project, the architect's office initiates the construction drawing phase for the construction of the project. This phase includes drawings with great detail and would typically include specifications and construction details in preparation for the client and contractor contract.

During the CD phase, architects determine which consulting engineers are required on a specific project if they have not determined this in the DD phase. The engineers may be employed directly by the architect, or they may have their own private practices. These consultants may include soils and geological engineers, structural engineers, mechanical engineers, electrical engineers, and civil engineers. Other consultants may include landscape architects, interior designers, LEED consultants, and cost estimators. Periodic conferences with the client are recommended during this phase to attain approvals on the various phases of the construction drawings. These phases or stages may include lighting layout and electrical designs, cabinetry, reflected ceiling, and many other features for which client review and approval are needed.

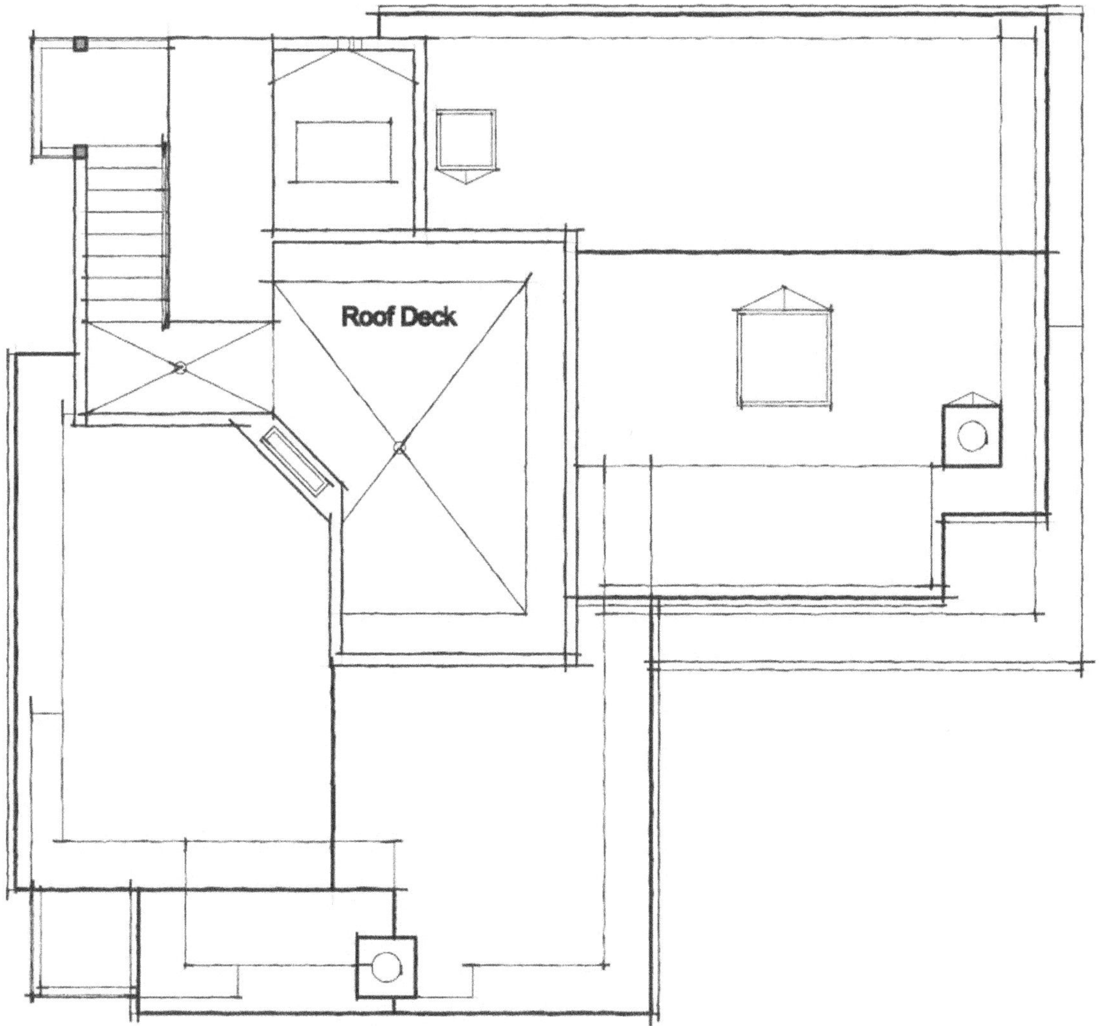

Figure 1.5 Roof plan schematic design.

Upon completion of the construction drawings and specifications, which are now termed CDs, the architect and/or client may submit the CDs to financing institutions for building loans, to various construction firms for building cost proposals, and to governing agencies for their final approvals. Finally, the architectural firm will submit the CDs to the local planning and building department to obtain the required building permits.

Bidding and Negotiating

Once the CDs have been developed, plans are put out to bid. Often accompanying the plans are the instructions to bidders, the bid form, bid documents, the owner-contractor contract agreement, bond requirements, and any added data that is required for completion of the bid process. For public projects, such as schools or state and federal buildings, an unlimited number of bidders can propose a price for completing the work. A public project is typically advertised and provides the minimum qualifications required for the contractor to meet in order to be eligible to bid the construction project. On private projects, the clients may choose who may bid and how many bidders they would like for the job. Often, as many as four or five contractors will bid a job, allowing for a high, mid, and low bid and the opportunity to eliminate an unqualified bid or a bidder that has not met the bid submission deadline.

Negotiation of bids can occur for a project on which a specific price or timeline must be met. A single contractor may be asked to propose a budget and make revisions to replace expensive items or omit items from a project. The result of bid negotiations, ideally, is a modified contract document that will meet the budget and/or time requirements.

In this stage, it is the architect's responsibility to help the owner evaluate the bids and select a winning contractor. Any of the negotiation of scope and bid should be

Figure 1.6 North elevation schematic design.

Figure 1.7 West elevation schematic design.

completed prior to the contract execution to minimize the confusion of scope. A letter of intent and a signed contract will be the trigger to allow construction to begin.

Construction Administration

When the construction firm has been selected and construction has commenced, the architect and consulting engineers, according to their agreement in the contract, observe the various phases of construction. This phase in the architecture contract is termed **construction administration (CA)**. At this point, the architect's role may change to one that is more field active. These periodic observations generally correspond to the construction phases, such as field-visiting construction of the foundation, framing, and so forth. The services

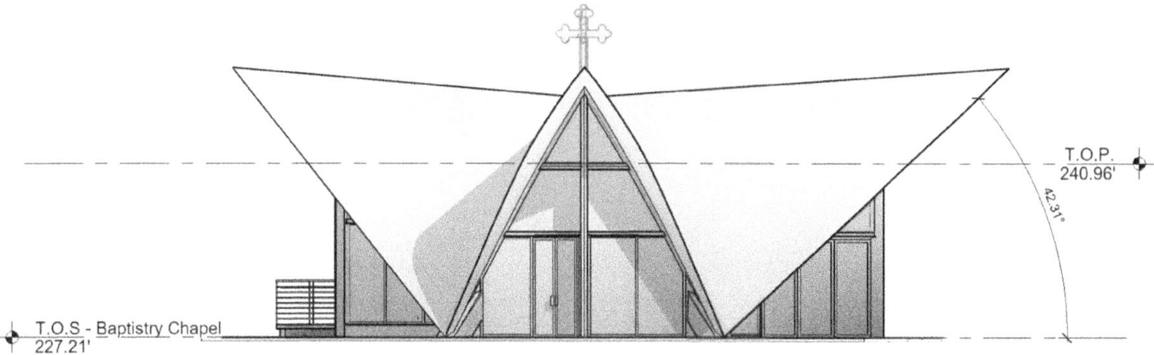

Figure 1.8 North elevation schematic design.

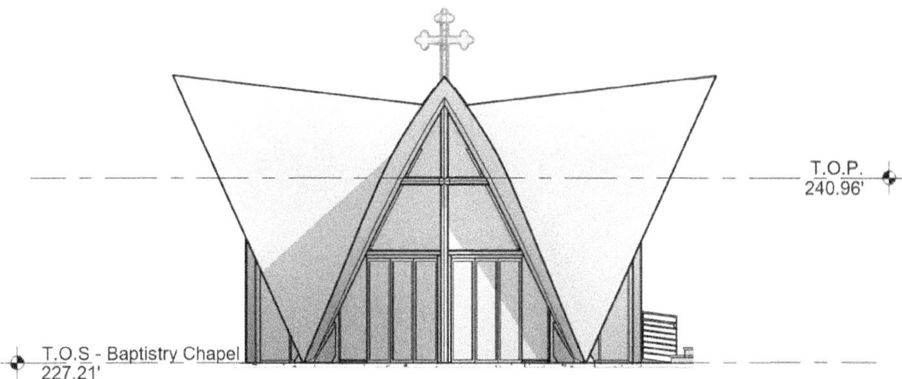

Figure 1.9 West elevation schematic design.

are determined and outlined in the owner–architect agreement or contract and can be a variety of levels of services. Following their observations, the architect and consulting engineers provide written reports to the client and contractor describing their observations, along with any recommendations or alterations they deem necessary for the success of the project. Performing site visits, making field revisions and clarifications, and responding to **requests for information (RFIs)** enhance opportunities for better design, budget, and schedule results. The primary role of the architect in this stage is to assist the contractor to build the project as specified in the CDs.

At the completion of the project, the architect and consultants make a final inspection of the construction of the building and prepare a **punch list**. This punch list, which is in written form, includes graphics indicating to the client and construction firm any revisions, reports, or alterations the architect or consultant deems pertinent and reasonable for a successful building project. After the construction firm makes the revisions, the architect and the consultants again inspect the project. If acceptable, a final notice of approval is sent to the client and the construction firm.

BUILDING CODE REQUIREMENTS

Building Codes

The purpose of building codes is to safeguard life, health, and the public welfare. Building codes are continually being revised to incorporate additional regulations based on tests or conditions caused by catastrophic events, such as hurricanes, earthquakes, and fires. In most cases, the governing building codes are similar in organization and context.

Building codes exist to establish the minimum requirements for life safety. Components of a code cover areas such as exiting, fire resistivity, occupancy, sustainability, and disability access. Although some things are specified in great detail, such as the maximum rise of a stair and the minimum depth of a tread, some aspects are more general, such as a requirement of two exits for a specific occupancy group. An understanding of these codes aids the architect in the decision-making process.

It is extremely important that you research building code requirements, as they are updated regularly and new requirements are implemented. In multiple housing projects as well as in residential projects, building codes

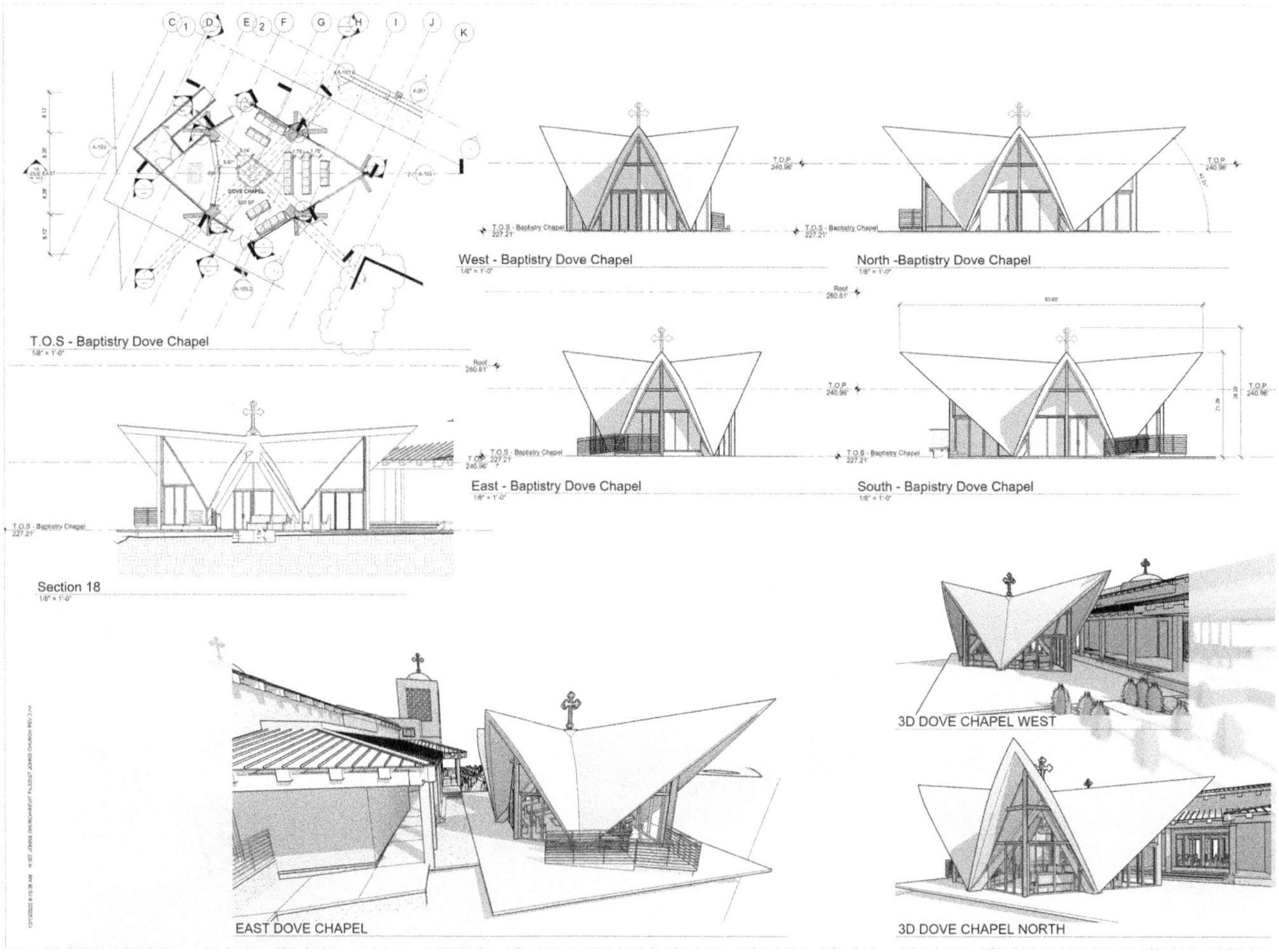

Figure 1.10 Presentation of the schematic design.

establish minimum physical requirements for various rooms such as sleeping room areas and ceiling heights to meet code guidelines.

Remember that the building department sets minimum standards. An architect sets standards (often above minimum) to satisfy or enhance health and safety. For example, the maximum slope for a disability ramp is 1:12. An architect may choose to use 1:14 as the slope of the ramp to be more accommodating to the individual with a disability.

Figure 1.11 Rendering schematic design.

A new integration of sustainable architecture is becoming a larger part of the code requirements. The direction of green or environmentally friendly design is less driven by common sense and under more scrutiny by public officials. Currently, the review process is fundamental; as time passes, there will be added pressures for architects to exceed the green code minimums. As in all good design, it should be your goal to surpass the demands of city review minimum requirement and address the demands of good design with the incorporation of great environmental design.

The requirements of various agencies and codes influence the design and detailing of today's structures. A great number of codes govern and regulate the many elements that are integrated into the construction of a building. The major codes that are used in the design and detailing of buildings are the building

Figure 1.12 North elevation revised schematic design.

code, mechanical code, electrical code, plumbing code, fire code, energy code, and accessibility design criteria for compliance with the **Americans with Disabilities Act (ADA).**

Procedures for Use of Building Codes

Step I. *Building use and occupancy.* The first step is to classify the building use and to determine the occupancy group for the building. When the occupancy classification has been determined, the building is assigned a group designation letter, which determines the description of the occupancy and the group it falls under. For instance, "A" is utilized for an assembly occupancy group or "E" for education.

Step II. *Fire-rated wall assemblies.* Most codes provide a chapter on acceptable fire-resistive standards for assemblies, so that the architect is able to select an assembly that satisfies his or her specific condition. For example, a one-hour fire-rated wall is constructed with 2″ × 4″ wood stud partition with 5/8″ type "X" gypsum wallboard on both sides. Often the size of the building in square footage determines if the building will need sprinklers or if corridors are fire rated.

Step III. *Building location on the site.* The location of the building on the site and the clearances to the property lines and other structures on the site determine the fire-resistant construction of the exterior walls. The openings are based on the distances from the property lines and other structures. As you can imagine if the building has no to little setback the assembly system will need to be fire rated.

Figure 1.13 West elevation revised schematic design.

Step IV. *Allowable floor areas.* The next step is to determine the proposed and allowable floor areas of the building based on the occupancy group, such as theater or assembly room, and the type of construction. If the building size exceeds the allowable square footage, building construction materials may have to be varied or sprinklers have to be introduced to allow the next level of footage allowed.

Step V. *Height and the number of stories or floors in the building.* The architect computes the maximum height of the building and determines the number of stories and/or floors. The maximum number of stories and the height of the building are determined by the building occupancy and the type of construction.

Code Influence on Building Design

An example of code-related design requirements is provided by a site plan for a proposed two-story office building. The architect desires that all four sides of the building have windows. To satisfy this design factor, the minimum building setback from the property line will be a minimum 10 feet for openings in exterior walls. Figure 1.18 depicts the proposed site plan for the two-story office building, showing property line setbacks satisfying one design requirement.

As the design program is developed, it is helpful to provide code-required assemblies in graphic form as a visual means for reviewing what is required for the various elements of the office building. An example of such a graphic aid appears in Figure 1.19. Building codes specify the wall assemblies that meet the fire-resistive requirements for the various elements of the building type selected.

Another very important part of a building code is the chapter dealing with egress requirements. This chapter sets forth the number of required exits for a specific

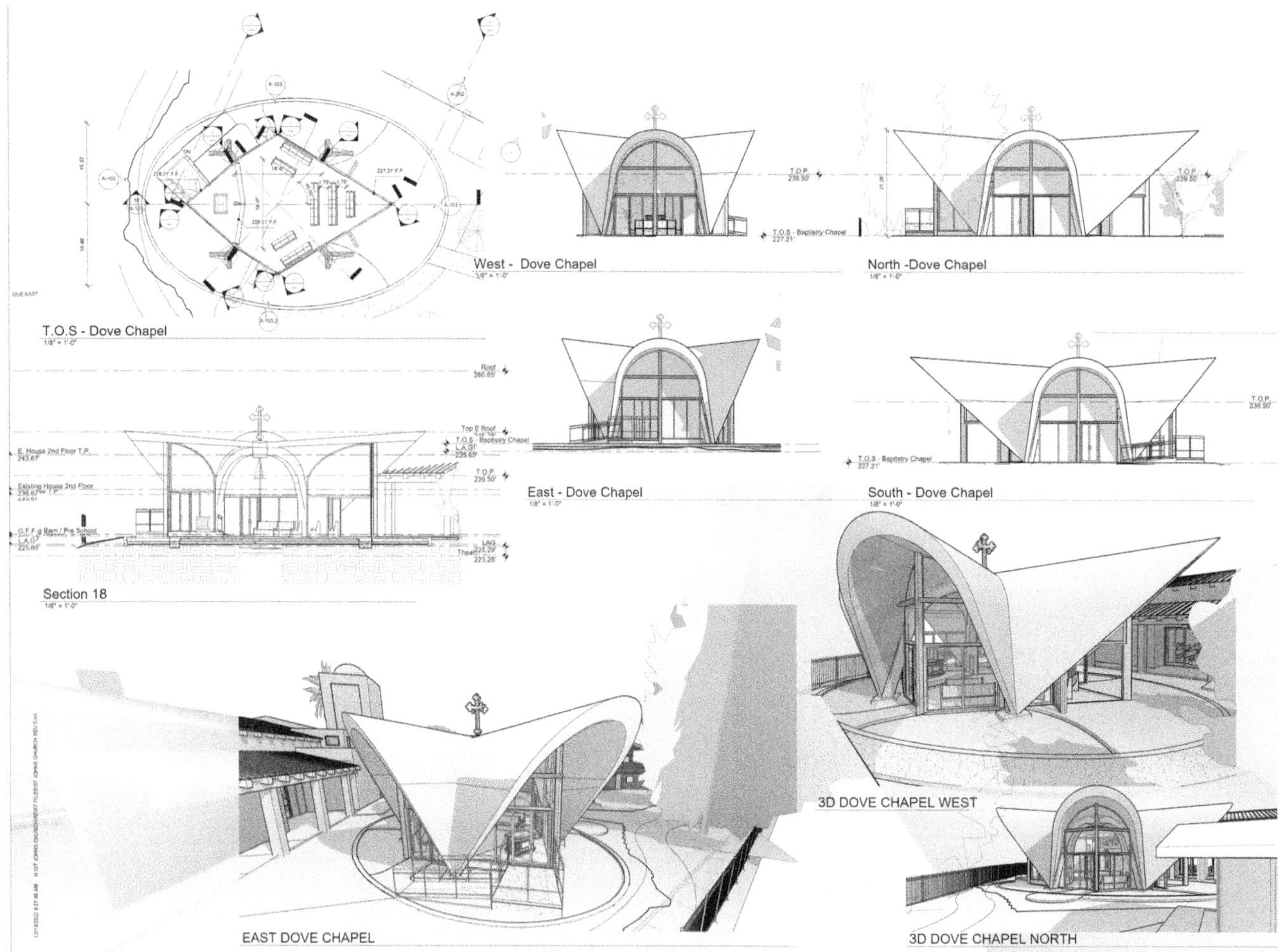

Figure 1.14 Presentation of the revised schematic design.

occupancy use, based on an occupant load factor. The occupant load will depend on the use of the building. In the case of a two-story building that is designed for office use, the occupant load factor is 1 person per 100 square feet. To determine the number of exits required, the 100-square-foot occupant load factor is divided into the office floor area of 10,000 square feet. The resulting occupant factor of 100 exceeds the factor of 30, therefore requiring a minimum of two exits.

The next step in the design program is to plan the location of the required exits, required stairs, and an acceptable **egress travel** (the path to a required exit). Building codes regulate the minimum distance between exits, the minimum width of exit corridors, and the entire design of required exit stairways and the proposed occupancy determines the minimum width of the corridor. Figure 1.20 depicts the second-level floor plan of the proposed office building, illustrating an acceptable method for the planning of required exits and stair locations. An acceptable egress travel will terminate at the first-floor level, exiting outside the structure to a public right-of-way. A public right-of-way may be a sidewalk, street, alley, or other passage. On the first-level floor plan, illustrated in Figure 1.21, the egress travel path terminates outside the building through an exit corridor at the east and west walls of the building.

REGIONAL CONSIDERATIONS

Regional differences in construction techniques are controlled or influenced primarily by climatic conditions, soil conditions, and natural events and forces such as high winds and seismic activity.

In brief, regional differences influence:

1. Soils or geological requirements
2. Environmental impacts
3. Structural assembly
4. Climatic impacts
5. Material availability

Figure 1.22 illustrates a type of foundation used in regions with cold climatic conditions: an exterior

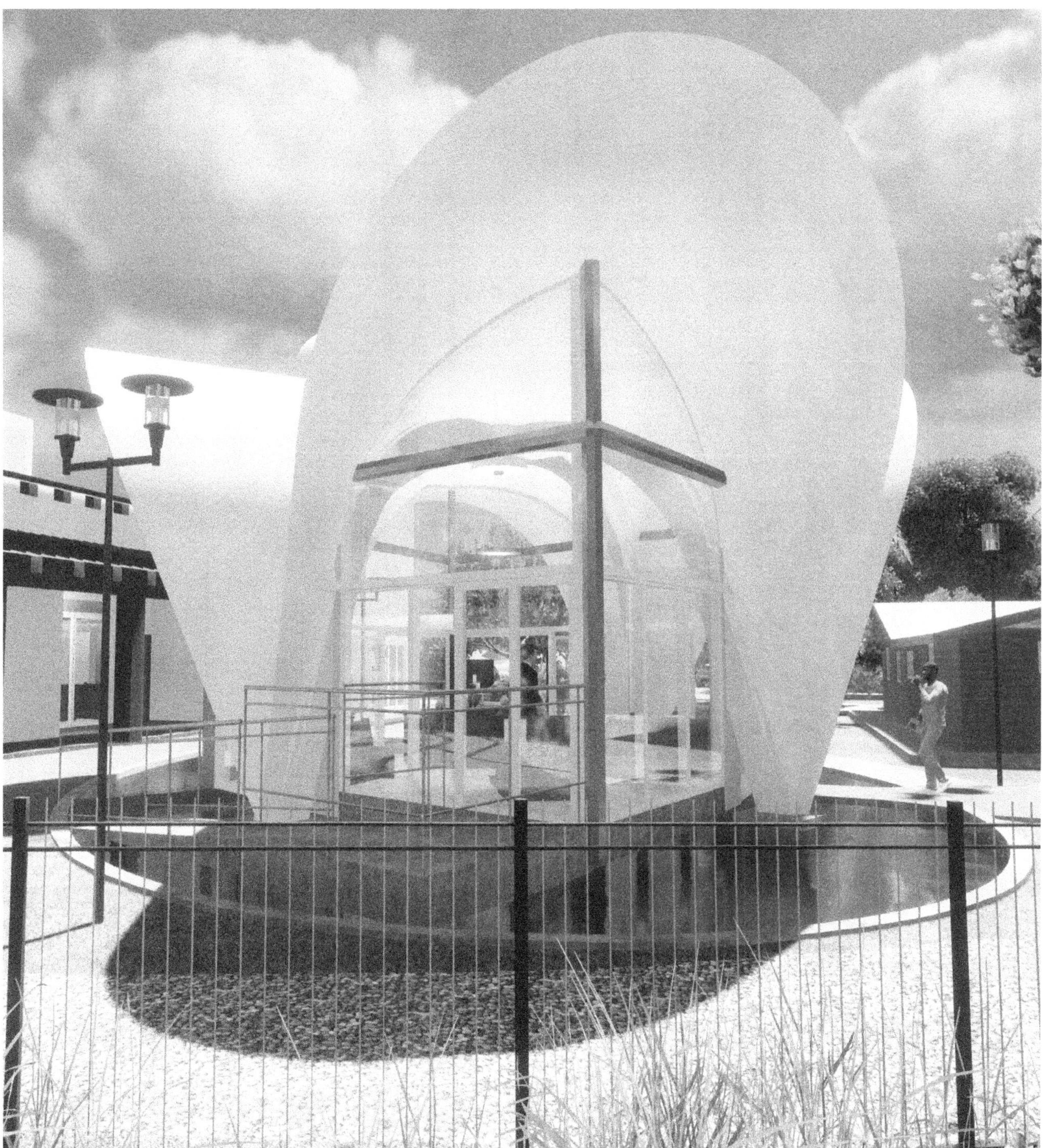

Figure 1.15 Revised rendering schematic design.

foundation wall and footing with a concrete floor. The depth of the foundation is established from the frost line, and insulation is required under the concrete floor.

Where temperatures are mild and warm, the foundation design and construction techniques are primarily shown in Figure 1.23. Here, solid sheathing is used, and this in turn requires the wood studs to be set in from the face of the foundation wall. This one regional difference can affect many procedures and detailing throughout the CDs, such as wall dimensioning, window details, and door details.

Not every material is available in every region. For example, if a specific species of lumber is available

Figure 1.16 Revised rendering schematic design.

Figure 1.17 Revised rendering schematic design.

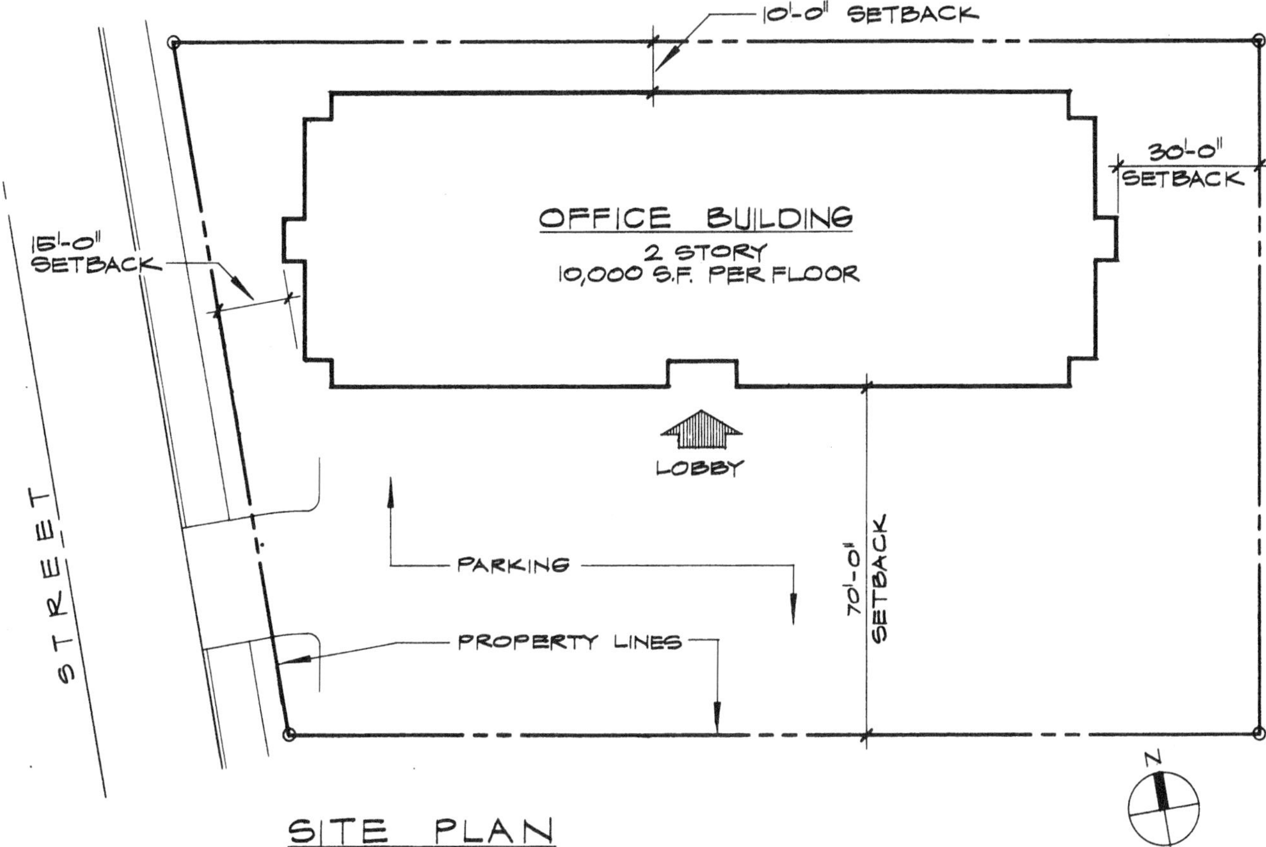

Figure 1.18 Site plan with setbacks illustrated.

only on the East Coast, it may not be environmentally or economically feasible to ship that lumber across the country; hence, these regional considerations would mandate selection of a different timber specification.

Locations also determine what you must do to satisfy local and federal energy conservation requirements, you must complete preliminary research. These requirements can affect exterior wall material and thickness, amount and type of glazing, areas of infiltration (leakage of air), amount of artificial lighting to

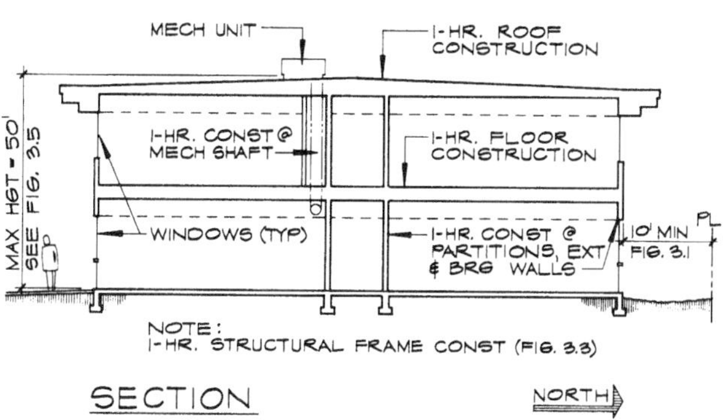

Figure 1.19 Graphic building section with fire-rated assembly.

be used, thickness and type of insulation, mechanical engineering design, and so forth. For example, a wood building requires exterior walls to be 2 × 6 studs instead of 2 × 4 to allow for the thickness of governed by seismic, wind, and local building codes. Figure 1.23 illustrates an exterior foundation detail where the depth of the footing is established to a recommended depth below the natural grade.

Another example of regional influence is change in exterior wall design. Figure 1.24 shows a section of an exterior wall with wood frame construction. This open-frame construction is suitable for mild climates. A wood frame exterior wall recommended for eastern regions utilizes building insulation see Figure 1.25. This particular requirement dictates procedures in the CD process, such as floor-plan wall thickness and dimensioning, window and exterior door details, and other related exterior wall details. Figure 1.26 shows a segment of a floor plan that indicates the thickness of walls and the locations of required insulation. Fattened stud walls are required to allow for the added resistance for insulation.

An excellent example of an award-winning mechanical system that produces energy savings is an ice bank. The use of storage tanks in the design of a

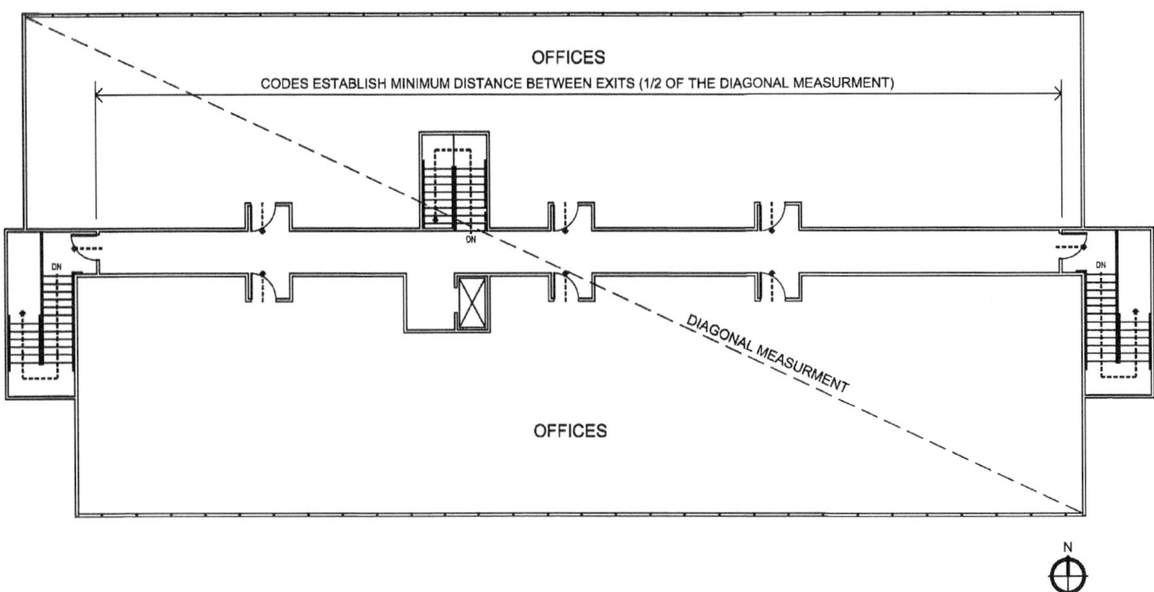

Figure 1.20 Second-level floor plan.

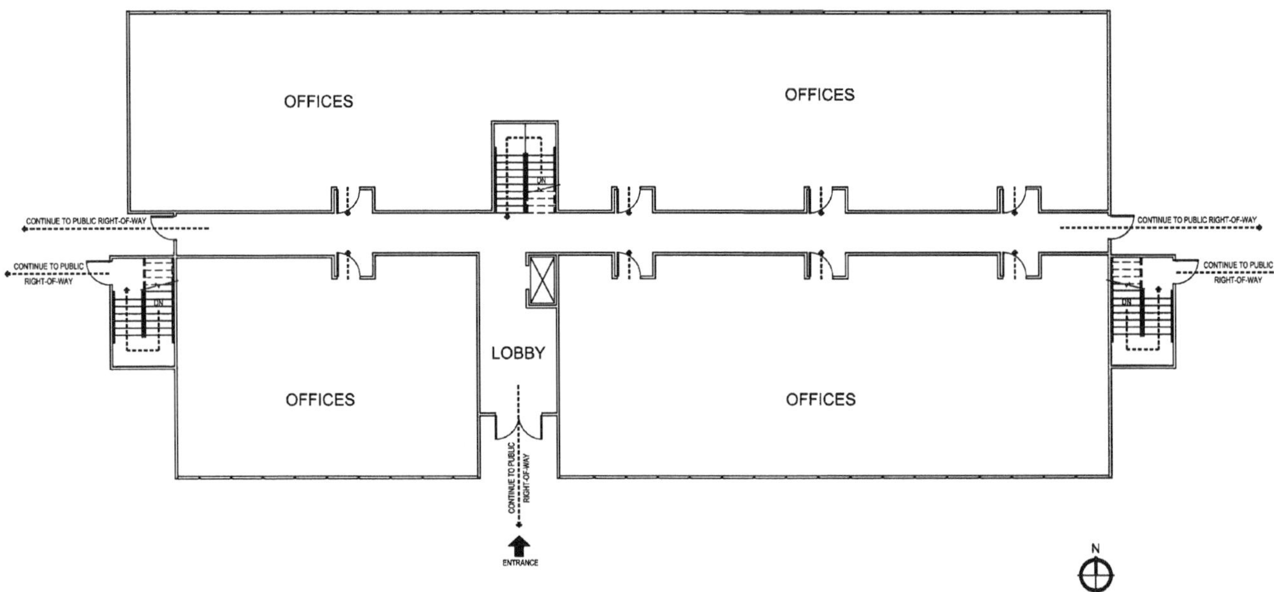

Figure 1.21 First-level floor plan.

mechanical system can increase operating efficiency and considerably reduce both the electrical costs and the amount of energy used. An example of this storage-tank approach is the use of ice storage tanks to produce cooling for a large office building. Ice usually forms around the piping that carries the refrigerant located in a tank. The ice is produced during off-peak hours, such as during the night, when energy costs are at their lowest. This then provides the necessary coolant during the following day's peak-use hours. See Figure 1.27.

AMERICANS WITH DISABILITIES ACT (ADA)

Public building accessibility is a result of legislation for the protection of persons with disabilities. The Americans with Disabilities Act, or ADA, is a civil rights law, not a building code. This law is divided into four major titles that prohibit discrimination against those who are disabled: Title I, Employment; Title II, Public Services and Transportation; Title III, Public Accommodations; and Title IV, Telecommunications.

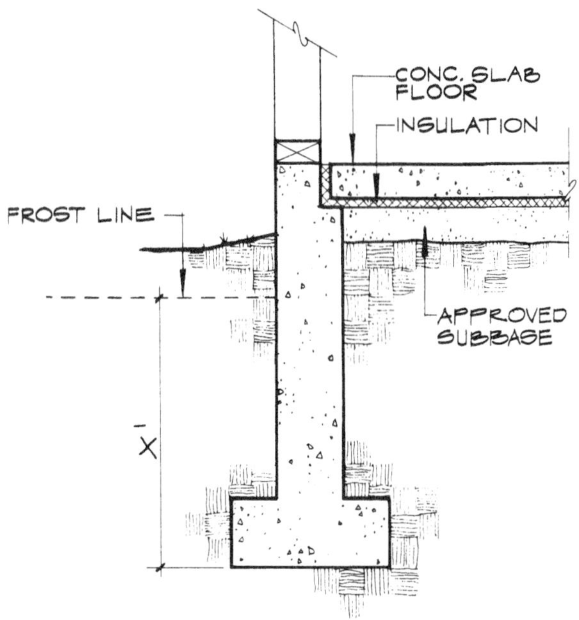

Figure 1.22 Cold-climate foundation conditions.

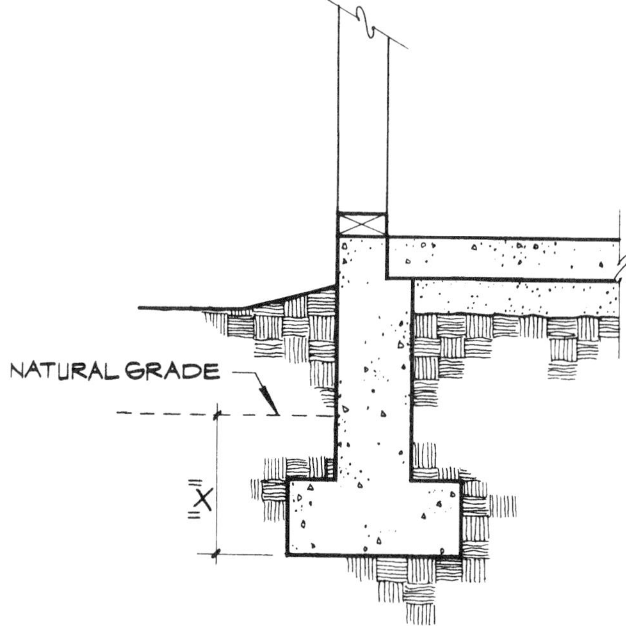

Figure 1.23 Recommended foundation depth in warm climate.

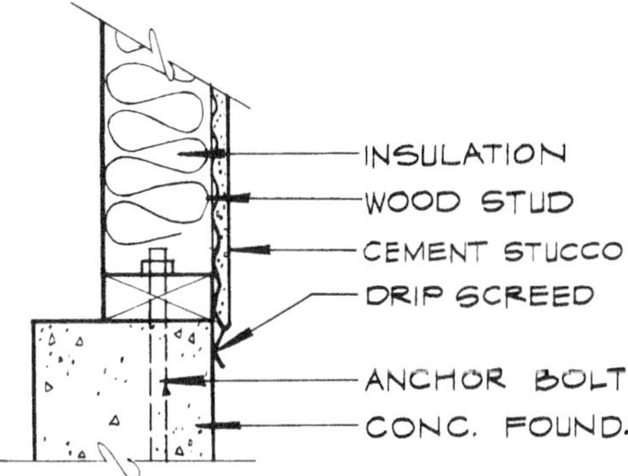

Figure 1.24 Exterior wall: Open-frame construction.

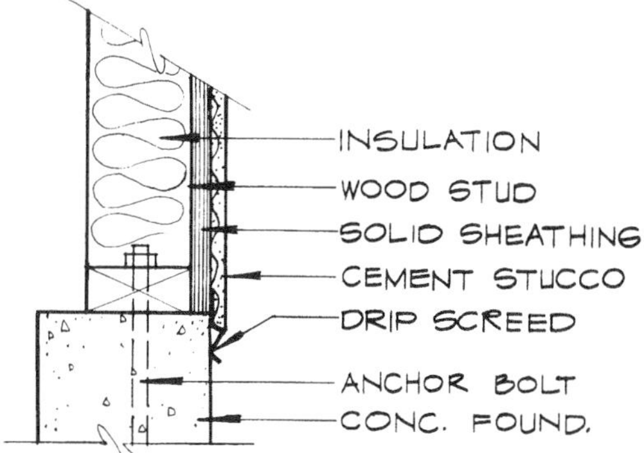

Figure 1.25 Exterior wall: Sheathed frame construction.

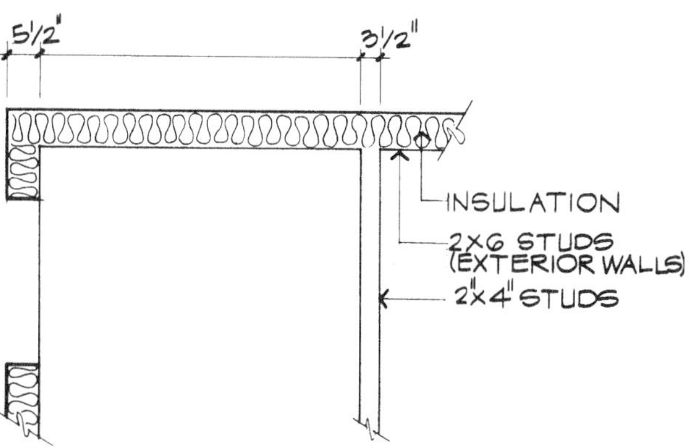

Figure 1.26 Floor-plan wall thickness.

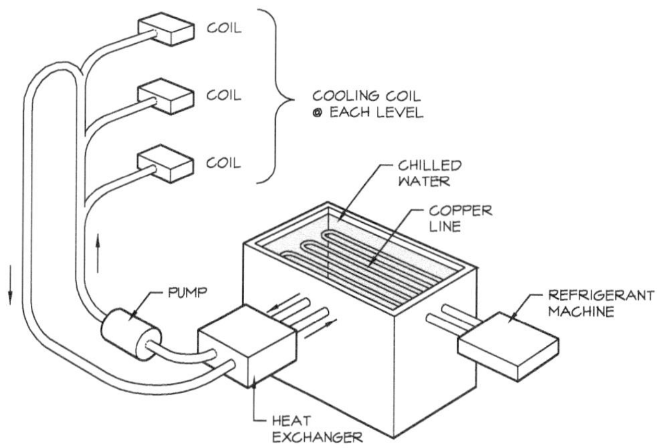

Figure 1.27 Ice bank system.

Given that the focus of this book is on building design and construction detailing, this chapter discusses Title III, Public Accommodations, and provides graphic illustrations of methods required to be used in public buildings and facilities to accommodate the needs of persons who are disabled.

The dimensions with maximums and minimums are shown only to allow readers a glimpse into the type of

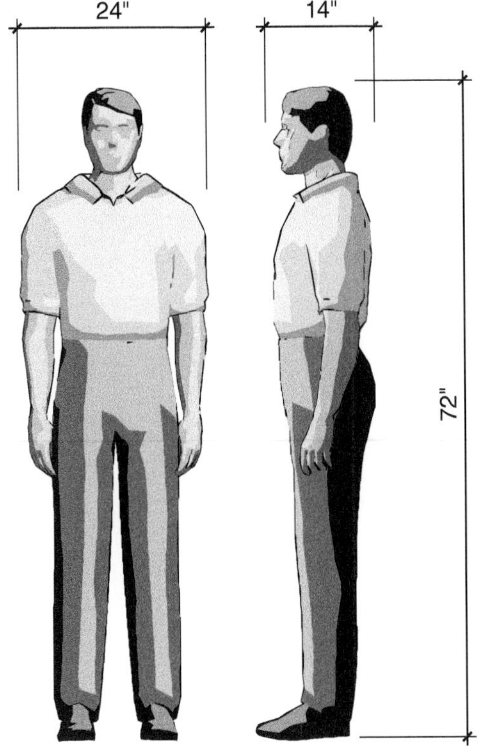

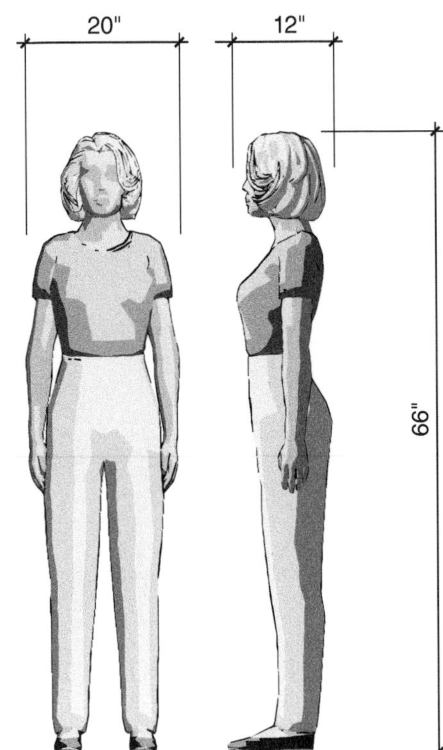

Figure 1.28 Understanding the human figure: average dimensions.

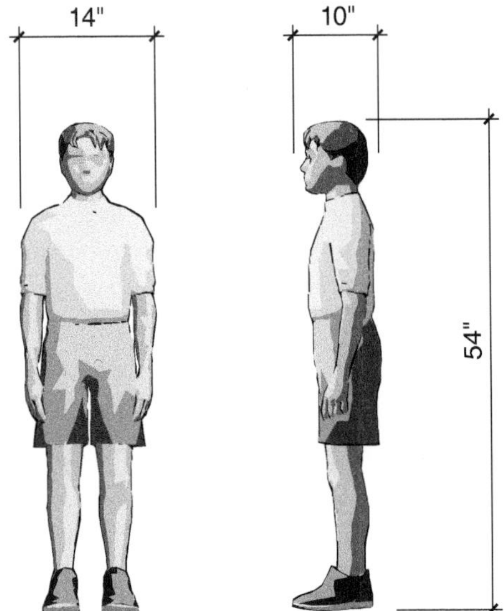

Figure 1.28 *(Continued)*

concerns we have as a profession. See Figures 1.28–1.30 to get a better understanding of typical human size, reach, and visibility. For example, Figure 1.31 shows a wheelchair going up a ramp in a curb. A designer, drafter, office manager, or architect will have to seek out the national standard and always follow that up with a check of state and local municipality regulations. Local or state regulations may be more stringent than federal guidelines and requirements.

The federal law also provides an order on importance when converting non-conforming buildings. New buildings must conform 100% to all current ADA guidelines. As time passes and codes change, buildings become less conforming and the code states that a portion of the proposed renovation all work must be allocated to upgrade ADA non-conformance. You can imagine some buildings would be near impossible to get into compliance. The guidelines state that a minor renovation or tenant improvement under ($184,000, verify in your region) only 20% has to be allocated to the budget for compliance. If this number is exceeded 100% is required.

To offer greater accessibility to and better accommodations in public buildings for those with disabilities, various

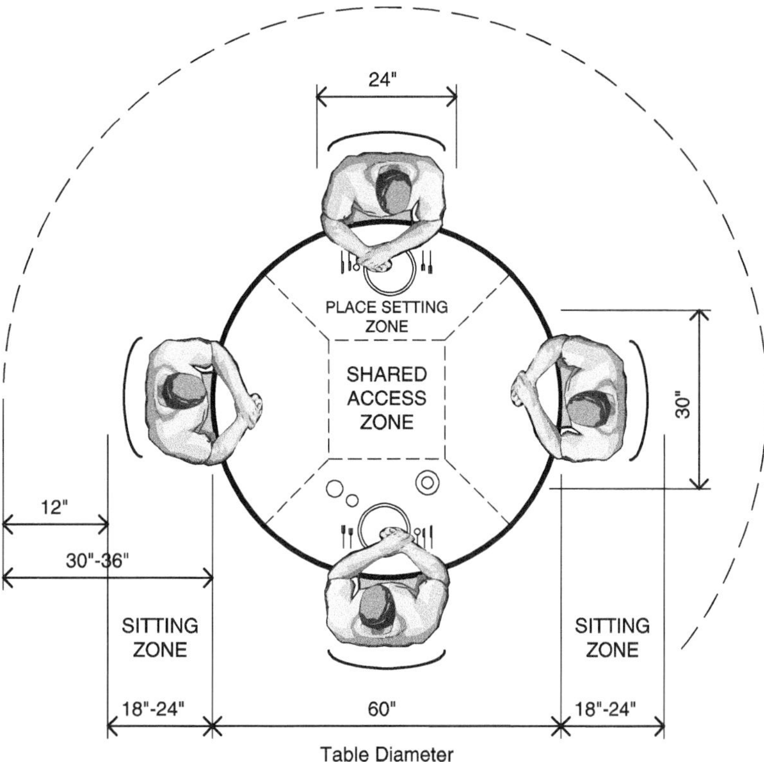

60"-Diameter Circular Table for Four / Optimum Seating

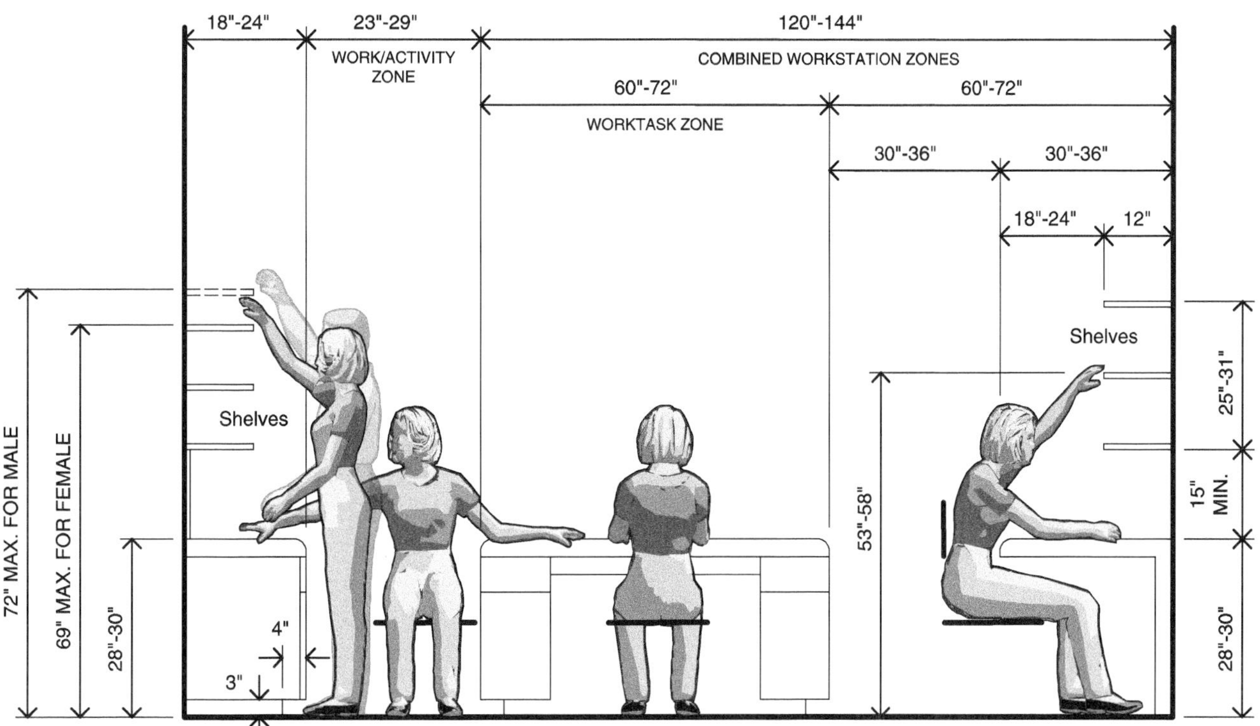

Desk and Workstation Considerations with Shelves

Figure 1.29 Reach.

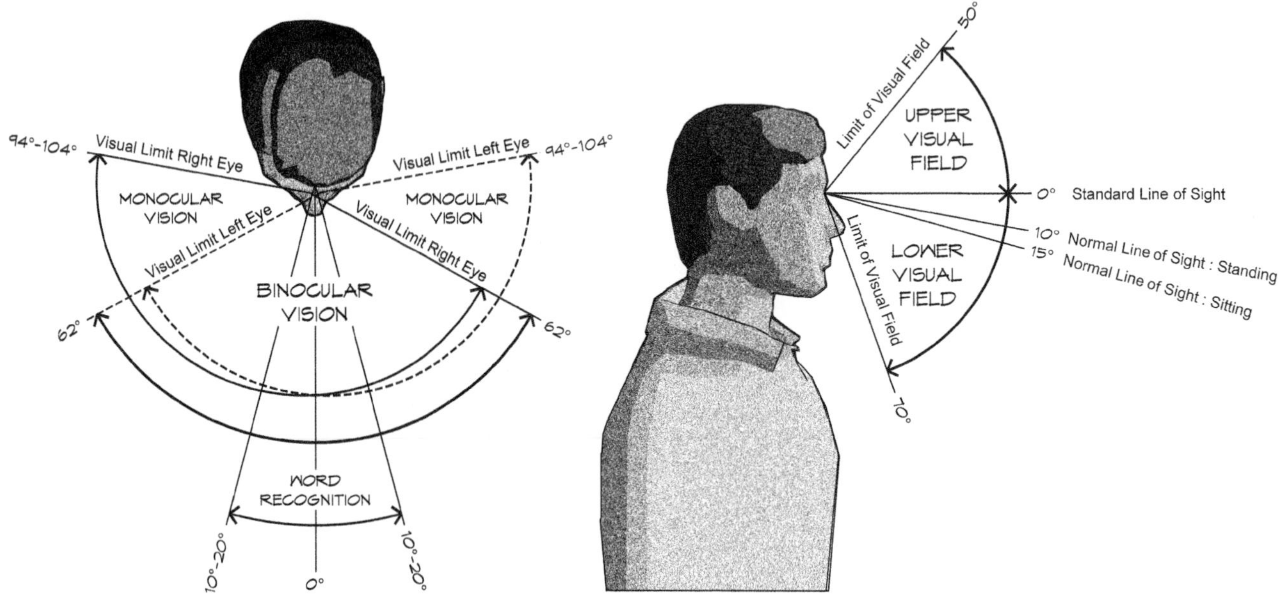

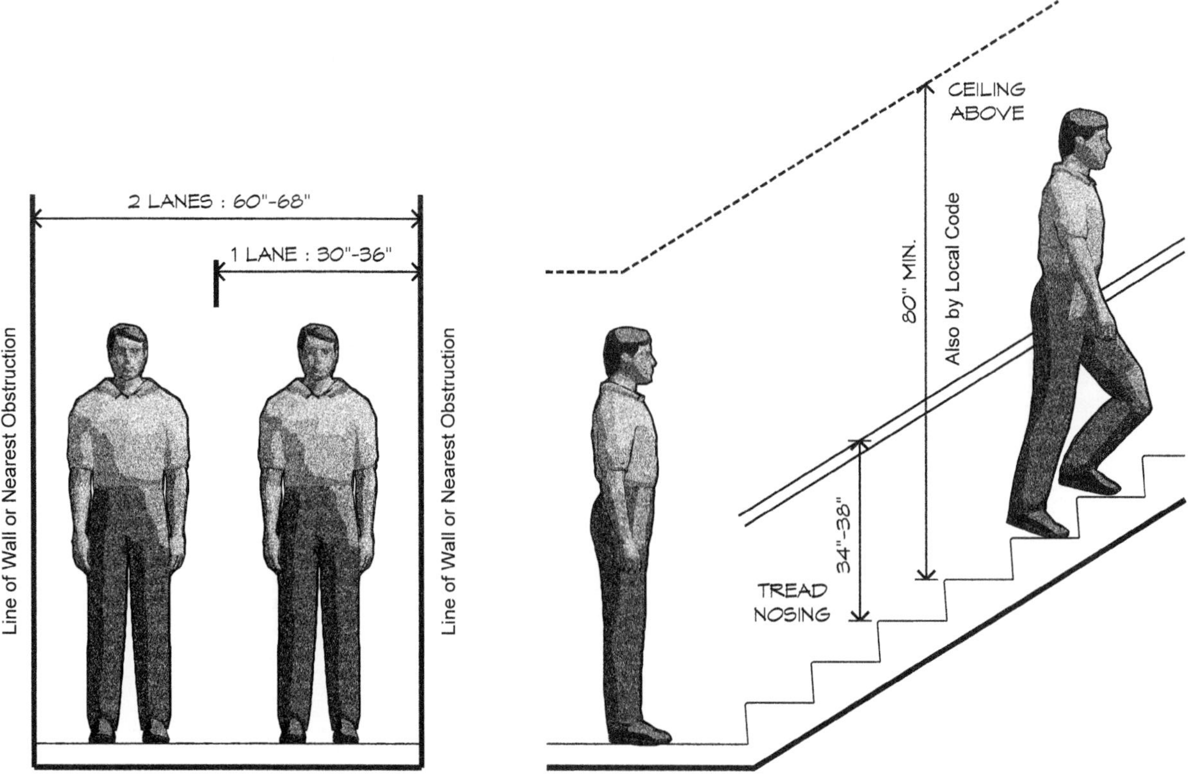

Figure 1.30 Space relative to sight and movement.

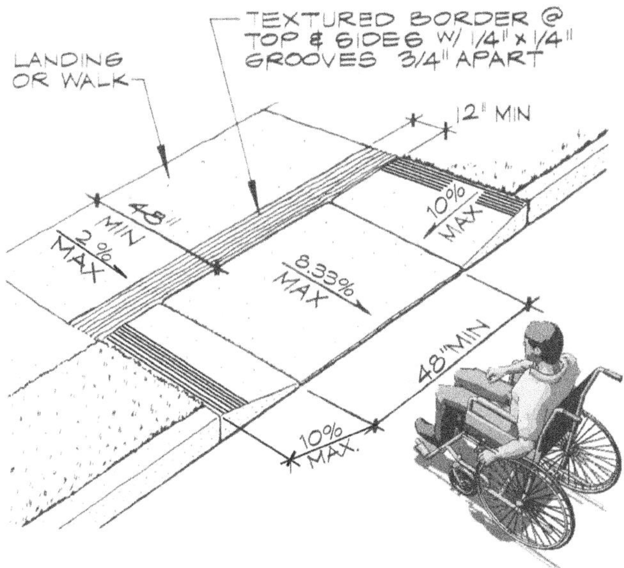

Figure 1.31 Curb ramp.

representatives of organizations for disabled persons have worked with federal agency officials to establish recommended standards. Requirements implementing these standards have been compiled in a list of elements that will be of concern to you as you prepare drawings and details to satisfy the various required/recommended design criteria:

1. Path of travel from a public transit path—exterior accessibility route to the facility
2. Accessible parking for van or vehicle
3. Accessible path from parking to front door
4. Ramps that meet code
5. Stairs and rails that meet code
6. Accessible doors/thresholds/door hardware
7. Accessible restrooms/water closets/urinals/lavatories and mirrors
8. Interior access route
9. Elevators or Platform lifts
10. Push–pull clearance for doors
11. Drinking fountains
12. Bathtubs
13. Shower stalls
14. Grab bars
15. Tub/shower seats
16. Assembly area seating
17. Alarms
18. Signage
19. Public telephones
20. Seating and tables
21. Automatic teller machines
22. Dressing and fitting rooms
23. Register counters
24. Floor materials/finishes
25. Electrical fixture heights

There are also requirements and recommendations for special applications in the following types of buildings:

Assembly buildings
Business and mercantile facilities
High-rise buildings
Libraries
Medical care facilities
Restaurants and cafeterias
Theatre buildings
Transient lodging facilities

Accessible Requirements

For specific buildings, the required number of parking spaces for those with disabilities is determined by the total number of spaces provided for that facility. This determination is based on ratios of the cars to be accommodated. An example of ratios for disabled parking is 5% disabled spaces per total parking spaces, this can increase based on the occupancy of the building for instance if it is medical this number is higher. See Figure 1.32. Note that there are provisions for a marked access aisle, a curb ramp, a disabled parking sign, and a parking-surface disabled symbol. Figure 1.33 depicts separately the freestanding disabled sign and the parking-surface disabled symbol. In most municipalities, a large fine is imposed on non-disabled persons who use these parking spaces without proper decals.

Another way of providing exterior accessibility to a facility is through the use of ramps. Figure 1.31 showed a curb ramp detail—one example of providing an accessible exterior route of travel to a specific facility. Ramps have proven to be a desirable method of enhancing accessibility when there are grade changes in the path of travel to a building. Figure 1.34 illustrates an example of an acceptable ramp with various changes in levels. Handrails are required on both sides of a ramp if the rise exceeds 6 inches or the horizontal projection exceeds 72 inches. If handrails are required, they will have to be drawn and detailed in accordance with the applicable requirements. Figure 1.35 depicts handrail requirements for the ramp shown in Figure 1.34.

In cases where there are no specific rules for a particular planning situation, it is prudent for the architect or designer to be aware of the space needed for maneuverability by someone using a wheelchair. Figures 1.36–1.40 give some examples of floor space areas and reaching dimensions that are desirable for those who function from a wheelchair.

As shown in Figures 1.36–1.40, there are dimensional limitations in various directions for a person using a wheelchair. Therefore, controls such as thermostats, window controls, electric switches, pull cords, convenience

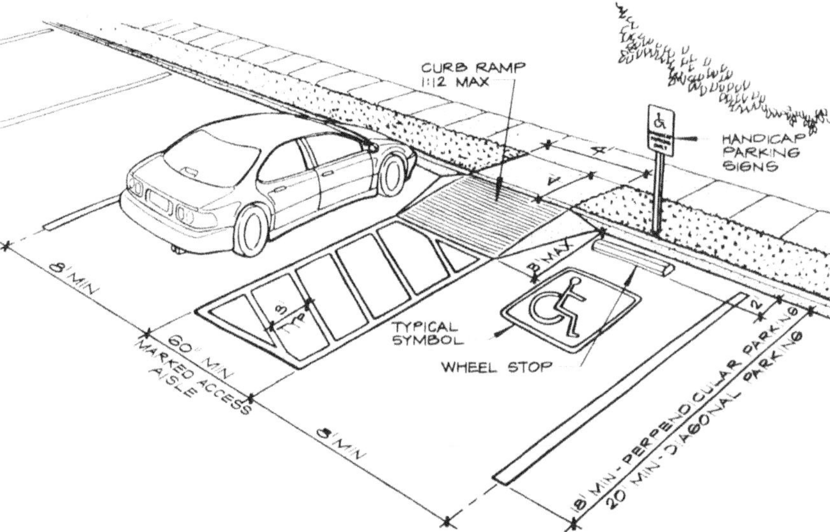

Figure 1.32 Parking spaces.

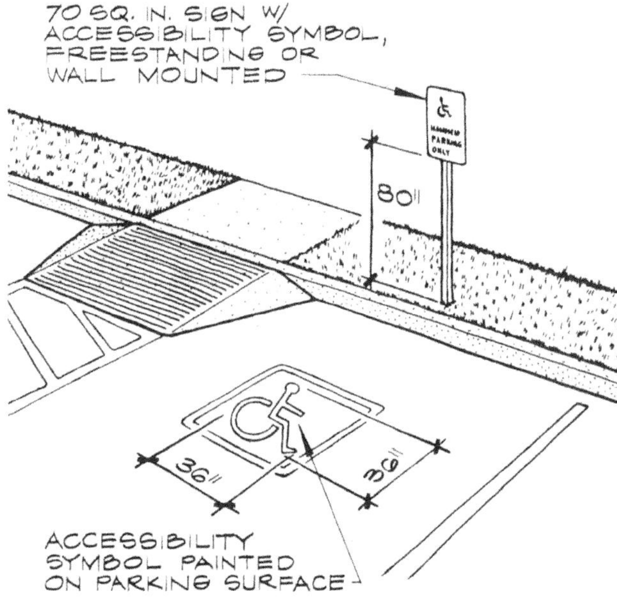

Figure 1.33 Parking sign and symbol.

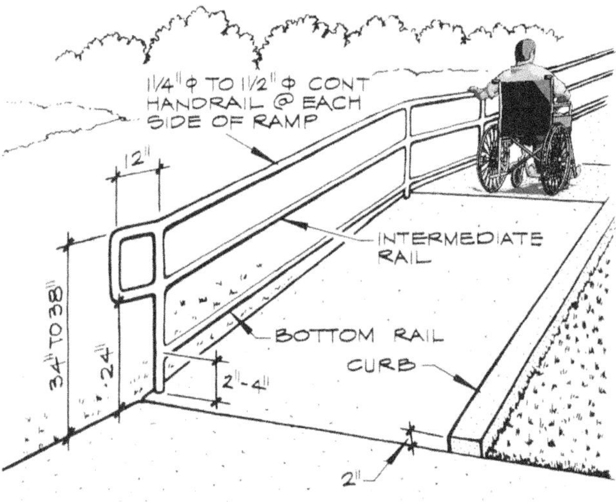

Figure 1.35 Ramp handrail.

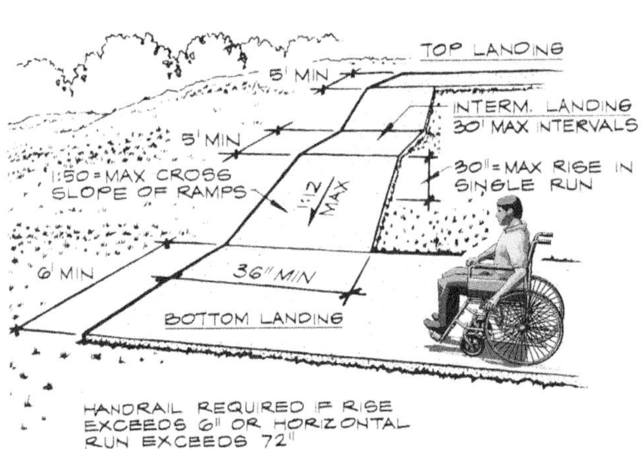

Figure 1.34 Ramp.

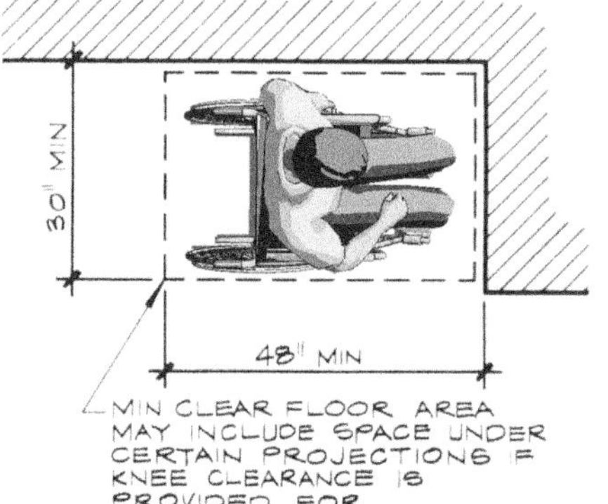

Figure 1.36 Wheelchair space requirements.

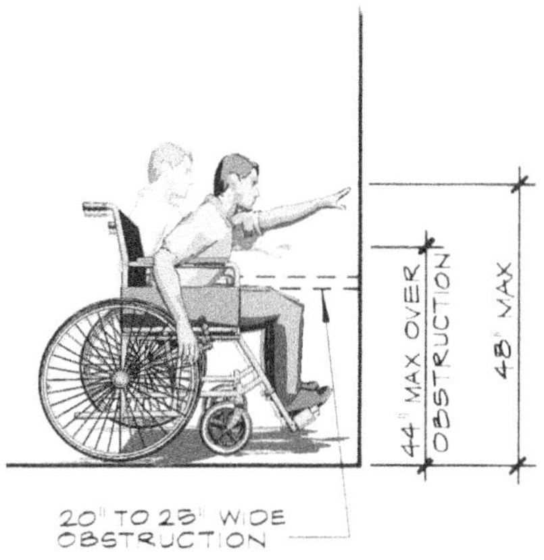

Figure 1.37 Wheelchair space requirements.

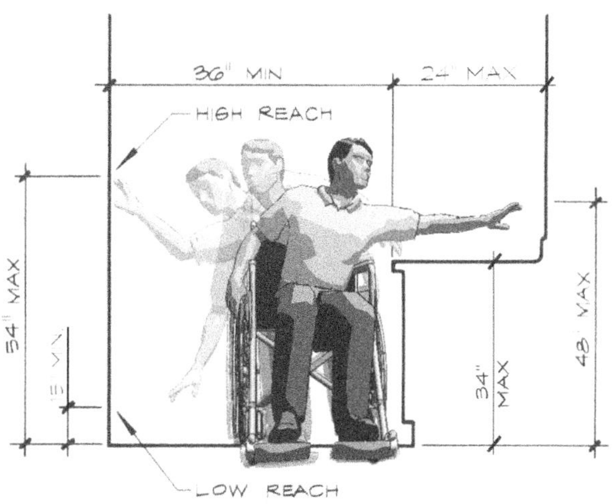

Figure 1.38 Wheelchair space requirements.

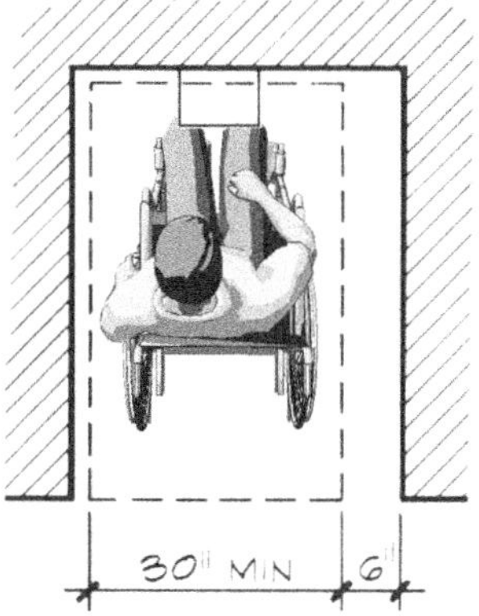

Figure 1.39 Wheelchair space requirements.

outlets, and the like will have to be located within these reach limitations. Figure 1.41 illustrates such controls. Another concern in regard to reach limitations is accessibility to the bookshelves found in educational and library facilities. Figure 1.42 illustrates maximum shelf heights and passage dimensions for various types of aisles.

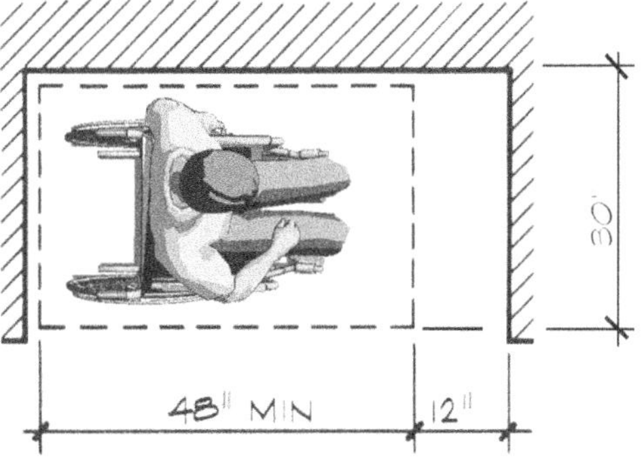

Figure 1.40 Wheelchair space requirements.

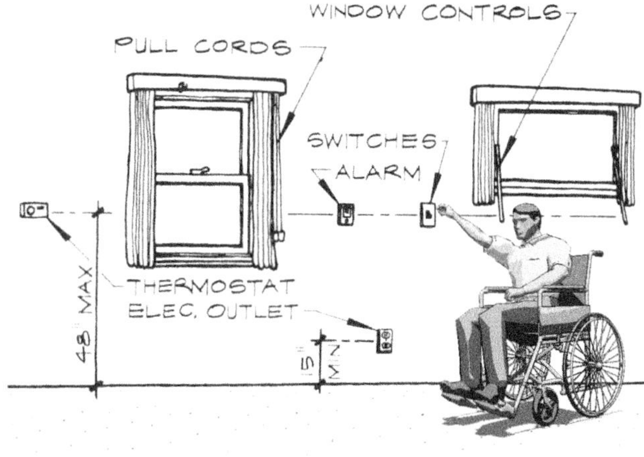

Figure 1.41 Control heights.

The maneuvering capabilities of a person in a wheelchair are important considerations when dealing with accessibility of doors and doorways. These capabilities determine the minimum required floor-plan dimensions. An example of a floor-plan configuration involving a door and doorway access is depicted in Figure 1.43. Note that the door clearance does not include the door thickness or any hardware. Door-swing direction in access corridors will be dictated by required minimum clearances for maneuvering a wheelchair to access doors. If building code requirements specify that certain doors have to swing into corridors, then corridor dimensions may have to be adjusted to satisfy wheelchair clearances. Figure 1.44 illustrates two examples of door-swing directions that affect the dimensional width of a corridor.

Access doors and the various hardware assemblies required for their functioning must also meet certain requirements. For example, regulations confine the selection of door handle hardware to a lever-type U-shaped handle with a minimum and maximum

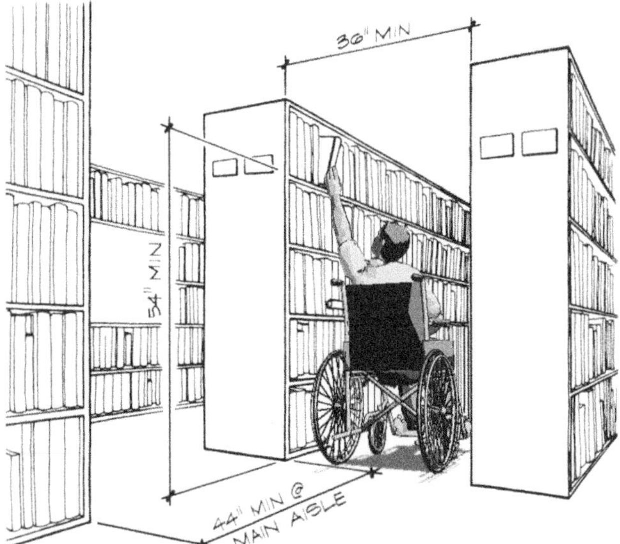

Figure 1.42 Shelf heights.

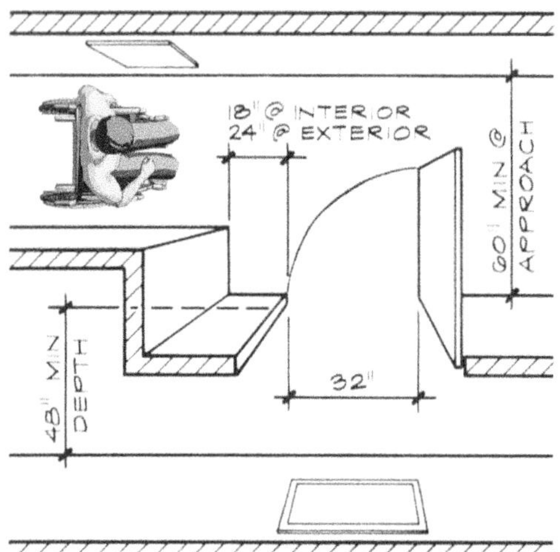

Figure 1.43 Doorway maneuvering clearances.

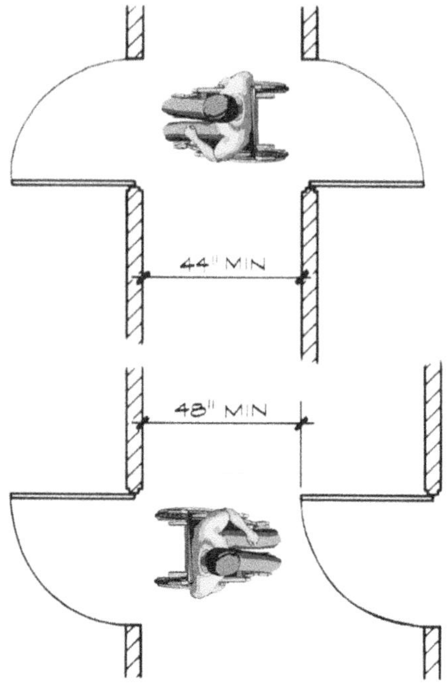

Figure 1.44 Doorway maneuvering clearances.

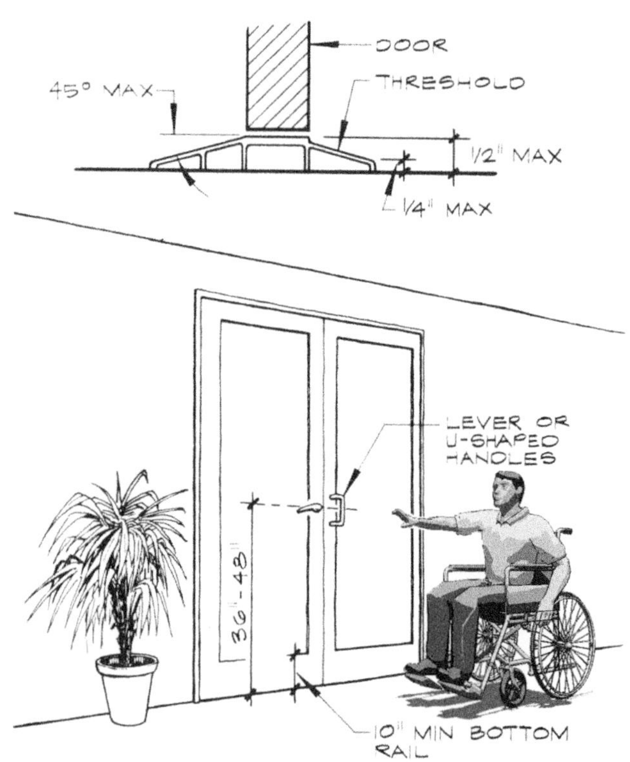

Figure 1.45 Threshold and door hardware.

dimensional location above the floor. Similarly, the slopes and heights of door thresholds must satisfy accessibility requirements. An illustration of hardware for door handles and an example of an acceptable threshold are shown in Figure 1.45.

When planning drinking fountain locations, the architect will have to be aware of minimum required dimensions for recessed or projected installations. Figure 1.46 provides a view of these two types of installation, illustrating dimensional clearances as well as the maximum height to the spout and clearance for knee space.

An important facet of the building design process is the provision of accessible plumbing facilities that accommodate persons with disabilities. These facilities, which include such fixtures as water closets, lavatories, and urinals, are planned to ensure accessibility for those who have disabilities. A floor plan must be designed to provide at least the minimum required space clearances and accessibility to specific plumbing fixtures. Figure 1.47 illustrates an overall pictorial view of a proposed restroom facility that incorporates minimum access clearances for the various plumbing fixtures. Note the required grab bar

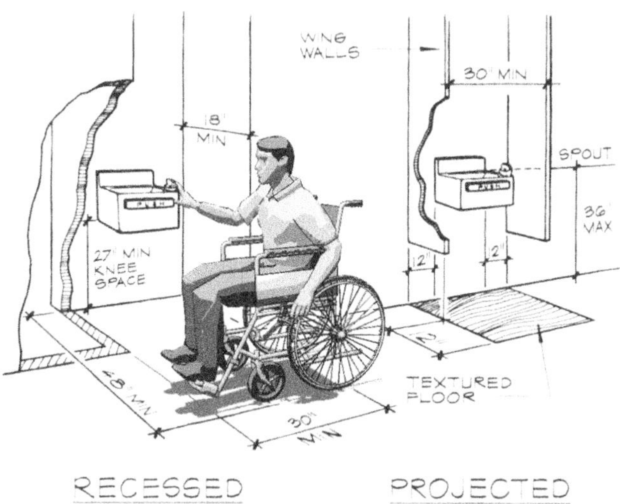

Figure 1.46 Drinking fountains.

sizes and locations relative to the water closet. The installation of the various plumbing fixtures is regulated with reference to their dimensional height above the floor, side-wall clearances, and knee and toe spaces for the use of lavatories. See Figure 1.48.

Note that hot-water and drain pipes are required to be insulated to protect against contact. Lavatory clearances are most important, because the knee will project under the lavatory fixture and will therefore require additional clearance. For a clearer illustration of the required clearances beneath the lavatory; see Figure 1.49. In planning for accessibility to toilet compartments, the location of the door to the compartment will dictate the required fixture layout. See Figure 1.50.

These illustrations are examples of the elements within a public building that the architect must plan for in order to accommodate persons with disabilities.

We have included a few samples of CDs (partial plans and elevations) showing how ADA information must be displayed and what types of notes might accompany the drawings. If these drawings confuse you, try reading Chapter 6 on floor plans, and Chapter 9 on exterior and interior elevations, before looking at these sample plans, elevations, and notes again.

Typically, notes such as the ones seen in Figure 1.53 would be found adjacent to the images found in Figures 1.51 and 1.52. It is also possible that the notes could be included in the specification section of the architectural documents.

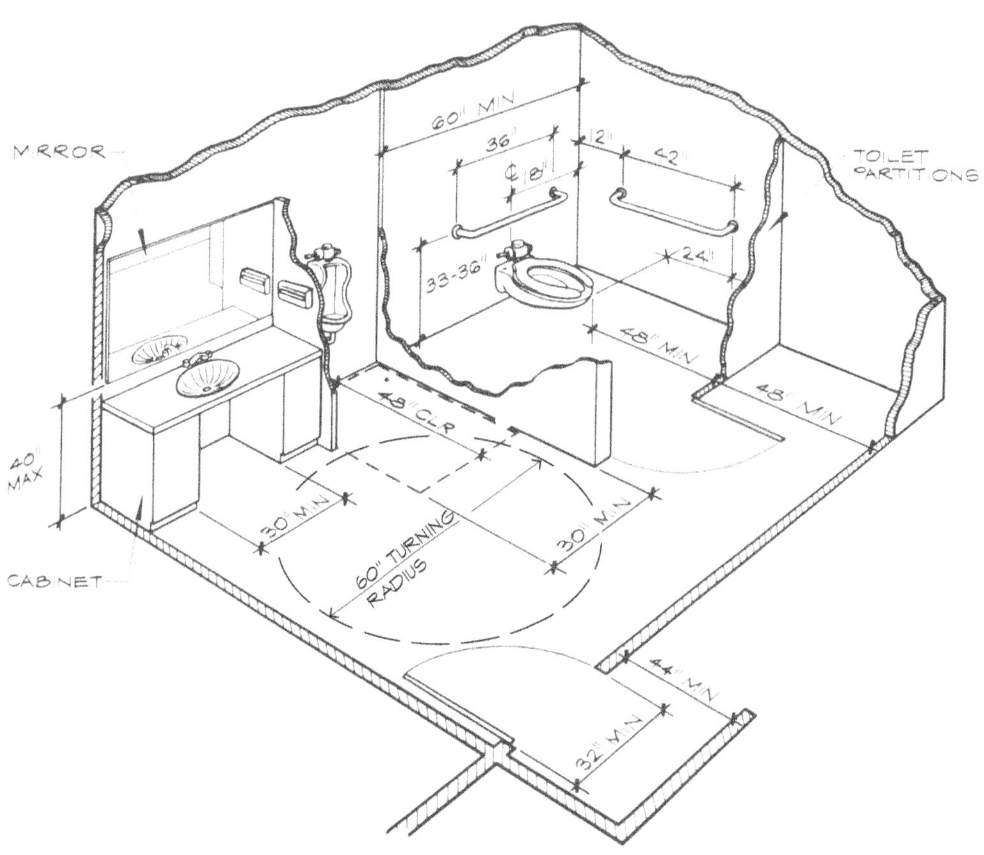

Figure 1.47 Restroom facilities.

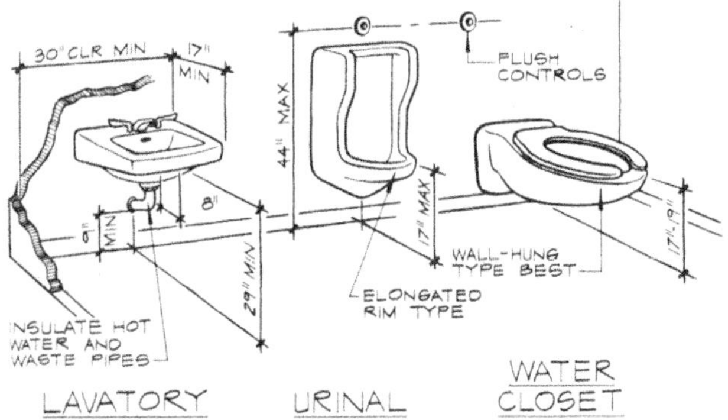

Figure 1.48 Plumbing fixtures.

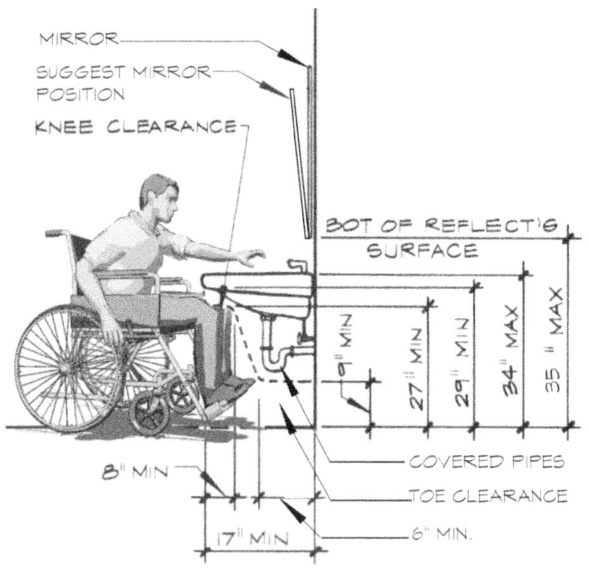

Figure 1.49 Lavatory access.

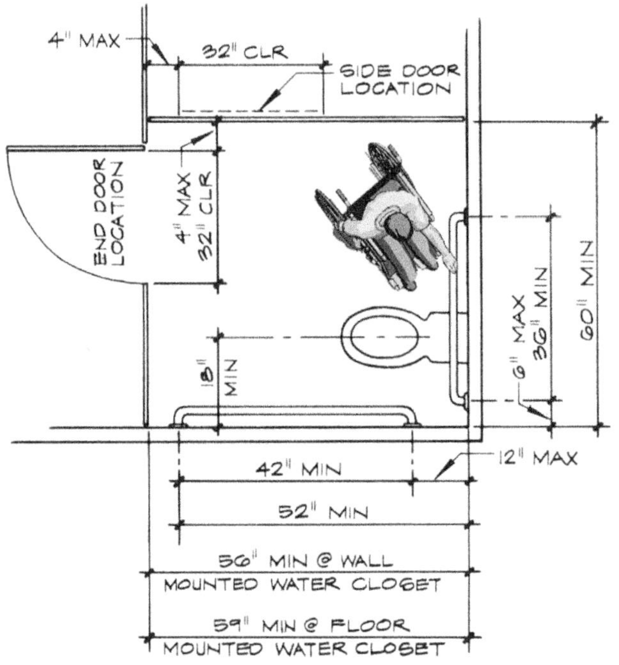

Figure 1.50 Toilet compartment plan.

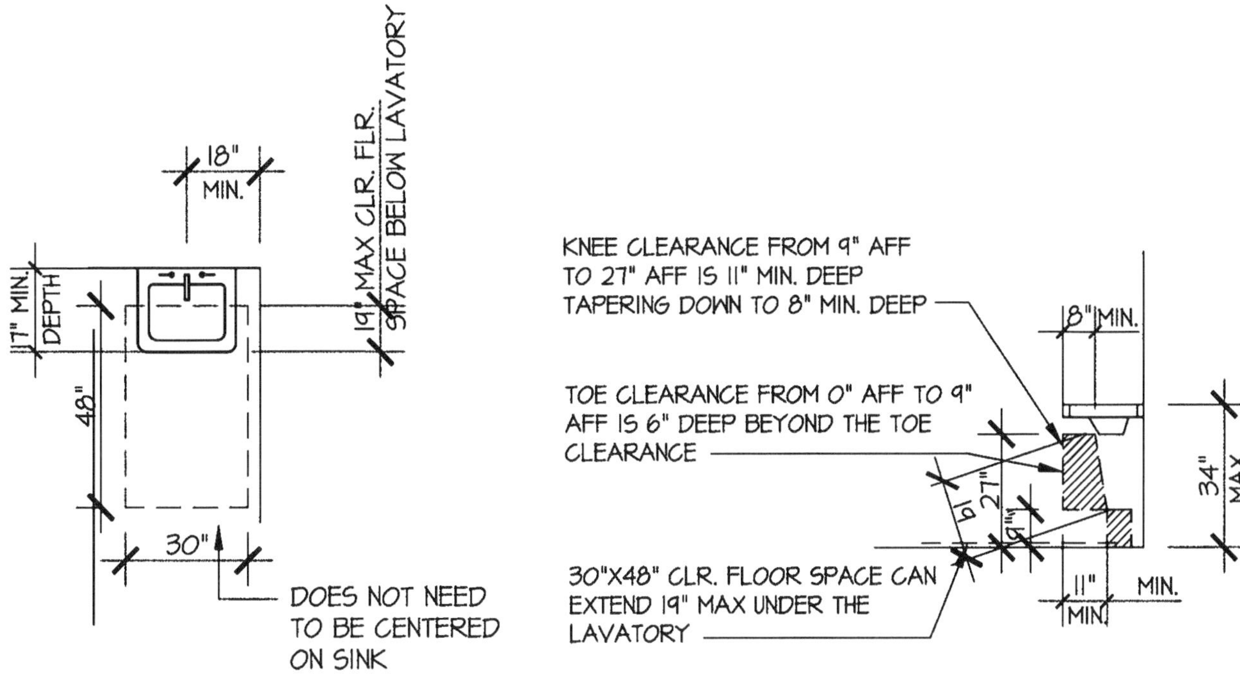

Figure 1.51 Lavatory drawings and specifications.

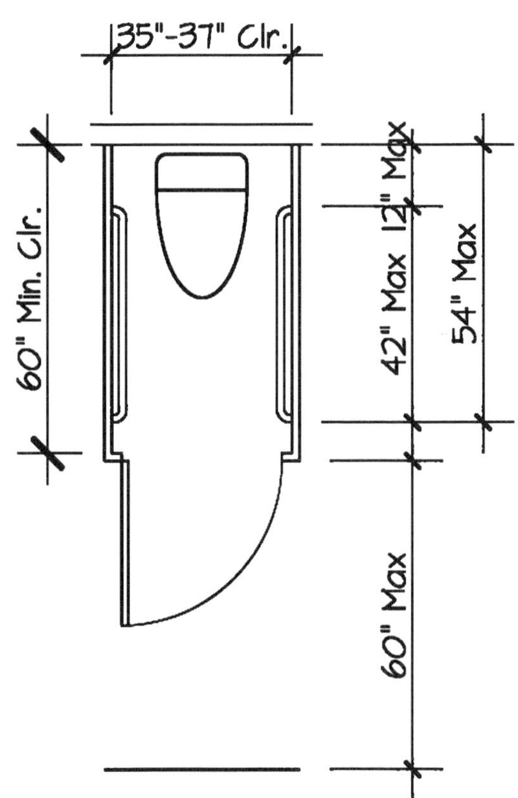

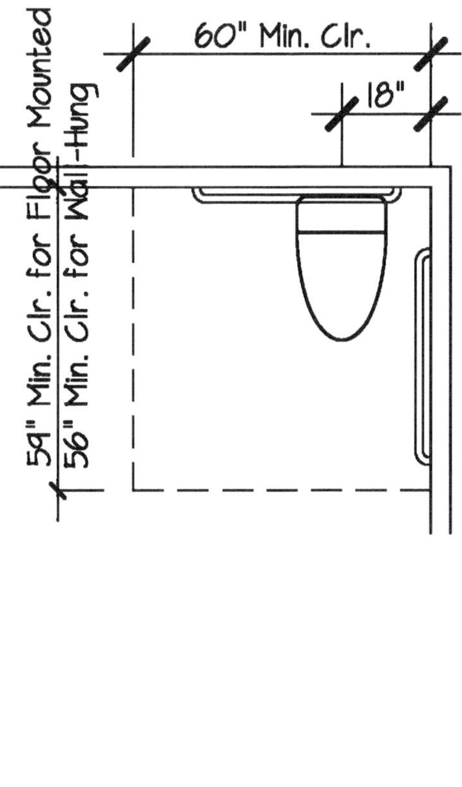

Figure 1.52 Construction documents for a water closet (ambulatory).

Notes:

Lavatory:
- All drain and hot-water pipes under the lavatory must be insulated or covered with a boot or shield to prevent contact.
- All sharp and abrasive surfaces under the lavatory must be covered to prevent contact.
- Doors should not swing into the required clear space.

Faucets:
- Faucets must be operable with one hand and should not require tight grasping, pinching, or twisting of the wrist; lever-operated, push-type, and electronically controlled faucets need to be ADA compliant.
- Force necessary to operate faucet controls is 5 pounds maximum.
- Self-closing valves are to remain open for 10 seconds maximum.

Water Closet:
- Toilet (single or multiple accommodations):
  - Toilet is located 18″ from the side wall to its centerline.
  - Flush valve is located on wide side of toilet.
  - Flush valve requires 5 pounds of maximum force to operate, is operable with one hand, and does not require tight grasping, pinching, or twisting of the wrist.
  - The top of the seat is 17″–19″ above the finish floor (AFF).
  - The seat does not automatically spring into an open position.
  - The toilet paper dispenser allows for a continuous paper flow and does not control delivery.
  - The toilet paper dispenser is located between 7″ and 9″ from the front of the toilet to the center of the dispenser and 15″–8″ AFF.
- Single accommodation toilet:
  - Provide a turning space of 60″ diameter in the restroom, with a clearance height of 27″ minimum.
  - Above the finish floor, the turning space can overlap clear spaces of other fixtures, and doors can swing into the turning space.
  - Or provide a "T"-shaped turning space of 60″ × 60″ with two 12″ × 24″ notches; the turning space can overlap clear spaces of other fixtures and can use the 27″ clear height for knee and toe clearance on one side only.
  - Doors cannot swing into the required clear space of any fixture.
  - Operable parts of hardware are located 34″–45″ AFF.
  - Doors within 10″ AFF should have smooth kick plates the full width and 10″ high.
  - Provide one minimum accessible lavatory.
  - If separate restrooms are provided for each sex, then an accessible restroom should be provided for each sex.
  - If a unisex restroom is provided, it should be accessible.

Figure 1.53 Minimum requirements for fixtures, door, and clearance.

Key Terms

American Institute of Architects (AIA)
Americans with Disabilities Act (ADA)
Architecture Registration Examination (ARE)
building information modeling (BIM)
computer-aided drafting (CAD)
construction administration (CA)
construction documents (CD)
corporation
design development (DD)
egress travel
human resources (HR)
internship
Intern Development Program (IDP)
Leadership in Energy and Environmental Design (LEED)
MasterFormat
National Architectural Accrediting Board (NAAB)
National Council of Architectural Registration Boards (NCARB)
partnership
program, programing
project architect
punch list
redlines
requests for information (RFIs)
schematic design (SD)
sole proprietorship
space planning

chapter

2

STANDARDS AND TECHNIQUES

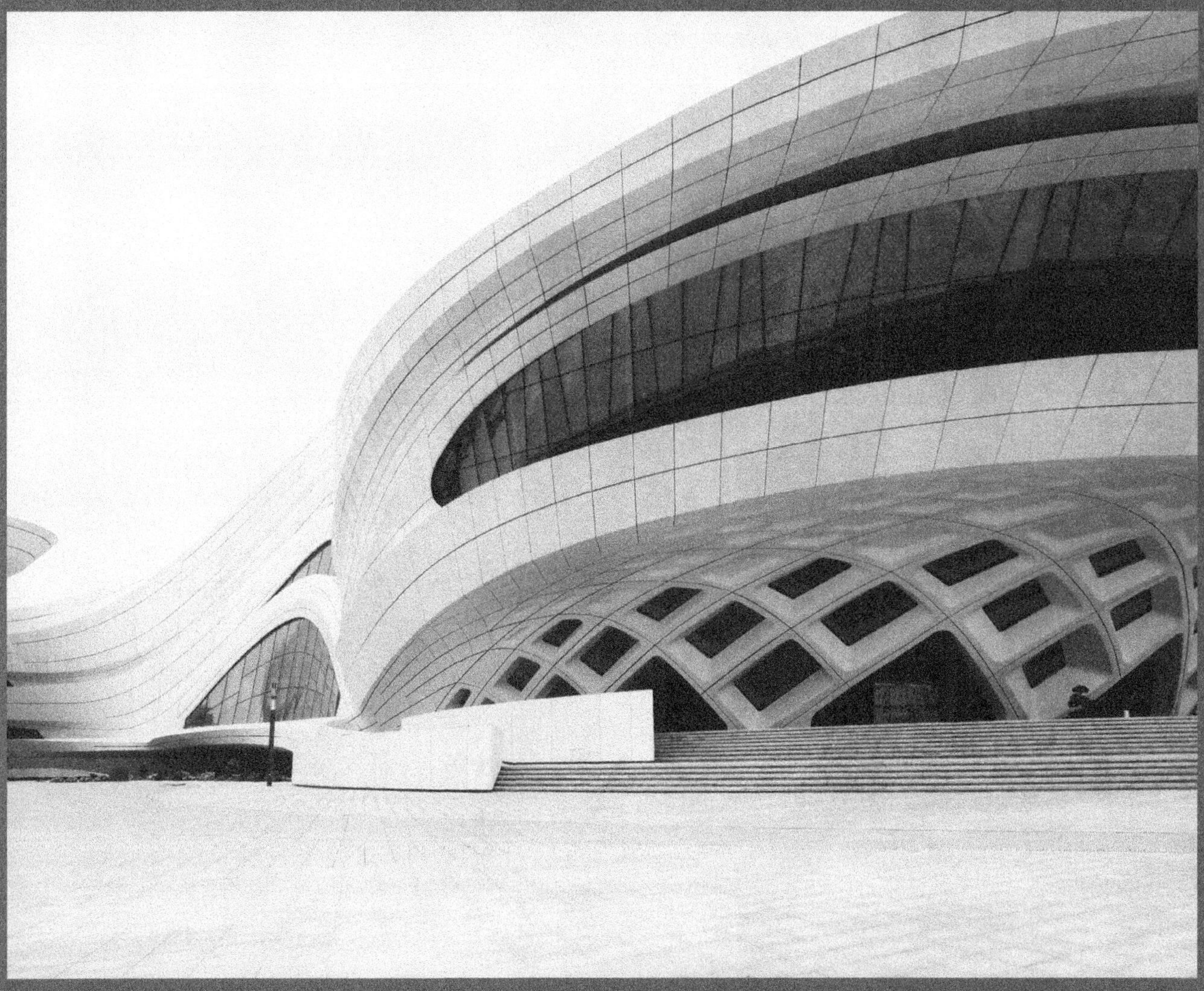

(Frankie/Unsplash.)

The Professional Practice of Architectural Working Drawings, Sixth Edition. Nagy R. Bakhoum and Osamu A. Wakita.
© 2024 John Wiley & Sons Inc. Published 2024 by John Wiley & Sons Inc.
Companion website: www.wiley.com\go\bakhoum\theprofessionalpracticeofarchitecturalworkingdrawings

OFFICE STANDARDS

Standards and techniques are used to create a uniform system both nationally and internationally. This action maintains a uniform approach throughout our profession, while maintaining control over the drawings, and ensures craftsmanship and workmanship in architecture.

These standards are based on the American Institute of Architects (AIA) standards prescribed here and throughout the text.

This chapter covers four points:

1. Hand drafting and equipment
2. Computer-aided drafting (CAD) & building information modeling (BIM)
3. Understanding the vocabulary of our profession
4. Building materials and methods

The process of architectural technology is continually changing, from hand drafting to BIM, and even in the technical aspects of architecture such as the use of new materials and methods of construction, which have an impact on the way information is organized.

FREEHAND AND HAND DRAFTING

Any new idea for assembly should be sketched (freehand) and studied before it is hard-lined manually or drafted on the computer. These detail sketches **(design sketches)** are then sent to the drafter to draw formally. This ability to sketch and communicate puts the employee at a management/supervision level, not at the design level. When we refer to freehand detail, scale is still used, especially at critical intersections.

Drafting. Manual drafting also develops many positive attributes and skills that are needed to sustain employees in the future. These come in the form of:

Patience. Drafting manually produces a high degree of understanding of one's own limits and timing.

Flexibility. CAD drafters possessing manual drafting skills are more flexible in their ability to create drawings.

Presentational drawings. Many CAD drafters are not proficient in the use of standard drafting equipment. Thus, they are not effective in formatting and producing presentation boards and cutting mats.

Basic Equipment. The drafting tools needed by a beginning draftsperson and the basic uses of those tools are shown in Figure 2.1 and are as follows:

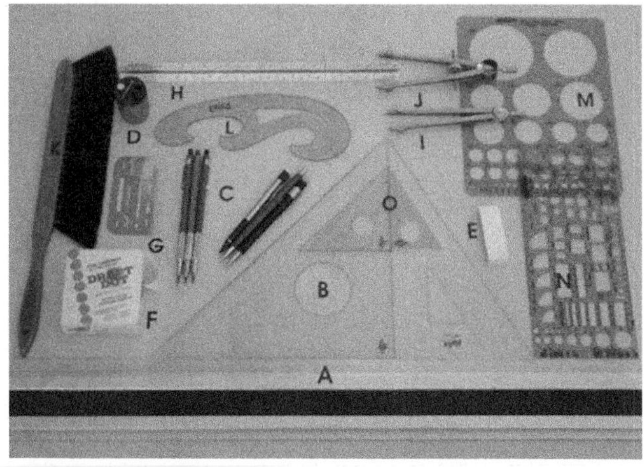

Figure 2.1 Basic drafting equipment.

- **A. Parallel bar.** A straightedge used to draft horizontal lines and base for the use of triangles. Runs on a wire cable at the sides of the bar.
- **B. Triangle.** A three-sided guide used in conjunction with a parallel bar to draft vertical lines and angular lines. The 30°/60° and 45° triangles are basic equipment.
- **C. Drafting pencil and lead holders.** Housing for drafting leads.
- **D. Lead pointer.** A device used to sharpen the lead in a lead holder.
- **E. Dusting brush.** A brush used to keep drafting surfaces clean and free of debris/**Eraser.** A rubber or synthetic material used to erase errors and correct drawings.
- **F. Drafting dots.** Circular-shaped tape/**drafting tape.** Tape used to hold paper while drafting.
- **G. Erasing shield.** A metal or plastic card with pre-punched slots and holes used to protect some portions of a drawing while erasing others.
- **H. Scale.** A measuring device calibrated in a variety of units for ease of translating large objects into a small proportional drawing.
- **I. Divider.** A device resembling a compass, used mainly for transferring measurements from one location to another.
- **J. Compass.** A V-shaped device for drafting arcs and circles.
- **K. French curve.** A pattern used to draft irregular arcs.
- **L. Circle template.** A pre-punched sheet of plastic punched in various sizes, for use as a pattern for circles without using a compass.
- **M. Plan template.** Pre-punched patterns for shapes commonly found in architectural plans.
- **N. Triangle, small.** A three-sided guide used to draft vertical lines when lettering.

In addition to the tools previously listed, a number of others aid in and simplify the drafting process. They are shown in Figure 2.2.

1. **Parallel bar.** Straightedge.
2. **Adjustable triangle.** A triangle used to draft odd angles such as those found in the pitch (slope) of a roof.

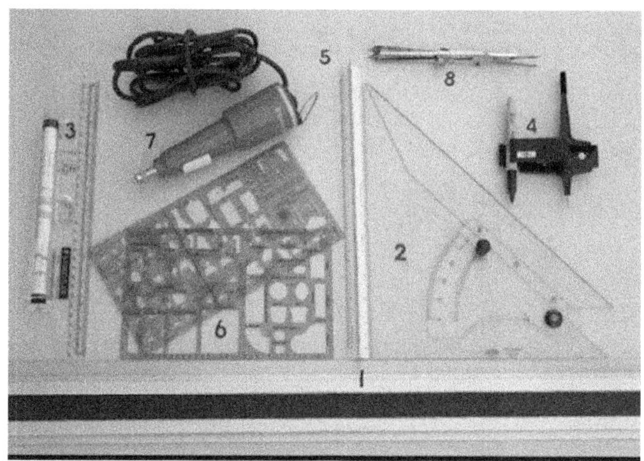

Figure 2.2 Additional drafting equipment.

Figure 2.3 Parallel straightedge.

3. **Rolling ruler.** Draws horizontal, angular, and vertical lines, has a protractor function, and can be used as a compass.
4. **Clip compass.** Can be used to hold cutting knives, pencils, inking devices, paintbrushes, felt pens, and the like. Has a 9″ diameter capacity.
5. **Metric rule.** Scale for international work.
6. **Specialty templates.** Include furniture, trees, electrical and mechanical equipment, geometric shapes, and standard symbols. Enables the drafter to show, for example, plumbing fixtures in elevation.
7. **Electric eraser.** Particularly useful when one is working with erasable sepias or ink. Models available include hard-wired, battery-operated, and portable (with power charger).
8. **Proportional dividers.** Used to enlarge or reduce a drawing to any proportion. Many have golden mean proportions.

Figure 2.3 shows the correct way of using a straightedge. The lead holder is being rotated as a horizontal line is drawn.

Using Triangles. Triangles are generally used in conjunction with a straightedge such as a parallel bar, a T-square, or even another triangle (see Figure 2.4). A combination of triangles can produce 15° and 75° lines in addition to a perpendicular 90° angle, a 45° line, and 30° and 60° lines.

Using Erasing Shields and Erasers to Draw Dotted Lines. Dotted lines, which are usually called **hidden lines** in drafting, can be drawn rapidly by using an erasing shield and an eraser. An electric eraser is more effective than a regular eraser.

First, draw the line as if it were a solid line, using the correct pressure to produce the desired darkness. Second, lay the erasing shield over the line so that the row of uniformly drilled holes on the shield aligns with the solid line. Next, erase through the small holes. The results will be a uniform and rapidly produced hidden (dotted) line.

This technique is particularly effective for foundation plans, which use many hidden lines.

Using the Scale. The most convenient scale to purchase is a triangular scale, because it gives the greatest variety in a single instrument. There are usually eleven scales on a triangle scale, one of which is an ordinary 12″ ruler.

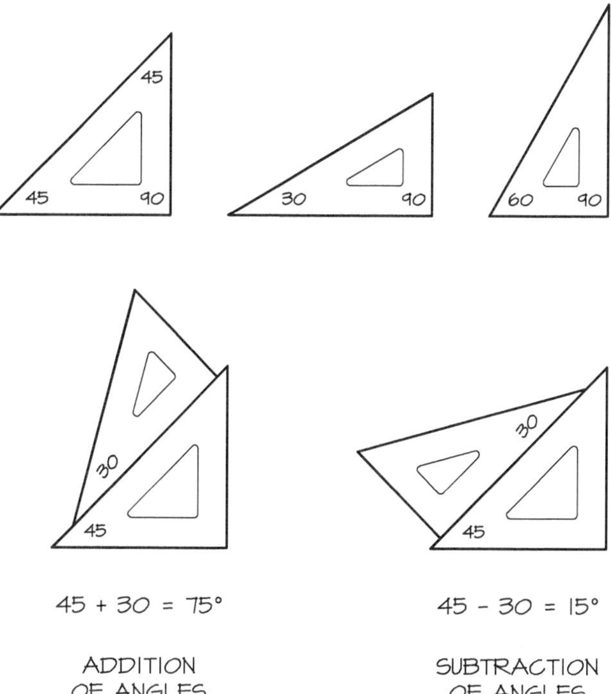

Figure 2.4 Triangles and combinations of triangles.

If you look at a triangular scale (see Figure 2.5A), you will see a side marked 16 on the edge. It measures 12 inches using 1/16″ increments. If you can read this, you can read the rest of the information printed on the tool.

Let us say you were assigned to do a drawing at 1/8″ = 1′-0″. This means that 12 inches is now equal to 1/8 inch. So let us look at Figure 2.5B. One-eighth of an inch has been printed as a 12″ ruler as shown by "X." The area next to this 12″ ruler ("X") has large numbers on it starting with "0" and small numbers in between. We must stay with the small numbers. Note that from "0" to the 12 has been marked as "Y." If you wanted 12′-6″, you would first measure the "Y" and then add the 6″ or half of the "X" area.

The large numbers previously mentioned belong to the 1/4″ scale, shown in Figure 2.5C. In this instance, the "Y" area measures 6′-0″ and additional inches can be added from the 12″ scale marked "X."

The most difficult scale to comprehend is the 3″ scale. It is not listed as a fraction, as this might confuse you in the beginning (see Figure 2.5D). The "X" on this figure shows the length corresponding to 12 inches; just like a 12″ ruler. A 3″ scale is also called 1/4″ (quarter) scale, not to be mistaken for a 1/4″ scale. Other scales are:

3/12″ on one end and 3/16″ on the other
1 1/2″ on one end and 3″ on the other
3/4″ on one end and 3/8″ on the other

It is easy to make an error by reading the wrong number, because the "32" on the 1/8″ scale is so close to the "32" on the 1/4″ scale. Similar pitfalls occur in other pairs of scales on the triangle scale.

Using Drafting Tape. A simple but effective method of taping original drawings is to keep the edges of the tape parallel with the edges of the **vellum** (a translucent, high-quality tracing paper), as shown in Figure 2.6. This prevents the straightedge from catching the corner of the tape and rolling it off. Drafting supply stores sell tape in a round shape (dot), which is even better.

Rolling Original Drawings. Most beginners begin rolling drawings in the wrong direction. In their attempt to protect the drawings, they often roll the print or the original so that the printed side is on the *inside,* as shown in Figure 2.7B. However, the correct way is to roll the sheet so that the artwork is on the *outside,* as shown in Figure 2.7A.

When a set of prints is unrolled and read, the drawings should roll toward the table and should not interfere with easy reading by curling up. If originals are rolled correctly, the vellum curls toward the drafting table, preventing it from being torn when drafting equipment slides across it or when it is being reproduced.

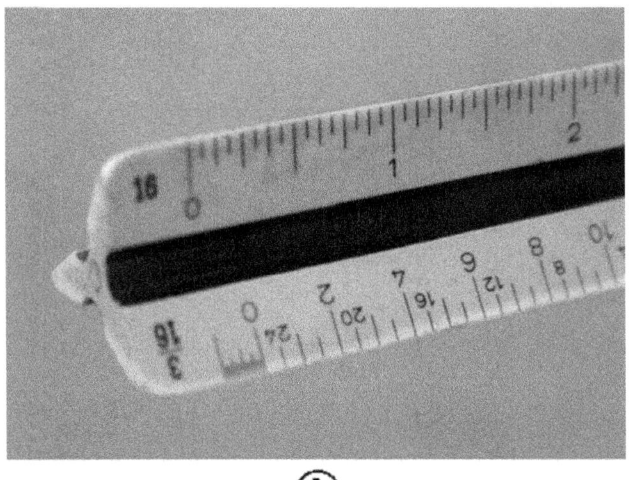

(A)

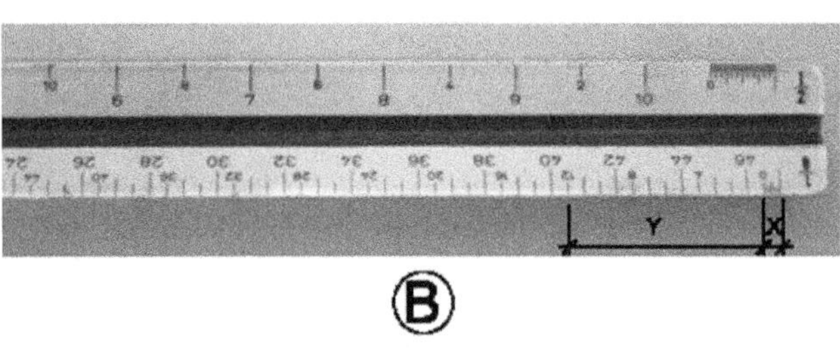

(B)

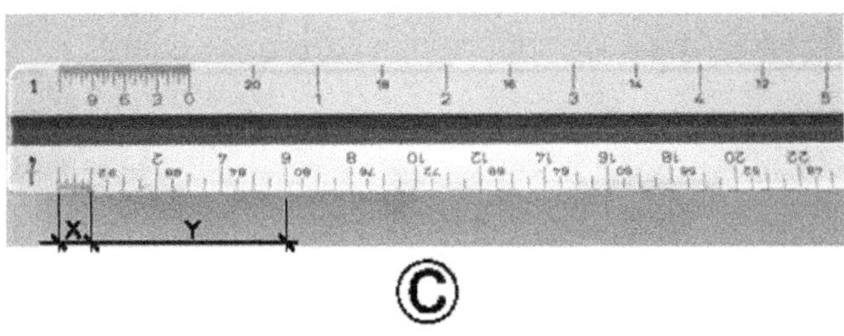

(C)

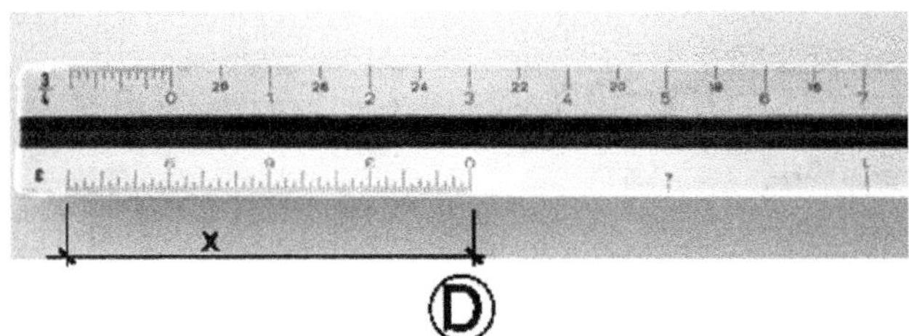

(D)

Figure 2.5 Reading a scale.

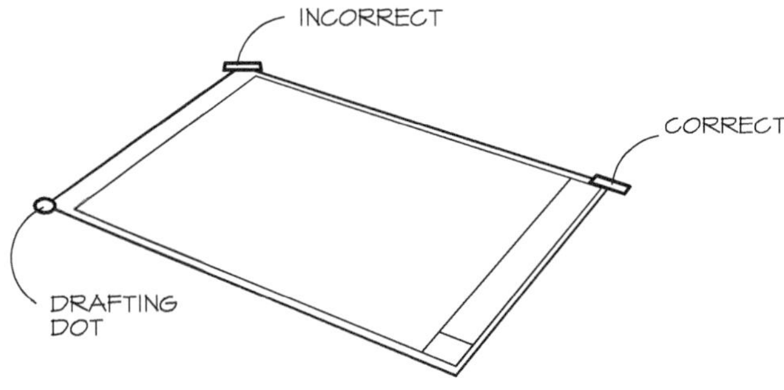

Figure 2.6 Correct placement of drafting tape.

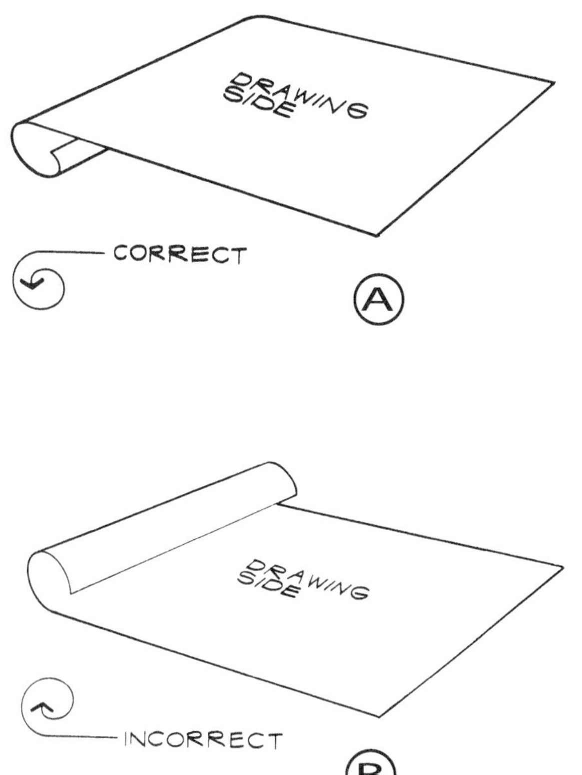

Figure 2.7 A. Correct way to roll a drawing. B. Incorrect way to roll a drawing.

Types of Leads. Harder leads are given an "H" designation, whereas softer leads are given a designation of "B." Between the "H" and "B" range are "HB" and "F" leads. (See Figure 2.8.)

Only the central range of leads is used for drafting. 2H, 3H, and 4H are good for drafting, while H is good for a medium and dark object lines.

However, many other factors also determine the choice of pencil. Temperature and humidity may dictate that certain leads be used. Also, the natural pressure that the drafter places on the pencil varies from individual to individual.

Pencils Versus Lead Holders. Wood pencils are fine, but serious drafting requires mechanical lead holders. See Figure 2.9. Wood pencils do not hold the point shape as long and require sharpening more often which is time consuming. More important, a lead holder allows you the full use of the lead, whereas a wood pencil does not.

A **lead pointer** is a tool used to sharpen drafting leads. Sandpaper can be used for both wood pencils and lead holders, but it is not nearly as convenient, consistent, or rapid as a lead pointer. Take the sharpened lead and hold the pointer perpendicular to a hard surface such as a triangle; crush the tip of the lead slightly; then hone the tip by drawing a series of circular lines on a piece of scratch paper. This stops the lead from breaking on the first stroke. Roll the pencil as you draw to keep a consistent tip on the lead. Draw either clockwise or counterclockwise, depending on whichever produces the best line and is the most comfortable for you. Note the position of your fingers and thumb at the beginning and end of the line.

Computer Drafting. CAD has significantly affected the field of architecture. This section does not instruct you on how to use the computer or the various CAD programs (there are books solely devoted to CAD that do), but rather teaches you how CAD programs can best be used to become an effective tool in an architectural office.

CAD does *not* refer to what the computer allows you to do; rather, it refers to the process of taking the conventions, symbols, and the drawing dimensions and incorporating them into the computer to be adjusted for the task at hand. Literally, we are talking about design that uses the computer as just another tool, albeit a very powerful and convenient one. In this section, we discuss:

Lines and Line Quality

Lines can be broken down into three types: light, medium, and dark. Each of these types can be broken down further by variation of pressure and lead or computer line thickness.

Light lines are drawn for less significant data or background items. The lightest lines used are usually the guidelines drawn to help with lettering height or organizational lines that help align portions of the design. These lines should be only barely visible and

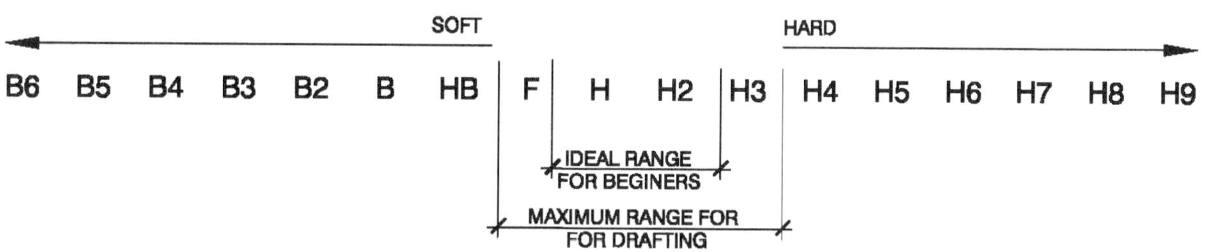

Figure 2.8 Lead hardness.

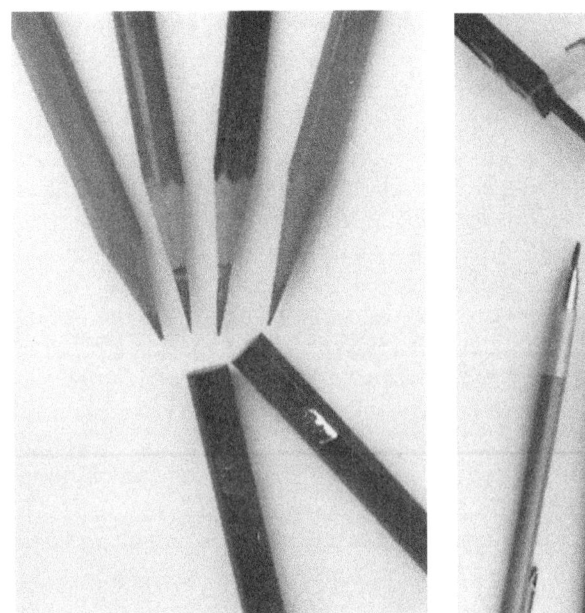

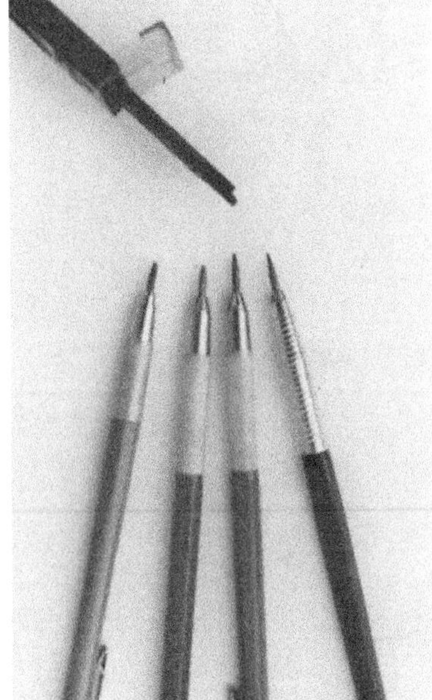

Figure 2.9 Types of lead holders and pencils.

should completely disappear when the final output is plotted. See Figure 2.10A. At the darker end of the light line spectrum are lines for door swings or other less significant objects.

Medium-weight lines are used for dimension lines and extension leaders. Leaders and break lines also use medium-weight lines. See Figure 2.10B. They can also be used for such nonstructural components as bath fixtures, cabinets, or other similar objects. The majority of the lines on an architectural set are medium quality lines.

Medium to dark (darkest of this group) lines are used to describe objects (object lines) and for centerlines. Medium to slight dark lines are used for hidden or dashed lines and utilized to make more emphasis to an object. See Figure 2.10C.

The darkest lines are used to profile objects, for border lines or for cutting plane lines. See Figure 2.10D. Walls or structural components of a building would be at the lighter end of the spectrum of dark lines, but darker than most of the lines other than the aforementioned.

Line quality depends on the use of that particular line. An intense line is used to profile and emphasize, an intermediate line is used to show elements such as walls and structural members, and a light line is used for elements such as dimensioning and door swings.

Another way to vary line quality is to increase the width of the line. A thicker line can represent the walls on a floor plan, the outline of a building on a site plan, or the outline of a roof on a roof plan. For line-quality examples and uses, see Figure 2.11, which shows a sample of the types of lines used to indicate property lines and easements. See the clarity of the drawing produced, it demonstrates

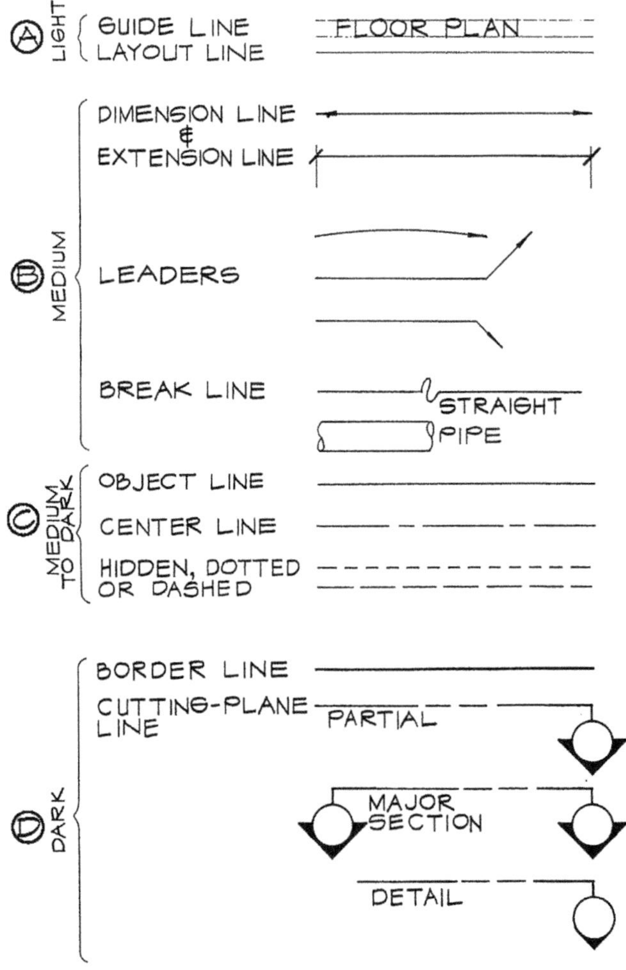

Figure 2.10 Vocabulary of architectural lines.

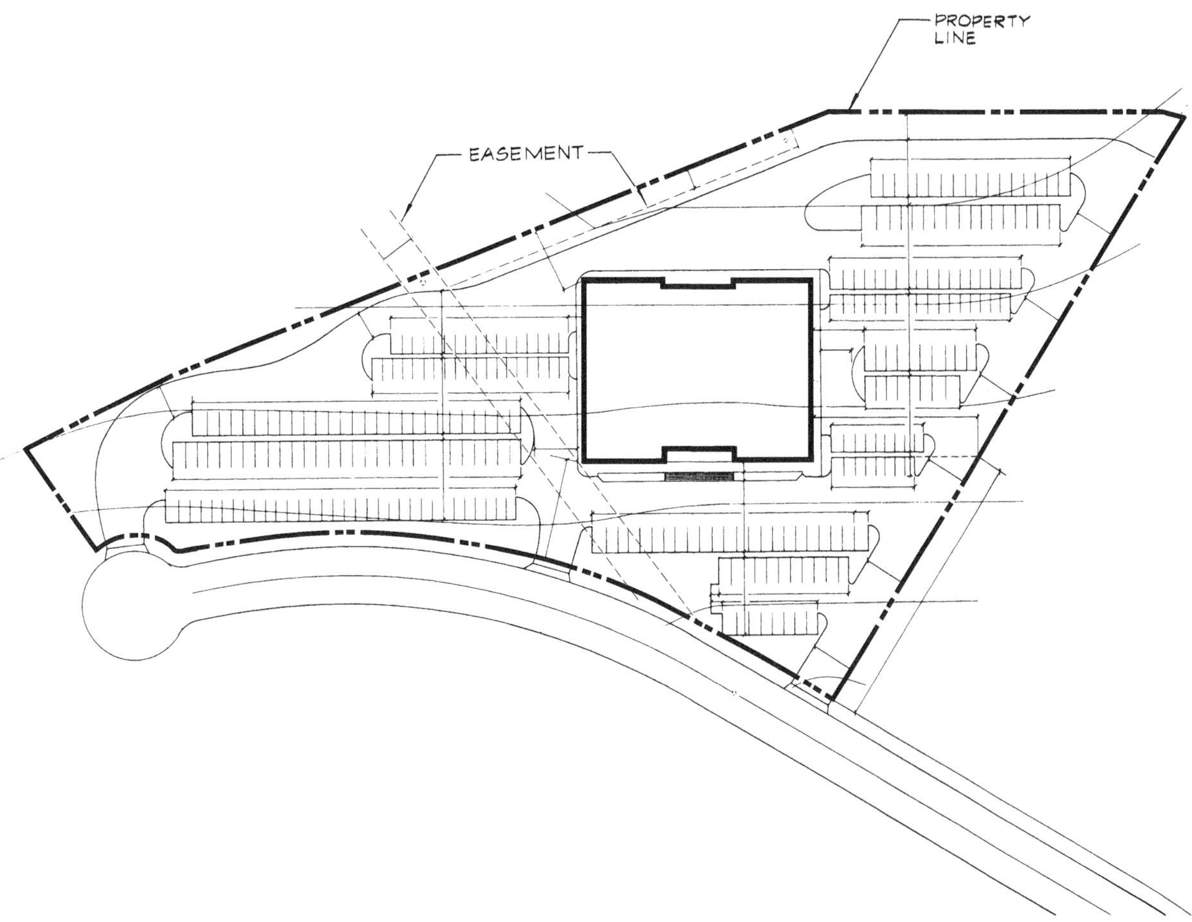

Figure 2.11 Types of lines used for property lines and easements.

that dark lines communicate important features and lighter lines become secondary to the viewer of the drawings.

Hidden or dotted lines are used to indicate objects hidden from view. They can be items that either above or below the viewing plane of the plan. Solid objects covered by earth, such as foundations, can be indicated with hidden lines. This type of line can also depict future structures, items that are not in the contract, public utility locations, easements, a wheelchair turning radius, or the direction of sliding doors and windows. Such lines are often used to delineate walls that are to be removed or demolished.

A floor plan will often show the roof outline, a balcony above, or a change in ceiling height with a dotted line. On a site plan, dotted lines indicate the existing grades on the site. A hidden line on a kitchen floor plan indicates the upper cabinets that are hidden from view since the cutting plane is lower than the upper cabinets, the hidden line will indicate that there is an object, unseen, above the cutting plan in this instance.

Different types of arrowheads are used in dimensioning. These are shown in Figure 2.12. The top one is used architecturally for leaders and dimensioning radial arcs more often than for dimension lines. The second one, with the dark tick mark, is the arrowhead most prevalently used in our field. The dot is used in conjunction with the tick mark when you are dimensioning two systems. For example, the dot can be used to locate the center of steel columns, and the tick mark can be used to dimension the secondary structure within a building built of a varying material. The final wide arrowhead is used as a design arrowhead and in structural drawings indicating the duration of structural element.

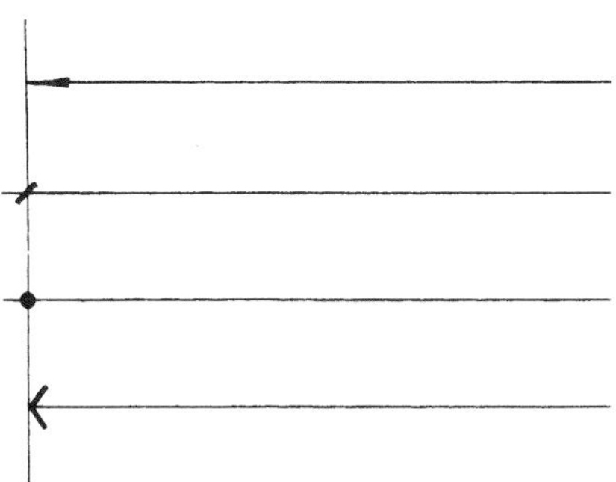

Figure 2.12 Types of arrowheads used in dimensioning.

Material designation lines are used to indicate the building material used. See Figure 2.13 for a sample of tapered or lighter lines. (This device saves time; complete lines take longer to draw.) In BIM material designations are integral to the program but in some instances, these need to be changed to meet the office standard representation. Utilizing AutoCAD, a hatch pattern has to be selected to complete the image materiality. Also note the cross-hatched lines between the parallel lines that represent the wall thickness on Figure 2.14. These diagonal lines represent masonry. Hatch patterns can fill an entire area but you can limit or lighten the hatching if the drawing gets too busy or unclear.

Architectural **profiling** is the process of taking the most important features of a drawing and outlining or darkening them. Figure 2.15 shows four applications of this concept.

Example A illustrates the darkening of the lines that represent the walls of a floor plan. The dimension lines or extension lines are drawn as medium-weight lines not only to contrast with the walls but also to allow the walls of the particular floor plan to stand out.

In example B, a footing detail is profiled, because the concrete work is cut through and the outline is drawn darker than any other part of the detail. It signifies the most important portion of the specific drawing.

Example C shows the top portion, head, of a window. The light lines at the bottom of the detail represent the side, or jamb, of the window. Note how the head section is outlined and the interior parts plus the sides of the walls are drawn lightly. The light lines indicate objects that are farther away and not cut through and not as important as the other parts of the drawing.

Example D represents another form of profiling, called **poché,** which enhances the profile technique by using shading. The technique of using shading is limited to design drawings; in construction documents, poché on a wall indicates a bearing wall, or a new wall in an addition or alteration. This shading can be done by pencil shading or by hatching lines. Example B also uses this principle: In this instance, the dots and triangles that represent concrete in section are placed along the perimeter (near the profiled line) in greater quantity than toward the center.

In a section drawing, the items most often profiled are cut by the cutting plane line. A footing detail, for example, is nothing more than a theoretical knife (a cutting plane) cutting through the wall of the structure. The portion most often cut is the concrete, so it is profiled.

On an elevation, the main outline of the structure should be darkened. See Figure 2.16. This type of profiling is used to simplify the illusion of the elevation to show that the structure is basically an L-shaped structure and that one portion does actually project forward. This technique is used to pull you eye to the object that is most near to the viewer.

In the plan view, often the outline of the main structure is heavily outlined (profiled) in order to make the main area stand out more than any other feature of the property. See Figure 2.17 for a finished plan and elevation that have been properly profiled.

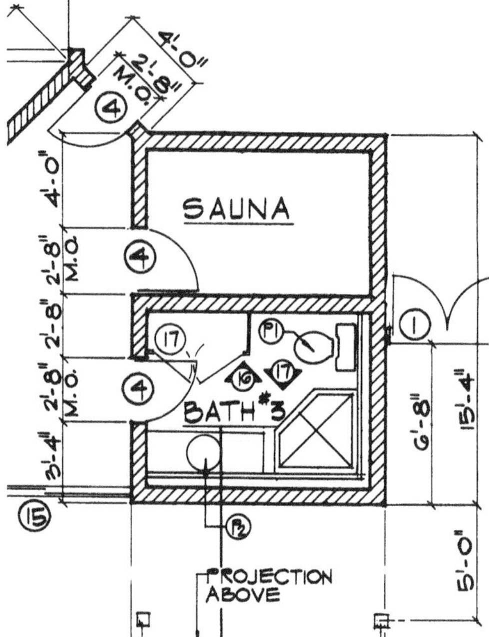

Figure 2.14 Lines representing masonry.

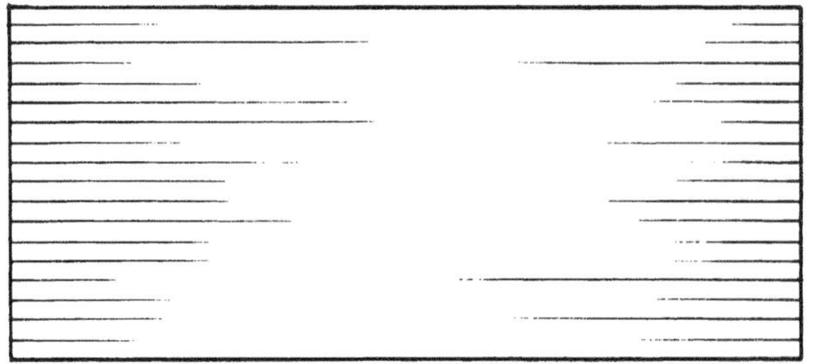

Figure 2.13 Tapered lines.

Lettering

Being able to hand letter well becomes very important to maintain accurately communicate by handwritten notes with an office and particularly when correcting drawings. This is especially true when correcting computer-generated construction documents. The process of noting items that need further work or corrections, redlining, is a critical portion of an architect's work. Additionally, if field notes are taken,

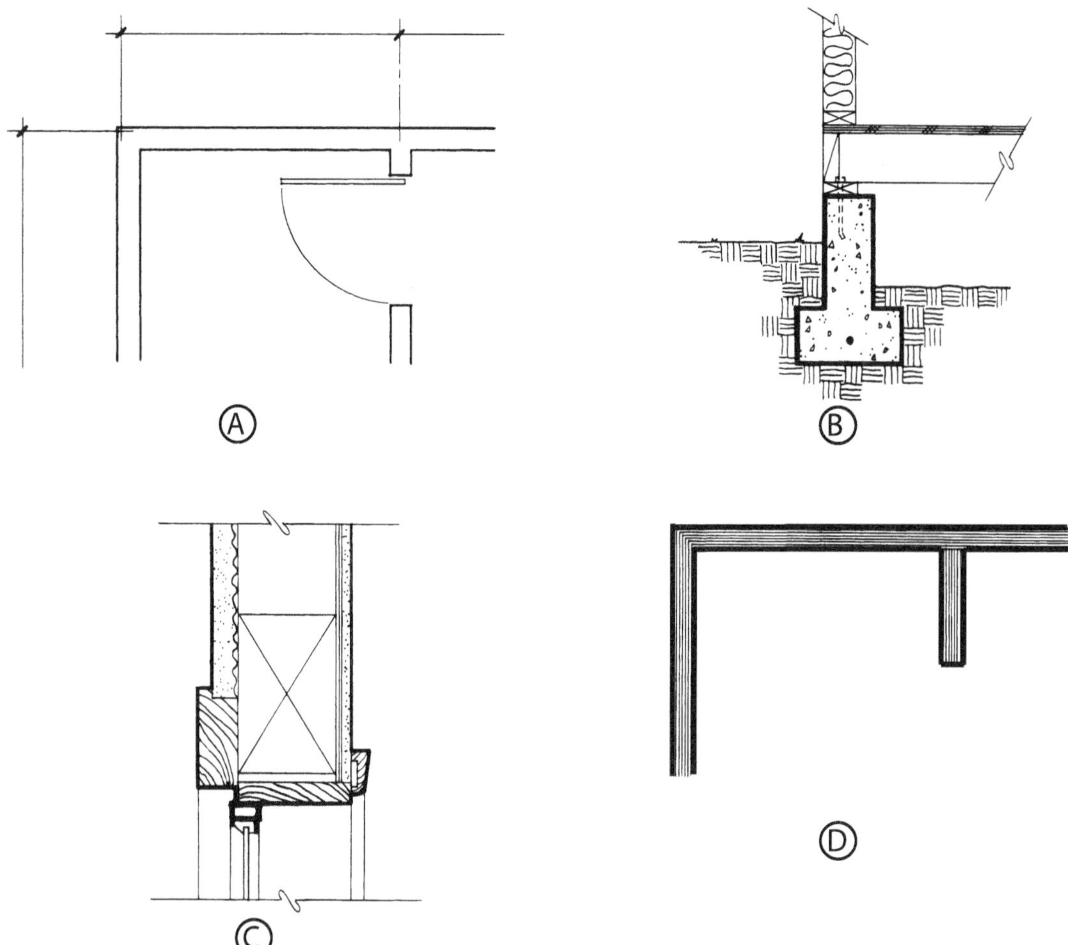

Figure 2.15 Profiling.

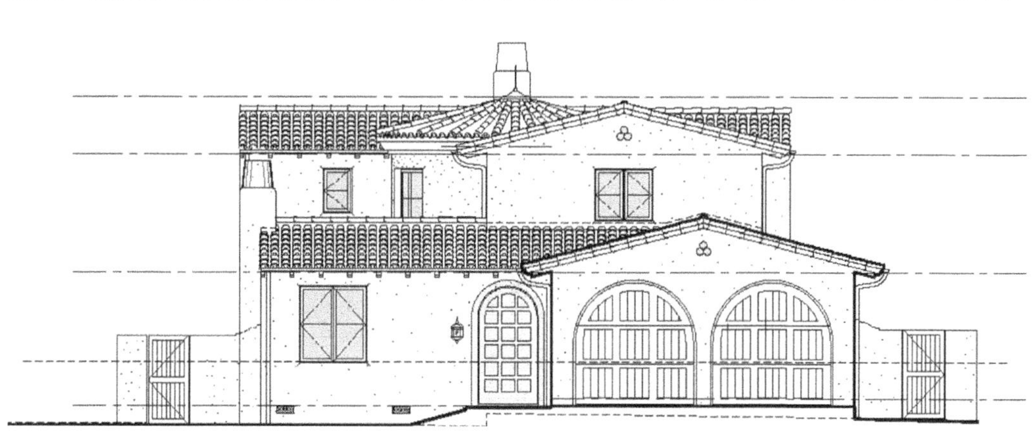

Figure 2.16 Correctly profiled elevation.

these notes are distributed to the client and the contractor for records sake.

Architectural lettering differs somewhat from the Gothic-type letters developed by C. W. Reinhardt about 90-plus years ago and now called *mechanical lettering*. Architectural lettering has evolved from a series of influences, including the demand for speed. We must not, however, interpret speed to mean or allow sloppiness.

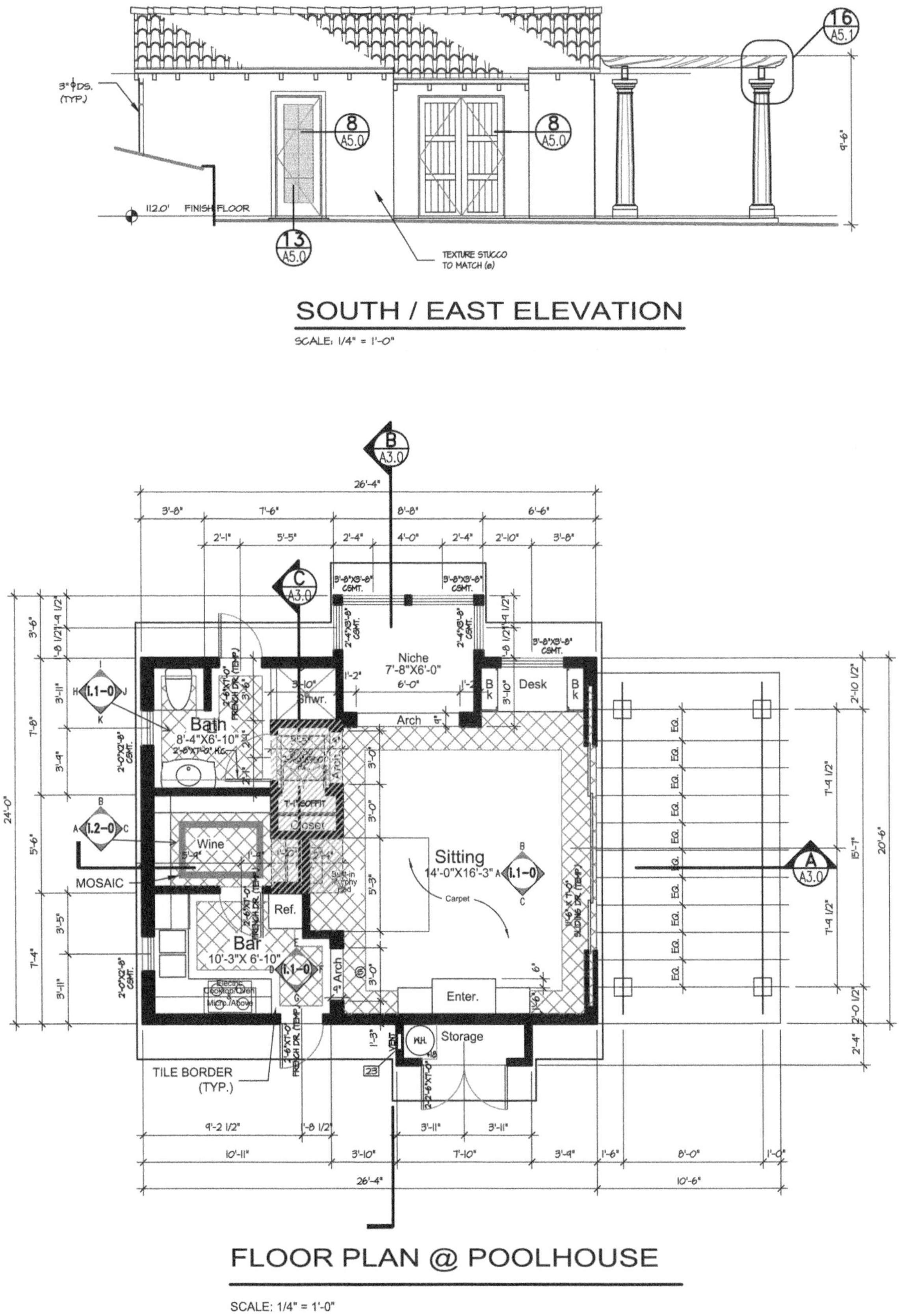

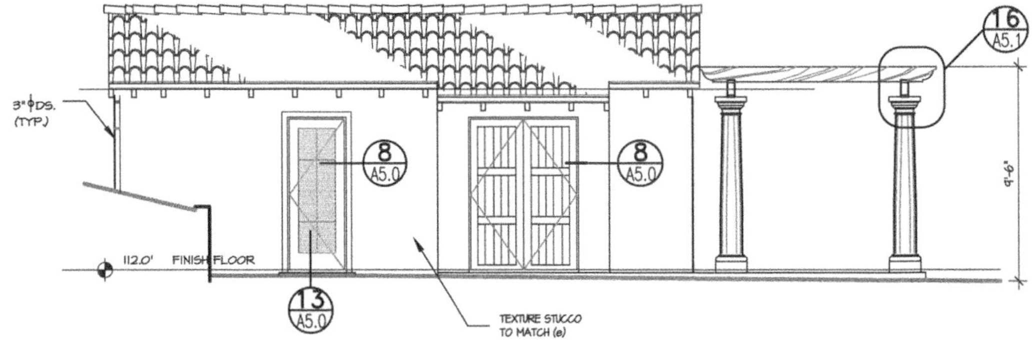

SOUTH / EAST ELEVATION

SCALE: 1/4" = 1'-0"

FLOOR PLAN @ POOLHOUSE

SCALE: 1/4" = 1'-0"

Figure 2.17 Profiled plan and elevation.

Following are a few simple rules for lettering and numbering:

1. Learn to letter with vertical strokes first. Sloping letters may be easier to master, but most architectural offices prefer vertical lettering. It is easier to change from vertical to sloping letters than the reverse. See Figure 2.18.
2. Practice words, phrases, and numbers—not just individual letters.
3. The shape of a letter should not be changed. The proportion of the letter may be slightly altered, but one should never destroy the letter's original image. Although the middle example "W" in Figure 2.19 is in a style used for speed, it can be misconstrued as an "I" and a "V."
4. Changing the proportions of letters changes their visual effect. See Figure 2.20.
5. Certain strokes can be emphasized so that one letter is not mistaken for another. This also forces the draftsperson to be more definitive in the formation of individual strokes. The strokes emphasized should be those most important to that letter; for example, a "B" differs from an "R" by the rounded lower right stroke, and an "L" from an "I" by the horizontal bottom stroke extending to the right only. The beginning or end of these strokes can be emphasized by bearing down on the pencil to ensure a good reprint of that portion. See Figure 2.21.
6. Maintain all uppercase lettering. Do not pick up the bad habit of mixing upper- and lowercase letters.
7. Maintain proper spacing between letters and do not leave space within the letter that is not properly there. See Figure 2.22.
8. Consistency produces good lettering. If vertical lines are used, they must all be parallel. A slight variation produces poor lettering. Even round letters such as "O" have a center through which imaginary vertical strokes should go. See Figure 2.23.
9. Second only to the letter itself in importance is spacing. Good spacing protects good letter formation. Poor spacing destroys even the best lettering. See Figure 2.24.
10. Use guidelines. Let your letters touch the top and bottom guideline but not extend beyond it. See Figure 2.25.
11. Horizontal lines are easier for a beginner than vertical lines, and shapes appear better formed when all of the vertical strokes are perfectly perpendicular and parallel to each other. Curved and round strokes are done without the aid of an instrument. Placing lined paper under the vellum is also a good trick to use, as well as using grid vellum.

ANCHOR BOLT ANCHOR BOLT
VERTICAL LETTERS SLOPING LETTERS

Figure 2.18 Comparison between vertical and sloping lettering.

MECHANICAL ARCHITECTURAL
M W ← (Poor)
M W ←(Good)

Figure 2.19 Overworking architectural letters.

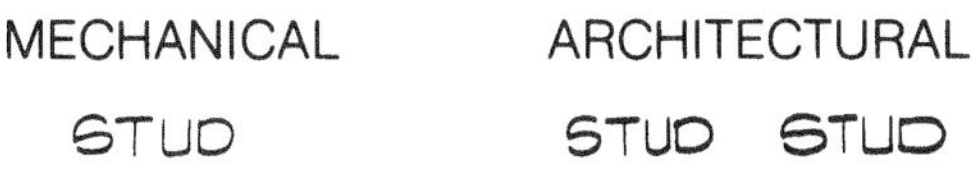

MECHANICAL ARCHITECTURAL
STUD STUD STUD

Figure 2.20 Changing letter proportions to produce architectural effect.

EXAMPLE:
B L I T R K

Figure 2.21 Emphasis on certain strokes.

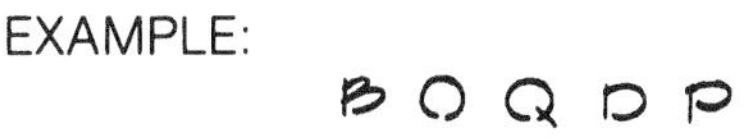

EXAMPLE:
B O Q D P

Figure 2.22 Spaces incorrectly left within letters.

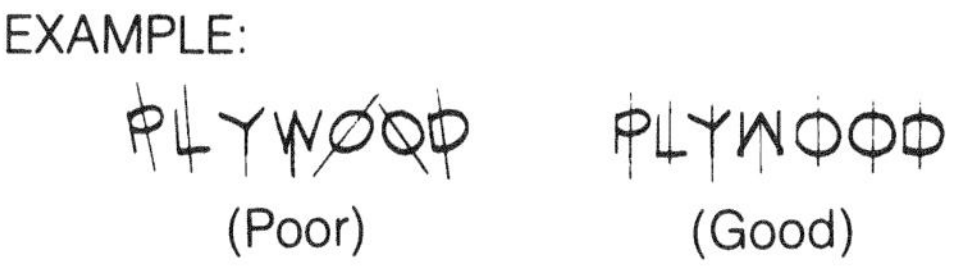

EXAMPLE:
PLYWOOD PLYWOOD
(Poor) (Good)

Figure 2.23 Producing consistency.

EXAMPLE:
PLYWOOD P LY WO OD
(Good) (Poor)

Figure 2.24 Importance of good spacing.

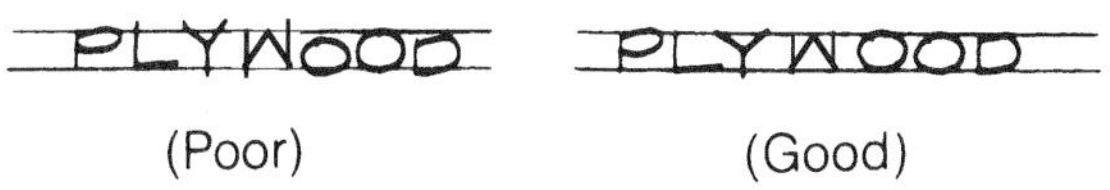

PLYWOOD PLYWOOD
(Poor) (Good)

Figure 2.25 Full use of guidelines.

After drawing the guidelines, place a parallel about 2 or 3 inches. Relocate the straightedge below the lines. Place the triangle to the left of the area to be lettered, with the vertical portion of the triangle on the right side. See Figure 2.26. "Eyeball" the spacing of the letter. Position your pencil as if you were ready to make the vertical line without the triangle. Before you make the vertical stroke, slide the triangle over against the pencil and make the pencil mark. See Figures 2.27 and 2.28. Draw nonvertical lines freehand. See Figure 2.29. If you are left-handed flip all the directions noted above.

Using a straightedge helps build your skills. Eventually, you should discontinue its use as practice improves your lettering skills.

Drafting Conventions and Dimensions

Many architectural offices have adopted the practice of separating the **net size** and the **nominal size** of lumber in their notations. The *net size* is the size of the actual piece of wood drawn and used. The *nominal size* (call-out size) is used to describe or order a piece of lumber. For example, the nominal size of a "two by four" is 2 × 4, but the net or actual size is $1\frac{1}{2}'' \times 3\frac{1}{2}''$. The distinction between the two sizes is accomplished by the use of inch (″) marks. Figure 2.30A would be very confusing because the nominal size is listed but inch marks are used. Compare this notation with that of Figure 2.30B. The 16″ o.c. (on center) is to be translated as precisely 16 inches, whereas the 2 × 4 is used to indicate nominal size.

Dimensions in feet are normally expressed by a small mark to the upper right of a number (′), and inches by two small marks (″) in the same location. To separate feet from inches, a dash is used. See Figure 2.31. The dash in this type of dimensions becomes very important because it prevents dimensions from being misread and adds to clarity. If space for dimensions is restricted, an acceptable abbreviated form can be used. This is illustrated in Figure 2.32. The inches are raised and underlined to separate them from the feet notation.

Dimension lines can be broken to show the numerical value, but it is faster simply to put numerical values

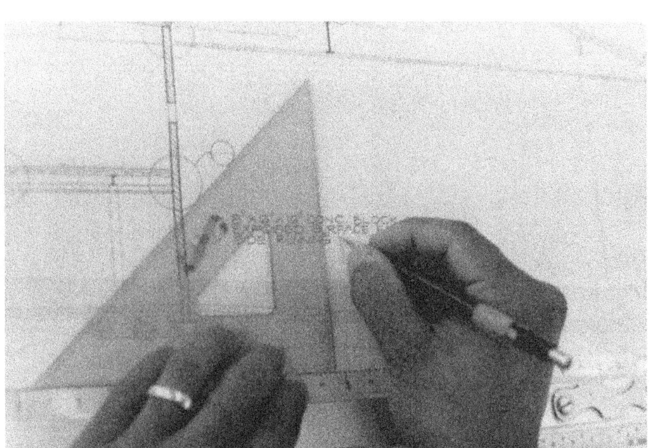

Figure 2.26 Pencil placement for vertical lettering.

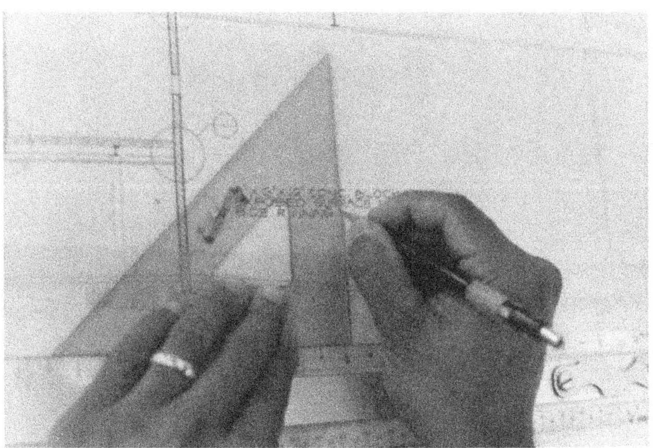

Figure 2.27 Placing the triangle against the pencil.

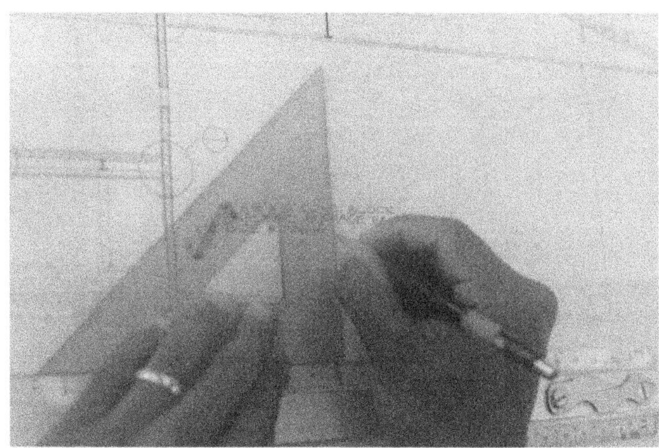

Figure 2.28 Drawing the vertical pencil line.

Figure 2.29 Completing the letter.

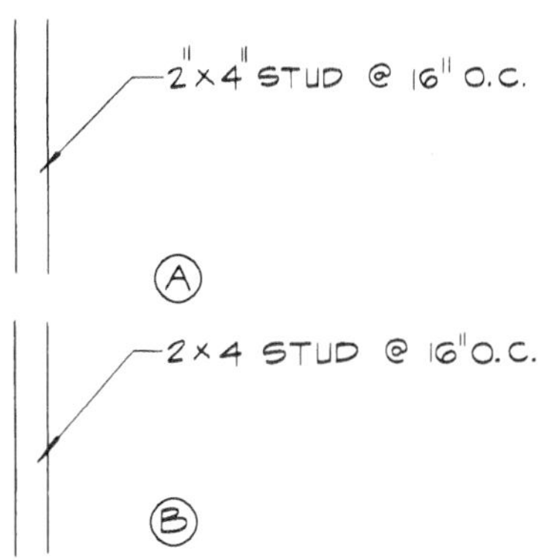

Figure 2.30 Net and nominal notation.

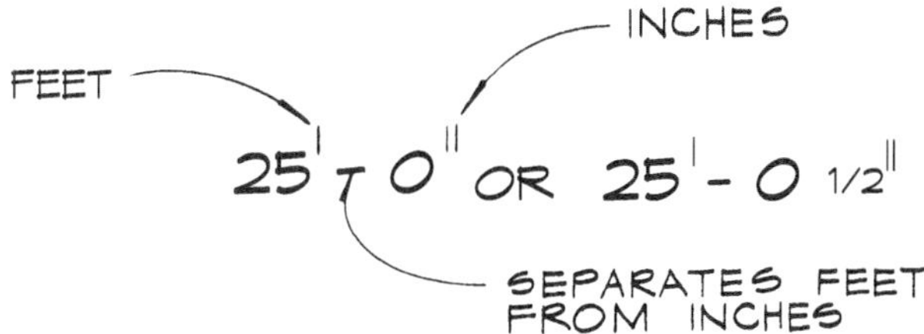

Figure 2.31 Expressing feet and inches.

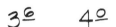

Figure 2.32 Dimensions in a restricted area.

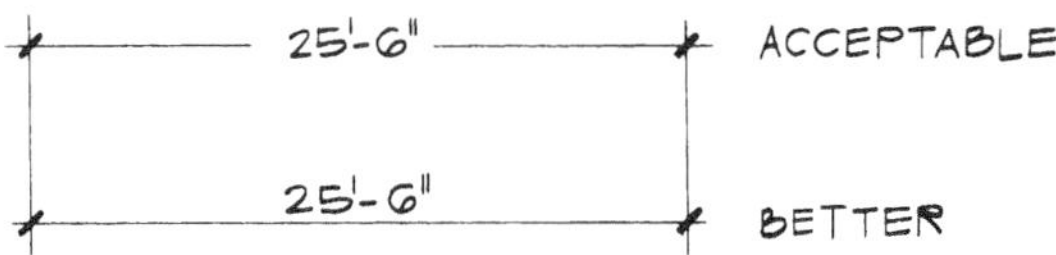

Figure 2.33 Placement of dimensions above or between dimension lines.

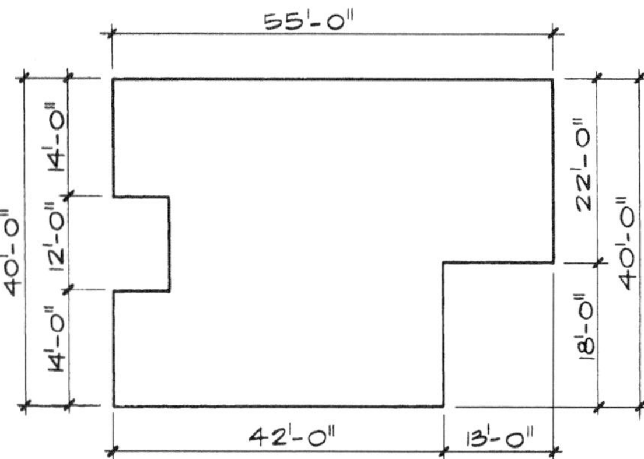

Figure 2.34 Dimensions read from bottom and from the right.

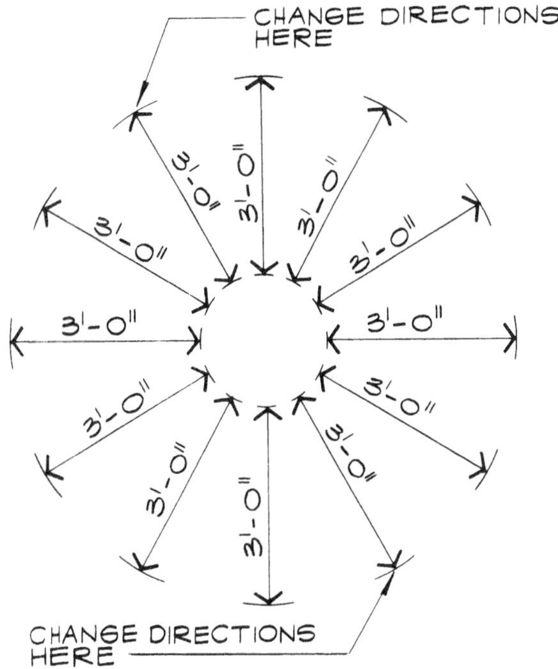

Figure 2.35 Dimension placement.

above the lines. See Figure 2.33. When dimension lines run vertically, place the numbers above the dimension line as viewed from the right. See Figure 2.34.

Not all dimension lines, however, are horizontal or vertical. Often, dimension lines are angled, and this can cause problems when you position the numerical value. Figure 2.35 suggests a possible location for such values. When working with BIM or AutoCAD, these don't always default to the ideal location and must be moved or adjusted for proper viewing.

Architectural Drafting

The architectural version of **orthographic projection** is an object projected at 90° as you view the object, as shown in Figure 2.36. The top view (as viewed from a helicopter) is now called the **plan**, and the views all the way around from all four sides are referred to as **elevations**. Each of these elevations has a special name, as will be discussed in the chapter on exterior and interior elevations.

In brief, a top view of the total property is called the **site** or **plot plan.** A horizontal section (drawn as if the structure were cut horizontally, the top portion removed, and the exposed interior viewed from above) is simply called a plan. There are many types of plans: **floor plans**, **electrical plans** (showing electrical features), **framing plans** (showing how a floor, ceiling, or roof is assembled), and **foundation plans**, to mention just a few (Figure 2.36).

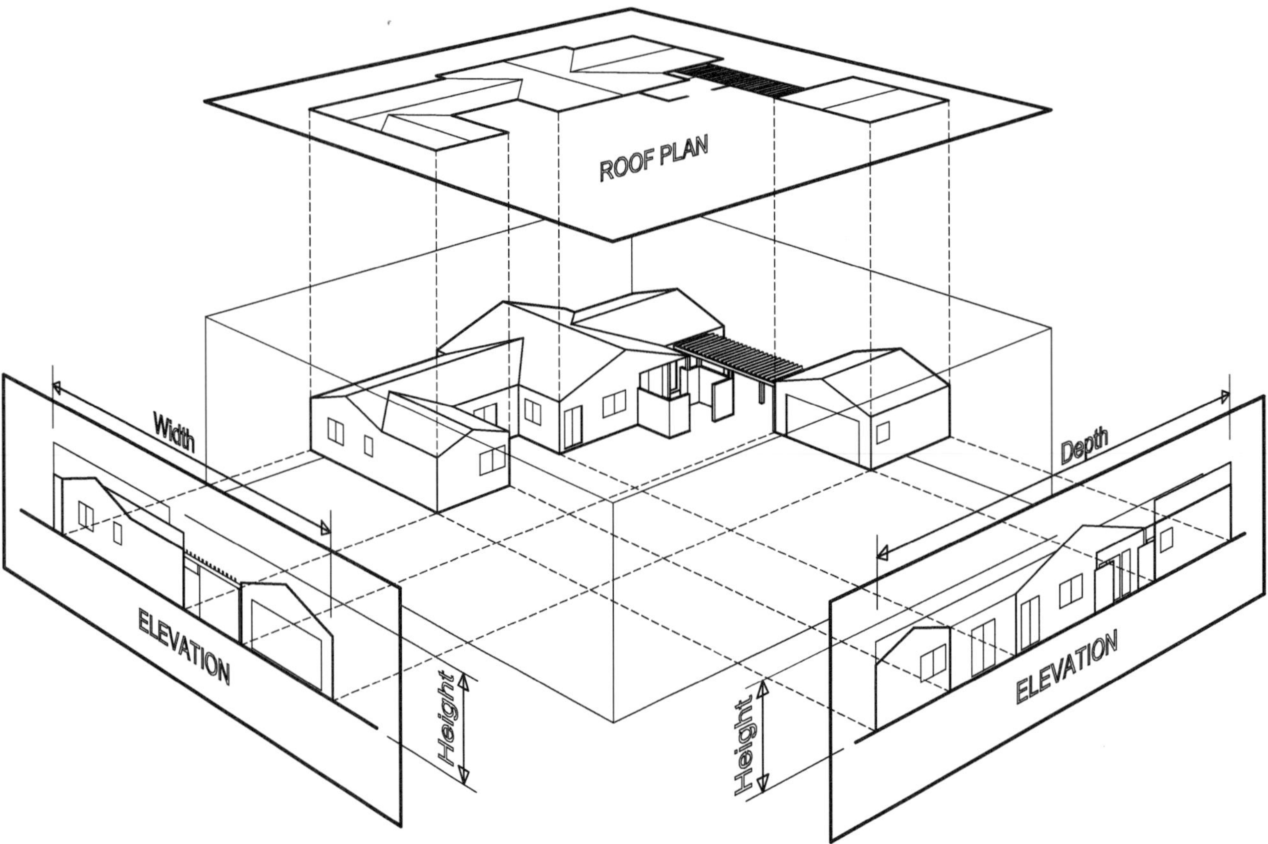

Figure 2.36 A multi-view drawing of a structure.

A vertical cut through a structure is called a **cross-section** or a **longitudinal section**, depending on the direction of the cut. The cross-section is a cut taken through the short end of a structure. As of the turn of the century (and for some architects), the architectural term for cross-section, longitude section transverse, has been replaced with the term **building section.**

Printing to an Accurate Scale on AutoCAD or Revit

Step I. Determine the scale you want your drawing to be printed on. If you will be printing at ¼″ = 1′-0″, you will need to specify this on your Properties pallet. See Figures 2.37A or 2.38A.

Step II. Under the application menu, select Print and a dialogue box will open. See Figures 2.37A or 2.38B. Under this dialogue box the most important part to select is the Setup Settings, and a second dialogue box will open. See step 3.

Step III. This is the most important portion while printing to make sure your drawing will be printed to scale. See Figure 2.37B. Under Zoom you MUST check zoom 100%. Your drawing will not print to scale if you check Fit to page. Under this dialogue box you can also select the paper size and paper placement.

Step IV. Use your scale and measure to make sure your drawing printed to scale.

Shortcut Procedures

One of the best shortcuts you can learn is freehand drawing. You still should use a scale to maintain accuracy and adhere to the drafting vocabulary of lines and techniques. Freehand skill is useful in field situations, for informal office communications, and for communications with contractors, building department officials, and clients.

Reprodrafting is a term used to describe a number of approaches to improving or revising drafted material in a way that takes advantage of photographic or photocopying processes. These approaches have spawned a number of new terms, including eraser drafting, paste-up drafting, photo drafting, overlay drafting, pen drafting, and scissors drafting. Reprodrafting, then, actually consists of many processes.

Restoration refers to the process of taking a photograph of an old original or an old print and, by repairing the negative, producing a new master.

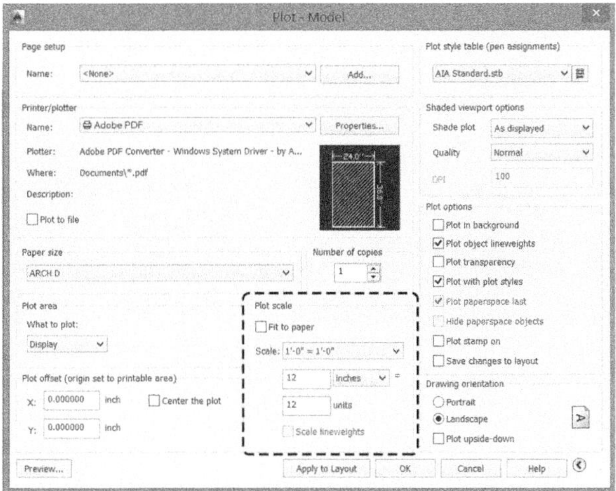

Ⓐ **Page setup managemet (plot scale)**

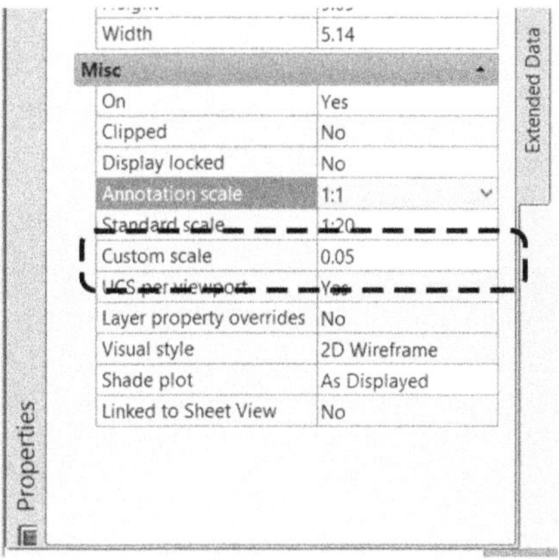

Ⓑ **Properties tab (standard scale)**

Figure 2.37 Setting an accurate scale in AutoCAD. (©Autodesk, Inc. All rights reserved.)

Composite drafting is the photographic process of making a single drawing from many, or of taking parts of other drawings to make a new drawing.

Paste-up drafting simply refers to the process of pasting pieces onto a single master sheet, and then photographing and reproducing the master. The lines on the edges of the pieces can be eliminated by a photo retoucher.

Scissors drafting takes an existing drawing and eliminates undesirable or corrected portions by cutting them out before the paste-up process. **Eraser drafting** is similar, but the unwanted portions are simply erased. In both cases, the original is never touched.

Photo drafting, as the name indicates, uses both drafting and photography. It begins with a photograph of any drawing, such as a plan, elevation, or detail. The drawing is printed on a matte-surfaced film, and additional information is drafted onto it. Photo drafting is an ideal method for dealing with historical restoration drawings. Editing an image digitally with editing software is ideal for generating a new master.

Make a copy of all the early stages of the different parts of a building. If there are no significant changes, tape the drawing to a piece of bond paper, copy it onto the vellum, and then finish the process. If, for example, the **pitch** (roof slope) is different, then simply cut out the roof portion, tape it to a sheet of bond paper, and print onto vellum. Manually correct the new roof pitch and proceed to finish the process.

To achieve the enlargement using a computer, the first thing to do is to scan the image into the computer and import it into AutoCAD.

Step I. **Scan** the desired plan and **import** it into AutoCAD. Make sure that your AutoCAD at this time has been set up with the correct units and limits.

Step II. Select a known dimension on the drawing that you just scanned and create a reference line. Now you will need to create a second reference line that is drawn to scale. You can now superimpose these two lines or bring them close together to change the scale. (It may be easier to identify if these two lines have different colors.) See Figure 2.37.

Step III. Next go to the **Scale** command and select the drawing and the drawing reference line. Click on the end point of your scaled lined and type R for reference. Next, click the end point of the drawing reference line, and, finally, click the end point of the scale line. This will give you a scale drawing to be used in AutoCAD that can then be transferred to Revit if necessary.

Step IV. **Verify** by printing your drawing to scale and double-check that the dimensions are accurate.

Sheet S ize

The drawing sheet size varies from office to office depending on the type of work performed, size of the job, and the system of drafting used in the office. The most common sheet sizes are 24″ × 36″, 30″ × 42″, and 36″ × 48″.

When sheets are used horizontally, they are usually bound on the left side. Because of this, the border is larger on the left side. A typical border line is 3/8″ to 1/2″ around the three sides and 1″ to 1 1/2″ on the left side.

Title blocks can run the full height of the right side rather than simply filling a square in the bottom right corner, as in mechanical drafting. The long title band contains such information as sheet number, client's name or project title, name of firm, name or title of the drawing, person drafting, scale, date, and revision dates.

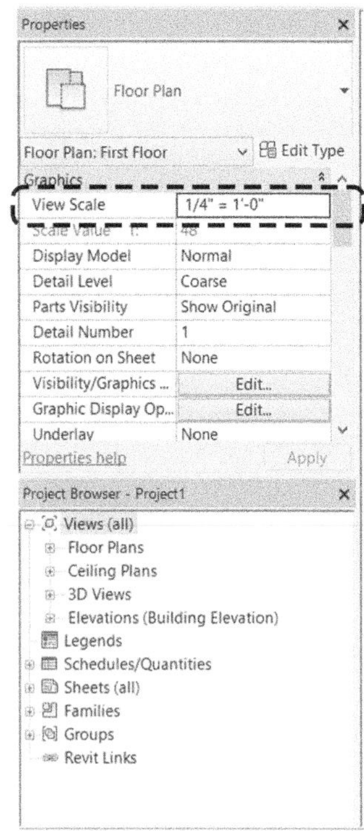

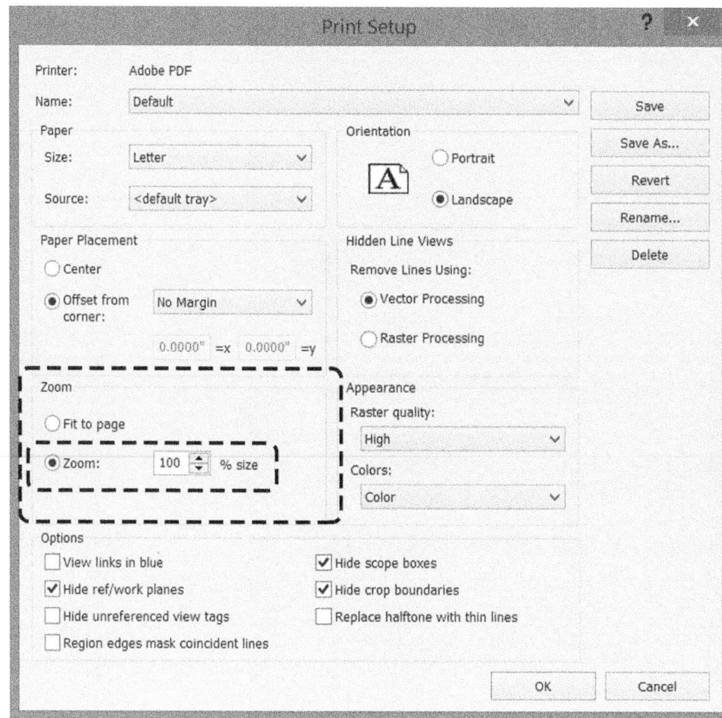

(A) Properties Pallet

Figure 2.38 Printing to an accurate scale in Revit. (©Autodesk, Inc. All rights reserved.)

When drawings are rolled up, the title block and all the important information is left exposed. Many offices establish a sheet module. Here is an example of this method with a 24″ × 36″ sheet:

Binding side	1½″ border
Other three sides	½″ border
Title block	1½″ wide

This leaves a drawing area of 23″ by 32½″. The vertical 23″ distance can be divided into four equal parts, while the horizontal 32½″ can be divided into five equal parts. This provides 20 spaces 6½″ wide by 5¾″ high. This office procedure may be followed so that each sheet has a consistent appearance. Whether the sheet is full of details or a combination of a plan and details and/or notes, the module gives you parameters within which to work. For larger details, cells can be combined to allow for clarity. You should draft from the right side of the sheet so that any blank spaces remaining are toward the inside (on the binding side). Although some office go from right to left find the office standard and follow its example.

Lettering Height

The height of lettering depends on the scale of reproduction. Use the following standards as a rule of thumb:

Main titles under drawings ″	½″ maximum
Subtitles	3/16″
Normal lettering	3/32″ – 1/8″
Sheet number in title block	½″–1″

Increase these sizes when you are reducing drawings. For example, increase normal lettering from 3/32″ to 3/16″, depending on the reduction ratio. If projects are done for government contracts—they will establish the guidelines for you.

One of the most important office standards to which a drafter must subscribe is lettering. Many offices use a combination of uppercase and lowercase letters for the main titles, such as for room names. Certain fonts, such as Arial, Helvetica, and Garamond, are very popular. When selecting a font, be sure to find one based on a simple stroking system so as not to impede the printing process. There can be a marked difference in plotting time for different fonts, especially when the text is very long, as in general notes, framing notes, or energy notes.

The height of the letters is also very important for legibility. Lettering that is 1/8″ or 3/32″ tall is very readable. Using letters ½″ tall (maximum) for main titles produces enough contrast between notes and titles to enhance the construction documents.

A problem caused by the infusion of electronic equipment into our field is the difficulty in maintaining the lettering size from computer terminal to terminal. Copy and paste functions often stand out as a result of font variations.

Scale of Drawings

The scale selected should be the largest practical scale based on the size of the structure and the drawing space available. The following are the sizes most commonly used by offices.

Site plan. 1/8″ = 1′-0″ for small sites. Drawings are provided by a civil engineer and scales are expressed in engineering terms such as 1″ = 10′, 1″ = 20′, etc. See Figure 2.39 where a graphic scale is also included.
Floor plan. 1/4″ = 1′-0″, 1/8″ = 1′-0″ for larger structures.
Exterior elevations. Same as the floor plan.
Building sections. 1/4″ = 1′-0″; 1/8″ for larger projects.
Interior elevations. 1/4″ = 1′-0″, 3/8″ = 1′-0″, 1/2″ = 1′-0″.
Architectural details. 1″ = 1′-0″ to 3″ = 1′-0″, depending on the size of the object being drawn or the amount of information that must be shown. Footing detail: 1″ = 1′-0″ or 1½″ = 1′-0″. 3″ = 1′0″ for smaller items

Materials in Section

Figure 2.40 shows the various methods used throughout the United States to represent different materials in section. These conventions were developed by the Committee on Office Practice, AIA (National), and published in Architectural Graphic Standards.

Clearly, there is standardization and there are variations. For example, all groups agree on the method of representing brick in section, yet there is a great deal of variation in the way concrete block is represented in section. The last figure shows specialty items from a variety of sources.

Graphic Symbols

The symbols in Figure 2.41 are the most common and acceptable, to judge by the frequency with which the architectural offices surveyed use them. This list can be and should be expanded by each office to include those symbols generally used in its practice and not indicated here.

Abbreviations

Suggested abbreviations compiled by Task Force #1 National Committee on Office Practice AIA and published in the *AIA Journal* can be found as a resource on the internet. Many offices utilize standards that are available with the BIM program and AutoCAD hatch patterns.

Dimensioning is the act of incorporating numerical values into a drawing as a means of sizing various components and also locating parts of a building. This is accomplished on dimension lines, in notes, and by reference to other drawings or details.

Group dimensions whenever possible, in order to provide continuity. This takes planning. Try running a print of the drawing in question and dimension it on this check print first. This will allow you to identify dimensions and decide how they can be effectively grouped.

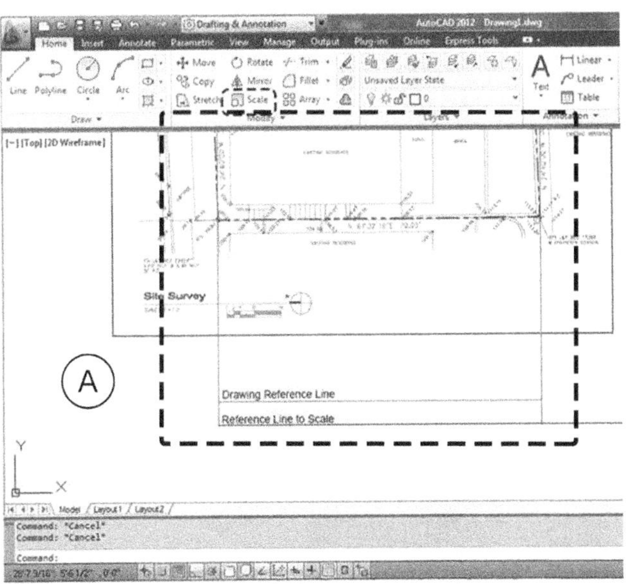

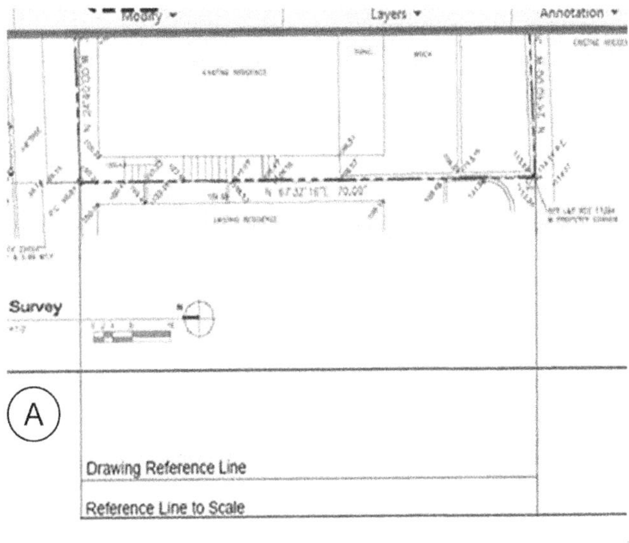

Figure 2.39 Using graphic scale on a drawing. (©Autodesk, Inc. All rights reserved.)

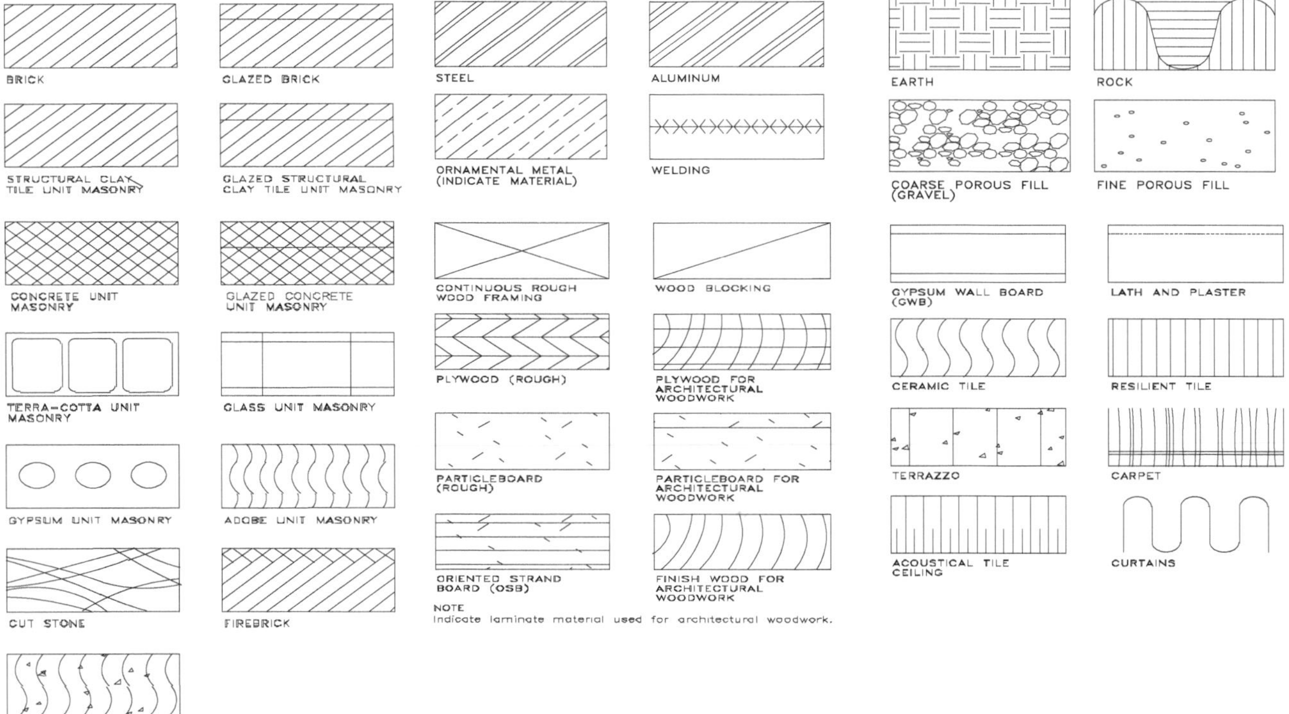

Figure 2.40 Graphic symbols for materials in section. (Hoke 2000. Reproduced by permission from The Professional Practice of Architectural Detailing, 3rd edition, © 1999 by John Wiley & Sons, Inc.)

The most important dimensions dictate subsequent dimensions. For example, if a wall is dimensioned to the center of the wall first, all subsequent dimensions using this wall as a reference point should be dimensioned at its center.

The two basic kinds of dimensions are size and location. See Figure 2.42. Size dimensions indicate overall size. Location dimensions deal with the actual placement of an object or structure, such as a wall, a window, or a planter.

Offices have a set of standards that employees must follow. This is essential in the industry, not only because many drafters may be working on the same project, but also to ensure uniformity of the language that the drafters speak. Adhering to standards helps coordinate drawings for a firm's associates both inside and outside the office.

Standards establish sheet size, scales used, standard line and symbol conventions, placement and positions of drawings, and sheet modules, to mention a few items.

These standards are often kept on the drafter's desk and are referred to as the **drafting manual**, the office procedure manual, or something similar. Computers have their standards, and although standards may differ slightly from job to job or office to office, they should be rigidly followed. Standards do change, as new and better methods are created.

National CAD Standards

For a number of years, we have had the US national CAD standards (NCS); however, an office must now subscribe to the latest NCS-V6 edition, as it now includes BIM. This inclusion of BIM is critical because it is the natural evolution of architecture in all phases: designing, construction documents, and the building of structures that will ultimately create a process missing in the past.

Although standards are established by individual offices and are often based on existing drafting manuals, the introduction of computers to the arsenal of production tools has created a need for national and international standards. Associations such as the AIA, National Institute of Building Sciences, Construction Specifications Institute, and even the military, to mention just a few, have in fact produced national CAD standards.

When applying standards, a drafter should not be so dependent on existing standard templates that they are unable to develop new ones if the job calls for them. If a drafter is knowledgeable and flexible and knows how to set up line types, lettering size, sheet size, and scales. A managing body will take note and assess the value of the employee accordingly.

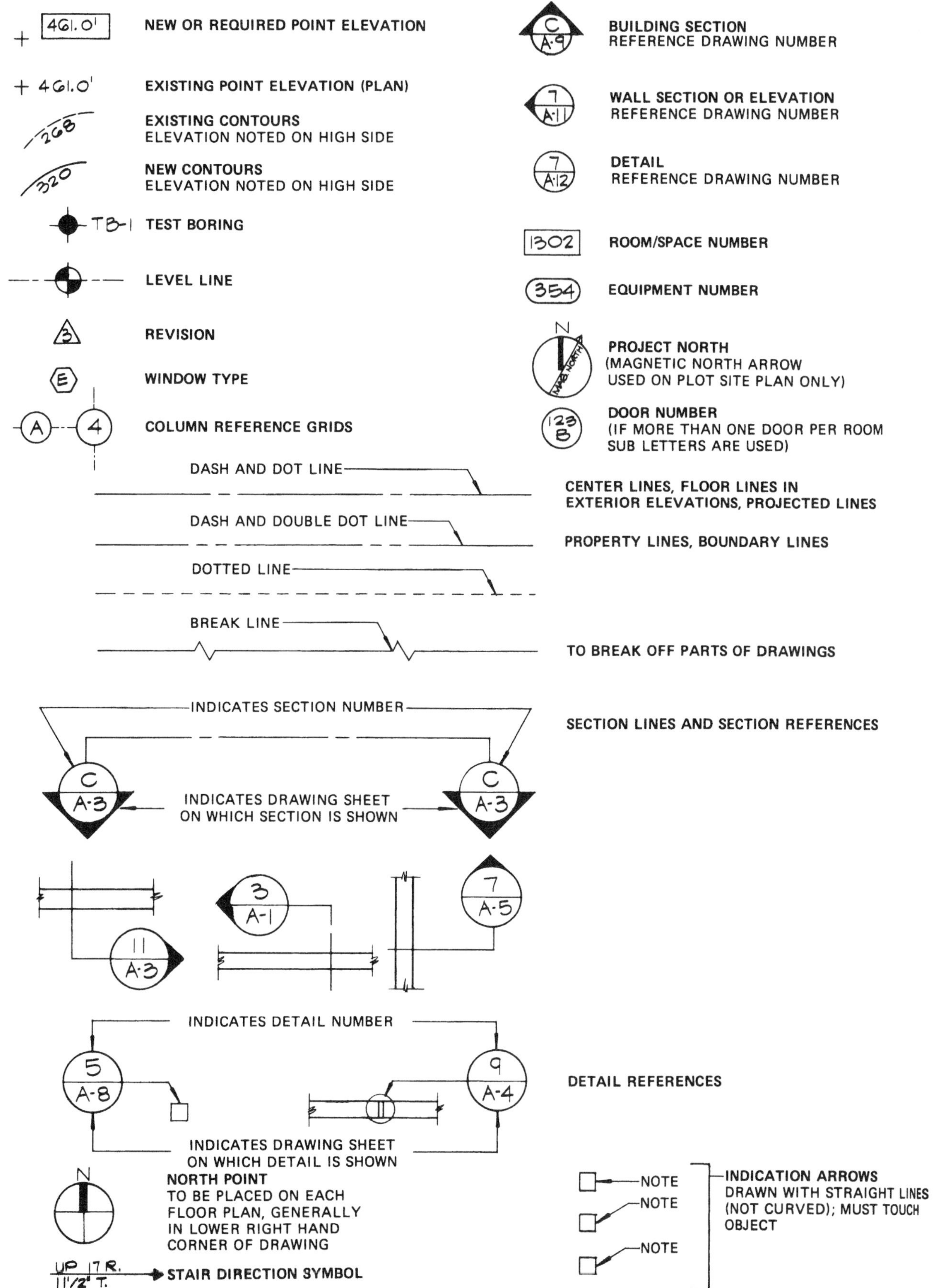

Figure 2.41 Graphic symbols from AIA standards.

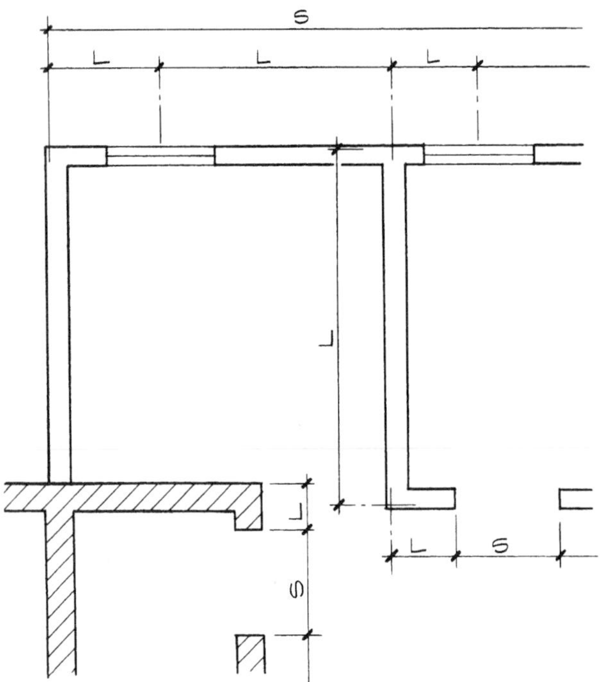

Figure 2.42 Size and location dimensions.

In this section, we discuss the following topics with regard to standards and CAD, BIM, or hand drafting:

1. Standards in the drafting world
2. Vector versus raster
3. X-referencing (XREF)
4. Oddly scaled drawings
5. Paper
6. Paper space/virtual space (model space)
7. Scaling factor
8. Layering
9. Pen setting/line weights/color
10. Lettering size
11. Disadvantages
12. Advantages

With the use of CAD or BIM, structures should be drawn at full scale. This is made possible because we are working in virtual space (model space), which is unlimited.

When designing and drawing in full scale on the computer, you can look around the space you are occupying and draw relationships based on real-world sizes. The monitor becomes a window through which you are viewing this full-size structure. The printer/plotter becomes a photograph of this image displayed on the monitor screen in a scaled print out.

The architecture industry is based on communicating ideas. We can do this only if each of the participants—architects, drafters, associates (mechanical, structural, electrical engineers), and so forth—speak the same language.

When drawings are drawn by layers, the titles of these layers become critical for identification. To aid in identification, the office subscribes and plot them out onto a chart similar to that found in Figure 2.43.

Generally speaking, drawings are categorized by subject—for example, A, architectural, M, mechanical, S, structural, C, civil, and the like. See Figure 2.44 for such a breakdown. Notice the 13 "A" drawings listed in the left column. The walls of the floor plan are drawn on one layer and given the name A-WALL. All of the appliances (such as plumbing) are drawn on another layer called A-FLOR, windows and doors on A-GLAZ and A-DOOR, dimensions on A-ANNO-DIMS, and so on. To produce a drawing for construction, layers can be turned on and off as needed. To print a furniture plan for the client, you would most certainly need layers A-WALL, A-FURN, and A-ANNO.

If the structural engineer is producing a roof framing plan or a ceiling joist plan, they will initially need the wall layer. In this way, the wall (A-WALL) layer is used as a base for a multitude of other drawings. A quick look at Figure 2.44 reveals that the A-WALL layer is used for the floor plan, ceiling plan, furniture plan, and finish plan, as well as the floor framing plan, roof framing plan, and, on the simplified chart, the power plan, lighting plan, and the reflected ceiling plan. This is called cross-referencing, or X-referencing.

Vector Versus Raster. It is imperative that all CAD drafters know the difference between vector drawings and raster drawings because of the ways in which each file format can be used. Both raster and vector images can be manipulated. **Raster** images are made up of pixels; a photo manipulation program must be used with a raster image. You can remove items from the image and elongate, stretch, or compress the image. You can even change the position of the image relative to the paper and format for presentation. However, you cannot easily change the geometry.

Vector drawings are done both two-dimensionally and three-dimensionally. Vector drawings are actually lines, planes, and geometric shapes drawn in virtual space. Height, width, and depth are described as X, Y, and Z directions, respectively. This means you can rotate a three-dimensional (3-D) form and look at it from any of the six principal directions—front, back, left, right, top, and bottom (or underside)—and an unlimited number of views in between.

For importing a digital drawing from a vendor, you should request a vector drawing. Figure 2.45 shows a single-hung window with a transom made of vinyl and imported as a vector file. Such drawings represent the basic manufacturer's configuration, which can be placed with the header, exterior finish, interior finish, and waterproofing methods to produce a construction detail for a specific application.

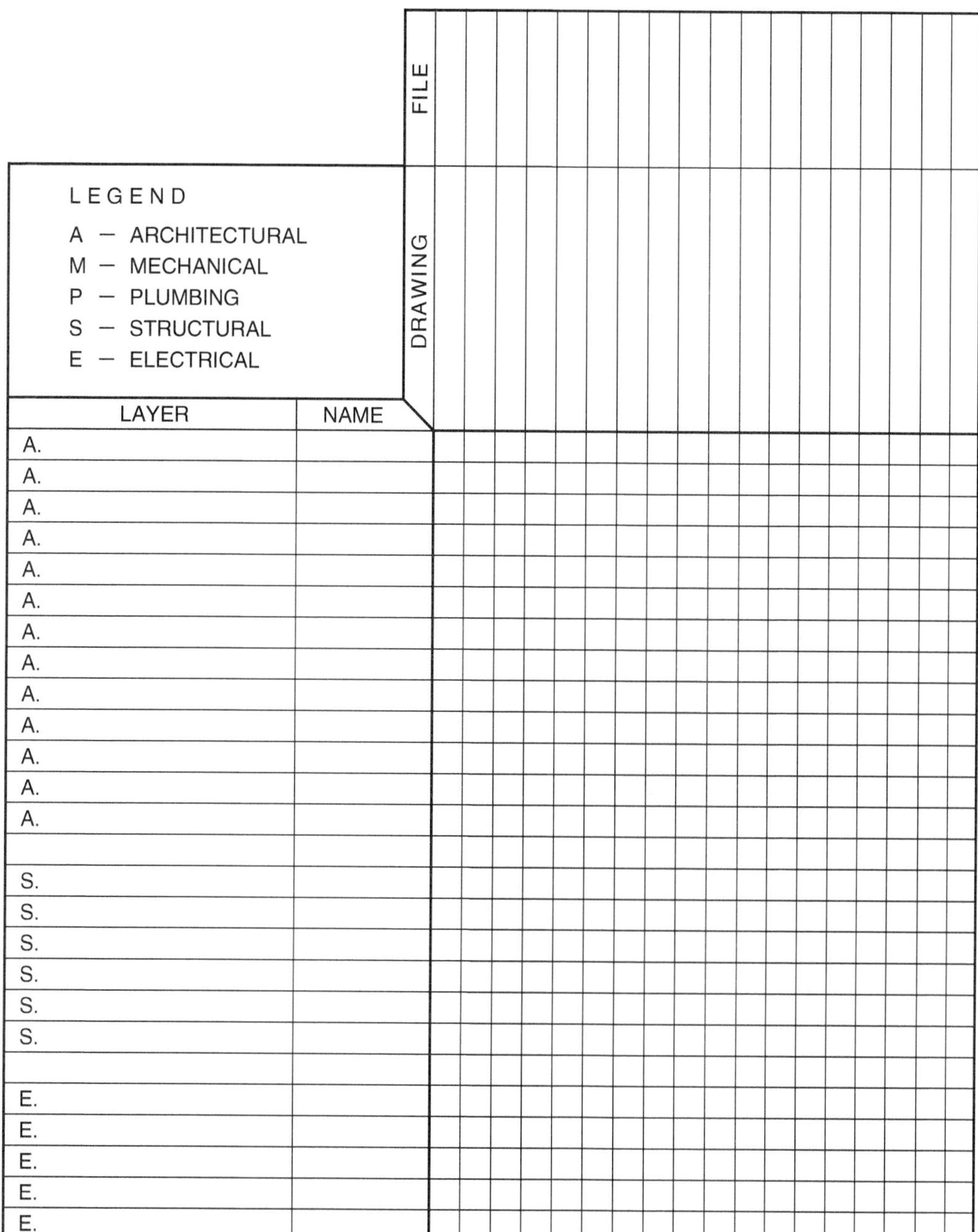

Figure 2.43 Sample layout for layers.

Figure 2.46 shows a recommended installation detail. The drafter can take this detail and adapt it to a specific application while adding pertinent design features. When requesting both basic shapes and installation details, ask for the file format your office typically uses. Usually, that will be DXF, DWG, or RVT. The majority of CAD programs can easily manipulate these file types.

DWG Versus DXF. If a drawing is to be sent or received electronically, it must be formatted. Although there are other formatting methods, DXF and DWG are most typically used.

The **DWG** format, which is the most desirable, is the easiest for the AutoCAD and other programs drafter to use, change, or correct because it has all the ingredients needed to produce the end result.

The **DXF** (short for *drawing exchange format*) strips down the total drawing sequence in a way that makes it easier to translate. Because it is a stripped-down form, you cannot perform certain tasks; although the final visual image is complete, pertinent information is missing and thus it cannot be easily manipulated. DXF is easier to exchange with other programs.

LEGEND

A — ARCHITECTURAL
M — MECHANICAL
P — PLUMBING
S — STRUCTURAL
E — ELECTRICAL

LAYER	NAME	A-1.0 SITE PLAN	A-2.0 FLOOR PLAN	A-2.1 CEILING PLAN	A-2.2 FURNITURE PLAN	A-2.3 FINISH PLAN	A-3.0 ELEVATIONS	A-4.0 SECTIONS	A-5.0 SCHEDULES	A-6.0 INT. ELEVATIONS		S-1.0 FOUNDATION	S-2.0 FLOOR FRAMING	S-3.0 ROOF FRAMING	S-4.0 WALL SECTION		E-1.0 POWER PLAN	E-2.0 LIGHTING PLAN	E-3.0 REFLECTED C.P.
FILE		2000_A-1.0	2000_A-2.0				2000_A-3.0	2000_A-4.0	2000_A-5.0	2000_A-6.0		2000_S-1.0	2000_S-2.0	2000_S-3.0	2000_S-4.0		2000_E-1.0	2000_E-2.0	2000_E-3.0
A. SITE	A-SITE	●																	
A. WALL	A-WALL		●	○	○	○							○	○			○	○	○
A. FIXTURES	A-FLOR		●		○	○													
A. DOORS	A-DOOR		●		○	○												○	
A. WINDOWS	A-GLAZ		●		○	○												○	
A. DIMENSIONS	A-ANNO-DIMS		●			○							○	○					
A. CEILING PLAN	A-CEIL			●															●
A. FURNITURE	A-FURN				●														
A. NOTES	A-ANNO					●													
A. BORDER & TITLE	A-TBLK		●	●	●	●	●	●	●			●	●	●	●		●	●	●
A. EXTERIOR ELEVATION	A-ELEV-EXTR						●								○				
A. INTERIOR ELEVATION	A-ELEV-INTR							●											
A. BUILDING SECTION	A-SECT								●										
S. NOTES	S-ANNO											●							
S. DIMENSIONS	S-DIMS											●							
S. FOUNDATION WALLS	S-WALL											●							
S. FOOTING CONVENTIONS	S-FNDN											●							
S. FRAMING MEM. FLOOR	S-FRAM-FLOR												●						
S. FRAMING MEM. ROOF	S-FRAM-ROOF													●					
E. NOTES	E-ANNO																●		
E. EQUIPMENT	E-EQUP																●		
E. WALL FIXTURES	E-FIXT-WALL																	●	
E. CEILING FIXTURES	E-FIXT-CEIL																		●
E. SUSPENDED CEILING	E-CEIL																		●

Figure 2.44 Example of layers and their titles.

X-Referencing (XREF). Cross-referencing, in the architectural industry, refers to the process of referencing one drawing to another by means of reference bubbles. In the computer industry, the term *X-referencing* (**XREF**) sounds like cross-referencing, but it is not the same. XREF means "externally referenced" drawings. XREF is used to combine drawings and keep the entire set of construction documents updated with the most recent version of a drawing. A secondary datum is now being used to produce drawings. The example shown in Figure 2.47 is an electrical plan. The floor plan (master) becomes the externally referenced drawing and is not directly a part of the electrical plan layers.

Computer-generated drawings, with their intricate network of finely tuned layers, titles, and patterns, are produced almost as if they were a family. Base drawings, such as exterior and interior walls showing some of the basic fixtures and stair locations, are often referred to as *masters* or **parent drawings**. Their offshoots, such as framing plans, electrical plans, building sections, and so on, are commonly referred to as *children* or *submasters*.

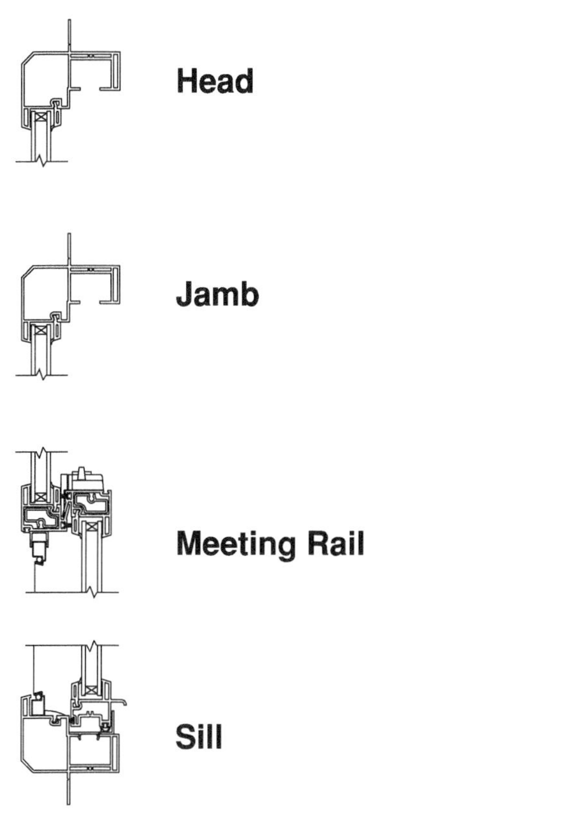

Figure 2.45 Vinyl window configurations. (Courtesy of Certainteed Windows.)

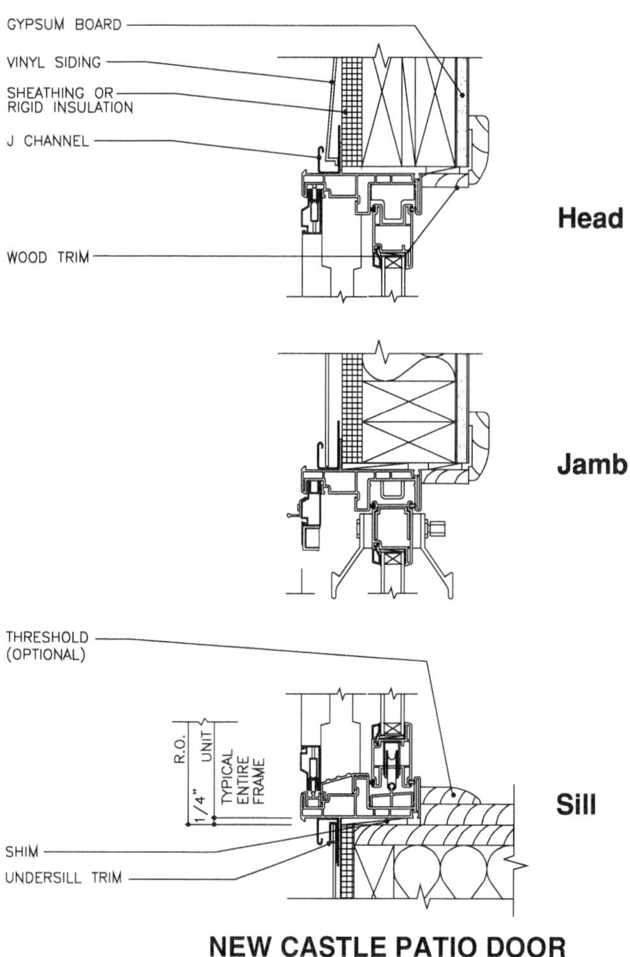

Figure 2.46 Manufacturers' installation details in DWG format.

The plot sheets serve the parents and children by presenting specific drawings and information (*maids* or *servants*).

Figure 2.48 shows a sampling of an XREF standard for a hypothetical office. Figure 2.49 provides examples of a master, submaster, and servant. This cross-referencing has the same meaning in manual drawings as it does in CAD drawings, whereas XREF refers to a special process unique to computer-generated drawings.

Oddly Scaled Drawings. A peculiar group of computer-generated drawings that are beginning to find their way into the construction industry are drawings without a specific or known scale. These are drawings that may have been drawn to scale initially, but were resized to fit the paper on which they were plotted.

The reduction process has found its way into the CAD system with a command called "Print to Fit," which prints the drawing on a sheet of paper regardless of scale. If the drafter anticipates how much the drawing will be reduced, office standards for lettering height can be maintained.

If a floor plan would fit a 24 × 36 piece of paper at ¼″ = 1′-0″ and the office standard is to maintain all lettering and ¼″ tall titles, the drafter must produce lettering at 6″ in height (at ¼″ scale) and titles 12″ tall.

Paper comes in various sizes. The standard and nonstandard sizes are listed in Figure 2.50. Nonstandard-sized paper is listed with asterisks. When drafting manually, the drafter has the entire sheet of paper to work with. Such is not the case with computer-generated drawings. The drafter must be aware of the limits of the printer or plotter. For example, an 8½″ × 11″ paper may have a printable area of only 8″ × 10½″. This proportion holds true with all paper. When you add border lines and title blocks to the drawing sheet, the actual drawing area of the sheet will be reduced to a given standard used in the office. Figure 2.50 shows a diagram of the printable area and the drawing area of an 8½″ × 11″ sheet of paper.

Knowing that the printable area for an 8½″ × 11″ sheet of paper can be 8″ × 10½″, ideally, we would set the margins at ¼″ and use a 1″ or ¾″ strip for a title block.

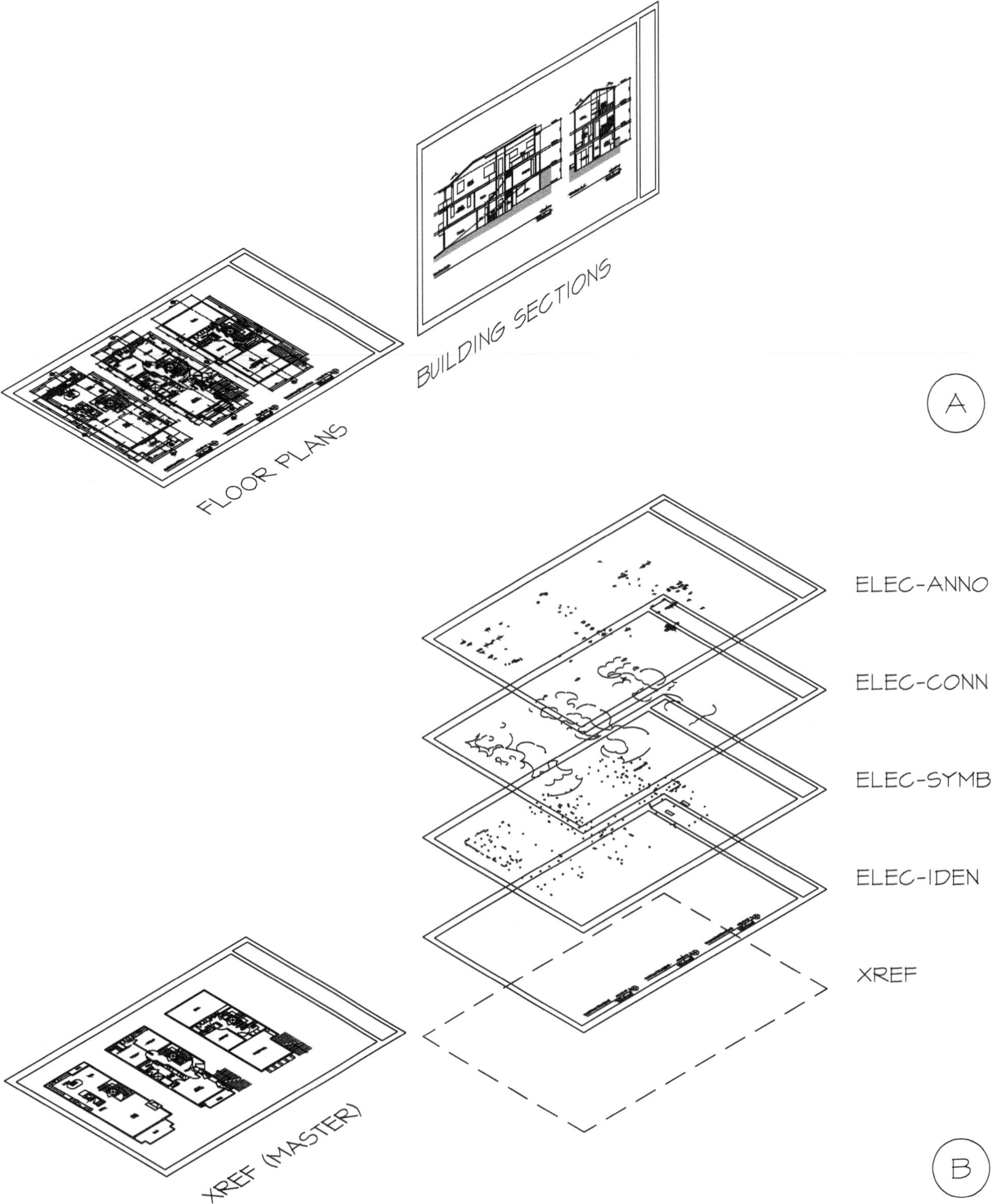

Figure 2.47 XREF the external reference system.

Some offices do not even print the borders, but only the title block. If the drawing will be bound, the binding edge is increased to 3/4″, leaving a drawing area of 7 1/2″ × 9 3/4″ (see Figure 2.51B and C, respectively).

Because most computer drawings are done in layers, one layer may contain the limits within which the drafter must stay. These borders may or may not be printed in the final drawing (see Figure 2.51A and C, respectively).

Preliminary Documentation of Office XREF Standard

Schematic Design/Design Development (MASTER) Naming: YearMonthProjectNumber-MAST.dwg (YYMM##-MAST.dwg) 000101-MAST.dwg			
	MAST	Master Design Drawing	Walls, Doors, Windows, Stairs, Fireplaces, Room Labels,
			Plumbing Fixtures, Closets (What you need for the Client)

Design Development/Construction Documents (Sub-Masters) Naming: YearMonthProjectNumber-FLOR.dwg (YYMM##-FLOR.dwg) 000101-FLOR.dwg			
XREF	**Listed in order of importance**		**Description**
MAST	**NBHD**	Neighborhood Compatibility	If needed
MAST	**FLOR**	Floor Plans	Poche, Hatching, Notes, Dimensions
MAST	**ROOF**	Roof Plan	
MAST	**ELEV**	Elevations	
MAST	**SECT**	Building Sections	
MAST	**SITE**	Site Plan	Modify TOPO to start Could also include a separate Grading Plan
MAST	**FRAM**	Framing/Foundation	All Structural Drawings
MAST	**ELEC**	Electrical Plans	
MAST	**OTHR**	Other Architecture	If in project program
	TBLK	Titleblock	XREF'd to ALL plotsheets
	TOPO	Survey/Topography	Produced by surveyor

PLOTSHEETS or Layouts w/ modelspaces. It is possible to have all sub-masters drawn on their respective plotsheet modelspaces.			
XREF	**Sheet**	**Sheet Title**	**Description**
	T-1.0	Title Sheet	
	T-1.1	General Notes	
	CF-1R	Title 24/Energy Calcs	
SITE	**A-1.0**	Site Plan	
TOPO	**A-1.1**	Survey/Topography	
NBHD	**A-1.2**	Neighborhood Compatibility	If required for submittal
SITE	**A-1.3**	Grading Plan	If not included in Site Plan
FLOR	**A-2.0**	Floor Plans	
	A-2.1		
ELEV	**A-3.0**	Exterior Elevations	
	A-3.1		
SECT	**A-4.0**	Building Sections	
	A-4.1		
MAST	**A-5.0**	Roof Plan	
INTR	**A-6.0**	Interior Elevations	
	A-6.1		
OTHR	**A-7.0**	Other Architecture	
	A-7.1		
	A-8.0	Schedules	
	A-8.1		
	A-D.1	Architectural Details	
	A-D.2		
FRAM	**S-1.0**	Foundation Plan	
FRAM	**S-1.0B**	Basement Framing Plan	If needed for space reasons
FRAM	**S-1.1**	First Floor Framing	
FRAM	**S-1.2**	Second Floor Framing	
	S-1.3		
FRAM	**S-2.0**	Roof Framing	
	S-2.1		
	S-D.1	Structural Details	
	S-D.2		
ELEC	**E-1.0**	Electrical Plans	
	E-1.1		

Figure 2.48 A sample XREF standard.

MASTER
(PARENT)

SUBMASTER
(CHILD)

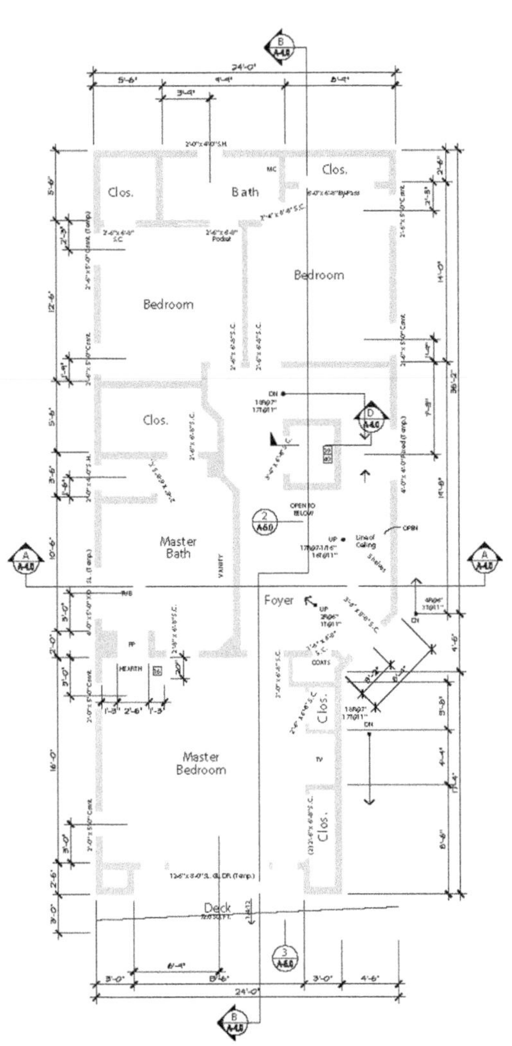

SLAVE
(SERVANT)

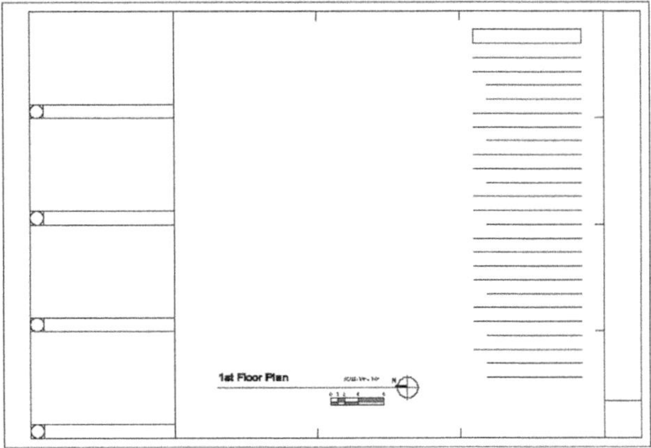

Figure 2.49 A floor plan developed through XREF.

Typical Paper(s)

"A" Paper (16)
- a. 11" x 8.5"
- b. 12" x 9"
- c. 10.5" x 7.5" **

"B" Paper (8)
- a. 17" x 11"
- b. 18" x 12"
- c. 15" x 10.5" **

"C" Paper (4)
- a. 22" x 17"
- b. 24" x 18"
- c. 21" x 15" **

"D" Paper (2)
- a. 34" x 22"
- b. 36" x 24"
- c. 30" x 21" **

"E" Paper (1)
- a. 44" x 34"
- b. 48" x 36"
- c. 42" x 30" **

(#) = sheets in an "E" size sheet
** = nonstandard

Figure 2.50 Typical standard and nonstandard paper sizes.

Paper larger than 8½″ × 11″ is subdivided into drawing modules. In Figure 2.50, a 24″ × 36″ sheet of paper is shown with a 1½″ left binding border and a ½″ border for the top, bottom, and right side. It will use a 1½″ title block. The remaining drawing area is divided into five horizontal and five vertical spaces, each of which is 4″ × 6½″. This now becomes the office standard for all drawings. Notes will be typed so as not to exceed 6½″ in width (or 13″ if two modules are used) and a vertical height of 4 5/8″, 9¼″, 13¾″, 18″, or 22 5/8″ (Figure 2.52).

Architectural details are drawn to this module of 4 5/8″ × 6½″. This space may be further divided into drawing areas and keynote areas to further exploit paper usage.

Plans, elevations, building sections, and site plans should be drawn within this established matrix so as to allow the remaining space to be used by details, notes, charts, and schedules. Figure 2.51 shows a site plan, general notes, details, vicinity map, and an index formatted to a 24″ × 36″ sheet of paper with a matrix of five vertical and five horizontal modules (Figure 2.53).

Figure 2.54 shows this formatting process using a 24″ × 36″ sheet divided into a 5 × 5 module and a 4 × 5 module, and a 30″ × 42″ sheet divided into a 5 × 5 module and a 6 × 6 module. Once the formatting process decision is made in the office, the drafter must comply with these limits when drawing, writing notes, and even detailing. If many drafters are working on one set of working drawings and all subscribe to a single format pattern, not only will the entire set look well organized to the client, clear, precise drawings reduce office liability and increase the visual impact of office documents.

As described earlier, a structure is drawn at full scale on the computer and viewed through a window that is actually the monitor. By filling this entire screen area with a standard-size sheet of paper, you have a formatted screen ready to import drawings. The interior of this drawing sheet is now your new window, which is called a **viewport.** Each module can also be a viewport. Thus, a viewport becomes a window on the paper through which you can see a full-size building. The computer allows you to zoom up close or fill the viewport with a graphic image such as a floor plan. In this way, you can fill to the extents of the viewport, but you will not be displaying to any given scale.

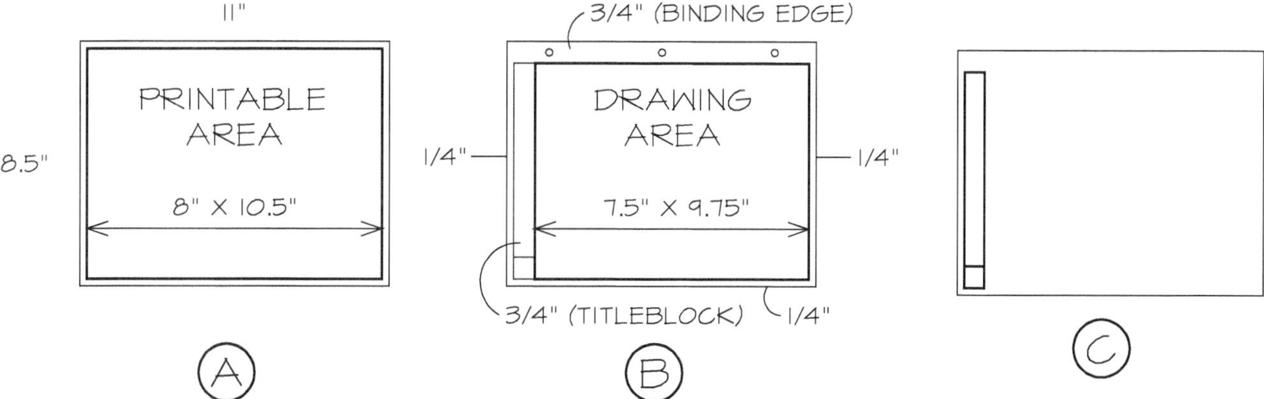

Figure 2.51 Printable and drawing area for a sheet size of 8.5″ × 11″.

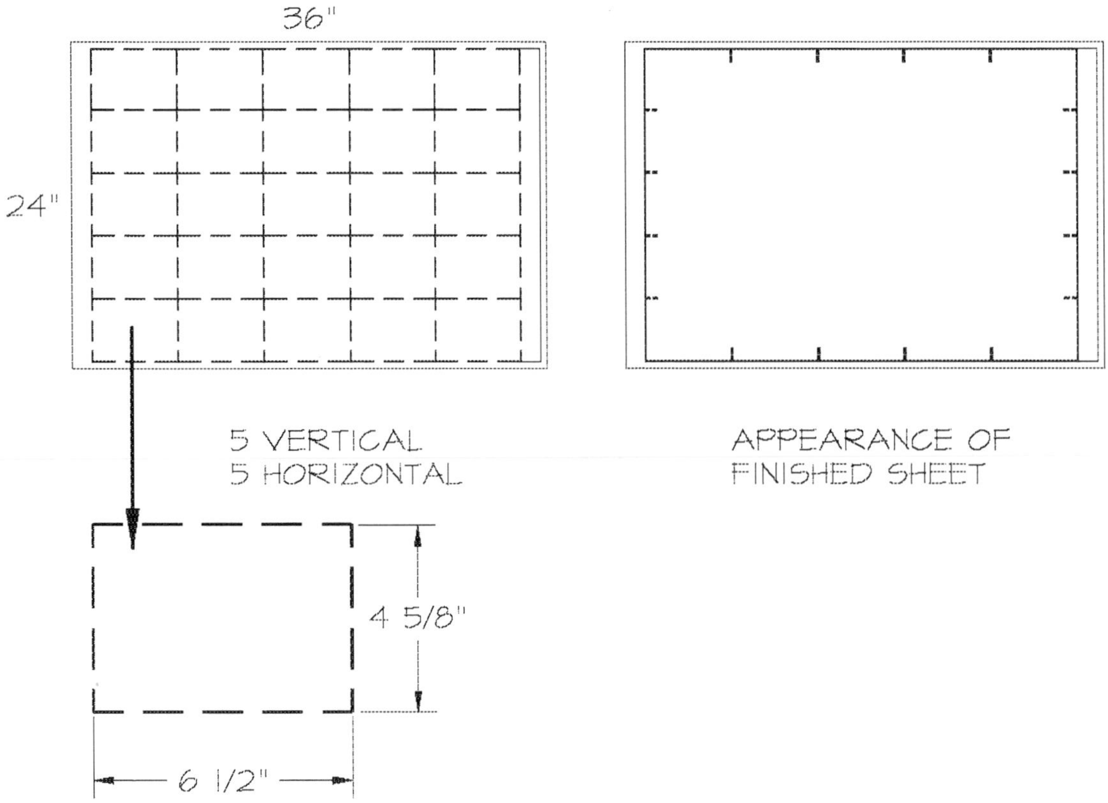

Figure 2.52 Drawing modules for 24″ × 36″.

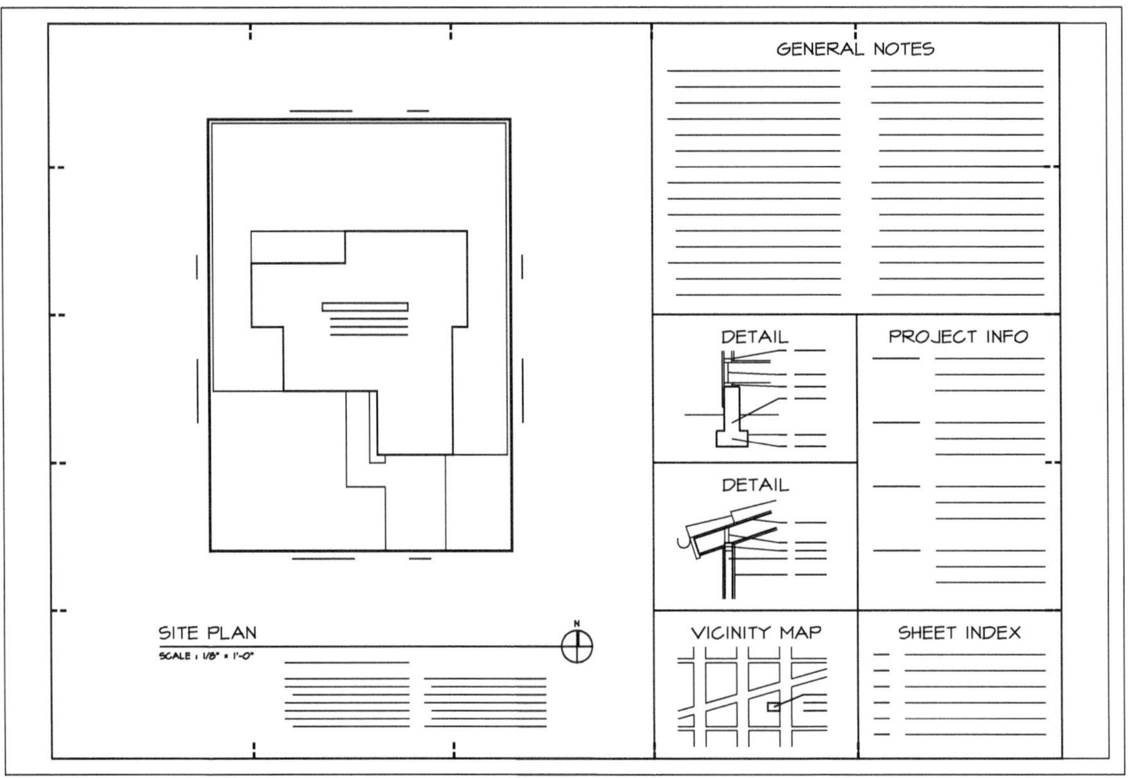

Figure 2.53 Drawing modules for 24″ × 36″ registered.

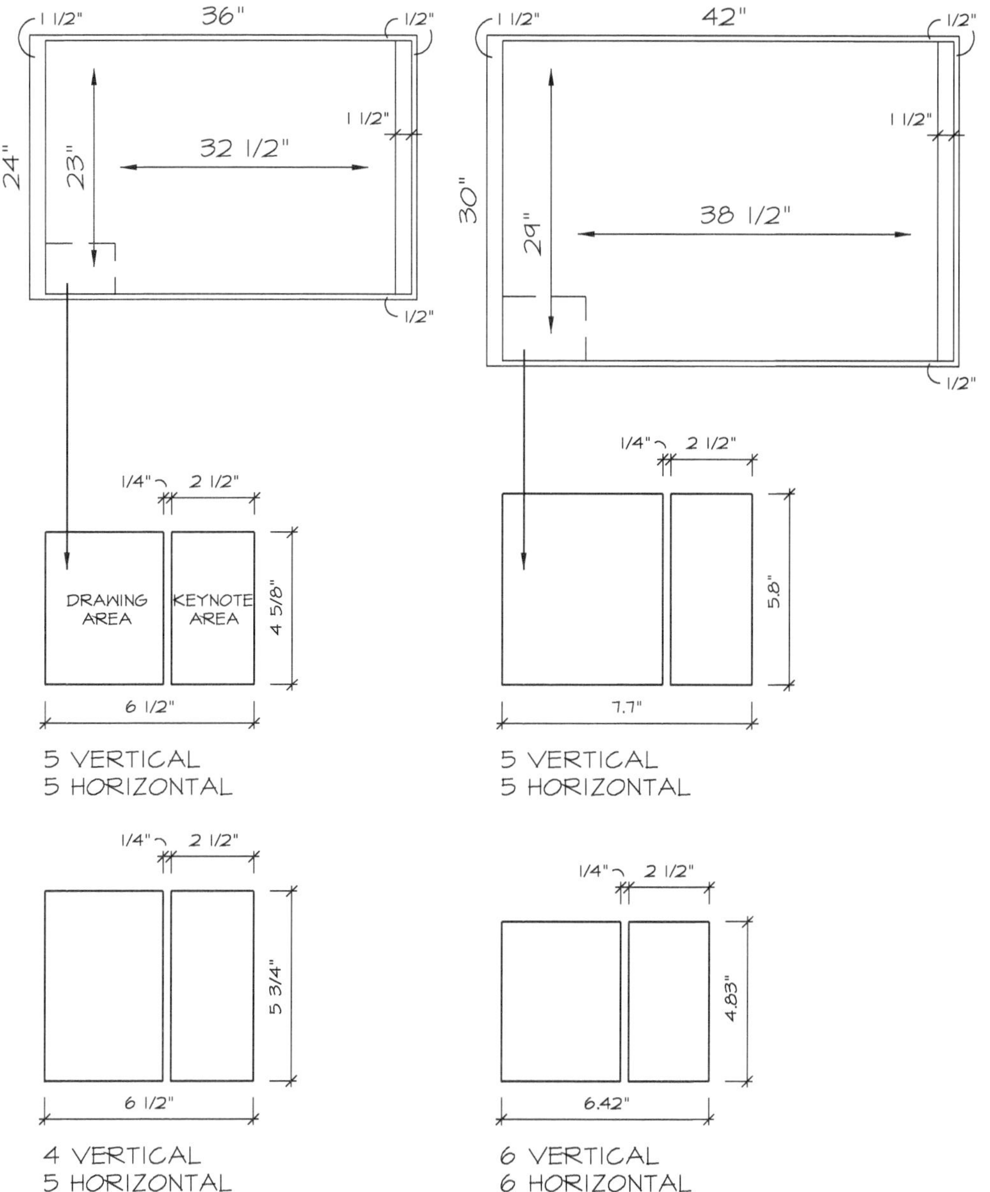

Figure 2.54 Detailing modules for 24″ × 36″ and 30″ × 42″.

The best solution to this non-scaled drawing is to fill the viewport with the largest image possible, but to a known scale. This scale may be an architectural scale such as ⅛″ = 1′-0″ or ¼″ = 1′-0″.

2-D (Paper) Versus 3-D (Virtual or Model) Space. The difference between two-dimensional (2-D) and 3-D space can be compared to the difference between manual drafting and CAD. In paper (2-D) space, you fill the monitor with a theoretical piece of paper. This theoretical piece of paper is already unrealistic, because it is an image of the actual piece of paper reduced to fit the screen. In manual drafting, the paper is actual size.

In model space or virtual space (3-D), you are drawing full size. When you are "modeling" a drawing, you measure the size of the building exactly. You do not work at a reduced scale.

When printing or plotting a drawing, you must reduce this full-size drawing or model to a scale that will fit on the actual paper size. For this reason, we encourage you to draw structures in model space and draw them full scale. Model space, also called **virtual space**, is the closest thing to the real thing.

Figure 2.55 shows various sizes of paper and their drawing areas based on scale, sizes of paper range from a standard 8½″ × 11″ to a 36″ × 48″. These are listed

	AP		BP		CP		DP		EP		FP	
(width) X"	11	8	17	14	24	21	36	33	48	45	42	39
(height) Y"	8.5	7.5	11	10	18	17	24	23	36	35	30	29
Scale	TRUE	ADJ	TRUE	ADJ	TRUE	ADJ	TRUE	ADJ	TRUE	ADJ	TRUE	ADJ
3"=1'	3'8x2'10	2'8x2'6	5'8x3'8	4'8x3'4	8'x6'	7'x5'8	12'x8'	11'x7'8	16'x12'	15'x11'8	14'x10'	13'x9'8
1 1/2"=1'	7'4x5'8	5'4x5'	11'4x7'4	9'4x6'8	16'x12'	14'x11'4	24'x16'	22'x15'4	32'x24'	30'x23'4	28'x20'	26'x19'4
1"=1'	11'x8'6	8'x7'6	17'x11'	14'x10'	24'x18'	21'x17'	36'x24'	33'x23'	48'x36'	45'x35'	42'x30'	39'x29'
3/4"=1'	14'8x11'4	10'8x10'	22'8x14'8	18'8x13'4	32'x24'	28'x22'8	48'x32'	44'x30'8	64'x48'	60'x46'8	56'x40'	52'x38'8
1/2"=1'	22'x17'	16'x15'	34'x22'	28'x20'	48'x36'	42'x34'	72'x48'	66'x46'	96'x72'	90'x70'	84'x60'	78'x58'
1/4"=1'	44'x34'	32'x30'	68'x44'	56'x40'	96'x72'	84'x68'	144'x96'	132'x92'	192'x144'	180'x140'	168'x120'	156'x116'
1/8"=1'	88'x68'	64'x60'	136'x88'	112'x80'	192'x144'	168'x136'	288'x192'	264'x184'	384'x288'	360'x280'	336'x240'	312'x232'
1/16"=1'	176'x136'	128'x120'	272'x176'	224'x160'	384'x288'	336'x272'	576'x384'	528'x368'	768'x576'	720'x560'	672'x480'	624'x464'
1/32"=1'	352'x272'	256'x240'	544'x352'	448'x320'	768'x576'	672'x544'	1152'x768'	1056'x736'	1536'x1152'	1440'x1120'	1344'x960'	1248'x928'
3/32"=1'	117'6x90'6	85'6x80'	181'6x117'6	149'6x107'	299' x 192'	224' x 181'6	384'6x 256'	352'6x 245'6	512'6 x 384'6	480'6x373'6	448'6 x 326'	416'6x309'6

Architectural

	AP		BP		CP		DP		EP		FP	
(width) X"	11	8	17	14	24	21	36	33	48	45	42	39
(height) Y"	8.5	7.5	11	10	18	17	24	23	36	35	30	29
Scale	TRUE	ADJ	TRUE	ADJ	TRUE	ADJ	TRUE	ADJ	TRUE	ADJ	TRUE	ADJ
1/10"=1'	110'x85'	80'x75'	170'x110'	140'x100'	240'x180'	210'x170'	360'x240'	330'x230'	480'x360'	450'x350'	420'x300'	390'x290'
1/20"=1'	220'x170'	160'x150'	340'x220'	280'x200'	480'x360'	420'x340'	720'x480'	660'x460'	960'x720'	900'x700'	840'x600'	780'x580'
1/25"=1'	275'x212'6	200'x187'6	425'x275'	350'x250'	600'x450'	525'x425'	900'x600'	825'x575'	1200'x900'	1125'x875'	1050'x750'	975'x725'
1/30"=1'	330'x255'	240'x225'	510'x330'	420'x300'	720'x540'	630'x510'	1080'x720'	990'x690'	1440'x1080'	1350'x1050'	1260'x900'	1170'x870'
1/40"=1'	440'x340'	320'x300'	680'x440'	560'x400'	960'x720'	840'x680'	1440'x960'	1320'x920'	1920'x1440'	1800'x1400'	1680'x1200'	1560'x1160'
1/50"=1'	550'x425'	400'x375'	850'x550'	700'x500'	1200'x900'	1050'x850'	1800'x1200'	1650'x1150'	2400'x1800'	2250'x1750'	2100'x1500'	1950'x1450'
1/60"=1'	660'x510'	480'x450'	1020'x660'	840'x600'	1440'x1080'	1260'x1020'	2160'x1440'	1980'x1380'	2880'x2160'	2700'x2100'	2520'x1800'	2340'x1740'
1/75"=1'	825'x637'6	600'x562'6	1275'x825'	1050'x750'	1800'x1350'	1575'x1275'	2700'x1800'	2475'x1725'	3600'x2700'	3375'x2625'	3150'x2250'	2925'x2175'
1/100"=1'	1100'x850'	800'x750'	1700'x1100'	1400'x1000'	2400'x1800'	2100'x1700'	3600'x2400'	3300'x2300'	4800'x3600'	4500'x3500'	4200'x3000'	3900'x2900'

Engineering

Adjusted Margins	
Top	0.5"
Bottom	0.5"
Left	1.5"
Right	0.5"
Title Rt.	1"
Title Bot.	0"

Figure 2.55 Paper space maximum.

across the top of Figure 2.55, and the various scales (architectural and engineering) are shown to the left. For example, if you were preparing a floor plan for a building 90′ deep and 135′ wide at a ¼″ = 1′-0″ scale (shaded area on chart) and wanted to find a paper sheet size, note that at the intersection of a 24″ × 36″ column and ¼″ = 1″ row, a 96″ × 144″ figure appears. This means that at a ¼″ scale, and using a 24″ × 36″ piece of paper, a 96′ × 144′ space is available. If a 70′ × 90′ building were to be drawn, it would occupy approximately 18″ × 24″ of the 24″ × 36″ sheet. The rest could be used for details, notes, or schedules.

Scaling Factor. Some computer programs are programmed to deal with scale. With these programs, the drafter can size or scale a drawing simply by typing in the scale desired or selecting a scale from a menu. For example, if you wish to print or draw a floor plan at ¼″ = 1′-0″ scale, you simply select this scale and the computer does the rest of the work.

Other programs call for a scaling factor to be used. Scaling factor is computed in reference to a foot (12 inches). For example, if a drawing is to be scaled at ¼″ = 1′-0″, you divide 12″ by ¼″. Forty-eight becomes the scaling factor for ¼″ = 1′-0″.

Figure 2.54 lists scaling factors for a variety of the most typically used architectural and engineering scales. Figure 2.56 shows a 9″ × 12″ and a 24″ × 36″ piece of paper. Using a scaling factor (48) for a ¼″ scale, the numbers in the parentheses indicate how many feet (at ¼″ scale) are available on the 24″ × 36″ sheet of paper. Now go back to Figure 2.57 and see the figures repeated for a number of different-sized sheets of paper and a variety of scales. Next, the drafter must know the same information for the drawing area. See Figure 2.58 and compute.

Scale	Factor
1'=1'	1
3"=1'	4
1 1/2"=1'	8
1"=1'	12
3/4"=1'	16
1/2"=1'	24
1/4"=1'	48
1/8"=1'	96
1/16"=1'	192
1/32"=1'	384
1"=10'	120
1"=20'	240
1"=25'	300
1"=30'	360
1"=40'	480
1"=50'	600
1"=60'	720
1"=75'	900
1"=100'	1200
1"=200'	2400

Figure 2.56 Scaling factors.

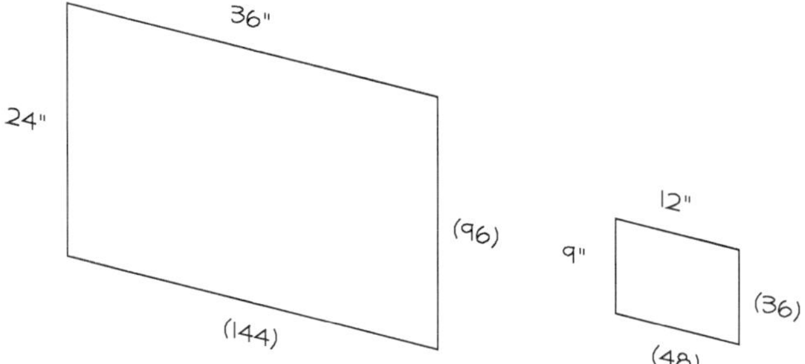

Figure 2.57 Scaling factor (¼") for 24" × 36" and 9" × 12".

Figure 2.59 shows the drawing area for a variety of scales and sheet sizes. The drawing area is now called the *viewport*.

Layering is what makes computer drafting so superior to manual drafting. Layering is the process of creating a series of overlays on which you display different functions and different types of lines and conventions. The alignment of computer-generated layers is perfect. Selection of the proper layers is done in seconds. Layers may be turned on and off, frozen in place, plotted or not plotted. They can also be grouped and XREFed from other drawings.

Let us now look at a typical set of layers for a construction document. The first layer is often considered the base, unless you are using XREF drawings as a base. This first layer contains the matrix that will act as a datum for the entire drawing. A matrix locates and positions the columns. The matrix will be drawn on the base layer, with the columns possibly on the subsequent layer.

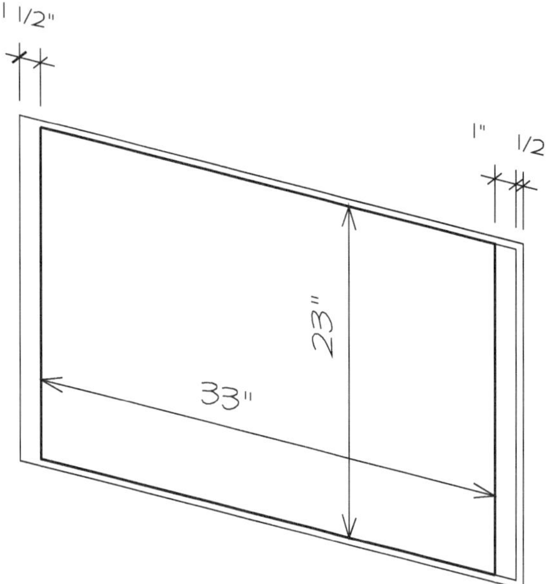

Figure 2.58 Printable area for 24" × 36" sheet.

This base (the datum) can be used for other drawings, so different views subscribe to the same system. Therefore, it becomes even more important that the drafter of tomorrow become familiar with 3-D datum drawings (described earlier) so that elevations, building sections, framing plans, and foundation plans can use the same base (datum) layer. In this way, we can cross-reference drawings from the very beginning (XREF drawings).

Each layer can be done in a different color. The use of various colors helps the drafter stay focused on the specific layer on which a particular task is to be accomplished. Colors also help in identifying drawings. Color also has an impact on the quality of lines, as explained in the next section.

If there is an inherent geometry present in the drawing but not used in the finished drawing, the construction lines can be drawn on a layer but never printed, A-NOH plotting layer. Take the case of drawing a winding stair, as shown in Figure 2.60. The construction lines are on one layer, and the drawing of the stair is on another. One need only outline the required portions of the geometry to produce a base drawing, and then repeat the forms to produce the finished drawing.

Setting Up Layers. Look again at the sample of layers and their specific titles in Figure 2.61. Although this is a simplified plan, it does follow many of the examples found in the national CAD standards pamphlet. Notice the legend and the letter designations for architectural, mechanical, structural, and so on. Learn to identify the standards so that you can tell the difference between correctly and incorrectly drawn documents.

			AP		BP		CP		DP		EP		FP	
		(width) X"	11	8	17	14	24	21	36	33	48	45	42	39
		(height) Y"	8.5	7.5	11	10	18	17	24	23	36	35	30	29
Factor	*Feet in 1"*	*Scale*	TRUE	ADJ	TRUE	ADJ	TRUE	ADJ	TRUE	ADJ	TRUE	ADJ	TRUE	ADJ
4	1"=0'-4"	3"=1'	3'8x2'10	2'8x2'6	5'8x3'8	4'8x3'4	8'x6'	7'x5'8	12'x8'	11'x7'8	16'x12'	15'x11'8	14'x10'	13'x9'8
8	1"=0'-8"	1 1/2"=1'	7'4x5'8	5'4x5'	11'4x7'4	9'4x6'8	16'x12'	14'x11'4	24'x16'	22'x15'4	32'x24'	30'x23'4	28'x20'	26'x19'4
12	1"=1'-0"	1"=1'	11'x8'6	8'x7'6	17'x11'	14'x10'	24'x18'	21'x17'	36'x24'	33'x23'	48'x36'	45'x35'	42'x30'	39'x29'
16	1"=1'-4"	3/4"=1'	14'8x11'4	10'8x10'	22'8x14'8	18'8x13'4	32'x24'	28'x22'8	48'x32'	44'x30'8	64'x48'	60'x46'8	56'x40'	52'x38'8
24	1"=2'-0"	1/2"=1'	22'x17'	16'x15'	34'x22'	28'x20'	48'x36'	42'x34'	72'x48'	66'x46'	96'x72'	90'x70'	84'x60'	78'x58'
48	1"=4'-0"	1/4"=1'	44'x34'	32'x30'	68'x44'	56'x40'	96'x72'	84'x68'	144'x96'	132'x92'	192'x144'	180'x140'	168'x120'	156'x116'
96	1"=8'-0"	1/8"=1'	88'x68'	64'x60'	136'x88'	112'x80'	192'x144'	168'x136'	288'x192'	264'x184'	384'x288'	360'x280'	336'x240'	312'x232'
192	1"=16'-0"	1/16"=1'	176'x136'	128'x120'	272'x176'	224'x160'	384'x288'	336'x272'	576'x384'	528'x368'	768'x576'	720'x560'	672'x480'	624'x464'
384	1"=32'-0"	1/32"=1'	352'x272'	256'x240'	544'x352'	448'x320'	768'x576'	672'x544'	1152'x768'	1056'x736'	1536'x1152'	1440'x1120'	1344'x960'	1248'x928'

Architectural

			AP		BP		CP		DP		EP		FP	
		(width) X"	11	8	17	14	24	21	36	33	48	45	42	39
		(height) Y"	8.5	7.5	11	10	18	17	24	23	36	35	30	29
Factor	*Feet in 1"*	*Scale*	TRUE	ADJ	TRUE	ADJ	TRUE	ADJ	TRUE	ADJ	TRUE	ADJ	TRUE	ADJ
120	1"=10'	1/10"=1'	110'x85'	80'x75'	170'x110'	140'x100'	240'x180'	210'x170'	360'x240'	330'x230'	480'x360'	450'x350'	420'x300'	390'x290'
240	1"=20'	1/20"=1'	220'x170'	160'x150'	340'x220'	280'x200'	480'x360'	420'x340'	720'x480'	660'x460'	960'x720'	900'x700'	840'x600'	780'x580'
300	1"=25'	1/25"=1'	275'x212'6	200'x187'6	425'x275'	350'x250'	600'x450'	525'x425'	900'x600'	825'x575'	1200'x900'	1125'x875'	1050'x750'	975'x725'
360	1"=30'	1/30"=1'	330'x255'	240'x225'	510'x330'	420'x300'	720'x540'	630'x510'	1080'x720'	990'x690'	1440'x1080'	1350'x1050'	1260'x900'	1170'x870'
480	1"=40'	1/40"=1'	440'x340'	320'x300'	680'x440'	560'x400'	960'x720'	840'x680'	1440'x960'	1320'x920'	1920'x1440'	1800'x1400'	1680'x1200'	1560'x1160'
600	1"=50'	1/50"=1'	550'x425'	400'x375'	850'x550'	700'x500'	1200'x900'	1050'x850'	1800'x1200'	1650'x1150'	2400'x1800'	2250'x1750'	2100'x1500'	1950'x1450'
720	1"=60'	1/60"=1'	660'x510'	480'x450'	1020'x660'	840'x600'	1440'x1080'	1260'x1020'	2160'x1440'	1980'x1380'	2880'x2160'	2700'x2100'	2520'x1800'	2340'x1740'
900	1"=75'	1/75"=1'	825'x637'6	600'x562'6	1275'x825'	1050'x750'	1800'x1350'	1575'x1275'	2700'x1800'	2475'x1725'	3600'x2700'	3375'x2625'	3150'x2250'	2925'x2175'
1200	1"=100'	1/100"=1'	1100'x850'	800'x750'	1700'x1100'	1400'x1000'	2400'x1800'	2100'x1700'	3600'x2400'	3300'x2300'	4800'x3600'	4500'x3500'	4200'x3000'	3900'x2900'

Engineering

Figure 2.59 Paper sizes at specific scales (½″ top, bottom, and right border, 1½″ left border, 1″ right title-block space).

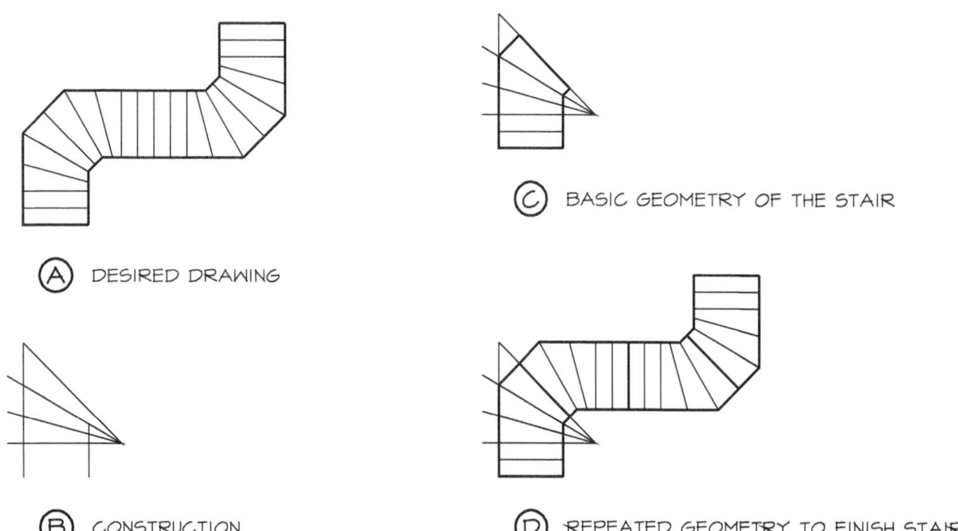

Figure 2.60 Diagnosing geometry (stair).

Correct and uniform titles are important, because as you are laying out the structural members of a building, these members must be cross-referenced with the electrical conduit on the electrical drawing, or the heating or air-conditioning ducts found on the mechanical set, that may occupy the same space.

The strategy employed might be staged similarly to that in Figure 2.61. Note the number of layers produced on the left side, the composite drawing for construction in the center, and the drawing used for client consumption on the right side. Note the inclusion of the furniture layer for client consumption and the voiding of the dimensioning layer on the same set.

In the multifile strategy illustrated in Figure 2.62, an example of a three-file system is shown. File #1 is the architectural file, which we just looked at in Figure 2.61. File #2 is a structural set, and File #3 is a lighting plan. Note how various layers are selected to produce still

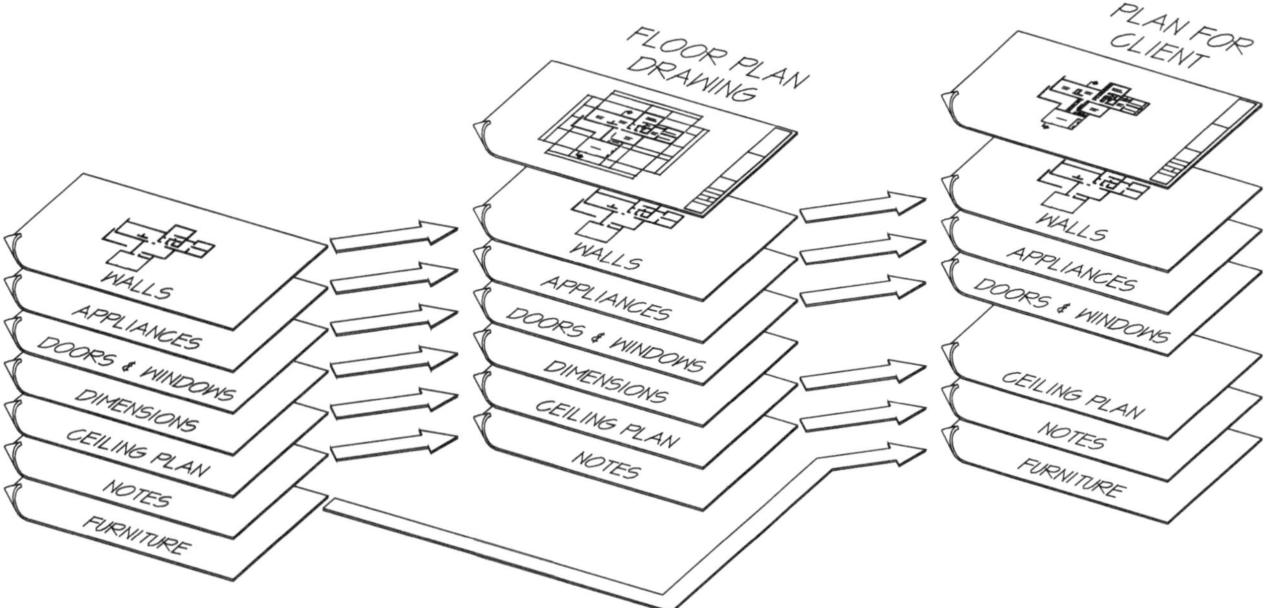

Figure 2.61 Example of the planning for a single file.

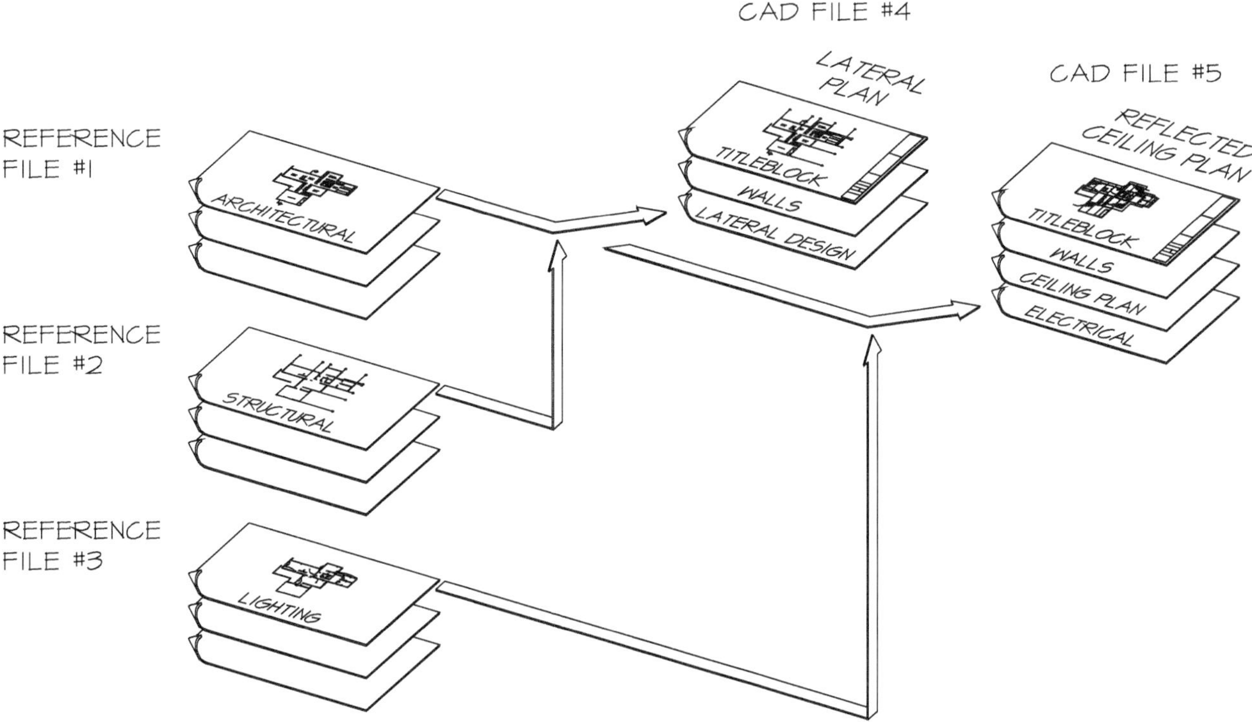

Figure 2.62 Example of planning for multiple files.

another file. In this example, File #4 becomes a lateral plan, and File #5 becomes the reflected ceiling plan. As indicated earlier, this process is called "XREFing."

The use of BIM and the families utilized in that system does an outstanding job of simplifying the complex system of layer that simple CAD utilize. The system of BIM understands that a simple line is a symbol of a specific object constructed a particular way and that representation of that object is tracked by the BIM program.

Pen Setting and Line Weights. Line weights can be produced by establishing and assigning certain colors as

Pen Settings

color	name	width
1	red	0.008
2	yellow	0.012
3	green	0.008
4	cyan	0.010
5	blue	0.012
6	magenta	0.030
7	white (high ink)	0.020
8	dark gray	0.015
9	light gray	0.015
15	dark red	0.012
30	orange	0.008
174	dark blue	0.010
250	dark gray	0.015
251	med. dark gray	0.015
252	med. gray	0.015
253	med. light gray	0.015
254	light gray	0.015
255	white (low ink)	0.015

Figure 2.63 Pen settings, line weights, and colors.

desired pen settings. Figure 2.63 shows common AutoCAD pen settings. The number assigned to the pen can be found on the extreme left side of the chart. Directly adjacent to the pen number is the name of the pen. The names are names of colors. As you can see by the width of the pens, magenta is the strongest and should be used for object lines. The thinnest line is red.

The office may have already established these standards, which may be based on a national standard. You need to know the source and why the office standards were established in this fashion. Knowing why allows you to know the office's game plan.

Pen settings and line weights should be saved on the computer when establishing the layers so that you can employ them as needed.

Figure 2.64 is a summary chart of the items discussed in this section. Sample standard titles are listed to the left, and then the colors used, followed by the line types and descriptions of their uses.

Lettering Size. One advantage of a computer is its ability to change scale rapidly. The disadvantage appears, for example, in drawing a floor plan at 1⁄4″ = 1′-0″ scale with 1⁄8″ tall lettering, then reducing it to a 1⁄8″ = 1′-0″ scale without any regard to the final height of the lettering. The lettering in this example will be 1⁄16″ tall and very difficult to read, not to mention that it will not follow the office standard and will look peculiar in a set of drawings.

Graphic scales are often used in lieu of expressing the scale in a proportion (see Figure 2.65A).

Because we are drawing in model space (virtual space), we are able to draw the structure at full scale. However, every drafter must realize the scale to which the drawing will be reduced and printed. For example, a floor plan can be drawn at full scale but may be reduced to 1⁄4″ = 1′-0″ scale when printed on a 24″ × 36″ sheet of paper. Knowing the final display scale is important because when notes and dimensions are placed on the final print, they must be readable. If the office standard is to have lettering that is 1⁄8″ tall, with titles 1⁄4″ tall, this lettering height must be translated into a measurement that is full size because we are drawing in full size. At 1⁄4″ = 1′-0″, all lettering (1⁄8″ in height) must be scaled at 6″ tall and the titles (1⁄4″ tall) at 1′-0″ because the lettering height is measured in scale. For your convenience, two charts, an engineering scale and an architectural scale, are included to help translate various lettering heights to specific heights (see Figure 2.66).

The scale in which you will print/plot your drawing is read across the top of each chart. The desired height of the final text is read down the left column. The intersection of these columns will tell you the height of the lettering. See the shaded area for the 1⁄8″ tall lettering at 1⁄4″ = 1′-0″ scale for the previous example.

The decimal conversion chart in Figure 2.65 includes the height of lettering in decimals. As every schoolchild knows, 1⁄2″ is equal to 0.5″, but equivalents for fractions such as 3⁄16 and 3⁄32 are hard to remember; they are 0.1875 and 0.09375, respectively.

Standards are established for general noting, room titles, and the title of the drawing. For example, it is a prevalent practice to use upper- and lowercase lettering for the title of a drawing, such as "Floor Plan." The font may be Helvetica. Room titles may be in all caps, using the same Helvetica font (Figure 2.67).

Advantages of a Computer

The first advantage with a computer is that you are drawing full size. Fifty-foot-long buildings are drawn 50 feet in length. This is possible because we are drawing in model (virtual) space, which is unlimited. Drafters can now think and measure full-size buildings in actual dimensions, rather than in a reduced scale.

Another advantage is the computer's ability to enlarge or reduce a drawing instantly. A single drawing can be reproduced in a variety of different scales. The computer has the capability to enlarge and reduce, much like a paper copier.

NAME	COLOR	LINETYPE	DESCRIPTION
0	WHITE	Continuous	For making Blocks and Unknown
ANNO	CYAN	Continuous	Text (annotation)
ANNO-DIMS	RED	Continuous	Dimensions
ANNO-IDEN	YELLOW	Continuous	Identification (rooms)
ANNO-KEYN	CYAN	Continuous	Keynotes
ANNO-LEGN	CYAN	Continuous	Legends and Schedules
ANNO-NOTE	CYAN	Continuous	General Notes
ANNO-PATT	RED	Continuous	Hatches (all)
ANNO-PCHE	8 (lt) or 9 (dk)	Continuous	Poche (all)
ANNO-REDL	RED	Continuous	Redlines (corrections to be made)
ANNO-SYMB	YELLOW	Continuous	Symbols (scale, north, section)
ANNO-TTLB	CYAN	Continuous	Title block
ANNO-VIEW	RED	Continuous	Viewports
DOOR	CYAN	Continuous	Doors (plan and elevation)
ELEC	YELLOW	Continuous	Electrical Symbols
ELEC-CONN	CYAN	CENTER2	Electrical Connections
ELEV	CYAN	Continuous	Elevation (colors can vary)
ELEV-BYND	BLUE	Continuous	Objects Beyond
ELEV-OTLN	WHITE	Continuous	Building Outline/Profile
FLOR	CYAN	Continuous	Floor plan (secondary information)
FLOR-DECK	YELLOW	Continuous	Deck
FLOR-HIDD	RED	HIDDEN	Hidden
FLOR-HRAL	RED	Continuous	Handrails and Balcony Railings
FLOR-STRS	CYAN	Continuous	Stairs
FNDN	YELLOW	HIDDEN	Foundation (footings and pads)
FNDN-SHRW	MAGENTA	Continuous	Shearwall
FNDN-SLAB	WHITE	Continuous	Slab
FRAM	YELLOW	Continuous	Framing (posts, headers, rafters)
FRAM-BEAM	WHITE	CENTER	Beams (wood, steel, prefab)
FRAM-JOIS	CYAN	CENTER2	Ceiling Joists
FRAM-SHRW	MAGENTA	Continuous	Shearwall
GLAZ	CYAN	Continuous	Windows (plan and elevation)
ROOF	WHITE	Continuous	Roof Outline (ridges, hips, valleys)
ROOF-BLDG	RED	DASHED	Building Outline
ROOF-OTHR	CYAN	Continuous	Roof (vent, chimney, skylight, etc.)
SECT	CYAN	Continuous	Section (colors can vary)
SECT-BYND	BLUE	Continuous	Objects Beyond
SECT-OTLN	WHITE	Continuous	Objects at Section Cut/Profile
SITE	CYAN	Continuous	Site
SITE-BLDG	WHITE	Continuous	Building Outline
SITE-EXST	RED	Continuous	Existing Information
SITE-PLNT	GREEN	Continuous	Plants/Landscape
SITE-PROP	MAGENTA	PHANTOM	Property Line
SITE-RTWL	YELLOW	Continuous	Retaining Wall
TOPO	GREEN	DASHED	Topography (from surveyor)
TOPO-OTHR	BLUE	DASHED2	Topography (faded)
WALL	WHITE	Continuous	Wall (full height)
WALL-HALF	YELLOW	Continuous	Wall (partial height)
XREF	WHITE	Continuous	Cross-Referenced Files (XREFs)
XREF-GHST-OTHER	BLUE	Continuous	Ghost - faded (fixtures, labels, etc.)
XREF-GHST-WALL	RED	Continuous	Ghost - light (walls, stairs, etc.)

Figure 2.64 Sample preliminary documentation of office layering standard.

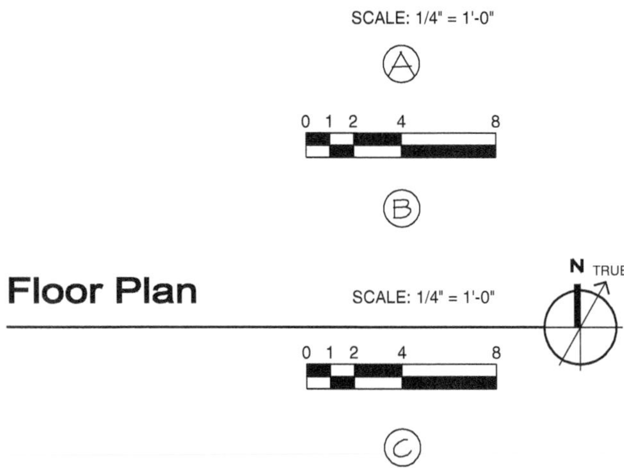

Figure 2.65 Numerical scale versus graphic scale.

A drawing can be displayed on the monitor as a single drawing, or the screen can be split and the original drawing can be displayed adjacent to an enlargement (see Figure 2.68). Two monitors can also be used simultaneously: one displaying the original drawing and the second monitor zooming in to show an enlargement of a given area (see Figure 2.69).

The computer was made for repetitive and redundant tasks. The accuracy and speed with which a computer carries out these tasks is far superior to the abilities of even the best manual drafter.

Computers can be networked so that if many drafters are working on one project, they can communicate with each other. As one drafter changes an element of a drawing—say, a window size—the change will be reflected on the drawing of the computers that are networked (this feature is particularly valuable when XREFed drawings are changed).

With BIM a window change will update all subsequent drawings and schedules such as the elevations and the window schedule, an updated set of drawings in an instant. The client directed change that is billable, but only takes moments to do the actual work. The computer programs of today can perform many tasks simultaneously. As a drafter is outlining a floor plan, for example, the computer is also computing the perimeter and the square footage of this polygon. Additionally in BIM a schedule table of floor area by level can be automatically generated

Architectural

Scale:	3"=1'	1 1/2"=1'	1"=1'	3/4"=1'	1/2"=1'	1/4"=1'	1/8"=1'	1/16"=1'	1/32"=1'
Feet in 1":	1"=0'-4"	1"=0'-8"	1"=1'-0"	1"=1'-4"	1"=2'-0"	1"=4'-0"	1"=8'-0"	1"=16'-0"	1"=32'-0"
Scale Factor:	4	8	12	16	24	48	96	192	384
1" Text	4"	8"	12"	16"	24"	48"	96"	192"	384"
3/4" Text	3"	6"	9"	12"	18"	36"	72"	144"	288"
1/2" Text	2"	4"	6"	8"	12"	24"	48"	96"	192"
3/8" Text	1.5"	3"	4.5"	6"	9"	18"	36"	72"	144"
1/4" Text	1"	2"	3"	4"	6"	12"	24"	48"	96"
3/16" Text	0.75"	1.5"	2.25"	3"	4.5"	9"	18"	36"	72"
1/8" Text	0.5"	1"	1.5"	2"	3"	6"	12"	24"	48"
3/32" Text	0.375"	0.75"	1.125"	1.5"	2.25"	4.5"	9"	18"	36"
1/16" Text	0.25"	0.5"	0.75"	1"	1.5"	3"	6"	12"	24"

Engineering

Scale:	1/10"=1'	1/20"=1'	1/25"=1'	1/30"=1'	1/40"=1'	1/50"=1'	1/60"=1'	1/75"=1'	1/100"=1'
Feet in 1":	1"=10'	1"=20'	1"=25'	1"=30'	1"=40'	1"=50'	1"=60'	1"=75'	1"=100'
Factor:	120	240	300	360	480	600	720	900	1200
1" Text	120"	240"	300"	360"	480"	600"	720"	900"	1200"
3/4" Text	90"	180"	225"	270"	360"	450"	540"	675"	900"
1/2" Text	60"	120"	150"	180"	240"	300"	360"	450"	600"
3/8" Text	45"	90"	112.5"	135"	180"	225"	270"	337.5"	450"
1/4" Text	30"	60"	75"	90"	120"	150"	180"	225"	300"
3/16" Text	22.5"	45"	56.25"	67.5"	90"	112.5"	135"	168.75"	225"
1/8" Text	15"	30"	37.5"	45"	60"	75"	90"	112.5"	150"
3/32" Text	11.25"	22.5"	28.125"	33.75"	45"	56.25"	67.5"	84.375"	112.5"
1/16" Text	7.5"	15"	18.75"	22.5"	30"	37.5"	45"	56.25"	75"

Figure 2.66 Text size for architectural/engineering drawings.

Standard Text Sizes

Standard Text		Optional Text	
1"	1	3/4"	0.75
1/2"	0.5	3/8"	0.375
1/4"	0.25	3/16"	0.1875
1/8"	0.125	3/32"	0.09375
1/16"	0.0625	3/64"	0.046875
1/32"	0.03125		

Figure 2.67 Conversion chart for simple fraction to decimal.

and updated on a set of drawings for inclusion on a cover sheet and a total can be calculated in real time as well.

New computer programs that are rapidly being introduced require the new breed of computer technologist to thoroughly be aware of BIM, sustainable/green architecture, and the computer engine to make this a possibility in our industry. This means that you cannot depend on any old information that you may have, specifically seek out new information about architecture in general.

The impact of BIM is now beginning to be fully realized by the large offices and working its way into the smaller offices. The larger offices have the ability to redesign the various programs, such as Bentley, ArchiCAD, and Revit, and are beginning to hire their own specialists to redesign the programs and customizing to fit in their own practice by using AIA and national standards as their office datum. Earlier exposure of our associates to the national (even global) interest in green architecture and the implementation of LEED in buildings should introduce architecture to a new era.

Governmental agencies are now beginning to require architectural firms to use CAD programs such as Bentley, VectorWorks, ArchiCAD, and Revit. Although

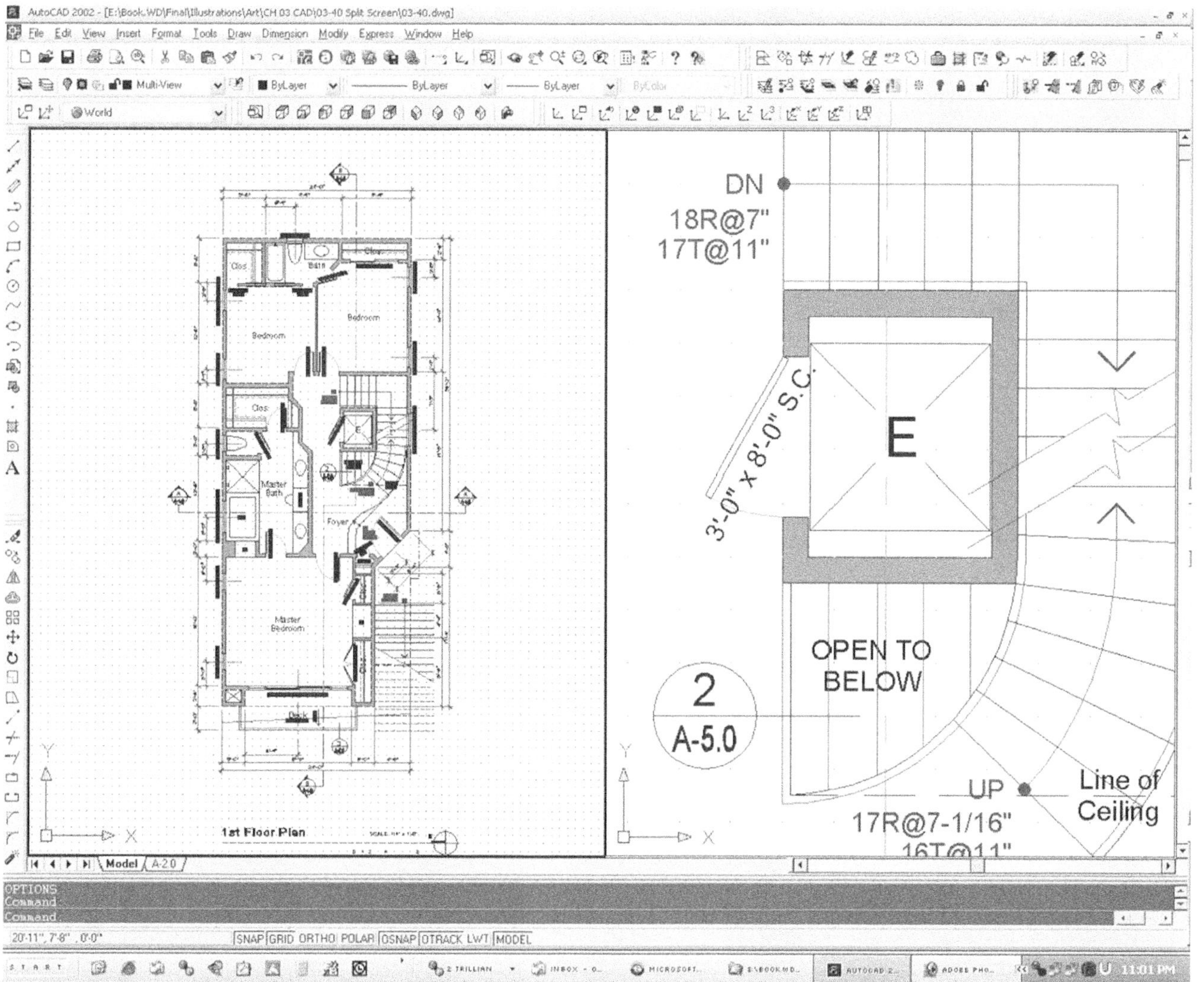

Figure 2.68 Split screen.

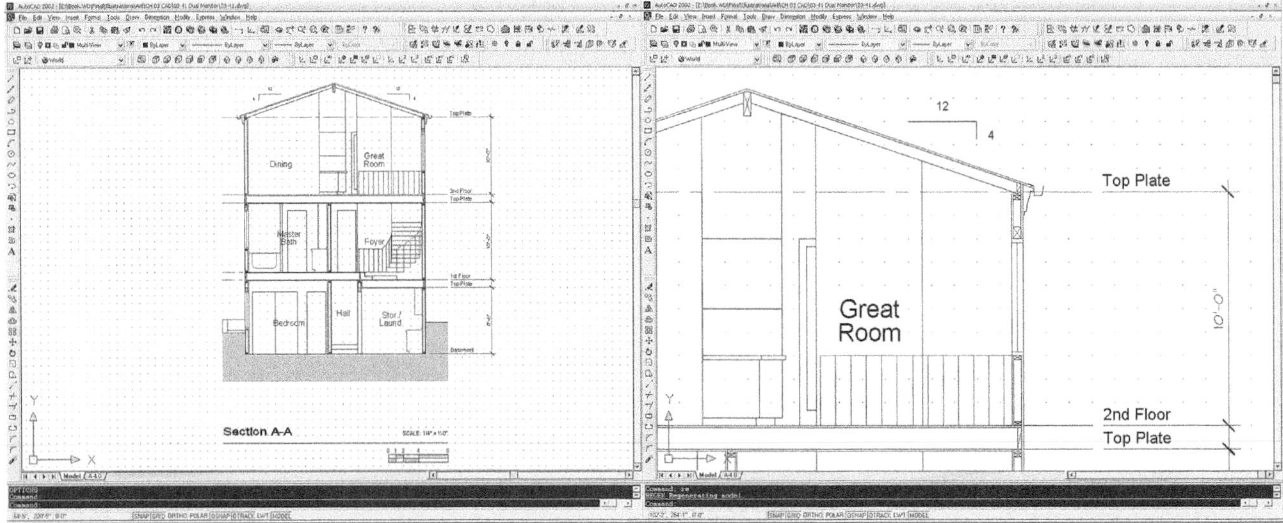

Figure 2.69 Dual screen.

programs other than Revit are available, large firms appear to favor Revit. Many school districts, hospitals, and large commercial projects are also requiring successful contract bidders to use BIM as the instrument for building design and construction. Thus, it behooves architects and designers to be familiar and comfortable with both BIM and Revit.

THE DIMENSIONAL REFERENCE SYSTEM

The **Dimensional Reference System** is based on a 3-D axis. See Figure 2.70. Critical planes are located by a series of reference bubbles and used as **planes of reference.** Figure 2.71 shows a box; reference bubbles describe the three planes of height, width, and depth. Now examine this box sliced in two directions, as shown in Figures 2.72 and 2.73. The first slice produces a **horizontal control plane**, and the second a **vertical control plane.**

The shaded area in Figure 2.74 represents a horizontal plane at a critical point on the structure, such as the floor line. The shaded area in Figure 2.75 represents a vertical plane at a critical point of the structure, such as the location of a series of columns or beams. There is a definite relationship between the vertical control plane and the horizontal control plane. Compare the plan and the section shown in Figure 2.76. The section is a vertical cut as in Figure 2.75 and the plan is a horizontal cut as in Figure 2.74. The two vertical and one horizontal reference bubbles on Figure 2.75 are an attempt to show this relationship.

Sketching. **Sketching** is the process of drawing the design of a structure to a specific architectural detail. This is a way of conveying to the CAD drafter the ideas you are trying to deliver to the contractors in the field. Details, in particular, must be resolved before the plans, elevations, and building sections are drafted, as they will dictate the shape and configuration of structural components.

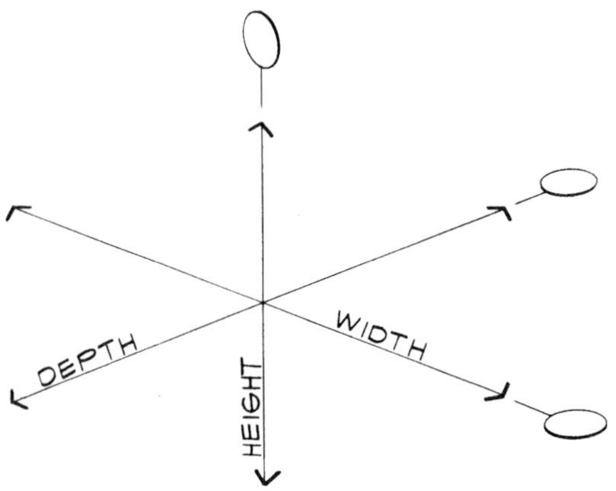

Figure 2.70 Dimensional reference system.

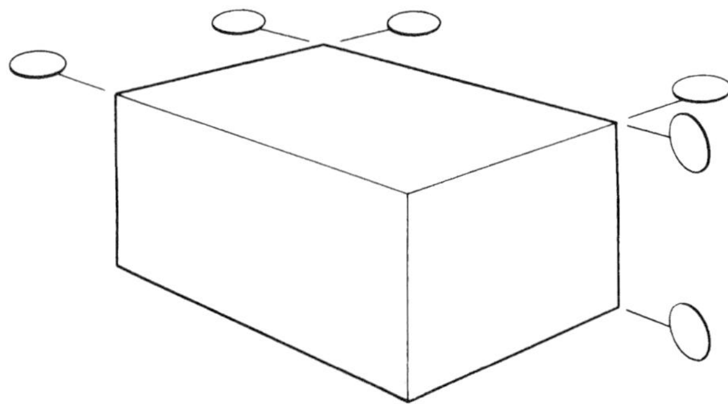

Figure 2.71 Three principal planes using dimensional reference system.

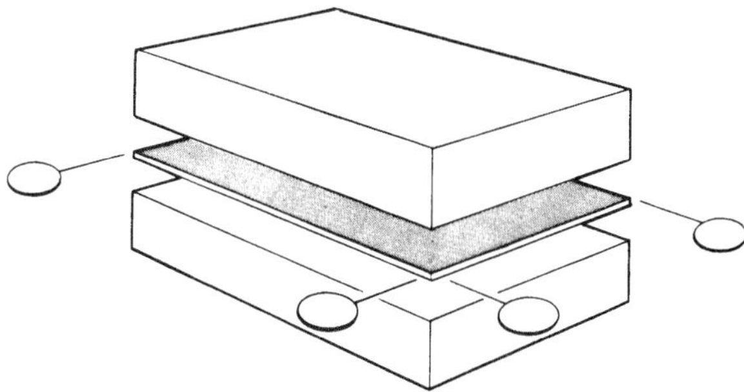

Figure 2.72 Horizontal control plane.

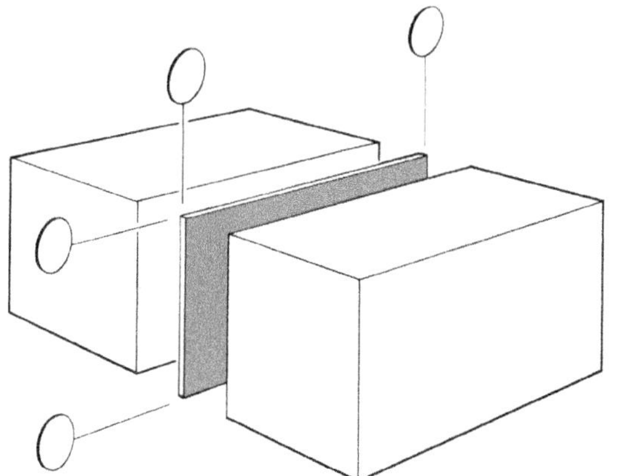

Figure 2.73 Vertical control plane.

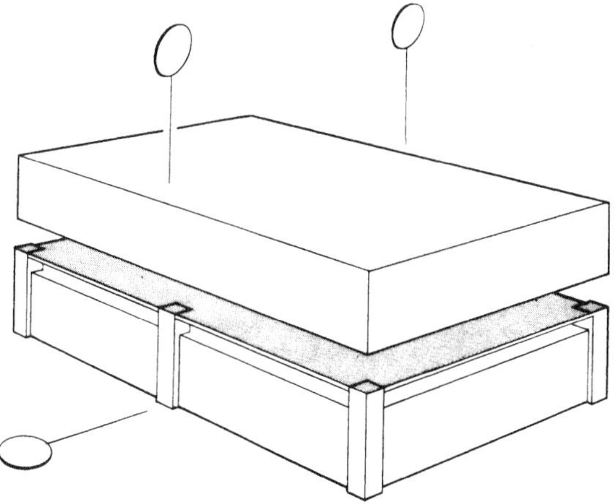

Figure 2.74 Horizontal plane.

Types of Planes

There are two types of planes. The first is the **axial plane**, which goes through the center of critical structural items as shown in Figure 2.77. Note how the columns are dimensioned to the center. When **pilasters** (widening of a masonry wall for support) are used, they become a good location for control dimensions, as they support the structural members above.

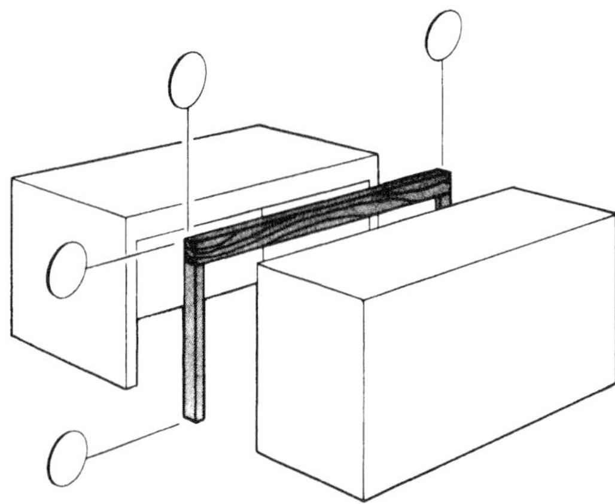

Figure 2.75 Vertical plane.

The second type of plane is called a **boundary control plane.** See Figure 2.78. In this case, columns and walls are not dimensioned to the center; instead, their boundaries are dimensioned. Figure 2.79 shows examples of columns and walls located in the **neutral zone.** These neutral zones are especially valuable in dealing with the vertical dimensions of a section and with elevations. See Figure 2.80. A neutral zone is established between the ceiling and the floor above. The floor-to-ceiling heights can be established to allow the structural, mechanical, and electrical consultants to perform their work. Once that dimension is established, the neutral zone and floor-to-floor dimensions follow. See Figure 2.81 for a practical application for the **vertical control dimension** and **control zone** (another term for neutral zone).

■ SPECIFICATIONS

Specifications are the written portion of the contract documents that describe the work to be performed by the hired contractor. Specifications complete the drawing portion of the CDs. The AIA defines the specifications as that portion of the contract documents consisting of the written requirements for materials, equipment, systems, standards, and workmanship for the work and performance of related services in its A201 contract. Many manufacturers will provide you specifications for your use. Primarily they do this to provide opportunities for increased sales; if an architect specifies Benjamin Moore paints, it is likely the contractor will purchase for the application of paint, Benjamin Moore. Providing the architect data results into direct sales. The specifications are an integral part of the contract and know that the written word supersedes the graphic representations on CDs.

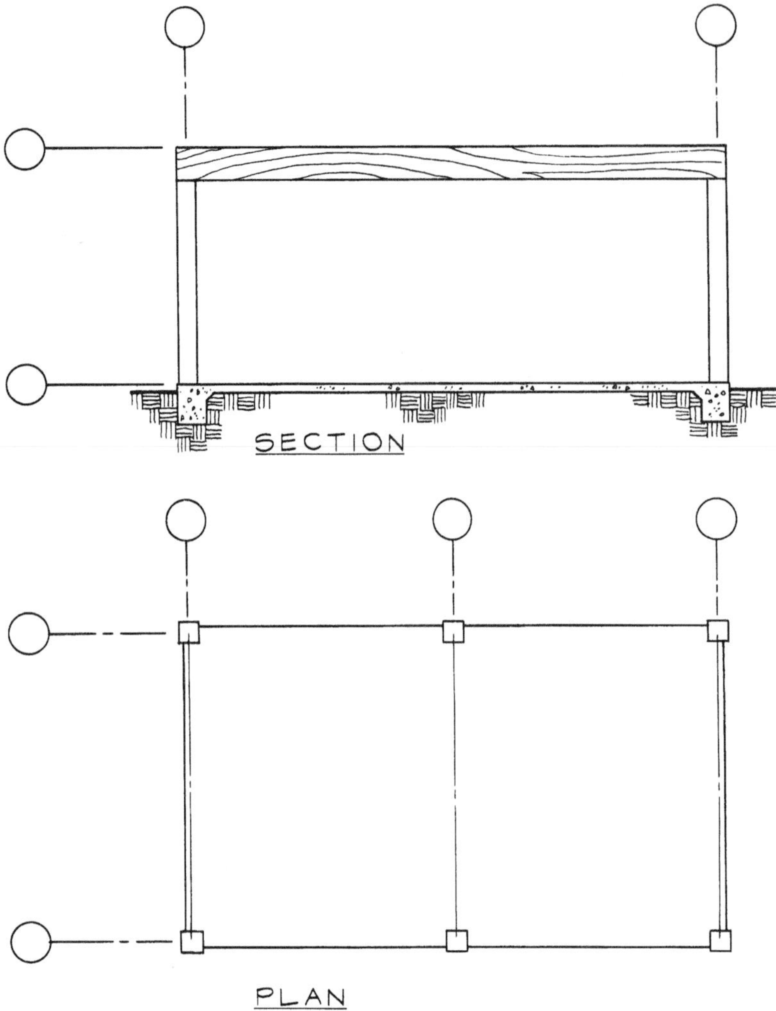

Figure 2.76 Section and plan.

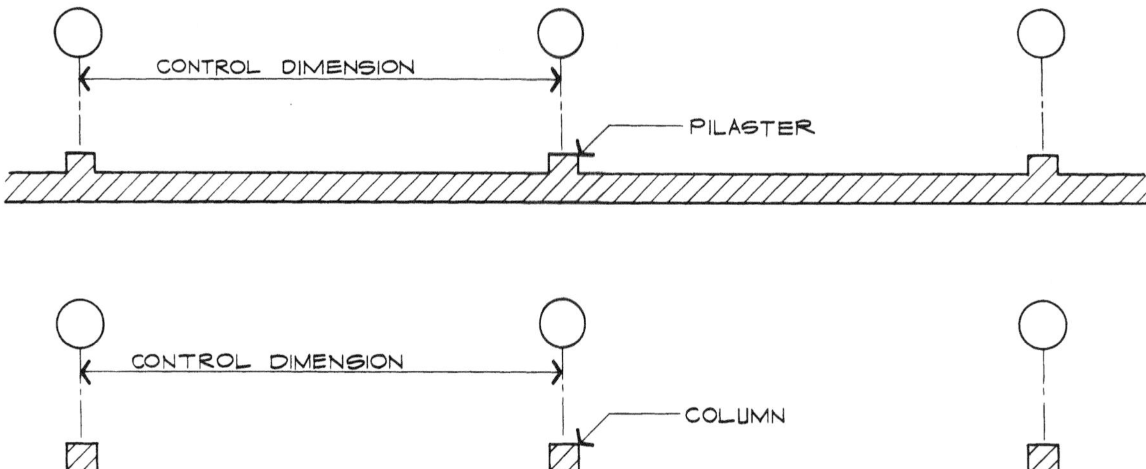

Figure 2.77 Axial control planes.

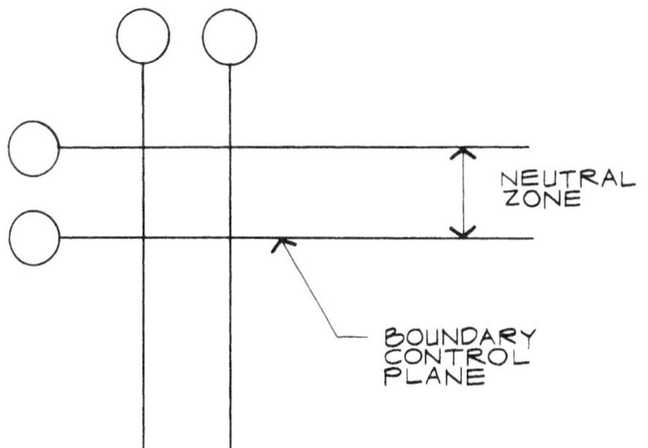

Figure 2.78 Boundary control planes.

BUILDING MATERIALS AND METHODS

Materials and Systems

Building construction incorporates various building systems, materials, and construction principles. These systems, materials, and principles are generally selected for the following reasons:

1. The type and use of the proposed structure
2. Governing building code requirements
3. Architectural design and planning solutions
4. Structural concepts
5. Economic considerations
6. Environmental influences
7. Energy requirements

The use of one or more materials for a proposed building may be predicated on reasons such as building code requirements or the building occupancy; architectural design; energy and climatic conditions; and the influence of natural forces, including high winds, seismic events, infestation, and moisture. For most structures, the main materials used are wood, concrete, structural steel, masonry, light steel framing, and composite materials. For many structures, a combination of materials may be utilized. The primary components of construction systems include the foundation and floor systems, and the wall and roof systems.

The primary materials utilized in construction systems are the following:

1. Wood—sawn lumber and manufactured lumber, often called **engineered lumber**
2. Concrete
3. Structural steel and light steel framing
4. Masonry, brick, or block
5. Composite systems with a combination of materials
6. Recycled/reclaimed
7. Tensile structures

Wood Materials

The layout of a floor plan using a wood stud framing system is very flexible in comparison to that of a floor plan using another material. This is because openings in the exterior and interior walls are not restricted by a modular unit or other material constraints. Wood also performs well in environmental conditions such as seismic events or hurricanes.

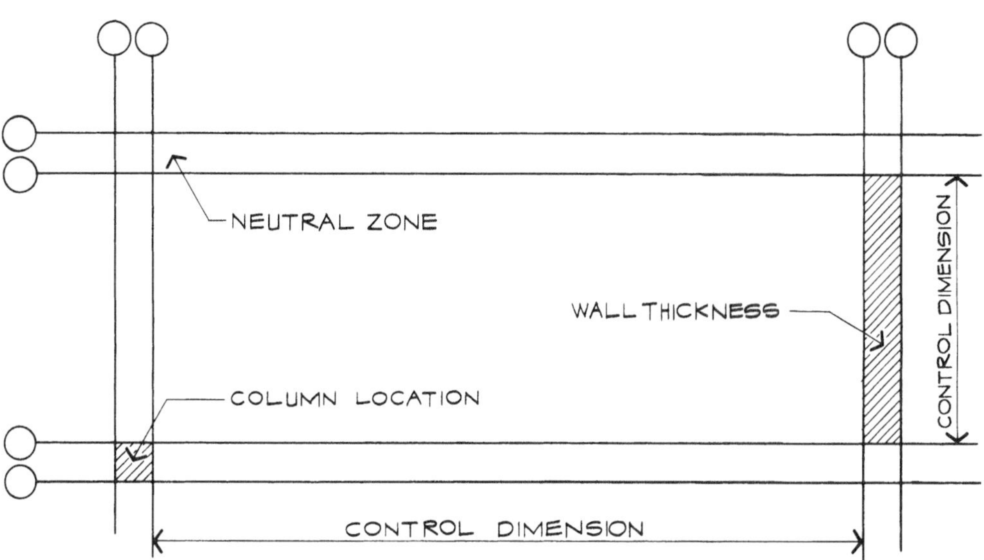

Figure 2.79 Column location in a neutral zone.

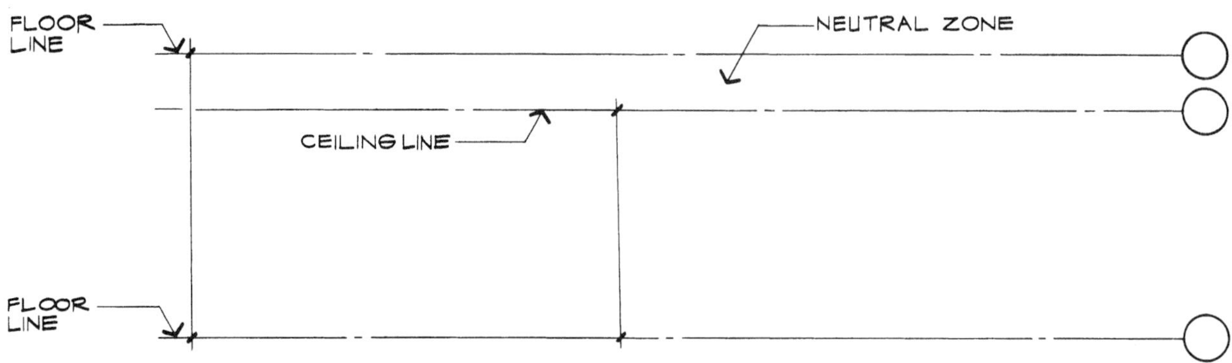

Figure 2.80 Neutral zone in a vertical dimension.

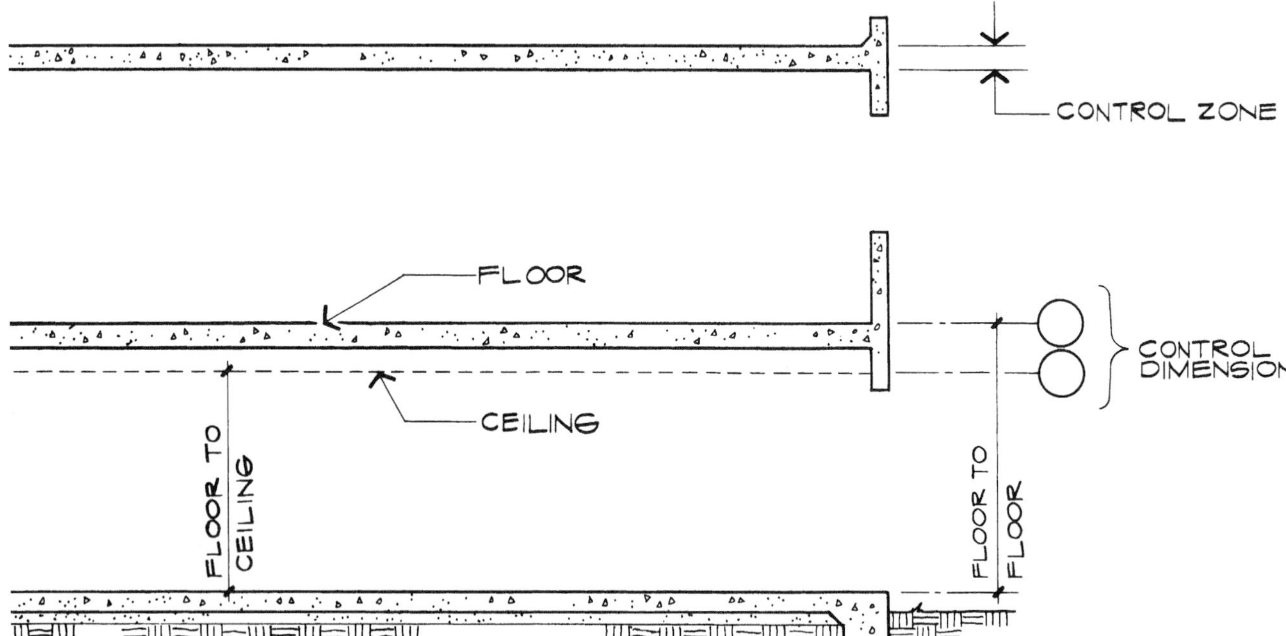

Figure 2.81 Vertical control dimension.

When a conventional wood stud framing system has been selected for the floor, walls, and roof systems, the floor plan drawings must be graphically correct. For example, a wood stud wall system is presented with the use of two parallel lines, which may be drawn to scale, incorporating the wood stud size in combination with the exterior and interior finishes. An example of a floor plan for a small dwelling, using two parallel lines to represent a conventional 2 × 4 wood stud wall in plan view, is illustrated in Figure 2.80. The exterior walls are dimensioned from the face of the wood stud as abbreviated with the letters **"FOS,"** indicating **"face of stud."** This method of dimensioning will correspond to the face of the concrete foundation footing, thus providing a good dimensional check for both the floor plan and the foundation plan. For layout purposes, the width of the two parallel lines will be the stud width of 3½″ plus the thickness of the exterior and interior wall finishes. Interior wall finish can be ½″ or ⅝″ gypsum wall board often called drywall. Another common interior finish is ¾″ thick lath and plaster. Exterior wall may consist of ½″ thick plywood, ½″-¾″ siding or shingles, ⅞″ cement plaster often termed stucco. Brick, tile, and stone veneer are also finishes often seen in variations of sizes and finishes. With BIM, these are all pre-selected in the wall family or customized as need for your specific situation. The interior walls are dimensioned to the centerline of the walls, as indicated in Figure 2.82. Note that the 4 × 4

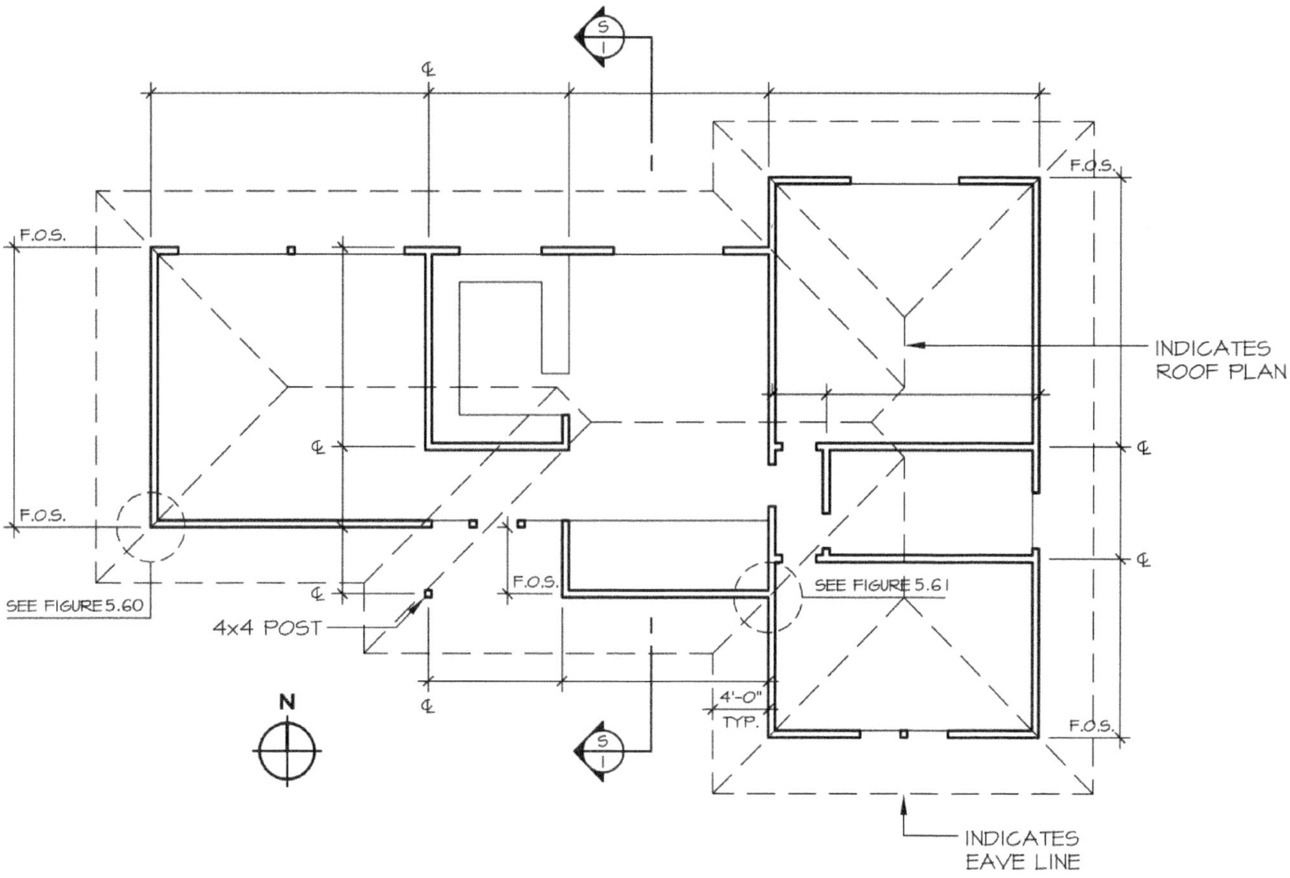

Figure 2.82 Floor plan with 2 × 4 stud framing.

post is dimensioned to the centerline in both directions. With AutoCAD it is difficult (or let's say more time consuming to dimension to center of stud wall,) so often it is dimensioned to the face of stud, though this is not a standard convention.

Figure 2.83 represents a view of the corner framing condition for this small dwelling. This is shown to illustrate the actual dimension line as it relates to the stud face dimension. The corner layout is intended to maximize strength and accommodate the connection of the finish materials to the studs. In this example, gypsum board can be screwed to two of the interior corner studs, while the cement plaster can be nailed to the exterior corner stud.

In laying out the interior walls of the floor plan, the two parallel lines are drawn to scale, incorporating the width of the wood stud plus the thickness of the interior wall finishes. See Figure 2.84.

Wood Post and Beam

Another project to be built with wood may use a different format with a conventional wood stud construction system. For example, a wood modular system may be selected for the structure. This system will incorporate the use of posts and beams spaced at a preferred dimensional distance. The modular distance will depend on the type and size of the floor and roof members that will span between the modular beam systems. These members may use solid tongue-and-groove planking, sawn lumber joists, or engineered lumber joists. Modular post-and-beam systems may be used in light construction projects, such as a residence, or in the heavy timber construction of a public building. See Figure 2.85.

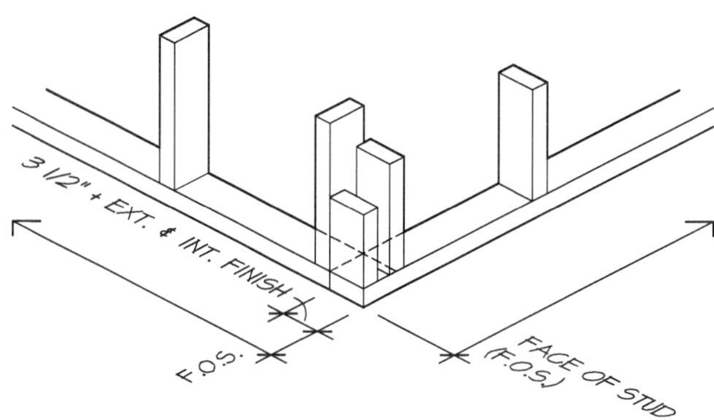

Figure 2.83 Corner framing layout.

Fire Resistant Wood

Recently, a product was introduced to the architectural world that is worth investigating. It uses the entire tree and produces a product somewhat like engineered lumber. However, there is one major difference. The lumber that is produced uses glass as one of the ingredients, resulting in lumber that will not burn.

Concrete Material

Once concrete has been selected as the structural material for a building project, it is necessary to decide whether the concrete will be poured in place or precast concrete will be used. If precast concrete units have been selected for construction of the exterior and interior walls and the roof system, it is of paramount importance to consult with the project's structural engineer. From the approved preliminary building design, the structural engineer will determine the thickness of the interior and exterior walls. The thickness of a wall will depend on whether it is a load-bearing or non-load-bearing wall and whether it will have to resist wind, snow, or lateral loads. These determinations will allow the architect to lay out the exact wall thickness on the floor plan. See Figure 2.86. This initial drawing of the floor plan establishes the wall thickness for the load-bearing and non-load-bearing precast concrete walls. The walls shown on matrix lines A, B, and D are non-load-bearing walls and have been determined to be 5″ thick. The wall thickness for the load-bearing walls along matrix lines 1–9 is to be 7″ thick. The load-bearing walls have been engineered

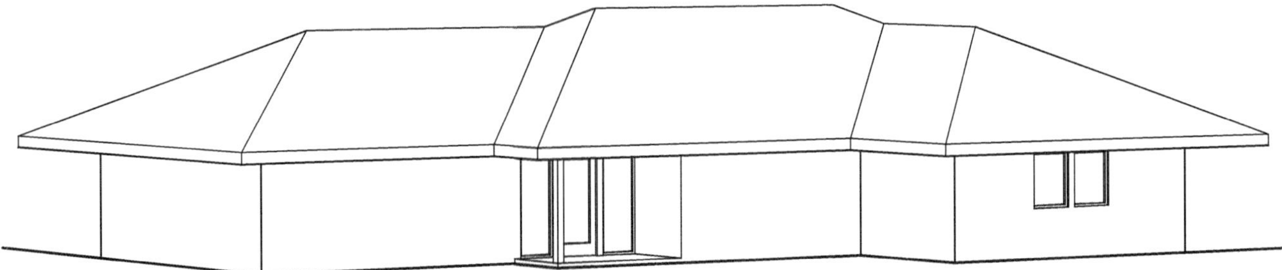

Figure 2.84 Perpendicular wall intersection.

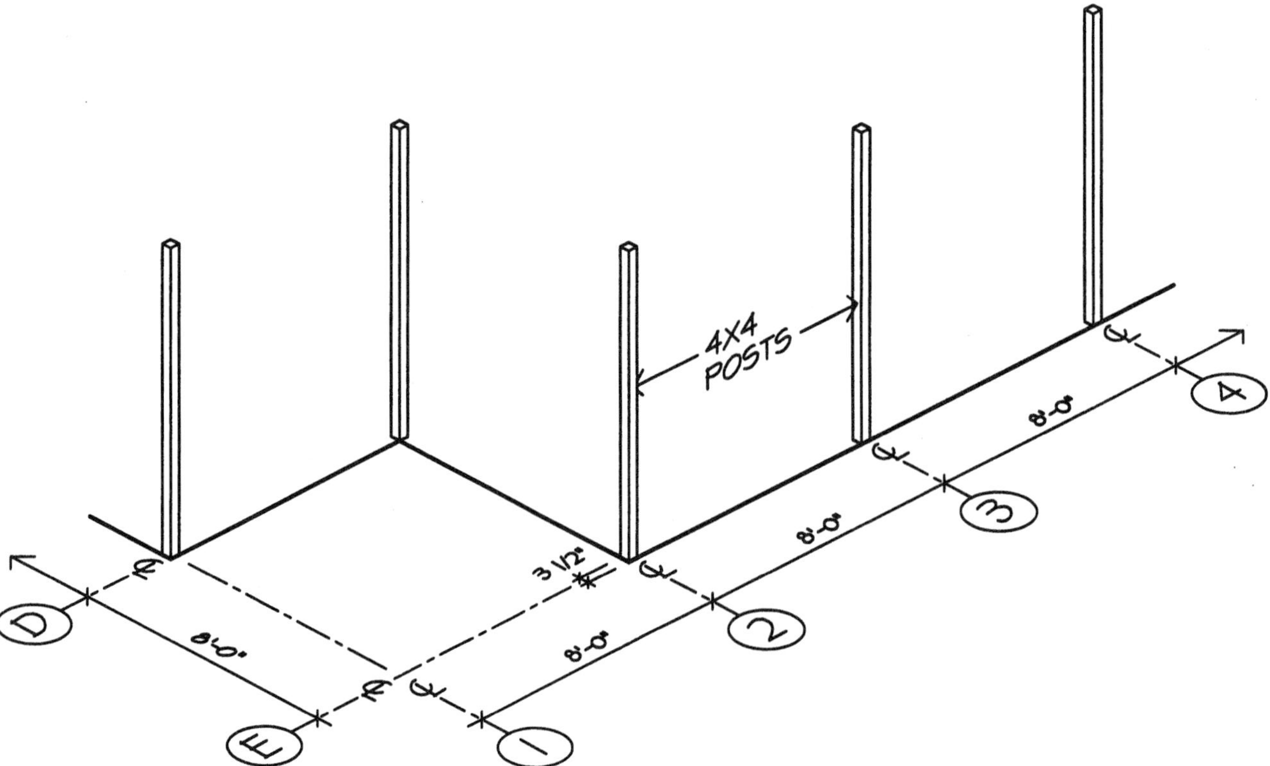

Figure 2.85 Partial modular post layout.

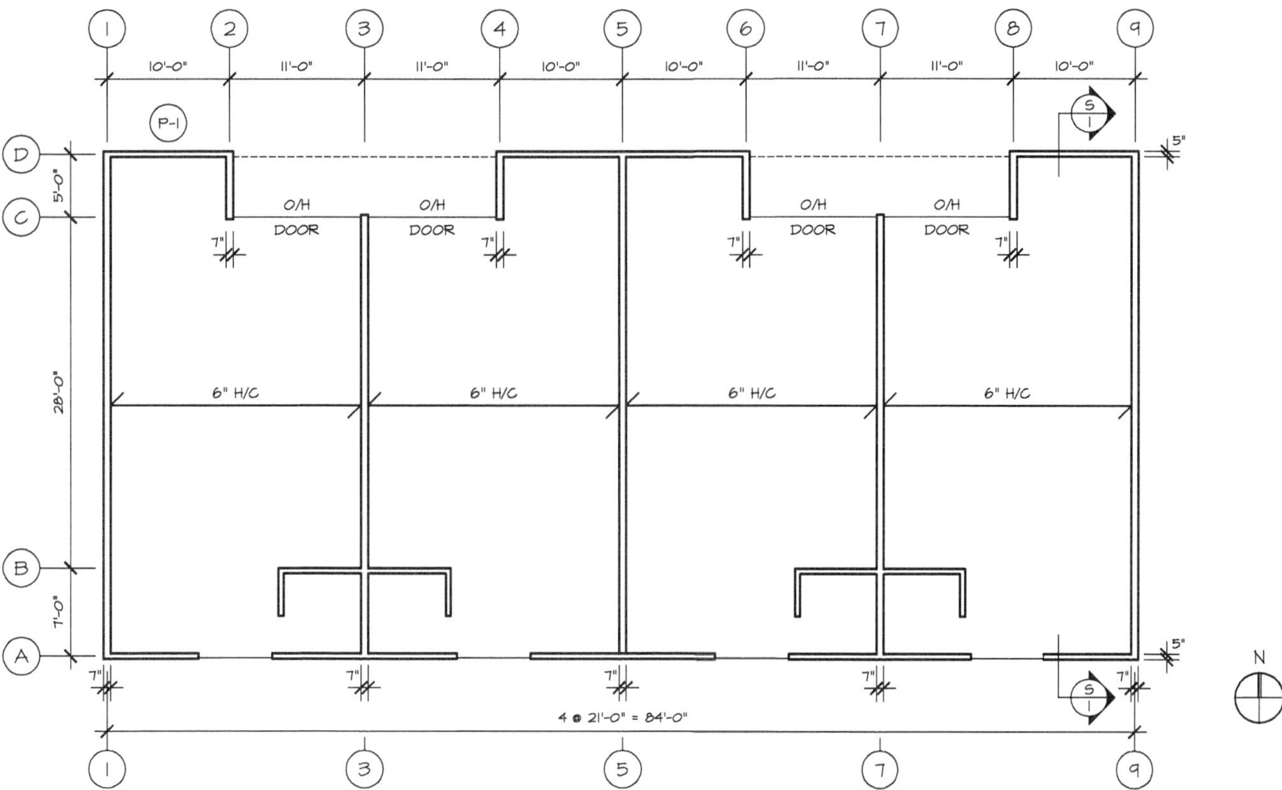

Figure 2.86 Plan layout—precast concrete walls.

to support 6″ precast concrete cored slab panels, which will span 21′. The use of a matrix system provides clarity for identifying the various precast concrete panel locations. See Figure 2.86.

The next step in developing the floor plan layout is to provide the building dimensions and the various wall thickness dimensions. Also noted at this time are the directional arrows for the spans of precast hollow-core panels that will support the roof. Indicated on the span directional arrows are the thickness of the concrete cored slab panels, which is 6″, and the abbreviation HC, which means hollow core. A directional arrow is drawn between the matrix symbols and ① to further illustrate the bays that the hollow-core precast panels are spanning. On this arrow are noted four bays at 21′, with an overall length of 84′. At this stage, the basic floor plan layout shows the primary structural members.

A commonly used concrete wall system that is poured in place is called a **concrete retaining wall**. As with most poured-in-place concrete, wood forms are constructed on both sides of the wall and tied together to resist the weight and force of the poured concrete. Steel reinforcing bars are required and are attached to the wood forms before the concrete is poured. See Figure 2.87.

Concrete walls are also utilized in basements for below-ground conditions, and can be manufactured as described earlier with wood forms. Metal forms are used in a manner similar to the wood forms but are best for a more repetitive dimensional system. If the measurements are uniform, the use of modular metal forms is a more efficient system of forming. These forms can be rented and are intended for frequent use. In either case, any basement wall must be waterproofed.

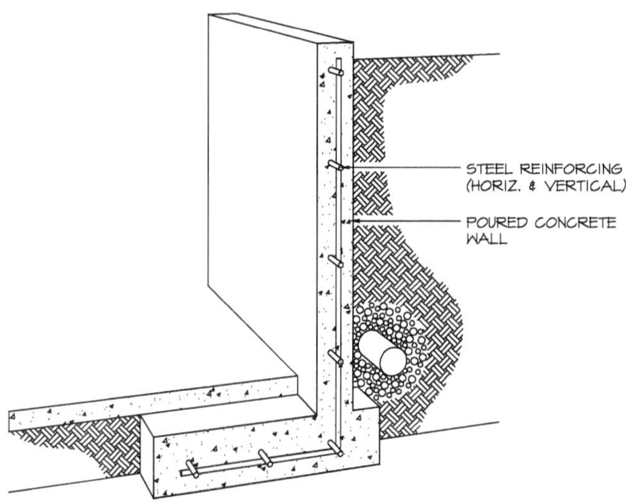

Figure 2.87 Poured-in-place concrete retaining wall.

Concrete Tilt-Up Wall System

Tilt-up wall panels are used to support roof and floor loads and serve as shear walls to resist movement due to earthquakes and high wind conditions. See Figure 2.88.

Tilt-up wall construction is a precast construction method in which the wall panels are cast on the job site. In most cases, the concrete floor of the building serves as the casting platform for the wall panels. The panels may be of high-strength concrete and relatively thin. Tilt-up construction is especially suitable for commercial and industrial structures.

Generally, fabrication of a tilt-up wall is accomplished with the use of wood forms, reinforcing steel, and a bond-breaker liquid suitable to release the precast panel from the casting platform. After the concrete meets the curing specifications, the panels are lifted into place by a mobile truck crane. See Figures 2.89 and 2.90.

A detailed wall section for a two-story concrete tilt-up wall is illustrated in Figure 2.91. Note that a concrete pour strip is used to connect the wall and the casting slab after the tilt-up wall panel is erected (Figure 2.92).

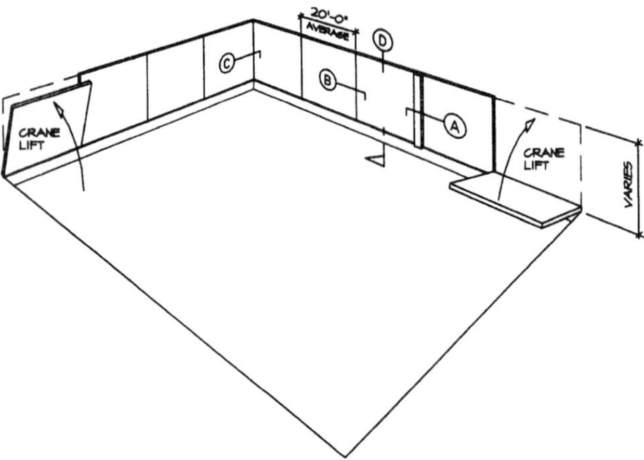

Figure 2.88 Tilt-up wall diagram.

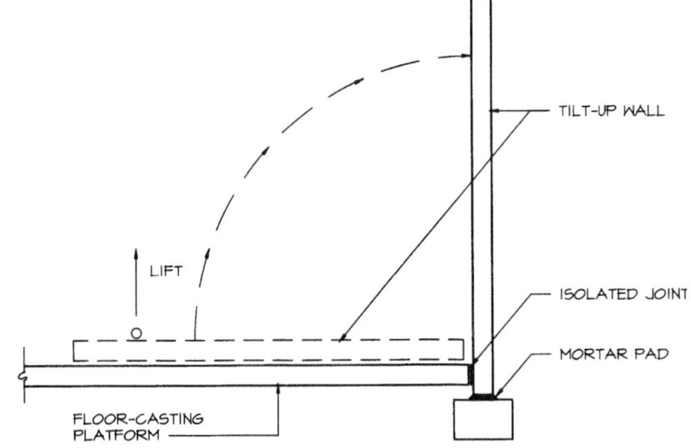

Figure 2.89 Tilt-up wall installation.

Precast Concrete Wall System

A highly successful construction method for concrete walls is the use of precast concrete bearing and non-bearing walls. These walls are manufactured at a casting plant and delivered to the building site for erection. The walls may be cast with various openings in them, such as for doors and windows. The wall sizes and shapes vary, based on the designs of the architect and the structural engineer. Figure 2.90 depicts a precast concrete wall arrangement with the use of a precast concrete hollow-core floor system. Note that when wall openings are required, they may be incorporated into the internal and external planning. The connections for precast concrete elements, such as for walls, are dictated by the consulting structural engineer's detail. A wall-to-floor connection (section A) is shown in Figure 2.93. This detail does not show the steel reinforcing and grouting required to connect the walls to the floor system to maintain the structural integrity of the building. There are various methods of meeting these structural requirements.

Steel Systems

When selecting steel as a construction material for a building project, it is necessary to decide whether the steel components are to be structural steel members or light steel framing members. The use of structural steel members, such as "W" shapes, "S" shapes, tubes, or channels, will probably dictate the use of a matrix identification system. See Figure 2.94. For a light steel framing system, the approach will be similar to that used for a wood stud framing system.

If an architectural firm has been commissioned to design and prepare working drawings for an office building incorporating structural steel members, then the game plan is to establish a matrix identification system. A matrix system will identify the column and beam

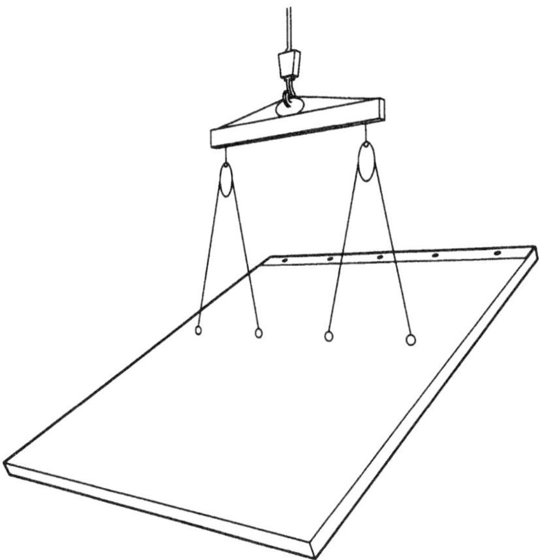

Figure 2.90 Tilt-up wall section.

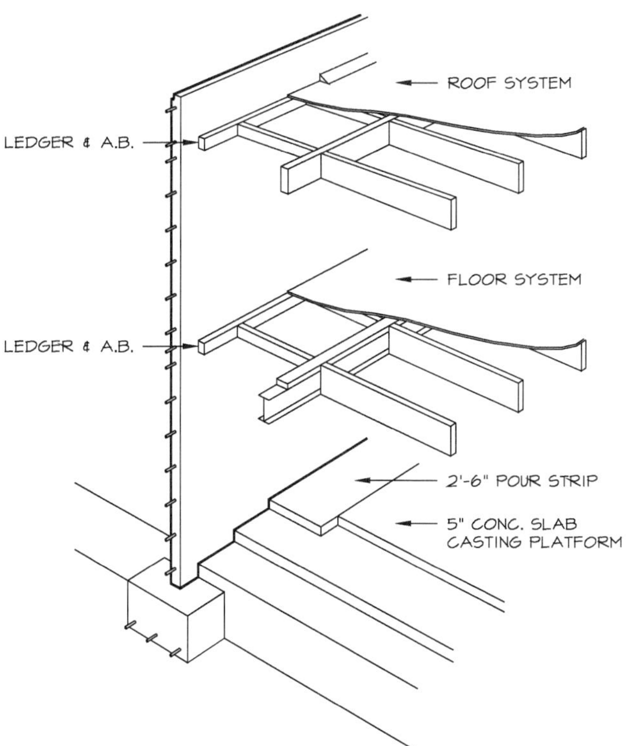

Figure 2.91 Concrete tilt-up wall.

locations as well as spread concrete footings and concrete piers. Before formulating a floor plan layout with the steel column locations, it is necessary to consult with the project's structural engineer for his or her recommended span lengths between the supporting steel columns. With the structural engineer's preliminary recommendations, the architects may proceed with the preliminary studies, incorporating the client's requirements and all the other design considerations necessary in designing a building. See Figure 2.95.

Steel Studs

The use of lightweight, cold-formed steel stud members provides a wall framing system for load-bearing and non-load-bearing walls. These walls provide a noncombustible support for fire-related construction and are well suited for preassembly. Moreover, shrinkage is not a concern with steel stud walls. The material of the studs varies from 14- to 20-gauge galvanized steel, with sizes ranging from 1½″ to 10″ in depth. These walls are constructed with a channel track at the bottom and top of each wall and steel studs attached to the channels. Horizontal bridging is achieved with the use of a steel channel positioned through the steel stud punch-outs and secured by welding. See Figure 2.96. Wood sheathing may be attached to steel framing members with self-tapping screws. See Figure 2.97.

Masonry

Masonry has proven to be a versatile and durable construction material. Various types of masonry products are available for the construction of buildings. In general, reinforced grouted brick masonry units and reinforced **concrete masonry units (CMUs)** are widely used in the construction of residential, commercial, and industrial structures.

Wall thickness and modular layout will depend on whether reinforced grouted brick masonry or CMUs are selected. Brick masonry units are manufactured in a great range of sizes, starting with the standard brick size of 2½″ × 3⅓″ × 8¼″ and ranging to a brick block size of 7⅝″ × 5½″ × 15½″. CMUs are often referred to as *concrete block units*. Though sizes vary, a typical modular concrete block unit is rectangular with dimensions of 8″ wide, 8″ high, and 16″ long.

Masonry is widely used for exterior structural walls. The main masonry units are bricks and concrete blocks, which are available in many sizes, shapes, textures, and colors. A primary advantage is that the masonry acts as the formwork for concrete.

Masonry is fire resistant and provides excellent fire ratings, ranging from two to four hours or more. The hour rating is based on the time it takes a fire-testing flame temperature to penetrate a specific wall assembly. Masonry also acts as an excellent sound barrier. When solid brick units are used for an exterior structural wall, the primary assembly is determined by regional geophysical conditions, such as seismic activity and high winds. For example, steel reinforcing bars and solid grout may be needed to resist

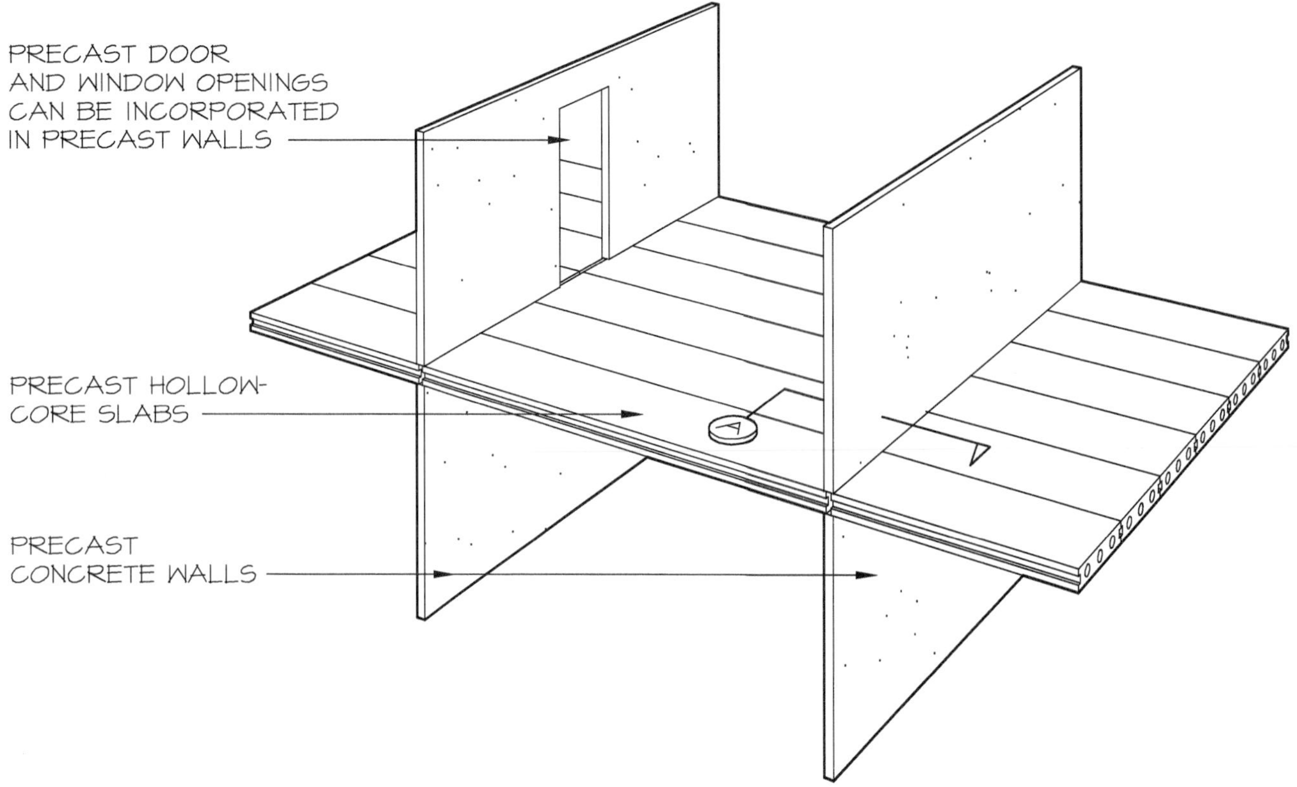

Figure 2.92 Precast concrete bearing walls.

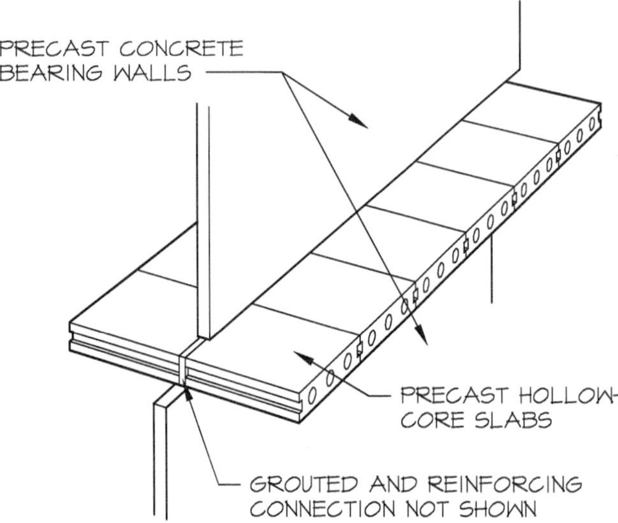

Figure 2.93 Precast walls and hollow-core slab.

lateral forces. Figure 2.98 shows a steel-reinforced brick masonry wall. The size and placement of the horizontal and vertical reinforcing steel are determined by the structural engineer and the governing building code. In regions without high wind conditions or seismic activity, reinforcing steel and grout are not needed. The unreinforced masonry wall or brick cavity wall is excellent for insulating exterior walls. Two 3″ or 4″ walls of brick are separated by a 2″ air space or cavity. This cavity provides a suitable

Figure 2.94 Photograph of a similar column and beam connection. (Courtesy of Rich Development.)

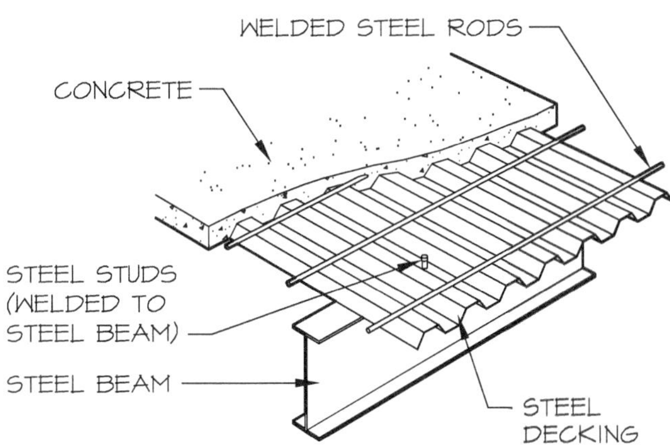

Figure 2.95 Composite steel decking floor system.

space for insulating materials, and the two masonry walls are bonded together with metal ties set in the mortar joints. See Figure 2.99.

CMUs for structural walls are generally 6″, 8″, 12″, or 16″ thick, depending on the height of the wall and the weight it carries. The hollow sections of these units are called **cells**. Vertical cells may be left empty or filled solid with grout and reinforcing steel; when required, horizontal cells can also include concrete and steel to add strength. As in brick wall construction, the use of unreinforced or reinforced walls will depend on the structural engineer's calculations and the building code requirements. In regions where reinforcing steel and grout are not required, the open cells may be filled with a suitable insulating material. When you utilize a concrete block wall, the dimensions of the blocks affect the height and width of the building; it is best to utilize the modular unit of the block. See Figure 2.100. Window and door openings must satisfy the dimensions of the modular units as well.

Masonry Veneer Wall

Masonry veneer includes the use of brick, CMU, or stone as a non-load-bearing component of the

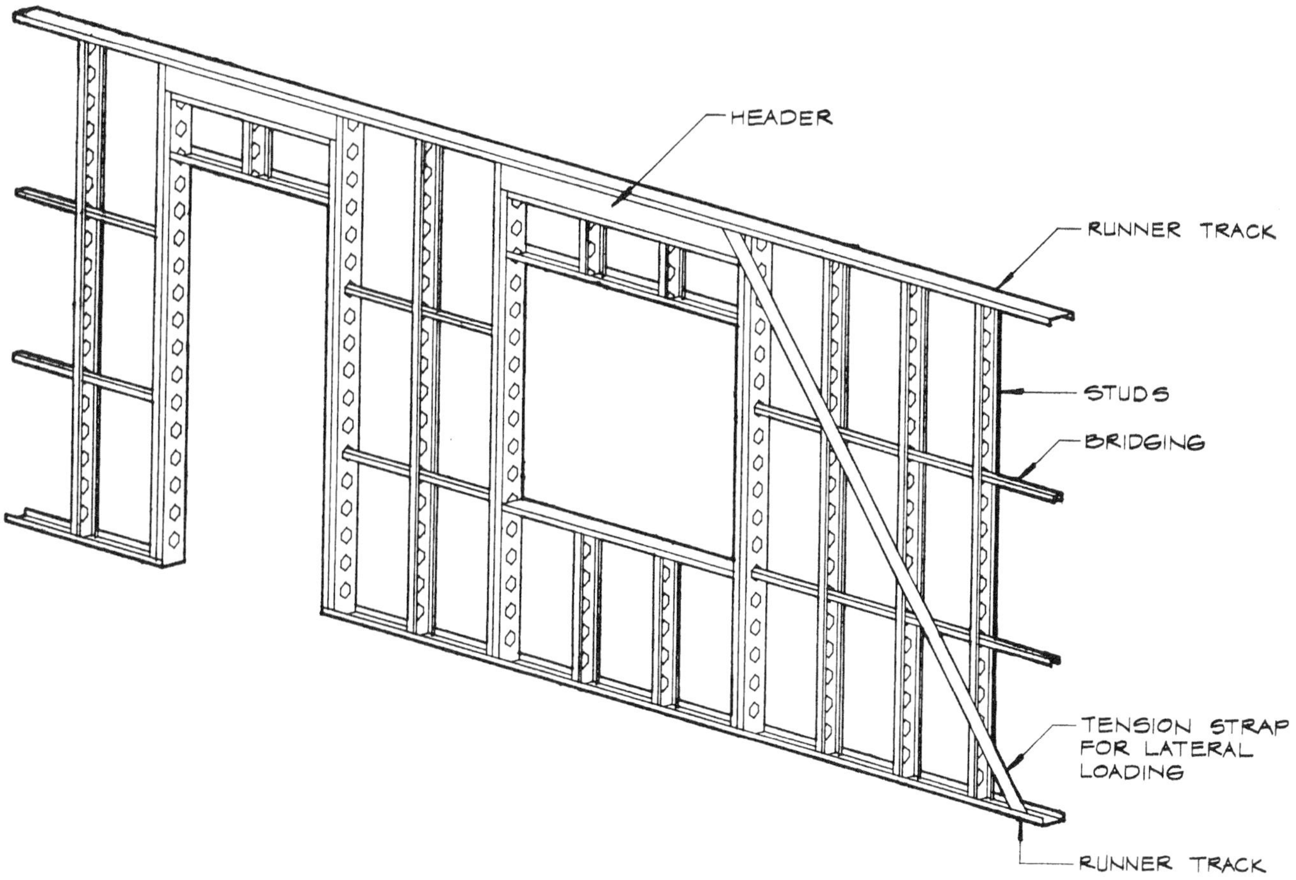

Figure 2.96 Isometric of steel stud wall.

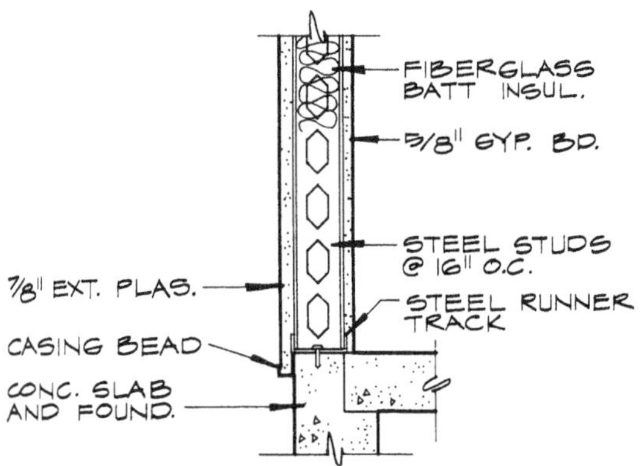

Figure 2.97 Partial steel stud wall section.

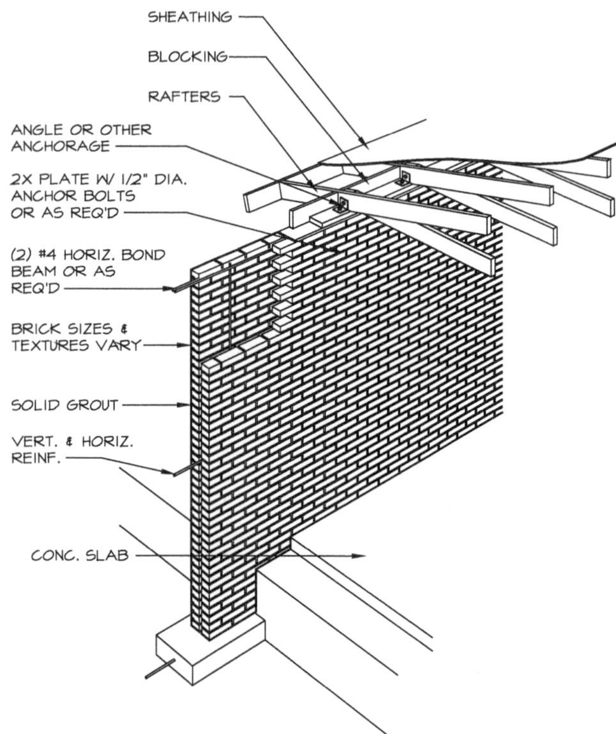

Figure 2.98 Section of reinforced grouted brick masonry wall.

building. The maximum thickness of masonry veneer is regulated by most building codes and is generally recognized as 5″ or less. **Masonry veneer** may be defined strictly as a masonry finish that is nonstructural and generally used for its architectural appearance. In regions with seismic disturbances, a positive bond between the veneer and a stud wall is required. See Figure 2.101.

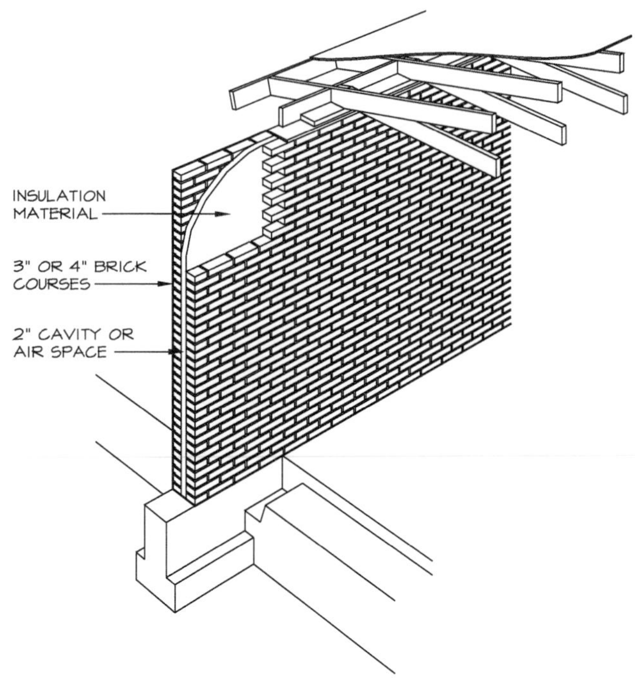

Figure 2.99 Brick cavity wall section.

Systems and Materials

Some construction methods incorporate systems that are assembled with various materials. These are called **composite systems** and may include a combination of materials

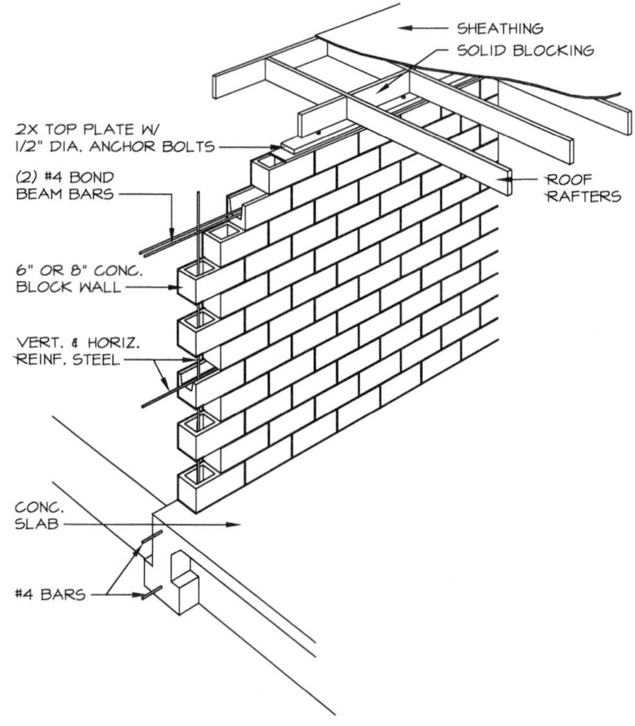

Figure 2.100 Reinforced concrete block wall section.

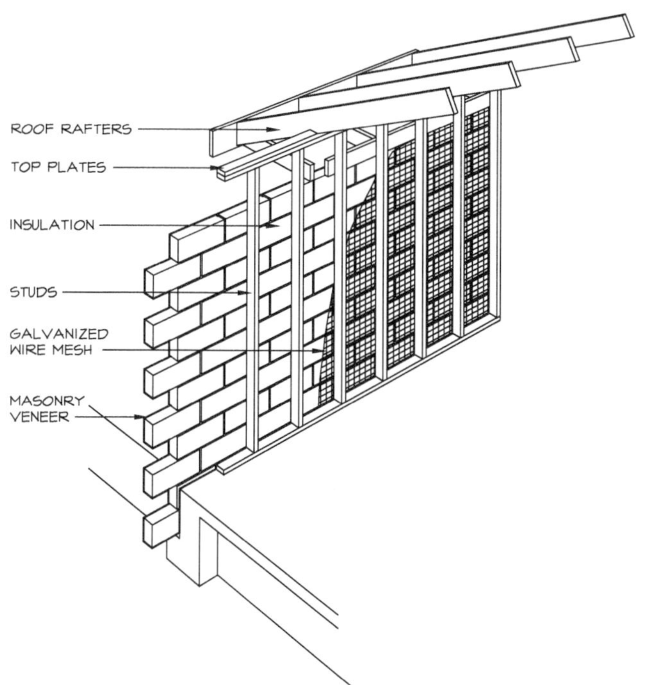

Figure 2.101 Masonry veneer detail.

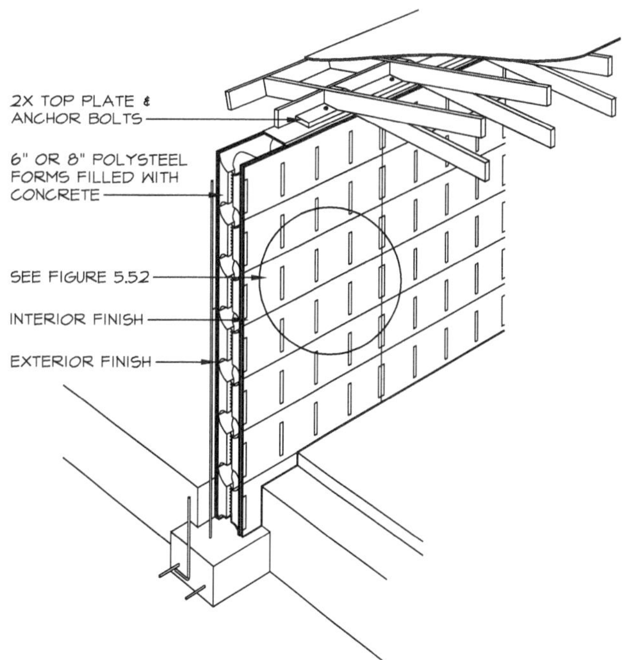

Figure 2.102 Polysteel forms and concrete wall. (Courtesy American Polysteel, Inc.)

such as steel and concrete; aluminum and insulation panels; polystyrene, galvanized steel, and concrete; and plastic and wood. These are just a few of the material combinations utilized in building construction. Another example of a composite system is the use of polystyrene and galvanized steel forms for construction of poured concrete walls. See Figure 2.102. This system provides a form for the poured concrete and also possesses excellent insulation qualities, as the polystyrene forms are retained in the structural wall. They are designed to serve as an anchor for the finish materials that will be applied to the exterior and interior faces of the wall. The exterior and interior finishes may be anchored to galvanized steel furring strips that are an integral part of the form unit. Figure 2.103 depicts a single polysteel form unit.

For structures that are designed to have exterior wall insulation, the architect may select a composite exterior wall system that utilizes a substrate material insulation board and a moisture-proof exterior finish. The thickness of an acceptable substrate may be at least ½″, and an expanded polystyrene insulation board may be from 1″ to 2″ in thickness. The selected thickness may be determined by the required or desired R factor. (The R factor designates the assigned insulation capability.) It is recommended that the supporting exterior wall members for this system be galvanized steel studs at 16″ center to center or 24″ center to center. This composite system can be attached to the steel studs and the approved substrate with an approved adhesive or a mechanical attachment. The mechanical attachment incorporates a metal screw and washer. See Figure 2.104.

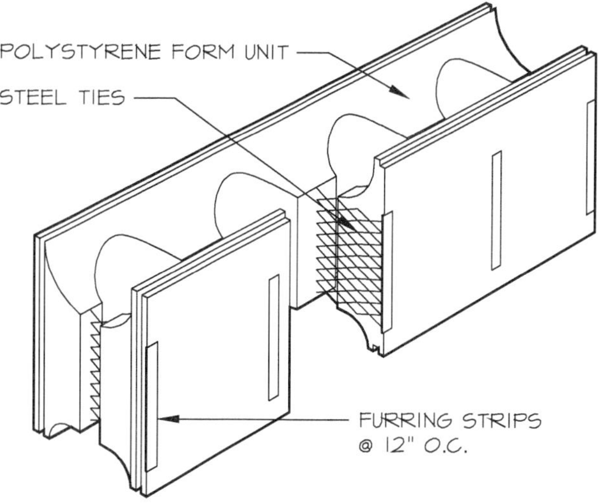

Figure 2.103 Polysteel form unit. (Courtesy American Polysteel, Inc.)

Figure 2.105 illustrates an exterior wall assembly utilizing the aforementioned wall panel. Note that the polystyrene selected is 2″ thick. The parapet detail in Figure 2.106 incorporates the various requirements for using this system.

Wood and plastic are found in a product developed for exterior decking and handrails in construction. This composite product requires virtually no maintenance and is manufactured from a sturdy wood composite. The decking material will not splinter, split, or crack; is resistant to

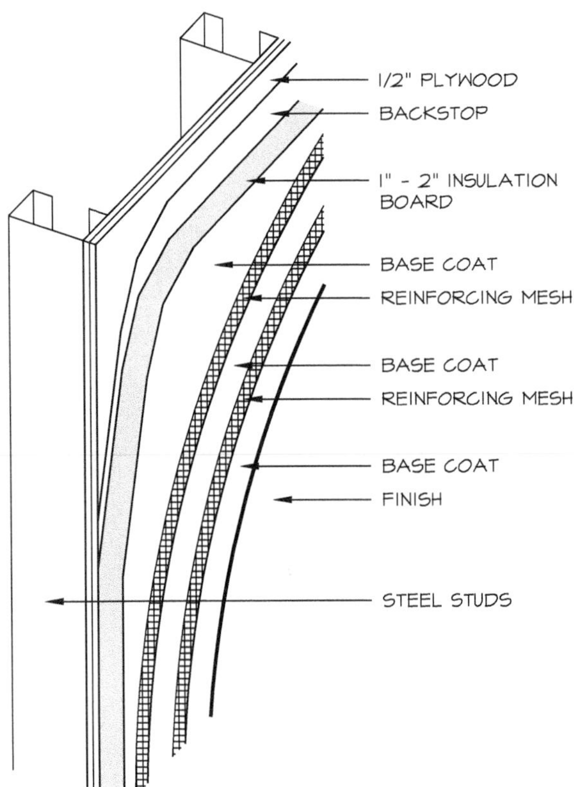

Figure 2.104 Composite wall panel. (Courtesy of Dryuit Systems, Inc.)

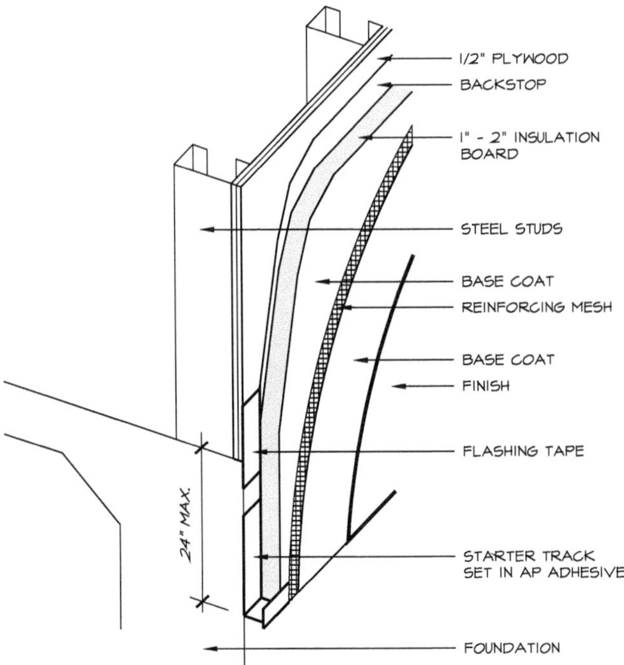

Figure 2.105 Composite wall panel attachment. (Compliments of Dryuit Systems, Inc.)

termites, dry rot, and decay; and is available in a wood-like finish. The individual members are straight and true, having a smooth or wood-grain finish. The members can be attached using the same method as for sawn lumber; however,

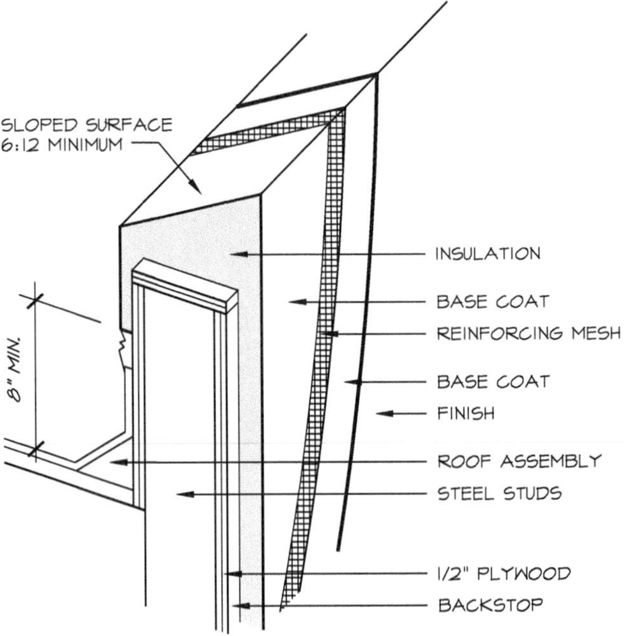

Figure 2.106 Composite parapet detail. (Compliments of Dryuit Systems, Inc.)

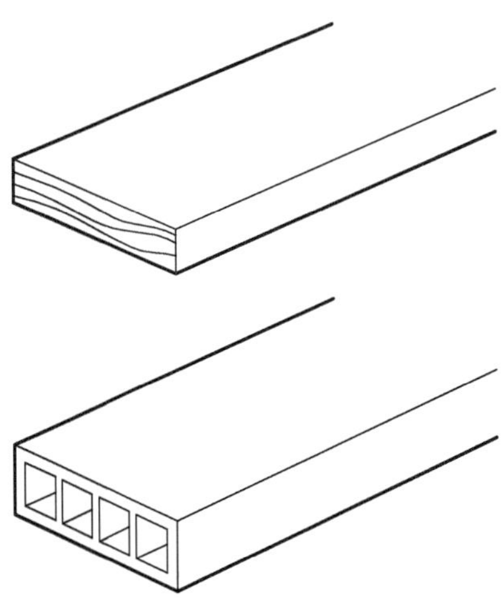

Figure 2.107 Composite decking members.

predrilling and the use of screws are recommended. This decking material is available in two types. One is a solid 4×6 unit that can be supported with structural members spaced at 16″ center to center. The other type is a 2×6 unit that is hollowed to provide a lighter weight for ease of handling. The hollowed member may span over the joists spaced at a maximum of 24″ center to center.

These two products do not require painting, staining, or sealing. Because all members are of exactly the same size and shape, the installation process is made easier. See Figure 2.107.

The composite handrail system incorporates 2 × 6 handrails, 2 × 4 side rails, and 2 × 2 balusters. The use of screws with countersunk-type heads is recommended

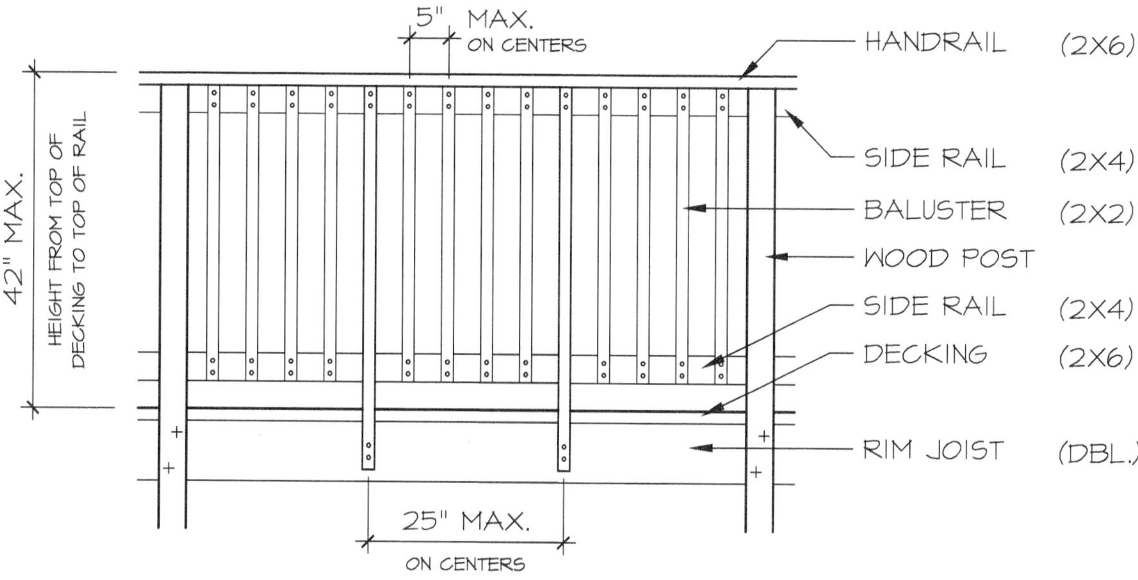

Figure 2.108 Composite handrail system. (Courtesy of Louisiana Pacific Corp.)

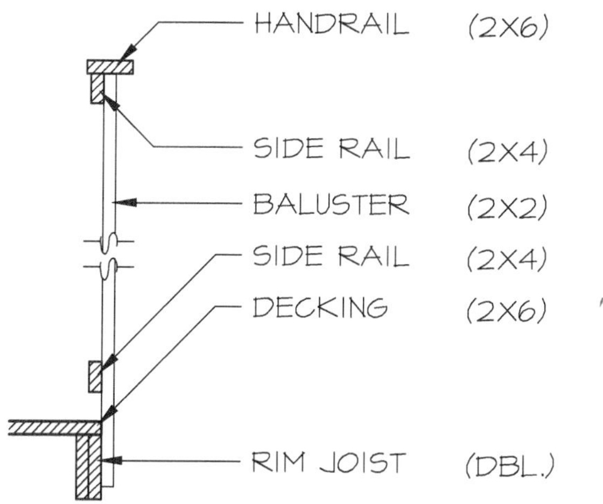

Figure 2.109 Section through handrail.

for connection of the various members. All screws must be predrilled. The composite handrail system is depicted in Figure 2.108. This handrail assembly shows the various member sizes that are available for construction of an exterior handrail system. See Figure 2.109.

Tensile Structure Awnings and Canopies

A unique form of architectural structure is what is known as *tension structure*. Picture your hands holding a rope and pulling it apart. This is the concept of using the strength of a material—in our case, steel. If it helps you can visualize a rubber band being stretched this pull apart action is called tension. Often used in conjunction with canvas, one can span large areas such as shown in Figure 2.110A and B. The first of these figures shows a large span covering the bleachers adjacent to the stadium, and the second shows a possible outdoor eating area.

Awnings are used to extend a roof plane to shade a particular area or a series of windows. See Figure 2.111A–C.

BUILDING INFORMATION MODELING (BIM)

The US National Building Information Model (BIM) Standard Project Committee has defined BIM as follows:

> Building Information Modeling (BIM) is a digital representation of physical and functional characteristics of a facility. A BIM is a shared knowledge resource for information about a facility forming a reliable basis for decisions during its life cycle; defined as an existing from earliest conception to demolition.

For centuries, architects have embraced new methods, new materials, and new technologies. This embrace accelerates the evolution of the field of architecture and shapes our built environment. BIM is such a technology, and it is setting new precedents in the world of architecture as we know it. Offering increased accuracy, productivity, collaboration, and organization—all while reducing repetition—BIM is a process of drafting in which almost every detail of a building assembly is included from its fundamental parts. For example, details such as stud, sheathing, building paper, lath, plaster, and gypsum are included to define a specific wall type. Where earlier programs established two lines to represent a wall, BIM identifies the entire wall with specificity.

BIM is basically the sum total of what we have learned about how to manage digital representation of both the physical and characteristics of a structure. It is a method that allows the designers and architects to be able to

Ⓐ

Ⓑ

Figure 2.110 Tensile structures. (Courtesy of Lawrence Fabric & Metal Structures, Inc.)

make changes rapidly because the entire structure and its related areas such as engineering, plumbing, air conditioning, and such are resolved early in the design phase of the building. BIM also looks to be a major step in defining the necessary work to be done in our industry. The vehicle used to process this information has been developed by many companies. In this chapter we will discuss a program called Revit, which will be described in detail later in this chapter. Revit is not the only program available to program BIM; programs such as ArchiCAD and Bentley are also vehicles of BIM.

If this is your first experience with BIM using Revit as the vehicle, BIM via Revit—the inclusion of every factor in the production of a building, especially during the design phase. As you begin to translate the needs, wishes, and dreams of your client, the architect in the firm will begin to develop a concept on which they will develop a field of play, and begin to diagram the site to locate the forms with which the original concept will begin to develop. The architect will need to contact their consultants and immediately begin incorporating structural forms, selecting materials, contacting the plumbing and electrical specialists, developing a way in which the mechanical equipment with the ducting does not change the design and develop a total approach, and using the forms that the designer is using, without interrupting the concept of the structure during the design phase. In a multistory structure, the designer must consider elevator shafts, skylights, and stair locations.

(B)

Figure 2.111 Awnings. (Courtesy Mapes Architectural Canopies.)

In the past, many architects and designers have not included the consultants or professional associates at the onset of the design, therefore causing a need to compromise the design and work these features in using "change orders" during construction because the air-conditioning ducts were intersecting the pass away of structural members at a point when the building was more than 50% complete. This often causes a compromise of the design and would force a rescheduling of the subcontractors and perhaps significant delays. We must incorporate all of the things that impact the design at the beginning, called "front loading" the contract, and the initial cost of the contract becomes higher at the beginning, but ultimately the cost of architectural construction will be much lower, which will please the client.

BIM standard is written in by cost estimators, facility managers, specifiers, designers, contractors, project managers, International BIM developments have appeared in globally.

The standard is developing patterns that will begin to include all related forms of architecture and incorporating them early, which will require not only great knowledge of the totality of architecture at an early stage but also a tremendous amount of front loaded knowledge, ultimately avoiding massive changes during construction, which in and of itself will change the process of construction and will require more preplanning and costs at the beginning of the project but will ultimately be lower cost on the total budget of the structure. This strategy will also demand a comprehensive understanding of the materials being used and their limits and strengths.

Programs such as Revit by Autodesk, ArchiCAD, and Bentley are designed to increase productivity in all phases of drawing documentation. Its primary advantage is its ability to produce drawings that are generated by defining floor, wall, and roof assembly types. In addition, BIM will develop schedules, identify doors and windows from the placement, and determine door and window sizes and types. Finish schedules are also established by using information on floor, wall, and roof materials. BIM will even go further in developing detailed sections, elevations, and details.

It is amazing how such a program can aid in development of a construction set of drawings. This advantage is further enhanced by its process capability to modify all the plans, schedules, and elevations to reflect the changes when modifications are made regardless to where the change is made plan, elevation, or schedule. A standard drafting program would require a technician to modify all the plans based on their own experience. The program is not perfect, but it does include a conflict detection element to aid in the process. Simply put, one can develop a more accurate, thorough, and coordinated set of drawings with the aid of Revit, Bentley, or other BIM technologies.

BIM has become universal in popularity and has recently spread its wings into not only the United States, Canada, and Central and South America but throughout Europe, the Middle East, most of the Orient, and in fact all over the world. It is a program that looks at the information and turns it into a 3-D mode. This model can be rotated and seen from above as a plan or look at it as an elevation. In fact, it can create a perspective view (3-D) that can be shown to contractors, expediting and clarifying estimating above all your clients (see Figure 2.112) can walk through the building before bidding on the project or the contract is given to a contractor. The 3-D walk through can be experienced by virtual reality (VR) glasses.

You must know all about the structural engineering and where the beams used will be located, the path of the ductwork throughout the building, the location of the plumbing lines and so on. In fact, the architect or the designer of the structure will need to know all of the facts of the building, early during the development of the project. The profession calls this "front loading," but it must be done to use BIM effectively.

Of the many technical programs available that will initiate BIM, it must be carefully selected, and then carefully reprogrammed to follow office standards that have previously been established must change the existing programs that you subscribe to and implement national standards.

One aspect that is usually missed is the printer or plotter. You can check by drawing a sample rectangle at a given scale and plot, then measure it with an actual scale. If it does not measure correctly, then the printer setup must be reprogrammed (please review this step in Chapter 2). Otherwise, you are sharing an incorrect drawing with your client, contractors, and all for the individual concerned with the building.

BIM is a new way to approach construction documents, particularly working drawings. BIM addresses the characteristic of a building, from material quantities to energy performance, from lighting to site disturbances (to mention just a few). BIM can be an integral part of sustainable design because it allows the architect/designer to explore, investigate, and implement designs that have the least impact on the environment.

In architecture, as in life in general, there is nothing as constant as change. Fortunately, BIM manages change for you. It also keeps you honest, although it does allow you to avoid a decision by temporarily inserting a "placeholder" unit in your design until you have determined the direction to completion. BIM is data driven. It allows

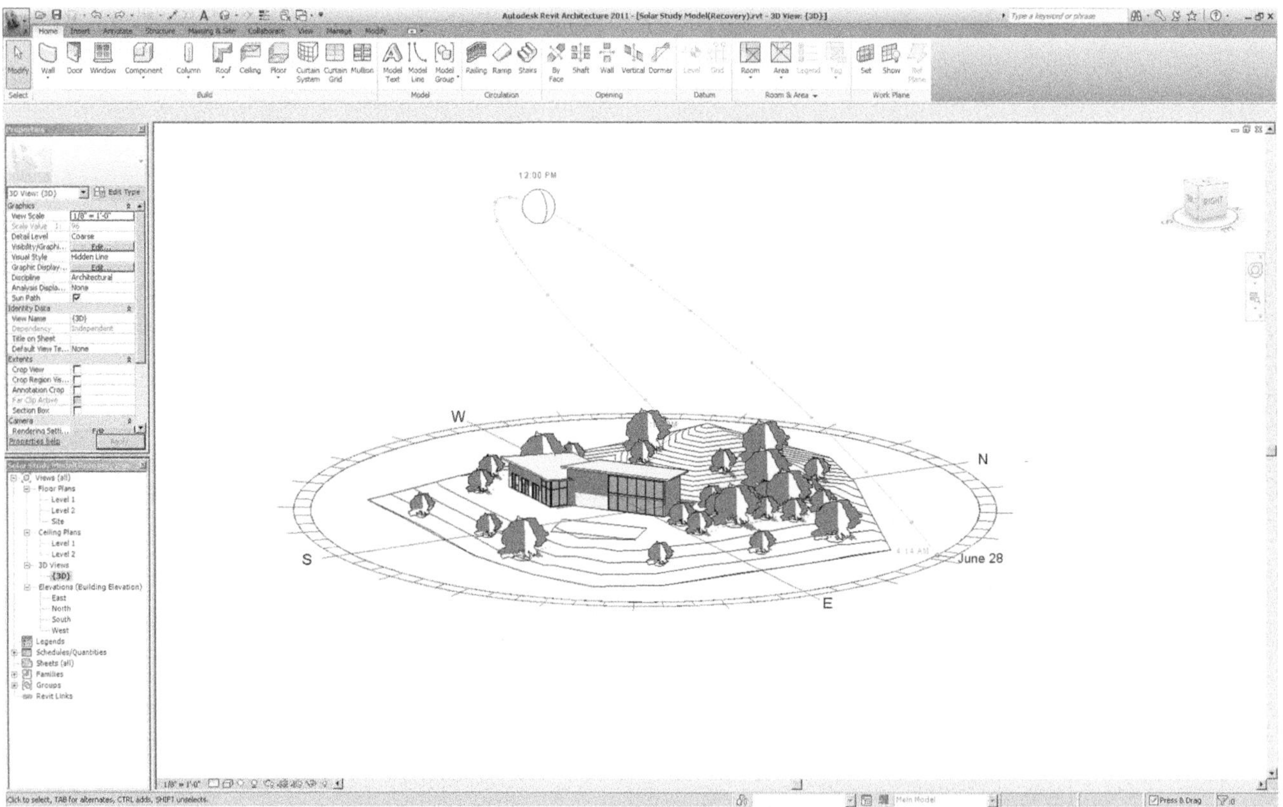

Figure 2.112 12:00 noon June 28. (Screenshots © Autodesk Inc. All Rights Reserved.)

you to take a design and enhance its data, but it does so in a holistic manner. This means you cannot be fickle: the change you make on any plan or elevation will be reflected in all drawings. For example, if you put a window on the first floor of a three-story building, using BIM, it will change the window alignment on the other floors to accommodate it. The program is "parametric" modular; that is, it creates and maintains relationships among elements. Therefore, you work in three dimensions. You must see the impact the floor plan has on other drawings and understand that changing the specifications of a window will be changed in all aspects of the drawings and schedules.

BIM can be used with software tools that analyze energy use. With these capabilities, we are able to quantify the green effect of our structures much earlier in the design stage. Those involved with the project (the design team and the client) will be able to "walk through" the virtual structure so as to actually visualize and see the results and effects of greener design.

For example, we can study lighting via tools that allow use of airport information about the weather at any given latitude and longitude on Earth. In this way, we can see the effects of daylighting. **Daylighting** refers to using natural lighting (sun) to illuminate the structure, thus reducing the use of electrical energy to light (and heat) the building. Thus, high-performance, sustainable design can be realized by using the multifaceted approach made possible with ease via BIM. This is critical in current design, because structures (both residential and commercial, of which there are approximately 81 million in the United States) account for about 40% of all energy consumption in this country.

Federal agencies, state governments, and local governments are all helping to finance green building design, whether by grants, tax credits, or other schemes. There are also regulatory incentives from state and local government entities. Architectural firms are eager to employ individuals who are Leadership in Energy and Environmental Design (LEED) certified, as that status enhances the chances of success when bidding on government-funded projects such as schools.

Autodesk **Green Buildings Studio (GBS)** is a tool used for building energy analysis. GBS creates a thermal model of the building and even applies local building code presumptions. This can (and should) be done throughout the design stages. Early use enables better orientation of the structure on the site. Daylight can be checked during the design stages. Also, GBS creates an input that, in turn, enables engineering analysis systems to be used in conjunction with Revit for detailed analyses. This automated input of geometric coordinates saves hundreds of hours of labor. Revit's hidden strength is its ability, when used correctly, to provide information effortlessly, accurately, and quickly.

You can even do estimates of LEED credits for use of recycled material in your draft specifications, as well as reducing waste and improving staff efficiency. You select what materials are to be used in Revit, it will automatically know what to draw; all it needs is for the drafter to input the size of the components.

Figure 2.113 the architect becomes the coordinator and resolver of conflicts. This is very difficult to do with a 2-D drawing. Even a trained eye may miss a duct that conflicts with a structural member or a plumbing or electrical line drawing that conflicts with a beam in the framing plan. Often, mechanical engineers will lay out their equipment while overlooking or ignoring the fact that the other engineers and trades need to use the same space. Such conflicts can be minimized by the use of BIM because it shows the structure holistically in 3-D. If all of the engineers would input their information into a single source, any conflict that arises would be shown immediately. In this way, Revit catches human errors in our construction documents that the senior drafter, the job captain, or any of the staff in an office might miss. See Figure 2.114 for a picture of this coordination of associates.

Because BIM is detail minded, many drafters fall back to using AutoCAD because they are comfortable there. Even when Revit, a powerful parametric modeling tool, gives

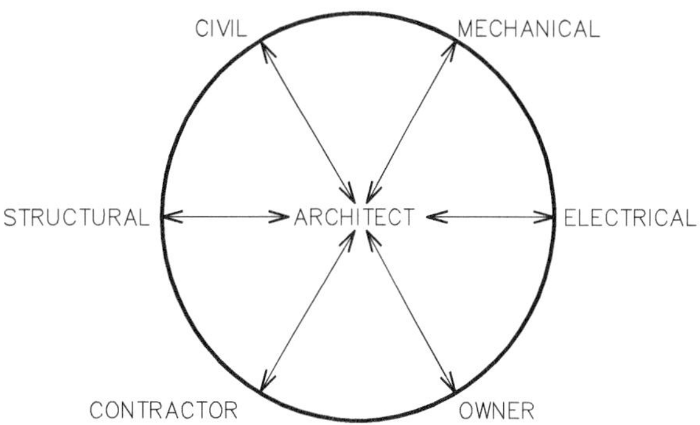

Figure 2.113 Disseminating project information to owner and professional associates.

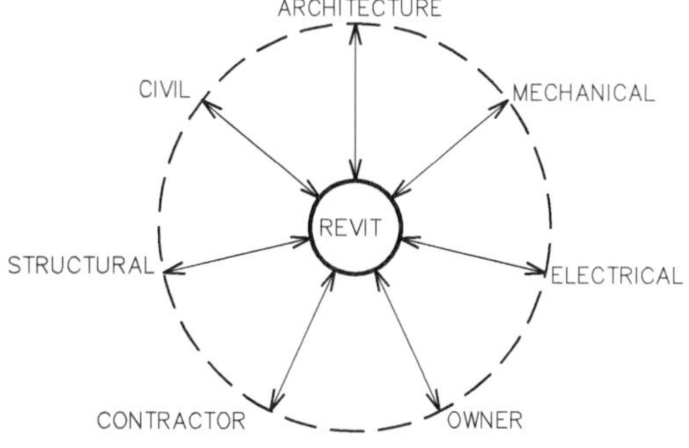

Figure 2.114 Coordination of drawings to catch conflicts.

them a significant advantage, eventually we hope that the entire profession will use 2-D drawing only when it is absolutely necessary, and even then, continue thinking in 3-D.

As for BIM, it creates a fine line between SD, DD, and CD. When design development is finished, the construction documents (working drawings) will also be all but finished.

The learning curve for the transition from AutoCAD to BIM is steep. BIM requires much more than a translation or acquisition of skills: It demands greater and deeper knowledge of architecture and construction. To complete a 3-D drawing, one must change what has been learned in 2-D to a finite 3-D drawing. The front-loaded drawing programs of today require the designer to solve architectural problems, such as conflicts in the positioning of air-conditioning ducts, plumbing, and structural components, up front, well before the construction documents stage and early in the BIM process. This is a disadvantage to the present CAD drafters, who often depend on their skill with AutoCAD rather than their architectural skills to solve their problems. This is why the offices using BIM/Revit must set up a template that the drafter can follow. Too much computer skill and too little architectural knowledge can be disastrous to an architectural project.

The BIM concept has revolutionized the design process and changed how production drawings are produced. At the same time, it has enhanced the use of sustainable/green architecture, thus allowing designers to earn as much as 20 LEED points in the process.

Changes have blurred the distinction between the functions of the designer and the drafter. In fact, many firms have eliminated the terms **draftsman** and **draftsperson** and instead train for their particular uses of Revit.

The entire thinking process has changed. Our drafters need to be able to understand how buildings are built and work in 3-D first, before they attempt to use Revit. To be useful in the BIM process, a drafter must be able to produce details in their final form, cut sections, and be more focused on drafting and drawing conventions. Learn how Revit works and understand how Revit can produce structures that are fully thought through.

Site Plan

The Site Plan

1. Check any field theory and datums that were established by the designer. Validate design patterns used by the designer.
2. Use the office standards or establish your own set of standards based on national standards, such as those produced by the AIA.
3. The site plan shows the contour of the property.
4. Confirm any structural, heating, and air-conditioning units adjacent to the structure as well as the location of the water meter, gas meter, and even the electrical lines and electrical panel.
5. The site information should be confirmed with the civil engineer's property line, true north, orientation north, existing structures, and existing trees.
6. Check for easements on the property.
7. Minimum setbacks for the property should be checked via the building department.
8. Locate and dimension the structure and locate any improvements around the structure from the building.
9. Locate all existing trees and identify the trees that are to be removed.
10. Indicate a minimum slope of the slabs or the direction and percentage of slabs.
11. Show the roof if it extends beyond the building.
12. Proper noting is an absolute must.
13. Proper attention should be paid to any special items such as sculptures, fountains, canopies, gazebos, and other such items.

CHECKLIST—Site Plan

1. Verify with the designer/architect.
2. Establish standards.
3. Check with associates.
4. Plot the contour of the property:
   a. Orientation
   b. Easements
   c. Setbacks
5. Locate and dimension improvements.
6. Identify existing trees and trees to be removed.
7. Show roof lines and anything that extends beyond the building.
8. Indicate finished grade elevation and indicate the height of concrete.
9. Identify special items:
   a. Vicinity map
   b. Lot description
   c. Roof slope and description
   d. Title and scale

■ FLOOR PLAN

When preparing construction documents, begin with verifying patterns used by the office. Modules that are used to design the building and/or shapes that are unique to this particular design comprise field theory. The designer may be using the patterns in a different way than you might understand. Review the standards that are used for the floor plan and not those that are already included on the computer.

Construct the perimeter of the floor plan. If the plan was drawn during the SD stage, remember the drawing was executed as a family. Your task will be to validate its size against the site plan, elevation, and building section. Drawing the correct wall thickness is also critical.

If the floor plan had no interior walls drawn, this should be your next step, along with validating the size and location of the windows, doors, and openings, checking to see that they do not conflict with the structural integrity of the building. Kitchen cabinets, appliances, bathroom fixtures and location of closets, indicating any built-in units within the closet or wardrobe, positioning, shelves, and poles will follow. If there is a game room or a built-in theater, how much room will need to be added? Is the seating formal? What will be required on the floor plan and any change in the floor plan regarding stairwells should be researched in terms of the size of the tread and riser plus the landing. The outline of the roof should be included, and what type and density should be used for the lines indicating the roof? If there is a structure within say 5′-0″, should a partial plan or outline be drawn adjacent to the floor plan that you are now drawing?

Show the proper material designation for the walls, the various changes in the ceiling plane, and soffits above the cabinets. Use proper notation throughout the drawing, including room titles. Many offices include floor materials in the floor plan. Include the proper title, north and orientation north, and the scale of the floor plan. All of these details must follow the office standard so that the floor plan will match all other drawings.

CHECKLIST—Floor Plan

1. Validate all design dimensions used in the structure.
2. Construct the outside and inside walls of the structure.
3. Show interior connections such as stairs and any change of the level in the floor.
4. Show any structural members such as columns.
5. Indicate windows, doors, and openings in the wall plane.
6. Add kitchen cabinets, built-in appliances, and closets.
7. Show all bathroom fixtures.
8. Indicate any change in the ceiling level, including soffits, and cabinets.
9. Indicate the proper standard for the material being used, such as wood, steel, masonry, or composites.
10. Include section lines, partial sections, and detail references.
11. Use proper notation, including room titles and sometimes floor material (possibly located in the schedule).
12. Show proper title, scale, dimensions, and north arrow.

Building Section

As before, you must establish the standard that applies to building sections. Check to discover the datum that have already been established. This can be done by checking the building section with the elevation. In most sets of drawings, the building section is done prior to the elevation and confirmed with the architect to find patterns that have already been established.

Continue by outlining the building beyond the structural form that you just performed. Since a section is visualized much like a knife slicing through the building, you should concentrate on that which was sliced and becomes the darkest lines on the drawing (all others should be much lighter based on how far they are behind the dark section lines.

If the section cut through a window, door, or opening, the framing should be shown. Do not show objects beyond the cutting plane unless the object has a direct impact on the structure itself.

If there are structural members coming toward the viewer, such as floor joists, be sure to show them with the same emphasis as the other structural members. If possible, add the outside cladding to the building, such as stucco, wood paneling, or dry wall. Depending on the scale of the drawing's cladding, it may be difficult to show on this drawing. Thus, you must use your own judgment to indicate the outside covering using just an indication of the material. To this end, you will be able to understand why a wood-framed structure is dimensioned to the stud line and the center of the stud on the floor plan. You should now add texture to the elevation portion of the section, but do not include the entire area; indicate only a small portion using a brake line, leaving it for the next stage, which is notation. Complete the drawing following the standard used on the entire set of drawings and position the title and scale.

CHECKLIST—Building Section

1. Verify standards.
2. Validate vertical and horizontal measurements.
3. Check with engineering drawing.
4. Construct a structural outline
5. Finish outlining the building.
6. Draw the rest of building outline not cut by the section.
7. Show the windows and doors cut by section.
8. Do not show furniture or objects beyond the cutting plane unless they impact the structure.
9. Add the end view of the structures that are seeing coming toward you.
10. Profile the structural parts and add texture to the inside of walls.
11. Add texture to those portions that will be seen as elevation.
12. Provide the required notation.
13. Provide the Title and scale of the drawings.

Elevation

After having dealt with the site plan and floor plan, which predominantly focused on two of the horizontal measurements—width and depth—our journey takes us to height and width or depth. You must begin to understand what standards we will incorporate herein. Check the standard used in drafting an elevation.

Finding the vertical datum becomes the major task on our journey through elevation while validating one of the two other dimensions (width or depth, depending on the direction that you are viewing the elevation).

The first vertical datum usually deals with the earth (bedrock, frost line, natural or finished grade). The floor line is then found. The structural and geological drawings are used to validate this, as is the building section if available. The floor line is based on the above and is showed as a datum. The plate line is usually next, followed by the next floor line, and this rhythm continues no matter how many floors we have in the structure.

CHECKLIST—Elevation

1. Verify the size of the structure with the site plan and floor plan.
2. Verify the vertical datums established by the building section.
3. Draft the vertical datums.
4. Locate bedrock, frost line, and natural and finish grade. Validate with structural and geological drawings.
5. Draw the floor line based on the previous step.
6. Position.
7. Roof pitch and Overall height.

When you open the program, you will be greeted with the recent file screen, as explained in the pre-Revit portion of this text. Here is one of the first areas where you can start modifying the way you interact with Revit. It is recommended that you follow a work flow. The first step is to open and create a template or modify a template that has been provided for you by Revit. Each individual template will have different functionalities. You can create your own template or use a predefined template by going under the project portion of recent file window to your left. See Figure 2.115. If you are already employed, a template may have been predetermined by your office. If you are creating a template from scratch, you will need to input a lot of information into the program at the beginning. It is sometimes recommended that you use an existing template and modify it to fit your needs. See Figure 2.115, which shows the different functionalities that are found in a few templates. These functionalities can be found under your project browser.

Think of a template as a predetermined drafting manual that will determine the pages to be used, title block, annotations, materials, and specifications. You can modify the standards predefined by Revit to comply with the actual architectural standards. One example in modifying the standards given to you by Revit is shown

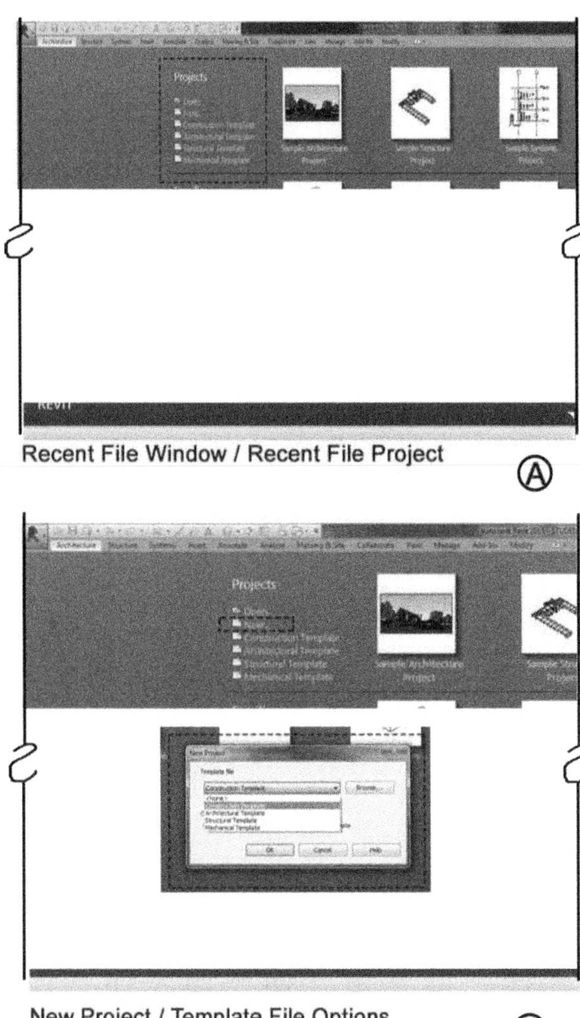

Figure 2.115 Working with templates. (Screenshots ©Autodesk, Inc. All Rights Reserved.)

in Figure 2.116. Please note that most of these modifications will be done under annotations.

For example, Revit uses a convention to cut a section in a drawing, as shown in Figure 2.117A, which represents a partial section. In the industry, this might work, but it is not technically correct. Figure 2.117B shows the correct symbol for a full section: a cutting plane line that has a broken dark line with two short dashes. The ends are made up of a pair of circles bound by darkened triangles. This section is a full section, cut through the entirety, as opposed to a partial section, which has the triangular form around a circle on one side only. The full section title has an "X" on both sides, and thus the title of that section is Section X-X. This also helps to alert the contractor and crew to look at both sides to see if it is a partial section or a full section. The arrowheads also show the direction one is looking when viewing the section. Figure 2.117C illustrates another section detail in which the darkened beak shows the direction in which

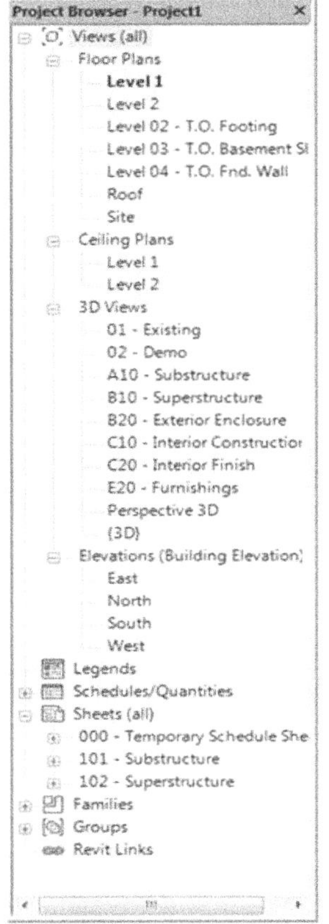

Construction Template

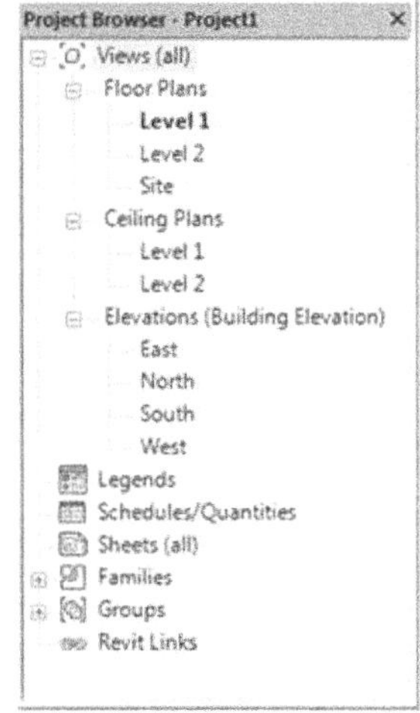

Residential Template

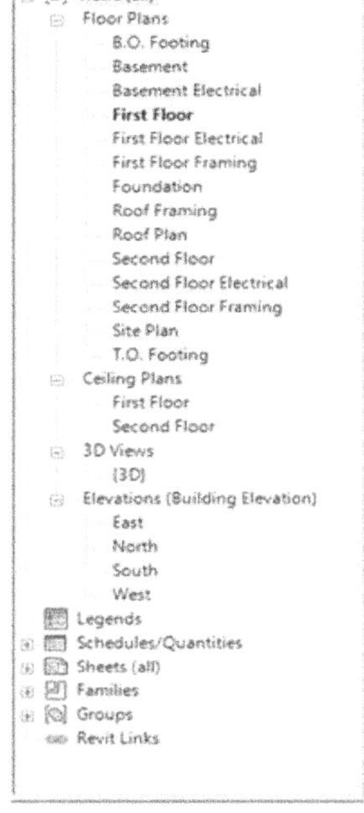

Architectural Template

Figure 2.116 Templates and project browser samples. (Screenshots ©Autodesk, Inc. All Rights Reserved.)

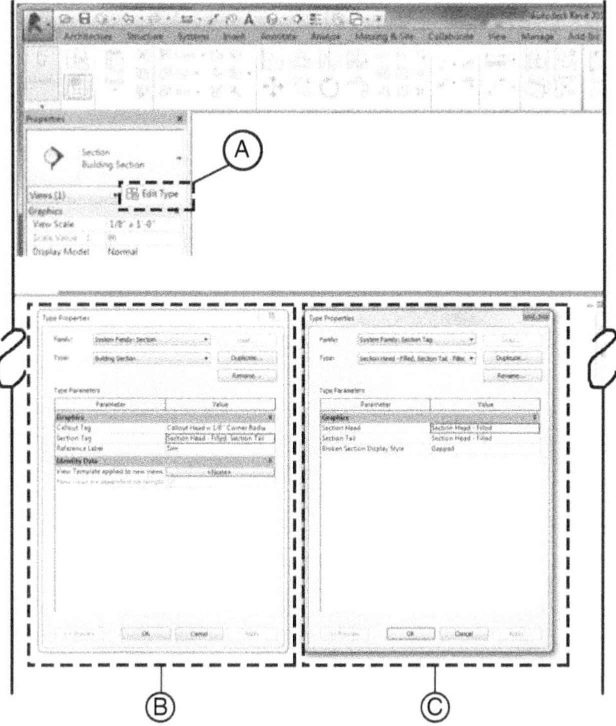

A. Start by selecting "Edit type"
B. Select "Section Tag", under "Type Properties"
C. Choose tail properties

Figure 2.117 Modifying section annotation. (Screenshots ©Autodesk, Inc. All Rights Reserved.)

the detail is being viewed. The outside of the building on a detail is always to the left.

One would think that since Revit is programmed by Autodesk its drawings are produced for national use, but these drawings must follow the standards that are indicated by deans and practicing architects from all over the United States, many of whom are Pritzker Prize winners. Individuals who are just entering the field of architecture can use the standards that are used throughout this text. The drafter must take into consideration the density of lines and the type of lines used for a section. Each line is drawn for a particular reason.

Modifying the way your drawing will be drawn and printed can be a task that can take some time, but once these changes are saved to your templates, you will be able to use them every time. One of the most important modifications that must be addressed, other than standard annotations, is line weights. Modifying your line weights will require some thinking since the lines that you see on your screen are actually 3-D forms rather than lines. In Revit, line weights are modified to the different type of scales you will be using. A quick view on modifying line weights is shown in Figure 2.118. This is done under the manage tab under object styles. Refer to Figure 2.118A. Pen settings are changed based on your object styles; these are your model objects. There are categories built into the system; see Figure 2.118B. Familiarize yourself with the object style window and review the way you want your lines to appear in projection and cut. Each of these line weights is assigned a number that can be modified under the line weight window; see Figure 2.118C. You can get to this window under the manage tab, and going to additional settings here you will find the line weight option. Under the line weights window, you will find the model line weights tab; this is where each number is assigned a line weight based on the scale you are working on. This is a quick

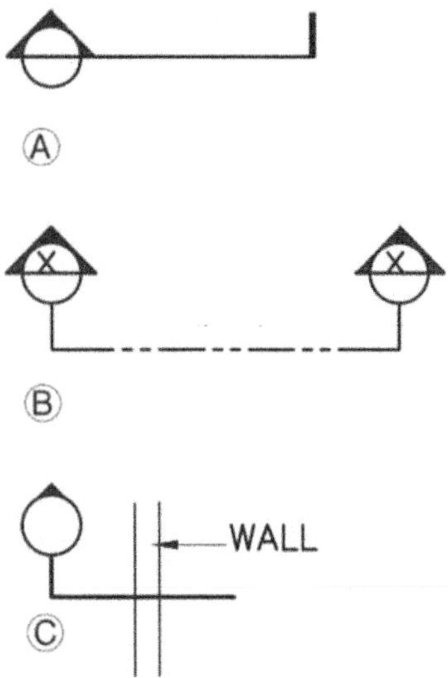

Figure 2.118 Standard section call-outs.

review on line weights, but it can be a very extensive learning experience. We recommend you explore this portion of Revit in more detail since your drawings will be greatly impacted by the way you manage your line weights.

With Revit a new language has to be learned, as may be the case with other software. The terminology used with Revit often does not match the terminology you are used to hearing in architecture or in using AutoCAD. To begin, the end user must become familiar with the terminology used in Revit. One of the first steps is to learn your Revit interface. See Figure 2.119, which shows the Revit interface window with a list of terms you will need to know that you will commonly hear while using Revit.

The term **Revit** comes from "Revise Instantly," which the program accomplishes as changes are made. Move one door and Revit will reflect the change in all other drawings. This is because Revit creates relationships within objects and between objects. If you were to call out (tag) a wall to be made of wood studs with stucco on the exterior and drywall on the inside, all walls would be affected (although you could change one particular wall from drywall to wood paneling).

In order to start a BIM model, you need to talk to all your associates, the engineer, and all the individuals that will have a direct impact on the structure prior to the design phase. How does one start? You can start by using one of the programs that are available. We will start by downloading a program called Revit. A novice in architecture must become a part of the Autodesk community. By doing so you will have access to Revit for a limited time at no cost. This means that if you are enrolled in an accredited college, authorized by the government, you can get the program by contacting Autodesk and validating your enrollment. There is no cost, of course, but use the time wisely. Of course, after you have had enough courses, you can make better use

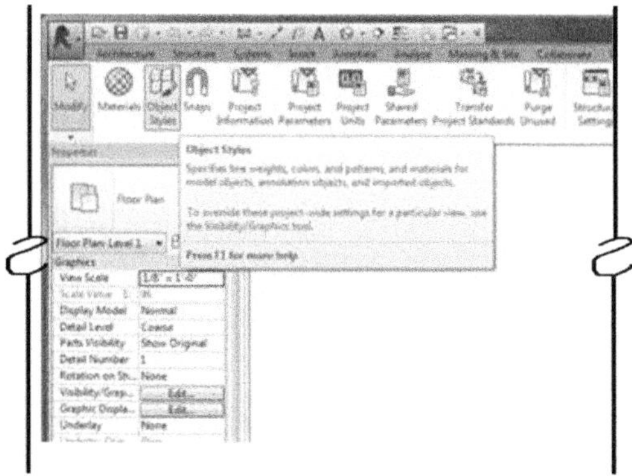

(A) Object styles under manage tab.

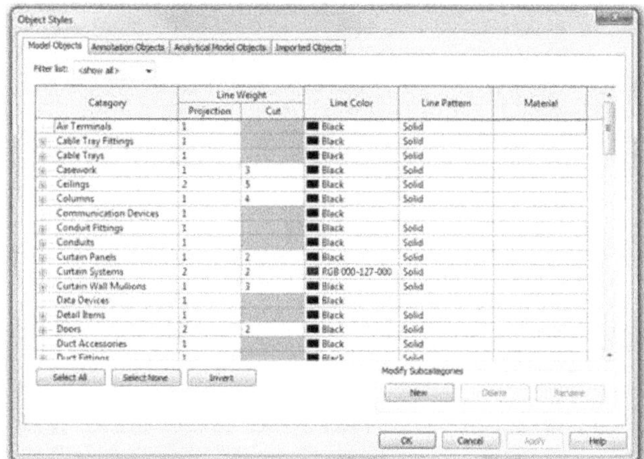

(B) Object styles window

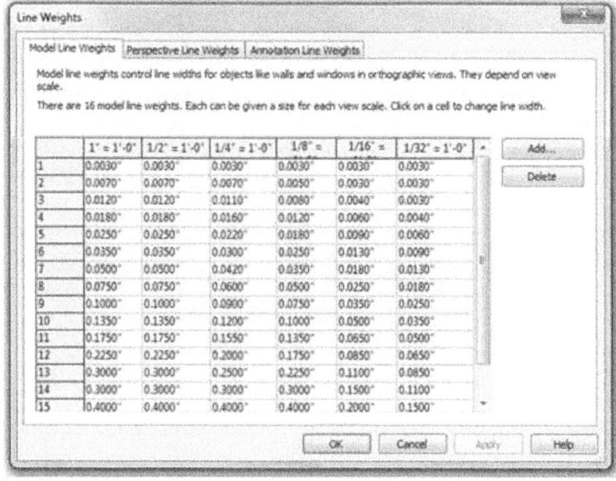

(C) Line weights window

Figure 2.119 Revit object styles and line weights. (Screenshots ©Autodesk, Inc. All Rights Reserved.)

of your enrollment on Revit. Go to the Autodesk web site and create an account and register for the Autodesk Education Community. At the top of your screen, you will be asked to input your personal information, including whether you are a student or a faculty member. If you are a professional, you can also download the Revit trial version, which allows you to use the program for 30 days. There are different types of Revit versions that you can download depending on your needs (different versions will have different functionality disciplines/tabs):

- Revit: Building Design Suite (Autodesk Revit)
- Revit: Architecture
- Revit: LT new comer (similar to Revit: Architecture)
- Revit: Engineering MEP (mechanical, electrical, plumbing)
- Revit: Structure

Building Design Suite is the version recommended, as it will have all of the functionalities from the versions listed earlier. You can turn off all of the functionalities you don't need and use only the parts of the program that fit your needs and your architectural education level. Use this trial version carefully; later, we will describe what, in reality, you need to know to go on in Building a 3-D Model by way of Revit. Beyond this point, you must realize that you need a bit more background in architectural theory before you start using Revit. This professional program subscription runs around $2,500 annually.

Go to Figure 2.121, which show the Revit icon as it may appear on your desktop after you have downloaded the program. When you click on this icon, the program will load and you will be greeted by the recent file screen. See Figure 2.120. On this screen you will find your Projects and Families and their respective templates. In the middle portion you will find a few thumbnails of your most recent files, and most importantly on the right-hand side you will find the resources window, which will become extremely helpful as make your way to become proficient in Revit. Under the resources tab you will find videos, tutorials, and forums. There are other resources outside Autodesk such as books, Internet course subscriptions, and a mobile application that will help you navigate through Revit. Remember to validate the source of the information. Many videos found on social media might have been created by amateurs in the profession. Good resources will be those found in Autodesk and those course subscriptions such as Lynda.com, to name a few.

So now you are ready to strike out on your journey through Revit. Remember that Revit is only as good as the user and the information the user puts into the program. As a Revit 3-D model is being developed during the design phase, develop guidelines during the design process, using standards that you may have developed earlier, or use the Office Drafting Room Manual if you are employed. The guidelines may also be called Architectural Design Standards.

If you come from an AutoCAD background, please understand there will be limitations that exist between the two programs. It's noteworthy that you will not be able to work the same way in Revit as you do in AutoCAD.

When you begin to draw a floor plan, include all interior walls, built of wood, masonry, or steel. Of those structures built of wood, you will begin to describe the exterior covering called cladding. Thus, you are drawing a floor plan that is now built around what is called a "Family." You must draw a minimum of four an additional drawings. So, as you draft a floor plan, validate the size and shape and be sure it will fit on the site properly. Revit will also draw a building section and elevations to ensure accuracy of the structure. A common way that this can be accomplished is to split the monitor into the images that you are drawing. In a large office, most computer stations are equipped with multiple monitors to enable the user to use multiple images of various drawings, which allows that technician to look at any drawings at. All of the drawings are integrated in such a fashion that changes in one drawing will immediately reflect in the other. For example, if you were to locate a window on the floor plan, it would show on the exterior elevation. A feature of the Revit program is that changes in each individual drawing are reflected in all other drawings. You can monitor your drawings and changes in different views by displaying all of the drawings on the screen. You will have the ability to zoom in and out of any drawing in progress. You will find all your drawings in the project browser and can view them simultaneously by clicking on the view tab under tile. See Figure 2.121, which shows drawings organized in a tile view.

As you work in Revit, you must periodically save your work as an RVT (Revit) file. A new template will be saved as an RTE extension. As you draw in Revit, you are simply adding more information to this complex 3-D model.

Construction Document Standards

As you change the BIM/Revit design model to construction documents, it is essential that you take the partial standards displayed below and develop them to meet your needs.

Generic Standards for Construction Documents

- Lettering height
- Max./Min. scale of document
- Materials in section
- Graphic symbols

ABBREVIATIONS

Dimensioning grouping of dimensions size and location

- Dimensional reference system
- Drawing sheet size
- Standardization used in the electronic world
- Human concerns—Americans with Disabilities Act (ADA)
- Use of energy—energy conservation
- Sustainable/green architecture

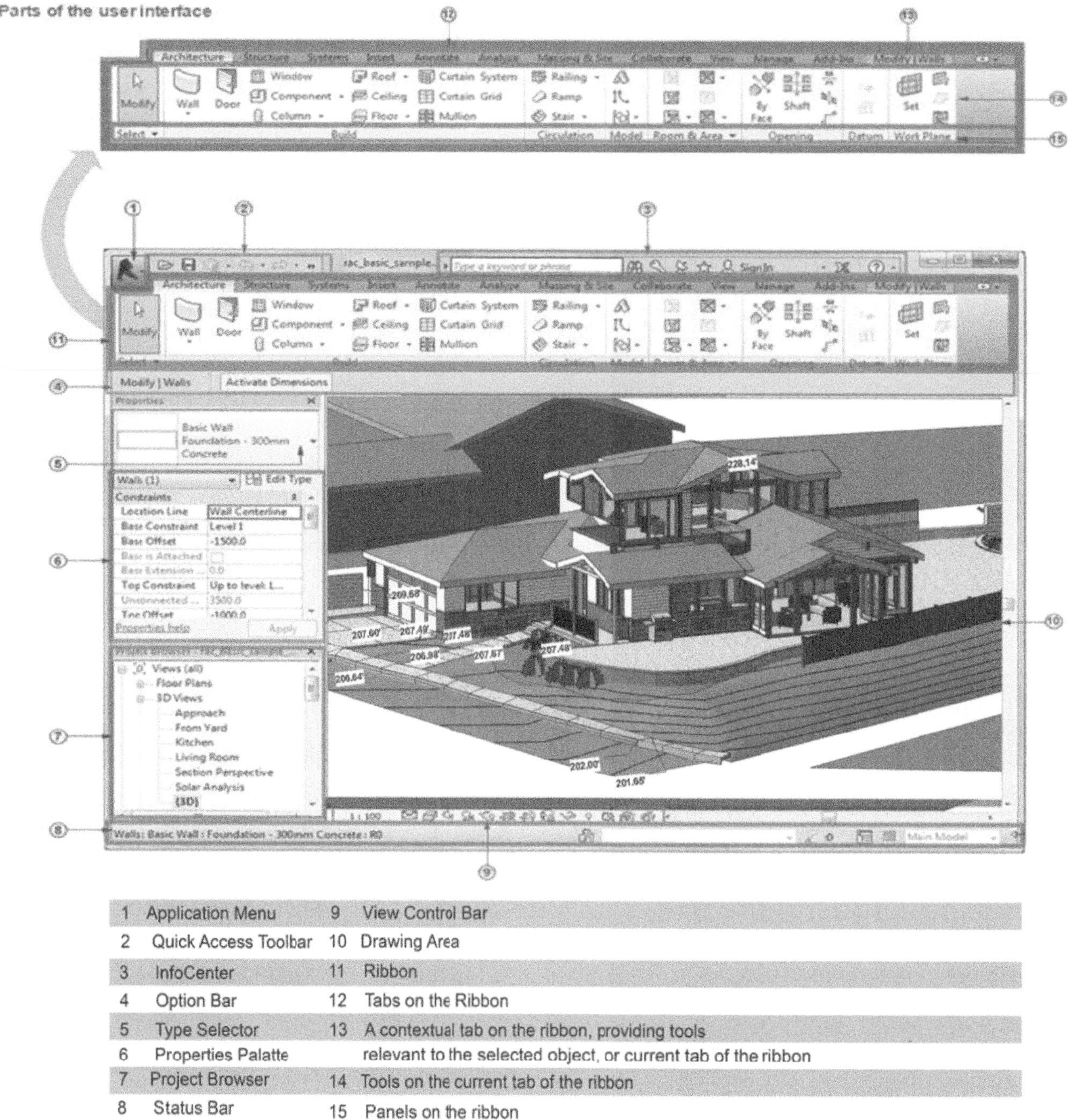

1	Application Menu	9	View Control Bar
2	Quick Access Toolbar	10	Drawing Area
3	InfoCenter	11	Ribbon
4	Option Bar	12	Tabs on the Ribbon
5	Type Selector	13	A contextual tab on the ribbon, providing tools relevant to the selected object, or current tab of the ribbon
6	Properties Palatte		
7	Project Browser	14	Tools on the current tab of the ribbon
8	Status Bar	15	Panels on the ribbon

Figure 2.120 User interface window. (Screenshots ©Autodesk, Inc. All Rights Reserved.)

This section is devoted to describing the use of Revit in the development of working drawings. Remember that the partial working drawings checklist is the subject we are addressing, and Revit is the technical tool that we are using. To start, we address the steps in preparing the necessary ingredients for working drawings for those beginning individuals who are working in the realm of Revit for the first time. Since working drawings have been discussed previously, we will limit our discussion to describing the use of Revit exclusively in developing a site plan, a floor plan, an exterior elevation, and a building section. Yes, we realize that there are other drawings, such as foundation plans, roof plans, floor and roof framing plans, grading plans, and so on, to complete a total set of working drawings. At this stage, we will presume that you have the information from the architect/designer who has provided you with the other drawings. This approach was used because the

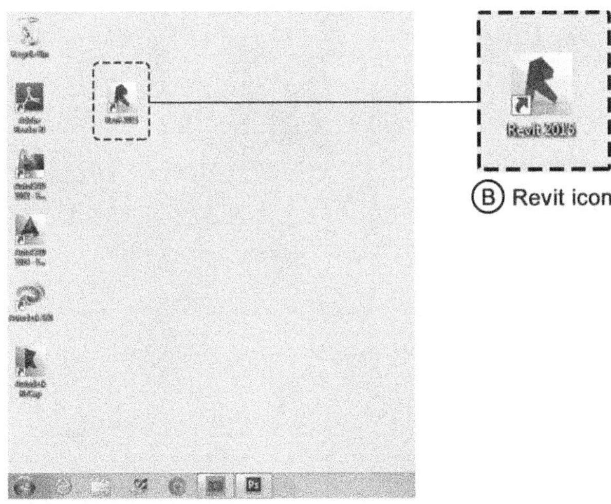

Figure 2.121 Loading Revit (Screenshots ©Autodesk, Inc. All Rights Reserved.)

purpose of this portion of the book was mainly to show a beginner in Revit the attitude needed in the formation of working drawings using Revit. There are other programs available that are being used in architecture such as Bentley, ArchiCAD, and VectorWorks, among the various programs that are available and used by architects. We have obviously selected Revit.

The attempt herein will be to expose the beginner to the correct separation of creating, designing, and the pure study of architecture and the pure technical skill of Revit. In this manner, the book weaves learning and technical scheduled knowledge in a manner called a deconstructive forming in education. Thus, we will pursue that which is needed in the technology of Revit as we develop a plan for our journey through the technical aspect of the creative part of architecture.

Therefore, it is critical that, before you go on this journey, you review the various parts of BIM and digest what will be expected of you in the production of working drawings. In this manner, the book will try to explain how working drawings are trying to convey to the contractor and their employees and subcontractors how the structure is to be built and how to articulate that knowledge in our drawings. Learn the language of architecture.

If you are hired by an architectural firm, you must reaffirm that the standards aligned themselves with the drafting room manual. Next, be ready to create a new project. Familiarize yourself with the Recent File screen, which is the first screen that appears when you first open Revit. Revit provides you with predetermined templates to start a project; you can use these templates to start your project, create your own, or use the templates that are provided to you at your workplace. These templates will have predetermined standards, and different information can be provided under different templates. If you are starting a template from scratch, you must review all standards.

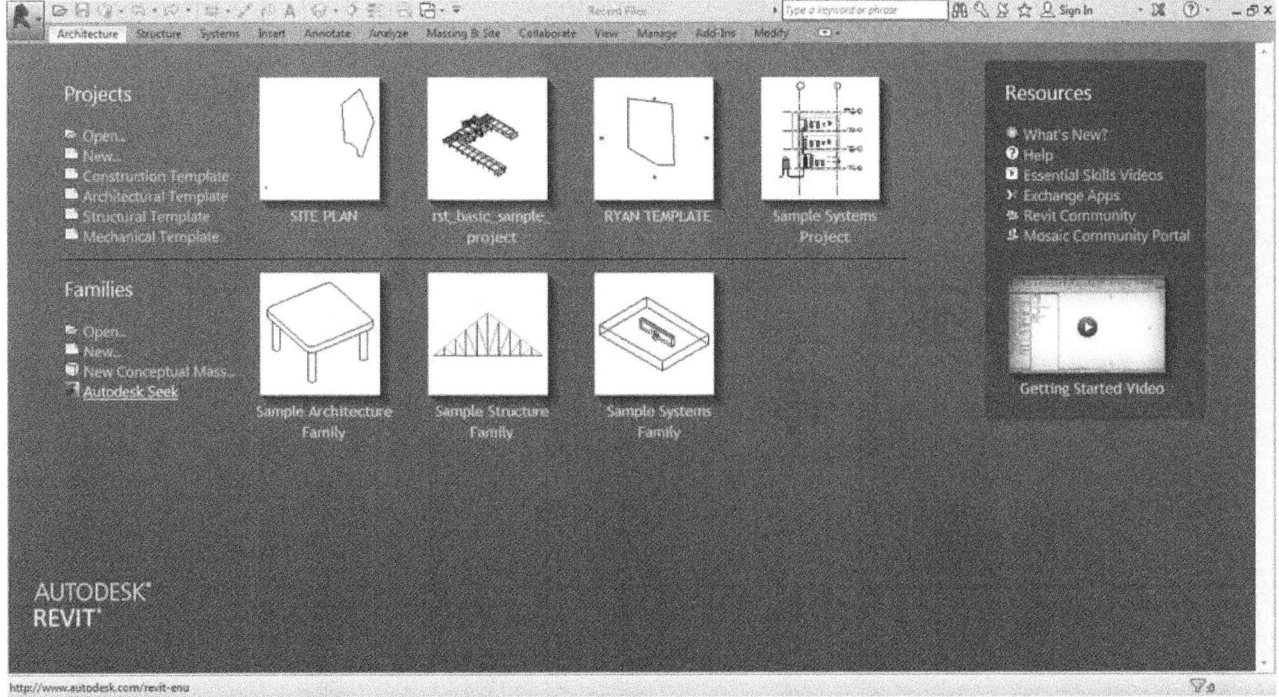

Figure 2.122 Recent file window. (Screenshots ©Autodesk, Inc. All Rights Reserved.)

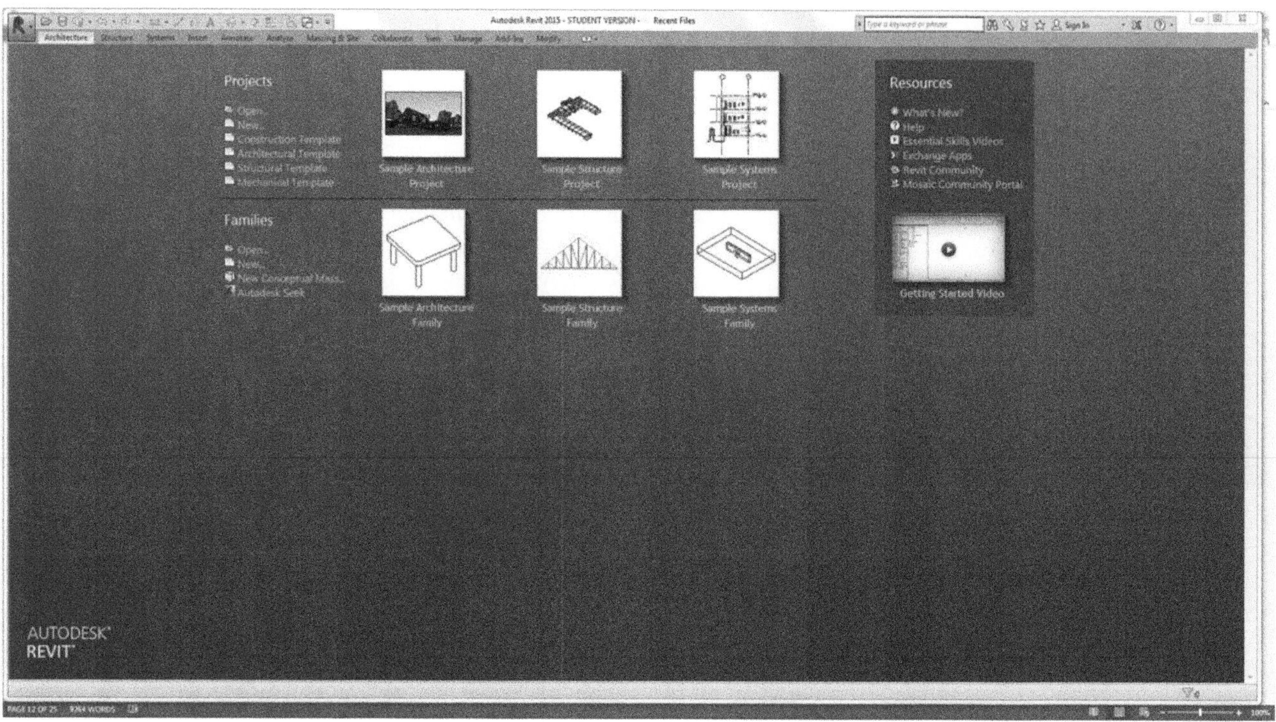

Figure 2.122 *(Continued)*

Site Plan

At this stage, locate the Revit icon after opening the Revit program, locate the construction template under the Projects section, and click on it with your mouse. See Figure 2.122. If you cannot locate the construction template, you can find it by going to Projects, New, and a window will open where you can choose the construction template under the template file window. See Figure 2.123. There are several steps in this preparation. At this time, a project file window will show on the screen. This is where your project will begin. Familiarize yourself with this window since this is where most of your work will be done; review all the tabs. At this point we will start setting up our project. We will start with the property information. Under the manage tab, you will find the icon called Project Information. See Figure 2.124. There you will give the project a title, name, status; most of this information will appear in the title block. Then you will need to set up site location. This will be an actual geographic location of the site, and you can check the accuracy of the site location if seen from above, called a bird's-eye view. Technically, this is referred to as pictometry. See Figure 2.123.

We now begin to work on the site! We will begin by going to the massing and site tab. See Figure 2.125. Begin to draw the site using the civil engineer's survey of the property, which can be transferred to your drawing from the civil engineer CAD drawing by tracing over it or starting from scratch. See Figure 2.126, which shows the start of a site plan by determining the bearing from scratch. The property lines will start with the bottom left corner of the site (site datum) and each property line counter clockwise. The property lines must close. See Figure 2.127. If the property does not close, there may be an error in your drawings when you translated the information. The property lines are not always north–south or east–west, and each leg of the property is expressed only in feet and decimal equivalents of parts of a foot and never in inches. Most residences are drawn at a scale of 1/8″ = 1′-0″; however, an even smaller scale might be needed for larger sites. Depending on the size and shape of the site, you may need to check all the drawings to be placed on the sheet and on the module of the sheet.

Project north and true north have to be determined the importance of true north comes when designing your building but when creating your working documents your north has to be set to project north. These two can be interchanged under the properties tab. See Figures 2.128 and 2.129. Remember that your true north will also be associated with your property line bearings. You can link your floor plan to your site plan, and both will correspond and share the correct information associated with true north and the position of your building on the site.

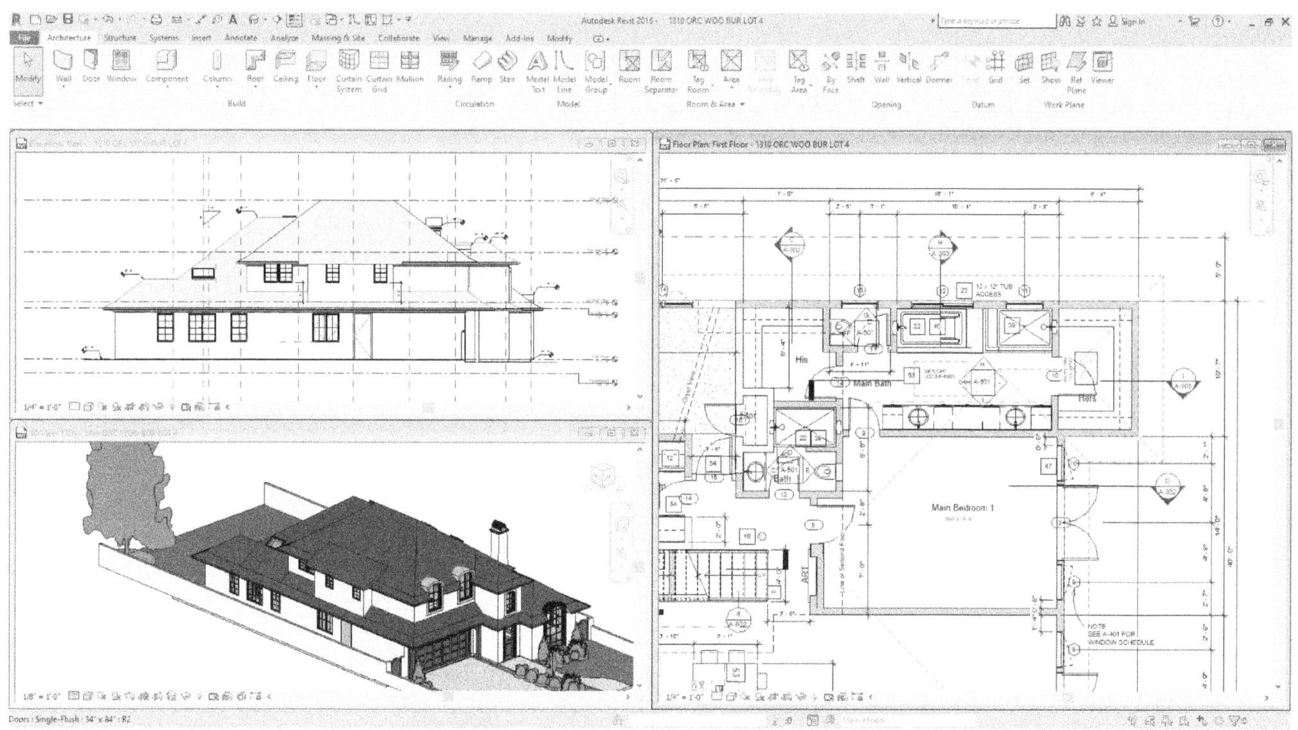

Figure 2.123 Multiple view windows. (Screenshots ©Autodesk, Inc. All Rights Reserved.)

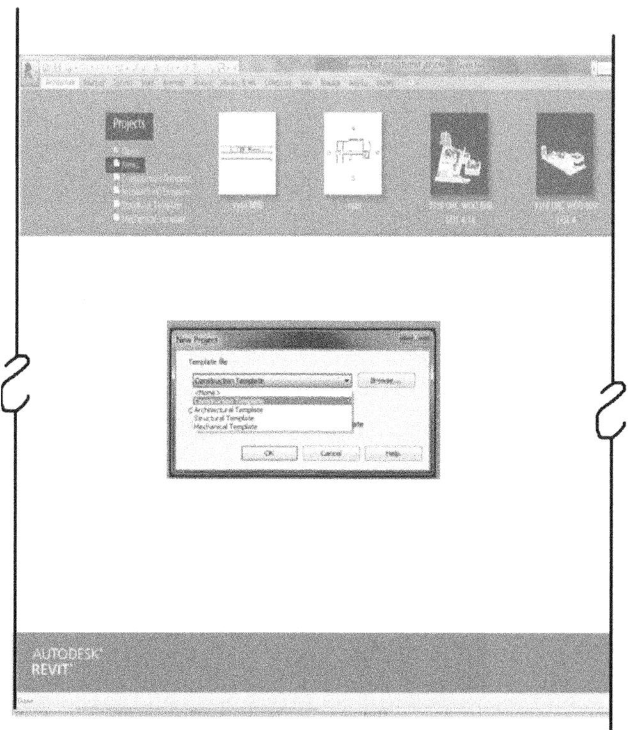

Figure 2.124 Starting a new project. (Screenshots ©Autodesk, Inc. All Rights Reserved.)

Floor Plan

Preparing construction documents must always begin with verifying patterns used by the designer—modules that are used to design the building and/or shapes that are unique to this particular grid is called Field Theory. The designer may be using the patterns in a different way than you might understand. Two typical examples of a field are shown—the Iowa field and one on the golden mean—in Figure 2.130. Review the standards that are used for the floor plan and not those that are already included on the computer.

Before you begin to draw a floor plan on Revit you must make sure that your project template contains all the information required for the project. First, make sure that you have updated all of the standard annotations to comply with the architectural standards. Next, make sure your template contains all of the families you will need for your project. Remember when you are drawing a wall, you will not just be drawing two simple lines but you will be drawing an actual wall; therefore, make sure to choose the correct walls. See Figure 2.131, which shows different walls.

Construct the perimeter of the floor plan, again noting that your exterior walls will be different from your interior walls; therefore, you must start with the perimeter of the building and then work on the interior walls. If the plan was drawn during the design stage, your task will be to validate its size against other drawings that

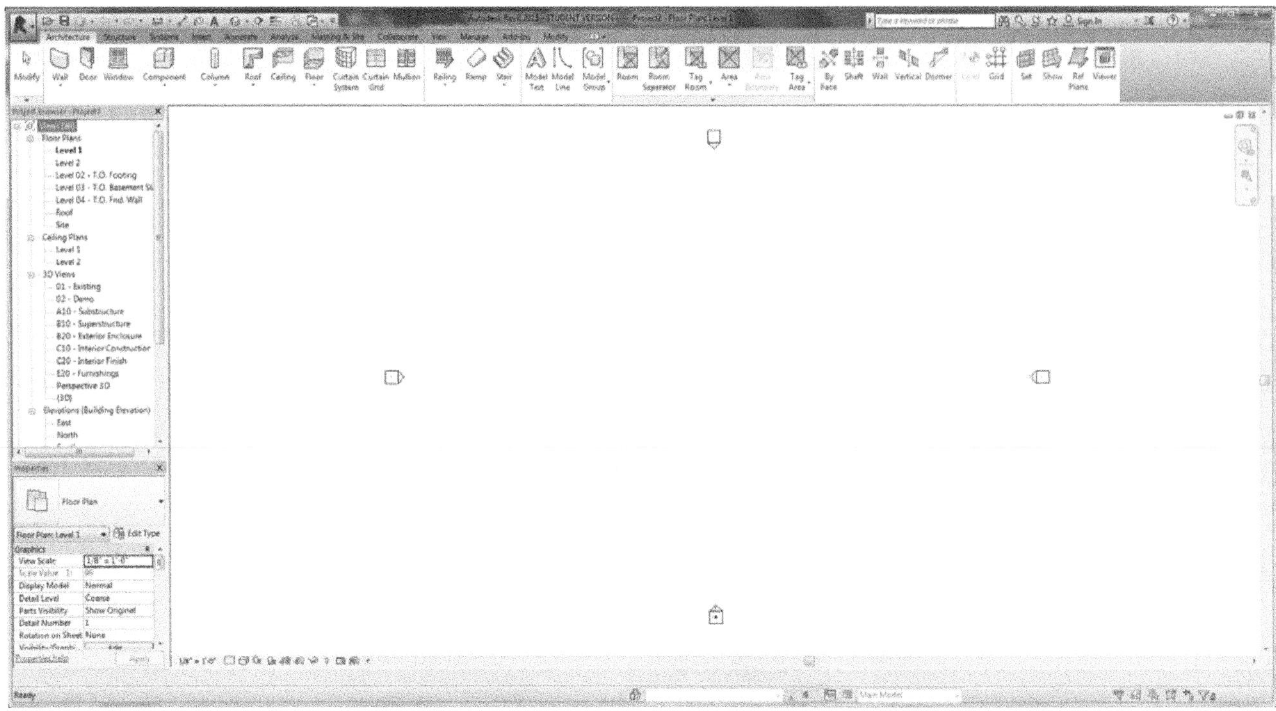

Figure 2.125 Project file window. (Screenshots ©Autodesk, Inc. All Rights Reserved.)

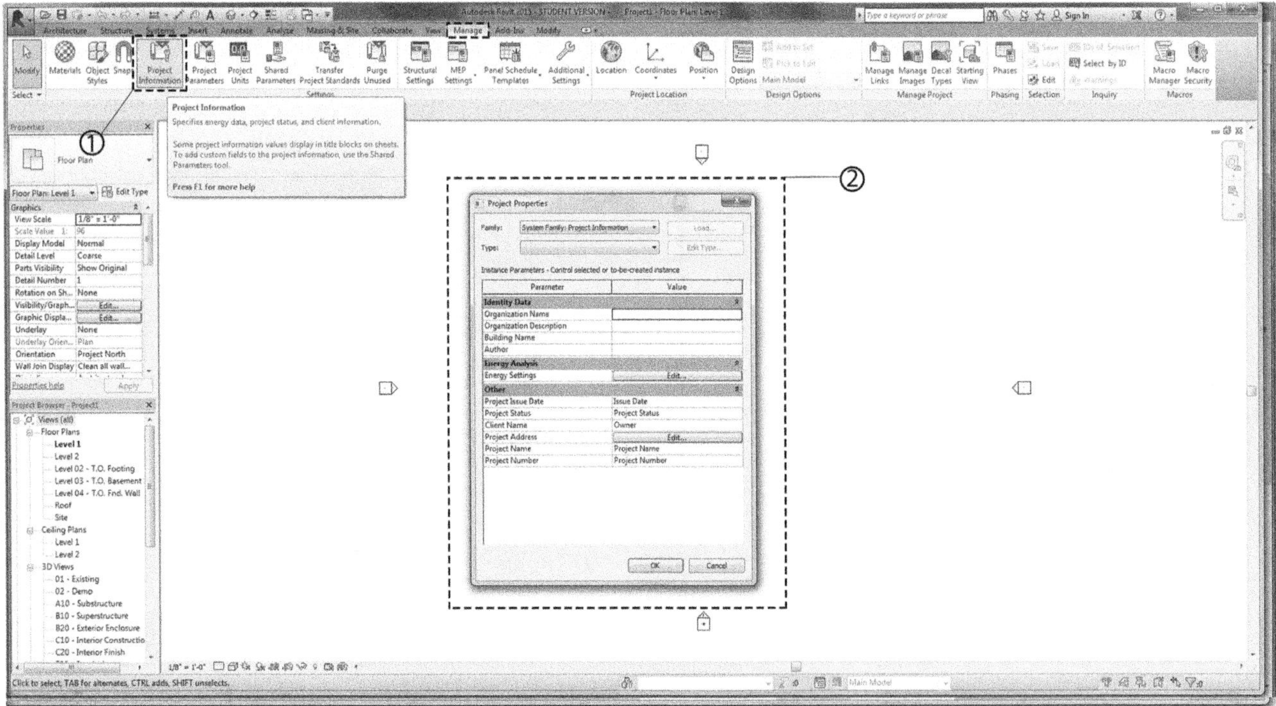

①Find the project information tab under the manage tab in order define your project information
②Define project, name address, project status under the project properties window

Figure 2.126 Project information.

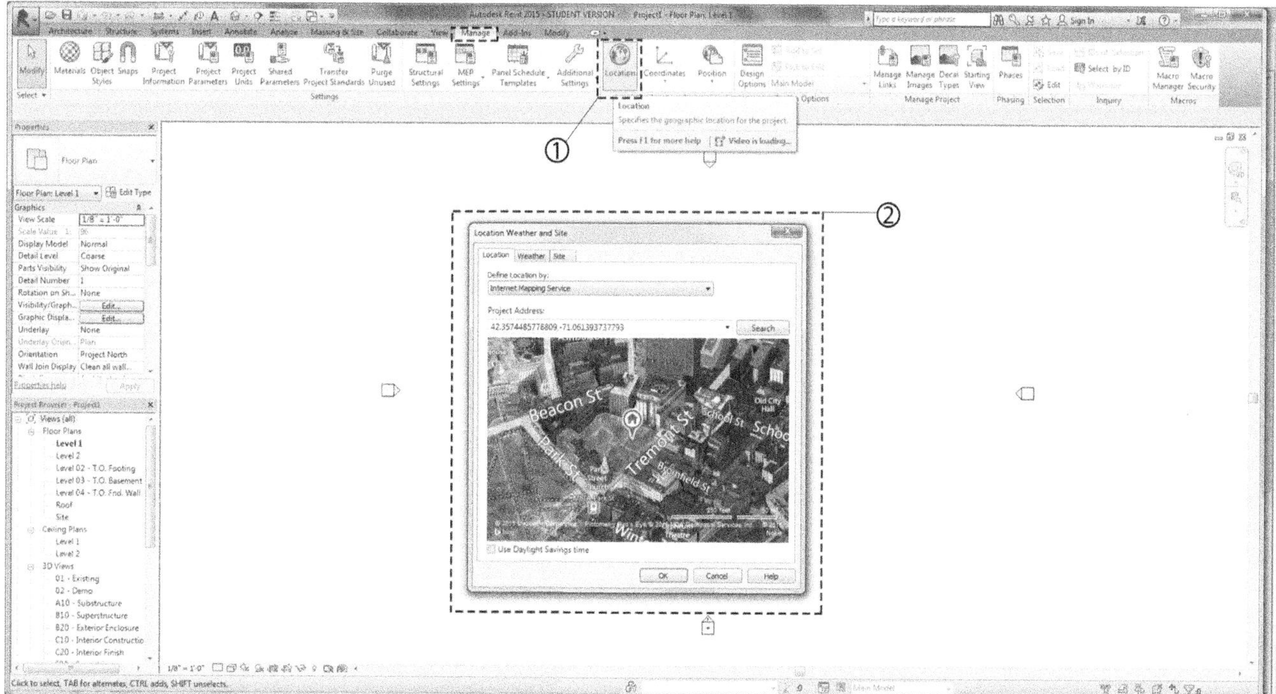

①Find the location tab under the manage tab in order define the location of the project
②Define the location of the project address by typing project address

Figure 2.127 Locating the project.

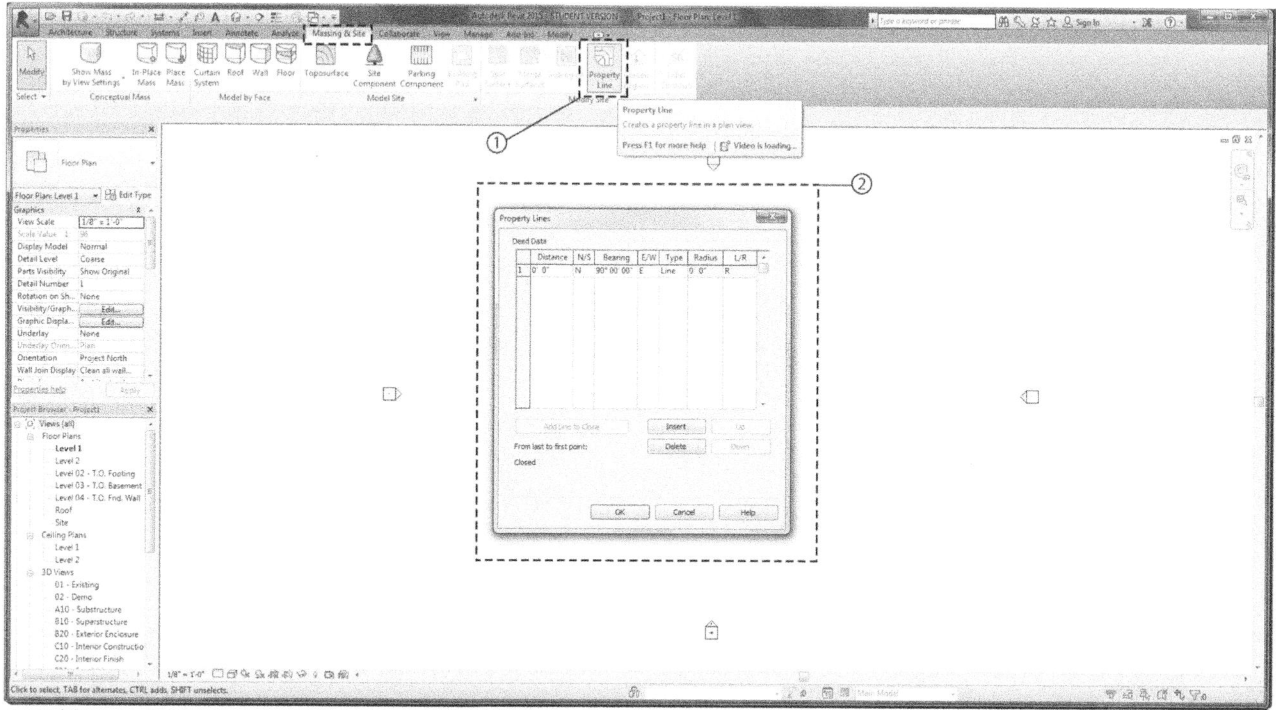

1 Find the property line command under the massing and site tab.
2 Under Property Lines window you can enter the bearings to create your site.

Figure 2.128 Site plan—property lines.

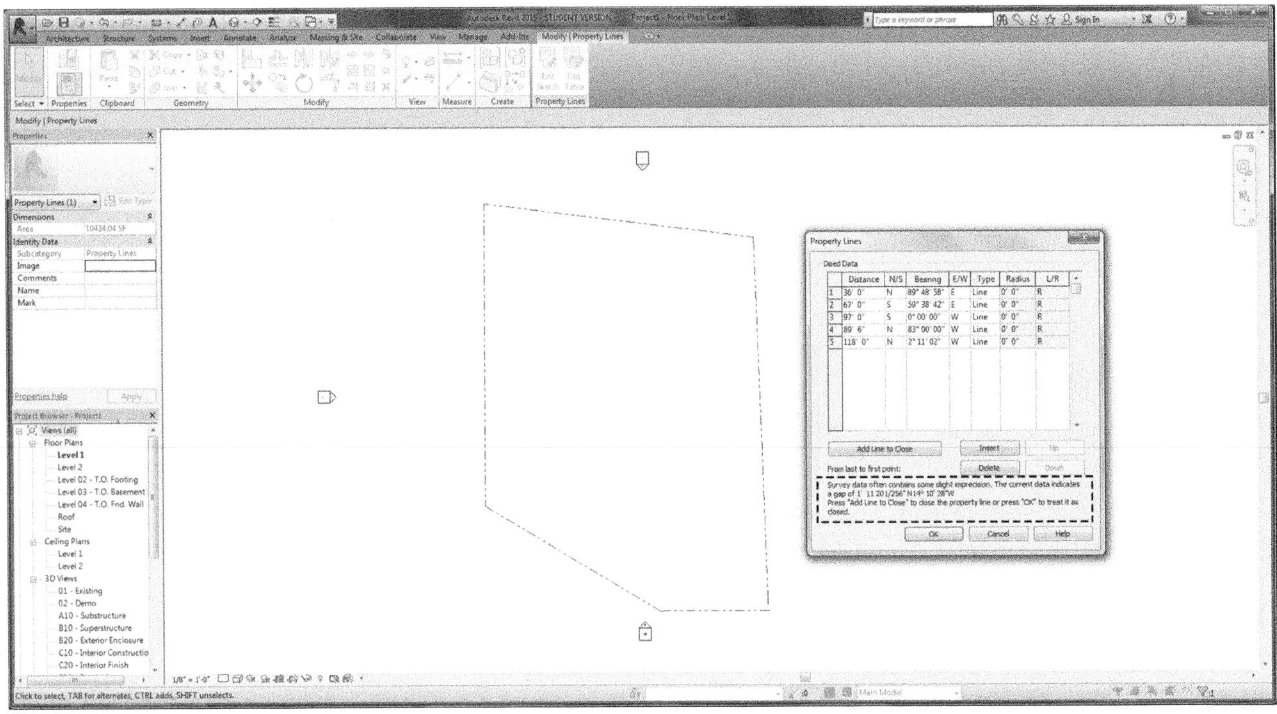

Figure 2.129 Site plan—property line not closing. (Screenshots ©Autodesk, Inc. All Rights Reserved.)

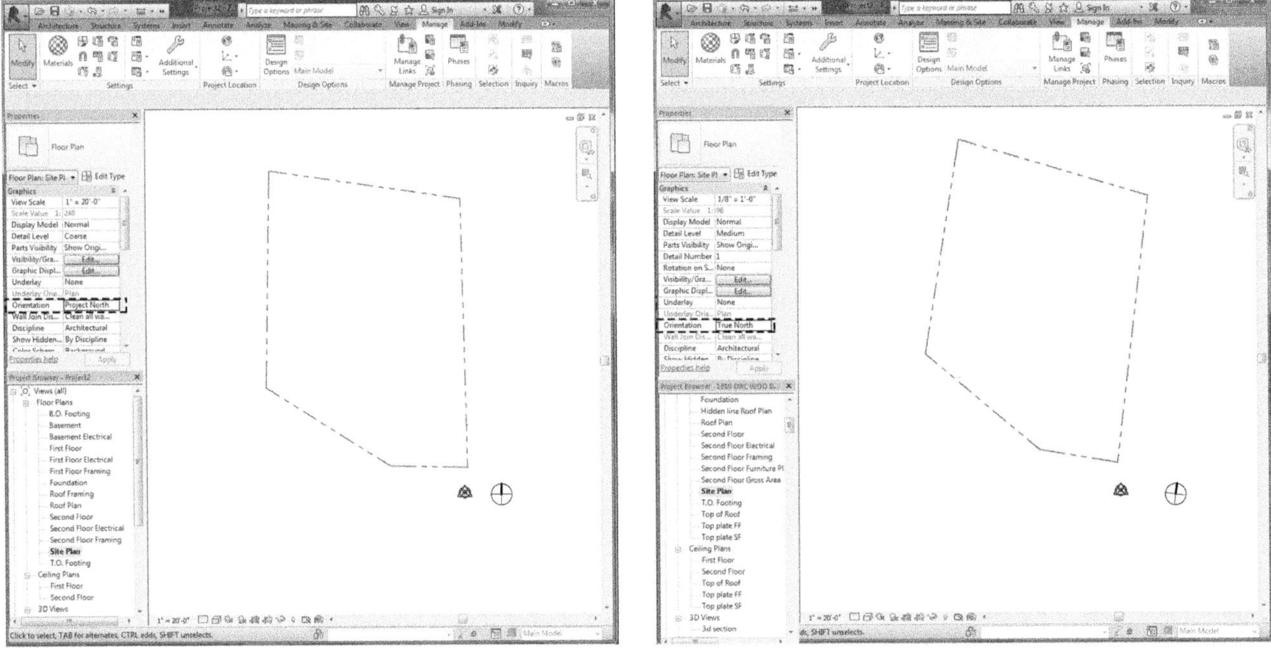

Figure 2.130 Site plan—true north versus project north. (Screenshots ©Autodesk, Inc. All Rights Reserved.)

are available to you, such as the site plan, elevation, and building section. If the floor plan was drawn during the design phase, but Revit was not used, the technical drafter must start from scratch, as Revit drawings require a greater amount of information describing the total wall. This is called a "Family," which includes all aspects of the ingredients of a floor plan. Therefore, the walls will include in a wood-framed structure the size,

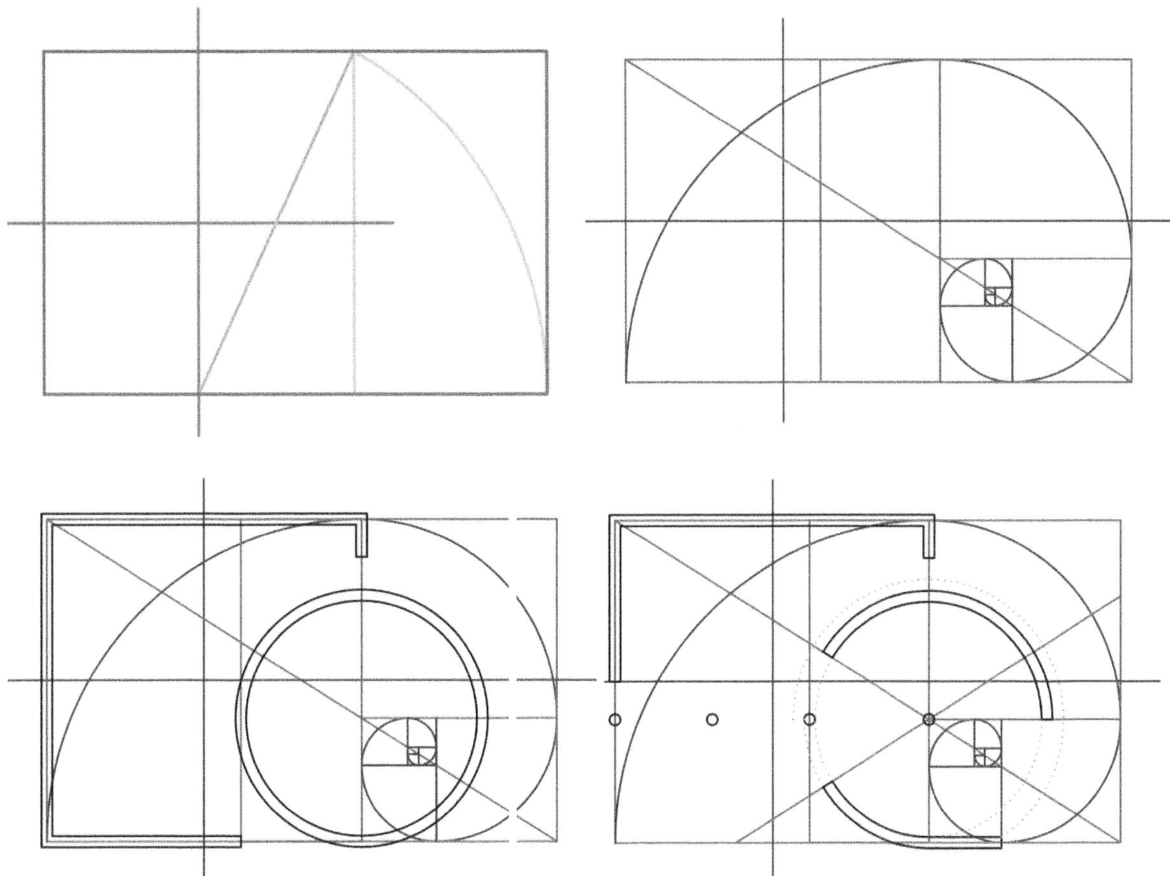

Figure 2.131 Golden mean field.

shape, and quality of the studs; a description of the covering used on the outside; and that which is used on the interior such as drywall. The information includes all aspects of the engineering, the type of building wrap which will include such items as the density, and its ability to allow what percentage of humidity at will allowed to penetrate and so on must be understood way up front. This is why Revit is often referred to as a front-loading program, and the information and takes much more time than previous drawings, drawn on programs such as AutoCAD.

Use the proper indication for wood, steel, masonry, and the correct standard for indicating composites. If at any time you are unable to do any of the above and it is asked of you, refer to the proper chapter in this book. Be sure to check your wall type and the correct application of wall for its condition as seen in Figure 2.132.

Imagine the floor plan, but be sure to leave an ample amount of space around the perimeter of the exterior walls and the first-dimension line for detail references, section lines, partial section symbols, and even structural notations and notes. Be selective for dimensions on the interior. If any dimension is not

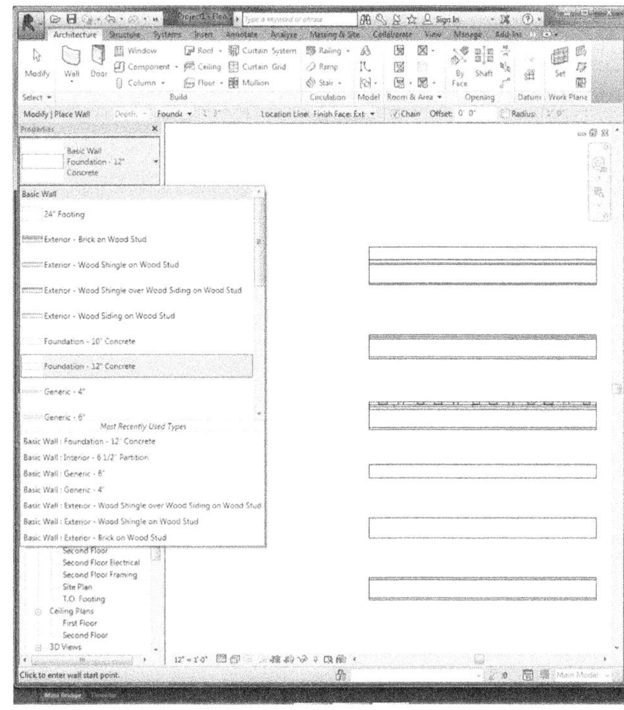

Figure 2.132 Types of walls in Revit.

done correctly, the building might not be at right angles as desired.

Elevation

Please note that your elevation as well as the section will be drawn automatically as you add more information to your drawing.

Provide proper title and scale as demonstrated in Figure 2.133.

Building Section

The preparation for drafting a building section begins with verifying the standard. Next, verify the size of the structure the materials to be used. The single most important documents to check are the structural engineer's drawings, as these will be used to start the building section.

In some offices, the drawing is almost complete with noting, dimensioning, and the necessary titles. While others draw the configuration of the building immediately adjacent to the section, and some item on the inside of the building section such as columns at support the structure vertical connectors such as stairs. The item most forgotten by the beginner are framing members that come toward the observer, such as floor joists and ceiling joists. See Figure 2.134.

In Revit you start by cutting a section through your drawing. You can set up how much of that section should cut through if you don't want to show a lot of information. You must plan where you will cut your section. See Figure 2.135. You may find that there is a lot of information on your section that you don't need. You can turn off the information you don't want to see. See Figure 2.136. You can also set the level of detail you want your drawing to show, and all of these can be saved as a view template; therefore, every time you are working on your sections, they will all show the same amount of information that you previously set. As mentioned before, the most forgotten items to be shown by a beginner are the framing members. You can show these framing members by going to your annotate tab and choose them under the components tab. See Figure 2.137. You can now start adding annotations by going to the annotation text tab. See Figures 2.138 and 2.139.

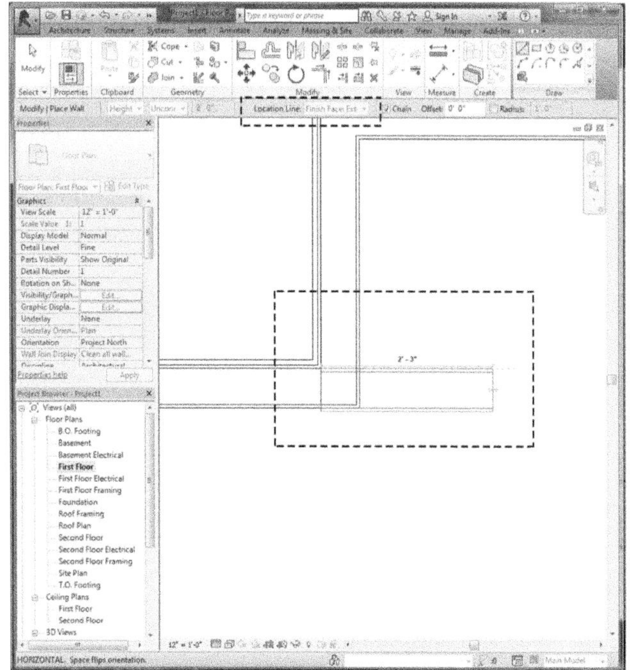

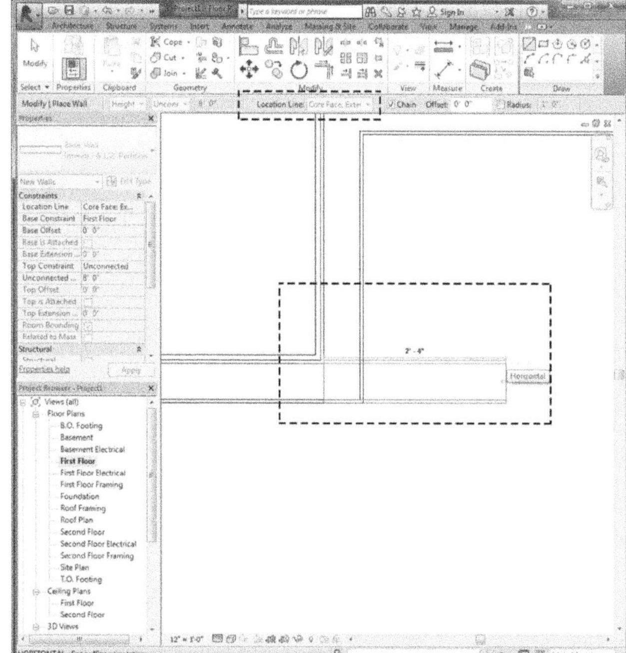

Incorrect location line. (Finish face exterior)

Correct location line. (Core face exterior)

Figure 2.133 Checking your work.

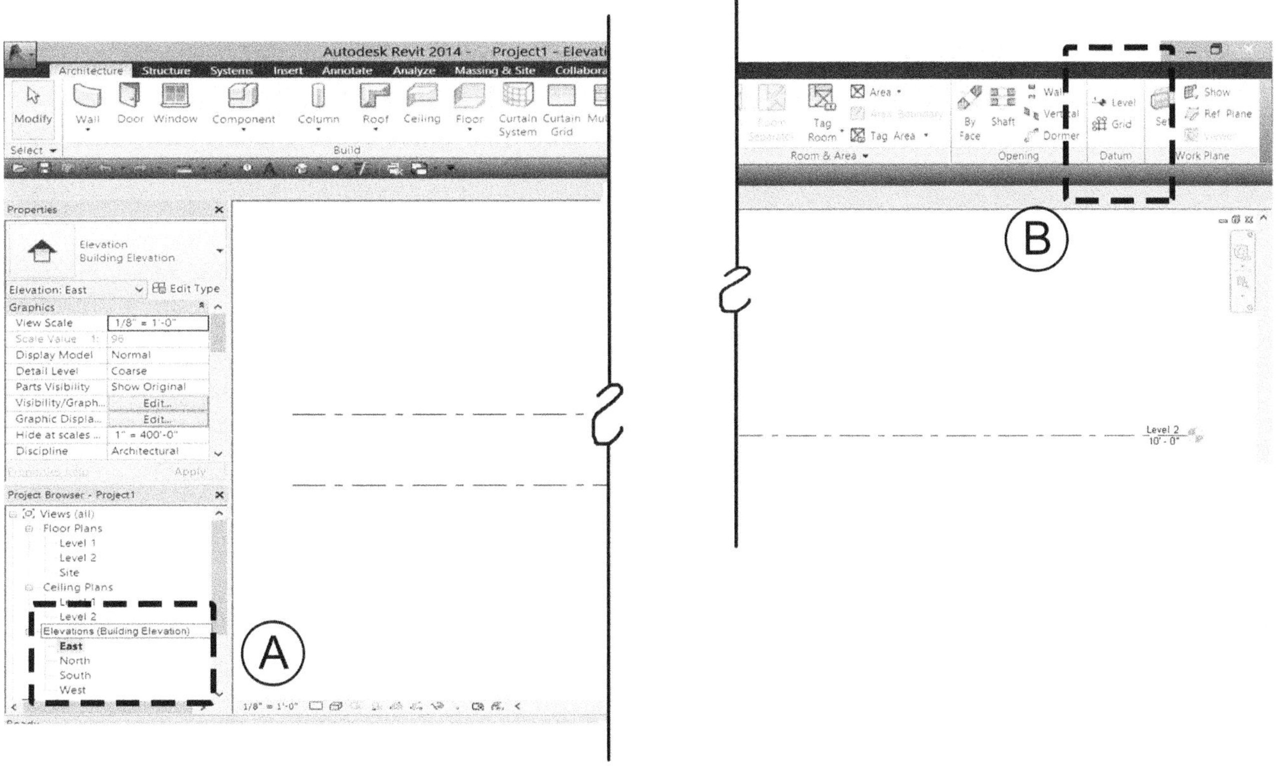

Figure 2.134 Defining datums in project. (Screenshots ©Autodesk, Inc. All Rights Reserved.)

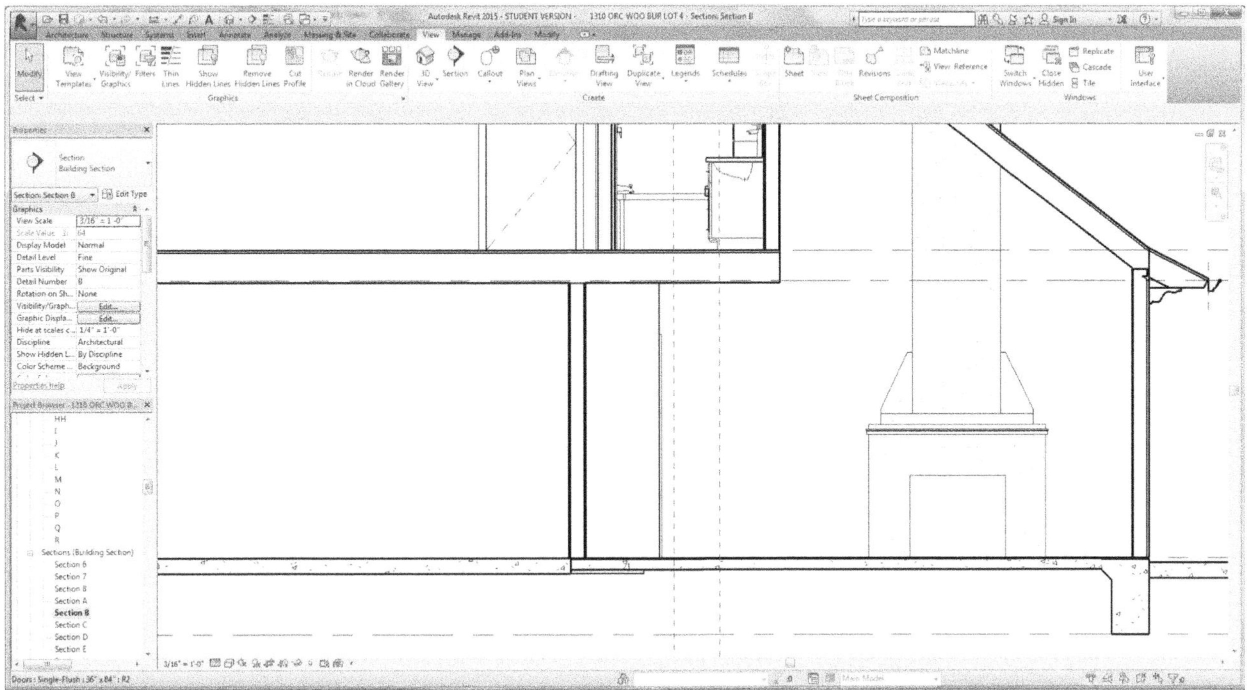

Figure 2.135 Section—cutting plane. (Screenshots ©Autodesk, Inc. All Rights Reserved.)

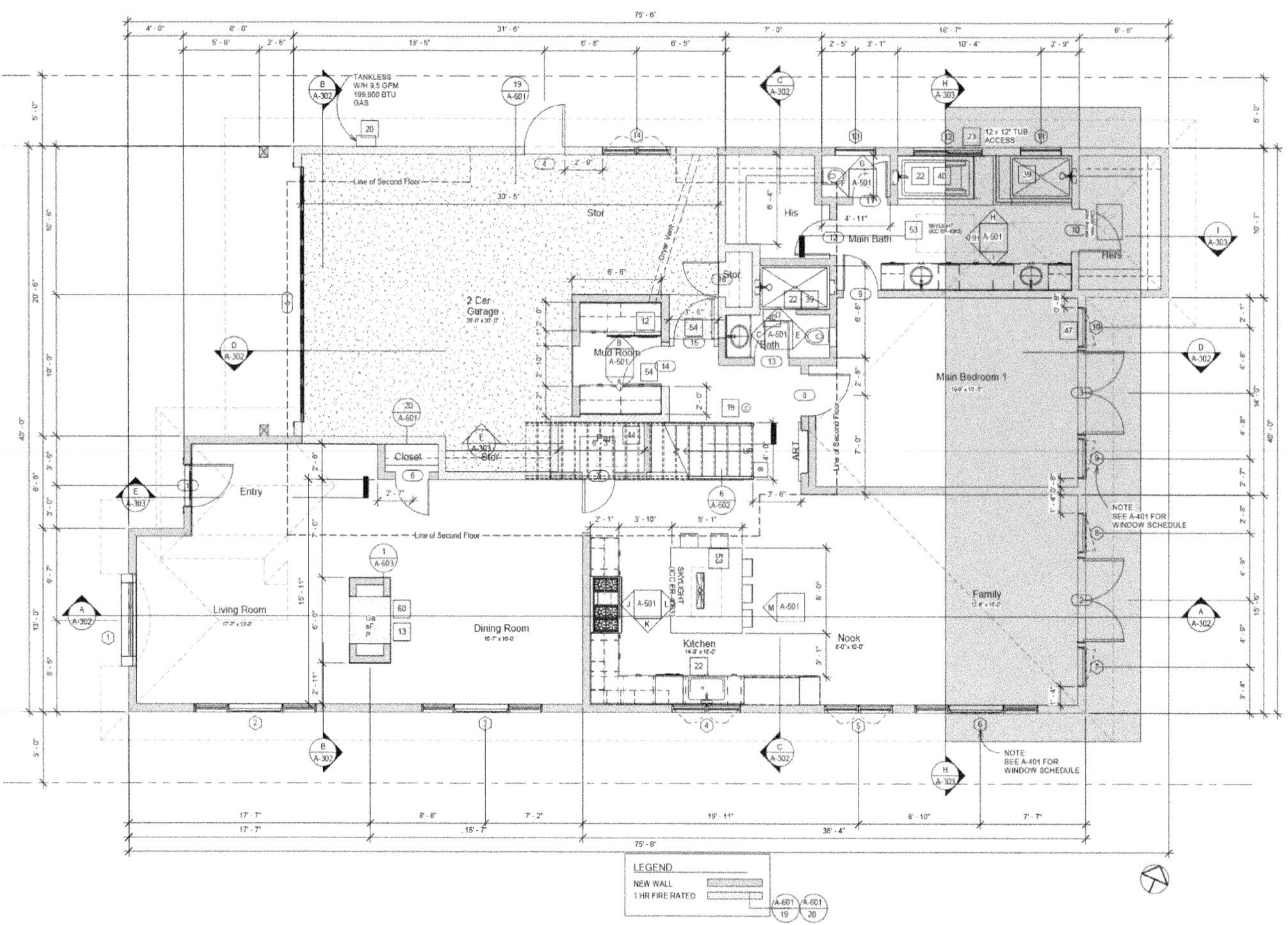

Figure 2.136 Section—determining cutting plane.

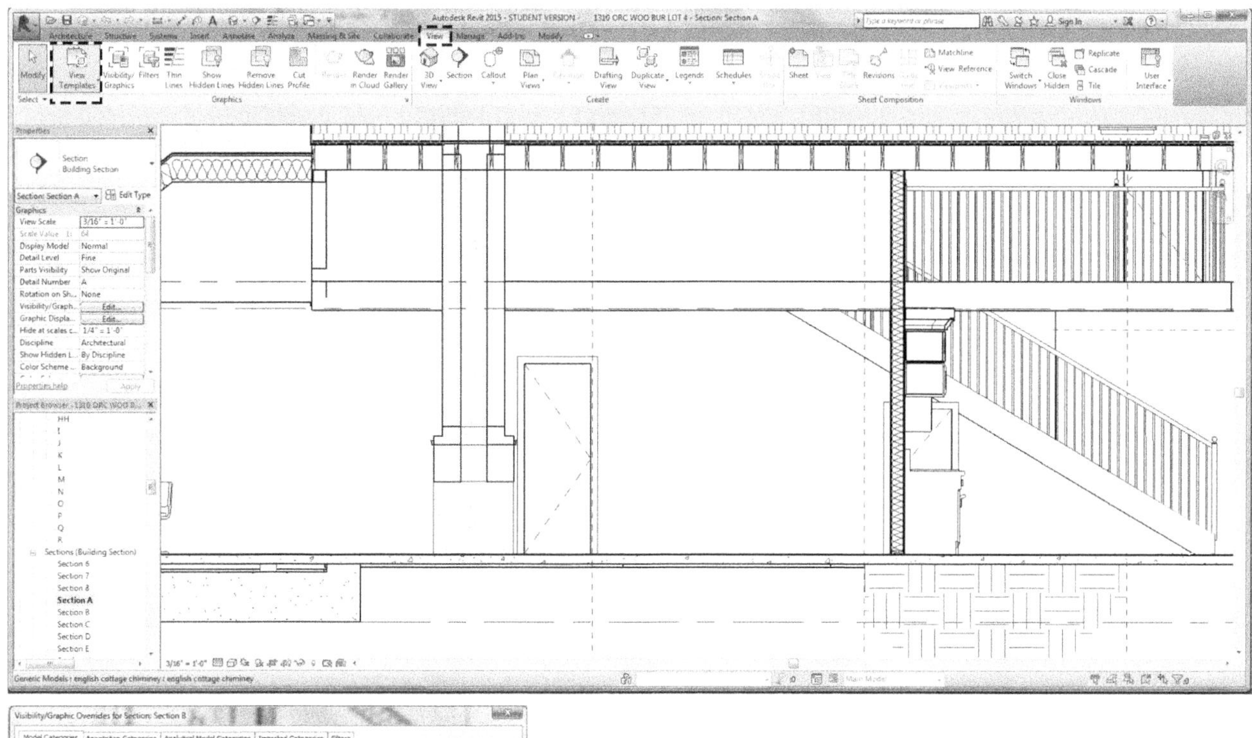

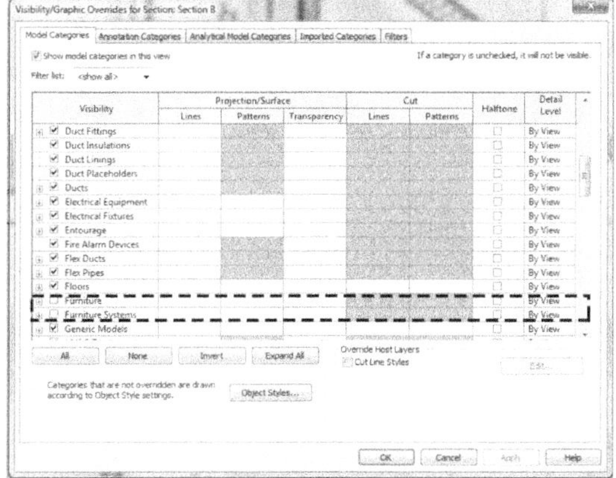

Hidding elements under visibility window

Figure 2.137 Section—cleaning up your section. (Screenshots ©Autodesk, Inc. All Rights Reserved.)

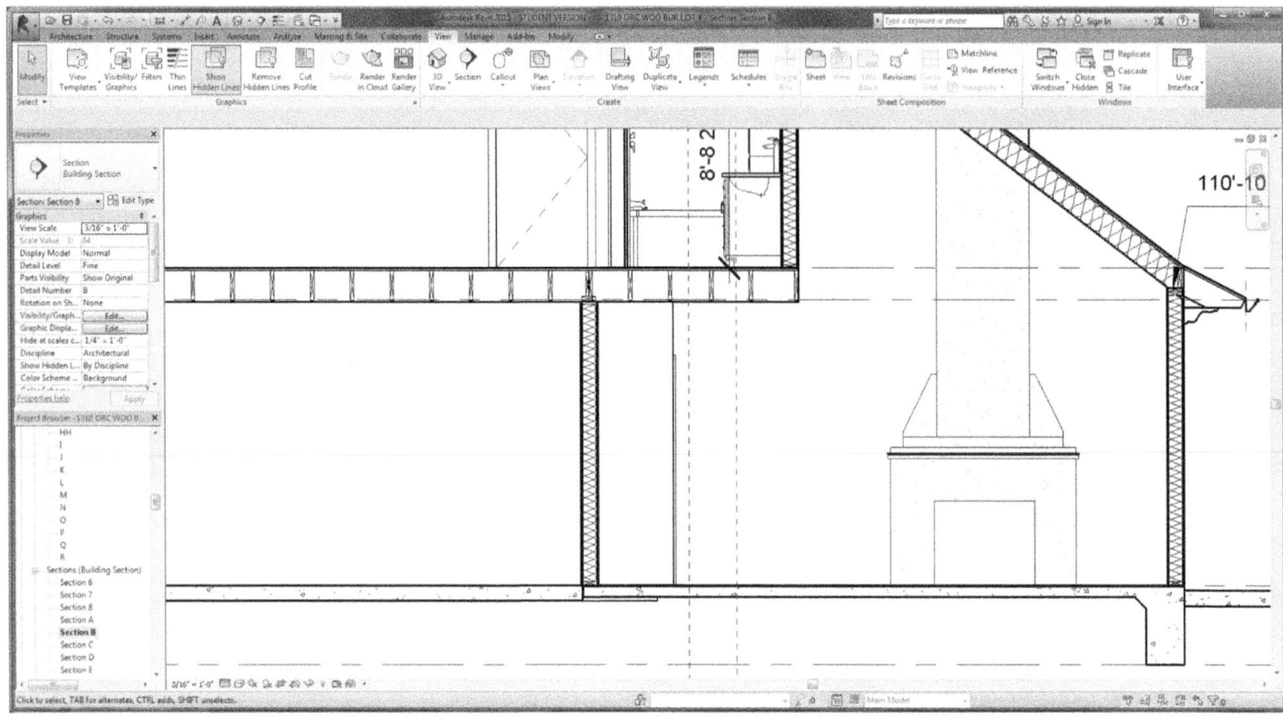

Figure 2.138 Section—showing framing members. (Screenshots ©Autodesk, Inc. All Rights Reserved.)

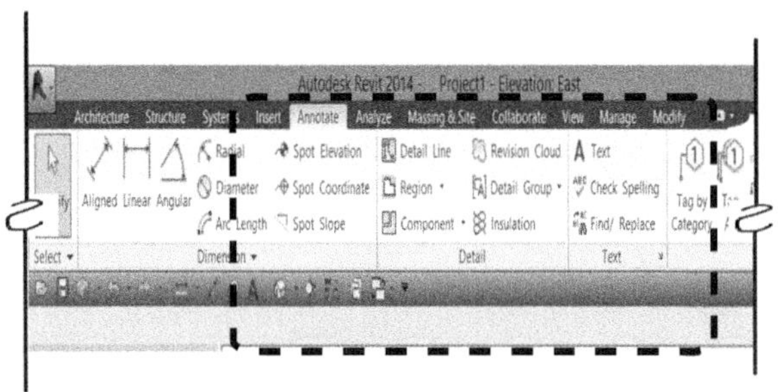

Figure 2.139 Menu options. (Screenshots ©Autodesk, Inc. All Rights Reserved.)

Key Terms

Architectural Graphic Standards
architectural profiling
axial plane
boundary control plane
Building Design Suite
Building information modeling (BIM)
building section
Cells
composite drafting
composite systems
computer-aided drafting (CAD)
concrete masonry units (CMUs)
concrete retaining wall
control zone
cross-referencing
cross-section
design sketches
dimensional reference system
Dimensioning
drafting room manual
DWF
DWG
electrical plans
engineered lumber
eraser drafting
floor plans
foundation plans
head
hidden lines
horizontal control plane
import
jamb
layering
lead pointer
longitudinal section
masonry veneer
module
net size
neutral zone
nominal size
office procedure manual
parent drawings
paste-up drafting
photo drafting
pilasters
pitch
plan
planes of reference
planking
plot plan
Revit

chapter

3

SUSTAINABLE ARCHITECTURE

(Zbyszek Nowak/Adobe Stock.)

The Professional Practice of Architectural Working Drawings, Sixth Edition. Nagy R. Bakhoum and Osamu A. Wakita.
© 2024 John Wiley & Sons Inc. Published 2024 by John Wiley & Sons Inc.
Companion website: www.wiley.com\go\bakhoum\theprofessionalpracticeofarchitecturalworkingdrawings

SUSTAINABLE ARCHITECTURE

The idea of sustainable design is not new; it has been available to us since the history of time. The definition or purpose of sustainable design is to reduce and minimize negative impacts on the environment and enhance the quality of life of its inhabitants. This can be applied locally within the building, experiencing one best life or more regionally where parks and open space enhance the quality of life and even globally where oceans are clean and healthy without plastics and contaminants. The objective is simple: to reduce the consumption of non-renewable materials and resources as a result of the minimization of waste we can enhance our environment and become more productive.

In the beginning of time, we gathered the plentiful resources that that were available to us. Consider the Great Pyramids of Giza and the locally quarried stone, mud bricks, sand, or gravel. The casing made of white limestone. Finding plentiful materials and building for longevity is the ultimate return on investment. Thousands of generations have experienced the historic ancient world wonder—it is perhaps the oldest sustainable building example in history.

Sustainable design is a balance of providing for human need without degrading or abusing natural resources. This process allows the needs to be met without exhausting the future of natural resources. As you can imagine buildings utilize many materials, from concrete and masonry foundations to steel and wood structures, to gypsum and glass in fill walls. These materials all come together and appear seamless, but for a moment imagine the waste that is created in the process—even in the manufacturing of the products, waste is a formidable challenge. Waste generates pollution and as pollution increases, our quality-of-life declines.

If one could learn one key component in sustainable design, it would be to build for longevity. There is a realignment that is key in an architect thinking that moles his field forward in leaps and bounds. If an architect can design a building to last for hundreds or even thousands of years, that is the ultimate testament to sustainable design.

What are the key components to sustainable design?

1. Design for generations include the flexibility for a building to change its use over its entire life cycle. This includes flexible MEP systems.
2. Utilize a selected site that can be optimized for its potential considering its life cycle relative to the adjacent communities. Develop or access public transit/pedestrian access and open space, green ways for wildlife.
3. Protect/preserve natural resources. Protect water and restore water to replenish gray water. With low flow fixtures, collection of rain water, or reuse of gray water incorporated into the SD, select materials that can be recycled or replenished such as replenishable forest wood. Non-toxic local sustainable materials should take priority over alternative materials.
4. Conserve energy and incorporate flexible life cycle systems for MEP consider daylight versus electrical lighting systems to improve quality of environment. This will also reduce the demand of power consider occupancy sensors to conserve power to optimize the efficiency of HVAC systems. Utilize sun power for items such as solar heating. All of these systems integrated improve the user's health and experience with the indoor environment.
5. Recycle in all aspects of the construction and occupancy of the building. In demolition, a builder can be broken down into parts and utilized. Designate the building locations to store/sort and recycle materials for the life of the building and its inhabitants.
6. Incorporation of appropriate plant materials. This overlaps water conservation but expands into plant selection that is nature to the climate of the region. This sensitivity allows for wildlife to inhabit and further sustain wildlife.

Sustainable design requires a long-term vision. Cost is the overwhelming concern to building sustainability. Logically, building to a budget is a great goal. Moreover, it is an architect's responsibility to design to a budget. Education is instrumental to surpass this hurdle. A sustainable building is more valuable as it is up front costs are quickly offset by its long-term operational costs.

The United States Green Building Council was created to change the standards in the industry. **Leadership in Energy and Environmental Design (LEED)** was among the first systems that were created to develop a Green Building rating. The lead system has been reworked and refined since its inception in 1993. The year was 2000 when it was introduced to the general public and it has been updated every three years since.

As architects conduct the orchestra of consultants, the sustainable practices allow for great opportunities. As building and parking lots displace open space, water infiltration into Earth's water table is diminished. Civil engineers can design stormwater management solutions to control water runoff and incorporate water where it is needed. Green roofs are a creative method of incorporating a vegetated surface allowing water infiltration and absorption and stormwater runoff into a secondary utilization back into groundwater table. The system is not complex, but also serves other purposes such as lengthening the life expectancy of the water proof roofing system.

Other effects include aesthetics, wildlife habitats, insulation buffer, and roof cooling. While it's not quite a green roof system, a great improvement to our vast parking lots and parking structures is the incorporation of native trees. The sheer size of parking areas without trees reflects heat in an island effect, where it is nearly unbearable. The shade of a tree canopy is a welcome find in a summer heat, since it is simple and effective and allows water to infiltrate to the groundwater (ideally via an oil separator).

As we discuss the life cycle of a building, consider the life cycle of specific materials in the selection process.

1. Is it recyclable, biodegradable, or salvageable?
2. Is it durable, low-maintenance, toxic, off-gas, or hazardous to install?
3. Is it shipped, local, or sustainably manufactured?
4. In the production process does it waste water, use recycled materials, or generate toxic emissions?
5. Is the material renewable, sustainable, salvaged, or recycled?

One cannot place a building on a site without considering the impact the structure will have on the immediate environment. In fact, there are many environmental concerns facing the architect, ranging from seismic to snow, from the effects of the sun to rainfall, and from the control of termites to frost-line depth in certain regions. An abbreviated list of the most common concerns includes the following:

1. Climate
2. Soil/geology
3. Seismic activity
4. Fire
5. Energy
6. Foundation design
7. Flooding
8. Distribution of loads/roof loads/vertical loading
9. Structural design
10. Frost depths
11. Drainage
12. Insulation
13. Americans with Disabilities Act (ADA)
14. Water table
15. Exterior finishes

This chapter specifically addresses sun (light, heat, and ultraviolet radiation), sound, deterioration of materials, termites, and underground gases (see Figure 3.1).

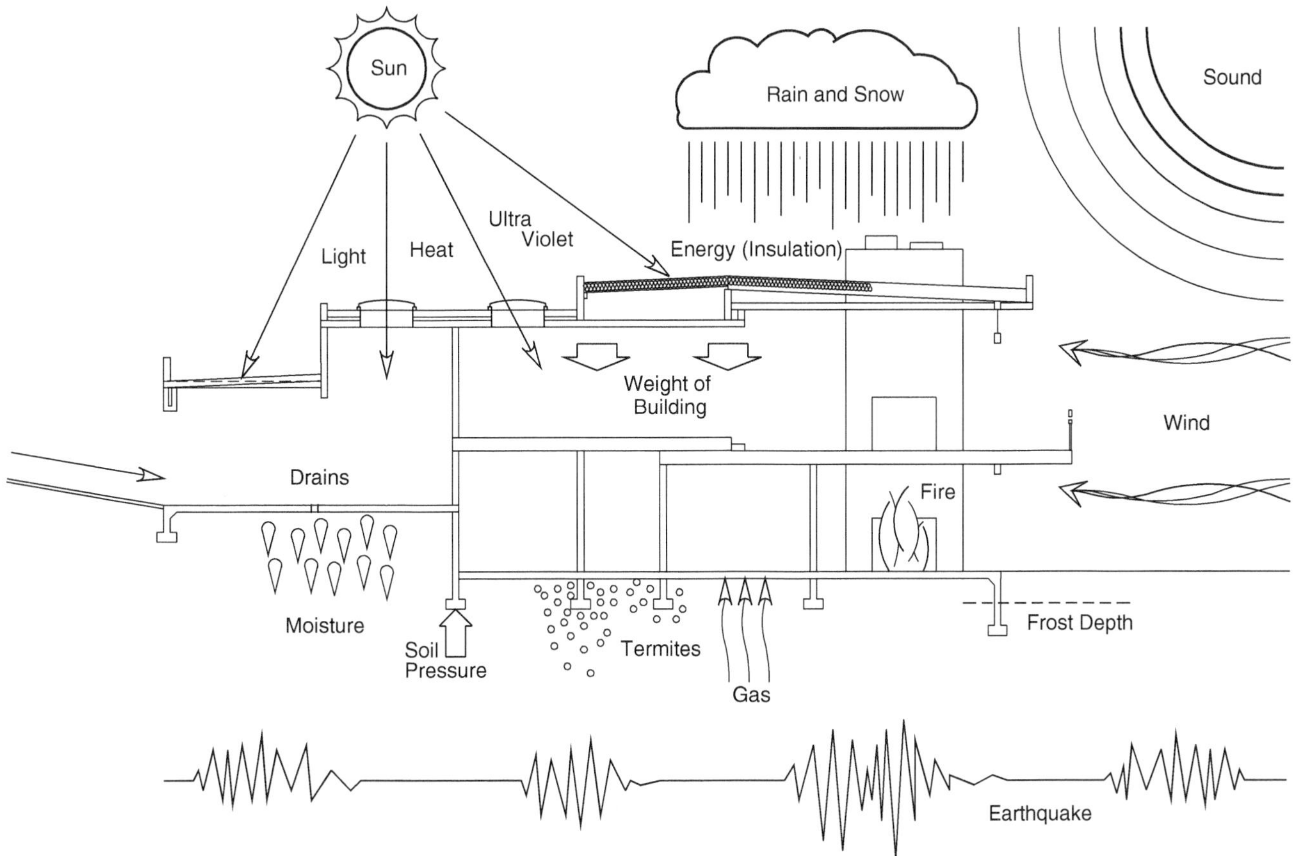

Figure 3.1 Natural forces.

Solar

We are now incorporating solar energy into our homes and business structures. Solar panels are not only very popular but can also be incorporated into the design a number of ways including the use of photovoltaic shingles into the roof during the initial designing preparation stages. To this end, we encourage manufacturers to produce solar shingles that blend with our existing configurations or in place of traditional roofing material, in such a manner that the roof looks natural in color and form. At the present time, there are a number of companies that design integrated tile-solar systems. However, they are expensive and people are shying away because of the initial cost. See Figure 3.2.

Energy Conservation

The architect, mechanical engineer, and electrical engineer will constantly be designing and providing methods to conserve energy. These methods will primarily deal with the use of insulation allocated to the roof, wall, and floor assemblies for a specific structure. The assemblies will handle both cold and heat, as well as mechanical and electrical systems, and any innovations that will assist in conserving energy.

Figure 3.3 illustrates a three-story residence in which the entire envelope will be calculated, detailed, and constructed with energy-conserving elements designed to address both warm and cold weather conditions. The first elements are the roof, ceiling, walls, and floors. These will be insulated with a material with an "R" value that will resist heat loss and heat gain. The R value is the value assigned to a specific insulating material or a combination of materials that have been tested for their resistive capabilities. One method of combating heat and cold is shown in an example of a roof and exterior wall assembly with insulation at the ceiling and wall locations (see Figure 3.4).

Figure 3.2 Solar shingles.

In areas where extreme cold weather conditions prevail in the winter, it is recommended that rigid insulation board be installed at the foundation, around the footing elements, and perhaps under floor slabs. This insulation will prevent excess cold from reaching the floor slab and, ultimately, the inside of the building. Figure 3.5 shows an example of a footing detail where 1″ rigid insulation board is incorporated at the footing and concrete slab connection. This detail would lower the need for heating and thus reduce the expenditure of energy.

For exterior wall openings, such as windows and doors, where extreme cold and hot weather conditions prevail, it is recommended—and in many municipalities required—that the windows have dual or triple glazing and be installed to prevent air infiltration. Doors should also be weather-stripped and installed to prevent air infiltration.

For many building projects, there may be methods and innovations for heating and cooling systems whereby energy conservation may be attained. One example of supplemental heating is the use of a Trombe wall. A **Trombe wall** is a large, massive wall that is typically oriented to absorb the most sunlight during the day; it then radiates the heat back into the living space in the evening when the heat is required to maintain a comfortable temperature.

As mentioned previously, the entire envelope in Figure 3.3 will be calculated and designed with energy savings in mind. **Envelope** is a term referring to the entire enclosure of the interior living space of a building. This enclosure may utilize insulation materials to prevent heat loss during the winter and heat gain during the summer. An example of a building section for a one-story residence that creates an insulated envelope is illustrated in Figure 3.6.

For the purpose of augmenting lighting conditions in interior spaces, devices such as manufactured skylights and a unit called a "Solatube" are recommended. The Solatube, a reflective tube, is attached to the roof, and a lens is directed to an interior space in the structure. The lens refracts the captured light and disperses it into a specific area. This device can reduce the demand for additional lighting energy.

These and other resources are available for conserving energy in building projects. In geographic areas with snow and prevailing cold climates, the various sections of a structure must be detailed to address these climatic conditions.

As shown in Figure 3.7, the roof structure initially will be designed based on the live load of the snow. This live load figure is usually established by the existing building code in the local municipality. The load may

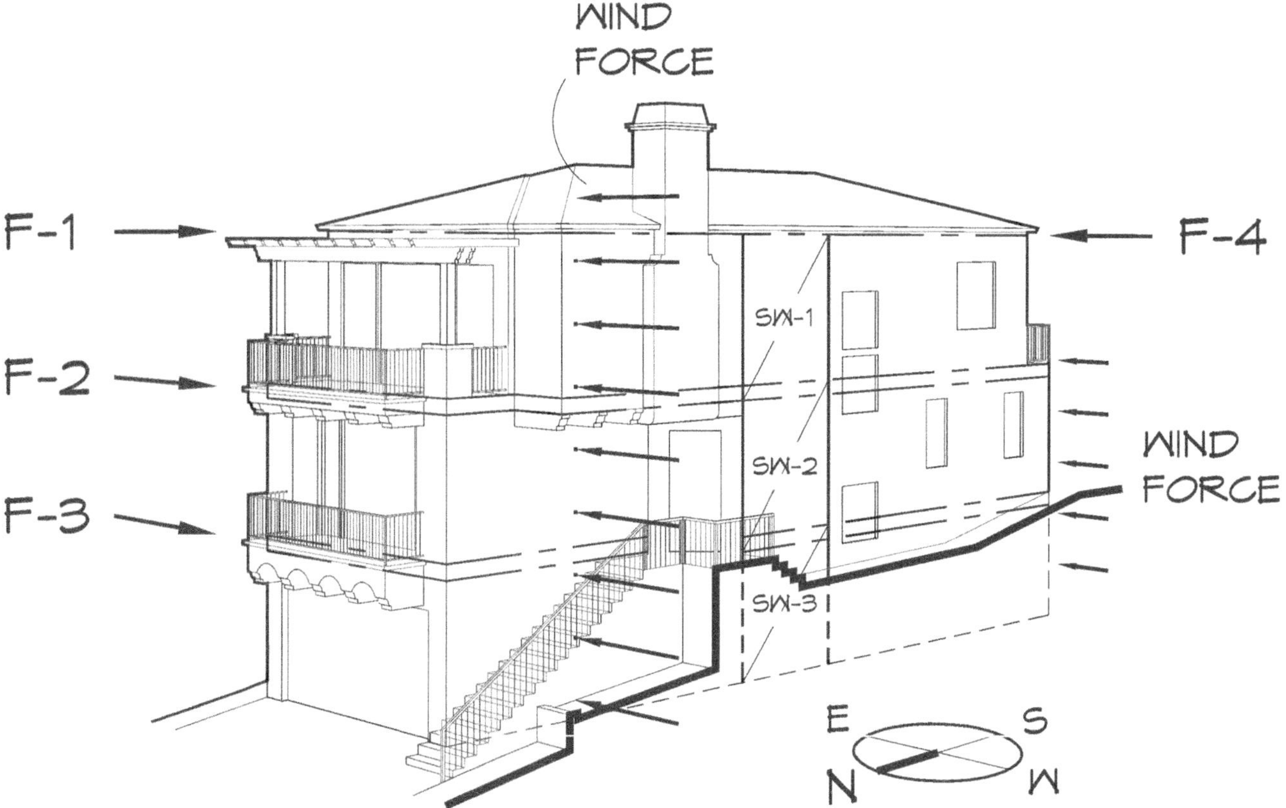

Figure 3.3 Weather conditions affecting energy conservation.

be reduced for each degree of a roof pitch that is more than 20° where snow loads are in excess of 20 pounds per square foot these are in addition to the normal 20 pounds per square foot for temporary live loads such as a person repairing something on the roof. Special eave requirements are set by the governing building codes. These requirements include a hot or cold underlayment of roofing material on all roofs from the edge of the eave for a distance of up to 5 feet toward the roof edge.

It should be noted that in areas that are subject to seismic activity, the building official of the municipality will ask that the snow live load also be calculated into the architect or engineer's lateral design.

It is a good practice, as well as a requirement of the building code, to protect all building exits from sliding ice and snow at the eaves. The use of heat strips and metal flashing at the exit areas in the eave

Figure 3.4 Roof/ceiling and wall insulation.

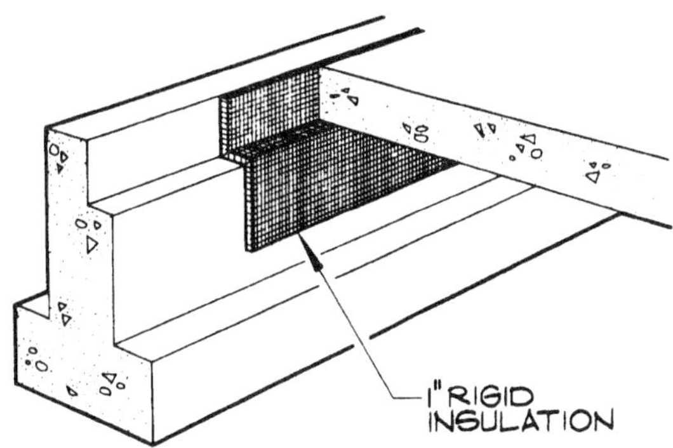

Figure 3.5 Footing insulation.

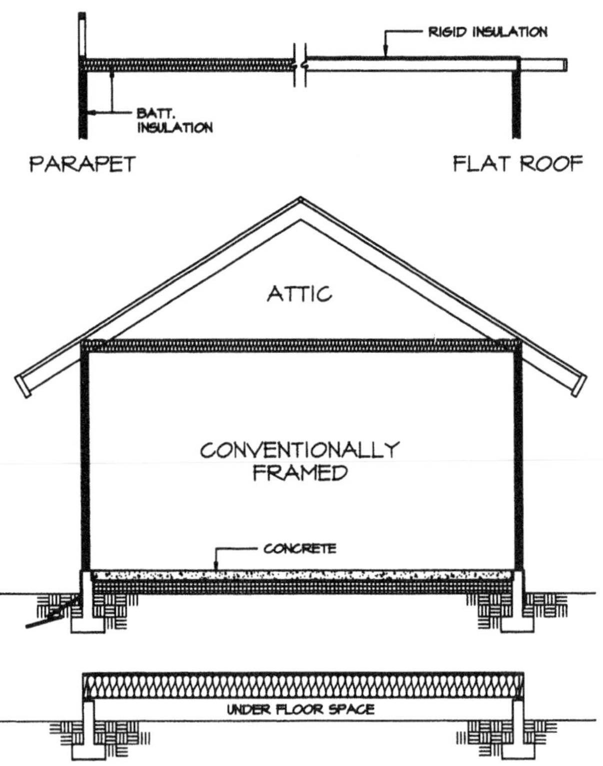

Figure 3.6 Creating an envelope.

assembly is an acceptable method of deterring ice dams and snow accumulation. Most roof structures with a roof pitch exceeding 70° are considered free of snow loads.

Insulation is required for roof, ceiling, wall, and floor locations. Rigid insulation board is installed at the exterior of the foundation to keep the utility spaces from freezing. See Figure 3.8.

Temperature

Outside temperatures affect the design of building structures. In areas with high temperatures, buildings are insulated and provided with various types of mechanical systems to control the temperature within the structure's habitable areas. Temperature also has a large effect on the structural integrity of a building. For example, buildings that are constructed with a concrete frame and a concrete floor system are detailed at various connections to allow for expansion and contraction of the various concrete elements affected by temperature fluctuations. Figure 3.9 shows a concrete column and a concrete floor beam connection that provides expansion joint clearances, as well as an electrometric pad for ease of movement. Such a pad need not be anchored; it is shock absorbent and returns to its original shape and dimension. Electrometric pads are best used for putting temporary gymnasium wood floor over concrete floor.

Another floor condition that may require an expansion joint appears when there is a large expanse of floor area, as shown in Figure 3.10. These expansion joints are placed in locations that are visually unobtrusive and will not require expensive covering methods. Concrete parking structures with vast areas of concrete floor require that various locations have expansion joints. The expansion joints are normally covered with an aluminum metal strip to allow easy passage of automobile traffic. These joints are referred to as **slip joints**. See Figure 3.11.

Figure 3.7 Snow conditions and concerns.

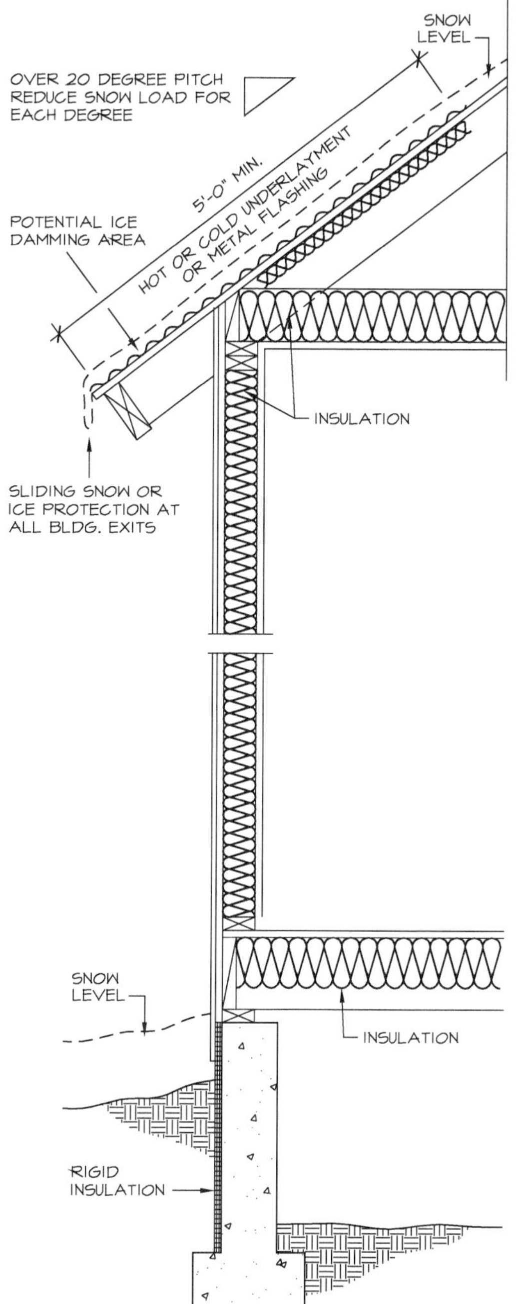

Figure 3.8 Roof/ceiling and wall insulation.

Underground Gas Control

Industrial and manufacturing buildings that are constructed on sites where there is evidence of underground gas, such as methane, will require a method of dissipating the underground gas. A recommended method is to install collector pipes below the concrete floor and vent these pipes to an outside area. Figure 3.12 illustrates the partial foundation plan for an industrial building. It shows the recommended locations of 4″ diameter perforated pipes and reference detail symbols

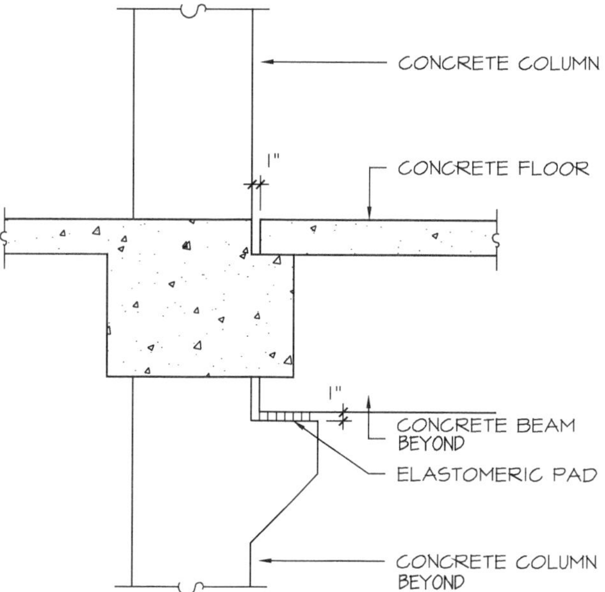

Figure 3.9 Expansion joint detail.

for the required pipe and venting installations. Note, in detail A, that a 24″ × 24″ gravel-filled trench encases the 4″ diameter perforated pipe as a means of collecting the gas. Detail B illustrates a method of venting the gas to the outside air through use of a 2½″ "0" vent in the exterior wall, terminating at a minimum distance of two feet above the roof.

Water Table

The term **water table** has two meanings. The first refers to the elevation (height) at which groundwater is atmospheric. The second refers to an aboveground projection that sheds water away from a structure. A sample detail of a water table at a foundation wall is shown in Figure 3.13.

First, let us establish some basic working facts about water, the movement of water, and water tables:

- **A.** Water will pass easily through clean gravel and sand and seek its own level.
- **B.** Perforated pipe in gravel provides an efficient means of travel for water. A good use for these pipes is under slabs and around basements.
- **C.** Water travels very slowly through silts and very little through clay. Thus, it is important to use gravel to encourage water to flow away from a structure.
- **D.** There are two basic ways of keeping water from penetrating a substructure when the substructure is below the water table. The first is through waterproofing with a barrier and draining the water by way of a **sump pit** (a tank for holding water that is under grade until it is pumped out) and a pump. Note that waterproofing is not 100% effective.

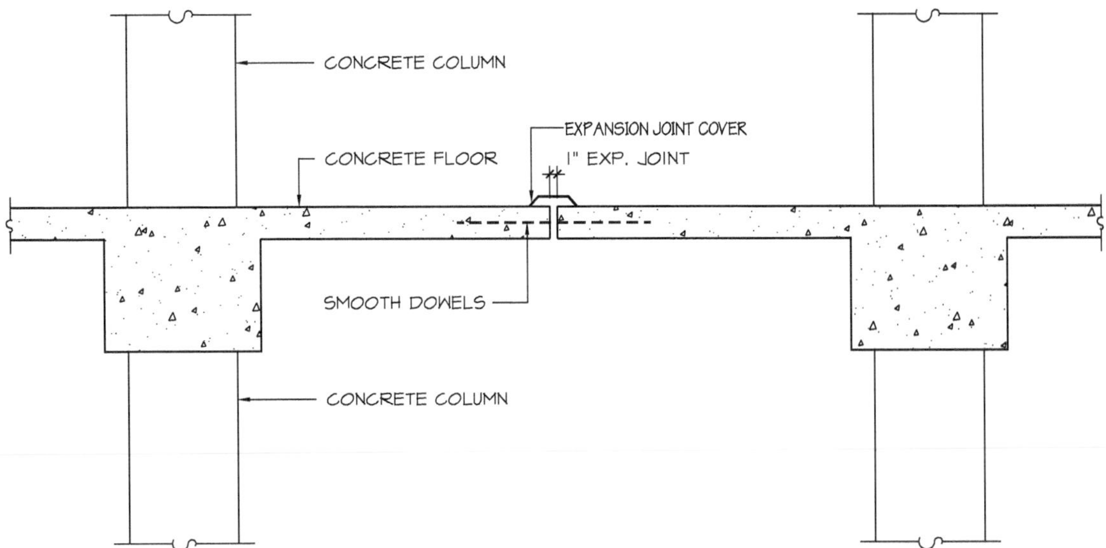

Figure 3.10 Floor expansion joint.

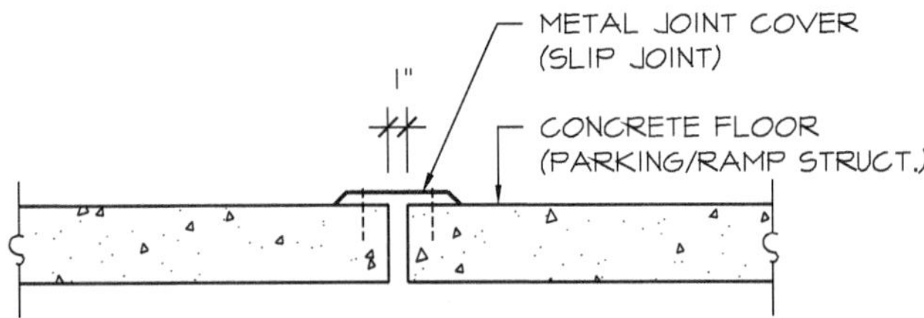

Figure 3.11 Expansion joint cover.

E. Municipalities require that when work is being done in an excavated area below the water table, the area must remain dry during construction. This can be accomplished with a pump or a series of pumps that change the water table configuration, as shown in Figure 3.14. An example of an area where this might occur is shown in Figure 3.15.

Frost Line/Frost Depth

In many parts of the world, temperatures fall below freezing. Thus, a new level of measurement is introduced in reference to existing grade. This measurement, called the **frost line** or **frost depth**, is a significant datum for building (see Figure 3.16). These lines and numbers on the map represent levels below the grade under which water no longer freezes. This is important, because at these levels the moisture will not become a solid, expand, and cause damage to a foundation system. The figures given on this map are in inches and are for general use only. Frost lines should always be checked, because they are established by local code. The national code requires that a footing be placed a minimum of 1′–0″ below the frost line (see Figure 3.17). The ground will not freeze below the frost line, making this a stable foundation.

To make us truly international and universal, rather than local or national, we must investigate cold climates in other parts of the world. There are climates such as these in the Arctic Circle, where we must deal with permafrost. We see this in one of the US states, Alaska. The existence of permafrost means that the annual mean temperature is 32°F. These areas are also subject to very high winds, extremely cold temperatures, snow drifts, continuous dark days, and very low sun angles (vertical angle), in addition to permafrost.

How do we deal with this? We raise the floor level or build a gravel bed upon which the building sits. See Figure 3.18. Figure 3.18A shows how a building on permafrost is configured, and Figure 3.18B shows a building built where there is sporadic permafrost.

Termites and Termite Treatment

The durability and longevity of wood are improved by preservative treatment techniques. The treatment of wood is usually recommended for two reasons: (1) the location of a member subjects it to an unsafe amount of moisture content, especially where the climate or site conditions promote decay; and (2) termite infestation.

Termites are a major problem in some of our states. California, Hawaii, and the southeastern states are some of the most heavily infested areas. Although not everyone practices in an infested area, architects should be familiar with the methods used to deal with termite infestation. Figure 3.19 shows the distribution of termite infestation in the United States. The chart is calibrated in modest, moderate, and heavy infestation areas,

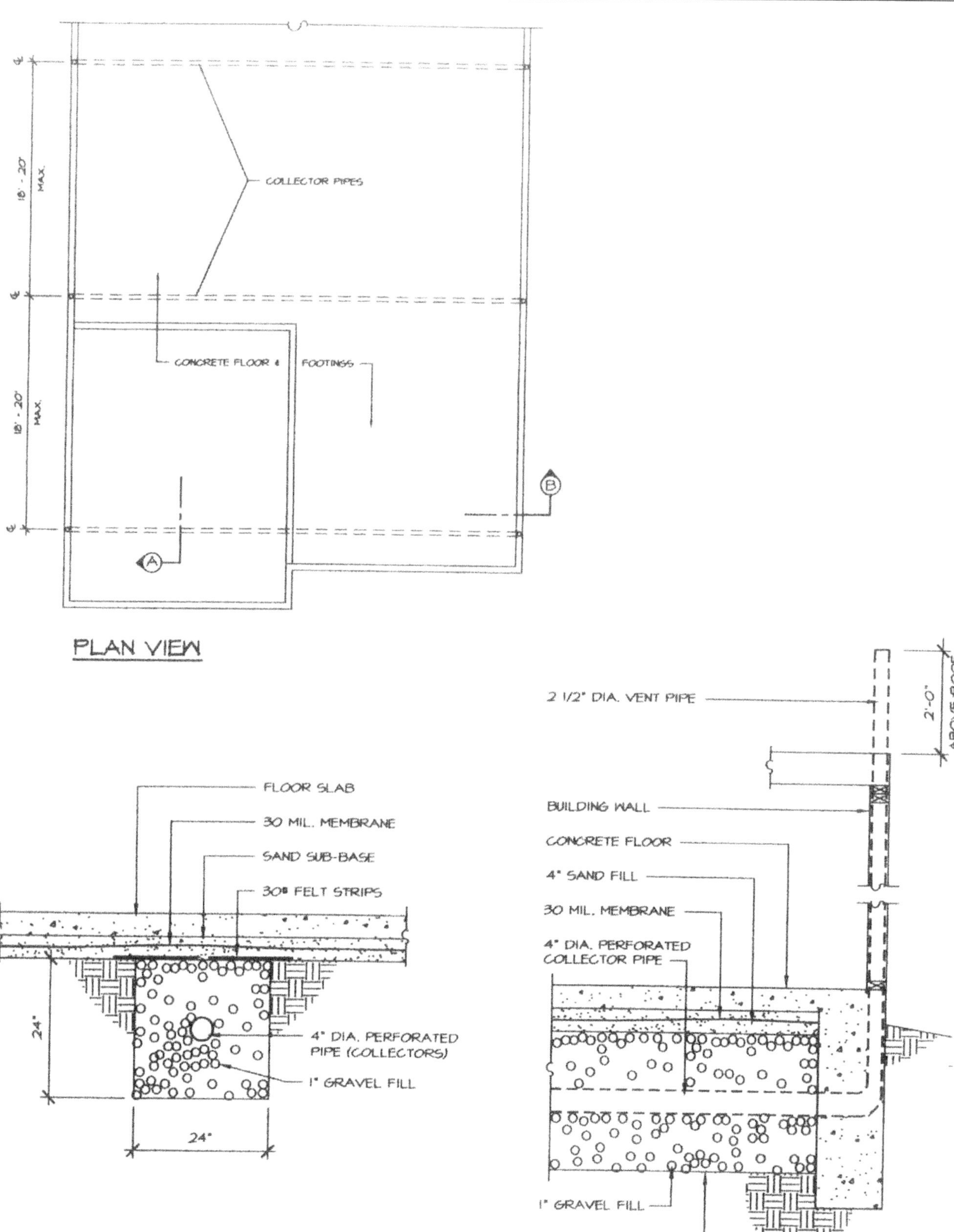

Figure 3.12 Partial building foundation plan.

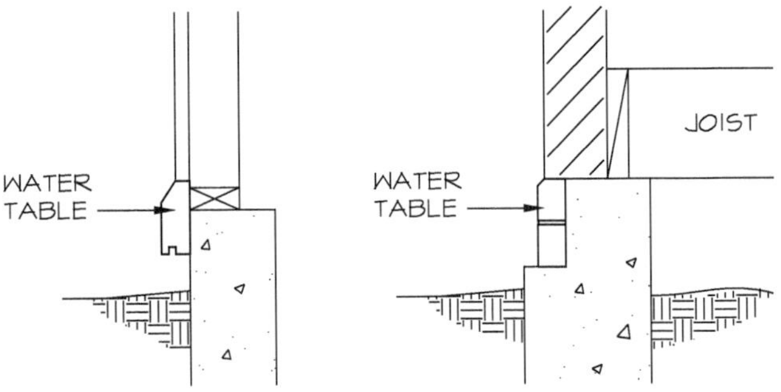

Figure 3.13 Water table at foundation plan.

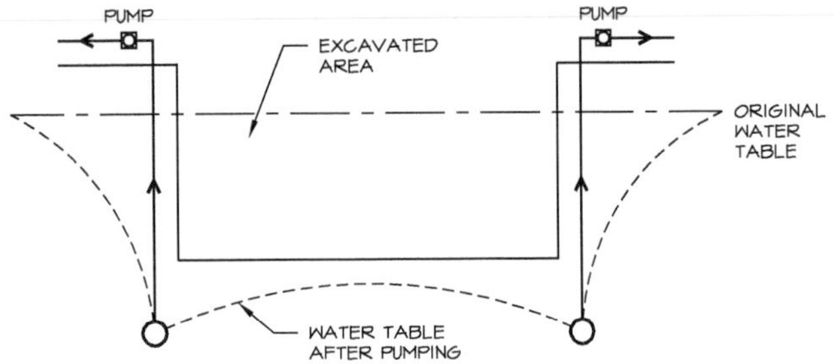

Figure 3.14 Diagram of dewatering.

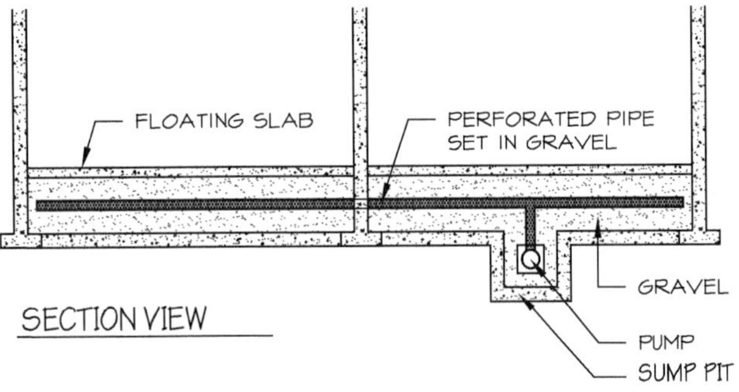

Figure 3.15 Removal of water table from substructure.

and reveals that the region's most heavily affected are in our southern states.

When a structure is supported by wood members embedded in the ground, the members should be of an approved **pressure-treated (PT)** wood. PT wood is impregnated with chemicals at elevated pressures and temperatures. One of the following classes of preservatives is commonly used: (1) oil-borne preservatives, (2) water-borne preservatives, or (3) water-repellent preservatives. Code standards for preservatives and treatments should be in accordance with those of the American Wood Preservers Association. Water-borne or water-repellent preservatives should be specified when members are to be painted or when finish materials are to be nailed to the members.

Wood members, such as sills, ledgers, and sleepers, that come in contact with concrete or masonry that itself is in direct contact with earth should be of an approved treated wood and approved by the local building department.

The effectiveness of treated wood depends on several factors: (1) the type of chemical used, (2) the amount of treatment penetration, (3) the amount of treatment retention, and (4) uniform distribution of the preservative.

In the course of detailing, the architect should be cognizant of the application of treated wood. Examples of details incorporating a treated wood mudsill, ledger, and sleeper are illustrated in Figure 3.20.

It should be emphasized that damage from moisture decay and termites develops slowly. Therefore, inspections should be done to ensure that proper clearances are being maintained and that termite barriers have been implemented and installed correctly. See Figure 3.21. Galvanized hardware can become corroded by pressure treated wood; therefore, verify type of wood and hardware prior to specifications.

OTHER SOURCES OF IMPACT

Sound

Various types of unpleasant (negative) sounds can enter a structure and cause discomfort to the occupants. Aircraft, vehicles, and trains are some of the sources of sound that create a need to construct buildings that address the problems of sound infiltration. Figure 3.22 depicts some of the major contributors of negative sounds that will be confronted in the detailing and construction of a three-story building. The negative sounds coming from above a building, like those created by various aircraft, will necessitate full sound insulation in the roof and ceiling members and the use of sound-rated windows. For a detail of an insulated wall and ceiling assembly, sound infiltration through the exterior walls can be controlled through required sound insulation techniques. Insulation of an exterior wall is achieved either with full insulation placed inside the wall or with sheets applied to the outside of the wall. An example of insulated sheets applied to the outside of exterior walls is shown in Figure 3.23.

In projects where concrete masonry units (CMUs) are used for the exterior walls, the open cells in the CMU may be filled with a metal baffle or a fibrous filler to deter or eliminate the infiltration of noise. A standard CMU with two types of insulation is depicted in Figure 3.24.

An effective method of deterring noise transmission through a floor assembly is to use lightweight concrete, carpet, and pad and batt insulation between the floor

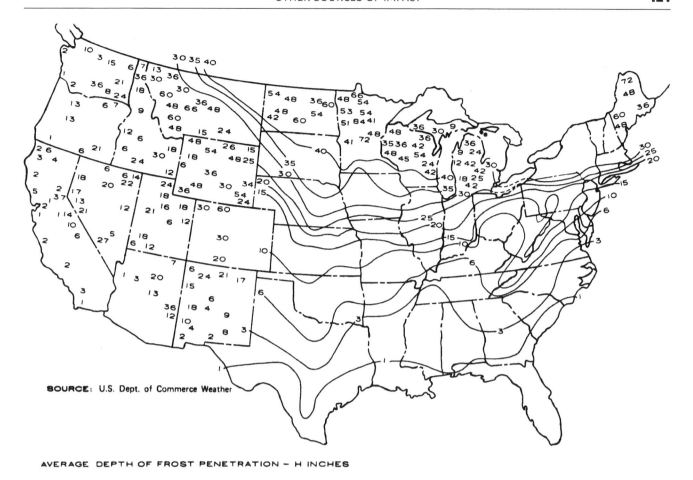

SOURCE: U.S. Dept. of Commerce Weather

AVERAGE DEPTH OF FROST PENETRATION – H INCHES

Figure 3.16 Frost depths. (Reproduced by permission from *Architectural Graphic Standards*, 9th edition, © 1994 by John Wiley & Sons, Inc.)

joists. The finished ceiling below may contain two layers of 5/8″-thick gypsum board attached to resilient channels, which are in turn attached to the wood joists. The resilient channels will provide a vibration isolation separation between the wood joist, which transmits sound, and the living space below. See Figure 3.25.

There are a few wood construction assemblies recommended for deterring sound transmission between the common walls of apartment units or other types of living units. One method is to provide a double-studded wall with a 1″ air space separating the individual stud walls, along with two layers of gypsum board on both sides of the party wall. Batt insulation is installed between the wood studs. See Figure 3.25.

Another method of interior wall insulation is to construct a wood wall with staggered studs and then continuously weave the sound insulation between the studs. The attachment of gypsum boards to the studs is accomplished with resilient clips. This construction method is shown pictorially in Figure 3.26. This type of assembly is less costly and slightly less effective than that shown in Figure 3.25.

An alternative method for deterring sound transmission through a floor assembly is to have a separate ceiling independent from the floor joist above. This will necessitate separate ceiling joist members with a higher wall plate line to support the floor joist above. The space

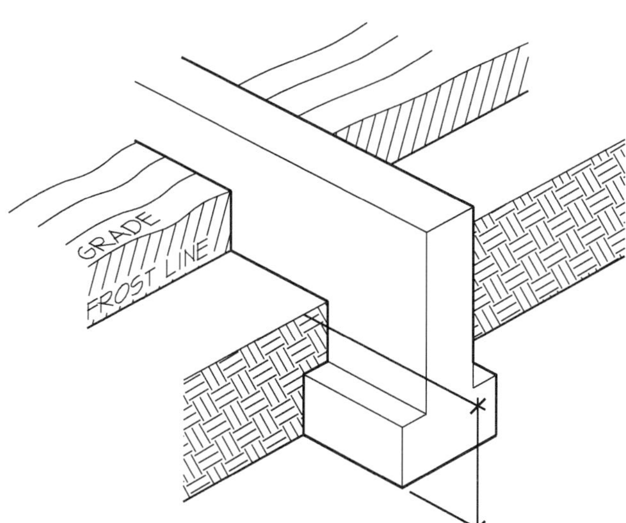

Figure 3.17 Frost line as a datum for footing depth.

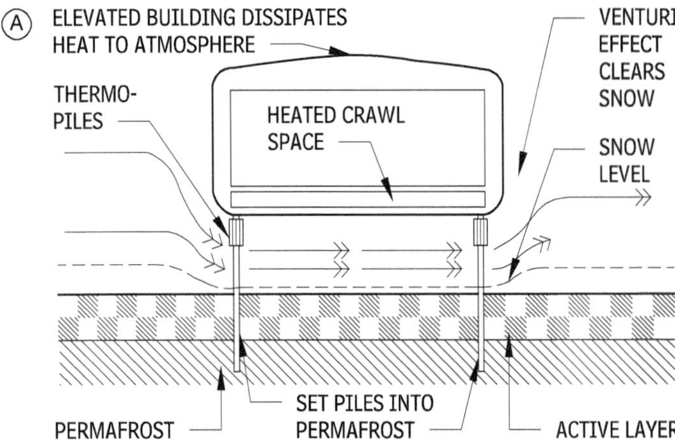

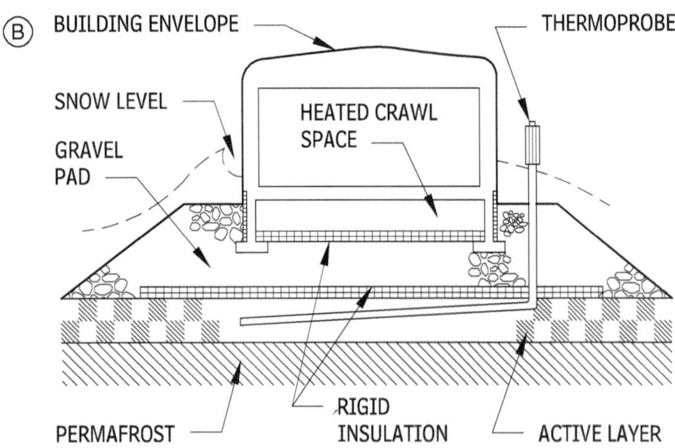

Figure 3.18 Building on permafrost. (Architectural Graphic Standards CD-ROM, © 2000 by John Wiley & Sons Inc.)

between the floor joist and the ceiling joist is an ideal arrangement for preventing sound transmission as well as allowing space for plumbing lines, heating ducts, and other equipment requirements. Resilient channels are recommended for the attachment of the gypsum board to the ceiling joist. This detailed assembly is illustrated in Figure 3.27 drawing depicting this assembly is shown in Figure 3.28.

Fire and Smoke

Fire and smoke are major concerns in the design of all types of structures. Building fires may be ignited by both external and internal causes, ranging from brush or forest fires to various internal causes, including electrical, vehicular, or heating fires.

Various methods and procedures are used to prevent the destruction of a building by fire. One method is to protect the various materials used in construction of the building. Underwriters Laboratory (UL) conditions, various materials, or a combination of materials are tested and given fire rating designations. These fire ratings are expressed as the number of minutes and hours it takes a material to catch fire. For example, a wall may be fire rated as a two-hour firewall, or a specific door may have a rating of 60 minutes. Structural columns can be assembled to provide a four-hour fire rating, whereas a glass panel may be manufactured with a 20-minute fire rating. Laboratory testing has produced results in a time/temperature chart illustrating temperature in degrees and time in hours.

Although all parts of a structure are vulnerable to fire, the safety of the occupants and the integrity of the structure can be enhanced by providing construction details that incorporate fire-rated materials to deter a fire or to minimize the spread of a fire. Buildings in high-risk brush fire areas can use exterior materials that will withstand high temperatures. This will give the building's occupants a longer time to evacuate the building in the event of a fire.

Smoke infiltration is a grave concern because most "fire" deaths are actually caused by the smoke rather than the flames or heat. Detailing the openings in walls, such as those for doors and windows, will reduce the potential of smoke infiltration.

Another concern in regard to fire is a building's stairs and exits. During the planning of a building, the architect must provide clearly defined pathways to fire exits. Fire exits and their layouts are determined by the governing fire protection agency and the requirements of applicable building codes. Distances between stair exits and the number of exits are also established by the governing agencies. In multilevel buildings, a correct stairwell design will allow people to move quickly down the stairs to an outdoor access without any interferences or obstructions in the exiting path.

A typical requirement for distance between stairwells is that it must exceed half the distance of the diagonal measure of the building. The local building code establishes requirements for the construction of the stairway walls. The stair tower is typically a fire-rated assembly. An example of a wood-constructed two-hour firewall assembly detail is illustrated in Figure 3.29; in this example, a two-hour wall construction encloses the stairwell.

All fire-rated doors must swing in the direction of the exit access. Note, too, in this example, the required two-hour wall construction that encloses the stairwell. The local building code establishes requirements for the construction of the stairway walls. An example of a pictorial view of a wood-constructed, two-hour, firewall assembly detail is illustrated in Figure 3.30.

A common method for exhausting smoke from a building that is on fire is to use automatic roof hatch

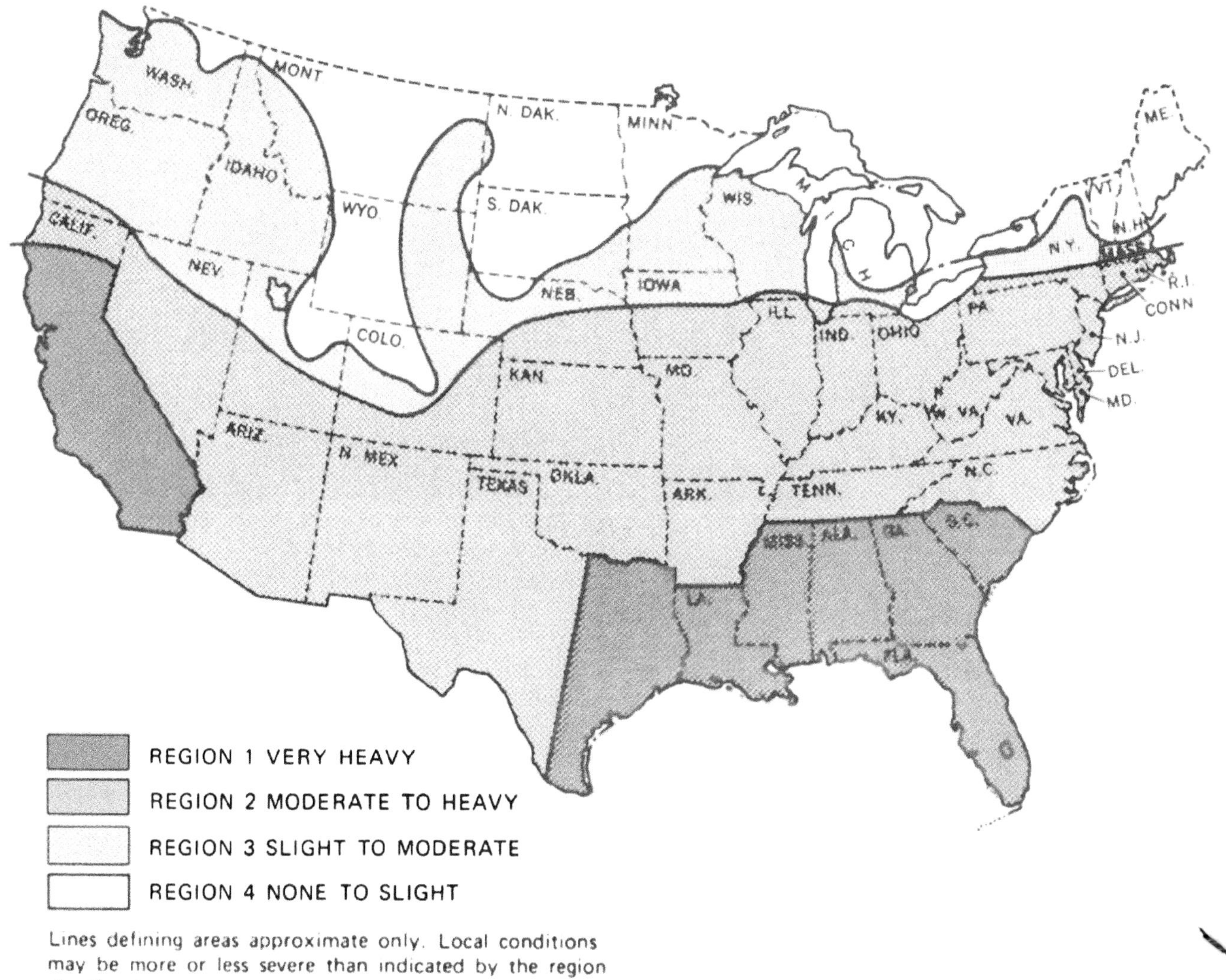

Figure 3.19 Regions of termite infestation. (Reproduced by permission from *Architectural Graphic Standards*, 9th edition, © 1994 by John Wiley & Sons, Inc.)

ventilators. These automatic ventilators, which are usually found in smaller buildings, open individually by means of a device that is activated by either smoke or heat. An example of a roof hatch ventilator that may be installed on a one-story industrial building is illustrated in Figure 3.31. The sizes and locations of these ventilators are determined by the governing fire protection agency and the building code.

Drainage/Rainfall

The accumulation of rainwater may lead to erosion or flooding problems. Because all regions of the country have specific and particular climatic conditions relative to the amounts of rainfall, the architect will need to anticipate and solve any problems of water drainage that may affect a building's structural areas and site conditions. As a general rule, water must drain away from the building to appropriate drainage devices or catch basins.

■ MOLD

Mold is a topic that is very rarely described but is necessary information for students and professionals in the field of architecture. There may be described, in all geographic locations in the United States and foreign countries, the existence of tens of thousands of different molds that affect a particular geographic area.

Real estate, site design, and any kind of investment in property require an understanding of how the various types of mold affect your geographic area. In Southern California, there are about 30,000 species of mold. Three types are considered dangerous to health: *Chaetomium,*

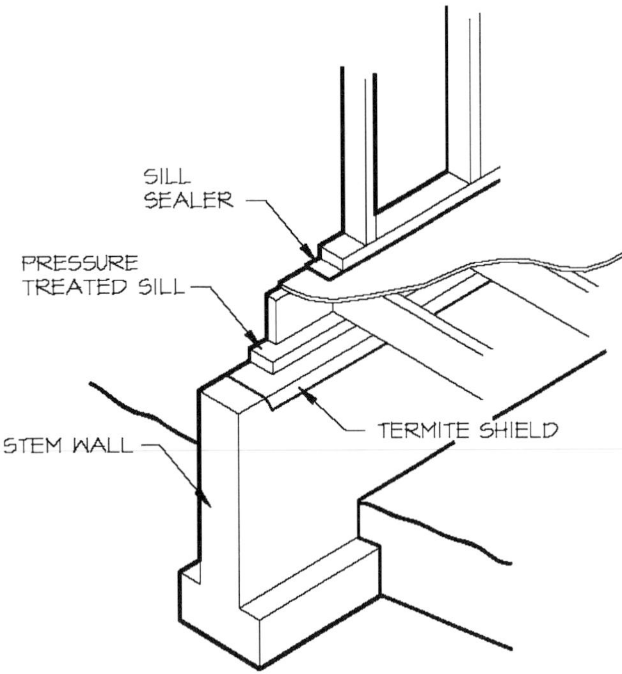

Figure 3.20 Mudsill area.

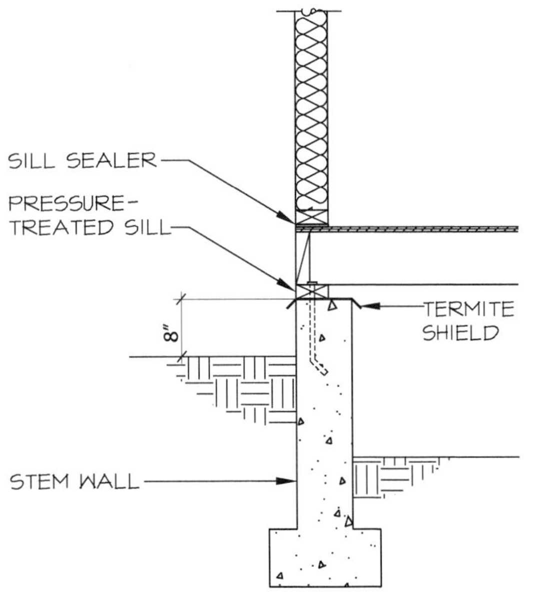

Figure 3.21 Detail of termite shield.

Stachybotrys (which is a black airborne mold), and mycelial fragments. In the state of Washington, there is a 30,000-acre parcel of land that started with one single family of mycelial fragments. If, as an investor, you purchased a few acres of this particular property, hired a land developer or an architect to develop it without researching and having a person from a mold abatement company evaluate the acreage, you would be jeopardizing the health and safety of all of the clients who use your facility, the individuals who built the new structure, and even the land developer/designer who designed this property and prepared construction documents for its erection. Imagine the lawsuits that would transpire—and the only winner would be the lawyers. Look at Figure 3.32, which shows an interior wall that has been infested with mold that now is beginning to leach out into the opposite side of the drywall. A reliable mold abatement company can remove the drywall and the mold and restore the wall to a condition similar to a brand-new framed wall.

We suggest that you explore and research various mold abatement companies in your area and find out what the dangers are in your particular geographic area.

ENERGY SOURCES

Wind

If you seek to use wind for energy and cannot use a propeller-type wing unit, there is now an alternative. The US military uses a hybrid form of what is called a **vertical axis wind turbine (VAWT),** which converts wind energy into electrical power. This omnidirectional, low-speed generator can be used practically anywhere that has good wind exposure. Presently, the unit size is 30″ in diameter and 8′ high, weighs 60 pounds, and rotates from a speed of 0 to a 600-rpm peak. It remains visible to birds as the speed increases. See Figure 3.33.

Because of its relatively small size and the fact that it can be effective in almost any vertical position, this application lends itself to designs that are curvilinear and kinetic in nature.

Geothermal

If you are one of the lucky inhabitants of an area that nature has provided with **geothermal** energy (a name that comes from the term **geothermic**, having to do with the heat of the earth's interior), you should look into the feasibility of tapping into this natural resource. Geothermal energy is accessible in many areas around the world; Figure 3.34 shows the locations of the best of these areas. If you are in one of these geothermal zones, you must first investigate the cost, how you can amortize the cost of installation, and the impact the equipment will have on the aesthetics of the structure. Remember that cost rebates may be available through the federal or state government or from a public utility. By sending down domestic water to match the earth's temperature, the cooled or warmed water can be radiated to cool or heat the interior of a space. See Figure 3.35.

In California, a production well is drilled in excess of a mile to reach the hydrothermal reservoirs, where 80% of the state's geothermal energy lies. Steam from these reservoirs, which can reach temperatures of 360°F, is

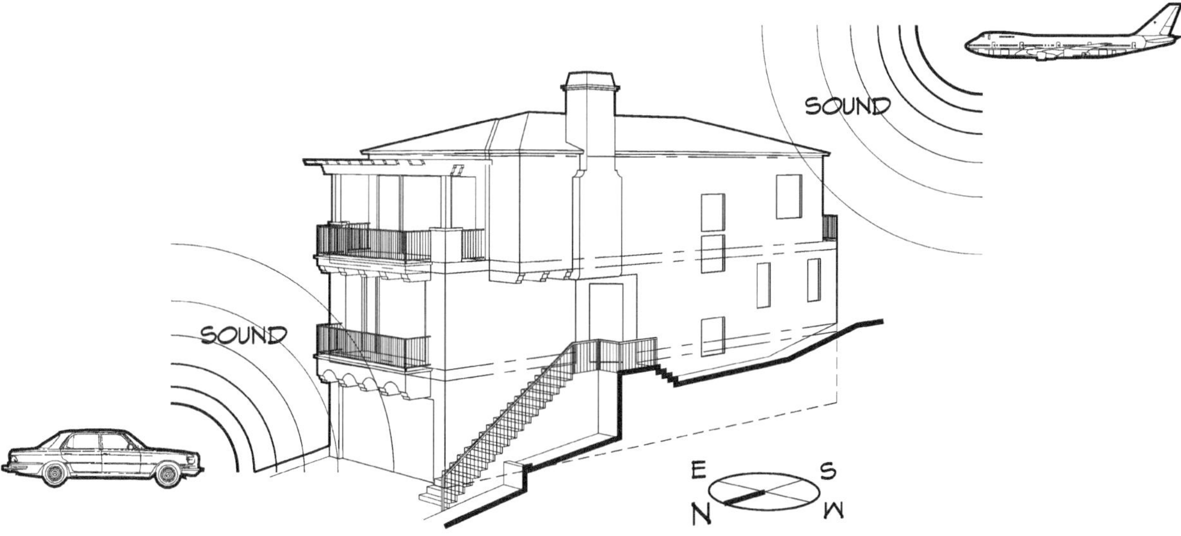

Figure 3.22 Sound-producing forces.

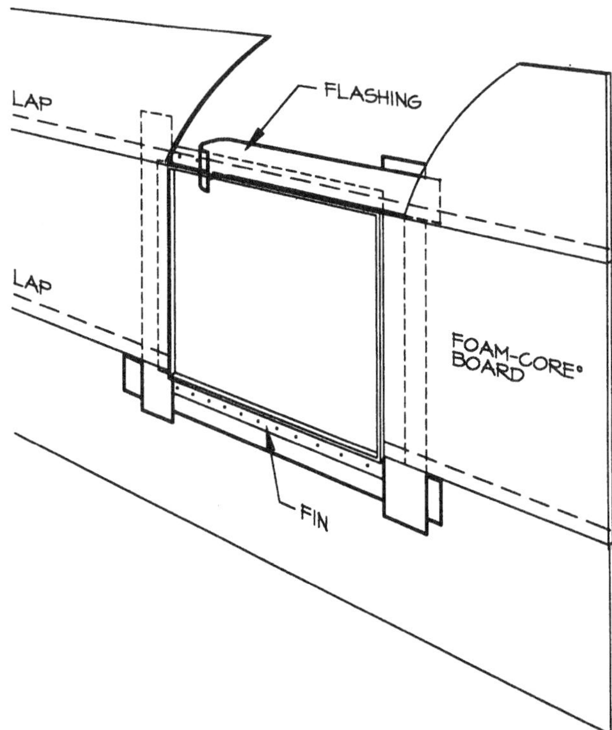

Figure 3.23 Foam-Core® board as a wrap. (Courtesy of International Paper.)

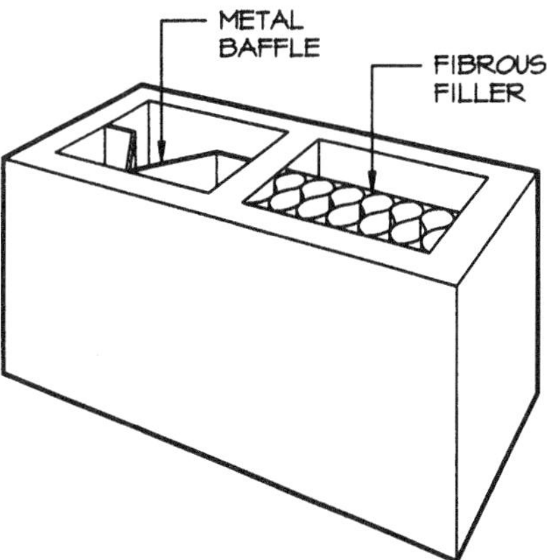

Figure 3.24 Sound insulation in concrete masonry units.

used to turn turbines; the electricity produced thereby is distributed via power lines. The cooled water returns to the reservoir by way of an injection well. Returned water is reheated and may be used over again. The whole process is shown diagrammatically in Figure 3.39.

Areas that have hot springs, such as Idaho, often simply use those springs to heat buildings in the winter. It might also be practical to go down into the earth some 80–100 feet and use the natural temperature of the earth to cool or warm a building.

Solar

Knowledge of the Sun. In its simplest form, the sun can be a negative in architecture. If, for example, we let direct sun into a structure in order to get light and heat, we also create a health hazard: prolonged exposure to the sun's ultraviolet rays is known to cause both basal cell carcinomas (skin cancer) and melanoma (a more serious form of cancer).

Position of the Sun. If you can control the temperature extremes and glare that the sun creates in the structure, you will have captured and made the best

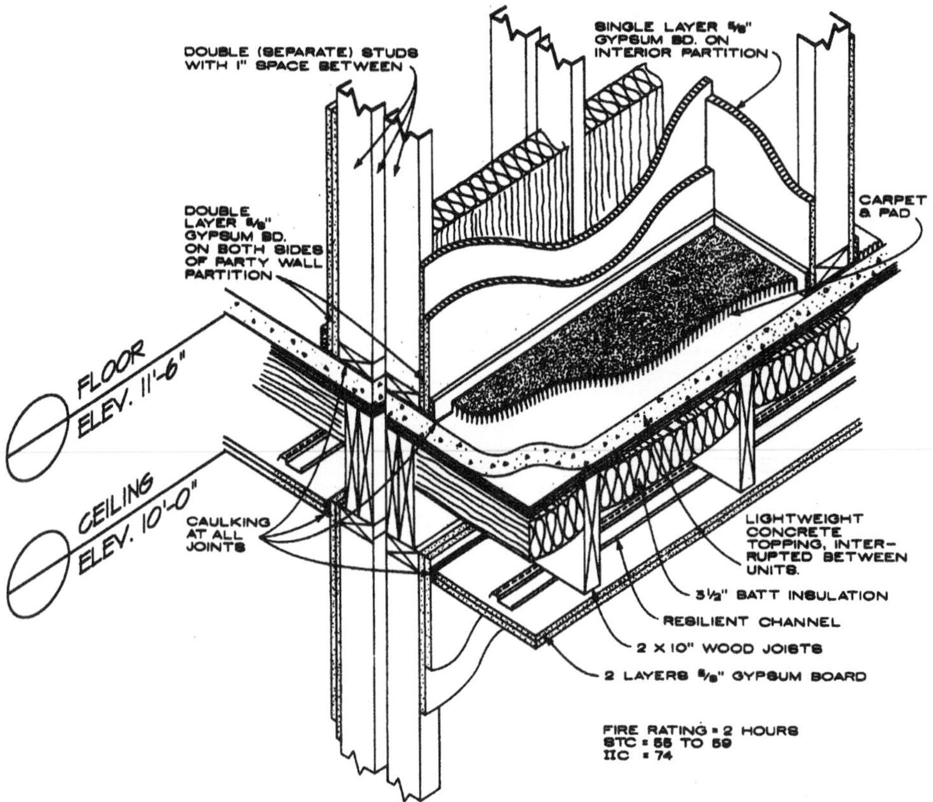

Figure 3.25 Soundproofing between floors.

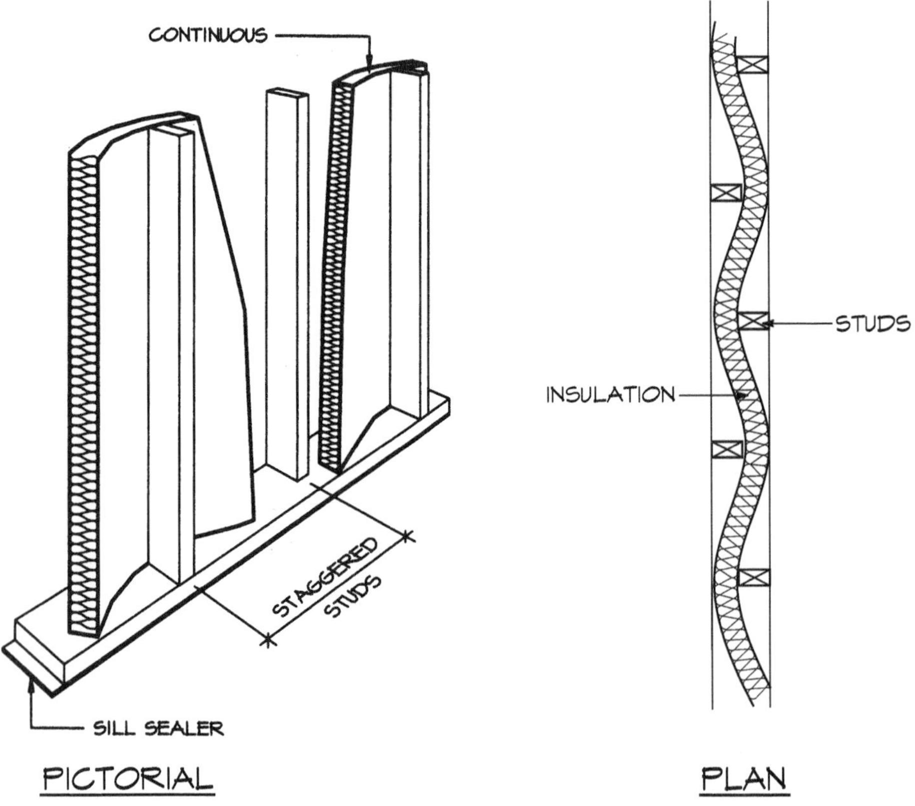

Figure 3.26 Interior wall sound insulation.

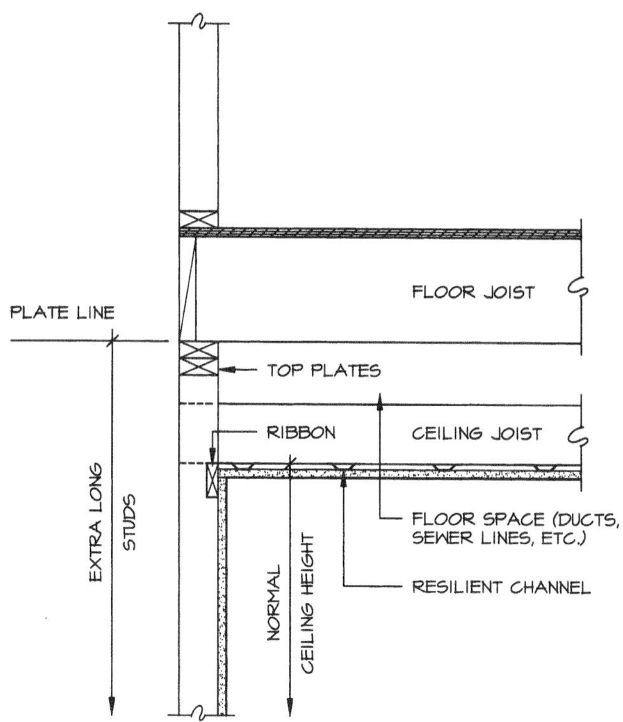

Figure 3.27 Detail of floor–ceiling separation.

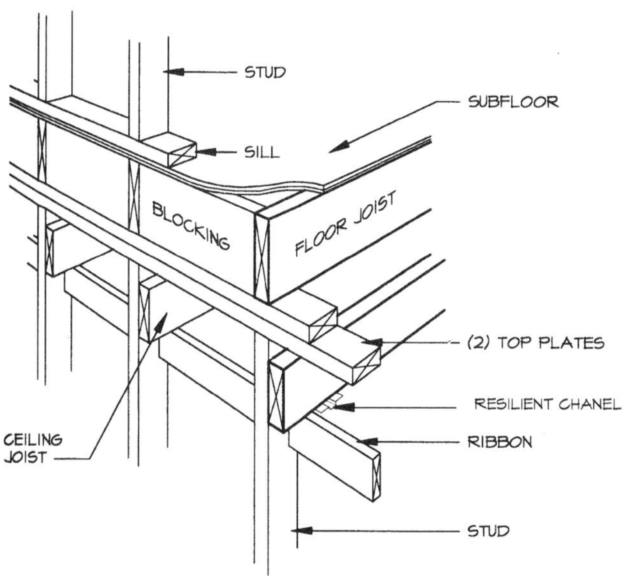

Figure 3.28 Separation of floor joist and ceiling joist.

use of the sun's solar energy. To attain this control, you must determine the longest day and the shortest day at the building site. June 21 and December 21, known as the summer and winter solstices, respectively, are what we as architectural designers must seek out prior to executing a design. The summer and winter solstices can best be determined by finding the sun's angles to the Earth and locating its latitude. **Latitude** refers to (artificial) horizontal markings we have placed on the Earth; **longitude** refers to the vertical markings we use as a datum. (It is easy to remember which is which when you pronounce these words: Note the shape of your mouth as you say *latitude* or *longitude*. Your lips will get wider when *latitude* is spoken, and the "long" of *longitude* will be pronounced with more vertically formed lips.) If you are not working in BIM, there are data banks that will give you the information you need to determine the environmental impact of the sun on you project. Figures 3.36–3.38 provide real data specific to the site location and allow the architect to design accordingly.

Plotting in 3-D Check your site and establish the bearing (N, S, E, W). Then plot the movement of the sun

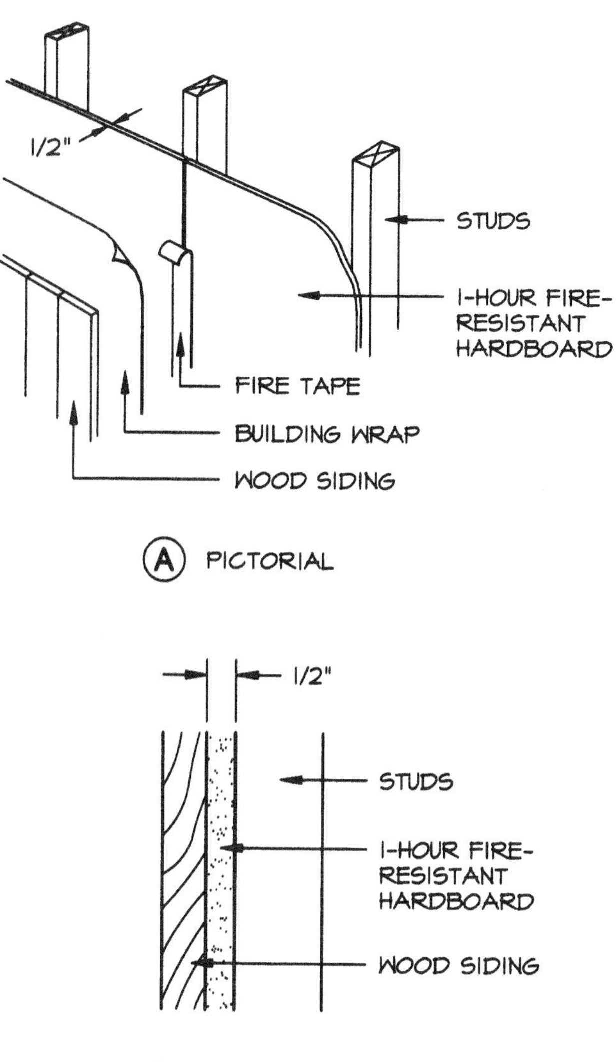

Figure 3.29 Fire-resistant stud walls.

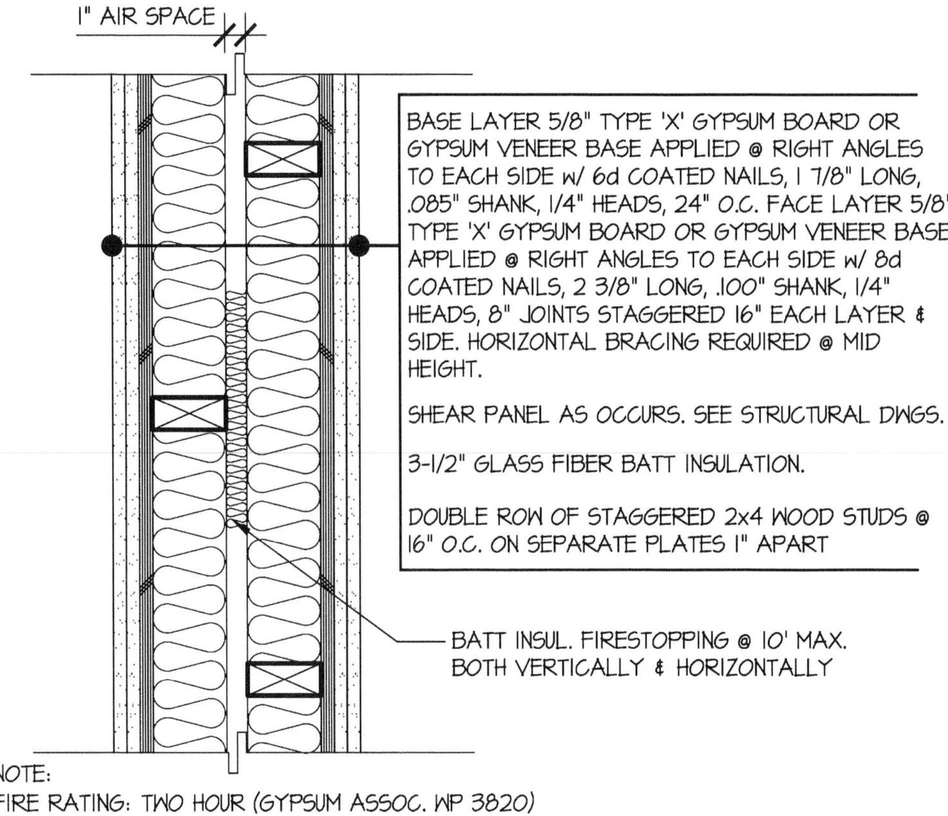
1" AIR SPACE
BASE LAYER 5/8" TYPE 'X' GYPSUM BOARD OR GYPSUM VENEER BASE APPLIED @ RIGHT ANGLES TO EACH SIDE w/ 6d COATED NAILS, 1 7/8" LONG, .085" SHANK, 1/4" HEADS, 24" O.C. FACE LAYER 5/8" TYPE 'X' GYPSUM BOARD OR GYPSUM VENEER BASE APPLIED @ RIGHT ANGLES TO EACH SIDE w/ 8d COATED NAILS, 2 3/8" LONG, .100" SHANK, 1/4" HEADS, 8" JOINTS STAGGERED 16" EACH LAYER & SIDE. HORIZONTAL BRACING REQUIRED @ MID HEIGHT.
SHEAR PANEL AS OCCURS. SEE STRUCTURAL DWGS.
3-1/2" GLASS FIBER BATT INSULATION.
DOUBLE ROW OF STAGGERED 2x4 WOOD STUDS @ 16" O.C. ON SEPARATE PLATES 1" APART
BATT INSUL. FIRESTOPPING @ 10' MAX. BOTH VERTICALLY & HORIZONTALLY
NOTE:
FIRE RATING: TWO HOUR (GYPSUM ASSOC. WP 3820)
SOUND RATING: STC-66 (NBCC WALL W15A)
Area Separation Wall
SCALE: 1 1/2"=1'-0"

Figure 3.30 Two-hour area separation wall detail.

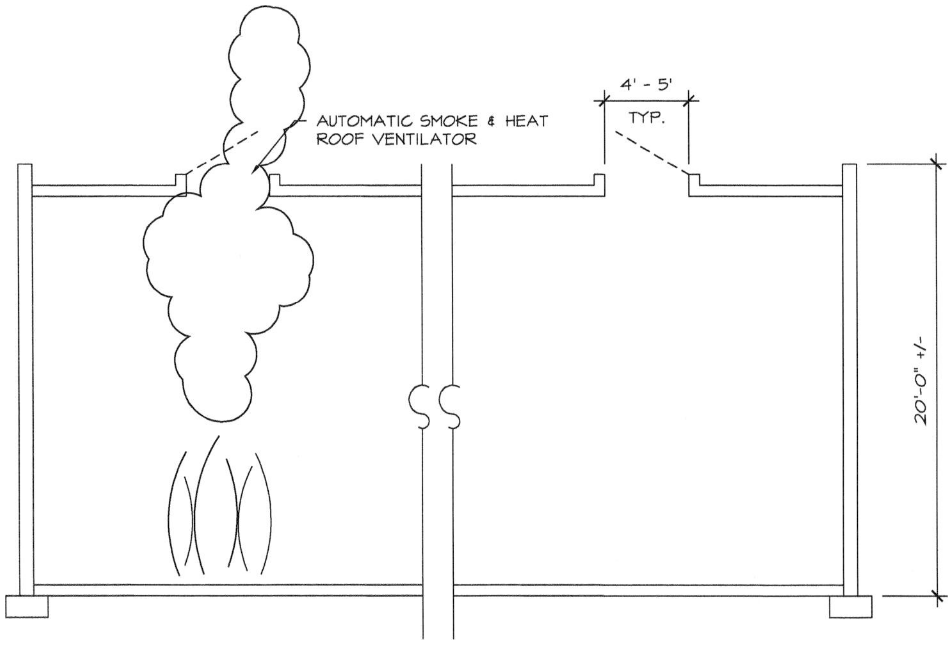
AUTOMATIC SMOKE & HEAT ROOF VENTILATOR
4' - 5'
TYP.
20'-0" +/-

Figure 3.31 Smoke and heat roof ventilators.

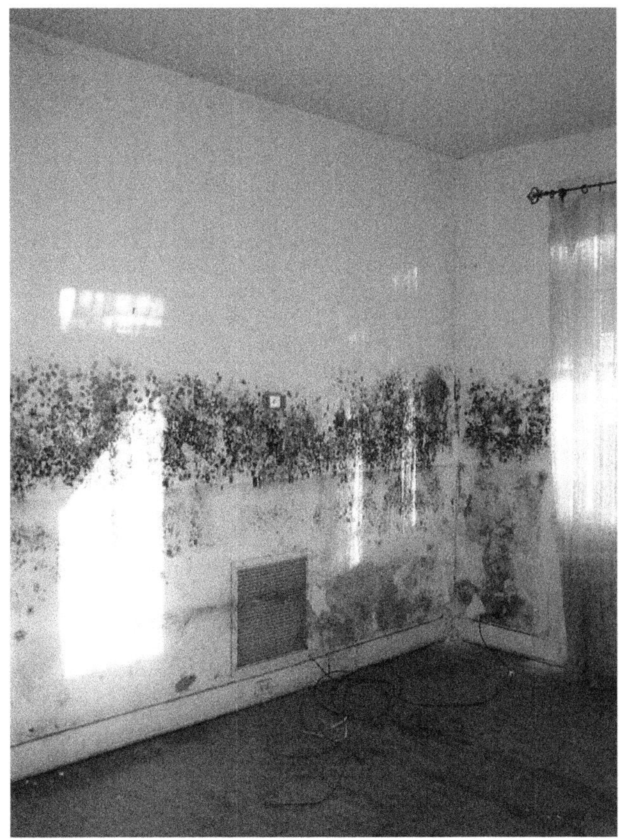

Figure 3.32 Mold infested interior. (Infrogmation/Wikimedia Commons/CC BY-SA 2.0.)

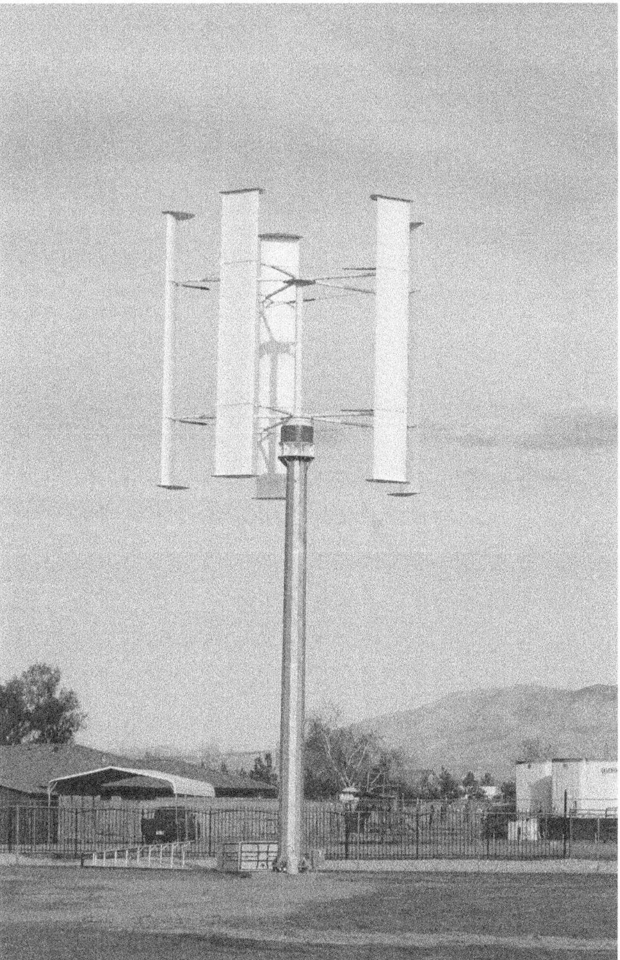

Figure 3.33 Wind-power air turbine. (Wepower LLC ©.)

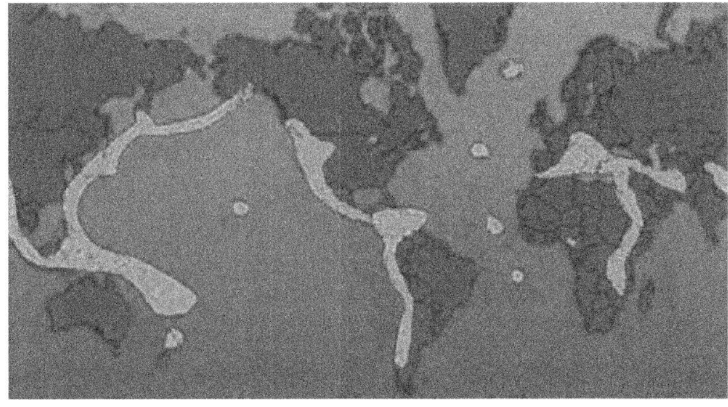

Figure 3.34 Hottest known geothermal areas. (Courtesy of Department of Energy, Geothermal Education Office, Earth Policy Institute.)

on June 21 and December 21 (see Figure 3.39). This will give you an idea of how the sun moves across the sky in the winter and the summer. Next, show the step, drawing your sets onto the grid. Now you are ready to design your structure—or maybe not! You will also want to explore the prevailing wind in conjunction with the sun, correlate the annual rainfall, noise, and so on. BIM suggests that you check all the elements in select materials by rotating a 3-D model of the structure on the site, to determine the effects of rain, wind, and other elements on the structure. As educators, we suggest that you study and learn about one design element at a time, even though you will eventually have to consider all of them when you execute a design.

Understanding the location of the sun allows for utilization of other design ideas to incorporate building shading resulting in building cooling. A key component is designing shading devices adjacent or above window and door openings allowing for building cooling reduction and heating reductions. Knowing that the south side of the building is the most impacted from the sunlight in the summer months encourages the designer to provide horizontal shading devices over the opening resulting in a shaded glazed area. This shaded area is protected from significant heat gain and the result is energy savings since the building does not need added cooling time to reduce the heat gain. Similarly

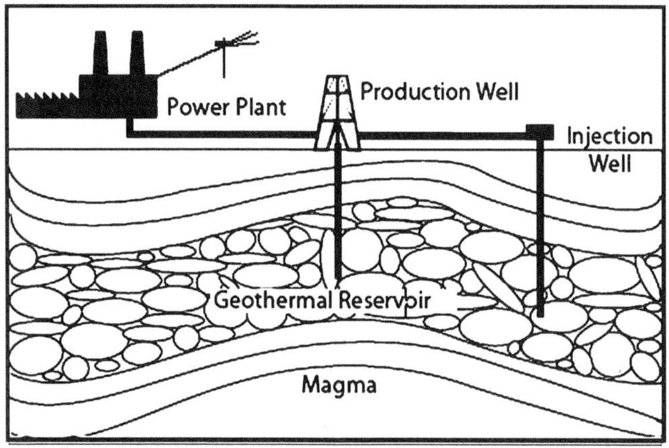

Figure 3.35 Tapping geothermal areas.

Winter Dec 21

	Vertical Angle	Horizontal Angle
Sunrise	0°	S 42°
10:00 AM	9°	S 30°
12:00 (Noon)	12°	S
2:00 PM	10°	S 31° W
Sunset	0°	S 42° W

Summer June 21

	Vertical Angle	Horizontal Angle
Sunrise	0°	E 49° S
8:00 AM	30°	E 21 1/2° S
10:00 AM	54-1/2°	E 35° S
12:00 (Noon)	64-1/2°	S
2:00 PM	56° S 57°	W
4:00 PM	37° W 1°	N
Sunset	0° E 48°	N

Figure 3.36 Berlin (52°–19±′).

knowing that the building is least impacted on the north face, there is seldom a reason to provide shading devices on that side of the building. The east and west side the sun angle is low and as a result, vertical shading devices (along the south side of the openings) are the best form of protection for direct sunlight impact. If you study the new architecture of Abu Dhabi, you will discover a second skin just outside the main structure of the building designed to shade the tall towers designed in an extreme heat environment. The building sits in its own shadow resulting in better building performance.

Overhangs of many types are affective in design solutions. Again, understanding where the sun impacts your site most of the day or year, a tree can be planted to impact lower building designs. In the heat of Arizona, a south facing buildings performance can be significantly improved by provide shade trees. Ideally these trees would be deciduous so that winter sun can warm up the glazing areas and warm up the interior when needed most, but any tree with a large canopy can impact positively the performance of the building environment. The tree can also be shaped to allow the lower angle of the winter sun by trimming up the bottom branches of the tree to allow the sun to enter the building only in the winter months. Trees are significantly under-utilized design feature in architecture. While trees are highly praised here, for midrise or high-rise buildings the prior shading devices are a better solution for shading.

Winter Dec 21

	Vertical Angle	Horizontal Angle
Sunrise	0°	E 34° S
10:00 AM	21°	E 60° S
12:00 (Noon)	27°	S
2:00 PM	21-1/2°	S 36° W
4:00 PM	6°	S 60° W
Sunset	0°	S 67-1/2° W

Summer June 21

	Vertical Angle	Horizontal Angle
Sunrise		E 3° S
8:00 AM	36°	W 11° N
10:00 AM	56°	E 21° S
12:00 (Noon)	80°	S
2:00 PM	62°	W 6° E
4:00 PM	37°	W 11° E
Sunset	0°	W 37-1/2° N

Figure 3.37 Las Vegas (36°–10±′).

Key Terms

envelope
frost depth
frost line
geothermal
geothermic
latitude
longitude
pressure-treated (PT)
slip joints
sump pit
vertical axis wind turbine (VAWT)
water table

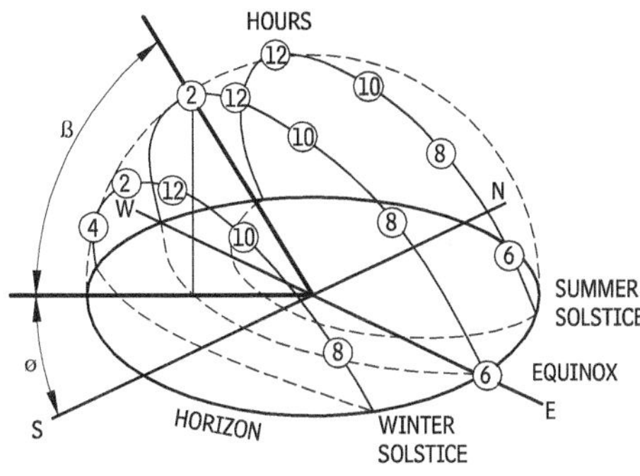

DWG # APP.1_12

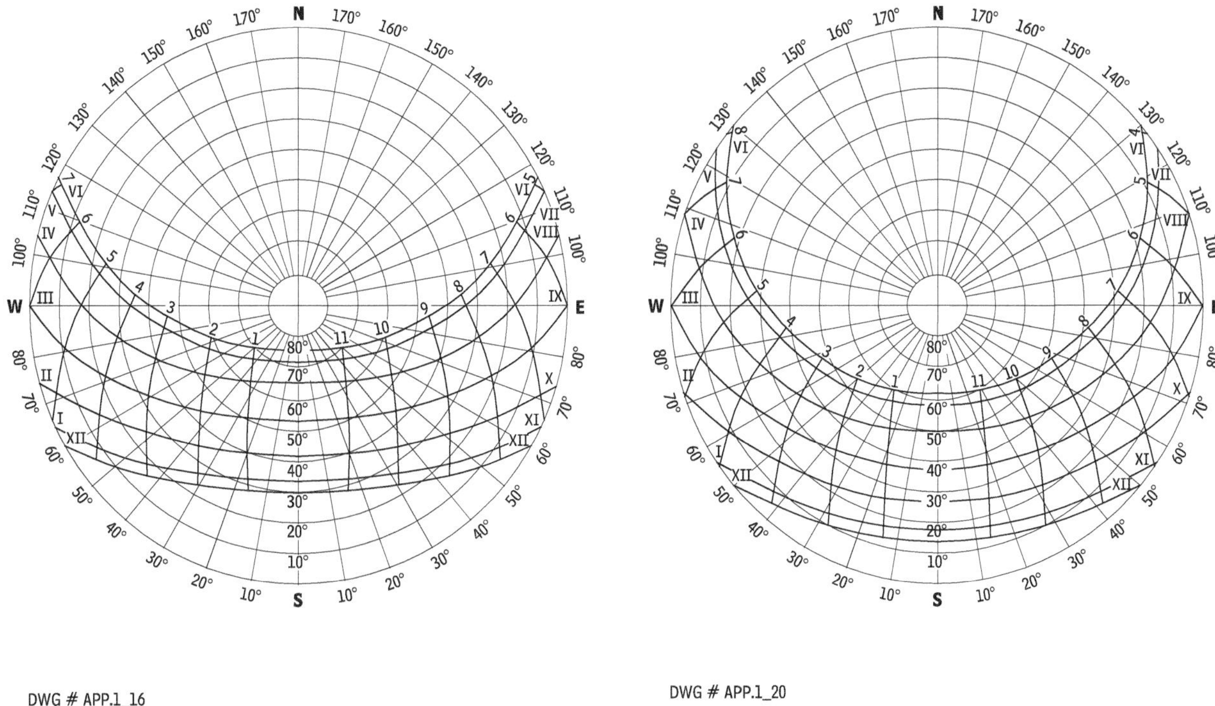

DWG # APP.1_16

DWG # APP.1_20

Figure 3.38 Sun position by latitude. (Architectural Graphic Standards CD-ROM, © 2000 by John Wiley & Sons.)

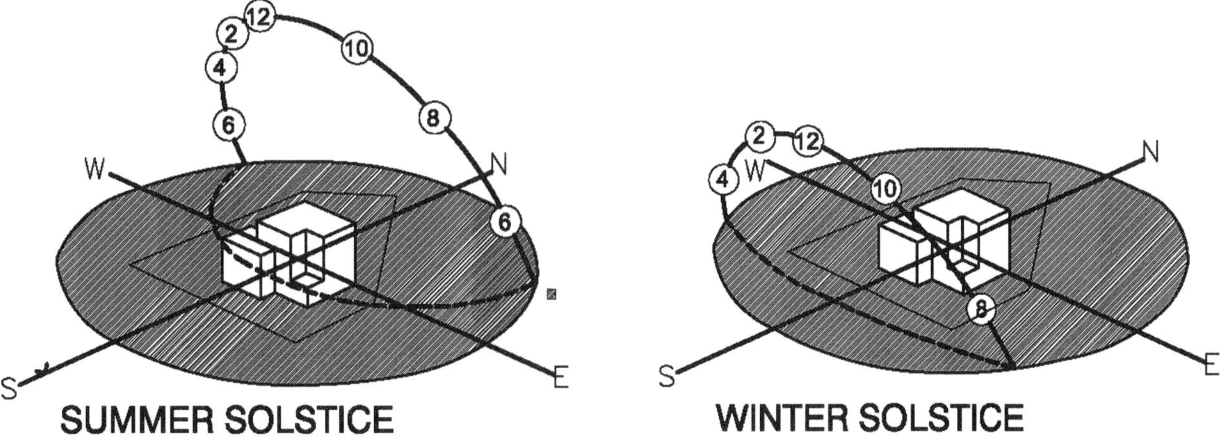

Figure 3.39 Checking massing forms with summer and winter solstices.

chapter

4

PREPARATION PHASE FOR CONSTRUCTION DOCUMENTS

The Professional Practice of Architectural Working Drawings, Sixth Edition. Nagy R. Bakhoum and Osamu A. Wakita.
© 2024 John Wiley & Sons Inc. Published 2024 by John Wiley & Sons Inc.
Companion website: www.wiley.com\go\bakhoum\theprofessionalpracticeofarchitecturalworkingdrawings

■ PHASES OF ARCHITECTURE

The American Institute of Architects (AIA) described in great detail what the five phases of architectural services are; don't be fooled, there are many more services that an architect can provide. However, most often the five phases are the most commonly contracted ones when engaging an architect. Among those five the first three described here are far and away the most common: schematic design (SD), design development (DD), and construction document (CD). The other two services are bidding and construction administration (CA). A detailed description of the five phases follows this section but let's expand on a few of the other services and some broad concepts at services. A program is typically established by a client, but in some cases an architect is hired to establish a program. This is an added phase of service that can be contracted; for instance, a municipality can approach an architect and ask for an airport expansion for 30 terminals. They may rely on the architect to better describe the area required, support buildings needed, additional parking, and public and private areas that need to be developed. All of this can happen before an architect is hired for the next five phases of the project. Site selection could be yet another service where a study is required to ensure the client has the required open space as in our prior example for the new terminal. An example of a service that can be contracted is providing an as-built drawing to demonstrate actual constructional dimensions and systems. As with all phases of service, architects must review changes to the program as phases have evolved from one to another and if scope increases, fees increase. A review of a contracted each phase will be required internally so billable time is not lost in the process, this can be the difference between profit and loss. Architecture is a service and extra services should be billed accordingly.

While it's nearly impossible to discuss all the services and terms architects can provide, it is ideal to become familiar with terms that are integral with the industry.

Schematic Design

The SD phase is the first of five phases of an architect's primary services that a client may contract for. The SD documents are the primary conceptual design drawings and diagrams prepared by an architect determining the preliminary layout and appearance of the architectural project. In simple terms, it's the beginning ideas the architect will present to the client for feedback and fine-tuning in order to achieve the collective goals and objectives established in the program.

The deliverables, the actual work produced for completion of this stage, include drawings and documents including a site plan, floor and roof plan, sections, and elevations. Renderings, 3D images, or even models can also be included to help convey the design concept. Preliminary material selections and outline specifications could be appropriate at this level. A preliminary budget estimate and most importantly client approval in order to move on to the next phase of the architectural contract.

Design Development

Based on the approval of the SD by the client, the second phase is DD. The DD document will further expand and detail the ideas established in SD. The development of the drawings and specifications will be more complete and more data will be documented in order to establish plans, like materials, methods, finish, and colors. A more comprehensive idea of structural systems, MEP, and other building systems include a more comprehensive deliverable package. These will include developed site plan, floor and roof plans, sections, elevations, typical construction details, and diagrammatic layout of building systems. The goal of these drawings is to provide a better description of the size and character of the proposed project. Additional renderings or models could be further added to get the approval of the client. An estimated cost of construction and client approval is needed to move to the next phase.

Construction Documents

Upon approval of the DD, the third phase is CDs. CDs are the largest portion of the work in the five phases of scope. It can be as much as 50% of the total contract and that is based on time required and scope of work to complete this phase. CDs are drawings and specifications completed by the architect and consultants that support the drawings of the building. After making all the adjustments in DD, the architect and subcontractors, such as MEP, civil engineers, and others, establish the contract between the client and the contractor, and therefore is completed. All the drawings and specifications become a graphic and written contract that will be constructed for the client by the chosen contractor for an agreed-upon cost.

The basic requirement for all CDs is clarity. It can incorporate any or all of the plans just discussed, depending on the complexity of the information that must be communicated and on office practice.

Bidding and Negotiations

The fourth phase is bidding or negotiations of a contract. Documents are developed specifically for the purpose of constructing the project. Seeking out qualified bidders can come by invitation to bid, advertising to the public for an opportunity to bid, and providing instructions to bidders. Bidding can begin even before CDs are completed. Bidding a job is an important step in selecting a contractor. If a project is bid via a negotiation of a preselected firm, the timeline can be significantly reduced.

A firm may decide to put plans out to bid at 95% completion. As long as all the bidders are given the same instruction and the same plan, bids can be compared by common scope. A bidder can be selected and given an opportunity to adjust his bid for that last 5% when plans are **ready to issue (RTI)**. This system allows the architect to submit plans to the revising agency, which could take months and allows the contractor a reasonable time to bid the scope of work.

Construction Administration

CA is the fifth phase of the architect's services. The beginning of this stage is determined by the execution of the contract between the client and the contractor. Once construction begins, the architect is involved in many aspects of construction such as **request for information (RFI)**, shop drawing review, change orders, application for payment, and monitoring project scheduling.

Let's expand on some of these specific items that are key terms to become familiar with. RFI is issued from the contractor to the architect to help with clarity of a specific issue or interpretation. An architect or the supporting engineers will respond to the RFI in writing to provide a clear response or provide a change if it is so desired as a result of the specific RFI.

The **application for payment** is a document provided by the contractor for the architect to confer with scope completed and billing provided to certify payment is due. If a loan is involved or in the client's behalf the lender may supersede the architect in processing included in the paperwork will include conditional and unconditional releases.

An **architect's field report** holds record of site visits, daily or weekly logs, and a record of construction activities.

The **architect's supplemental instructions** are intended to help the architect issue additional instructions on interpretations to order a minor change in work. This change should not alter the cost or time of the contract, just the scope.

A **change order** is an implementation of a change in the scope of work already contracted between the client and the contractor. This change order includes the financial sum, the contract time, and a change in the formal contract.

A **conditional release** is a document easily found on the Internet, and is the owner of a potential lien on the property. A simple description of how this works is a subcontractor who is owed $10,000, so he provides an invoice and a conditional release filled out and signed. The contractor will do the same totaling all the subcontractors. Once the contractor is paid and prior to the next billing (sometimes at the next billing) an **unconditional release** equal to the $10,000 must be signed. This document states the subcontractor has been paid in full and is no longer owed $10,000. The catch is if the contractor pays a subcontractor and a check bounces once the subcontractor signs the unconditional release, the subcontractor loses all of their lien rights, but it does secure the property for the client.

A **construction change directive** may be issued to modify and authorize a specific scope of work where the scope, cost, and time will be agreed upon. At the end of construction, a **certificate of substantial completion**, a written form of acceptance of the project completion date, is issued.

The **date of commencement** is the date of the beginning of the contract and a contract time begins to run.

The **list of subcontractors** is provided by the contractor to the architect for submission to the client. The list is comprehensive of the proposed employed for the proposed project.

Modifications are an effective change to the construction contract; these modifications can be accomplished by written amendments.

A **project checklist** is a listing of the tasks that need to be performed on a given project. Establishing this list will help the architect locate the data necessary to fulfill an assigned task.

A **punch list** outlines the items that need to be completed or corrected for the physical completion to be achieved.

Shop drawings are detailed drawings of how a specific item will be constructed. Review of staircases that are structural steel structures is one of the common shop drawing reviews. The architect or consulting team, as appropriate, will review, take action, date and sign, and then return to the contractor to proceed or alter any resubmit.

A properly selected and designed site comes from several variables that can be determined in order to help establish the ideal condition for development of a site. **Site analysis** is instrumental in understanding the positive and negative features of the specific site as it relates to the client's program. Generating a site plan will locate a building vertically and laterally on a site while a grading plan will demonstrate how the earth is moved to its final configuration to coincide with the building design.

A **work change proposal request** aids in obtaining cost quotations that are required for change orders. It is not a change order but a way to get information from the contractor specific to the proposed change with respect to cost.

PROJECT PROGRAMMING

Programming

As a professional architect, services are provided to establish a contract between the owner and the contractor hired to construct the design of the architect. The design process is a creative endeavor of fulfilling the client's program. A program is a comprehensive list of objectives and desires of the owner to establish a basis of needs for the fulfilled building design. A program is not necessarily static, it can and does evolve in the design process, but it is often reviewed to ensure the appropriate measures have been calculated for the design.

The AIA incorporates the program into its standard contracts under the heading of initial information. This would include additional items of relevant information including, but not limited to, project shop details, owners of budget for the cost of work, authorized representatives, owners' contractors and consultants, anticipated procurement methods, and other relevant information.

Programs can be quite simple or complex and anywhere in between. The format and layout will vary. See Figure 4.1 for a church campus program that was provided by the client and then refined further by the architect to adjust areas and determine if the building can be constructed within the size requirements established in the schematic phase of the process.

A client provides a list of requirements. In some cases, it is very specific, and in others it may be a list of words that evoke an emotion. In either case, it is the role of the architect to design a solution that meets or exceeds the goals set by the client. This list is called the program. Every phase of the design process requires the architect to review the program to determine if the design solution is consistent with the program needs and demands. Understand that a program is not static; it can, in fact, be evolving during the various phases of the design process. This process must be reviewed in every phase with the client to ensure that the goals have been met. In many offices, the program is updated as a component of the

Program for St. John Church Campus

Item	Church Building		Level 1	Level 2
1.1	Arcade		0	
1.2	Exo-Narthex		0	
1.3	Narthex	400	550	
1.3b	Balcony	1036		1500
1.4	Toilets	64	360	
1.4b	Toilets balcony	64	125	
1.5	Candle Storage	64		50
1.6	AV room	120	75	
1.7	Nursing	150	inc	
1.8	Bride	100	240	
1.10	Nave	2160	3360	
1.11	Choir Area	inc	inc	
1.12	Confession/off	inc		150
1.13	Soleas	450	480	
1.14	Sanctury/Alter	500	500	
1.15	Vestry	100	150	
1.16	Acolytes	100	100	
1.17	Toilet	60	120	
	Icon in lobby	0	50	
	Equipment room	0	50	
	Elevator	0	50	
	Stairs	0	200	
	Halls	0	100	
	subtotal	**5368**	**6510**	**1700**
	Chapel/Baptistry			
1.9	Baptistery	170	600	
	restroom	0	50	
	subtotal	**170**	**650**	
	Column Total	**5538**	**7160**	**1700**
		Church		

Item	Administration		Level 1	Level 2
2.1	Secretary	60		220
2.2	Copy/fax/files	180		120
2.3	Priest office	240		240
2.4	Priest off 2	100		150
2.5	Conference Rm	300		300
2.6	Coffee Niche	15		10
2.7	Storage	120		120
2.8		400		
	Hallways			200
	subtotal	**1415**	**0**	**1360**
	ED/Conf/Meeting		Revision	
3.1	Entry Foyer	400	100	200
3.2	mtg/class	2400		2500
3.3	Pre & Knd	1360	1800	
3.4	Youth	400		400
3.5	Café	100	200	
3.6	Ed Off	120		120
3.7	Toilets	300	100	200
3.8	Janitor	50	50	50
3.9	outdoor			
*	Accountant	0		50
	subtotal	**5130**	**2250**	**3520**
	Column Total	**6545**	**2250**	**4880**
	Admin/Office			

Item		Multi	Level 1	Level 2
4.1	Foyer	950	400	
4.2	Toilets	500	420	
4.3	Book store	120	200	
4.4	Large Hall	7500	6200	
4.5	Stage Alcove	200	inc	
4.6	Hall Storage	400	300	
4.7	Kitchen	850	600	
4.8	Kit Service	350	200	
4.9	Other Storage	675		400
4.10	Bethlehem rm	800	400	
	Information	0	150	
	Hallways	0	100	
	Elevator	0	50	
	Equip room	0	50	
	Balcony	0		125
	subtotal	**12345**	**9070**	**525**
	Existing House	3200	2300	900
	Existing Garages	600	200	
		3800	**2500**	**900**
	Column Total	**16145**	**11570**	**1425**
	Total Multi Building			

assumed number
revised number
revised number

Lot Area	157148.95	sq ft
Level 1 Max	15714.90	sq ft
Level 2 Max	12571.92	sq ft

Original program	**28228**	sq ft
1st level program	20980	sq ft
2nd level program	8005	sq ft
1st and 2nd level	**28985**	sq ft

Need to reduce x
5265.11 sq ft

Figure 4.1 Sample program for a new church campus.

project book or binder and the various evolutions of the program and memorialized as a study of the project changes. See Figure 4.1 for a sample program for a new church campus.

GUIDELINES FOR CONSTRUCTION DOCUMENTS

Construction Documents

Guidelines are too important to reduce to a series of steps and formulas to memorize. In fact, working guidelines for drafting are actually attitudes and ideals that are fundamental to good communication that will result in a smooth project. You may think that much of this material is obvious, common knowledge, or common sense. They have been arrived at through research in supervision, communication, human relationships, and field experiences, particularly with prospective employers. Remember, in an architectural firm you are not an individual; rather, you are an important part of a team, and as a team member, you must know how the team functions.

The Rules for Drafting Construction Documents

1. Plan the steps of your required drawings.
2. Establish a system in which you can check your work.
3. Understand the implications of decisions you make.
4. Know and understand the standards under which you will function.
5. Draft with an understanding of the other person's point of view.
6. Cooperate, communicate, document, and work with others.
7. Find out your primary and secondary responsibilities.
8. Think for yourself.
9. Concentrate on improving at least one aspect of your skills with each task.
10. Be sure to follow established office standards.

The Rules for Drafting Construction Documents, Expanded

1. *Plan the steps of your required drawings.* Each drawing has a distinct procedure and order. Make mental and/or written notes about the sequence and anticipated problems. Every sheet of a set of architectural plans subscribes to a basic system. The system may be based on the materials used, methods of erection, limits of the present technology, or even the limits of the builder, to mention a few. Whatever the controlling and limiting factors are, be aware, understand, digest them intellectually, and put them into effect. Know your options when you have an unusual problem.
2. *Establish a system in which you can check your work.* Every office has some method of checking drawings. Whatever the system, establish a method to check yourself before you submit a drawing to a senior in the firm. This does two things. First, it builds trust between you and your supervisor. If you are conscientious enough to double-check your work, the rapport built between you and your supervisor will be enhanced. Second, it builds the supervisor's confidence that you have done your best to perform your duty.

   This checking method differs with each person and each drawing. Accuracy transcends all checking systems—accuracy of representation as well as of arithmetic, grammar, and spelling. Nothing causes as many problems in the field as contradictory information, arithmetical tools that are not equal to their parts, or dimensions that do not reflect an established module.
3. *Understand the implications of decisions you make.* Know what decisions you will be allowed to make, and know when to ask a superior.

   If you ask a superior for help every time you are confronted with a decision, you are taking up that person's valuable time, reducing the superior's effectiveness, and demonstrating that you are not really ready for the job. Nevertheless, a production draftsperson cannot simply change a design decision; the **draftsperson** may not be aware of all the factors that led to that decision. It might seem obvious to the draftsperson that a particular change would produce a better effect, but the original may have been based on a code requirement, a client's request, cost of production, or any one of hundreds of reasons of which the draftsperson may not be aware.
4. *Know and understand the standards under which you will function.* You will encounter a multitude of standards. Just as there are various standards for office attire, ethics, and behavior, so there are drawing standards.

   Certain offices use certain sheet sizes. Title blocks, border lines, and sheet space allocation are usually set up in advance. In fact, some offices produce what is called a manual of "**office standards**." The standard may call for something as simple as a font style, or as professional as a standard based on building erection procedures. You must incorporate this standard into your documents.
5. *Draft with an understanding of the other person's point of view.* Your work involves many individuals who will interpret your drawings: people like the subcontractor, the client, and the contractor. All of these people influence your approach. For example, when you draft for the subcontractor, your work becomes a medium of communication between the

client's needs and the individuals who construct and execute the structure to meet those needs. Before drafting a detail, plan, or section, you must sufficiently understand the trades involved.

It is better to spend a few minutes with your supervisor at the beginning of a drawing, outlining your duties and the firm's objectives and needs, than to spend countless hours on a drawing only to find that much of the time you have spent is wasted.

If you know of a better solution or method, verify its appropriateness with a superior before you employ it.

6. *Cooperate, communicate, document, and work with others.* One of the main criticisms from employers is that employees do not know how to work as members of a team. Whereas education requires you to perform as an individual, each person in an office is a member of a team and has certain responsibilities, duties, and functions on which others rely. There may be many people working on a single project, and you must understand your part and participate with others toward achieving a common goal.

   Write memos and notes, write formal letters to other companies, and document correspondence. Keep in mind that you are a representative of your firm and that proper presentation, grammar, spelling, and punctuation reflect the abilities of the firm.

   Communication helps you know what the other people in the firm are doing, and it helps you to develop an appreciation of the attitudes, goals, and aims of the others with whom you will be working. Know what is going on in the office and allow others to easily track your progress.

7. *Find out your primary and secondary responsibilities.* Nothing gets an office or an employee in as much trouble as making assumptions. Phrases such as "I thought John was going to do it" not only break down the communication process in an office but can also create discord that disturbs office harmony and breaks down office morale.

   Know your responsibilities and how and whom to ask for guidance in case of a change in your responsibilities.

   A classic example of this was an office that had two divisions: an architectural division and a structural engineering division. On the architectural drawings there were notations that read, "See structural drawings for details." The details were never drawn, and when the total set was assembled and the lack of details was discovered, the omission caused a great delay and much embarrassment to the firm.

   Whenever more than one person works on a project, you need to understand not only your primary responsibilities but you're not-so-obvious secondary responsibilities as well.

8. *Think for yourself.* There is a natural tendency for a draftsperson to feel that all decisions should be made by a superior. However, your supervisor will tell you that certain decisions have been delegated to you.

   Your immediate supervisor or head draftsperson is earning two to five times as much as you are because of additional responsibilities and experience. Therefore, each time you ask a question and stop production, the cost is that of your salary plus that of your supervisor.

   Look through reference and manufacturers' literature, construction manuals, similar projects, reference books, and so on. Make a list of problems and questions and work around them until your superior is free and available to deal with them. THINK and be able to propose solutions or suggestions yourself.

   Above all, do not stop production and wait around for a superior to become available; employers react very negatively to this.

9. *Concentrate on improving one aspect of your skills with each task.* Constantly improve your speed or your accuracy. Work on your weakest aspect first, even though the tendency is to avoid or shy away from it. For example, if sections are your problem, view and study various sections from the office, texts, or publications.

   An employer wants an employee who is punctual, dependable, and accurate; has a high degree of integrity; and is able to work with a minimum amount of supervision.

10. *Be sure to follow established office standards.* Office standards are an integral part of the evolution of CDs. It is not sufficient merely to follow the standards; it is also necessary to understand why they are used. Layer titles, basic symbols, and conventions, while simple to implement, must be the same from a Los Angeles office to a New York office.

■ FROM SD, DD, TO CD

Making the transition from approved schematic drawings to DD drawings to CDs is important because it completes the process of making decisions about the physical characteristics of the building. When utilizing building information modeling (BIM), this system does not vary.

Accomplishing this transition—the DD phase—requires that the following basic requirements be satisfied and thoroughly investigated:

1. Building code, green code, and other requirements, such as those set by the zoning department, fire department, health department, planning department, engineering department, environmental department, and architectural committees

2. Primary materials analysis and selection
3. Selection of the primary structural system and materials
4. Requirements of consultants, such as mechanical, electrical, plumbing, and structural engineers
5. Regional and environmental considerations
6. Energy conservation considerations and requirements
7. Budget alignment
8. Project programming

Material Analysis

In any building project, among the most important building materials to be selected are those for foundations and floors, exterior and interior walls, and ceiling and roof structures. Several factors influence this selection, and many of these require considerable investigation and research:

1. Architectural design
2. Building codes
3. Economics
4. Structural concept
5. Region
6. Ecology
7. Energy conservation

The importance of selection is illustrated in Figure 4.2. Concrete masonry units have been selected as the material for the exterior walls of a structure. Using this material affects the exterior and interior dimensions, because concrete blocks have fixed dimensions. Establishing the exterior and interior dimensions before the production of CDs is most important because other phases, such as structural engineering, are based on these dimensions.

The importance of selecting primary building materials is further shown in Figure 4.3. The roofing material selected here actually governs the roof pitch. This, in turn, establishes the physical height of the building and also dictates the size of the supporting members relative to the weight of the finished roof material.

SELECTING THE PRIMARY STRUCTURAL SYSTEM

The selection of a structural system and its members is influenced by meeting building code requirements; satisfying design elements; and using the most logical system based on sound engineering principles, economic considerations, simplicity, and environmental factors. For most projects, the architect consults with the structural engineer about systems or methods that will meet these various considerations. A structural concept is required before CDs can be produced (see Figures 4.4 and 4.5). After a structural concept is established, the decision-making process is based on supporting that concept.

REQUIREMENTS OF CONSULTANTS

Early involvement of structural, electrical, mechanical, and civil engineering consultants is highly recommended. This is especially critical early in the design stage when using BIM. Their early involvement generally results in fewer adjustments having to be made to the finalized preliminary drawings to meet their design requirements. For example, the mechanical engineer's

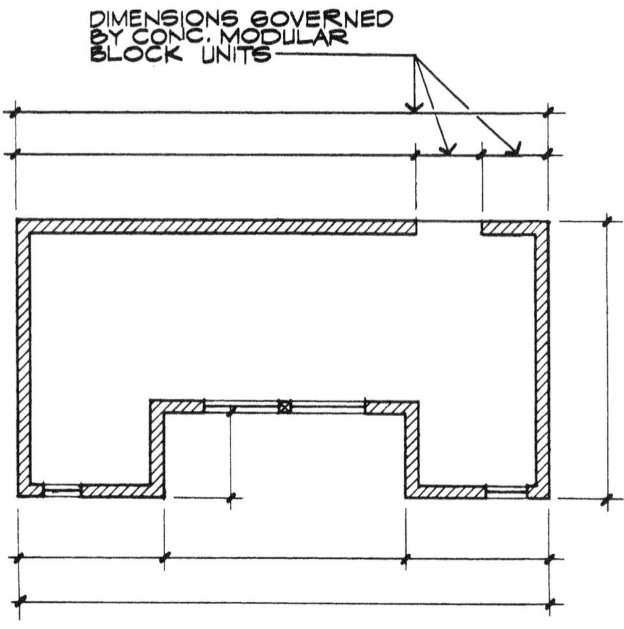

Figure 4.2 Exterior concrete block walls.

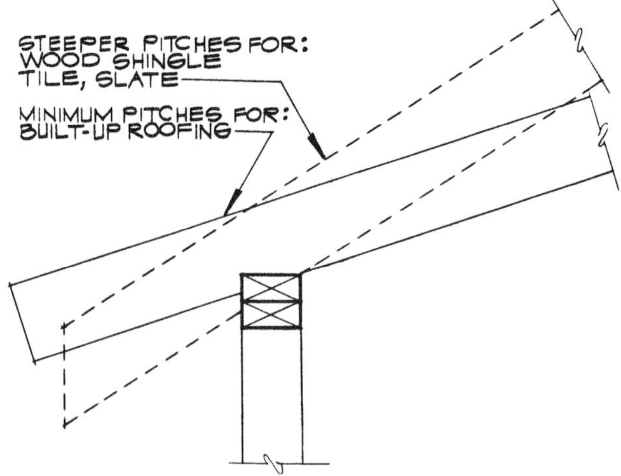

Figure 4.3 Roof material and roof pitches.

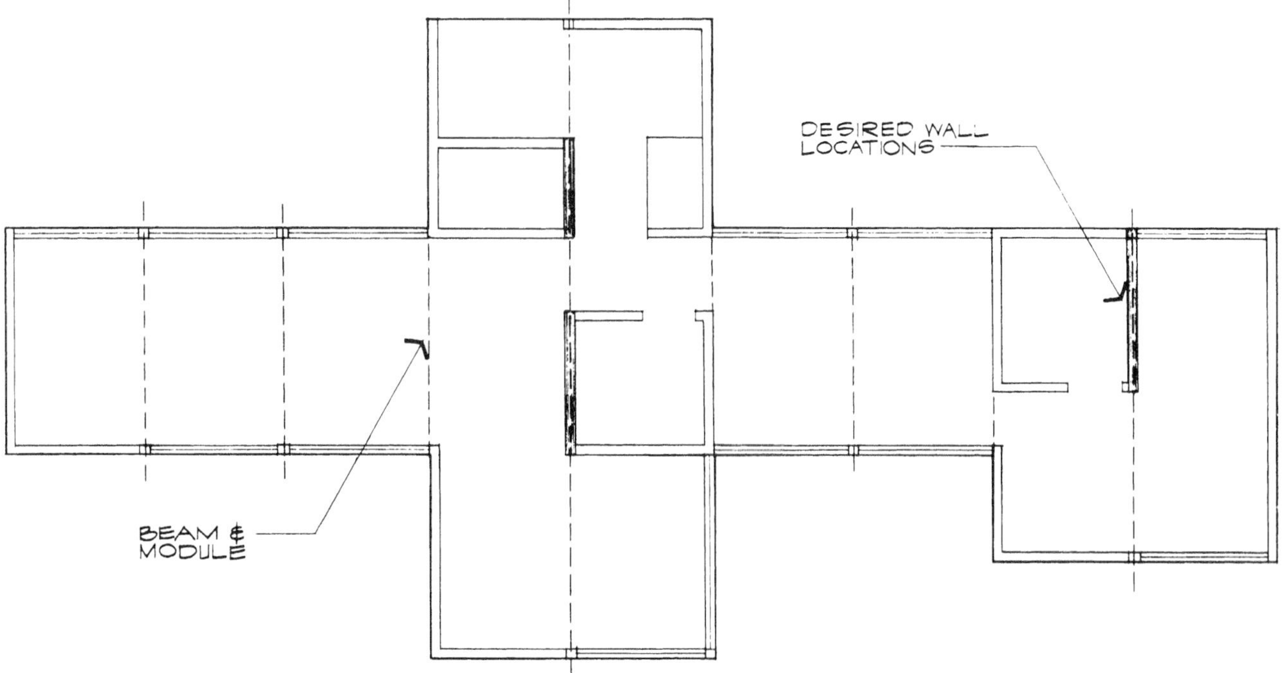

Figure 4.4 Wood post-and-beam structural system.

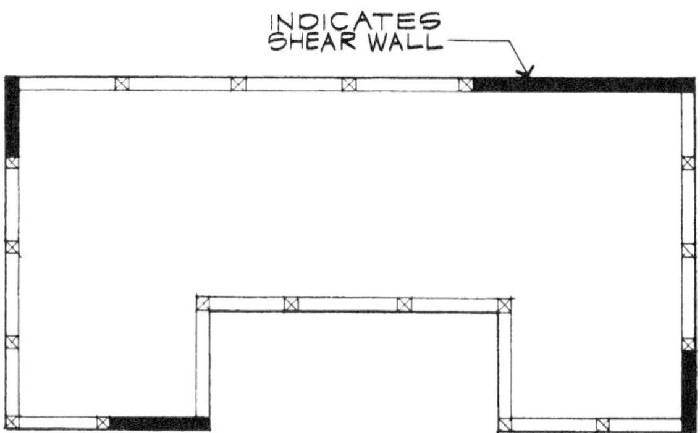

Figure 4.5 Plan view of shear wall locations.

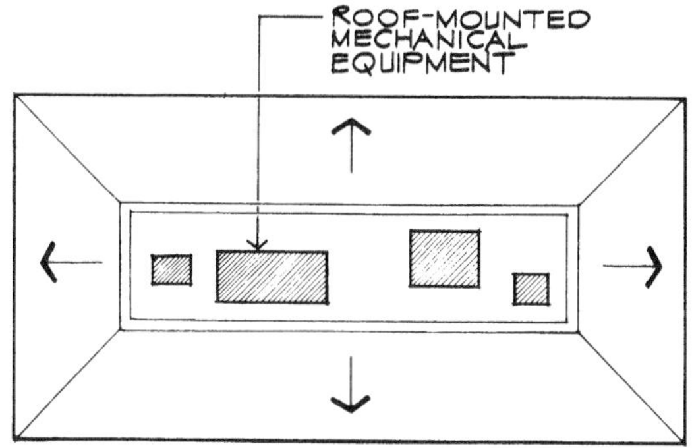

Figure 4.6 Roof plan with mechanical equipment area.

design may require a given area on the roof to provide space for various sizes of roof-mounted mechanical equipment. See Figure 4.6. For projects that require mechanical ducts to be located in floor and ceiling areas, necessary space and clearances for ducts must be provided. Figure 4.7 shows a floor and ceiling section with provisions for mechanical duct space.

The electrical engineer should also be consulted about any modifications to the building that may be required to provide space for electrical equipment. In most cases, the architect or project manager provides for an electrical equipment room or cabinet in the plans. However, with the increasing sophistication and size of equipment, additional space may be required. This increase in the electrical room dimensions may require a floor-plan adjustment, which can even result in a major or minor plan modification. Figure 4.8 illustrates

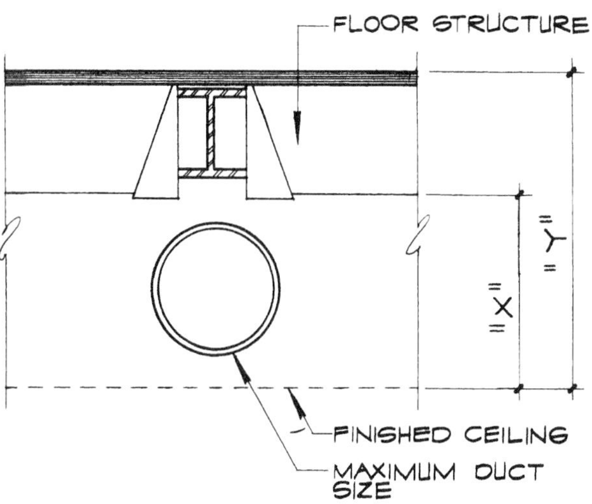

Figure 4.7 Mechanical duct space equipment.

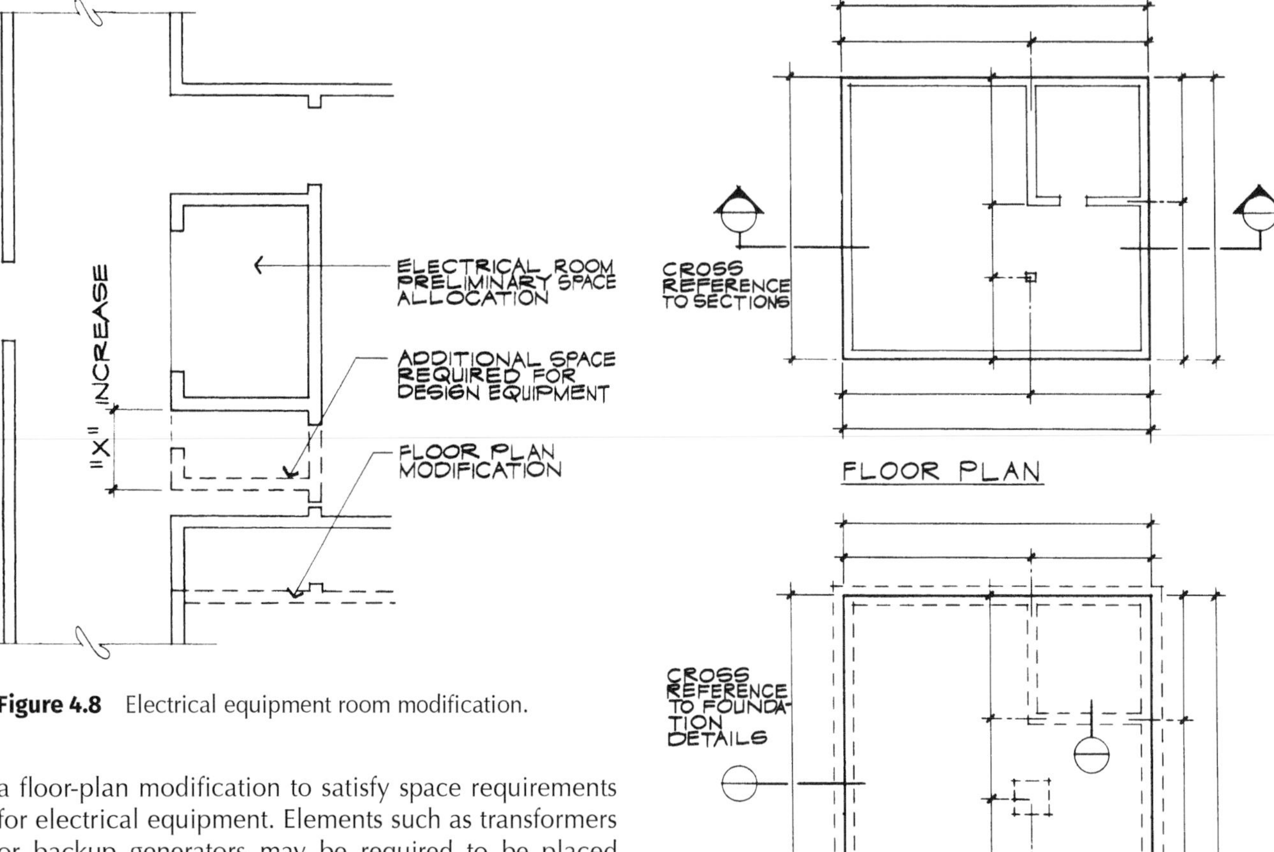

Figure 4.8 Electrical equipment room modification.

Figure 4.9 Relationship of foundation plan and floor plan.

a floor-plan modification to satisfy space requirements for electrical equipment. Elements such as transformers or backup generators may be required to be placed on the site, so the required clearances must also be accounted for.

INTERRELATIONSHIP OF DRAWINGS

When you develop CDs, you must have consistent relationships between the drawings for continuity and clarity. These relationships vary in their degree of importance.

For example, the relationship between the foundation plan and the floor plan is most important because continuity of dimensioning and location of structural components for both are required. See Figure 4.9. The dimensioning of the floor plan and the foundation plan are identical, and this provides continuity for dimensional accuracy.

The relationship between drawings for the electrical plan and the mechanical plan is also critical. The positioning of electrical fixtures must not conflict with the location of mechanical components, such as air supply grilles or fire sprinkler heads.

Cross-reference drawings with important relationships such as these and constantly review them during preparation of the CDs. The utilization of BIM programs identifies conflicts and aids in determining where revisions are required.

This cross-referencing and review is not as critical with drawings that are not so closely related, such as the electrical plans, the civil engineering plans, the interior elevations, and the foundation plan. Nevertheless, it is still be important.

Standards and Procedures

Most offices have a set procedure for planning the transition from schematic drawings to the development and execution of CDs. In a small office, it may be a simple matter of the principal giving verbal directives to employees until a specific system is understood. In a large office, the system may be an intricate network of preplanned procedures.

There are two items in any office with which the beginner will be confronted. These are described herein as **standards**, standard graphic and written patterns to which the office subscribes, and **procedures**, the methods that are instituted during this transition and by which the standards are implemented.

Many offices have a booklet called Office Standards or the **Drafting Room Manual**. These are critical to both the employee and the employer. In large architectural firms, employees are asked to study and learn these standards. See Figure 4.10. It contains such items as the following:

1. A "Uniform List of Abbreviations" for working drawings
2. Material designations in plan, section, and elevation
3. Graphic symbols
4. Methods of representing doors and windows in both plan and elevation
5. Mechanical, electrical, and plumbing symbols
6. Graphic representations of appliances and fixtures
7. Sheet layout and drawing modules
8. Line weights and layers
9. BIM

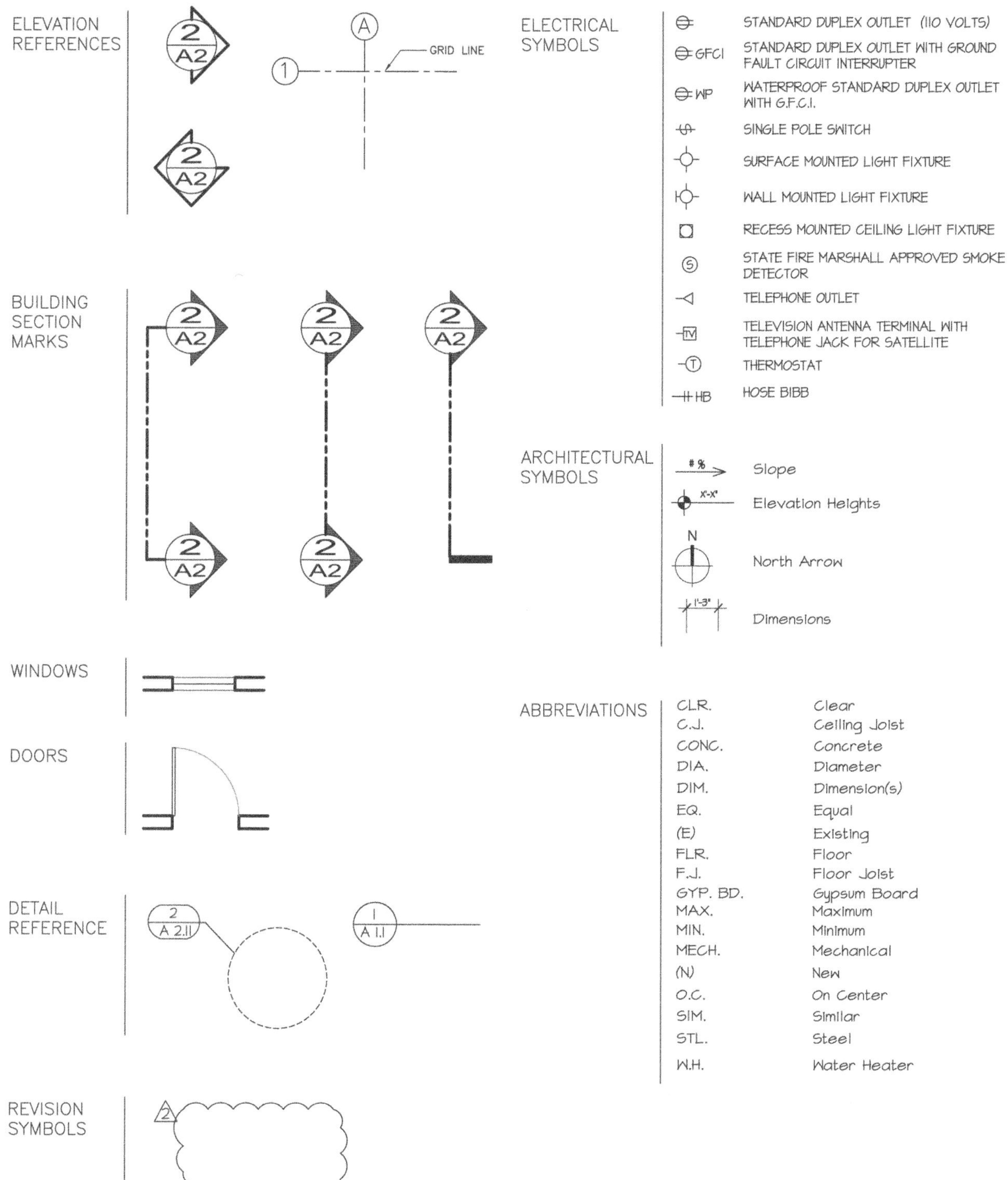

Figure 4.10 Sample of standard conventions.

PROJECT BOOK

Project Materials and Specifications

All information about a specific project—the materials selected, the structural system chosen, the exterior finishes, and interior finishes, plus all correspondence relating to the project—is documented, collected, and placed in a **project book.** This can be a simple three-ring binder or a series of binders. Lists of structural considerations, exterior finishes, and interior finishes are shown in Figures 4.11–4.13, respectively.

Exterior and Interior Finishes

In the development of the exterior elevation, the drafter must be able to identify the various materials to be used on the exterior surface, as well as the type of fenestration (windows and doors). As with structural considerations, a chart is again the instrument used to convey the information to the drafter. See Figure 4.12.

To allow an accurate drawing of the floor plan, interior elevation, and finish schedule, interior finishes are selected by the client, in conjunction with the architect. The drafter can find this information in the project book on a chart similar to the one shown in Figure 4.13. Although this list is called "Interior Finishes," it can include appliances and other amenities such as fireplaces, a security system, a safe, and so on.

Legal Description

Every project has some type of legal description. A simple description might look like this:

Lot #____________ Block #____________
Tract #___, as recorded in book ___, page ___,
of the ____________ County recorder's office.

This description must appear on the set of working drawings. It may be on the title sheet or on the site plan or survey sheet.

The legal description is used when researching your client's site: zoning requirements and limitations, setback requirements, height limits, or any other information you might need for a specific design feature of the project.

Job Number

Every office has its own way of identifying a specific project. Generally, each project is assigned a job number, which might incorporate the year of the project, the month a job was started, or even the order in which the project was contracted. For example, job number 2303 might reflect the third project received in an office in the year 2023. By using this system, an office can rapidly identify the precise year in which a job was contracted and never duplicate a number.

Task Number

All offices use time sheets, applications, or log data into a time spreadsheet; the data include keeping track of the drafter's performance. A drafter might log the time spent on a project by date, the job number, a written description of the task performed, and amount of time, such as:

07–30–23 Job #2303—Tylin Residence—Plans—SD 2.25hrs.

In a large office, each task is also numbered. Figure 4.14 displays a chart describing the work to be performed as "work packages"; the task number at the left is assigned to the specific package, and a column at right indicates the total man-hours planned for the particular work package. The task numbers jump by 10, allowing the flexibility, on a complex project, to have sub-work packages. For example, 140 Site Visit might use 141 as a task number for measuring an existing structure to be altered.

Figure 4.15 is an example of the total man-hours for a residence. Note the task numbers and the computer display of the corresponding work-package names.

STRUCTURAL

1. FOUNDATION	2. TYPICAL WALL FRAMING	3. TYPICAL FLOOR FRAMING	4. TYPICAL ROOF FRAMING
a. Conventional slab-on-grade	a. 2 x ___ wood studs	a. 2 x wood floor joists	a. Conventional (wood rafters & beams)
b. Post-tensioned slab	b. Lap with corner boards	b. 2 x wood floor joists per structural consultant	b. TJI
c. Wood floor	c. Other	c. TJI	c. Trusses
d. Other		d. 1-1/2" lightweight concrete over	d. Trusses and conventional framing
		e. Other	
		Note: Specify any minimum sizes	Note: Specify any minimum sizes

Figure 4.11 Listing of structural considerations.

EXTERIOR FINISHES

A. WALLS			
1. STUCCO	2. CEDAR SIDING	3. MASONITE SIDING	4. MASONRY VENEER
a. Sand texture	a. Lap with mitered corners	(specify other manufacturers)	a. Thin set brick (mfg.)
b. Other	b. Lap with corner boards		
		a. Lap with metal corners	b. Full brick (mfg.)
		b. Lap with corner boards	c. Stone
		c. V-groove with corner boards	d. Stucco stone
		d. Other	e. Other

B. TRIMS, BARGES, AND FASCIA	
1. SIZE	2. TEXTURE
a. X ___ Trim at windows and doors	a. S4S
___ Whole house	b. Resawn
___ Front elevation only	c. Rough sawn
b. X ___ Barge and fascia with ____ X ____Trim over	d. Other

C. ROOFING				
1. MATERIAL		2. GUTTERS	3. DIVERTERS AT DOORS	
a. Wood shakes		a. At whole house	Composition shingle	Only
b. Wood shingle		b. At doors only	Wood shake and shingle	
c. Concrete "s" tile	(mfg.)		Flat concrete tile	
d. Clay "s" tile	(mfg.)	*Note:* Gutters will be assumed at all tight eave conditions.		
e. Clay 2-piece mission tile	(mfg.)			
f. Flat concrete tile	(mfg.)			
g. Composition shingle	(mfg.)			
h. Built-up				
i. Built-up with gravel surface				
j. Other	(mfg.)			

D. DECKS AND BALCONIES	E. STAIRS	
1. TYPE	1. THREADS	2. STRINGERS
a. 2 X spaced decking	a. Open wood treads	a. Steel stringers
b. Dex-o-Tex waterproof membrane decking	b. Precast concrete threads	b. Wood stringers
c. Other	c. Conc.-filled metal pan treads	
	d. Dex-o-Tex waterprf. membrane	

F. DOORS		
1. ENTRY		3. PATIO / DECK
a. 3068 1-3/4" S.C.	(mfg.)	a. Aluminum sliding glass door
b. 3080 1-3/4" S.C.	(mfg.)	b. Aluminum French doors
c. Other		c. Wood sliding glass door
2. GARAGE		d. Wood French doors
a. Overhead		e. Other
b. Wood roll-up	(mfg.)	
c. Metal roll-up	(mfg.)	

G. WINDOWS			
1.	Aluminum	Wood	2. MUNTINS
a. Sliding			a. All windows
b. Single-hung			b. Front elevation and related rooms
c. Double-hung			3. Dual glazed
d. Awning			4. Single and dual glazing per Title 24
e. Casement			5. Other

H. SKYLIGHTS			
1. GLASS (mfg.)	2. ACRYLIC (mfg.)		3. GLAZING
Color	Color	Shape	a. Single
a. Bronze	a. Bronze	a. Flat	b. Double
b. Gray	b. Gray	b. Dome	c. Per Title 24 report
c. Clear	c. Clear	c. Pyramid	d. Other
d. White	d. White	d. Other	
e. Other	e. Other		

Figure 4.12 Listing of exterior finishes.

INTERIOR FINISHES

A. WALLS	
1. Drywall - Texture	
2. Plaster - Texture	
3. Other	
4. Bullnose Corners	

B. FLOORS	Carpet	Sheet Vinyl	Ceramic Tile	Other
Entry				
Living				
Dining				
Family				
Den				
Kitchen				
Nook				
Hall				
Master Bedroom				
Second Bedroom				
Master Dressing Room				
Second Bathroom				
Powder				
Service				

C. CEILING	
1. Drywall - Texture	
2. Plaster - Texture	
3. All dropped beams shall be drywall wrapped	
4. All dropped beams shall be exposed	
5. Other	

D. CABINET TOP AND SPLASH	Ceramic Tile	Corian	Cult. Marb	Cult. Onyx	Plastic Lam.	Wood	Other	Splash Hght.
Kitchen								
Service								
Wet Bar								
Powder								
Linen								
Master Bathroom								
Second Bathroom								

E. INTERIOR DOORS		
1. Passage		2. Wardrobe
Master Bedroom		a. 6'-8" high siding
a. 3068		b. 8'-0" high siding
b. 2868		c. 6-'8" high bifold
c. Other		d. 8'-0" high bifold
Secondary Bedrooms		e. Other
a. 2868		
b. 2668		
c. Other		
3. Mirrored		
a. Master Bedroom		
b. Secondary Bedroom		
c. Other		

F. BATHROOM FIXTURES	Master Bath	Second Bath
1. Tubs and Tub/Showers		
a. 3'-6"x5'-0" cast iron oval tub		
b. 3'-6"x5'-0" porc/stl. oval tub		
c. 3'-6"x5'-0" fiberglass oval tub		
d. 3'-6"x5'-0" 1-piece fiberglass oval tub and surr.		
e. 2'-8"x5'-0" cast iron tub		
f. 2'-8"x5'-0" porc./stl. tub		
g. 2'-8"x5'-0" 1-piece fiberglass oval tub and surr.		
h. Other		
Note : Specify surrounding material		
2. Showers		
a. Fiberglass pan and surround		
b. Hot mopped ceramic tile pan with ceramic tile surrounding material		
c. Precast pan with surround		
Specify: Type Pan		
Type Surround		
d. Shatterproof enclosure		
e. Curtain rod		
3. Mirrors		
a. 3'-0" high		
b. 3'-6" high		
c. 3'-8" high		
d. 4'-0" high		
e. Full height to ceiling		
4. Medicine Cabinets		

G. KITCHEN APPLIANCES
1. Sink
a. Double
b. Double with garbage disposal
c. Triple
d. Triple with garbage disposal
2. Built-In Oven
a. Double - gas
b. Double - electric
c. Single with microwave
3. Built-in Cooktop
a. Gas
b. Electric
c. Downdraft - gas
d. Downdraft - electric
e. Hood, light and fan above
f. Microwave above
4. Slide-in Range/Oven (30")
a. Gas
b. Electric
c. Downdraft - gas
d. Downdraft - electric
e. Hood, light and fan above
f. Microwave above

Figure 4.13 Listing of interior finishes.

	G. KITCHEN APPLIANCES (continued)
	5. Hi/Low Slide-in Range/Oven (30")
	a. Gas
	b. Electric
	c. Oven below and above
	d. Oven below, microwave above
	6. Dishwasher
	a. Included
	7. Trash Compactor
	a. Included
	Size
	8. Refrigerator
	a. 3'-3" wide space
	b. 3'-0" wide space
	c. Other
	d. Stub-out for ice maker
	e. Recessed stub-out for ice maker
H.	LAUNDRY
	1. Dryer
	a. Gas
	b. Electric 220V
	c. Both
I.	MECHANICAL
	1. F.A.U.
	a. Gas
	b. Electric
	c. Zoned - Specify number of units ________
	1. Air Conditioner
	a. Included
	b. Optional
J.	PLUMBING
	1. Water Heater - Gas
	a. Recirculating
	b. Water softener - included
	c. Water softener - loop only
	2. Exterior Hose Bibb
	a. Total Required ____________________
	b. Locations: ______________________

	K. ELECTRICAL	Surface Mounted	Rec. Can Light	Square Flush Light	Lum. Clg. (Fluor.)	Lum. Soffit (Fluor.)	Lum. Soffit (Incand.)	Wall Mounted	Pendant	Other
	1. Location									
	Entry									
	Living									
	Dining									
	Family									
	Den									
	Kitchen									
	Nook									
	Stair									
	Hall									
	Master Bedroom									
	Second Bedroom									
	Master Dress									
	Second Dress									
	Master Bath									
	Second Bath									
	Powder									
	Service									
	2. Outlet for Garage Door Opener									
	3. Exterior W.P. Outlets									
	a. Total Required:____________________									
	b. Location: ____________________									
	4. Phone Outlets - Locations									
	a. ______________________________									
	b. ______________________________									
	5. TV Outlets - Locations									
	a. ______________________________									
	b. ______________________________									
	6. Intercom System									
	a. Wired									
	b. Option									
	7. Security System									
	a. Wired									
	b. Option									

L.	FIREPLACES
	1. Prefab Metal
	a. Manufacturer
	b. Size
	c. Gas stub-out
	2. Precast Concrete
	a. Manufacturer
	b. Size
	c. Gas stub-out
	3. Masonry Sizes
	b. Size
	c. Gas stub-out

M.	Miscellaneous Amenities
	1. Safe
	a. Wall - location ____________________
	b. Floor - location ____________________
	2. Wet Bar - Plans
	Under-counter
	Ice maker ________________________
	Refrigerator,______________________
	3. Other (specify)
	a.
	b.

Figure 4.13 *(Continued)*

As the drafters turn in their time sheets, the project manager must ascertain the progress on a particular job or check to see if the project has been budgeted correctly. Figure 4.16 provides an example of such a spot check.

Document Numbering System

Although this book is mainly concerned with architectural working drawings, it also includes other drawings among those that constitute a complete set of CDs.

ADDITIONAL SERVICE CHECKLIST
SINGLE-FAMILY SUMMARY OF PLANNED MAN-HOURS

PROJECT NAME: ________________
PROJECT NO: ________________
PROJECT MANAGER: ________________
START DATE ________________

WORK PACKAGE NAMES	PLANNED MAN-HOURS
110 BUILDING DEPARTMENT PLAN CHECK	
120 BUILDING DEPARTMENT SUBMITTAL	
130 IN-HOUSE PLAN CHECK	
140 SITE VISIT	
150 PRODUCTION ASSISTANT/PRINTING	
160 CONSTRUCTION DOCUMENTS (DIR. & ASSOC DIR.)	
170 FOUNDATION LAYOUT (ARCHITECTURAL)	
180 FLOOR PLAN	
190 ARCHITECTURAL BACKGROUND	
200 EXTERIOR ELEVATIONS	
210 BUILDING SECTIONS	
220 DETAILS	
230 INTERIOR ELEVATIONS	
240 ROOF PLAN	
250 STAIRS PLANS	
260 NOT USED	
270 NOT USED	
280 FOUNDATION PLAN (STRUCTURAL INFORMATION)	
290 FRAMING PLAN (STRUCTURAL)	
300 TITLE SHEET	
310 SITE PLAN	
320 SCHEDULES	
330 PLAN CHANGE (SINGLE FAMILY)	
340 PROJECT MANAGEMENT (PROJECT MGR./ARCHITECT)	
350 PROJECT MEETINGS (TEAM MEMBERS)	
360 CAD COORDINATION (DIR. OF CAD SERVICES)	
370 CAN BE USED FOR ADDITIONAL WORK	
380 CAN BE USED FOR ADDITIONAL WORK	
390 CAN BE USED FOR ADDITIONAL WORK	
TOTAL PLANNED MAN-HOURS	

APPROVED BY:________________

Figure 4.14 Task numbers and summary of planned man-hours.

To keep all of the drawings in their proper spaces, they are numbered differently. For example, the set of architectural drawings can easily be identified by the letter A: Sheets A-100, A-200, A-300, and so on. In contrast, S can be used for structural drawings (S-100, S-200, S-300), E for electrical, L for landscape, and M for mechanical, to mention but a few categories.

While the letter indicates a particular discipline, the number may indicate a type of drawing series. For instance, the 100 series may represent the floor plans of a building and the 200 series may represent elevations and so on. The AIA has a recommendation for all of these letters and numbers for an architectural firm.

Summary of Planned Man-Hours		
	Project Name: The Professional Practice of Architectural Drawings Case Study—Mr. and Mrs. ____________________ Residence	
Task No.	Work Package Names	Planned Man-Hours
310	Site Plan Roof Plan, and Energy Notes	10
170	Foundation Plan and Details	20
180	Floor Plan and Electrical Plan	20
220/320	Door Window Details and Schedules	32
200	Exterior Elevations and Details	20
210	Building Sections	10
290	Roof Framing Details	20
230	Interior Elevations	16
130	Project Coordination and Plan Check	18
	Total Hours	166
	166 hours $________ Hr. =	$__________

Figure 4.15 Planned man-hours for a project.

	Summary of Man-Hours Through 12-15-10	
310	Site Plan	2 hrs. 40 min.
310	Vicinity Map	20 min.
310	Roof Plan	1 hr. 15 min.
170	Foundation Plan	3 hrs. 15 min.
320	Foundation details	3 hrs. 55 min.
180	Floor Plan	4 hrs. 5 min.
200	Exterior Elevations	3 hrs. 55 min.
210	Sections (Garage)	15 min.
290	Roof Framing Plan	40 min.
130	Projection Coordination	2 hrs. 5 min.
	Total	22 hrs. 25 min.

Figure 4.16 Progress for a specific time period.

A title sheet includes a legend of all the sheet titles, and page numbers are indicated so that recipients of a set of drawings will know if a page is missing.

Drawing Development

As indicated previously, most offices have a game plan. Although such plans may vary slightly from one office to another, Figure 4.17 displays what we feel is a rather typical sequence. The terms **layout** and **block out** in this list mean to roughly draw out so that changes and corrections can easily be implemented. Key or special notes (**keynotes**) refer to the fact that noting is vitally important and actually supersedes the graphic documentation or representations illustrated on the plans.

Preliminary Approach with Computer Model

Following the initial design stages of whatever process is chosen, a massing study is used as a bridge between the design and CDs (see Figure 4.18). The massing study is initially formed as a 3-D model on the computer, making the journey much easier. Review the steps described in Chapter 1 to better understand the process we will now embark upon.

Initially, the 3-D massing model is refined and adjusted to the client's needs (see Figure 4.19). The next step is to convert the refined 3-D model into a series of orthographic views. The top view becomes the roof plan, and the front, rear, and side views become the elevation (see Figure 4.20). This is the process of taking a building (drawn in 3-D) and slicing it. The horizontal slice produces a floor plan when the inside is detailed. The vertical slice becomes a building section when rotated into an ortho position (see Figure 4.23). A summary of the various views available via rotation can be seen in Figures 4.21 and 4.22.

Stages and Layers of Production Drawings

The pictorial and preliminary floor plan shown in Figure 4.24 can be scanned and used as a construction layer for computer drawings. If the 3-D model is digital, we can then rotate the object into the required views as described earlier.

Working Drawing Procedures

PROJECT

1. Lay out Unit Floor Plans – ¼"
   - __ Block out walls.
   - __ Door and windows.
   - __ Cabinets, appliances and fixtures.
   - __ Dimension overalls.
   - __ Calculate square footages.

2. Lay Out Roof Plan – ⅛"
   - __ Indicate exterior line of building.
   - __ Indicate roof lines and pitch.

3. Lay Out Building Sections – ¼"
   - __ Indicate type of framing.
   - __ Dimensions floor and plate heights.

4. Lay Out Exterior Elevations – ¼"
   - __ Indicate doors and windows.
   - __ Indicate exterior materials.
   - __ Dimension floor and plate heights.

5. Lay Out Addenda Plans – ¼"
   - __ Partial floor plans.
   - __ Exterior elevations (per step #4)
   - __ Roof plan (per step # 2)

6. Project Manager to Select Keynotes.
   - __ Floor plans.
   - __ Exterior elevations.
   - __ Interior elevations.
   - __ Sections.

7. Project Manager to Select Details
   - __ Doors and windows.
   - __ Exterior elevations
   - __ Interior elevations

8. Project Manager to Lay Out Framing and Mechanical Study.
   - __ Overlays.

9. Plot
   - __ Floor Plans.
   - __ Addenda plans/exterior elevations/roof plans.
   - __ Sections.
   - __ Submit package to structural, T-24 Engineers, and applicable consultants.
   - __ In-house back check of package (Designer and project Architect.)

50% COMPLETE

10. Floor Plans
    - __ Lay out electrical plan.
    - __ Finish interior/exterior dimensions.
    - __ Note plans.
    - __ Reference details.

11. Lay Out Interior Elevations and Fireplaces – ¼"
    - __ Indicate ceiling heights.
    - __ Dimension cabinet heights.
    - __ Dimension appliances.
    - __ Note interiors.
    - __ Dimension fireplaces.
    - __ Note fireplaces.

12. Architectural Detail Sheets
    - __ Finish all Details.

    Consultant design information due; in-house plan check and application to drawings.

13. Addenda.

    13.1 Partial Floor Plans
    - __ Electrical.
    - __ Dimension.
    - __ Note-Plans.
    - __ Reference details.

    13.2 Roof Plans – ¼"
    - __ Reference details.
    - __ Reference notes.

    13.3 Exterior Elevations
    - __ Reference details.
    - __ Reference notes.
    - __ Exterior materials finish schedule.

14. Sections
    - __ Reference notes.
    - __ Coordinate consultant design.

15. Title Sheet
    - __ Code tabulation.
    - __ Consultant information.
    - __ Vicinity map.
    - __ Sheet index.

16. Final Coordination
    - __ Building department submittal information.
    - __ Final plotting for building department.
    - __ Submit for plan check.

90% COMPLETE

17. Formal In-House Plan Check
    - __ Plan check.

18. Building Department Plan Check
    - __ Incorporate correction into plans.
    - __ Coordinate client/cyp in-house plan checks and incorporate into plans

19. Signatures
    - __ Upon building department approval (permit), route plan set for consultant approval and signatures

100% COMPLETE
Ready for plotting and submittal.

Figure 4.17 Working drawing procedure game plan.

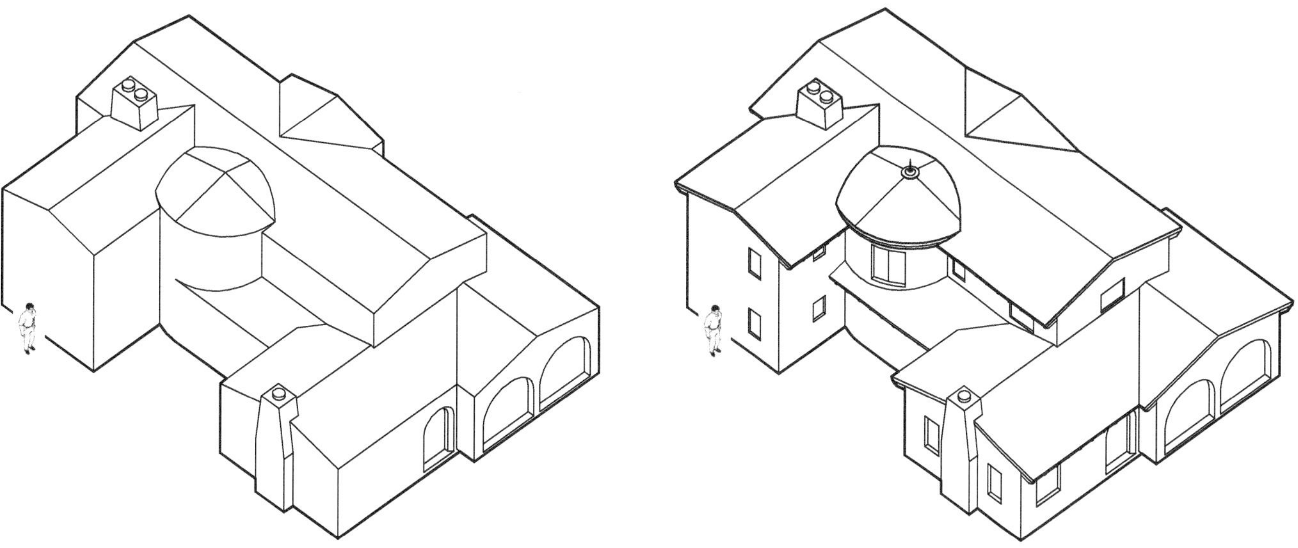

Figure 4.18 Preliminary massing model of the Clay residence.

Figure 4.19 Refined 3-D model of the Clay residence.

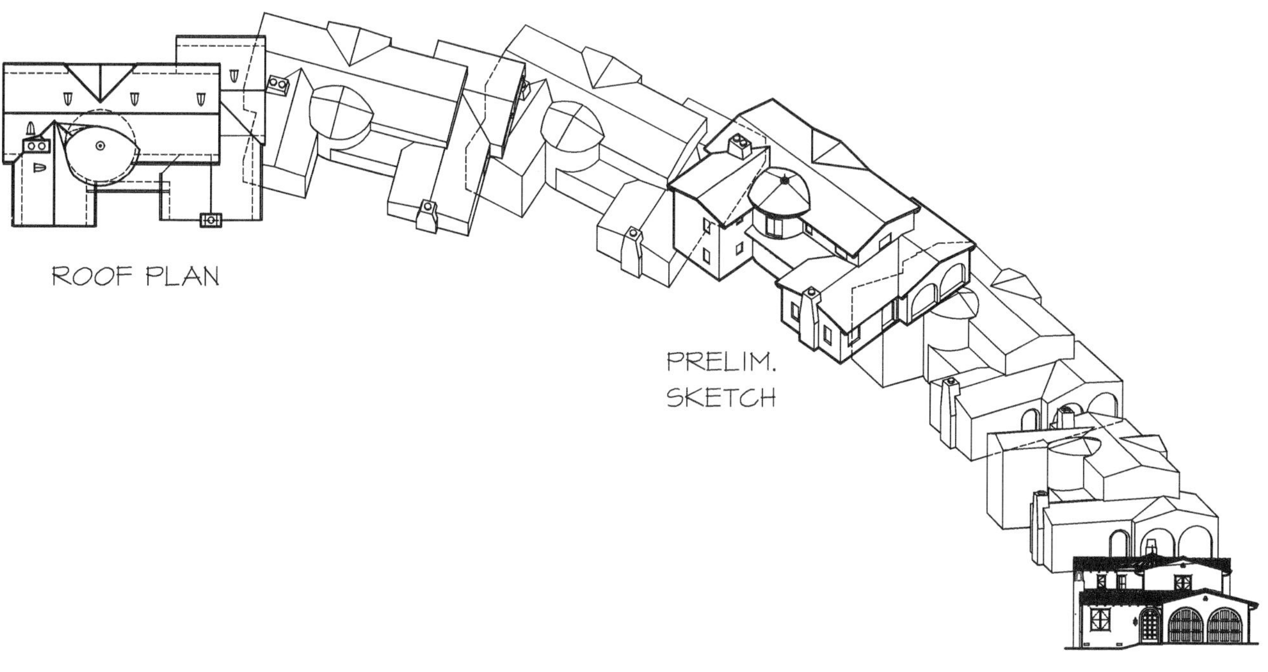

Figure 4.20 Rotation of massing model into orthographic view.

Producing the initial stage of working drawings by rotation sets the stage for the following five to six stages of layers to be produced by the CAD drafter. More complex projects may call for more stages, but we think that five is the absolute minimum number of stages for any set of construction drawings.

Stages

Stage I (Figure 4.25). The floor plan becomes the basic pattern for all other drawings in the set. If a computer is used, grids and snaps are set to produce the pre-established modules, such as a block module when masonry is used or a matrix for steel.

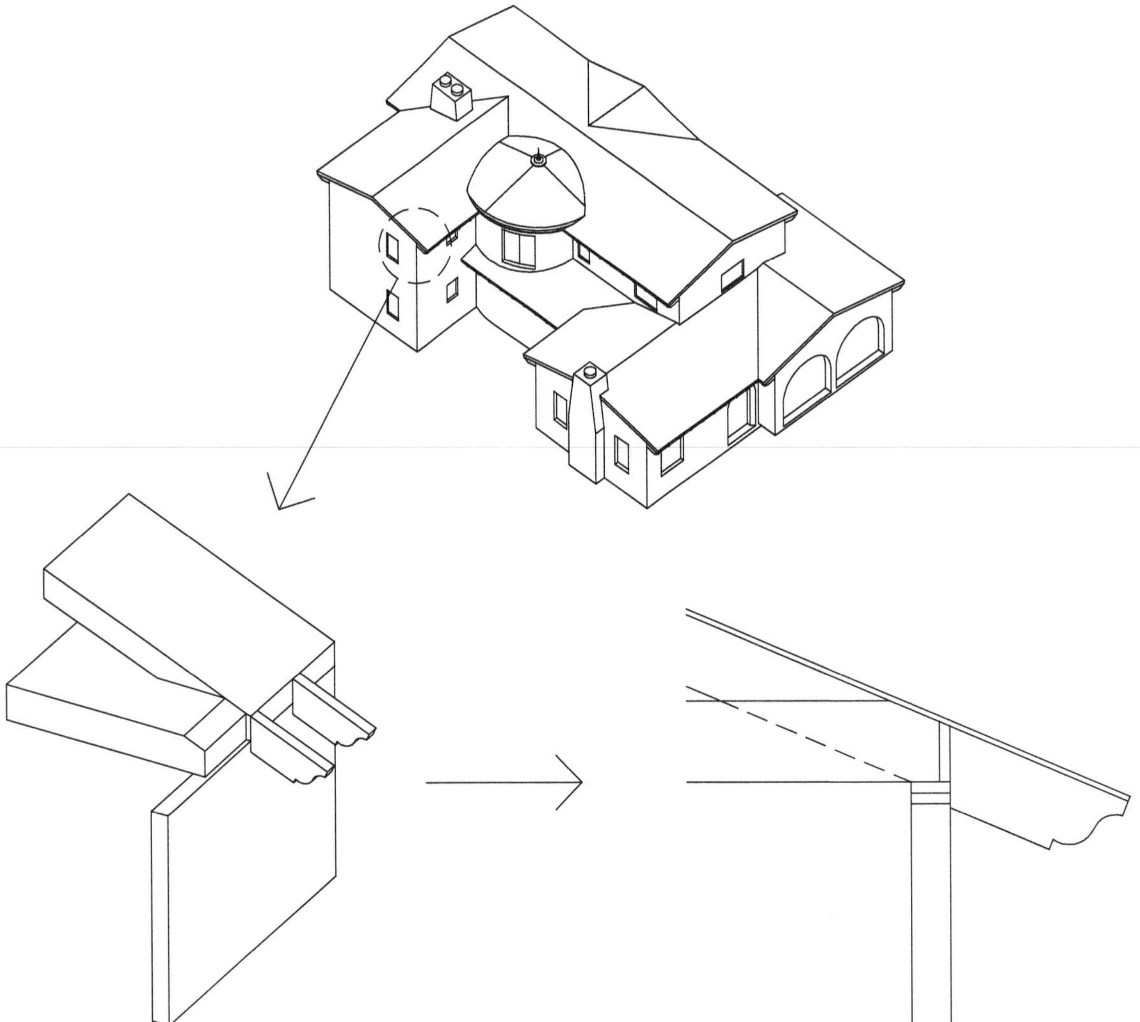

Figure 4.21 Isolation areas for detailing.

Stage II (Figure 4.26). The interior and exterior walls with their limits are drawn in this stage. Columns and openings should also be included at this stage. The designer called for rounded corners. Figure 4.27 shows a pictorial and a detail of how this is accomplished. This stage may become the datum stage for the foundation plan.

Stage III (Figure 4.28). Stair positioning is critical at this stage. Plumbing fixtures also become a critical part of the drawing. For an office, partitions are frequently drawn at this stage, as are non-load-bearing walls and the positions for openings and doors not previously positioned by rotation of the 3-D model.

Stage IV (Figure 4.29). Dimensioning, including values, is accomplished here. You must dimension to face or center of stud for wood, follow a block module for masonry, and position the columns correctly using the axial reference plane method for steel.

Stage V (Figure 4.30). The drawing is cross-referenced with other drawings, plans, sections, and details.

Stage VI (Figure 4.31). All text and titles should be placed on one layer. Refer to the standard for typeface, size, and positioning.

Stages and layers may appear to be the same to the beginning CAD drafter, but in reality, they are different.

An example is the floor plan shown in Figure 4.32. This is a drawing done in six or seven stages, but there are as many as 15 layers. The greater the number of layers, the easier it is to change or alter the drawing. As any office employee will tell you, there is nothing more

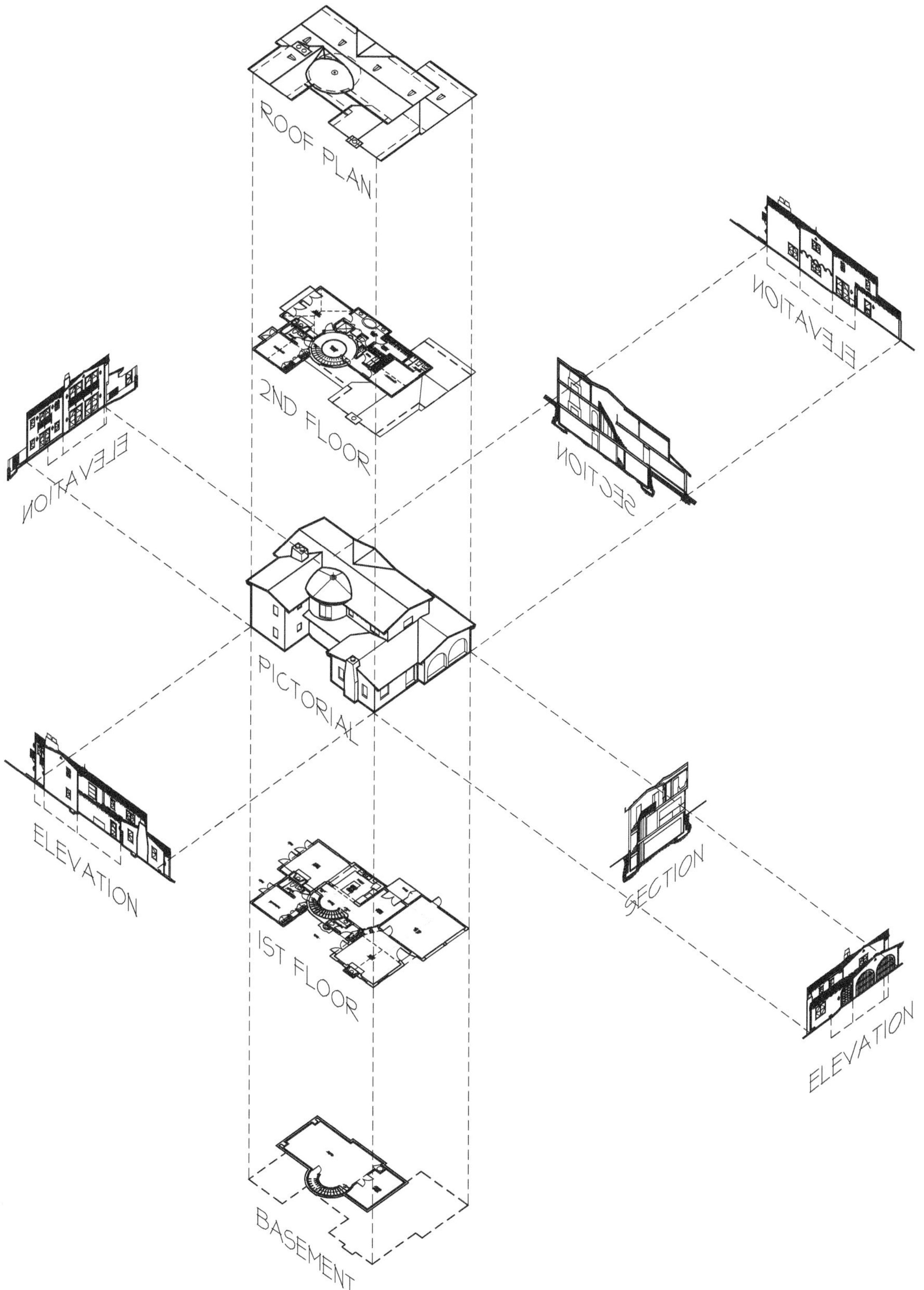

Figure 4.22 Evolution of construction documents.

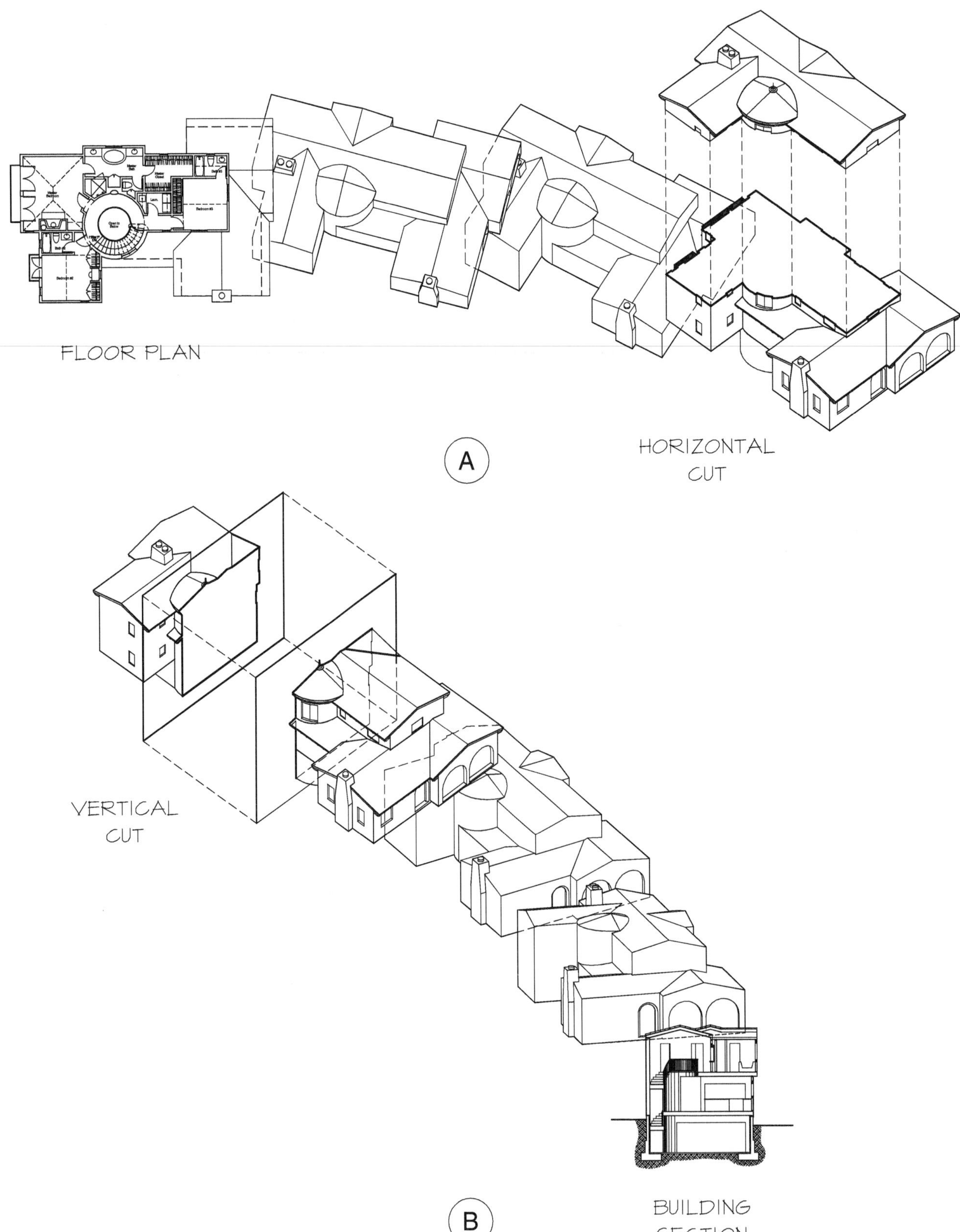

Figure 4.23 Horizontal and vertical sections through preliminary sketch.

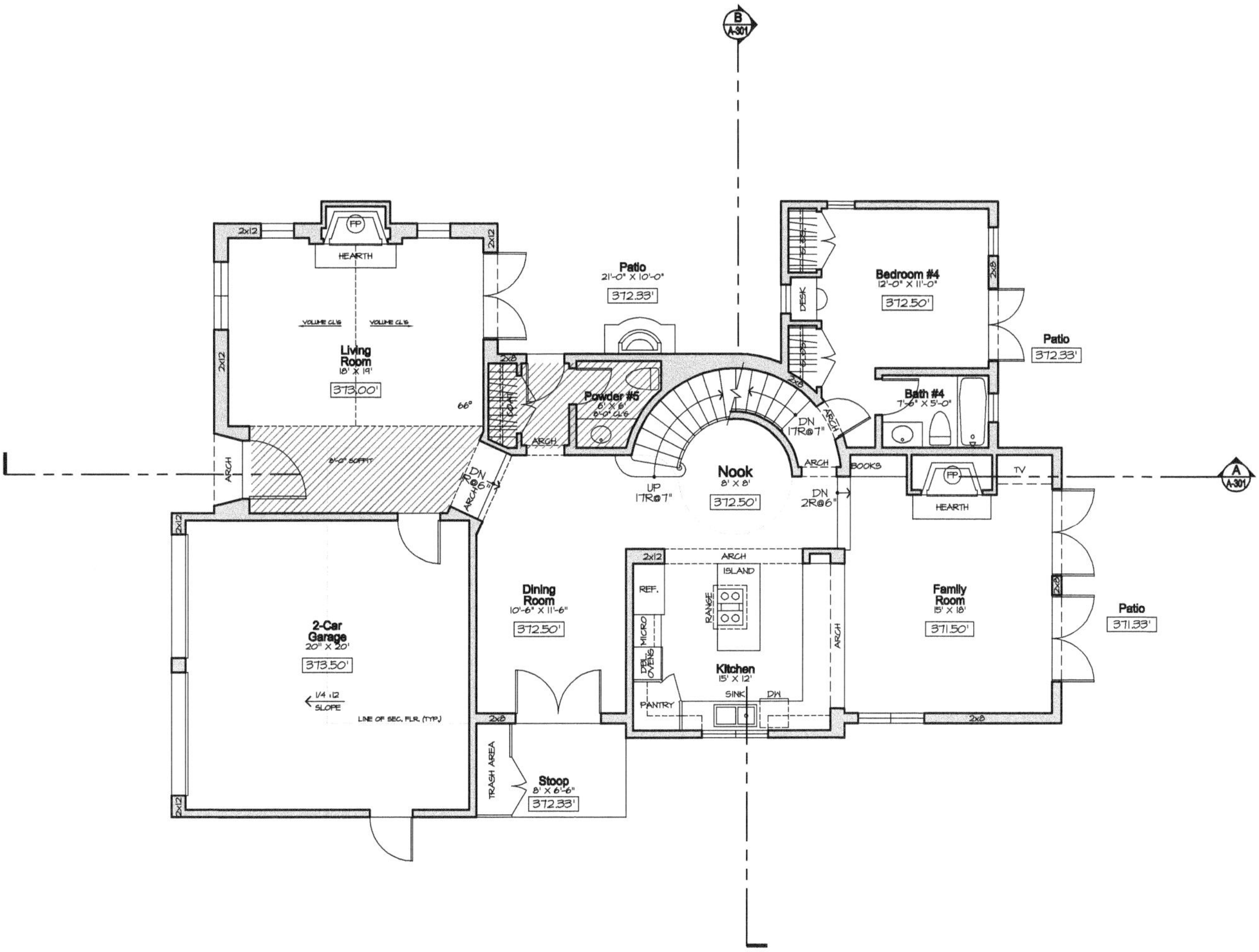

Figure 4.24 Pictorial and preliminary floor-plan layout.

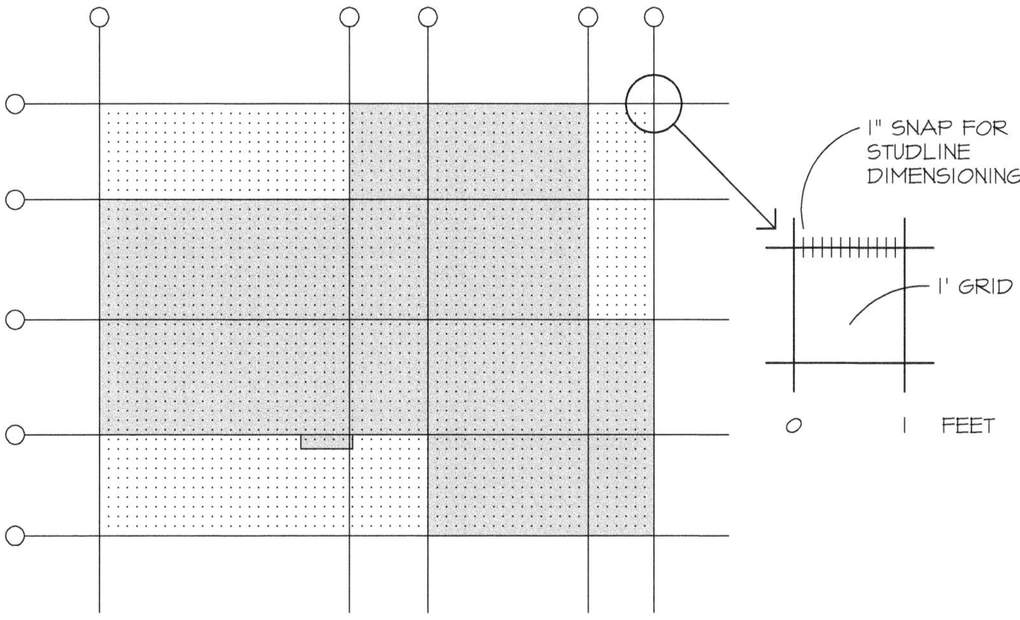

Figure 4.25 Stage I: Floor-plan datum layer.

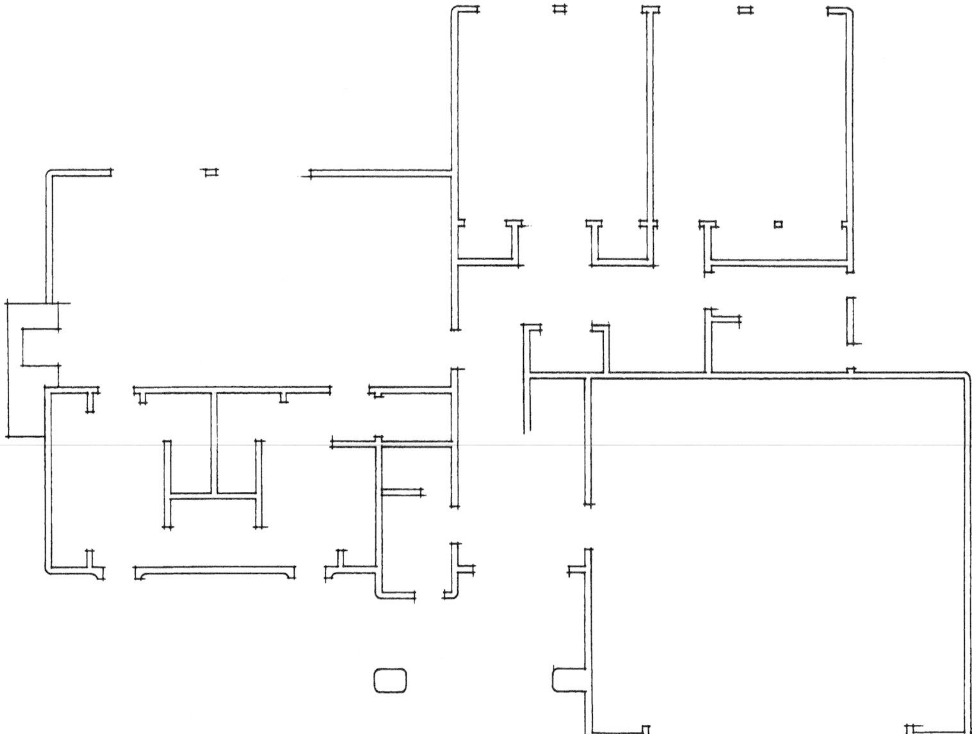

Figure 4.26 Stage II.

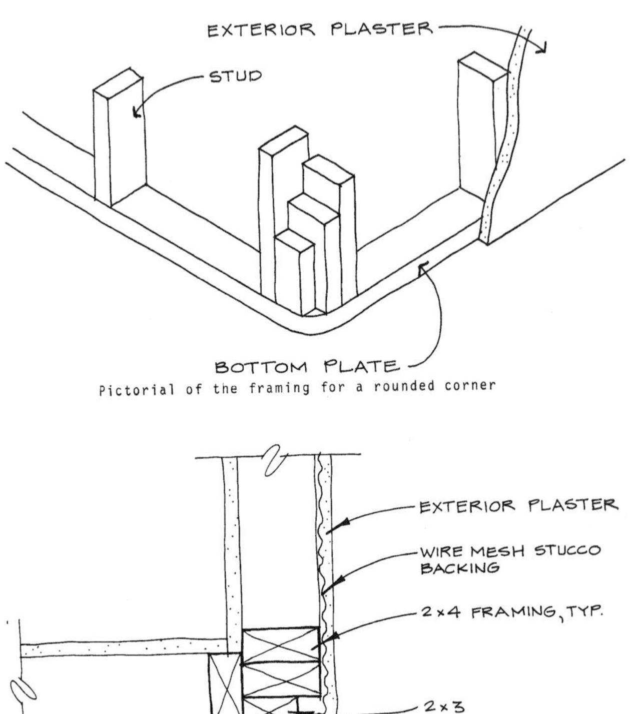

Figure 4.27 Framing at rounded corners.

constant than change. The importance of being able to alter a drawing easily then becomes paramount.

The stages are a guideline of how to create construction drawings. BIM does not follow a strict set of guidelines; it allows the drafter to provide data as the data are received and does not have to get input in a linear pattern. For instance, if it is determined that the exterior walls will be 2 × 6 studs and the interior walls are 2 × 4 studs, the wall type can be created without drawing a single line. This typically occurs in Stage 2 of CAD drawing. Also, with BIM, Stage 5 is automatically determined in the parametric referencing system built into the software and will aid in a more organized method of development.

Additional layers may have to be developed as needed. An example of this is the text titled "ANNO" (annotation). The text layer can be divided into a multiple number of layers. One layer may be used for room titles only, a second layer may be used for general construction notes, and all other incidental notes may be on a third. An architectural office may utilize a standard layering practice as proposed in the national standards, or it may develop its own office system method.

The final plot sheet of the first-floor plan of the Clay residence is shown in Figure 4.32. This sheet has

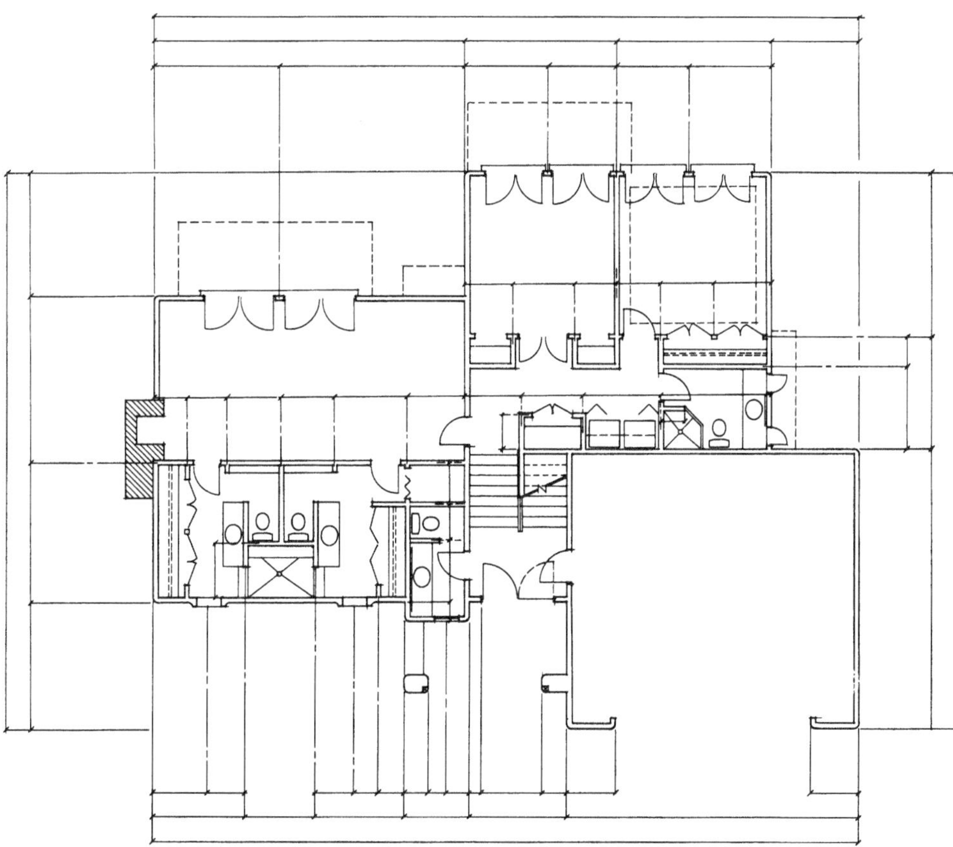

Figure 4.28 Stage III: Stairs and plumbing fixtures.

20 layers, but many of the layers have been combined, resulting in a set of drawings with 11 layers:

1. Plot sheet. Figure 4.32 includes the title block and the notes on separate sheets.
2. The floor plan is divided into the following layers:
   A. *Datum layer—Figure 4.33*. This layer shows the perimeter layout for a block module if the building is made of masonry. Space is plotted at the given module if a module is used (e.g., 50″module). If steel is used, the module at which the steel columns are set by the structural engineer appears (e.g., 10′-0″ o.c.). When the structure is to be framed in wood, the grid may be set at 1-foot increments and the snap at 1-inch increments for stud line dimensioning. Whatever the game plan is for the structure in question, the datum layer becomes the pattern by which all other drawings are established and on which they are based. This perimeter drawing can be used to estimate square footage or to estimate the perimeter of the form.

      Figure 4.34. All walls are drawn on this layer. It may be split further into two additional layers, one showing bearing walls only, and non-bearing walls on the other. If a wall is moved, one can see immediately whether it is a load-bearing wall that affects the structure or a non-bearing wall that does not affect the calculation or engineering of the structure.
   B. *Figure 4.35*. Plumbing fixtures, stairs, cabinets, and fireplaces are drawn on this floor layer. They can also be drawn on separate layers.
   C. *Figure 4.36*. All hidden lines are drawn on this layer. They may be outlines of cabinets, soffits, or ceiling level changes. Whatever the reason for using hidden lines, they are placed on this level, avoiding the need to change line types within a layer. This too can be divided into wall and floor layers.
   D. *Figure 4.37*. Because openings were positioned on a previous layer, the conventions used to identify doors, windows, and, in some instances, large cabinets are drawn at this point. As can be seen on this layer, the doors that lap are identified. It will also help later in the positioning of light switches to ensure that none are placed behind doors.
   E. *Figure 4.38*. This is the most critical of all of the layers in this set because it establishes the parameters and limitations for all the other drawings, elevations, sections, framing, and so forth. The numerical values must adhere to the

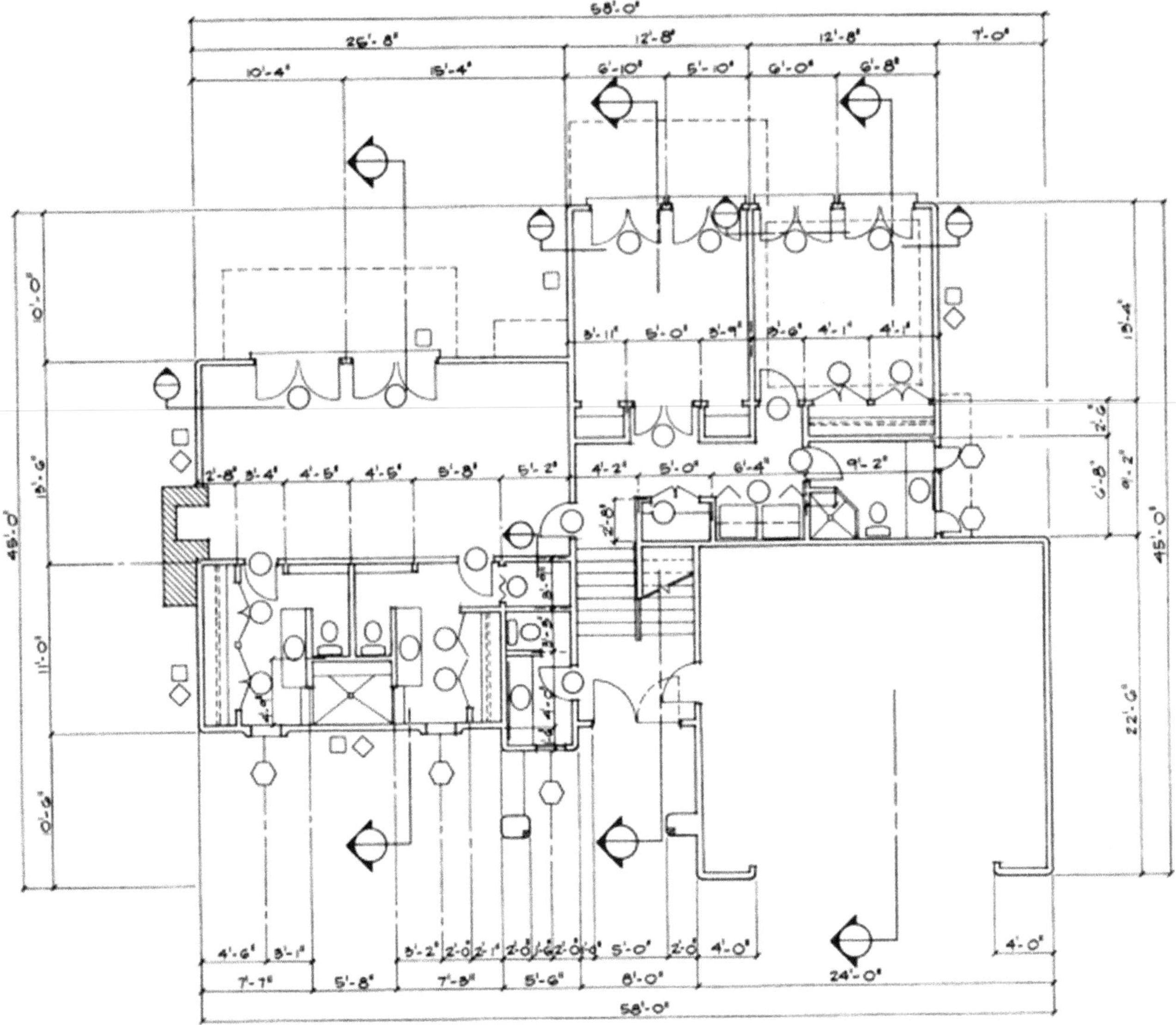

Figure 4.29 Stage IV: Dimensioning and material designation.

module being used. If the structure is a wood stud construction, the dimensions must be set to face of stud (outside walls) or center of stud (inside walls). They must be positioned so the workers in the field (carpenters in this instance) can immediately find them and use the measurements efficiently and accurately. Dimension everything. Do not force the carpenters to compute figures. Be sure the total equals the sum of its parts.

F. *Figure 4.39*. This is the lettering layer. In most instances, it is split into two layers, one for room titles and another for lettering. The name of the drawing, north arrow, scale, and any other office-standard titling identification can be placed on a third lettering layer.

G. *Figure 4.40*. Walls can be pochéd or hatched (darkened) on this layer. For the floor plan, all walls are shaded in the same intensity. On a framing plan, the bearing walls can be shaded dark and the non-bearing walls left unhatched. Patterns for furred ceilings, floor material, fireplace hearths, and any other patterns can be done on this layer or, again, as in previous layers, split into multiple layers if the patterns are complex.

H. *Figure 4.41*. This section and symbol layer is a critical communicative layer. It references one area of a drawing to a detail, schedule, or building section. You will notice reference bubbles for a variety of referrals. Each of these can be placed on a separate layer.

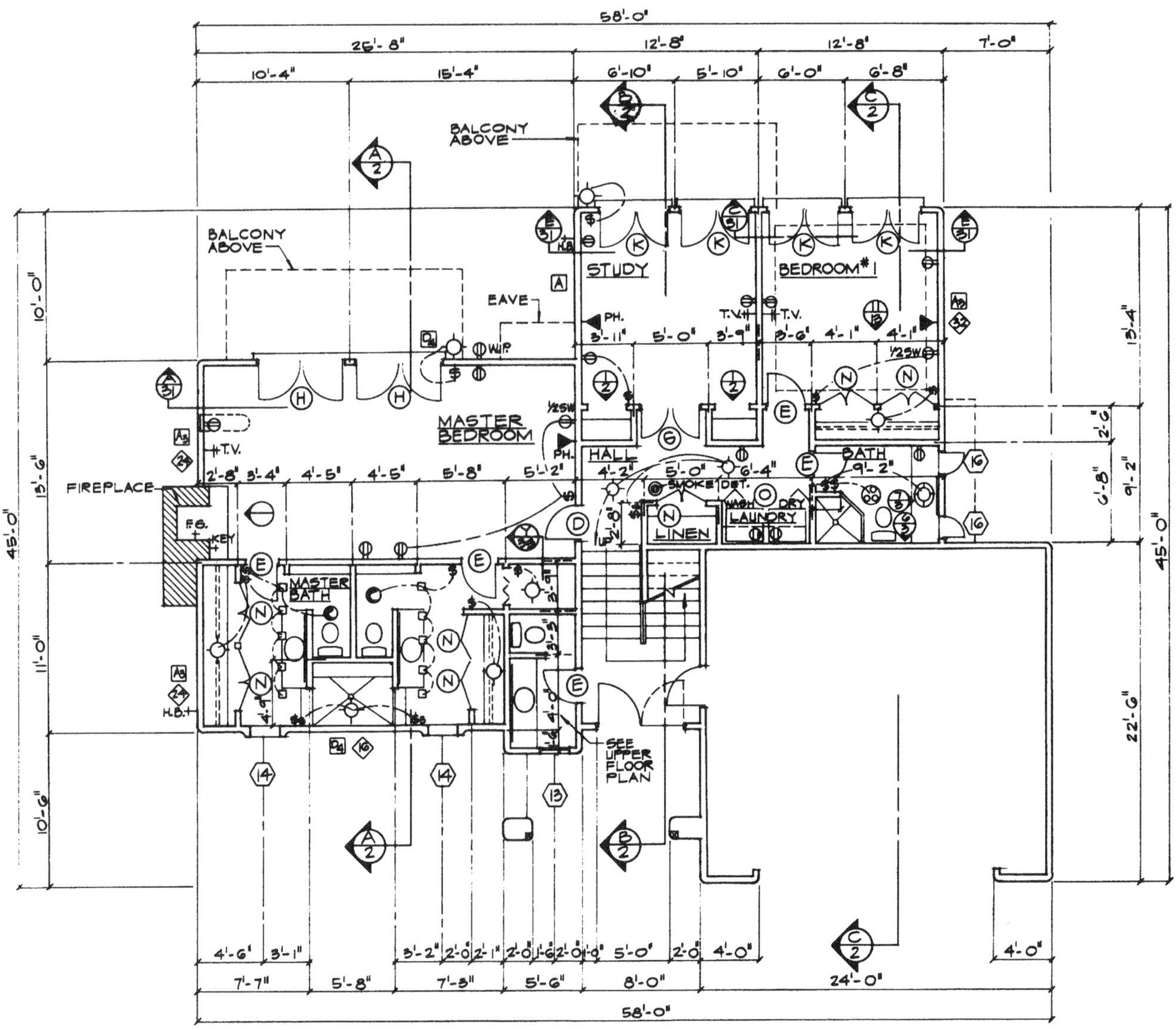

Figure 4.30 Stage V: Referencing.

I. Patios, barbeques, and other outside forms that do not affect the floor plan, yet set the proper context for the floor plan, can be placed on another layer. The outside forms on this floor plan were so minimal that an example is not shown.

J. *Figure 4.42.* XREF(ed) and positioned on all sheets is the standard office title block and notes (Figure 4.43).

K. As can be seen in Figure 4.32, a set of notes is positioned on the extreme right side. As with details, these may be pre-drawn or preformatted notes and should be placed on a layer by themselves.

L. Notice the revisions to the notes and in the revision portion of the title block on Figure 4.32. All revisions should be placed on a separate layer.

On the positive side,

1. Our consultants get the exact base sheet on which they can compute and draw the framing plans and structural details.
2. For an out-of-stage project, multiple copies can be at another location.
3. Corrections can be made instantly in the field and relayed to the home office.
4. There is no downtime for mail delivery, as was the case with hard copy.

On the negative side,

1. There is a potential for piracy of the drawings.
2. Building departments require wet-copy signatures for permits.

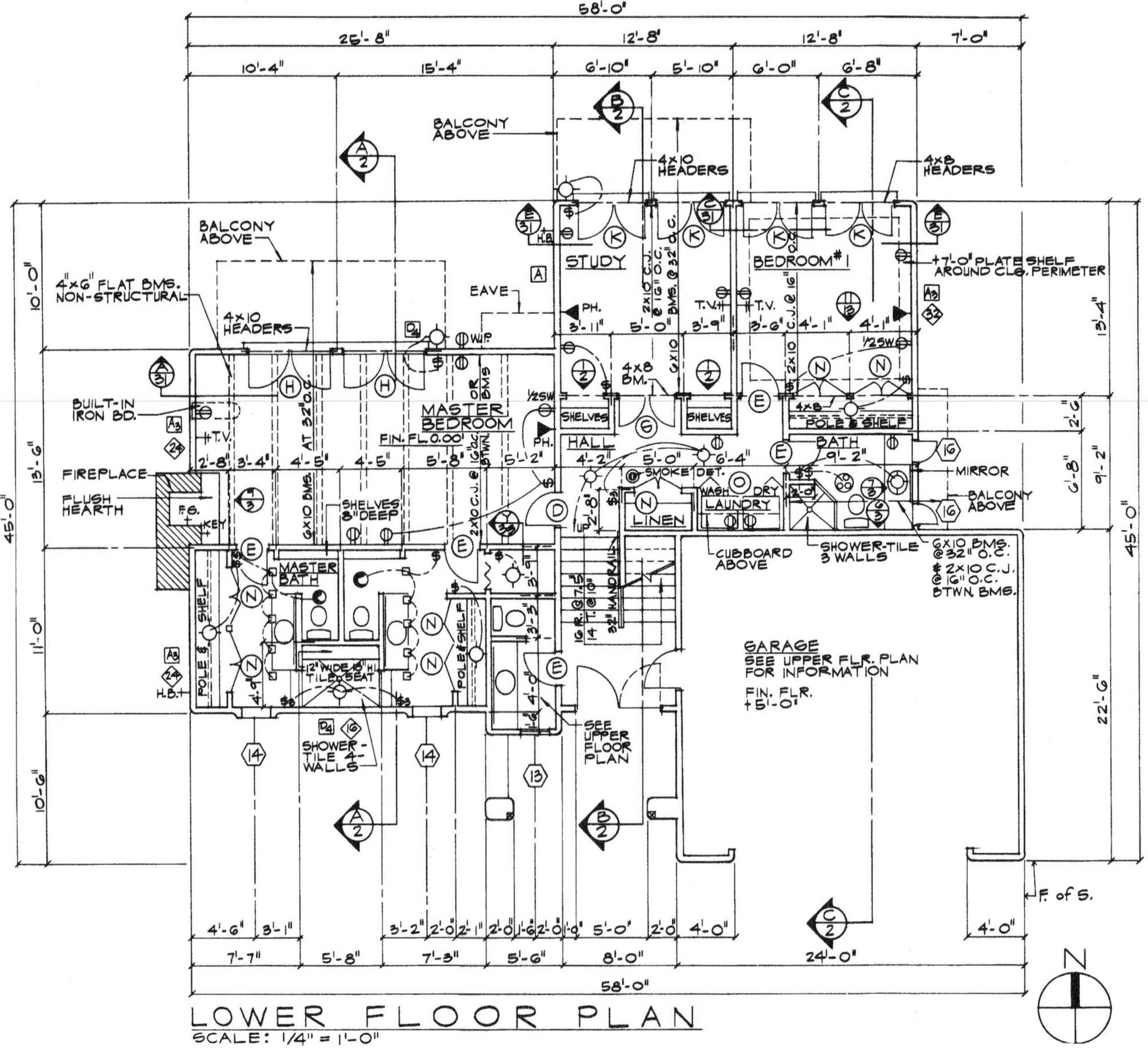

Figure 4.31 Stage VI: Final plot sheet of lower floor plan.

3. Viruses can destroy parts of an image, creating an incorrect set of drawings.
4. Someone can be working on a set of drawings that appears to be the original but is not.

■ ARCHITECT/CLIENT RELATIONSHIP

Working Relationship

The relationship between the architect and the client will vary. In general, the relationship for a specific building project and the responsibilities and procedures necessary to accomplish the goals of the project will be initiated with the selection of the architect. After the architect is selected, the architect and the client enter into a contract, which defines the services to be performed and the responsibilities of the architect and the client. The client can be an individual, couple, team, or board of individuals that give direction and goals for the development of the project. Many states require architects to use a written contract when providing professional services.

The form of the agreement will vary with the size and complexity of the project and the scope of services that the architect will provide. As you can imagine, the larger and more complex tasks require more dialogue or terms to address legal issues. A good contract can provide

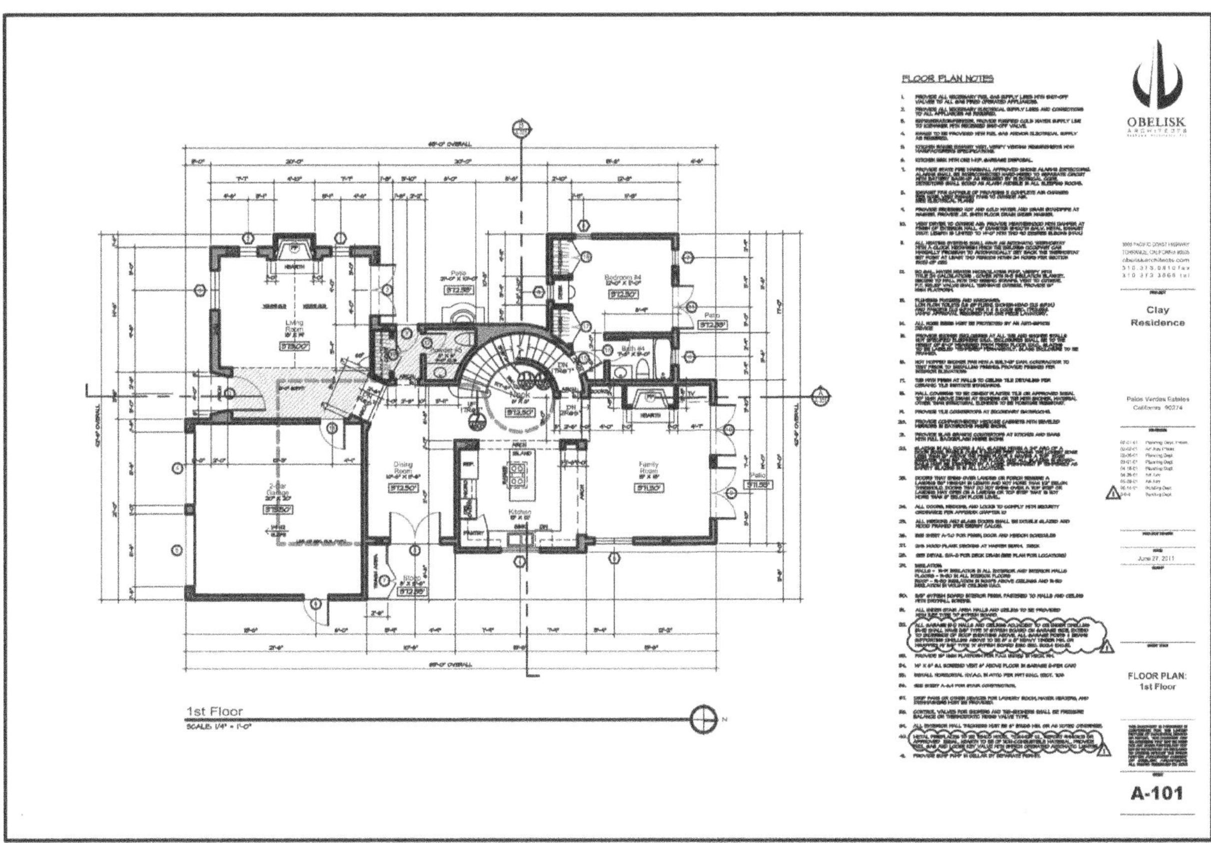

Figure 4.32 Plot sheet: First-floor plan.

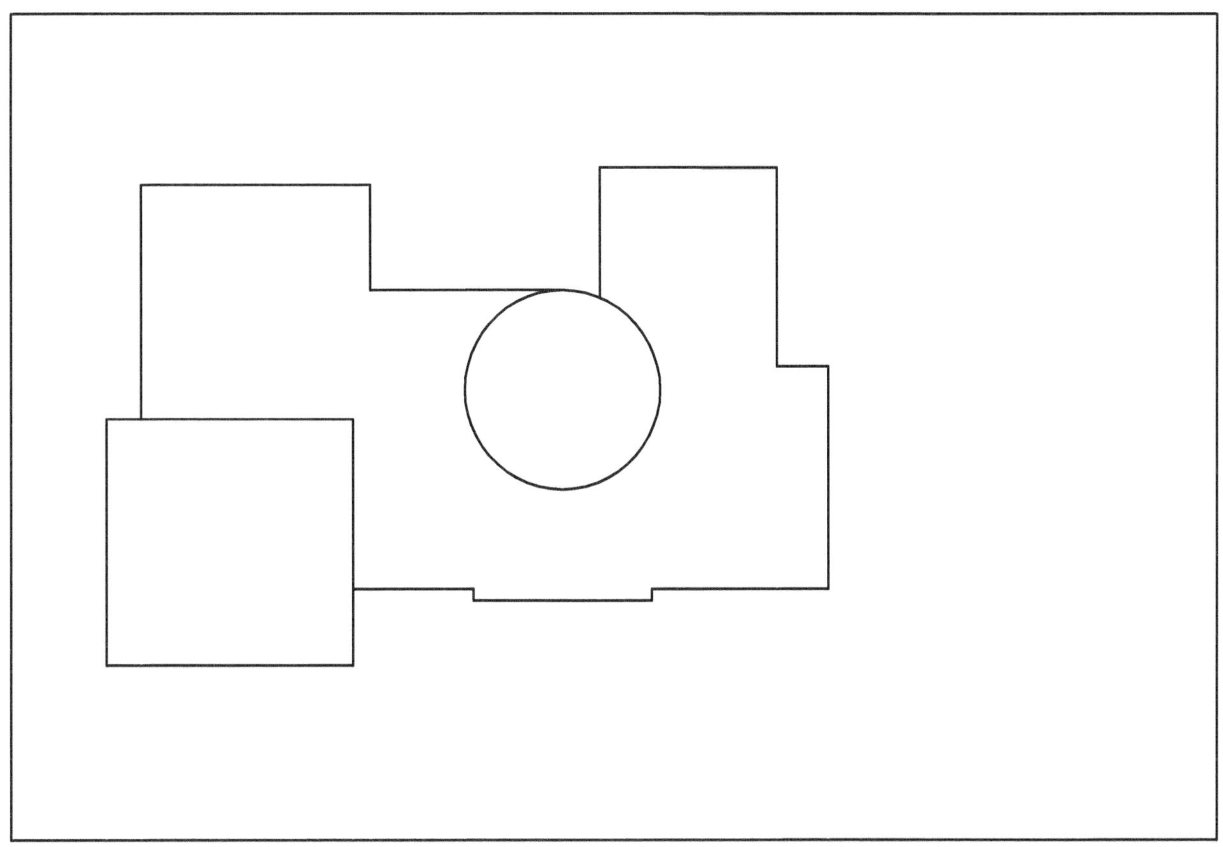

Figure 4.33 Master: Datum layer.

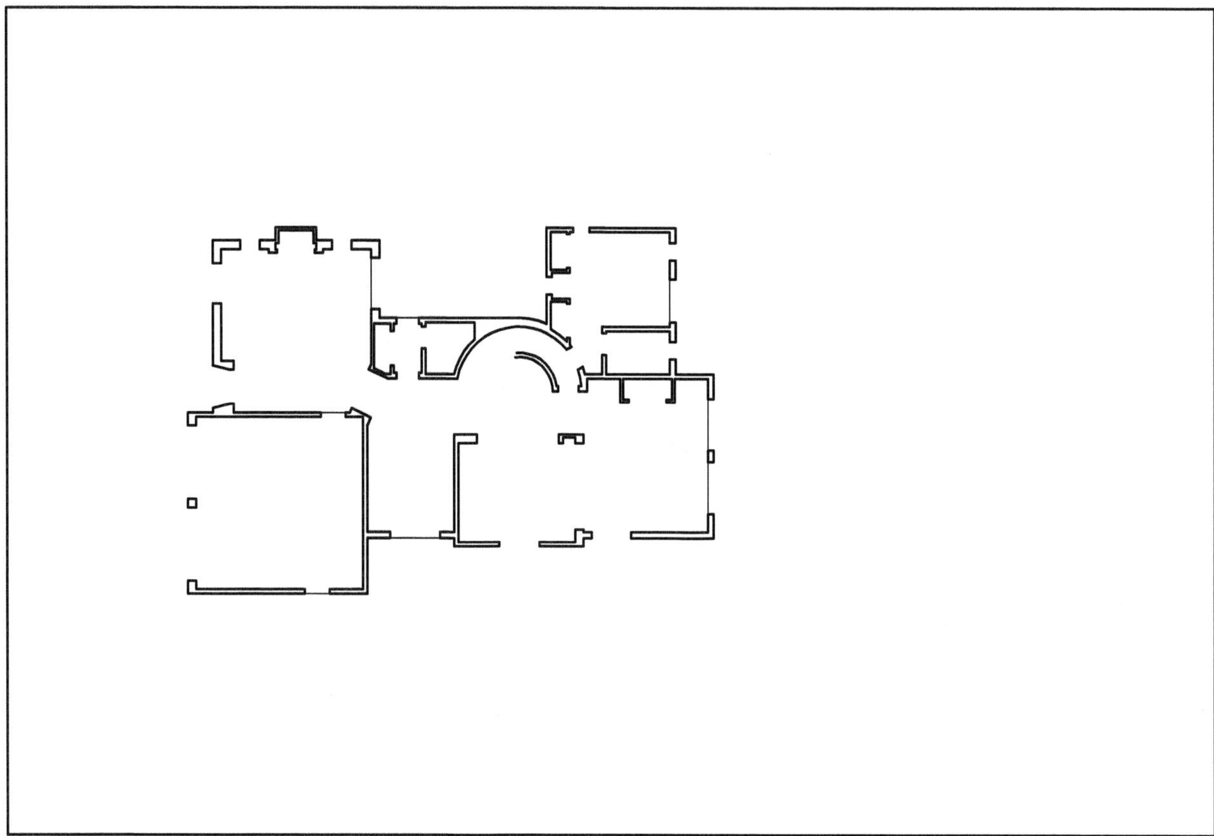

Figure 4.34 Master: Wall layer.

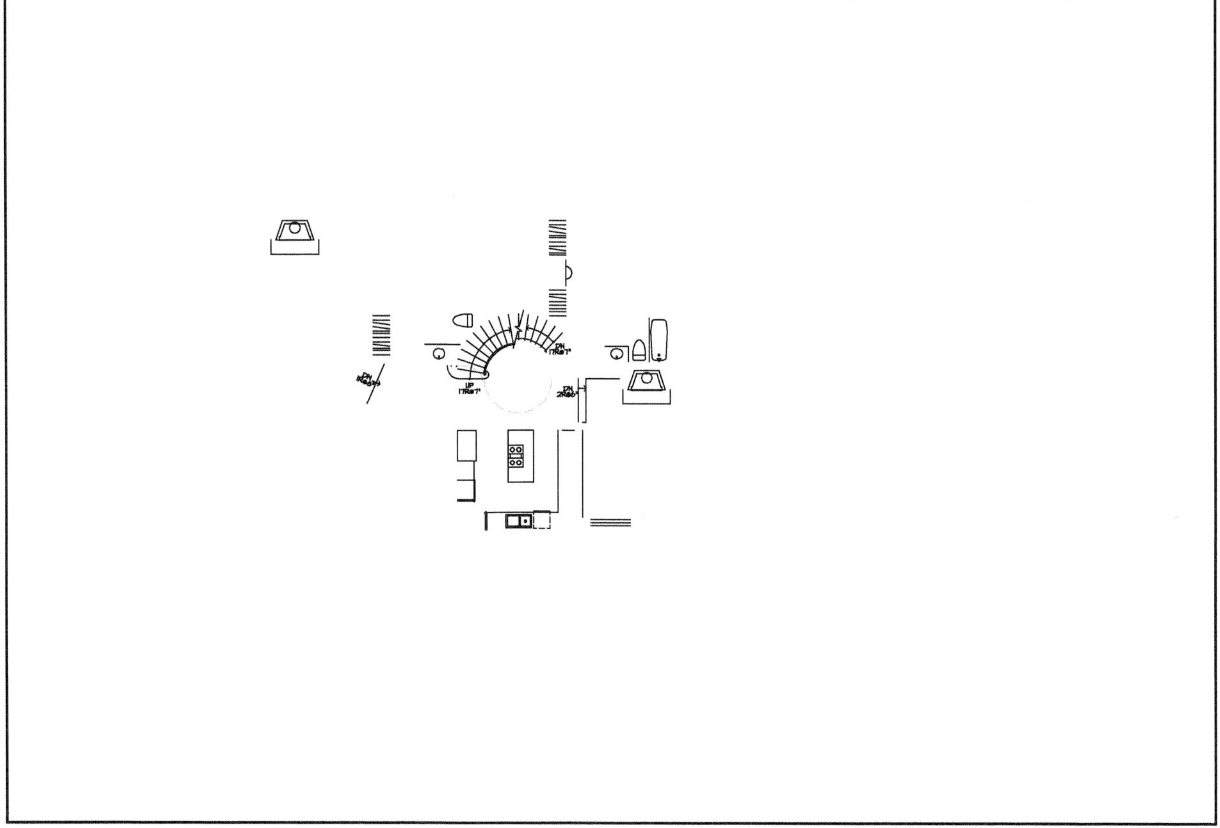

Figure 4.35 Master: Floor layer.

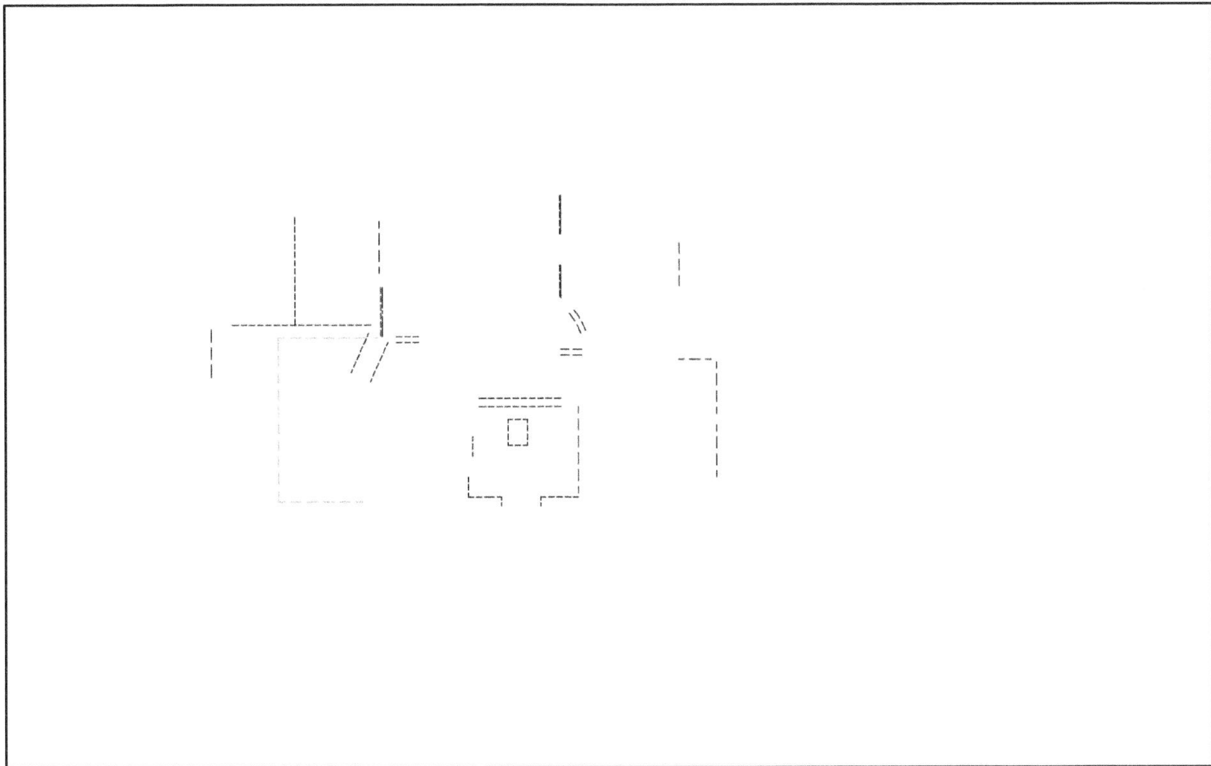

Figure 4.36 Master: Wall and floor hidden layer.

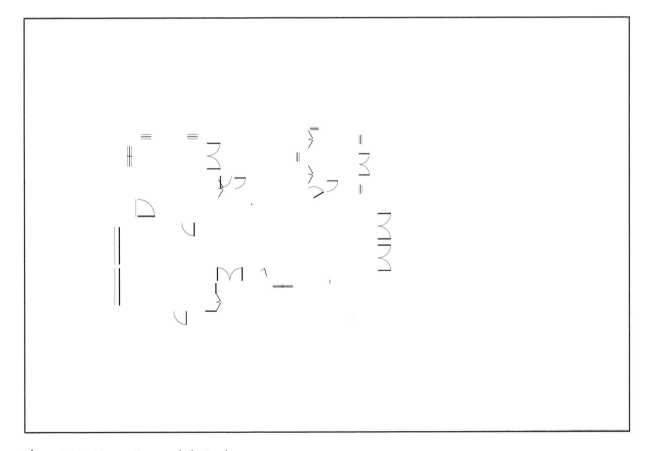

Figure 4.37 Master: Door and glazing layer.

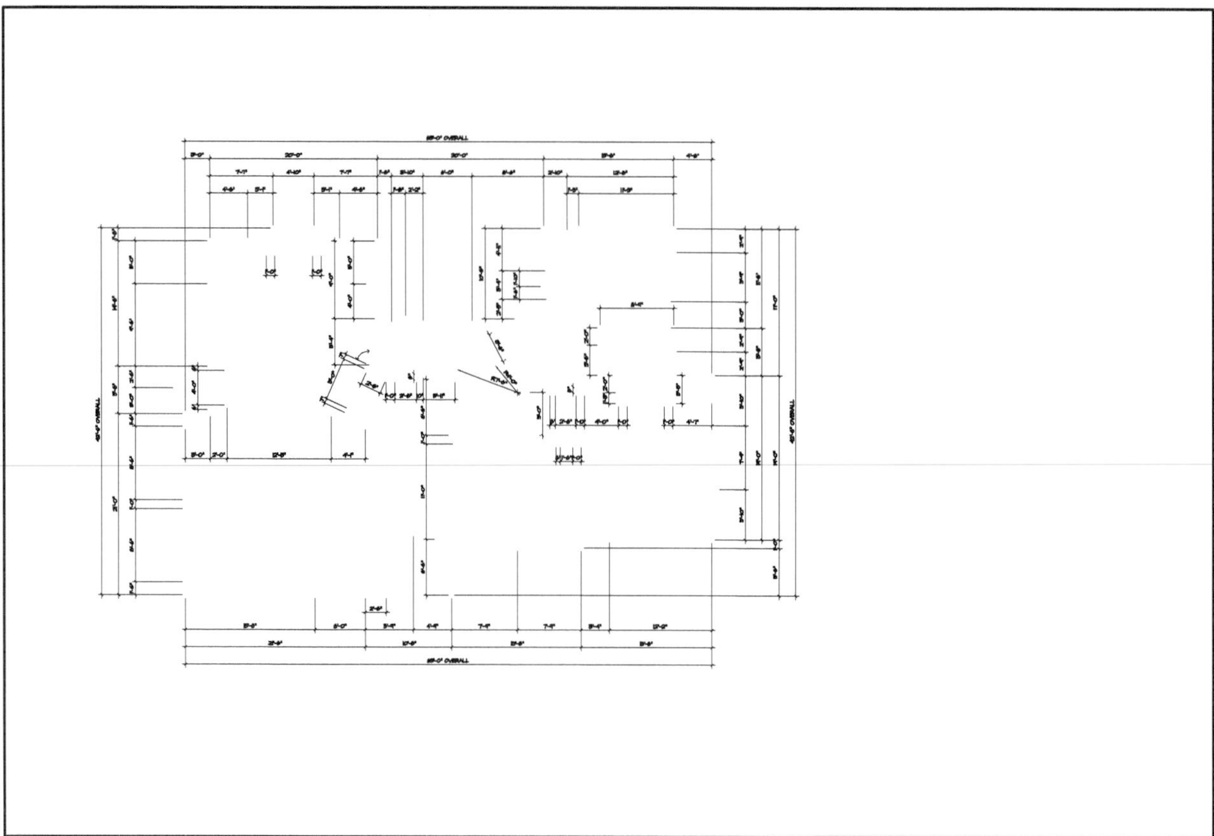

Figure 4.38 Master: Dimensions layer.

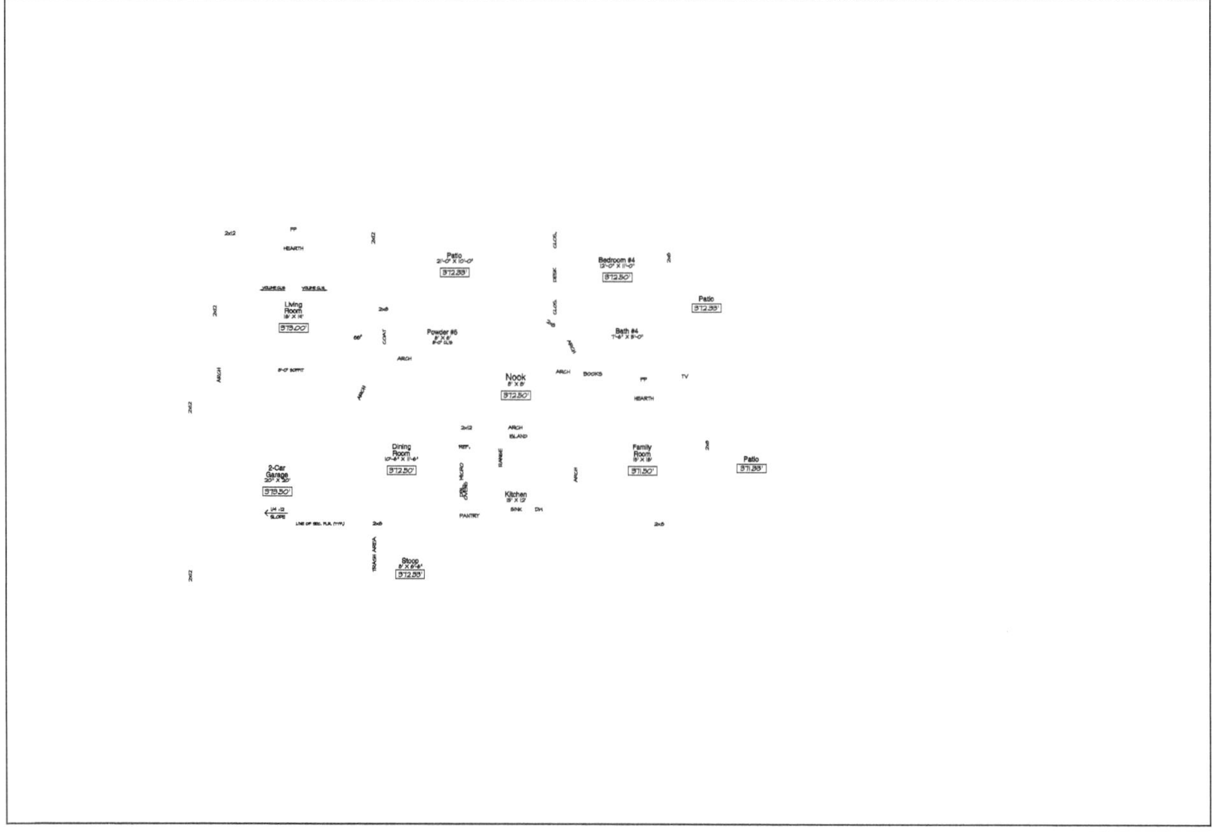

Figure 4.39 Master: Annotation layer.

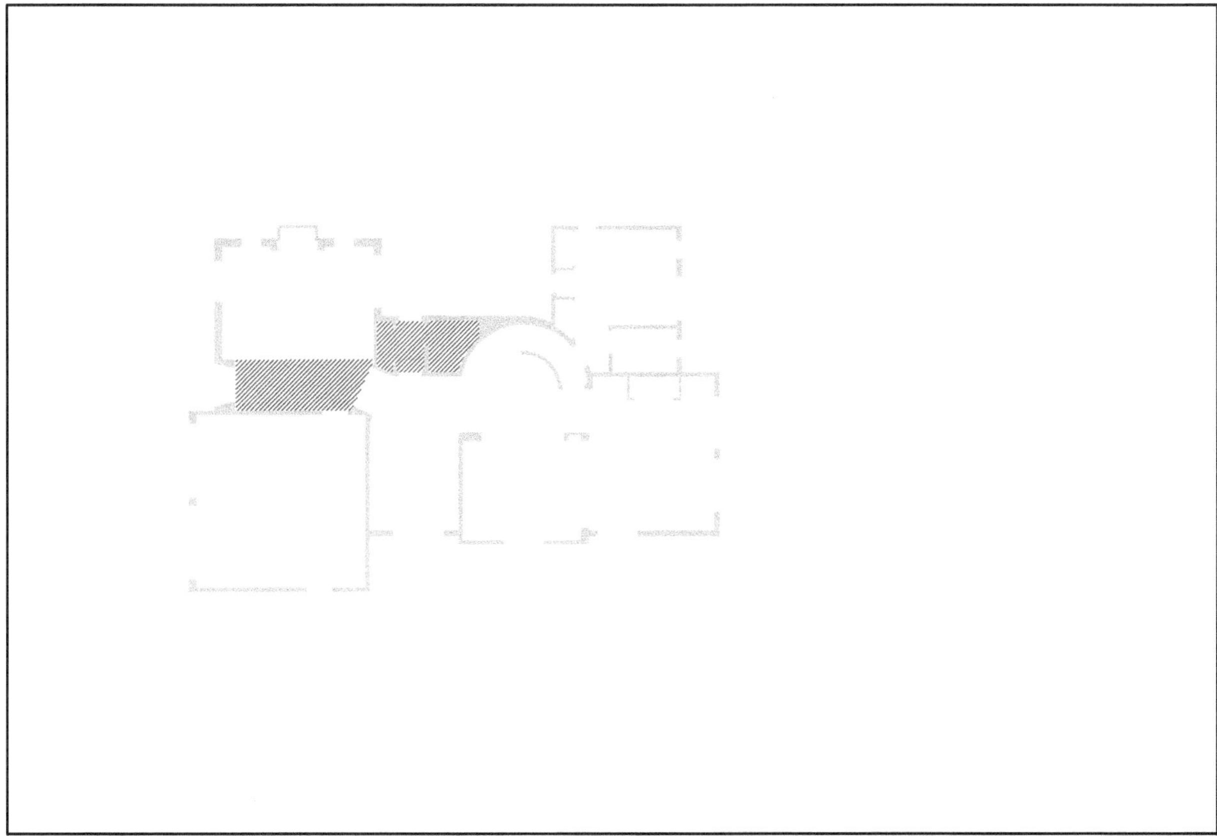

Figure 4.40 Master: Pattern and poché layer (hatch).

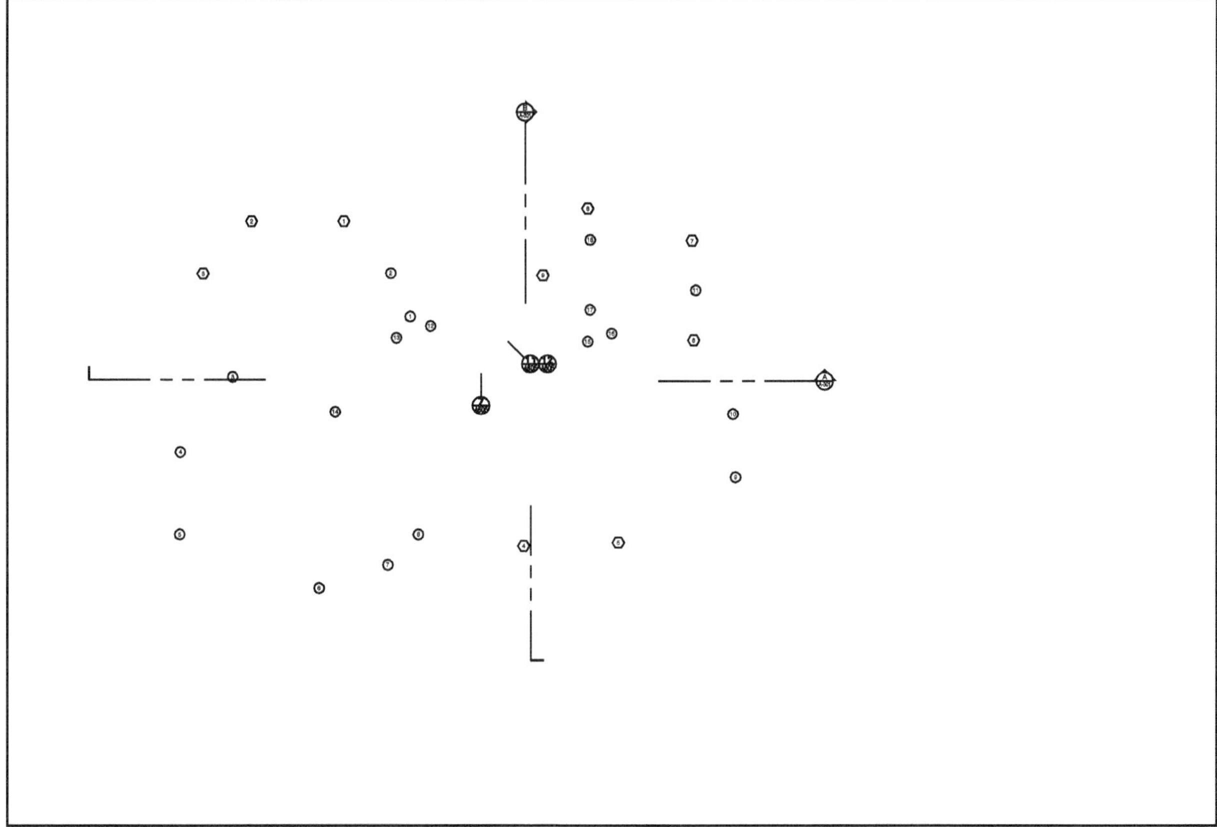

Figure 4.41 Master: Section and symbol layer.

Figure 4.42 XREF: Title block.

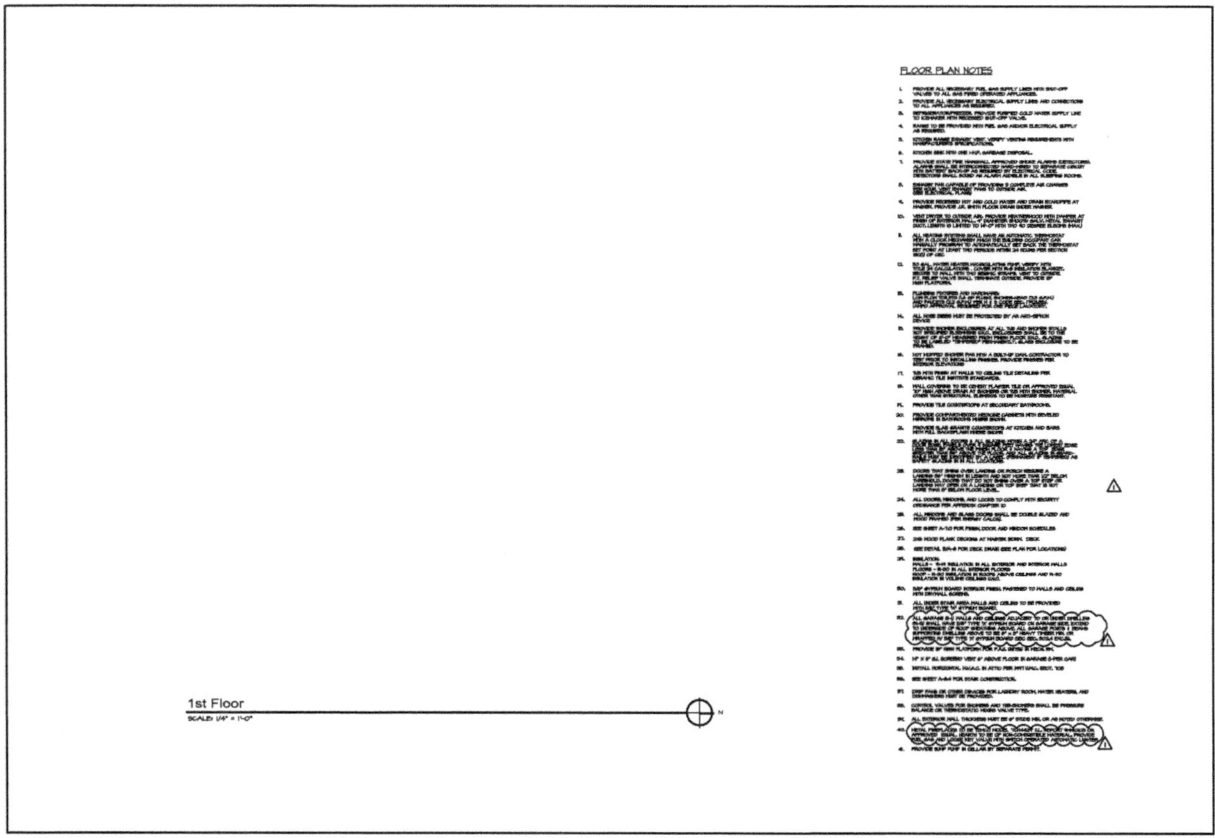

Figure 4.43 Plot sheet: Annotation.

clarity and remind all parties of the responsibilities that are shared to complete the goals that are required and define scope that is outside the contract that would be considered added scope for added costs.

After the contractual agreement is signed and a retainer fee is received, the architect reviews the building site and confers with the client to determine the goals of the building project. After establishing the project goals, there will be meetings with the governing agencies, such as the planning department, building department, and architectural committees. The primary goal of the architectural team at this point is to initiate the preliminary planning and design phases called schematic design.

Most architectural contracts and agreements include provisions for the architect and the consulting engineers to observe construction of the project during the various building stages. It is a standard practice for the architects to visit the site, determine if the construction is progressing correctly, and report their findings called construction administration.

Key Terms

block out
delivery
drafting room manual
draftsperson
keynotes
layout
office Standards
procedures
project book
sheet layout
standards

PART

Document Evolution

The information contained in Chapters 5–12 is meant to convey an in-depth study of the process of architectural working drawings. This area of the text elaborates on the three of the five main phases of the architect's scope of services and expanding in the knowledge base in order to produce a better set of construction documents. Understanding the scope and the deliverables at each stage will aid in meeting the project's, client's, and contractor's expectations and achieve the project goals as the final step for the working drawing that establish the contract set of drawings. A focus on the completeness of the drawings and notations in the deliverable drawings will aid to this end.

chapter

5

SITE ANALYSIS AND SITE DOCUMENTS

The Professional Practice of Architectural Working Drawings, Sixth Edition. Nagy R. Bakhoum and Osamu A. Wakita.
© 2024 John Wiley & Sons Inc. Published 2024 by John Wiley & Sons Inc.
Companion website: www.wiley.com\go\bakhoum\theprofessionalpracticeofarchitecturalworkingdrawings

INTRODUCTION

Site analysis is among the most important aspects of the preliminary design process. It is the evaluation of an existing or potential site to determine the fulfillment of the client's program. A properly selected site can significantly impact the success of a project. Proper analysis of a site can also take full advantage of the potential it offers.

Site plans locate a building on a specific site in a specific location both vertically in space and laterally. A grading plan assists the architect in the movement of earth in order to accommodate this task. In an ideal situation, the building can be accommodated without significant earth movement, specifically import and export of soil.

The overall goal for the architect is to generate a logical and sensitive development of the land. When the architect is engaged early in the process, they can help the client with the specific selection process. Architects, landscape architects, planners, and others often aid in the process of site selection and analysis and provide this specific service for the client.

Sites are a component of a project that directly affects the cost of a project and construction cost. The specific site may also affect the long list of factors that can help or hurt a specific program. We will outline specific examples in this chapter.

SITE ANALYSIS DEFINED

The purpose of a **site analysis** is to determine the best use of the site and find a layout that capitalizes on site attributes to optimize the fulfillment of the client's needs while respecting the inherent site conditions. A site analysis is a specific study of the project site and how it supports the program.

Important components of research in site analysis include, but are not limited to, determining the following:

- Boundaries
- Topography
- Drainage
- Traffic (vehicular, pedestrian, transportation)
- Setbacks
- Climate (rain, sun, snow, wind)
- Lot shape (orientation)
- Site utilities (electric, gas, telephone, TV, water, sewer, the Internet)
- Zoning (easements, covenants)
- Vicinity
- Neighborhood character (positive and negative elements)
- Past, present, and future conditions

Community and Neighborhood Research

The location within a country, county, state, province, and city is a factor in understanding a site. A large view of the site situated in its larger surroundings will aid in developing the site. In addition to the physical aspects of the site, become familiar with the activities that occur in the neighboring area, both positive and negative. These features range from a monthly festival or an annual parade to graffiti incidence and crime patterns.

Understand the site within the context of the neighborhood. This may require a two- to three-block study, in a refinement of the larger-scale study described earlier. For a larger building, this research might expand to five or six blocks around the site.

Sensory Research

Document and observe significant views to and from the site, both positive and negative. Understand the impact of building and window placement in relation to those views. Often, noise, such as from vehicles, trucks, trains, buses, or airplanes, can affect site conditions. Even smells should be taken into account: it takes only one design of a building downwind from a dairy farm or paper mill for the designer to learn never to overlook the "scentscape" of a site again!

Site-Specific Research

Each site is identified by a legal description. Some legal descriptions are written according to metes and bounds, but most sites in more developed areas are identified according to plats, subdivision maps, and area maps. Although the format will vary from one municipality to the next, a legal description will typically read something like: Lot **6**, Block **27**, Tract **4289**, as recorded in the Richmond County Map Page 5–69. Once you have this information, you can determine more specific information about the site, such as setbacks, zoning requirements and limitations, development covenants, building area, redevelopment district requirements, and required dedications and easements.

Site-specific climate research must include factors such as temperature range, rainfall and snowfall, humidity, prevailing winds, and sun direction, as well as regional concerns such as earthquakes, hurricanes, and tornadoes. All of these factors will affect the approach to site design and layout, although some will be more important than others in any given situation. See Figure 5.1.

Setbacks are predetermined restrictions that aid in determining the limits on a building footprint. For example, a site may require that the structure not encroach upon a strip of land 20′ in front, 5′ from each side, and 15′ in the rear; these are the required setback dimensions where building is not allowed. A height limitation will determine the maximum allowable height of a structure. In most cases, there are also limits on the maximum allowable area or square footage of a building.

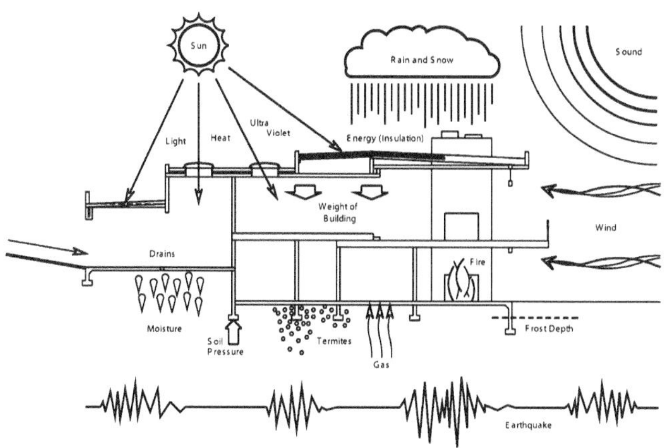

Figure 5.1 Climate impacts.

A **building footprint** is the total area of a building that covers the parcel. This footprint can be imagined as the dry outline that a rainfall will not touch as a result of the shape of the building on a parcel. Often a **floor area ratio** (FAR), or the gross area footage, is established so that the site cannot be completely covered from setback to setback. For example, a 1.5 FAR would limit an architect to a building area that is 1.5 times the total lot area.

Zoning—a municipal system of controlling what activities and structures are permitted on a piece of property—is determined by a governmental agency that has a primary purpose of public protection, implemented by rules harmonizing allowable land uses with owners' desires and the highest and best use of a site. This is what keeps high-rise office buildings and industrial production facilities from being built on a block of two-story residences. **Dedications** are portions of a site identified by the governing agency as a required contribution of land for an express public purpose. Most common is a dedication for a new road or a road expansion, which can vary in scale from a couple of feet to a strip 10 or 20 feet wide. Another example is a required greenbelt area. Often, site owners are not compensated for a dedication; it is considered a cost of development. A site may also be subject to *easements*, which are portions of the property that others have the right or permission to use in some way even though the owner retains title to the land; most common are utility right-of-way easements or access easements where driveways are shared.

Many city and county agencies have established **redevelopment districts** within their jurisdictions. Land use in redevelopment districts must, for various reasons, follow a different set of use and building guidelines to achieve an overarching, specific public goal. In many cases, these guidelines are more stringent than zoning requirements for other areas, but in some cases, they may be less restrictive. Consider an old main street; the guidelines could outline new buildings must match in scale and character.

Utility Research

In some areas, such as Manhattan, determining the availability of electricity, gas, sewer, water, telephone, internet, and cable television may be as simple as visiting a public works or engineering counter. In other areas, such as Wyoming, finding this information may be much more involved, and one may have limited utility options. In large cities, most utilities are immediately available, and typically are routed underground in the street or under sidewalks. In the Wyoming countryside, each site owner may have to have a well drilled to access fresh water and bear the cost of bringing in the lines for electrical and telephone service; natural gas, sewer, and cable TV may not even be options. Obviously, these considerations weigh heavily on the possible uses of the site and the type of structure. To fully understand the utilities of a specific site, one must also determine the depth, pipe diameter, pipe material, and pressure available. See Figure 5.2.

Circulation Research

Understanding how people will approach or access a site will affect your design for the site. Are there bus and train stops or metro stations near the site? Do service

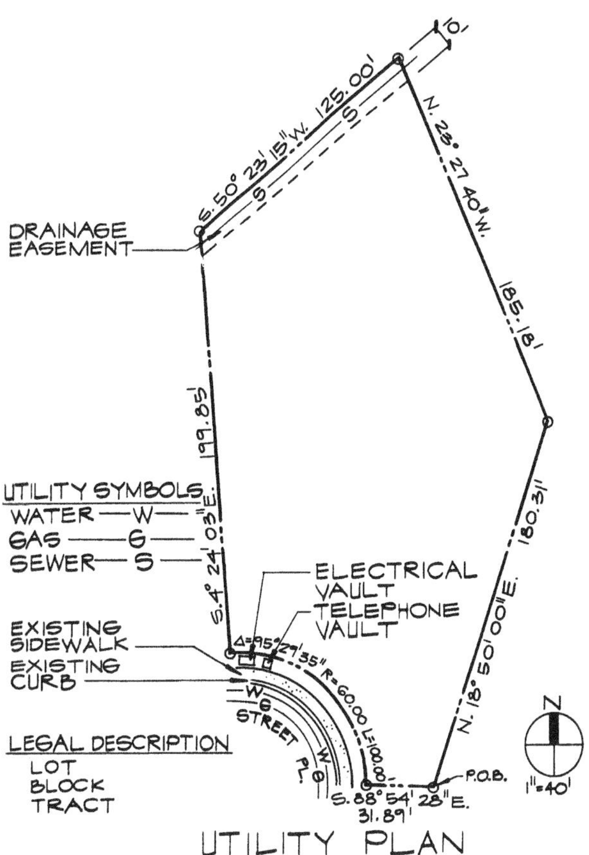

Figure 5.2 Utilities.

trucks or fire trucks figure prominently in the traffic pattern study? Perhaps there is an elementary school nearby, or vehicles can make a right turn only. Consider future development as well: Is there an electric trolley stop planned near the site or a future police or fire station adjacent to the site?

Features

Significant natural features often include the views, but natural elements such as a winter spring or creek, a rock outcropping, or a vertical bluff can strongly influence the layout of a site. See Figure 5.3.

The three natural elements that perhaps will most affect a site plan are the **existing contours**, or the slope of the site; the **soil type** (if it is sandy or expansive) and **bearing capacity** (how the soil supports the structure of the building); and the **geology**, the nature of the earth's structure beneath the soil elements. Geological concerns also include things like archeological/prehistoric sites that might affect the future building foundation or even location.

In some regions, native and preexisting trees are protected, whether by law or by covenant. In many cities in California, for example, the California live oak, walnut, and others are in this category and may not be removed or damaged and are typically protected in place.

Man-made features that are on a site or adjacent to the site should be documented as well. Elements such as existing structures, buildings, walls, curbs, gutters, sidewalks, power poles, light poles, and fire hydrants are often difficult to move or relocate. Even if they can be moved, it is usually very expensive to do so; alternatives should be explored before deciding to relocate an existing feature.

On occasion, man-made features will limit access to a site. (Perhaps there is a center divide on a street, with no left turn lane or median cut to allow vehicles into your site.) Document and record all of these features, as they will further shape the site plan layout.

Figure 5.3 Natural features. (Library of Congress, Prints & Photographs Division, Reproduction number LC-DIG-highsm-25344 (original digital file).)

SITE ANALYSIS APPLIED

Implementing Site Analysis

Accumulation of research on a specific site will allow the architect to establish a series of important supporting documents, some of which will require the consultation of a civil engineer. Many drawings may be needed to further develop the analysis of the site, including the following:

- Vicinity plan
- Location plan
- Plat map
- Topographic map
- Site plan/plot plan
- Grading plan
- Drainage plan
- Erosion control plan—storm water system mitigation plan (SWSMP)
- Utility plan
- Circulation plan
- Landscape/irrigation plan
- Sound study
- Traffic study
- Phasing plan

Not all of these drawings are created for every job, but the more complex jobs may require all of them.

Vicinity Map

A **vicinity map** provides an overall view of the region around the specific site to better introduce the surrounding neighborhood or district. Often, this map will be provided on the cover sheet of a set of working drawings. See Figure 5.4.

Location Plan

A **location plan** helps the viewer see the proposed project in relation to the specific area where the work is to be accomplished. This is particularly important on large-scale projects such as campuses or warehouse facilities. See Figure 5.5.

Plat Map

The site plan is developed in stages, each dealing with new technical information and design solutions. The first step in site plan development is the **plat map**. This map,

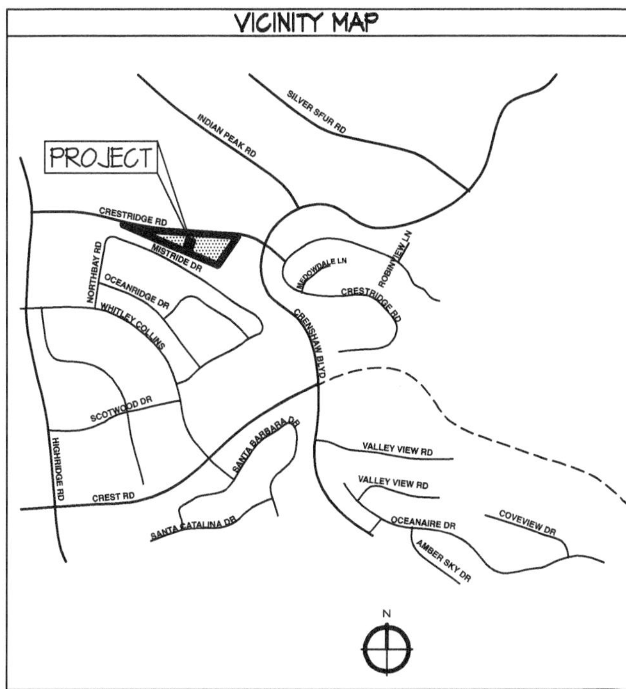

Figure 5.4 Vicinity map.

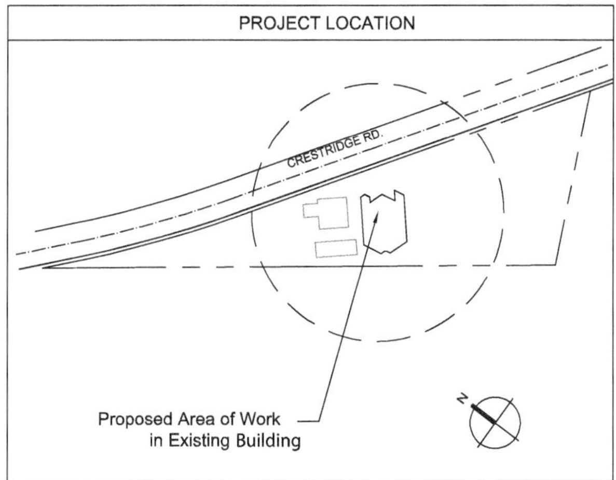

Figure 5.5 Location plan (map).

normally furnished by a civil engineer, is a land plan that delineates the property lines with their bearings, dimensions, streets, and existing easements. The information from the plat map forms the basis of all future site development. The property line bearings are described by degrees, minutes, and seconds; the property line dimensions are noted in feet and decimals. These are termed the **metes and bounds**. See Figure 5.6.

Even when the architect is furnished with only a written description of the metes and bounds of the plat map, a plat map can still be derived from this information.

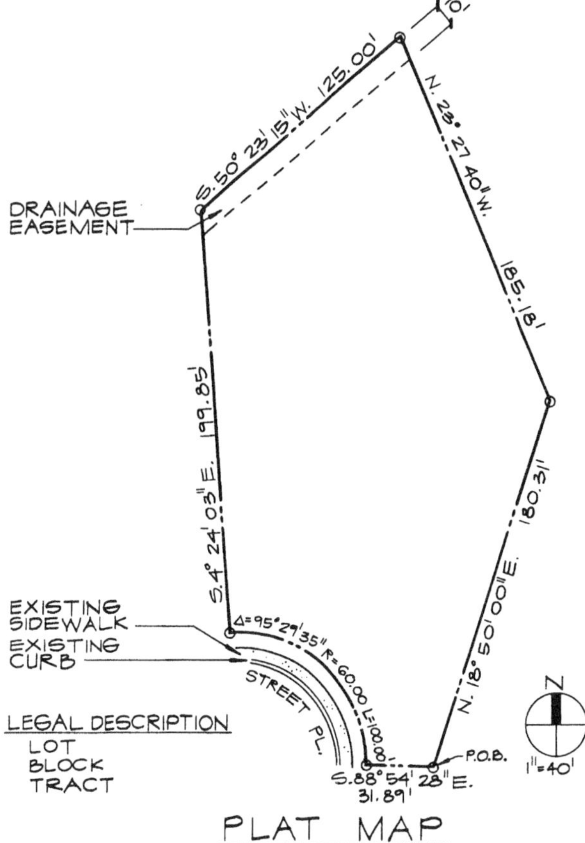

Figure 5.6 Plat map.

Lot lines are laid out by polar **coordinates**; that is, each line is described by its length plus the angle relative to true north or south. This is accomplished by the use of compass direction, degrees, minutes, and seconds. A **lot line** may read N 6° 49′ 29″ W (this describes the lot line as running north 6 degrees 49 minutes, 29 seconds westerly). See Figure 5.7. In some US counties, a boundary description can be retrieved via the Internet from the county in which the plat is located.

Figure 5.8A shows a plat map with the given lot lines, **bearings**, and dimensions. To lay out this map graphically, start at the point labeled **point of beginning** (POB). From the POB, you can delineate the lot line in the northeast quadrant with the given dimension. See Figure 5.8B. The next bearing falls in the northwest quadrant, which is illustrated by superimposing a compass at the lot line intersection. See Figure 5.8C. You can delineate the remaining lot lines with their bearings and dimensions in the same way, eventually closing at the POB. See Figures 5.8D–5.8F. For a plat map layout, accuracy is critical; thus, it is preferable to accomplish this task on a computer.

With the completion of the plat map layout, a specific plot of ground has been established. The boundary of a

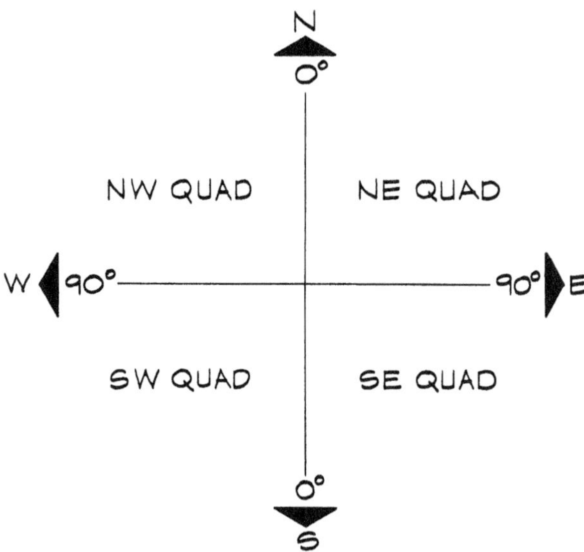

Figure 5.7 Compass quadrants.

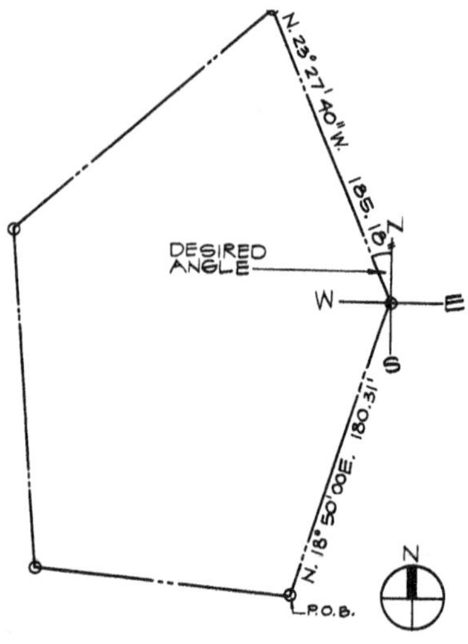

Figure 5.8C Point of beginning and second angle.

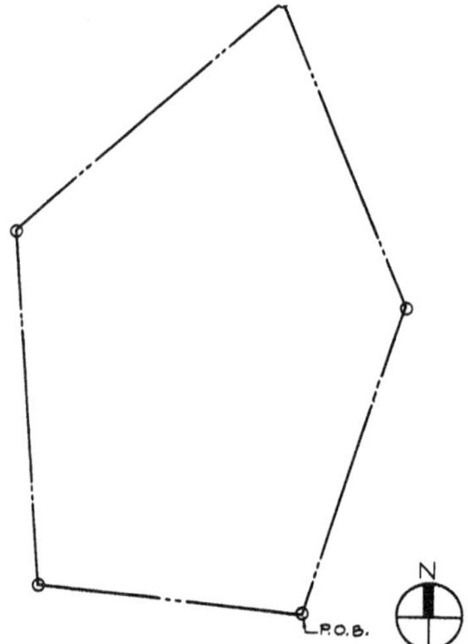

Figure 5.8A Point of beginning.

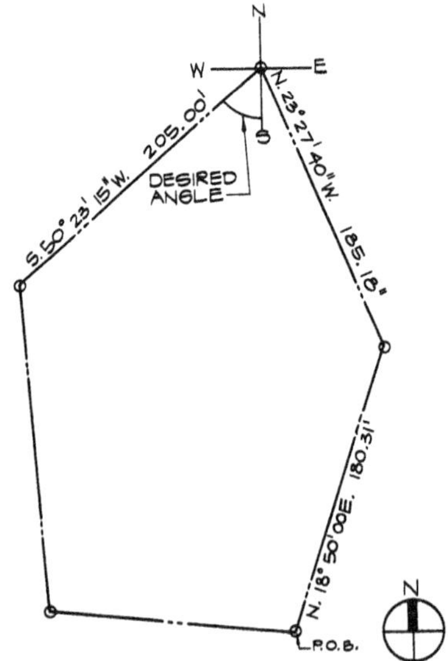

Figure 5.8D Point of beginning and third angle.

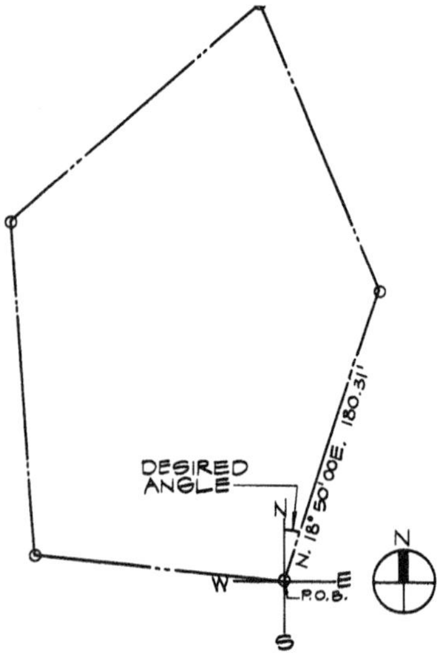

Figure 5.8B Point of beginning and first angle.

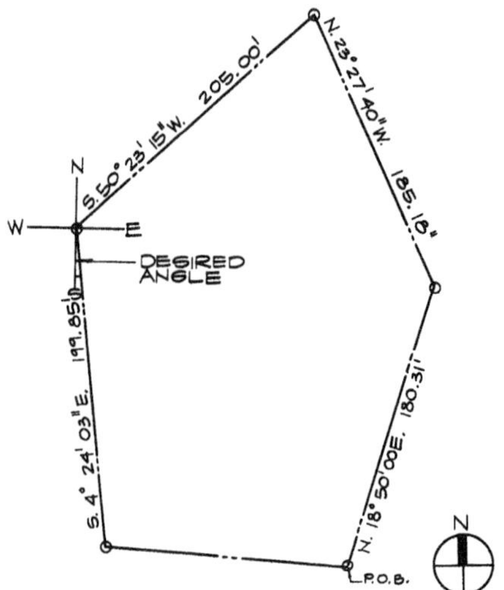

Figure 5.8E Point of beginning and fourth angle.

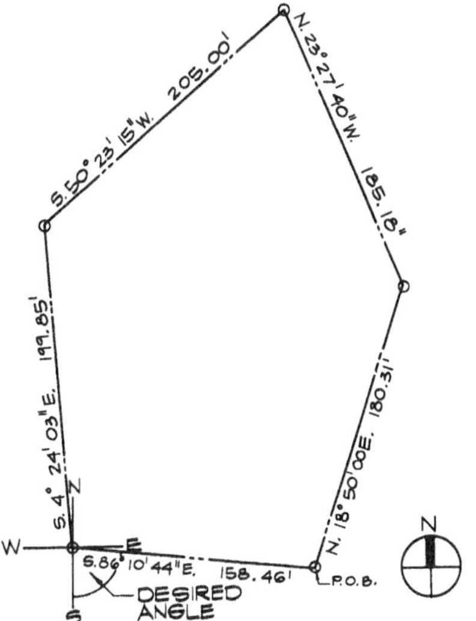

Figure 5.8F Point of beginning and fifth angle.

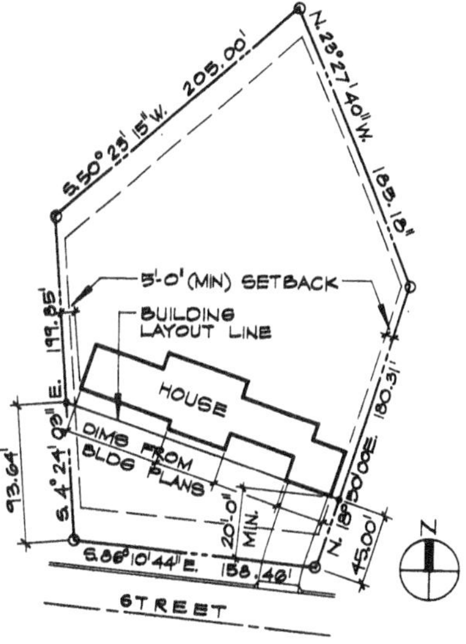

Figure 5.8H Site plan with building location.

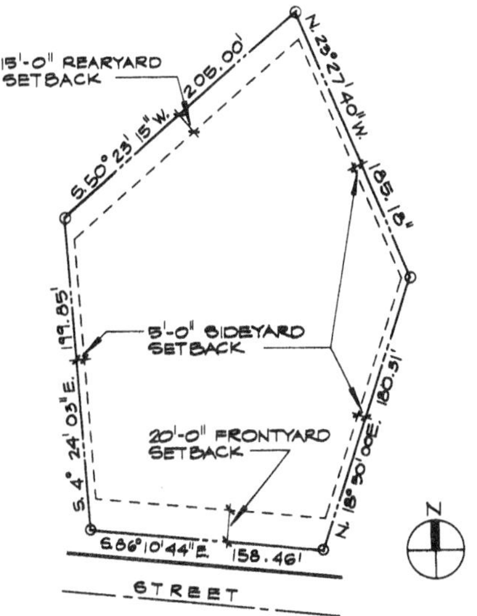

Figure 5.8G Site plan with building setbacks.

plat will also influence the development of the property. For the purpose of the architectural construction drawings, this portion of the drawings is called the **site plan** or **plot plan**. This drawing can now be utilized to determine the city-required setbacks required for aesthetics or life safety. In Figure 5.8G, the front yard, side yard, and rear yard setbacks are illustrated for the purpose of defining the governing building setback locations.

The next step in site plan development is to provide a dimensional layout for a proposed building. One method, as shown in Figure 5.8H, is to provide a dimension along the west and east property lines. Starting from the front property line, establish a line parallel with the front of the building, to determine the angle of the front of the house in relation to the front property line. In addition, from this parallel line, dimensional **offsets** of the building can be established. Note also in Figure 5.8H that all required yard setbacks will be maintained without encroachments.

Function of a Topography Map

For most projects, the architect adjusts the existing contours of the site to satisfy the building design and site improvement requirements. **Finish grading** is the process of adjusting existing contours so that they are in the desired position for the final stage of the site improvement process. Sometimes it is referred to as a topo, which is short for topography. The architect needs a topography or topographical map to study any slope conditions that may influence the design process. Usually, a civil engineer prepares this map and shows, in drawing form, the existing **contour lines** and their accompanying numerical elevations. Commonly, these contour lines are illustrated by a type of broken line. The **topography map** is actually a plat map, and its broken lines and numbers indicate the grades, elevations, and contours of the site. See Figure 5.9.

A topography map can appear complex. However, a **cross-section** or a cutaway view through any portion of the site can make the site conditions clearer; this will also be valuable for the finish grading. See Figure 5.10. The rise or fall of the contours will represent the change of elevation, from the front or rear of the site.

To make a cross-section, draw a line on the topography map at the desired location. This is called the **section line**. Next, draw a series of horizontal lines, using the same scale as the topography map and spacing equal to the grade elevation changes on the topography map. These lines represent the vertical elevation of the grade. Project each point

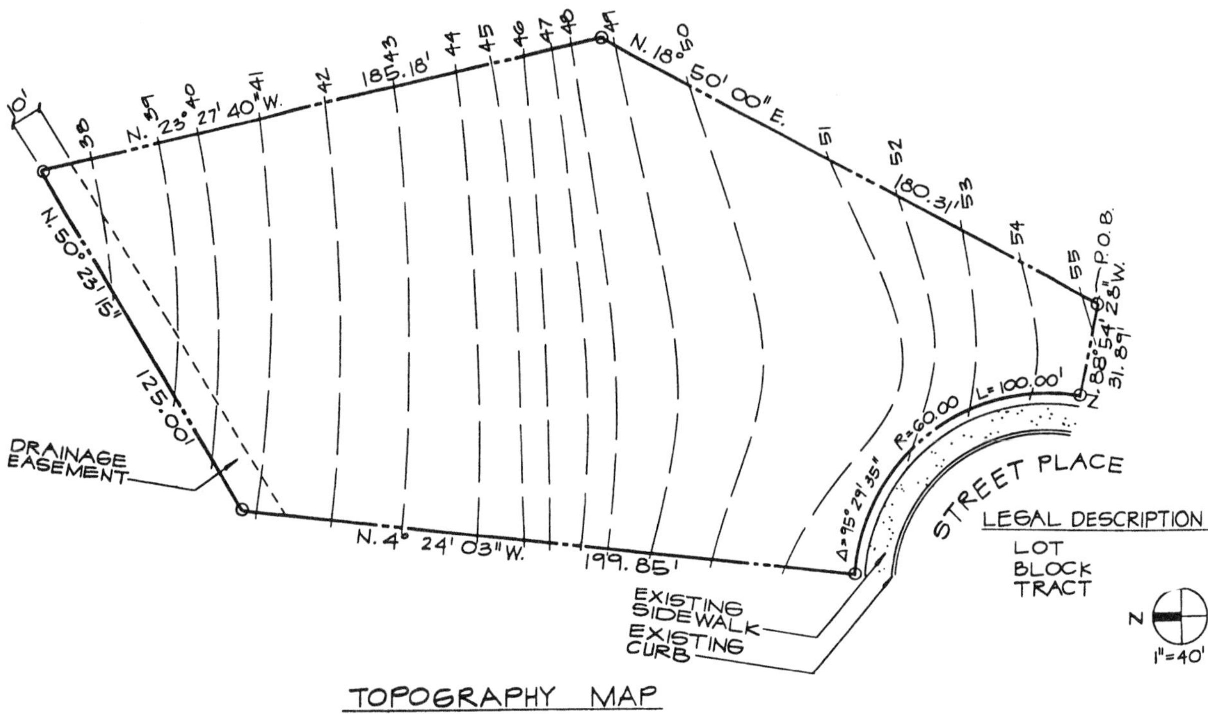

Figure 5.9 Topography map.

of grade change to the appropriate elevation line. Now connect the series of grade points to establish an accurate section and profile through that portion of the site. In many cases, multiple cross-sections are required to better understand the existing or proposed grade.

■ SOILS AND GEOLOGY MAP

Soils investigations evaluate soil conditions such as type of soil, moisture content, expansion coefficient, and soil bearing pressure. **Geological investigations** evaluate existing geological conditions such as fault lines and bedding planes, as well as potential geological hazards.

Field investigations may include test borings at various locations on the site. These drillings are then plotted on a plat map, with an assigned test boring identification and a written or graphic report. This report provides findings from the laboratory analysis of boring samples under various conditions. See Figure 5.11.

When there are concerns about geological instability and soil, the particular problem areas may be plotted on a **soils and geology map** for consideration in the design process. Figure 5.11 shows a plat map with each test boring identified. This map becomes a part of the soils and geological report. Borings are done close to the location of the proposed work established by the architect or the area of structural concern. Figure 5.12 shows a **boring log** in graphic form. Notice the different types of information presented in the sample boring log. Figure 5.13 shows a geological cross-section.

Architects are not significantly involved in preparing drawings for geology and soils information other than locating the proposed work on a site plan and perhaps a site section. However, it is important to have some understanding of their content and representation in order to understand how it may affect design. It will most directly affect the foundation design, system, and size of foundation. Within the soils or geological report, there is typically a recommendations sections, and the architect must become familiar with it and design according to the said recommendations.

■ SITE PLAN/PLOT PLAN

Drawing a Site Plan

When drawing a site plan, the easiest way to start is to call your civil engineer and ask for a digital copy of the site topography for the project. This drawing becomes the base drawing on which various layers are drawn, such as setbacks, building location, dimensions, noting, and so on. See Figure 5.14.

If a drawing is available as a hard copy but not digitally, you can scan the drawing into the computer, and then size and scale it. If you are fortunate enough to

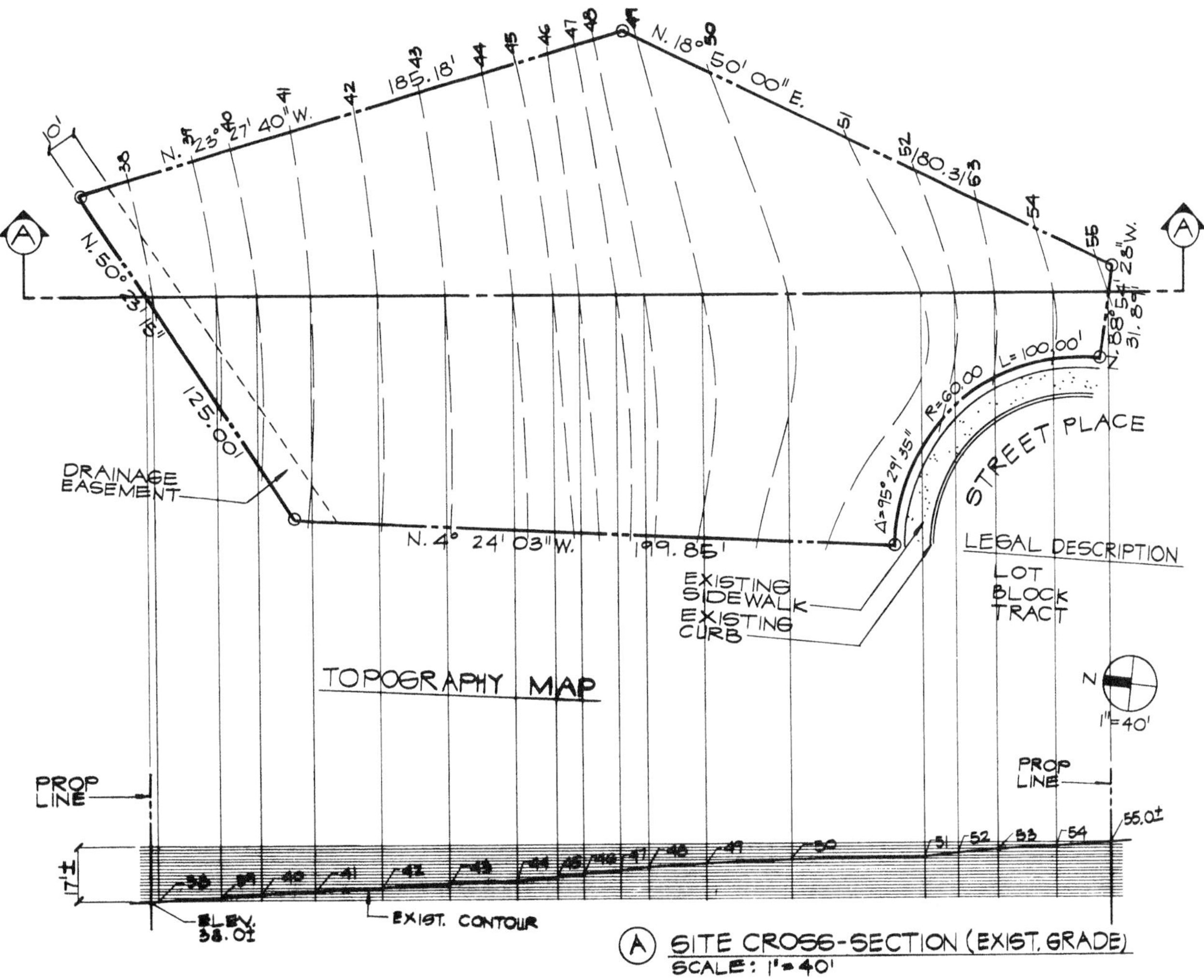

Figure 5.10 Topography map with section lines and cross-section.

have a building information modeling (BIM) program to draw site plans, then it's just a matter of following the procedure outlined in Figures 5.8A–5.8F.

In most CAD programs the drafter must adjust his or her thinking to accommodate the computer. For example, in the majority of instances, the computer has been programmed to view the east compass bearing as 0°, north as 90°, west as 180°, and south as 270°. If you need to draw a property line N 18° 50′ 00″ E, you must understand that line will be drawn in the wrong location if you do not adjust the computer orientation. For the purpose of giving the computer the proper command, you must subtract 18° 50′ from 90° and instruct the computer to draw a line 71° 10′. Let us continue drawing this lot (developed on Figure 5.8) and construct the second line of 23° 27′ 40″. Because north is 90°, we must add 27° 40′ 40″ to 90°, giving us 113° 27″ 40′, and relay this instruction to the computer. Understand that the computer bearing 0° is the east direction on a compass. It may prove to be simpler to develop the entire site boundary without correcting angles until you have closed back to the POB, and then rotate the drawing 90° to the correct orientation.

A final note: You will find no key for degree unless it has been programmed into the computer. Often, you can type in % % d to get the degree symbol. Once the final line is drawn, you must ensure that the polygon is totally closed.

BIM Site Plan

The first component to introduce is the existing topography or contouring of the building site. BIM programs allow you to create a three-dimensional site plan including the shape of the slope of the property. This can be accomplished by importing a topography map produced by the civil engineer, or you can develop it by selecting points around the footprint of the ground-floor plan. Once topography is established, modifying a "topo" is a matter of editing the data or shape. You can add trees, shrubs, plantings, and sod

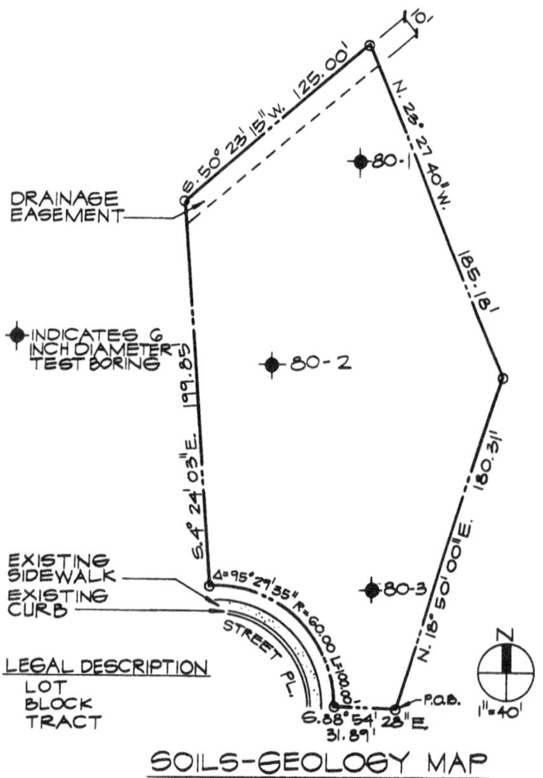

Figure 5.11 Soils–geology map.

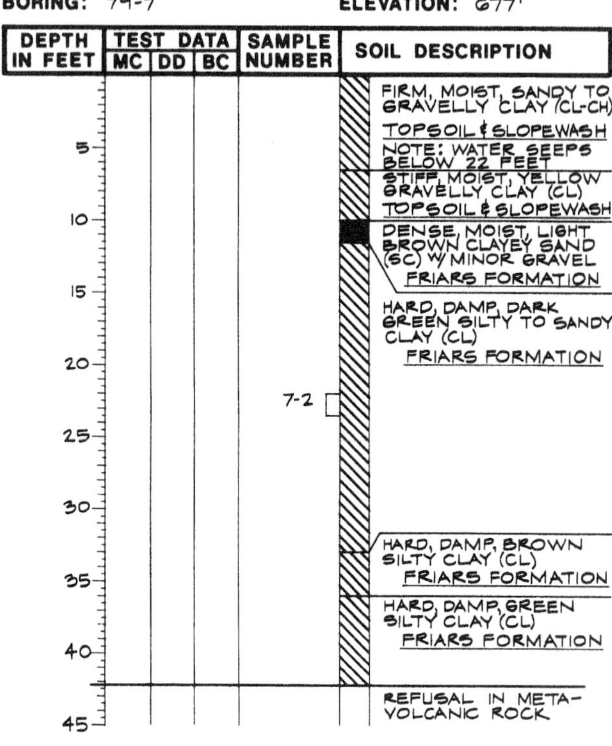

Figure 5.12 Example of a boring log.

by selecting the appropriate materials from the library and placing them. See Figure 5.15. At any stage, additional elements, such as property lines, setbacks, utilities, and dimensions, can be added to the site plan.

For most building designs, cutting and filling grade areas are required to be calculated. A shortfall of BIM, albeit one that is easily overcome, is that BIM will not recall the original topography. It is necessary to make a copy of the completed site and name it something different to keep track of the original data. Once this is done, cut and fill can be determined in reference to the original topography. See Figure 5.16.

Architects may choose to create a project with a north orientation, but when modeling in BIM true north must be accounted for so that solar studies can be accurately depicted and proper representation of shades and shadows can be viewed. In addition, the vertical height relative to sea level will be required (default set to 0 at sea level). Without these two critical adjustments, a site

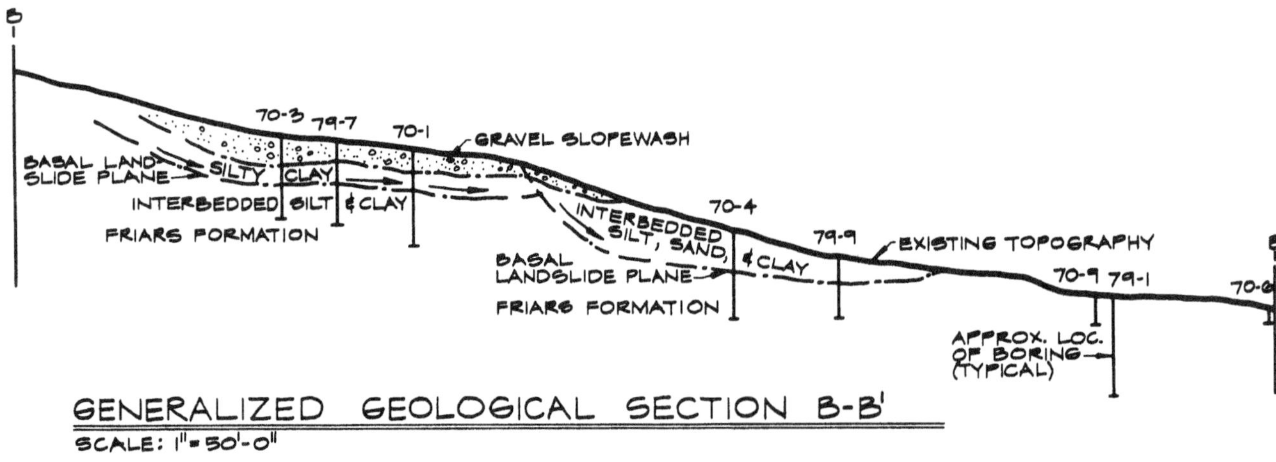

Figure 5.13 Geological cross-section.

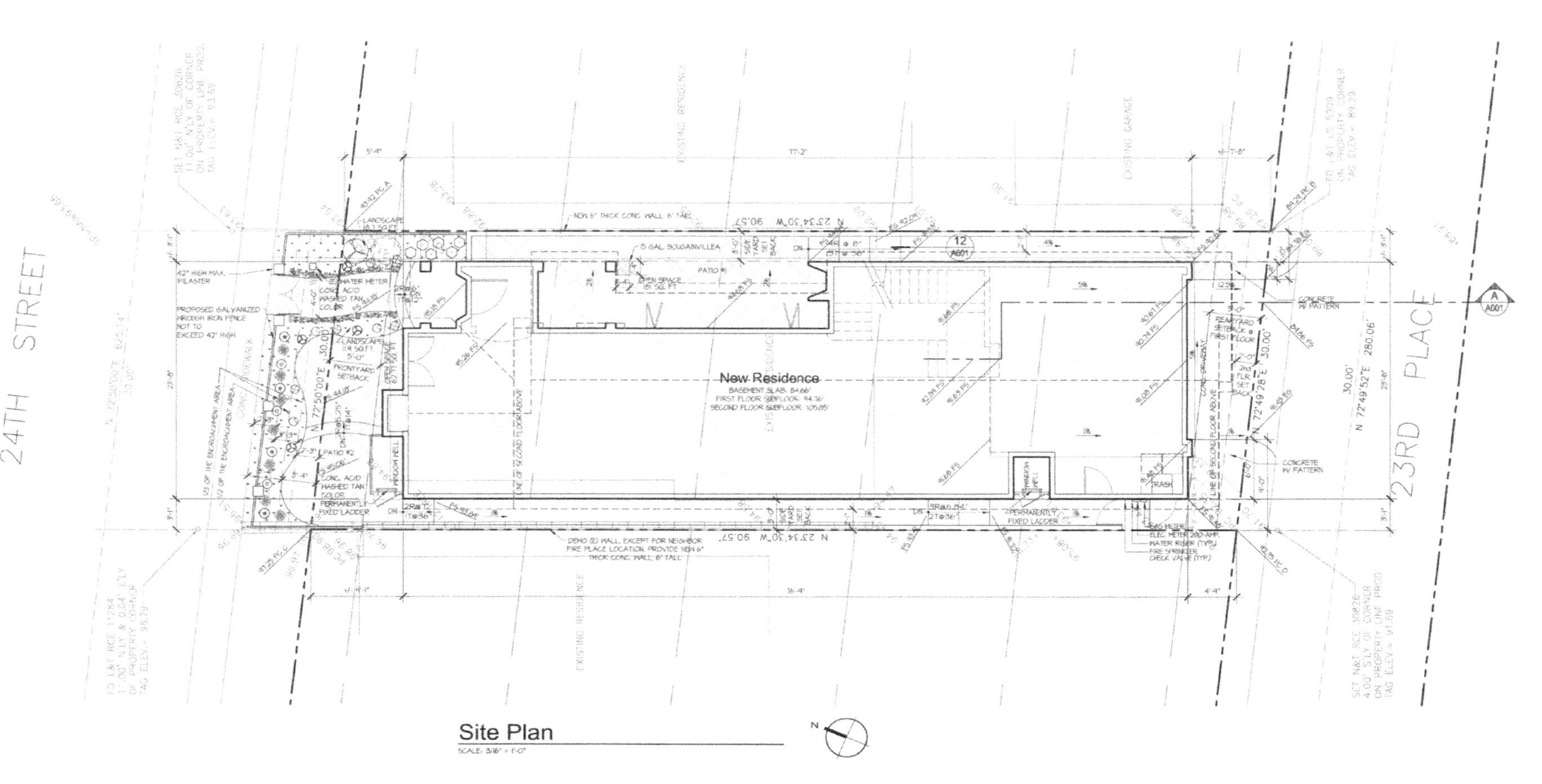

Figure 5.14 Site layout (site plan).

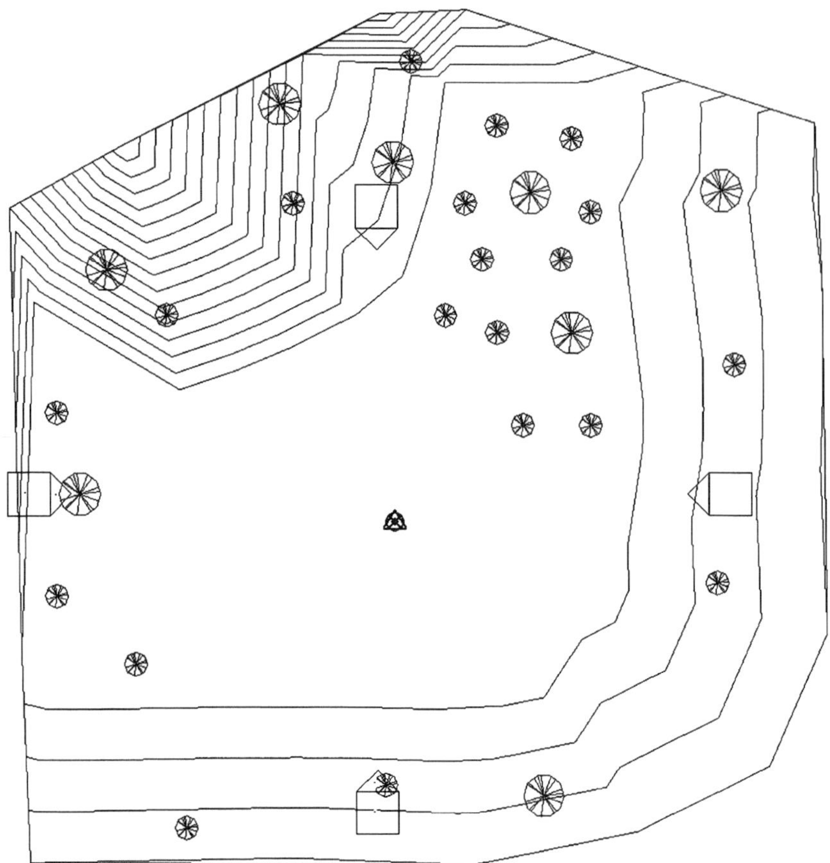

Figure 5.15 BIM site plan.

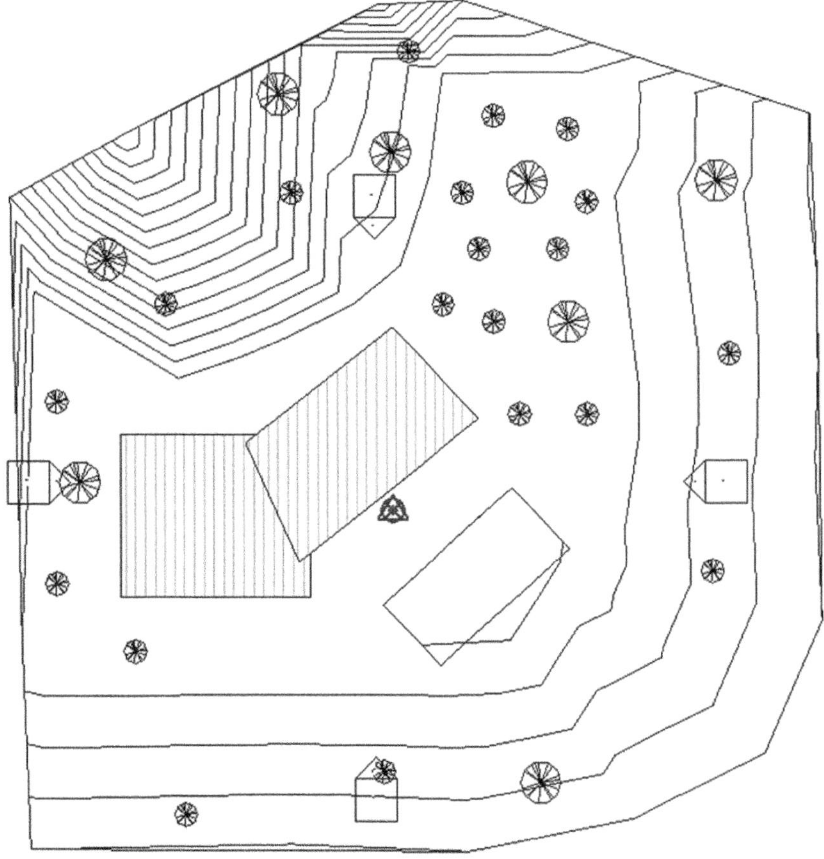

Figure 5.16 BIM developed site.

plan may be valid but models, shades, and shadow will not. See Figure 5.17.

Procedural Stages for Site Plan Development

Stage I. The architect requests a digital drawing of the site plan illustrating the property lines, existing grade contours, and any major physical features such as trees, utility poles, or any other feature that may dictate or influence the site plan process. This digital drawing is provided by a civil engineer (see Figure 5.18).

Stage II. Easements that are allocated for utility purposes, such as sewers, are depicted on the drawing with a broken line. This stage of the drawing also shows the adjacent streets, street curbs, sidewalks, and pathways (see Figure 5.19). After the final preliminary building designs and their relationship to the influencing factors of the building site are determined, the building is placed on the site plan.

Stage III. The placement of the building is derived from the final preliminary designs relative to the orientation of the sun, prevailing winds, governing setback requirements, and any existing easements. A solid line depicts the perimeter lines of the building, and a broken line indicates walls beneath. This is done to ensure that the setback dimension lines are to the perimeter wall lines. See Figure 5.20.

Stage IV. Items such as the driveway, patio slab, garage, and any other significant features are included on the site plan. See Figure 5.21.

Stage V. Provide the finish contour lines, which are drawn with a solid line and connected to their correlating grade elevations. The numerical elevation grades have been added, representing 1-foot intervals. Dimension lines and their values are now shown from the property lines to the

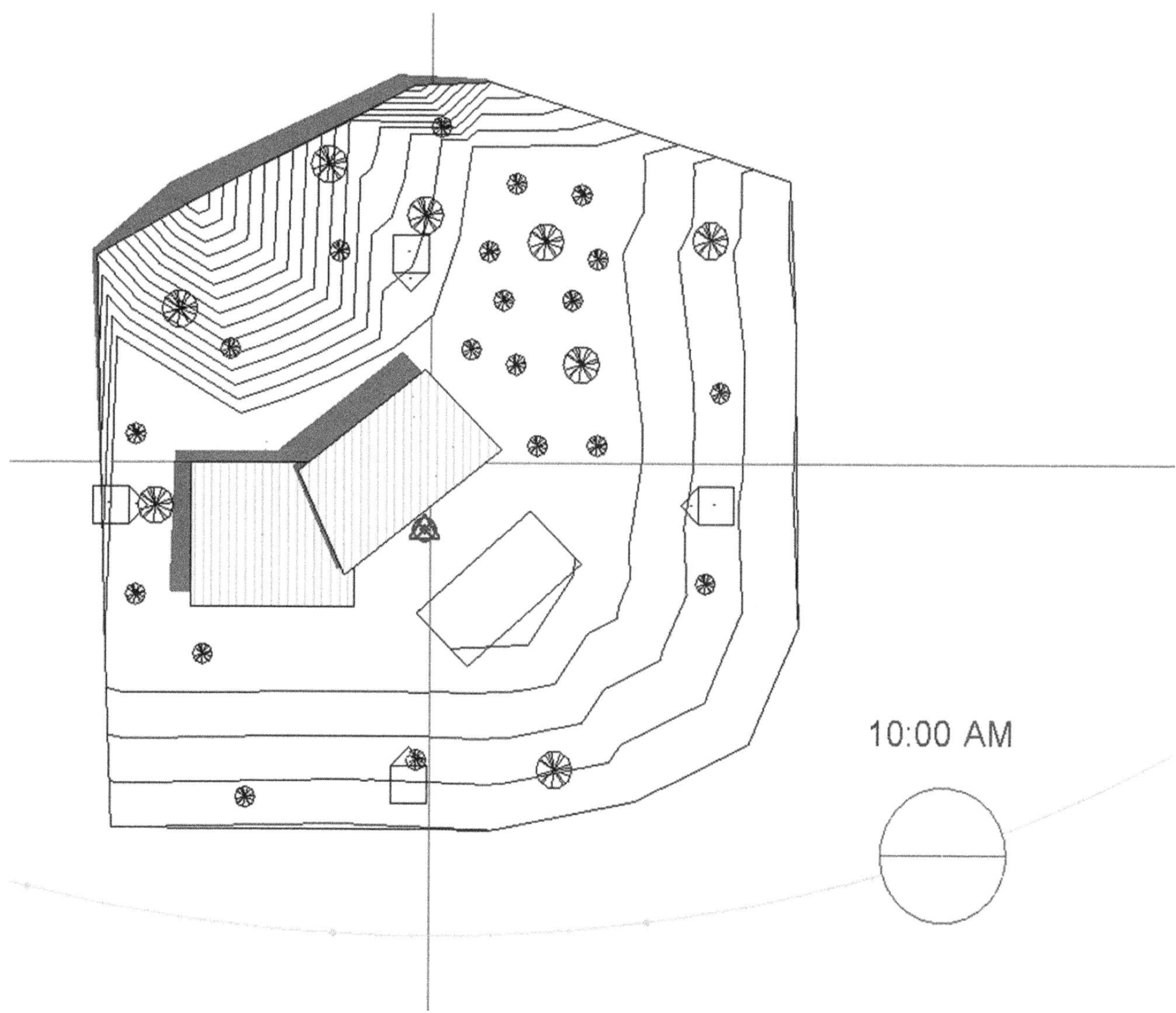

Figure 5.17 BIM shades and shadows.

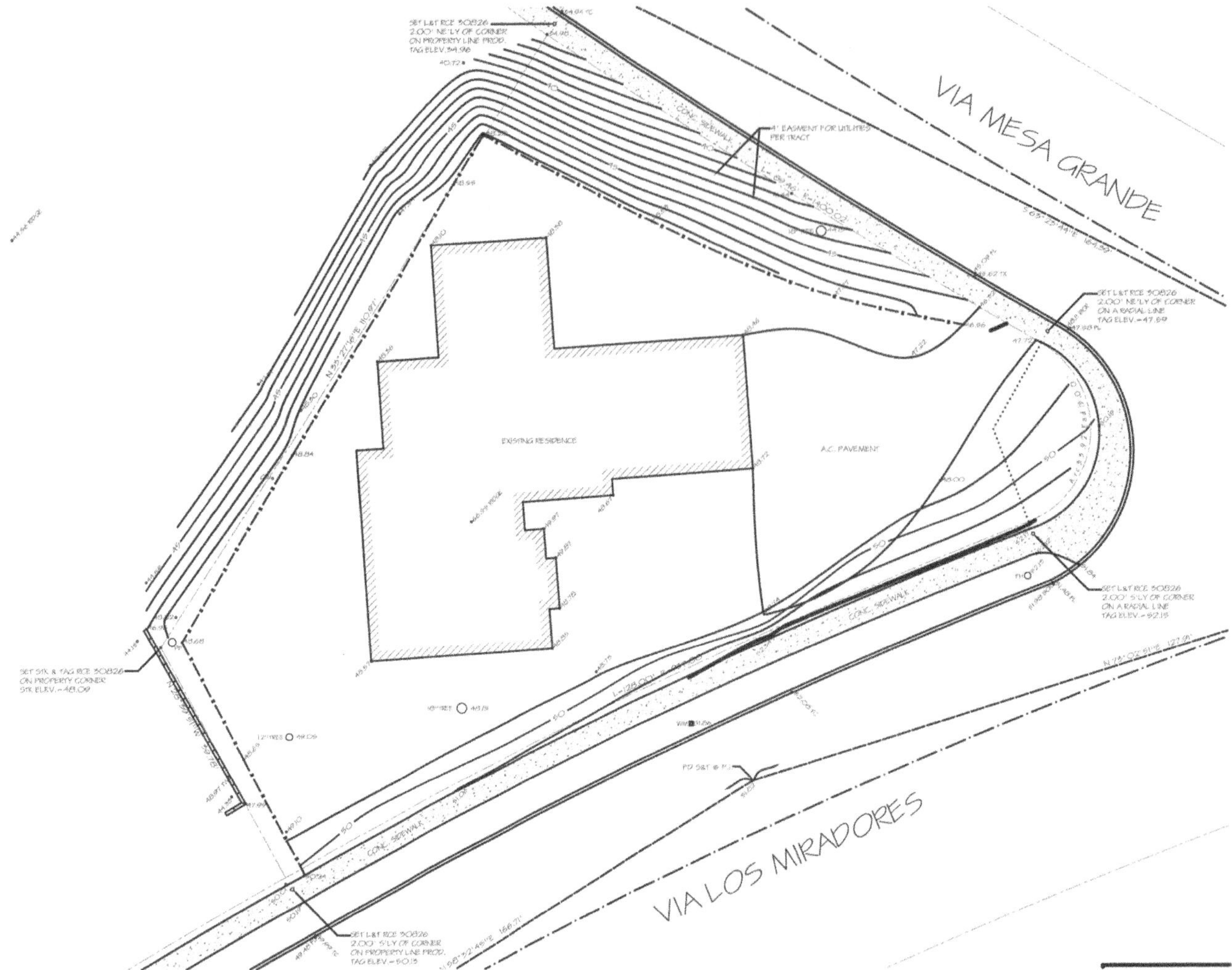

Figure 5.18 Site plan: Stage I.

perimeter wall lines of the building for layout purposes. Also shown in this stage are the property line dimensions and their bearings. See Figure 5.22.

When dimensioning a site plan, locating the building is the primary goal. There are no other plans in an architectural set of drawings that will position the building on the site. That is not to say other dimensions are not important: they are, but the locating of patios and other site features is secondary.

Stage VI. The final stage includes all the required noting. The finish noting on the site plan includes material finish, the walkway material, and any required specifications. In addition, the title and notes are included on the plot sheet. See Figure 5.23.

For clarity, all the various floor elevations should be labeled on the site plan. In addition, a symbol legend should be provided, to define those symbols used on the site plan. Finally, the title of the drawing is shown, along with the north orientation arrow, the street name, and the scale for the site and roof plan drawings.

GRADING PLAN

Grading

The grading plan shows how the topography of the site will be changed to accommodate the building design. This plan shows the existing grades and proposed grades, which are termed **finished grades**. It also indicates the finished grade elevations and the elevations of building floors, walks, and site walls. Existing grade lines are shown with a broken line, and proposed finished grades with a solid line. Finished grading lines represent the end result or desired layout once the site is graded. See Figure 5.24.

The grading plan drawing illustrates and defines the various alterations of the land contours that are needed to develop the site for a specific structure.

Floor Elevations

Once the orientation and location of the building have been established, the process of preparing a grading

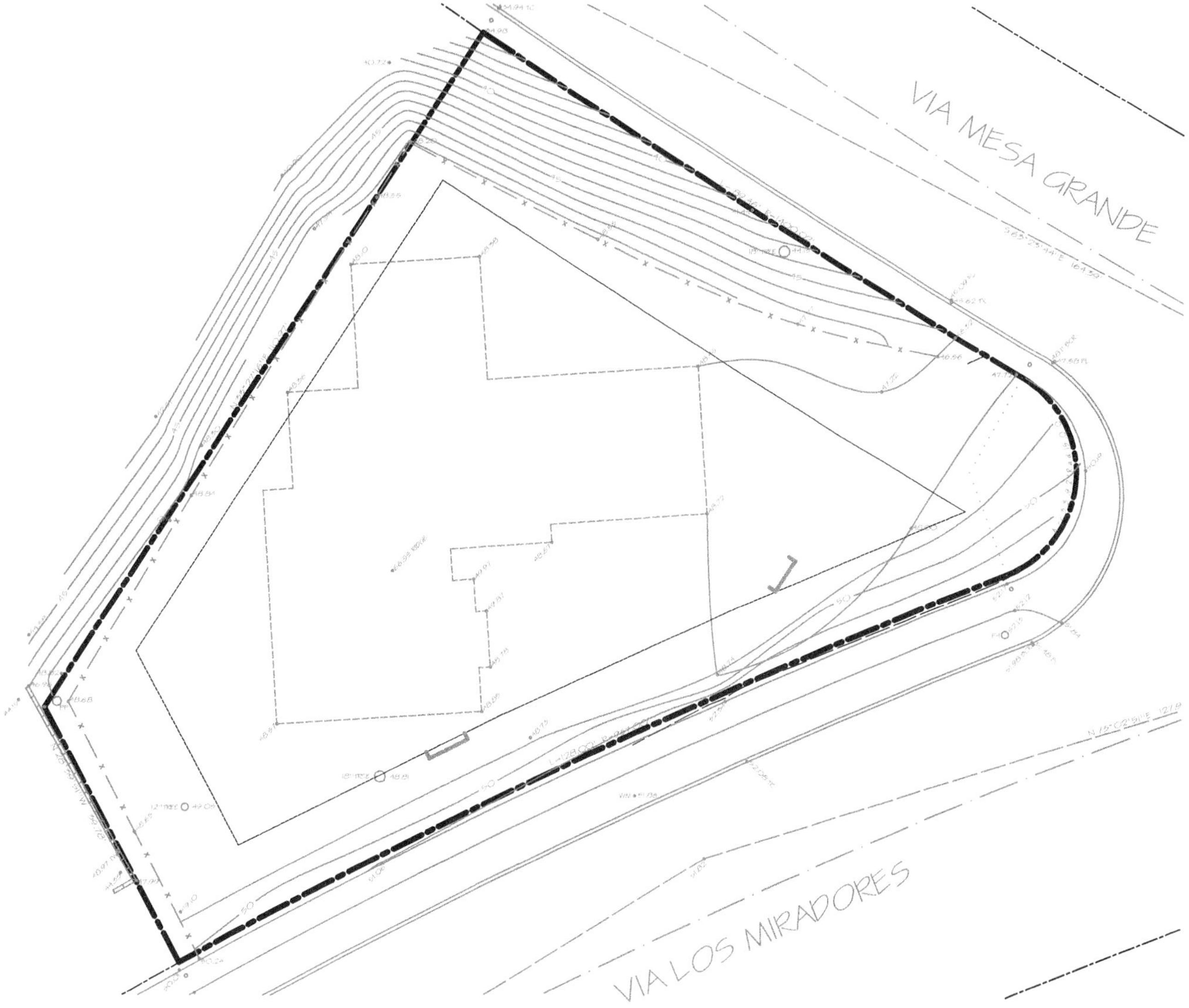

Figure 5.19 Site plan: Stage II.

plan may begin. The first step is to designate tentative floor-level elevations, which will be determined by the structure's location in relation to the existing grades. It should be noted that in the process of designing a grading plan, tentative floor elevations may have to be adjusted to satisfy the location of the finished contours and their elevations. With the establishment of the floor-level elevations, it will then be necessary to reshape the existing grade lines to satisfy floor clearances and site drainage control. See Figure 5.25.

For the purpose of providing proper drainage around the building, the designer should encourage surface drainage to flow to each side of the building and follow the natural slope of the site. Finished contour elevations will be shaped to provide a gentle slope around the front and sides of the building. A minimum of 2% slope is recommended for proper drainage of soil areas.

Orienting a structure on the site with a minimum amount of finished grading is the most environmentally sensitive response to a site. Once the primary location and floor elevation have been established for the garage, the formation and planning for the residence may now proceed, with the intention of ensuring compatibility with the existing grade elevations and the contour configurations of the existing grades. The architect may decide to develop a building configuration that will accommodate minimal finished grading conditions and provide a development that is more compatible with the natural terrain.

In designing a more severe slope, as in cases where a building pad must be enlarged, a maximum slope ratio is laid out. **Slope ratios** are laid out with horizontal scaled increments for the tentative slope ratio. For instance, in some counties a ratio of 2:1

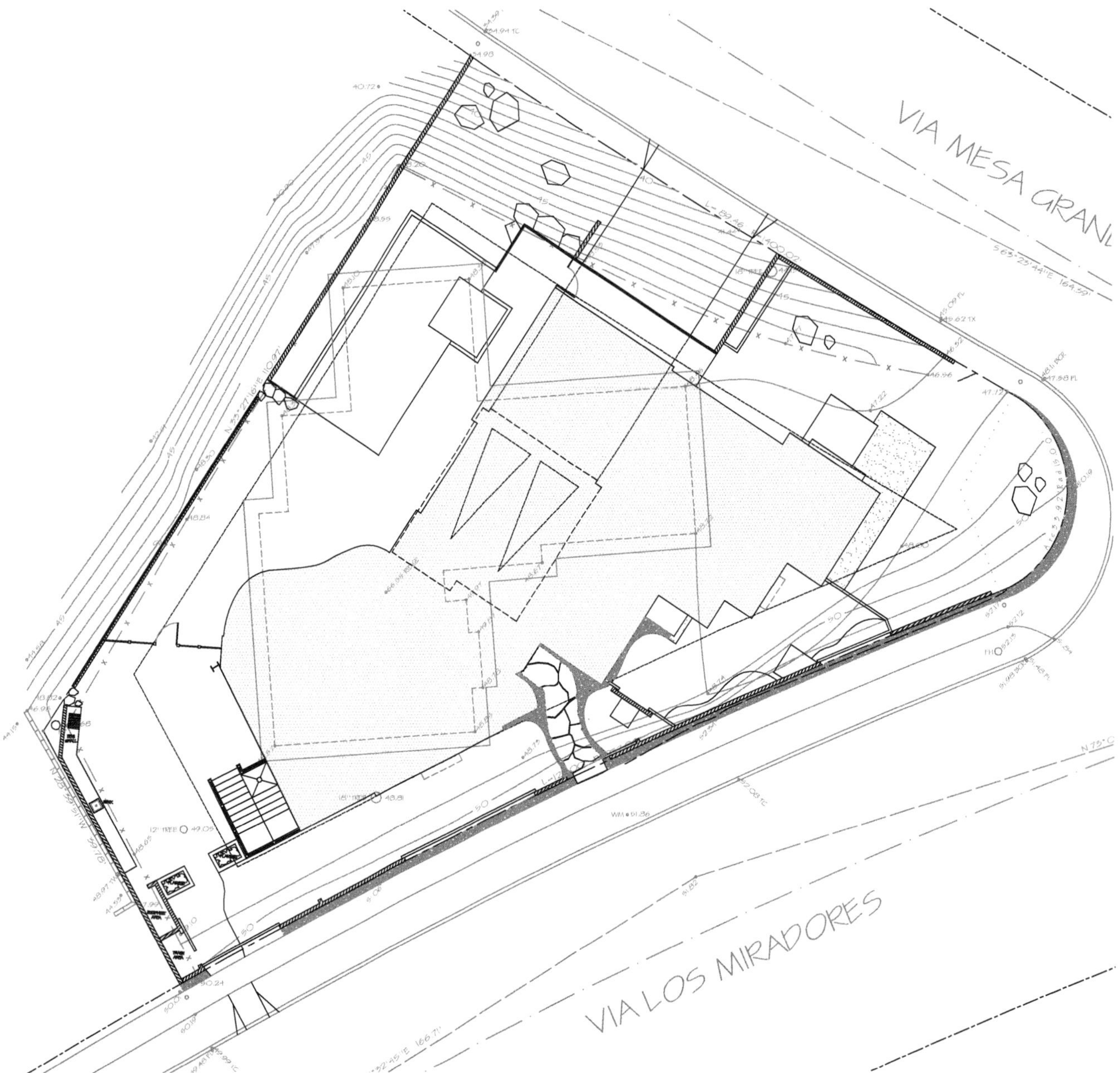

Figure 5.20 Site plan: Stage III.

is the minimum slope allowed for each site contour. This would allow a site to increase 1 foot in height for every 2 feet traveled in the horizontal direction. A slope ratio of 3:1 is a more gradual slope, and in many areas an ideal target for slope stability. Slope ratio is anticipated for the grade cut for the placement of the building. Increments will start from the established grades adjacent to the building. Once the various increments have been plotted, these points can be connected. In most cases, all finish grade elevations start at an existing or natural grade elevation and terminate at the respective existing grade elevation. See Figure 5.26.

Cut and Fill Procedures

Contour changes will require either the removal of soil—a **cut** into the existing contours—or the opposite, the addition of soil to the site; the latter is called **fill**. In reshaping contours with cut and fill procedures, one can provide a relatively level area for construction. Depending on the soil's condition and soil preparation, the maximum allowable ratio for cut and fill slopes may vary from 1½:1, 2:1, or 3:1. A ratio of 3:1 means that for each 3-foot distance on the horizontal, there is a minimum 1-foot change in vertical elevation. A slope of 3:1 establishes a stable slope that is less likely to slide. In some municipalities, a

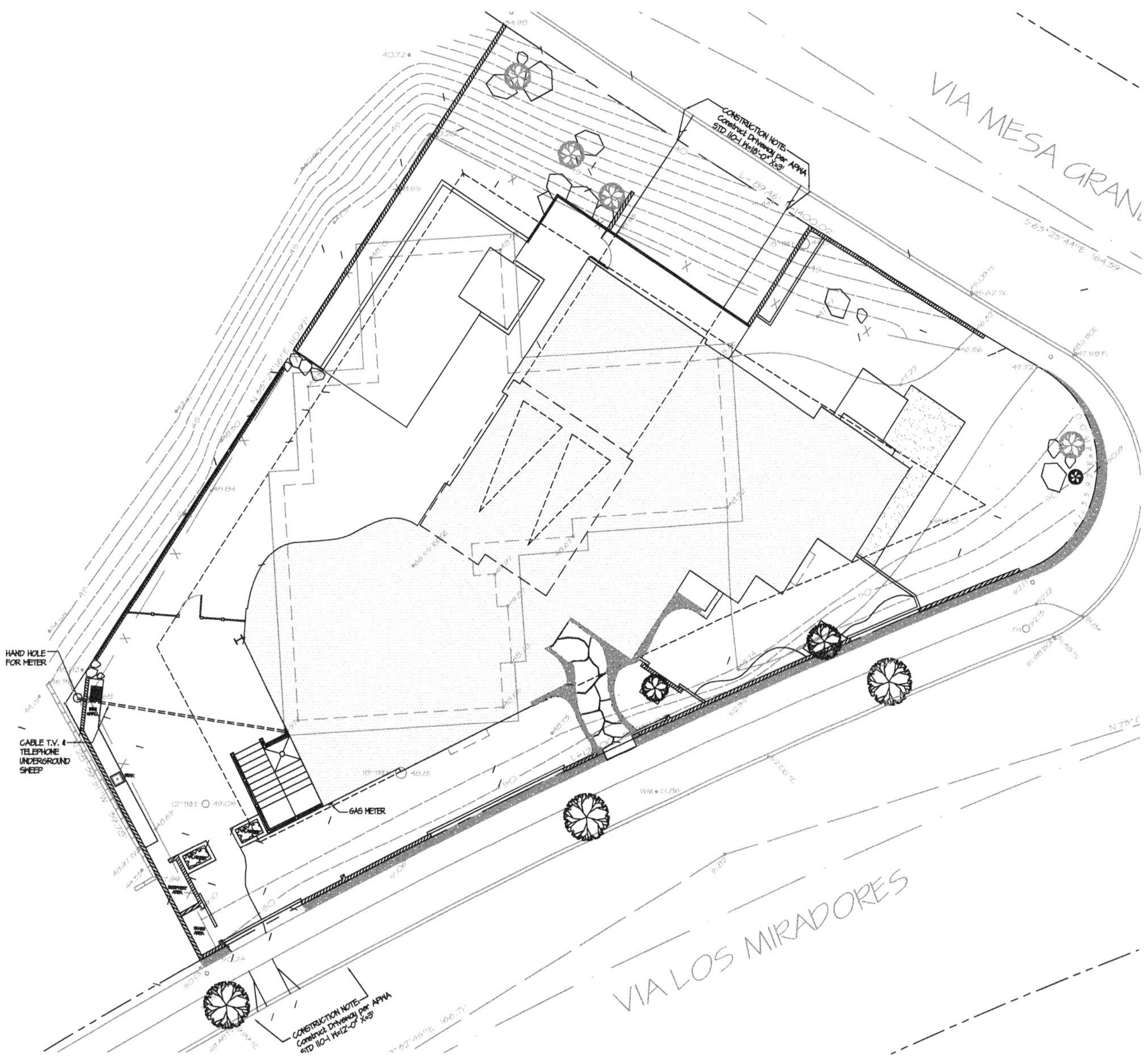

Figure 5.21 Site plan: Stage IV.

maximum slope of 3:1 is required for cut and fill. To clarify grading conditions, grading sections should be taken through these areas. See Figure 5.27.

Another approach is to develop a level area on a site for the construction of a residence. The level area, called a **building pad**, will have a minimal slope for drainage of approximately 2%. The creation of a building pad will provide the architect with more flexibility in the design, because he or she will not be constrained by grade elevations, floor transitions, building shapes, or other considerations.

One approach in developing a building pad is to try to create a balance cut and fill. In this approach, the earth that is cut from the site slope is dispersed and used as the fill material to increase the building pad site. The fill material must then be **compacted** to an acceptable soil-bearing capacity if a structure is to be founded in the fill area. To develop the size, shape, and grading for the building pad, it is recommended that an assumed pad elevation be established. This pad elevation may be determined by what is referred to as a **daylight grade elevation**, defined as that point or elevation where the cut and fill portions of the site grading intersect at a given grade elevation.

SITE AND GRADING PLAN

In this section, we discuss and illustrate another example of grading design and the various criteria that dictate design solutions, this time for a two-story

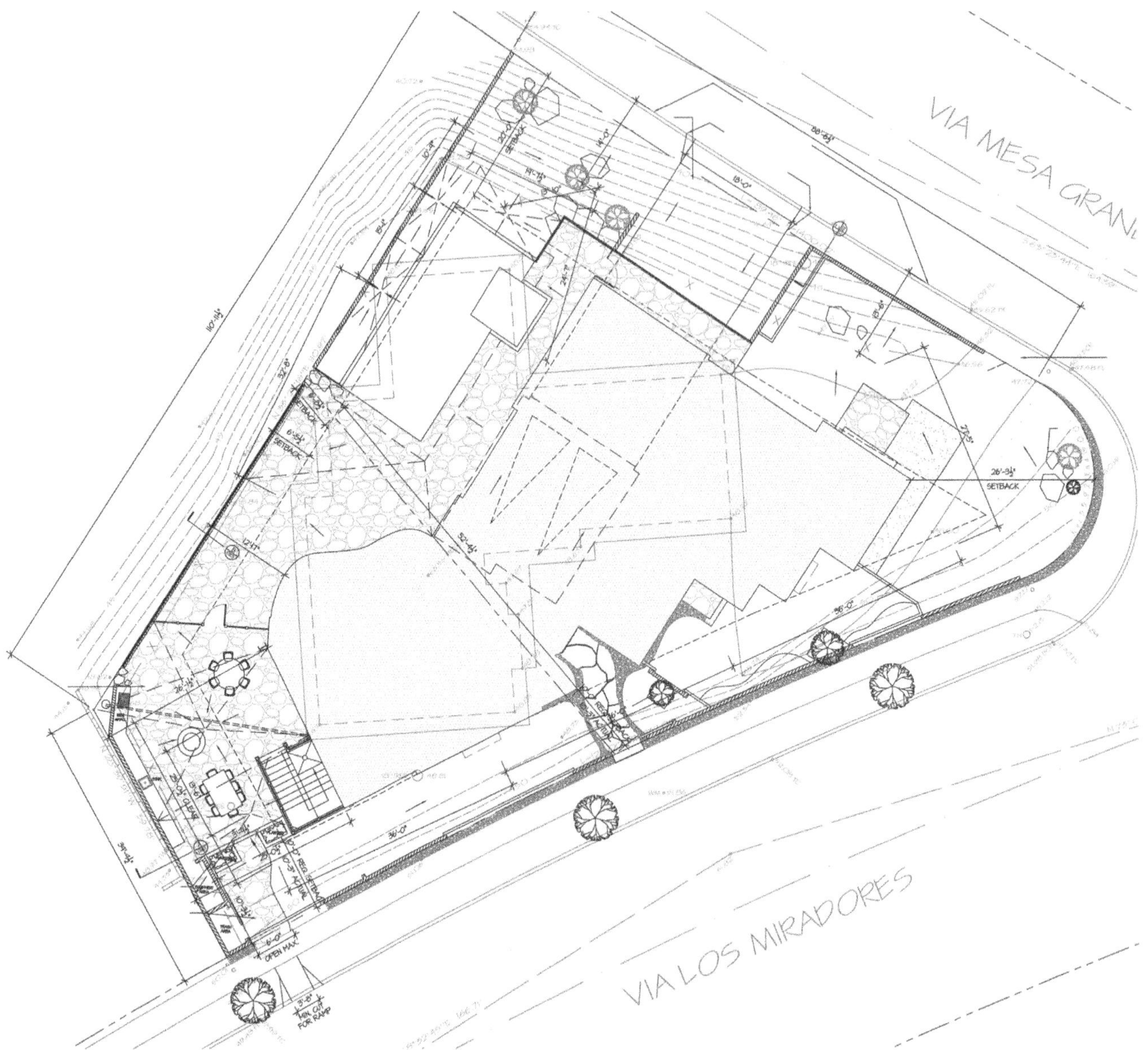

Figure 5.22 Site plan: Stage V.

residence. The topography map for this project is shown in Figure 5.28. Note that the natural or existing grades are indicated with a broken line and a designated number indicating the grade elevation of each contour line.

For this project, the initial concern was the driveway access and slope relative to the garage floor elevation. The desired maximum slope of the driveway does not exceed 1 foot in 10 feet (1:10). This translates into a slope of 10%. Starting at the southerly property line, which is the front property line, the existing contour grade elevation is 375.00′. From this existing grade elevation of 375.00′, it is desirable to maintain a maximum driveway slope of 10% within the 15′-0″ building setback area. This design solution then establishes the garage floor elevation at 372.50′. This condition is illustrated in Figure 5.29. Note that a trench drain is located in front of the garage to divert any water accumulation from the sloping driveway. This trench drain will have a grate cover and drain lines to dissipate the water.

Another concern in dealing with sloping driveways is the transition from the street and the driveway apron elevation to the sloping portion of the driveway. This concern is illustrated graphically in the driveway transition section shown in Figure 5.30. Note the hypothetical driveway transition, depicted with a broken line, which shows steep slope transitions that may cause under-car damage and/or bumper scraping.

The first step is to develop the grading for a driveway that will provide acceptable slopes for access to

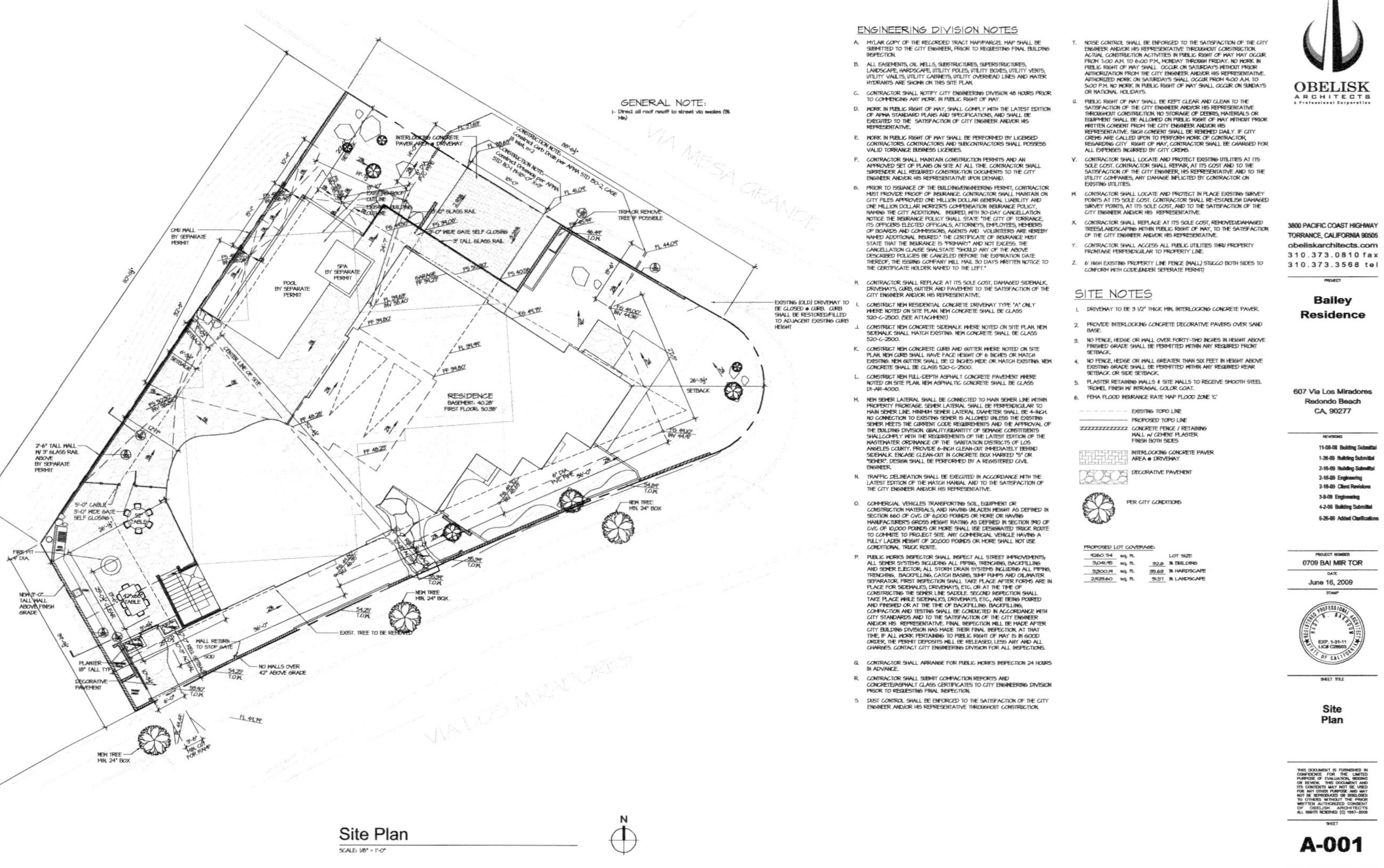

Figure 5.23 Site plan: Stage VI.

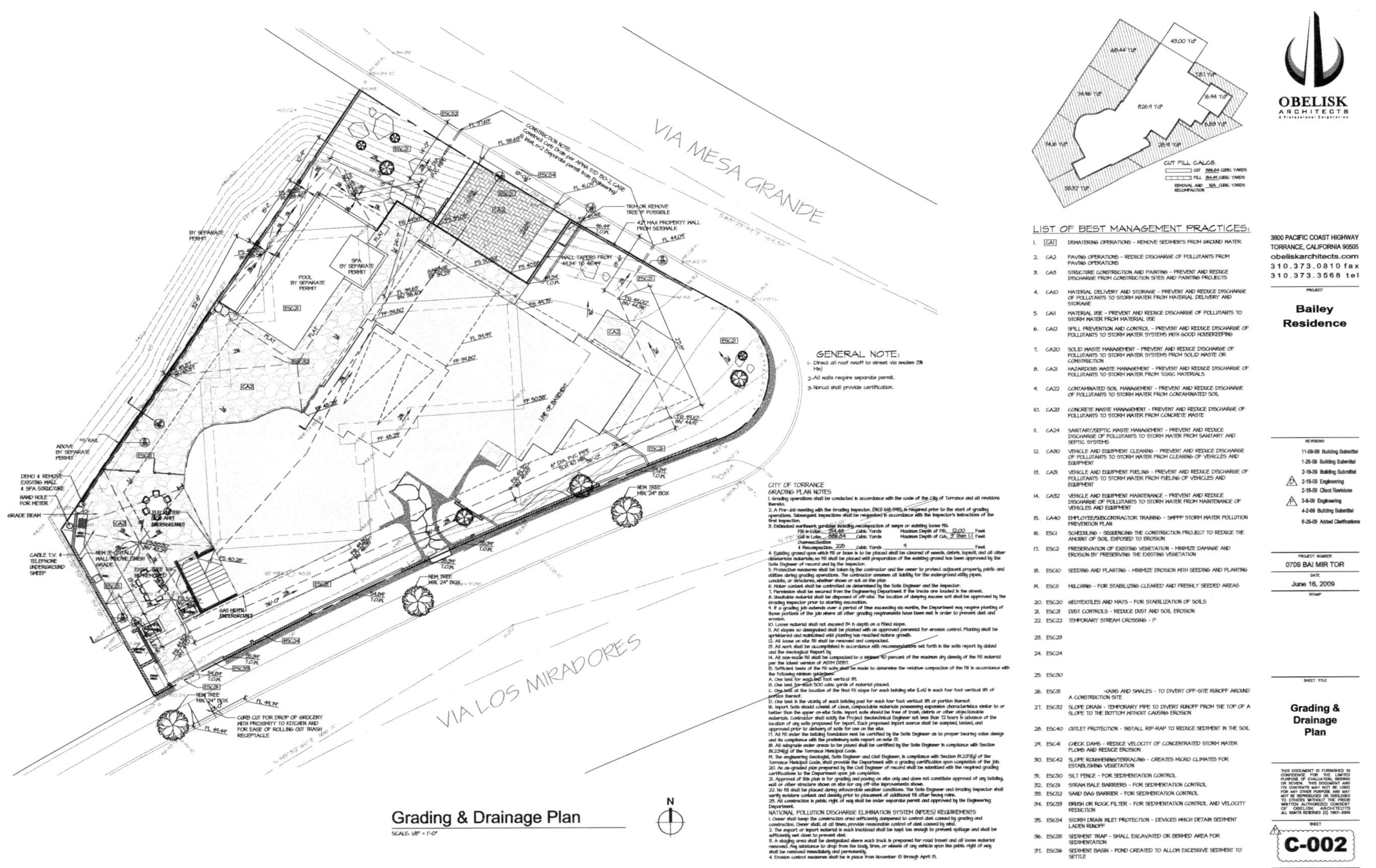

Figure 5.24 Grading plan.

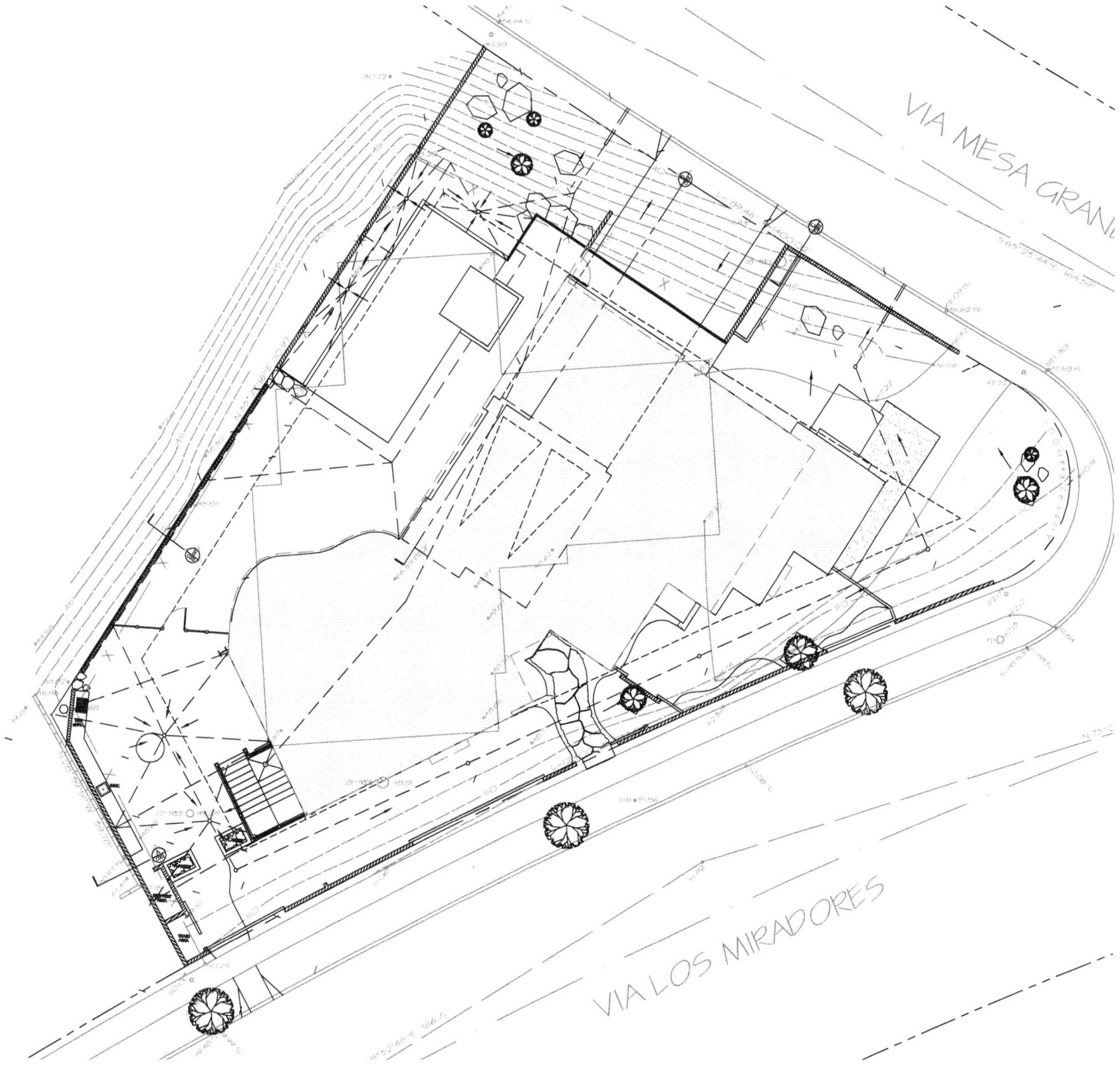

Figure 5.25 Initial grading.

the garage, which will in turn determine the garage location and floor elevation. Starting at the street grade elevation, the initial grade transition from the street to the driveway should not be so steep as to scrape the bumper of an automobile. The initial maximal slope ratio is approximately 1 foot vertically to 10 feet horizontally (1:10), or a 10% slope. A slope of 20% or a 1:5 ratio would be the maximum allowable in most jurisdictions.

Although a 20% driveway can be utilized with appropriate transitions of 10% at the beginning and ending of the 20% area, approximately 8–10 feet of 10% grade, then 20%, and then another 8–10 feet of 10% will allow a smoother transition for vehicles. A goal for a contoured lot is to work with the existing topography, but an ideal smooth slope of 12.5% or less is comfortable. In addition to the vertical slope, the length of a driveway maximum cross-slope, measured at the width, would be 10% (ideally, less than 5%). In each region of the country, the local municipality will establish the maximum for this condition.

It is not recommended that one exceed a 20% driveway slope. A maximum 4% slope is recommended for the side-to-side slope or **cross-slope** of the driveway. As mentioned previously, the garage floor elevation has been established at 372.50′. From the garage floor elevation, a 6″ floor transition will determine the first-floor elevation to be 373.00′. The garage floor and

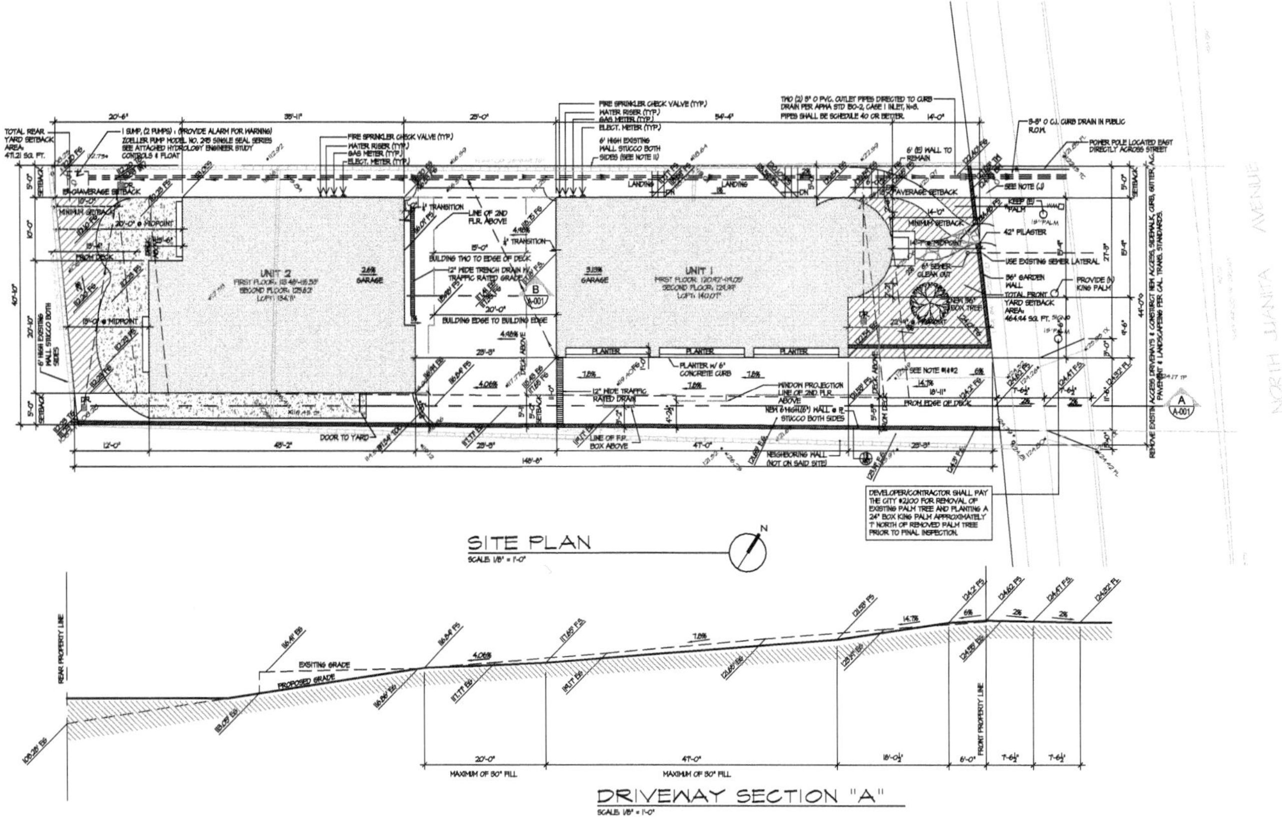

Figure 5.26 Finished slope design.

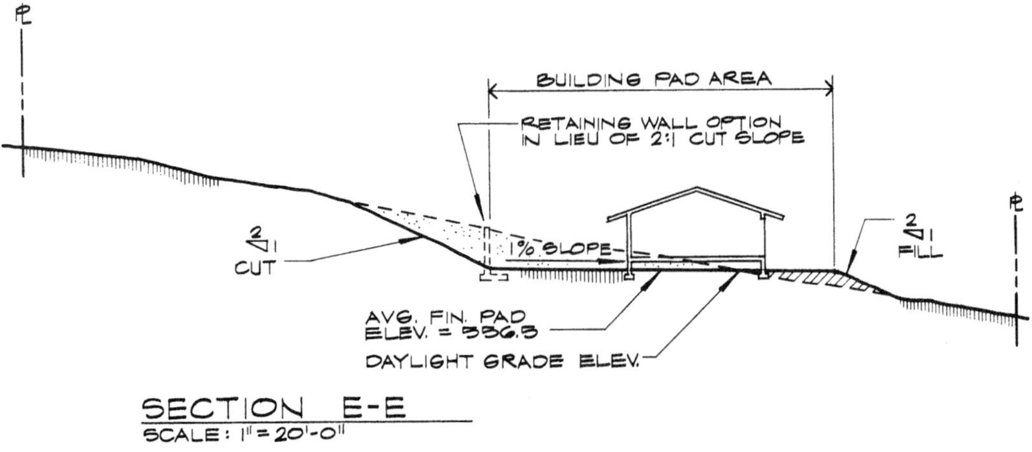

Figure 5.27 Cross-section with finish grades.

first-floor elevations will now become the basis for the finished grading design. See Figure 5.31. The existing grade lines of the site slope gently down from the southerly property line to the northerly property line. This condition, based on the established garage and first-floor elevations, will require an earth cut at the front or southerly area of the site, with the soil removed being relocated to the rear or northerly portion of the site, which becomes a fill area. The solid lines illustrate the finish grade contours, as depicted in Figure 5.31. Note that the finish grade line elevations connect to the existing grade line elevations. Figure 5.31 graphically illustrates a cross-section of the building site cut in a south-to-north direction. The broken line depicts the approximate existing grade, and the solid line and shaded areas show the finished grade line and fill areas. Additional cross-sections in relationship to abutting properties are illustrated in Figure 5.32.

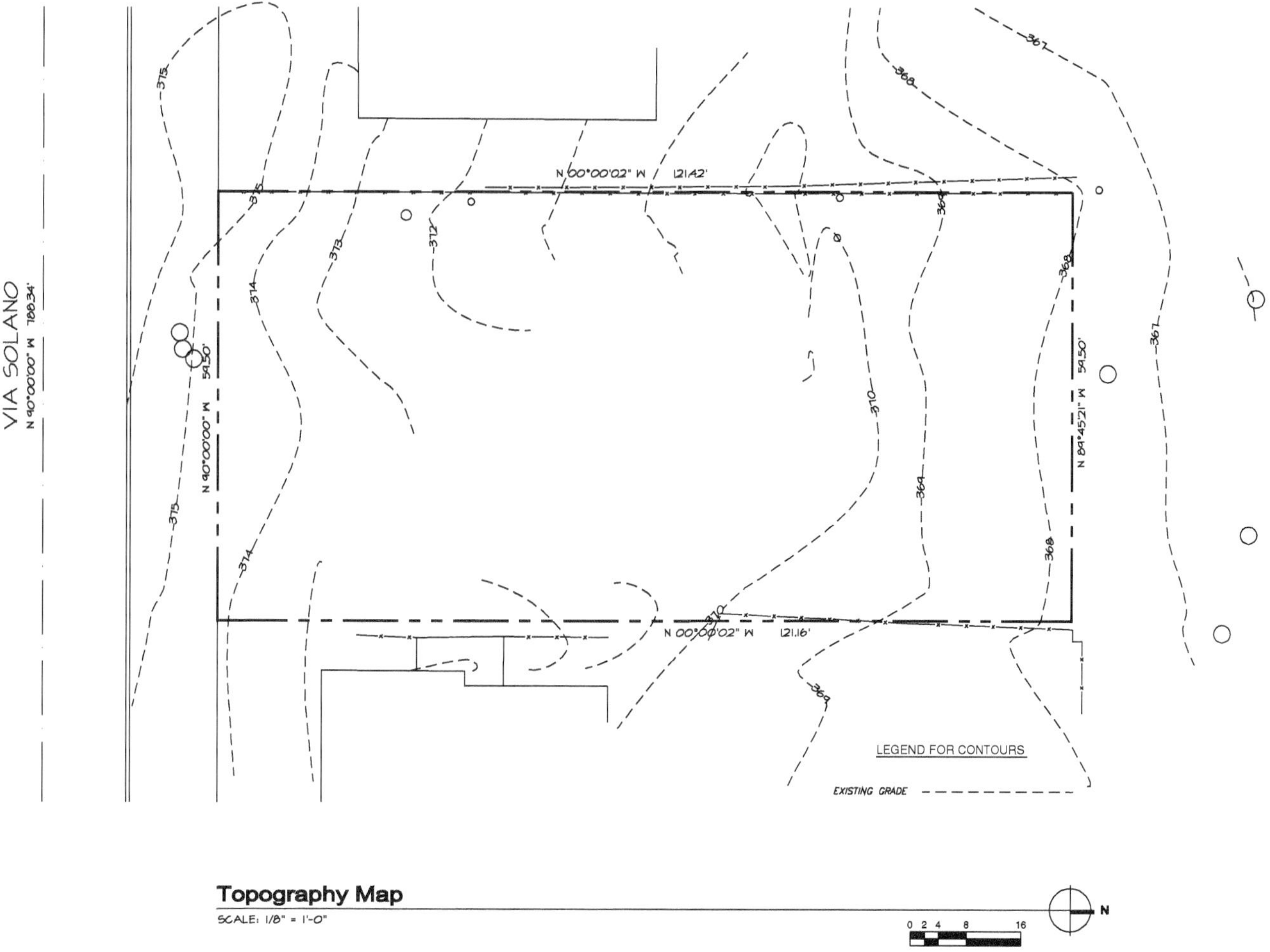

Figure 5.28 Topography map.

The maximum slope or gradient for cut and fill slope conditions may be determined by the type of soil found on the site and local agency requirements. Various soil types react differently to potential soil erosion. For most cases, the maximum slope or gradient may range from 1, to 1½:1, to 2:1. These ratios translate into 66% and 50% slope conditions, respectively. See Figure 5.33.

Driveway and Curb

Often, one side of your site will be bounded with a sidewalk, parkway, and a small curb. In most cities, this portion adjacent to a street is maintained by the Department of Public Works or some other such municipal agency. Permits are required to break the curb for a driveway; permits can be obtained from the appropriate agency or agency subdivision (perhaps the city's Road Department Bureau or engineering department). Based on the size of the curb, the agency will configure an angle at which you can cut the curb to form the driveway. See Figure 5.34.

For sloping sites that are going to be developed for commercial and office use, the grading design will have to address automobile and disabled pedestrian access to the building. The transition from the street to the parking area should provide easy access relative to the driveway slope and the slope of the parking area. Grade transitions that require stairs and landings will also require ramps for people with disabilities, which are regulated by the Americans with Disabilities Act (ADA) requirements. See Figure 5.35.

■ DRAINAGE PLAN

A **drainage plan** establishes the path by which water travels on a site, often in a controlled method via a nonerosive device. Such devices include pipes, area drains, sub-drains, drains, catch basins, drainage swales, diverters/interceptors, and bio-filters. Other controlled methods include shaping of grade, berms, driveways, splash walls, riprap, and velocity reducers.

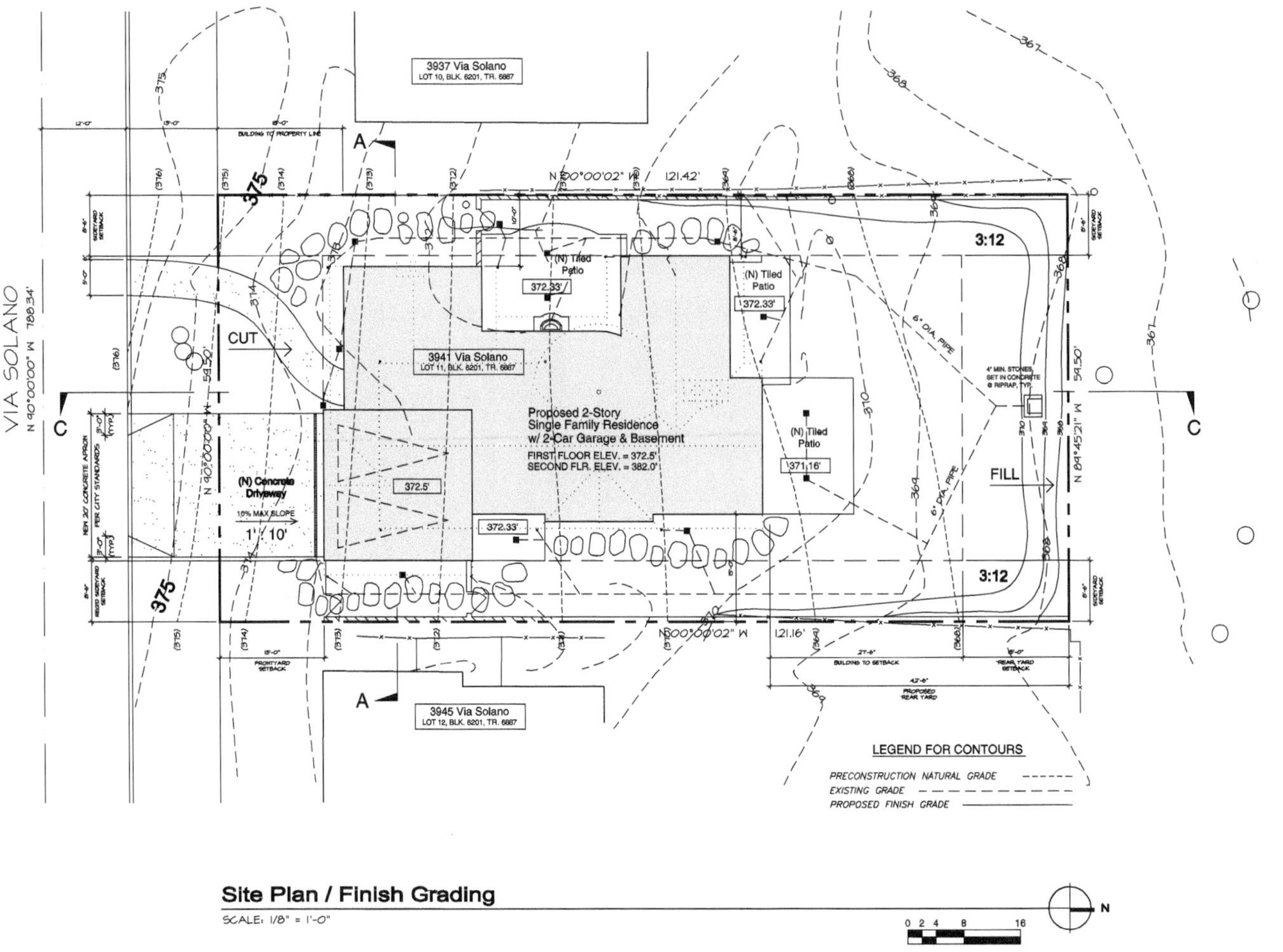

Figure 5.29 Site plan/finish grading.

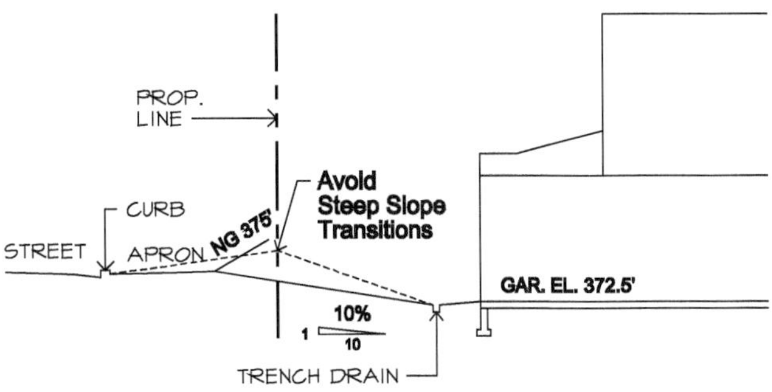

Figure 5.30 Driveway transition section.

Area drains are inlets that allow excess water collected on the surface of an area to be rerouted with pipes below grade. A drain is typically located in a hard paved area where a **sub-drain**, sometimes called a **French drain**, collects excess water below grade (for example, behind a retaining wall). These too are connected to a pipe and outlet. On large sloping sites, it is difficult to control water and channel the flow into area drains. In these cases, a **swale**, a "V"-shaped catching device, is used to divert the water flow. These swales will gather the excess water and carry it to a **catch basin**. **Bio-filters** are a new addition to the drainage arsenal. Bio-filters are devices designed to catch harmful chemicals or silt in surface runoff. There are many types of bio-filters; consult regional codes for proper choice and fabrication. Often, shaping the grade with berms or a 2% slope can route runoff in the right direction. Even a driveway can have a low point to guide water; splash walls and raised curbs are also effective methods. When water flow is excessive, implementation of a velocity reducer or a riprap area may be required. This slows the water flow and disperses the water in a fashion that limits erosion potential. See Figure 5.36.

The site may require that floor elevation changes be utilized to enhance the compatibility between the structure and the existing grades. The residence shape may follow the contours of the existing grade elevations and result in a unique shape or configuration. Note that some excavation will occur below the floor levels in order to

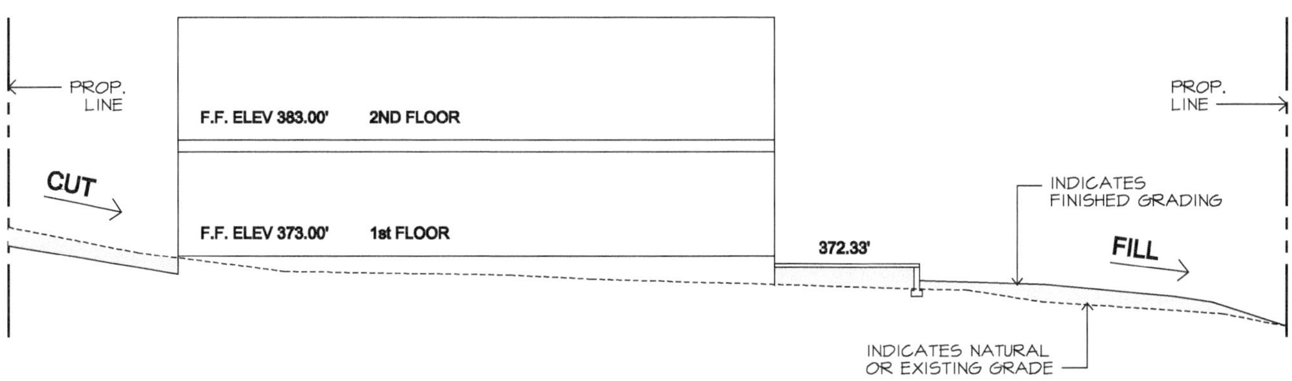

Figure 5.31 Site grading cross-section.

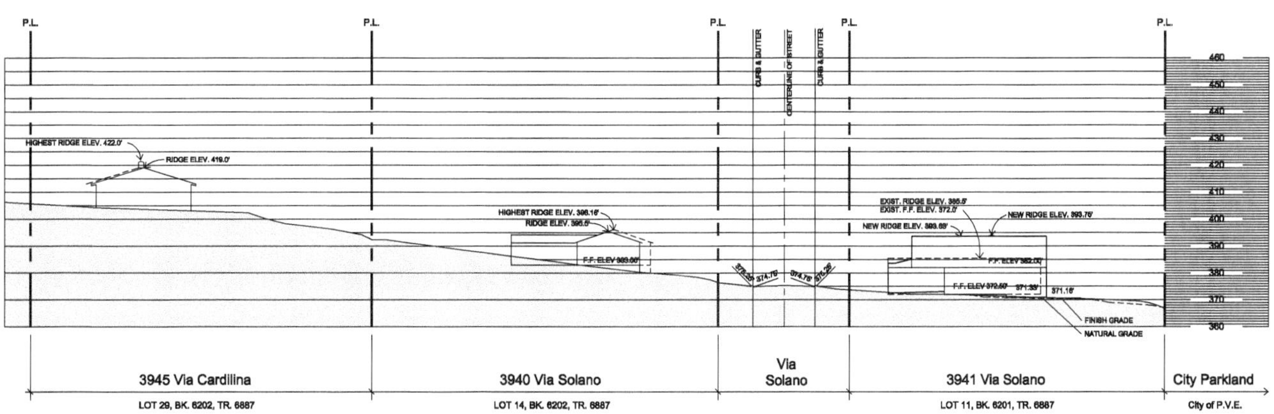

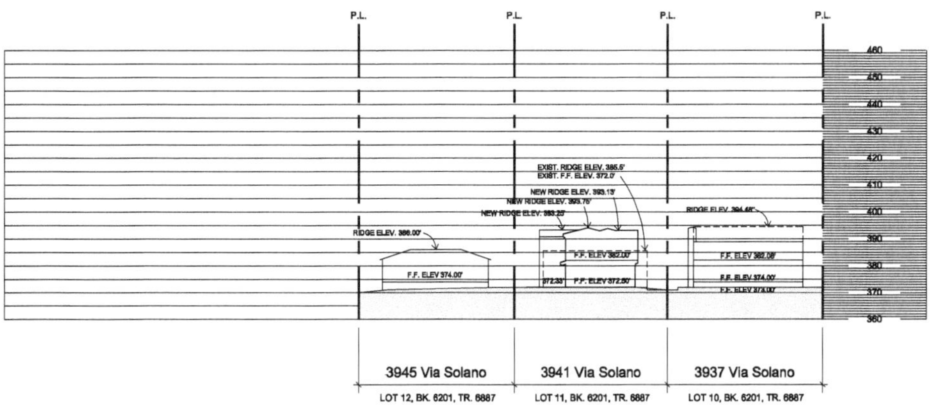

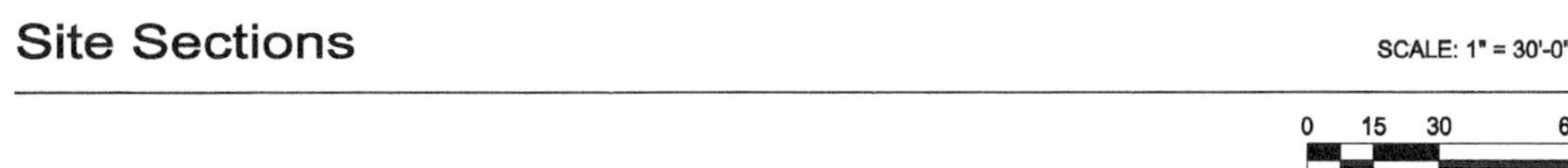

Figure 5.32 Site sections.

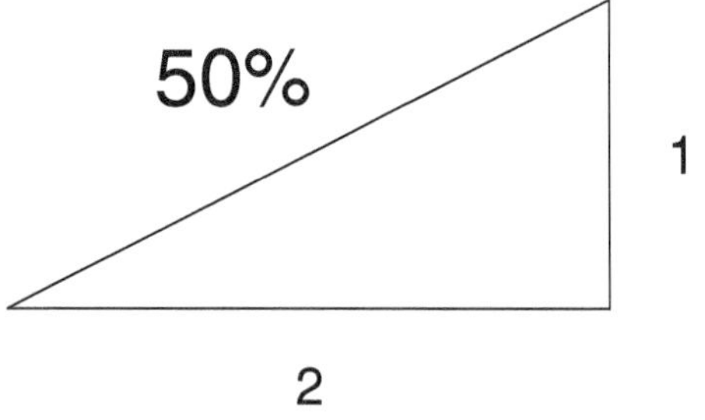

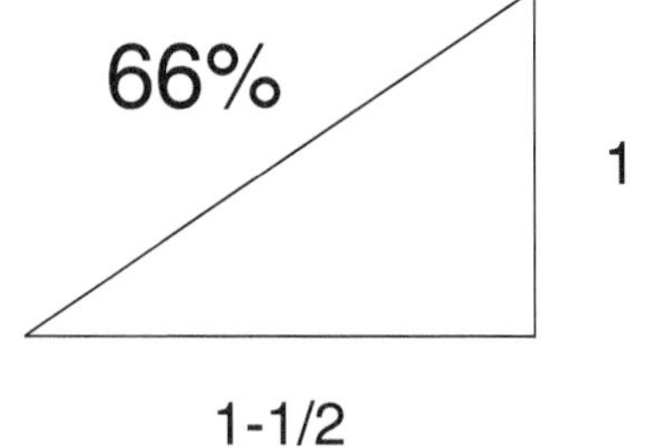

Figure 5.33 Slope ratios.

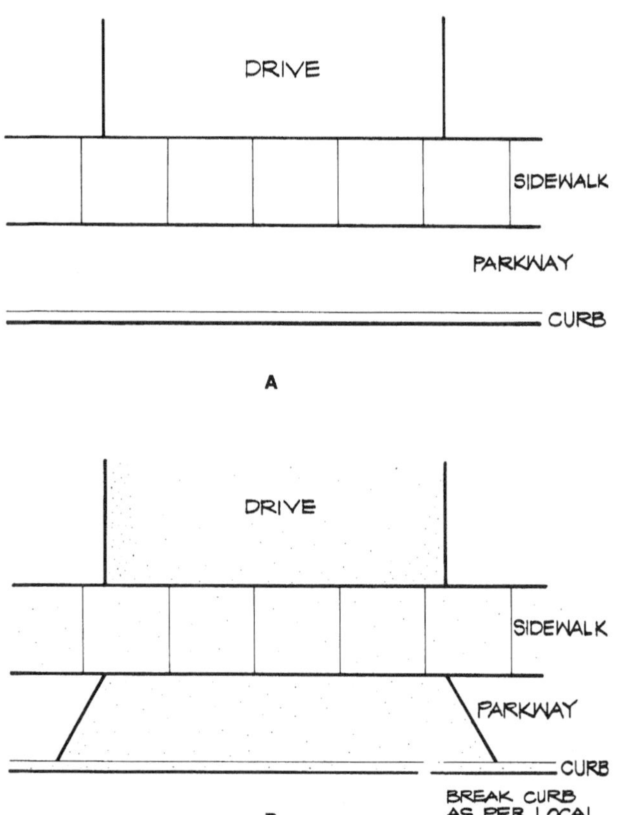

Figure 5.34 How to break a curb for a driveway.

provide the under-floor clearances required by building codes for wood floors.

After completing an analysis of the existing grades and their contours, in conjunction with the architectural planning of the residence, a grading plan can be prepared.

EROSION AND SEDIMENT CONTROL PLANS

When construction of a building occurs in winter months, the governing agency will require a plan that demonstrates how runoff is to be controlled onsite. This plan is called an **erosion control plan**. Such a plan graphically demonstrates that water will not carry off silt, dirt, or contaminants from a site into storm drains, waterways, or neighboring sites. These can be designed utilizing:

- Sediment control
- Silt fence
- Hay-bale barriers
- Sediment traps
- Silt curtain
- Sediment mat
- Filter logs
- Erosion control
- Temporary ditch checks
- Mulch
- Erosion control blankets
- Compost
- Erosion stabilization mats

These are a few methods that could be further researched when planning for erosion control. See Figure 5.37.

THE UTILITY PLAN

Plotting of existing utilities is necessary to the site improvement process. See Figure 5.2. Such a plan should show the location of all existing utilities, including sewer laterals, water and gas lines, and telephone, TV cable, and electrical service lines. This drawing then provides a basis for locating new utility connections. It may also influence the locations of transformers, generators, electrical rooms, and meter rooms in the structure itself.

CIRCULATION PLAN

In designing large complexes—more specifically, complexes with heavy vehicular circulation—it may become necessary to create a plan that articulates the flow of vehicular travel. These forms of plans are not complex to develop, but are informative to clients, city officials, and architects who are determining appropriate and efficient circulation design. See Figure 5.38.

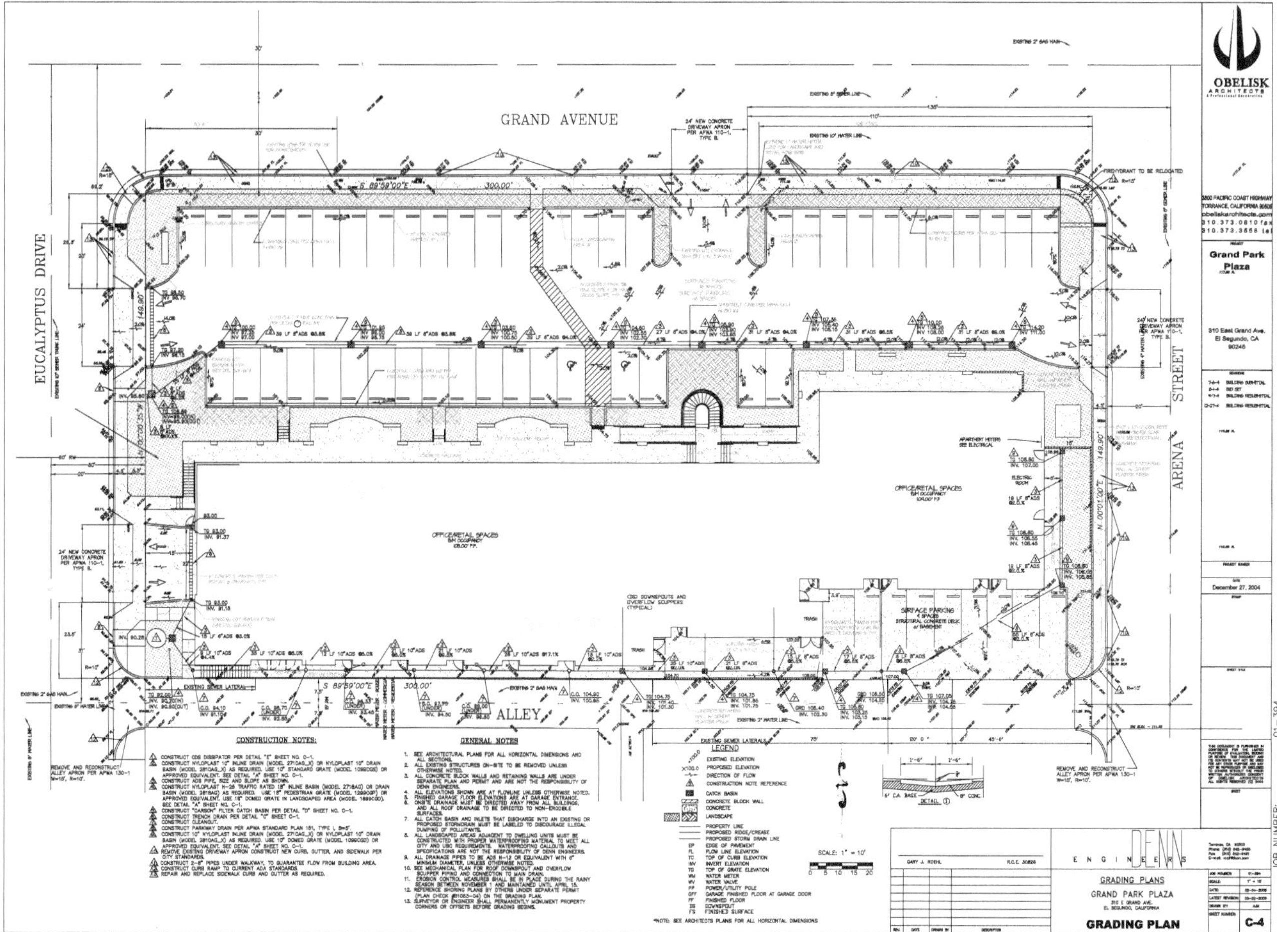

Figure 5.35 Existing grade. (Courtesy of Denn Engineers.)

LANDSCAPE, IRRIGATION, AND DRAINAGE PLANS

Landscape Plan and Plant List

The final stage of site development for most projects is landscaping. The landscape drawing shows the location of trees, plants, ground covers, benches, fences, and walks. Accompanying this is a **plant list**, identifying plant species with a symbol or number and indicating the size and number of plants. See Figure 5.39. Often, a landscape architect will be hired as a consultant to specify the ideal plant materials and make recommendations for the **hardscape** surrounding the project.

Irrigation Plan

An irrigation plan often accompanies the landscape plan. This drawing is typically separate from the landscape plan, but is directly influenced by the locations of plant material. This plan shows all water lines, points of connection, control valves, and types of watering fixtures required for irrigation. See Figure 5.40.

The primary information to be found in the site improvement plan is as follows:

1. Site lot lines with accompanying bearings and dimensions
2. Scale of the drawing
3. North arrows
4. Building location with layout dimensions
5. Paving, walks, walls with their accompanying material call-outs, and layout dimensions

Figure 5.41 shows the primary information found on a site improvement plan. The building layout dimension lines must be noted to their respective property lines, providing two measuring points at each side of the property lines. This, in turn, provides the location of the building on the site. This is helpful when the property lines do not parallel the building. This method may apply to patios, walks, paving, and walls, which are also dimensioned on the site improvement plan.

Site plans for large sites, such as multiple-resident housing projects, must show primary information, such as utility locations, driveway locations, and building locations. Further examples of site development plans

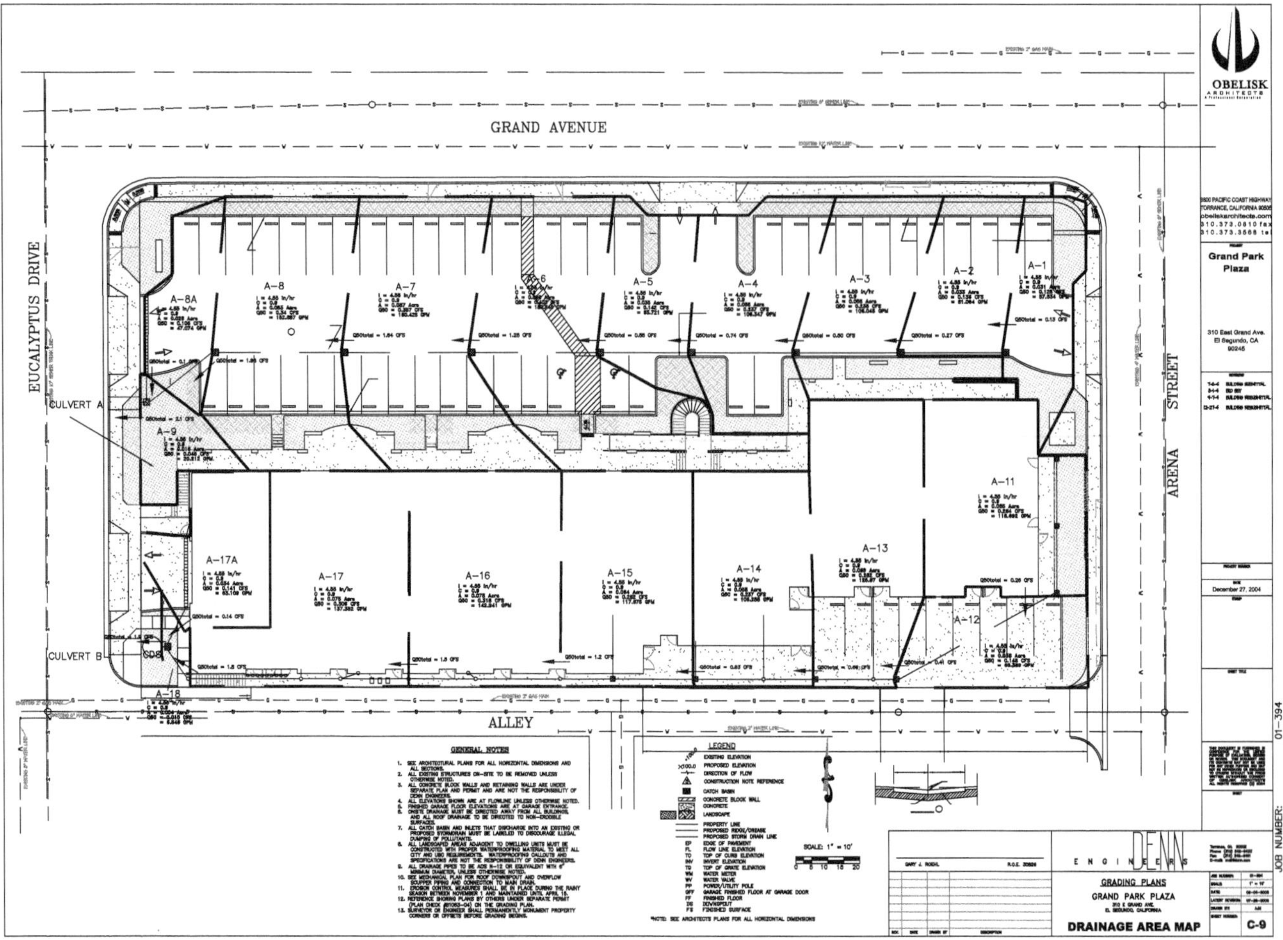

Figure 5.36 Drainage plan. (Courtesy of Denn Engineers.)

appear in later chapters. See Figure 5.42 for a site plan checklist. See Figure 5.43 for a finished example.

Key Terms

area drains
bearing capacity
bearings
bio-filters
boring log
building footprint
building pad
catch basin
compacted
contour lines
coordinates
cross-section
cross-slope
cut
daylight grade elevation
dedications
drainage plan
erosion control plan
existing contours
fill
finish grading
finished grades
floor area ratio (FAR)
French drain
geological investigations
geology
hardscape
location plan
lot line
man-made features
metes and bounds
offsets
point of beginning (POB)
plant list
plat map

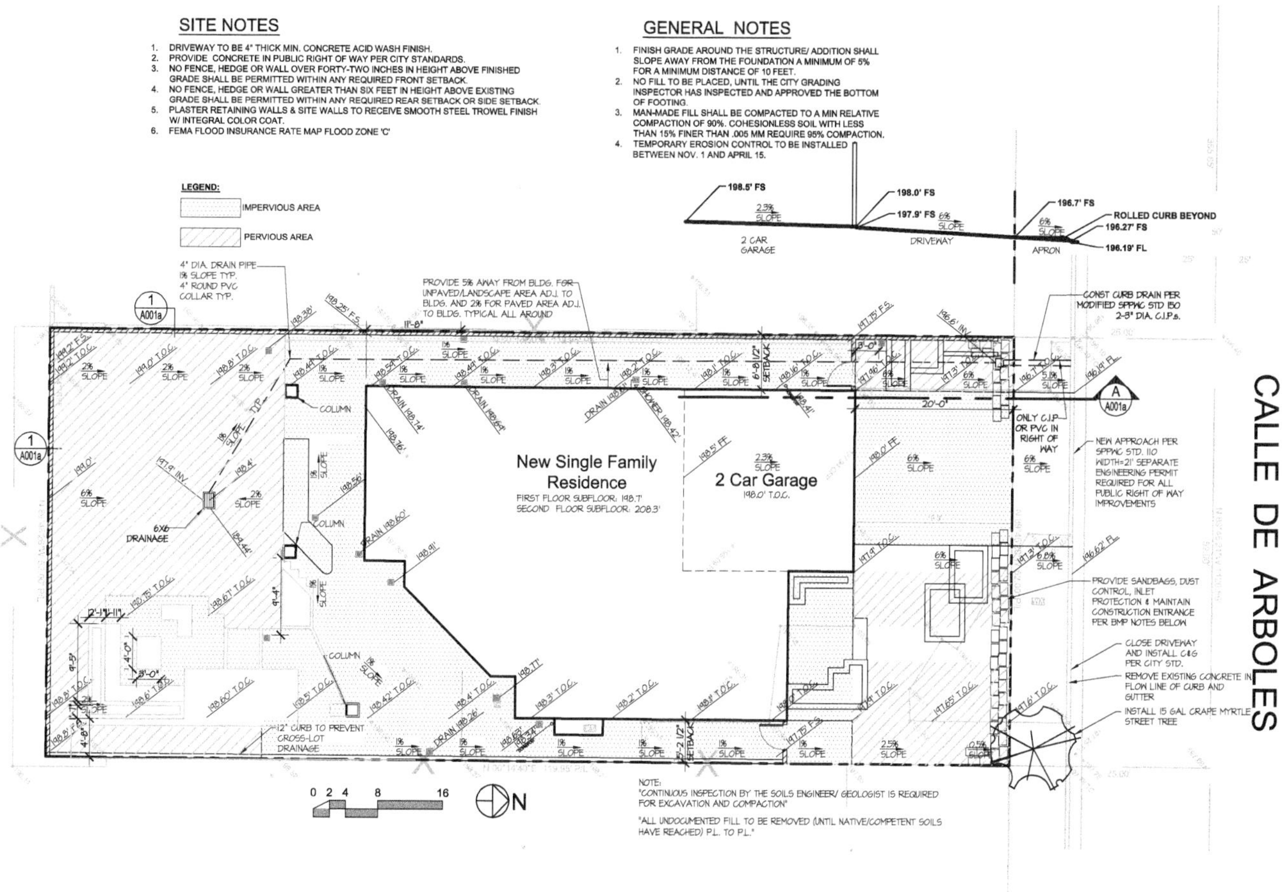

Figure 5.37 Erosion control plan.

plot plan
redevelopment districts
section line
setbacks
site analysis
site plan
slope ratios
soil type soils and geology map
soils investigations
sub-drain
swale
topography map
vicinity map
zoning

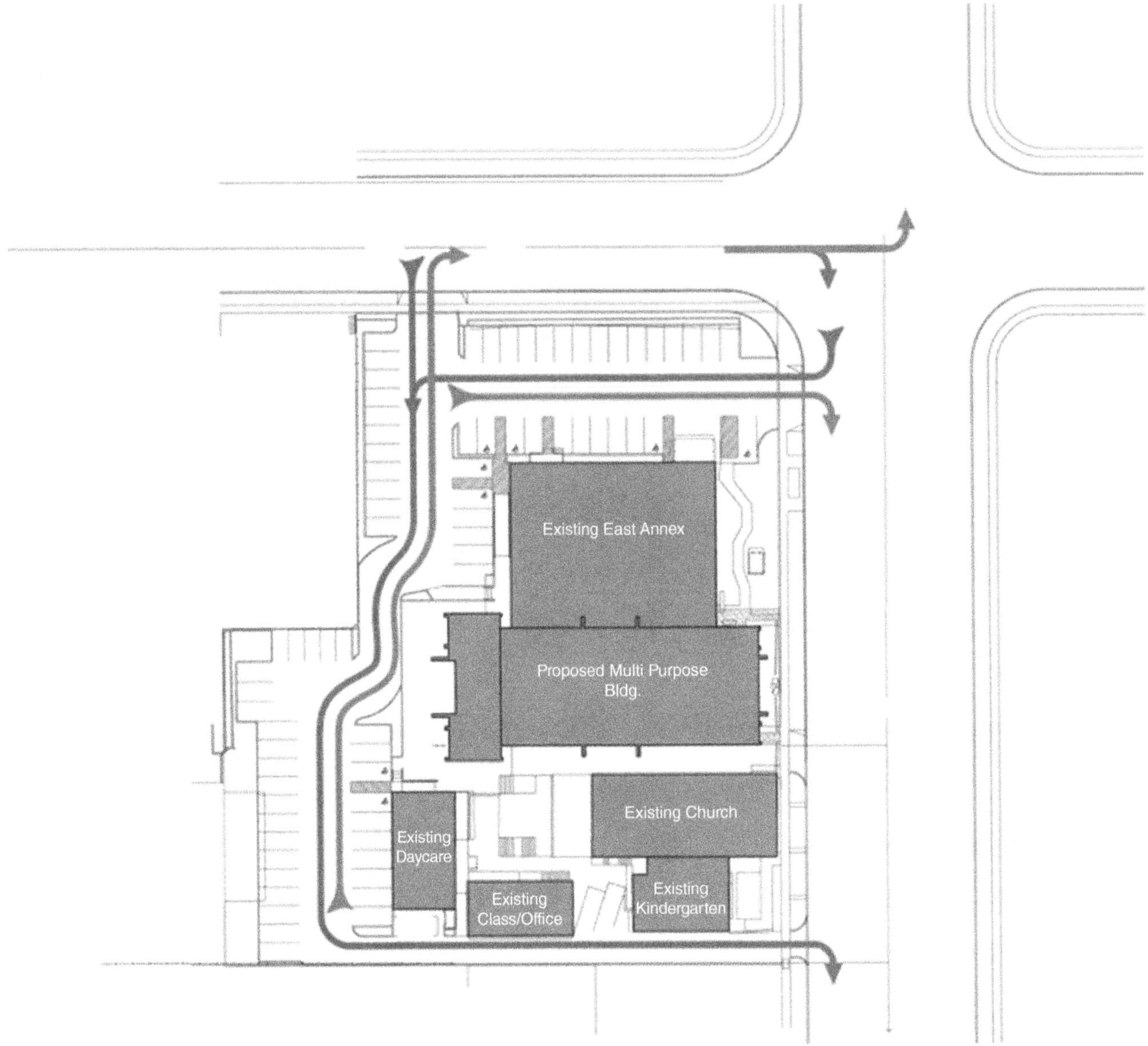

Figure 5.38 Circulation plan.

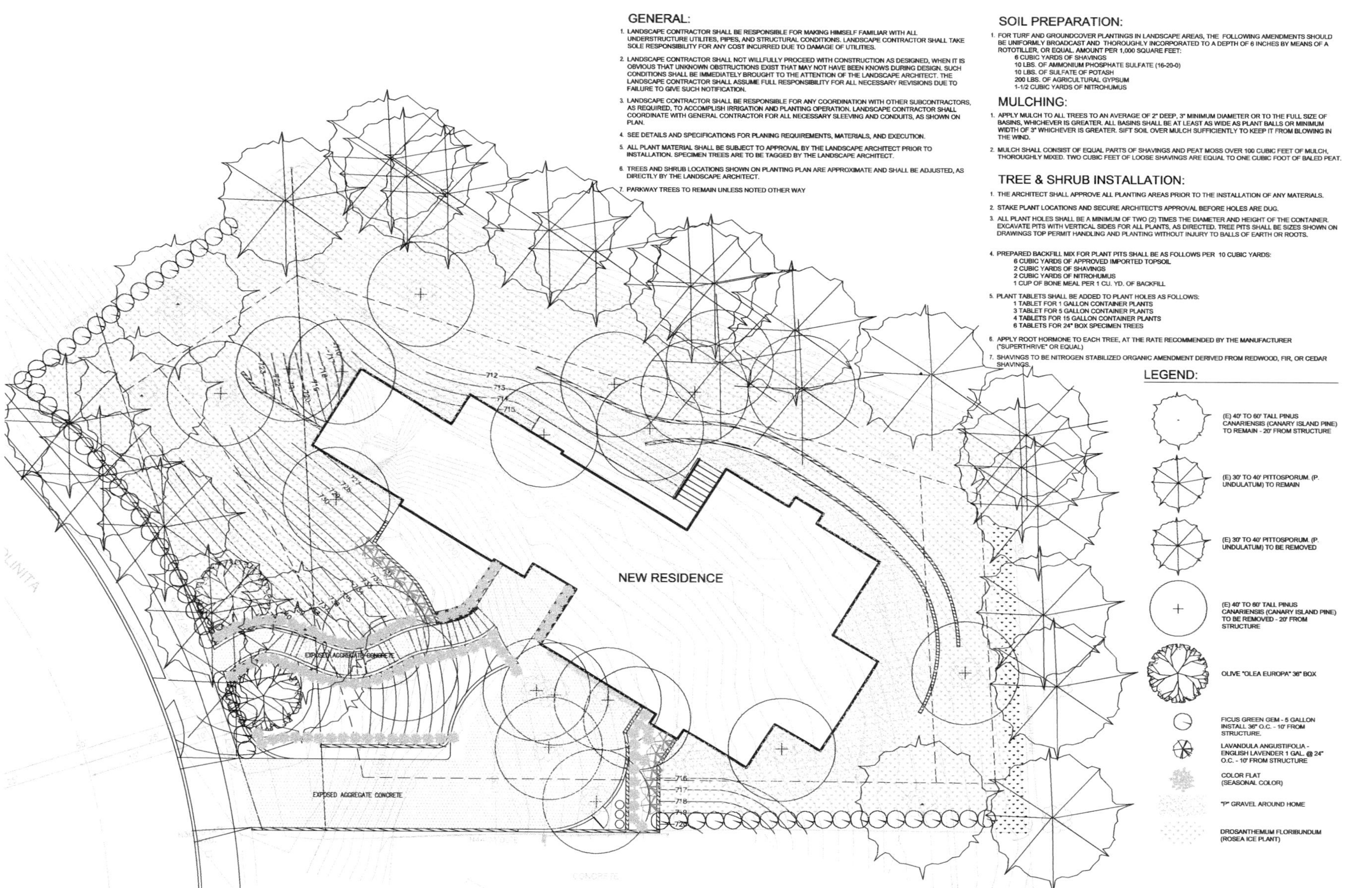

Figure 5.39 Landscape plan and material list.

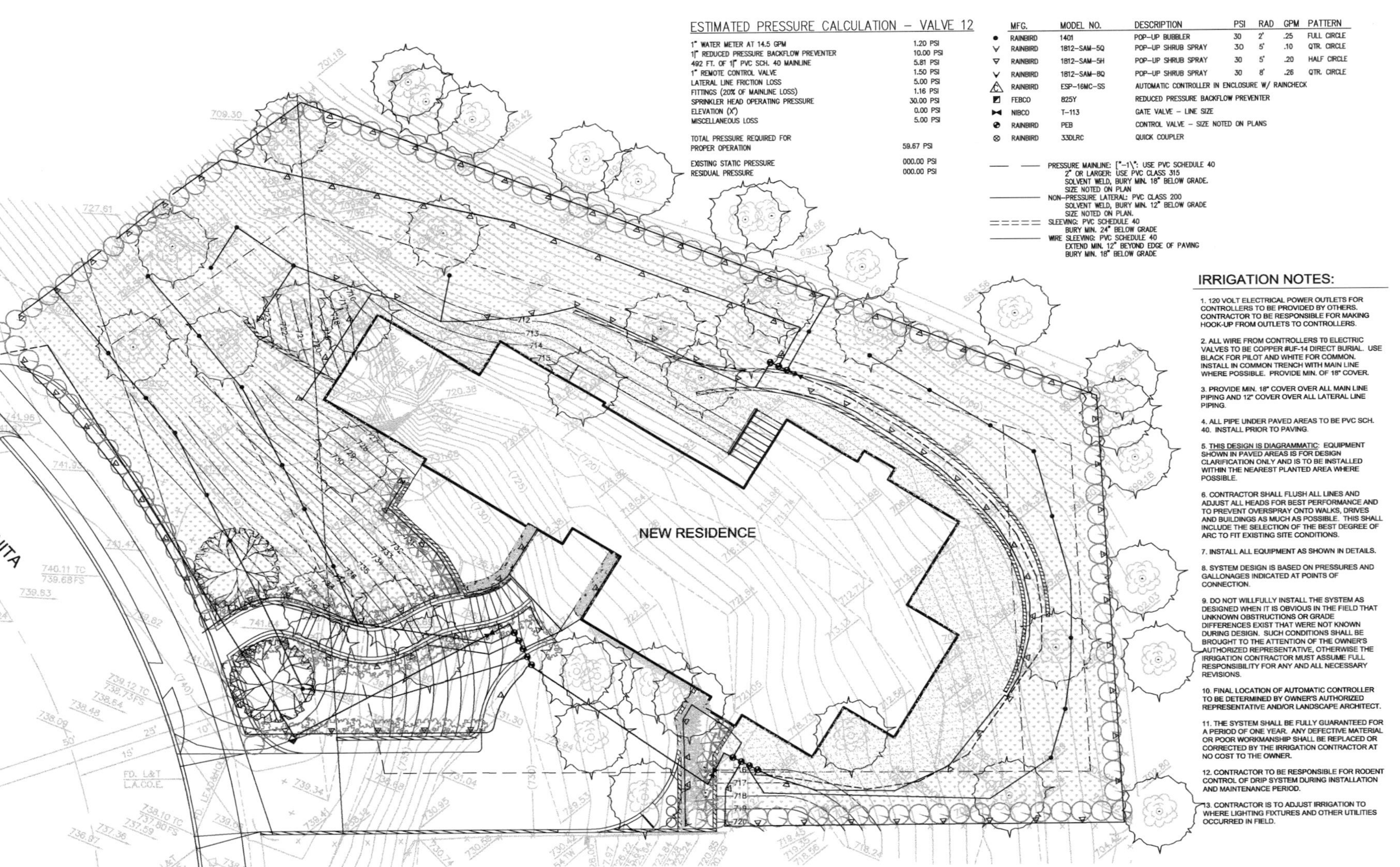

Figure 5.40 Irrigation plan.

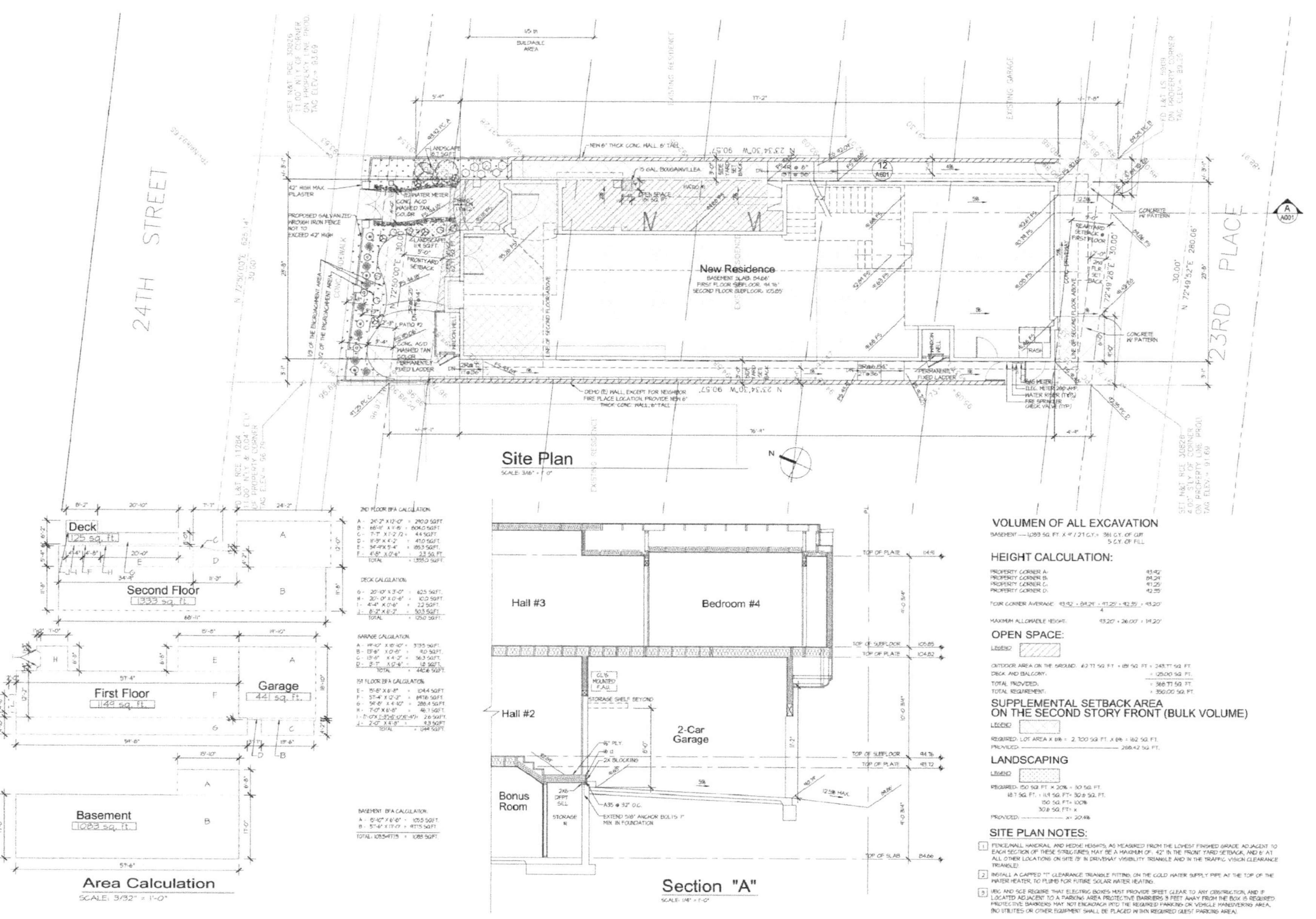

Figure 5.41 Site improvement plan.

1. Vicinity Map / Location Map
2. Property lines
   a. Lengths—each side
   b. Correct angles noted
   c. Direction of angle noted
3. Adjoining streets, sidewalks, parking, curbs, parkways, parking areas, wheel stops, lanes and lighting, trees
4. Existing structures, buildings, alleys, and trees
5. Structures and buildings to be removed / to remain
   a. Trees / Landscape
   b. Old foundations / Walls
   c. Walks / Patios
   d. Miscellanea
6. Public utilities locations
   a. Storm drain
   b. Sewer lines
   c. Gas lines
   d. Gas meter
   e. Water lines
   f. Water meter
   g. Power line
   h. Power pole
   i. Electric meter
   j. Telephone pole
   k. Lamp post
   l. Fire plugs
   m. Fire alarms
   n. Determine overhead / underground
7. Public utilities easements if on property
8. Grading and drainage plan
   a. Existing grade—dotted line
   b. Finish cut or fill—solid line
   c. Legend
   d. Slopes to street
   e. Slopes away from building
9. Grade elevations
   a. Finish slab or finish floor
   b. Corners of building (finish)
   c. Top of all walls
   d. Amount of slope for drainage
10. Roof plan
   a. Building—hidden line
   b. Roof overhang—solid line
   c. Garage located
   d. Slopes (arrows)
   e. Projecting canopies
   f. Slabs and porches
   g. Projecting beams
   h. Material for roof
   i. North arrow
   j. Title and scale
   k. Show ridges and valleys
   l. Roof drains and downspouts
   m. Parapets
   n. Roof jacks for TV, telephone, electric service
   o. Note building outline
   p. Dimension overhangs
   q. Note rain diverters
   r. Sky lights
   s. Roof accessways
   t. Flood lite locations
   u. Service pole for electrical
11. New construction
   a. Retaining walls
   b. Driveways and aprons
   c. Sidewalks
   d. Pool locations and size
   e. Splash blocks
   f. Catch basins
   g. Curbs
   h. Patios, walls, expansion joints, dividers etc.
12. North arrow (usually pointing up)
13. Dimensions
   a. Property lines
   b. Side yards
   c. Rear yards
   d. Front yards
   e. Easements
   f. Street center line
   g. Length of fences and walls
   h. Height of fences and walls
   i. Width of sidewalks, driveway, and parking
   j. Utilities
   k. Locations of existing structures
   l. Note floor elevation
   m. Dimension building to property line
   n. Setbacks
14. Notes
   a. Tract no.
   b. Block no.
   c. Lot no.
   d. House no.
   e. Street
   f. City, county, state, county
   g. Owner's name / address / #
   h. Materials for porches, terraces, drives, etc.
   i. Finish grades where necessary
   j. Slope of driveway
   k. Scale (1/8", 1"-30', 1"-20', etc.)
15. Landscape lighting, note switches
16. Area drains, drain lines to street
17. Show hose bibs
18. Note drying yard, clothes line equipment
19. Complete title block
   a. Sheet no.
   b. Scale
   c. Date
   d. Name drawn by
   e. Project address
   f. Approved by
   g. Sheet title
   h. Revision box
   i. Company name and address (school)
   j. Date printed

Figure 5.42 Sample site plan checklist.

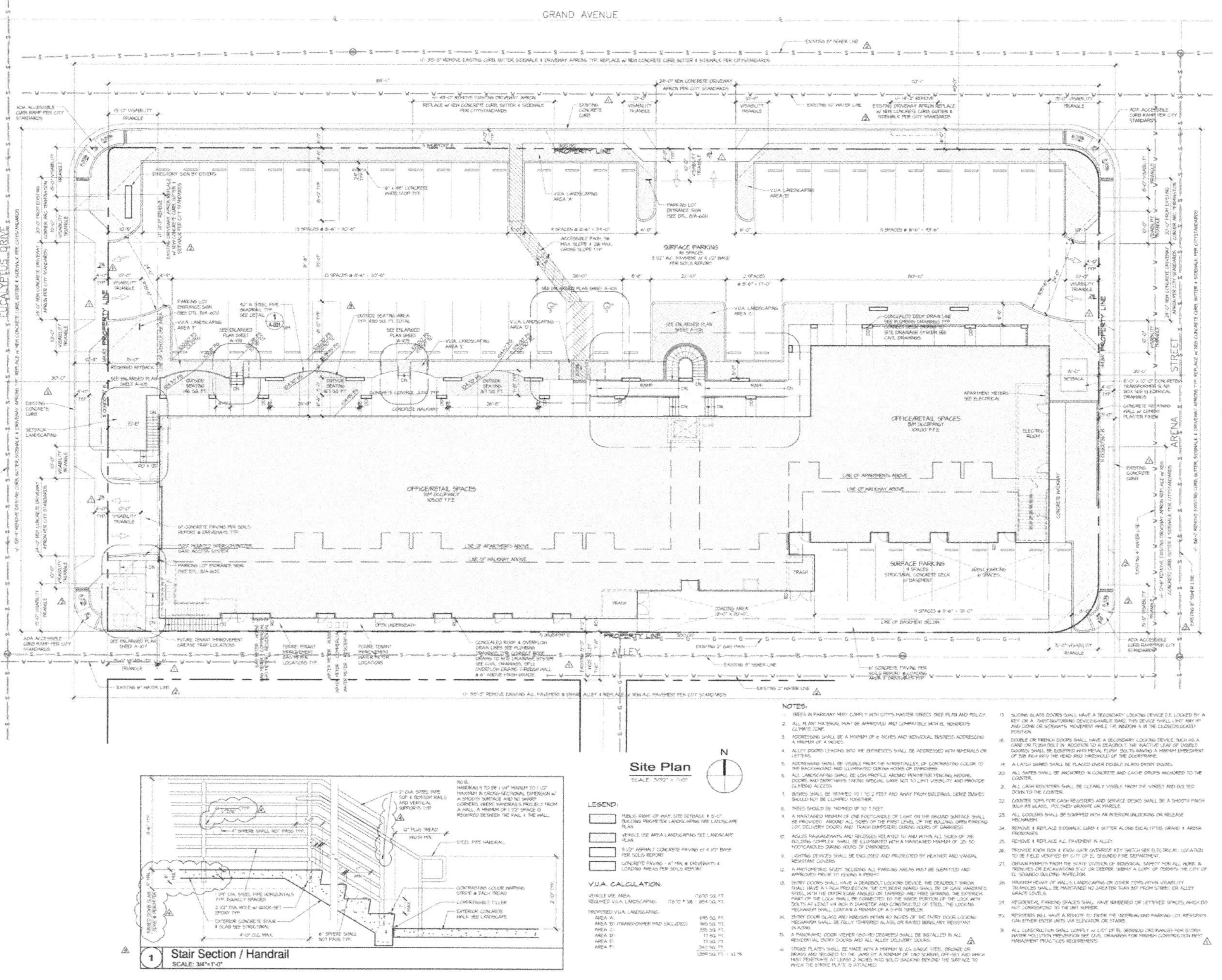

Figure 5.43 Commercial site plan.

chapter

6

FLOOR PLAN

The Professional Practice of Architectural Working Drawings, Sixth Edition. Nagy R. Bakhoum and Osamu A. Wakita.
© 2024 John Wiley & Sons Inc. Published 2024 by John Wiley & Sons Inc.
Companion website: www.wiley.com\go\bakhoum\theprofessionalpracticeofarchitecturalworkingdrawings

FLOOR PLANS

Defining the word floor plan can be simply described as a horizontal cut at eye level through a building with the upper portion of the roof portion removed and viewed from above. The floor plan is that and much more. It is also a representation of a 3-D building drawn to scale and demonstrates the rooms in a building and its adjacencies. It demonstrates the wall opening via symbolic representation of doors, windows, and other styles of passages. Including dimensions, fixtures, furnishings, finishes, specifications, notes, and appliances, the floor plan is among one of the most communicative illustrations an architect can develop.

The floor plan is such an important drawing that most consultants, such as interior designers, structural engineers, MEP, Title 24, and other consulting engineers, utilize as a datum or background for the development of their drawings. Clients also review and study the floor plans in three phases of architectural services, SD, DD, and CDs. Contractors rely heavily on plans to establish things like foundation layout, room layout, and placement of all fenestrations.

BIM does an outstanding job of giving the architect options for wall assemblies; if the exact option is not available, a quick customization or a generic wall type will do the job. This schedule feature offered in BIM will give you an exact calculation of the plaster, drywall, and linear feet of the lumber needed for bidding purposes and assignment advancement over AutoCAD drawing systems.

Circulation of space is best demonstrated by the floor plan (FP) if buildings consist of several levels; each floor requires an FP. If a building has floors that are identical, such as a high-rise one, a simple label describing floor levels can accommodate the job of demonstrating those levels.

A floor plan is a multi-faceted drawing that can require a legend describing wall types or types of construction methods. Understanding that the two lines symbolically represent a construction system or method of construction is imperative. For exterior walls and interior plumbing walls that are typically drawn as 2 × 6 studs with interior finishes such as gypsum drywall and exterior walls covered with siding or plaster and in between the studs is a cavity filled with insulation. Plumbing walls require an additional space for plumbing waste and water supply lines, providing two extra inches of space and maintaining the wall integrity. Interior walls can be drawn at 2 × 4 stud walls and if desired can be insulated as well.

When drawing a floor plan, occasionally materials such as wood studs do not work and metal studs are required. The building code states that all fireplaces must maintain a 2-inch clearance from the wood studs. In this scenario, metal studs can be used to meet the code requirement and achieve the desired outcome. Some building types do not allow the use of combustible materials, such as wood, so steel or masonry is required. Unlike wood studs, these wall types have a convention as well.

The point of reference for working drawings is the floor plan: a drawing viewed from above with the roof removed. Actually, it is a horizontal cut (section) taken at approximately eye level. See Figure 6.1.

To better understand this, imagine a knife slicing through a structure and removing the upper half (on a single-story structure, the half with the roof). The remaining half is then viewed from the air. This becomes the floor plan. See Figure 6.2.

Single- and Split-Level Floor Plans

The floor plan for a split-level residence is more complicated. In the following example, the entry, powder room, and garage are at the mid-level, which is also the level of the street and sidewalk. Use this level as a point of reference.

The stairs at the rear of the entry lead to the upper and lower levels. The lower level contains the master bedroom, master bath, study, bedroom, laundry, and bathroom. See Figure 6.3. The upper level contains the living room with a wet bar, and the dining room, kitchen, breakfast room, and foyer. See Figure 6.4.

When these are translated into a floor plan, they appear as in Figures 6.5 and 6.6. The mid-level is duplicated and common to both drawings.

A second approach is to use a **break line** (a line with a jog in it to indicate that a portion has been deleted), showing only a part of the garage on one of the plans. Another approach is to use a straight break line through the garage and draft it showing only part of the garage on one of the plans.

In a two-story building, a single room on the first floor is sometimes actually two stories high. If this room were a living room, for example, it would be treated as a normal one-story living room on the first-floor plan; however, the area would be repeated on the second-floor plan and labeled as upper living room or just labeled "open."

To simplify the image to be drafted, not every structural member is shown. For example, in a wood-framed structure, if every vertical piece of wood were shown, the task would be impossible. Simplifying this image of the wood structure is done with two parallel lines. Sometimes the insulation is shown in symbol form and is not shown through the total wall. See Figure 6.7. The same parallel series of lines can also be used to represent a masonry wall by adding a series of diagonal lines. See Figure 6.8. Steel frame can be represented as shown in Figure 6.9.

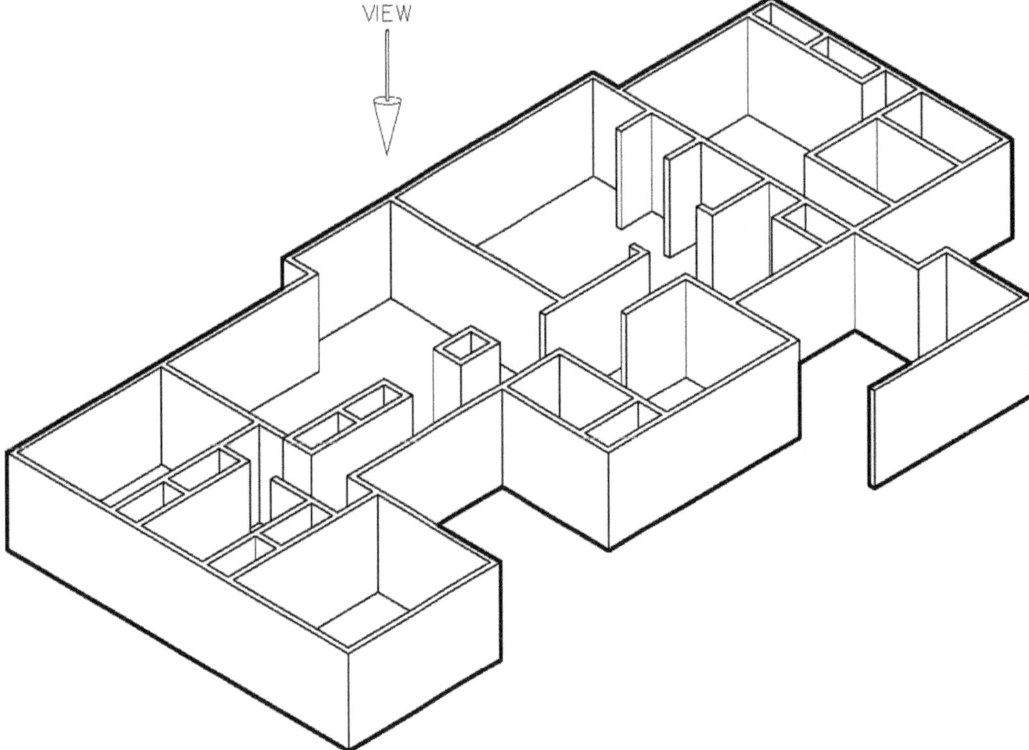

Figure 6.1 Cutaway pictorial floor plan.

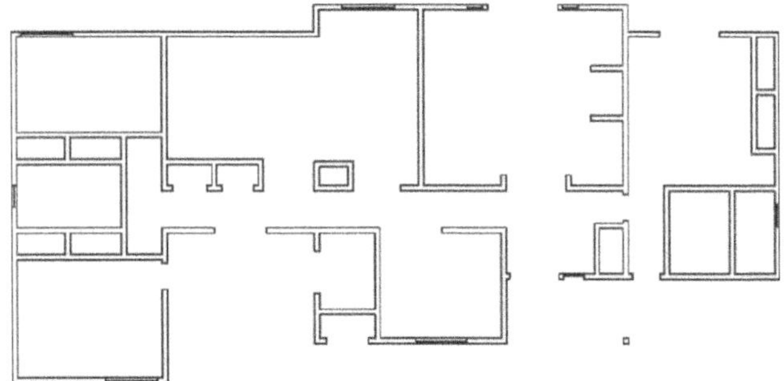

Figure 6.2 Floor plan.

TYPES OF FLOOR PLANS

Wood Framing

Figure 6.10 shows the appearance of a corner of a wood-framed structure. Each side of the wall is built separately. An extra stud is usually placed at the end of the wall; it extends to the edge of the building. It therefore acts as a structural support and gives a larger nailing surface to which wall materials can be anchored.

Figure 6.11 shows the pictorial intersection of an interior wall and an exterior wall, and a plan view of that same intersection.

Walls are not the only important elements in the framing process, of course. You must also consider the locations of doors and windows and the special framing they require. See Figure 6.12.

Interior Dimensioning. Because a wood-framed wall is a built-up system—that is, a wall frame of wood upon which plaster or another wall covering is added—dimension lines must sometimes be drawn to the edge of studs and sometimes to their center.

Figure 6.13 shows how the corner of a wood-framed wall is dimensioned to the stud line. Figure 6.14 shows how an interior wall intersecting an exterior wall is dimensioned. It is dimensioned to the center so that the two studs that the interior wall will join can be located.

The process of drawing each stud in a wall becomes tiresome. So, usually, two lines drawn 6″ apart (in scale) are used to represent wood. To make sure that the person reading this set of plans knows that the stud is being dimensioned and not the exterior surface, the extension is often brought inside the 6″-wide wall lines. Another way to make this clear is to take extension lines to the outside surface and write **face of stud (FOS)** adjacent to the extension lines. See Figure 6.13.

Dimensioning interior walls requires a centerline or an extension line right into the wall intersection, as

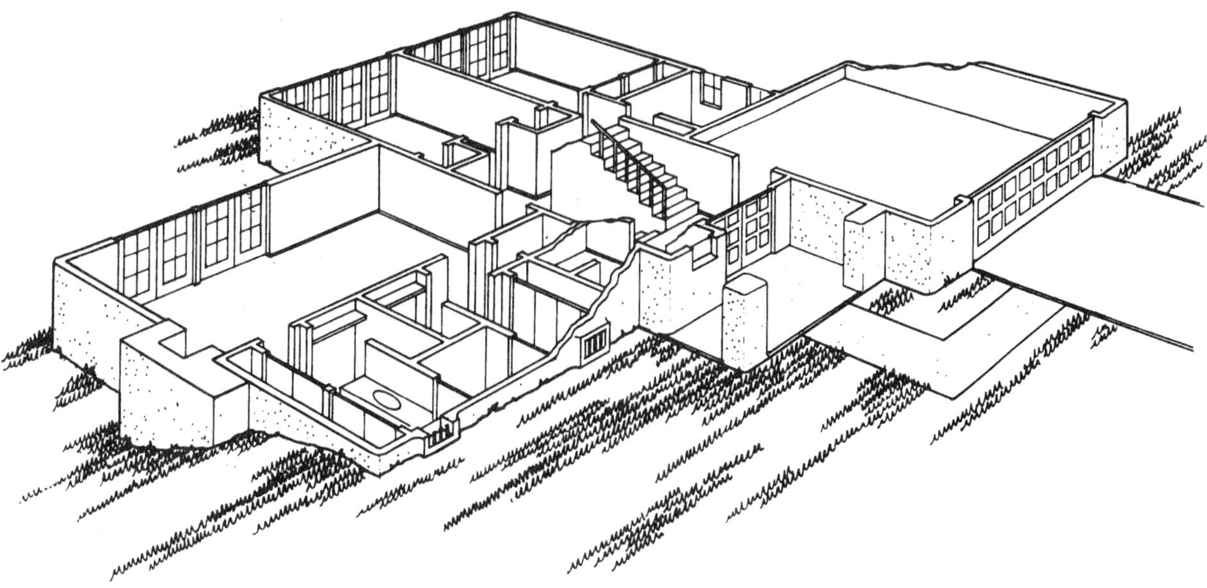

Figure 6.3 Pictorial of lower-level floor plan. (Courtesy of William F. Smith—Builder.)

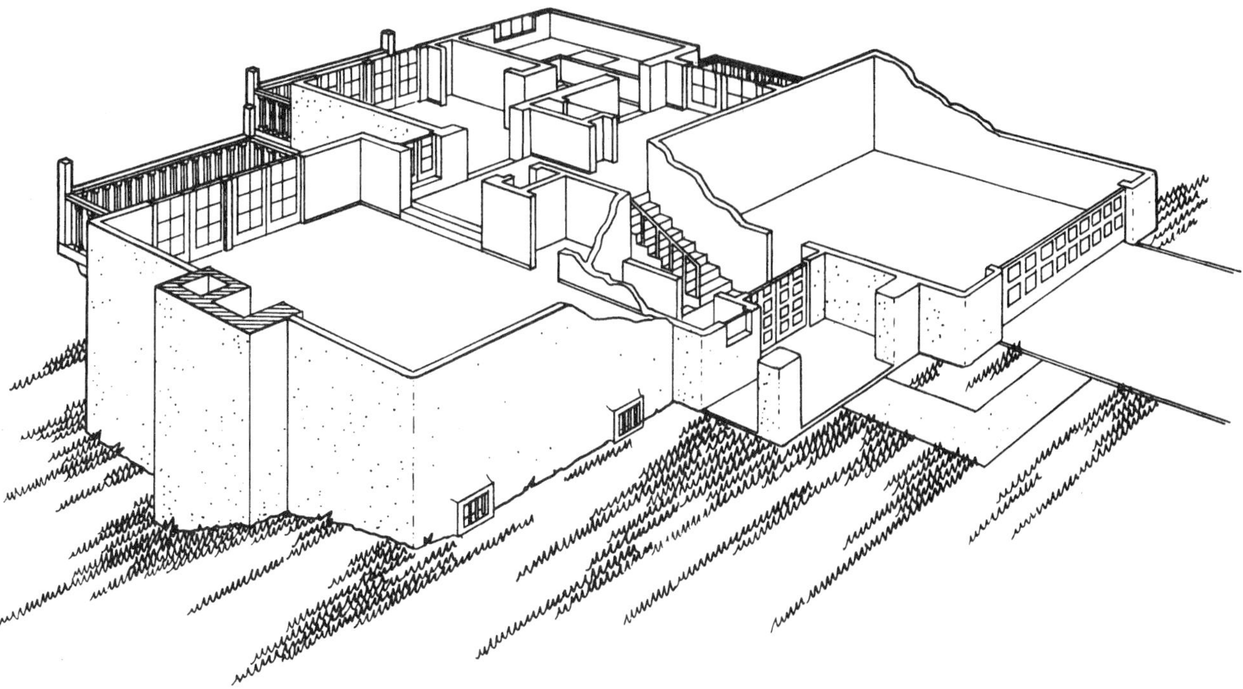

Figure 6.4 Pictorial of upper-level floor plan. (Courtesy of William F. Smith—Builder.)

shown in Figure 6.14. A centerline is more desirable than a solid line.

Windows and doors are located to the center of the object, as shown in Figure 6.15. When a structural column is next to a window or door, the doors and windows are dimensioned to the structural column. The size of a particular window or door can be obtained from a chart called a *schedule*. This schedule can be found by locating the sheet number on the bottom half of the **reference bubble** adjacent to the window or door. See Figure 6.16. (A reference bubble is a circle with a line drawn through it horizontally.) Depending on the office standard this notation can be a circle or square.

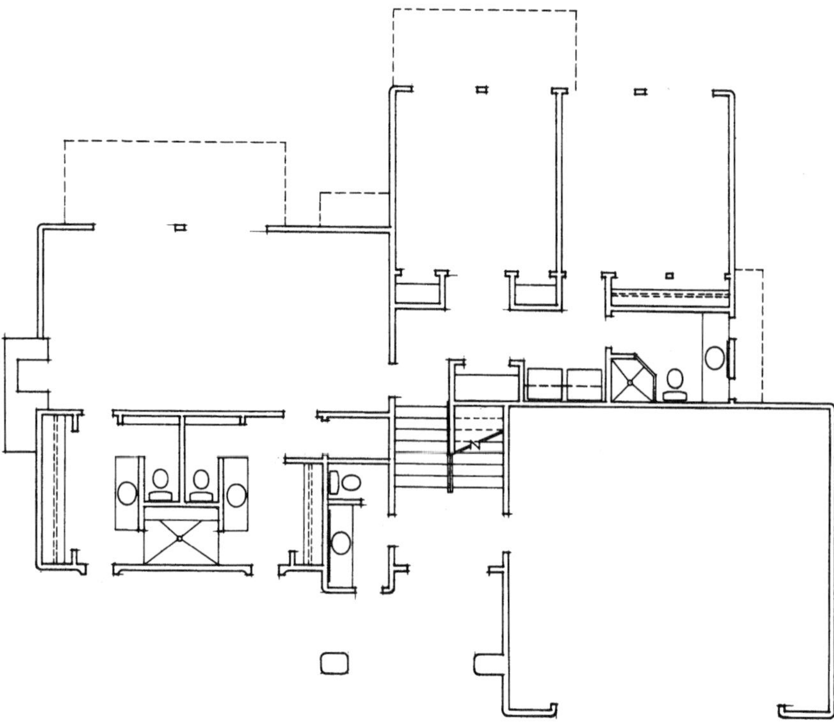

Figure 6.5 Lower-level floor plan. (Courtesy of William F. Smith—Builder.)

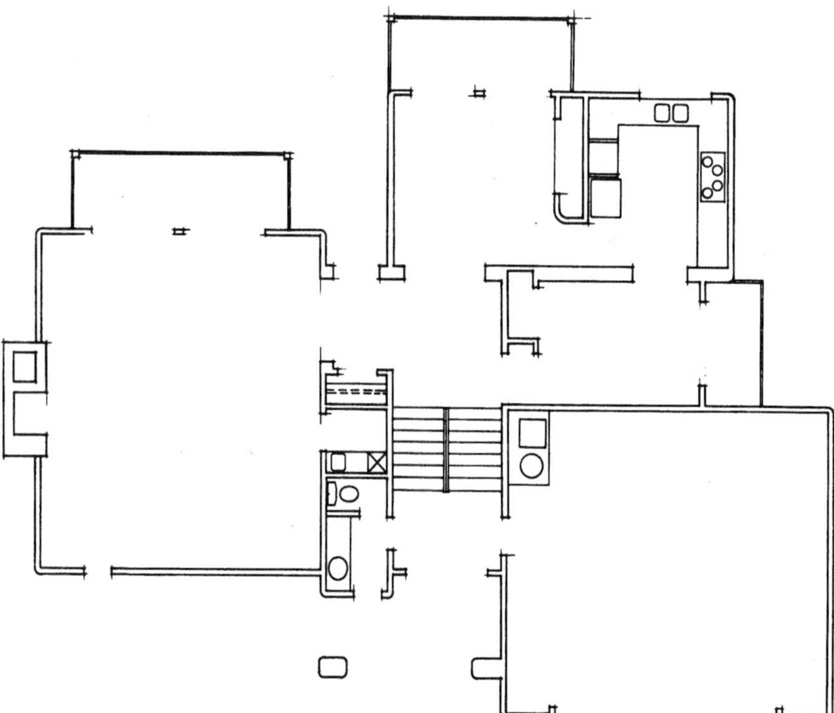

Figure 6.6 Upper-level floor plan. (Courtesy of William F. Smith—Builder.)

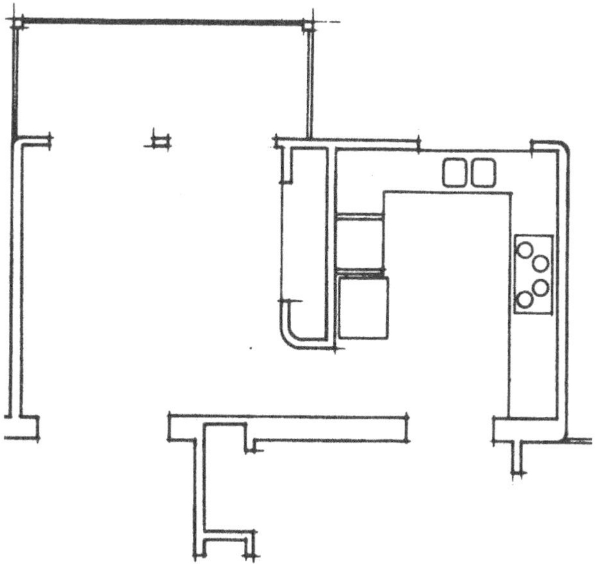

Figure 6.7 Representation of wood frame.

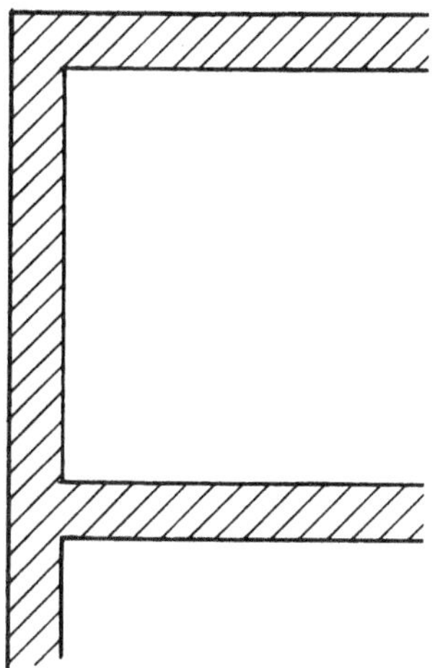

Figure 6.8 Representation of masonry.

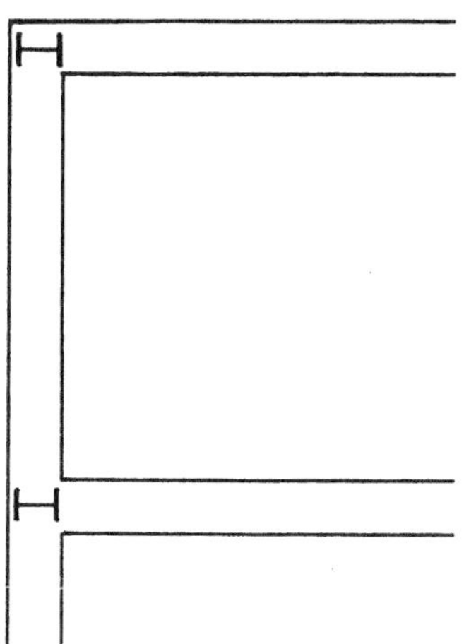

Figure 6.9 Representation of steel frame.

Exterior Dimensioning. Normally, three-to-four-dimension lines are needed on an exterior dimension of a floor plan. The first-dimension line away from the object includes the walls, partitions, centers of windows and doors, and so forth. See Figure 6.17. The second-dimension line away from the object (floor plan) includes walls and partitions only. If, in establishing the second-dimension line, you duplicate a dimension, eliminate the dimension line closest to the object. The third-dimension line away from the object is for overall dimensions. The first-dimension line away from the structure should be measured 3/4″ to 1 1/2″ from the outside lines of the plan to allow for notes, window and door reference bubbles, equipment that may be placed adjacent to the structure, and so on. The second-dimension line away from the structure should be approximately 3/8″ to 1/2″ away from the first-dimension line. The distance between all subsequent dimension lines should be the same as the distance between the first- and second-dimension lines.

A large jog in a wall is called an **offset**. Because the jog is removed from the plane that is being dimensioned, you must decide whether to use long extension lines or to dimension the offset at the location of the jog.

If the jog were lengthy, it would be better to dimension the jog on its own. See Figure 6.18 for a small jog. This would be dimensioned on the second- or third-dimension line, and the fourth-dimension line would become the overall.

Objects located independently or outside of the structure, such as posts (columns), are treated differently. First, the order in which the items are to be built must be established. Will the columns be built before or after the adjacent walls? If the walls or the foundation for the walls are to be erected first, then major walls near the columns are identified and the columns are located from them. See Figure 6.19.

Masonry/Concrete Block Structures

When walls are built of brick or concrete block instead of wood frame, the procedure changes. Everything here is based on the size and proportion of the masonry unit used. Represent masonry as a series of diagonal lines. See Figure 6.20. Show door and window openings in the same way as you did for wood-framed structures. You may represent concrete block in the same way as brick for small-scale drawings but be aware that some offices use different material designations. See Figure 6.21. Extension lines for dimensioning are taken to the edge (end) of the exterior surface in both exterior and interior walls. See Figure 6.22.

Pilasters, which are columns built into the wall by widening the walls, are dimensioned to the center. See Figure 6.23. The size of the pilaster itself can be lettered adjacent to one of the pilasters in the drawing. Another

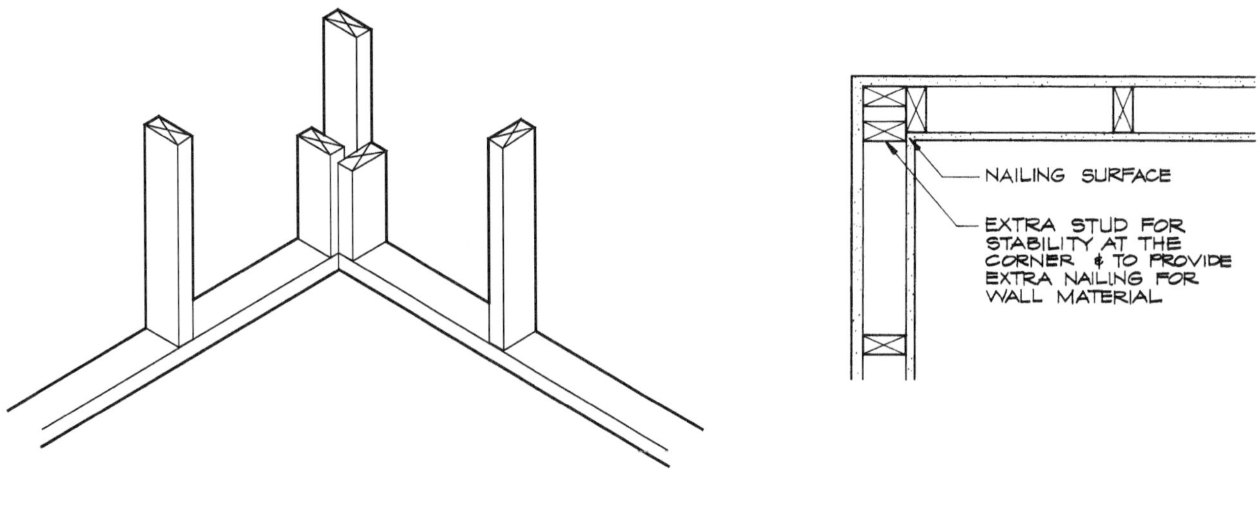

Figure 6.10 Corner at sill.

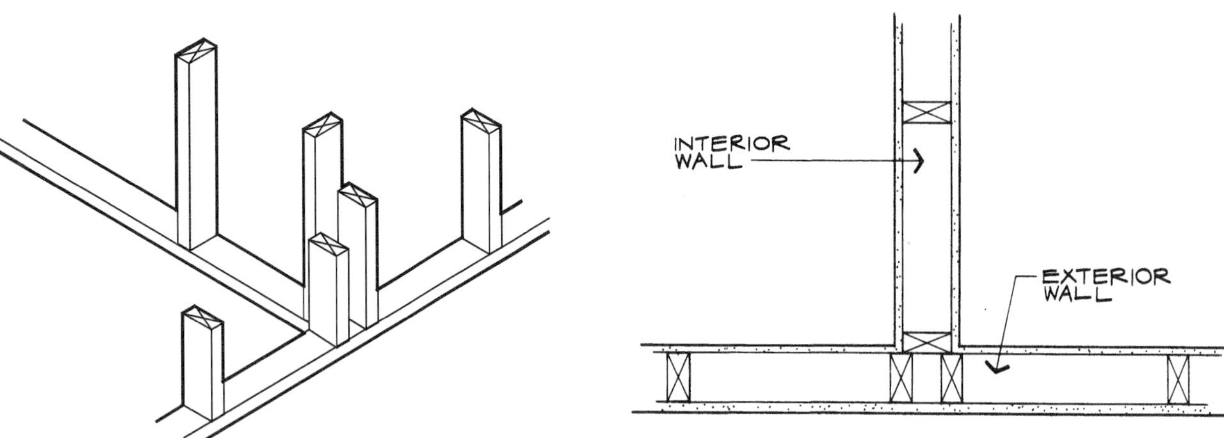

Figure 6.11 Intersection of exterior wall in interior wall.

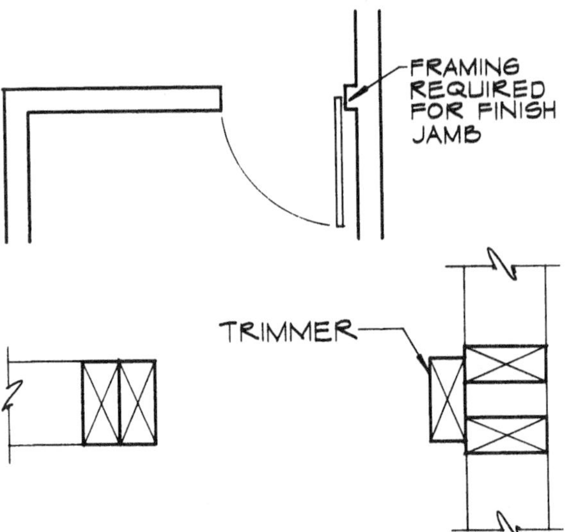

Figure 6.12 Framing for a door.

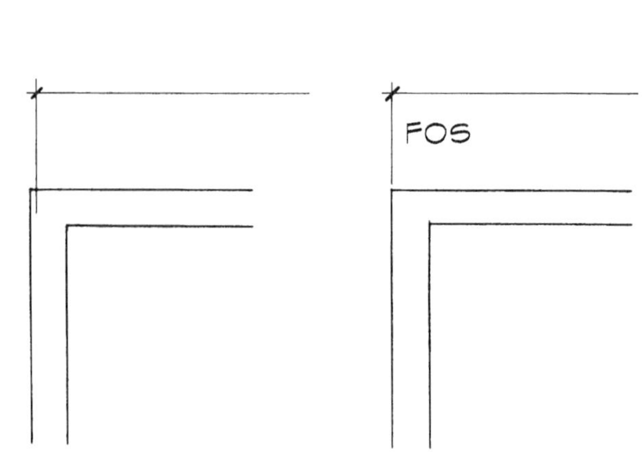

Figure 6.13 Dimensioning corners.

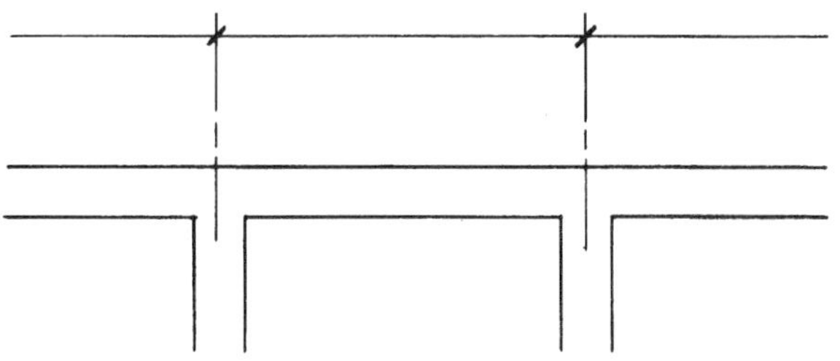

Figure 6.14 Dimensioning interior walls.

method of dealing with the size of these pilasters is to refer the reader of the plan to a detail with a note or reference bubble. All columns consisting of masonry or masonry around steel are also dimensioned to the center.

Windows and Doors. Windows and doors create a unique problem in masonry units. In wood structures, windows and doors are located by dimensioning to the center and allowing the framing carpenter to create the proper opening for the required window or door size. In masonry, the opening is established before installation of the window or door. This is called the **rough opening**; the final opening size is called the **finished opening**.

The rough opening, which is usually the one dimensioned on the plan, should follow the masonry block module. See Figure 6.24. This block module and the specific type of detail used determine the most economical and practical window and door sizes. See Figure 6.25. Therefore, you should provide dimensions for locating windows, doors, interior walls, and anything of a masonry variety to the rough opening. See Figure 6.26. A floor plan of a truck wash constructed of masonry is shown in Figure 6.27.

Steel Structures

There are two main types of steel systems: **steel stud** and **steel frame**. Steel studs can be treated like wood stud

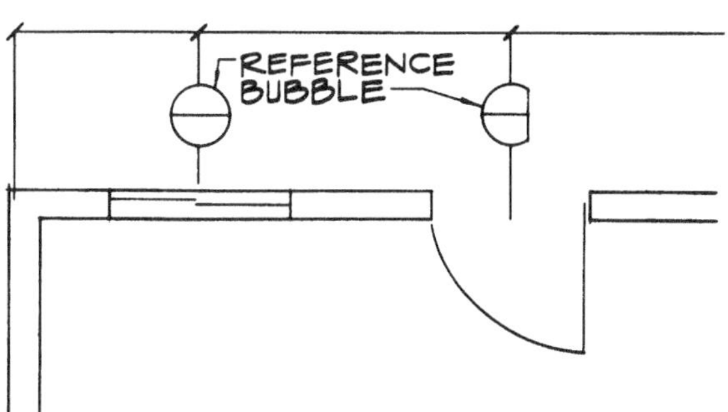

Figure 6.16 Use of reference bubbles on doors and windows.

construction. As with wood stud construction, you need to dimension to the stud face rather than to the wall covering (skin).

There are various shapes of steel studs. See Figure 6.28. Figure 6.29 shows how these shapes appear in the plan view. Drawing each steel stud is time-consuming, so two parallel lines are drawn to indicate the width of the wall. See Figure 6.28A, B, and C. Steel studs can be called out by a note.

If only a portion of a structure is steel stud and the remainder is wood or masonry, you can shade (*poché*) the area with steel studs or use a steel symbol. See Figure 6.30.

Dimensioning Columns. Steel columns are commonly used to hold up heavy weights. This weight is distributed to the earth by means of a concrete pad. See Figure 6.31. This concrete pad is dimensioned to its center, as Figure 6.32 shows. When you dimension the steel columns that will show in the floor plan, dimension them to the center. See Figure 6.33. This relates them to the concrete pads. Dimensioning a series of columns follows the same procedure. See Figure 6.34. The dimensions are taken to the centers of the columns in each direction.

Sometimes, the column must be dimensioned to the face rather than to the center. As Figure 6.33 shows, the

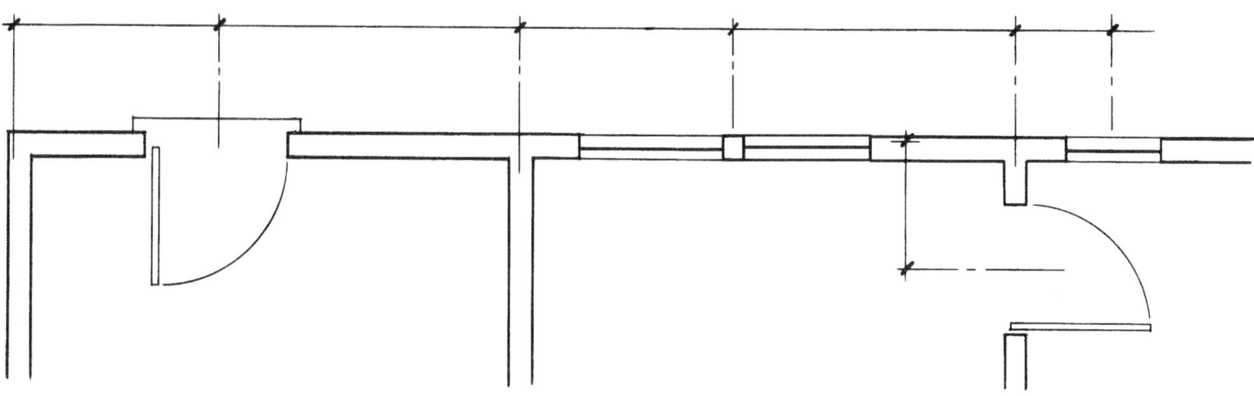

Figure 6.15 Dimensioning doors and windows.

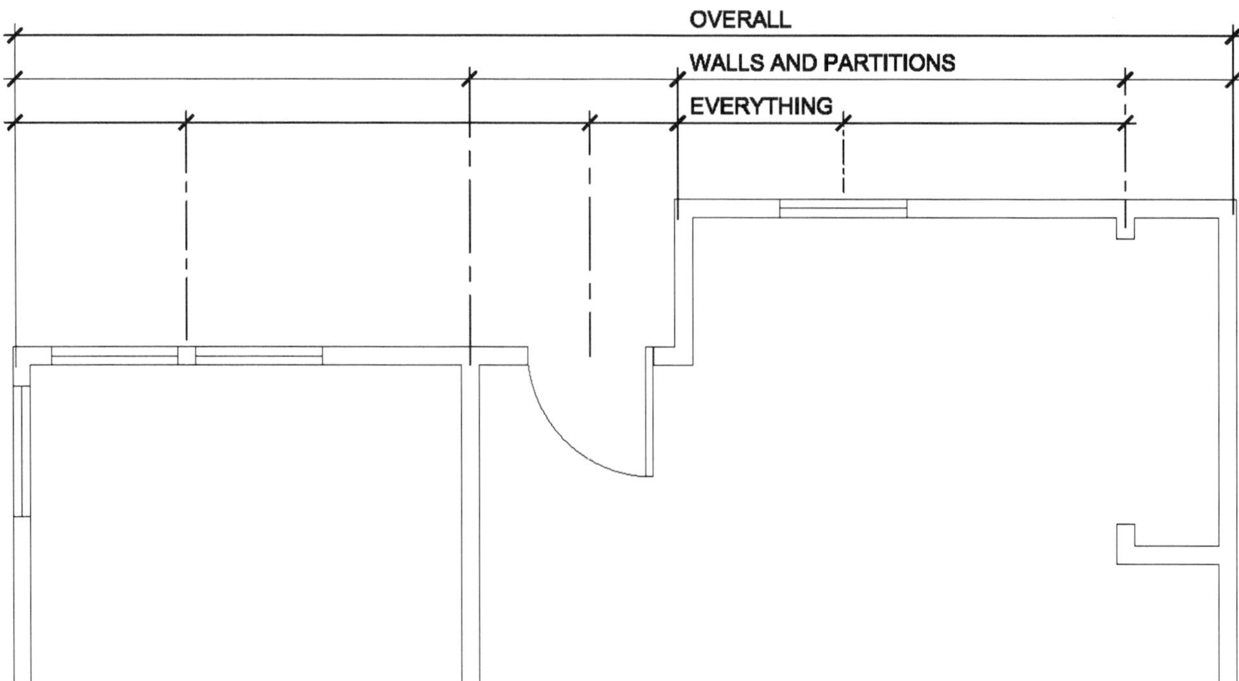

Figure 6.17 First dimension line away from the object.

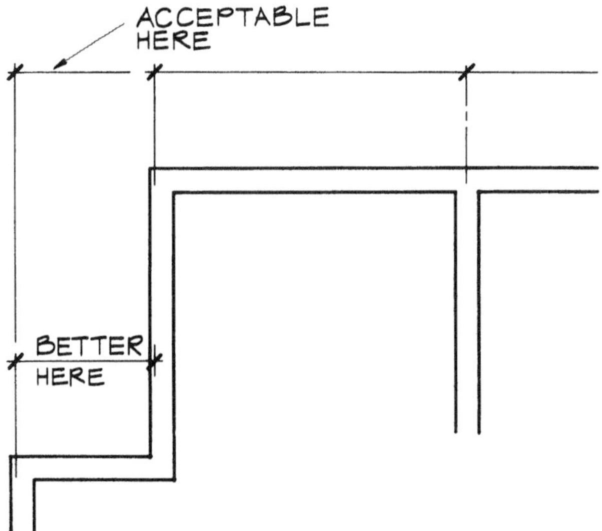

Figure 6.18 Offset dimension locations.

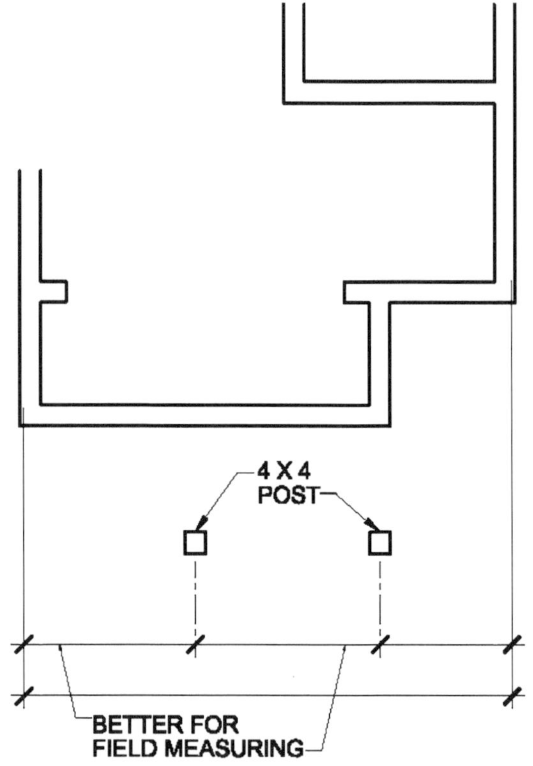

Figure 6.19 Locating columns from the structure.

extension line is taken to the outside face of the column. Axial reference planes are often used in conjunction with steel columns, as shown in Figure 6.34, and the column may be dimensioned to the face.

A sample of a portion of a floor plan dimensioned with and without a series of axial reference planes is shown in Figure 6.35A and B. Because of the **grid** pattern often formed by the placement of these columns, a centerline or a plus (+) type symbol is often used to simplify the drawing. See Figure 6.36.

Walls, especially interior walls that do not fall on the established grid, have to be dimensioned—but only to the nearest dimension grid line. Figure 6.37 is a good

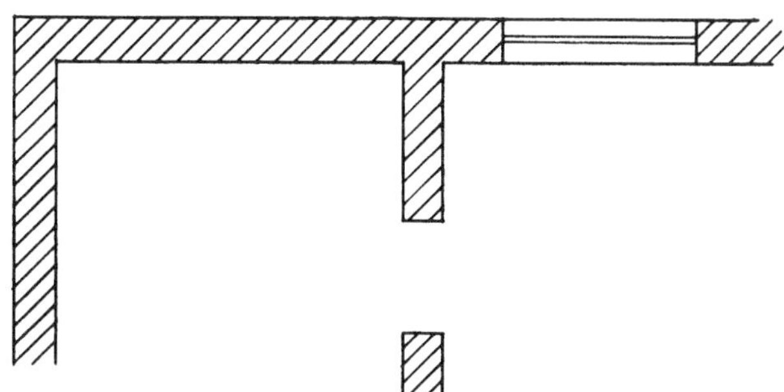

Figure 6.20 Masonry floor plan.

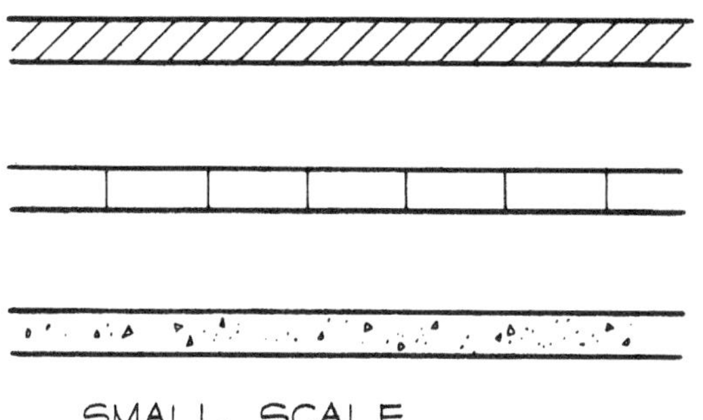

Figure 6.21 Concrete block material designations used on floor plans.

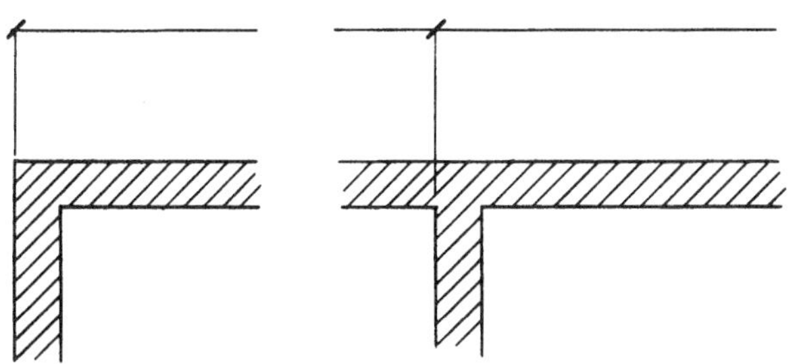

Figure 6.22 Dimensioning masonry walls.

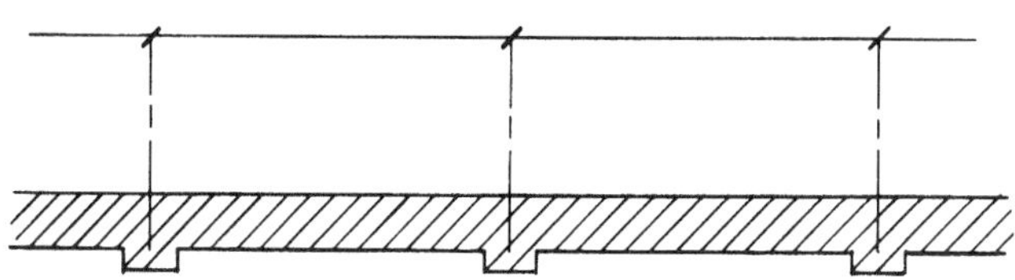

Figure 6.23 Dimensioning pilasters.

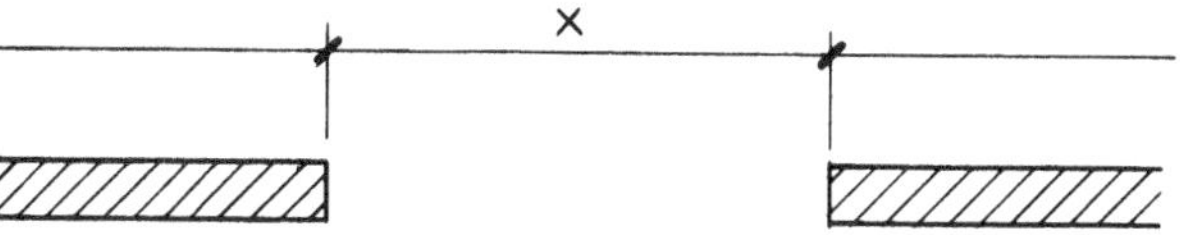

Figure 6.24 Rough opening in masonry wall.

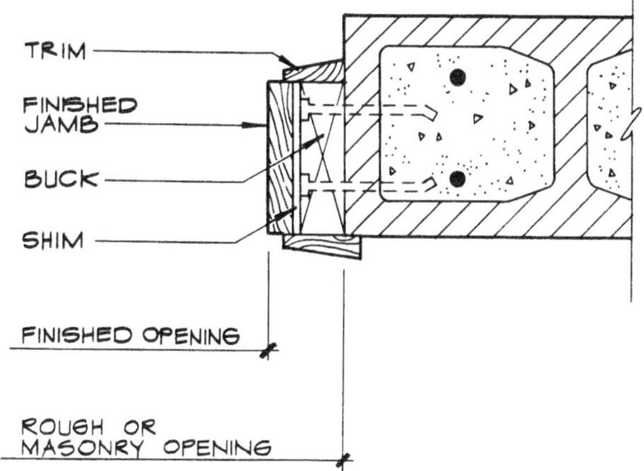

Figure 6.25 Door jamb at masonry opening.

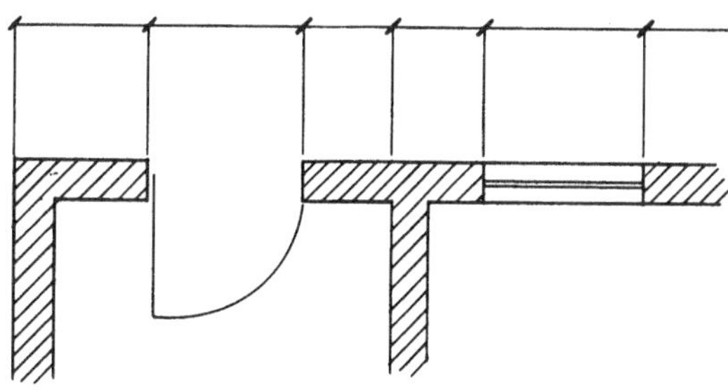

Figure 6.26 Locating doors and windows.

example of an interior wall dimensioned to the nearest column falling on a grid.

Because of design or code requirements for fire regulations or structural reasons, materials are often combined: concrete columns with wood walls; steel mainframe with wood walls as secondary members; masonry and wood; steel studs and wood; and steel and masonry, for example. Figure 6.38 shows how using two different systems requires overlapping dimension lines with extension lines. Because dimension lines are more critical than extension lines, extension lines are *always* broken in favor of dimension lines. The wood structure is located to the column on the left side once and thereafter dimensioned independently.

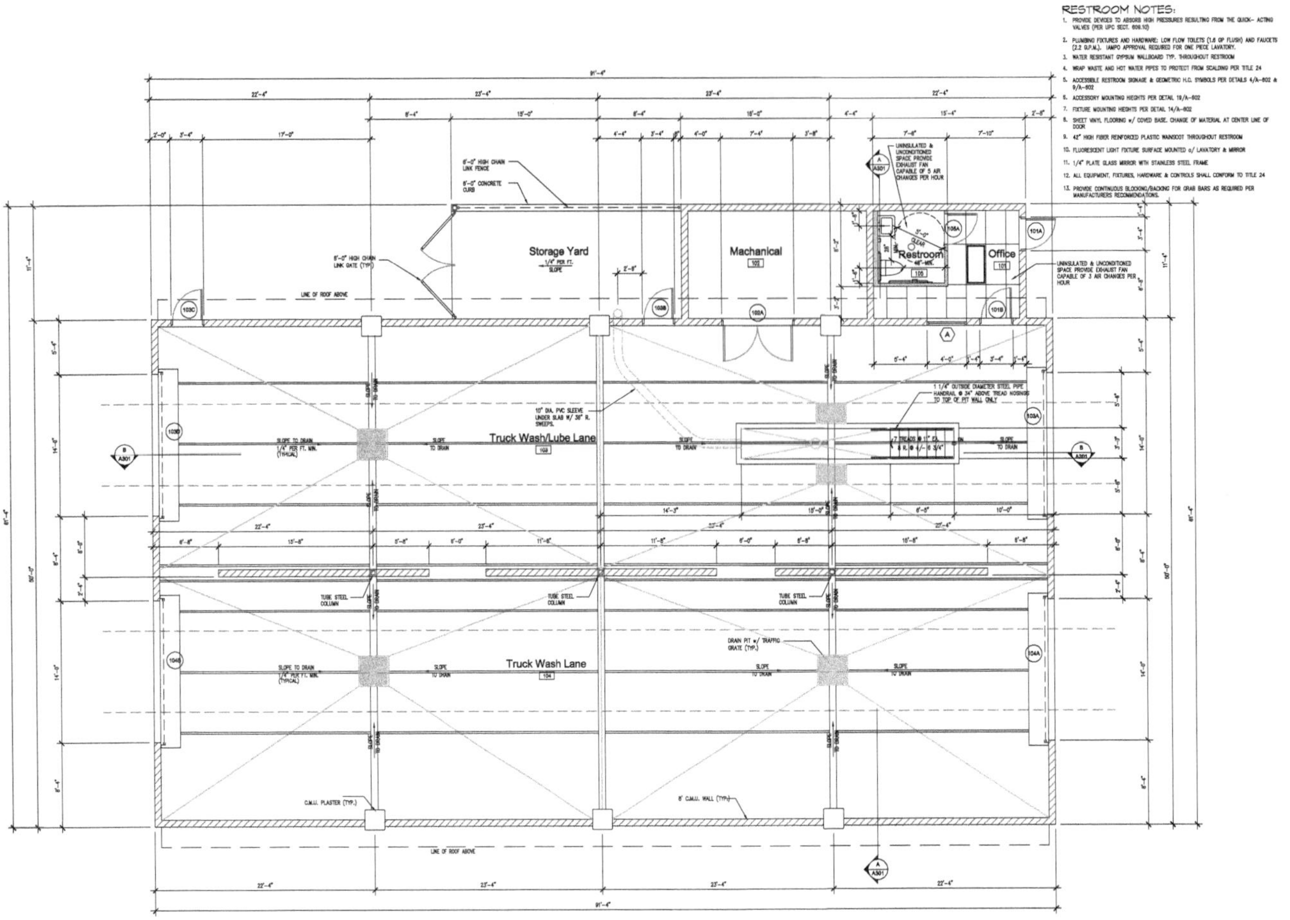

Figure 6.27 Masonry floor plan of a truck wash.

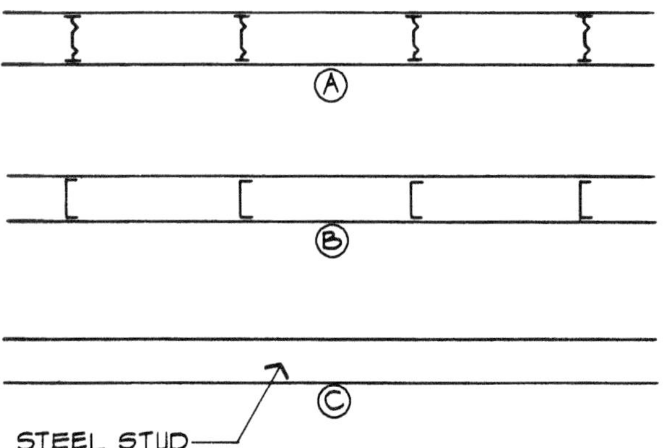

Figure 6.28 Basic steel stud shapes.

Wood and masonry, as shown in Figure 6.39, are dimensioned as their material dictates: the masonry is dimensioned to the ends of the wall and the rough opening of windows, while the wood portions are dimensioned to the center of interior walls, center of doors, and so forth. The door in the wood portion is dimensioned to the center of the door and to the inside edge of the masonry wall. This assumes that the block wall will be built first.

Masonry walls and concrete columns, shown in Figure 6.40, are treated in much the same way as wood and concrete columns. In both instances, the building sequence dictates which one becomes the reference point (datum). See Figure 6.41. Here, steel and masonry are used in combination. Using the dimensional reference system, the steel is installed first. The interior masonry wall is then located from the nearest axial reference plane and dimensioned according to the block module for that kind of masonry.

Additional axial reference plane sub-bubbles are provided. Numbers are in decimals. Because one face of the masonry wall is between 1 and 2, 7/10 of the distance away from axial reference plane 1, the number 1.7 is used in the sub-bubble. Also, because the same wall is also halfway between A and B, A.5 is used as a designation. Another example of the process is found

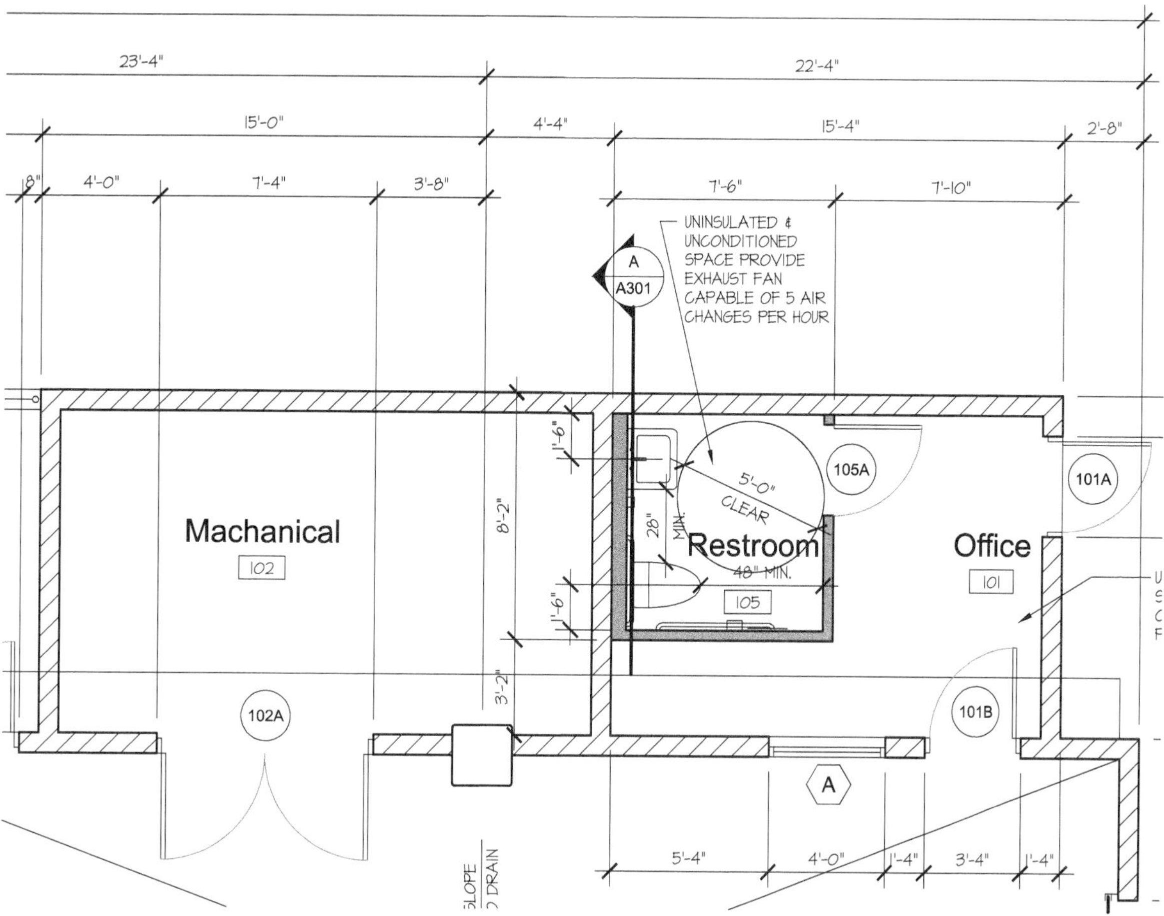

Figure 6.29 Representation of steel studs in a floor plan.

in Figure 6.42. The fabricators will locate the steel first, then the masonry wall. Dimension "X" relates one system to another.

The general method of dimensioning a window or a door was discussed earlier. Here, we examine a variety of doors and windows and how to draft them. Figure 6.43 shows a sampling of the most typically drafted doors.

Doors A and B in Figure 6.43 show the main difference in drafting an exterior **hinged door** versus an interior hinged door. A straight line is used to represent the door, and a radial line is used to show the direction of swing. Door "I" shows the same kind of door with its thickness represented by a double line. Doors A, B, and I are used in the floor plans to show flush doors, panel doors, and sculptured doors (decorative and carved).

Flush doors, as the name indicates, are flush on both sides. They can be solid on the interior (solid slab) or hollow on the inside (hollow core).

Panel doors have panels set into the frame. These are usually made of thin panels of wood or glass. A variety of patterns are available. See *Sweet's Catalog File* under "Doors" for pictures of door patterns. Also, see the earlier discussion of elevations for a drafted form of these doors.

Sculptured and decorative doors can be carved forms put into the doors in the form of a panel door or added onto a flush door in the form of what is called a **planted** door. Different types of trim can also be planted onto a slab door.

Door C in Figure 6.43 represents a double-action door, a door that swings in both directions. Double-action doors can be solid slab, panel, or sculptured.

Two types of sliding doors are shown in Figure 6.43. Door D, when used on the exterior, typically is made of glass framed in wood or metal. Pocketed sliding doors are rarely found on the exterior because the pocket is hard to weatherproof, and it is difficult to keep rain, termites, and wind out of the pocket.

Doors F and G are good doors for storage areas and wardrobe closets.

Where there is a concern about heat loss or heat gain, a revolving door is a good solution. See door H, which shows a cased opening, that is, an opening with trim around the perimeter with no door on it.

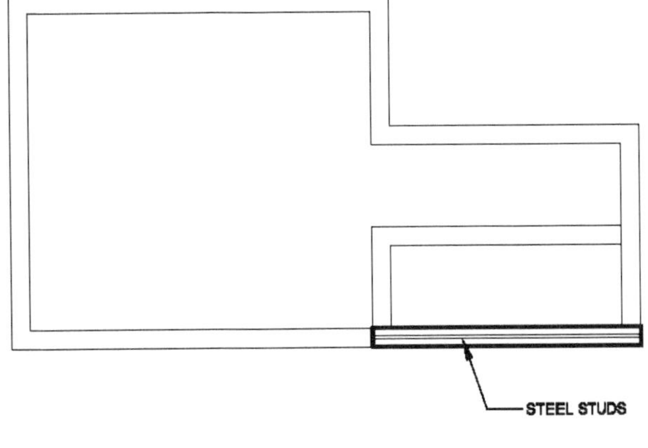

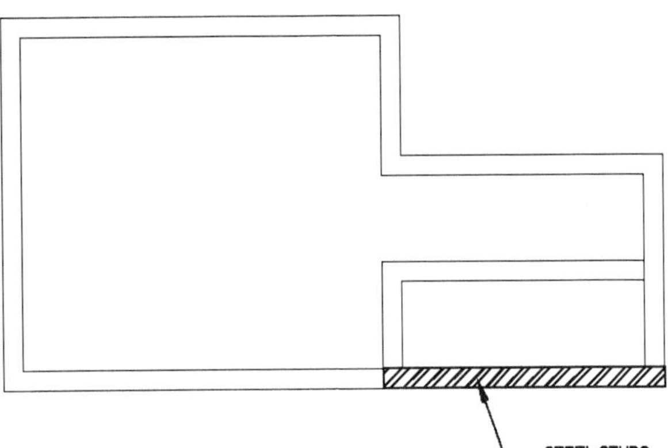

Figure 6.30 Combination of wood and steel.

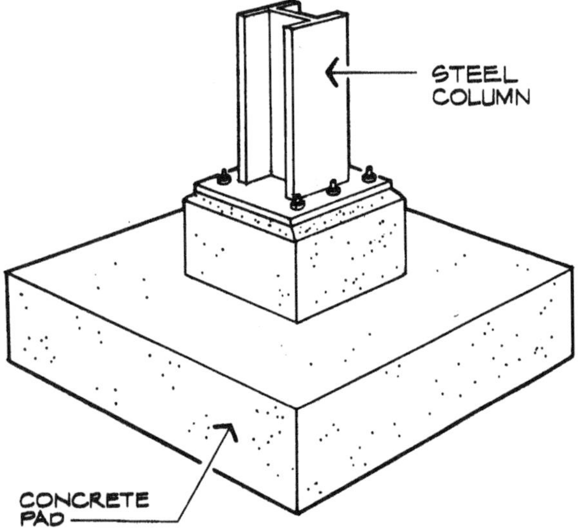

Figure 6.31 Steel column and concrete pad.

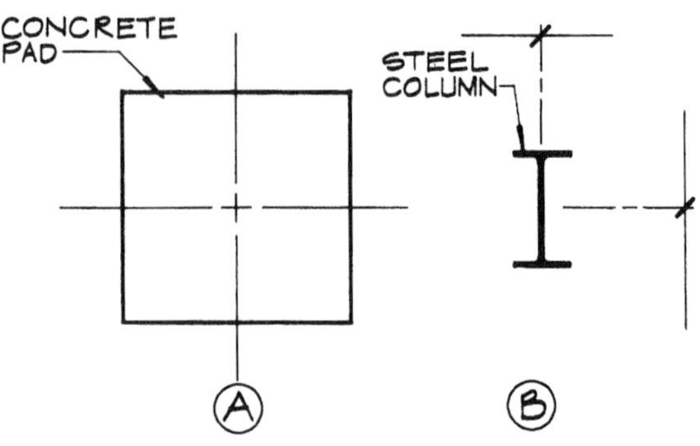

Figure 6.32 Dimensioning concrete pads and steel columns.

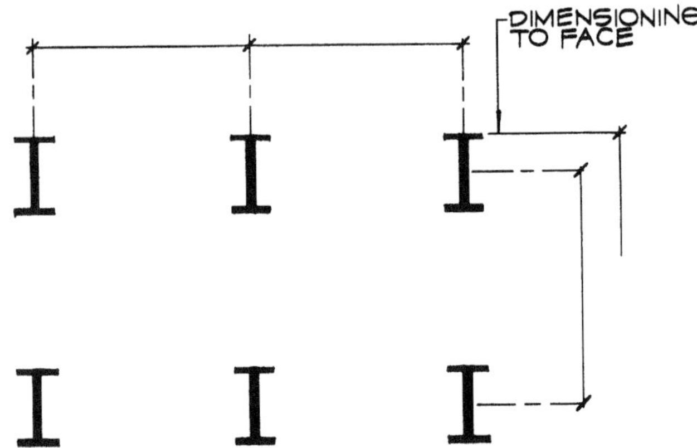

Figure 6.33 Dimensioning a series of columns.

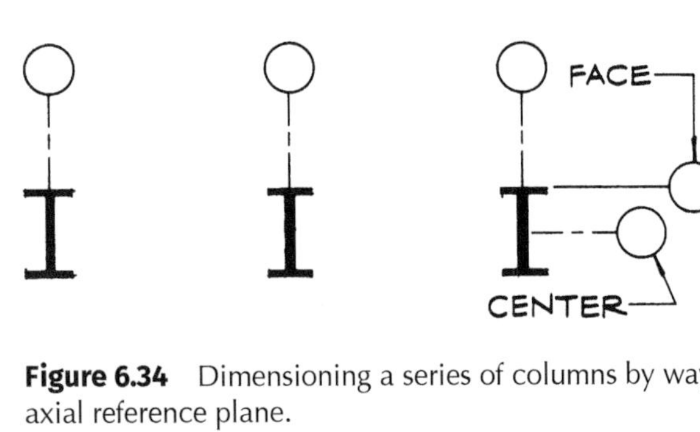

Figure 6.34 Dimensioning a series of columns by way of the axial reference plane.

Windows in Plan View

Typical ways of showing windows in the plan view are shown in Figure 6.44. When a plan is drawn at a small scale, each individual window, of whatever type, may simply be drawn as a fixed window (window A, Figure 6.44), depending for explanation on a pictorial drawing (as shown in Chapter 2). Ideally, casement, hopper, and awning-type windows should be used only on the second floor or above, for the sake of safety. If they are used on the first or ground floor, they should have planters or reflection pools or something else around them to prevent accidents.

The best way to find specific sizes of windows and doors (especially sliding glass doors) is to check the specific manufacturer's website. There, you will find interior doors ranging from 1′-6″ to 3′-0″ and exterior doors ranging from 2′-4″ to 3′-6″. Sizes of doors and

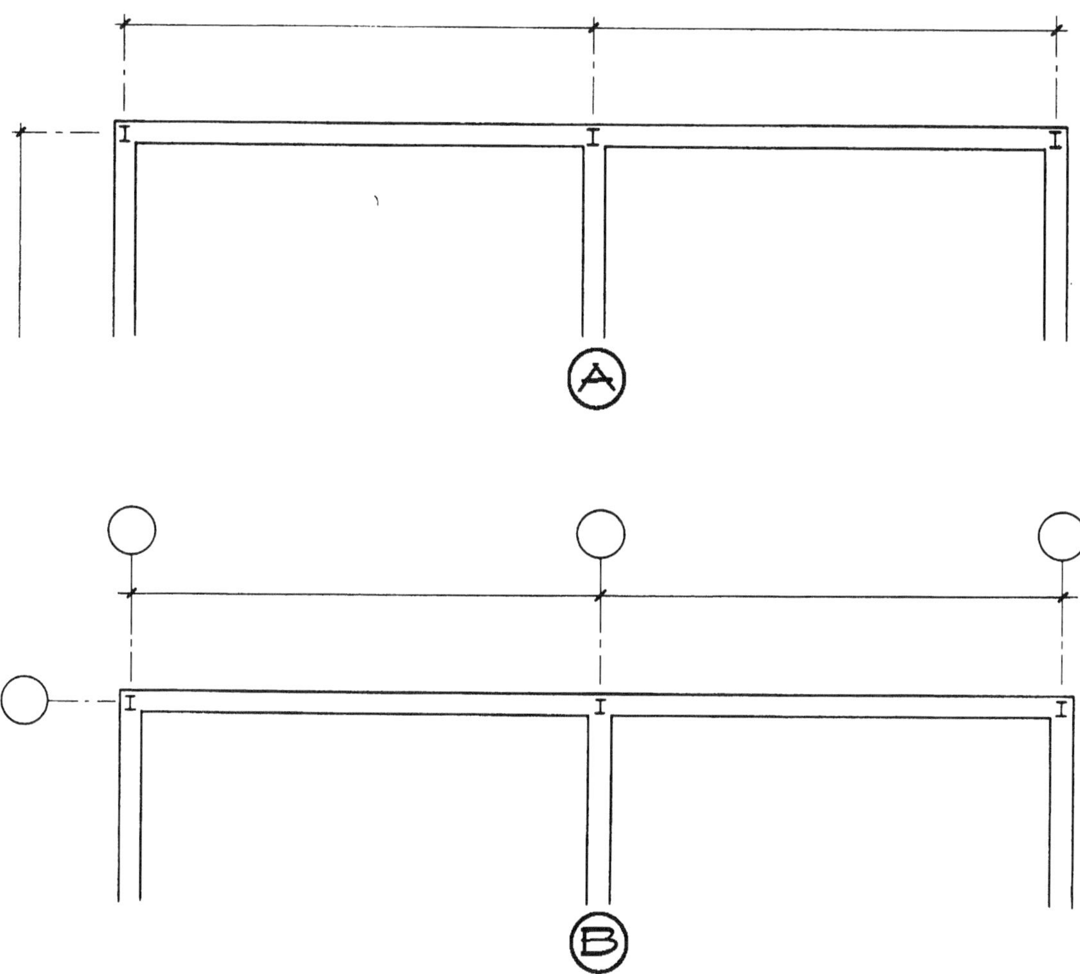

Figure 6.35 Dimensioning a floor plan with steel columns.

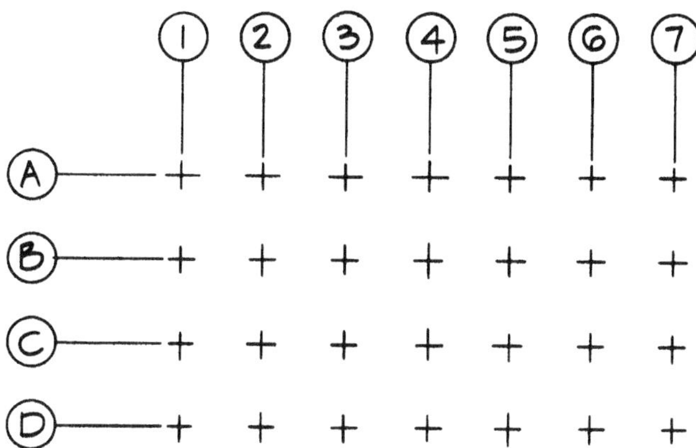

Figure 6.36 Columns forming a grid pattern.

windows also depend on local codes. Local codes require a certain percentage of the square footage to be devoted to windows and doors to provide light and ventilation. These percentages often come in the form of minimum and maximum areas as a measure of energy-efficient structures. Still, another criterion for door size is consideration of wheelchairs and the size required for building accessibility (Americans with Disabilities Act compliance).

■ SYMBOLS

Electrical and Utility Symbols

Just as chemistry uses symbols to represent elements, architectural floor plans use symbols to represent electrical and plumbing equipment. Figure 6.45 shows the ones most typically used. These are symbols only. They do not represent the shape or size of the actual item. For example, the symbol for a ceiling outlet indicates the *location* of an outlet, not the shape or size of the fixture. The description of the specific fixture is given in the specifications document.

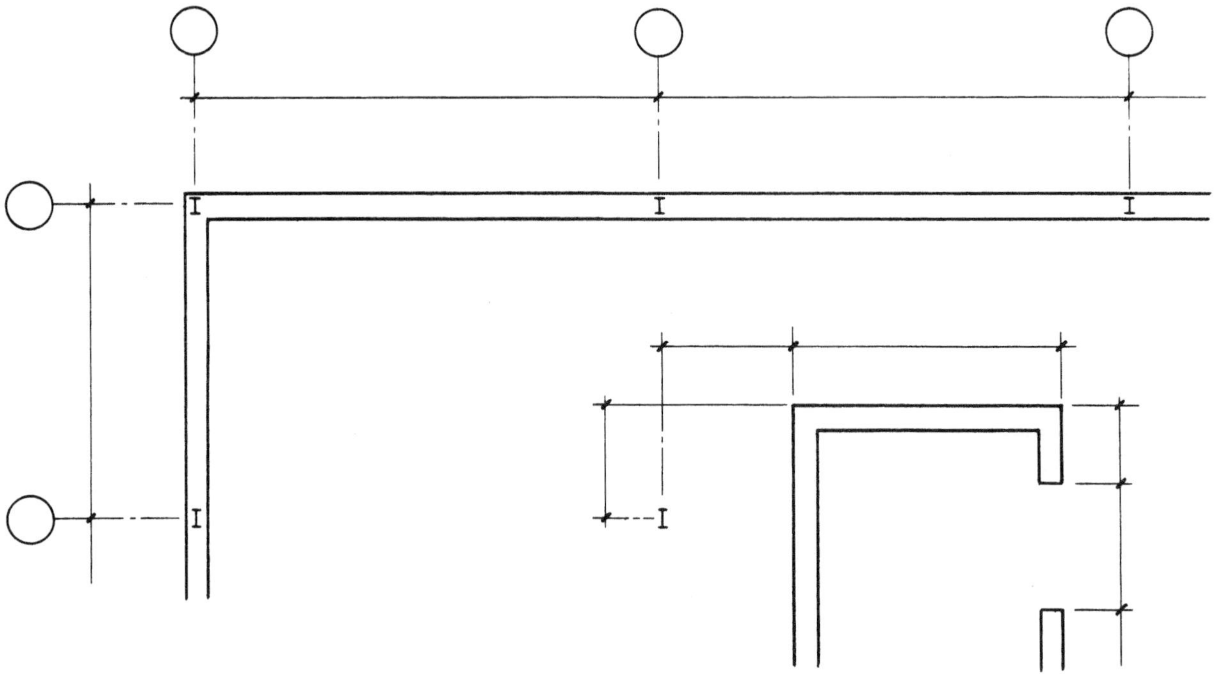

Figure 6.37 Locating interior walls from axial reference bubbles.

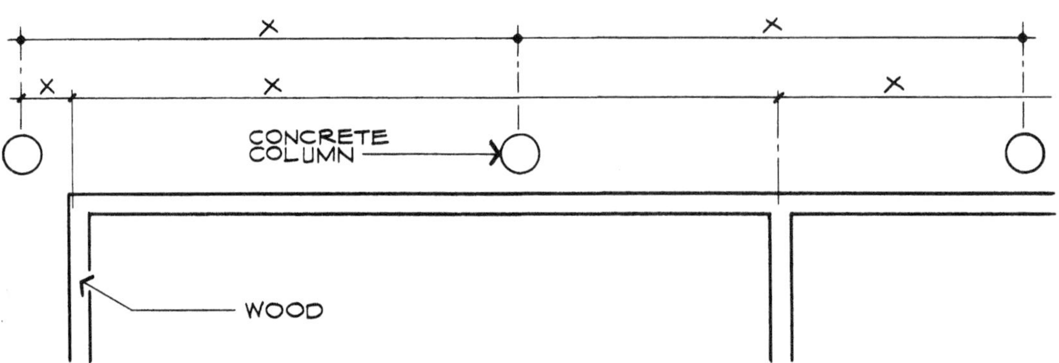

Figure 6.38 Concrete and wood.

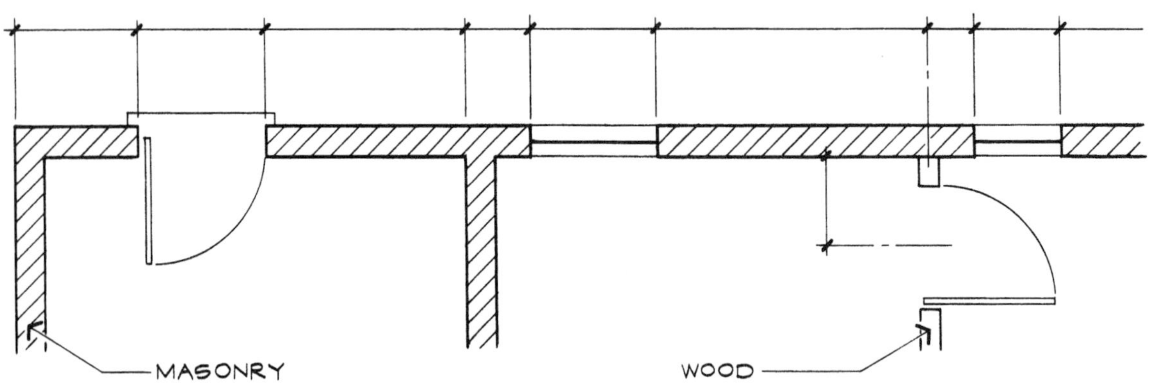

Figure 6.39 Wood and masonry.

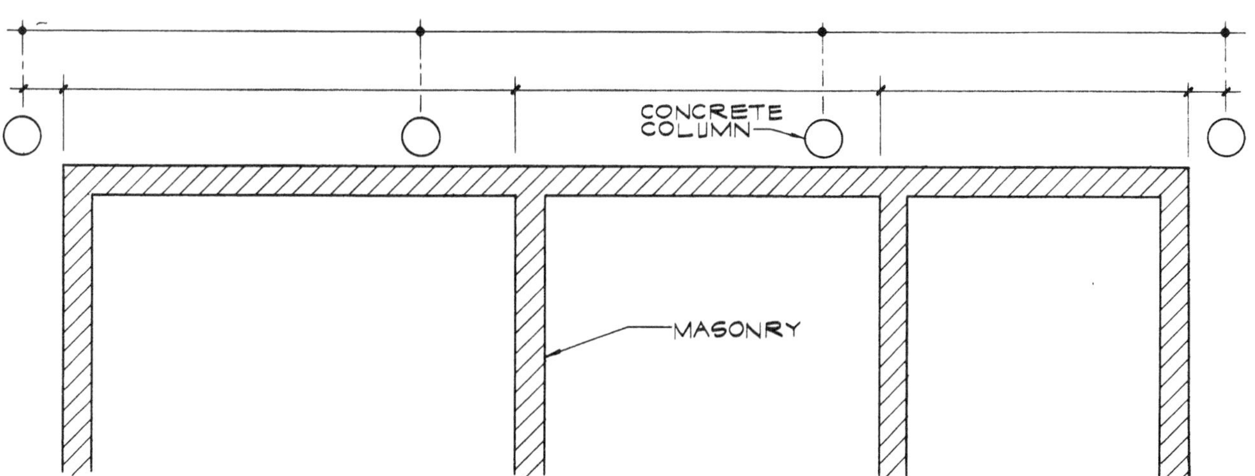

Figure 6.40 Concrete columns and masonry walls.

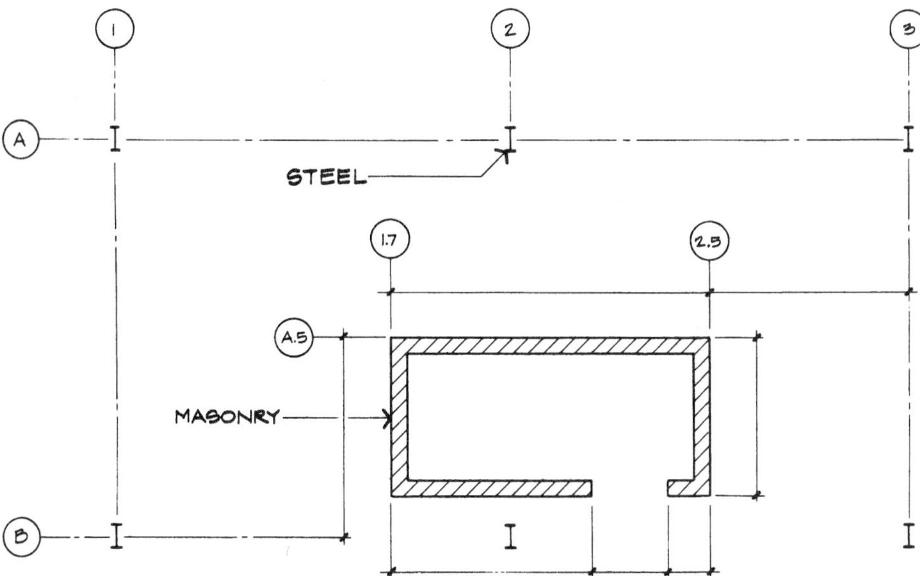

Figure 6.41 Steel and masonry.

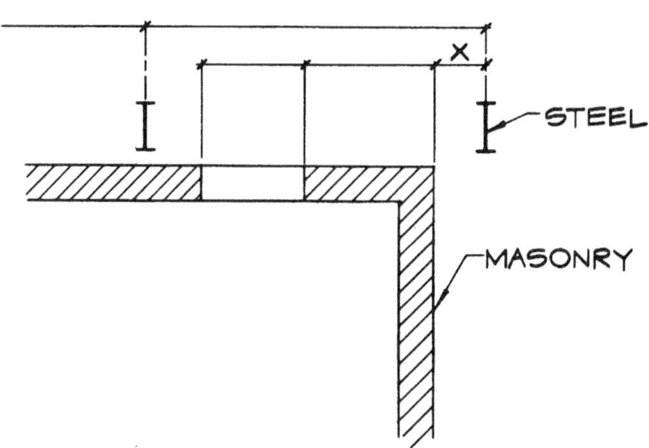

Figure 6.42 Steel and masonry.

Some symbols are more generally used than others in the architectural industry. A floor plan, therefore, usually contains a legend or chart of the symbols being used on that particular floor plan.

Number Symbols

Symbols 1, 2, and 3 in Figure 6.45 show different types of switches. Symbol 2 shows a weatherproof switch, and symbol 3 shows a situation in which there might be a number of switches used to turn on a single light fixture or a series of light fixtures. See Figure 6.46. A centerline-type line is used to show which switch connects with which outlet. This is simply a way of giving this information to the electrical contractor. (However, Figure 6.46

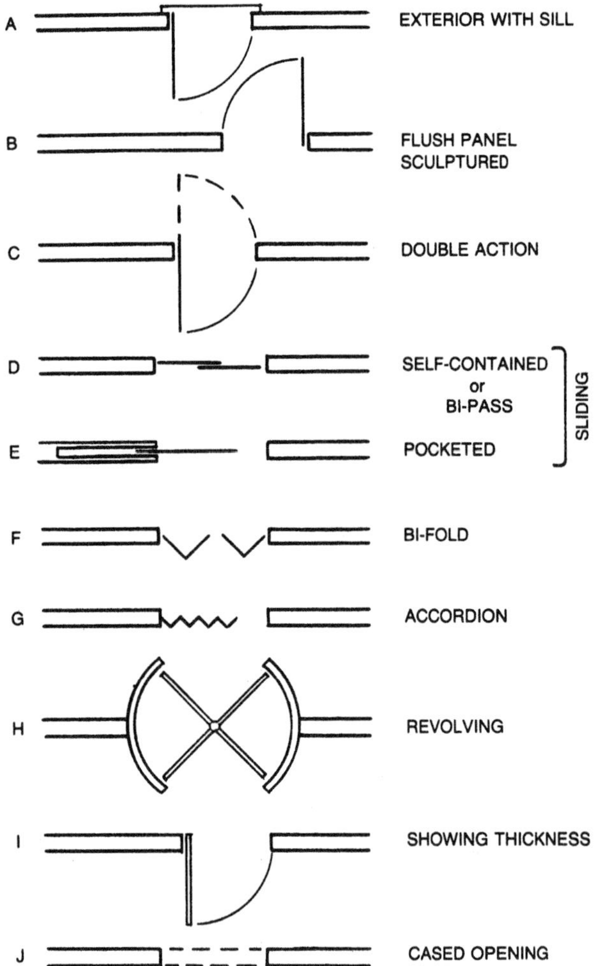

Figure 6.43 Doors in plan view.

is not a wiring diagram.) If one switch controls one or a series of outlets, it is called a two-way switch. A three-way switch comprises two switches controlling one outlet or a series of outlets. Three switches are called a four-way, and so on. Thus, you name switches by the number of switches plus one. For example, the number 3 is placed next to the switch when there are two switches, the number 4 for three switches, and so on. See Figure 6.46 for examples of switches, outlets, and their numbering system.

Symbol 4 in Figure 6.45 represents a duplex convenience outlet with two places to plug in electrical appliances.

Numbers are used to indicate the number of outlets available other than the duplex, the most typical. For example, if a triplex outlet is required, the number 3 is placed beside the outlet symbol. A number in inches, such as 48″, may be used to indicate the height of the outlet from the floor to the center of the outlet. See Figure 6.45, symbols 6, 7, and 9.

Letter Symbols

A letter used instead of a number represents a special type of switch. For example, "K" is used for key-operated, "D" for dimmer, "WP" for weatherproof, and so forth.

As with switches, letter designations are used to describe special duplex convenience outlets, for example, "WP" for waterproof. A duplex convenience outlet is generally referred to by the public as a wall plug.

The call letters "GFI" mean ground fault interrupt. They designate a special outlet used near water (bathrooms, kitchens, etc.) to prevent electric shock. "SP" designates special purpose—perhaps a computer outlet on its own circuit and unaffected by electrical current flowing to any other outlet.

A combination of a switch and a regular outlet is shown in Figure 6.45, symbol 8. This illustration shows a duplex convenience outlet that is half active (hot) at all times. In other words, one outlet is controlled by a switch and the other is a normal outlet. The switch half can be used for a lamp and the normal outlet for an appliance.

Other Symbols

A square with a circle within it and two lines represents a floor outlet. See symbol 13, Figure 6.45. The various types of light outlets are shown by symbols 14 through 18.

A **flush outlet** is one in which the fixture will be installed flush with the ceiling. The electrician and carpenter must address the problem of framing for the fixture in the members above the ceiling surface. See symbol 21, Figure 6.45.

A selection of miscellaneous equipment is shown in symbols 22 through 36.

Special Explanation

Symbols 24, 25, 26, 28, 31, and 32 in Figure 6.45 require special explanation as follows:

Symbol 24. Used for electrical connections (usually on the outside) for such things as outdoor lighting and sprinkler connections.

Symbol 25. A "J" box is an open electrical box that allows the electrician to install fixtures or tie wires together at that location.

Symbol 26. This is not the TV antenna itself, but the point at which you connect a television antenna line from cable or satellite dish.

Symbol 28. Location to push a button to ring a doorbell or chime.

Symbol 31. The connection between the utility company and the structure where the power panel is installed.

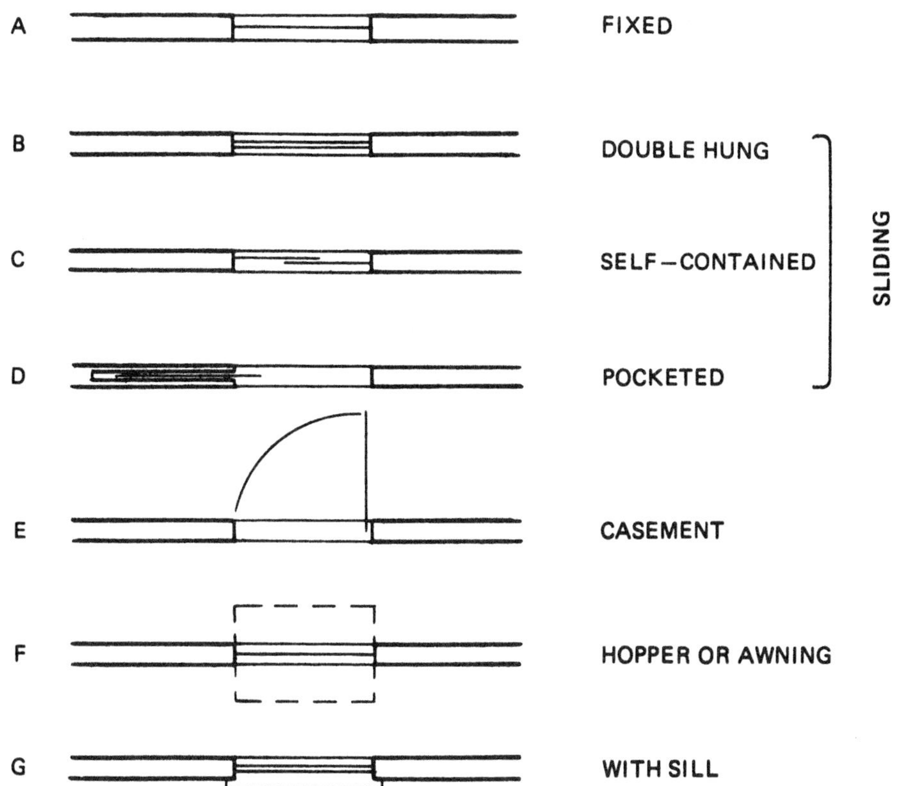

Figure 6.44 Windows in plan view.

Symbol 32. As the structure is zoned for electrical distribution, circuit breaker panels are installed. This allows you to reset a circuit at a so-called substation without going outside to the main panel or disturbing the rest of the structure.

Symbol 34 represents a gas outlet, and 35 is a control for fuel gas. Symbol 34 would be used to indicate a gas jet in a fireplace, and 35 would be used to indicate the control for the gas, probably somewhere near the fireplace. Symbol 36 is a hose bibb, a connection for a water hose.

Symbols 37 through 39 represent present-day symbols. Incandescent track lighting shown in 37 and 38 indicates a card reader for a security door, such as a hotel room door or conference room door, that is opened by a card reader. Symbol 39 represents an outlet through which to receive computer data. Symbol 40 indicates two wires mounted on the ceiling for attachment of the movable and repositionable light often referred to as *cable lighting*.

Electrical and Computers

Although most residences are still wired in the conventional manner, the use of the computer to control circuitry has found its way into the architectural construction world. Today, we are being asked to think in terms of the following:

1. What type of general lighting would be appropriate for a given structure?
2. What wall washes, by color and intensity, should be used in a specific area?
3. What specific tasks are to take place in an area, and what kind of lighting would satisfy the requirements of this task?
4. What type of mood do we wish to create, and how will we dim or employ colored lights to produce that specific mood?
5. How should the floor area be lit to facilitate the safe movement of people through a corridor at night or during the day, as in a school environment?
6. How can we efficiently light stairs, both to identify the positions of the steps and to show where they begin?
7. How will specialty lighting be employed, such as fiber optics or neon lighting to identify an entry area or light located to produce a light beacon to the sky at night?

Electrical wiring falls into three basic categories: conventional, retrofit, and centralized controller (computer).

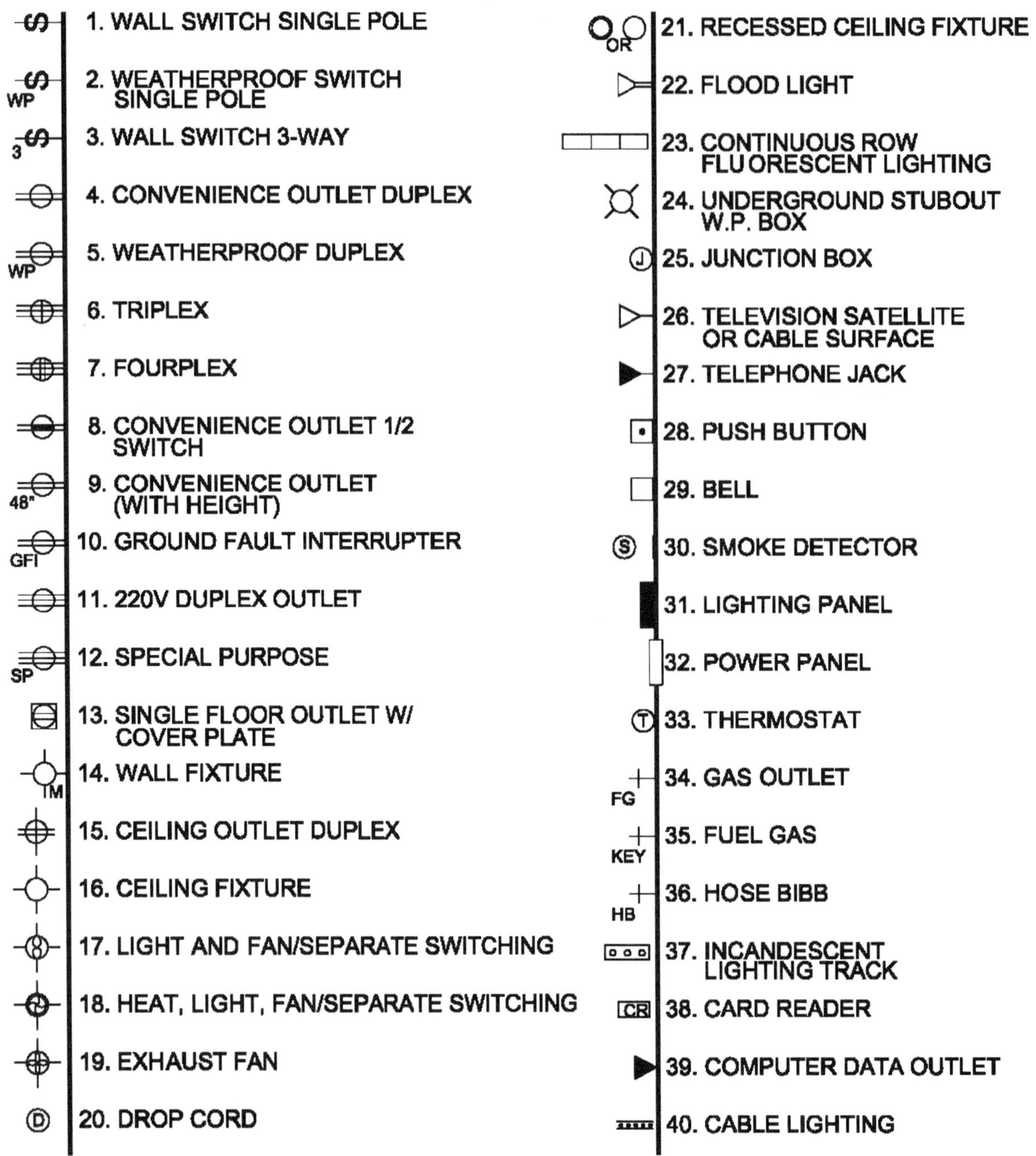

Figure 6.45 Electrical and utility symbols.

1. *Conventional.* This system presently exists in the majority of today's structures. Lights are hardwired from switch to outlet, and the system is not very flexible (see Figure 6.46).
2. *Retrofit:*
   a. *Radio frequency.* An old conventional toggle-style switch is replaced by what we will refer to as a "smart switch." The smart switch is capable of transmitting and receiving signals to and from other outlets (modules). This system is ideal in building additions and alterations where the cost of rewiring can become prohibitive. Radio-wave signals can be disturbed by steel studs, the chicken wire present in older walls as a base mesh for stucco or plastic, or by distance (approximately 25′ distance limit).
   b. *Power line carrier (PLC).* Also uses smart switches, but rather than sending a radio-wave signal, it sends an electrical pulse through the existing wiring. A single switch can be replaced with a

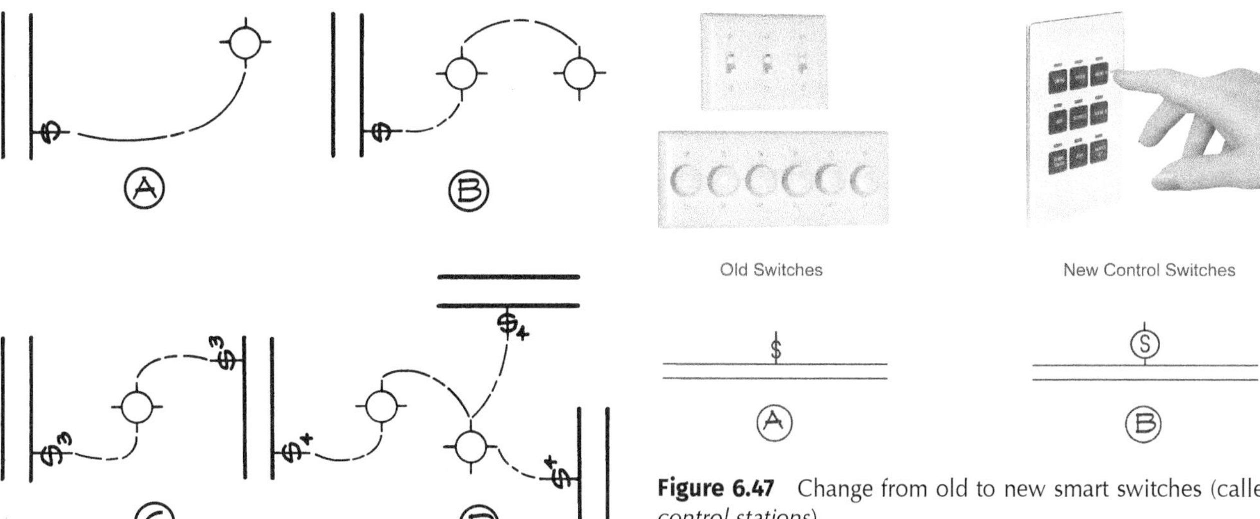

Figure 6.46 Switch to outlet (conventional).

smart switch with multiple controls. This enables one smart-switch location to control multiple outlets, fixtures, appliances, and so forth. Home-Touch by Lite-Touch, Inc. is an example of such a system.

3. *Centralized controller (computer).* Using low-voltage wires, the switches are connected to a central processor. We no longer think in terms of a single light switch controlling a bank of lights, but rather a single control station with as many as nine buttons that can control any or all lights in a structure. These *control stations*, which are wall-mounted keypads, replace the old-fashioned switches and dimmers (see Figure 6.47B). Note that nine switches and dimmers are replaced with one control station the size of a single-gang toggle switch.

Figure 6.47A is a conventional switch similar to that shown in Figure 6.45. With a simple circle added to an existing switch, a drafter can indicate that a smart switch should be installed. Thus, you can easily adjust an existing drawing. Figure 6.47B shows a slight variation of the same smart switch that is drafted from scratch.

The first major change is in the way we think about lighting. Do not think of a room with its lighting controlled by a single switch; instead, plan lighting scenes. Position the lighting to create a visual pathway through a structure. Consider how you would light the exterior

Figure 6.47 Change from old to new smart switches (called *control stations*).

of the structure for visual impact or to deter possible intruders (possibly motion-activated flashing lights). Think in terms of how best to secure your house electrically, by opening or closing windows or draperies. Controls can also be programmed to provide music throughout a structure, to activate a television, or even to dramatically showcase works of art.

The next step to take with your client is to decide from which locations you would like to control these various lighting scenes. Let us now look at the three basic components in this type of control system. As mentioned before, the first are the control stations, wall-mounted keypads suitable for use in both wet and dry areas of a structure. The second is the central control unit (CCU). The CCU is the brain of the system, that is, where the programming resides. It receives signals from the control stations and then processes them. Each control station is connected to the CCU with low-voltage wire. This is very different from the old system, in which the lights were hooked up to the control station. Once programmed, the CCU will maintain the information even during a power outage or spike—and, yes, the CCU can be programmed for times when the occupants are away on vacation. Lighting can be programmed to give the structure an appearance of being occupied and then returned to its original setting upon the owners' return. The client can be trained to program his or her own system, or the system installer can reprogram the system via the telephone. Thus, a technician need not come to the structure to reprogram the CCU.

Control modules make up the third component. These are self-contained modules that actually do the work. Receiving their instructions from the CCU, they dim lights; drive motorized devices to open skylights, windows, and draperies; raise or lower the screen in a home theater; or merely turn on the garden and pool lights (see Figure 6.48).

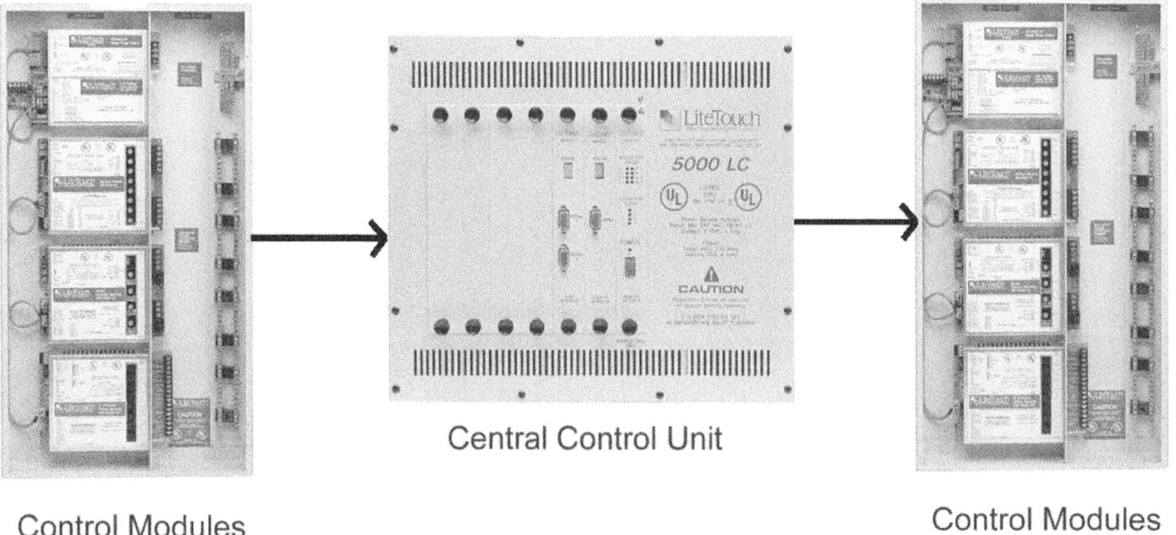

Figure 6.48 Three components of the Lite-Touch system.

Drawing for the Installer

The next task is to convey to the installer the information about the system you have designed, the location of the control stations, and the number of control points you have at one location. The number of control points at a given location can be dealt with using a chart. A **routing schedule** (a chart similar to that shown in Figure 6.49) can easily be developed and become part of the electrical plan. The first column identifies the location of the control station in the structure, and the second column actually tells the manufacturer the actual number of control points needed. Each control station in that location (say #1) is then labeled, such as 1A, 1B, 1C, 1D, and so on.

Each group of outlets—for example, six outlets in the ceiling in the living room—is then given a call letter. In this chart, the designation E-1 is used for the general light in the living room, E-3 is used for mood lighting, and E-2 may be used as a spotlight for paintings.

Control-station groups can be identified with a single number (see Figure 6.50A). The symbol should be a square. The outlets are connected as in the conventional method but are not connected to the control stations identified by a C and an S with a line through it. Now look at Figure 6.50B. The outlets are connected to a symbol that should be a square. The symbol should not duplicate those already used for the control stations.

The electrical symbols shown in this chapter are mostly used in residential applications, although most of them are similar in commercial, institutional, and industrial settings. For hospitals, you need a symbol for a nurse call system or signal center system and very specialized auxiliary systems. You may also need to run a multitude of equipment for surgery at one time and provide a system that cannot be compromised during surgery. In an office or school building, you may need an electrical door opener or interconnecting telephone service and in-floor ductwork for a computer room.

Appliance and Plumbing Fixture Symbols

Many templates are available for drafting plumbing fixture and kitchen appliances. A good architectural template contains such items as:

- Circles
- Various kitchen appliances
- Door swings
- Various plumbing fixtures
- Electrical symbols
- Typical heights marked along edges

Figure 6.51 shows some of these fixtures and appliances.

OTHER FLOOR PLAN CONSIDERATIONS

It is often necessary to show more than one or two building materials on a floor plan. Let us take a college music building as an example of a structure that has a multitude of walls of different materials, including the following:

1. Masonry
2. Wood studs
3. Two types of soundproof partitions
4. Low walls
5. Low walls with glass above

Routing Schedule								
	Number of Housed	Individual	Connected to System	Number of Outlets	Dimmer % (100% is Full)	Location	Type	Remarks
1	6	1A	E-1	4	100	LIVING	GENERAL	-
		1B	E-2	6	60	LIVING	SPOT	-
		1C	E-3	2	40	LIVING	MOOD	-
		1D	C	1	100	OUTSIDE	SECURITY	-
		1E	M	2	40	HALL	PATH	-
		1F	L	2	80	DINING	GENERAL	-
2	4	2A	E-1	2	100	DINING	GENERAL	
		2B	F-2	2	80	DINING	GENERAL	
		2C	L	4	80	OFFICE	SPOT	

Figure 6.49 Routing schedule.

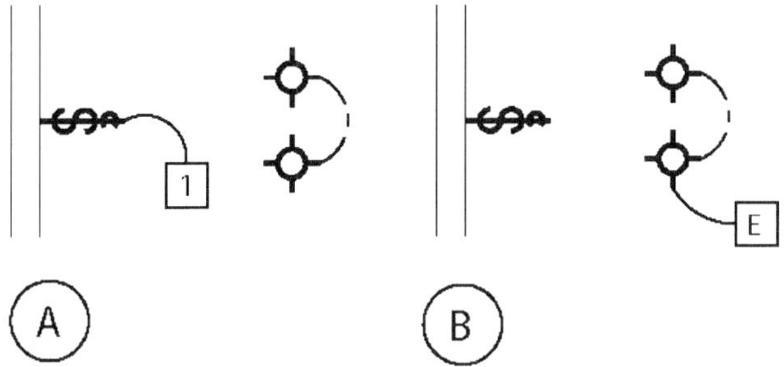

Figure 6.50 Routing symbol for control stations/outlets.

We need to establish an acceptable symbol for each material and to produce a legend similar to that in Figure 6.52. A sample of a partial floor plan using some of these materials symbols is shown in Figure 6.53.

Combining Building Materials

Because of ecological requirements (such as insulation), structural reasons, aesthetic concerns, and fire regulations, materials often must be combined. For example, insulation may be adjacent to a masonry wall, a brick veneer may be on a wood stud wall, and steel studs may be next to a concrete block wall. Figure 6.54 shows examples of what some of these combined-materials walls will look like on the floor plan.

Poché Walls

The word **poché**, mentioned earlier, refers to the process of darkening the space between the lines that represent wall thickness on a floor plan. A special pochéd wall can easily be done on the computer with lines or dots. However, each line type must mean something. It might mean an existing wall, a wall to be, or even a new wall. Figure 6.54 shows an example of pochéd walls.

Stairs

An arrow is used on the plan of the stair to show the direction in which the stair rises. See the partial floor plan in Figure 6.55. Notice how the arrowheads show direction and how the number and size of the treads and risers are indicated.

Noting Logic

The basic approach used for noting (notation) logic is to show a complete set of working drawings as if a complete set of specifications were included. **Specifications** are the written documentation of what is drafted; they give information that is not given in the drawings. Brand names, model numbers, installation procedures, and quality of material are just a few of the items included and discussed in a set of specifications.

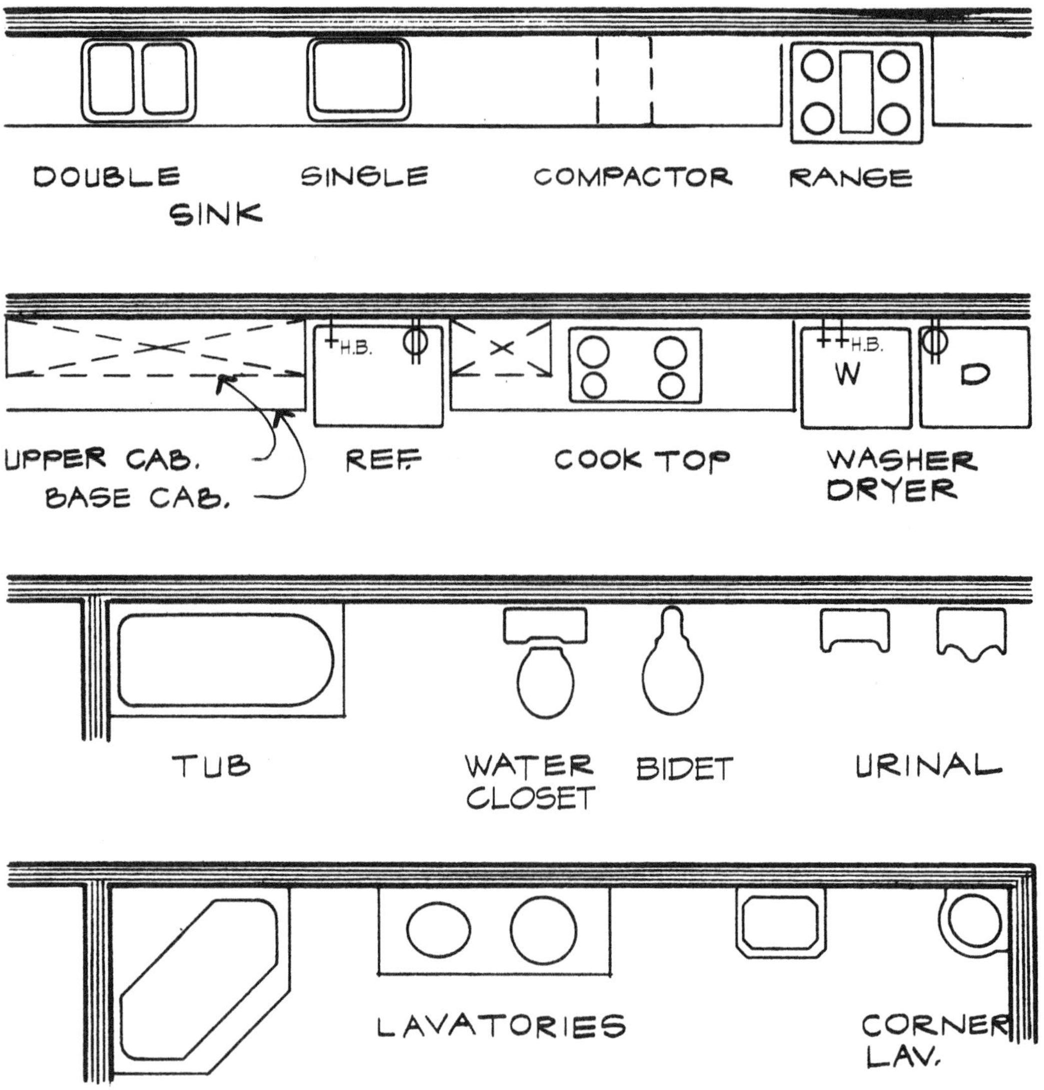

DOUBLE SINK
SINGLE
COMPACTOR
RANGE
UPPER CAB.
BASE CAB.
REF.
COOK TOP
WASHER DRYER
W
D
H.B.
TUB
WATER CLOSET
BIDET
URINAL
LAVATORIES
CORNER LAV.

Figure 6.51 Appliance and plumbing fixtures.

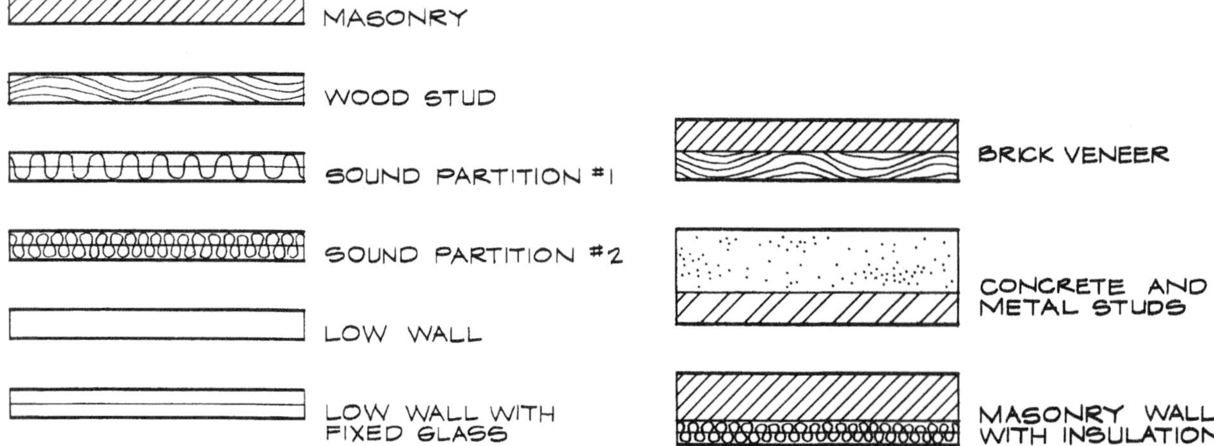

Figure 6.52 Legend for music building floor plan.

Figure 6.53 Partial floor plan: Music building.

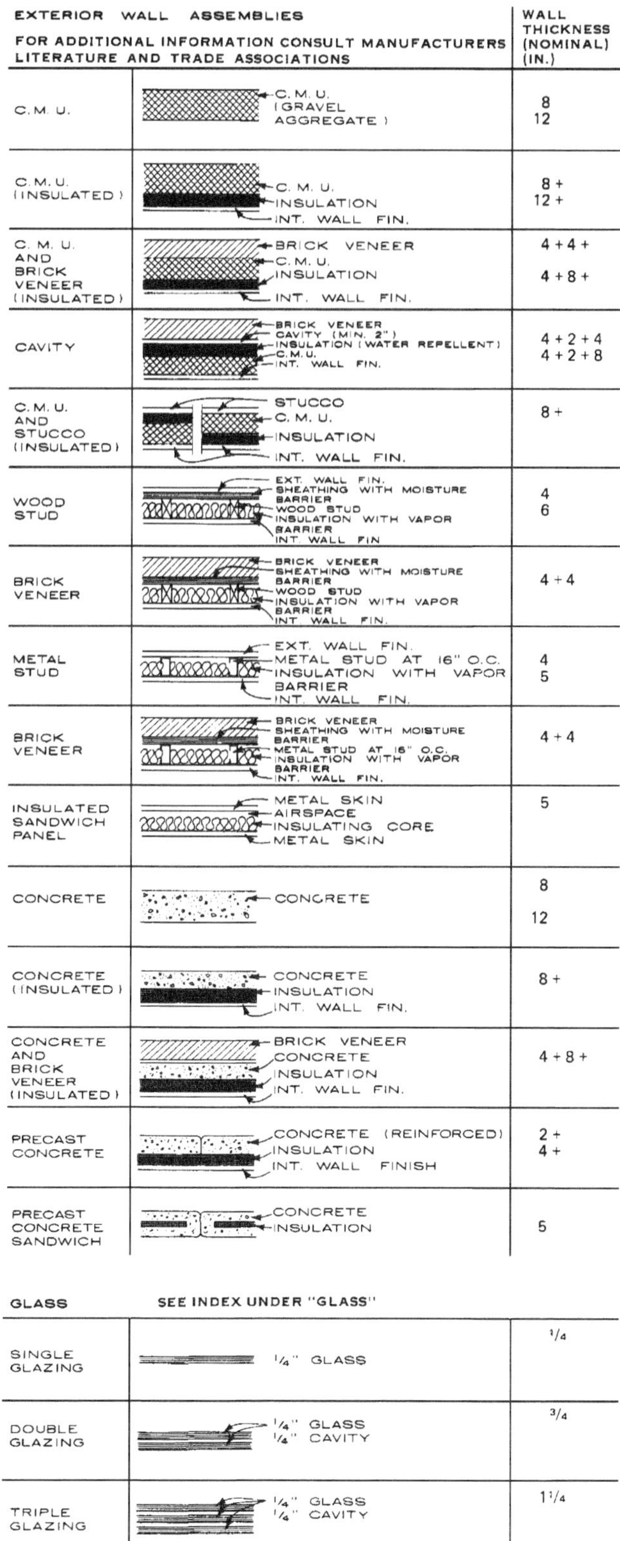

EXTERIOR WALL ASSEMBLIES FOR ADDITIONAL INFORMATION CONSULT MANUFACTURERS LITERATURE AND TRADE ASSOCIATIONS		WALL THICKNESS (NOMINAL) (IN.)
C. M. U.	C. M. U. (GRAVEL AGGREGATE)	8 12
C. M. U. (INSULATED)	C. M. U. INSULATION INT. WALL FIN.	8 + 12 +
C. M. U. AND BRICK VENEER (INSULATED)	BRICK VENEER C. M. U. INSULATION INT. WALL FIN.	4 + 4 + 4 + 8 +
CAVITY	BRICK VENEER CAVITY (MIN. 2") INSULATION (WATER REPELLENT) C. M. U. INT. WALL FIN.	4 + 2 + 4 4 + 2 + 8
C. M. U. AND STUCCO (INSULATED)	STUCCO C. M. U. INSULATION INT. WALL FIN.	8 +
WOOD STUD	EXT. WALL FIN. SHEATHING WITH MOISTURE BARRIER WOOD STUD INSULATION WITH VAPOR BARRIER INT. WALL FIN	4 6
BRICK VENEER	BRICK VENEER SHEATHING WITH MOISTURE BARRIER WOOD STUD INSULATION WITH VAPOR BARRIER INT. WALL FIN.	4 + 4
METAL STUD	EXT. WALL FIN. METAL STUD AT 16" O.C. INSULATION WITH VAPOR BARRIER INT. WALL FIN.	4 5
BRICK VENEER	BRICK VENEER SHEATHING WITH MOISTURE BARRIER METAL STUD AT 16" O.C. INSULATION WITH VAPOR BARRIER INT. WALL FIN.	4 + 4
INSULATED SANDWICH PANEL	METAL SKIN AIRSPACE INSULATING CORE METAL SKIN	5
CONCRETE	CONCRETE	8 12
CONCRETE (INSULATED)	CONCRETE INSULATION INT. WALL FIN.	8 +
CONCRETE AND BRICK VENEER (INSULATED)	BRICK VENEER CONCRETE INSULATION INT. WALL FIN.	4 + 8 +
PRECAST CONCRETE	CONCRETE (REINFORCED) INSULATION INT. WALL FINISH	2 + 4 +
PRECAST CONCRETE SANDWICH	CONCRETE INSULATION	5
GLASS	SEE INDEX UNDER "GLASS"	
SINGLE GLAZING	¼" GLASS	¼
DOUBLE GLAZING	¼" GLASS ¼" CAVITY	¾
TRIPLE GLAZING	¼" GLASS ¼" CAVITY	1¼

Figure 6.54 Combinations of building materials.

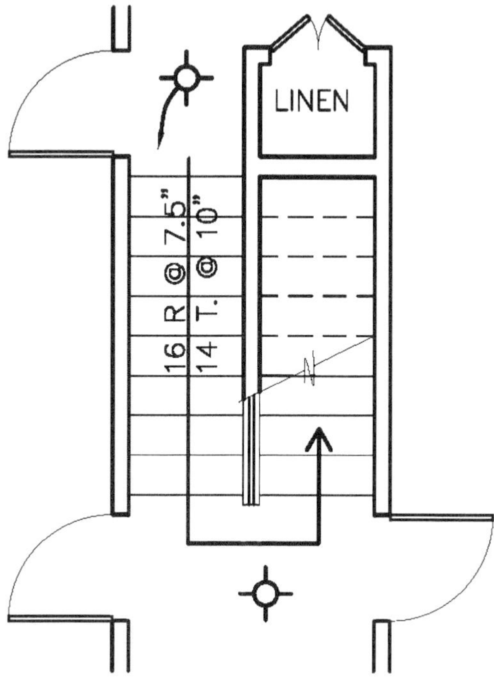

Figure 6.55 Stair directions and number of treads.

Thus, inclusion of the specifications affects the noting on the floor plan.

Because of the precise descriptions contained in the specifications, only general descriptions are necessary on the floor plan. For example, it is sufficient to call out a "cooktop" as a generic name and let the specifications take care of the rest of the description. "Tub" and "water closet" are sufficient to describe plumbing fixtures.

Because further description would only confuse the drawing, these items should be described in the specifications (*specs*). In other words, specific information should not be duplicated. If it is, changes can present problems. For example, suppose brand "A" is selected for a particular fixture and is called out as brand "A" on the floor plan rather than by its generic term. Later, it is changed to brand "B." Now both the floor plan and specs must be changed; if one is missed, a discrepancy that can cause confusion results.

Many architectural firms that superimpose the electrical plan on top of the floor plan note the **electrical rating** necessary for a particular piece of equipment; for example, range 9 KW, oven 5 KW, dishwasher 1.5 KW, and refrigerator 110V. Electrical ratings can also be included in an electrical appliance schedule if one exists. It is important to track electrical ratings so as not to overload a circuit and trip the circuit breaker, or cause snow to appear on the TV screen every time you use, say, a dishwasher.

Because sizes of rooms are often found on presentation drawings (scaled drawings), some people think that sizes of rooms (9 × 12, 10 × 14) belong on a floor plan. *They do not*. These approximate sizes are fine for client consumption but are useless in the construction process.

Providing Satisfactory Dimensions

One of the most common criticisms from the field (workers on the job) is that the floor plans do not contain enough dimensions. Because these people cannot scale the drawings (something we would not want them to do anyway), they are dependent on dimensions; be sure they are all included! Remember that notes take precedence over the drawing itself. If a member is called a 2 × 10 but is drawn as a 2 × 8, the note takes precedence.

Sampling of Other Types of Floor Plans

Not all floor plans fit on a sheet, even a 36 × 48 sheet. The Vista del Largo structure is a good example. To maintain readability, the plan was cut in half, and it uses a key plan at a very small scale located on the bottom right corner of the sheet to show how the cut was made and how to reassemble it. Look at Figure 6.56.

A structure such as the Costa home, which falls into the category of a restoration drawing, is seldom seen in the field of architecture relative to the percentage of drawings produced. See Figure 6.57.

Also rarely used is a space plan that shows furniture for a residence; this does, however, give the client a better understanding of the physical constraints and benefits of the structure. See Figure 6.58. However, it is a good plan to superimpose an electrical plan over such a space plan for the simple reason that, based on the furniture layout, an electrical plan can be developed from it. For an example, see Figure 6.59.

A good example of a small commercial plan appears in Figure 6.60. In this figure, we are looking at Grand Park Plaza, which is a steel structure of mixed use; it ties in a commercial venture and residential that is why we call it mixed use.

Checklist: Checking Your Own Drawing

There are so many minute details to remember in the development of a particular drawing that most offices have worked out some type of checking system. A **checklist** (or check sheet) is frequently used to mitigate missing information. It lists the most commonly missed items in chart form, making it easy for you to precheck your work before a checker is asked to review a particular drawing. See Figure 6.61 for a floor-plan checklist.

DRAWING A FLOOR PLAN WITH A COMPUTER

The procedure for drawing a floor plan on a computer is somewhat different from that normally used only a few years ago to draw a floor plan manually. However, the information placed on the floor plan, as well as the dimensioning techniques and the formal representations used, remain valid for construction purposes.

The floor plan should be layered out on the grid the architect used. The structure may be built on a 4- or 5-foot grid, and this grid should be drawn on the datum layer. If there is no set module, the datum grid can be set to 1- or 2-foot increments (see Figure 6.62). If the structure is built of masonry, there may be a block module to which this grid can be set.

Multiples of 16″ have become a favorite spacing, inasmuch as most building products come in multiples of 16″. Thus, 16, 32, and 48 become easy modules to locate. In working with steel, the columns may be set to a larger grid, such as 12′-6″ spacing. If the grid is this large, set your snaps (spacing where the cursor will momentarily stop) to a smaller spacing. If you are rounding off walls to the nearest 3″, then 3″ will be a good distance to set your snaps. In dimensioning conventional stud construction, the snap should be set at 1″, allowing the drafter to dimension to the FOS (see Figure 6.63).

Let us take a look at the computer drawings, done in six stages, for the first-floor plan of the Adli residence. Remember, you may need more than 10 layers to accomplish these six stages.

Stage I (Figure 6.64). This is the most critical stage because it sets the field of work and the basic outlines for the structure. If we were working with steel, the columns would be set and positioned during this stage. The properties of the outline can be listed, so that plan users can immediately find the square footage of the structure and its perimeter. This outline can be used to position the structure on the site, to verify the required setbacks, or to compare this figure with the allowable buildable area of a particular site.

Stage II (Figure 6.65). All walls are established at this stage. Exterior walls and interior bearing walls can be

FLOOR PLAN

MAIN BEDROOM #1

MAIN BATH #1

WEST GARDEN ENTRY

BATH #3

BEDROOM #3

TERRACE

HIS/HERS CLOSET #1

HIS/HERS CLOSET #2

HALL

STOR #2

LAUNDRY

BATH #4

BEDROOM #4

MAIN BATH #2

BEDROOM #5

BATH #5

MAIN BEDROOM #2

POWDER

VESTIBULE #1

ENTRY

LIVING ROOM

VESTIBULE #2

A-101

A-102

KEY PLAN

Figure 6.56 Vista del Largo: Split floor plan with key plan.

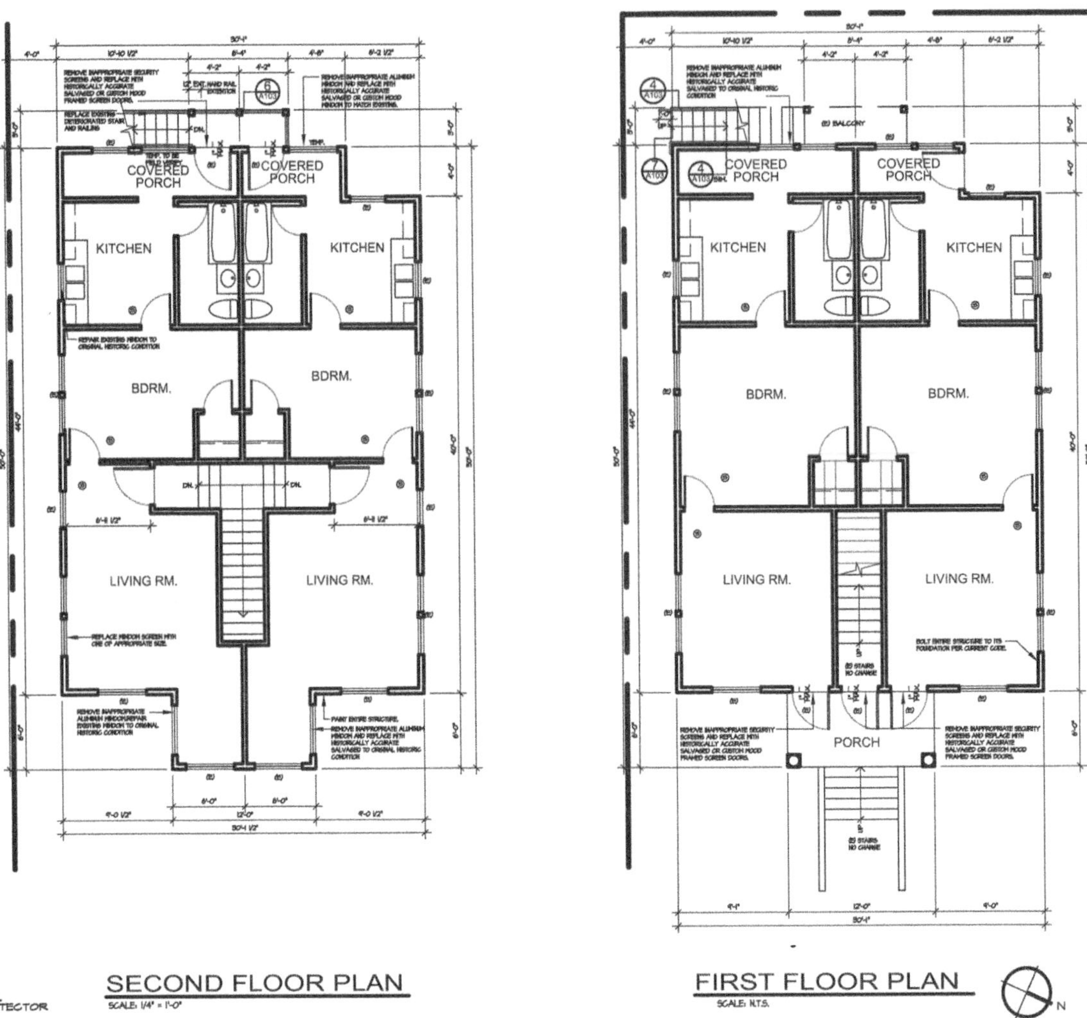

LEGEND
⊛ STATE FIRE MARSHALL APPROVED SMOKE DETECTOR

Figure 6.57 Historical building restoration drawings.

put on one wall layer, and all nonbearing walls can be placed on a secondary wall layer. Column locations and all openings are drawn on still another layer. Openings for doors and windows may also be placed on separate layers. Completion of this stage may produce four to six layers. Preliminary energy calculations can be done easily at this stage.

Stage III (Figure 6.66). At this stage, door and window conventions are drawn, along with any connectors such as for stairs, ramps, escalators, elevators, and lifts. Partitions for office layouts are done now, as well as indications for plumbing fixtures such as sinks and toilets, and built-in cabinets such as kitchen cabinets, shelves, and poles in wardrobe closets, built-in bookcases, reference tables, and the like.

Stage IV (Figure 6.67). This is the sizing and location stage. All the necessary dimensioning is done now. You must verify block modules and stud-line dimensioning, or adhere to the dimensional reference system if one is being used. Work to numerical values (maximum and minimum) and tolerances to which the workers in the field can build.

Stage V (Figure 6.68). This could easily be called the communication stage, because what is produced in this stage must communicate with all the other drawings. Reference symbols are used to connect one drawing with another. Detail references, reference to schedules, and building section reference bubbles are drawn at this stage. This allows the reader to look to other sources for additional information about a portion of the floor plan. Section symbols refer us to the multiple building sections throughout this plan. Detail reference bubbles explain in greater detail the nature of the cabinets and columns and how they are connected with other structural members. Interior elevation reference bubbles show, for example, how a

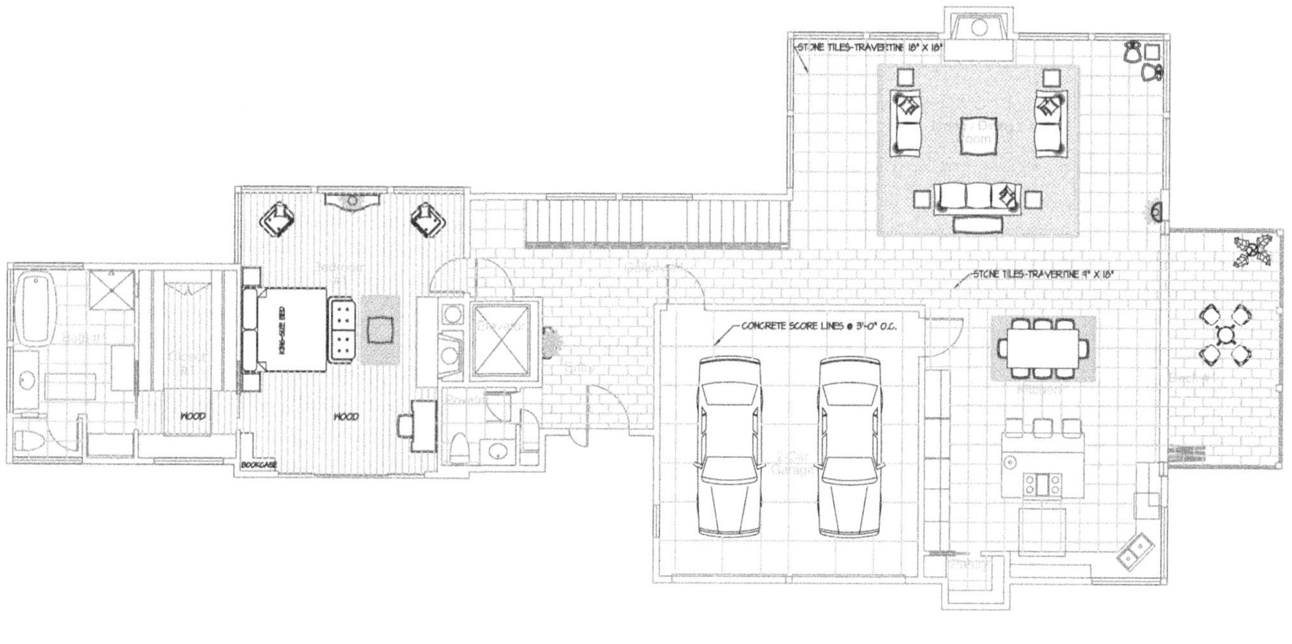

Figure 6.58 Colinita residence: Furniture plan.

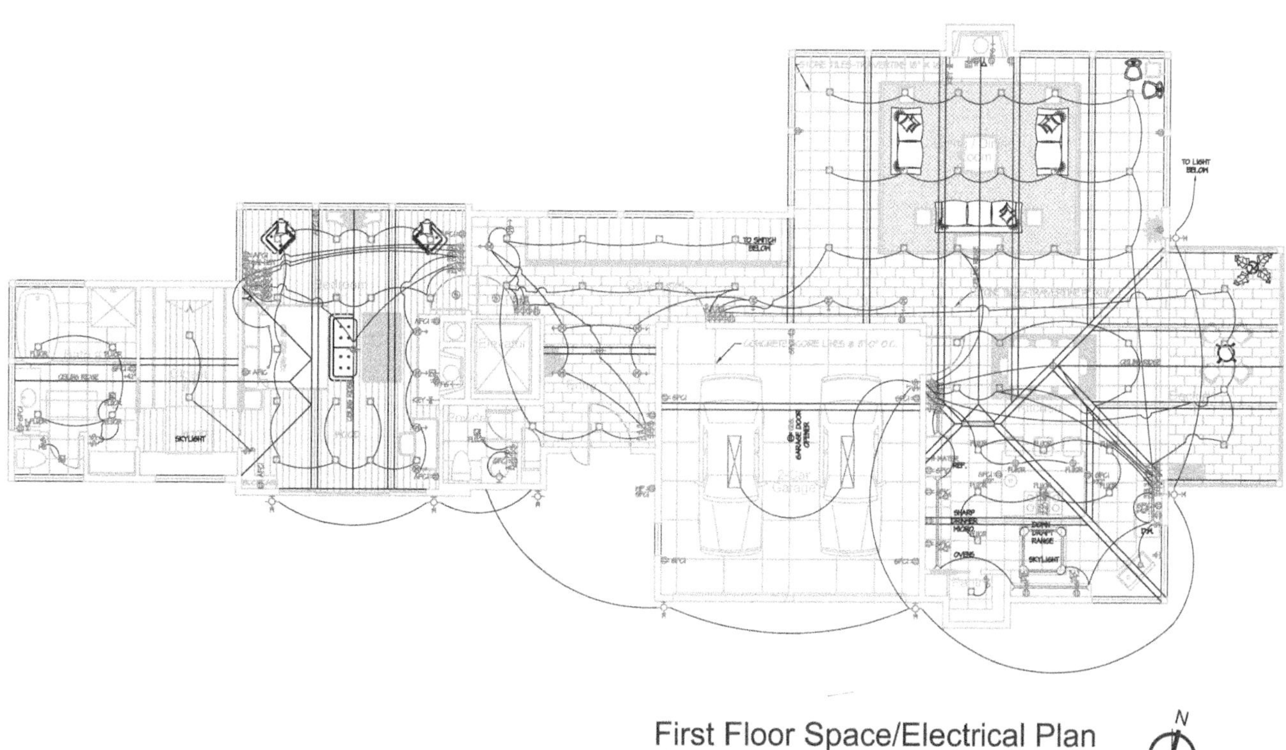

Figure 6.59 Colinita residence: Electrical plan based on furniture plan.

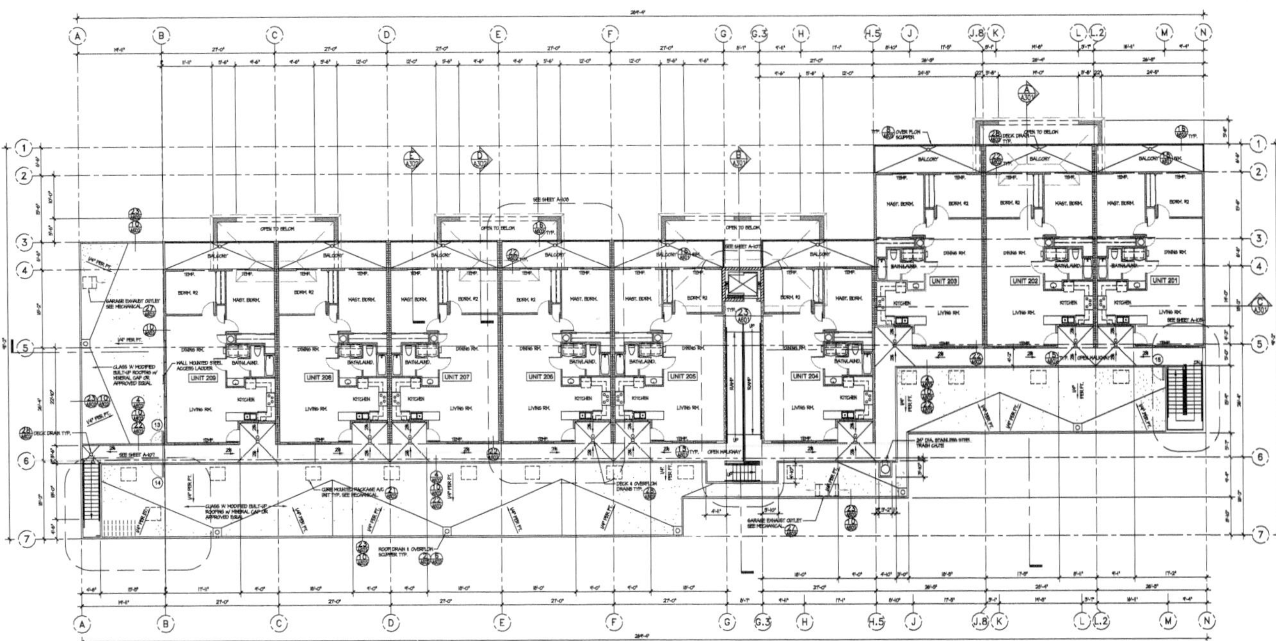

Figure 6.60 Commercial plan: Grand Park Plaza. (Courtesy of Mr. Kizirian.)

fireplace may be finished, or the appearance of cabinets in an examination room of a medical facility; they can also be used to reference windows and doors to schedules for size or for details on the physical makeup of a particular window or door.

Stage VI (Figure 6.69). All noting and titles are added in this stage, but in many instances, the designer may have inserted the room titles when presenting the floor plan to the client. These titles may be relocated at this stage, for clarity, so that they do not interfere with the dimensions, appliances, and so forth. Room titles can be placed on one layer, and other notes, such as those identifying columns or materials, can be placed on another layer. Lettering size may be a determinant for the different layers or the font being used. Main titles should be of existing fonts in the computer program, and all construction notations should be done with an architectural lettering font for ease of correction.

Producing the Floor Plan

One will think that if you were familiar with AutoCAD that the technological information would transfer to the new programs that are being used. The new programs are using a completely different vocabulary and are asking the technical drafter to know more about architecture. Most noteworthy about the new programs is their ability to catch human error. This is because the newer programs do not draw plans individually but draft the entire building three-dimensionally, including a description of the individual components that make a wall, such as the studs and the insulation. In AutoCAD, you draw individual drawings (floor plan, elevations, sections, etc.), whereas in Revit you draw the entire model of the building in 3-D and then develop, for example, the floor plan, dimensioning, and notes; validate wall locations; and so on. You do this two-dimensionally while thinking in three dimensions, so all of the information in this chapter is valuable. The conventions are standard.

Catching human error is not as easy or complete as it might sound. If you put in the wrong dimension, as in Figure 6.70, and your original intent was to make wall "A" parallel with "B" and "C," Revit will not do so. In keeping with the dimensions, you entered, the top wall will be dimensioned from FOS to center of wall, whereas the dimension on the bottom is dimensioned from FOS to FOS. On a 2 × 4 system, this creates a discrepancy of 1¾″. In trying to position this wall, the computer will slide the one wall over 1¾″. To repair this, the original walls ("B" and "C") must be drawn parallel in the original building model and dimensioned later. However, unlike AutoCAD, Revit will dimension to a stud line.

If a change is made to a floor plan, such as the location of a door or window, Revit will reflect this change in all other drawings, such as the elevation section, framing plans, and so on. However, if the building were a six-story structure, a change in the first-floor plan window would not carry over to or appear on the second-floor plan or other floor plans. If you intended for the windows to be aligned vertically, it would be best to make the change on the exterior elevation, whereupon all subsequent floor plans would be changed.

OTHER FLOOR PLAN CONSIDERATIONS

1. Walls
   a. Accuracy of thickness
   b. Correctness of intersections
   c. Accuracy of location
   d. 8-inch wall
   e. Openings
   f. Pony walls designated
   g. Poché
2. Doors and windows
   a. Correct use
   b. Location
   c. Correct symbol
   d. Schedule reference
   e. Header size
   f. Sills, if any
   g. Show swing
   h. Direction of slide if needed
3. Steps
   a. Riser and treads called out
   b. Concrete steps
   c. Wood steps
4. Dimensioning
   a. Position of line
   b. All items dimensioned
   c. All dimensions shown
   d. All arrowheads shown
   e. Openings
   f. Structural posts
   g. Slabs and steps
   h. Closet depth
   i. Check addition
   j. Odd angles
5. Lettering
   a. Acceptable height and appearance
   b. Acceptable form
   c. Readable
6. Titles, notes, and call-outs
   a. Spelling, phrasing, and abbreviations
   b. Detail references
   c. Specification references
   d. Window and door references
   e. Appliances
   f. Slabs and steps
   g. Plumbing fixtures
   h. Openings
   i. Room titles
   j. Ceiling joist direction
   k. Floor material
   l. Drawing title and scale
   m. Tile work
      (1) Tub
      (2) Shower
   n. Attic opening—scuttle
   o. Cabinet
   p. Wardrobe
      (1) Shelves
      (2) Poles
   q. Built-in cabinets, nooks, tables, etc.
7. Symbols
   a. Electric
   b. Gas
   c. Heating, ventilating, and air conditioning
8. Closets, wardrobes, and cabinets
   a. Correct representation
   b. Doors
   c. Depths, widths, and heights
   d. Medicine cabinets
   e. Detail references
   f. Shelves and poles
   g. Plywood partitions and posts
   h. Overhead cabinets
   i. Broom closets
9. Equipment (appliances)
   a. Washer and dryer
   b. Range
   c. Refrigerator
   d. Freezer
   e. Oven
   f. Garbage disposal
   g. Dishwasher
   h. Hot water
   i. Forced draft vent
10. Equipment (special)
    a. Hi-Fi
    b. TV
    c. Sewing machine
    d. Intercom
    e. Game equipment (built-in)
    f. Other
11. Legend
12. Note exposed beams and columns
13. Special walls
    a. Masonry
    b. Veneers
    c. Partial walls, note height
    d. Furred walls for plumbing vents
14. Note sound and thermal insulation
15. Fireplaces
    a. Dimension depth and width of fire pit
    b. Fuel gas and key
    c. Dimension hearth width
16. Mail slot
17. Stairways
    a. Number of risers
    b. Indicate direction
    c. Note railing
18. Medicine cabinet, mirrors at bath
19. Attic and underfloor access ways
20. Floor slopes and wet areas
21. Hose bibbs
22. Main water shut-off valve
23. Fuel gas outlets
    a. Furnace
    b. Range
    c. Oven
    d. Water heater
    e. Fireplace
24. Water heater: gas fired
    a. 4″ vent through roof
    b. 100 sq. in. combustion air vent to closet
25. Furnace location: gas fired
    a. Exhaust vent through roof
    b. Combustion air to closet
26. Electric meter location
27. Floodlights, wall lights, note heights
28. Convenience outlets, note if 220V, note horsepower if necessary
29. Note electric power outlets
    a. Range 9 KW
    b. Oven 5 KW
    c. Dishwasher 1.5 KW
    d. Refrigerator 110V
    e. Washer 2 KW
    f. Dryer 5 KW
30. Clock, chime outlets
31. Doorbell
32. Roof downspouts
33. Fire extinguishers, fire hose cabinets
34. Interior bathroom, toilet room fans
35. Bathroom heaters
36. Kitchen range hood fan and light
37. Telephone, television outlets
38. Exit signs
39. Bathtub inspection plate
40. Thermostat location
41. Door, window, and finish schedules
42. Line quality
43. Basic design
44. Border line
45. Title block
46. Title
47. Scale

Figure 6.61 Floor-plan checklist.

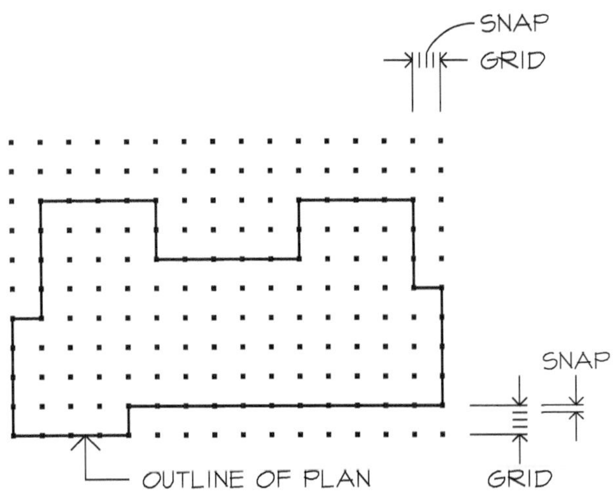

Figure 6.62 Setting grids and snaps to a module.

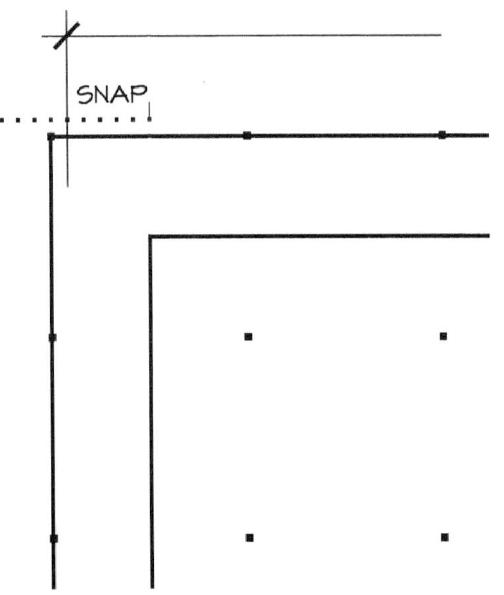

Figure 6.63 Grid versus snap.

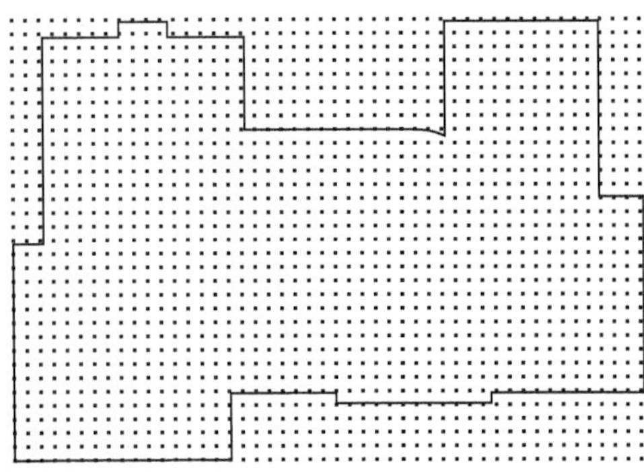

Figure 6.64 Stage I: Setting the datum and building outline.

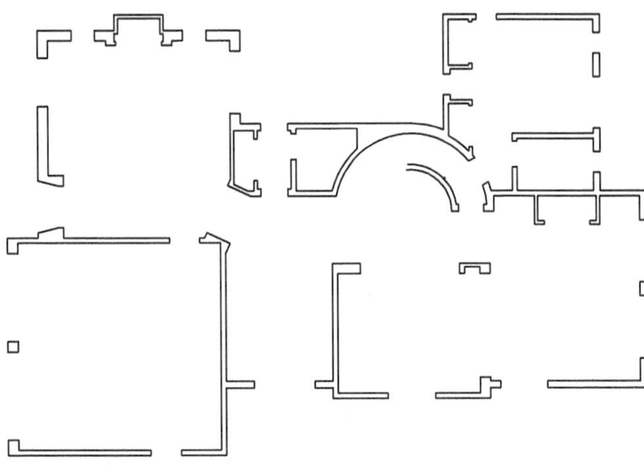

Figure 6.65 Stage II: Exterior/interior wall and openings.

You must build the template of a floor plan based on what is standard in our industry. A template should work as well in New York as in California, in Alabama as in England, and in France as in China. You may work on buildings in Texas, but what you draw should be understood all over America or Asia or Europe if you are to become a master of our profession.

Checklist—Floor Plan

1. Visualize the task at hand. Is it modeling or annotation? If you are a drafter or designer, be sure you understand the important parts of this structure that should not be compromised.
2. If there is a module or pattern, set the grid.
3. Refine the grid by setting up a snap.
4. If annotating, set up your monitor so you can see if there is any impact on the model-use viewports, and/or use two monitors.
5. Review AIA standards and align drawings with its standards.
6. Be sure to make a drawing template.
7. You cannot create a template as you build your first set of drawings on Revit. Build a template before you begin your first Revit drawings.
8. Be sure the massing model is complete before you begin construction drawings.
9. Check special items that are required by the planning department and/or building department.

Troubleshooting a Floor Plan

1. Always enlarge the drawings to locate walls that are misaligned. Make any necessary corrections before you dimension.
2. Check to see that the floor plan, along with its dimensions, notes, and title, will fit on the drawing sheet.

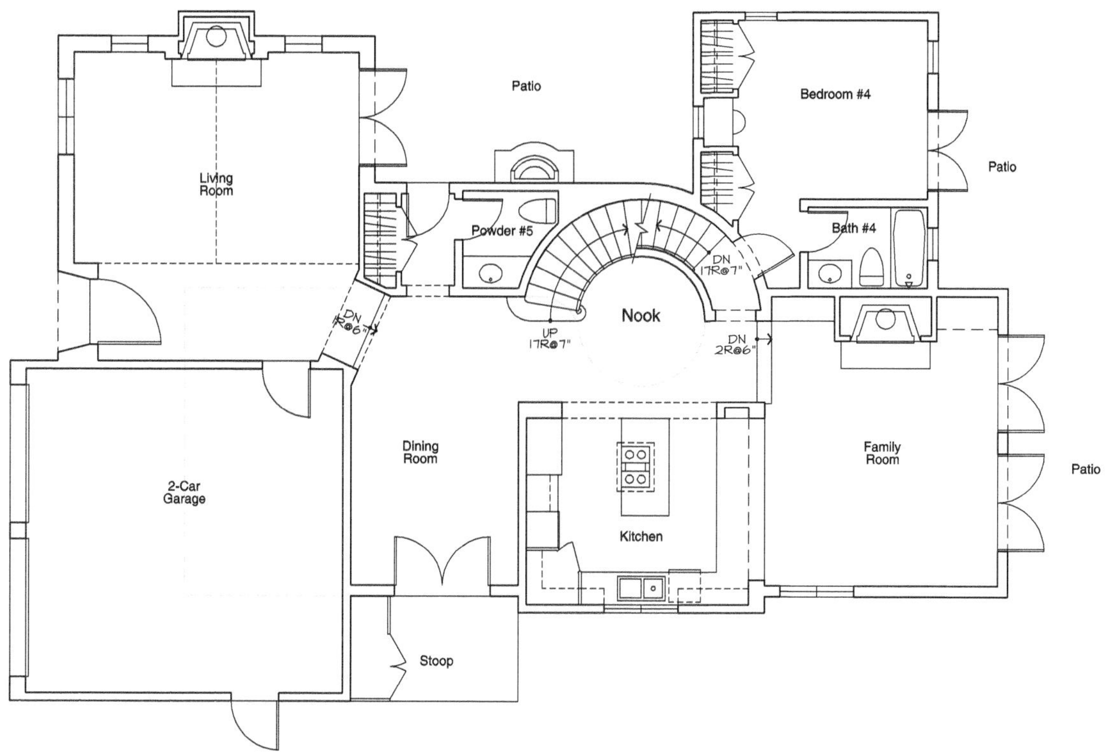

Figure 6.66 Stage III: Plumbing fixtures, stairs, windows/doors, and partitions.

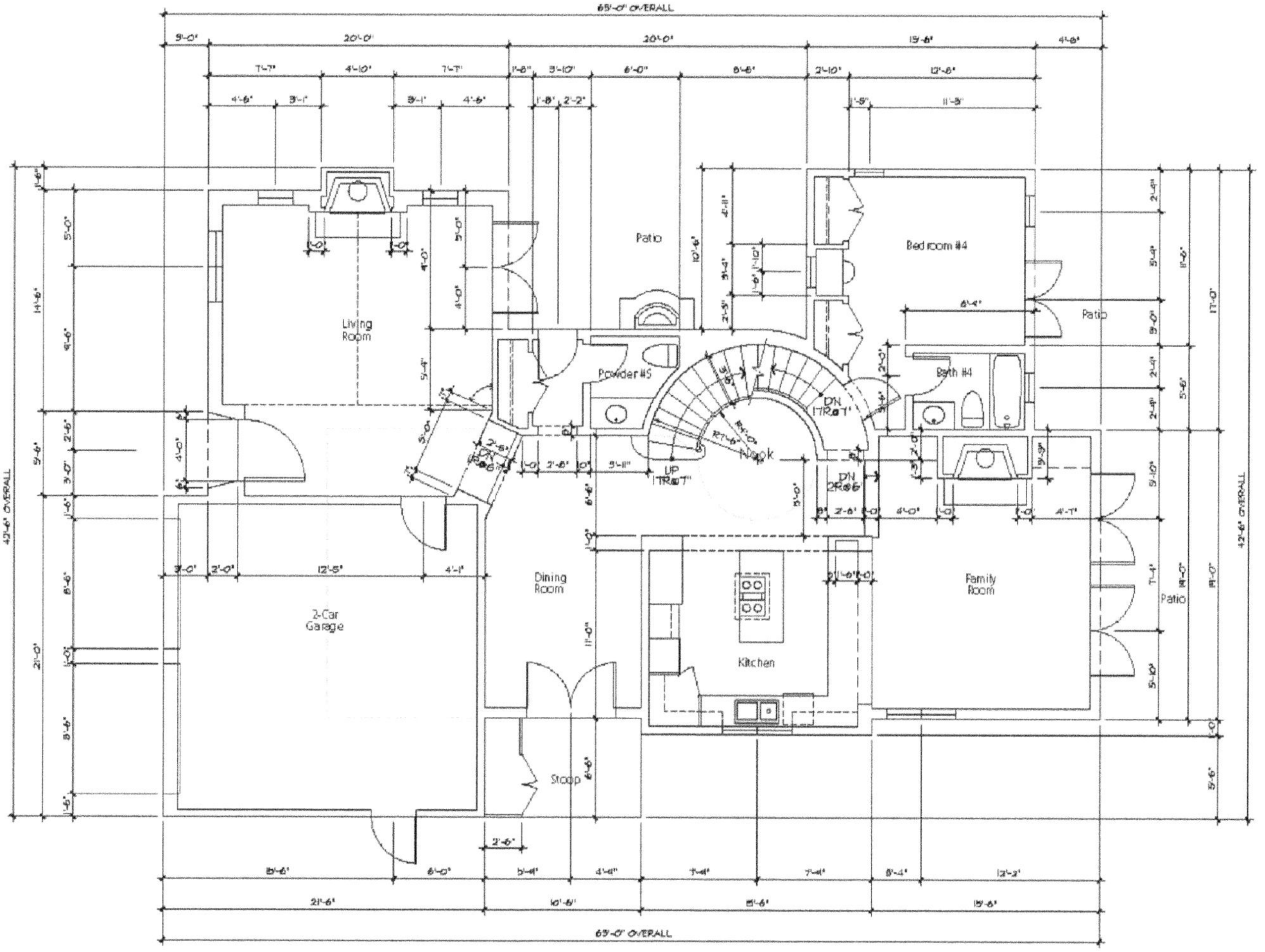

65'-0" OVERALL

Patio
Bedroom #4
Patio
Living Room
Powder #5
Bath #4
DN 17R@7"
Nook
UP 17R@7"
DN 2R@6"
Dining Room
2-Car Garage
Kitchen
Family Room
Patio
Stoop
42'-6" OVERALL
65'-0" OVERALL

Figure 6.67 Stage IV: Dimensioning.

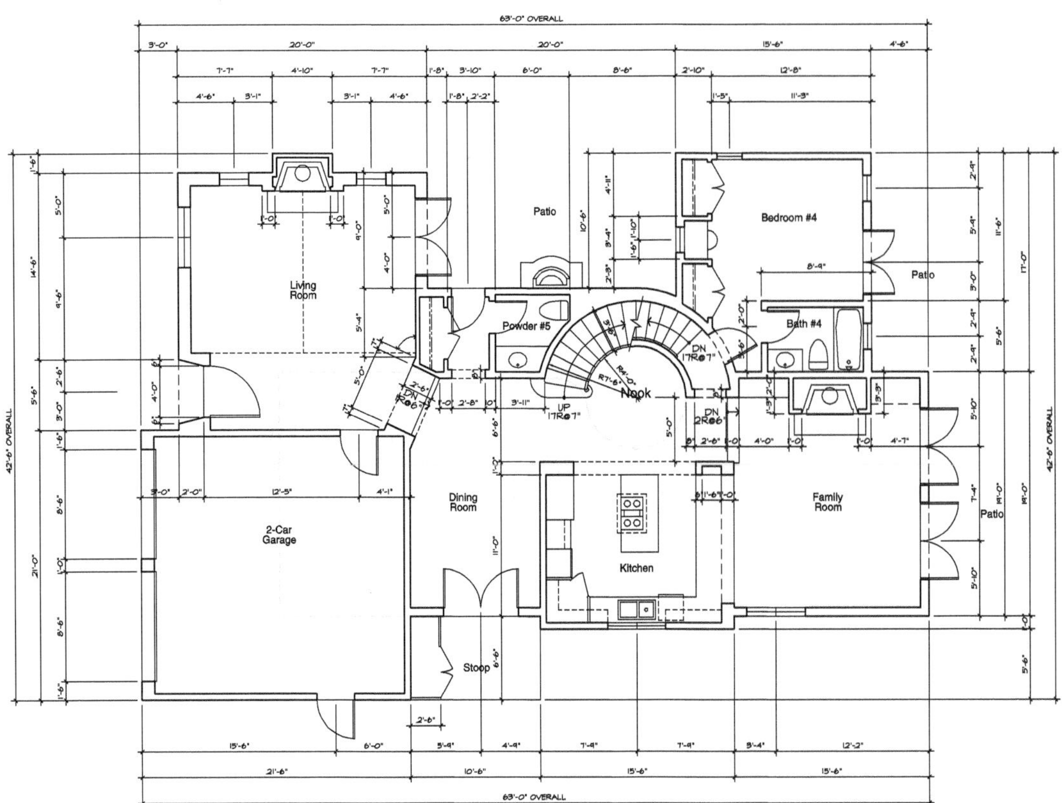

Figure 6.68 Stage V: Noting and references, both detail and section.

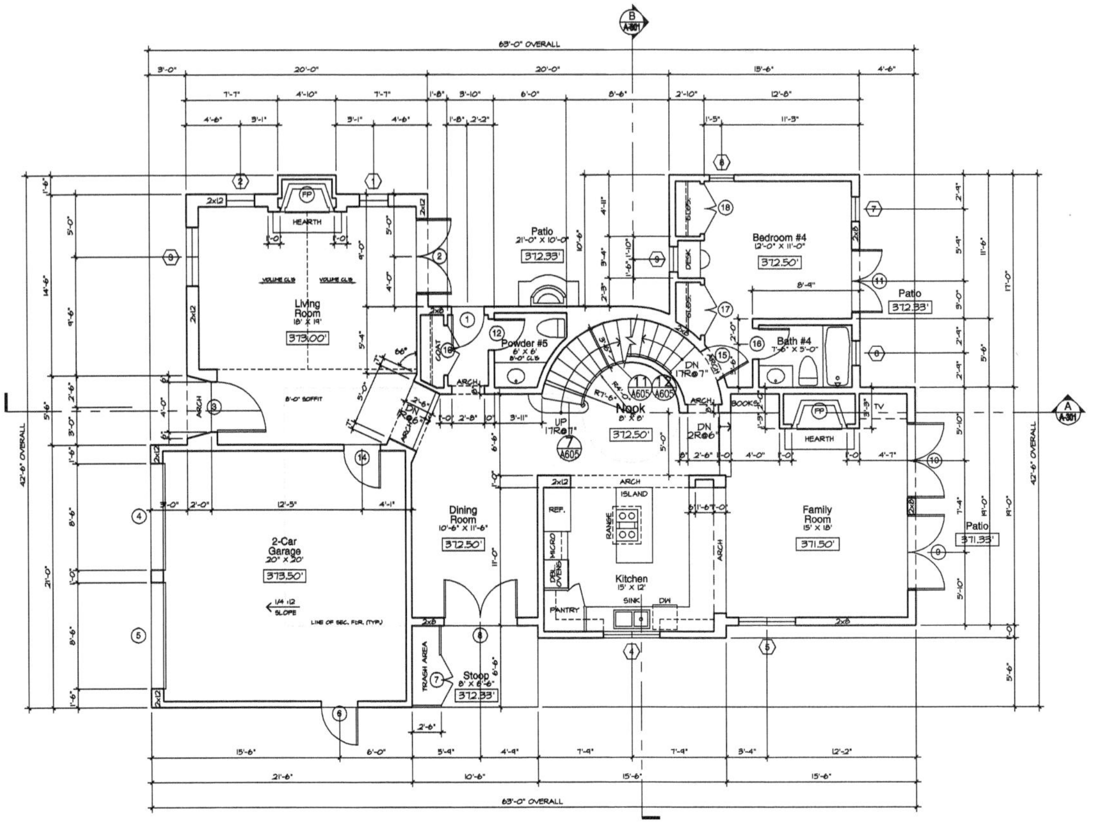

Figure 6.69 Stage VI: Finish work—titles, poché, scale.

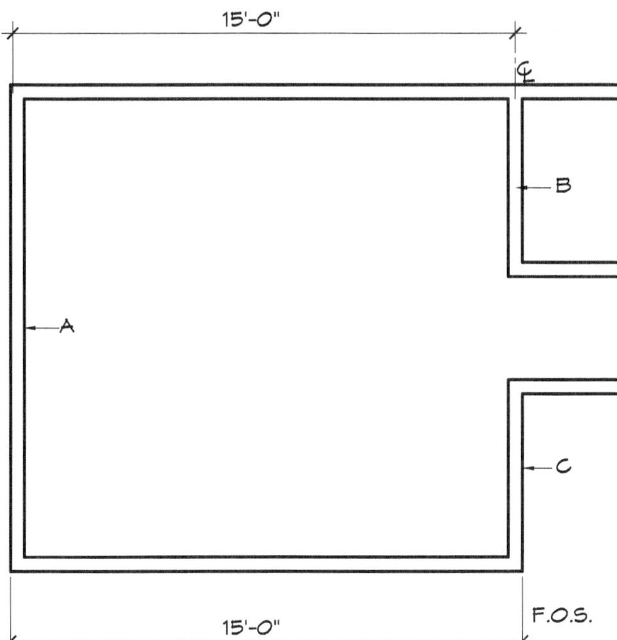

Figure 6.70 Positioning a wall on the floor plan.

If it does not, a scale change is one option; drawing the two halves of the plan on two separate sheets with a key plan is an alternate choice.

3. Make sure you have the proper material designations to complete a specific job.
4. Ensure that you have enough space to comply with the axial reference. Plan on the correct spacing between the dimension lines and the structure.
5. Check that you have correctly employed line qualities.
6. Ensure that section lines and other conventions were used correctly.

CASE STUDIES: WORKING DRAWING DEVELOPMENT

In this section, we discuss the development of the floor plan working drawings for the Clay Theater a Steel and Masonry Building.

Design Development

Even in the development stage, you need to know more about the finished product than about drawing methods. For example, for this theater project, we needed to learn (to mention just a few items):

- What the client can supply, such as the proper slope of the stage, and other knowledge derived from years of building theaters
- Volume and size of the concession area
- Whether the client approves of video games (determines whether a game arcade becomes part of the theater)
- The local and regional building codes applicable to the proposed site
- Fire truck turn around
- All about cars:
- Turn radius
- Parking requirements
- Ratio of compact versus regular stalls
- Aisles required between rows of cars
- Parking required for disabled patrons
- Dedicated green space—minimum required and optimum
- Environmental concerns and elements to be designed in anticipation of the future

Of course, this is above and beyond the aesthetic building form, "normal" environmental concerns, concepts, essence, and so on that dictate the spirit and parti (essence in drawing form).

Clay Theater—Steel/Masonry Structure

Ground-Floor Plan. The floor plan is the base datum from which all other drawings are established. It is also the first preliminary drawing to be used. It must be done comprehensively and adhere to all of the principles of drawing.

Stage I The floor plan is taken from the preliminary floor plan because it is usually the first to be laid out. Thus, this stage must acknowledge the material that will be used to construct the building. In this instance, 8″ × 8″ × 16″ concrete blocks are used. Thus, when drawing the floor plan on the computer, a grid and snap must be built to the block module. See Figure 6.71 for an example of a block module chart. A chart similar to this one can be obtained from any of the manufacturers or associations that produce masonry units. A suggested layer might be set up with the grid set to 16″ increments and the snap set to 8″. The layout of Stage II will conform to this module.

Stage II Clients may supply prototype plans based on their experience in a particular business. This particular client stated that this would be a six-theater structure

BLOCK MODULE

(3/8″ HORIZONTAL AND VERTICAL MORTAR JOINTS)

LENGTH	NO. 16″ LONG BLOCKS	LENGTH	NO. 16″ LONG BLOCKS
0′–8″	1/2	20′–8″	15 1/2
1′–4″	1	21′–4″	16
2′–0″	1 1/2	22′–0″	16 1/2
2′–8″	2	22′–8″	17
3′–4″	2 1/2	23′–4″	17 1/2
4′–0″	3	24′–0″	18
4′–8″	3 1/2	24′–8″	18 1/2
5′–4″	4	25′–4″	19
6′–0″	4 1/2	26′–0″	19 1/2
6′–8″	5	26′–8″	20
7′–4″	5 1/2	27′–4″	20 1/2
8′–0″	6	28′–0″	21
8′–8″	6 1/2	28′–8″	21 1/2
9′–4″	7	29′–4″	22
10′–0″	7 1/2	30′–0″	22 1/2
10′–8″	8	30′–8″	23
11′–4″	8 1/2	31′–4″	23 1/2
12′–0″	9	32′–0″	24
12′–8″	9 1/2	32′–8″	24 1/2
13′–4″	10	40′–0″	30
14′–0″	10 1/2	50′–0″	37 1/2
14′–8″	11	60′–0″	45
15′–4″	11 1/2	70′–0″	52 1/2
16′–0″	12	80′–0″	60
16′–8″	12 1/2	90′–0″	67 1/2
17′–4″	13	100′–0″	75
18′–0″	13 1/2	200′–0″	150
18′–8″	14	300′–0″	225
19′–4″	14 1/2	400′–0″	300
20′–0″	15	500′–0″	375

HEIGHT	NO. 4″ HIGH BLOCKS	NO. 8″ HIGH BLOCKS	HEIGHT	NO. 4″ HIGH BLOCKS	NO. 8″ HIGH BLOCKS
0′–4″	1		10′–4″	31	
0′–8″	2	1	10′–8″	32	16
1′–0″	3		11′–0″	33	
1′–4″	4	2	11′–4″	34	17
1′–8″	5		11′–8″	35	
2′–0″	6	3	12′–0″	36	18
2′–4″	7		12′–4″	37	
2′–8″	8	4	12′–8″	38	19
3′–0″	9		13′–0″	39	
3′–4″	10	5	13′–4″	40	20
3′–8″	11		13′–8″	41	
4′–0″	12	6	14′–0″	42	21
4′–4″	13		14′–4″	43	
4′–8″	14	7	14′–8″	44	22
5′–0″	15		15′–0″	45	
5′–4″	16	8	15′–4″	46	23
5′–8″	17		15′–8″	47	
6′–0″	18	9	16′–0″	48	24
6′–4″	19		16′–4″	49	
6′–8″	20	10	16′–8″	50	25
7′–0″	21		17′–0″	51	
7′–4″	22	11	17′–4″	52	26
7′–8″	23		17′–8″	53	
8′–0″	24	12	18′–0″	54	27
8′–4″	25		18′–4″	55	
8′–8″	26	13	18′–8″	56	28
9′–0″	27		19′–0″	57	
9′–4″	28	14	19′–4″	58	29
9′–8″	29		19′–8″	59	
10′–0″	30	15	20′–0″	60	30

Figure 6.71 Grid and snap set to block module/block module chart.

with 200 seats in each theater. The level for each row of seats and fire restrictions were all design factors prior to the preliminary drawings.

Compare the aerial photograph in Figure 6.72 with Figure 6.73 to see what was actually being constructed.

These figures show the construction sequence in relationship to the floor plan found in Figure 6.74.

In Figure 6.74 the columns toward the center of the theater support the upper floor. (The upper floor accommodates the projectors and allows projectionist to move from one projector to another.) Near the rear of the building are the restrooms and snack bar storage. The two partial rectangles near the front of the theater are stairwells.

Stage III At the bottom of the left and right sides of the plan, we added a planter and a ramp for disabled people. See Figure 6.75. Stairs were added throughout the plan and we added a set of dotted lines in each auditorium to represent the motion picture screens. The size of the screen was determined by the seating capacity and the client needs. Dividing walls were drawn within the stairs at the front. Notice at the front and rear of the building are brick pavers as described in the foundation plan (see Chapter 7). These pavers were drawn with textured concrete within them.

At the center of the structure is the concession stand. The textured area represents a tile floor and the black

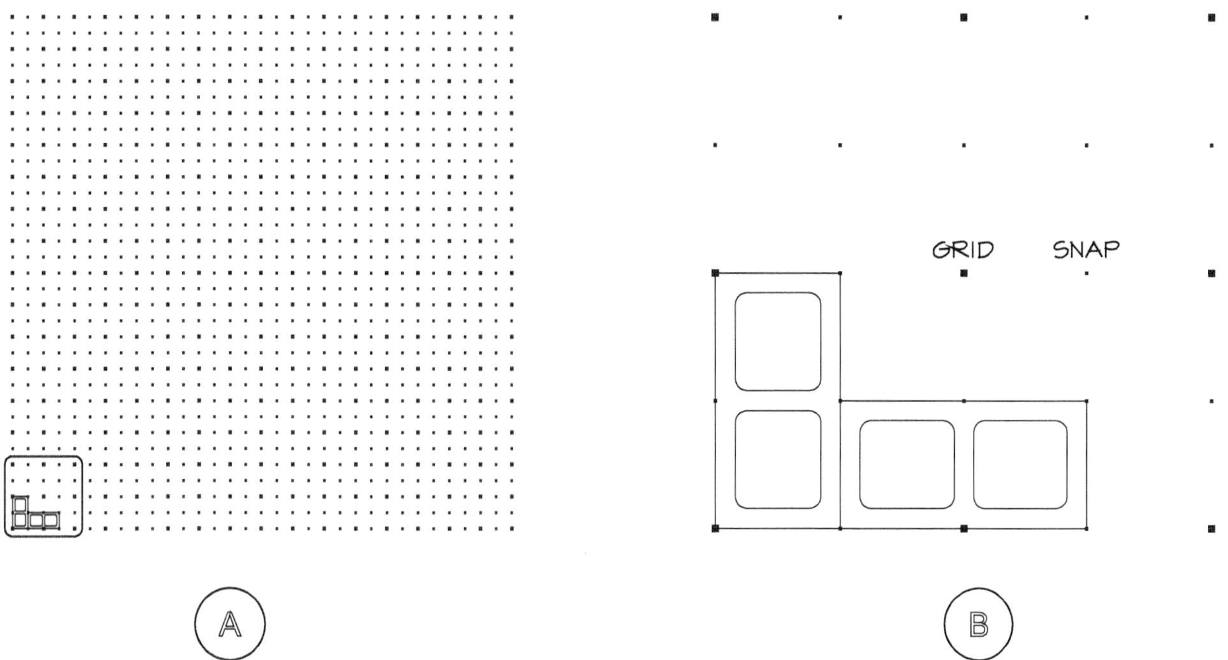

Figure 6.71 *(Continued)*

Figure 6.72 Aerial view of completed wall. (Reprinted with permission of William Boggs Aerial Photography.)

Figure 6.73 View of entry, lobby, and back of theaters.

space, the counter. We added toilet partitions and lavatories to the restrooms, leaving large stalls for persons with disabilities. Toilets can be added here later.

At the center of each restroom entry, the small area for telephones also accommodates disabled people. The small circles with a darkened cross indicate fire extinguishers. We added fire sprinkler symbols in the trash area at the rear of the building. Line quality becomes important here to differentiate between walls, floor patterns, and fixtures.

Stage IV Interior and exterior dimension lines were now added, as shown in Figure 6.76. These dimension lines must always be double-checked with the foundation plan, to ensure proper alignment of walls with the foundation. As the floor plan was dimensioned first, the concrete block module was followed.

The axial reference plane bubbles across the top and the right correspond with walls, columns, and any structural members above. From the reference plane matrix, we also indicated door swings.

Stage V All of the reference bubbles have now been added. See Figure 6.77. Full architectural section references, wall sections, door reference bubbles, and interior elevation reference symbols were included. Each room would later receive a number as well as a title, so we drew in underlines for the names and rectangular boxes for the numbers.

We drew plants in the planters at the entry to clearly differentiate the planter areas from the ramps. The planters and plants were later included in the elevations for clarity and consistency.

The material designation for the walls indicated by hatching lines in the wall lines was drafted next.

For the final stage of the ground floor working drawing, refer to Figure 6.77, where numerical values for the dimension lines were included, as well as the noting of items such as the pilaster size and location of screens, area, and room titles.

Finally, the drawing title, scale, and north arrow were also added at the final stage.

Upper-Floor Plan

Stage I We included the six auditoriums in the upper-floor plan, as shown in Figure 6.78, because the upper portions of the auditorium were adjacent to the upper floor. The center of the structure is the lobby, which extends to the roof.

We located the projection windows according to their required angle. See Figure 6.78, which shows the interior of the structure. Note the projection windows and the connectors below to attach the upper floor. We took care to align the walls of the upper floor with the walls below.

Another view of this relationship can be seen in the structural section.

Stage II This stage (Figure 6.79) shows the restroom facilities, two fire extinguishers (one circle on each side), and, most important, the projectors and the space they occupy. A rectangle with a line through it next to the circle was the symbol selected to represent the projectors.

Stage III The main difference in this stage and previous stages is the addition of most of the dimension numbers.

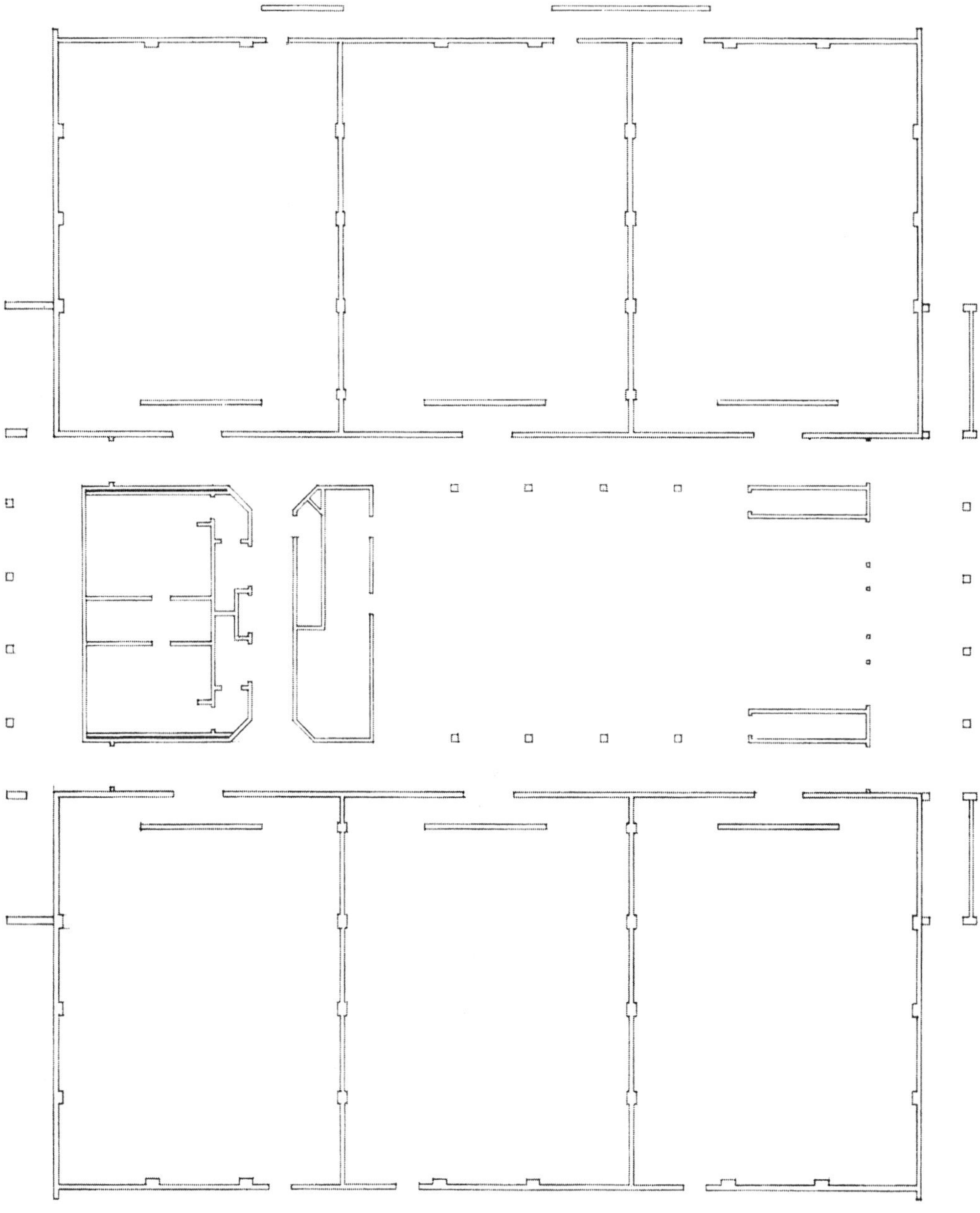

Figure 6.74 Clay Theater—Stage II: Working drawing—ground-floor plan.

See Figure 6.80. The dimensions had to be checked against the floor plan of the floor below, and both had to be checked to ensure correct concrete block modules dimensions. For the final stage of the second-floor plan working drawing, refer to Figure 6.80.

Madison—Steel Building

Ground-Floor Plan

Stage I The first step in the evolution of the working drawings was to precisely lay out the site plan, incorporating the parking stalls, traffic lanes, handicapped parking stalls, and spaces for public access locations. These accurately scaled areas were predicated on the schematic studies of the site plan and the ground-floor plan.

Once the accurately scaled parking stalls were located, the locations of the steel supporting columns could be established. From this drawing, a matrix identifying system designating the various column and wall locations was created. Refer to Chapters 2 and 3 for detailed information and explanations of the use of a matrix system. Figure 6.81 illustrates a site plan, parking layouts,

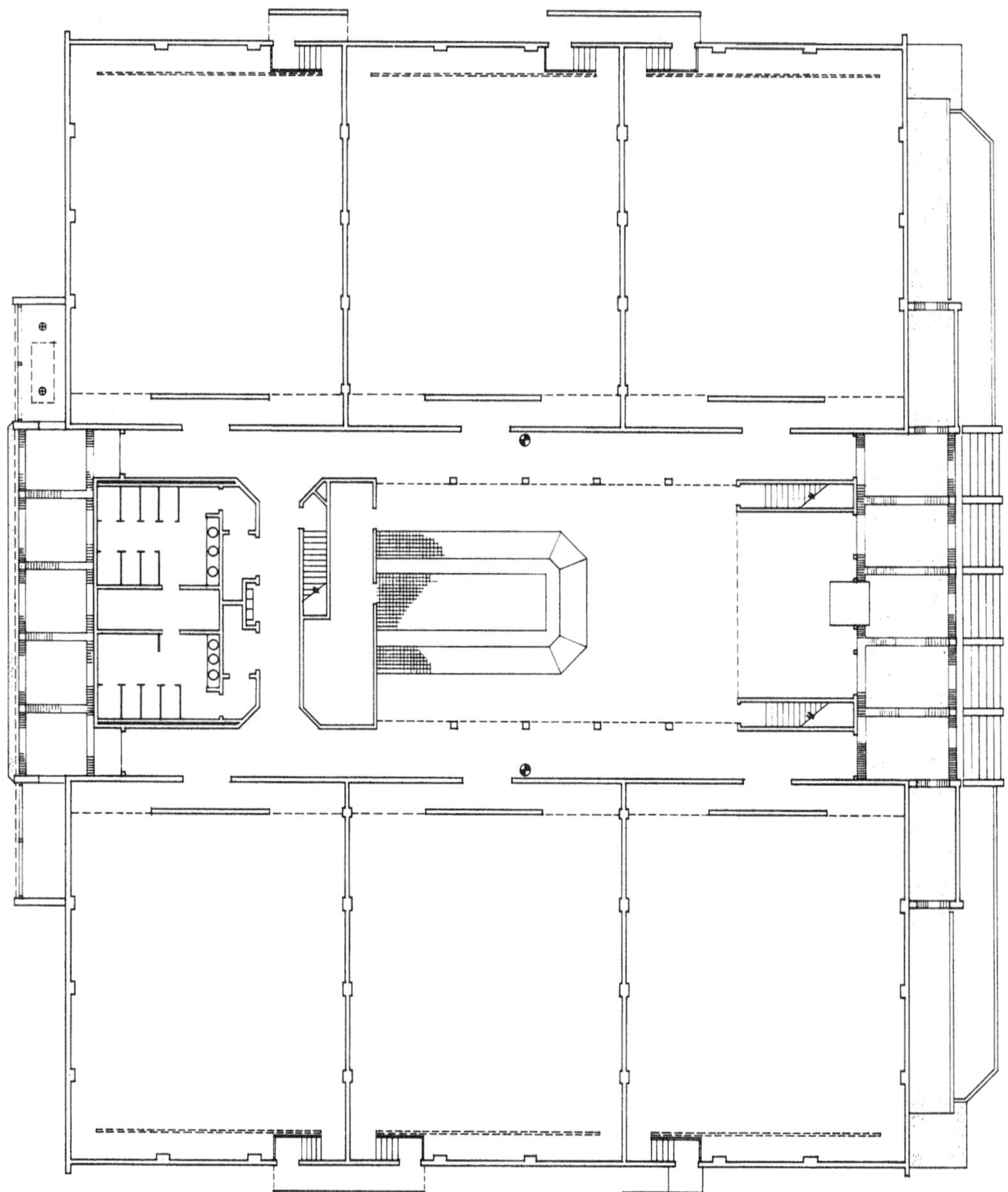

Figure 6.75 Clay Theater—Stage III: Working drawing-ground floor plan.

and the initial structural matrix system with bubbles for the purpose of identifying the locations of the steel columns and wall. This drawing, which was prepared by the computer-aided drafting (CAD) operator for the project, was the first and the basis for the additional layering of succeeding drawings that were used in developing the various floor levels for the completion of the working drawings. In general, the layering process for drawings is the evolution of a series of drawings that have been formatted from initial drawings, which become the basis for all succeeding drawings.

Stage II From Stage I, a basic matrix system layout for all structural members was established in Stage II. This drawing became the primary structural template for all succeeding floors, incorporating the floor and roof framing plans, exterior elevations, and building sections. Note that on the west side matrix, there are symbols with a specific letter designation that may be followed by a number. This tells the viewer that there is an identifying wall located north of column "D." The basic matrix layout template is depicted in Figure 6.82.

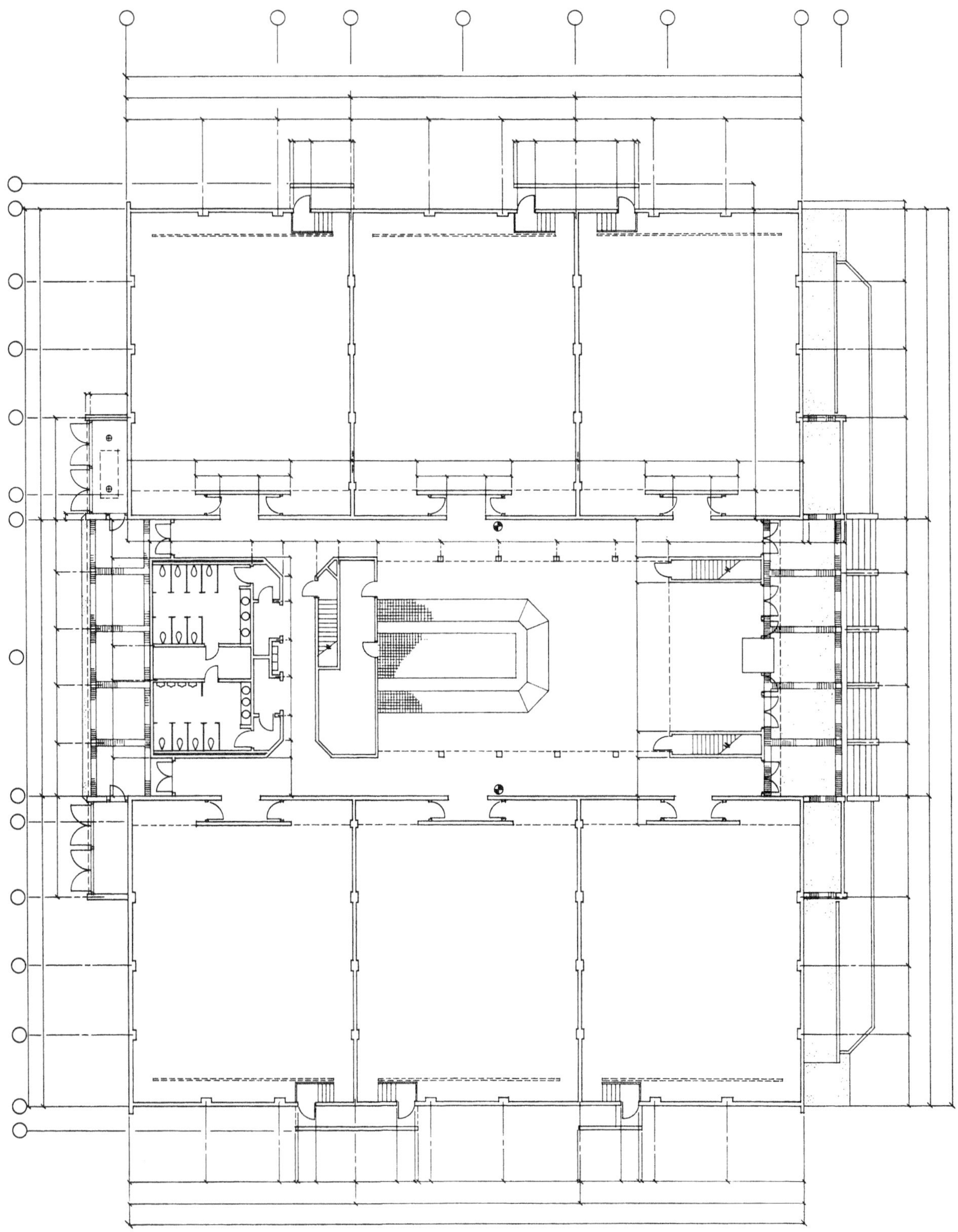

Figure 6.76 Clay Theater—Stage IV: Working drawing—ground-floor plan.

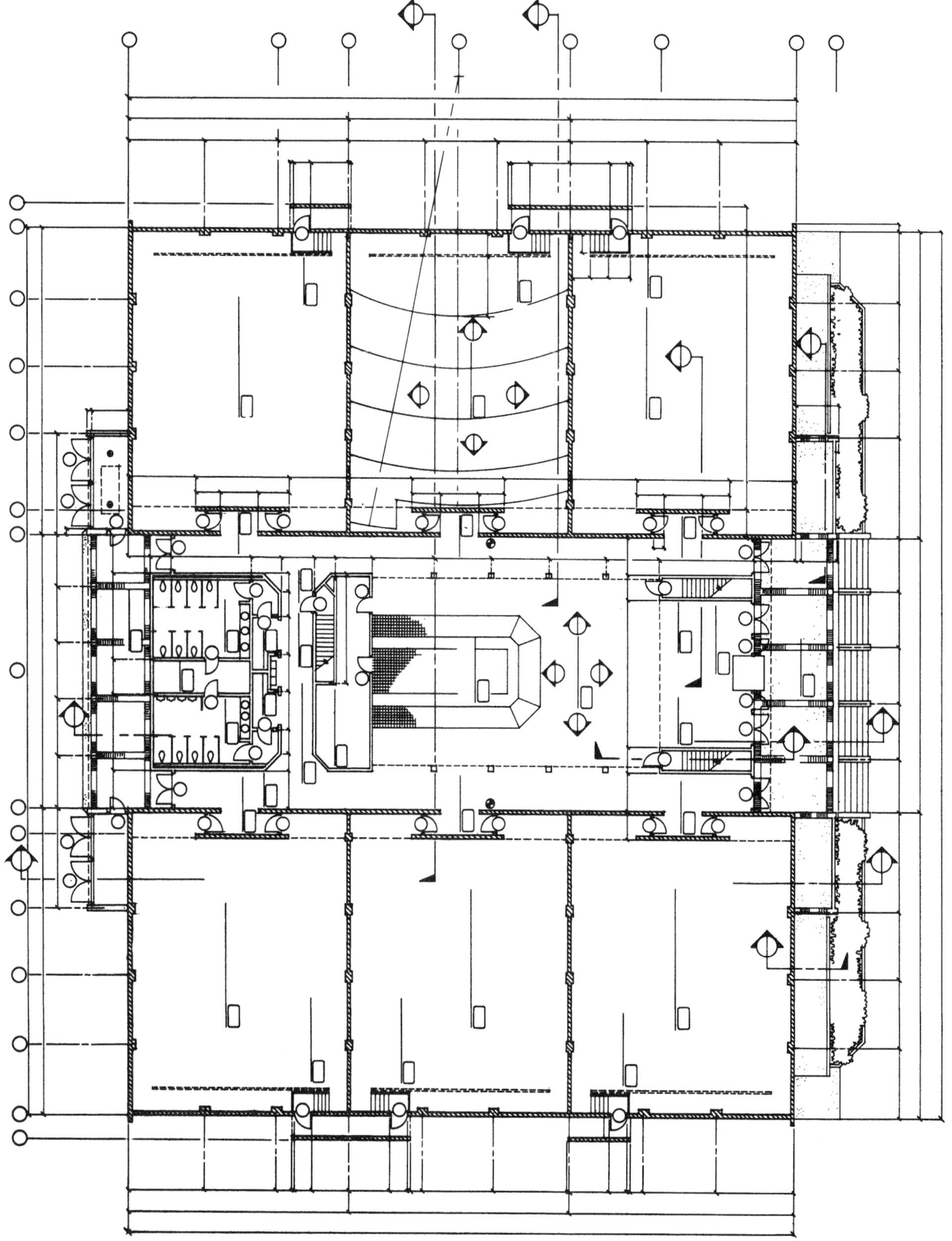

Figure 6.77 Clay Theater—Stage V: Working drawing—ground-floor plan.

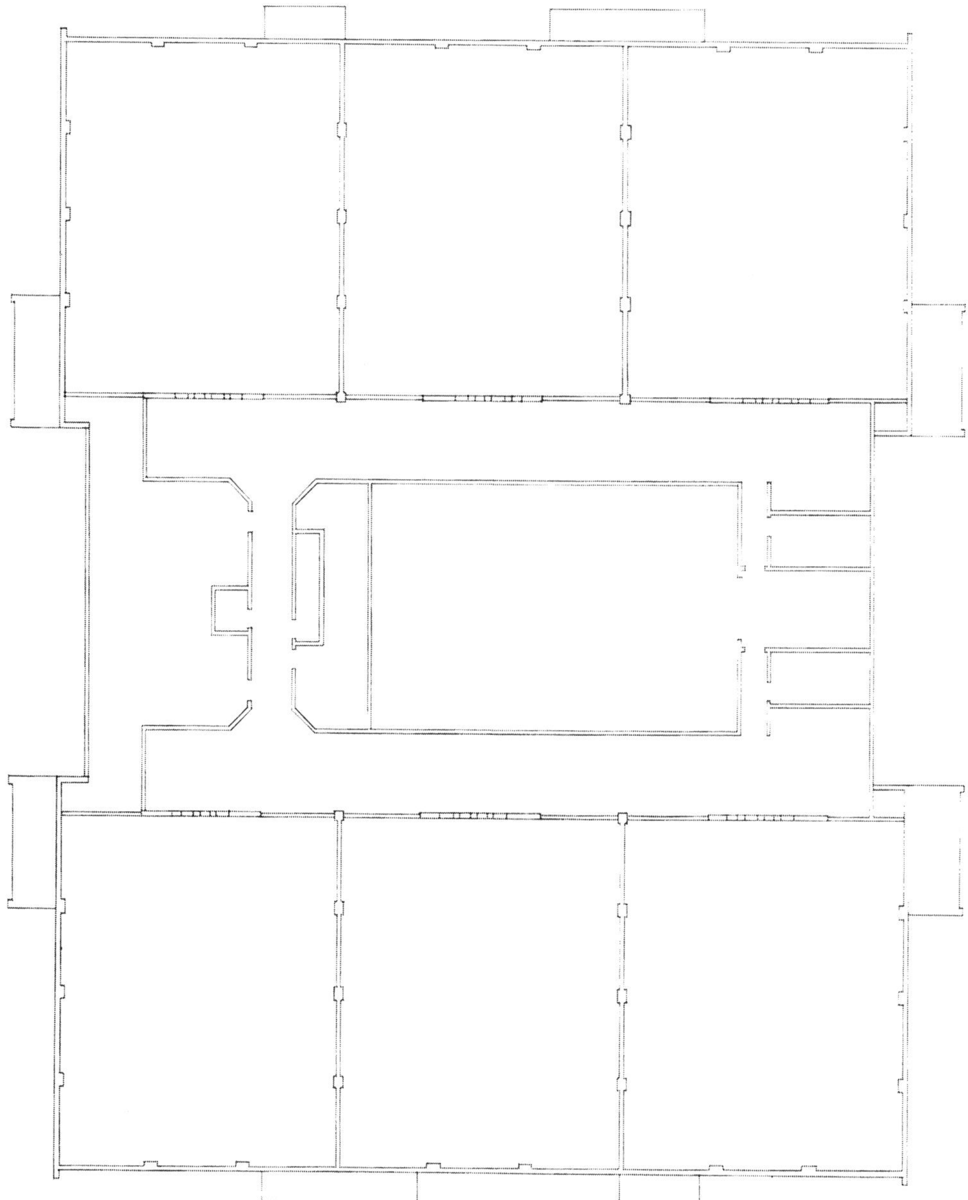

Figure 6.78 Clay Theater—Stage I: Working drawing—upper-floor plan.

Stage III With the combination of layering from Stages I and II, a third stage for the ground-floor plan was developed. This drawing illustrated the combination of the parking stalls, the matrix system, the supporting steel column locations, and the wall locations for public access and structural considerations. The drawing also defined the wall boundary location for the succeeding upper-floor levels. As a result of the early schematic drawings, elliptical wall shapes were incorporated into the stair-well walls and lobby locations at the west and east sides of the structure. In the main lobby area, which is located approximately in the center of the building, other spaces were established for facilities such as an elevator, stairwell, and machine and utility rooms. This drawing is shown in Figure 6.83.

Stage IV The drawing for Stage IV incorporated the required number of risers and treads for the stairs while establishing the elevator size. The CAD operator designated the doors and the glass areas that are adjacent to the lobbies, along with the room numbers, for the various areas. These room numbers were eventually defined for their use on a room schedule.

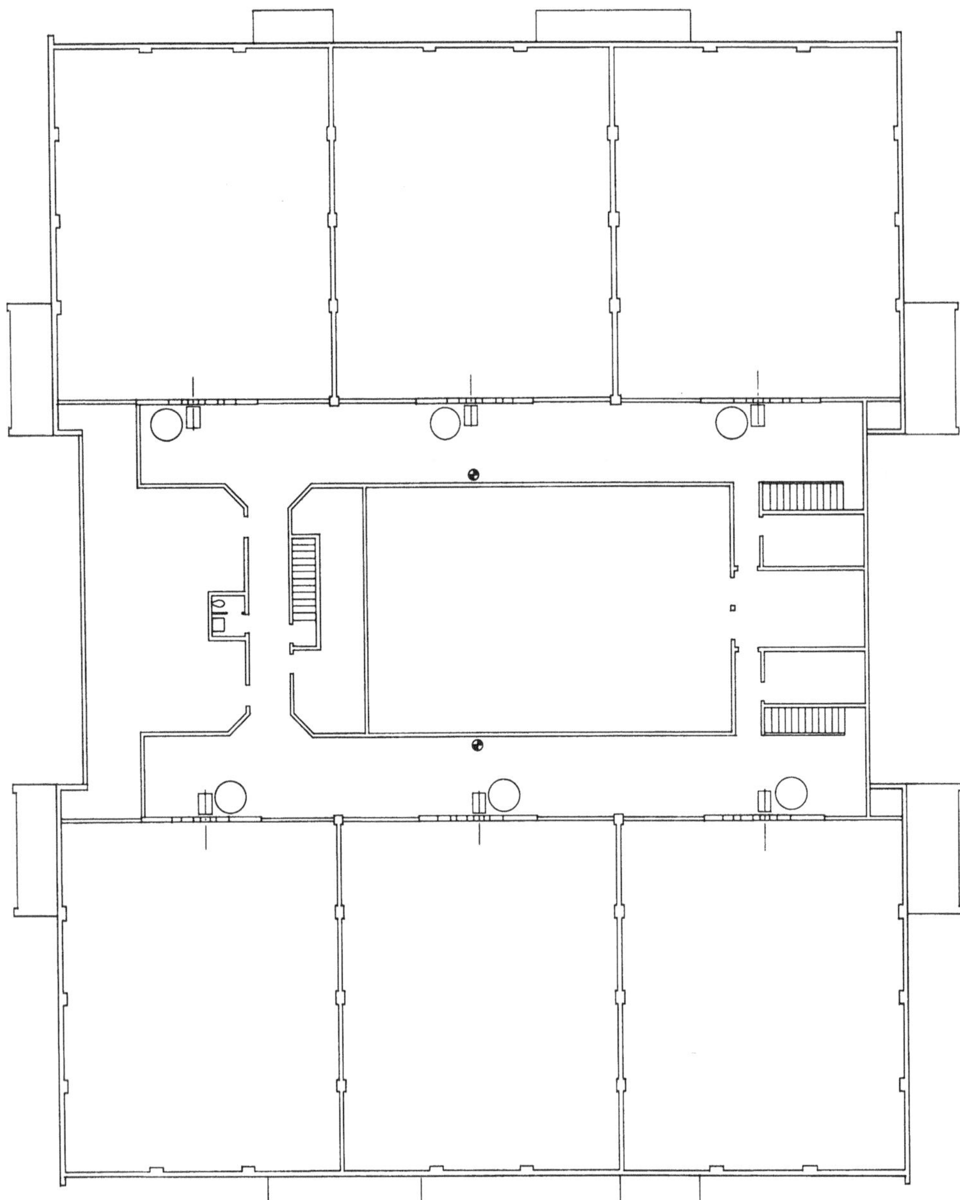

Figure 6.79 Clay Theater—Stage II: Working drawing—upper-floor plan.

As mentioned earlier in regard to the schematic studies, the architect and the mechanical engineer decided to incorporate an "off-peak cooling system," which can also be referred to as an "ice bank" system.

This system requires a pool for the storage of the coolant. The pool is now shown at the matrix lines of D and E. The purpose of the off-peak cooling system is to save energy and costs by developing the coolant necessary for daily use.

The system produces coolant in the late night or early morning hours when the demand for and cost of electricity is at a minimum. Finally, the title and the scale were established for this drawing. Figure 6.84 depicts the first-floor plan for Stage IV.

Stage V At Stage V, dimension lines and dimensions were established for the column and wall locations. These particular dimension lines related to the matrix system and provided a basis for the dimensioning of the various spaces. Parking stalls and automobile access areas were dimensioned, along with the handicapped parking access areas. The dimensioning of the walkways, trash areas, and the off-peak cooling pool was shown

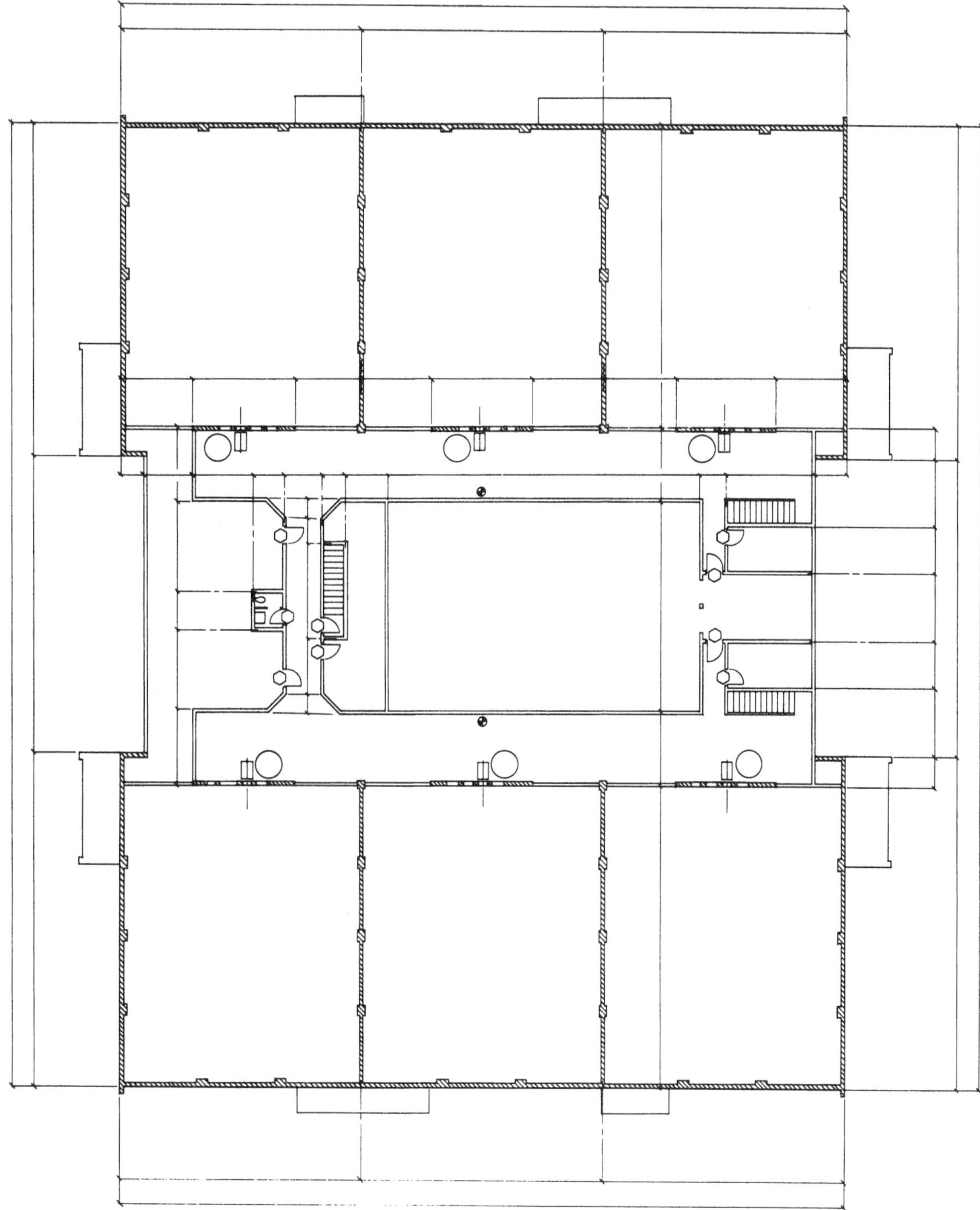

Figure 6.80 Clay Theater—Stage III: Working drawing—upper-floor plan.

at this stage. The drawing also defined the various curb radius dimensions within the parking and automobile access areas. This drawing stage is shown in Figure 6.85.

Stage VI In Stage VI, the principal information added includes the various locations of the building's structural sections. This is done at this time in order to allow the structural engineering firm to commence with the initial structural design and calculations. Note the bubble designations and the direction from which the building section will be viewed. This stage is illustrated in Figure 6.86.

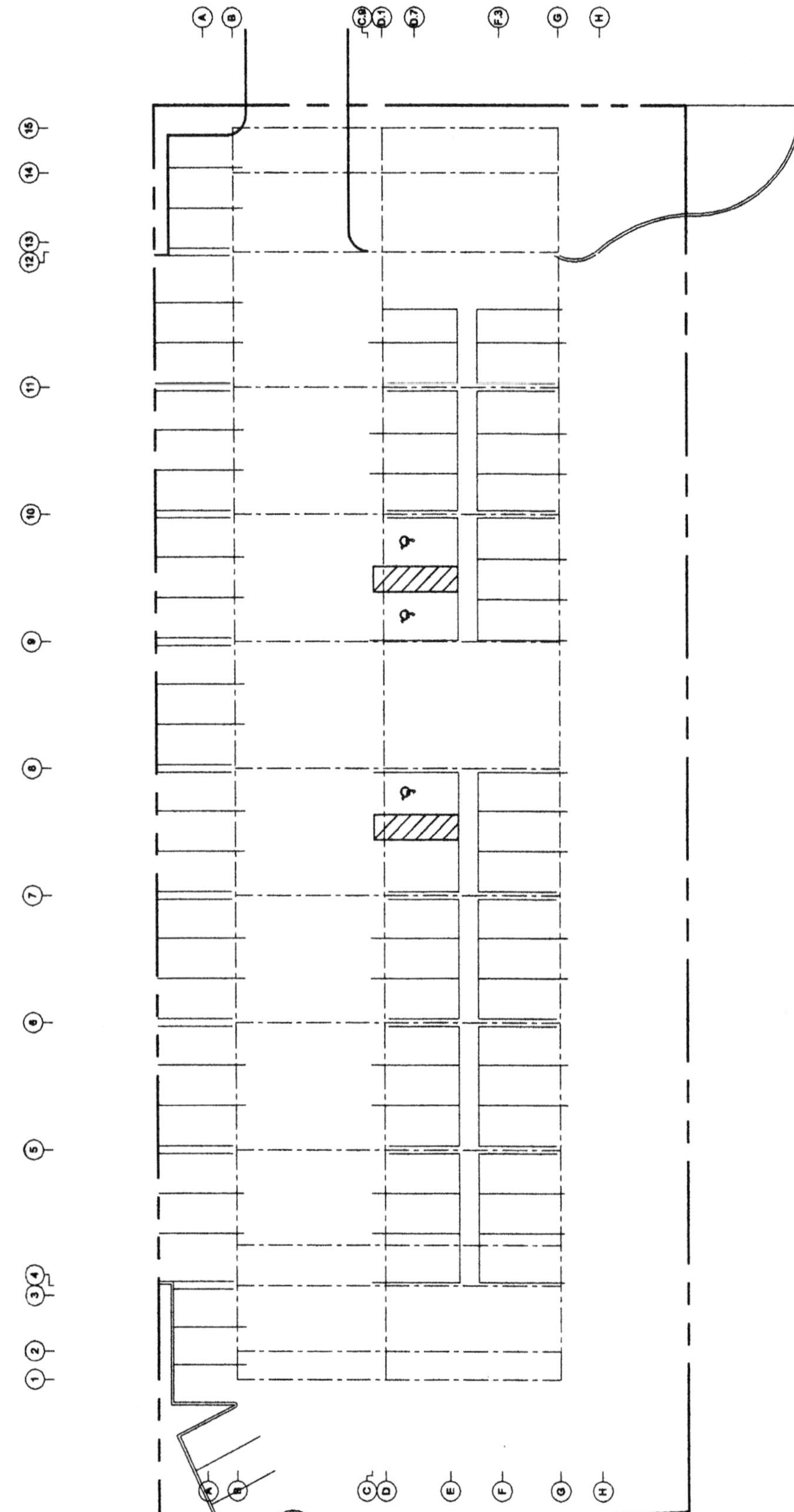

Figure 6.81 Madison Building—Stage I: Matrix system.

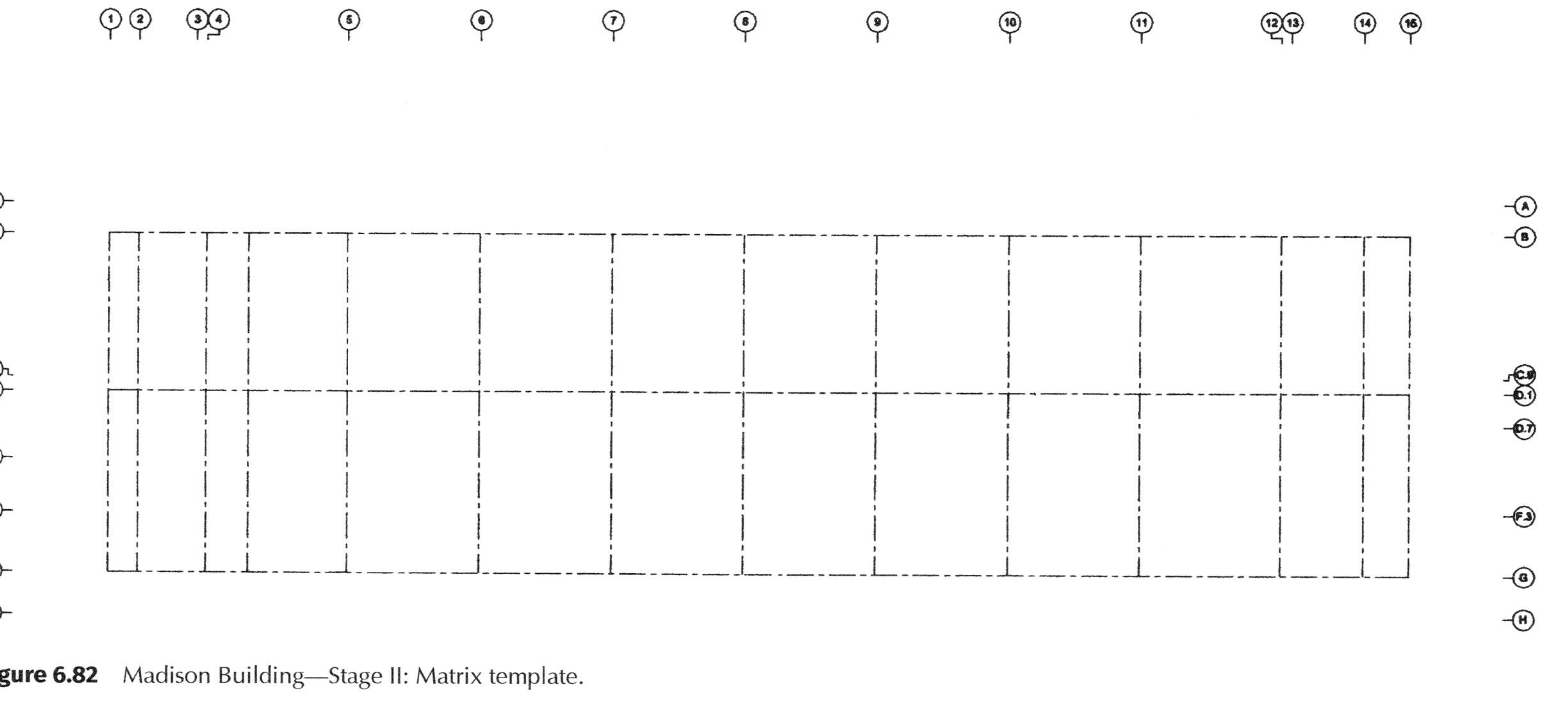

Figure 6.82 Madison Building—Stage II: Matrix template.

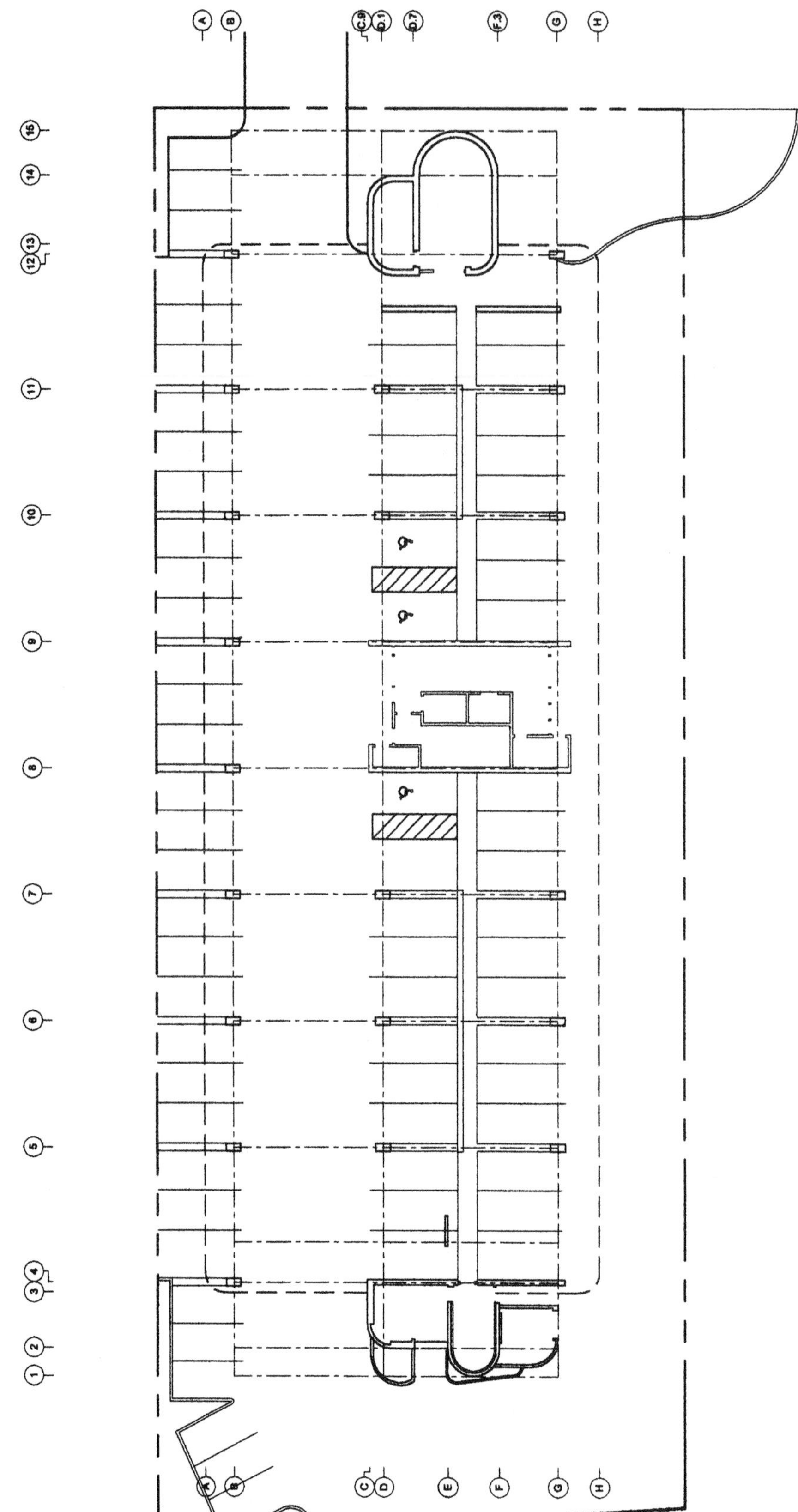

Figure 6.83 Madison Building—Stage III: Working drawing—ground-floor plan.

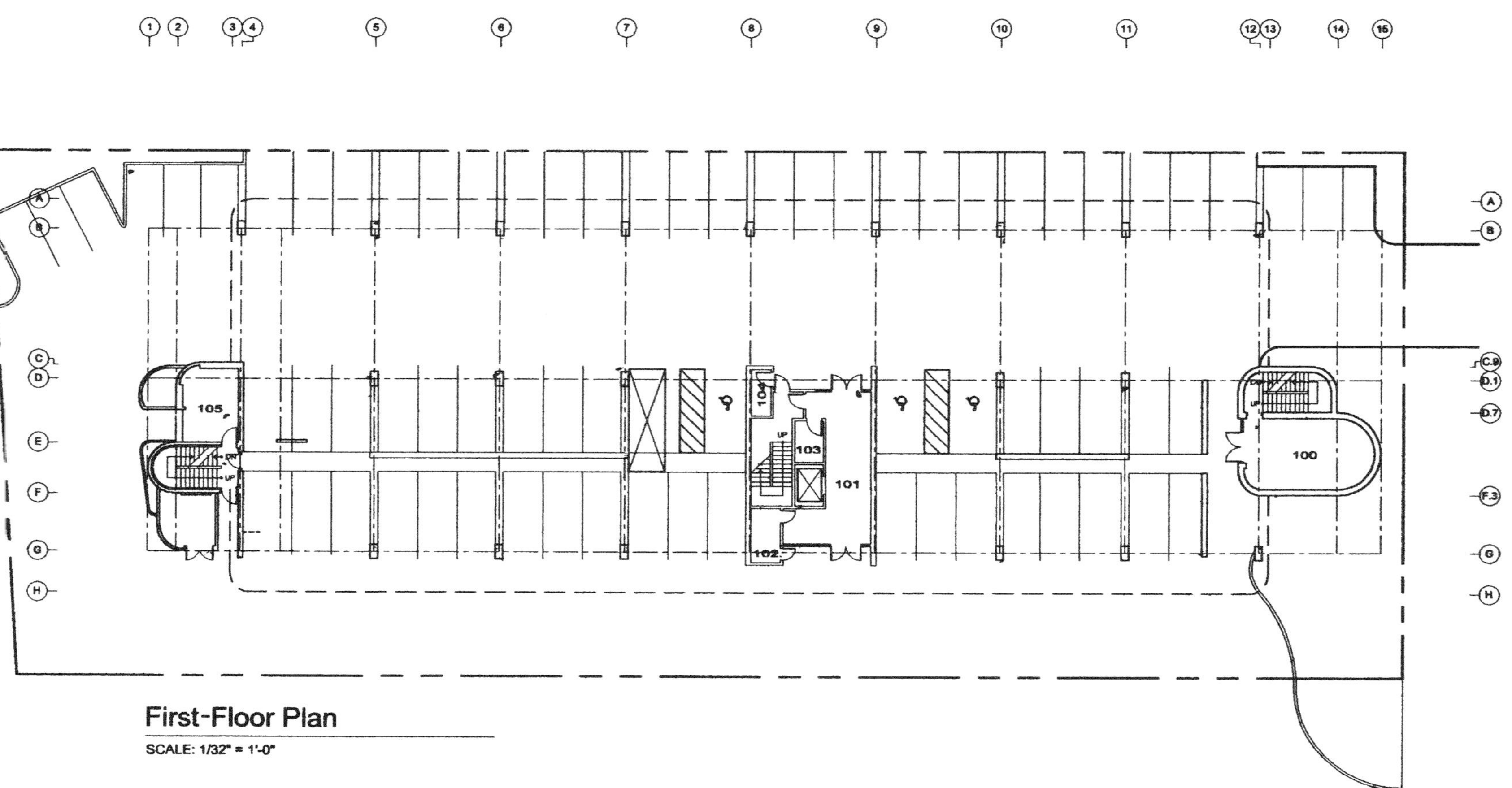

Figure 6.84 Madison Building—Stage IV: Working drawing—ground-floor plan.

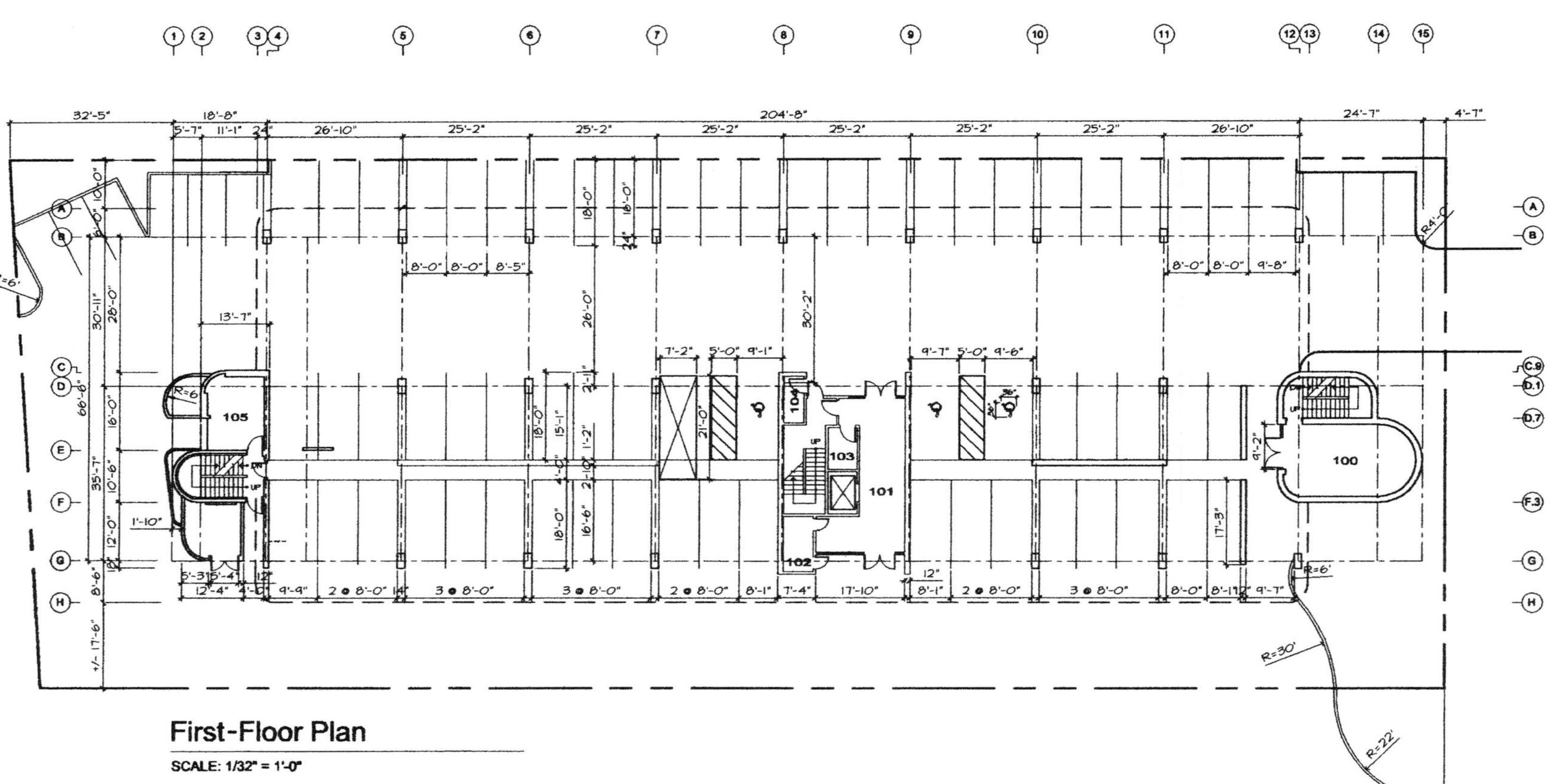

Figure 6.85 Madison Building—Stage V: Working drawing—ground-floor plan.

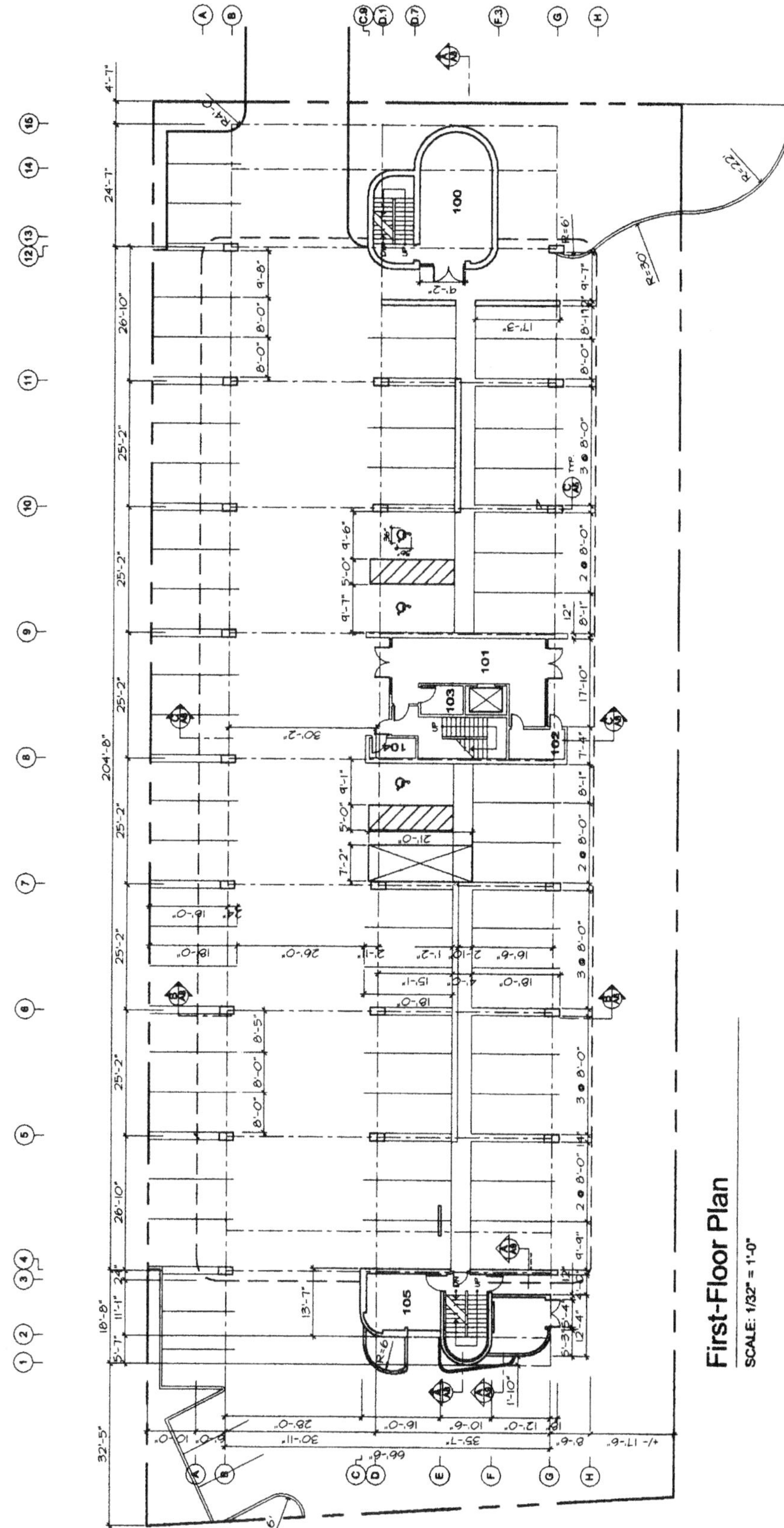

Figure 6.86 Madison Building—Stage VI: Working drawing—ground-floor plan.

Second-Floor Plan Working Drawing Development

Stage I The first task for Stage I of the second-floor plan is to review and finalize the matrix symbolizing for all structural steel columns and exterior walls. This completed drawing is a culmination of a series of drawings evolving from the initial matrix that was shown in Figure 6.81. The finalized matrix drawing is depicted in Figure 6.87.

Stage II With the use of the finalized matrix developed in Stage I as a basis for identifying the locations of steel columns and walls, a floor plan is developed that is primarily an overlay of the finalized first-floor plan. This plan indicates the wall locations from the final first-floor plan, including the walls for the elevator shaft and stairwells and the exterior wall extremities. This stage also shows the locations for all the vertical window mullions around the perimeter of the exterior walls. The drawing for Stage II is illustrated in Figure 6.88.

Stage III The purpose of Stage III for the second-floor plan is to delineate the risers and treads for all the stairwells, the elevator location, and the required vertical shafts for the housing of mechanical ducts. Restroom locations are also included in this stage. The room number designations are indicated, as well as door locations and the door swing directions. Finally, the second-floor plan title and drawing scale are shown graphically. This drawing is shown in Figure 6.89.

Stage IV Stage IV of the second-floor plan deals mainly with dimensioning and notes pertaining to the spacing of the vertical window mullions. The dimensioning values have been established primarily in the final stage of the first-floor plan, with the main supporting columns aligning with the floors above. In addition, the referencing matrix symbols are identical to those of the first-floor plan. This stage is depicted in Figure 6.90.

Stage V The next step in completing the second-floor plan is to designate the locations for the structural cross-sections and to provide a symbol for the referencing of these structural sections. These sections are taken in the north/south and east/west directions. Other details that are symbolized with a bubble and a detail reference are shown for a steel column and steel beam connection. These reference bubbles occur at the center supporting columns. Further detail symbols are indicated for the exterior window and wall assembly, while providing a reference detail symbol for the steel columns at the exterior walls. Notes for the exterior window mullion spaces are shown for the glazing areas found on the east/west walls and the north/south walls. The completion of Stage V is illustrated in Figure 6.91.

Third-Floor Plan Working Drawing Development

Stage I The first step in Stage I for the development of the third-floor plan is to start and work from the governing matrix system, as done for the second-floor plan. The only difference between the matrix system for the second-floor plan, as shown in Figure 6.87, and the matrix system for the third-floor plan is the addition of two matrix symbols identified as D/5 and F/1, which are located at two interior walls. Figure 6.92 illustrates the matrix system that is used for the third-floor plan.

Stage II Stage II for the third-floor plan is a duplicate of the CAD drawing used in Stage II for the second-floor plan.

The only variation from the second-floor plan drawing is the addition of matrix symbols D/5 and F/1, as indicated in Figure 6.93. The locations of the vertical window mullions, corresponding to the second-floor glazing, are also shown at this stage.

Stage III Stage III shows the risers and treads for all the stairwells, which include an additional stair for access to a mezzanine level. The mezzanine level will be accessible only from the third floor. Broken lines are added to this drawing to depict the mezzanine floor area above. Also incorporated at this stage are the men's and women's restrooms, the elevator, the vertical mechanical shafts required for the air-conditioning ducts, and the room numbering for the various areas. The title identifying the third-floor plan and the scale of the drawing are added at this stage as well. Figure 6.94 illustrates Stage 3 of the third-floor plan.

Stage IV The initial step for Stage IV is to lay out all the necessary dimension lines for all sides of the structure and the numerical values within the dimension lines. The drawing for Stage 4 of the third-floor plan is depicted in Figure 6.95.

Stage V The main difference between Stage V and the previous stage is the addition of various detail reference symbols. These symbols illustrate where the building cross-sections are to be taken and the viewing direction. Detail bubbles indicating the detail number and sheet number are also shown. These particular bubbles are located at the steel column and steel beam connection in the center of the building and at the exterior walls. Figure 6.96 illustrates the drawing for Stage V.

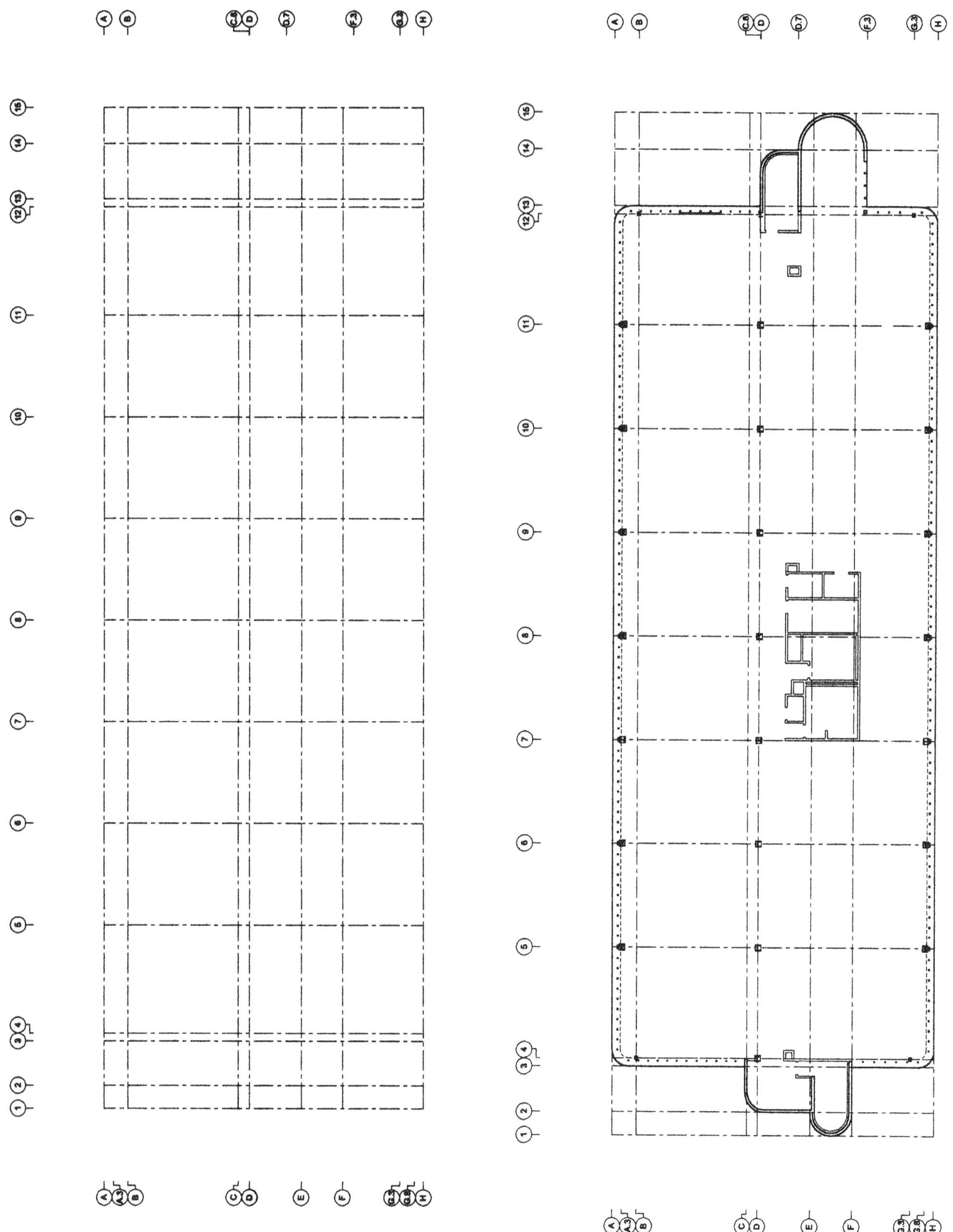

Figure 6.87 Madison Building—Stage I: Second-floor matrix.

Figure 6.88 Madison Building—Stage II: Working drawing—second-floor plan.

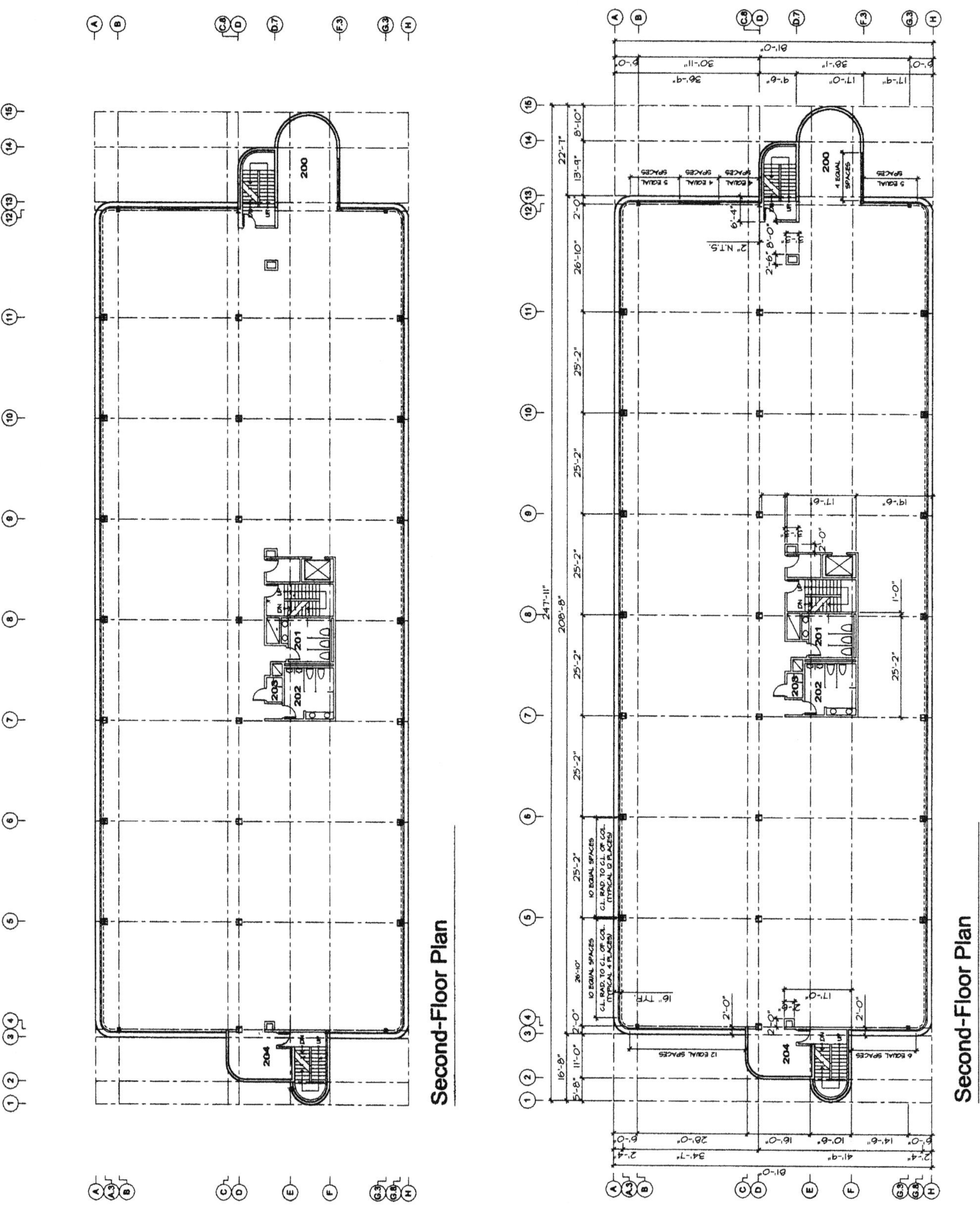

Figure 6.89 Madison Building—Stage III: Working drawing—second-floor plan.

Figure 6.90 Madison Building—Stage IV: Working drawing—second-floor plan.

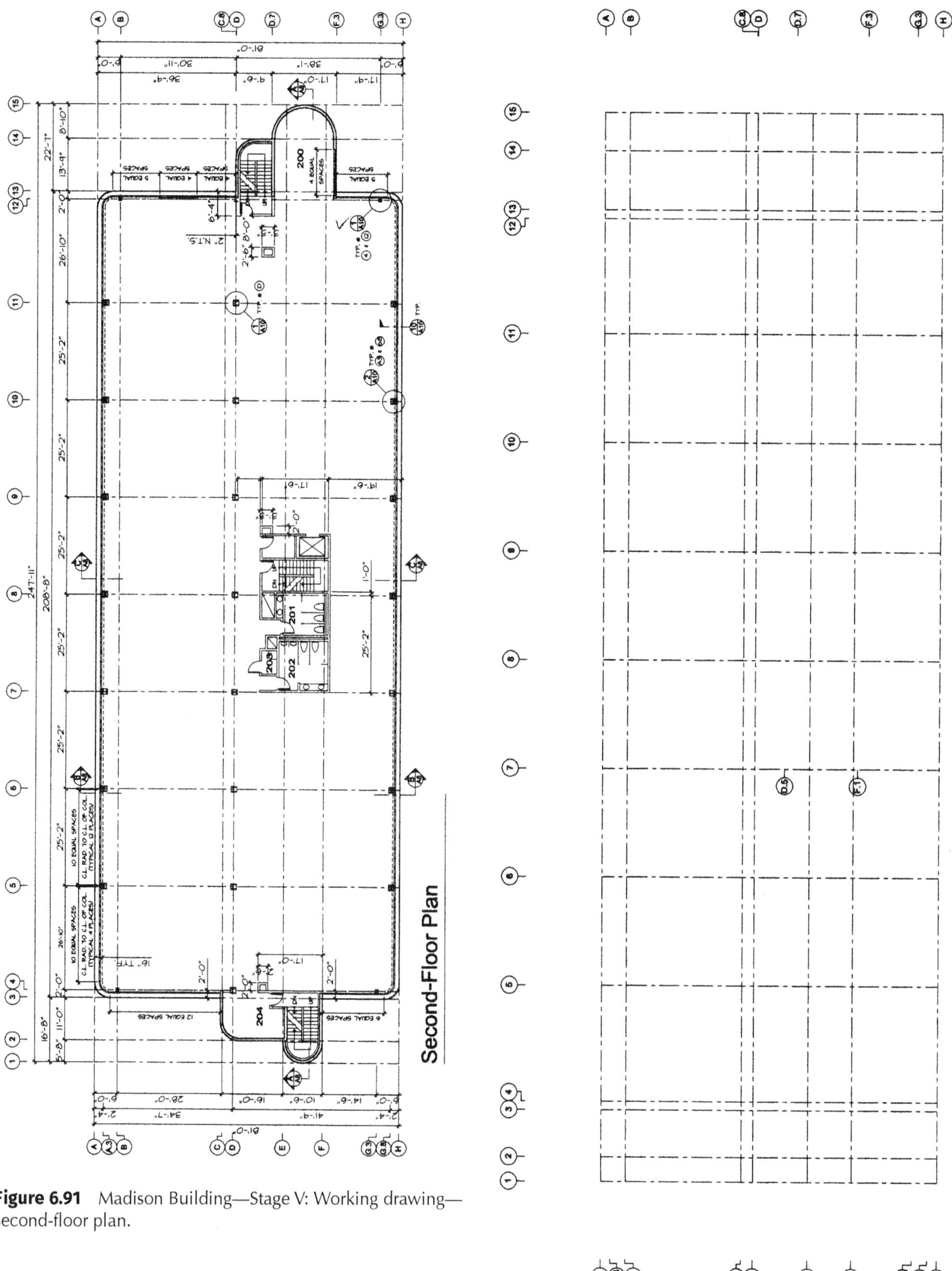

Figure 6.91 Madison Building—Stage V: Working drawing—second-floor plan.

Figure 6.92 Madison Building—Stage I: Third-floor matrix.

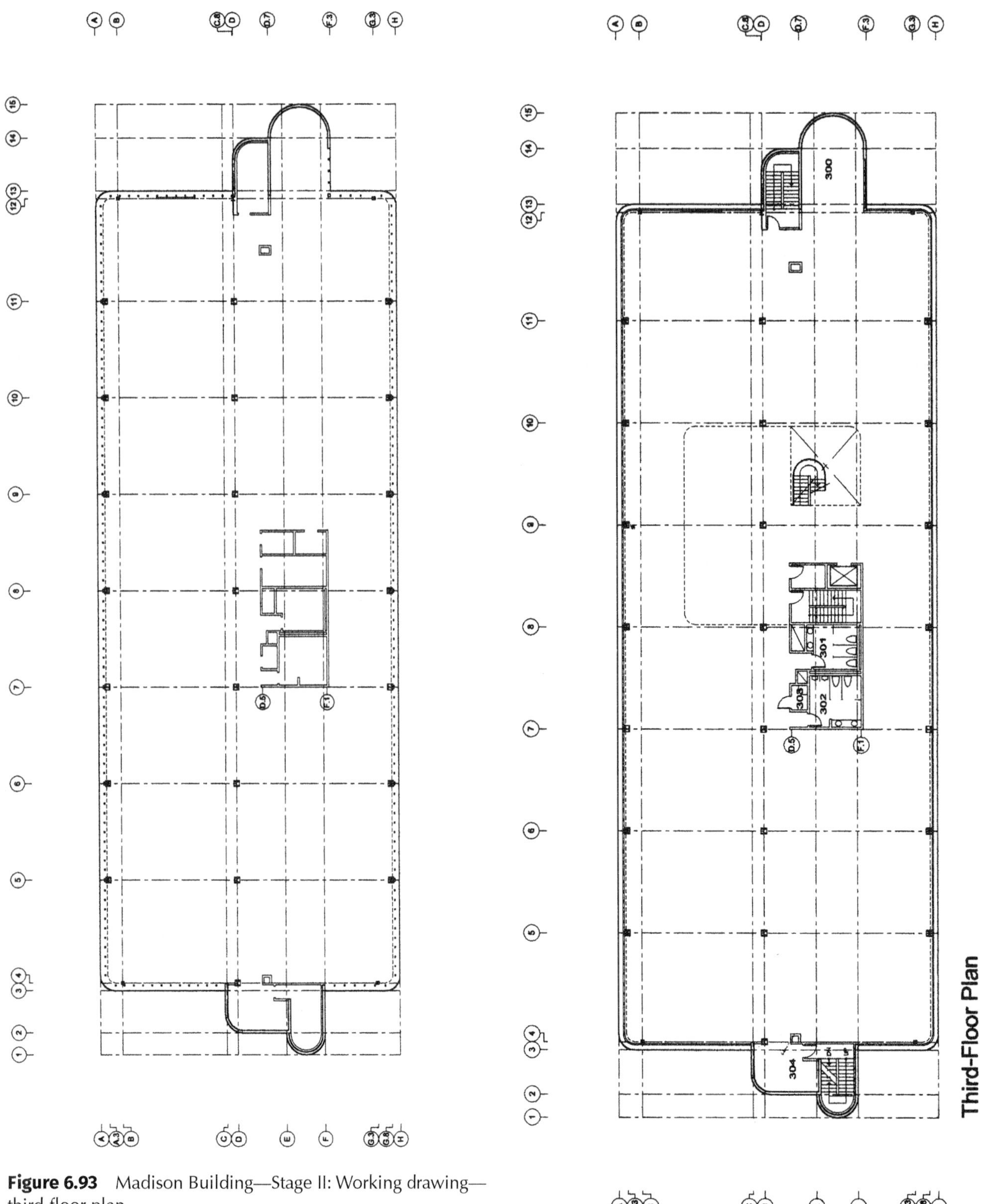

Figure 6.93 Madison Building—Stage II: Working drawing—third-floor plan.

Figure 6.94 Madison Building—Stage III: Working drawing—third-floor plan.

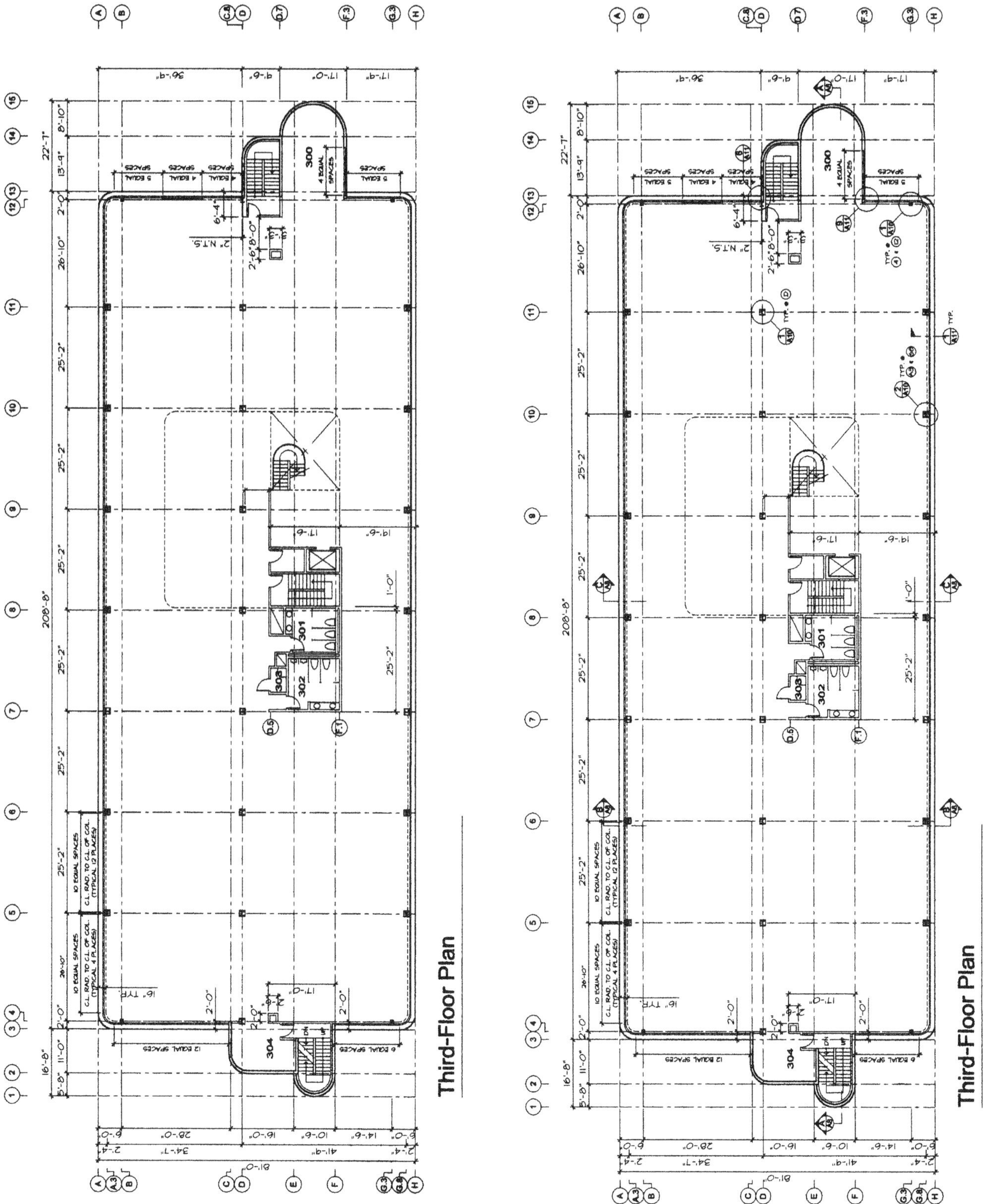

Figure 6.95 Madison Building—Stage IV: Working drawing—third-floor plan.

Figure 6.96 Madison Building—Stage V: Working drawing—third-floor plan.

Key Terms

break line
checklist
electrical rating
face of stud (FOS)
finished opening
flush outlet
grid
hinged door
offset
pilasters
planted
poché
reference bubble
rough opening
routing schedule
specifications
steel frame
steel stud

chapter

7

ROOF PLANS

(Jorge Gascón/Unsplash.)

The Professional Practice of Architectural Working Drawings, Sixth Edition. Nagy R. Bakhoum and Osamu A. Wakita.
© 2024 John Wiley & Sons Inc. Published 2024 by John Wiley & Sons Inc.
Companion website: www.wiley.com\go\bakhoum\theprofessionalpracticeofarchitecturalworkingdrawings

■ ROOF PLANS

A roof plan is a simple look at the top view of a structure, as if you were aboard a helicopter. Unless you are looking at a flat roof, the view is usually distorted, because a roof plan cannot reveal the entire surface of the roof in its true shape and size if there are slopes involved.

There are a multitude of roof forms. Among the most commonly known are flat parapet, gable, hip, and shed roofs.

Most small structures, especially residential structures, use a flat, gable, or hip roof; the determination of roof type is influenced by the prevailing rain or snowfall. Throughout this section, we will devote most of our attention to the hip roof. If you can configure a hip roof, a gable or flat roof will be a simple task.

Our approach will be to create a roof system that is geometrically correct and consistent in pitch, while avoiding flat areas that can entrap rain, thus causing leaks through the roof structure. Note the roof structure in Figure 7.1. Between the two roof systems, you will notice a flat (parallel to the ground) line. This space can trap water, causing deterioration of the roof material and, eventually, leaks. A short-term solution is to place a triangular metal form to induce the water to travel outward. Figure 7.2 shows a standard solution for a roof that was configured incorrectly to begin with. See Figure 7.3 for the geometrically correct way to solve the problem in this roof outline.

We describe here the procedure you should follow for even the simplest of roof outlines. With this knowledge, you will be able to create even the most complex outline. Once you know the system, you may even alter the building configuration slightly to avoid problematic roof areas in your plan.

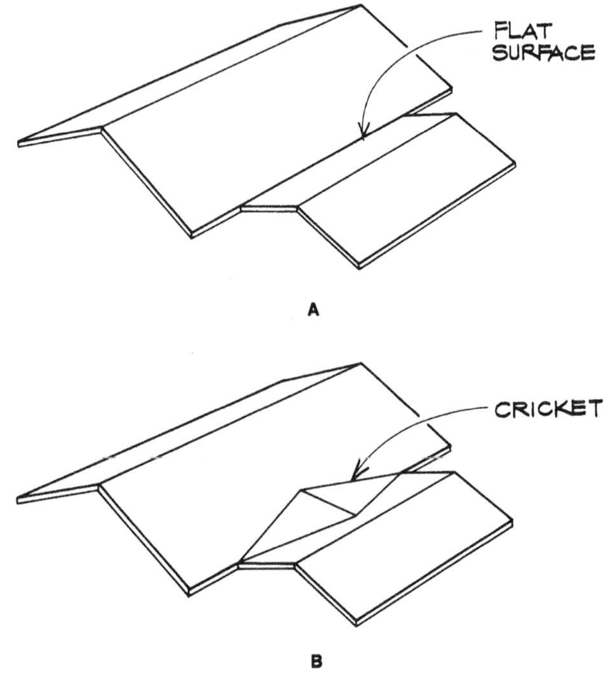

Figure 7.1 Incorrectly configured roof.

■ ROOF PLANS EXERCISES

Solution to Problem 1

Step I. Identify the perimeter of the roof as shown in the plan view in Figure 7.3. Be sure to dimension the overhang.

Step II. Reduce the shape to rectilinear zones. Find the largest rectilinear shape that will fit into the roof configuration. Figure 7.4A shows an outline of a roof, and Figure 7.4B shows the selection of the major area, as designated by the number "1." The major area is not

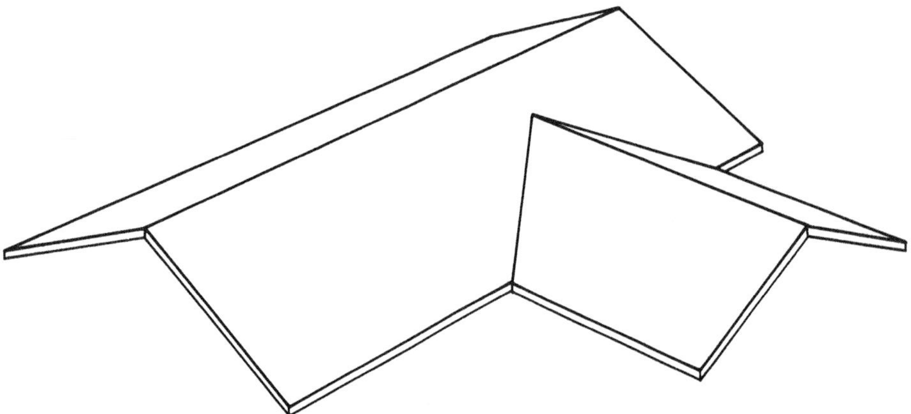

Figure 7.2 Ideal solution to avoid water problems. It might be, but remember, the major zone is the zone with the greatest width.

selected according to square footage, but by greatest width. Look at another shape, similar to the preceding outline, in Figure 7.5A. Because the dimension of the base designated by the letter "B" is larger than base A, the major zone is zone 1, as shown in Figure 7.5B.

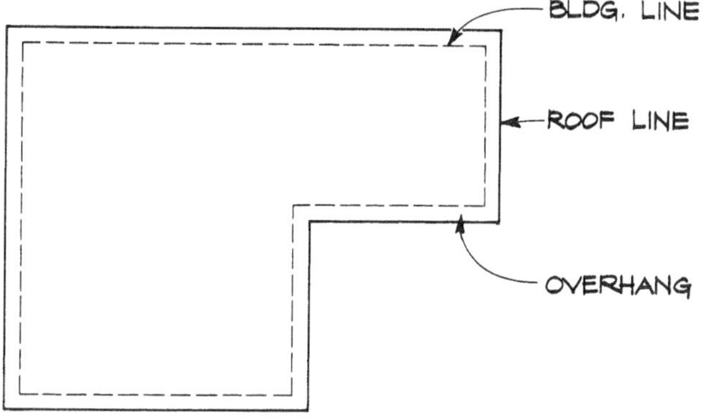

Figure 7.3 Draft the perimeter of the roof to be configured.

Step III. Locate both the hip rafter and the ridge. See Figure 7.6A. A 45° triangle is used to ensure the same pitch (angle of roof) on both sides of the roof, as shown in Figure 7.6B. This is possible when the corners are at 90° to each other.

Note, in Figure 7.7, that the outline has been organized into three zones: the main zone (1) in the center, with zones 2 and 3 above and below. These angles have been identified by the letters "A," "B," and "C." For the sake of this solution, any angle such as A, which is 90°, will be called an inside corner. The other two corners (nos. 2 and 3) have angles greater than 90° and are referred to as *outside* corners.

Step IV. Configure the roof. Let us take this configuration and develop it into a hip roof with the information already learned.

Taking the major zone identified as zone 1 in Figure 7.8A, we strike 45° hip lines from each of the inside corners to form the main structure around which the other two zones will appear.

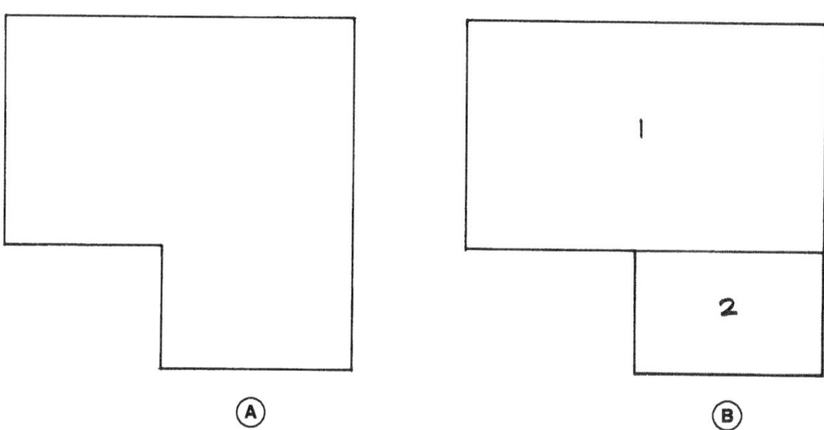

Figure 7.4 Find the major zone.

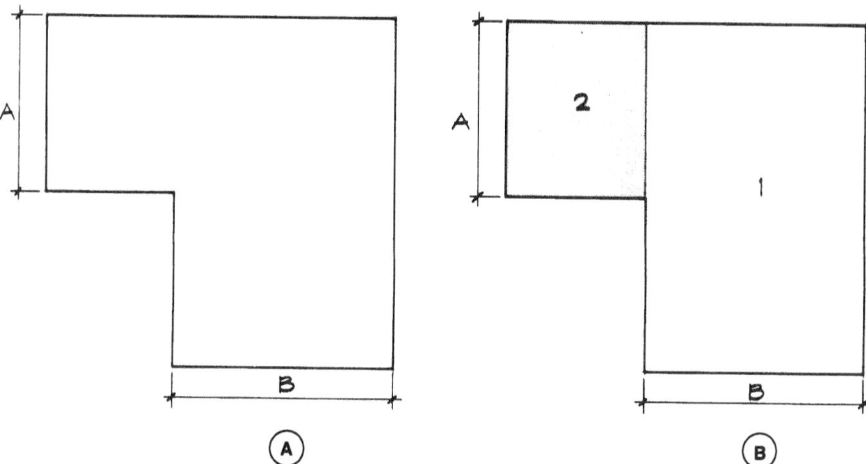

Figure 7.5 Letting the largest width determine the major zone.

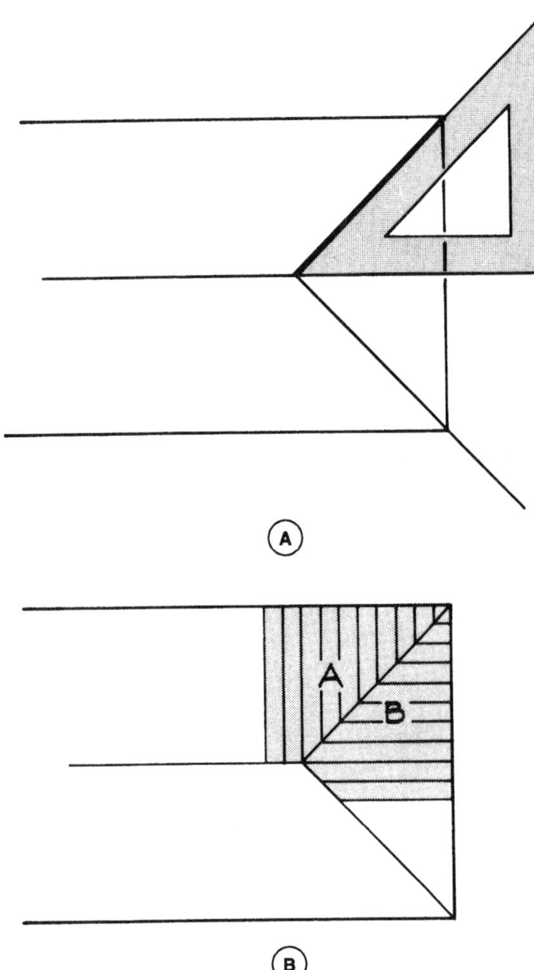

Figure 7.6 Use of 45° triangle to maintain pitch.

We now approach zone 2 in Figure 7.8B with an eye out for inside and outside corners. There are two of each. The inside corners at the top are drawn toward the center of the rectangle. The outside corners have their 45° lines going away from the zone 2 rectangle, thus forming the valleys of the roof.

The same approach is used for zone 3 as was used for zone 2. In the process of drawing the outside corners, you will notice that the one on the right overlaps an existing line (see Figure 7.8C). When this happens, the lines cancel each other, creating a continuous plane. See Figure 7.8D, which displays the final roof shape.

As you look at the final roof form, it may appear foolish to have gone through such an elaborate system because you may have been able to visualize the finished roof from the beginning. Let's reinforce and validate the procedure by attempting roofs of varying complexities.

Solution to Problem 2

Step I. Figure 7.9A displays an area in the center that appears to be the major zone. By square footage,

Step II. In Figure 7.9B, notice the relocation of the major zone by greatest width. Compare zone 1 with zone 2. The one with the greatest width will produce the highest ridge because it takes longer rafters in the framing of this roof.

Step III. Figure 7.9C shows all of the zones with roofs outlined. Remember the outside/inside corner rule.

Step IV. As can be seen in the previous step, many of the lines overlap. In Figure 7.9D, we show them side by side for ease of understanding, but in reality, they are on top of each other. This means they cancel each other and are erased.

To continue this exploration of problems, we have selected an outline in which the major roof configuration will all but disappear as we develop the roof.

Solution to Problem 3

Step I. In Figure 7.10A, the main zone is situated vertically through the center of the total form. Check this area, in width, with a horizontal rectangle drawn through the top.

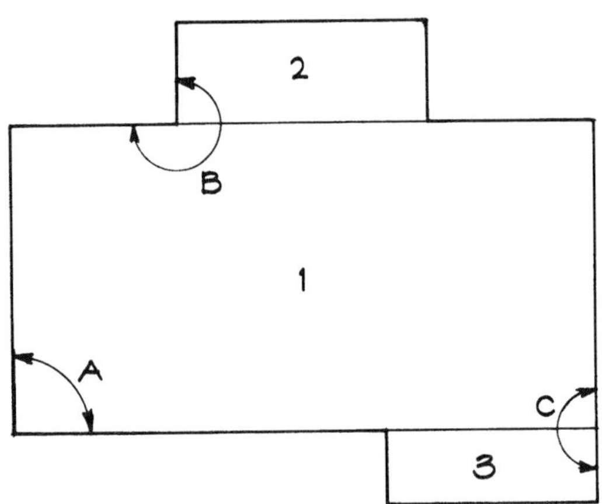

Figure 7.7 Defining inside and outside corners.

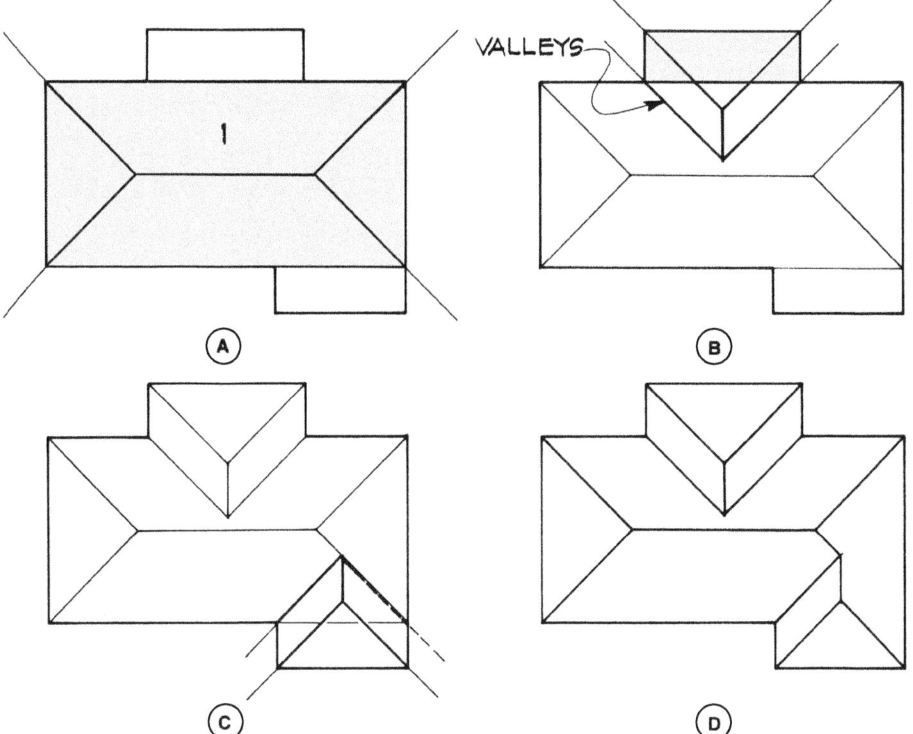

Figure 7.8 Solving hip roof Problem 1.

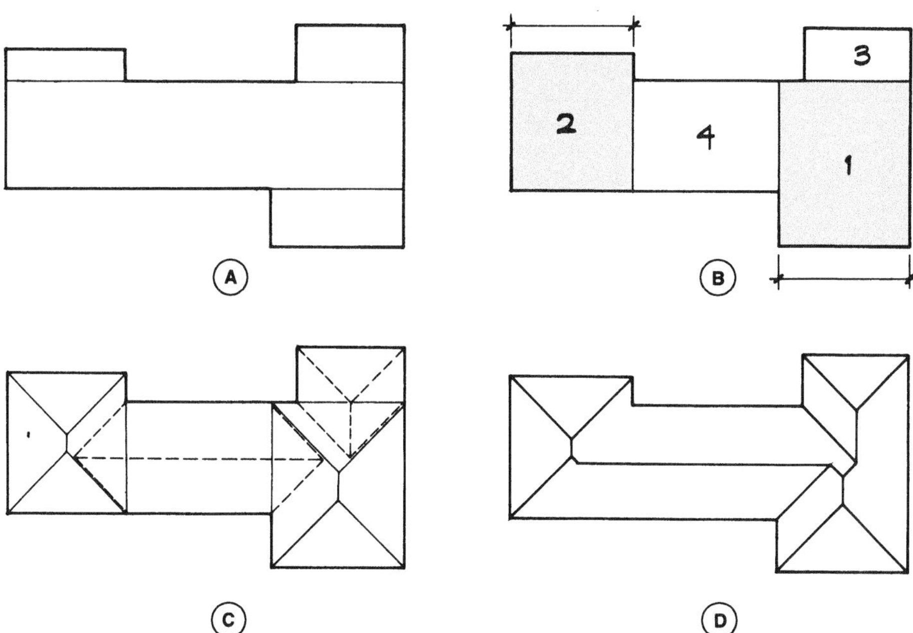

Figure 7.9 Problem 2.

Step II. Draw the hip and ridge lines as shown in Figure 7.10B. Identify inside and outside corners, and proceed with drawing both the hip and valley lines.

Step III. As the lines overlap each other, which happens in three locations, these locations are identified with dotted lines (see Figure 7.10C). Notice that three of the four hip lines of the major zone are eliminated in the process.

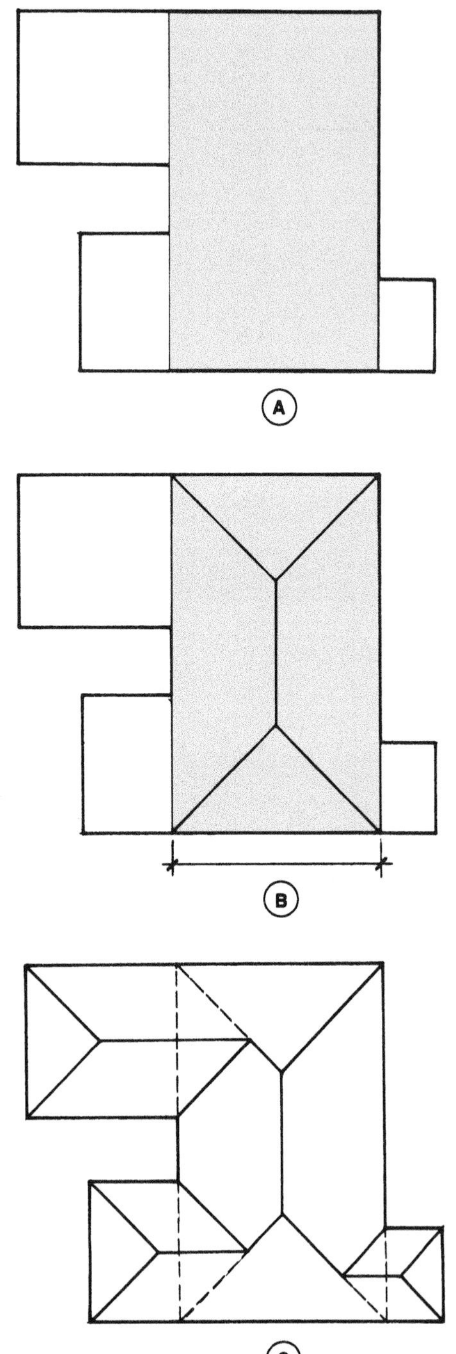

Figure 7.10 Problem 3.

There are configurations in which the major zones are well hidden. There are also shapes that have overlapping zones. These are by far the most difficult challenges. The following five-step example demonstrates a solution for such cases.

Solution to Problem 4

Step I. Covering all but the top illustration, see if you can identify the major zone on this outline of the structure in Figure 7.11A.

Step II. Validate your initial selection with Figure 7.11B. Next, identify the second largest zone, which has been "X"ed out. Notice the overlap of zones 1 and 2.

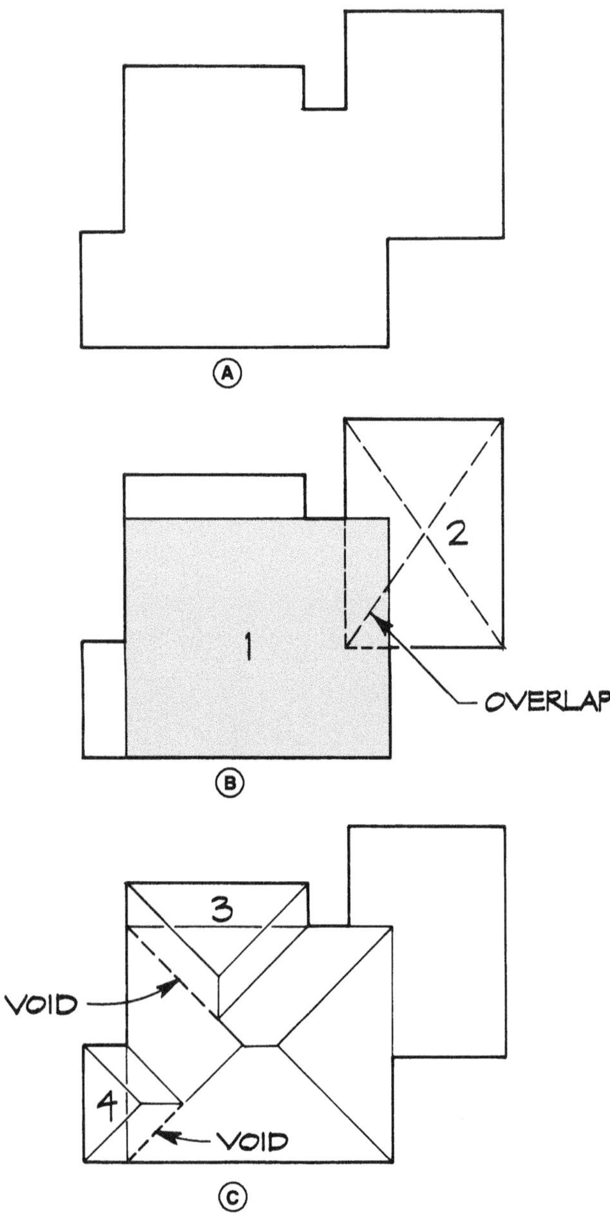

Figure 7.11 Problem 4.

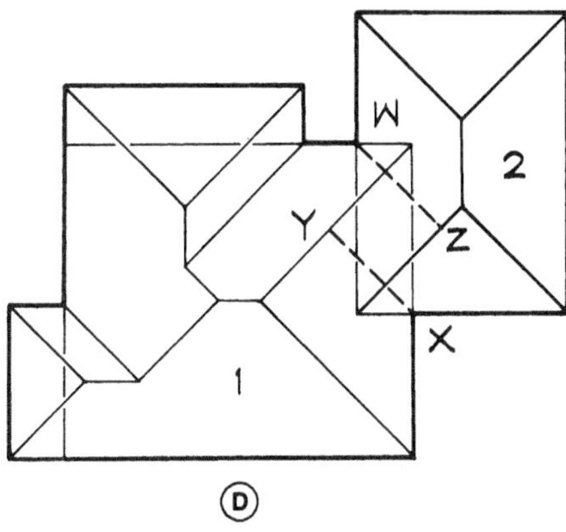

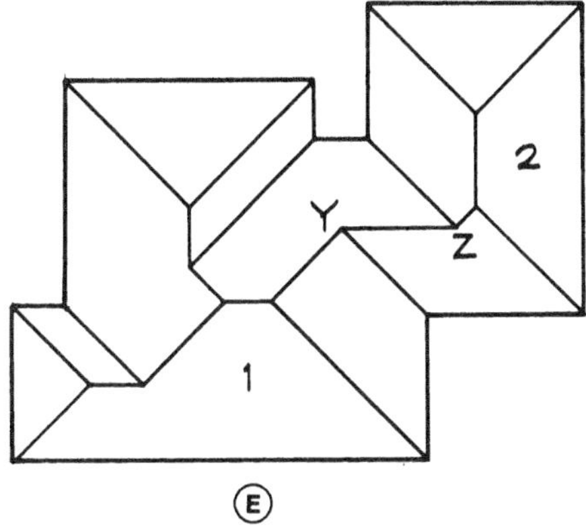

Figure 7.11 *(Continued)*

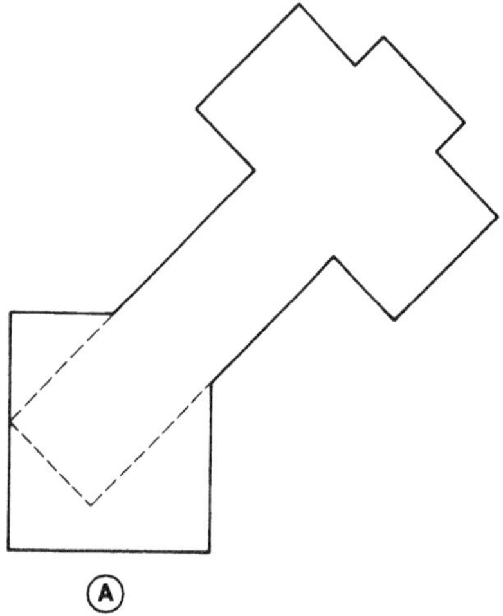

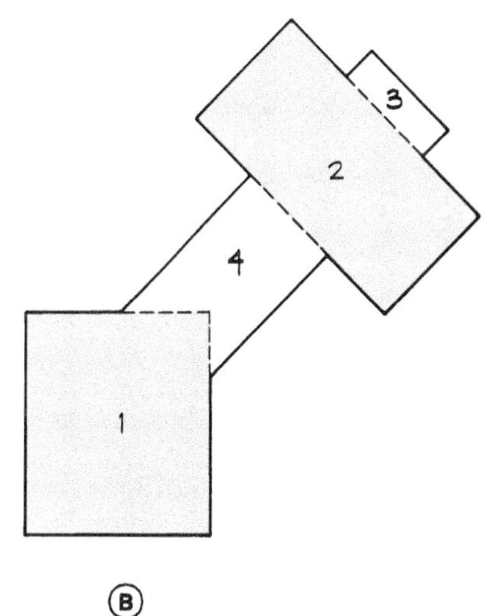

Figure 7.12 Problem 5.

Step III. Solve zones 3 and 4 next. Two lines will overlap, causing their removal, as shown in Figure 7.11C.

Step IV. Zone 2 has inside corners only, as shown in Figure 7.11D. Solve zone 2 as you did zone 1. The points that overlap have been identified with the letters "W" and "X." These are outside corners, which become valleys. Extend point X toward zone 1, and W toward zone 2. These lines will intersect a hip line, identified by the letters "Y" and "Z," respectively.

Step V. Y, and Z are connected to form a ridge (see Figure 7.11E). This ridge is slightly lower than the ridge of zones 1 and 2. The hip lines below points Y and Z are also eliminated to form the final roof configuration.

Saving the most challenging for last, we encounter a shape that includes an angle other than 90° around the perimeter. At first glance the task of roofing this outline seems difficult, but if you apply the principles set out in this chapter, the solution is easier than it may first appear.

Solution to Problem 5

Step I. Extending the center portion toward the left (Figure 7.12A) does not produce the rectangle with the largest width, so change your approach and solve the major zoning as explained in the next step.

Step II. After you have checked the various possible zones, we hope you have selected zones 1 and 2 as shown in Figure 7.12B.

Step III. With all inside corners in zones 1 and 2, the solution is simple (see Figure 7.12C). Zone 3 should also be easy, with two inside and two outside corners, and thus will be shown as a finished section in the next step.

Step IV. Zone 4 has four outside corners, two of which overlap zone 1. To find the ridge, use the upper two outside corners and extend the ridge well into zone 1, as shown in Figure 7.12D. The valleys will start at points X and Y.

Because points X and Y are not the normal outside angles (180° or 270°), they must be bisected. It is

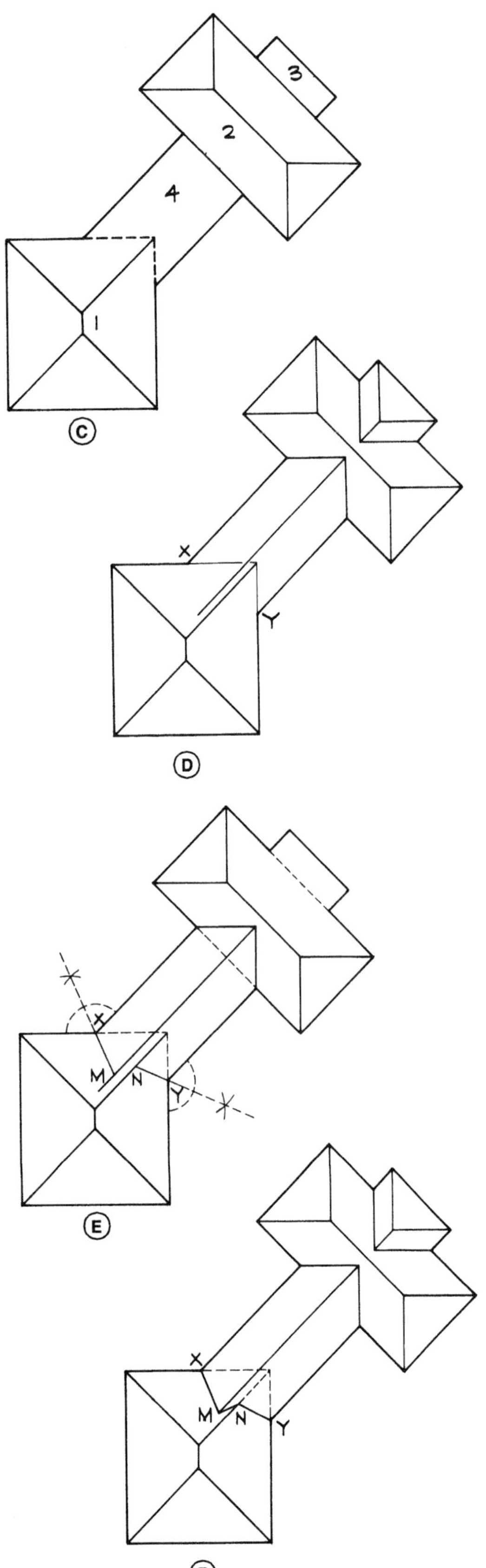

Figure 7.12 *(Continued)*

easier to bisect the outside rather than the inside angle around points X and Y because these angles are less than 180°. This can be accomplished by measuring the angle with a protractor and mathematically dividing the angle, or by using a method, which you may have learned in a basic drafting class or in a geometry class, that requires use of a compass.

The compass is set at any radius and an arc is struck, using X and Y as the center of the arc. See Figure 7.13A. Next, open the compass wider than the original settings and strike two more arcs, starting where the original arc struck the angular lines. See Figure 7.13B. Let's call this new intersection Z. When a line is drawn through Z and X (or Z and Y, depending on which angle you are bisecting), you have bisected the angle.

Step V. Extend the bisecting lines from X and Y to the inside until they hit the ridge. We have identified these points as M and N in Figure 7.12E.

Step VI. Next, connect M and N, as shown in Figure 7.12F. This line represents another valley at a different angle and defines the true geometric shape of zones 1 and 4 as they intersect each other. The dotted line, which is the underside of the hip of zone 1, is eliminated in a roof plan but may be shown on a subsequent roof framing plan.

ODD GEOMETRY ROOF DESIGN

Changing Configuration

After having configured an outline of a roof to its correct geometric shape, you can readily convert it to other than a hip roof. For example, consider the roof shown in Figure 7.14A.

To change this roof to a gable roof, you simply extend the ridges to the edge of the roof, as shown by the arrows. The final gable roof is displayed in Figure 7.15B. Notice the return of the valley lines (marked X).

In the next example, found in Figure 7.15, the arrows provide the slight bit of interpretation needed for the top right corner of the structure.

Skylight Attic Location—Ventilation

A roof plan in conjunction with an exterior elevation gives the designer a perfect opportunity to position and check the appearance of such things as an attic ventilating system that must comply with energy standards. Standards have been instituted by local, state, and even federal commissions for energy conservation. An effective system may be as simple as a screened opening or a screened opening enhanced with a mechanical device.

Because heat rises, it is best to place ventilating systems as high as possible, at the ends of a roof, for thorough

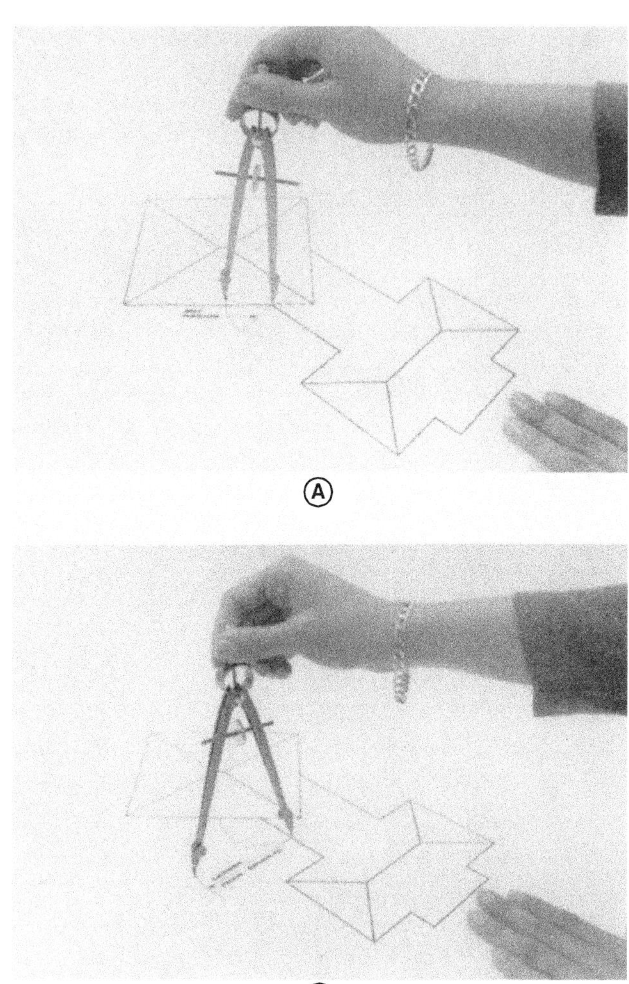

Figure 7.13 Bisecting an angle.

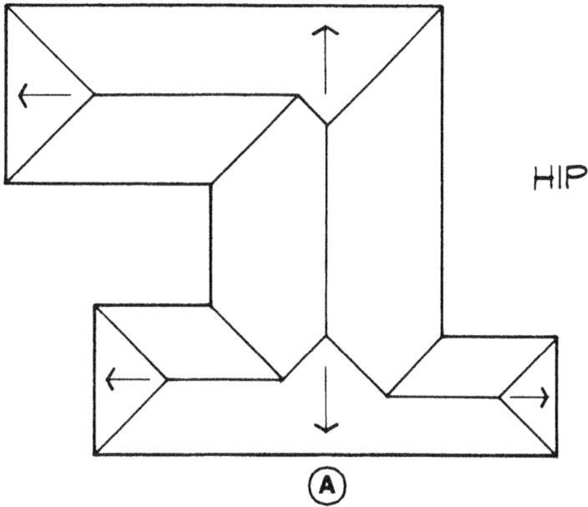

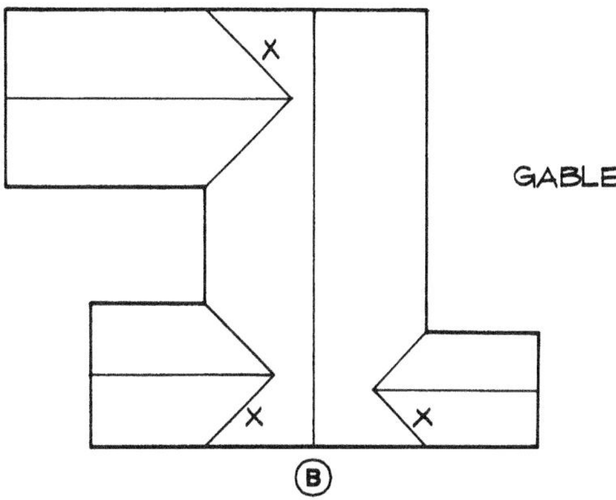

Figure 7.14 Changing configuration.

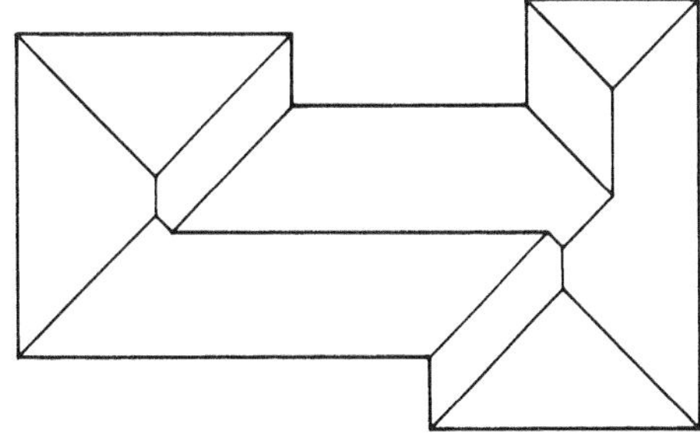

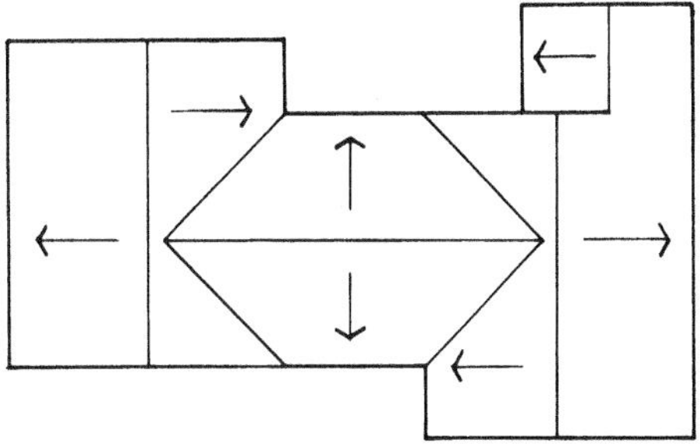

Figure 7.15 Hip to gable conversion.

ventilation—also taking into consideration the prevailing winds and any other environmental factors that may dictate their position. Code may also allow a reduction of required venting for a combination of high and low vents that encourages **convection**, which is the drafting of the cool air in place of the hot air and vice versa.

Traditionally, ventilation systems were placed on the ends of gable roofs, on the gable portion of a roof, or at the eaves of a hip roof. Today, roof-surface-mounted units and ridge ventilating systems are presently available, as well as numerous mechanical systems for industrial, commercial, and residential structures.

The position of skylights must always be verified on the roof plan. This will ensure that you are not cutting through a strategic area, such as a hip or valley of the roof. For example, the skylight shown at the bottom of Figure 7.16 does not bridge any structural roof member, so it can be placed in the desired location directly above the room below. However, this is not the case with the skylight at the top of this figure, because it crosses a hip

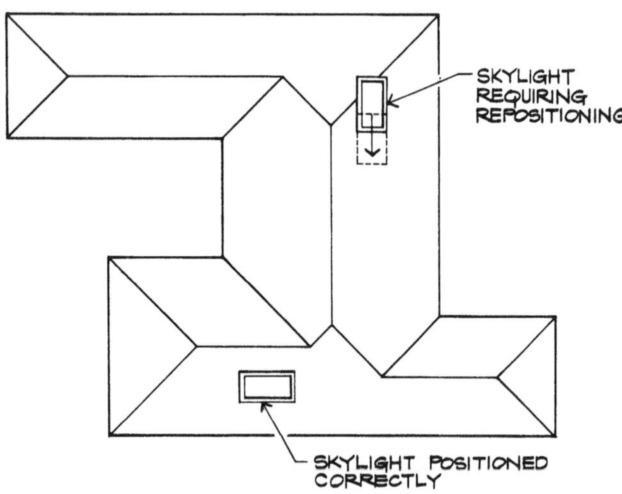

Figure 7.16 Verifying skylight location.

member (a pleated plane); therefore, it must be moved to another area, which is shown as a dotted line. The opening below may be in the original position, but with the skylight shifted, the light shaft will be bent. See Figure 7.17.

A Newly Built Major Roof Zone

Rather than restricting yourself to a particular outline, you can alter the configuration with porches, balconies, colonnades, and so on. Simply following the outline of the structure would produce an unusual roof that is difficult to frame. The simple addition of a roof over the entry can protect the entry, create the basis for a better structural form, and even simplify the roof form. See Figure 7.18. A simpler roof allows easier construction

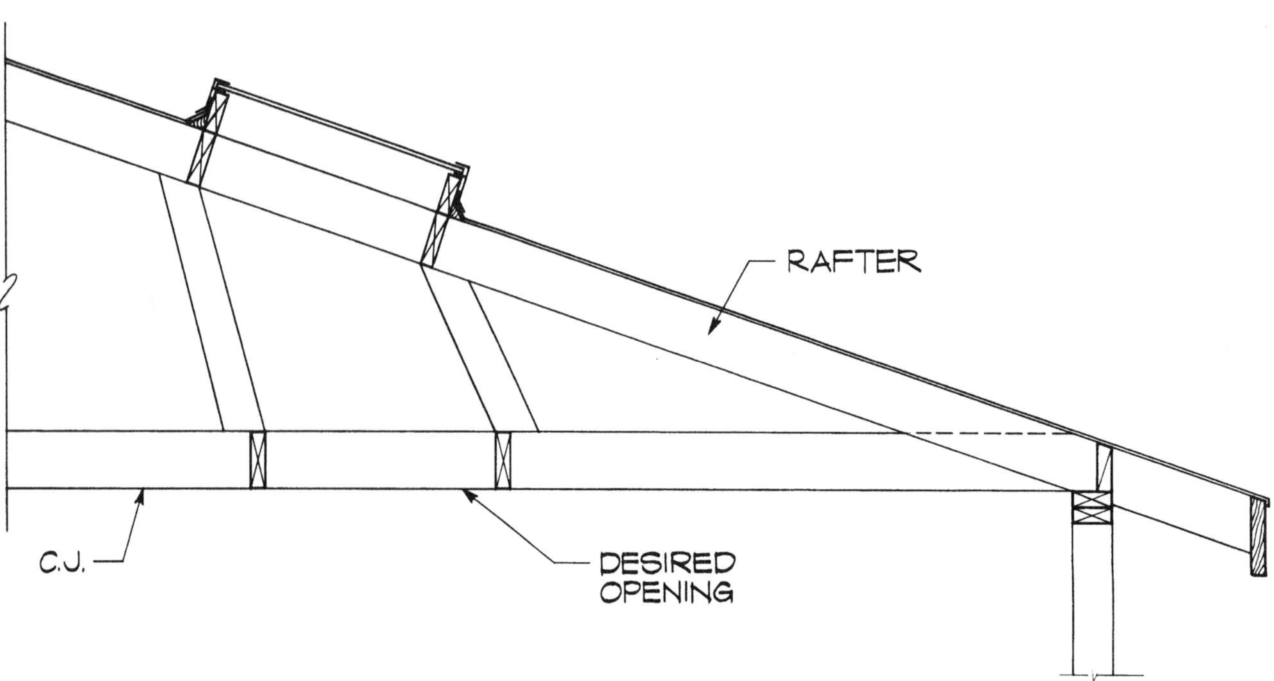

Figure 7.17 Skylight with bent light shaft.

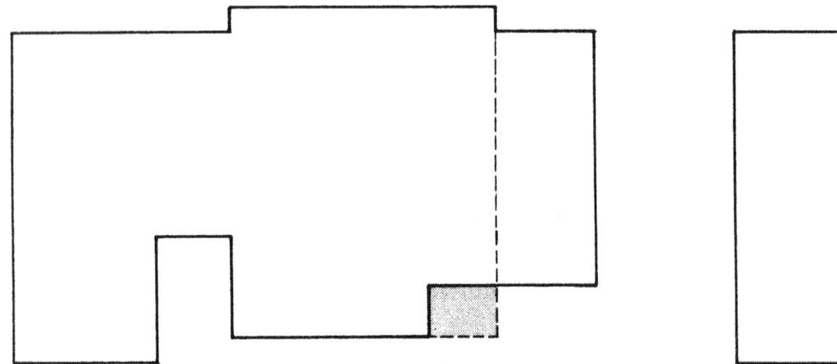

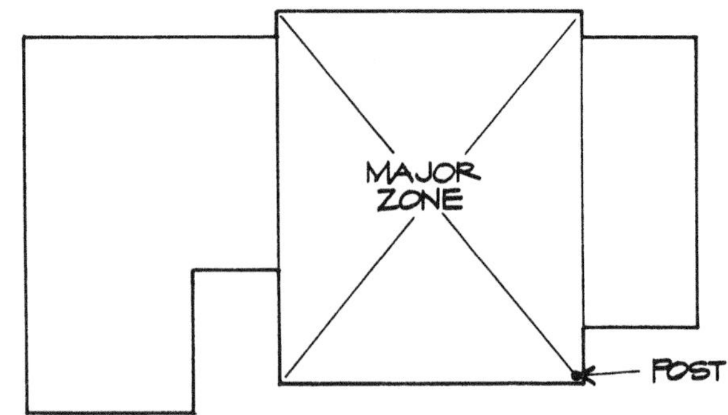

Figure 7.18 Changing the outline.

and creates a system that is structurally stable; thus, if it answers a functional need (covered entry), it is the best of all solutions. See Figure 7.19.

■ COMPUTER DRAWN ROOF PLANS

Stage I The roof plan shown in Figure 7.20 requires an accurate drawing of the perimeter of the structure. One of the initial stages of the floor plan becomes the datum and should be XREFed into the system.

Stage II (Figure 7.21). Add to the outline the various zones to be roofed by isolating the geometry used by the designer and later used by the structural engineer to properly structure this geometric form with its component parts.

Stage III (Figure 7.22). The chimney to the fireplace and skylights are positioned, and the roof ridges and valleys are added to the roof structure.

Stage IV (Figure 7.23). Skylights and chimneys that cut through ridges and valleys are resolved through detailing. Roof slopes and venting of the attic are done at this stage. Heat rises, so it is recommended that the ridge vents be placed as high atop the roof as possible. A portion of the roof may be hatched or delineated to show the roof material covering this structure. Show downspouts, gutters, and scuppers as needed for the roof design.

Stage V (Figure 7.24). The plotting and titling stage may include elevation **call-outs** of the top of the roof. This is typically required when the municipality has height restrictions.

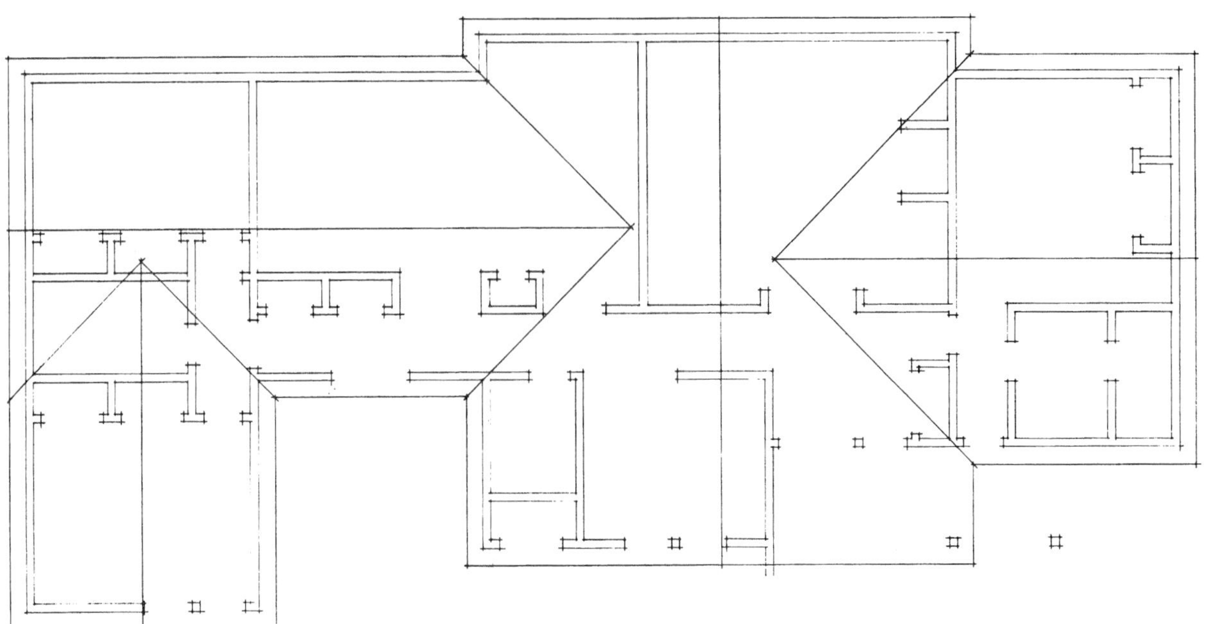

Figure 7.19 Roof to match zoning.

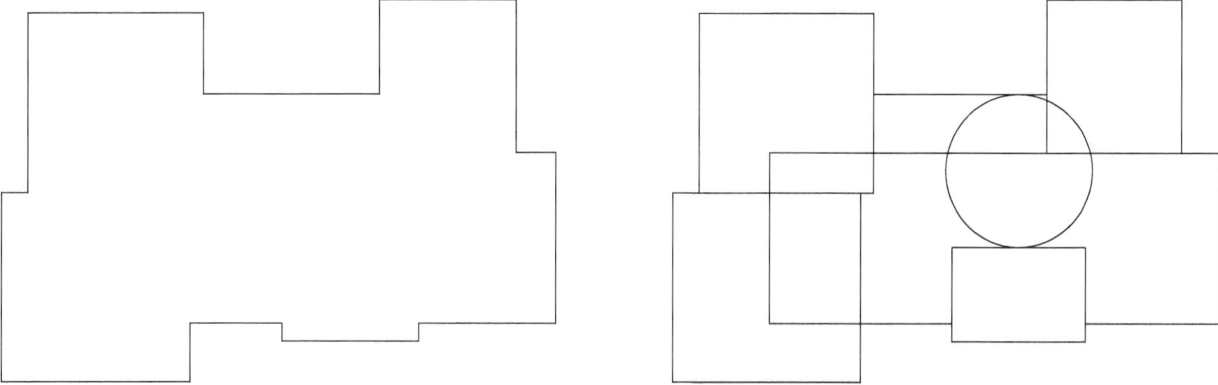

Figure 7.20 Stage I: Base.

Figure 7.21 Stage II: Isolating geometry.

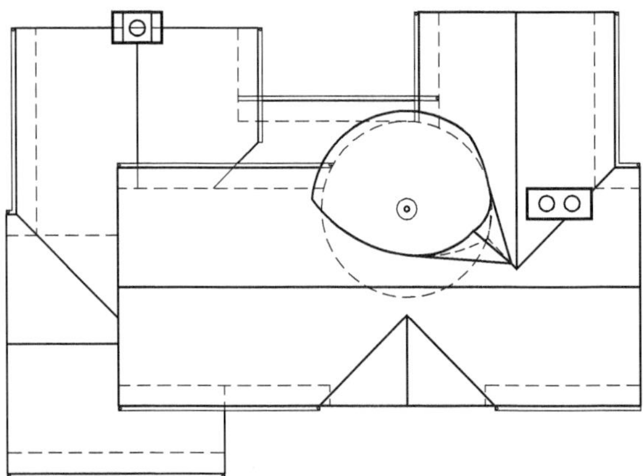

Figure 7.22 Stage III: Defining roof shape.

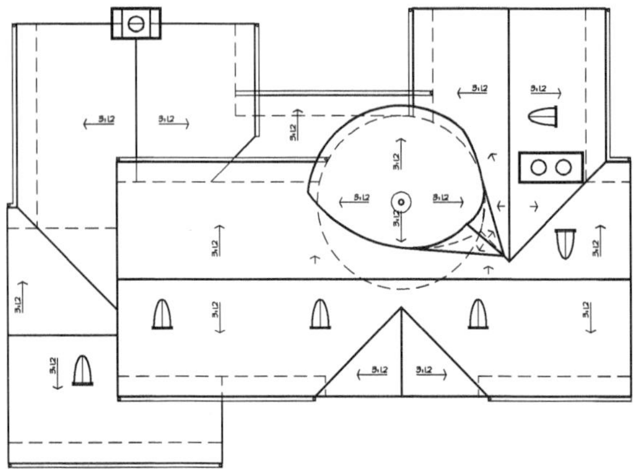

Figure 7.23 Stage IV: Chimney, slope direction, and vents.

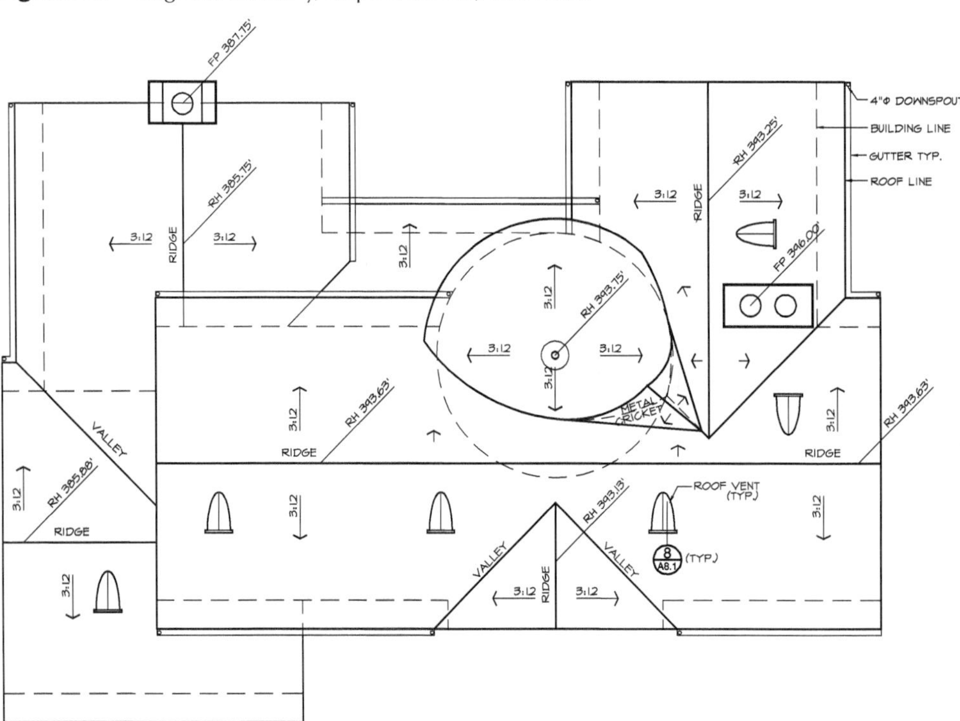

Figure 7.24 Stage V: Noting.

■ DRAWING A BIM ROOF PLAN

The roof plan may be drafted on the computer, and in BIM, it can be automatically generated by the software. Now don't get too excited often this automatically generated drawing often needs hours of reworking and adjusting to get the entire roof system to close property, but it does help out when you have an overly complex roof shape. It often helps to visualize a water droplet landing on the roof in various locations and determining how it will work its way down the roof system and into a non-erosive devise to the ground or to the curb gutter. In various regions, ground water is a significant concern and replenishing the ground with roof water is a priority in those regions. As seen in Figure 7.24 beyond the roof edge is a roof gutter with downspouts taking down the water to the ground line or into collection units such as rain storage drums. The idea of recycling the water is ideal for draught concerned regions. Most of the roof plans are quickly generated drawings to help the engineer design the system of structure which will be discussed in the Roof Framing chapter of the text.

Key Terms

call-outs
convection

chapter

8

BUILDING SECTIONS

(Christian Perner/Unsplash.)

The Professional Practice of Architectural Working Drawings, Sixth Edition. Nagy R. Bakhoum and Osamu A. Wakita.
© 2024 John Wiley & Sons Inc. Published 2024 by John Wiley & Sons Inc.
Companion website: www.wiley.com\go\bakhoum\theprofessionalpracticeofarchitecturalworkingdrawings

■ BUILDING SECTIONS

A **building section** cuts a vertical slice through a structure in much the same way a floor plan is a horizontal slice through the building. For the computer, a section is a cut along the *z*–*x* axis or the *z*–*y* axis. It is also an integral part of the dimensional reference system described earlier in this book. Figure 8.1 shows a vertical slice cut through a wood-framed, two-story residence. To further examine the various roof, floor, and wall conditions found at the location of that particular slice, we can enlarge the elements and then call it a **detail**, as seen in Figure 8.2.

The building section is second only to the floor plan in importance, because it reveals how the building is assembled, describes the collective parts of the building, and demonstrates the volume of each specific building area. The building section allows the discovery of essential details. In many instances, for example, the building section reveals potential problems in the intersection of walls, floors, stairs, ceilings, and roof.

To draw a building section, select a cross-section location with relevant architectural and structural information. When given the task of drawing a building section, you first need to gather basic information, including the following:

1. Type of foundation
2. Floor system
3. Exterior and interior wall construction
4. Beam and column sizes and their material
5. Plate or wall heights
6. Floor elevations
7. Floor members, size, and spacing
8. Ceiling joist direction
9. Floor sheathing, material, and size
10. Ceiling members, size, and spacing
11. Floor system direction
12. Roof pitch and member direction
13. Roof sheathing, material, and size
14. Insulation requirements
15. Finished roof material
16. Ceiling heights

Although it may not be possible to gather all of this data early in the design stage, it is possible to construct the parts that are known and add data as the information comes in. When you have gathered this information, select a suitable architectural scale. Usually, the scale ranges from 1/8″ = 1′-0″ to 1/4″ = 1′-0″. The scale depends on the size and complexity of the project and should be chosen to maintain clarity. Most commercial jobs use 1/8″, and most residential jobs 1/4″.

As you draw the building section, visualize the erection sequence for the structure and the construction techniques for the material(s) being used. See Figure 8.3.

The first step is to show the concrete floor and foundation members at that particular location. Although foundation details should be drawn accurately, they need not be dimensioned or elaborated upon; all the necessary information will be called out in the larger-scale drawings of the individual foundation details.

Next, establish a **plate height**. (A **plate** is a horizontal timber that joins the tops of studs.) Here the plate height is noted, measuring from the top of the concrete floor to the top of the two plates (2 – 2 × 6 continuous) of the wood stud wall. This height also establishes the height to the bottom of the floor joist for the second-floor level. Once the floor joists are drawn in at the proper scale, repeat the same procedure to establish the wall height that will support the ceiling and roof framing members. The height is typically selected based on the desire of

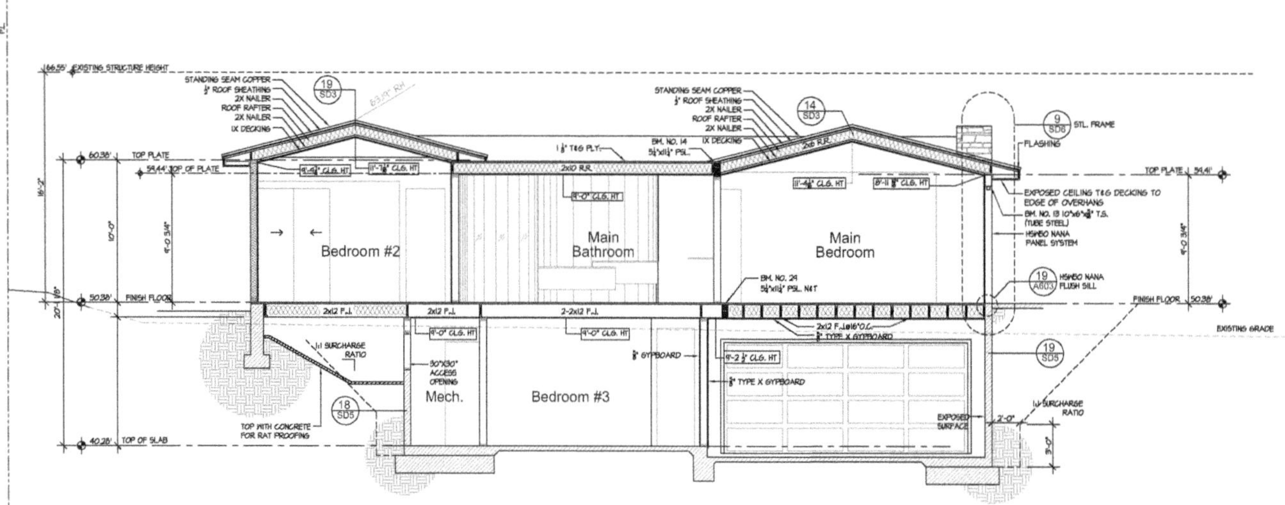

Figure 8.1 Vertical slice through a building.

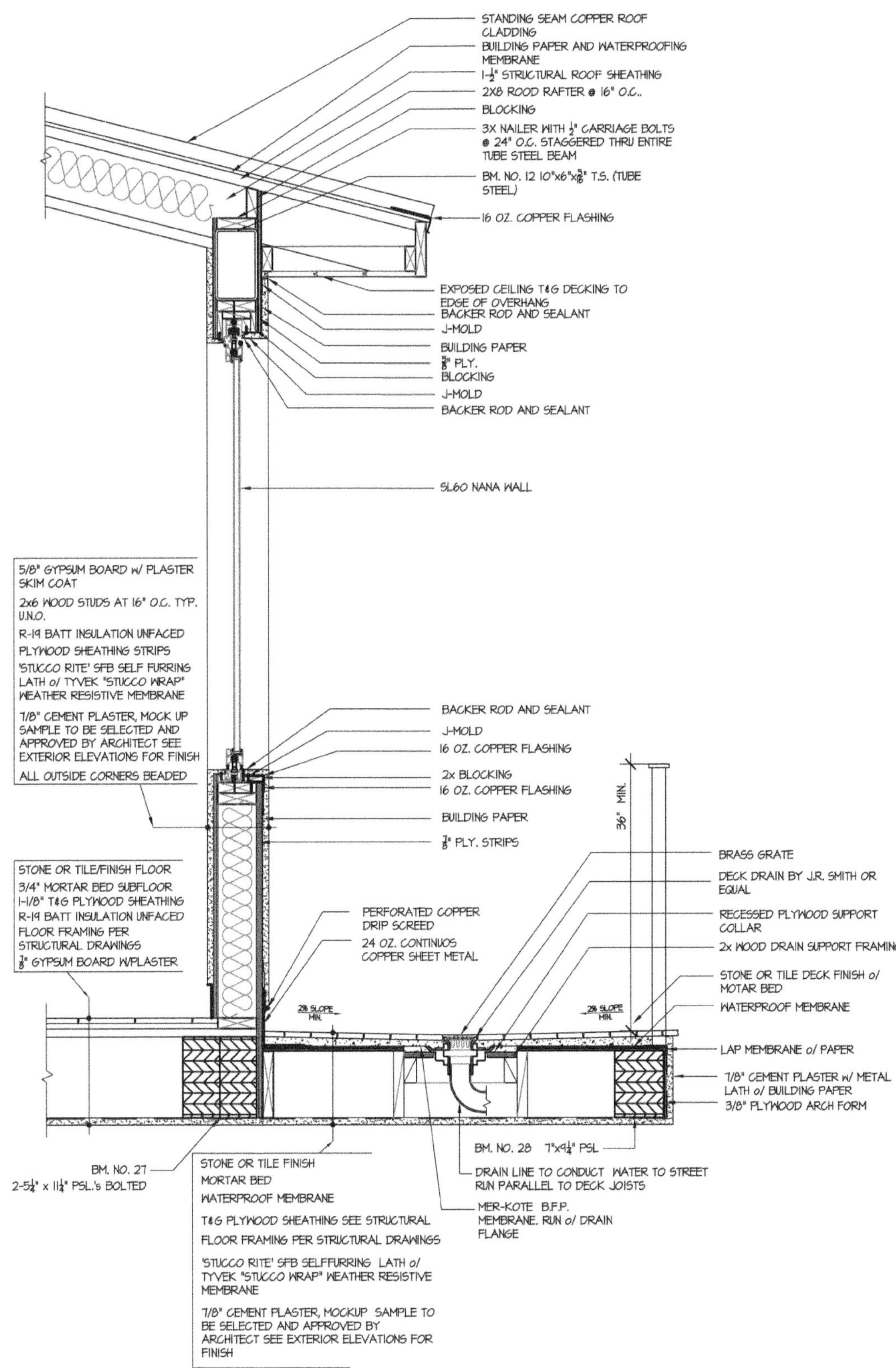

STANDING SEAM COPPER ROOF CLADDING
BUILDING PAPER AND WATERPROOFING MEMBRANE
1-1/2" STRUCTURAL ROOF SHEATHING
2X8 ROOD RAFTER @ 16" O.C.
BLOCKING
3X NAILER WITH 1/2" CARRIAGE BOLTS @ 24" O.C. STAGGERED THRU ENTIRE TUBE STEEL BEAM
BM. NO. 12 10"x6"x3/8" T.S. (TUBE STEEL)
16 OZ. COPPER FLASHING
EXPOSED CEILING T&G DECKING TO EDGE OF OVERHANG
BACKER ROD AND SEALANT
J-MOLD
BUILDING PAPER
3/8" PLY.
BLOCKING
J-MOLD
BACKER ROD AND SEALANT
SL60 NANA WALL
5/8" GYPSUM BOARD W/ PLASTER SKIM COAT
2x6 WOOD STUDS AT 16" O.C. TYP. U.N.O.
R-19 BATT INSULATION UNFACED
PLYWOOD SHEATHING STRIPS
'STUCCO RITE' SFB SELF FURRING LATH o/ TYVEK "STUCCO WRAP" WEATHER RESISTIVE MEMBRANE
7/8" CEMENT PLASTER, MOCK UP SAMPLE TO BE SELECTED AND APPROVED BY ARCHITECT SEE EXTERIOR ELEVATIONS FOR FINISH
ALL OUTSIDE CORNERS BEADED
BACKER ROD AND SEALANT
J-MOLD
16 OZ. COPPER FLASHING
2x BLOCKING
16 OZ. COPPER FLASHING
BUILDING PAPER
7/8" PLY. STRIPS
36" MIN.
BRASS GRATE
DECK DRAIN BY J.R. SMITH OR EQUAL
RECESSED PLYWOOD SUPPORT COLLAR
2x WOOD DRAIN SUPPORT FRAMING
STONE OR TILE DECK FINISH o/ MOTAR BED
WATERPROOF MEMBRANE
LAP MEMBRANE o/ PAPER
7/8" CEMENT PLASTER W/ METAL LATH o/ BUILDING PAPER
3/8" PLYWOOD ARCH FORM
STONE OR TILE/FINISH FLOOR
3/4" MORTAR BED SUBFLOOR
1-1/8" T&G PLYWOOD SHEATHING
R-19 BATT INSULATION UNFACED
FLOOR FRAMING PER STRUCTURAL DRAWINGS
7/8" GYPSUM BOARD W/PLASTER
PERFORATED COPPER DRIP SCREED
24 OZ. CONTINUOS COPPER SHEET METAL
2% SLOPE MIN.
2% SLOPE MIN.
BM. NO. 27
2-5¼" x 11¼" PSL.'s BOLTED
STONE OR TILE FINISH
MORTAR BED
WATERPROOF MEMBRANE
T&G PLYWOOD SHEATHING SEE STRUCTURAL
FLOOR FRAMING PER STRUCTURAL DRAWINGS
'STUCCO RITE' SFB SELFFURRING LATH o/ TYVEK "STUCCO WRAP" WEATHER RESISTIVE MEMBRANE
7/8" CEMENT PLASTER, MOCKUP SAMPLE TO BE SELECTED AND APPROVED BY ARCHITECT SEE EXTERIOR ELEVATIONS FOR FINISH
BM. NO. 28 7"x9¼" PSL
DRAIN LINE TO CONDUCT WATER TO STREET RUN PARALLEL TO DECK JOISTS
MER-KOTE B.F.P. MEMBRANE. RUN o/ DRAIN FLANGE
Wall Section through Master Bedroom
SCALE: 1"=1'-0"

Figure 8.2 Portion of a section.

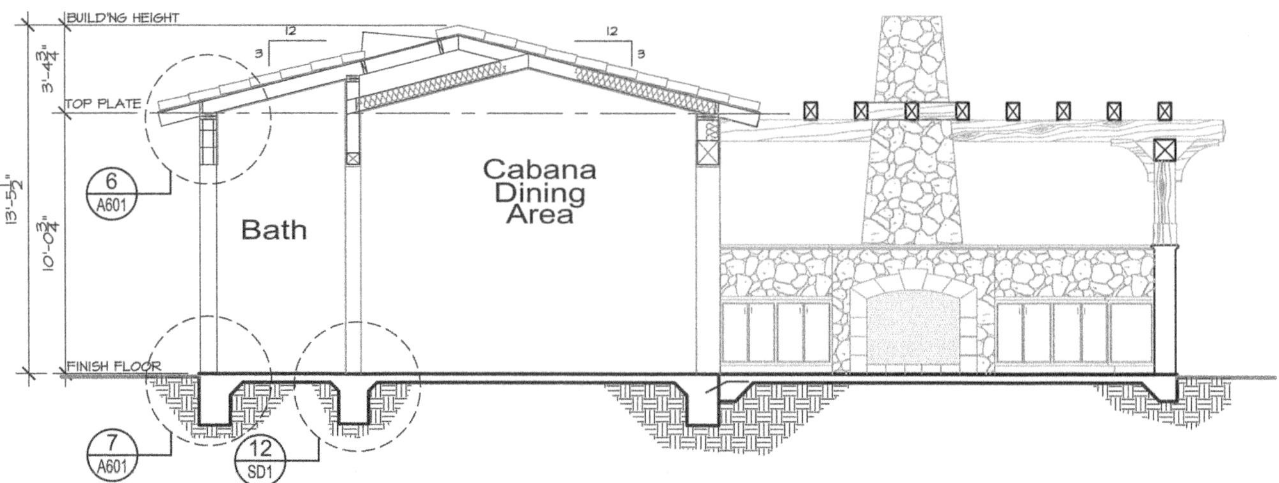

Figure 8.3 Building section.

the client, the building height constraints, or the budget. There is a current trend where the plate heights have increased from standard residential heights of around 8′ to 9′ or even 10′. Commercial buildings can vary but are between 12′ and 15′ high to allow for mechanical chases and equipment to be located above the drop ceiling line.

As indicated, the roof pitch for this particular project is a ratio of 3 to 12; the roof rises 3 inches for each 12 inches of horizontal measurement (the roof rises 3 feet for every 12 feet). You can draw this slope or angle with an architectural scale, or you can convert the ratio to an angle degree. Draw the roof at the other side of the building in the same way, with the intersection of the two roof planes establishing the ridge location. Mission clay tile was chosen for the finished roof material for this project.

When you have drawn in all the remaining components, such as stairs and floor framing elevation changes, note all the members, roof pitch, material information, and dimensions. See Figure 8.4.

Figure 8.5 shows various reference symbols. These symbols refer to an enlarged drawing of those particular assemblies. To demonstrate the importance of providing enlarged details, Figure 8.5 shows a building section of a wood-framed structure with critical bolted connections. A reference symbol (the number 1 over the number 8, in a reference bubble) is located at the roof framing and wall connection. This connection is made clear with an enlarged detail, showing

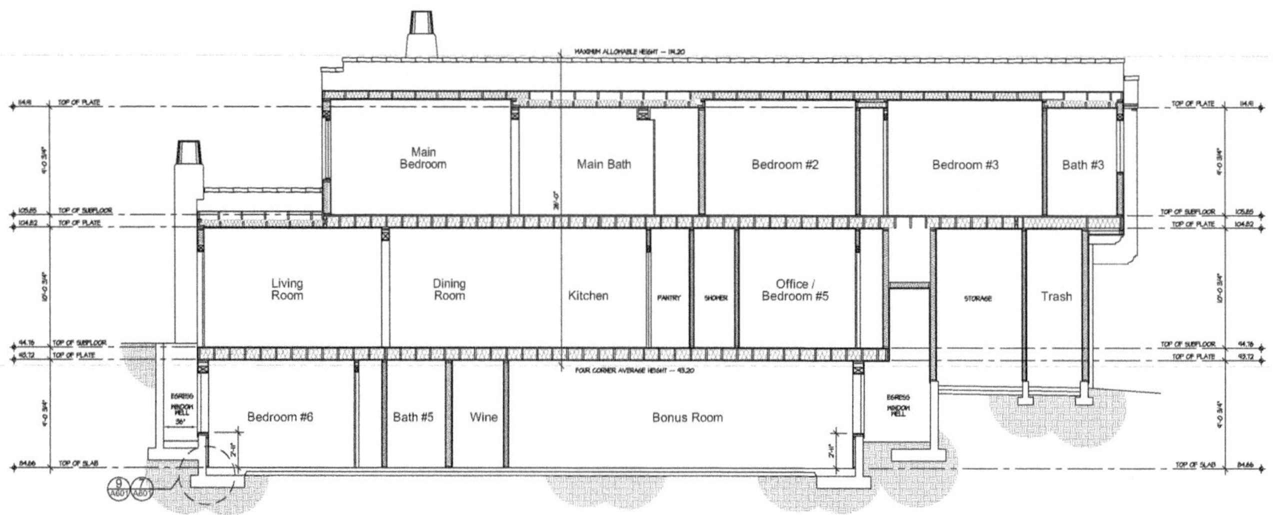

Figure 8.4 Building section.

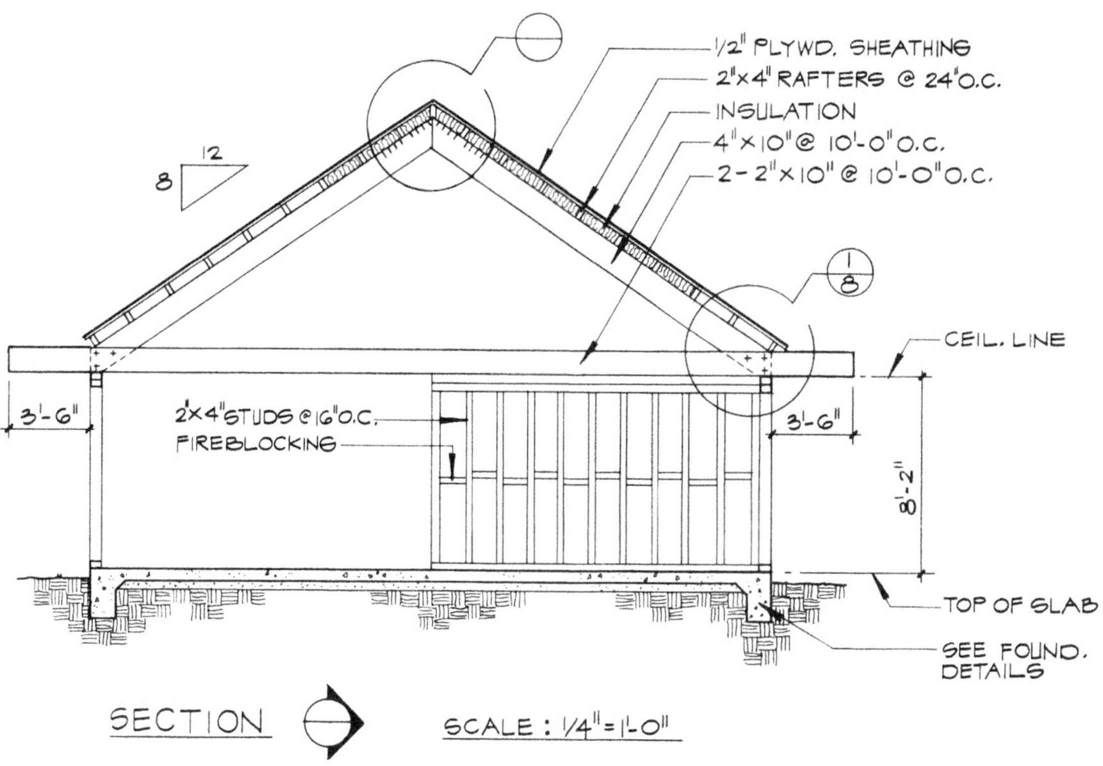

Figure 8.5 Structural section.

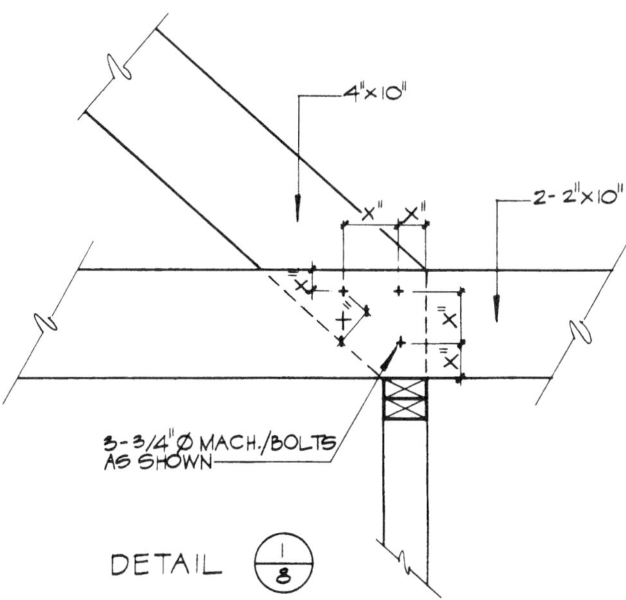

Figure 8.6 Bolted connection.

the exact location and size of bolts needed to satisfy the engineering requirements for that assembly. See Figure 8.6.

In BIM or a three-dimensional model, the building section can be sliced or sectioned or flattened. The various construction members, such as the studs and rafters, can then be rotated in a three-dimensional model to reveal and explain the construction features that are not readily obvious in a two-dimensional drawing.

Number and Place of Sections

Draw as many building sections as you need to convey the necessary information, with the greatest possible clarity, to the contractors building the structure. The building department typically requires a minimum of two sections, one cross-section and one longitudinal section often one must cut through the stairs.

Building sections are used to investigate various conditions that prevail in a structure. These sections can point out flaws in the building's structural integrity, and this information can lead to modifications in the initial design.

The number of building sections required varies according to the structural complexity of the particular building. For a simple rectangular building, you may need only two building sections to clearly provide all the required information. However, for a building with a more complex shape, you may require five or more sections to provide all the structural and architectural information. See Figure 8.7.

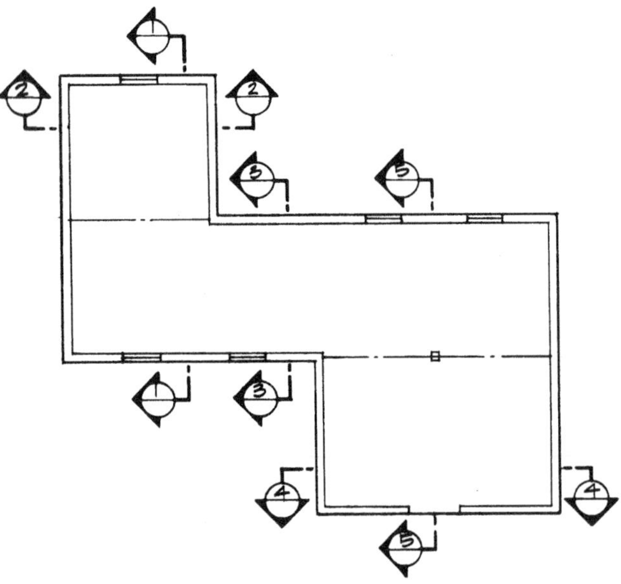

Figure 8.7 Building section locations of interest.

■ DRAFTING A BUILDING SECTION

After deciding where a section is to be taken so as to reveal the greatest amount of information, a grid pattern is drafted. The horizontal lines of the grid represent the floor line and the plate line (at the top of the two top plates). All of the vertical lines represent the walls of the structure or column locations. See Figure 8.8.

A scale of ¼″ = 1′-0″ is ideal, but because of the size of the structure or the limits of the sheet, a scale of ⅛″ = 1′-0″ might be used.

Before you decide on a smaller scale, explore the possibility of removing redundant portions of the building by virtue of break lines. See Figure 8.10. If the building is symmetrical, a partial section, as shown in Figure 8.18, may suffice.

If the building section is to be drawn at the same scale as the floor plan, the drafter need only transfer measurements by projecting or extending lines down from the floor plan to section. If the building section is drafted at twice the size of the floor plan, you can simply transfer the measurements and double the scale.

With the computer, you do not have a problem with scale because the floor plan and the building section, along with the entire set of construction documents, are drawn at full scale in model space. Only when you import the drawings into paper space do you need to add a scaling factor.

If the floor plan was drawn in paper space at a scale of ¼″ = 1′-0″ rather than at full scale in model space, you can quickly change the scaling factor, using the computer, from the ¼″ plan to another scale.

Pitch

If a pitch (an angle) is involved and it is constant, an adjustable triangle is handy. Another option is to actually measure the pitch. If you have a template, look for a pitch scale printed on its side. If you are in the market for a plan template, check the various brands carefully because there are templates that will measure pitch; have markings for typical heights of equipment from the floor; and even plot spacing, such as for 4″ and 6″ tile, 16″ spacing for stud and joist position, and door swings, among other items.

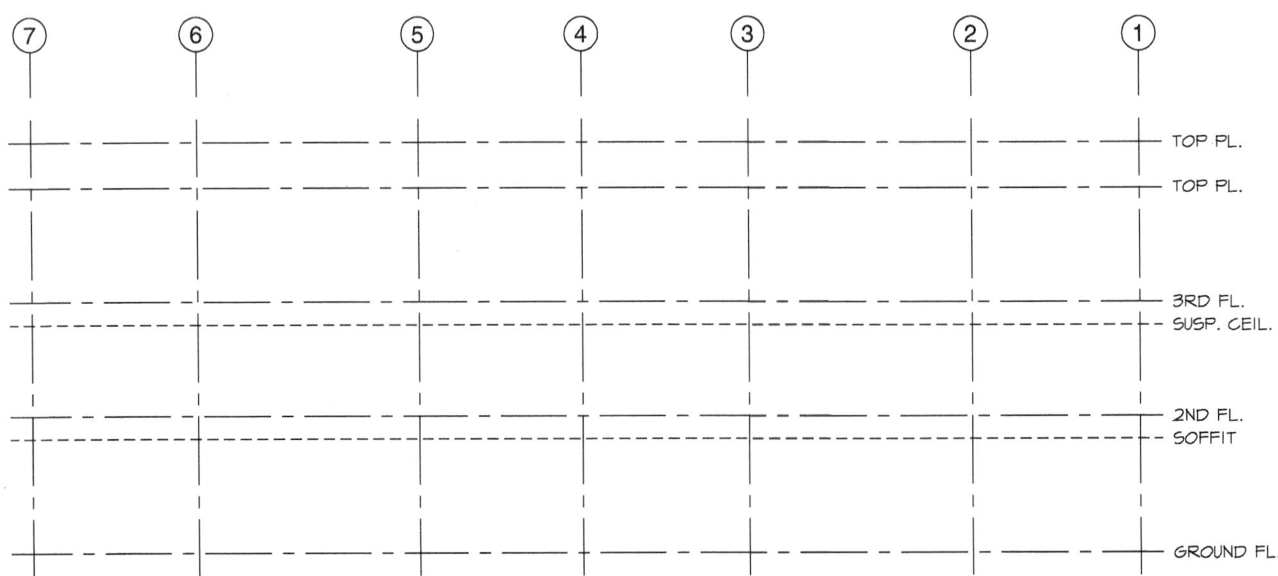

Figure 8.8 Layout of the grid pattern.

If you understand the process of drafting a building section, you might develop a shortcut method. For example, if you have access to a plain-paper copier that enlarges and reduces, it would be a simple matter to reproduce an eave detail to the proper scale. Then, with the same pitch on a sheet, place it under the building section and trace.

TYPES OF BUILDING SECTIONS

Because the design and complexity of buildings vary, types of sections also vary. The type of section that will best demonstrate the required data is the determining factor in choosing the required types of sections.

Wall Sections

Simple structural conditions may only require wall sections to convey the necessary building information. Structural sections for a small industrial building, for example, might use wall sections.

In most cases, wall sections can be drawn at larger scales, such as ½″ = 1′-0″. These larger-scale drawings allow you to clearly elaborate building connections and call-outs without having to draw separate enlarged details.

Figures 8.9–8.12 are for an industrial building and show how wall sections are incorporated into a set of construction documents. Figure 8.9 shows the floor plan

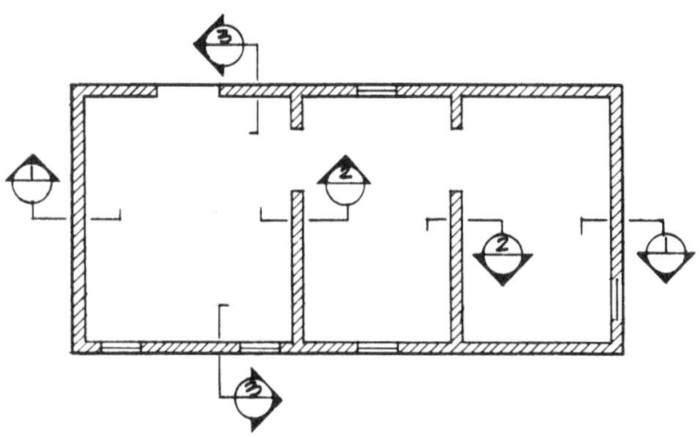

Figure 8.9 Floor plan of an industrial building.

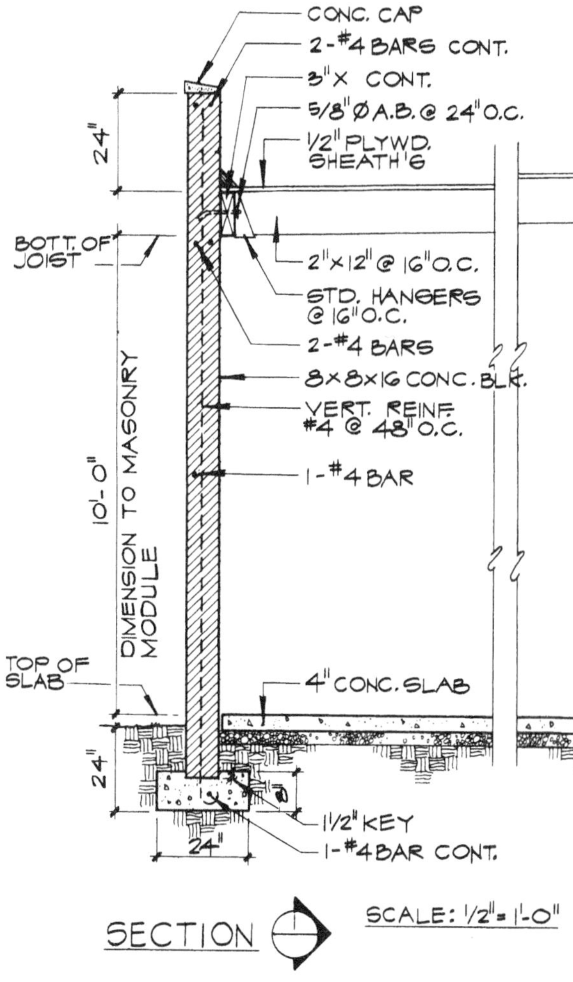

Figure 8.10 Exterior wall section 1.

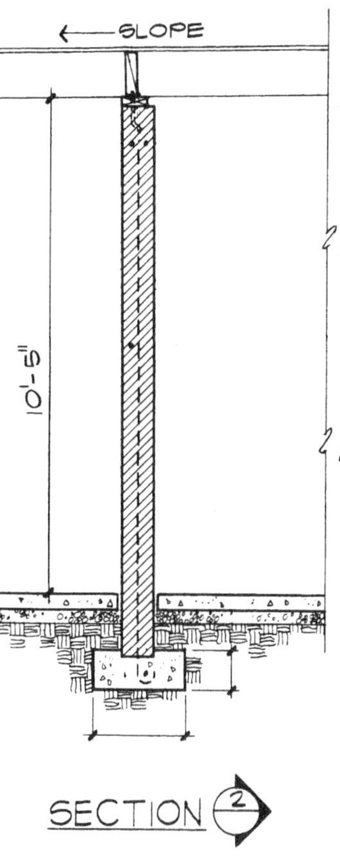

Figure 8.11 Interior wall section 2.

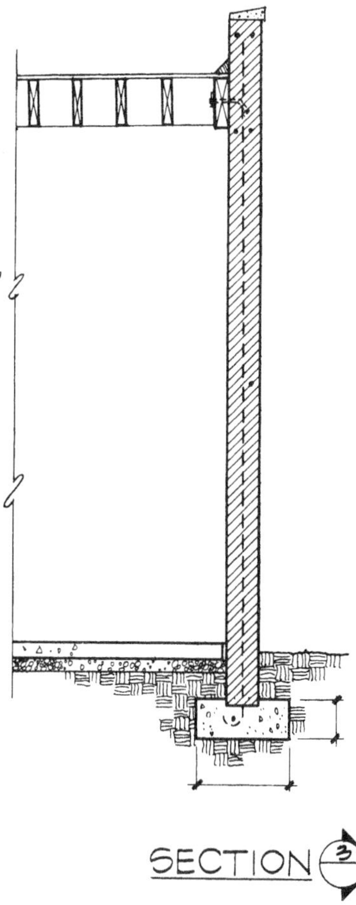

Figure 8.12 Exterior wall section 3.

with two main exterior and one interior bearing wall conditions. These wall conditions are referenced to wall sections and are shown in Figures 8.10–8.12.

When drawing at a large scale, you can note all the footing information directly on the wall section, thereby making separate foundation details unnecessary. Next, draw the masonry wall using 8 × 8 × 16 concrete block as the wall material. Because a modular unit is being used for the wall construction, a wall height is established that satisfies the 8″ concrete-block increments. Draw the roof-to-wall assembly at the desired height above the concrete floor, with the various framing connections and members needed to satisfy the structural requirements. After you finish the drawing, add notes for all members, steel reinforcing, bolts, and so forth. Other wall sections, as shown in Figures 8.11 and 8.12, are drawn and noted similarly. Note that while Figure 8.12 is similar to Figure 8.10, different roof framing conditions exist.

In short, large-scale wall sections allow the structural components and call-outs to be clearly drawn and usually make larger-scale details, such as framing connections and foundation details, unnecessary.

Full Sections

For projects with complex structural conditions, you should draw an entire section. This gives you a better idea of the structural conditions in that portion of the building, which can then be analyzed, engineered, and clearly detailed.

Figure 8.13 shows a building section through a residence that has complex framing. Here, you can clearly understand the need for a full section to see the existing conditions. When doing a full section, you should draw this type of section in a smaller architectural scale, 1/4″ = 1′-0″. Again, when you use a smaller scale for drawing sections, you must provide enlarged details of all relevant connections. The circled and referenced conditions in Figure 8.13, for example, will be detailed at a large scale.

Whether in the area of schematic design or design development, a design section can be created to aid in the design process. A design section utilizes no structural detail; in fact, it is a drawing that describes volume within a building and graphically holds space for the future structure. See Figures 8.14 and 8.15.

Notice the level of interior detail in Figures 8.16 and 8.17. The option of providing interior detail within the section allows the client to better understand the relationship of the elements inside the room. In this regard, a design section also serves another important purpose: it is one of the few drawings that explain the volume of the rooms. This is also helpful to the consultants, such as mechanical, electrical, and structural engineers. With this kind of section, the mechanical engineers can best determine the space allotted for them to work in, the

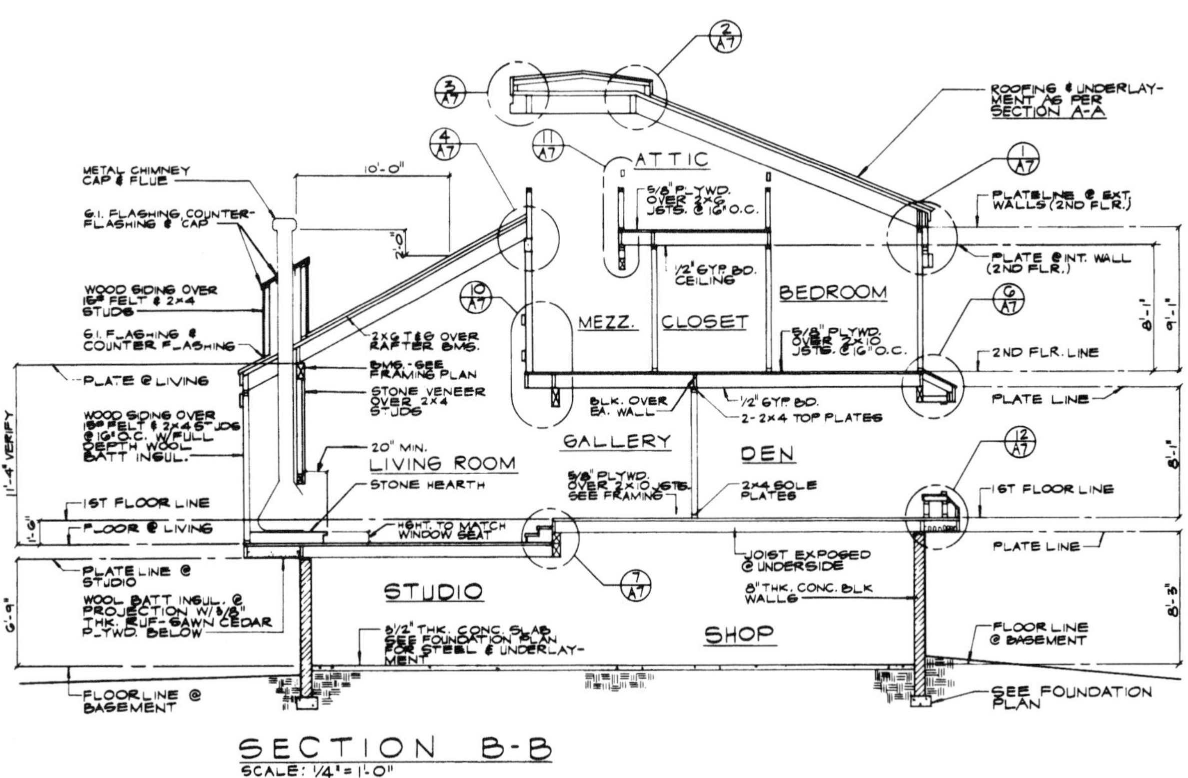

Figure 8.13 Full section. (Courtesy of Steve L. Martin.)

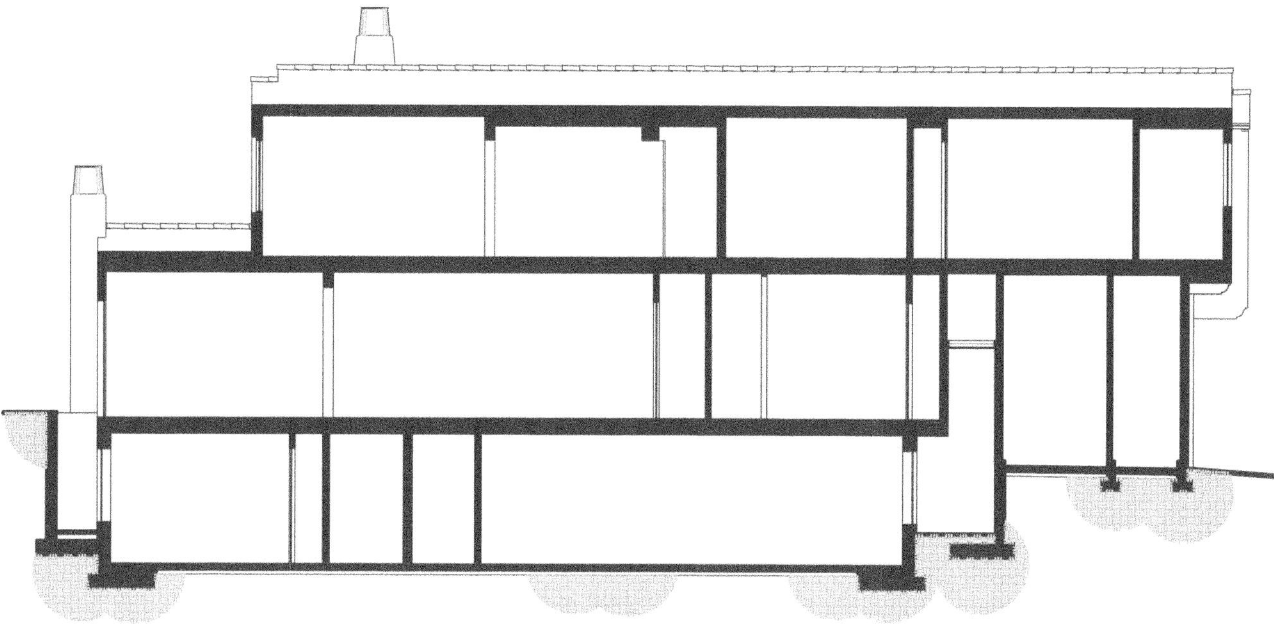

Figure 8.14 Building design section.

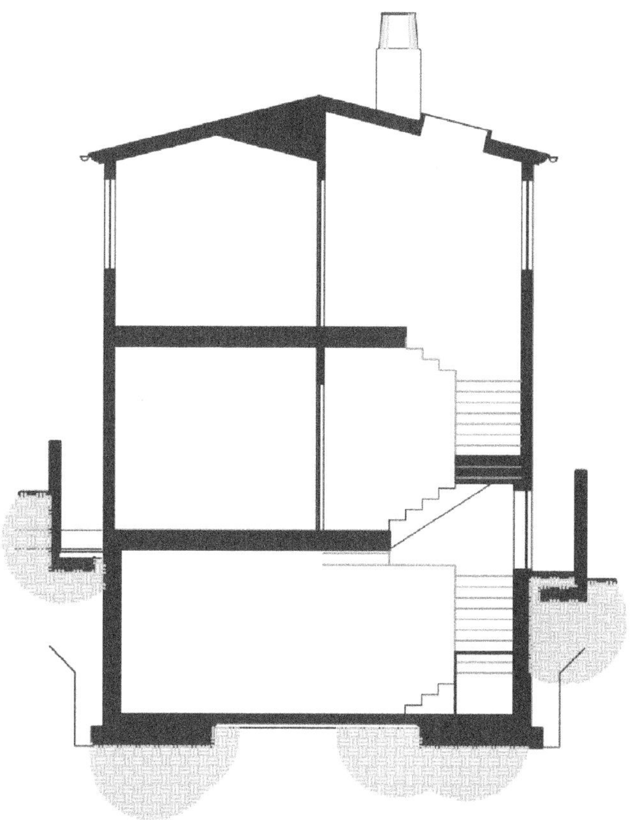

Figure 8.15 Building design section.

electrical engineers can determine which types of fixtures will best light the room, and structural engineers can shape the structure to achieve the shape concept designed by the architect.

Partial Sections

Many projects have only isolated areas that are structurally complex. These areas are drawn in the same way as a cross section, but they stop when the area of concern has been clearly drawn. This results in a partial section of a structural portion.

In addition to the structural aspect of sections, the designed shape of the building is exposed to better demonstrate the 3-D aspect of the space. The section is an aid in realizing the space, for both the builder and the client.

The partial section shown in Figure 8.18 illustrates the structural complexities existing in that portion. Additional detailing is required to make other assemblies clear.

One of these assemblies, for example, may require a partial framing elevation to show a specific roof framing condition. This condition may be referenced by the use of two circles—each with direction arrows, reference letters, and numbers—attached to a broken line. Figure 8.19 shows this partial framing elevation, as referenced on Figure 8.18.

Steel Sections

For buildings built mainly with steel members, use elevations to establish column and beam heights. This approach coincides with the procedures and methods for the shop drawings provided by the steel fabricator. Both the architect and the structural engineer will review the shop drawings for intent and approve them prior to fabrication.

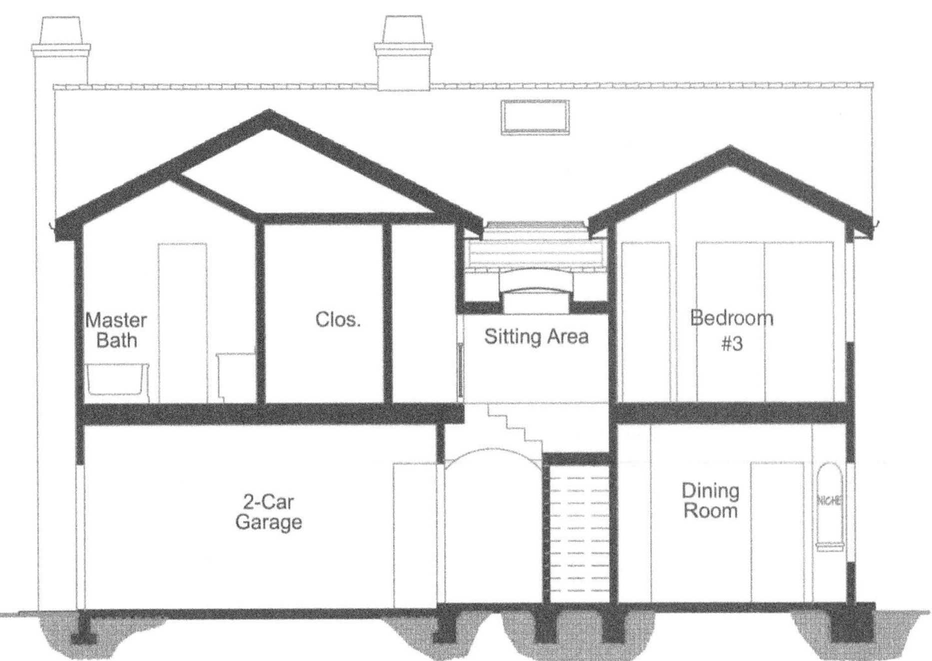

Figure 8.16 Building design section.

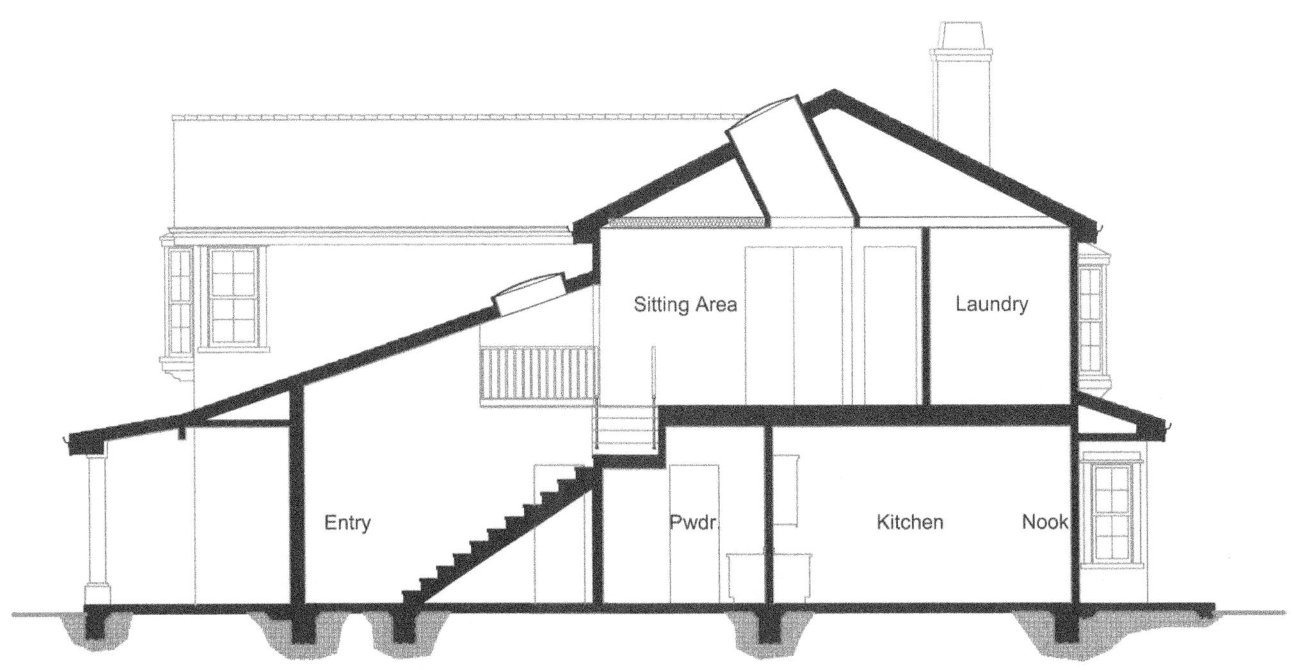

Figure 8.17 Building design section.

Figure 8.20 shows a structural section through a steel-framed building. In contrast to sections for wood-framed buildings, where vertical dimensions are used to establish plate heights, this type of section may establish column and beam heights using the top of the concrete slab as a beginning point. Each steel column in this section has an assigned number because the columns are identified by the use of an axial reference matrix on the framing plan, shown in Figure 8.21.

Building Sections Checklist

1. Sections that clearly depict the structural conditions existing in the building
2. Sections referenced on plans and elevations
3. Dimensioning for the following (where applicable):
   a. Floor to top plate
   b. Floor to floor
   c. Floor to ceiling

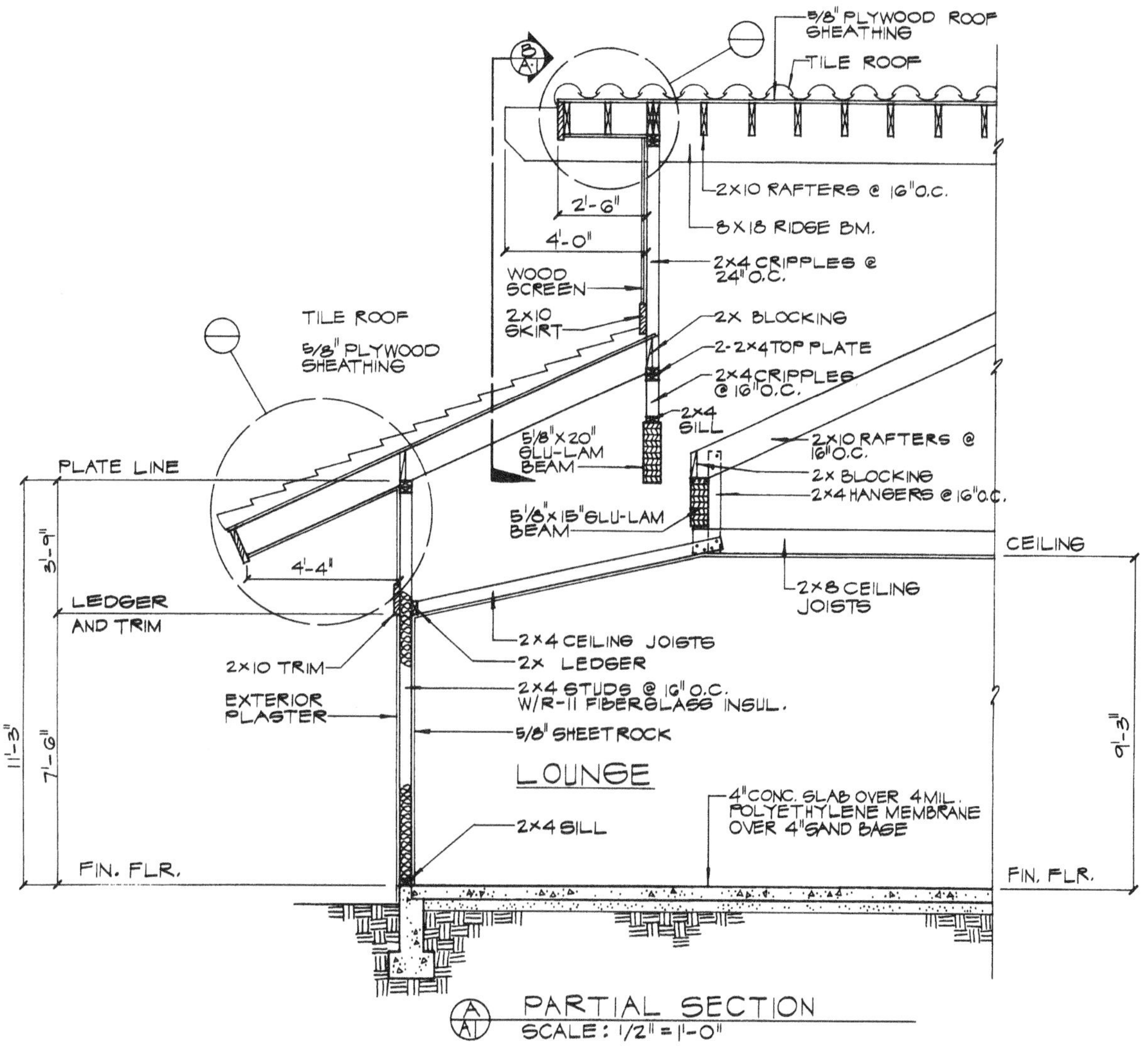

Figure 8.18 Partial section.

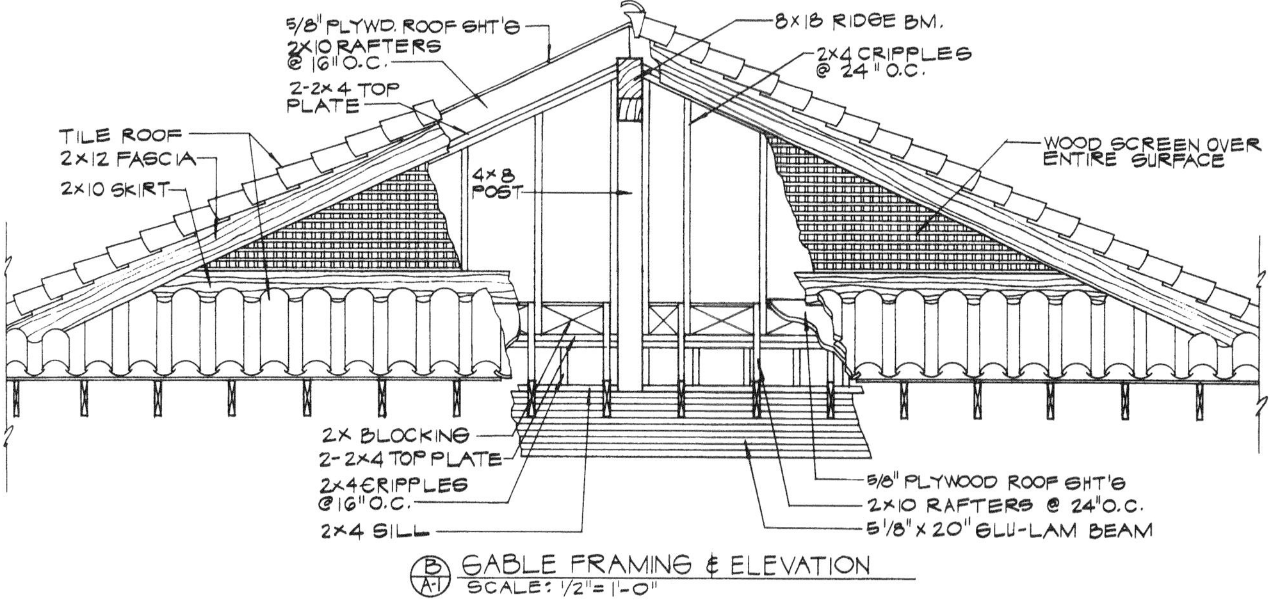

Figure 8.19 Framing elevation.

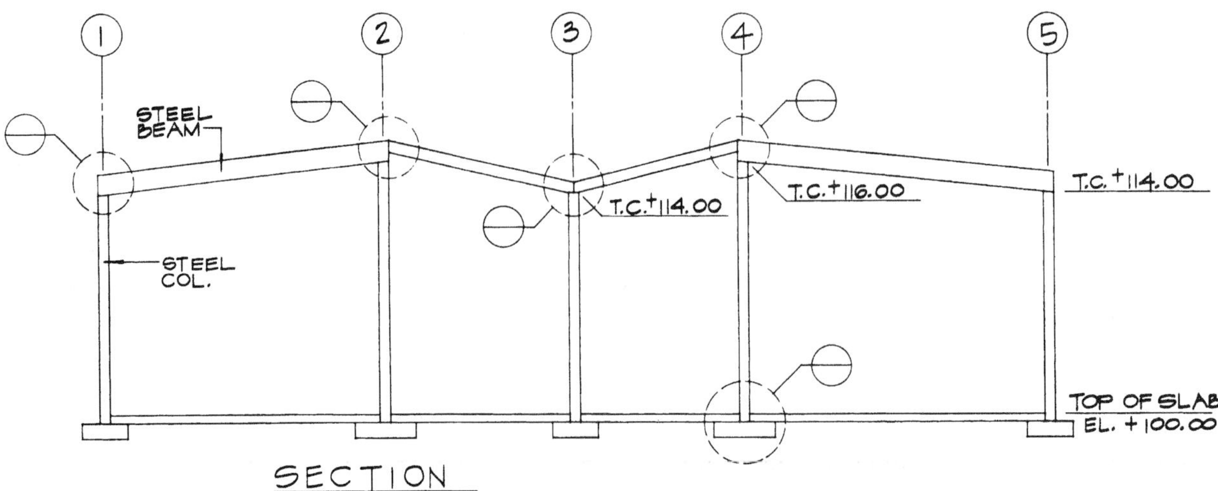

Figure 8.20 Steel frame section.

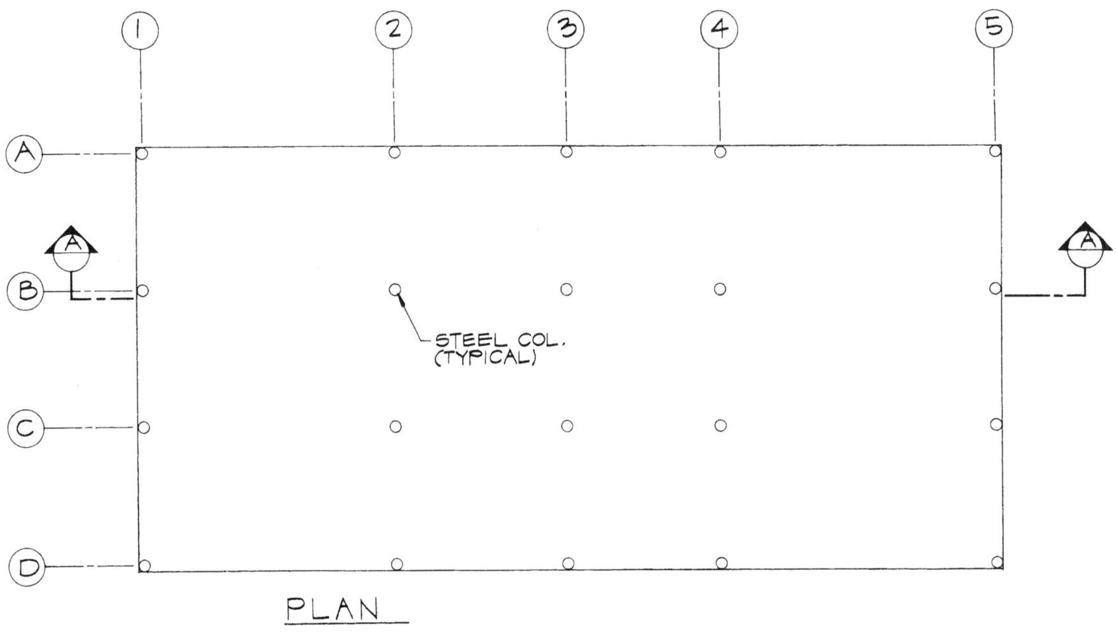

Figure 8.21 Column matrix.

   - **d.** Floor to top of wall
   - **e.** Floor to top of column or beam
   - **f.** Cantilevers, overhangs, offsets, etc.
   - **g.** Foundation details
4. Elevations for top of floor, top of columns and beams
5. Call-out information for all members, such as the following:
   - **a.** Size, material, and shape of member
   - **b.** Spacing of members
6. Call-out information for all assemblies, including fire assembly rating (if enlarged details are not provided)
7. Column and beam matrix identification, if incorporated in the structural plan
8. Call-out for subfloor, insulation location and size, and sheathing assembly
9. Roof pitches and indication of all slopes
10. Reference symbols for all details and assemblies that are enlarged for clarity
11. Designation of material for protection of finish for roof, ceiling, wall, and structural members
12. Structural notes applicable to each particular section, such as the following:
    - **a.** Nailing schedules
    - **b.** Splice dimensions
    - **c.** Structural notes

13. Structural sections corresponding accurately to foundation, floor, and framing plans
14. Scale and title of drawing section

■ SAMPLE DESIGN AND DETAILED BUILDING SECTIONS

Building Section Stages

In this study example, a simple one-story residence with multiple floor levels is demonstrated in the section. Note the various heights of the floors and the plate heights. These are established early in the process and are critical in the initial layout of the sections.

Stage I (Figure 8.22). This stage establishes heights. As the floor plan controls the width and depth of the residence, the building sections control the heights. The floor line and plate line are the most critical from a building perspective. The Jadyn residence has three floor lines because of the change of level that occurs at the bearing wall located in the center of the structure. Many planning departments require that the top of the ridge be dimensioned to make sure it does not obstruct views for neighbors.

Stage II (Figure 8.23). The outline of the roof and the positioning of the bearing walls are incorporated at this stage.

Stage III (Figure 8.24). The building section is receiving detail at the various intersections such as the top and bottom plates, as well as the seat in the stem wall for the slab, are drafted.

Stage IV (Figure 8.25). This stage establishes all of the structural components, their position and direction, and even the direction in which the section was taken. Note the inclusion of the material designation and the makeup of the foundation with its insulation and sand. Walls show drywall, and the ceiling reveals the direction of the ceiling joist.

Stage V (Figure 8.26). Noting of the component parts and dimensioning become the most important tasks for this stage. All the parts should be identified. Material designations for insulation, roof material, and concrete are done at this stage, as well as referencing to reveal footing details and eave details.

Stage VI (Figure 8.27). The final stages of the details and the building section are merged at this point and positioned onto the title block sheet in the final plotting.

In this study example, a more complex multistory residence is demonstrated in the cross-section. Note the various floors and the plate heights, which are ideally established early and are critical in the initial layout of the sections.

Figure 8.22 Stage I: Building sections.

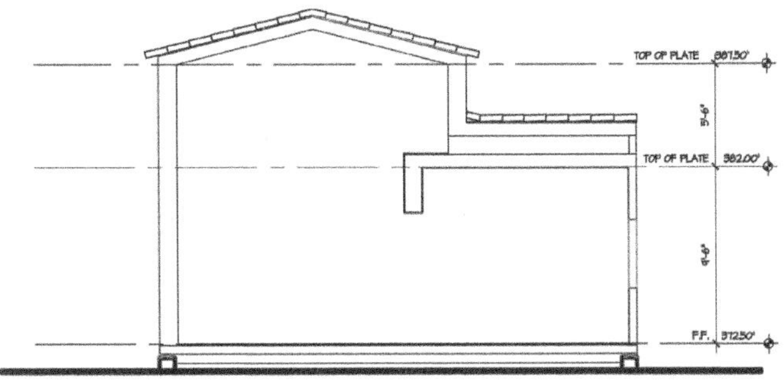

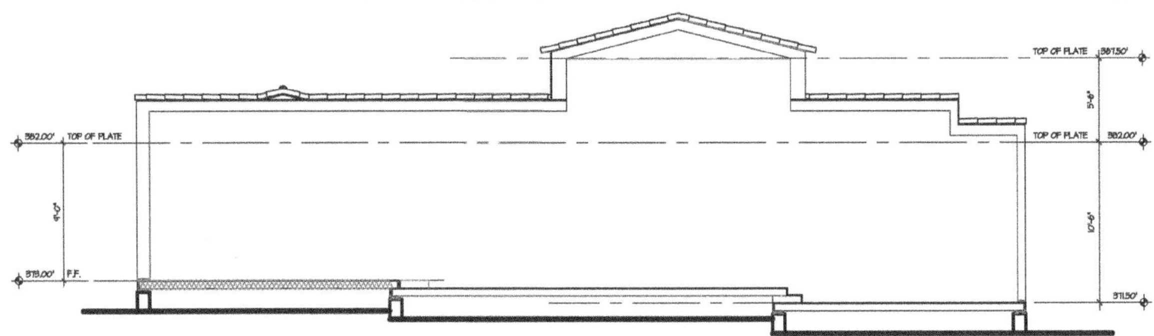

Figure 8.23 Stage II: Building sections.

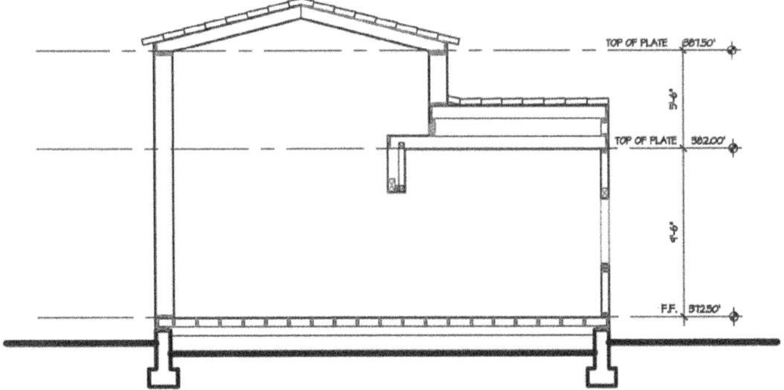

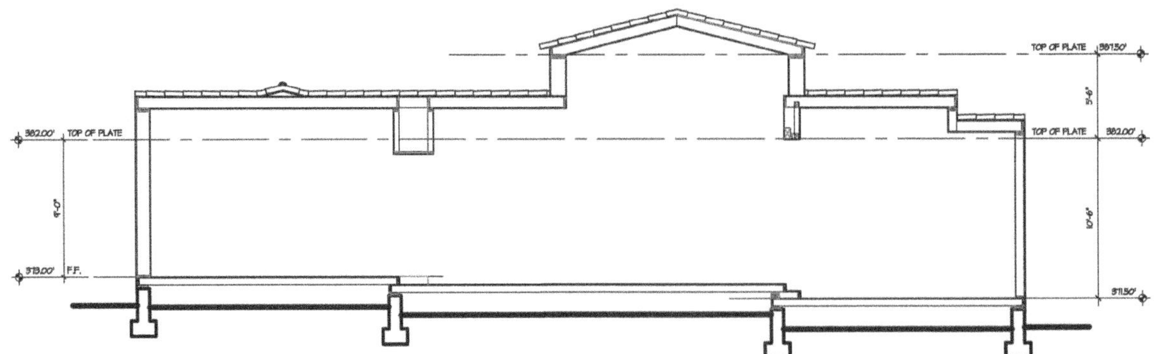

Figure 8.24 Stage III: Building sections.

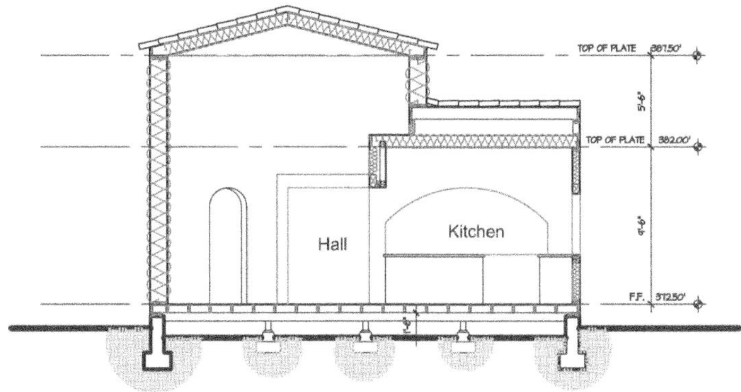

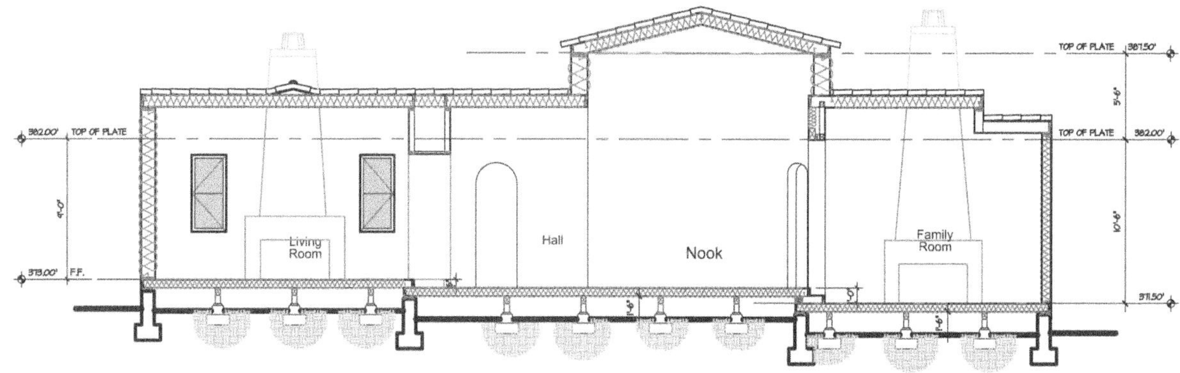

Figure 8.25 Stage IV: Building sections.

Stage I (Figure 8.28). If a flattened 3-D section is available, use this as the datum for future stages. All wall locations, plate heights, and level changes must be verified and corrected at this stage. If a flattened model is not available, the first stage of a 2-D drawing will establish the base or datum. Start by establishing the grade and its relationship with the floor line. Using this floor line as the main baseline, establish and measure the plate lines and floor lines of subsequent floors. In larger buildings, measurement may be in decimals. This is particularly true in steel structures, where the tips of the columns and tops of the floor girders are critical during installation.

Stage II (Figure 8.29). The outline of the structure is now positioned, including the roof. On 3-D drawings, the walls are already positioned, but on 2-D drawings the walls must be positioned by aligning the datum lines with a partial floor plan where the cut occurs (see Figure 8.30). In the schematic stage of design, a section may look very similar to the one in Figure 8.29.

Stage III (Figure 8.31). The thicknesses or widths of the foundation, walls, ceiling, and roof are drawn at this stage. Everything is drawn to net or actual size, not nominal size, to produce an accurate assembly drawing. Previously drafted details showing similar shapes and parts can be imported and used. This stage, which is actually a refinement of the Stage II drawing, constitutes the design development stage of a section.

Stage IV (Figure 8.32). This is said to be the most enjoyable stage because the building begins to take on character with the addition of material designations and the array of the end views of ceiling joists, floor joists, and rafters. Concrete takes on its own character adjacent to grade (soil).

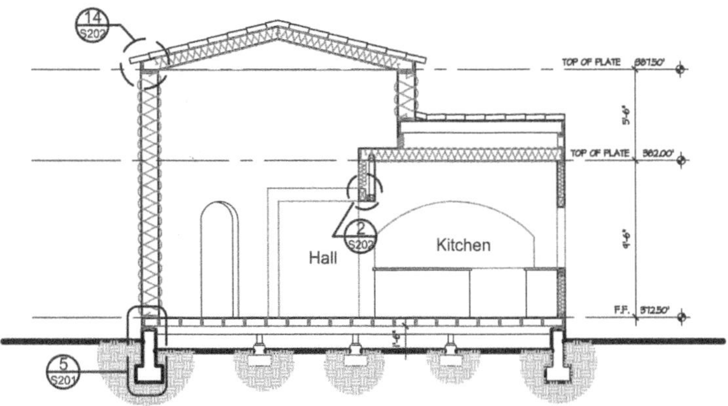

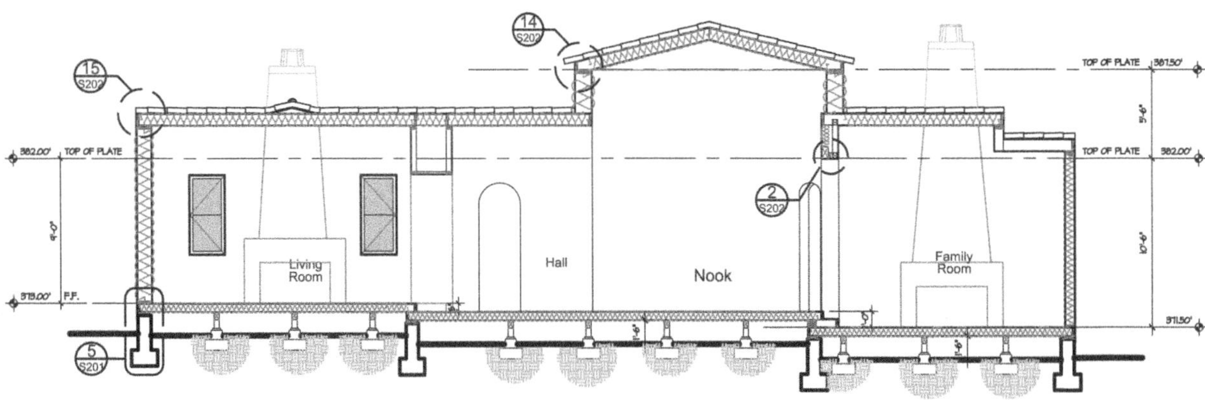

Figure 8.26 Stage V: Building sections.

Stage V (Figure 8.33). Stage V is the most critical to the accuracy of the project. All vertical dimensions are included at this stage. The most critical aspects are the dimensions for the floor to plate and definition of the neutral zones on the project. Horizontal dimensions should not appear in this stage, but rather on the floor plan, with the exception of describing the shape of a soffit or any other feature not seen in the floor plan. Note the call-out of elevation heights such as the top of subfloor 372.50′ (see Figure 8.33).

Stage VI (Figure 8.34). All notes and referencing are included in this stage. Notes should be generic if the specific materials are described in the specifications. Titles must be given to all of the parts, including the names of rooms through which the section cut occurs. Reference bubbles are positioned and are referred to footing details, eave details, stair details, and so on. Remember, the **title** is a name given to this building section. If it is a full section, as in our example, two letters are used—for example, A–A, B–B, and C–C. The first letter indicates the beginning of the section, and the second letter indicates the end of the cut.

The following two examples are completed sections that started as the design sections seen in Figures 8.13–8.16. Figures 8.35 and 8.36 are the completed sheets as presented to the client and to the Department of Building and Safety.

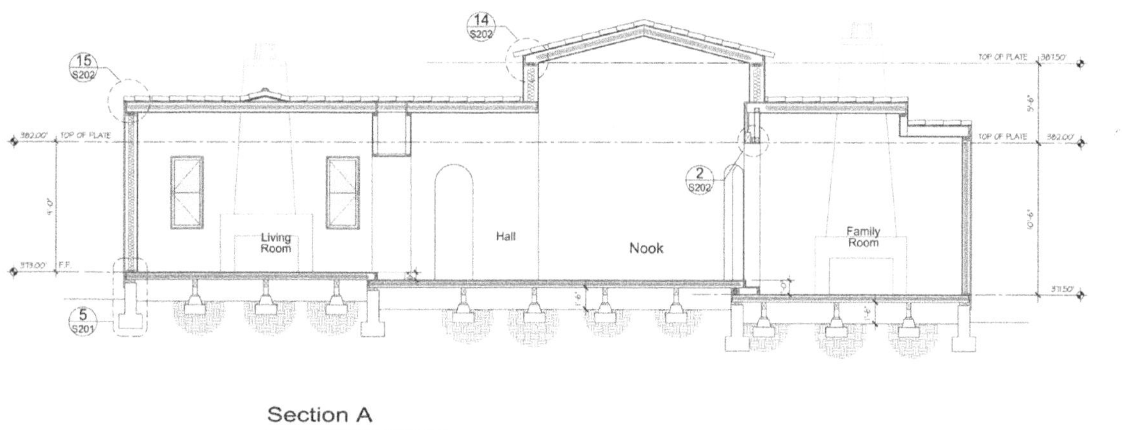

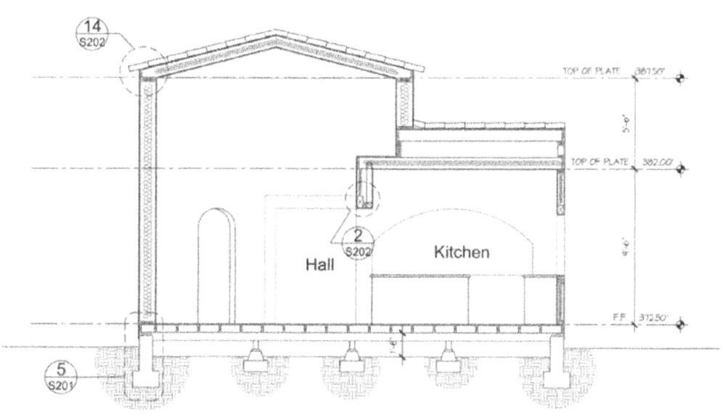

Figure 8.27 Stage VI: Building sections.

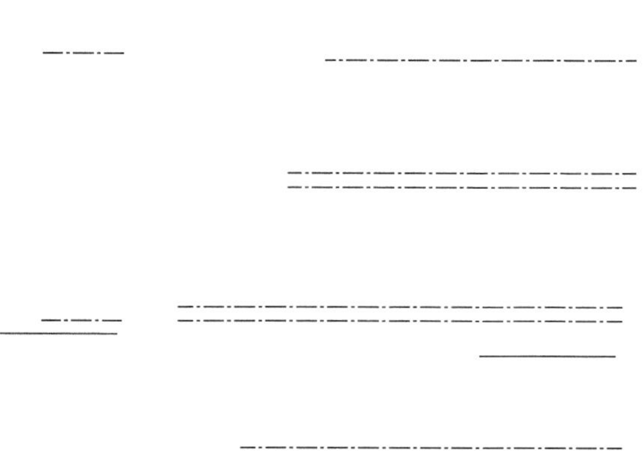

Figure 8.28 Stage I: Establishing datum.

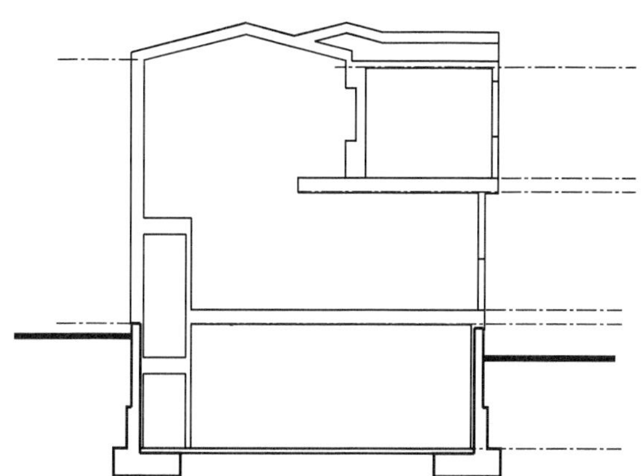

Figure 8.29 Stage II: Outlining of foundation, walls, and roof.

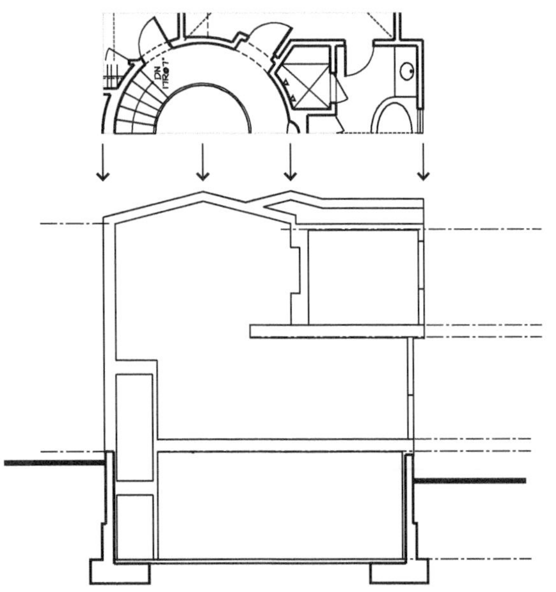

Figure 8.30 Stage II: Aligning datum with floor plan.

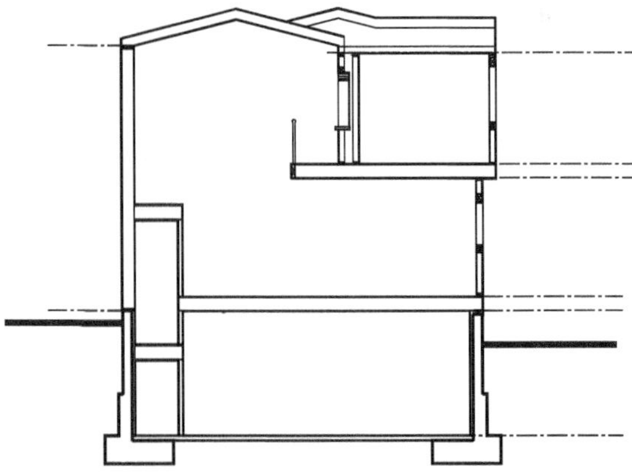

Figure 8.31 Stage III: Sizing members and outlining configuration.

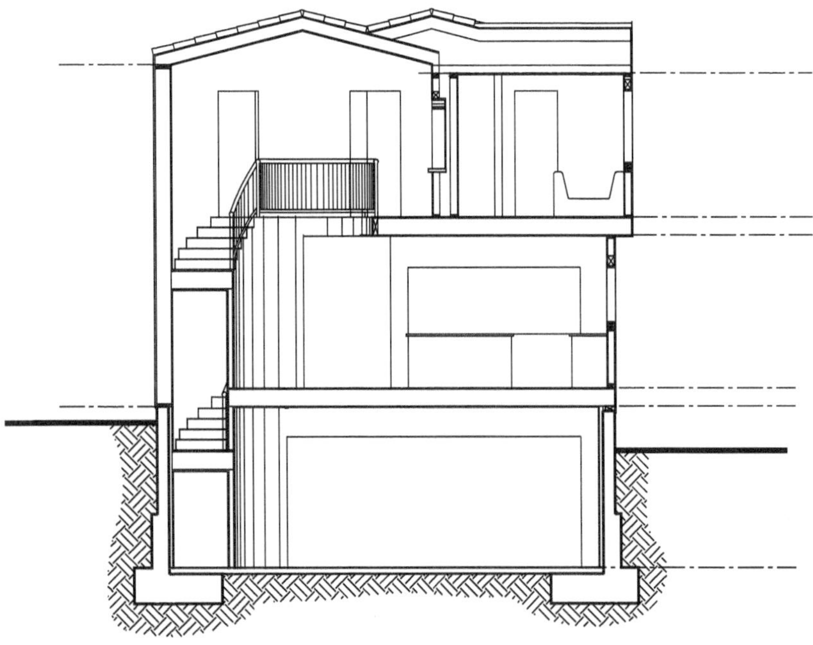

Figure 8.32 Stage IV: Materials designation, array joists.

MATERIALS AND BUILDING SECTIONS

It is recommended that you study a preliminary building section before developing the exterior elevations. The architect determined a roof pitch, an eave overhang, and a soffit so as to terminate the finish soffit material directly above the exterior window and door trims. This design requirement also established a 9′ plate height dimension from the top of the concrete floor to the top plate. Generally, the plate heights for light residential wood structures are from 8′-0¾″ to 10′-0″. A wood stud framing system provides flexibility in the design and construction process. Figure 8.38 illustrates a building section that is cut through the floor plan at the building section symbol location on the floor plan in Figure 8.37. As indicated by the building section symbol, the section cut is looking in a westerly direction.

Note that the horizontal soffit at the roof eave terminates just above the normal window and door height of 6′-8″.

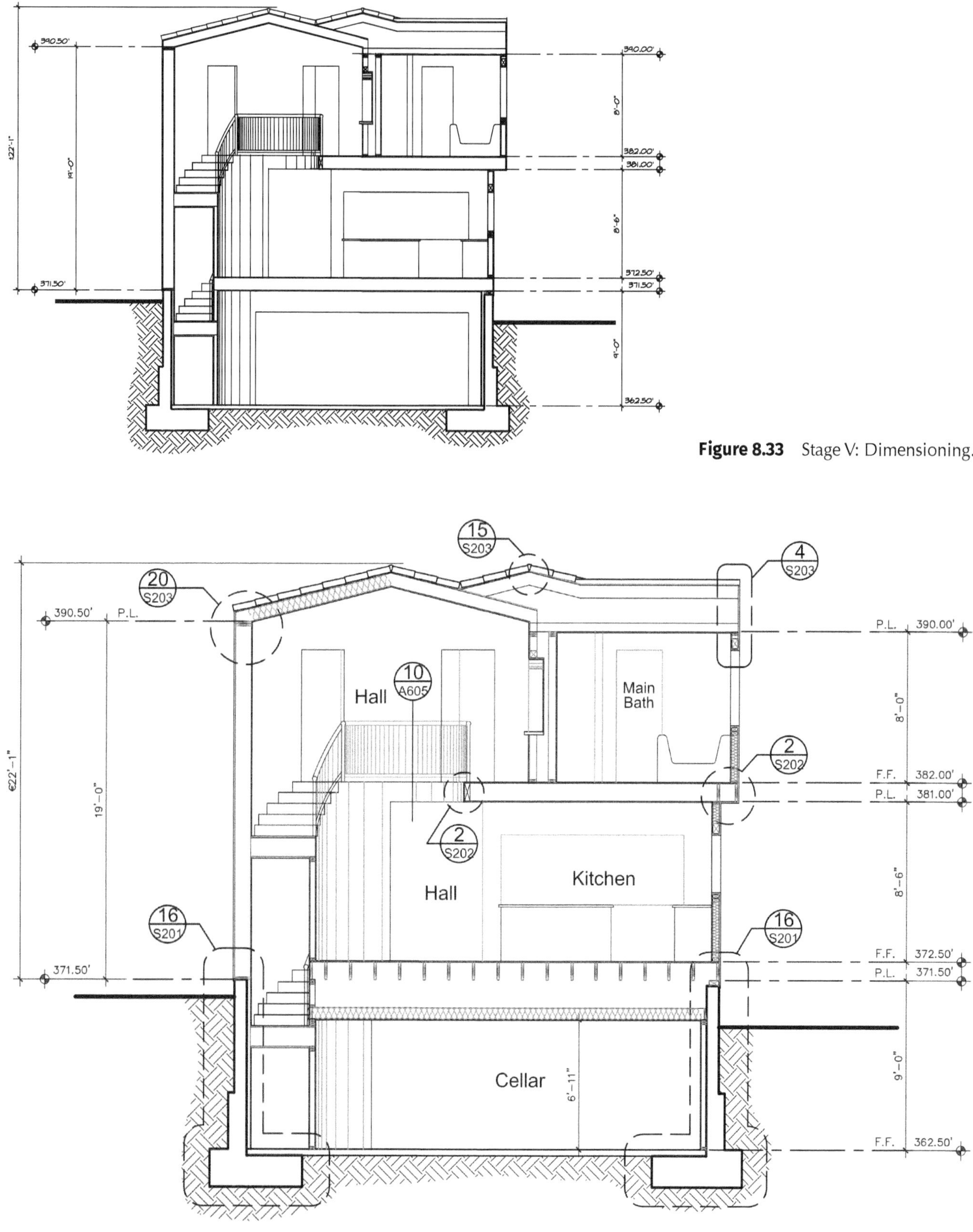

Figure 8.33 Stage V: Dimensioning.

Figure 8.34 Stage VI: Noting, referencing, and titles. (Courtesy of Mike Adli.)

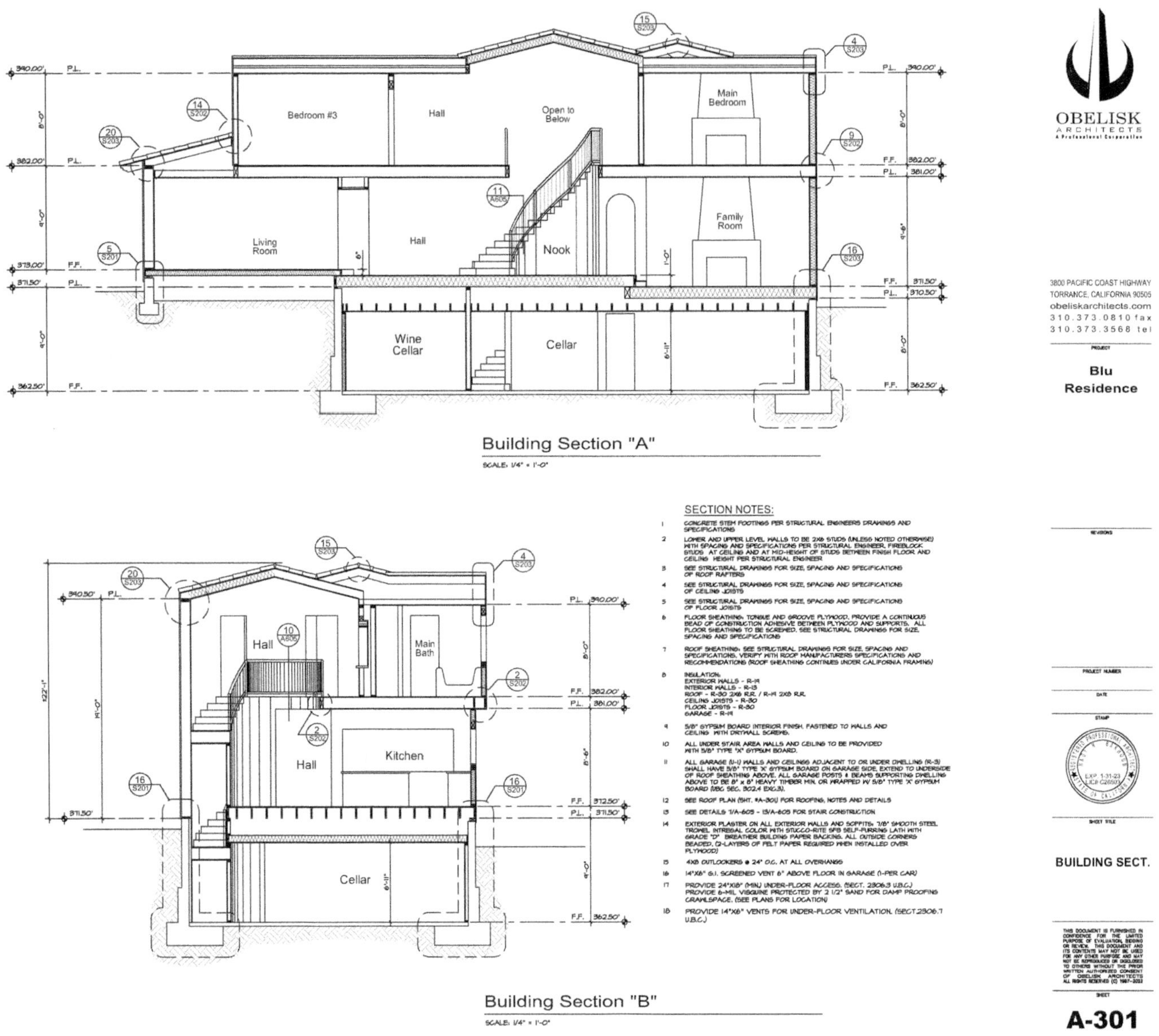

Figure 8.35 Completed sheet of building sections.

The size and grade of the wood supporting members in the roof system will be determined later in the working drawings by the architect or the structural engineer.

The next major item to consider and analyze is the building sections for the post-and-beam wood framing method. For this project, the architect decided to use tongue-and-groove planking spanning over the exposed beams, which are to be spaced 8′ center to center. Nailed directly over the tongue-and-groove planking will be one layer of 3/8″ exterior-grade plywood. To meet energy conservation standards, one layer of insulation board, such as urethane, will be applied over the plywood and will be the substrate for the application of a built-up roofing system. See Figure 8.39. This building section is viewed along the matrix axis line. Figure 8.40 depicts pictorially a view along the matrix line.

In conjunction with the necessary drawings for the building sections, it will be important to develop the precast panel drawings illustrating the wall dimensions and wall thickness for each specific panel. These panels should be identified with an elevation drawing and a panel identification number. See Figure 8.41.

The precast panel to be placed between matrix numbers ① and ② from Figure 8.42 is defined as panel P-1. Panel identification may be shown on the floor plan, or a key plan may be provided.

The number of building sections to be illustrated on a set of working drawings will be the number needed to

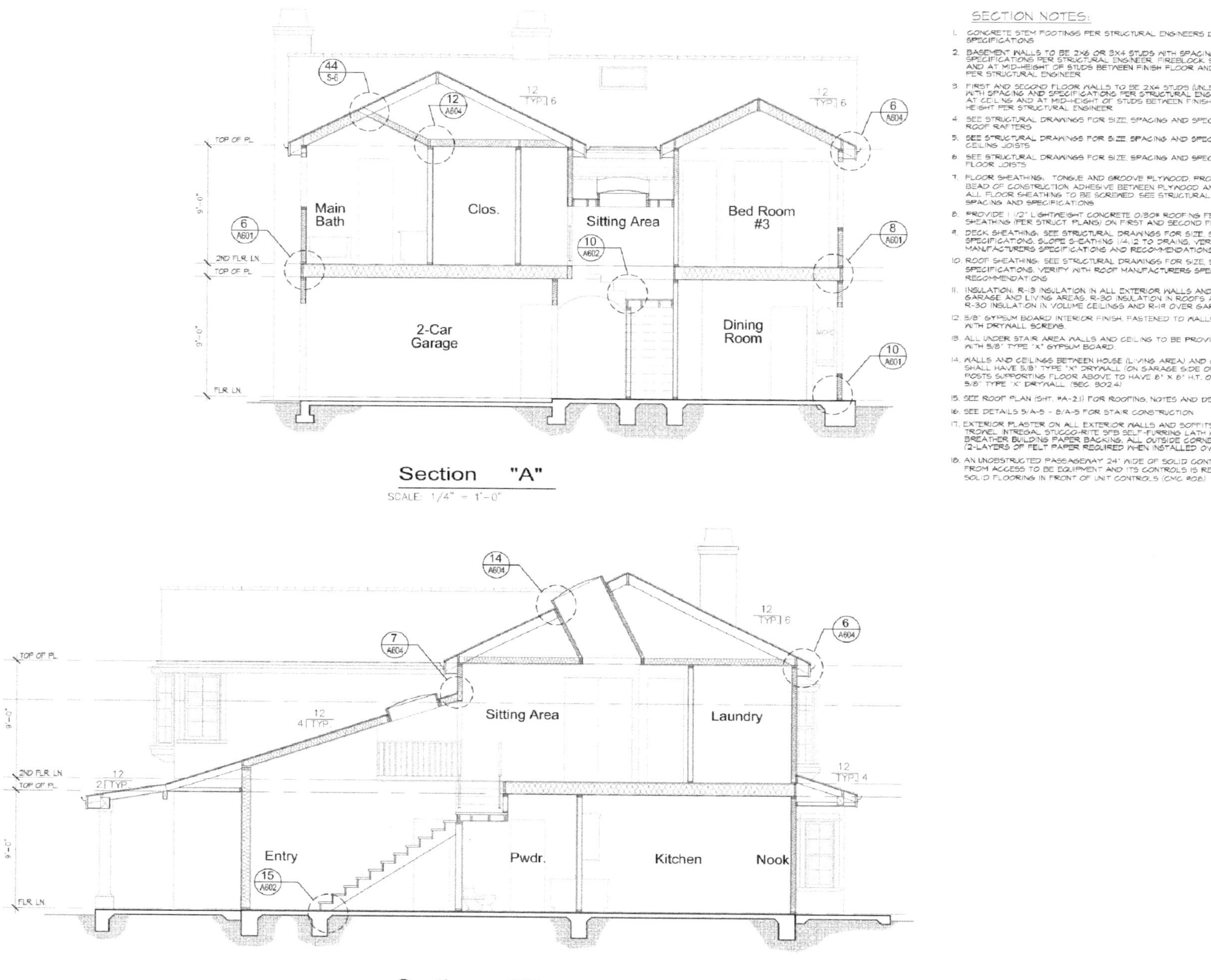

Figure 8.36 Completed sheet of building sections.

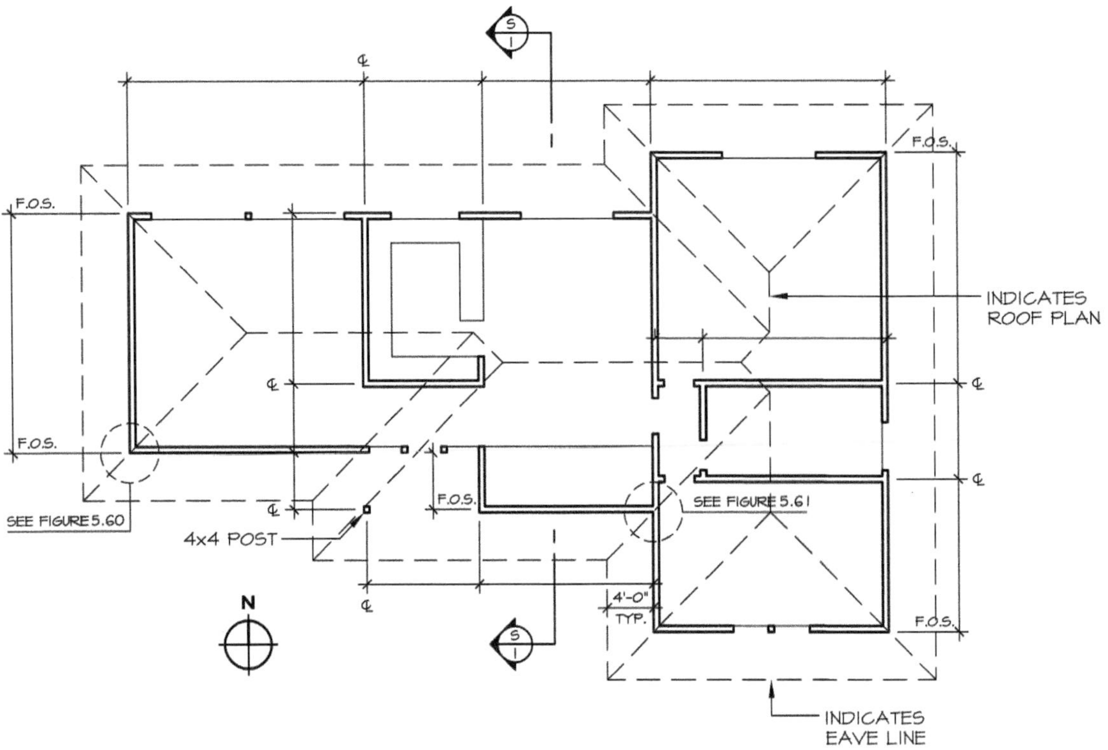

Figure 8.37 Floor plan with 2 × 4 stud framing.

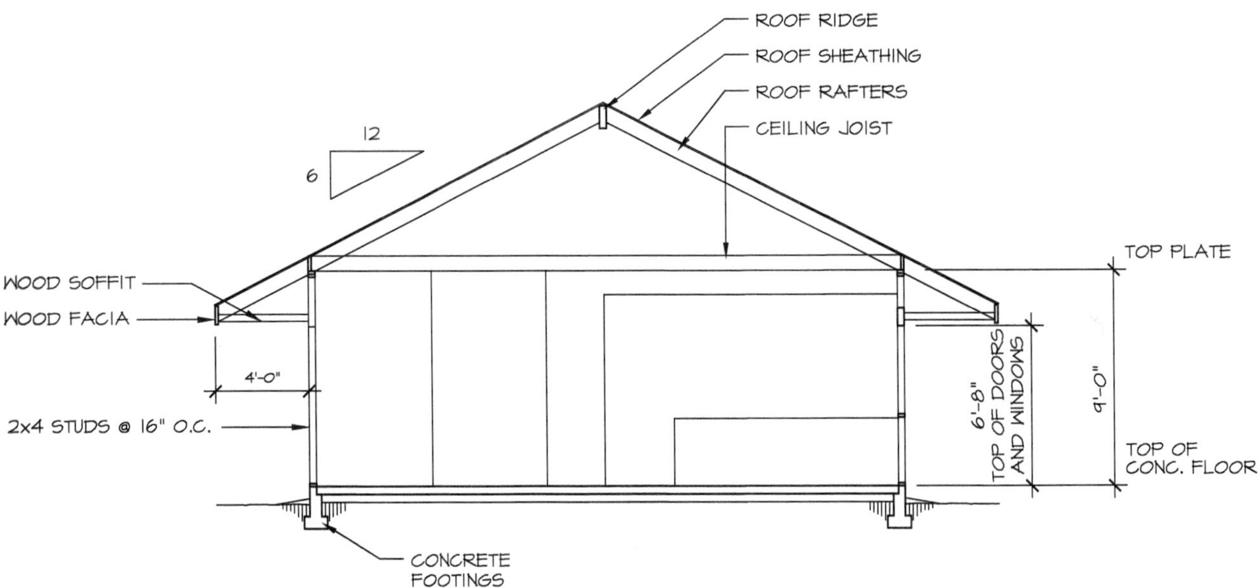

Figure 8.38 Building section.

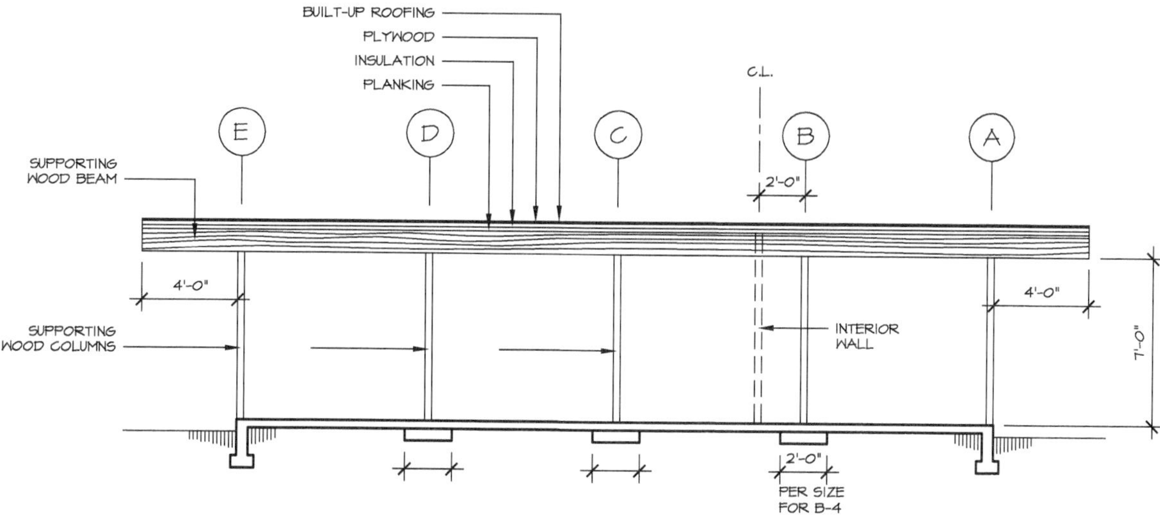

Figure 8.39 Building section on axis 4.

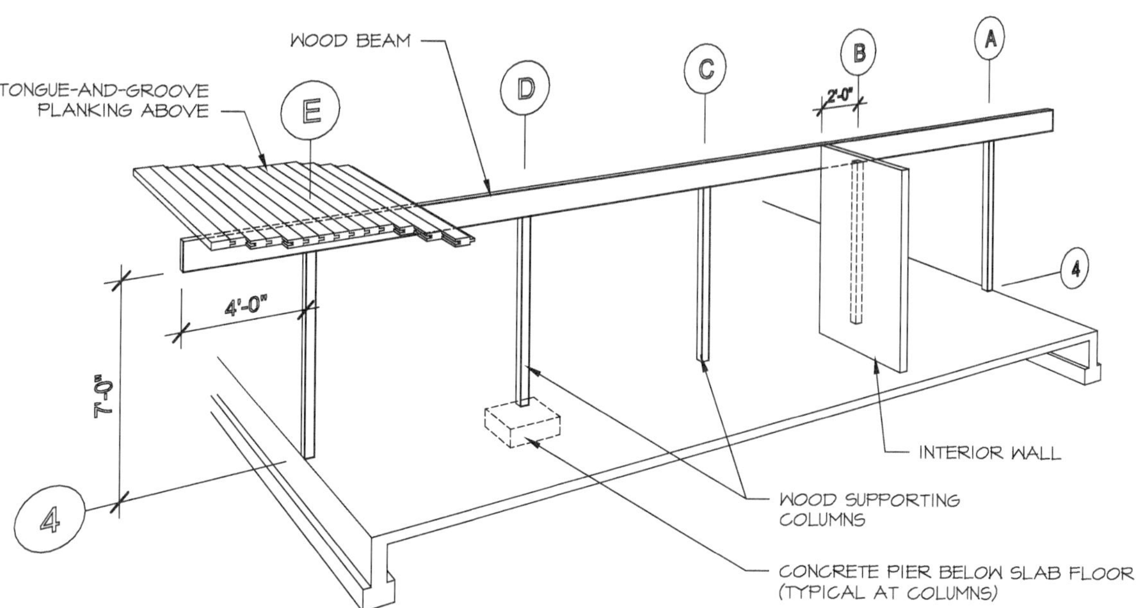

Figure 8.40 Pictorial view along matrix 4.

clearly explain and show the various conditions that exist for a specific building. Figure 8.43 depicts a building section cut in the north–south direction as referenced on the floor plan. The figure illustrates the dimensional heights for the ceiling and parapet and identifies the direction of the precast concrete cored roof panels. At the east and west outside walls, a corbel or haunch, which is formed in the precast wall panel, will be necessary to support the precast cored panels at the end wall conditions. See Figure 8.44. Similar requirements and drawings will be necessary for a project using a poured-in-place concrete construction method. These requirements will pertain to wall height dimensions, wall thickness, steel reinforcing, and any type of architectural feature.

The initial layout dimensionally illustrates the recommended floor-to-finished-ceiling height, while also showing the recommended dimensional space for the plenum area. Preliminary engineering calculations provide the approximate steel column and beam sizes necessary for development of the building sections.

Figure 8.47 is taken along matrix line ③, which is in the north–south direction looking eastward. Refer to the ground-level floor plan in Figure 8.45 for the building section designation symbol the elevation is also

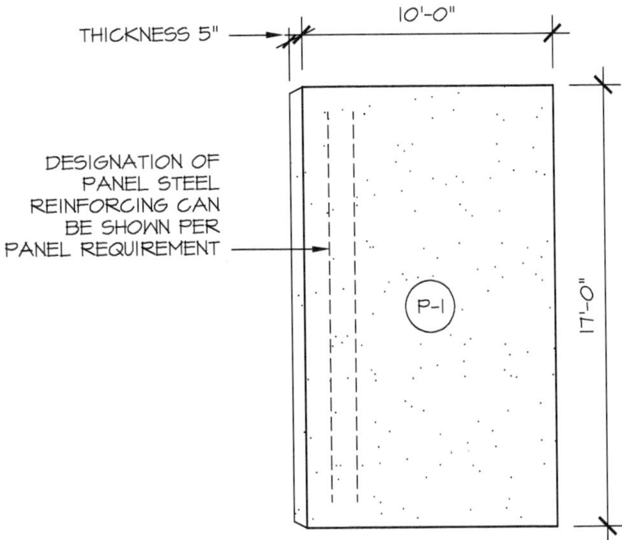

Figure 8.41 Precast concrete panel.

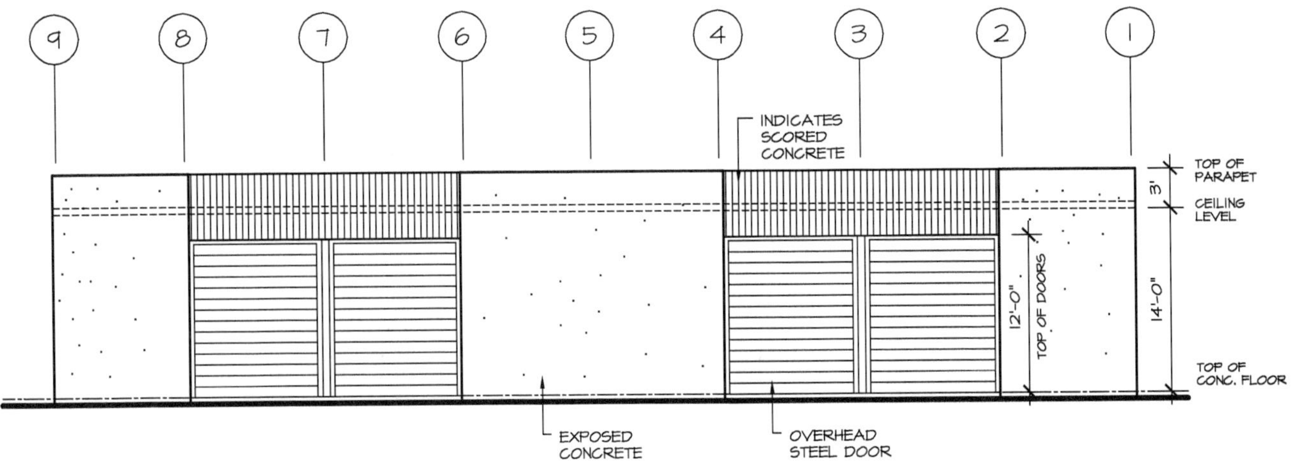

Figure 8.42 North elevation.

provide to aid with the visualization of the building. See Figure 8.46.

Here, the architect decided to use a composite floor and roof system utilizing corrugated steel decking and concrete fill as indicated on the building section. As shown in Figure 8.47, dimensions are provided for the heights of the concrete floor to the bottom of the second floor and the top of the second floor to the bottom of the roof beams. This may also be achieved with the use of vertical elevations relative to the ground-floor concrete slab elevation. A pictorial view of the building section is given in Figure 8.48.

Key Terms

building section
detail
plate
plate height
title

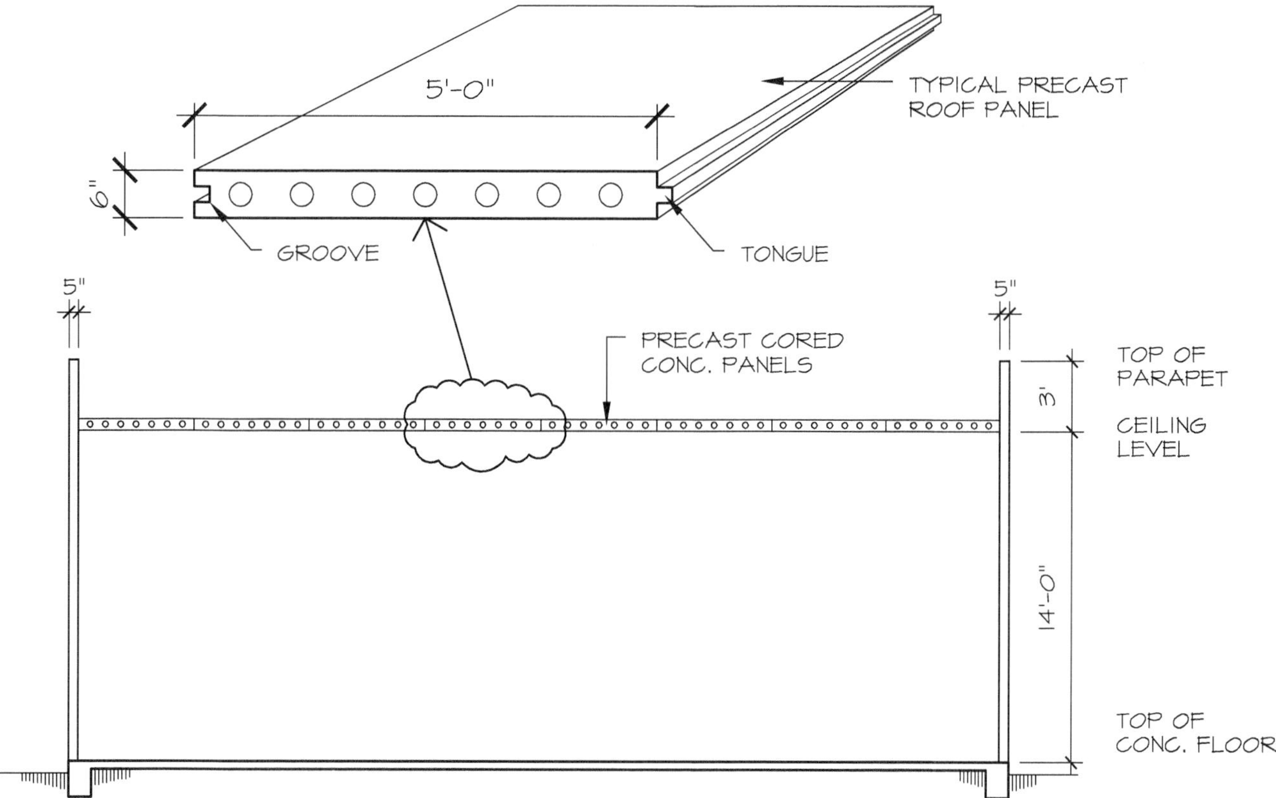

Figure 8.43 Building section on S-1.

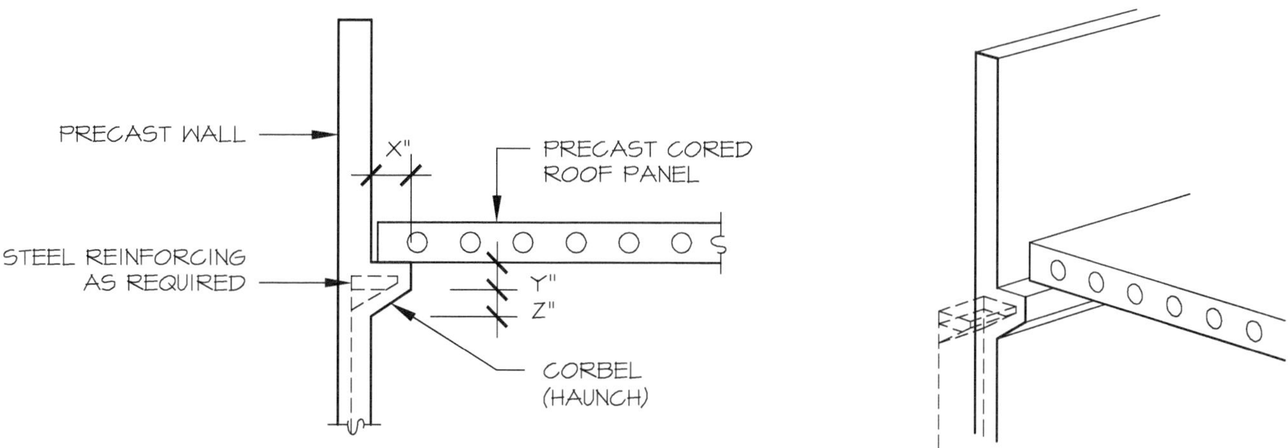

Figure 8.44 Wall corbel.

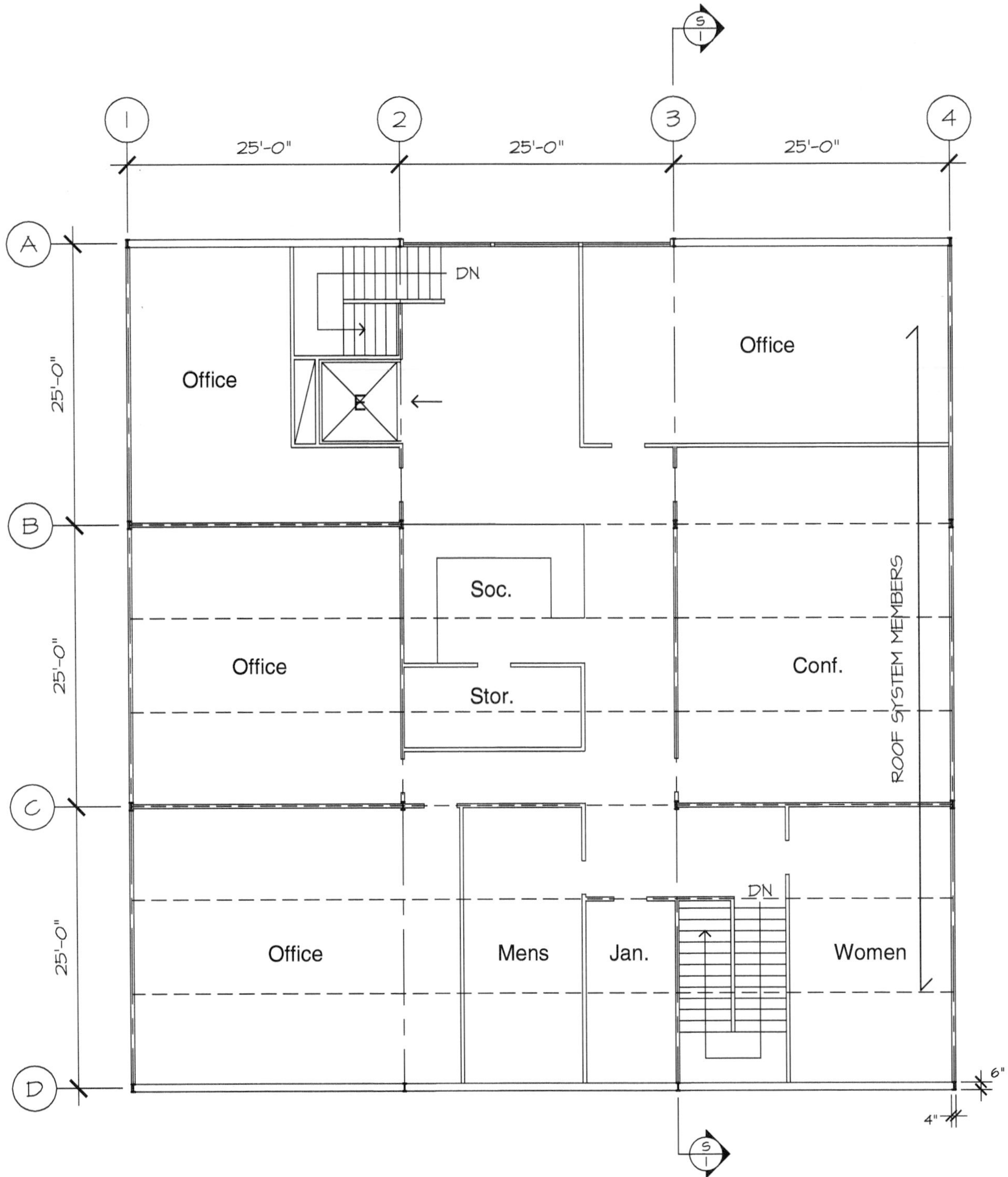

Figure 8.45 Second-level floor plan.

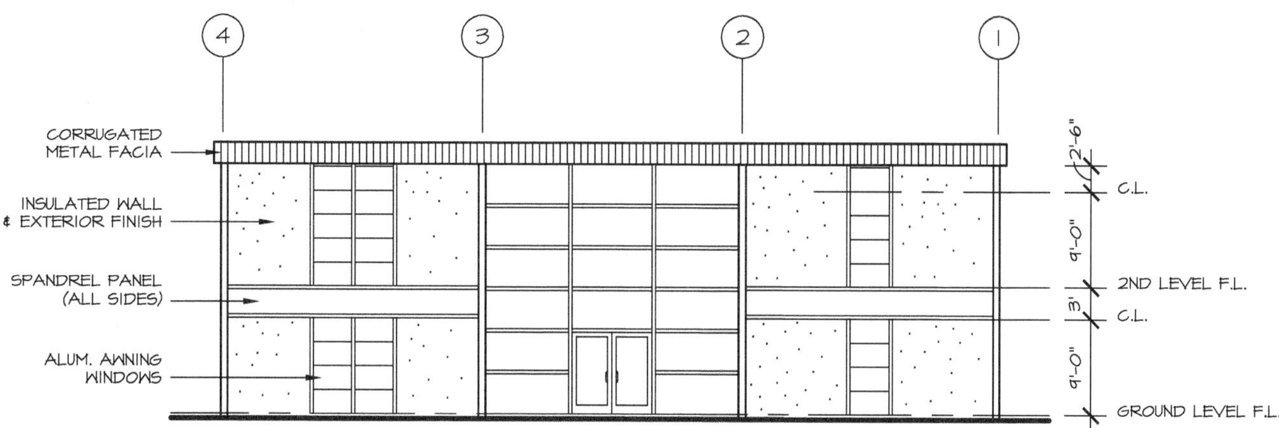

Figure 8.46 North elevation.

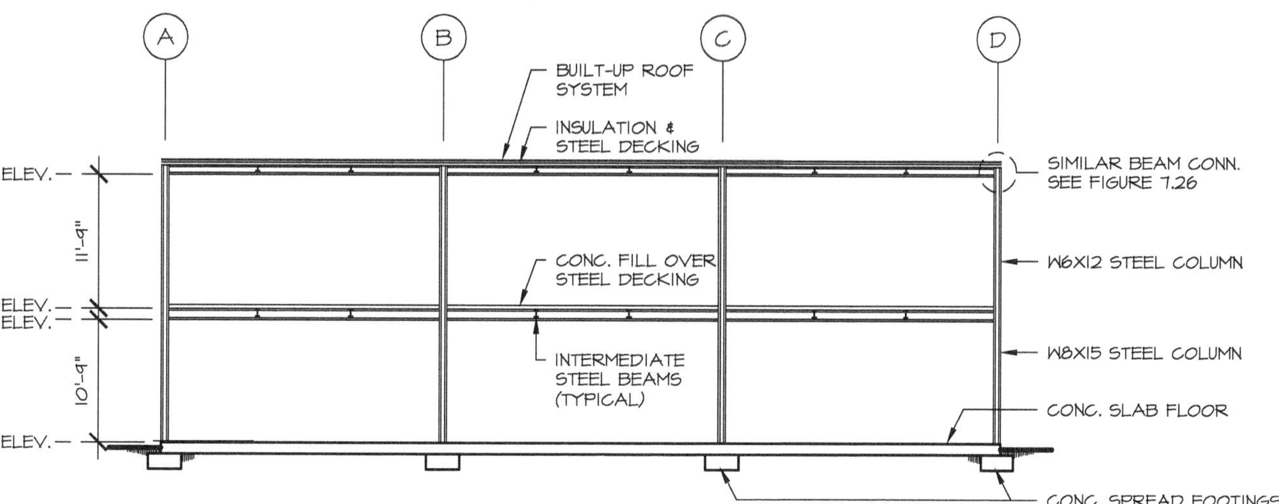

Figure 8.47 Building section.

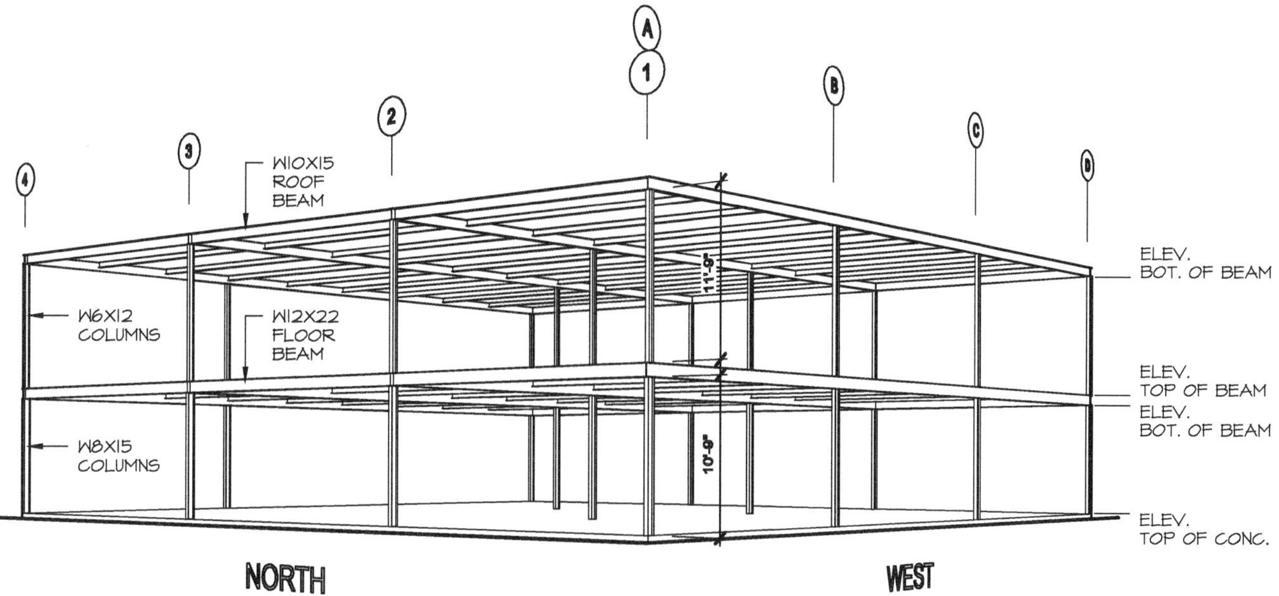

Figure 8.48 Steel frame building system.

chapter

9

EXTERIOR AND INTERIOR ELEVATIONS

The Professional Practice of Architectural Working Drawings, Sixth Edition. Nagy R. Bakhoum and Osamu A. Wakita.
© 2024 John Wiley & Sons Inc. Published 2024 by John Wiley & Sons Inc.
Companion website: www.wiley.com\go\bakhoum\theprofessionalpracticeofarchitecturalworkingdrawings

■ PURPOSE OF EXTERIOR ELEVATIONS

The main purpose of **exterior elevations** is to describe the outer skin, and often the subskin, of the structure and show vertical dimensions that do not appear on any other drawing specifically floor-to-floor measurements and/or floor-to-plate measurements and overall height.

Throughout this chapter, you will find examples of drawings done to meet this purpose. Hand drawing and computer applications will be described. Here is a simple list of what you should do—and what drawing users will expect to find—on an exterior elevation of a simple residence:

1. Describe exterior materials found on the structure.
2. Provide a location for horizontal and vertical dimensions not found elsewhere.
3. Show, by using hidden lines, structural members found inside the walls. (Diagonal bracing is a good example of such hidden members.)
4. Show the relationship of elements, such as the height of the chimney in relationship to the roof of the structure.
5. Incorporate reference bubbles for building, window, and door sections.
6. Show any exterior design elements that cannot be shown elsewhere.
7. Show stepped footings, if there are any.
8. Describe building finishes and colors.

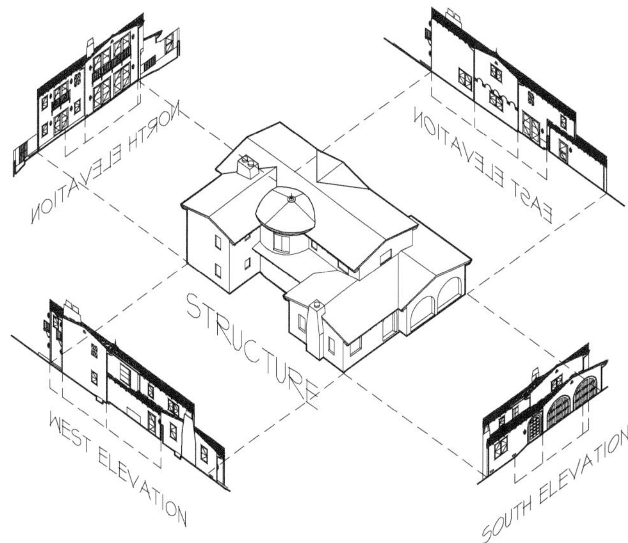

Figure 9.1 Multiview drawing of a structure.

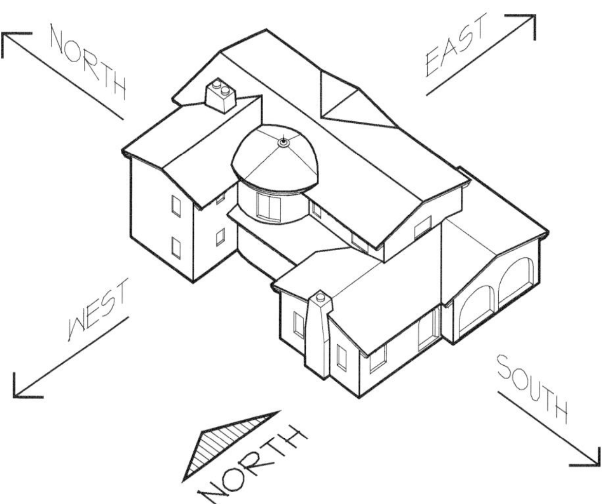

Figure 9.2 Names of elevations.

Basic Approach

In mechanical or engineering drafting, the elevations are described as the front, side, and rear. In architecture, exterior elevations are called *north*, *south*, *east*, and *west*. See Figure 9.1. Figure 9.2 shows how we arrive at the names for exterior elevations.

Orientation

The north, south, east, and west elevations may not be true directions (e.g., not true north or true east). They may have been taken from an "orientation north," or, as it has been called in other regions, *plan north*, which may not be parallel to true north. When the boundaries of a structure are not parallel with true north, an orientation north is established, and used from then on to describe the various elevations. See Figure 9.3.

These terms, then, refer to the direction the structure is facing. In other words, if an elevation is drawn of the face of a structure that is facing south, the elevation is called the *south elevation*; the face of the structure that is facing west is called the *west elevation*, and so on. Remember, the title refers to the direction the structure is facing, *not* to the direction in which you are looking at it.

Finally, because of the size of the exterior elevations, they are rarely drawn next to the plan view as in mechanical drafting. See Figure 9.4.

Method 1: Direct Projection. You can draft exterior elevations by directly projecting sizes from the plan views or sections. Figure 9.5 shows how elevations can be directly projected from a plan view (a roof

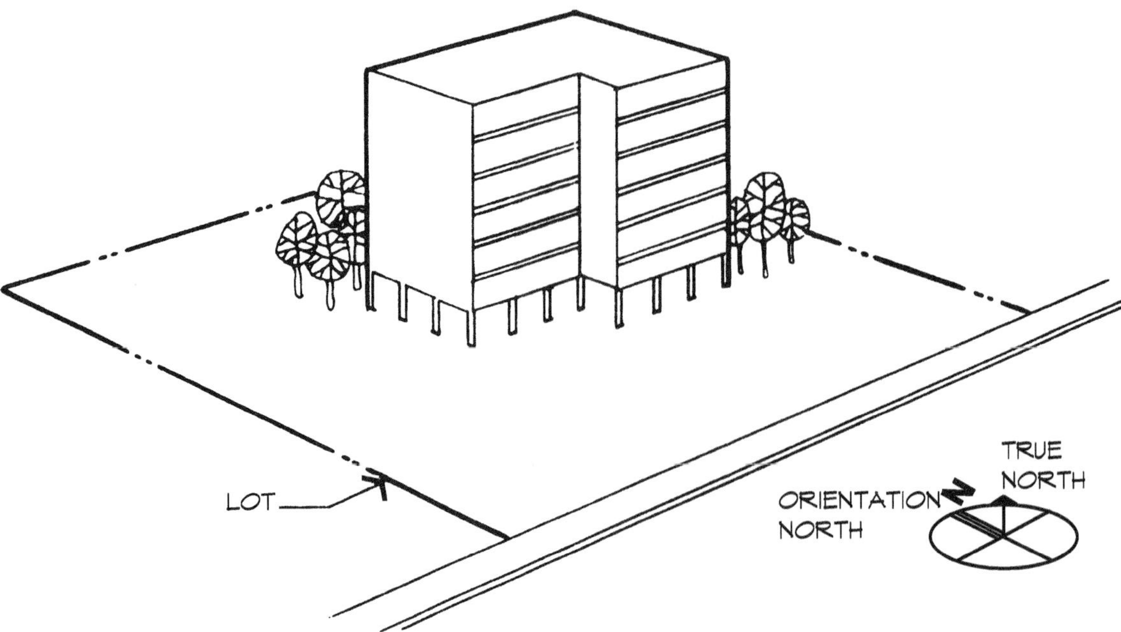

Figure 9.3 Use of orientation north.

Figure 9.4 Elevation arrangement.

plan, in this case). Figure 9.6 shows how the heights are obtained. Locations of doors, windows, and other details are taken from the floor plan. Figure 9.7 shows a slightly more complex roof being used to form the roof shape on an elevation.

Method 2: Dimensional Layout. You can also draft exterior elevations by taking the dimensions from the plans and sections and drafting the elevation(s) from scratch. First, lightly lay out the critical vertical measurements. In the example shown in Figure 9.8, these

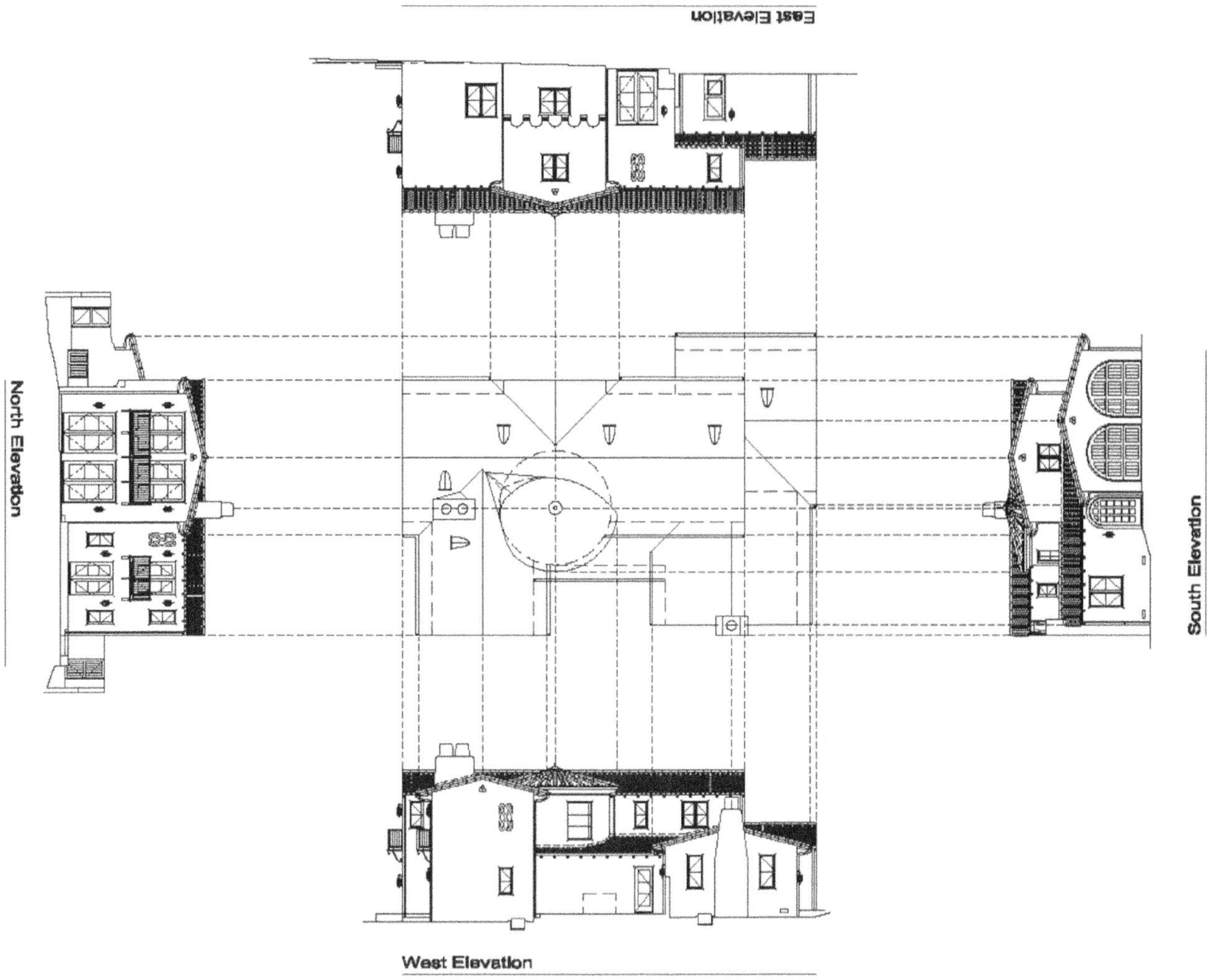

East Elevation
North Elevation
South Elevation
West Elevation

Figure 9.5 Obtaining width and depth dimensions.

West Elevation
Wall Section
Wall Section

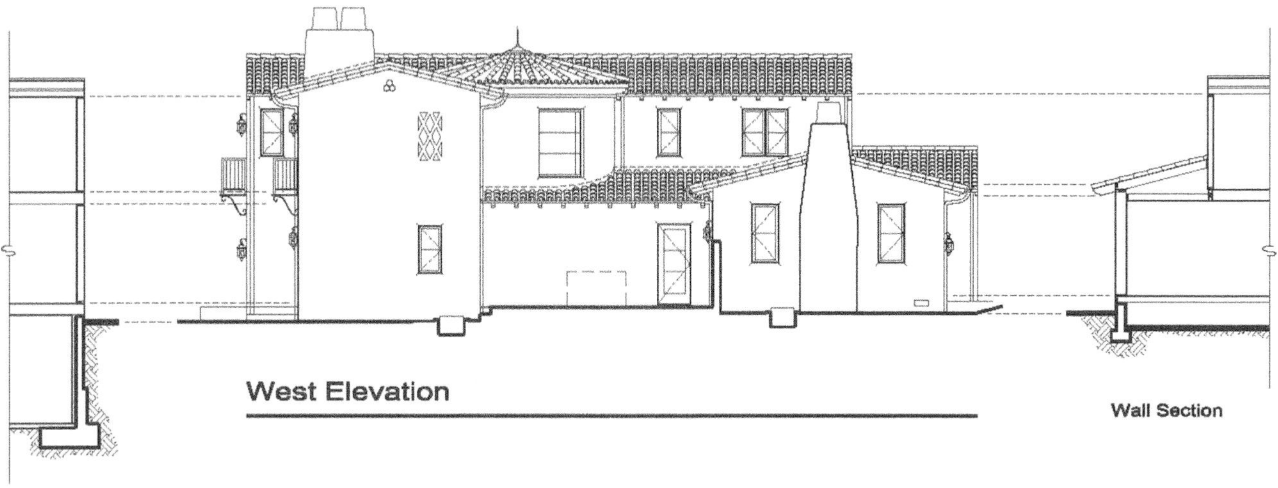

Figure 9.6 Heights from wall sections.

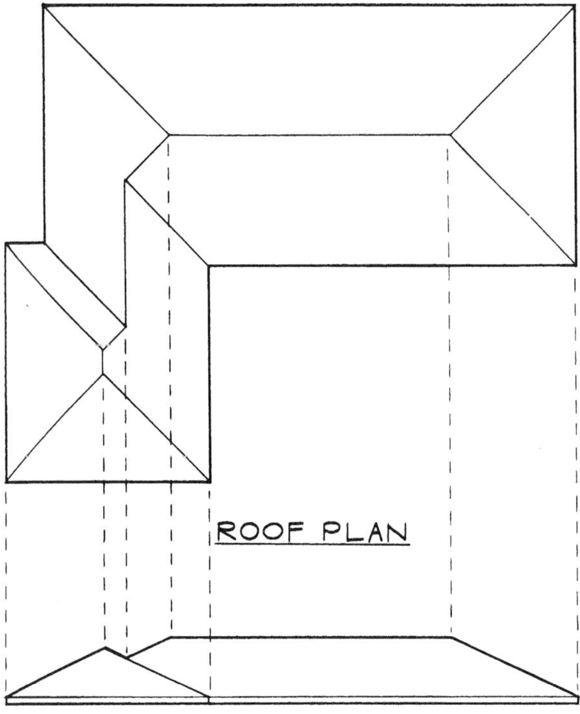

Figure 9.7 Roof elevation from roof plan.

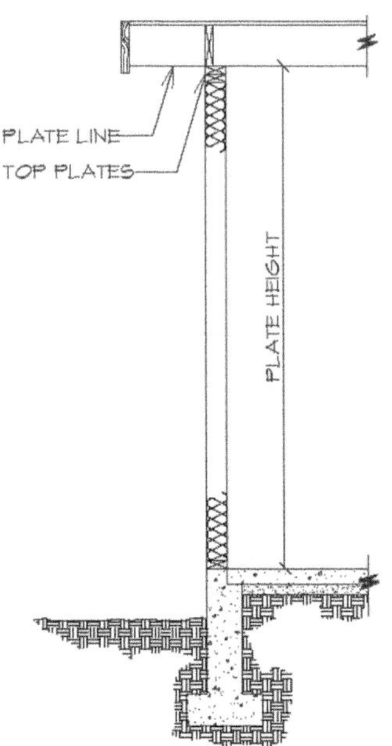

Figure 9.8 Establish plate height.

measurements are the *subfloor* (top of plywood or concrete) line and the *plate line* (top of the two top plates above the studs). See Figure 9.9A. This measurement is taken directly from the building section.

The second step establishes the location of the walls and offsets in the structure from the floor plan. Draw these lines lightly, because changes in line length may be required later. See Figure 9.9B.

Third, establish the grade line (earth) in relationship to the floor line. See Figure 9.9C. This dimension is from the building sections or footing sections.

Next, as Figure 9.9D shows, add the roof configuration. To better understand the relationship between the roof and the rest of the structure, draw the **eave** (portion of a roof that extends beyond the wall) in a simple form, as shown in Figure 9.9E. These dimensions are found on the building section. The finished roof shape depends on the roof framing plan or the roof plan for dimensions. See Figure 9.9F.

Finally, windows and doors are located. Sizes are found on the window and door schedule, and locations on the floor plan. Material designations, dimensions, notes, and structural descriptions complete the elevation. See Figure 9.9G.

Figure 9.10 shows a typical example of an exterior elevation. Go back to the beginning of the chapter and compare Figure 9.10 with the simple list of elements.

Choice of Scale

Selection of the scale for elevations is based on the size and complexity of the project and the available drawing space. For small structures, 1⁄4″ = 1′–0″ is a common scale. For a larger project, a smaller scale can be used. The exterior elevation is usually drawn at the same scale as the floor plan. For medium and large elevations, you may have to decrease the scale in relationship to the floor plans.

Because we are dealing with small structures, two to four stories in height, we are using the largest scale allowed by the available drawing space not exceeding 1⁄4″ = 1′–0″.

Odd-Shaped Plans

Not all plans are rectangular; some have irregular shapes and angles. Figure 9.11 shows several building shapes and the north designation. For these kinds of conditions, all elevations are drawn.

Shape A. Figure 9.12 shows the exterior elevations for a relatively simple L-shaped building and how these elevations were obtained using the projection method.

Shape B. The elevations for Shape B in Figure 9.13 present a unique problem on the east and particularly the south elevation. Because the fence is in the same plane as the south side of the structure, include it in the south elevation. Had the fence been in front of the structure,

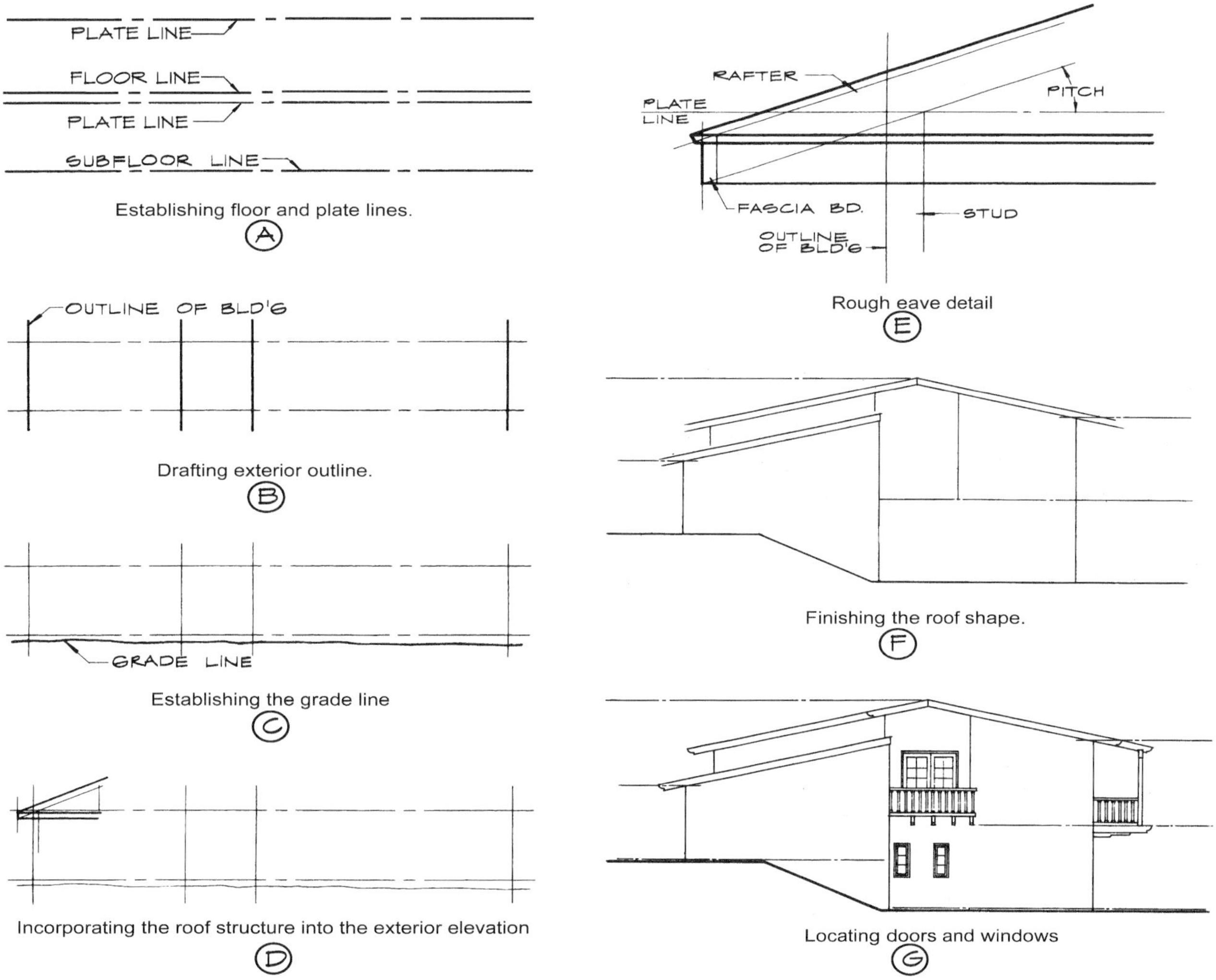

PLATE LINE
FLOOR LINE
PLATE LINE
SUBFLOOR LINE
Establishing floor and plate lines.
A
OUTLINE OF BLD'G
Drafting exterior outline.
B
GRADE LINE
Establishing the grade line
C
Incorporating the roof structure into the exterior elevation
D
RAFTER
PITCH
PLATE LINE
FASCIA BD.
STUD
OUTLINE OF BLD'G
Rough eave detail
E
Finishing the roof shape.
F
Locating doors and windows
G

Figure 9.9 Using a visual and written checklist.

EXTERIOR PLASTER OVER BRICK
12
2½
4
30
MISSION TILE ROOFING
EXTERIOR PLASTER
TOP PLATE
EXTERIOR PLASTER
TOP PLATE
5
30
3'-0"
TYP.
1X6 LET-IN DIAGONAL BRACING
COMMON PARTY WALL WITH UNIT "B"
3'-0"
6'-8"
3'-0"
SEE CROSS SECTION
BALUSTRADE/BALCONY SEE DET.
8
30
6'-8"
DIAGONAL BRACING
SEE CROSS-SECTION
EAST ELEVATION
SCALE: 1/4"=1'-0"

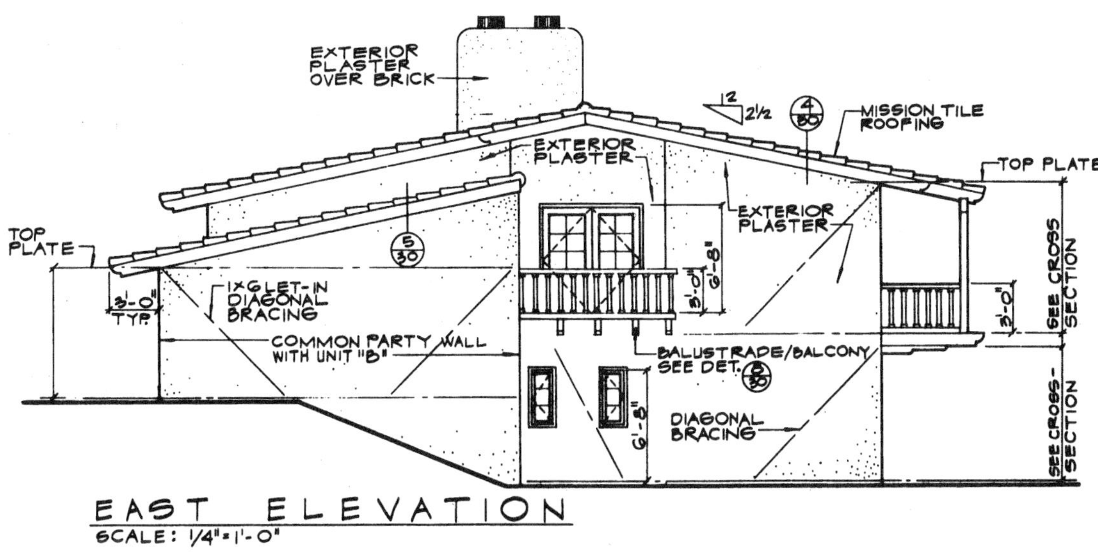

Figure 9.10 Drafted east elevation of a condominium.

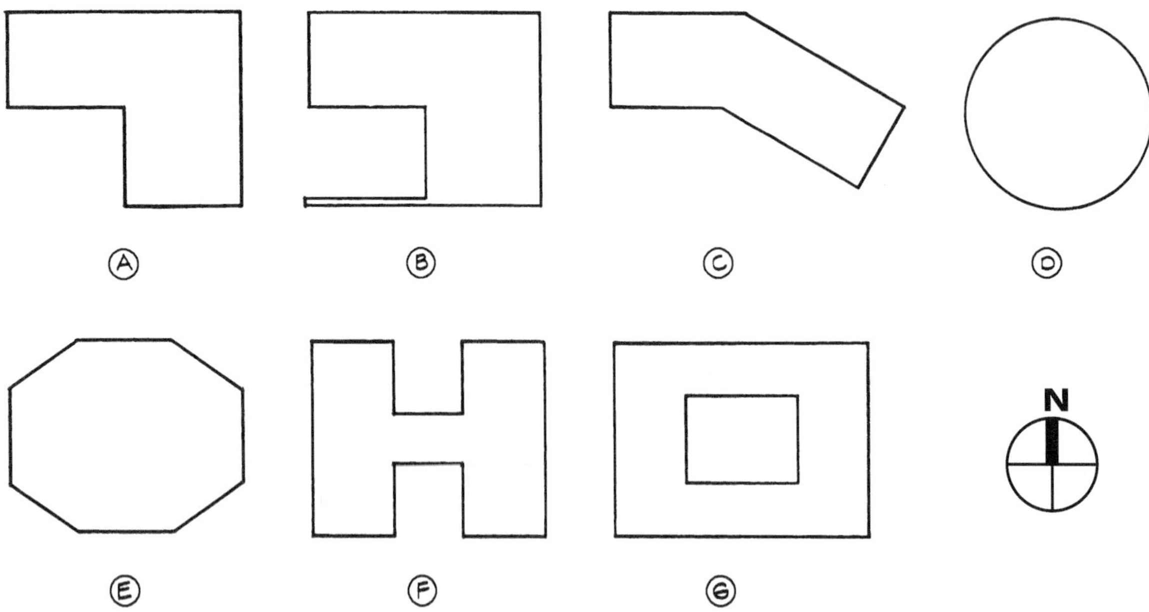

Figure 9.11 Irregularly shaped plans.

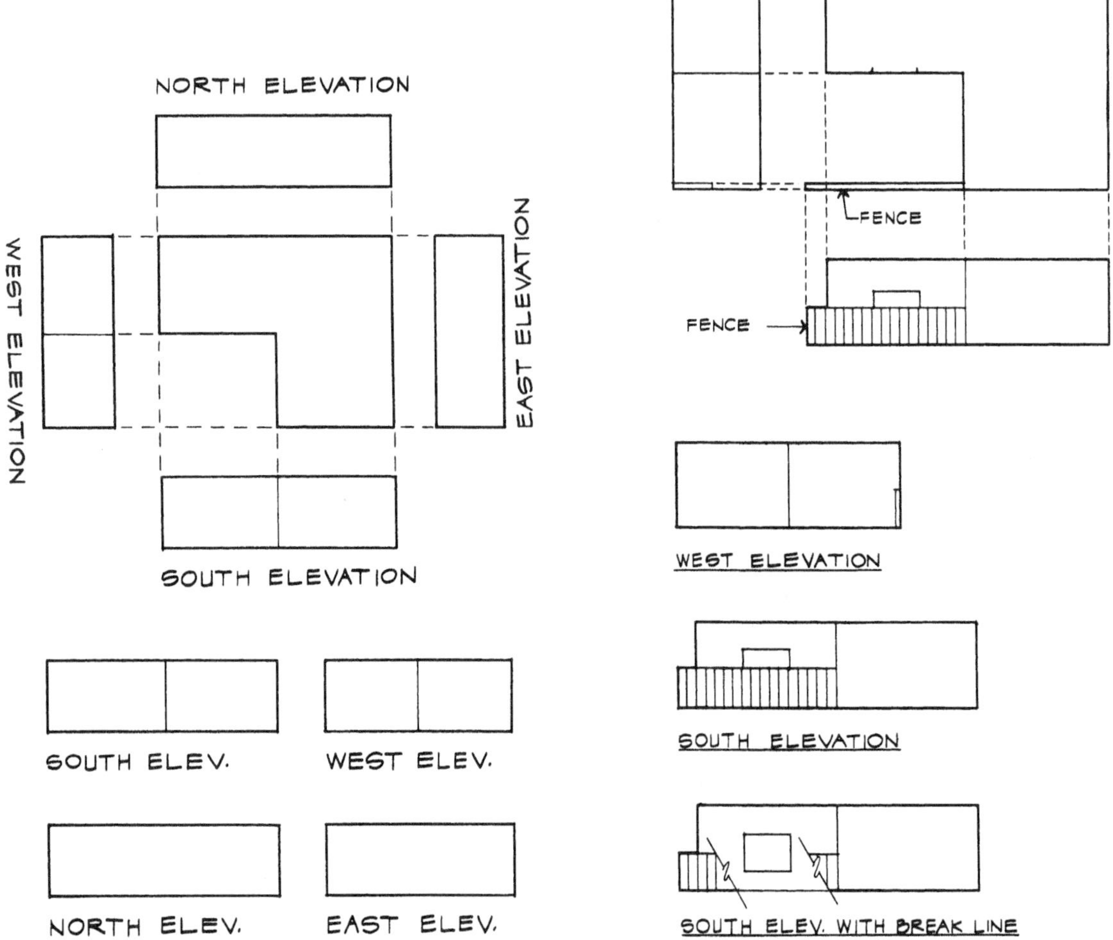

Figure 9.12 Elevations for Shape A.

Figure 9.13 Elevations for Shape B.

you could either delete it or include it in order to show its relationship to the structure itself.

The inclusion of the fence may pose additional problems, such as preventing a view of portions of the structure behind. You can overcome this difficulty in one of two ways: either eliminate the fence altogether (not show it) or use a break line, as shown in Figure 9.13. This allows any item behind it, such as the window, to be exposed, referenced, and dimensioned. Break lines still allow dimensioning and descriptions of the fence.

Shape C. The two portions on the right of the south elevation and all of the east elevation are *not* true shapes and sizes because they are drawn as direct 90° projections from the *left* portion of the plan view. This is sometimes a problem. See Figure 9.14. The west and north elevations will also be distorted. See Figure 9.11.

To solve this problem, we use an *auxiliary view*: a view that is 90° to the line of sight. The elevations are projected 90° to the sight lines, and a break line is used to stop the portion that is not true. Notice on Figure 9.15 how the break line splits the south elevation into two parts. Each part is projected independently of the other, and its continuation, which is not a true shape, is voided.

The south elevation in Figure 9.14 appears to have three parts rather than two, as in Figure 9.15. In the latter case, the third part will be left to the east elevation. With a more complex shape, a break line beyond the true surface being projected can be confusing. See Figure 9.16. To avoid confusion, introduce a *pivot point* (PP) (the point at which the end of one elevation becomes the beginning of another elevation), and show it as a dotted (hidden) line or a centerline-type line (dots and dashes). See Figure 9.17.

PP can cause a problem in selecting a title for a particular elevation. To avoid confusion, introduce a **key plan**. The key plan is usually drawn on the bottom right corner of the drawing sheet. See Figure 9.18.

Draw and label a reference bubble for every necessary elevation. These reference bubbles will become the titles for the elevations. If the surface contains important information about the structure or surface materials, it deserves a reference bubble. Figure 9.19 shows how these elevations are represented with titles and pivot-point notations.

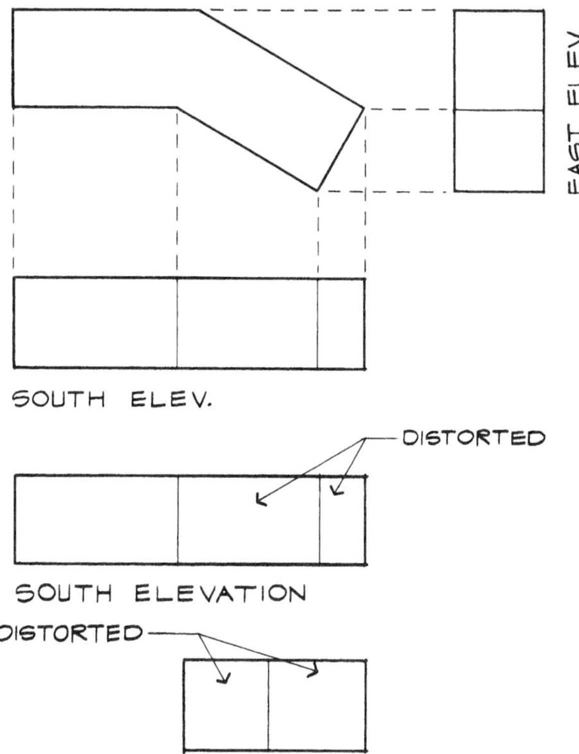

Figure 9.14 Elevations for Shape C.

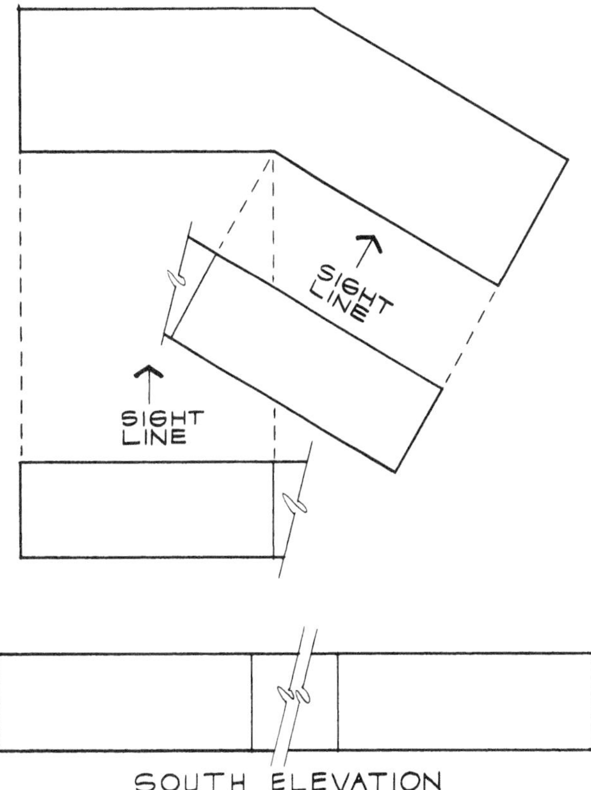

Figure 9.15 Elevations with new sight line.

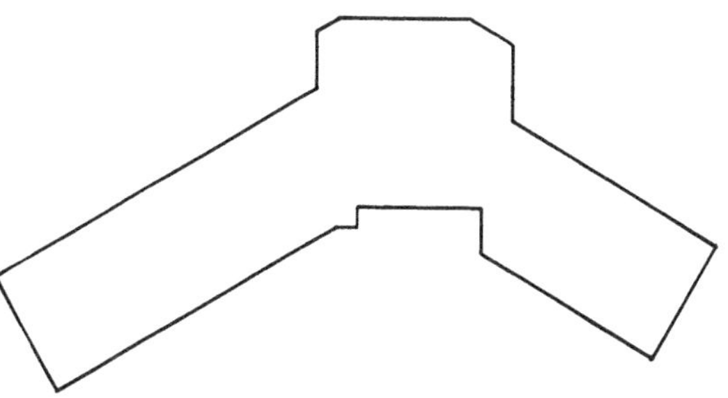

Figure 9.16 Complicated shape.

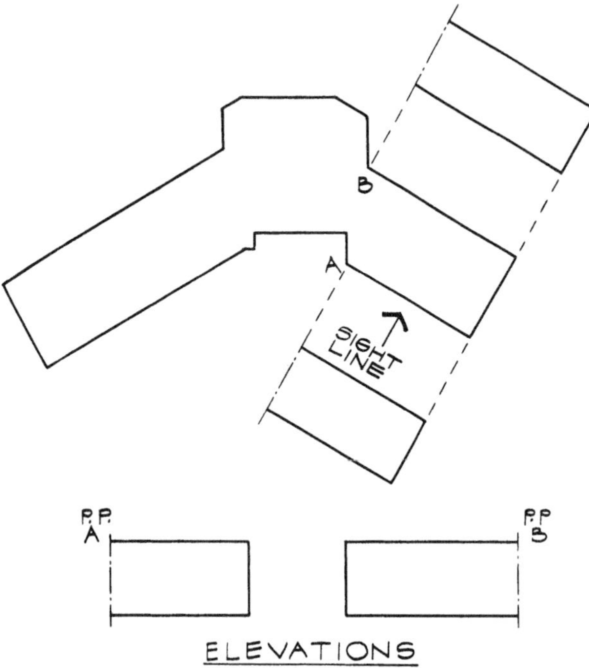

Figure 9.17 Use of pivot point in exterior elevations.

Shape D. With shape D from Figure 9.11, nothing is true shape or size, regardless of the direction of the elevation. See Figure 9.20. Figure 9.21 shows a PP together with a **fold-out** (called a **development drawing** in mechanical drawing).

Shape E. Shape E in Figure 9.11 can be drawn in one of three ways: first, by drawing it as a direct projection so that one of the three exposed faces will be in true shape and size; second, by using a key plan and drawing each surface individually; and third, by drawing it as a fold-out similar to Figure 9.21. Choose the method that will best explain the elevations. For example, if all other sides are the same, the direct-projection method may be the best. If every wall surface is different, then the key plan or fold-out method would be best.

Shape F. Surfaces that will be hidden in a direct projection, such as some of the surfaces of shape F in Figure 9.11, can effectively be dealt with in one of two ways. The first uses a key plan and the second uses a combination of an elevation and a section. Both methods are shown in Figure 9.22.

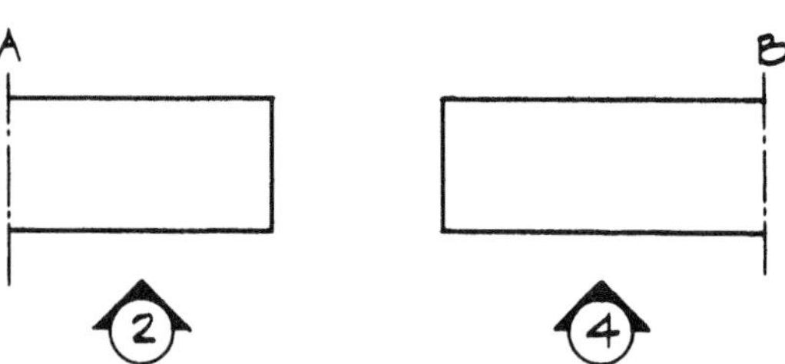

Figure 9.19 Elevations using key plan.

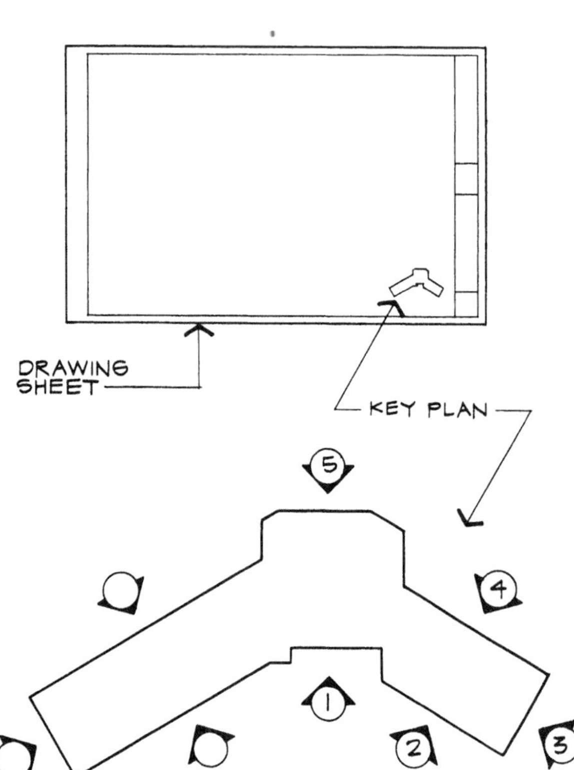

Figure 9.18 Using a key plan.

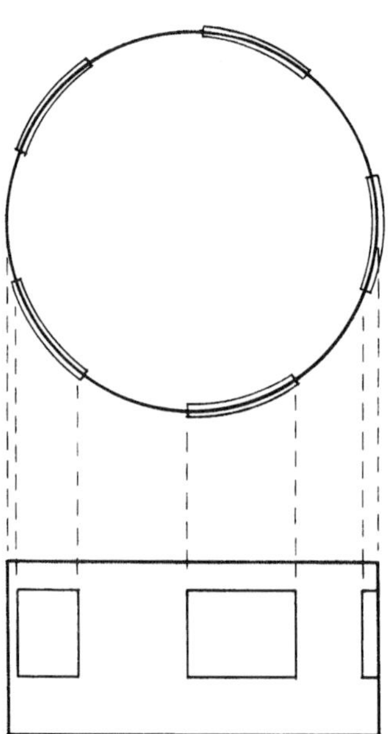

Figure 9.20 Elevations of a cylinder.

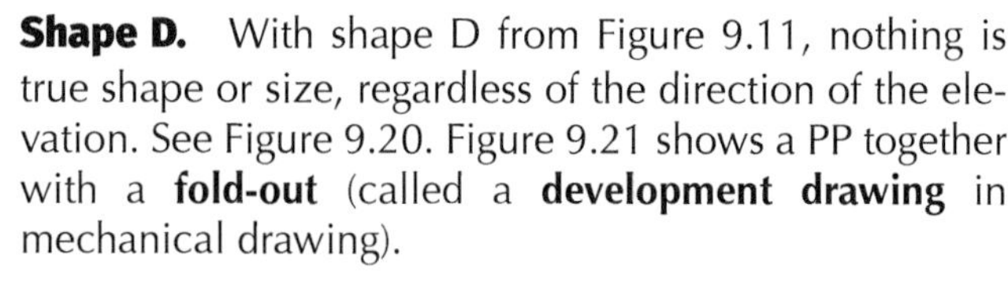

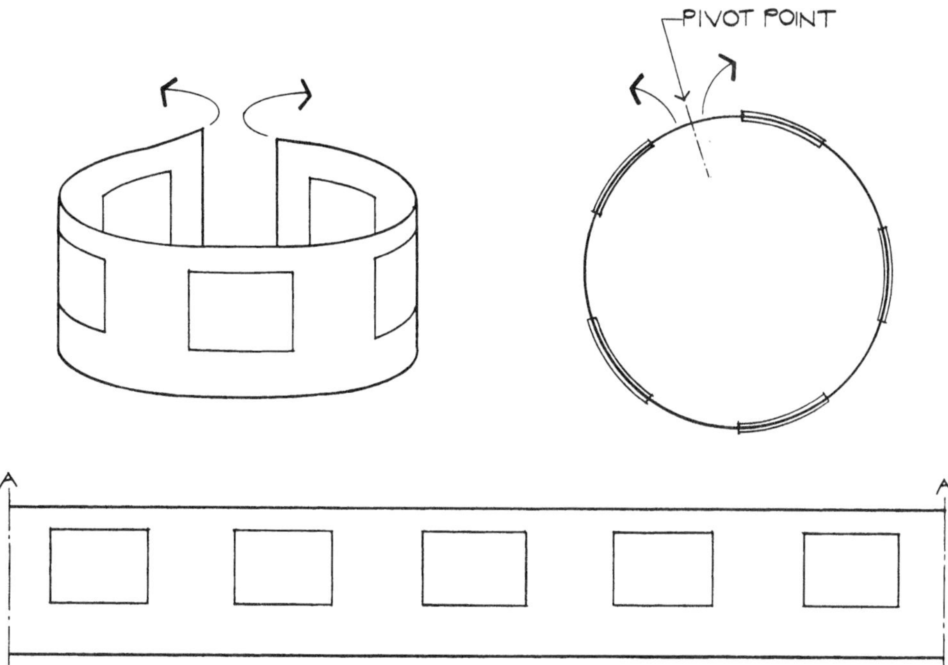

Figure 9.21 Elevation of cylinder using pivot point.

The combination of the section and the elevation shows the structure and its relationship to the elevation more clearly.

Shape G. Shape G in Figure 9.11 can be drawn simply as the south elevation, north elevation, east elevation, and west elevation using a direct-projection method. The interior space (atrium) can also be drawn as a direct projection with titles "Atrium North Elevation," "Atrium South Elevation," "Atrium East Elevation," and "Atrium West Elevation." A way to simplify this is shown in Figure 9.23.

Drawing Doors and Windows. Draw doors and windows on elevations as close as possible to the actual configuration. Horizontal location dimensions need not be included, because they are on the floor plan; likewise, door and window sizes are contained in the door and window schedule. However, vertical location dimensions are shown with indications of how the doors and windows open.

Doors. Doors and their surface materials can be delineated in various ways. Illustrations A and B in Figure 9.24 show the basic appearance of a door with and without surface materials—wood grain, in this instance. Illustration C shows the final configuration of a dimensioned door. Note that the 6′–8″ dimension is measured from the floor line to the top of the floor. The other line around the door represents the trim. For precise dimensions for the trim, consult the door details. Illustrations D and E of Figure 9.24 show how a door opens or slides. Panel doors are shown in illustration F, and *plant-on doors* (doors with decorative pieces attached) are shown in illustration G.

Windows. Windows are drafted much like doors. Their shape, their operation, and the direction in which they open are represented. Double-hung windows and louver windows are obvious exceptions because of their operation. See Figure 9.25.

On double-hung and sliding windows, one portion of the window is shown in its entirety, whereas the moving section shows only three sides of the window. Using the sliding window in Figure 9.25 as an example, the right side of the window shows all four sides because it is on the outside. The left section shows only three sides, because the fourth side is behind the right section.

Fixed Windows. If the window is *fixed* (non-opening), as shown in Figure 9.26, you must know whether the window is to be shop made (manufactured ahead of time) or constructed on the job. If the frame can be ordered—in aluminum, for example—treat it like other manufactured windows and include it in the window schedule. If the window is to be job made (made on the site), provide all the necessary information about the window on the window schedule or exterior elevations, as shown in Figure 9.27. However, keep all this information in one place for consistency and uniformity.

Referencing Doors and Windows. Reference doors and windows with bubbles. Bubbles can refer to details or to a schedule for size. See Figure 9.27. If, for some reason, there are no schedules or details for a set of drawings, all information pertaining to the windows or doors will be on the exterior elevations near or on the windows and doors or on the floor plan at the door or window location. See Figure 9.26.

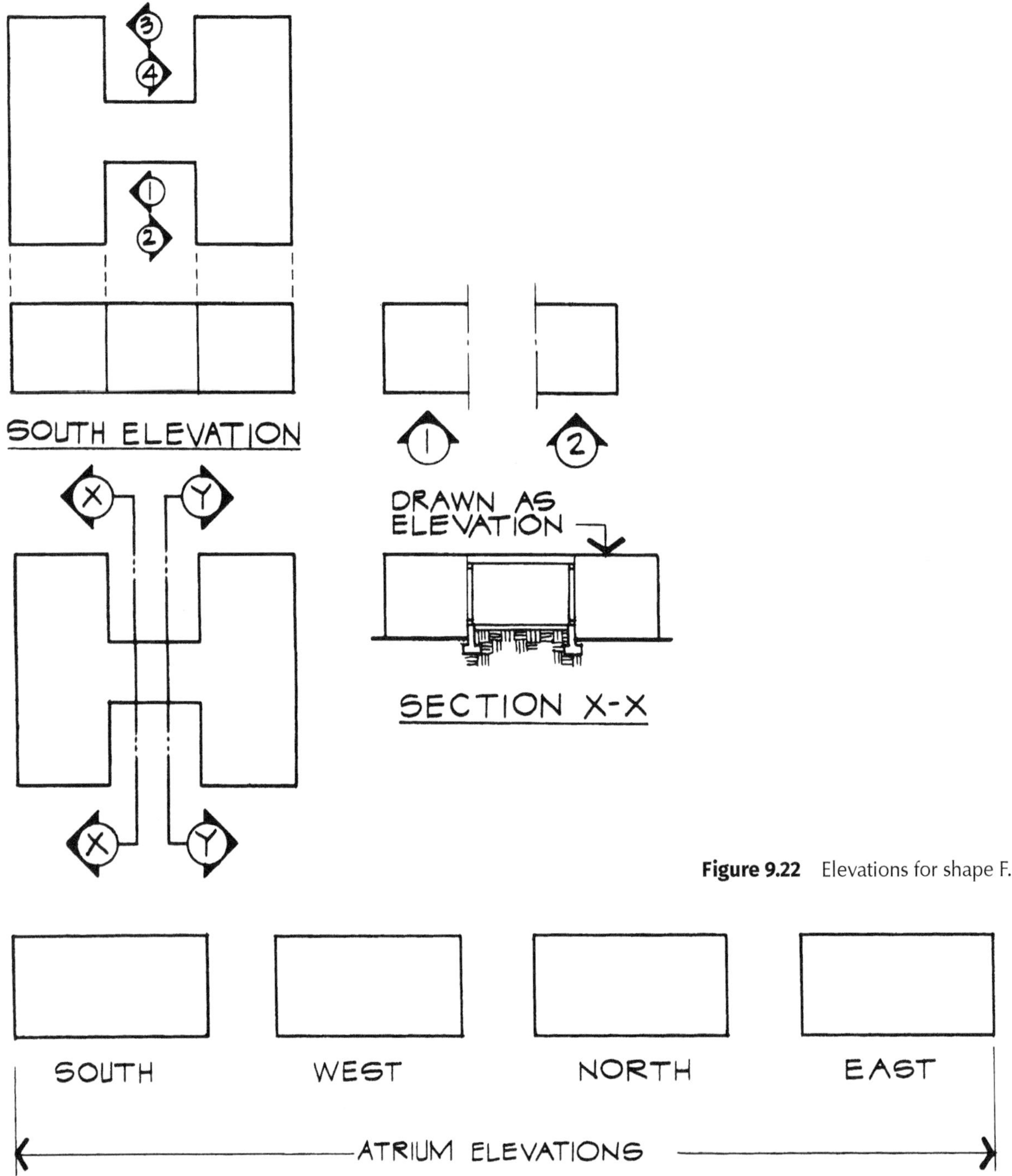

Figure 9.22 Elevations for shape F.

Figure 9.23 Simplified elevation titles.

■ MATERIAL DESIGNATIONS

Describing the Materials

The exterior elevations also describe the exterior wall surface material. For a wood structure, describe both the surface covering and any backing material. Wood siding, for example, is described with the backing behind it. See Figure 9.28.

In some cases, one word, such as stucco, describes the surface adequately unless a special pattern is to be applied. Here, the drafter assumes that the contractor understands that the word **stucco** implies building paper (black waterproof paper), mesh (hexagonal woven wire), and three coats of exterior plaster. Often, a more detailed description of the material is found in the specifications. The "stucco" finish, for example, might be described as "20/30 steel trowel sand."

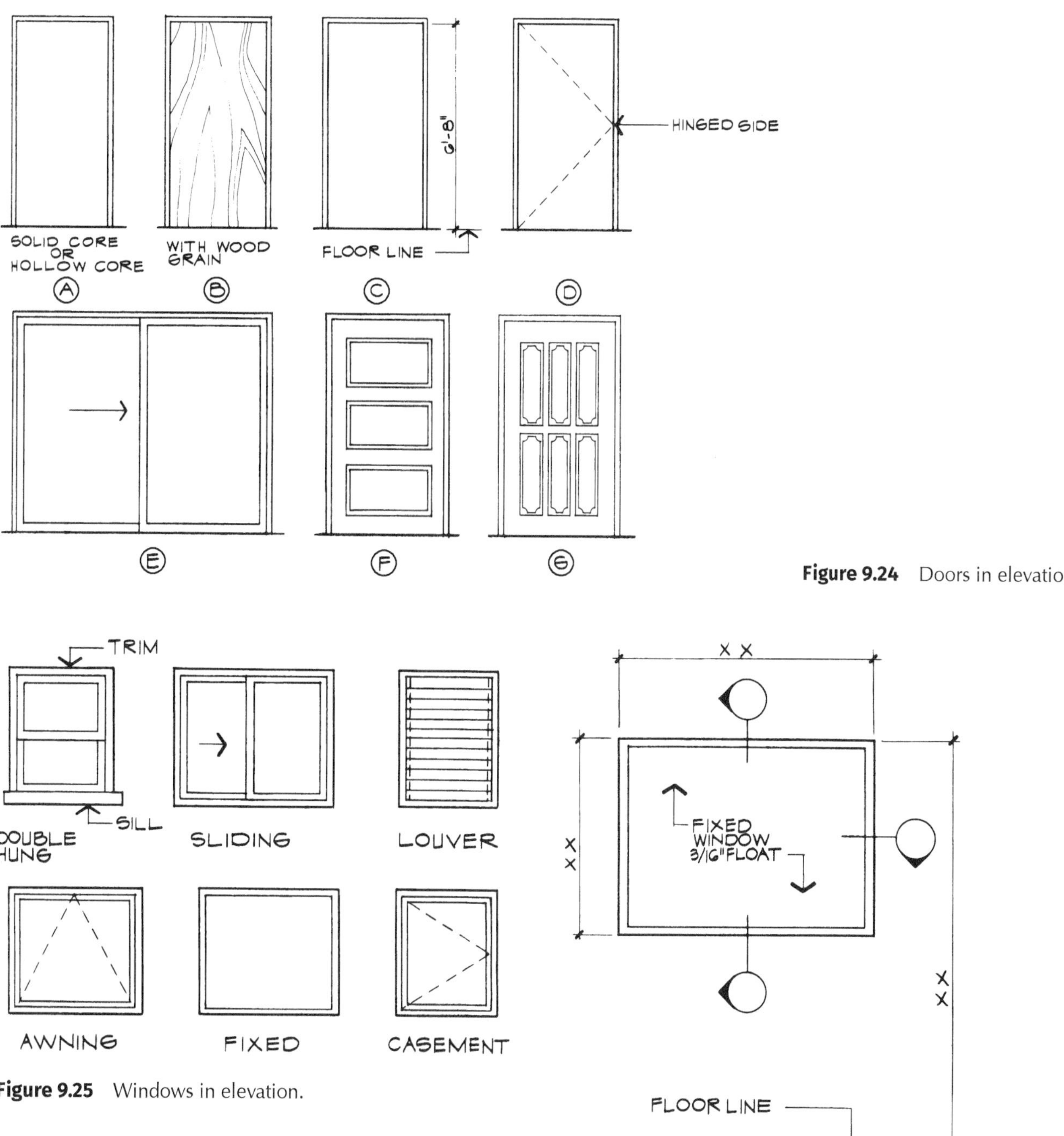

Figure 9.24 Doors in elevation.

Figure 9.25 Windows in elevation.

Figure 9.26 A fixed window.

Even if the complete wall is made up of one material, such as concrete block (as opposed to a built-up system as in wood construction), describe the surface. See Figure 9.29.

Drawing the Materials

A facsimile of the material is shown in both Figures 9.28 and 9.29. The material representation does not fill the complete area but is shown in detail around the perimeter only, which saves production time. Figure 9.30 shows more of the area covered with the surface material, but in a slightly more abstract manner. Another method is to draft the surface accurately and erase areas for notes.

Figure 9.31 shows other materials as they might appear in an exterior elevation. These are only suggestions. Scale and office practice dictate the final technique. See Figure 9.32.

Eliminating Unnecessary Information

Because exterior elevations are vital in the construction document process, unnecessary information should be

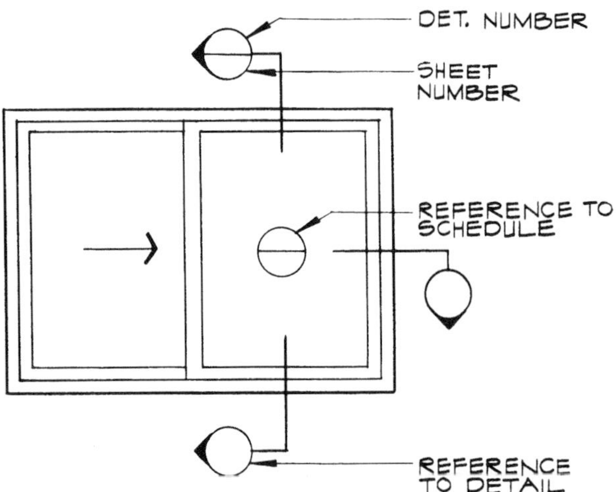

Figure 9.27 Wood window details.

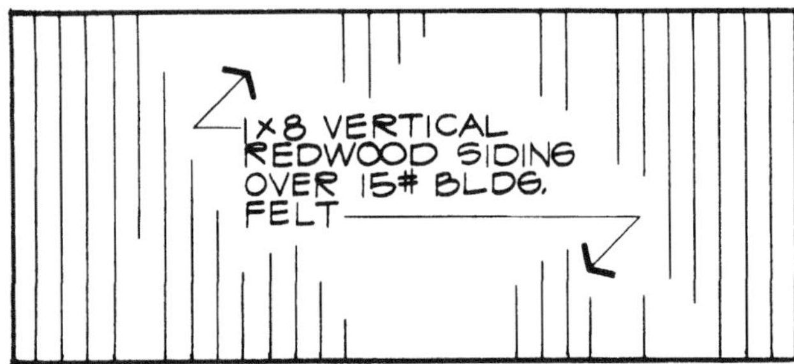

Figure 9.28 Wood siding in elevation.

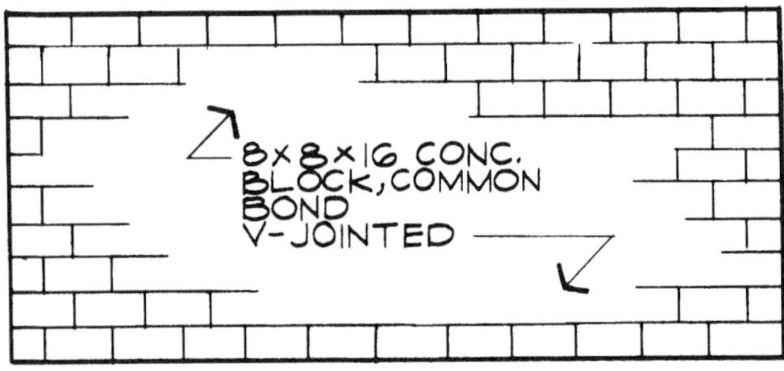

Figure 9.29 Concrete block in elevation.

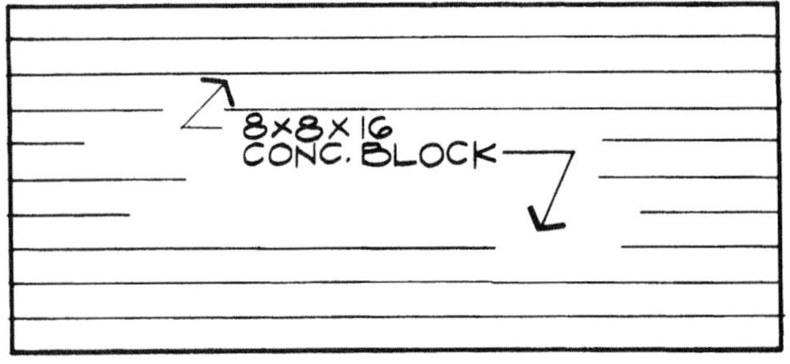

Figure 9.30 Abbreviated concrete-block pattern.

eliminated. Shades and shadows, cars, bushes and trees, people, and flowers add to the look of the drawings but serve no purpose here. These components are utilized for presentation elevations, client documents, city preliminary revisions, or landscape plans. If AutoCAD or Revit is used, layers can be voided to accomplish this.

Notes

Order of Notes. Notes on elevations follow the same rules as notes on other drawings. The size of the object is first, then the name of the material, and then any additional information about spacing, quantity, finish, or methods of installation. For example,

1×8 redwood siding, rough sawn over 15# (15lb)
building felt
or
Cement plaster over concrete block, smooth finish
or
Built-up composition gravel roof
or
1×6, let-in bracing

In the second example, no specific sizes are needed, so the generic name comes first in the note.

Noting Practices. Noting practices vary from job to job. A set of written specifications is often provided with the construction documents. Wall material on a set of elevations may be described in broad, generic terms, such as "concrete block," when the specific size, finish, stacking procedure, and type of joint are covered in the specifications.

If there are differences between the construction documents and the specifications, the specifications have priority (the specs control). In the construction documents, often the same material note can be found more than once. If an error is made or a change is desired, many notes must be revised. In the specifications, where material notes are mentioned once, only a single change has to be made.

There are exceptions. When there are complicated changes and variations of material and patterns on an elevation, it is difficult to describe them in the specifications. In this case, the information should be located on the exterior elevations. See Figure 9.32.

Hidden Lines (Dotted Lines)

Doors and Windows. Hidden lines (dotted lines) are used on doors and windows to show how they operate. See illustration D of Figure 9.24 and the awning and casement windows in Figure 9.25. These dotted lines show which part of the door or window is hinged. See Figure 9.33. Not all offices like to show this on an elevation. One reason is showing door swings using hidden

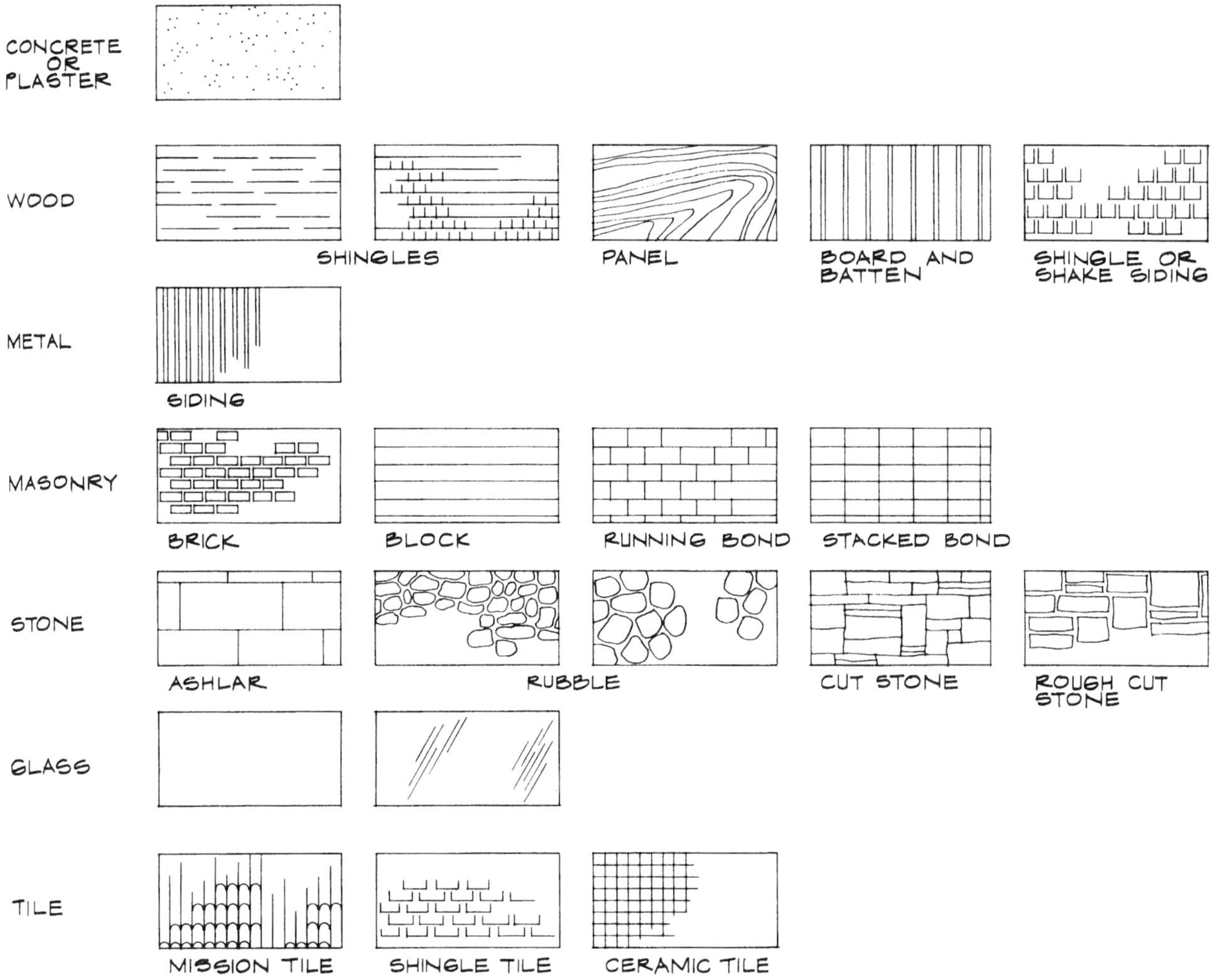

CONCRETE OR PLASTER
WOOD
SHINGLES
PANEL
BOARD AND BATTEN
SHINGLE OR SHAKE SIDING
METAL
SIDING
MASONRY
BRICK
BLOCK
RUNNING BOND
STACKED BOND
STONE
ASHLAR
RUBBLE
CUT STONE
ROUGH CUT STONE
GLASS
TILE
MISSION TILE
SHINGLE TILE
CERAMIC TILE

Figure 9.31 Material designations.

FLUTED CEMENT
EXTERIOR PLASTER
6X24 SCORED BLK. IN STACK BOND
6X12 CONC. BLK.
6X12 CONC. BLK.
4" RADIUS BLK.
4'-0" RADIUS BLOCK
6X24 CONC. BLK. IN RUNNING BOND
4" RAD. BLK.
ELEVATION

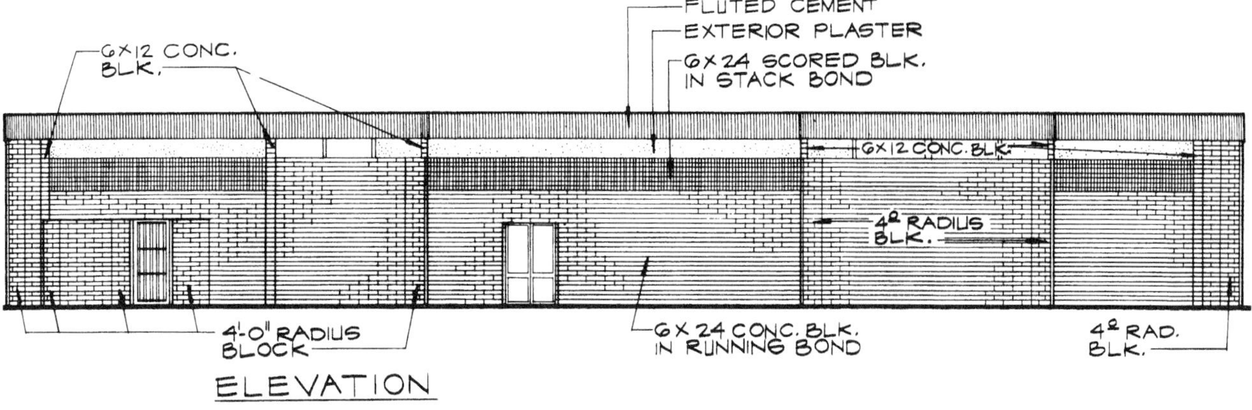

Figure 9.32 Masonry structure with variations in building patterns.

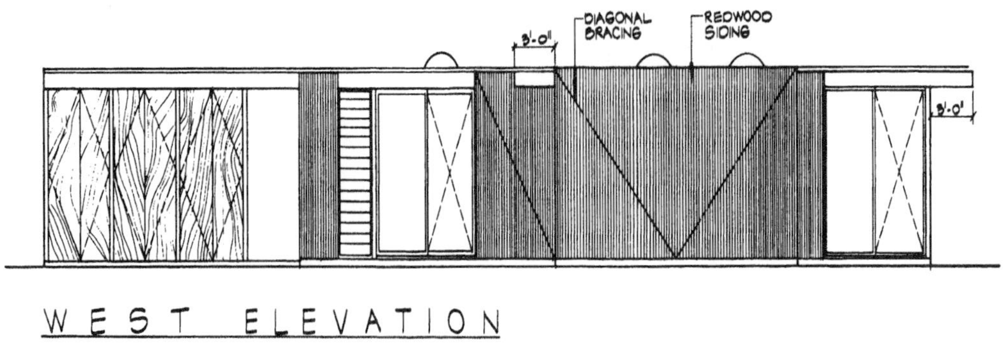

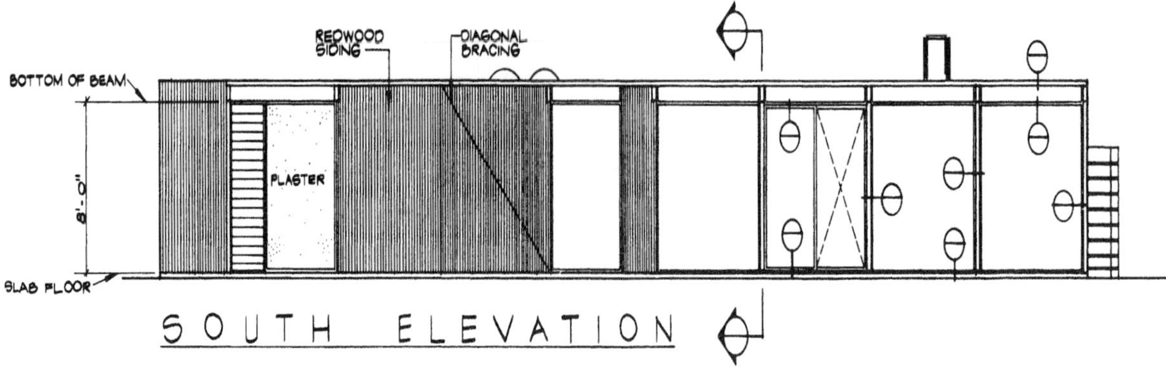

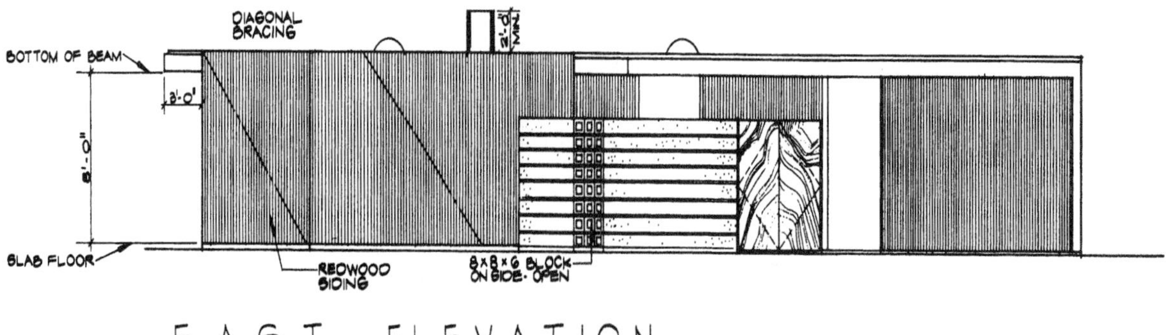

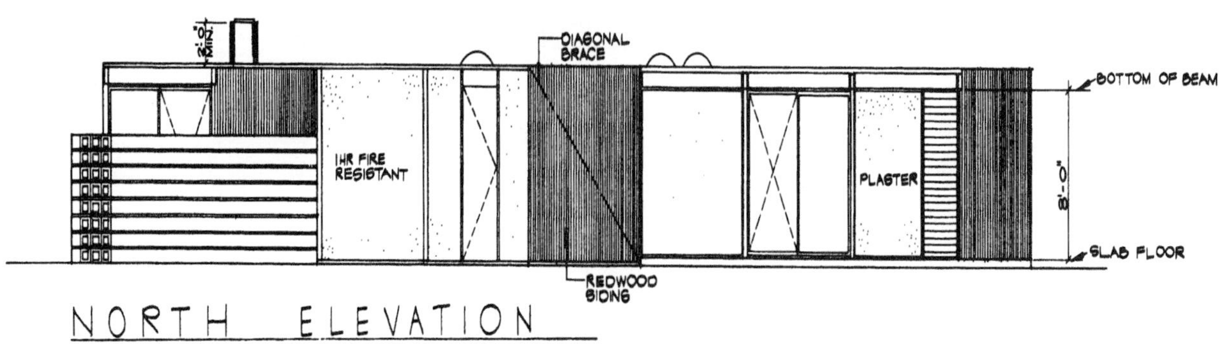

Figure 9.33 Elevation in wood.

lines has been a common practice to alert the craftsman on the job that the door does not interfere with any electrical fixture, columns, and so on. Some offices have selected not to show door swings on the elevations because the floor plan shows the door swing.

Foundations. At times, you may have to delineate the foundation on the elevations in order to explain the foundation better. Dotted lines are used in various ways relating to the foundation. Dotted lines (center line type lines are also used) show the top of a slab, as in Figure 9.34. They are also used to show the elevation of the footings. See Figure 9.35 for elevations of a two-pour footing and a one-pour footing or to delineate a basement.

Dotted lines are also used to describe a **stepped footing**. When the property slopes, the minimum depth of the footing can be maintained by stepping the footing down the slope. See Figure 9.36.

Structural Features. Structural features below the grade can be shown by dotted lines if this helps to explain the structure. See Figure 9.37. Dotted lines can also be used to help show structural elements of the building. In Figure 9.10, centerline-type lines (which can also be used) show **let-in braces** (structural angular braces in a wall). (The plate line is the top of the two horizontal members at the top of the wall, called **top plates**.) In Figure 9.34, dotted lines show the top of the roof, which slopes for drainage; a **pilaster** (a widening of the wall for a beam); and a beam (a laminated beam) for window wells.

As with doors and windows, the footing on an elevation can be referenced to the foundation plan, details, and cross-sections. The system is the same. Reference bubbles are used. See Figure 9.38.

Whatever the feature, the dotted line is used for clarity and communication. How can you keep the message clear for construction purposes? How can you best communicate this on the drawings?

Controlling Factors

Each type of construction has unique restrictive features that you need to know about to effectively interpret the transition from design elevations to production of exterior elevations in the construction documents.

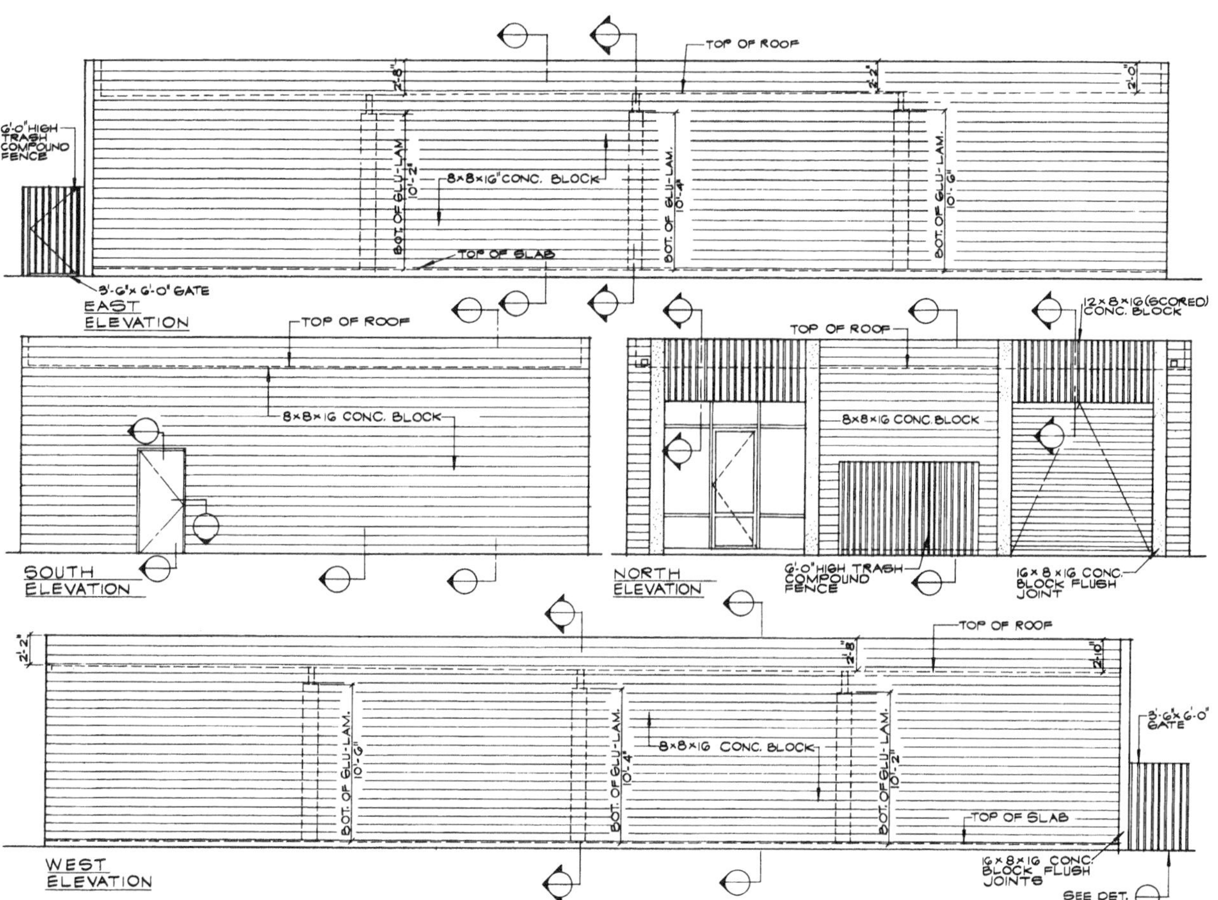

Figure 9.34 Elevation in masonry.

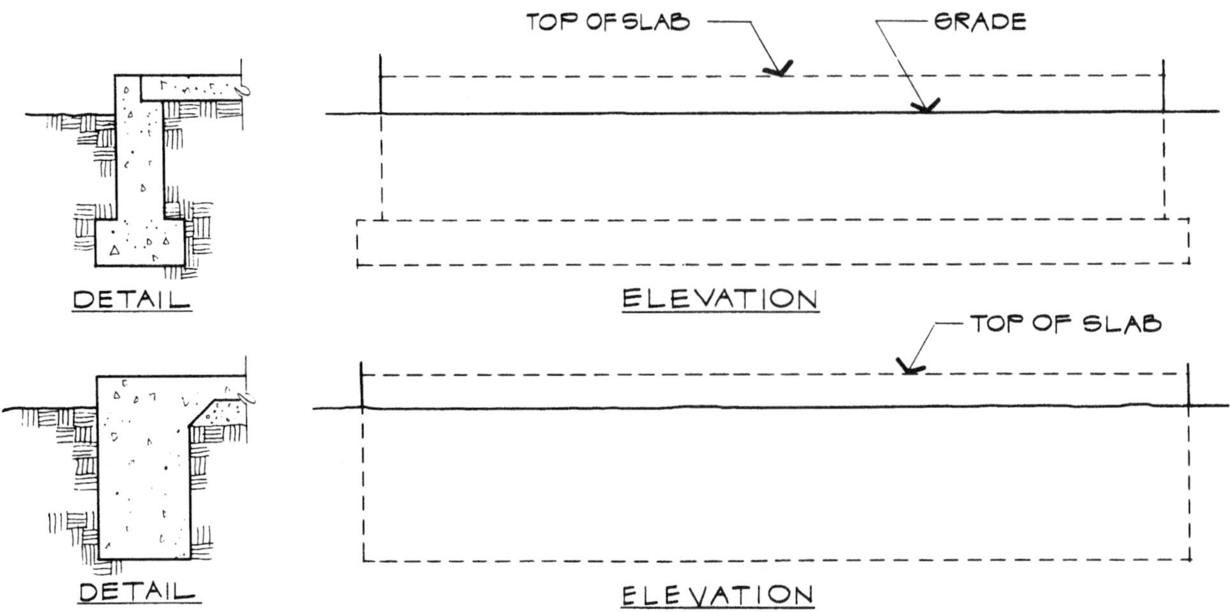

Figure 9.35 Showing the foundation on an elevation.

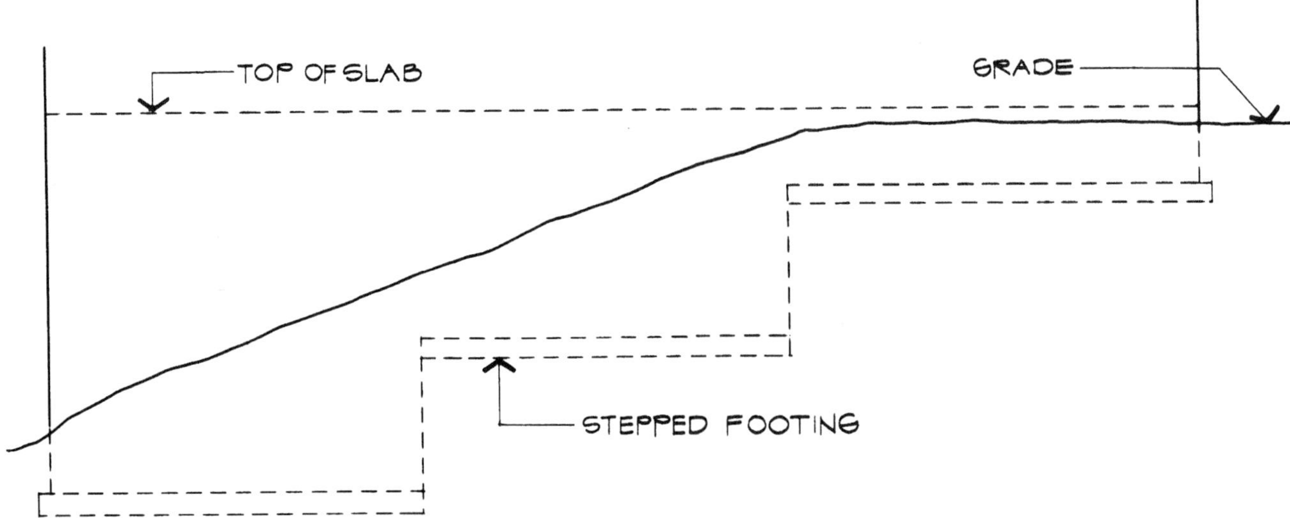

Figure 9.36 Stepped footings in elevation.

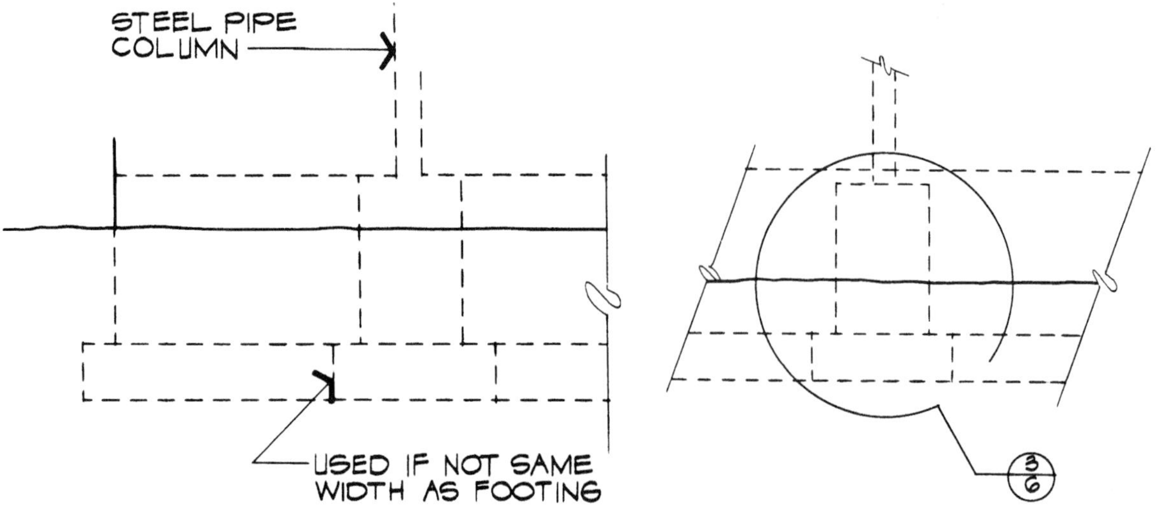

Figure 9.37 Structural features below grade.

Figure 9.38 Referencing hidden lines.

Wood Frame Structures

With wood frame structures, elevations are usually dictated by plate line heights. The *plate height* is measured from the floor to the top of the two top plates. See Figure 9.8. Efficient use of material is dictated by this dimension because studs are available in certain lengths and sheathing usually comes in 4′×8′ sheets.

Floor, Plate, and Grade Lines. When the floor elevations and plate heights are established, the first thing to draw is the floor line and its relationship to the grade. Next, draw the plate line. If the structure is of post-and-beam construction, measure from the floor line to the bottom of the beam. Some offices prefer to put these dimensions on the building sections.

Find the distance between the floor line and the grade line from the grading plan, foundation plan, footing details, and building sections. If the lot is relatively flat, just draw a grade line with the floor line measured above it and the plate line height above the floor as a start. If the site is not flat, carefully plot the grade line from the grading plan, foundation plan, and details or the site plan.

Some site plans, grading plans, and foundation plans indicate the grade height, marked F.G. (finished grade), in relation to the structure at various points around the structure. In Figure 9.39, the grade line is figured by making a grid where the horizontal lines show grade heights and vertical lines are projected down from the structure. Once this grade line is established, the top of the slab—that is, the floor line—is drawn. The plate line is then measured from the floor line. There is no need to measure the distance between the grade and the floor line. See Figure 9.40.

Masonry Structures

Masonry structures, such as those of brick or **concrete masonry units (CMU)**, must be approached differently. The deciding factor here is the size of the concrete block or brick, the pattern, the thickness of the joint, and the placement of the first row in relationship to the floor. Unlike wood, which can be cut in varying heights, masonry units are difficult to cut, so cutting is minimized. As Figure 9.32 shows, dimensions of the masonry areas are kept to a minimum. In a wood frame structure, the lumber can be cut to size on the job. In masonry, the size of the masonry units often dictates such things as the location of windows and doors, the modular height, and so on. Some of the controlling factors in steel construction are the size of the structural members; the required ceiling heights; and the **plenum** area (the space necessary to accommodate the mechanical equipment and ductwork). See Figure 9.41. Refer to the discussion of noting, earlier in this chapter, for suggested practices and sample illustrations.

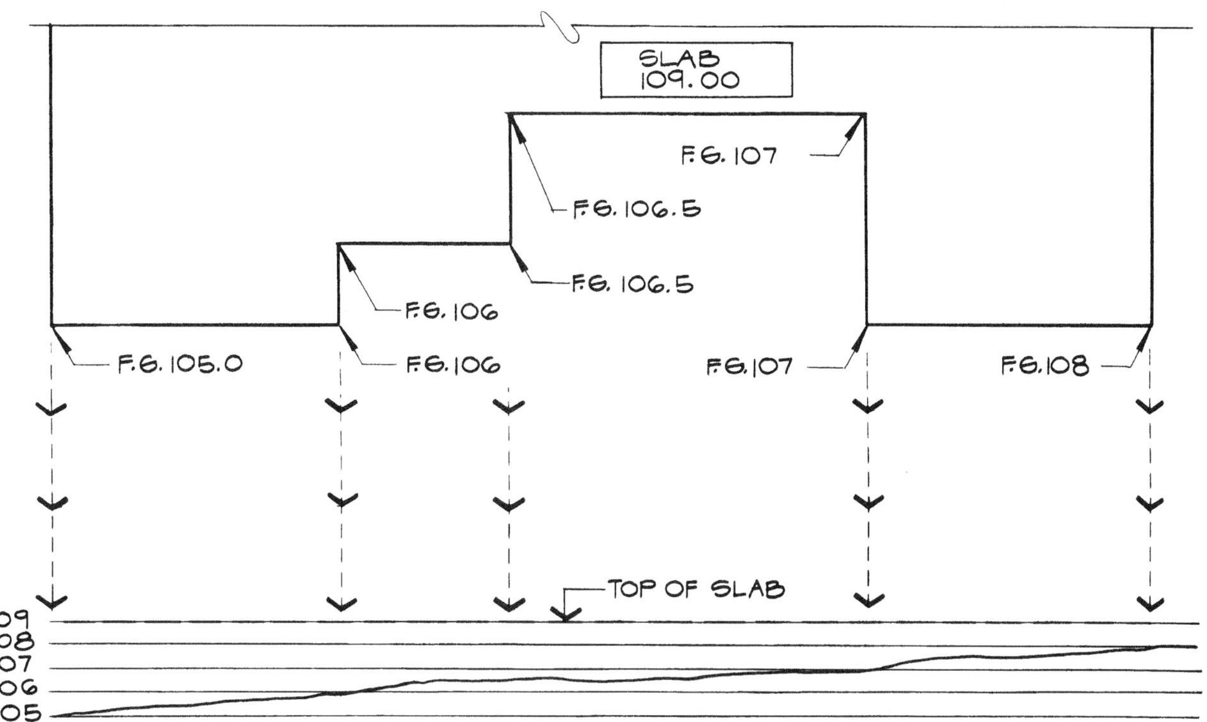

Figure 9.39 Plotting grade lines for an elevation.

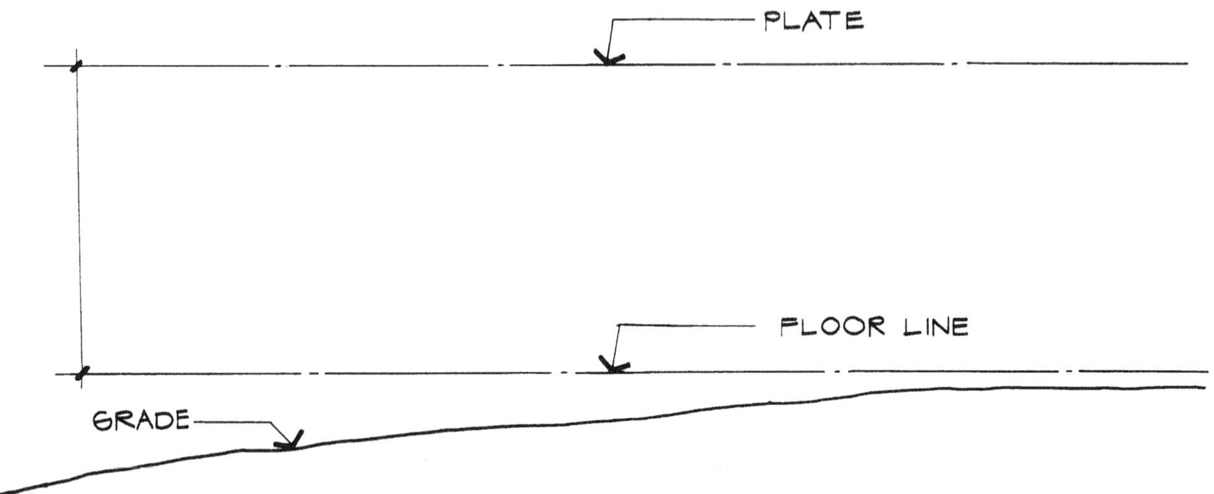

Figure 9.40 Preliminary steps for drafting an elevation with grade variation.

Steel Structures

Structures in which the main members are steel and the secondary members are, for example, wood are treated differently from wood structures or masonry. The configuration is arrived at in the same way and representation of material is the same, but dimensioning is completely different.

Drawing an exterior elevation for a steel structure is a relatively simple task. Usually, the floor elevations on a multistory structure of steel are established by the architect. The building section usually provides the necessary height requirements. See Figure 9.41. Figure 9.42 is a checklist for exterior elevations.

■ DRAFTING AN EXTERIOR ELEVATION

Drawing an exterior elevation is a straightforward procedure, because most of the structural and shape descriptions have been completed by the time it is drafted. The shape of the roof, the size of the site component parts, the shape and size of the foundation, and all of the vertical heights were determined when drafting the building section. For a small structure, such as those contained in this book, we believe it is the easiest drawing to accomplish.

Guide to Dimensioning

Do not dimension anything on the exterior elevation that has been dimensioned elsewhere, unless you are using Revit. For example, the distance between the floor line and the plate line is dimensioned on the building section and should not be repeated on the exterior elevation. In contrast, windows have been described (width and height) on the schedule, yet their positions in relation to the floor line have not. This makes the exterior elevation an ideal place to dimension these positions, as well as such architectural features as signage on a commercial building.

Descriptions

Anything that can be described better by drawing should be drawn, and anything that would be better as a written description should be included in the specifications. Noting should use generic terms. It would be sufficient to label the exterior covering (called *skin*) "redwood siding" or "stucco" (exterior plaster), rather than describing the quality of the siding or the number of coats and quality of the stucco.

Concerns

Compare the exterior elevation to the human body. In both instances, the outside cover is called the *skin*. Directly below the skin is the muscle. The muscle might be comparable to the substructure that strengthens a structure, such as metal straps, let-in braces, and shear panels. See Figure 9.43. The purpose of these members is to resist outside forces, such as wind, hurricanes, and earthquakes. The skeleton within a human body is analogous to the "bone structure" of a building, which is in the form of a network of wood pieces called *studs*.

The exterior elevation addresses the "skin and muscle," and the building section emphasizes the skeletal form.

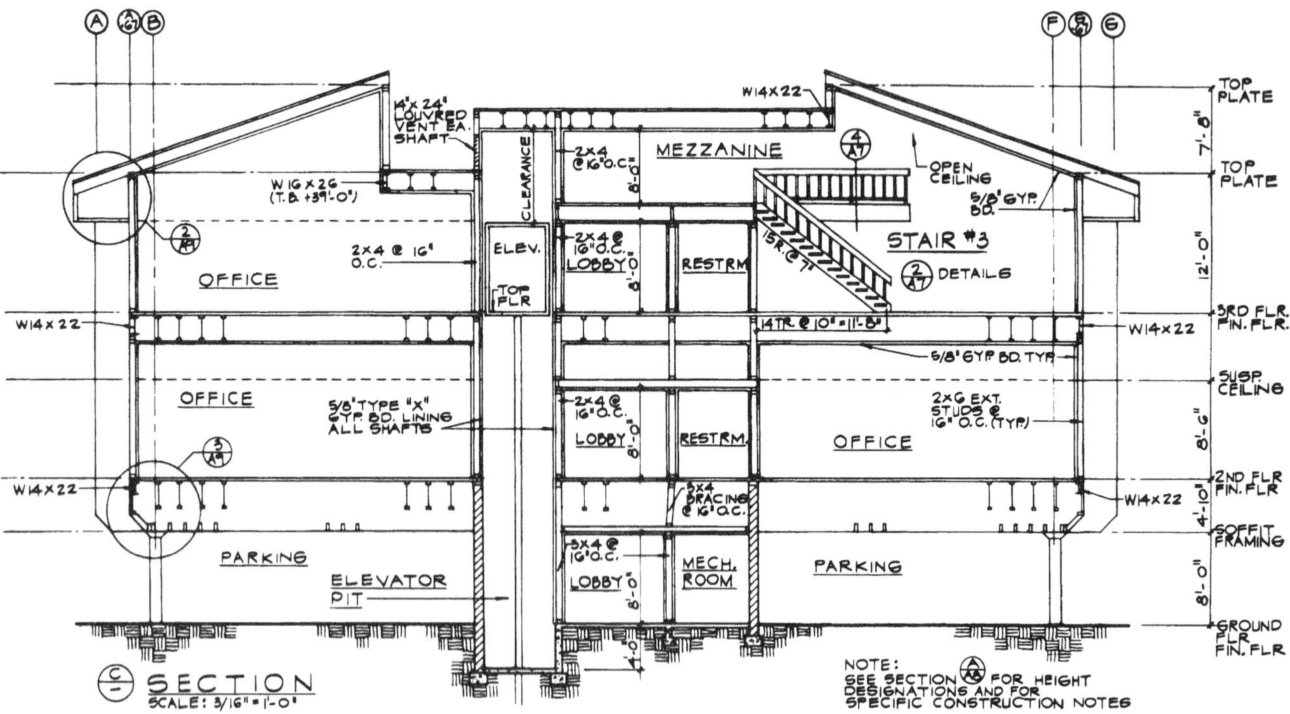

Figure 9.41 Section of a steel and wood structure. (Courtesy of Westmount, Inc., Real Estate Development.)

EXTERIOR ELEVATIONS CHECKLIST

1. Natural grade
2. Finish grade
3. Floor elevations
4. Foundation (hidden lines)
   a. Bottom of footing
   b. Top of foundation (stepped footing)
   c. Detail reference
5. Walls
   a. Material
      (1) Wood
      (2) Stucco
      (3) Aluminum
      (4) Other
   b. Solid sheathing
      (1) Plywood
      (2) 1 × 6 diagonal
      (3) Other
   c. Diagonal bracing (hidden lines)
6. Openings
   a. Heights
      (1) Door and window min. 6' - 8"
      (2) Post and beam special
   b. Doors
      (1) Type
      (2) Material
      (3) Glass
      (4) Detail reference
      (5) Key to schedule
   c. Windows
      (1) Type
      (2) Material
      (3) Glass—obscure for baths
      (4) Detail reference
      (5) Key to schedule
   d. Moulding, casing and sill
   e. Flashing (gauge used)
7. Roof
   a. Materials
      (1) Built-up composition, gravel
      (2) Asphalt shingles
      (3) Wood shingles or shake
      (4) Metal-terne-aluminum
      (5) Clay and ceramic tile
      (6) Concrete
   b. Other
8. Ground slopage
9. Attic and subfloor vents
10. Vertical dimensions
11. Window, door fascia, etc. detail references
12. Roof slope ratio
13. Railings, note height
14. Stairs
15. Note all wall materials
16. Types of fixed glass and thickness
17. Window and door swing indications
18. Window and door heights from floor
19. Gutters and downspouts
20. Overflow scuppers
21. Mail slot
22. Stepped foundation footings—if occur
23. Dimension chimney above roof

Figure 9.42 Exterior elevations checklist.

Use of Hidden Lines

Hidden lines are used on an exterior elevation to reveal structural members behind the surface. See Figure 9.34. Notice, in this figure, the use of hidden lines to show the slope of the roof, the pilaster, and the hinged side of doors and windows; in Figure 9.33, hidden lines are used to show diagonal bracing.

Now look at Figure 9.44. The outline of a gable roof (roof plan) is translated into elevations. Notice that in the front view the small bend in the roof at the top right corner does not show, whereas in the rear view the entire shape is shown and the right-side view shows only a single roof but nothing behind it. Hidden roof lines are not shown.

Pictorial Versus Written Description

It often takes a combination of a drawing and a generic description to describe a material used for covering the outer surface of a structure. For example, a series of horizontal lines is used to describe siding, a row of masonry units, or possibly a texture pattern on exterior plaster.

■ WEATHERPROOFING

Weatherproofing a structure basically means keeping out wind, rain, and ultraviolet rays (UVRs) of the sun. UVR reduction is necessary because these rays are harmful to human skin and will fade the color of drapery, furniture, and carpets. In a residence, the solution is rather simple. Large overhangs on roofs can eliminate these harmful rays, as can the newly developed high-performance glass utilized in windows.

Windows and doors are now made, or can be retrofitted, with weatherstripping. This keeps the structure energy efficient and prevents dust from entering the structure as a result of driving winds.

As you may have learned in a science course, the structure of water is different in its various phases: solid, liquid, and vapor. Therefore, a variety of materials are used to combat the migration of moisture from the outside to the inside of structures.

Generally, a cover is placed over the structure (especially the walls), much like a raincoat on a human. Yet, depending on the material of the raincoat, the wearer's body heat, the temperature of the air, and especially the humidity (moisture in the air), the inside surface of the raincoat will react differently. So, it is with buildings. Buildings do perspire. Consider the following scenario: Driven by wind, moisture migrates from the outside to the inside of a structure in the form of vapor. This moisture changes its state through condensation because of temperature change and is unable to leave the inside of the wall. As night approaches, the temperature drops drastically, and the moisture now expands as it becomes a solid (ice). If this moisture happens to be inside the wood or insulation within the wall, it can cause terrible deterioration and damage. Had a vapor barrier been used, moisture might come from the inside of the structure and condense along this membrane as it tried to escape.

Figure 9.43 Revealing let-in brace.

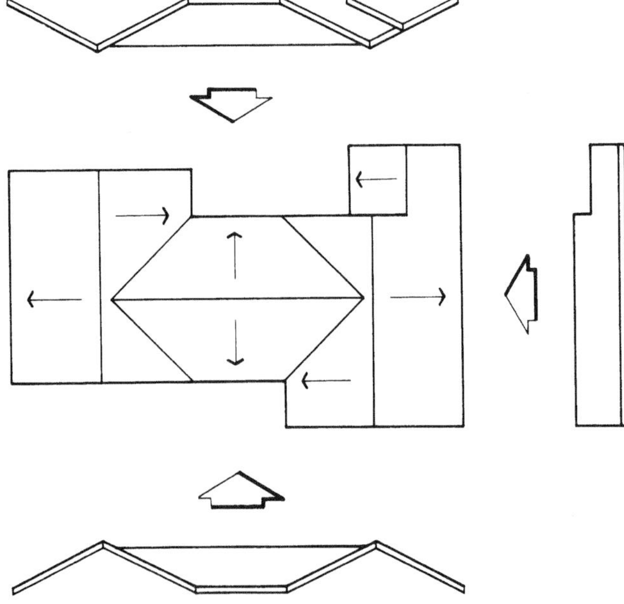

Figure 9.44 Visualizing roof in elevation.

Solution to Condensation

A solution to condensation in the attic and under-floor space in a wood floor system can easily be achieved by proper ventilation and recirculation of the air. This is done with small openings through which venting can take place, using the wind as an ally, or the air can be recirculated mechanically, as is often done for bathroom ventilation.

Figure 9.45 is a map of the United States. Notice how it is divided into three major zones. Zone A experiences severe damage to structures as a result of condensation. Zone B experiences moderate damage, whereas the damage in Zone C is slight to almost none. This does not mean that there will never be moderate-to-severe damage in mountainous areas in Zone C; rather, this is a more generalized look at large geographic areas. Therefore, the drafter must be aware that a building in Southern California will *not* be dealt with in the same way as a building in the Dakotas, nor can a building in southern Texas be treated the same as one in Colorado.

Waterproofing can be achieved in the following four ways:

1. The use of admixtures that render concrete impermeable.
2. Hydrolytically, by applying a waterproofing coat of asphalt or plastic to a surface.
3. Chemically, by applying a specially formulated paint to a basically porous surface such as concrete. Upon contact with water, this chemical crystallizes, sealing the pores. Such products are used more often for a retro-fix than initial construction.
4. The use of a membrane. Older houses used **bituminous-saturated felts** (also called **building felts**), which have recently been replaced with asphalt-saturated kraft paper.

For a structure in Zone A, you may wish to select a material that will keep the colder side of the wall wind resistant and airtight and require that the material be a vapor retardant. On the warm side of the wall, you might wish to stop the migration of moisture into the wall by using a foil-backed lath product. There are a number of products on the market today that can be specified by the project architect, including a vapor-proof membrane, a membrane that can breathe, and a self-sealing membrane for ice and water, as shown in Figure 9.46.

A drafter must know what is being used to properly ensure that he or she uses the correct convention and notation for drawings and details.

Counterflashing

Anytime you break the surface of a waterproof membrane, whether it is plastic or paper, a second sheet (usually of heavier weight) is used. This sheet, called **counterflashing**, is found around openings and at the ends of the membrane, inasmuch as these are the places most likely to leak. In Zone C, for example, where asphalt-saturated (grade D) kraft paper is often used, a heavier-grade band of kraft paper, called **sisal-kraft**, is used. In other instances, a strip of self-sealing vapor membrane may be used around the opening. In either

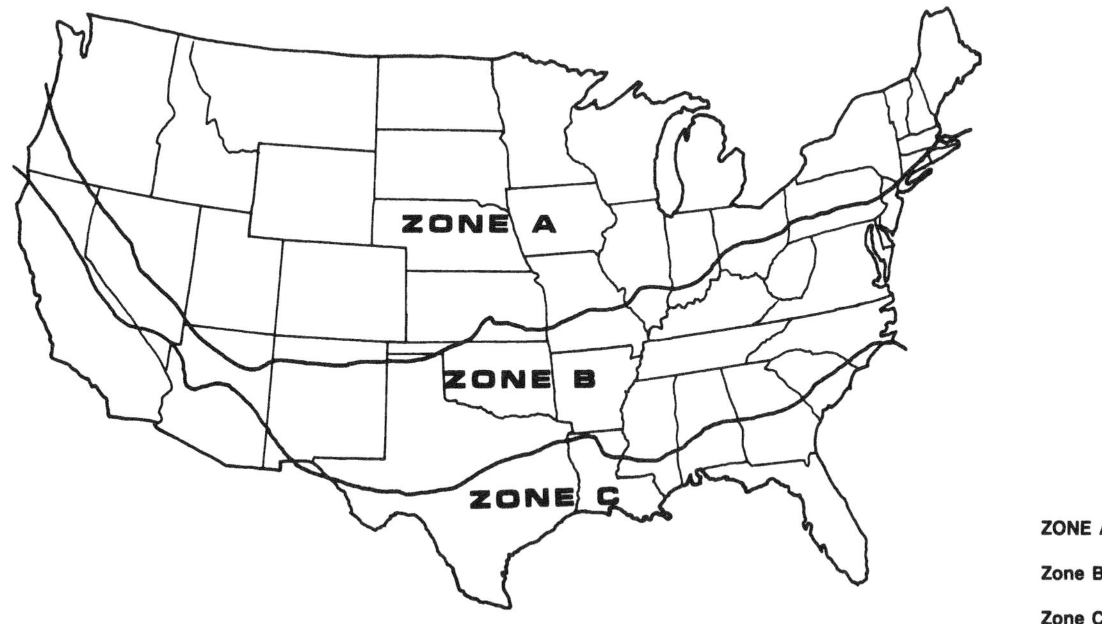

Figure 9.45 US condensation hazard zones.

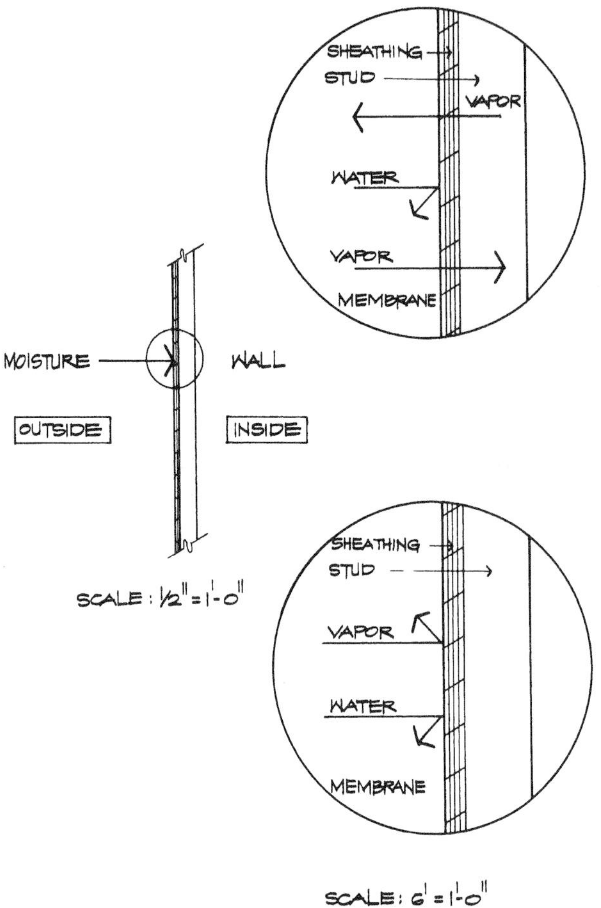

Figure 9.46 Breathing membranes and vapor membranes.

case, it should be done carefully so as to shed water lapping and overlapping so as to let gravity take its natural course and help eliminate moisture.

Referencing

Referencing is the process of referring a specific area to an enlarged detail. Thus, the top half of the reference bubble indicates the name of the detail, and the bottom number indicates the sheet on which the particular detail can be found. On a complete set with details of all conditions, you would see detail reference bubbles around all windows, doors, beam connections, and so on.

Noting

Whenever possible, noting is done outside the elevation within the right margin. You cannot fit all of the notes in one place without having to use long leaders pointing to the subject. Therefore, certain notes are made inside the elevation to reduce the length of the leaders. A good rule of thumb in regard to leaders is not to allow them to cross more than one object line, never cross a dimension line, and keep the leader length to a minimum.

Many offices use **keynoting**, a procedure of numbering and placing all of the notes on one side (usually the right). You then place a leader in the desired location and, rather than placing the note at the end of the leader, you use a reference bubble that refers to the correct note.

The advantage of keynoting is the standardization of the notes. Keynoting also allows the drafter to make direct references to the specification numbers right on the notes. Numbering systems recommended by the American Institute of Architects are similar to the numbering system used by libraries and can be incorporated here.

■ DRAWING AN ELEVATION WITH AND WITHOUT A MODEL

With a three-dimensional (3-D) model, the drafter needs only to rotate the image into an ortho mode and flatten it to create a base form for the elevation.

If a 3-D model is unavailable, the CAD drafter should use the base layer of the building section for the geometry layer under the base layer (datum layer) for the elevation.

Because we are drawing the structure full-scale, the drawings will transfer directly. If the drawings are prepared in paper space and/or the scale of the building section and elevation are to be drawn differently, the first stage of the building section must be changed in scale to suit the elevation.

Stage I The next move is to import the floor plan and position the walls as shown in Figure 9.47. The floor plan is temporarily positioned above the datum elevation drawing and rotated for each of the respective north, south, east, and west elevations. This drawing constitutes the base or datum stage of a set of elevations.

Stage II (Figure 9.48). The total outline of the structure is accomplished in this stage. The geometry of the roof and additional floor lines and plate lines is also incorporated as they change throughout the structure.

Stage III (Figure 9.49). Doors and windows are positioned. It is best to get digital images from the manufacturer, and then size and position them. If the structure is subject to lateral loads, shear walls may be included at this stage, as would stepped footing or any other structural components.

Stage IV (Figure 9.50). Line weight should be adjusted at this stage while adding texture. Adding texture may be fun, but restraint is recommended, so as not to disturb any notes or dimensions.

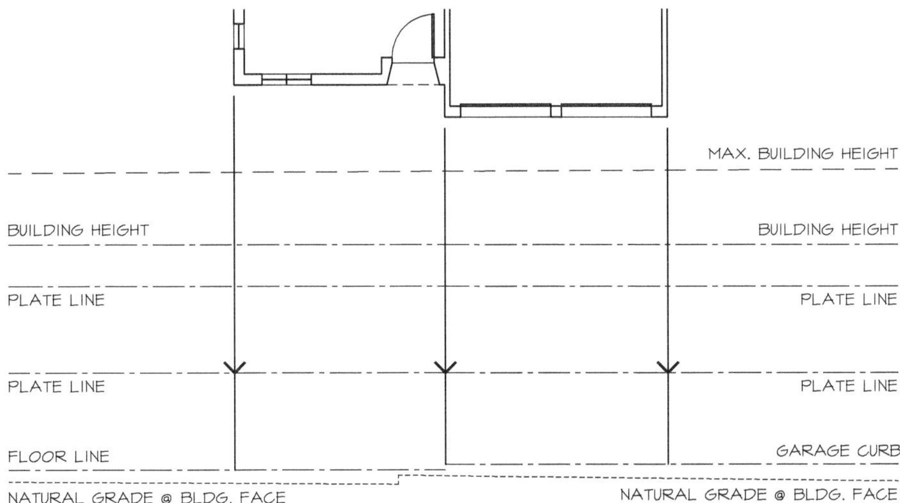

Figure 9.47 Stage I: Establishing a base.

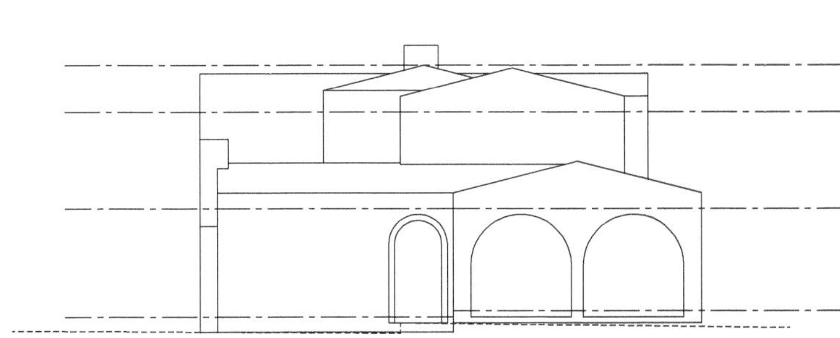

Figure 9.48 Stage II: Outline of structure.

Figure 9.49 Stage III: Positioning doors, windows, and the like.

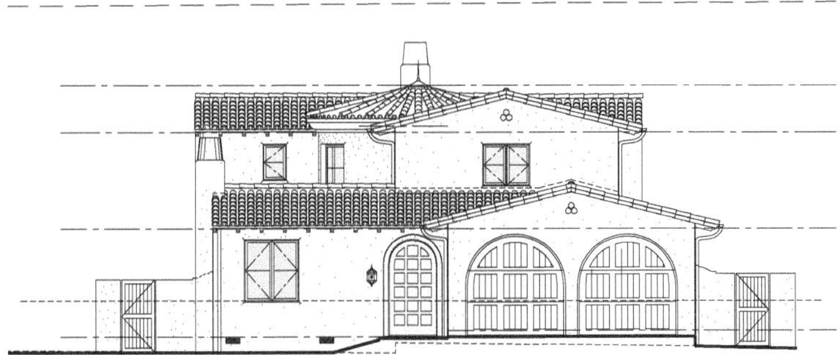

Figure 9.50 Stage IV: Adding texture and adjusting line quality.

Stage V (Figure 9.51). This is the dimensioning stage. Remember, the dimension for floor line to plate line should be noted once on the building section and should not be repeated here. Simply refer the floor-to-plate-line dimension to the section. Only those vertical dimensions that do not appear on the building section should appear here. Header height, ridge heights, handrail and guardrail dimensions, and heights of fences and walls adjacent to the structure are examples of actual dimensions that will appear on the exterior elevation.

Stage VI (Figure 9.52). This is the noting, titling, and referencing stage, as well as final stage of the exterior elevations. Notes should be generic; only the specifications should cite the precise quantity, brand names, model numbers, and so forth.

CASE STUDIES: WORKING DRAWING DEVELOPMENT

In this section, we discuss the development of the exterior elevation working drawings for the Clay Theater steel and masonry building (Chapter 18) (see Figure 9.53A and 9.53B).

Clay Theater—Steel/Masonry Structure

Exterior Elevations. Elevations are developed from scratch, and are not traced from any other drawings unless extremely accurate preliminary drawings have been prepared. Figure 9.53 demonstrates the menu used for exterior elevations. In most sets of drawings, the

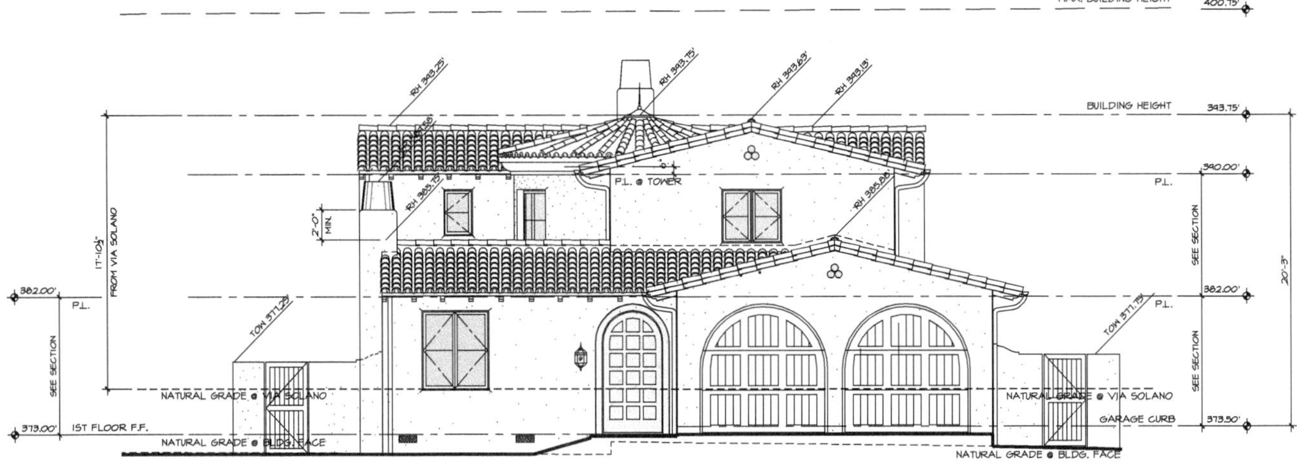

Figure 9.51 Stage V: Dimensioning stairs, handrails, and similar elements.

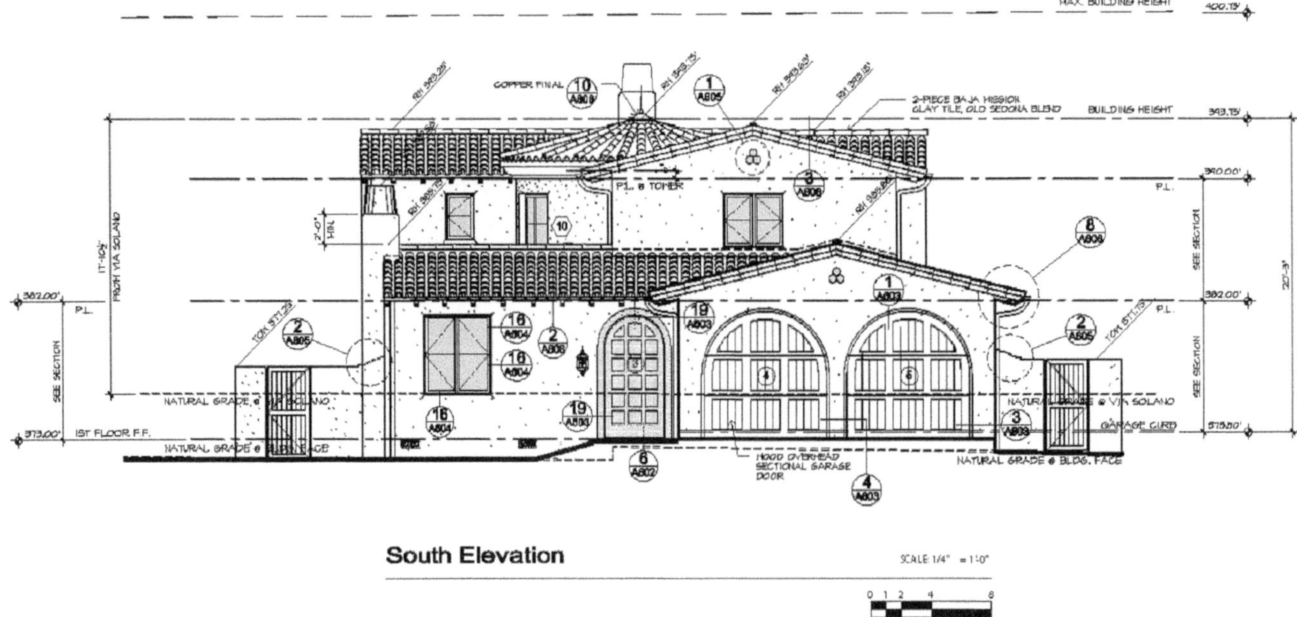

Figure 9.52 Stage VI: Noting and referencing.

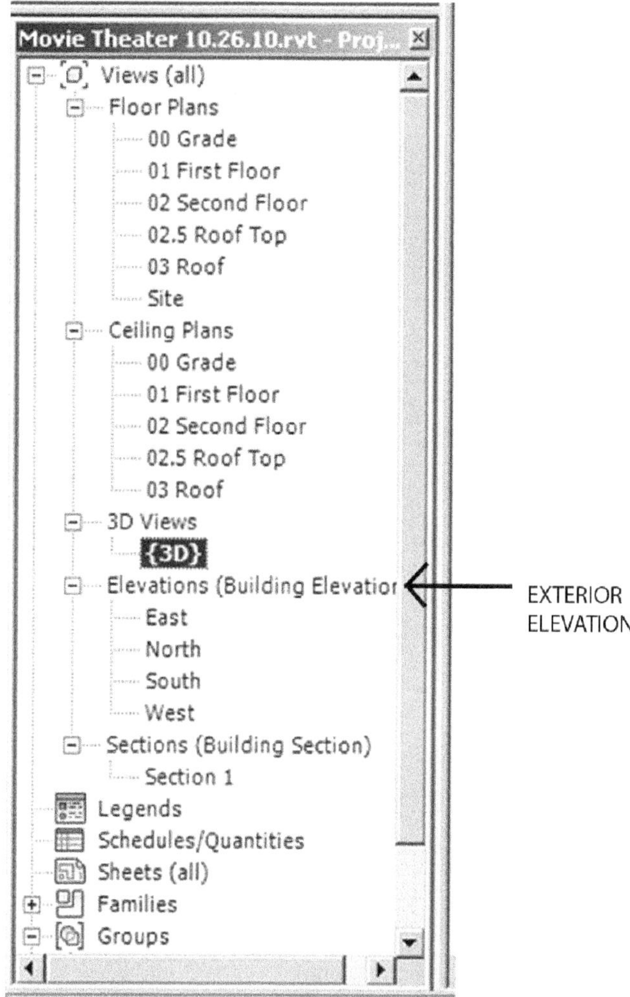

Figure 9.53A Exterior elevation menu. (Screenshots © Autodesk Inc. All Rights Reserved.)

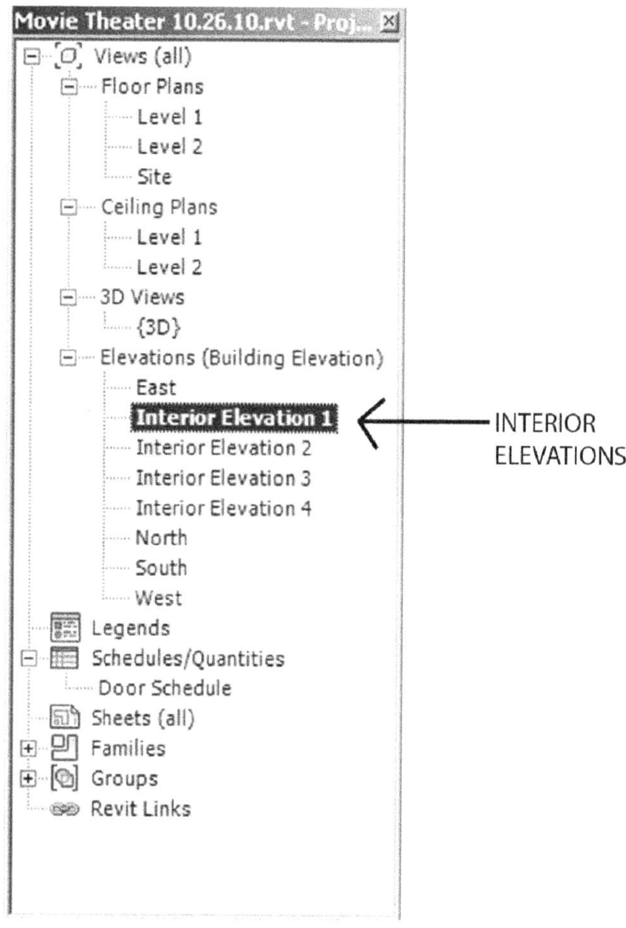

Figure 9.53B Interior elevation menu. (Screenshots © Autodesk Inc. All Rights Reserved.)

elevations are among the last to be completed because they are dependent on the floor plan, sections, roof plan, and so on. To better see how exterior elevations evolve, first read the chapter on building sections. Figures 9.54 and 9.55 show how the exterior of the project actually appears as the construction proceeds, and Figures 9.56 and 9.57 show front and rear views of the construction when completed.

Stage I

We decided to draft only three exterior elevations rather than the normal four because the structure is symmetrical and the north and south elevations are similar. The horizontal lines in Figure 9.58 represent several items: the two floor levels, the top of the parapet, the tops of the beams, and the tip of the beam at the canopy over the door. (The sloped, dotted line on the bottom elevation is the angle of the ramp for persons with disabilities.)

Stage II

The small, light vertical lines shown in Figure 9.59 locate the various beams and columns. These locations were taken from the reference bubbles on the floor plan. The complete structure would later be referenced by the column locations.

Stage III

Where Stage II indicated the vertical heights, Stage III established the outline of the building itself. See Figure 9.60. Column locations, wall thicknesses, and independent walls at the exit were all established at this point. These measurements were obtained from the various plans, such as the floor plan, foundation plan, and the architectural sections. Each of these drawings used

Figure 9.54 Front of theater.

a dimensional system. This was helpful in the development of this structure because it gave specific points of reference. Heights, width, and depth of the structure were all referenced to this system. For orientation purposes, the top elevation is the north elevation; the center is the west elevation; and the bottom is the east elevation and entry to the theater. The two rectangular shapes toward the center of the north elevation represent the walls protecting the patrons at the exit.

The top centerline on the west elevation is a point of reference. It is the top of the parapet wall extending above the roof plan. The series of vertical lines toward the center represent columns, and the two horizontal lines above the columns represent the fascia. The ramp on either side of the entry is indicated with dotted lines. See the east elevation in Figure 9.60. At the center are columns with handrails drawn in front of them. Stairs would be added later.

Stage IV

Now that we had a basic configuration, we could describe some of the smaller shapes. See Figure 9.61. We added the arbor, or shaded walk, to the north elevation. Refer back to Figure 9.57. The line above the wood arbor is the wood frieze (band of wood). The opening is located at the left. To the west elevation we added rear doors, the doors for the storage area, and the arbor at each end. We positioned steps and doors on the east elevation.

Madison—Steel Building

Exterior Elevations.

Stage I The initial preparation for developing the exterior elevations begins with drawing in light broken lines, which will indicate the floor line level for the

Figure 9.55 Front of theater showing ramp for disabled persons.

Figure 9.56 Front view of finished structure.

Figure 9.57 Rear view of finished structure.

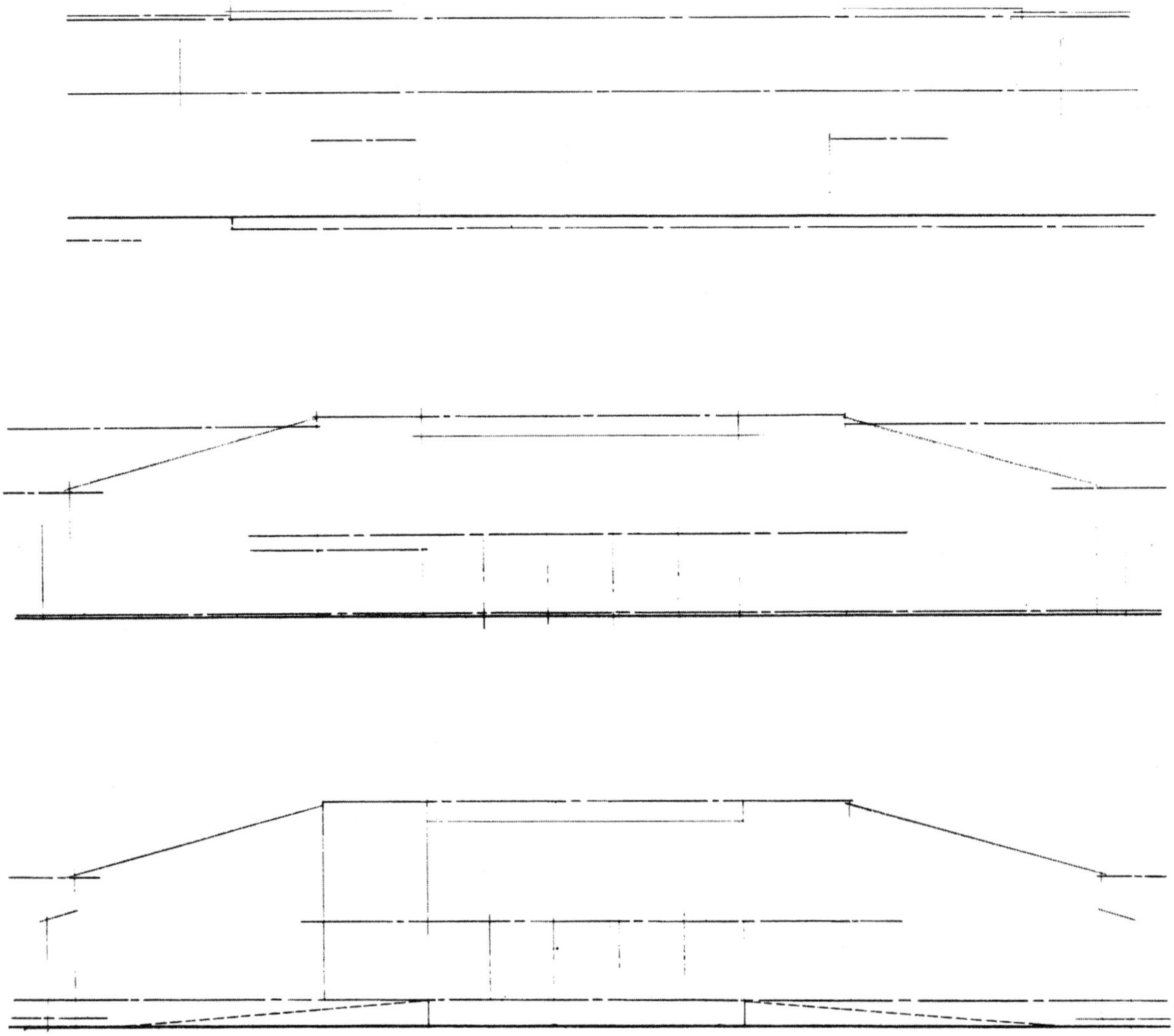

Figure 9.58 Elevation Stage I.

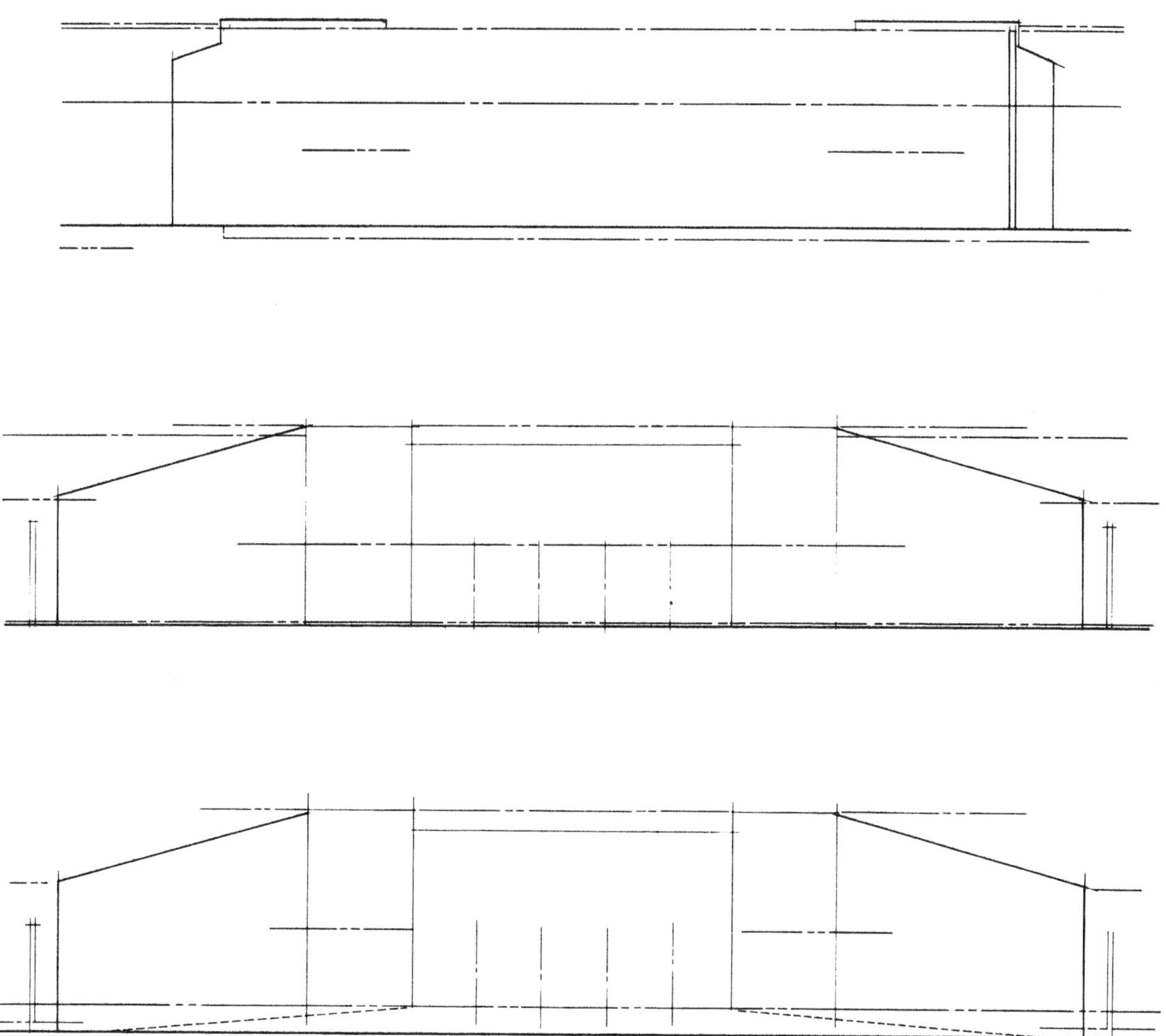

Figure 9.59 Elevation Stage II.

various floors. This is done for all four of the exterior elevations. In this stage, the ground level is represented with a solid line. The CAD operator uses this drawing for the layering or tracking of all future drawings of the exterior elevations. The initial drawing for Stage I of the exterior elevations is depicted in Figure 9.62.

Stage II After determining the ground level and the other floor levels, we use a solid vertical line to identify the exterior wall extremities on the various sides of the exterior elevations.

This drawing indicates the general massing of the building. Stage II is shown in Figure 9.63.

Stage III In Stage II, the various exterior wall extremities for the building elements were established. Stage III is drawn to refine all the horizontal and vertical masses of the structure. This refined dimensional drawing illustrates the heights of the roof and floor masses while indicating the height of the continuous window band. Many design refinements are created at this stage. These refinements include avoiding square edges at the roof, floor, and wall masses. This was done to give the building a sculptured appearance. To provide compatibility with the sculpting of the building, it was decided to encase the exposed rectangular steel columns in concrete for two primary reasons.

First, the fluid nature of concrete could be utilized in sculpting the columns. Second, the concrete could provide a larger proportional mass to the main supporting columns. Note the two vertical lines representing the main supporting columns. This particular column detail is illustrated later in the chapter. The roof and window elements for the mezzanine level above the third floor are shown at this stage. Stage III of the exterior elevations is illustrated in Figure 9.64.

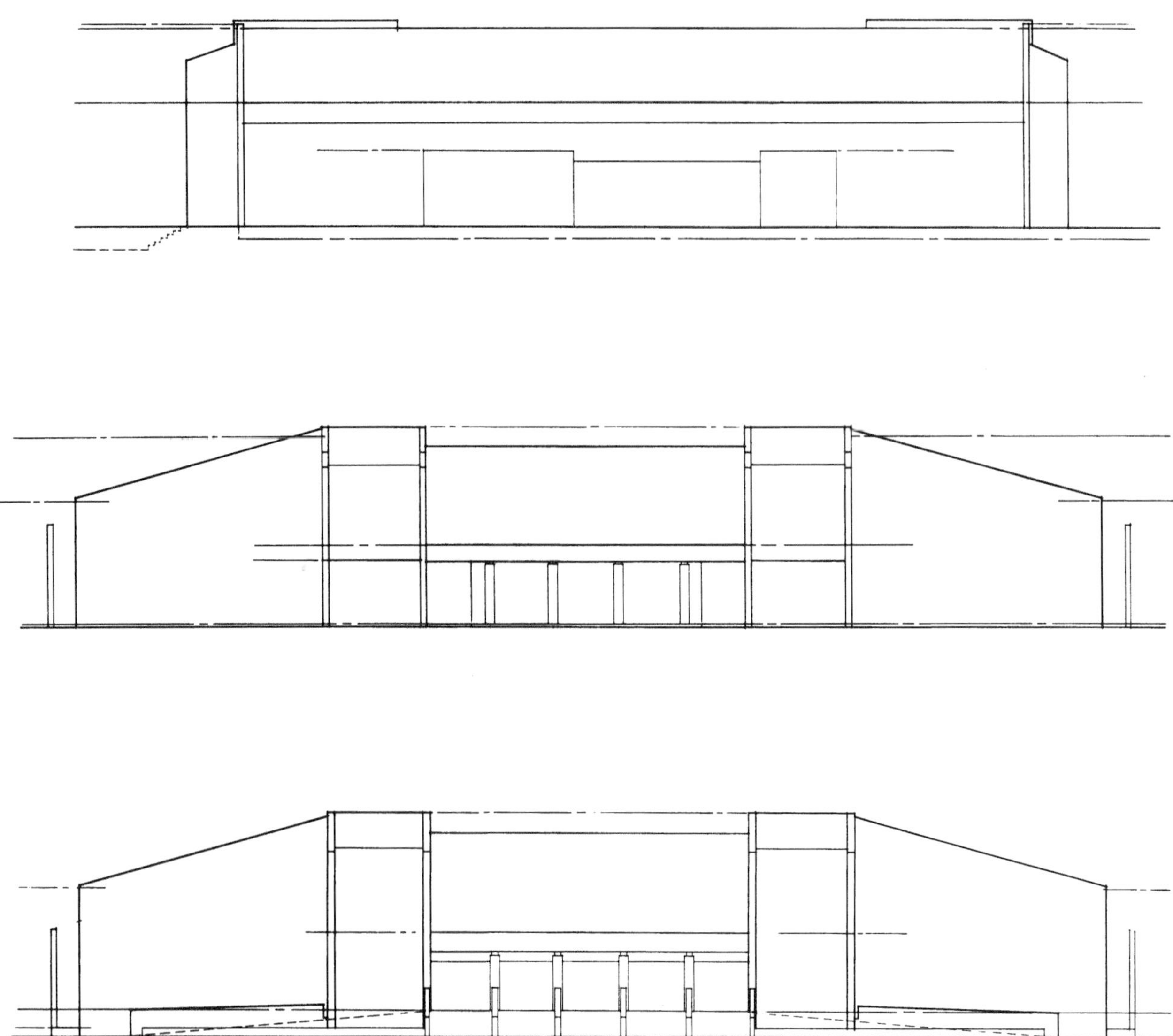

Figure 9.60 Elevation Stage III.

Stage IV After establishing the basic elements for the four exterior elevations, refinements within those elements are added. These include the vertical window mullions, glass entry doors, and the adjacent glazing in the lobby area, and the access gates at the trash area. It was decided to provide round sculptured openings in the masonry shear walls at this stage. This was done after consulting with the structural engineer. Figure 9.65 depicts Stage IV.

Stage V The drawing of Stage V depicts the shading of all the glazing areas and the gradation of vertical lines that are simulating the curved wall edges, corners of the roof sections, and the floor masses. It was decided to shade the glazed areas for the purpose of providing greater clarity (Figure 9.66).

INTERIOR ELEVATIONS PURPOSE

The whole purpose of **interior elevations** is to expose the interior walls so as to locate fixtures, appliances, and cabinets and reveal any additional framing necessary to accommodate fixtures. Interior elevations are necessary when the architect wants to control the visual effects of the interior walls of the structures. Although normally such elevations are not part of the submission, building departments do require an interior elevation showing Americans with Disabilities Act (ADA)-compliant elements.

This section gives many examples of interiors, from residential structures as well as commercial and industrial buildings.

For interior elevations, you draw an outline of what you see, based on the measurements of the ceiling

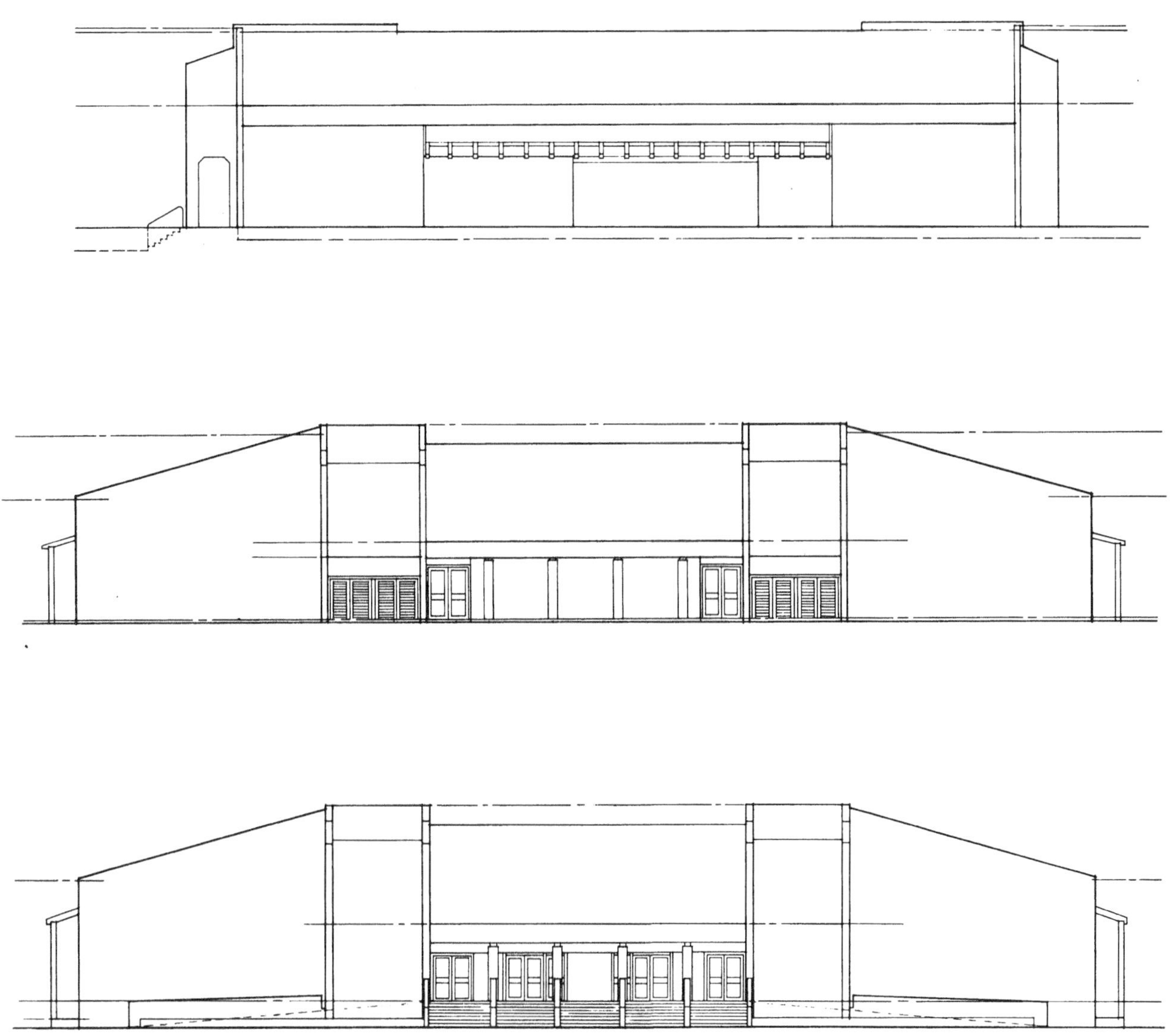

Figure 9.61 Elevation Stage IV.

height and the width of the walls. Things that are not in the contract (NIC) are not drawn solid. For example, a refrigerator often is not included in the contract; neither are the washer and dryer. Hence, these should be drawn with a hidden (dotted) line so as to reveal the wall behind, to show the construction of the base molding and/or the outlets needed to power the particular appliance. If there are no cabinet details, the cabinet form coming toward the viewer should be shown in profile instead of voided out, as previously discussed. Do not forget to show the base molding!

Sources of Measurements

Use the floor plan and building sections for accurate measurements of the width and height of an interior elevation wall. When you use these plans, remember that these dimensions are usually to the stud line or center line of the wall. Interior elevations are drafted to the plaster line.

Interior elevations may not always be drafted at the same scale as the floor plans or sections. Because this requires a scale transition, use caution to avoid errors. In some of the examples in this chapter, the same scale is used and the drawings are directly projected from the plan and section; this is done only to show the theory of where to obtain shapes and configurations.

Information Shown on Interior Elevations

Some architectural offices draft interior elevations for every wall of every room. Although this very careful approach can avoid errors, many wall surfaces are so simple that they do not require a formal drafted interior

Figure 9.62 Madison Building—Stage I: Working drawings—exterior elevations.

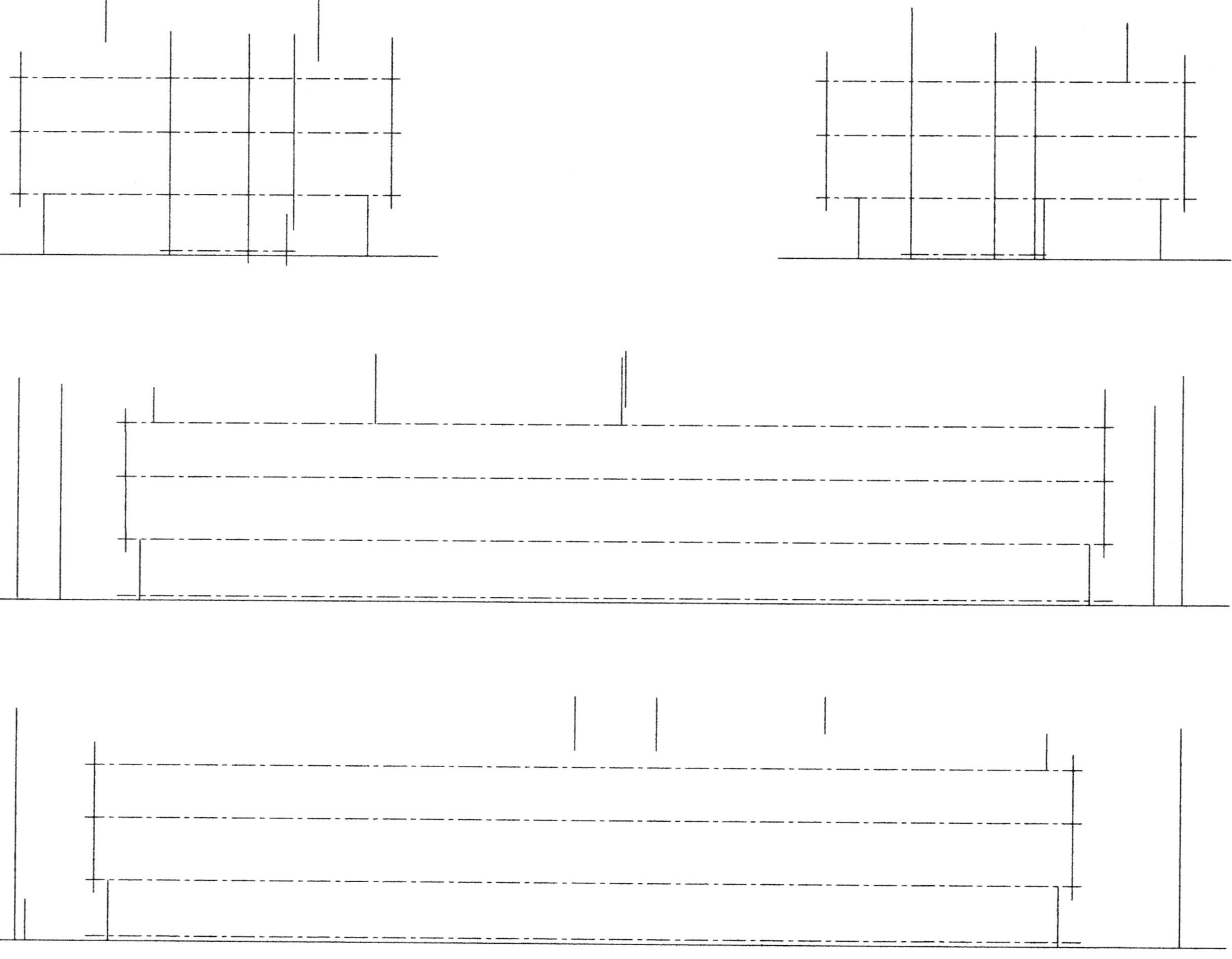

Figure 9.63 Madison Building—Stage II Working drawings—exterior elevations.

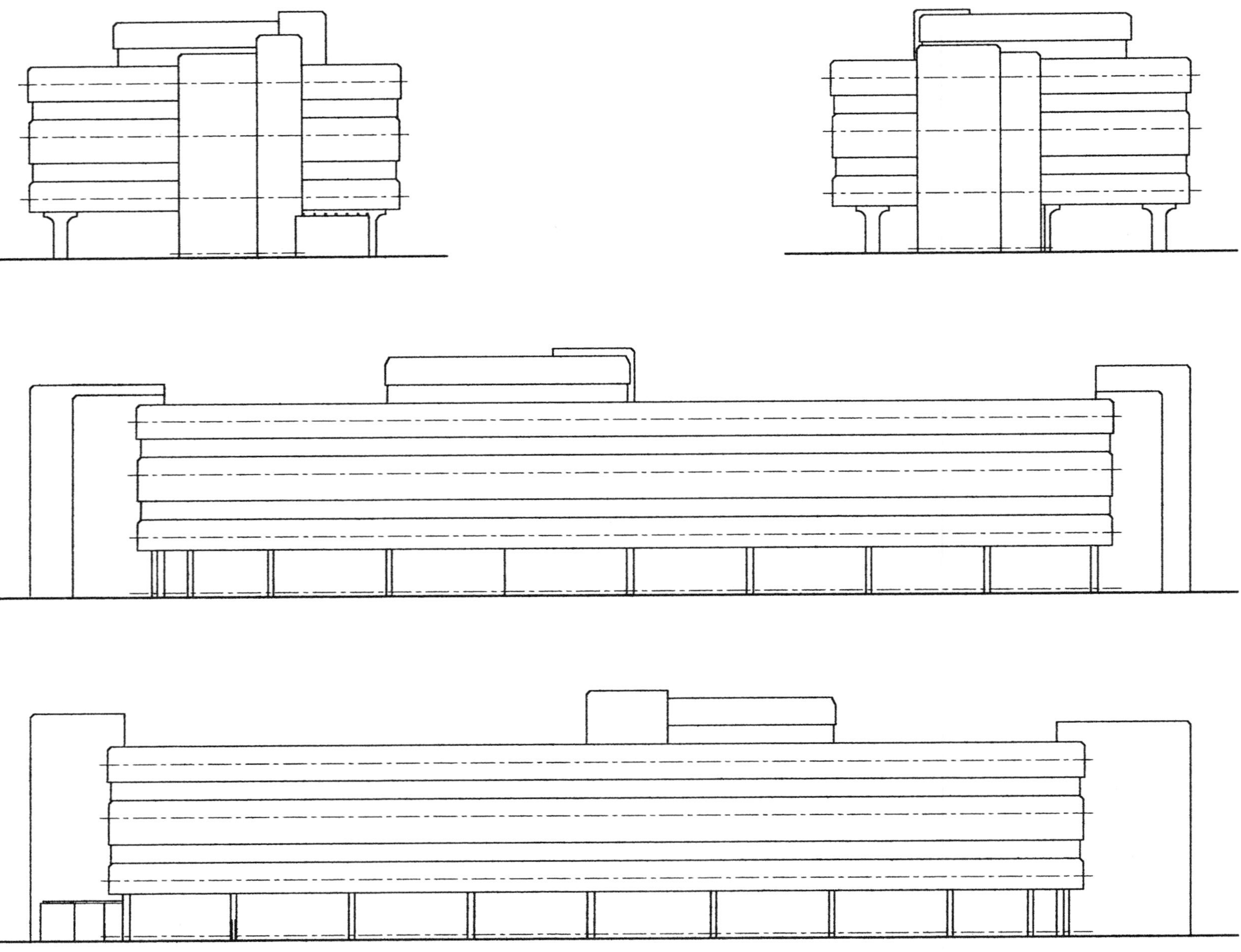

Figure 9.64 Madison Building—Stage III: Working drawings—exterior elevations.

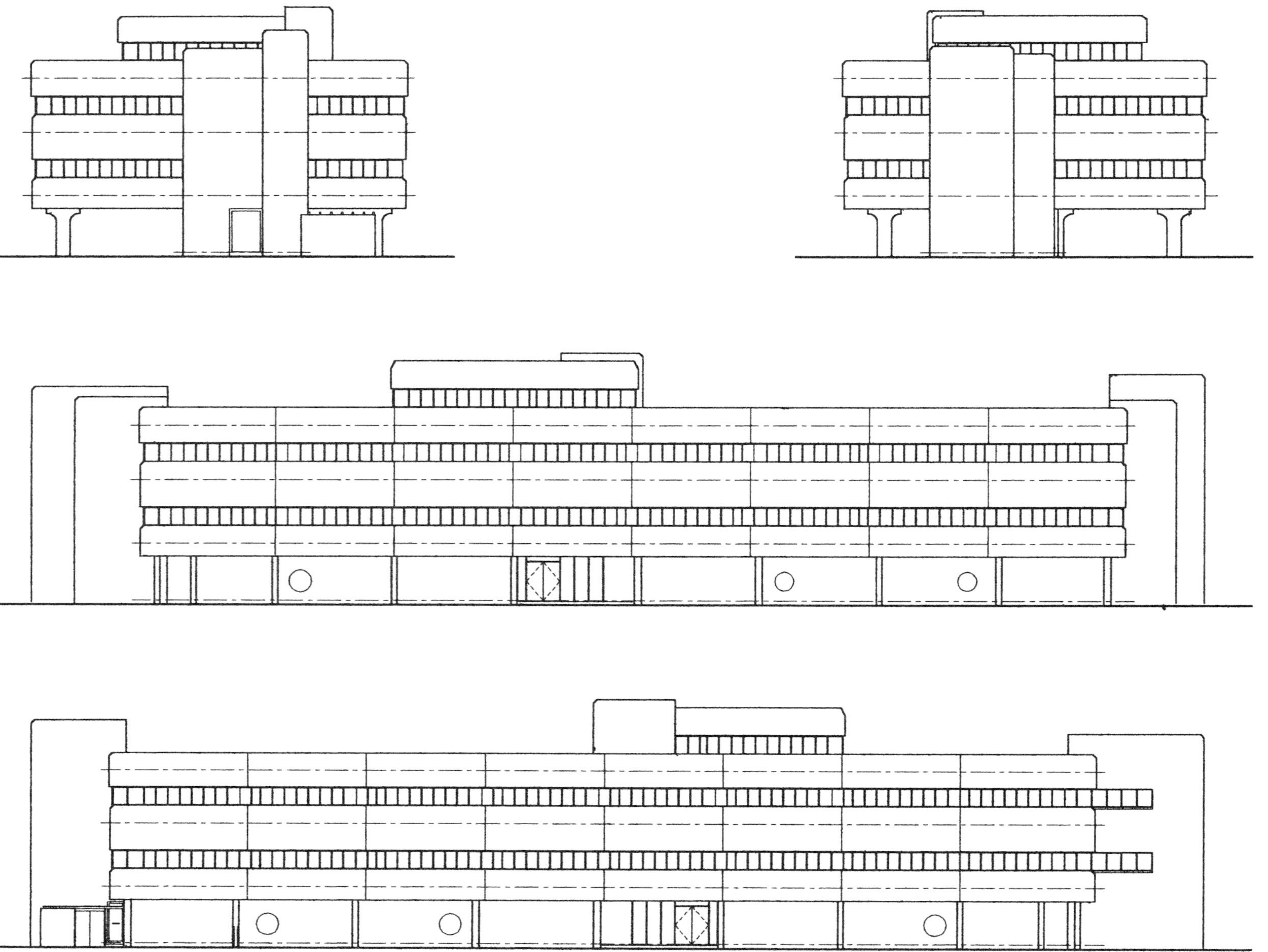

Figure 9.65 Madison Building—Stage IV: Working drawings—exterior elevations.

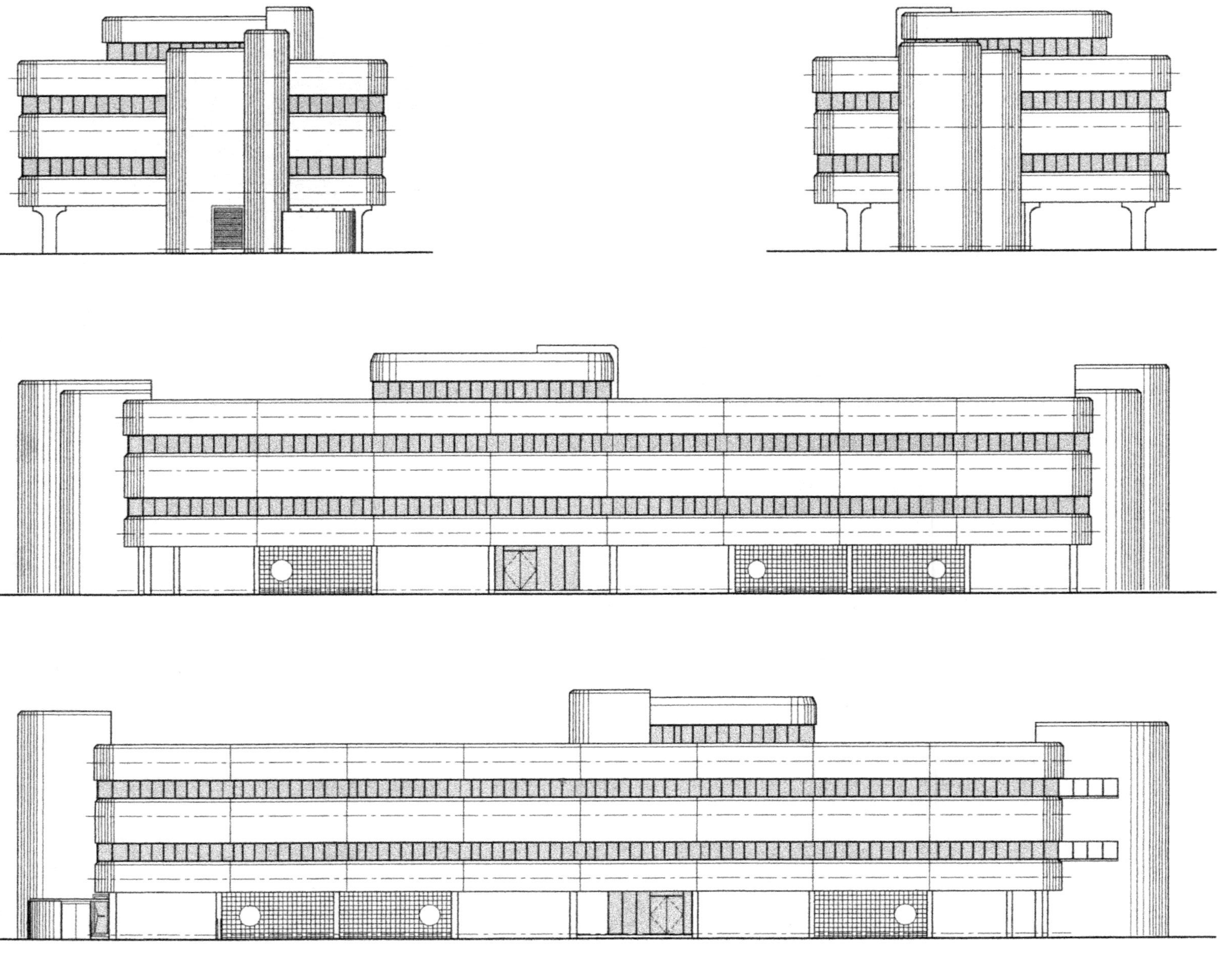

Figure 9.66 Madison Building—Stage V: Working drawings—exterior elevations.

elevation. These simple walls depend primarily on the interior finish schedule for their proper description.

Use interior elevations when you need to convey an idea, dimension, construction method, or unique feature that is better described by drafting than by a written description in the specification. For example, in a residence, the kitchen, bathrooms, special closets, and wet bars have walls that are usually drafted. On a commercial structure, you may select typical office units, showing bookcases, cabinets, display cases, and so on. In an industrial structure, you may draw the locations of equipment, conveyor belts, and special heights for bulletin boards or tool racks.

In short, interior elevations are the means of controlling the construction and surface finishes of the interior walls of a structure, and of providing information to contractors. If the contractor does not have the expertise or personnel to do a specific task, specialists (*subcontractors*) will be brought in to assist.

Naming Interior Elevations

In exterior elevations, the titles assigned—North, South, East, and West—are based on the direction the structure faces. In interior elevations, this is reversed: The title is based on the direction in which the viewer is looking. For example, if you are standing in a theater lobby facing north, the interior wall you are looking at has the title "North Lobby Elevation" (see Figure 9.67). To avoid confusion when you are naming an interior elevation, use reference bubbles like those shown in Figure 9.68.

The reference symbol shown on the left is the same as the one used in the foundation plans and framing plans to refer to details. Remember that the reference bubble is a circle with a darkened point on one side, which points to the elevation being viewed and drawn.

The reference symbol shown on the right in Figure 9.68 shows a circle with a triangle inside it. The point of the triangle tells the viewer which elevation is being viewed, and the placement of the triangle automatically divides the circle in half. The top half is filled in with a letter or number, which becomes the name of that interior elevation. The lower half contains the sheet number on which the interior elevation can be found (see also Figures 9.69 and 9.70).

Figure 9.69 shows a floor plan and a symbol used to show multiple elevations. Letter "A" is for the north elevation, "C" is for the south elevation, "B" for the west elevation, and "D" for the east elevation. Figure 9.70 shows two types of **title references** (manner in which the interior elevations are titled for ease of cross-references with the floor plan).

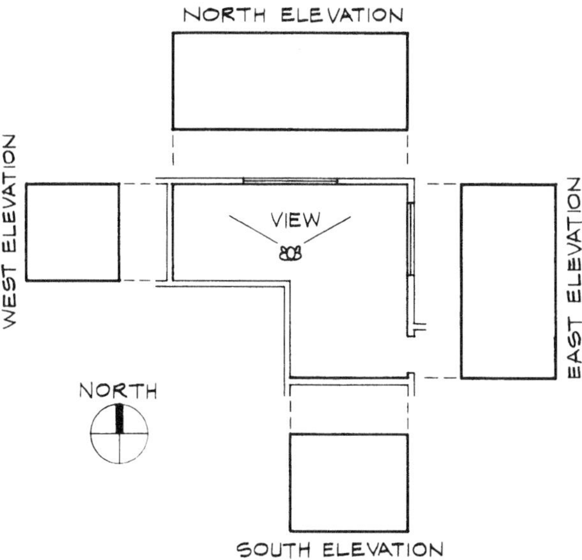

Figure 9.67 Naming interior elevations.

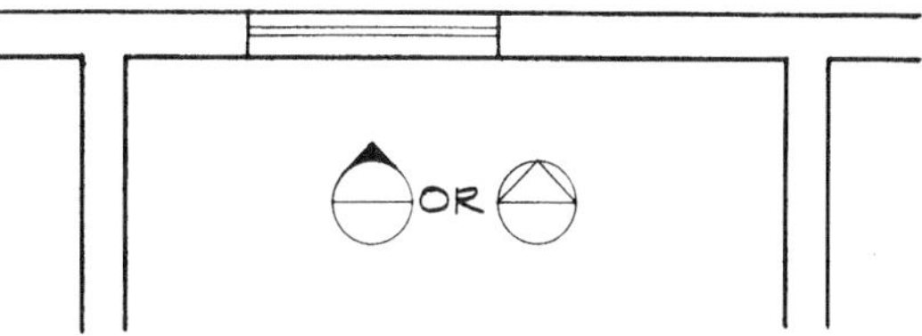

Figure 9.68 Interior elevation reference bubbles.

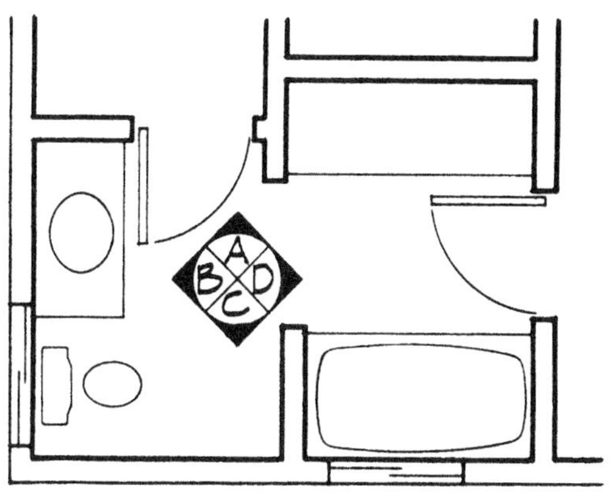

Figure 9.69 Symbol used to show multiple interior elevations.

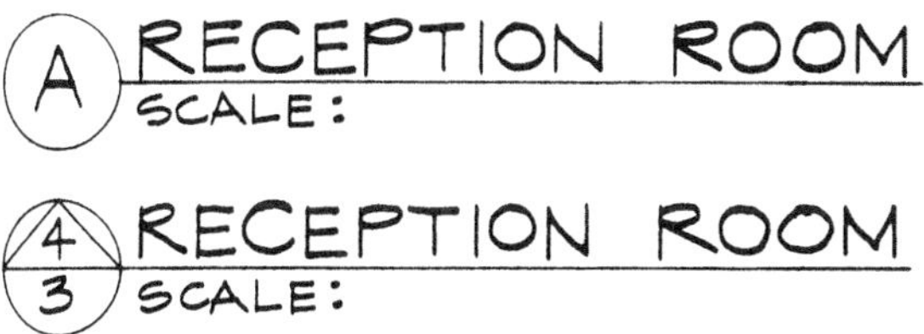

Figure 9.70 Interior elevation titles.

Choosing a Scale

The most desirable scale for an interior elevation is ½″ = 1′–0″. Most floor plans are drafted at ¼″ = 1′–0″, so using the half-inch scale makes the translation from floor plan to interior elevation easy: You only need to use a pair of dividers and double every measurement. Interior elevations are seldom drawn larger than this.

If the drawing space does not permit you to use a ½″ = 1′–0″ scale, or if the scale of the drawing calls for a smaller interior elevation, you may use a ⅜″ = 1′–0″ or ¼″ = 1′–0″ scale. The scale could also depend on the complexity of the wall to be shown.

Using Hidden Lines (Dotted Lines)

Dotted lines are used extensively on interior elevations. As in the drafting of exterior elevations, the dotted line is used to show door-swing direction—for example, for cabinets or for bifold doors on a wardrobe closet. See Figure 9.71. Dotted lines are also used to represent items hidden from view, such as the outline of a kitchen sink, shelves in a cabinet, or the vent above a hood vent, range, or cooktop.

Dotted lines are also used to show the outline of objects to be added later or those *not in the contract* (designated as *NIC*). For example, the outline of a washer and dryer or refrigerator is shown; even though the appliances themselves are NIC, space must be allowed for them. The wall behind the appliance is shown, including duplex convenience outlets, and molding or trim at the base of the wall.

Other Drafting Considerations

To draft interior elevations of cabinets, you must know the type, countertop material, heights, general design, and number of cabinet doors.

There are three main types of cabinet doors: **flush**, **flush overlay**, and **lip**. As Figure 9.72 shows, flush overlay doors cover the total face of the cabinet. The front surface of the cabinet, called the **face frame**, does not show. The flush door is shown in Figure 9.73 and the lip door in Figure 9.74. Because the face frame of the cabinet shows when either lip or flush cabinet doors are used, the face frame appears the same in the interior elevation.

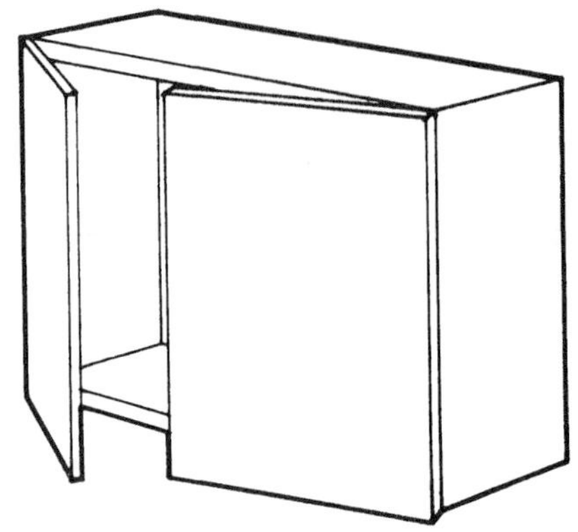

Figure 9.72 Flush overlay doors.

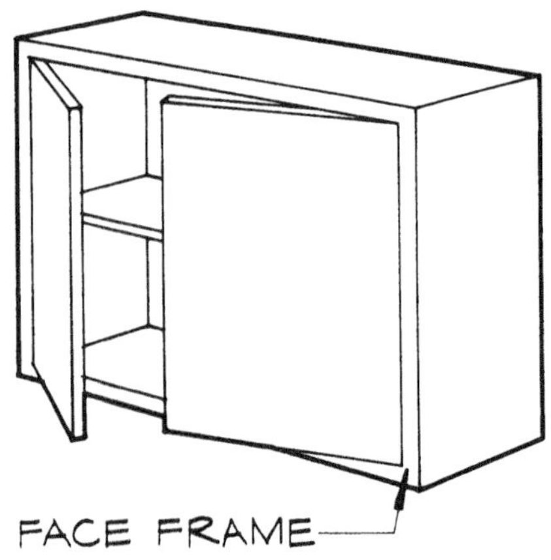

Figure 9.73 Flush doors.

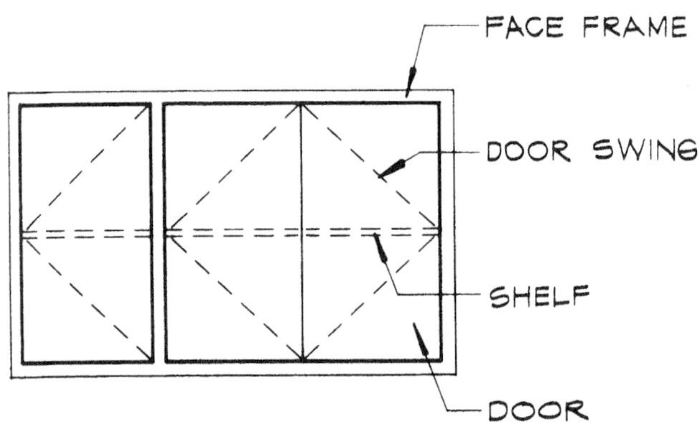

Figure 9.71 Typical elevation of cabinet.

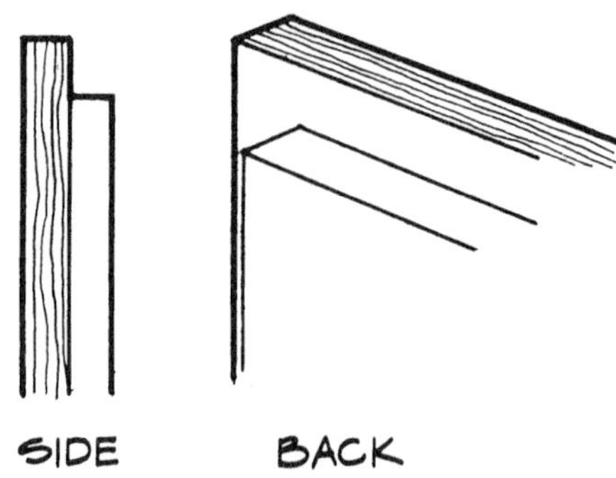

Figure 9.74 Lip door.

Material Designation and Noting

Materials for interior elevations are represented similar to the materials for exterior elevations. Noting is kept simple, and generic terms are often used. Specific information, brand names, workmanship notes, procedures, applications, and finishes are placed in the specifications. Later in this chapter you will see examples of generic noting for such items as ceramic tile countertops, an exhaust hood (with a note to "see specs"), and metal partitions.

Outline of Interior Elevations

The outline of an interior elevation represents the outermost measurement of a room. Objects that project toward the viewer, such as cabinets, beams, and air-conditioning ducts, are drawn. Some architectural offices deal with these as if they were in section, but most prefer to treat them as shown in Figures 9.75 and 9.76. Note in Figure 9.76 that the tops of the cabinets have been eliminated in drafting the outline of the cabinet.

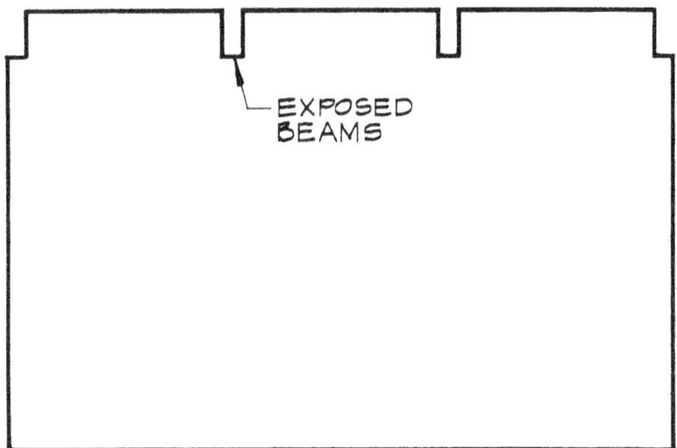

Figure 9.75 Exposed beams.

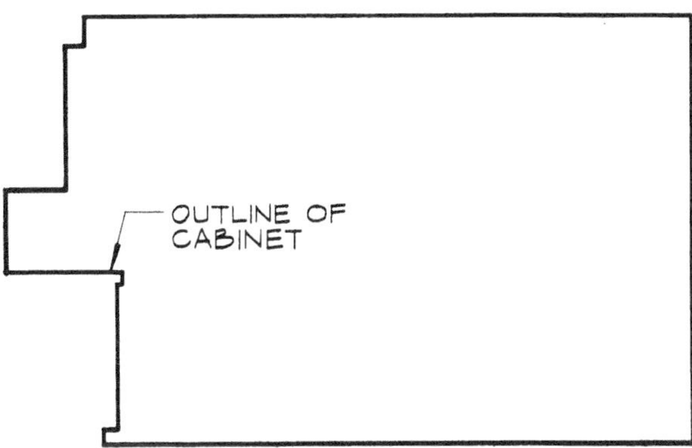

Figure 9.76 Outline of cabinet.

Planning for Children and Persons with Disabilities

Always have information available on standards affecting facilities that should be usable by children and persons with disabilities. Here are some of the standards established by several states for disabled persons:

1. Door opening: minimum size 2′–8″ clear
2. Restroom grab bars: 33″ to 36″ above the floor
3. Towel bars: 3′–4″ maximum above floor
4. Top of lavatory: 34″ maximum above floor
5. Drinking fountains: 3′–0″ maximum

Many standards can be obtained by writing to the proper authority, such as the state architect's office. Most standards are presented in the form of a drawing. See Chapter 1 for specifics, and see Figures 9.94 and 9.95 for examples.

■ DIMENSIONS AND INTERSECTIONS

Dimensions

When you draft a set of interior elevations, do not repeat dimensions that appear elsewhere. For example, you need not indicate the width of rooms on the interior elevation. In fact, avoid repeating dimensions at all costs.

In a similar way, you do not need to dimension the interior elevation of the counter shown in Figure 9.77, because it will occupy the total width of the room. The boundaries, which are the walls, are already dimensioned on the floor plan.

The interior elevations for Figure 9.77 will show a counter, walls, window, and an opening. The portion of the counter that returns toward the opening should be dimensioned either on the floor plan or on the interior elevations, but not on both. See Figure 9.78.

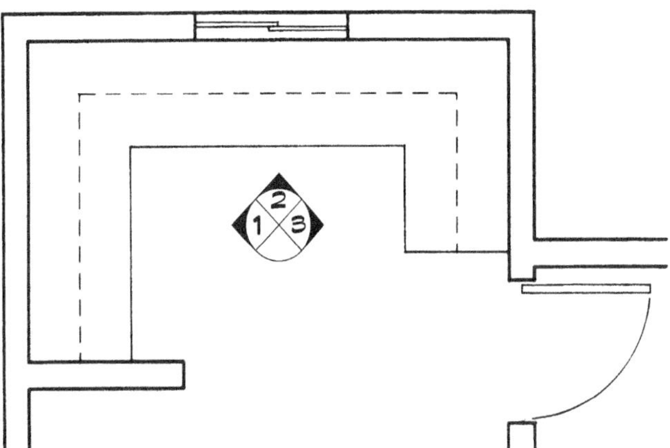

Figure 9.77 Partial plan of food preparation area.

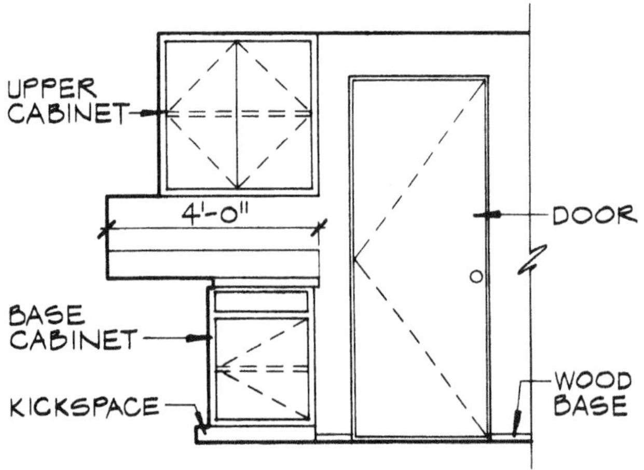

Figure 9.78 Partial interior elevation.

Notice how the base cabinet is dimensioned; in fact, the space between the door and the cabinet could have been dimensioned instead. Deciding whether to dimension the space or the cabinet is based on which is more important. If the space is left for an appliance or some other piece of equipment, then the space should be dimensioned.

The interior elevation is also the place to provide such information as the location of medicine cabinets, the heights of built-in drawers, the locations of mirrors, the required clearance for a hood above a range, and the heights of partitions.

Intersection of Wall and Floor

Interior elevations can also show, in a simple way, the wall and floor intersection. This can be achieved by applying a topset, covering the floor, or using a base or a base and a shoe. This creates a transition between the floor and wall planes. **Topset** is made of flexible material such as rubber and placed on the wall where it touches the floor. With **coving**, the floor material is curved upward against the wall. A **base** is used to cover, or as a guide to control, the thickness of the plaster on the wall, and a **shoe** covers the intersection between the wall and floor. See Figure 9.79.

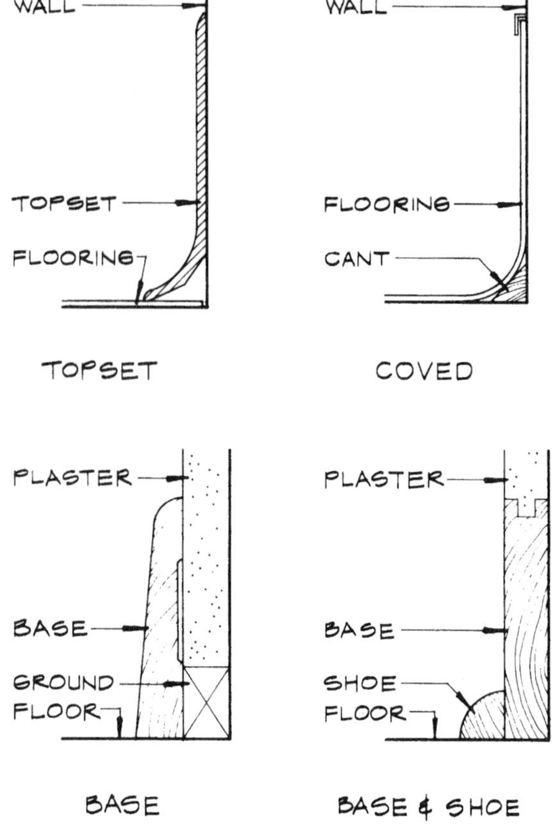

Figure 9.79 Intersection of wall and floor.

DRAFTING AN INTERIOR ELEVATION: EXAMPLES

A Kitchen

Figure 9.80 shows a perspective view of a kitchen. The main portion has lip doors on the cabinets, and the extreme left side (not shown in the perspective) has flush overlay doors. Different types of cabinet doors are not usually mixed on a single project; here the intention is simply to show the different methods used to represent them on an interior elevation. Figure 9.81 shows a floor plan of the perspective drawing in Figure 9.80. Note the flush overlay cabinet on the left and the lip or flush cabinets on the right. The upper and base cabinets, slightly to the left of center, project forward.

Figure 9.82 shows the drafted interior elevation of one side of the floor plan of the kitchen. You should take careful note of these points:

1. The difference in the method of representing a flush overlay and a lip door on the cabinets
2. The outlining of the cabinet on the extreme right side of the drawing
3. The use of dotted lines to show door swing, shelves, and the outline of the sink
4. The handling of the forward projection of the upper and base cabinets slightly to the left of center
5. Dimensions and, eventually, the location of notes

A Lobby and Restroom

Figure 9.83 shows a partial floor plan for the lobby and restroom area of an office building. Figure 9.84 shows

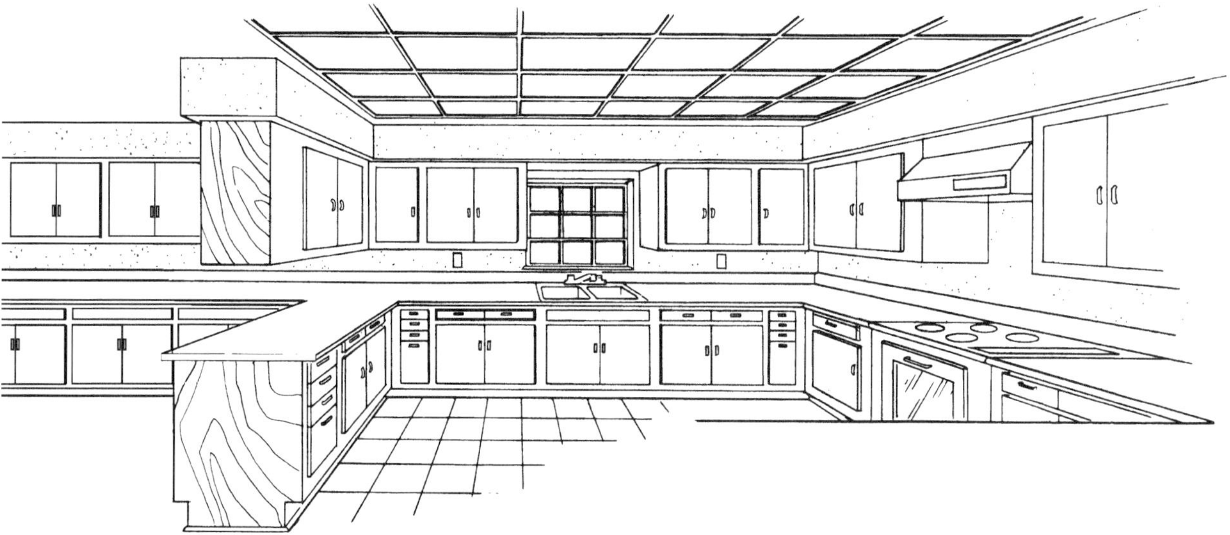

Figure 9.80 Perspective view of a kitchen.

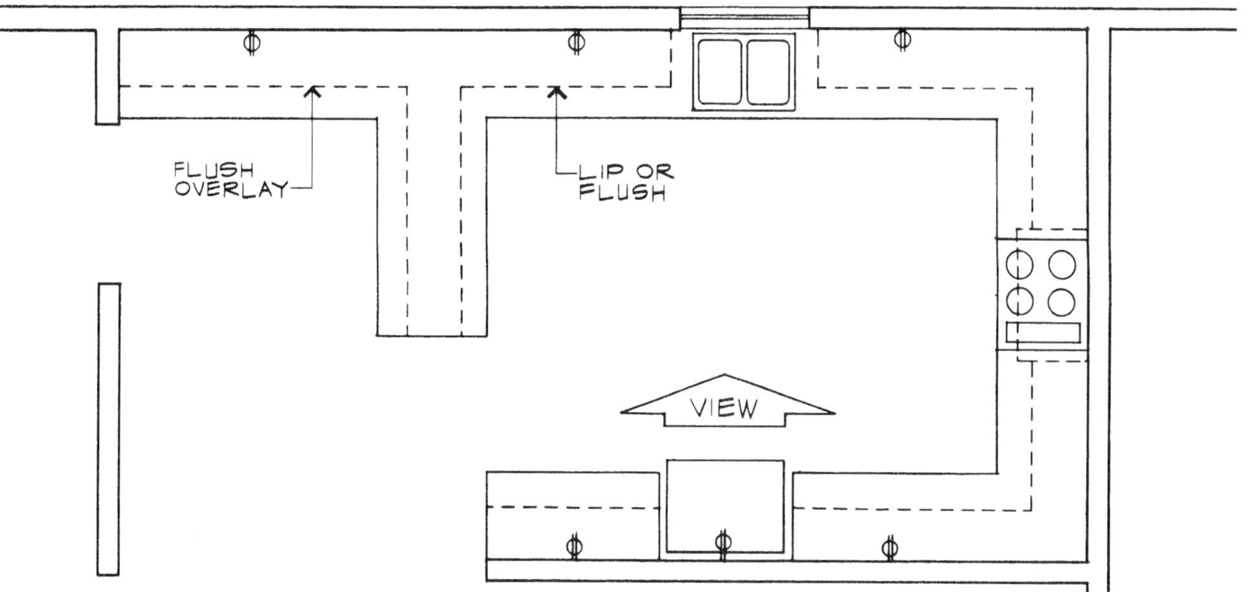

Figure 9.81 Partial floor plan of kitchen.

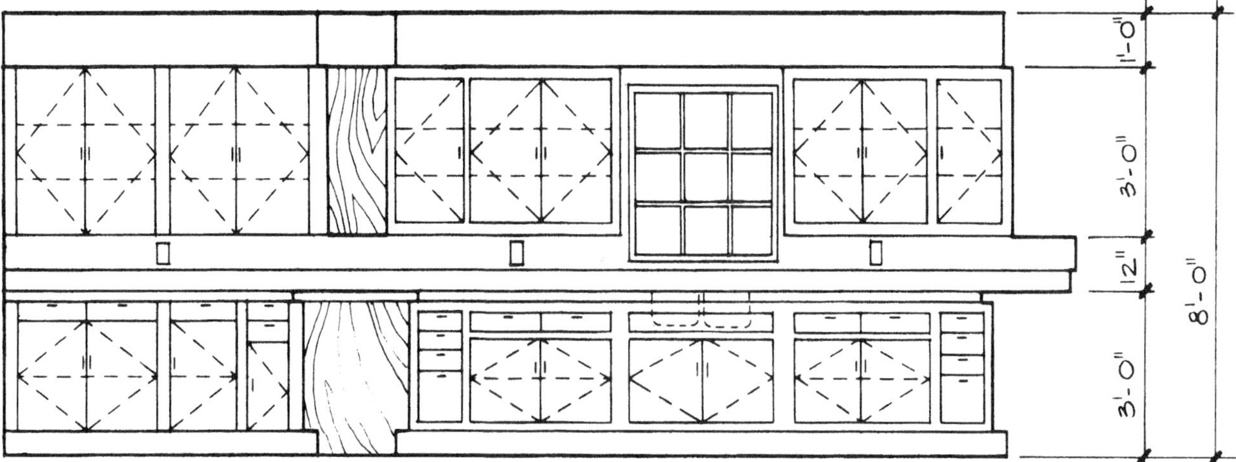

Figure 9.82 Interior elevation of Figure 9.80.

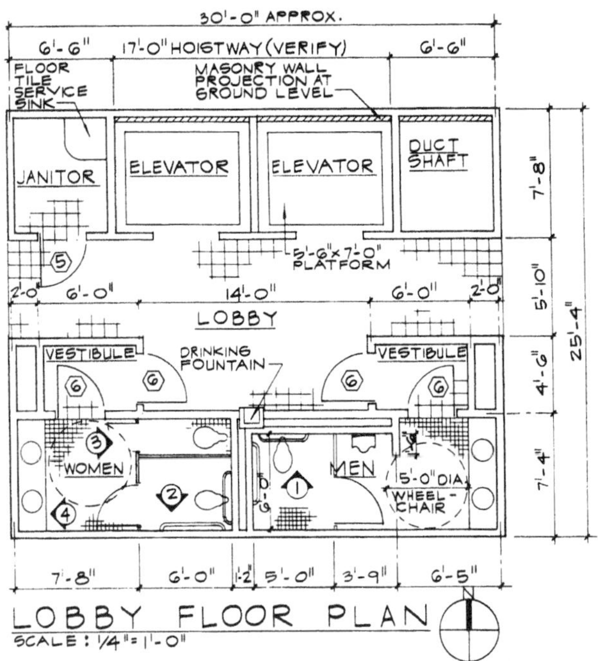

Figure 9.83 Partial floor plan of lobby and restroom. (Courtesy of Westmount, Inc., Real Estate Development.)

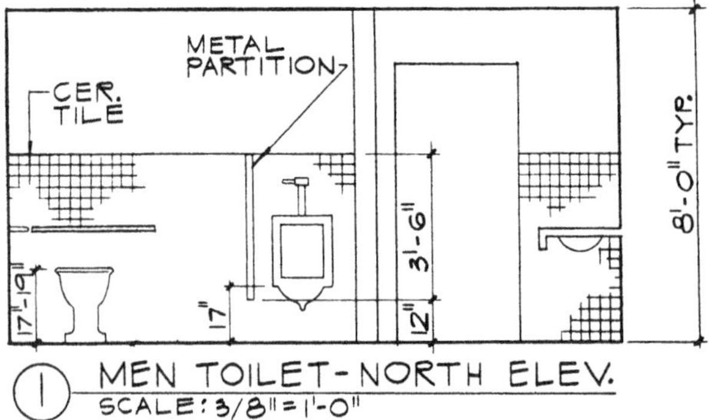

Figure 9.84 Men's toilet: North elevation. (Courtesy of Westmount, Inc., Real Estate Development.)

the north elevation of the men's toilet. Because this is a public facility, access for persons with disabilities is shown on both the partial floor plan and the interior elevation.

■ COMPUTERS AND INTERIOR ELEVATIONS

The drafting of a set of interior elevations for any structure, be it commercial, industrial, or residential, becomes a relatively painless task when you enlist the aid of a computer. Textures are easily applied to a drawing by using the appropriate commands. If you are drawing full scale in model space, you can transfer heights from the datum layer of the sections and the width and depth of a room from the floor plan.

Cabinet outlines, plumbing fixtures, and many other outlines can be imported from a set of previously developed drawings, or frequently can be found in a collection of shapes. A collection may include configurations and conventions for electrical, cabinetry, plumbing, and other categories, all stored in a library file of symbols and conventions.

The unique shapes of fireplaces, elevators, lifts, handrails, stairs, and so on can be purchased in a generic format, or exact sizes can be obtained from the manufacturers.

EVOLUTION OF A SET OF INTERIOR ELEVATIONS

This section is devoted to the various developmental stages of interior elevations. The Kavanaugh residence was selected to illustrate this. It has an exposed ridge and vaulted ceilings in some of its rooms, including the master suite, dining room, family room, library, kitchen, living room, and guest room. See Figure 9.75 and its accompanying text for a description of how to pictorially draw exposed beams in an interior elevation. The early stages of the floor plan are shown in Figure 9.85.

Stage I (Figure 9.86). Stage I, called the **ease** or **datum stage**, sets the parameters. These include the width from wall to wall and the height, and the changes that may occur in the floor or ceiling level. Before beginning this stage, the drafter should consult the project book and become familiar with the sizes and shapes of the various kitchen appliances, plumbing fixtures, cabinets, washer and dryer, and so forth.

Stage II (Figure 9.87). Once the maximum size of the room is determined, the real outline of the interior elevation is established by drawing in the soffits, cabinets, fireplaces, and so on. Doors and windows may also be included in this stage. The total outline is now converted to a dark outline.

Stage III (Figure 9.88). This is the stage at which various products are added to what is basically an empty room: bathtubs, toilets, built-in bookshelves, fireplaces, and so on.

Stage IV (Figure 9.89). Material designations and patterns, such as ceramic tile wainscots, fire extinguishers, bulletin boards, and decorative added forms, are included along with texturing. Some of the shapes for such items as plumbing fixtures can often be obtained from the manufacturer. Swings on cabinet doors and outlines (dotted) of fixtures behind the exposed face, such as a sink, flues from fireplaces, and shelves, are also added at this stage.

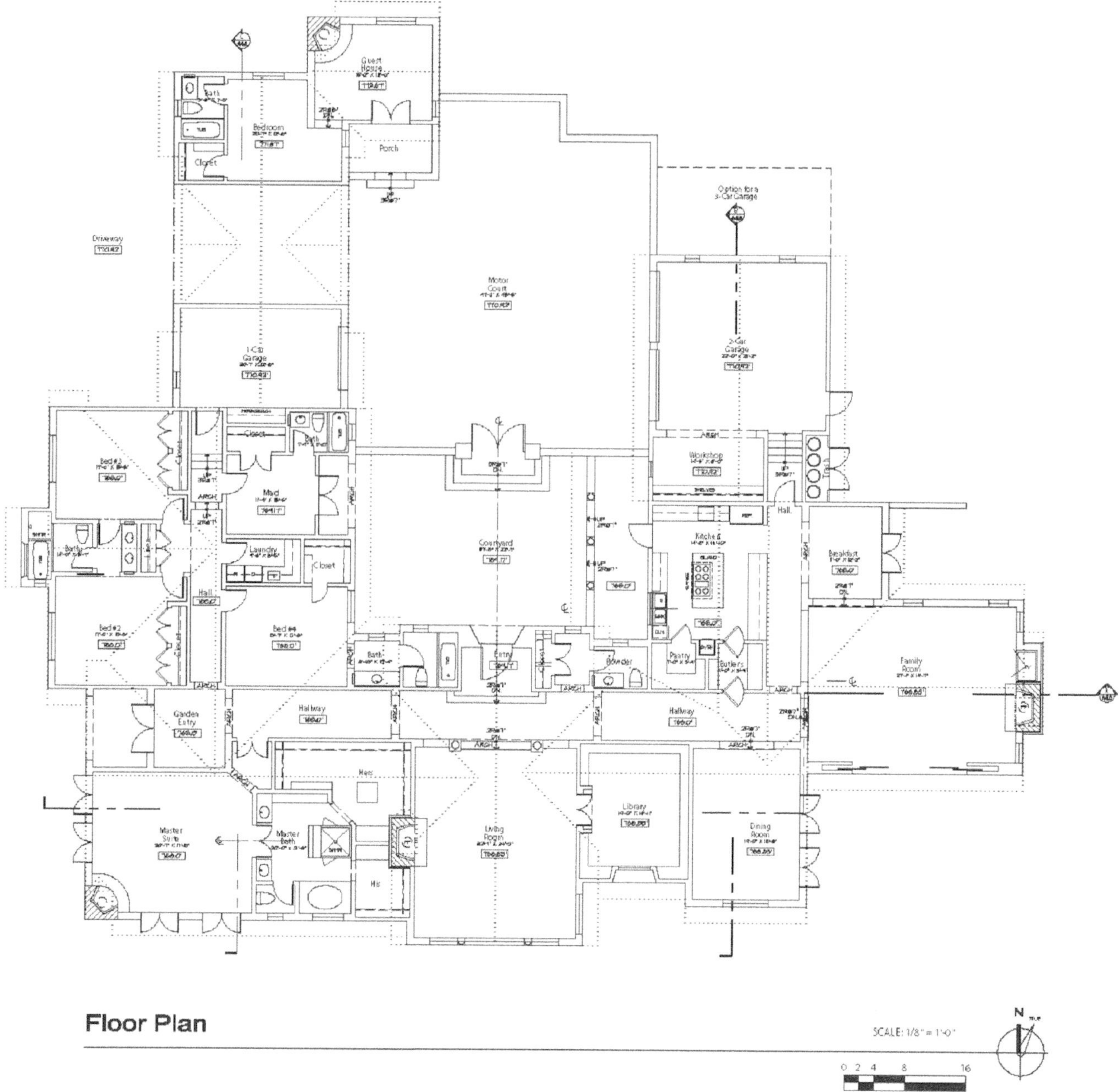

Figure 9.85 Reference floor plan.

Stage V (Figure 9.90). This is the dimensioning stage. Remember, we must locate and size all items. A good example is a mirror. It must first be sized, and its placement or position on a wall must be given to the installer. If the installation is at all complex, a detail should be drawn. If a description is needed, the detailer must know whether the item is described in the specifications. If it is, a generic title is all that is needed at this stage.

Dimensioning also calls for setting limits, such as the clearance of a water closet (toilet) between a wall and a cabinet. Some building codes require a minimum 15″ distance between the center of the water closet and the adjacent wall.

Stage VI (Figure 9.91). Notes, references, and titles are included at this stage. Use the following checklist as a guide, or develop your own.

A. Call-outs for all surface materials, other than those included on the finish schedule.

B. A description of all appliances, even those that are not on the surface facing the observer: for example, sinks, garbage disposals, and recessed medicine cabinets.

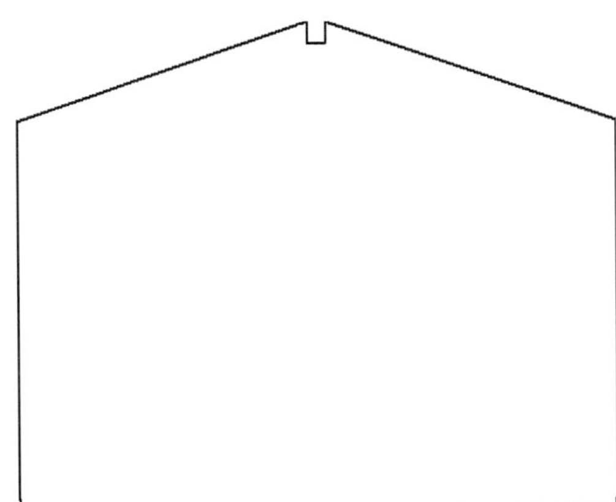

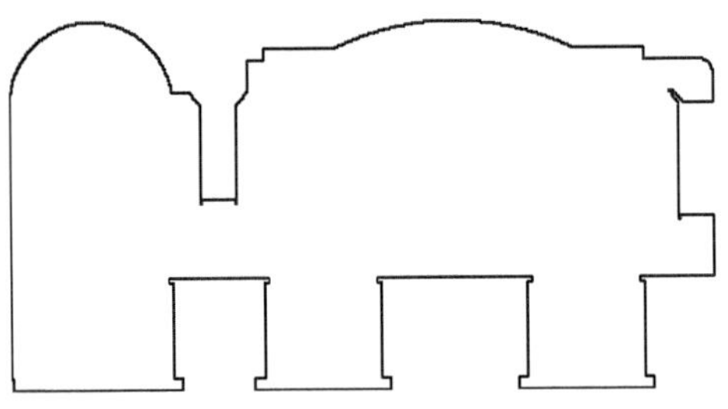

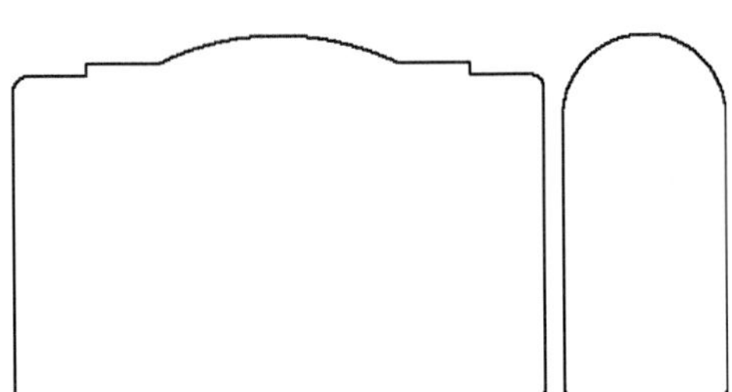

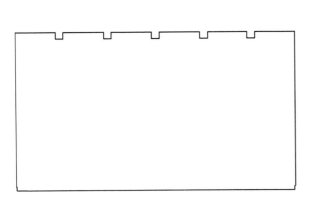

Figure 9.86 Stage I: Datum.

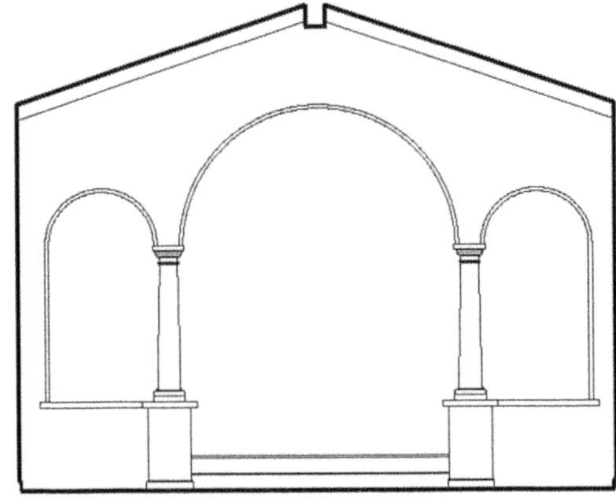

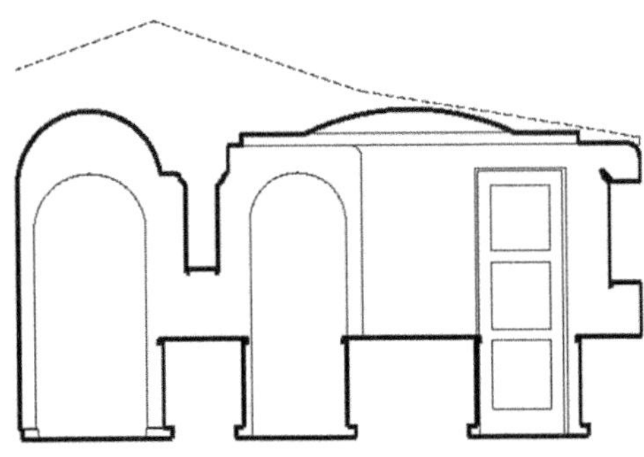

Figure 9.87 Stage II: Real outline and doors and windows.

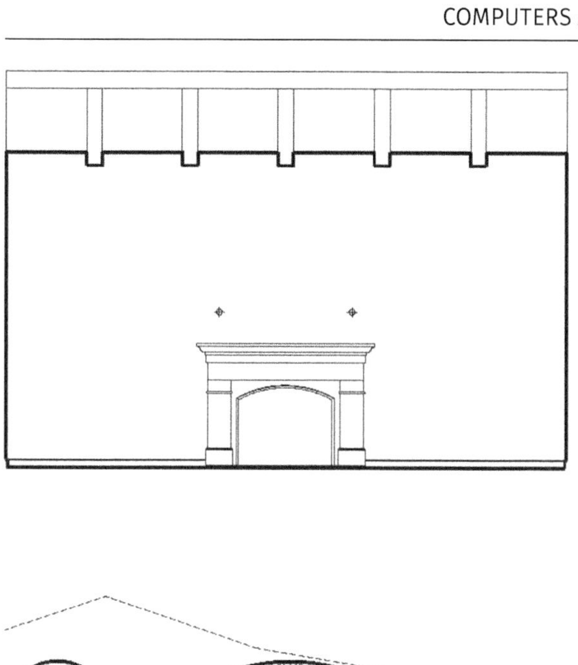

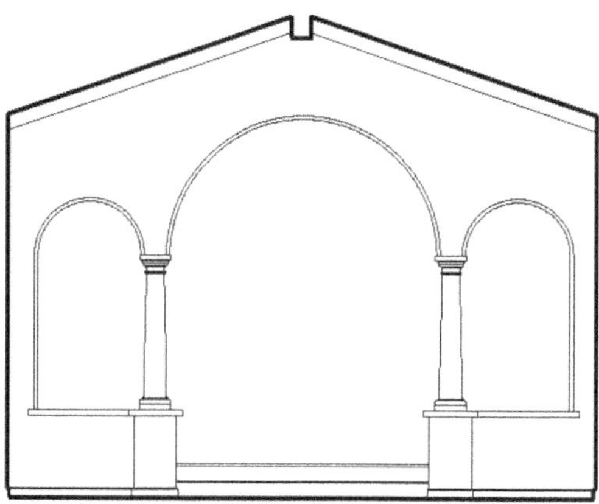

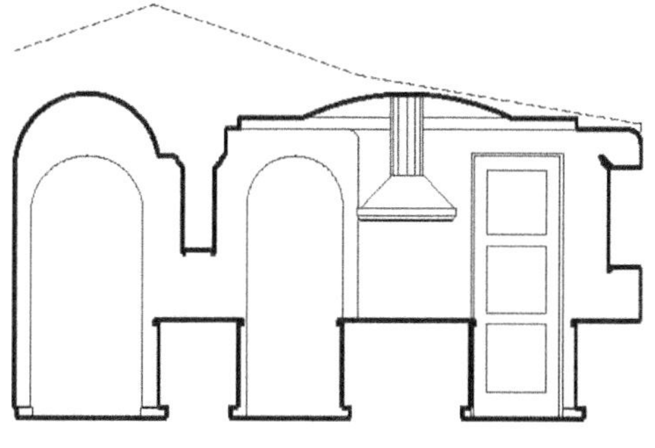

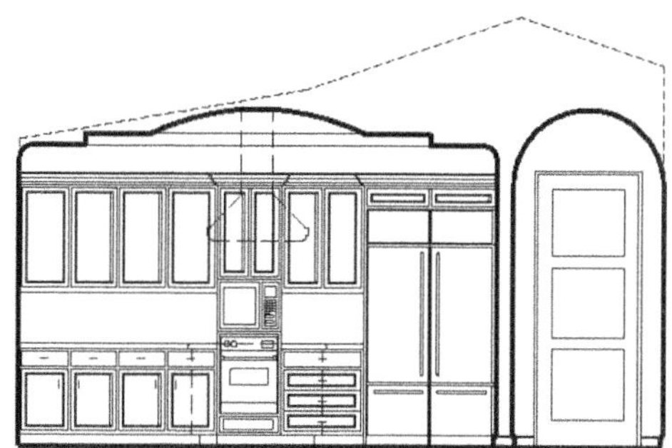

Figure 9.88 Stage III: Products and appliances.

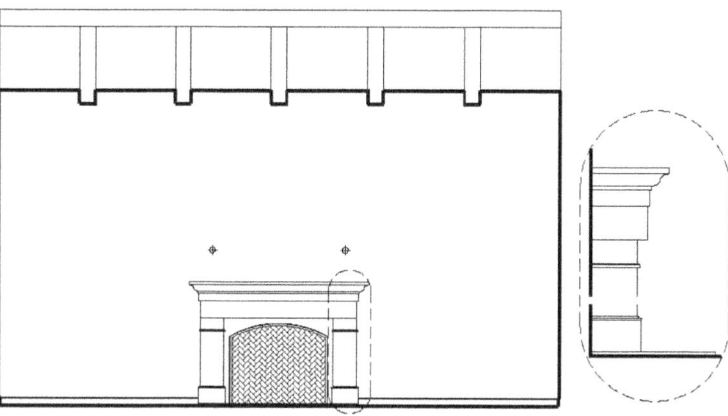

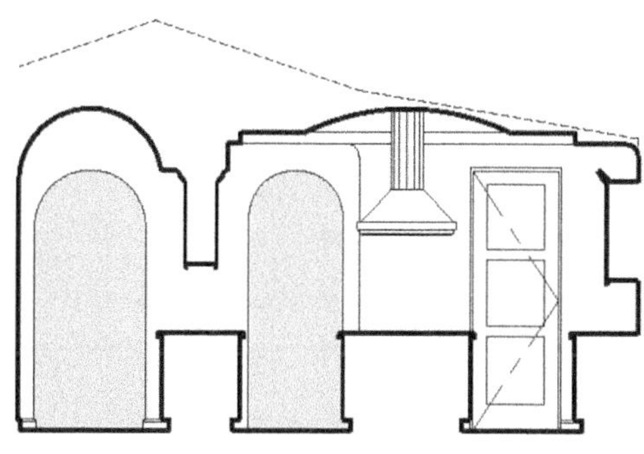

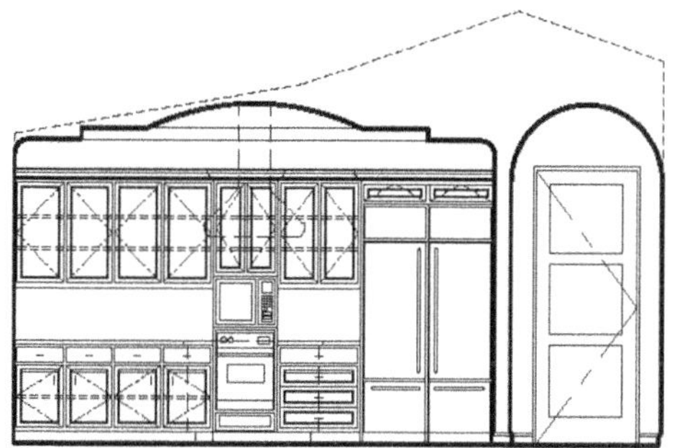

Figure 9.89 Stage IV: Material designation and patterns.

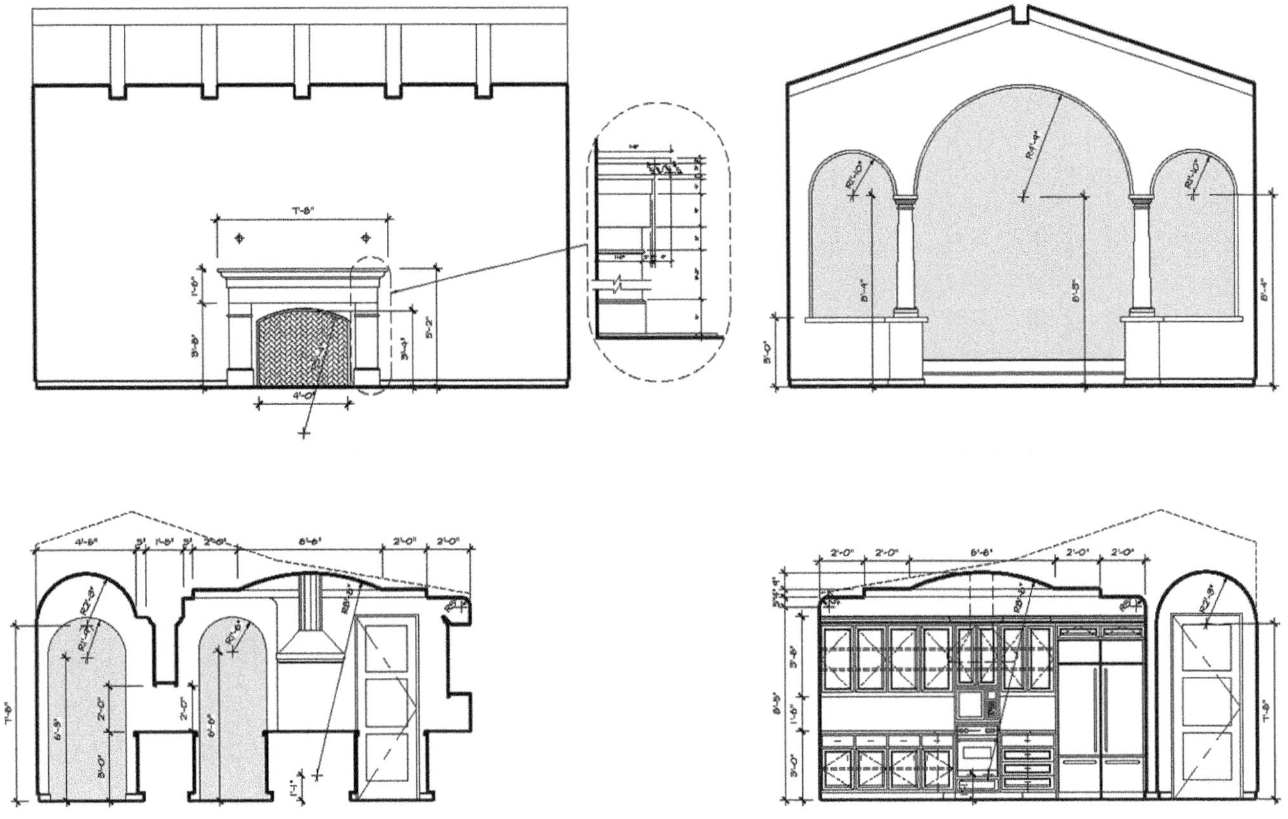

Figure 9.90 Stage V: Dimensioning.

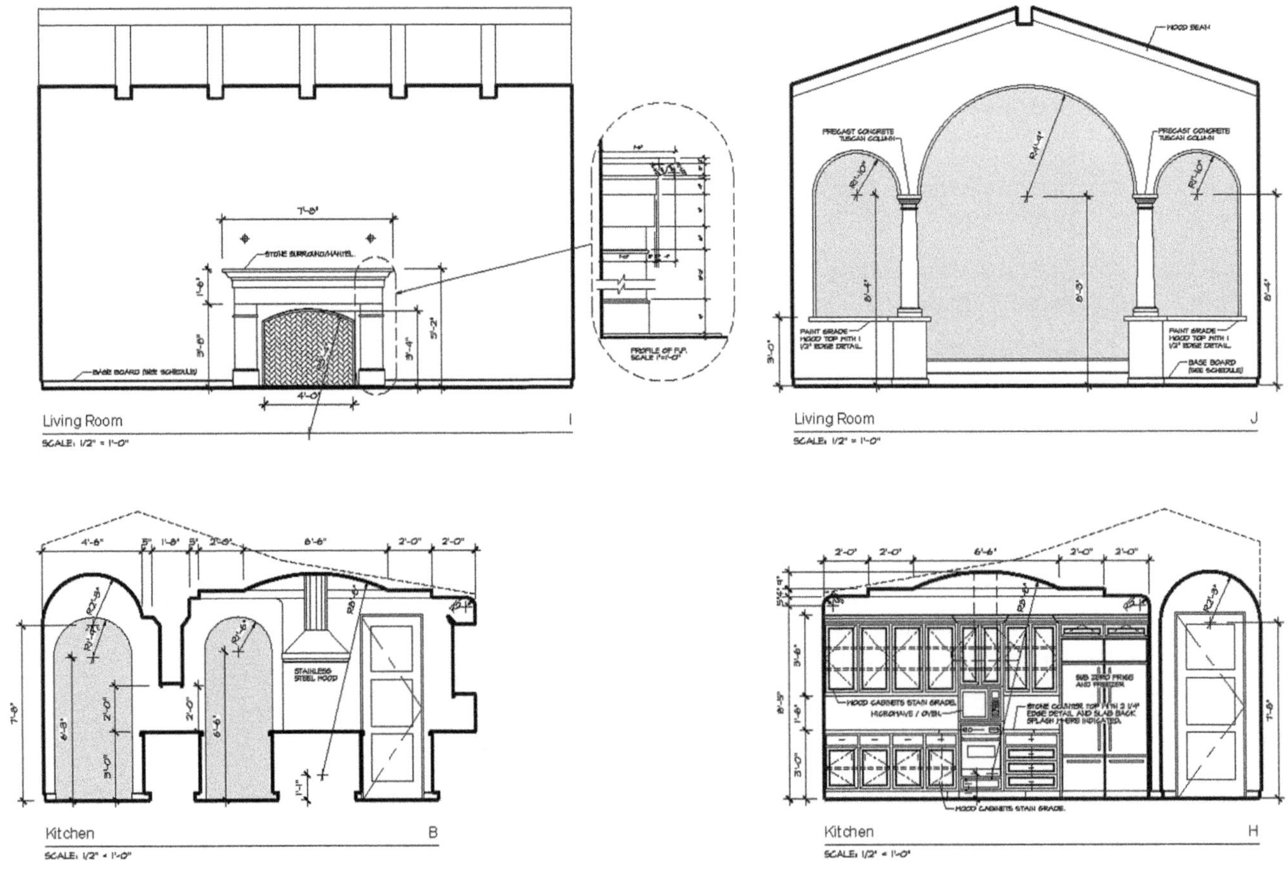

Figure 9.91 Stage VI: Noting, referencing, and titles.

C. A description of items that are not standard. The open shelves in a master bedroom are a classic example.
D. The use of standard conventions to denote shelves, cabinet door swings, drawers, and so forth.
E. Any clearances that must be maintained; those needed for refrigerators and microwave ovens or any client-specific equipment.

Interior Elevations Using BIM

A 3-D model is already produced when you are using building information modeling (BIM). The beginning form of the interior elevation already exists in a simplified pattern and is accessed via a pull-down menu. The drafter's job now is to complete the image, add detail, reference to existing details, do dimensioning when necessary, and note the materials used.

The pull-down menu is used again to obtain the designed outline form of the interior elevation. Before you begin enhancement of the interior elevations, double-check the existing datums, especially for the width and height of each room. The objects that are closest to the viewer are dark. The objects farther away from the viewer are just a bit lighter, but still dark in relation to such things as doors, windows, dimensions, and so on. Remember, this is not just a technical drawing with standard line types; it is also a piece of artwork putting the design into visual images so that the draftspersons in the field can easily visualize their task.

The second stage is to put in the appliances and fixtures. In the third stage, you add material designations and patterns. Fourth is dimensioning as needed to help the draftsperson. Finally, you will add noting, referencing, and of course titles and scale.

Review Figure 9.92 for a complete interior elevation sheet completed with manufacturer provided Revit files, in this example, for all of the appliances and even the furniture which enhances the interior elevations.

BIM programs are rather complex in their ability to provide a significant level of detail for the client to better imagine the end product. While most architects provide this as an additional service and charge added fees for the generation of 3-D renderings, it can be a great tool for communication. Often clients have trouble visualizing the flat 2-D line drawings and a perspective image helps fill in the missing information. See Figures 9.94 and 9.95 for examples of this image. Note the kitchen in the Figure 9.93 and see how it comes to life in the rendering. Many offices outsource this service when staffing is limited or if timeline for a project is tight with the current staffing situation.

The computer/scanner combination is a great partnership, making it possible to draw complex buildings and structures in three dimensions. Using BIM is a good example of turning 3-D drawings into workable and precise construction documents, via computer-aided design software, such as Revit.

CASE STUDIES FOR INTERIOR DEVELOPMENT

Interior Elevations

Stage I. The partial floor plan shown in Figure 9.96 was drawn at a larger scale than the other plans. It includes the concession areas and restrooms. Only a few interior elevations are drafted here.

Here, the partial floor plan is drawn twice the size of the first-floor plan. We took the measurements from the first-floor plan. At this scale, we could also show the double wall for the plumbing. (See the wall with toilets.) The four rectangles at the bottom of the drawing represent columns. Two more columns appear to be located next to the walls but are actually inside the walls. They were included for visual continuity and have no structural implications. The left half of the drawing was blocked out to receive the interior elevations, with one exception: the floor plan of the toilet on the upper-floor level located slightly left of center on the drawing. The rectangle to the right of the upper floor toilet would become the interior elevation for that toilet, while the long rectangle at the bottom would become the interior elevation of the entry to the restrooms and telephone area.

Stage II. The partial floor plan now shows the plumbing fixtures and the floor material in the restrooms. See Figure 9.97. The rectangles at the center near the entry to the restrooms are drinking fountains. Across the hall are the stairs to the upper level. The wall material was now added to the interior elevations. Various fixtures such as urinals, paper towel dispensers, grab bars for disabled persons, and drinking fountains were also added.

Stage III. All of the necessary dimension lines not included on the ground floor plan were located on this sheet (see Figure 9.98), as well as some of the critical dimensions on the interior elevations. Door swings were shown by dotted lines. We added the designation of floor material in the concession area.

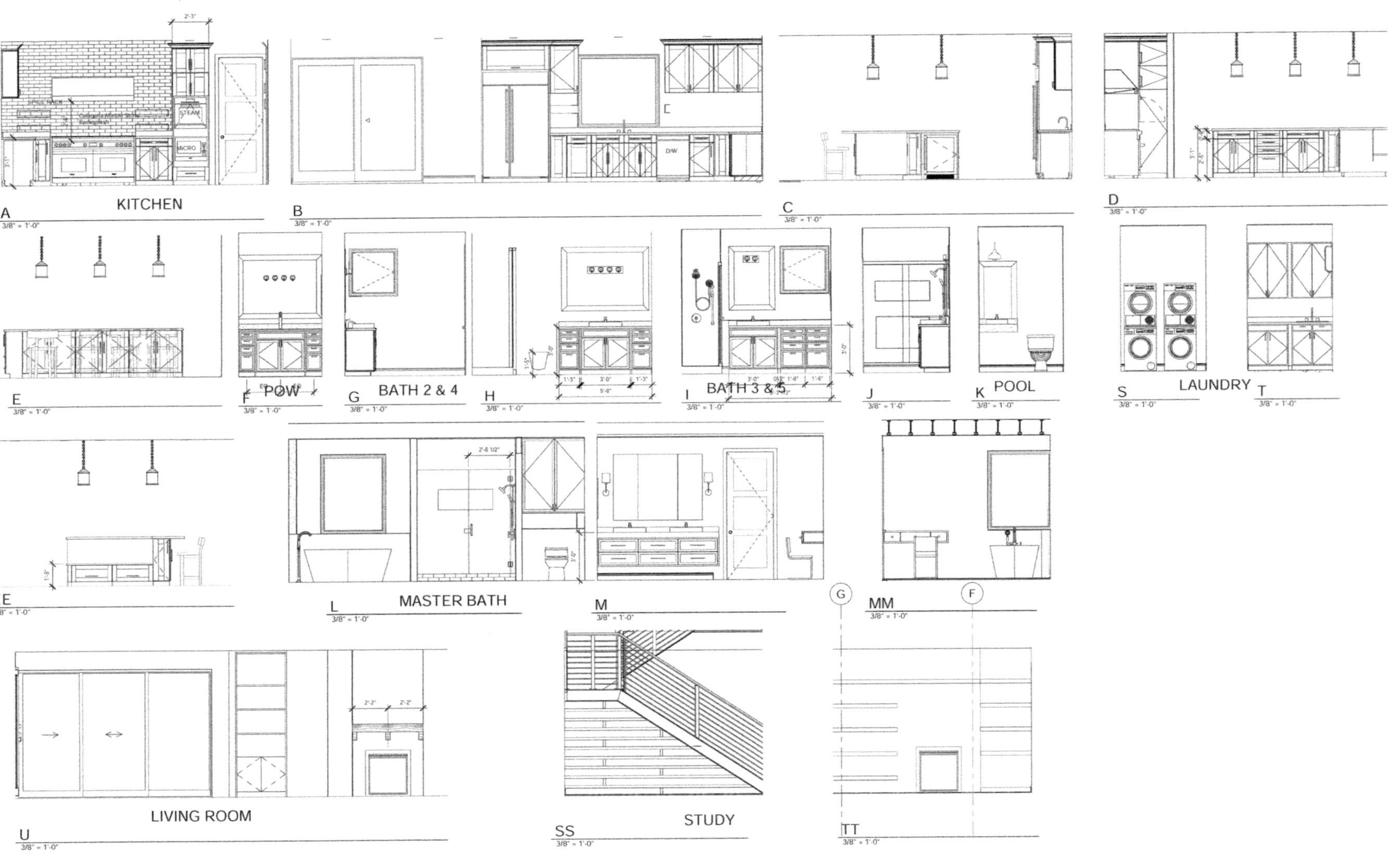

Figure 9.92 Sample BIM interior elevation sheet.

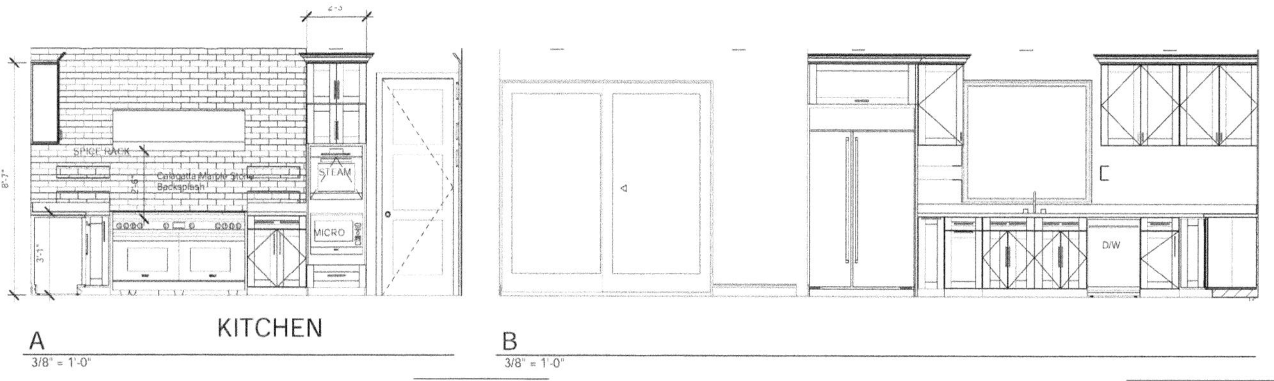

Figure 9.93 BIM Kitchen interior elevation sheet.

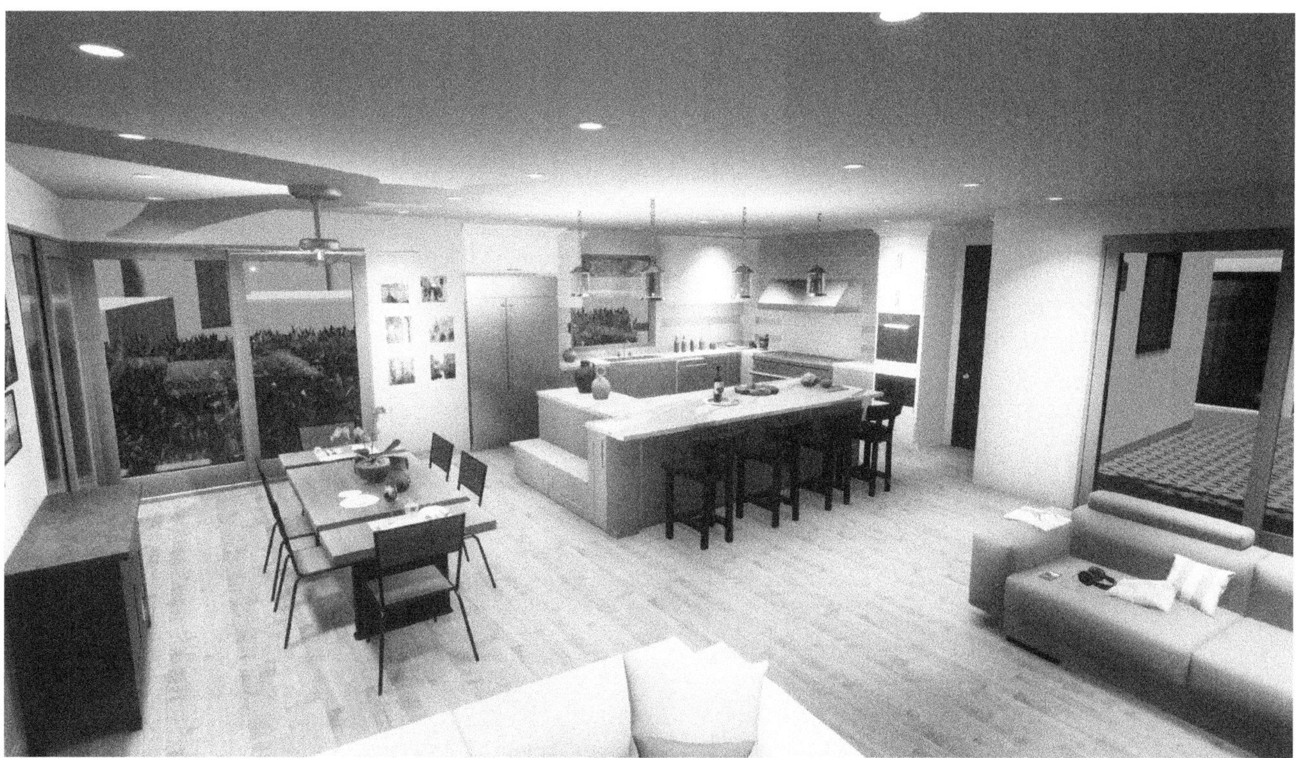

Figure 9.94 BIM kitchen interior rendering.

Figure 9.95 BIM Study interior rendering.

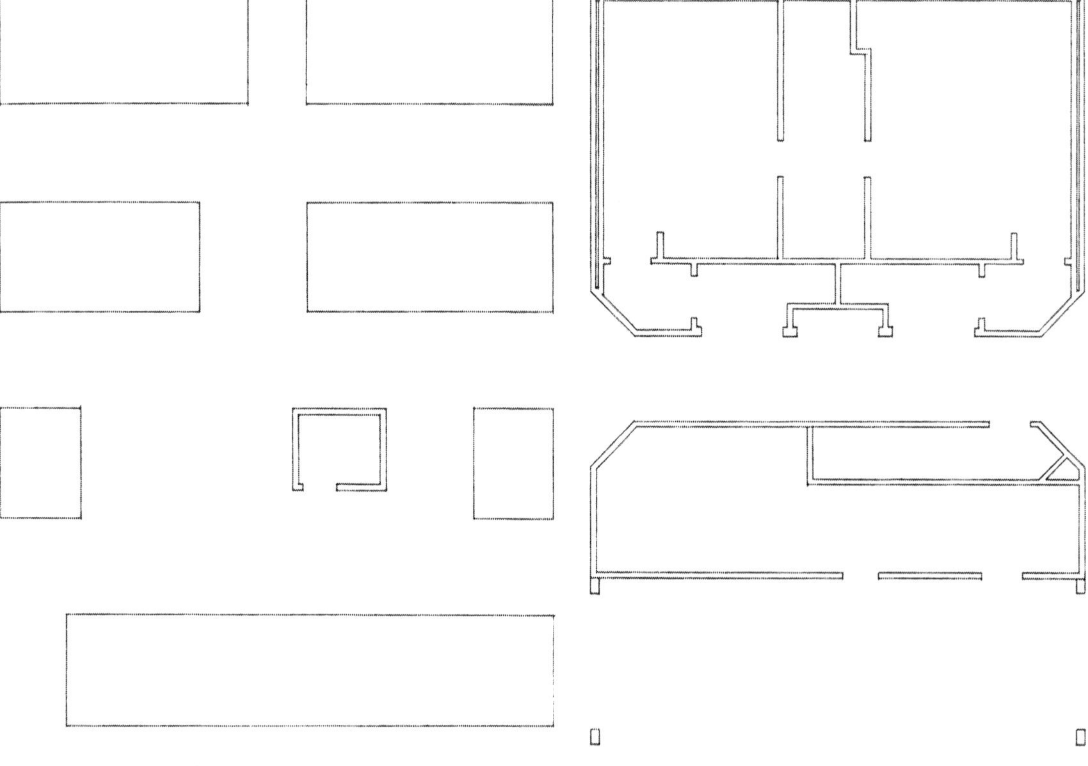

Figure 9.96 Clay Theater—Stage I Working drawings—interior elevations.

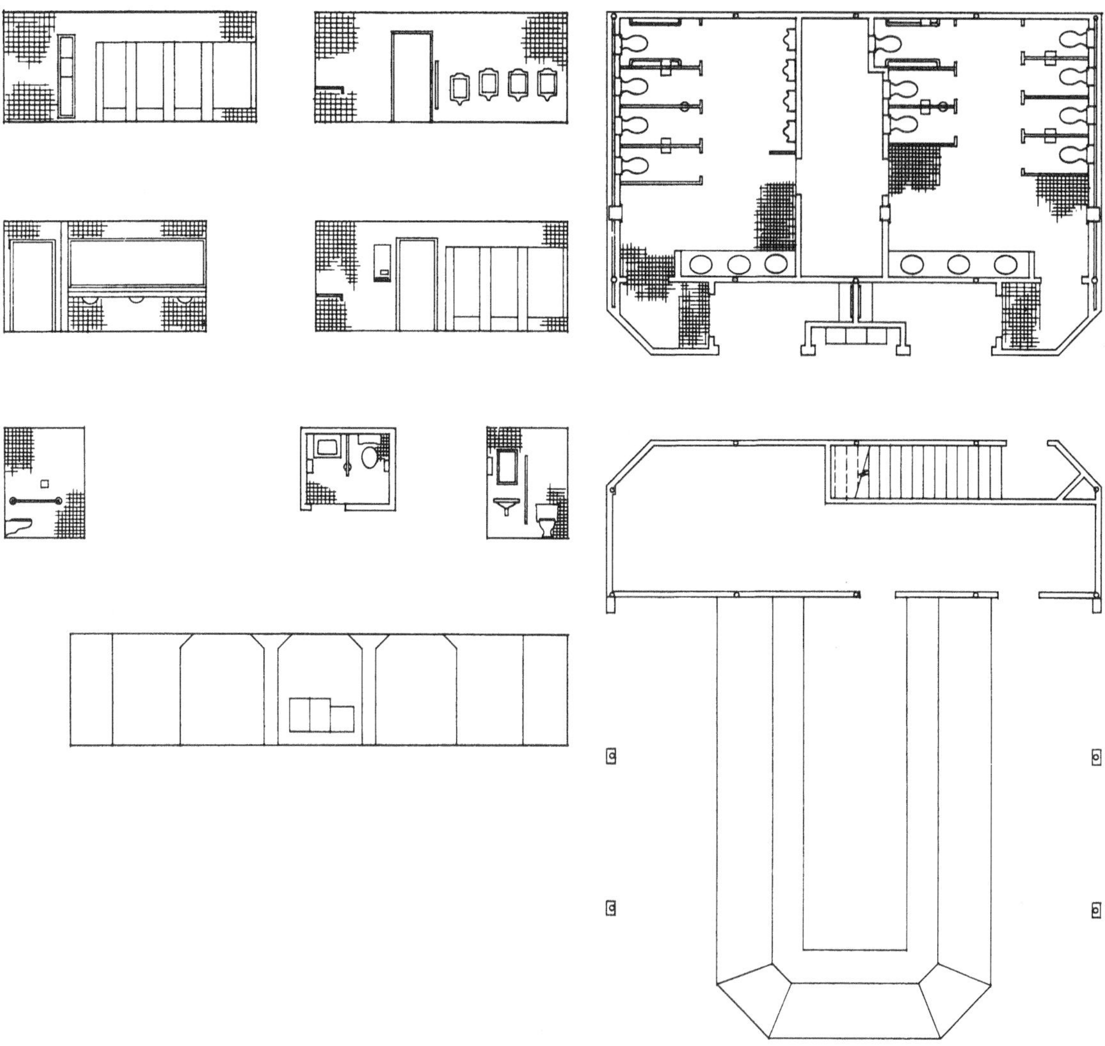

Figure 9.97 Clay Theater—Stage II Working drawings—interior elevations.

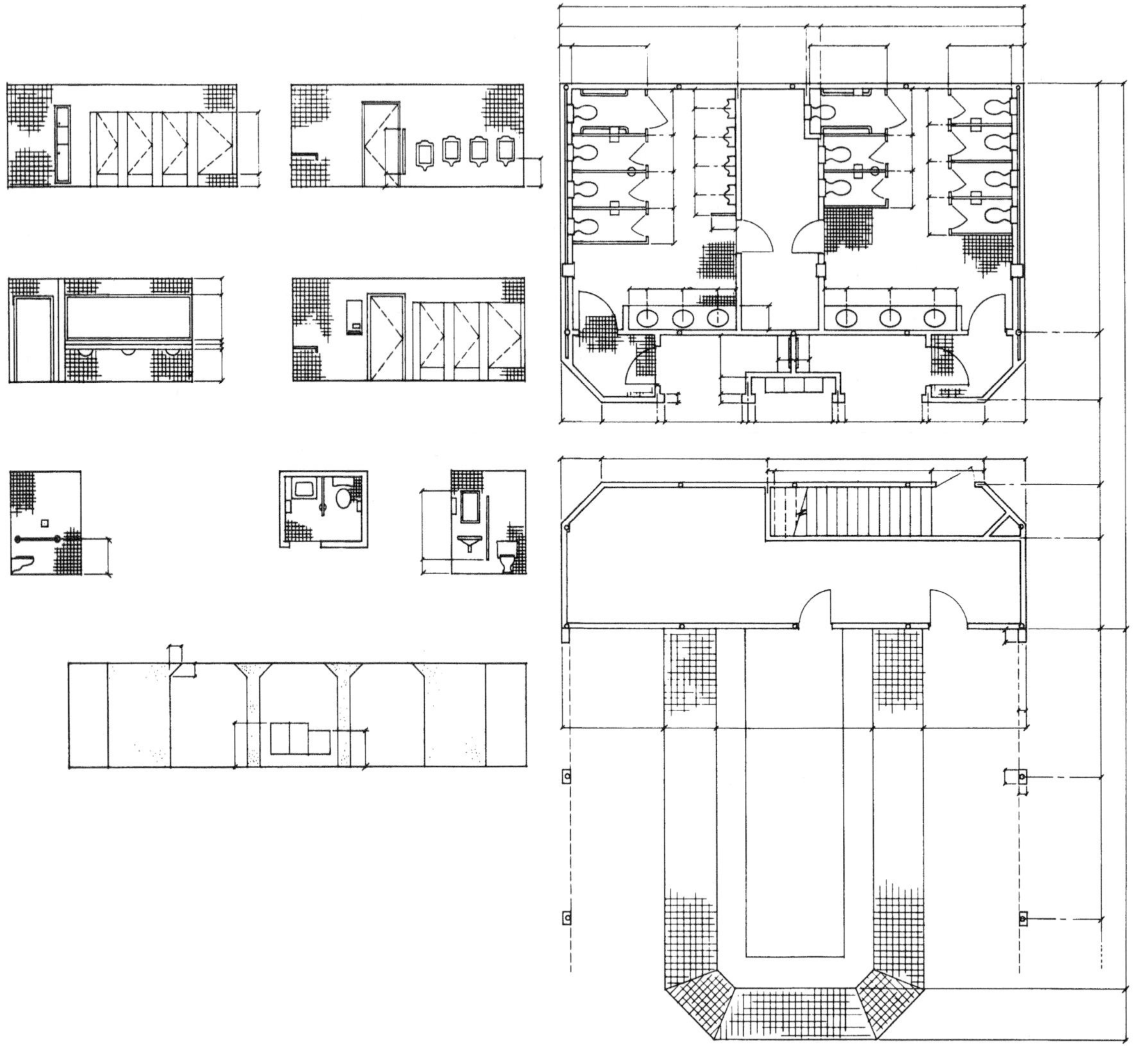

Figure 9.98 Clay Theater—Stage III Working drawings—interior elevations.

Key Terms

base
bituminous-saturated felts
building felts
cement plaster
concrete masonry units (CMU)
counterflashing
coving
datum stage
development drawing
dimensional layout
direct projection
ease
eave
exterior elevations
face frame
flush
flush overlay
fold-out
interior elevations
key plan
keynoting
let-in braces
lip
pilaster
plenum
referencing
shoe
sisal-kraft
stepped footing
stucco
title
top plates
topset

chapter

10

SCHEDULES: DOOR, WINDOWS, FINISH, AND OTHERS

(dr_verner/Adobe Stock.)

The Professional Practice of Architectural Working Drawings, Sixth Edition. Nagy R. Bakhoum and Osamu A. Wakita.
© 2024 John Wiley & Sons Inc. Published 2024 by John Wiley & Sons Inc.
Companion website: www.wiley.com\go\bakhoum\theprofessionalpracticeofarchitecturalworkingdrawings

SCHEDULES

A schedule is a list or catalog of information that defines a specific object with significant details such that the object can be purchased/manufactured and installed to meet the architects desired objective. The main purpose of incorporating schedules into a set of construction documents is to provide clarity, location, sizes, materials, and information for the designation of doors, windows, room finishes, plumbing and electrical fixtures, and other such items.

Schedules may be presented in tabulated or pictorial form. Although tabulated schedules in architectural offices vary in form and layout from office to office, the same primary information is provided.

Figures 10.1 and 10.2 are examples of tabulated door and window schedules. The door schedule provides a space for the symbol, the width and height, and the thickness of the door. It also indicates whether the door is to be **solid core (SC)** or **hollow core (HC)**. The "type" column may indicate that the door has raised decorative panels, a slab door, French door, and so forth. If a glazed area is provided in a door, it would need to be tempered and that can be seen under the glazing heading in Section 10.1.

The material space may indicate what type of material is to be used; it could be vinyl, aluminum, wood, or composite. If wood is to be used for the door, such as birch or beech, and if it is paint-grade or stain-grade quality. Space for remarks is used to provide information, such as the closing device or hardware to be used, or the fire rating required for the door. In some cases, where there is insufficient space for remarks, an asterisk (*) or symbol number may be placed to the left of the schedule or in the designated box and referenced to the bottom of the schedule with the required information. Information must under no circumstances be crowded or left out. For any type of schedule that includes lettering, provide sufficient space in each frame so that your lettering is not cramped or unclear. BIM programs have numerous options to select from and a significant level can be very quickly achieved utilizing this aspect of BIM.

Symbol designations for doors and windows vary in architectural offices and are influenced by each office's procedures. For example, a circle, a hexagon, or a square may be used for all or part of the various schedules; these are the most commonly used. Typically, we do not use triangles, as these symbols are used for revision numbers or for shear walls. Figure 10.3 illustrates symbol shapes

DOOR SCHEDULE							
KEY	WIDTH	HEIGHT	THICK.	TYPE	MATERIAL	GLAZING	REMARKS
①	16'-0"	7'-0"	1 3/4"	A	STAIN		ROLL-UP SECTIONAL GARAGE DOOR.
2	3'-6"	7'-0"	1 3/4"	B	PAINT GRD. WOOD		
3	2 - 2'-6"	7'-0"	1 3/4"	C		TEMP.	FRENCH DOORS
4	2 - 2'-6"	7'-0"	1 3/4"	C		TEMP.	FRENCH DOORS
5	2 - 2'-6"	7'-0"	1 3/4"	C		TEMP.	FRENCH DOORS
6	2 - 2'-6"	7'-0"	1 3/4"	C		TEMP.	FRENCH DOORS
7	2'-8"	7'-0"	1 3/4"	D	PAINT GRD. WOOD		
8	2'-8"	7'-0"	1 3/8"	D	PAINT GRD. WOOD		SELF-CLOSING, TIGHT FITTING 20 MINUTE RATED DOOR
9	2'-8"	7'-0"	1 3/8"	D	PAINT GRD. WOOD		
10	2 - 1'-9"	7'-0"	1 3/8"	D	PAINT GRD. WOOD		
11	2'-6"	7'-0"	1 3/8"	D	PAINT GRD. WOOD		
12	2'-6"	7'-0"	1 3/8"	D	PAINT GRD. WOOD		
13	2'-0"	7'-0"	1 3/8"	D	PAINT GRD. WOOD		
14	2'-6"	8'-0"	1 3/8"	D	PAINT GRD. WOOD		
15	2 - 2'-6"	8'-0"	1 3/8"	E	PAINT GRD. WOOD		BY-PASS
16	2'-8"	8'-0"	1 3/8"	D	PAINT GRD. WOOD		
17	2'-8"	8'-0"	1 3/8"	D	PAINT GRD. WOOD		
18	2 - 3'-6"	8'-0"	1 3/8"	E	PAINT GRD. WOOD		BY-PASS
19	2'-6"	8'-0"	1 3/8"	D	PAINT GRD. WOOD		
20	2'-6"	8'-0"	1 3/8"	D	PAINT GRD. WOOD		
21	2'-8"	8'-0"	1 3/8"	D	PAINT GRD. WOOD		
22	2 - 3'-0"	8'-0"	1 3/8"	E	PAINT GRD. WOOD		BY-PASS
23	2'-8"	8'-0"	1 3/8"	D	PAINT GRD. WOOD		
24	2 - 2'-6"	8'-0"	1 3/8"	D	PAINT GRD. WOOD		
25	2'-6"	8'-0"	1 3/8"	D	PAINT GRD. WOOD		
26	2'-6"	8'-0"	1 3/8"	D	PAINT GRD. WOOD		
27	2'-6"	8'-0"	1 3/8"	D	PAINT GRD. WOOD		
28	2'-6"	8'-0"	1 3/8"	D	PAINT GRD. WOOD		

Figure 10.1 Door schedule.

WINDOW SCHEDULE							
KEY	WIDTH	HEIGHT	TYPE	MATERIAL	GLAZING	HEAD HGT. FROM F.F.	REMARKS
1	6'-0"	5'-6"	A	VINYL		7'-0"	SINGLE HUNG
2	2'-0"	5'-0"	B	VINYL		7'-0"	SINGLE HUNG
3	2'-0"	5'-0"	B	VINYL		7'-0"	SINGLE HUNG
4	6'-0"	5'-0"	A	VINYL		7'-0"	SINGLE HUNG
5	4'-0"	5'-0"	J	VINYL		7'-0"	SINGLE HUNG
6	4'-6"	5'-0"	J	VINYL		7'-0"	SINGLE HUNG
7	4'-0"	5'-0"	J	VINYL	TEMP.	7'-0"	SINGLE HUNG
8	2'-0"	5'-0"	B	VINYL	TEMP.	7'-0"	SINGLE HUNG
9	2'-0"	5'-0"	B	VINYL	TEMP.	7'-0"	SINGLE HUNG
10	6'-0"	5'-0"	A	VINYL		7'-0"	SINGLE HUNG. EGRESS
11	1'-6"	3'-8"	E	VINYL	TEMP.	8'-0"	SINGLE HUNG
12	1'-9"	5'-6"	B	VINYL		8'-0"	SINGLE HUNG
13	3'-8"	5'-6"	F	VINYL		8'-0"	SINGLE HUNG
14	1'-9"	5'-6"	B	VINYL		8'-0"	SINGLE HUNG
15	2'-6"	5'-0"	G	VINYL		8'-0"	SINGLE HUNG. EGRESS
16	4'-0"	3'-8"	C	VINYL		8'-0"	SINGLE HUNG
17	6'-0"	5'-0"	A	VINYL		8'-0"	SINGLE HUNG. EGRESS
18	2'-0"	3'-8"	E	VINYL	TEMP.	8'-0"	SINGLE HUNG
19	2'-6"	5'-0"	G	VINYL	TEMP.	8'-0"	SINGLE HUNG. EGRESS
20	6'-0"	5'-0"	A	VINYL		8'-0"	SINGLE HUNG. EGRESS
21	3'-0"	5'-0"	D	VINYL		8'-0"	SINGLE HUNG
22	1'-9"	5'-6"	B	VINYL		7'-0"	SINGLE HUNG
23	3'-8"	5'-6"	F	VINYL		7'-0"	SINGLE HUNG
24	1'-9"	5'-6"	B	VINYL		7'-0"	SINGLE HUNG
25	2'-6"	5'-0"	G	VINYL		8'-0"	SINGLE HUNG. EGRESS
26	2'-6"	5'-0"	G	VINYL		8'-0"	SINGLE HUNG. EGRESS
27	5'-0"	3'-8"	H	VINYL	TEMP.	8'-0"	SINGLE HUNG
28	3'-0"	3'-8"	I	VINYL	TEMP.	8'-0"	SINGLE HUNG
29	3'-0"	3'-8"	I	VINYL	TEMP.	8'-0"	SINGLE HUNG
30	3'-6"	3'-6"					SKYLIGHT
31	3'-6"	3'-6"					SKYLIGHT

Figure 10.2 Window schedule.

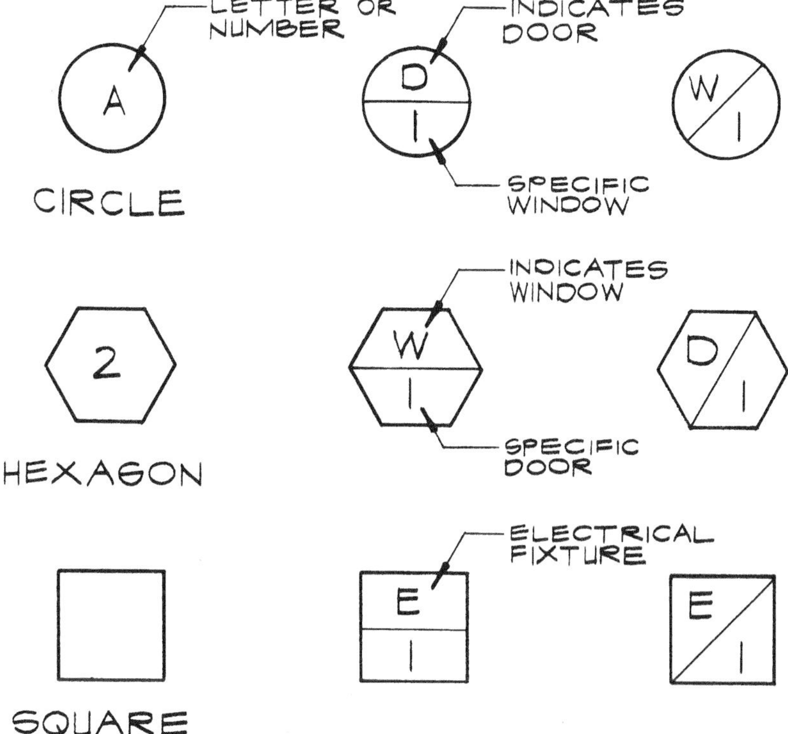

Figure 10.3 Symbol designations.

and how they may be shown. There are various options, such as using a letter or number, or both, and various shapes. Door and window symbol shapes should be different from each other. To clarify reading the floor plan, the letter "D" at the top of the door symbol and the letter "W" at the top of the window symbol are used. The letter "P" is used for plumbing fixtures, "E" for electrical fixtures, and "A" for appliances. Place the letter in the top part of the symbol. Whatever symbol shape you select, be sure to make the symbol large enough to accommodate the lettering that will go inside the symbol shape.

When you provide lines for the anticipated number of symbols to be used, allow extra spaces for door and windows that may be added as the project develops and evolves.

Your specific choice of a tabulated schedule may involve the following factors:

- Specific office procedures
- Standardization or variety of doors and windows selected
- Items with different dimensions
- Ease of changing specifications
- Format layout on plot pages
- Repetition of call-outs

In many cases, tabulated schedules cannot clearly define a specific door or window. In this case, you can add to a schedule a reference with a pictorial drawing of a door or window adjacent to the schedule, as shown in Figure 10.4. Door 1 is difficult to explain, so a pictorial representation makes it clearer.

A **pictorial schedule**, as distinct from a pictorial representation, is totally pictorial. Each item is dimensioned and accompanied by data such as material, type, and so forth. Figure 10.5 shows a pictorial schedule of a window. A pictorial schedule provides section references for the **head**, **jamb**, and **sill** sections, so you no longer need to reference the exterior elevations. (The *head* is the top of a window or door, *jamb* refers to the sides of a window or door, and the *sill* is the bottom of the window.)

Choice of a pictorial schedule may involve the following factors:

- Specific office procedures
- Unusual and intricate door or window design requirements

DOOR SCHEDULE

SYM.	WIDTH	HEIGHT	THK.	HC/SC	TYPE	MATERIAL	REMARKS
⟨1⟩	PR.3'-2"	7'-0"	1 3/4"	HC	NL	STEEL	1-HR. SELF CLOSING, PANIC HDW.
⟨2⟩	3'-0"	"	"	"	FLUSH	"	" " " NO GLASS
⟨3⟩	"	"	"	SC	SLAB	WOOD	
⟨4⟩	"	6'-8"	"	"	"	"	1-HR, SELF CLOSING, MTL. JAMBS
⟨5⟩	"	"	"	"	"	"	
⟨6⟩	"	"	"	"	"	"	SELF CLOSING, PUSH PLATES

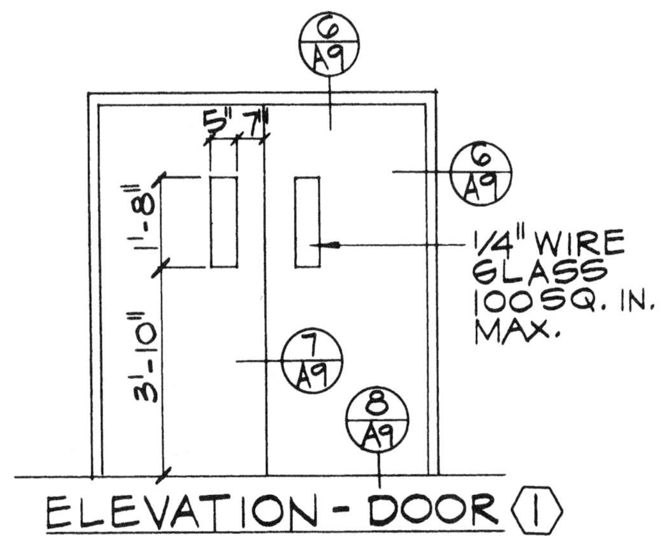

Figure 10.4 Pictorial representation on a tabular schedule.

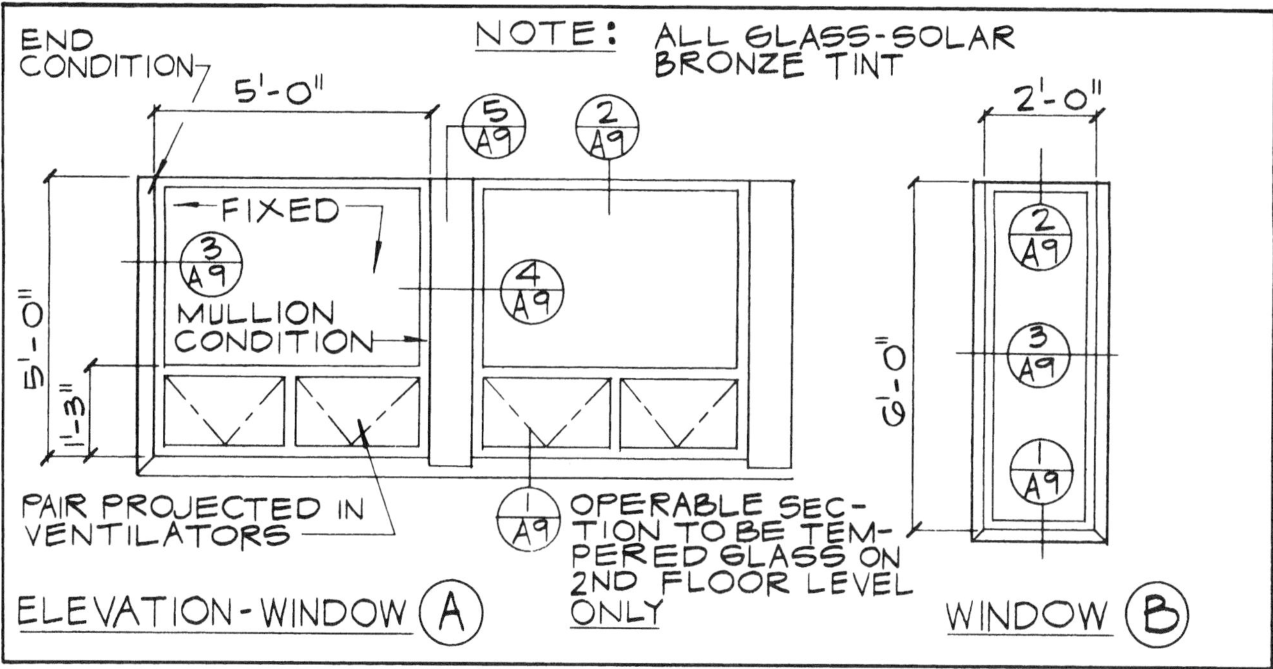

Figure 10.5 Pictorial schedule.

- Very few doors and windows in the project, or very few types used
- Desired clarity for window section referencing
- Irregular shapes
- Mixing types and shapes within a specific assembly
- Internal doors and windows not shown on external elevations

■ INTERIOR FINISH SCHEDULES

Interior finish schedules provide information such as floor and wall material, trim material, and ceiling finish. The layout of an interior finish schedule varies from office to office because of prevailing office philosophy and specific information the firm receives for various types of projects, and if an interior designer is developing that scope of work.

Figures 10.6 and 10.7 show interior finish schedules. The column allocated for room designation may show the room name or an assigned space number or both. Commercial buildings typically utilize room numbers, as many room names may be duplicated. Imagine a school or multistory building where classrooms or office spaces are utilized in repetition. This selection may be dictated by the project itself. Another method of defining finishes combines the room finish schedule with a room finish key, which uses numbers and letters to indicate the various materials to be used for floors, walls, and so forth. An example of this type of schedule is shown in Figure 10.8. Using space numbers is more logical for a large office building, for example, than for a very small residence. Once again, when extensive information is required in the remarks section of the schedule, use an asterisk (*) or footnote number for reference at the bottom of the schedule.

There are other forms of schedules that can be utilized to established clarity on a project. For example, if a project has many types of plumbing and appliance fixtures in various areas, provide additional schedules to clarify and to locate items with their designated symbols.

Figure 10.9 shows a plumbing fixture schedule, and Figure 10.10 shows an appliance schedule. This is an alternative method of identifying the fixtures and appliances that are required for a specific project scope. If these types of schedules are not used in a project, the fixture types, manufacturers, catalog numbers, and other information needed must be included in the project specifications.

For most projects, the specifications will augment information found in the schedules. Examples of information usually found in the specifications include the window manufacturer, the type and manufacturer of the door hardware, and the type and manufacturer of paint for the trim.

For building projects that may require various structural components, such as shear walls resisting lateral forces or spread concrete footings of various sizes

INTERIOR FINISH SCHEDULE

ROOM	FLOOR: CARPET	FLOOR: HARDWOOD	FLOOR: STONE TILE	FLOOR: CERAMIC TILE	FLOOR: CONCRETE	BASE: PAINT GRADE 8" BASE	BASE: PAINT GRADE 5" BASE	BASE: STAIN GRADE 8" BASE	BASE: STONE	BASE: CERAMIC TILE	BASE: NONE	WALLS: 5/8" GYP. BD.	WALLS: 5/8" TYPE "X" GYP. BD.	WALLS: WAINSCOT	WALLS: STAIN-GRADE WOOD PANELING	WALLS: BACK SPLASH CERAMIC TILE	WALLS: CEMENT PLASTER	CEILINGS: 5/8" GYP. BD.	CEILINGS: 5/8" TYPE "X" GYP. BD.	CEILINGS: STAIN GRD. T&G AND BEAMS	CEILINGS: STAIN GRD. WOOD BEAMS/PLAST.	CEILINGS: CEMENT PLASTER	CEILINGS: RED BRICK	CEILINGS: CROWN MOLDING	CABINETS: WOOD	CABINETS: STAIN GRADE ALDER	CABINETS: PAINT GRADE	CABINETS: MELAMINE	PAINT AND STAIN: WALLS: PAINT	PAINT AND STAIN: WALLS: ENAMEL	PAINT AND STAIN: WALLS: FAUX FINISH	PAINT AND STAIN: WALLS: WALL PAPER	PAINT AND STAIN: WALLS	PAINT AND STAIN: CEILING: PAINT	PAINT AND STAIN: CEILING: ENAMEL	PAINT AND STAIN: CEILING: STAIN	PAINT AND STAIN: CEILING: NOT APPLICABLE	PAINT AND STAIN: TRIM: PAINT	PAINT AND STAIN: TRIM: ENAMEL	PAINT AND STAIN: TRIM: STAIN	PAINT AND STAIN: TRIM	PAINT AND STAIN: CABINET: PAINT #	PAINT AND STAIN: CABINET: ENAMEL	PAINT AND STAIN: CABINET: STAIN #	PAINT AND STAIN: CABINET	REMARKS
ENTRY																																														
LIVING RM.																																														
PWDR.																																														
DINING RM.																																														
KITCHEN																																														
NOOK																																														
FAMILY RM.																																														
MAST. BDRM.																																														
MAST. BATH																																														
BDRM. #2																																														
BATH #2																																														
BDRM. #3																																														
BATH #3																																														
BDRM. #4																																														
BATH #4																																														
BDRM. #5																																														
BATH #5																																														
LAUNDRY ROOM																																														
SITTING AREA																																														
GARAGE																																														

Figure 10.6 Interior finish schedule.

INTERIOR FINISH SCHEDULE

ROOM	FLOOR: CARPET	FLOOR: HARDWOOD	FLOOR: MARBLE	FLOOR: CERAMIC TILE	FLOOR: CONCRETE	BASE: PAINT GRADE 2 1/4" BASE	BASE: STAIN GRADE 4" BASE	BASE: MARBLE	BASE: STONE	BASE: CERAMIC TILE	BASE: NONE	WALLS: 5/8" GYP. BD.	WALLS: 5/8" TYPE "X" GYP. BD.	WALLS: WAINSCOT	WALLS: STAIN-GRADE WOOD PANELING	WALLS: FULL-HEIGHT CERAMIC TILE	WALLS: CEMENT PLASTER	CEILING: 5/8" GYP. BD.	CEILING: 5/8" TYPE "X" GYP. BD.	CEILING: STAIN GRD. T&G AND BEAMS	CEILING: STAIN GRD. WOOD BEAMS/PLAST.	CEILING: CEMENT PLASTER	CEILING: RED BRICK	CABINET: STAIN GRADE SOLID WOOD	CABINET: PAINT GRADE	CABINET: MELAMINE	CABINET	PAINT AND STAIN: WALLS: PAINT	PAINT AND STAIN: WALLS: ENAMEL	PAINT AND STAIN: WALLS: FAUX FINISH	PAINT AND STAIN: WALLS: WALL PAPER	PAINT AND STAIN: WALLS	PAINT AND STAIN: CEILING: PAINT	PAINT AND STAIN: CEILING: ENAMEL	PAINT AND STAIN: CEILING: STAIN	PAINT AND STAIN: CEILING: NOT APPLICABLE	PAINT AND STAIN: TRIM: PAINT	PAINT AND STAIN: TRIM: ENAMEL	PAINT AND STAIN: TRIM: STAIN	PAINT AND STAIN: TRIM	PAINT AND STAIN: CABINET: PAINT #	PAINT AND STAIN: CABINET: ENAMEL	PAINT AND STAIN: CABINET: STAIN #	PAINT AND STAIN: CABINET	REMARKS
B01 MECHANICAL ROOM																																													
B02 CONFERENCE ROOM																																													
B03 CONFERENCE ROOM																																													
B04 HALL																																													
B05 EXISTING LOBBY	NO WORK																																												
B06 EXISTING OFFICE	NO WORK																																												
B07 COPY ROOM																																													
B08 EXISTING OFFICE	NO WORK																																												
B09 EXISTING OFFICE	NO WORK																																												
B10 EXISTING CORRIDOR	NO WORK																																												
B11 EXISTING OFFICE	NO WORK																																												
B12 EXISTING OFFICE	NO WORK																																												
B13 EXISTING RESTROOM	NO WORK																																												
B14 EXISTING CHIOR ROOM	NO WORK																																												
B15 OFFICE																																													
B16 KITCHEN																																													
B17 EXISTING CORRIDOR	NO WORK																																												
B18 MULTI-PURPOSE ROOM																																													
B19 STORAGE																																													
B20 WOMEN'S																																													
B21 MEN'S																																													
B22 HALL																																													
B23 EXISTING JANITOR	NO WORK																																												
B24 STORAGE																																													
B25 EXISTING NURSERY RROM																																													
B26 OFFICE																																													
B27 EXISTING CRIB ROOM	NO WORK																																												
B28 EXISTING RESTROOM	NO WORK																																												
B29 EXISTING MECHANICAL ROOM	NO WORK																																												

Figure 10.7 Interior finish schedule.

ROOM FINISH SCHEDULE								
NO.	ROOM	FINISHES				CEIL. HGT.	ROOM AREA	REMARKS
		FLOOR	BASE	WALLS	CEILING			
101	RECEPTION	B	1	A	2	9'-0"	110□'	
102	OFFICE	A		B	2	8'-0"	170□'	
103	OFFICE	A		B	2	"	180□'	
104	OFFICE	A		B	2	"	185□'	
105	WOMENS TOIL.	C	1	A	1	7'-6"	30□'	
106	MENS TOILET	C	1	A	1	7'-6"	25□'	

ROOM FINISH KEY							
FLOORS		BASES		WALLS		CEILINGS	
A	CARPET	1	WOOD	A	5/8" SHEETROCK	1	5/8" SHEETROCK
B	OAK PARQUET			B	1x6 T&G CEDAR	2	SUSP. AC. TILE
C	CERAMIC TILE						

Figure 10.8 Room finish schedule—key type.

FIXTURE SCHEDULE				
SYMB.	EQUIPMENT DEASCRIPTION	MOUNTING LOCATION	MFR / MODEL NO.	FIN NOTES
1	WATER CLOSET FLUSH VALVE	SURFACE / FLOOR	AMERICAN STD 3043.102	WHITE
2	URINAL FLUSH VALVE	SURFACE / WALL	AMERICAN STD 6541.132	WHITE
3	LAVATORY (SEE 8/501) (SELF-RIMMED)	SURFACE / COUNTERTOP	AMERICAN STD 0410.021	WHITE
4	FLUSH VALVE		SLOAN OPTIMA	CHROME
5	FAUCET	CENTER SET	SLOAN OPTIMA	CHROME

ACCESSORY SCHEDULE				
SYMB.	EQUIPMENT DESCRIPTION	MOUNTING LOCATION	MFR / MODEL NO.	FIN NOTES
1	PAPER TOWEL DISPENSER	SURFACE / WALL	BRADLEY 237-11	STAINLESS STEEL
2	SOAP DISPENSER	SURFACE / COUNTERTOP	BRADLEY 6326-68	STAINLESS STEEL
3	PAPER TOWEL DISPENSER	SEMI-RECESS WALL	BRADLEY 237-10	STAINLESS STEEL
4	SANITARY NAPKIN/ TAMPON DISPENSER	SURFACE/ WALL	BRADLEY 426-FREE	STAINLESS STEEL
5	1 1/4" DIA. GRAB BAR (SEE DTL. 9/501)	SURFACE / WALL	BRADLEY 812-7	STAINLESS STEEL
6	TOILET SEAT COVER DISPENSER	SURFACE/ WALL	BRADLEY 583	STAINLESS STEEL
7	TOILET TISSUE DISPENSER	SURFACE/ WALL	BRADLEY 5402	STAINLESS STEEL
8	SANITARY NAPKIN DISPOSAL	SURFACE/ WALL	BRADLEY 4722-15	STAINLESS STEEL
19	GEOMETRIC HC SYMBOLS (SEE DETAIL 3/501)	SURFACE/ WALL		PLASTIC
20	ACCESSIBLE RESTROOM SIGN (SEE DETAIL 1/501)	SURFACE/ WALL		PLASTIC

Figure 10.9 Plumbing fixture schedule.

carrying different loads, it is good practice to provide schedules for the various structural entities so as to maintain clear drawings.

Figure 10.11 is an example of a shear wall finish schedule. This schedule and the various finishes reflect the need for this kind of schedule to provide clarity when reviewing the structural drawings. A partial lateral floor plan is shown in Figure 10.12 to illustrate how shear walls are drawn.

Another example of a schedule that is related to a structural entity is a pier and/or spread footing schedule. This type of schedule is recommended when there are numerous spread footings of various sizes. This occurs on many commercial buildings. Figure 10.13 illustrates an example of a pier/spread footing schedule. Note the variances in the steel reinforcing requirements, the sizes of the base plates, the number and sizes of the anchor bolts, and other items. Figure 10.14 depicts how the schedule symbols may be shown on a structural foundation plan.

A template of a schedule can be made and attached to a set of drawings as required by the scope of work. As a project is altered, a new template can replace the earlier one to represent the changes. In most cases, a spreadsheet or the computer program will aid in the development of a schedule (Figure 10.15).

APPLIANCE SCHEDULE				
SYM.	ITEM	MANUFACTURER	CATALOG NO.	REMARKS
1	COOKTOP	APPLIANCES INC.	RU38V	WHITE
2	MICROWAVE	"	JKP65G	
3	DISHWASHER	"	GSD2500	WHITE
4	DISPOSER	"	GFC510	

Figure 10.10 Appliance fixture schedule.

Shear Wall Finish Schedule						
Sym	Wall Material	Blocked / Unblocked	Nailing Size & Spacing	Stud Size	Anchor Bolts & Number	Remarks
S 1	1/2" GYPSUM WALLBOARD	UNBLOCKED	5d COOLER @ 7" O.C.	2 X 4	(6) 1/2" DIA. X 10"	-
S 2	5/8" GYPSUM WALLBOARD	BLOCKED	6d COOLER @ 7" O.C.	2 X 4	(8) 1/2" DIA. X 10"	-
S 3	3/8" PLYWOOD STRUCT - I	BLOCKED	8d @ 3"	2 X 4	(5) 5/8" DIA. X 10"	FIELD NAILING : 8d @ 12" O.C.
S 4	1/2" PLYWOOD STRUCT - I	BLOCKED	10d @ 3"	3 X 4	(8) 5/8" DIA. X 10"	FIELD NAILING : 8d @ 12" O.C.
S 5	- -	-	- -	-	-	-
S 6	- -	-	- -	-	-	-
- -	- -	-	- -	-	-	-
- -	- -	-	- -	-	-	-

Figure 10.11 Shear wall finish schedule example.

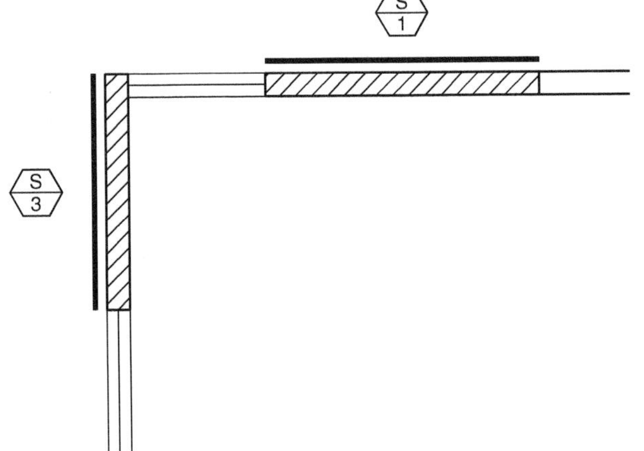

Figure 10.12 Shear wall in plan view.

CAD AND BIM GENERATED SCHEDULES

To illustrate a project utilizing the abilities of a computer-aided drafting (CAD)-generated schedule system in developing layouts, three examples are given in the following figures.

Figure 10.16 shows an example of a computer-generated interior finish schedule. This schedule can be revised quickly with a computer while still preserving the basic layout for future projects.

Figure 10.17 depicts a window schedule with drawings of some of the window types that will be incorporated into this project. As discussed previously in this chapter, the pictorial form adds clarity and demonstrates

Pier/Spread Footing Schedule						
Sym	Size	Depth	Reinforcing	Base Plate Size	Anchor Bolts & Number	Remarks
P 1	1'-6" X 1'-6"	10"	(3) 1/2" DIA. BARS ONE WAY	N.A.	N.A.	KEEP STEEL 3" CLR. OF EARTH
P 2	2'-6" X 2'-6"	12"	(4) 1/2" DIA. BARS EACH WAY	6" X 6" x 1/4"	(2) 5/8" DIA.	KEEP STEEL 3" CLR. OF EARTH
P 3	3'-6" X 3'-6"	12"	(5) 1/2" DIA. BARS EACH WAY	7" X 7" X 3/8"	(4) 5/8" DIA.	KEEP STEEL 3" CLR. OF EARTH
P 4	-	-	- -	-	-	-
- -	-	-	- -	-	-	-
- -	-	-	- -	-	-	-

Figure 10.13 Pier/spread footing schedule example.

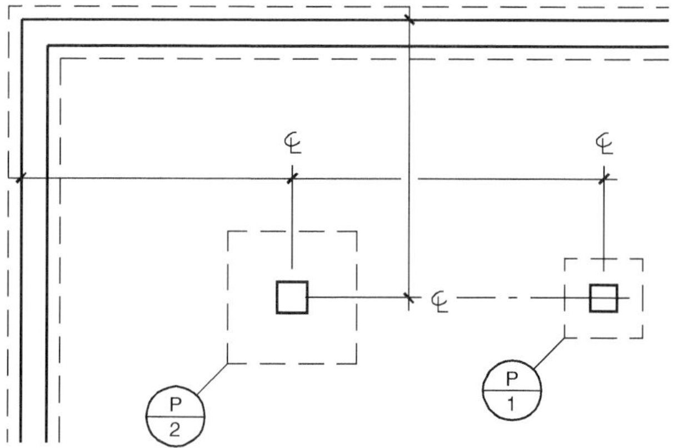

Figure 10.14 Pier/spread footing example.

the symbology for window sections. Note in the glazing column the areas refer to tempered glass. This has been done to satisfy a building department requirement that is required for a building department safety requirement. The architect has also added notes to indicate the alignment of the windows and doors. Notes relating to building code requirements are shown below the window types.

The types of doors specified for this project are shown in pictorial form (see Figure 10.18). Types of doors have been depicted pictorially for clarity and referencing. These types of doors are keyed with a letter on the door schedule. The computer offers the flexibility to alter or revise the schedule layouts types and sizes for projects that may have different requirements.

Schedule templates can be produced on the computer by simply drawing lines and arranging them horizontally and vertically. The text for the main title and the column titles is entered by typing a placeholder in each position. If the first phrase is positioned and centered carefully, the remaining columns will also be centered. Next, edit the placeholder to reflect the desired column titles and change the size if necessary. The text will automatically center the new titles. An alternative option is to link an excel file to a CAD program. Look at Figure 10.19. Because we are producing a generic schedule, put a hyphen (dash) in the unused spaces as a placeholder. The user of this schedule need only replace the hyphens with the desired information: height, width, material, and so on. All of the information will be automatically centered or placed with the margin to the left, as shown in the "Material" column in Figure 10.20.

Figure 10.21 is a depiction of a completed series of schedules as presented to the building department for review. Depending on the size of the project, all schedules can be placed on the same sheet for organization's sake. BIM takes schedules to a different level. Items such as building areas, materials, doors, and windows can be created edited and utilized with one major advantage. If you alter the size of door a schedule, it will automatically modify all the instances of the door in all drawings.

If a set of construction documents was produced using BIM, odds are the schedules can be generated automatically. The schedules are tied to the parametric design of the software, which will generate the table for you. This is the ideal situation, as the software's capabilities improve the accuracy of the schedules for both the size and quantity of windows, doors, and finishes. Previously, it was common for a drafter to spend hours reviewing a series of schedules; here the software does much of the thinking for you. There are opportunities to customize the schedules and the data on the schedule, but it is truly amazing how far we have come from the traditional methods of scheduling. See Figures 10.22 and 10.23.

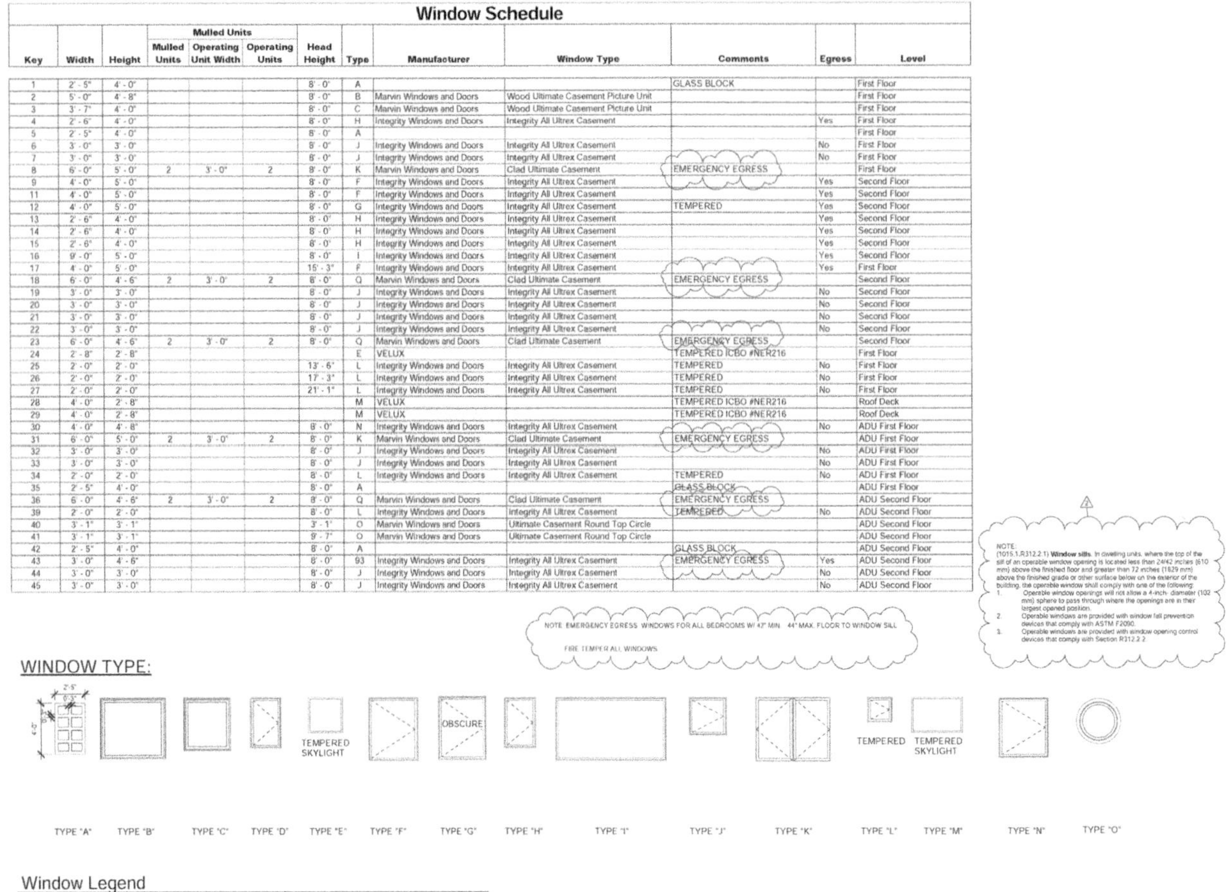

Window Schedule

Key	Width	Height	Mulled Units: Mulled Units	Mulled Units: Operating Unit Width	Mulled Units: Operating Units	Head Height	Type	Manufacturer	Window Type	Comments	Egress	Level
1	2' - 5"	4' - 0"				8' - 0"	A			GLASS BLOCK		First Floor
2	5' - 0"	4' - 8"				8' - 0"	B	Marvin Windows and Doors	Wood Ultimate Casement Picture Unit			First Floor
3	3' - 7"	4' - 0"				8' - 0"	C	Marvin Windows and Doors	Wood Ultimate Casement Picture Unit			First Floor
4	2' - 6"	4' - 0"				8' - 0"	H	Integrity Windows and Doors	Integrity All Ultrex Casement		Yes	First Floor
5	2' - 5"	4' - 0"				8' - 0"	A					First Floor
6	3' - 0"	3' - 0"				8' - 0"	J	Integrity Windows and Doors	Integrity All Ultrex Casement		No	First Floor
7	3' - 0"	3' - 0"				8' - 0"	J	Integrity Windows and Doors	Integrity All Ultrex Casement		No	First Floor
8	6' - 0"	5' - 0"	2	3' - 0"	2	8' - 0"	K	Marvin Windows and Doors	Clad Ultimate Casement	EMERGENCY EGRESS		First Floor
9	4' - 0"	5' - 0"				8' - 0"	F	Integrity Windows and Doors	Integrity All Ultrex Casement		Yes	Second Floor
11	4' - 0"	5' - 0"				8' - 0"	F	Integrity Windows and Doors	Integrity All Ultrex Casement		Yes	Second Floor
12	4' - 0"	5' - 0"				8' - 0"	G	Integrity Windows and Doors	Integrity All Ultrex Casement	TEMPERED	Yes	Second Floor
13	2' - 6"	4' - 0"				8' - 0"	H	Integrity Windows and Doors	Integrity All Ultrex Casement		Yes	Second Floor
14	2' - 6"	4' - 0"				8' - 0"	H	Integrity Windows and Doors	Integrity All Ultrex Casement		Yes	Second Floor
15	2' - 6"	4' - 0"				8' - 0"	H	Integrity Windows and Doors	Integrity All Ultrex Casement		Yes	Second Floor
16	9' - 0"	5' - 0"				8' - 0"	I	Integrity Windows and Doors	Integrity All Ultrex Casement		Yes	Second Floor
17	4' - 0"	5' - 0"				15' - 3"	F	Integrity Windows and Doors	Integrity All Ultrex Casement		Yes	First Floor
18	6' - 0"	4' - 6"	2	3' - 0"	2	8' - 0"	Q	Marvin Windows and Doors	Clad Ultimate Casement	EMERGENCY EGRESS		Second Floor
19	3' - 0"	3' - 0"				8' - 0"	J	Integrity Windows and Doors	Integrity All Ultrex Casement		No	Second Floor
20	3' - 0"	3' - 0"				8' - 0"	J	Integrity Windows and Doors	Integrity All Ultrex Casement		No	Second Floor
21	3' - 0"	3' - 0"				8' - 0"	J	Integrity Windows and Doors	Integrity All Ultrex Casement		No	Second Floor
22	3' - 0"	3' - 0"				8' - 0"	J	Integrity Windows and Doors	Integrity All Ultrex Casement		No	Second Floor
23	6' - 0"	4' - 6"	2	3' - 0"	2	8' - 0"	Q	Marvin Windows and Doors	Clad Ultimate Casement	EMERGENCY EGRESS		Second Floor
24	2' - 8"	2' - 8"					E	VELUX		TEMPERED ICBO #NER216		First Floor
25	2' - 0"	2' - 0"				13' - 6"	L	Integrity Windows and Doors	Integrity All Ultrex Casement	TEMPERED	No	First Floor
26	2' - 0"	2' - 0"				17' - 3"	L	Integrity Windows and Doors	Integrity All Ultrex Casement	TEMPERED	No	First Floor
27	2' - 0"	2' - 0"				21' - 1"	L	Integrity Windows and Doors	Integrity All Ultrex Casement	TEMPERED	No	First Floor
28	4' - 0"	2' - 8"					M	VELUX		TEMPERED ICBO #NER216		Roof Deck
29	4' - 0"	2' - 8"					M	VELUX		TEMPERED ICBO #NER216		Roof Deck
30	4' - 0"	4' - 8"				8' - 0"	N	Integrity Windows and Doors	Integrity All Ultrex Casement		No	ADU First Floor
31	6' - 0"	5' - 0"	2	3' - 0"	2	8' - 0"	K	Marvin Windows and Doors	Clad Ultimate Casement	EMERGENCY EGRESS		ADU First Floor
32	3' - 0"	3' - 0"				8' - 0"	J	Integrity Windows and Doors	Integrity All Ultrex Casement		No	ADU First Floor
33	3' - 0"	3' - 0"				8' - 0"	J	Integrity Windows and Doors	Integrity All Ultrex Casement		No	ADU First Floor
34	2' - 0"	2' - 0"				8' - 0"	L	Integrity Windows and Doors	Integrity All Ultrex Casement	TEMPERED	No	ADU First Floor
35	2' - 5"	4' - 0"				8' - 0"	A			GLASS BLOCK		ADU First Floor
36	6' - 0"	4' - 6"	2	3' - 0"	2	8' - 0"	Q	Marvin Windows and Doors	Clad Ultimate Casement	EMERGENCY EGRESS		ADU Second Floor
39	2' - 0"	2' - 0"				8' - 0"	L	Integrity Windows and Doors	Integrity All Ultrex Casement	TEMPERED	No	ADU Second Floor
40	3' - 1"	3' - 1"				3' - 1"	O	Marvin Windows and Doors	Ultimate Casement Round Top Circle			ADU Second Floor
41	3' - 1"	3' - 1"				9' - 7"	O	Marvin Windows and Doors	Ultimate Casement Round Top Circle			ADU Second Floor
42	2' - 5"	4' - 0"				8' - 0"	A			GLASS BLOCK		ADU Second Floor
43	3' - 0"	4' - 6"				8' - 0"	93	Integrity Windows and Doors	Integrity All Ultrex Casement	EMERGENCY EGRESS	Yes	ADU Second Floor
44	3' - 0"	3' - 0"				8' - 0"	J	Integrity Windows and Doors	Integrity All Ultrex Casement		No	ADU Second Floor
45	3' - 0"	3' - 0"				8' - 0"	J	Integrity Windows and Doors	Integrity All Ultrex Casement		No	ADU Second Floor

NOTE: EMERGENCY EGRESS WINDOWS FOR ALL BEDROOMS W/ 47" MIN 44" MAX. FLOOR TO WINDOW SILL
FIRE TEMPER ALL WINDOWS
NOTE:
(1015.1,R312.2.1) Window sills. In dwelling units, where the top of the sill of an operable window opening is located less than 24/42 inches (610 mm) above the finished floor and greater than 72 inches (1829 mm) above the finished grade or other surface below on the exterior of the building, the operable window shall comply with one of the following:
1. Operable window openings will not allow a 4-inch- diameter (102 mm) sphere to pass through where the openings are in their largest opened position.
2. Operable windows are provided with window fall prevention devices that comply with ASTM F2090.
3. Operable windows are provided with window opening control devices that comply with Section R312.2.2.
WINDOW TYPE:
2'-5"
4'-0"
TEMPERED SKYLIGHT
OBSCURE
TEMPERED
TEMPERED SKYLIGHT
TYPE "A"
TYPE "B"
TYPE "C"
TYPE "D"
TYPE "E"
TYPE "F"
TYPE "G"
TYPE "H"
TYPE "I"
TYPE "J"
TYPE "K"
TYPE "L"
TYPE "M"
TYPE "N"
TYPE "O"
Window Legend
1/4" = 1'-0"

Figure 10.15 Sample window schedule for a residential project.

INTERIOR FINISH SCHEDULE

ROOM	FLOOR					BASE						WALLS						CEILINGS						CABINETS				PAINT AND STAIN																	REMARKS
																												WALLS					CEILING				TRIM				CABINET				
	CARPET	HARDWOOD	STONE	CERAMIC TILE	CONCRETE	PAINT GRADE 8" BASE	PAINT GRADE 5" BASE	STAIN GRADE 8" BASE	STONE	CERAMIC TILE	NONE	5/8" GYP. BD. W/SKIM-COAT	CERAMIC TILE WAINSCOT	WAINSCOT	STAIN-GRD. WOOD PANELING	FULL-HEIGHT CERAMIC TILE	STUCCO	5/8" TYPE 'X' GYP BD.	STAIN GRD. WOOD PANELING	STAIN GRD. T&G AND BEAMS	STAIN GRD. WOOD BEAMS/PLAST	STUCCO	RED BRICK	STAIN GRADE ALDER	PAINT GRADE	MELAMINE		PAINT	ENAMEL	FAUX FINISH	WALL PAPER		PAINT	ENAMEL	STAIN	NOT APPLICABLE	PAINT	ENAMEL	STAIN		PAINT #	ENAMEL	STAIN #		
LIVING RM.		X				X						X						X												X			X												
DINING RM.		X				X						X						X												X			X												2X6 WOOD PLANK DECKING AT FAM. RM. DECK
FAMILY RM.	X					X						X						X										X					X												
KITCHEN				X		X						X						X						X					X						X								X		
NOOK				X		X						X						X										X					X												
POWDER			X			X						X						X							X			X					X								X				
LAUNDRY				X						X		X	X					X								X			X				X												
2-CAR GARAGE					X						X	X						X										X																	
STAIRWELL		X				X						X						X										X																	
HALL	X						X					X						X										X					X												
MAST. BDRM.	X					X						X						X										X					X												
MAST. BATH			X						X			X						X						X						X				X									X		
WALK-IN CLOSET	X						X					X						X						X				X					X								X				
BED RM. #2	X						X					X						X										X					X												
BATH #2				X						X		X	X					X							X				X					X								X			
BED RM. #3	X						X					X						X										X					X												
BATH #3				X						X		X	X					X							X				X					X							X	X			
BED RM. #4	X						X					X						X										X					X												
BATH #4				X						X		X	X					X							X				X					X								X			
CELLAR					X						X	X						X										X					X												
WINE					X						X	X						X										X					X												

Figure 10.16 Interior finish schedule.

WINDOW SCHEDULE							
KEY	WIDTH	HEIGHT	TYPE	MATERIAL	GLAZING	HEAD HGT. FROM F.F.	REMARKS
1	2'-4"	5'-0"	D	PAINT GRD. WOOD		8'-0"	CASEMENT
2	2'-4"	5'-0"	D	"		8'-0"	CASEMENT
3	4'-8"	5'-2"	A	"		8'-0"	FRENCH CASEMENT
4	4'-8"	4'-0"	A	STAIN GRD. WOOD	TEMPERED	6'-8"	FRENCH CASEMENT
5	4'-8"	5'-0"	A	PAINT GRD. WOOD		8'-0"	FRENCH CASEMENT
6	2'-0"	4'-0"	D	"	TEMPERED	6'-8"	CASEMENT
7	2'-0"	4'-0"	D	"		6'-8"	CASEMENT
8	2'-0"	4'-0"	D			6'-8"	CASEMENT
9	2'-0"	3'-0"	B	"		8'-0"	CASEMENT
10	6'-0"	4'-0"	C	"		6'-8"	FIXED
11	2'-0"	4'-0"	D	"		6'-8"	CASEMENT
12	4'-0"	4'-0"	A	"		6'-8"	FRENCH CASEMENT, EGRESS (12.25 SQ. FT.)
13	4'-0"	3'-6"	A	"		6'-8"	FRENCH CASEMENT
14	2'-0"	3'-0"	B	"	TEMPERED	6'-8"	CASEMENT
15	2'-0"	4'-0"	E	"		6'-8"	FIXED, SEE ELEV
16	4'-0"	4'-0"	A	"	TEMPERED	6'-8"	FRENCH CASEMENT
17	2'-0"	4'-0"	D	"		6'-8"	CASEMENT
18	2'-0"	4'-0"	E	"	TEMPERED	6'-8"	INSWING CASEMENT, SEE ELEV
19	2'-0"	4'-0"	D	"	TEMPERED	6'-8"	CASEMENT
20	2'-0"	4'-0"	E	"		6'-8"	INSWING CASEMENT, SEE ELEV
21	2'-0"	3'-0"	B	"		6'-8"	CASEMENT

WINDOW TYPES

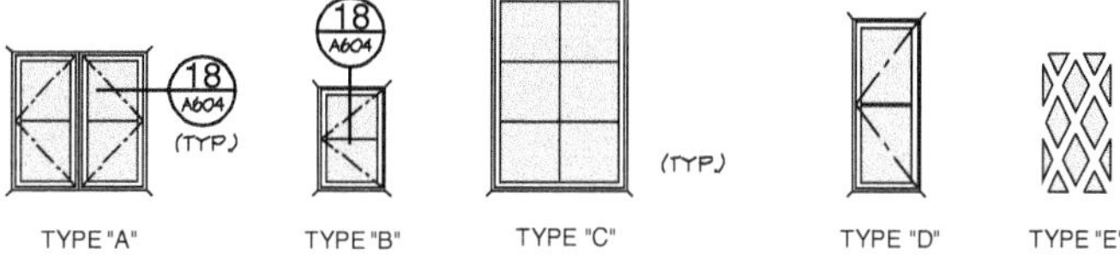

NOTES:

1. ALIGN TOP OF WINDOWS WITH TOP OF DOORS SO THAT TOP EDGES OF DOORS AND WINDOWS ALIGN IN A LEVEL PLANE ABOVE FINISH FLOOR.

2. ALL ESCAPE OR RESCUE WINDOWS SHALL HAVE A MINIMUM NET CLEAR OPENABLE AREA OF 5.7 SQ. FT.. THE MINIMUM NET CLEAR OPENABLE HEIGHT DIMENSION SHALL BE 24". THE MINIMUM NET CLEAR OPENABLE WIDTH DIMENSION SHALL BE 20" WHEN WINDOWS ARE PROVIDED AS A MEANS OF ESCAPE OR RESCUE. THEY SHALL HAVE A FINISHED SILL HEIGHT NOT MORE THAN 44" ABOVE FIN. FLR..

3. SKYLIGHTS SHALL HAVE A NON-COMBUSTIBLE FRAME GLAZED WITH DUAL GLAZING OF HEAT STRENGTHENED OR FULLY TEMPERED GLASS OR SHALL BE A 3/4-HOUR FIRE-RESISTIVE ASSEMBLY

4. WINDOWS WITH SILLS LESS THAN 5'-0" ABOVE TUB OR SHOWER FLOOR SHALL BE TEMPERED

Figure 10.17 Window schedule and types of windows.

The program is designed to create schedules of many components of a building, not just windows, doors, fixtures, and finishes. For example, when you place a new window, the program automatically numerates it in the floor plan and cross-references it to the window schedule. Most of the data you need for the schedule is already built into the software. The schedule will report with absolute accuracy the data you input. That is great news—provided the input information is correct. However, if it is determined that a change is desired (say, a window would be better in a larger size), you can simply enlarge it and the program will automatically update the schedule, and in the floor plan and elevations.

You will have to spend some downtime with BIM customizing the schedules to look the way you want them to look.

A view tab is utilized to bring up specific schedules. The lengthy list of options is almost limitless, ranging from building areas to electric equipment, to fascia or even eave gutters. All of these tabs are broken down even further to allow you to select or mark the fields you require for your customized schedule. Additional data can be customized by building level. Though this function may not be required for door or windows, it is ideal for floor area calculations.

Once the schedule is formatted as desired, it is simply a matter of dragging and dropping it onto the desired sheet and location to plot it.

OTHER SCHEDULES

What if a client is not sure which appliances or plumbing fixtures are desired? A great tool to utilize is an allowance schedule. Perhaps not really a schedule visually, it is more of a list of items that will be differed to

DOOR SCHEDULE							
KEY	WIDTH	HEIGHT	THICK.	TYPE	MATERIAL	GLAZING	REMARKS
①	2'-8"	6'-8"	2 1/4"	C	PAINT GRD. WOOD	TEMP.	FRENCH DOORS (SEE ELEVATIONS)
2	(2)-3'-0"	8'-0"	2 1/4"	E	"	TEMP.	FRENCH DOORS (SEE ELEVATIONS)
3	4'-0"	8'-0"	2 1/4"	A	STAIN GRD. WOOD		
4	8'-6'	8'-3"		D			GARAGE OVERHEAD SECTIONAL DOOR (SEE ELEVATIONS)
5	8'-6"	8'-3"		D	"		GARAGE OVERHEAD SECTIONAL DOOR (SEE ELEVATIONS)
6	3'-0"	6'-8"	2 1/4"	K	PAINT GRD. WOOD		
7	(2)-2'-0"	5'-0"		F	"		TRASH AREA, GATE
8	(2)-3'-0"	8'-0"	2 1/4"	E	"	TEMP.	FRENCH DOORS (SEE ELEVATIONS)
9	(2)-3'-0"	8'-0"	2 1/4"	E	"	TEMP.	FRENCH DOORS (SEE ELEVATIONS)
10	(2)-3'-0"	8'-0"	2 1/4"	E	"	TEMP.	FRENCH DOORS (SEE ELEVATIONS)
11	(2)-2'-6"	6'-8"	2 1/4"	E	"	TEMP.	FRENCH DOORS (SEE ELEVATIONS)
12	2'-6"	6'-8"	1 3/4"	J	"		
13	(2)-2'-0"	6'-8"	1 3/4"	G	"		
14	3'-0"	6'-8"	1 3/4"	J	"		20 MIN. RATED, SELF-CLOSING & TIGHT FITTING
15	2'-8"	6'-8"	1 3/4"	J	"		
16	2'-6"	6'-8"	1 3/4"	J	"		
17	(2)-2'-0"	6'-8"	1 3/4"	G	"		
18	(2)-2'-0"	6'-8"	1 3/4"	G	"		
19	2'-6"	6'-8"	1 3/4"	J	"		
20	(2)-2'-6"	6'-8"	1 3/4"	G	"		
21	(2)-3'-0"	8'-0"	1 3/4"	E	"	TEMP.	FRENCH DOORS (SEE ELEVATIONS)
22	(2)-3'-0"	8'-0"	1 3/4"	E	"	TEMP.	FRENCH DOORS (SEE ELEVATIONS)
23	(2)-2'-6"	6'-8"	1 3/4"	E	"	TEMP.	FRENCH DOORS (SEE ELEVATIONS)
24	(2)-2'-0"	6'-8"	1 3/4"	G	"		
25	(2)-2'-0"	6'-8"	1 3/4"	G	"		
26	2'-6"	6'-8"	1 3/4"	J	"		
27	2'-8"	6'-8"	1 3/4"	J	"		
28	2'-8"	8'-0"	1 3/4"	J	"		
29	2'-6"	8'-0"	1 3/4"	J	"		
30	(2)-1'-6"	8'-0"	1 3/4"	G	PAINT GRD. WOOD		
31	2'-6"	8'-0"	1 3/4"	J	PAINT GRD. WOOD		
32	(2)-1'-0"	8'-0"	1 3/4"	G	"		
33	2'-6"	8'-0"	1 3/4"	J	"		
34	2'-8"	6'-8"	1 3/4"	H	"		
35	2'-8"	6'-8"	1 3/4"	J	"		
36	(2)-4'-0"	6'-8"	1 3/4"	B	"		
37	2'-6"	6'-8"	1 3/4"	J	"		

NOTES:
1. ALL DOORS TO BE SOLID CORE.
2. BOTTOM OF INTERIOR DOORS TO BE 3/8" ABOVE FIN. FLR..

Figure 10.18 Door schedule and types of doors.

Window Schedule					
Key	Width	Height	Type	Material	Glazing
⬡ -	-	-	-	-	-
-	-	-	-	-	-
-	-	-	-	-	-
-	-	-	-	-	-
-	-	-	-	-	-
-	-	-	-	-	-
-	-	-	-	-	-
-	-	-	-	-	-
-	-	-	-	-	-
-	-	-	-	-	-

Figure 10.19 Partial template of a schedule with placeholder.

Window Schedule					
Key	Width	Height	Type	Material	Glazing
⬡ 1	2'-4"	5'-0"	D	PAINT GRADE WOOD	-
2	2'-4"	5'-0"	D	-	-
3	4'-8"	5'-2"	A	-	-
4	4'-8"	4'-0"	A	STAIN GRADE WOOD	TEMPERED
5	4'-8"	5'-0"	A	PAINT GRADE WOOD	-
6	2'-0"	4'-0"	D	-	TEMPERED
7	2'-0"	4'-0"	D	-	-
8	2'-0"	4'-0"	D	-	-
9	2'-0"	3'-0"	B	-	-
10	6'-0"	4'-0"	C	-	-

Figure 10.20 Replacing the placeholder with live information.

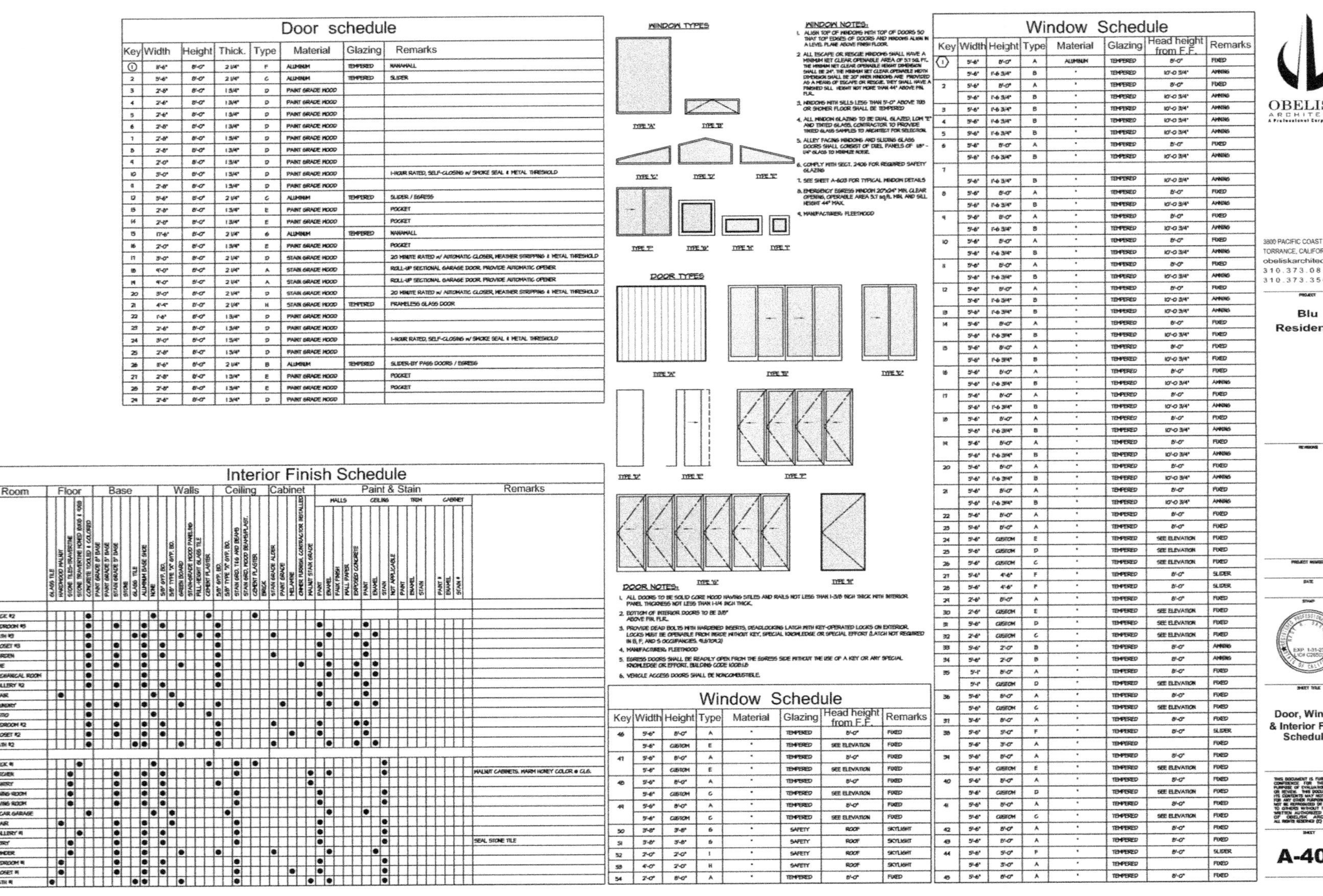

Figure 10.21 Completed door, window, and finish schedules on a plot sheet.

Window Schedule								
Mark	Type	Width	Height	Head Height	Sill Height	Family	Family and Type	Description
1	36" x 48"	3' - 0"	4' - 0"	6' - 0"	2' - 0"	Casement 3x3	Casement 3x3 with Trim: 36"	
2	16" x 72"	1' - 4"	6' - 0"	9' - 0"	3' - 0"	Fixed	Fixed: 16" x 72"	
3	36" x 60"	3' - 0"	5' - 0"	8' - 0"	3' - 0"	Casement 3x3	Casement 3x3 with Trim: 36"	
4	24" x 24"	2' - 0"	2' - 0"	5' - 0"	3' - 0"	Fixed	Fixed: 24" x 24"	
5	36" x 24"	3' - 0"	2' - 0"	5' - 0"	3' - 0"	Fixed	Fixed: 36" x 24"	
6	24" x 48"	2' - 0"	4' - 0"	11' - 0"	7' - 0"	Fixed	Fixed: 24" x 48"	
7	36" x 48"	3' - 0"	4' - 0"	7' - 0"	3' - 0"	Casement 3x3	Casement 3x3 with Trim: 36"	

Figure 10.22 Completed window schedule utilizing BIM.

Door Schedule					
Mark	Width	Height	Head Height	Family and Type	Description
1	6' - 0"	7' - 0"	7' - 0"	Sliding-2 panel: 72" x 84" Metal	
2	6' - 0"	7' - 0"	7' - 0"	Sliding-2 panel: 72" x 84" Metal	
3	6' - 0"	7' - 0"	7' - 0"	Sliding-2 panel: 72" x 84" Metal	
4	6' - 0"	7' - 0"	7' - 0"	Sliding-2 panel: 72" x 84" Metal	
5	6' - 0"	7' - 0"	7' - 0"	Sliding-2 panel: 72" x 84" Metal	
6	6' - 0"	7' - 0"	7' - 0"	Sliding-2 panel: 72" x 84" Metal	
7	2' - 6"	7' - 0"	7' - 0"	Single-Flush: 30" x 84"	
8	2' - 6"	7' - 0"	7' - 0"	Single-Flush: 30" x 84"	
9	2' - 6"	7' - 0"	7' - 0"	Single-Flush: 30" x 84"	
10	2' - 6"	7' - 0"	7' - 0"	Single-Flush: 30" x 84"	

Figure 10.23 Completed door schedule utilizing BIM.

be determined at a later date. It is necessary to establish line item for contractors to plug into the bidding process an ideally all contractors will plug in the same material cost, so they are able to bid the cost of labor. This makes it possible for the architect to review the bids and compare one contractor to another—apples to apples. The **allowance** is a set amount of money the client plans to spend on a specific item. For instance, a client would like engineered wood floors but is not ready to commit to a width/length/color. We can provide an allowance for $8.00 per square foot and the contractor will calculate the required square feet including waste and create an allowance for wood. Say, 1,000 square feet of flooring is required and because it will be set at 45° the builder estimates 15% waste. A total of 1,150 square feet will be budgeted at $8.00 square foot for a total of $9,200. That is a material cost only. The contractor will outline that line item as an allowance item. If, when the time comes, the client selects a wood floor that is $9 per square foot, the contractor will be owed an additional $1,150 or the difference between the original $8 budget and the actual $9 spent. The converse is also true if the client gets a great deal on the wood and only selects a wood for $7.00. The client holds back from the contractor $1,150 saved in this allowance item.

Now take this a level further, if the contractor charges the client a cost-plus contract, say, 15%, in the excess scenario, the contractor will additionally charge 15% on top of the $1,150 or $1322.50. In the cost saving option we have to hold back $1322.50 from the contractor as the client gets a credit toward the savings. This is why it is so important to get as close as possible to the actual allowance item.

See a typical list of allowance items on Figure 10.24. Note these are just a few options of many possible differed items that can be created.

Key Terms

allowance
head
hollow core (HC)
jamb
pictorial schedule
sill
solid core (SC)

ALLOWANCE SCHEDULE

1. ELECTRICAL FIXTURES - ALLOW $2,000 (CANS INCLUDED IN BASE BID NOT ALLOWANCE ITEM)
2. PLUMBING FIXTURES - ALLOW $6,000 (TUBS, LAVATORIES AND FIXTURES)
3. FINISH FIXTURES - ALLOW $500 (TOWEL BARS ETC.)
4. STONE FLOORS AND WALL TILES - ALLOW $8.00 SQ. FT.
5. SLAB AT KITCHEN AND TUB DECK - ALLOW $15.00 SQ. FT.
6. BASE SHOE MOULDING - ALLOW $2.00 LINEAR FEET (MATERIAL INSTALLATION IN BASE BID)
7. OWNER TO CONTRACT COST OF ALARM (CONTRACTOR RESPONSIBLE TO COORDINATE)
8. OWNER TO CONTRACT COST OF SURROUND SOUND (CONTRACTOR TO COORDINATE)
9. SHOWER DOOR - ALLOW $1,000 EA.
10. FIREPLACE SURROUND - ALLOW $1,500 PER EACH
11. HARDWOOD FLOORING $12 SQ. FT.
12. KITCHEN EQUIPMENT - ALLOW $18,000
13. CABINETS BY OWNER, INSTALLED BY MFG. (CONTRACTOR TO COORDINATE)
14. YARD DRAINAGE- ALLOW $1,000
15. BATH ACCESSORIES ALLOW $2,000, MIRRORS $1,500, SHOWER DOORS $500 EACH
16. LANDSCAPE & DRAINAGE ALLOW $20,000
17. POOL REPAIR ALLOW $10,000
18. SMART ELECTRICAL CONTROL - ALLOW $25,000
19. OWNER TO CONTRACT COST OF CLOSETS (CONTRACTOR TO COORDINATE)
20. MIRROR ALLOWANCE $2,000
21. PROVIDE ALLOWANCE FOR CLOSETS (SHELVES & POLES) $5,000
22. PROVIDE 2-NEW BATTERY BACK UP GARAGE DOORS $1,500
23. PROVIDE CABINET ALLOWANCE FOR KITCHEN CABINETS
24. PROVIDE CABINET ALLOWANCE FOR LAUNDRY ROOM
25. AC FOR HOME
26. PROVIDE AN ALLOWANCE/ COST FOR UNDERGROUND ELECTRICAL LINE
27. PROVIDE ALLOWANCE FOR SIDEWALK REPAIR
28. PROVIDE AN ALLOWANCE FOR NEW SEWER CONNECTION
29. PROVIDE AN ALLOWANCE FOR ABOVE GROUND SPA POWER
30. PROVIDE AN ALLOWANCE FOR SOLAR PANELS

Figure 10.24 Sample allowance schedule for a residential project.

chapter

11

FOUNDATION, FLOOR, AND ROOF FRAMING SYSTEMS

The Professional Practice of Architectural Working Drawings, Sixth Edition. Nagy R. Bakhoum and Osamu A. Wakita.
© 2024 John Wiley & Sons Inc. Published 2024 by John Wiley & Sons Inc.
Companion website: www.wiley.com\go\bakhoum\theprofessionalpracticeofarchitecturalworkingdrawings

FOUNDATION

A **foundation plan** is a drawing that shows the location of all concrete footings, concrete piers, and structural underpinning members required to support a structure. The main purpose of all the foundation footings is to distribute the weight of the structure over the soil in a manner that can support the significant weight of the structure.

Foundation systems are perhaps one of the most important structural components in a structural system. The foundation connects the structure to the ground and relies on the earth bearing pressure to support the entire weight of the building and the extended loads such as wind, snow, or seismic on the structure and transfers them down to the Earth.

The architect relies on a soils engineer and/or a geologist to make recommendations to the foundation system. If a report is not required in your jurisdiction the local building codes makes recommendations with respect to depth and width of footings. Within the soils/geological report, as you read through you will find a recommendation page. This part of the report will give you specific and numeric recommendations to aid you in the design of the foundation system. Let's discuss some generic ideas about foundations, in typical soil conditions if there is such a thing. If you were required to design a foundation for a 1, 2, or 3 level home the typical width of footings for a one-story is 12″ wide, two-story 15″ wide, and a three-story 18 in wide.

With respect to depth, it may rain from 12″ to 24″ depending on many factors, but most often it is between 12″ and 24″. Now if a frost line level is a consideration footing depth will be below that level an added depth, again become familiar with your region.

The building code requires that all exterior walls have footings. This makes the beginning of a foundation plan easy to block out. Interior footings are typically located where internal spans are required for sealing or roof support. Depending on span—structural members size—you can plan out interior footings.

In a soils/geology report, a foundation system can also be recommended. As in the earlier example of a frost line, a retaining wall system for a foundation may prove to be the best idea and the resulting basement area could be utilized for storage, mechanical, or other space uses. There are slab floors tied to conventional foundations or raised wood floor foundations. These three systems are the most prevalent systems in areas where "bad soil" exist—such as loose-fill or high water table. Here, a pile or caisson foundation system may be required. This is a more complex system or even the slab floor cannot rest on the soil—as it has no bearing capacity to support any structure—even a slab. In this example, you should be required to provide a structural slab. There are other systems that are very specialized such as rolling foundations. A system that is becoming more mainstream is a slab foundation, which is a foundation and a slab approximately 12 in thick under the entire building footprint. This is utilized in areas where the bedrock or very strong earth is difficult to cut into, and this system is a great option for that soils condition.

Foundation Selection

While there are many types of foundation systems, two primary types of floor systems are used in foundation plans. These floor systems are constructed of concrete or wood or a combination of both. Each floor system requires a foundation to support the floor system and the structure.

As with all working drawings, standards must be established from office standards, if you are presently employed foundations are determined based on things like water line or the level at which the moisture will not affect the structure, and the frost line, the level at which freezing temperatures will not affect the building.

Let's expand on the most common systems—slab on grade and raised wood floor systems. Depending on the cost of materials one system may be more cost-effective than another. A slab foundation system is not labor-intensive but is material heavy, specifically in volume of concrete. A raised wood floor foundation system utilizes less concrete, more forming or labor, more lumber and framing labor. Cost can be higher due to labor costs and this labor must be regionally determined. An additional advantage of a raised wood floor system is that items such as MEP can be modified by crawling under the floor system. With a slab system, once MEP is set up under the slab, it has to be cut and repoured to make changes.

In all the foundation system options, it is important to understand the strengths and limits of the materials you use. Concrete is ideal in compression. Steel rebar or reinforcing bars are great in tensile (tension) strength. Foundations utilize the strength of both these materials combined together to get a foundation that is strong in both compression and tension. In areas with significant water in the ground, the rebar may be additionally coated with epoxy to keep the bars from rusting away and failing the system. In areas where the soil is okay but not great, post tension or pretensioned cables can be incorporated in place of rebar. Retaining walls incorporate rebar in both vertical and horizontal to strengthen the wall and help resist the earth and water pressure that is exerted upon it.

TYPES OF FOUNDATIONS

Concrete Slab Floor: Foundation Plans

If you have selected concrete as the floor material for a specific project, first investigate the types of **foundation footing details** required to support the structure before drawing

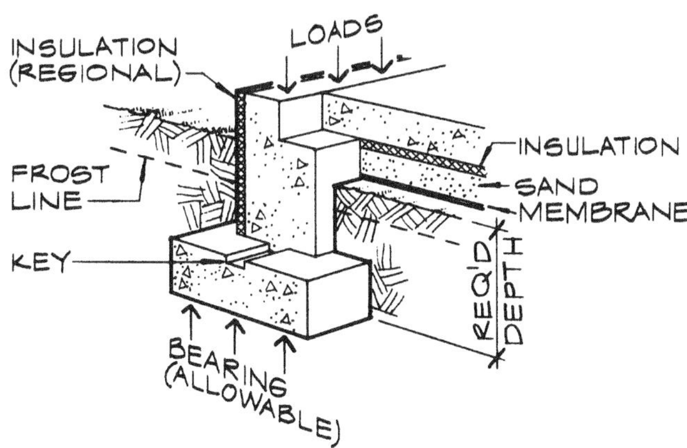

Figure 11.1 Concrete footing and floor with various influencing design factors.

the foundation plan. The **footing design** will be influenced by many factors, such as the vertical loads or weight it is to support, regional differences, allowable soil-bearing values, established frost-line location, and recommendations from a soils and geological report for reinforcing requirements. Figure 11.1 illustrates a concrete footing and concrete floor with various factors influencing design.

A broken line represents the footing and foundation wall, located under the concrete slab or grade. This broken line is referred to as a **hidden line**. The solid line shows the edge of the concrete floor slab as projected above the grade level. Broken lines are mainly used to show footing sizes, configurations, and their locations below grade level or below a concrete floor; solid lines show those above.

An interior bearing footing might look like Figure 11.2. If it does, draw the plan view of this detail only with broken lines because all the configurations are under the concrete slab floor and grade.

Often, concrete curbs above the concrete floor levels are used to keep the garage floor within a few inches above the driveway while keeping the wood 8 inches or more from the ground. Curbs are ideal in areas where wood studs must be kept free of floor moisture. See Figure 11.3.

When you are faced with drawing concrete steps and a change of floor level, you may draw a plan view reflecting this section. See Figure 11.4.

To aid in visualization of the foundation of the structure and its various components, a three-dimensional (3-D) image was produced. Two major segments were enlarged to help readers visualize the interior shapes and connections. One can actually see the exterior bearing footing and the change in level in Figure 11.5.

Drawing the Foundation Plan

Lay your tracing or create a new drawing layer over the floor-plan drawing, then draw the configuration of the

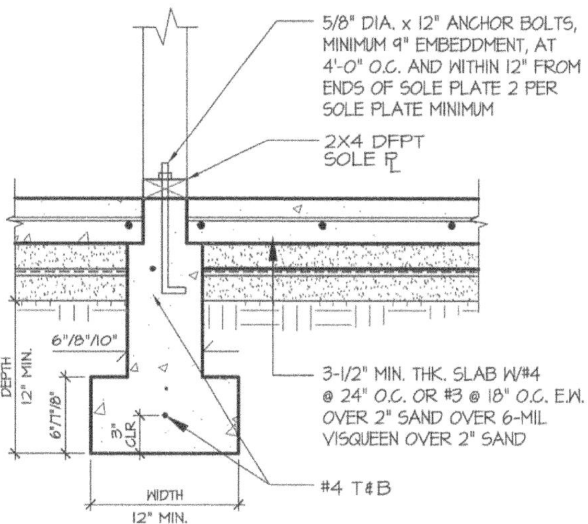

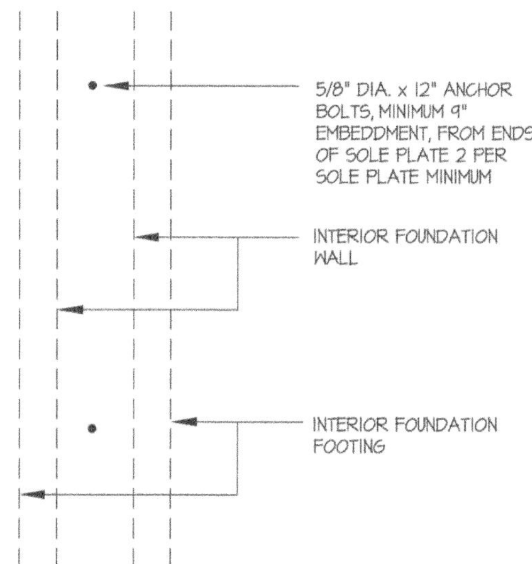

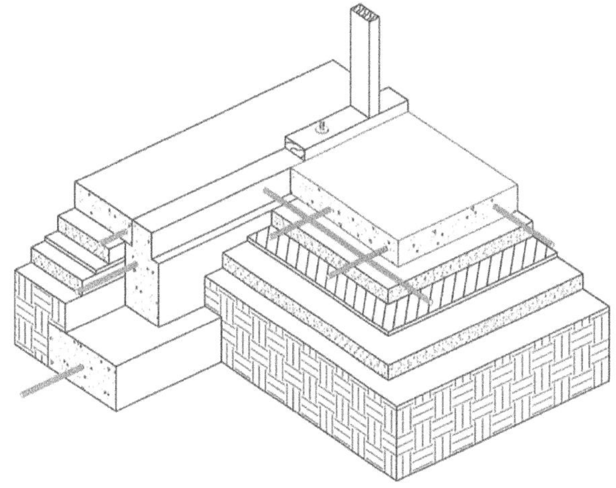

Figure 11.2 Detail of interior bearing footing.

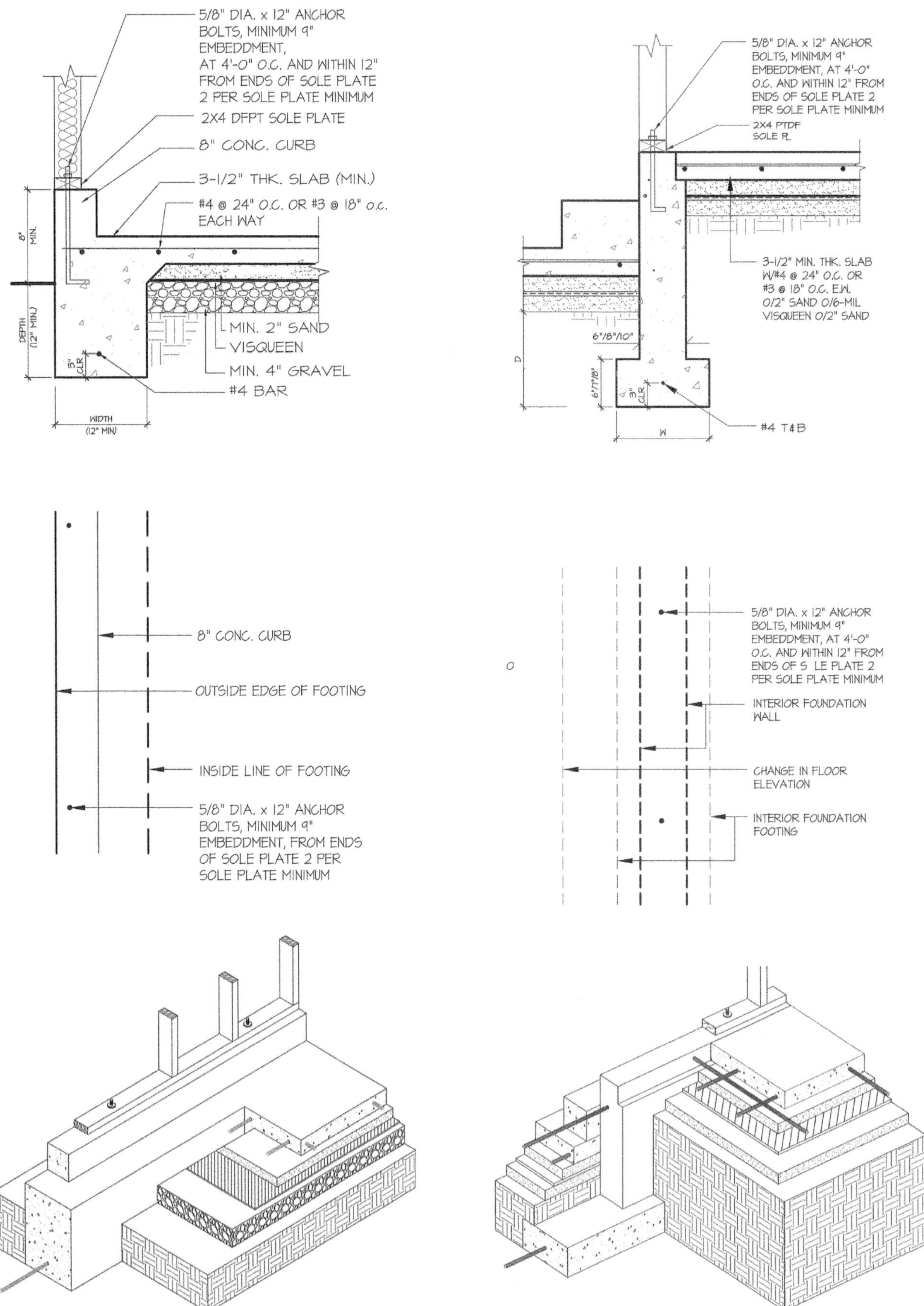

Figure 11.3 Exterior bearing footing with raised curb.

Figure 11.4 Interior bearing footing.

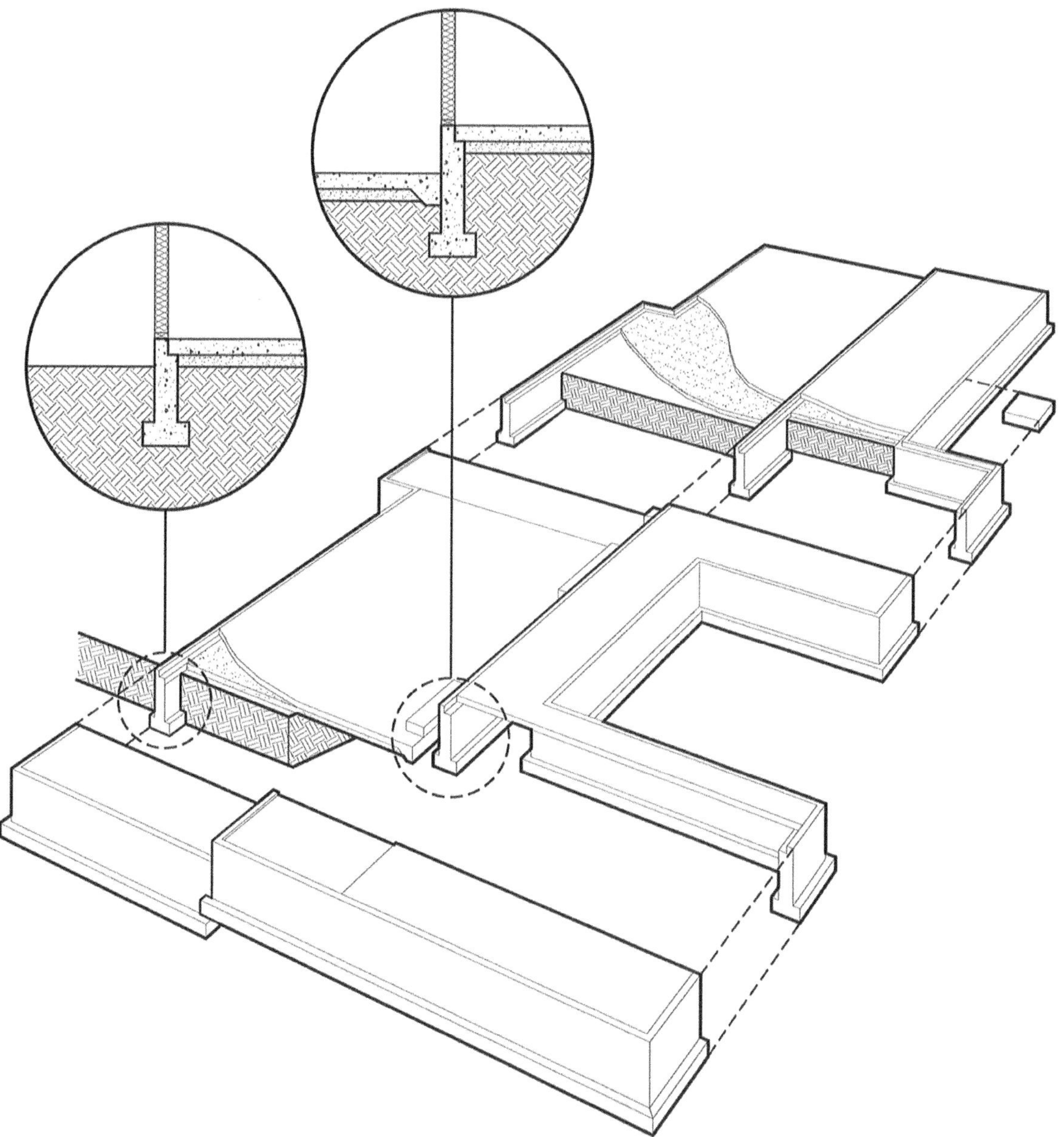

Figure 11.5 3-D foundation image.

floor plan, as well as the internal walls, columns, fire places, and so on, that require foundation sections. After this light tracing, you are ready to finalize the drafting.

The final drafting is a graphic culmination, in plan view, of all the foundation walls and footings. Start with all the interior bearing and non-bearing foundation conditions. Represent these with a dotted line according to the particular sections in plan view. Figure 11.6 shows an example of a foundation plan for a residence, incorporating the plan views similar to Figures 11.2–11.5, as previously discussed.

Usually, various notes are required for items to be installed before the concrete is poured. An item like a **post hold-down** or column base (a U-shaped steel strap for bolting to a post and embedded in concrete so as to resist lateral forces; see Figure 11.7) should be shown on the foundation plan, because its installation is important in this particular construction phase. Note the *call-out* (identification reference system) for this item in Figure 11.6.

Drawing Fireplaces. A drawing of a masonry fireplace on the foundation plan should have the supporting walls crosshatched. (To **crosshatch** is to shade with crossed lines, either diagonal or rectangular.) Show the fireplace footing with a broken line. When numerous vertical reinforcing bars are required for the fireplace, it is necessary to show their size and location, because they are embedded in the fireplace.

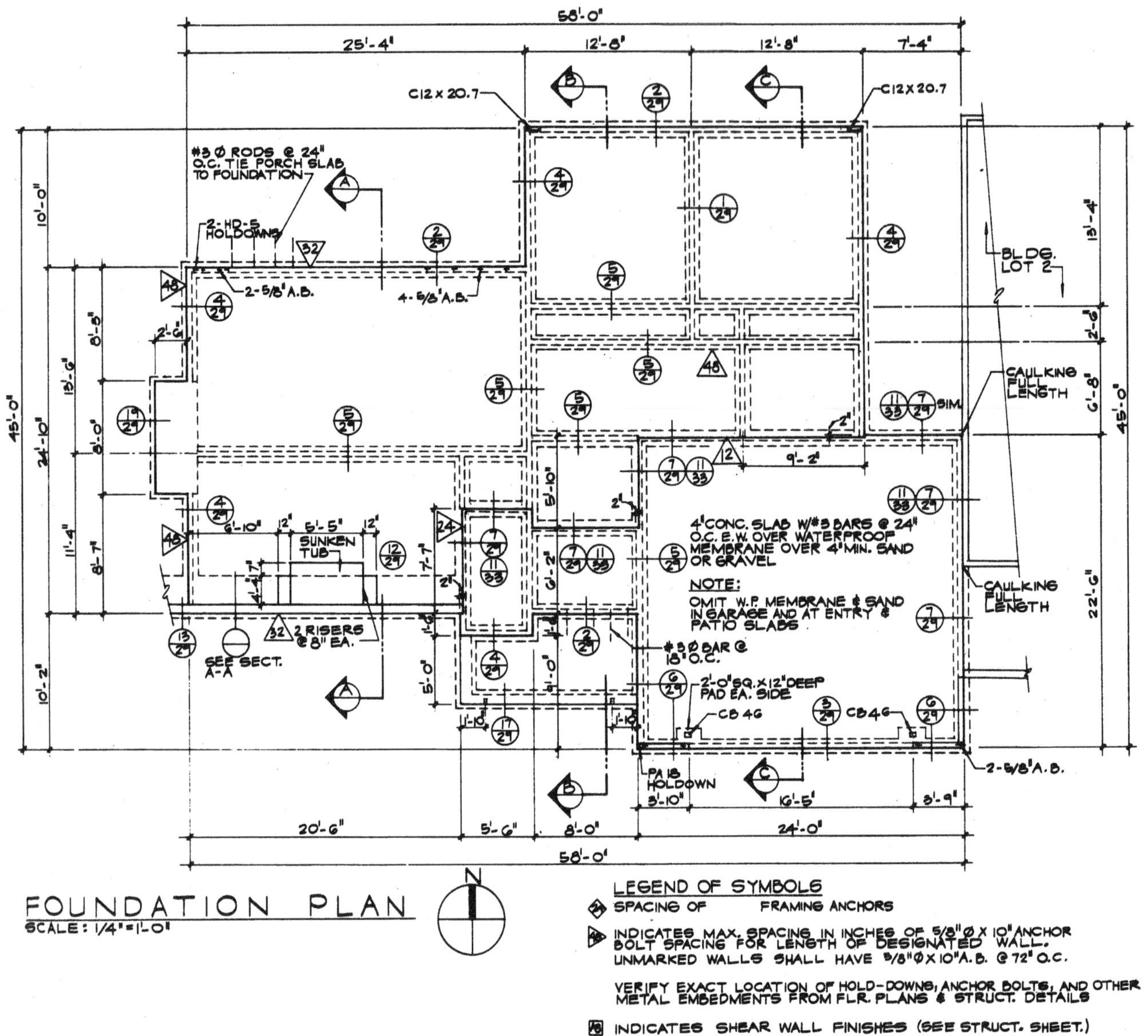

Figure 11.6 Foundation plan for a concrete floor.

Strengthening Floors. Requirements for strengthening concrete floors with reinforcing vary by project, so it is important to show their size and spacing on the foundation plan. The foundation plan in Figure 11.6 calls for a 6×6×10×10 welded wire reinforcing mesh to strengthen the concrete floor. This call-out tells us that the mesh is in 6″×6″ squares and made of number 10-gauge wire in both directions. Figure 11.8 shows how the reinforcing mesh and a plastic membrane are placed before the concrete is poured. Deformed reinforcing bars are also installed to strengthen the concrete slab floors. The size and spacing of these bars are determined by factors such as excessive weights expected to be carried by the floor and unfavorable soil conditions.

Sloping Concrete Areas. When concrete areas have to be sloped for drainage, indicate this on the foundation plan. You can do this with a directional arrow, noting the number of inches or 1% slope for the concrete. See Figure 11.6, in which a garage slab is sloped to a door.

Your foundation plan dimensioning should use the identical dimension-line locations of the floor plan. For example, centerline dimensions for walls above should match centerline dimensions for foundation walls below. This makes the floor and foundation plans consistent. When you lay out dimension lines, such as perimeter lines, leave space between the exterior wall and first dimension line for foundation section symbols. As Figure 11.6 shows, you must provide dimensions for every

Figure 11.7 Post hold-down at the base of a column.

Figure 11.8 Reinforcing mesh and plastic.

foundation condition and configuration. Remember, the people in the field do not use measuring devices; rather, they rely on all the dimensions you have provided on the plan.

Provide reference symbols for foundation details for all conditions. Provide as many symbols as you need to remove any guesswork for the contractors in the field. As Figure 11.6 shows, the reference symbol will have enough space within the circle for letters and/or numbers for detail and sheet referencing.

Foundation Details for Concrete Slab Floor

For most cases, foundation details are drawn using an architectural scale of ¾″ = 1′-0″, 1″ = 1′-0″, 1½″ = 1′-0″, or 3″ = 1′-0″.

Scale selection may be dictated by office procedure or the complexity of a specific project. The more complex a detail is, the larger the scale you will require to provide the additional information.

Different geographic regions may necessitate variations in footing depth, size, and reinforcing requirements. Check the specific requirements for your region to determine all of the variables required.

Foundation details for the residence shown in Figure 11.6 are drawn to incorporate a **two-pour system**; that is, the foundation wall and footing are poured first and the concrete floor later. Figure 11.6 shows the exterior bearing footing drawn in final form. In colder regions, the joint between the foundation wall and concrete floor slab is filled with insulation. In severe climates, one could also insulate the underside of the entire slab or even the footings themselves.

The interior bearing footing detail should also be drawn to reflect a two-pour system with call-outs for all the components in the assembly.

Powder-actuated nails, or **shot-ins**, as they are often called, can be used to replace the bolt in some municipalities. Because the nails are only a few inches long, a footing may not be required. However, they should be used only on non-bearing walls in the interior of a structure. These can often be found in tenant improvement projects where non-bearing partition walls are used for space layout. Shot-ins are not used for exterior or bearing walls because under stress the connection will fail.

Raised Wood Floor: Foundation Plans

Prepare a foundation plan for a wood floor the same way you do for a concrete slab floor. First, determine the different footing types required to support the structure. Include in the design the footing width, stem wall dimensions, and the depth below grade. Show earth-to-wood clearances, sizes and treatment of wood members, floor sheathing, and the exterior wall and its assembly of components above the sheathing or subfloor level. See Figure 11.9. Interior bearing footing requirements can be done the same way, as they are very similar to the exterior footing system. In the plan view, the interior bearing footing will look similar to the exterior bearing footing in Figure 11.9.

When laying out the foundation plan for a wood floor system, provide intermediate supporting elements located between exterior and interior bearing footings.

You can do this with a pier and girder system, which can be spaced well within the allowable spans of the floor joists selected. (This layout will be reviewed later in the discussion of the foundation plan.) The girder-on-pier detail can be sketched in the same way as the previous details. Figure 11.10 describes the concrete pier in plan view. The pier spacing depends on the size of floor girder selected. With a 4×6 girder, a 5′ to 7′ spacing is recommended under normal floor loading conditions. Regional building codes help you to select floor joists and girder sizes relative to allowable spans.

Drawing the Foundation Plan

Begin the foundation plan by drawing the outside line of the exterior walls, the centerline of the interior load-bearing walls (walls supporting ceiling, floor, and roof), and curb and stud edges that define a transition between the wood floor members and the concrete floor. It is not necessary to locate non-bearing wall conditions for wood floors, because floor girders can be used to support the weight of the wall or double floor joists.

As a review of this procedure, Figure 11.11 shows a foundation with wood floor construction, incorporating the plan views shown in Figures 11.9–11.10. The floor plan is the same one used for the concrete floor foundation plan. The spacing for floor girders and the concrete piers supporting the girders is based on the selected floor joist size and girder sizes. The floor girders can be drawn with a broken line; the piers, being above grade, should be drawn with a solid line. Dimension the location of all piers and girders. Wherever possible, locate floor girders under walls. Show the direction of the floor joists and their size and spacing directly above the floor girders. The fireplace foundation and reinforcing information can be designated as indicated earlier.

The foundation plan in Figure 11.12 shows a concrete garage floor connected to a house floor system with #3 dowels at 24″ on center (or as local code dictates). This call-out should also be designated for other concrete elements, such as porches and patios. If a basement exists, the supporting walls can be built of concrete block. The concrete-block wall will be crosshatched on the foundation plan to indicate masonry construction. See Figure 11.13. Detail ①, as designated on the foundation plan in Figure 11.14, is an isometric drawing of an exterior concrete foundation wall utilizing a wood floor joist and a plywood subfloor. Note the exterior foundation vent for the under-floor ventilation. See Figure 11.15.

Incorporate dimensioning and foundation detail symbols the same way you did for a concrete foundation. In this instance, however, the detail reference symbol shows arrowheads on the circular symbols, as recommended by state and national standards. An important note to be located on the foundation plan drawing is the number of foundation vents required, and their sizes, material, and location. This requirement is established by governing building codes.

The foundation plan is ideally suited for computer drawing. There are two main reasons for this. As every trained manual drafter knows, the repetitious drawing of piers and girders is a thing of the past, as is the drawing of dotted or hidden lines around the perimeter of the stem wall on the foundation. On the computer, you just change the layer and line type, and offset the lines, and you immediately have the outline of a footing or foundation.

Internal Load-Bearing Foundation. Internal load-bearing foundation assemblies are designed to support heavy loads from the floor system, load-bearing walls, and ceiling and roof loads. Such a foundation assembly may be designed as a concrete wall and footing similar to that in Figure 11.14, or with the use of wood girders and concrete piers. The size of the wood girders and the spacing of the concrete piers are predicated on the amount of structural loading they are required to support. Whenever possible, it is recommended that the wood girders be located directly beneath the load-bearing wall. It is good practice not to extend floor joists to their maximum span, because this approach may cause deflection or movement in the floor system. It is also good practice to include additional rows of girders and piers to provide a stiffer floor system. Figure 11.16 shows an internal pier and wood girder assembly. Note the required solid blocking between the floor joist and its placement directly above the girder and under the wall partition.

Moisture Protection. As mentioned in the list of construction principles for a wood floor system, it is paramount to protect wood members against moisture. Moisture can cause dry rot, swelling, and buckling of

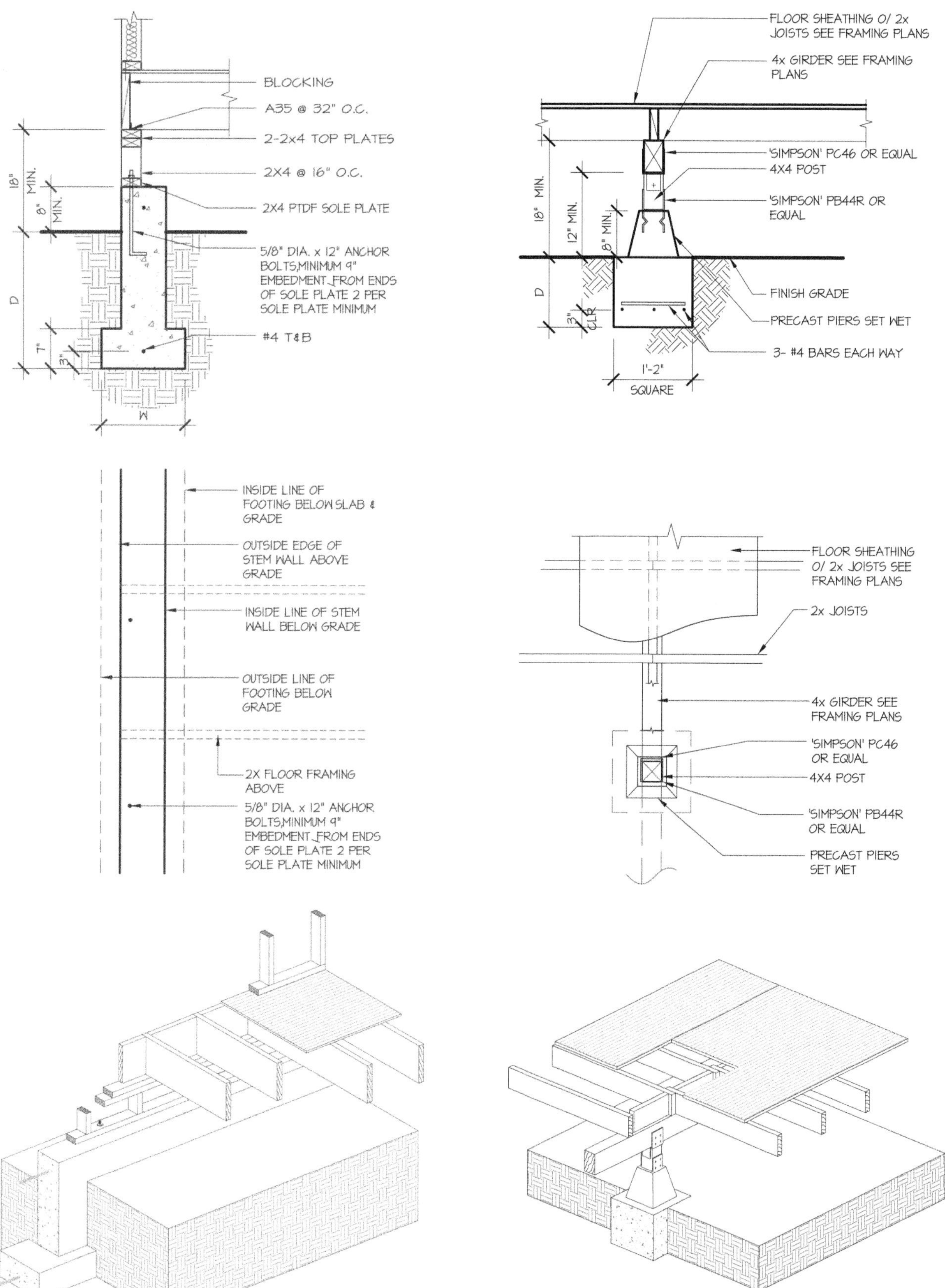

Figure 11.10 Pier and girder detail.

Figure 11.9 Raised wood exterior bearing footing detail.

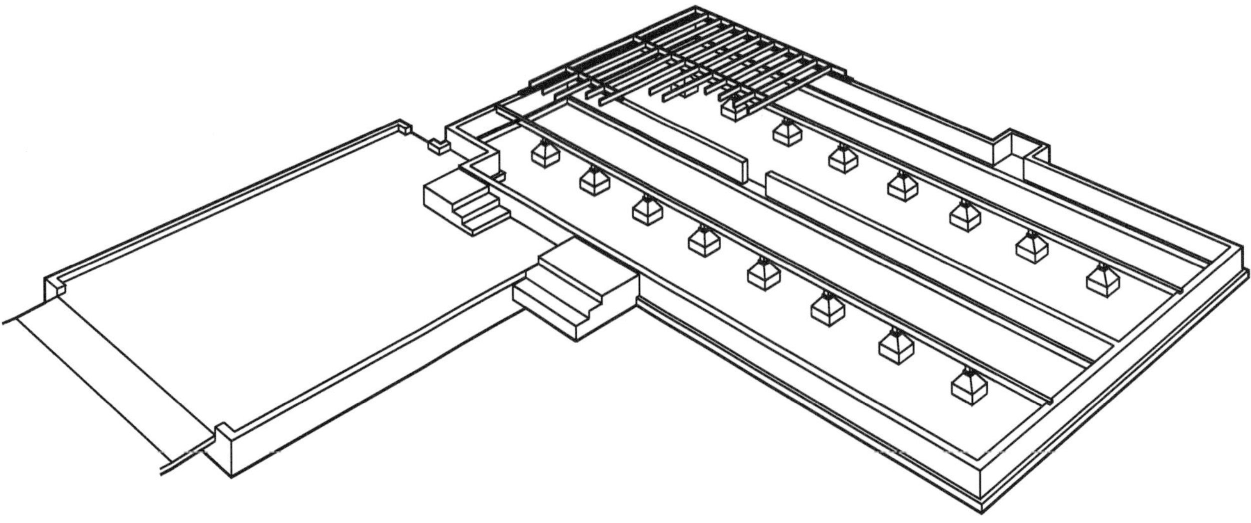

Figure 11.11 Foundation plan for a raised wood floor.

wood members. One method of deterring moisture is to provide an adequate sheet-metal flashing system in areas subject to water seepage.

Figure 11.17 illustrates a recommended sheet-metal flashing assembly positioned between a concrete porch and a wood floor system.

■ EXAMPLES

Example 11.1 A Building with Masonry Walls

When projects use concrete or masonry for exterior and interior walls, the walls may continue down the concrete footing. Figure 11.18 shows an exterior masonry wall and concrete footing. If interior walls are also constructed of masonry, the foundation section is similar to Figure 11.19. Drawing the foundation plan using masonry as the foundation wall requires delineation of the foundation walls by crosshatching those areas representing the masonry. If a change in floor elevation occurs, the detail can look similar to Figure 11.20. This detail indicates a slab on grade on one side and a raised wood floor system on the other. Figure 11.21 demonstrates a raised wood floor system to porch connection. There can be a numerous variations on a detail like this.

The foundation plan, shown in Figure 11.22, defines all the masonry wall locations as per Figure 11.18. The footings are drawn with a broken line. For this project, pilasters are required to support steel roof beams. A **pilaster** is a masonry or concrete column designed to support heavy axial and/or horizontal loads. The footing width is not called out, but rather refers to the foundation plan for a specific pilaster footing dimension. Many projects use a schedule, because the total loads acting on the pilaster vary based on location.

An example of a pad schedule is shown in the chapter of schedules, but the concept is that there is a significant repetition of sizes, and a legend is a better way to track the pad sizes. Locate the pad schedule directly on the foundation plan sheet for ease of reference. It should show dimensions for all footings, walls, and pad locations, with reference symbols clearly defined for specific conditions. Similar notes are provided for items such as ramp and floor slopes, pilaster sizes, and required steel reinforcing.

Example 11.2 A Foundation Using Concrete Pads and Steel Columns

The way foundation plans are drawn varies, depending on the method of construction for a specific structure. The example here is of a structure requiring concrete pads to support steel columns, with a continuous footing to support masonry walls.

Steel columns are also required to support heavy axial loads, and they, in turn, require a foundation. These foundation members are commonly referred to as concrete piers or **concrete pads**. The size of these pads varies with different loading conditions. Because of the

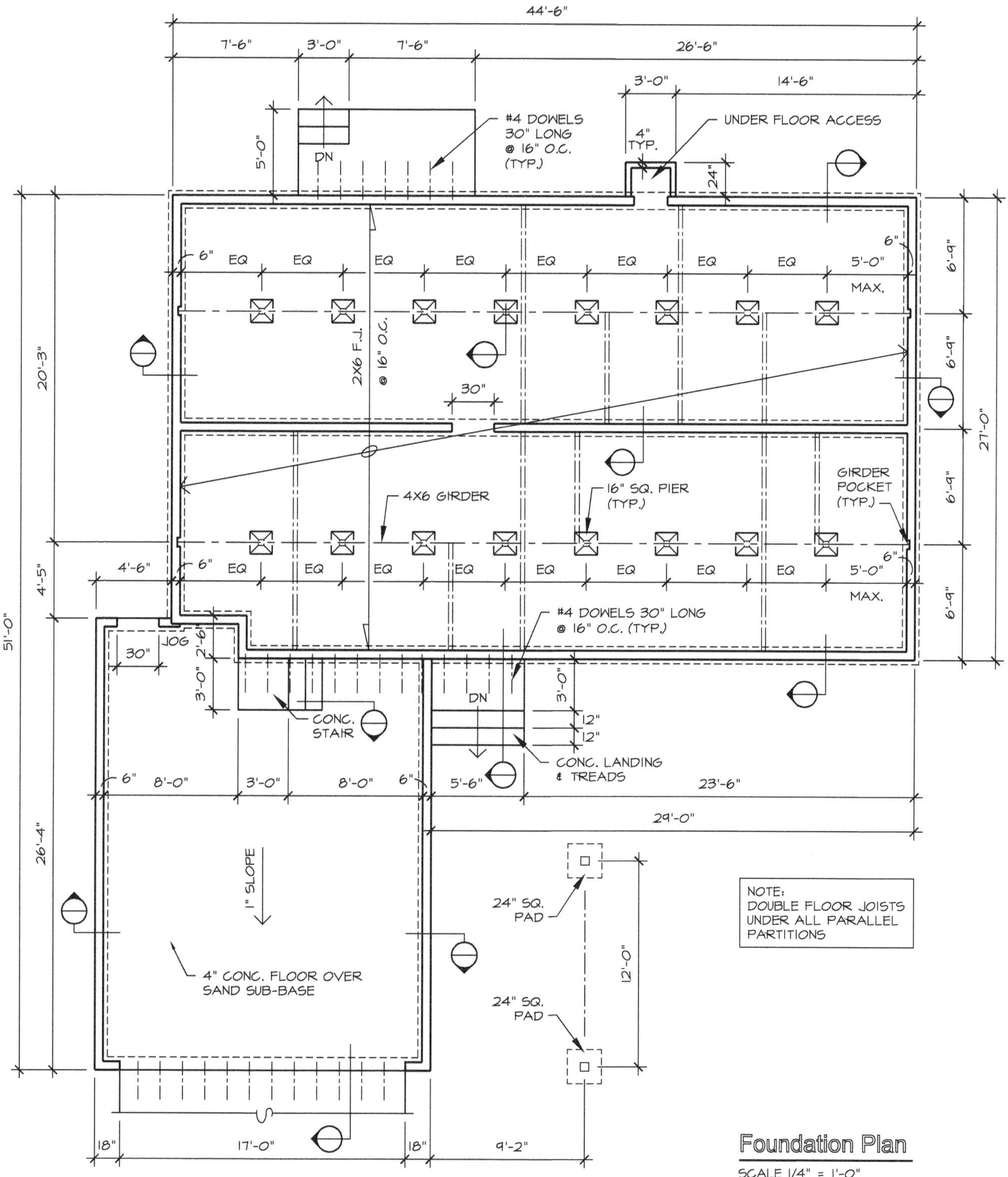

Figure 11.12 Foundation plan showing dowel ties.

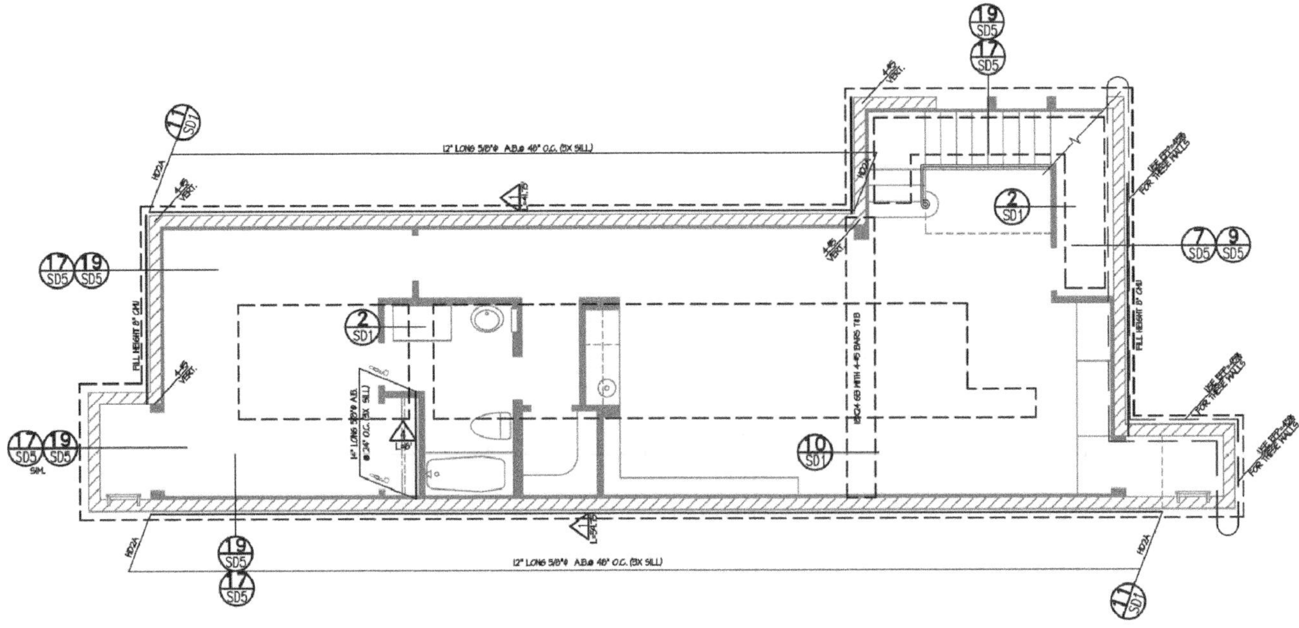

Figure 11.13 Basement foundation plan.

various pad sizes, you may need to use a column pad schedule. This schedule should note the column designation, size, depth, and required steel reinforcing.

This foundation plan, as Figure 11.23 shows, is handled differently from the foundation plan in Example 11.1. First, establish the column locations as they relate to the **axial reference locations**; then draw and delineate masonry walls. Concrete pads located under a concrete floor are represented with a broken line. See Figure 11.23. Figure 11.24 provides a visual example of this column pad footing detail in section. The column pad sizes may vary due to varying loads, and may be sized using a pad schedule or noted directly on the foundation plan. In this case, sizes are noted on the foundation plan. At the bottom of the foundation plan drawing, provide a **legend** defining the size and shape of the steel column and the base stem that supports it.

Because of all the critical information required in the field, a schedule for column base plates and their required anchorage may be necessary. Put this on the plan. Dimensioning this type of foundation depends on the axial reference locations, which are identical to the floor-plan referencing. Other foundation conditions are dimensioned from these axial reference lines.

After you complete all the necessary dimensioning, show section reference symbols and notes. Figure 11.23 has a double broken line representing a continuous footing underneath, which connects to all the concrete pads. The main purpose of this footing is to provide continuity for all the components of the foundation.

The concrete pads are the main supports for this structure. Figure 11.25 shows the trenching and some formwork for a concrete pad. Note particularly the placement of the reinforcing steel and the footing, which is used to tie all the pads together. After the concrete is poured and anchor bolts embedded, the steel column with the attached base plate is bolted to the concrete pad. See Figure 11.26.

When columns are used for structural support, concrete caissons may be needed in unfavorable soil conditions. A **concrete caisson** is a reinforced column designed specifically for the loads it will support and is located at a depth that has good soil-bearing capacity. The concrete caisson shown in Figure 11.27 is used on a sloping site to provide firm support for a wood column, which in turn is part of the structural support for a building. Figure 11.28 shows a job site drilling rig making holes for concrete caissons.

Most construction sites that require caissons use them in multiple locations where they are all tied together. The system of caissons is tied at the top with a **grade beam**. This beam acts as a grid of beams that ties all the caissons together and provides the foundation for walls or posts that will sit on top of them. The idea is to provide support for walls where the foundation does not rely on soil-bearing capacity up high but down low, at the bottom of the caisson, where soil-bearing capacities

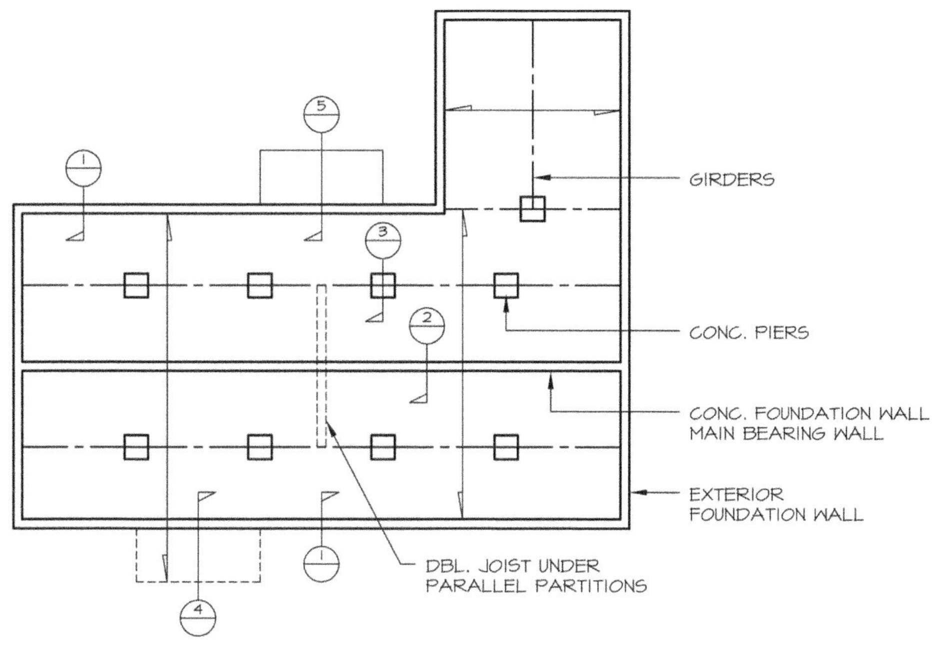

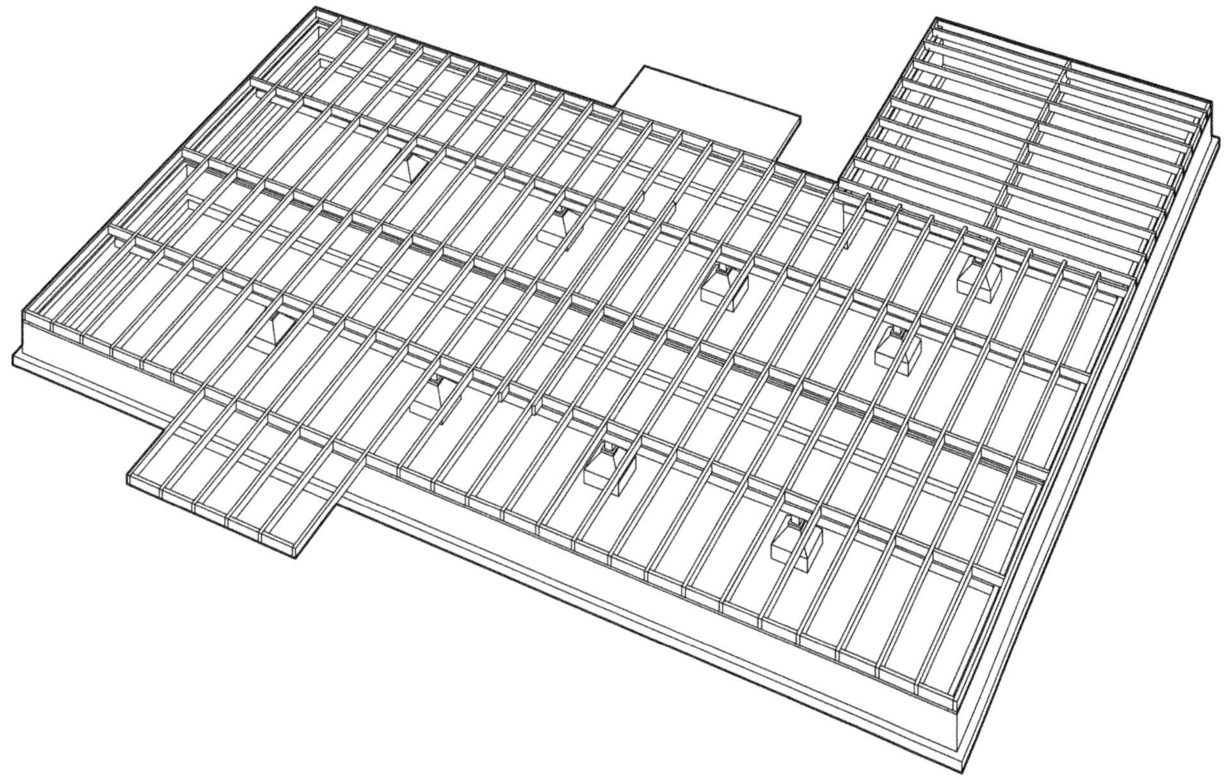

Figure 11.14 Foundation plan: Wood floor joist system.

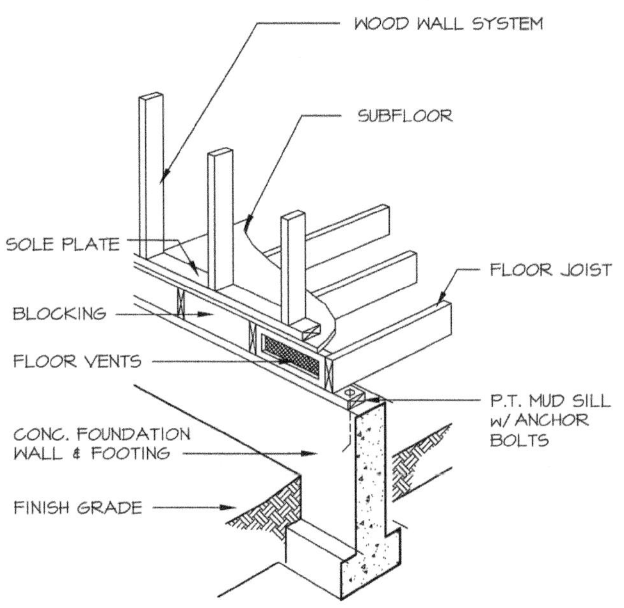

Figure 11.15 Exterior foundation wall with wood floor joist.

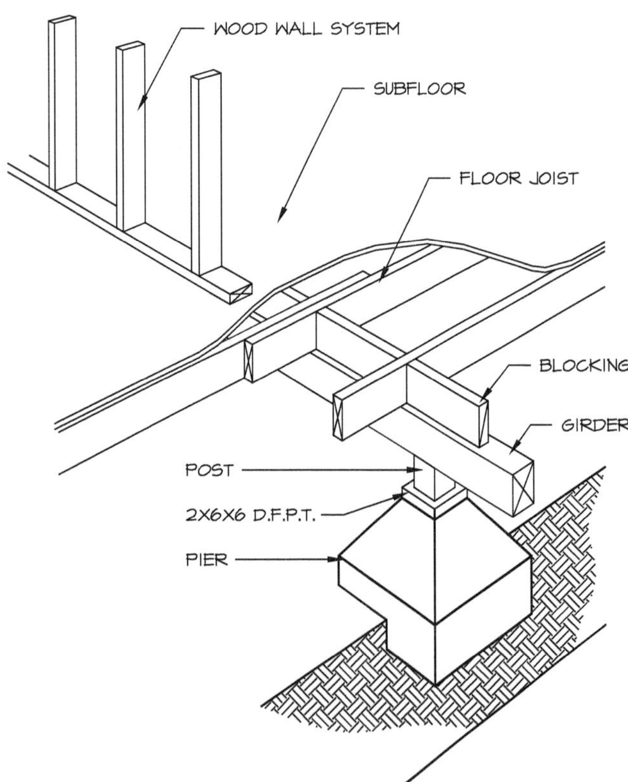

Figure 11.16 Internal pier and girder assembly.

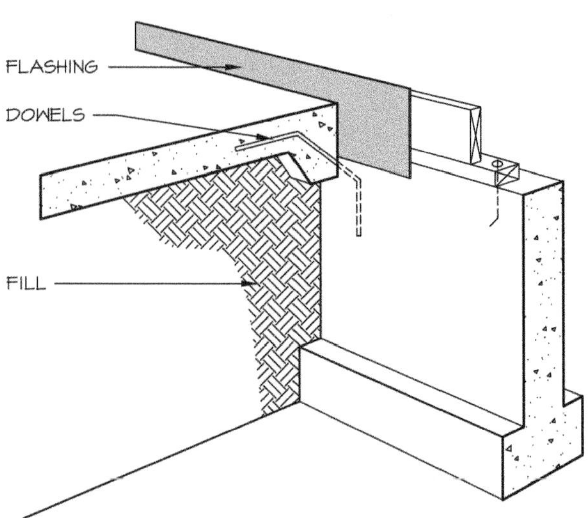

Figure 11.17 Flashing assembly (porch slab and wood floor).

are more ideal. If you visualize a table and its legs, the grade beam is the table top and the legs of the table are the caissons. See Figure 11.29.

Example 11.3 A Concrete Floor at Ground-Floor Level

The foundation plan in Figure 11.30 is for a small two-story residence with a concrete floor at the ground-floor level. The plan view drawing of the foundation sections is similar to those in Figures 11.2 and 11.3.

Everything that is to be installed prior to the pouring of the concrete must be noted on the foundation plan. If items are located on other drawings, the foundation contractor may miss them, causing problems after the pouring. Specific locations call for anchor bolt placement, steel column embedment, post hold-down hard-ware, and other symbols, all explained in the legend. Dimensions for the location of all foundation walls and footings are shown with reference symbols for the various footing conditions.

Figure 11.31 demonstrates the importance of noting all the required hardware or concrete accessories on the foundation plan. You can well imagine the problems that would arise if these items were not installed before the concrete was poured. Trenching and formwork for the foundation are shown photographically in Figure 11.32. The next step in completing the foundation phase of this residence is the pouring of the concrete and finishing of

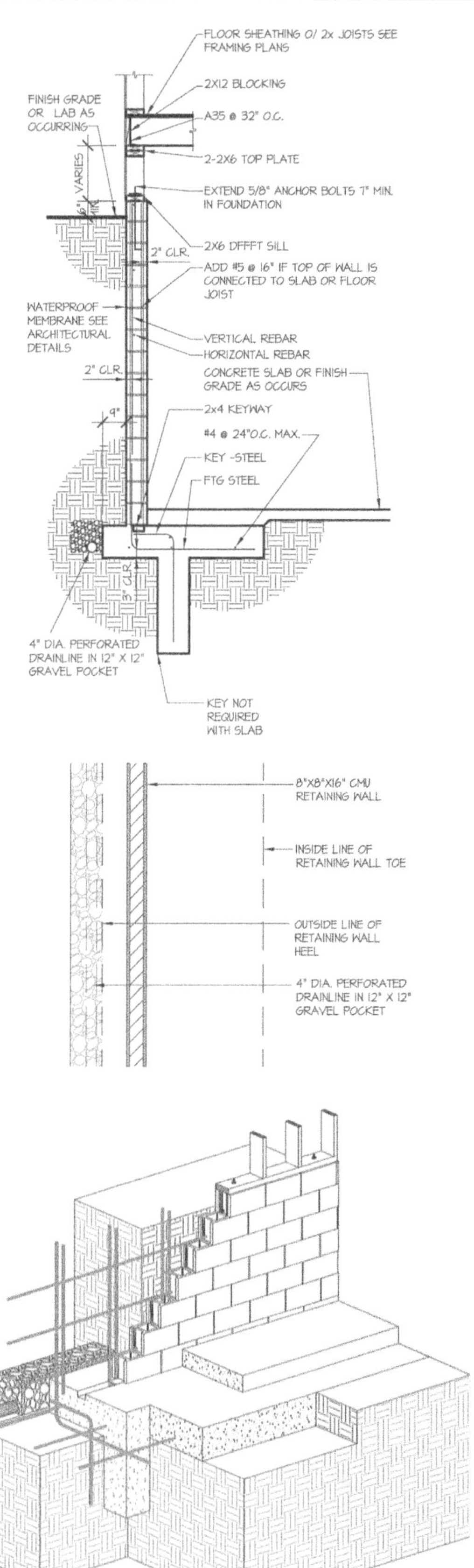

Figure 11.18 Concrete-block retaining wall at basement.

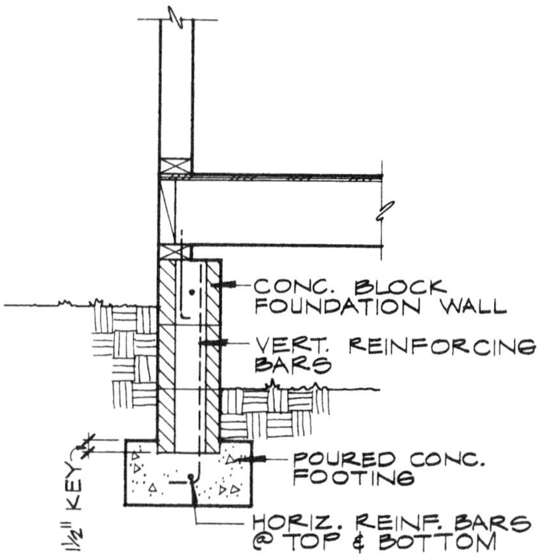

Figure 11.19 Concrete-block foundation wall supporting a wood floor.

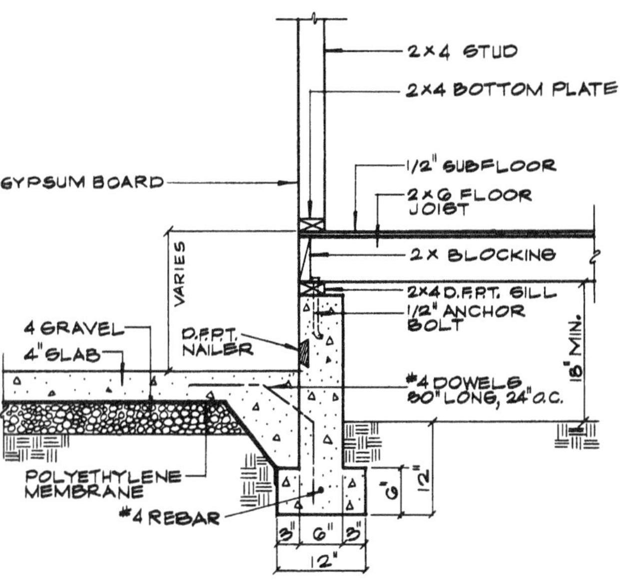

Figure 11.20 Drafted detail of change of level from a wood floor to a concrete slab.

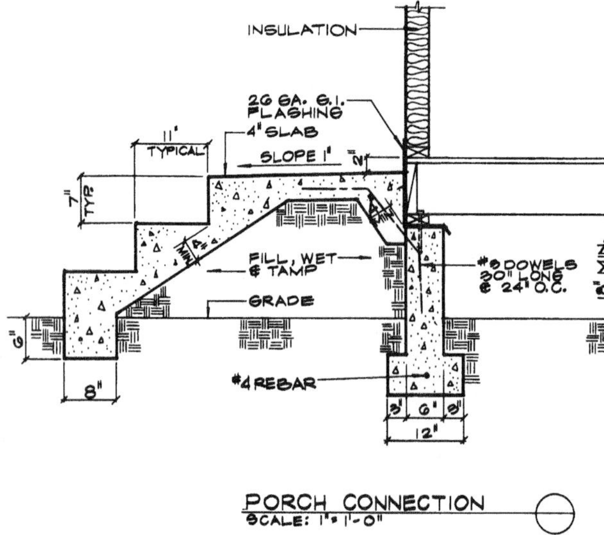

Figure 11.21 Drafted detail of a porch connection.

the concrete floor in preparation for the wood framing. Often, a checklist is also furnished to provide specific information required for a project. See Figure 11.33.

SUMMARY OF TYPICAL CONVENTIONS FOR FOUNDATION PLANS

Refer to Figure 11.34 as you review the items in the following list.

- **A.** Plan view of an exterior bearing footing for a slab-on-grade.
- **B.** Plan view of a footing with a concrete curb, such as a garage. Also represents bearing footing for a wood floor system.
- **C.** Plan view of an interior bearing footing for a slab-on-grade system.

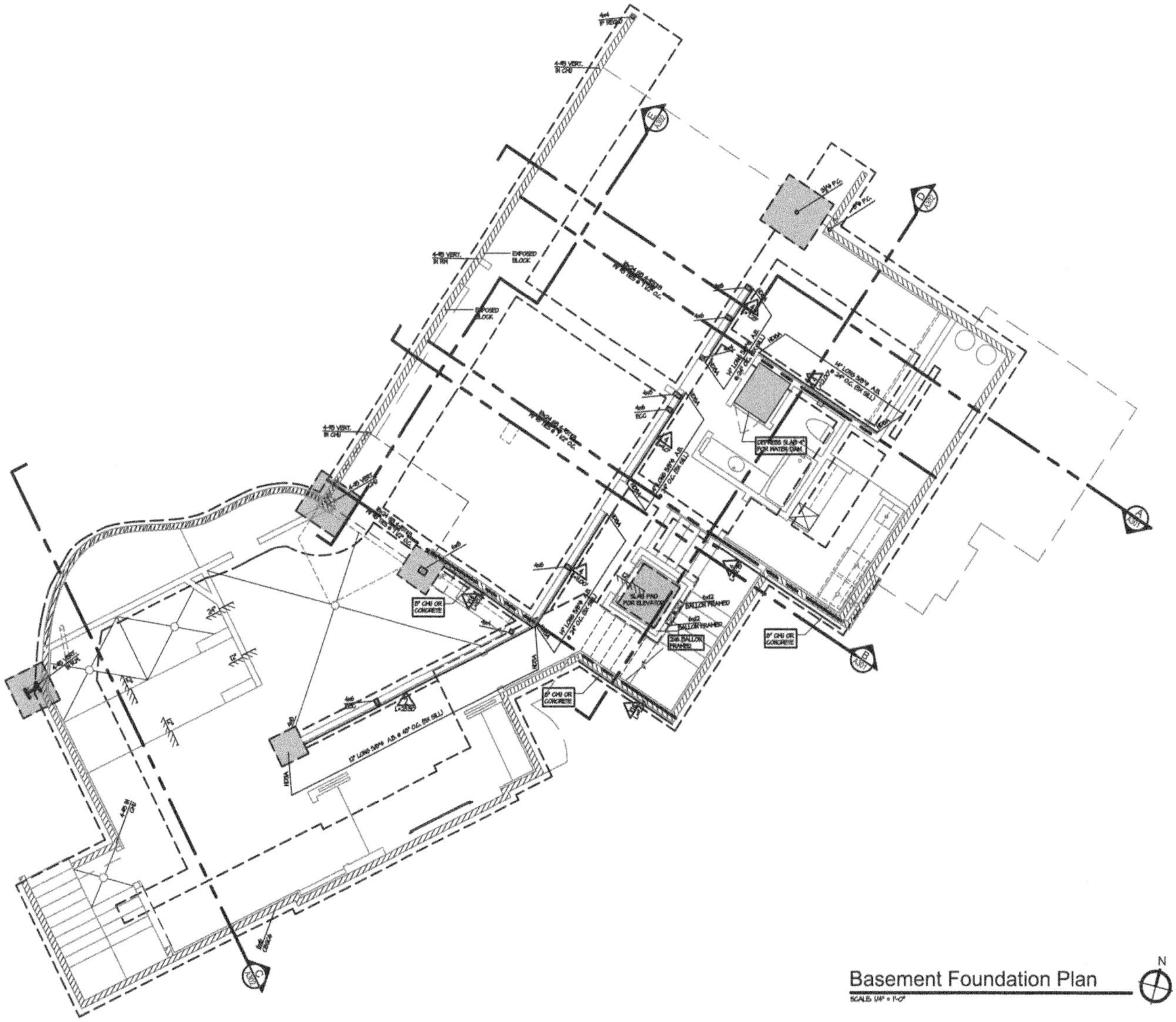

Figure 11.22 Foundation plan layout with masonry walls.

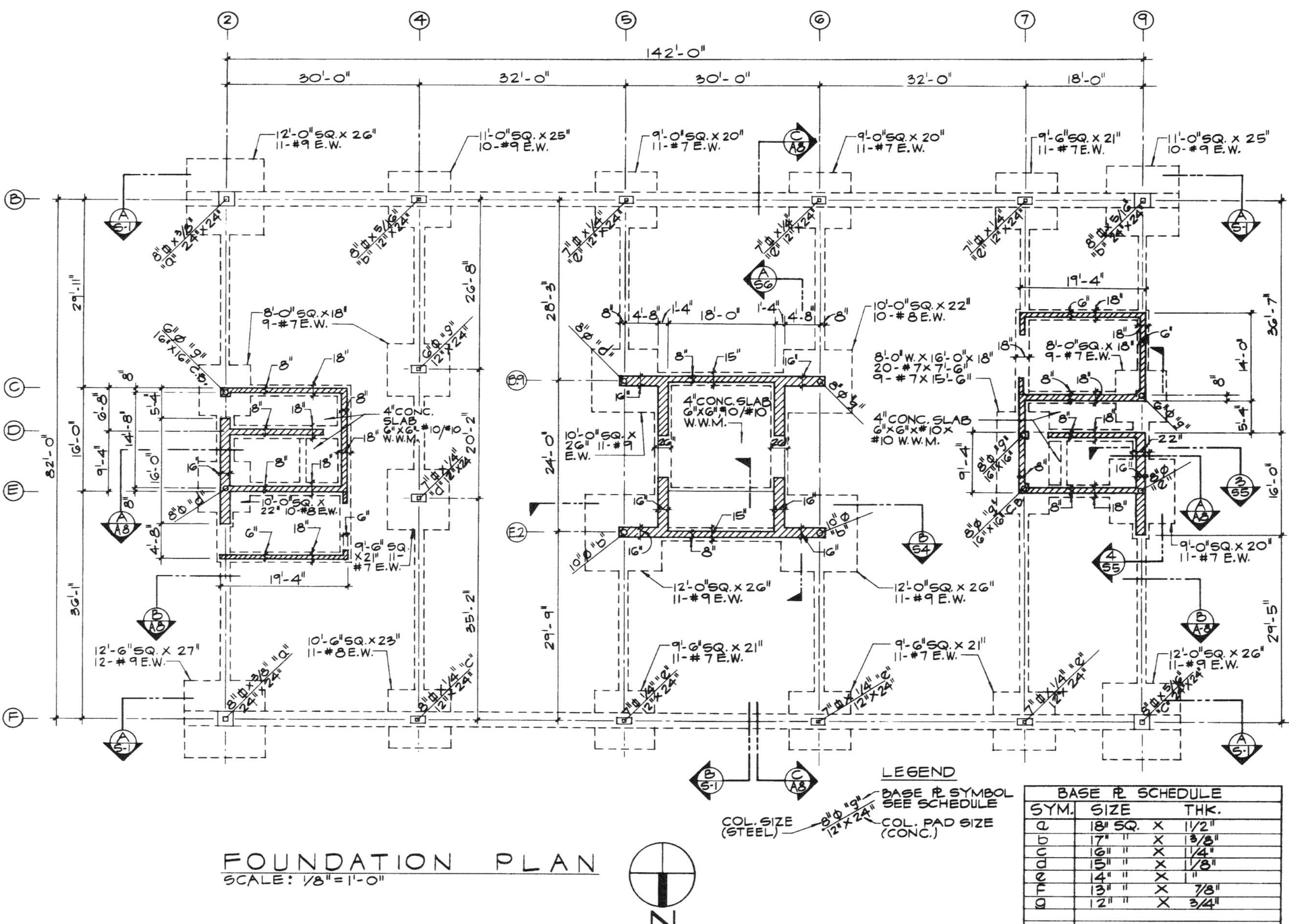

Figure 11.23 Foundation plan: Concrete pads. (Courtesy of Westmount, Inc. Real Estate Development.)

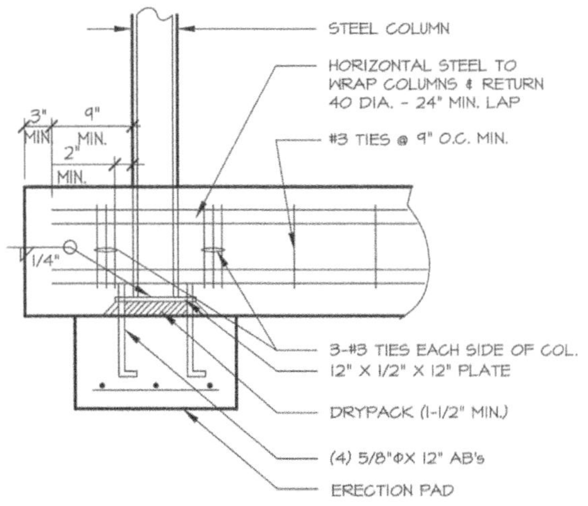

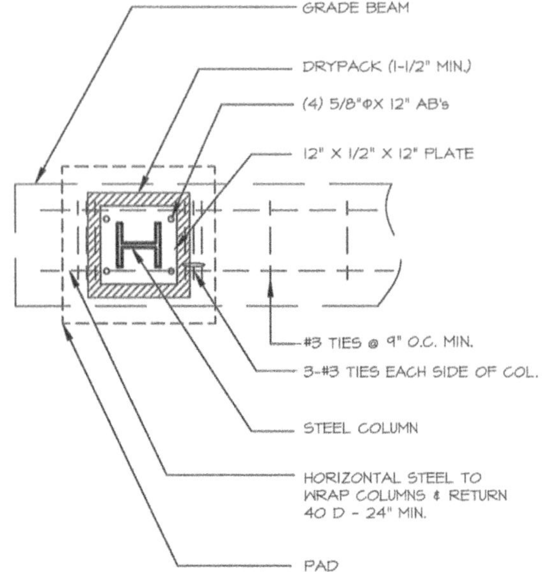

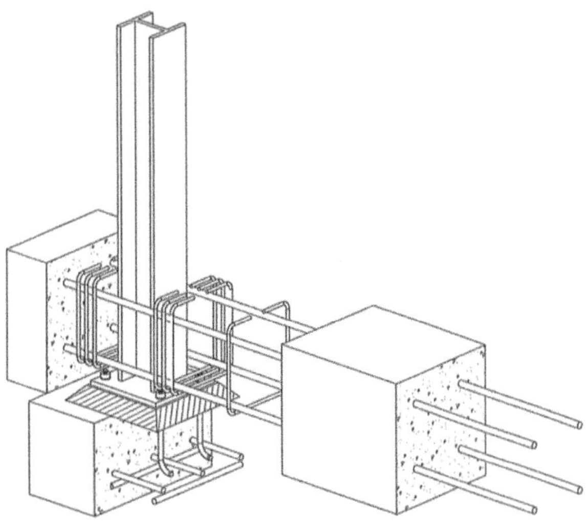

Figure 11.24 Column-to-footing detail.

Figure 11.25 Forming for concrete pad. (Courtesy of William Boggs Aerial Photography. Reprinted with permission.)

Figure 11.26 Steel column on concrete pad.

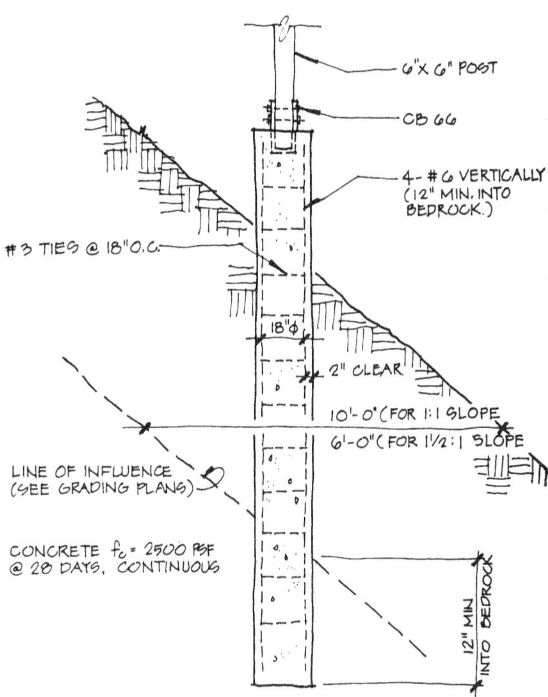

Figure 11.27 Concrete caisson.

D. Convention could represent a pier or a concrete pad for a column.

E. A widening of the footing portion of a foundation for a column; actually, a combination of B and D.

F. A plan view of a masonry wall and footing.

G. A system showing a pier and girder convention.

H. Centerlines as shown here represent dowels.

I. The diamond shape, triangle, and rectangle are used to identify such things as anchor bolt spacing, shear wall finishes, and spacing of framing anchors.

J. A multiple convention, indicating pad, pedestal, steel column, and base plate sizes. The letter refers you to a schedule in which the plate size, pad size, or even the reinforcing is described.

K. The (+) symbols represent anchor bolt locations for shear walls. This symbol should be accompanied with a note similar to the following: ½″ dia. A.B. @ 12″ o.c. (shear wall).

L. The ([) shapes represent hold-downs at shear walls.

M. Shows the location of under-floor vents and/or crawl hole from one chamber of under-floor space to another. As shown, the rectangle should be dimensioned.

N. The four hidden lines shown in this convention represent an interior bearing footing for a slab-on-grade system. If the stem wall and width of the footing vary from location to location, dimensions for them are indicated right at the location on the foundation plan.

O. A masonry retaining wall. As in the previous example, the plan view could be dimensioned if these walls are of varying sizes throughout a structure.

P. A non-bearing footing for a slab-on-grade system.

Q. Matrix used to represent concrete slab reinforcement. The size of the reinforcing is noted; for example, #4 @ 18″ o.c. each way. It is not shown throughout the foundation plan, but only on a portion of it and noted as typical.

R. An under-floor access, with the rectangle having an X as the actual opening through the foundation wall. This symbol can also be used for a window well in a basement area.

EXTERIOR AND INTERIOR WALLS

Figure 11.35 shows a partial floor plan of the living room wall adjacent to the bedroom that begins as an exterior wall and turns into an interior wall. The problem reveals itself when we remove the slab, as seen in Figure 11.36. Note that although the stem wall is not aligned, the plates are. If we align the foundation, the plates (sills) are out of alignment, resulting in a framing problem.

There are a couple of ways of representing this condition. One, as shown in Figure 11.37A, is to actually show the offset by jogging the hidden lines. Another method, as shown in Figure 11.37B, is to show the exterior/interior foundation wall as continuous and identify the jog with a note.

Drafting a Foundation on the Computer

Stage I (Figure 11.38). The first stage is always the datum or base stage. The floor plan must be used for the base or datum stage. XREF the floor plan.

Stage II (Figure 11.39). The second stage involves outlining the structure with a single line and positioning the interior bearing walls. Take care in identifying any exterior walls that become interior walls for sill (bottom plate) placement.

Stage III (Figure 11.40). Locate additional items such as concrete pads and establish the configuration of the footing.

Stage IV (Figure 11.41). If depressed slabs are needed to accommodate materials such as ceramic tile or

Figure 11.28 Drilling holes for concrete caissons. (Courtesy of William Boggs Aerial Photography. Reprinted with permission.)

brick pavers, concrete steps or stairs, or elevator shafts, they are shown at this or an earlier stage. Solid lines may be changed to dotted lines at this point. It is just a matter of changing layers and changing line type.

Stage V (Figure 11.42). Dimensioning takes place at this stage. Remember, the dimensions on the floor plan are to face of stud (FOS), and dimensions here should be the same as those on the foundation plan.

Stage VI (Figure 11.43). All noting takes place at this point, the final stage. Remember that main titles should conform to the standard office font, and all other noting should be done with an architectural lettering font that allows for easy manual correction.

■ A STEEL STRUCTURE

The foundation plan for a steel building is presented in this section as an example of a foundation plan for a commercial building.

Stage I

For this all-steel building, all drawings were produced using the dimensional reference system (see Figure 11.44). Thus, the datum or base for the foundation plan is the matrix.

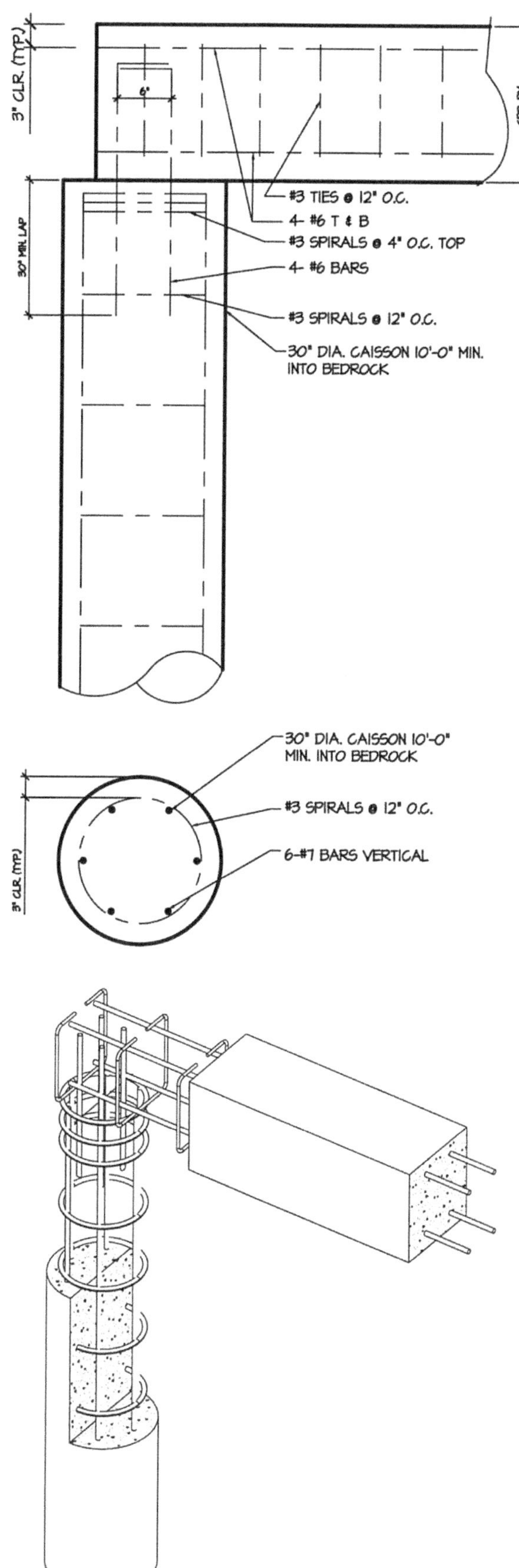

Figure 11.29 Caisson design with grade beam system.

Stage II

The structural engineer has established the size of the various concrete pads and pipe columns and provided us with engineering details (see Figure 11.45). These important pieces of information would be translated into a drawing in the next stage.

Stage III

As you compare the beginning stages of the ground-level plan and the ground-floor plan, you will see differences at the stair area (see Figure 11.46). When the complete set of drawings was submitted for building department plan check, changes were made. We next drafted columns (circles) and their respective support pads (squares). We obtained their sizes and shapes from the structural engineer.

Stage IV

Dimension lines were the first addition to the drawing at this stage. We used the reference plane system (see Figure 11.47). All subsequent dimensions were referenced to this basic set on the top and to the left. In the lobby area (central portion of the plan), where the walls do not align with the existing reference bubbles, we added new bubbles. We showed partial and full section designations.

Stage V

Dimensions were added for the concrete-block foundation walls. We also dimensioned the width of all footings (see Figure 11.48). A single detail is used for all of the foundation walls and footings. The material designation for the concrete-block walls and variations in dimensions in the footing and width of the walls were added. Also, the section reference notations were filled in, using the section designation symbols.

Stage VI

At this stage we added all remaining numerical values and filled in the reference bubbles on the matrix in the dimensional reference system (see Figure 11.49). The reference B.9, for example, indicates that there is a column at an intermediate distance between B and C of the axial reference plane. B.9 is approximately 9/10 of the distance between B and C. If there were another column that was 8/10 of the way between B and C, it would be designated B.8.

Around the perimeter of the structure is a series of squares drawn with dotted lines. These represent concrete

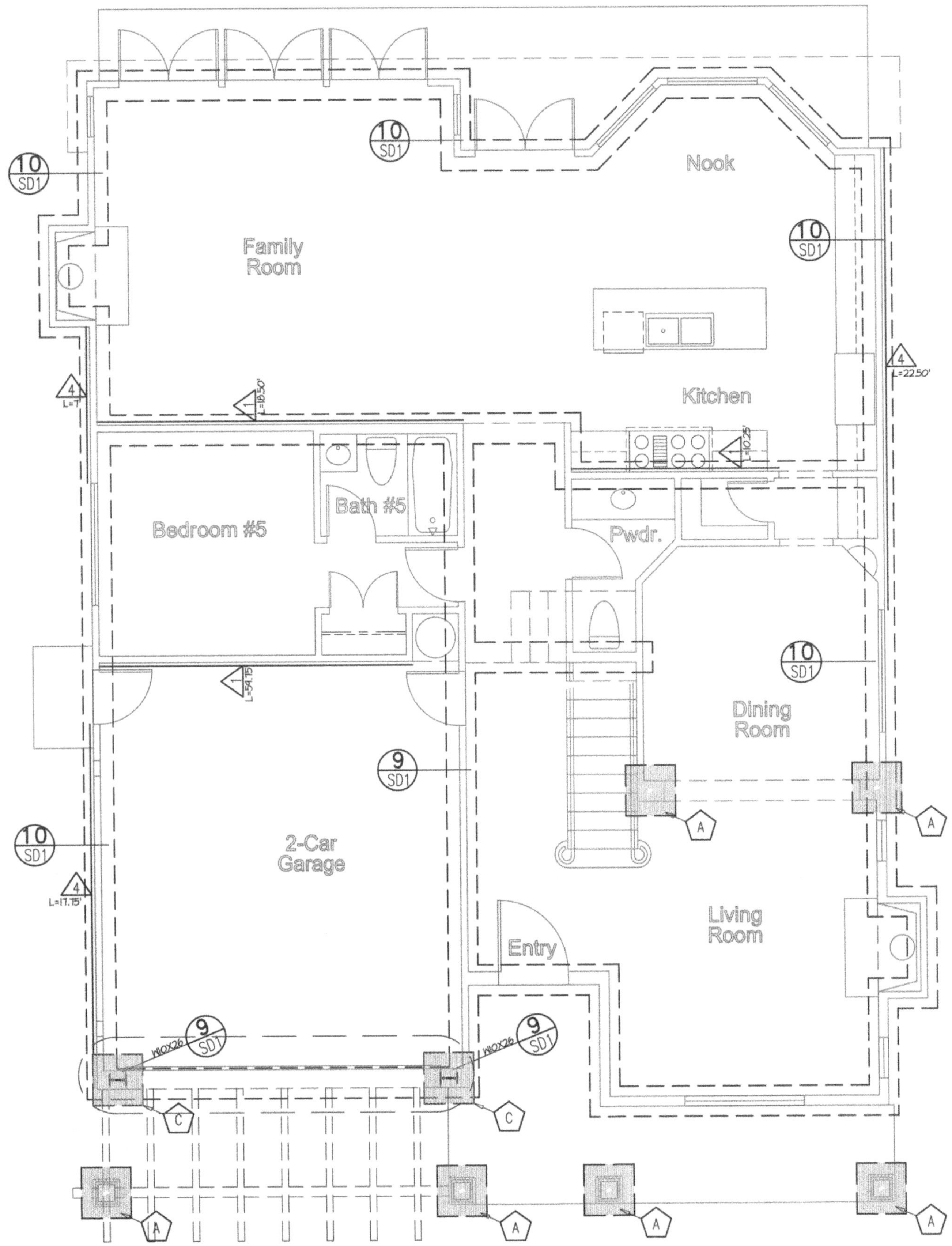

Figure 11.30 Foundation plan with concrete slab floor.

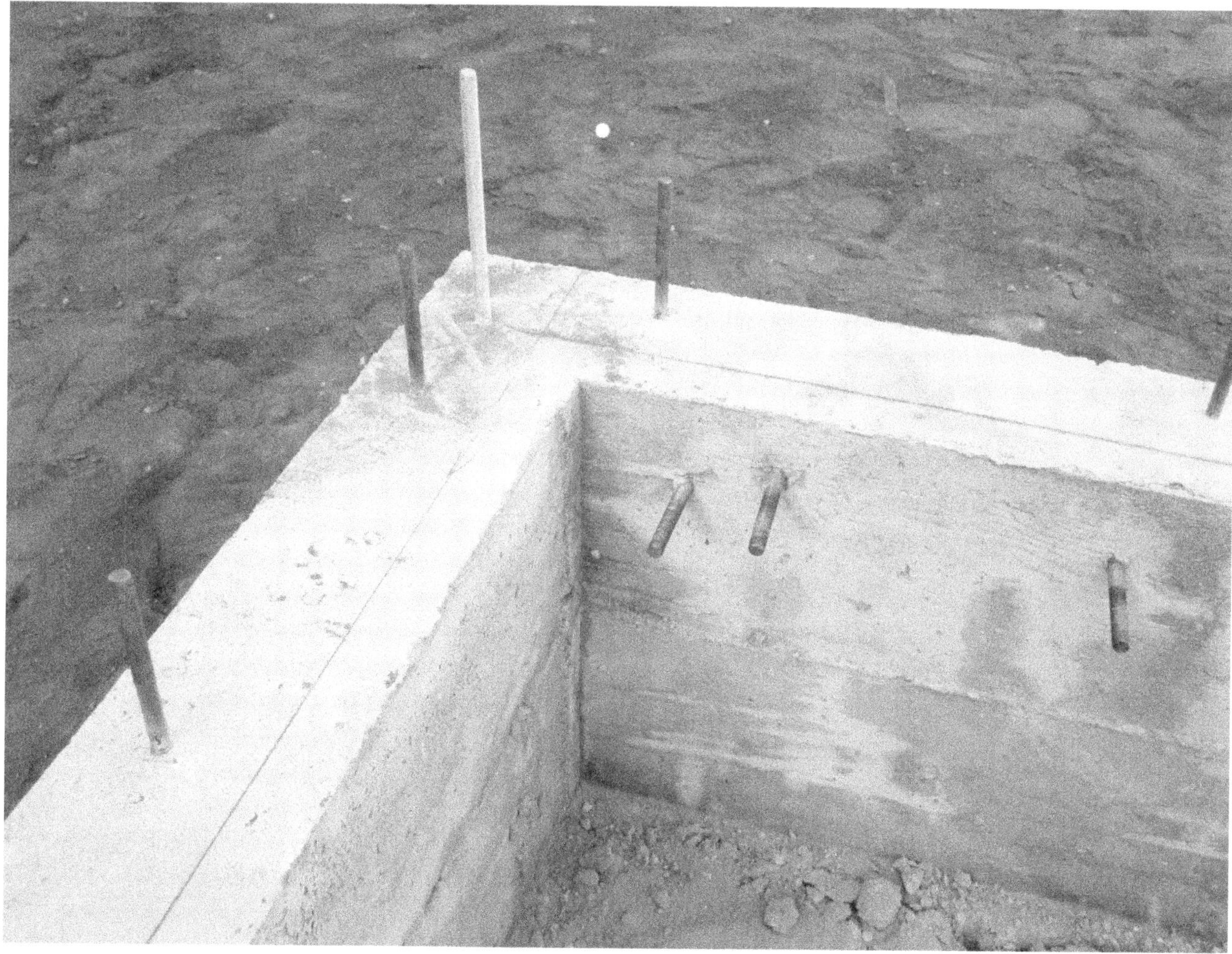

Figure 11.31 Foundation with embedded hardware.

pads that distribute the weight bearing down on the columns. The leader pointing to the hidden line indicates the size and thickness of the concrete pad and reinforcing.

At the center of these hidden lines is another rectangle with a smaller rectangle inside, representing a steel column. The leader pointing to this area explains these. For example, 7×7×¼, 12″×24″, means that the column is a 7″-square column, ¼;″ thick (wall thickness), mounted onto an "e" base plate. This "e" base plate size can be found in the base plate schedule at the lower right of Figure 11.49. Here, "e" is equal to a 14″-square by 1″-thick plate. This plate rests on another concrete pad, often called a **pedestal**, 12″ by 24″ thick.

Contained within the masonry walls are some steel columns, with concrete pads that are also noted using the schedule. Next to the schedule is a legend explaining the noting method. The title and north arrow finished this sheet.

See the process of the actual construction methods in the following Figures 11.50–11.55. Note the order of the work performed and consideration of the scale of the project does not change the process of trenching for footings it may change the frequency.

CASE STUDIES FOR DEVELOPMENT

Steel/Masonry Structure

Foundation Plan. The floor plan is used as a base when drawing the foundation plan (see Figure 11.56). Size and opening locations must conform to the block module.

Stage I. If you start a foundation drawing before you have these required sizes, you can still block out the walls and indicate the tentative location of the columns and pilasters with light cross lines to show the center. Figure 11.56 shows the first stage in the preparation of

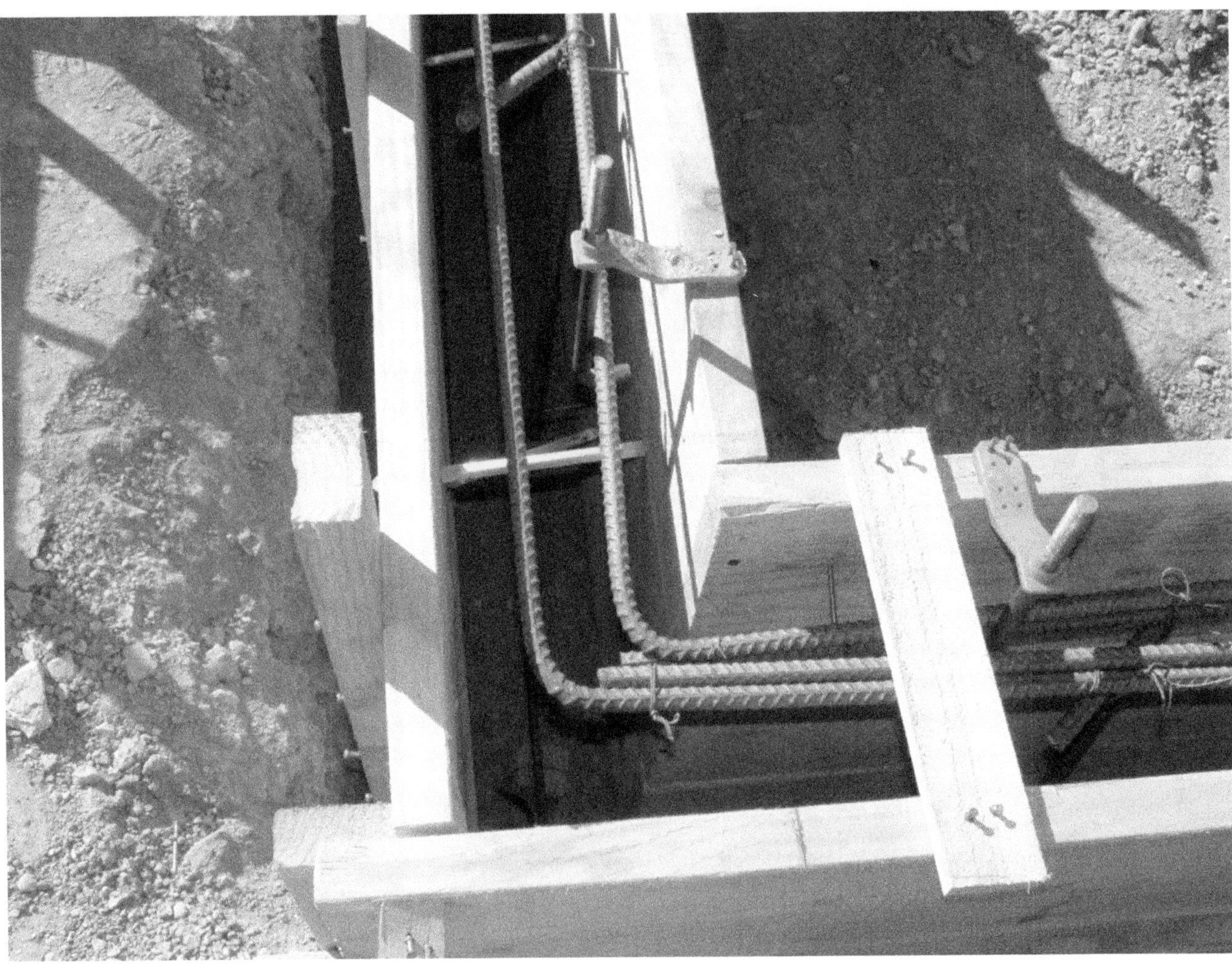

Figure 11.32 Foundation trenching, forming, reinforcement bar, and anchor bolt locating.

the foundation plan. In this drawing, lines are dotted lines, but often, at this initial stage, the outline is drawn with light solid lines. Four lines are needed to represent the walls of concrete block and the footing below the grade. At some locations, where the footing is continuous but the wall is not, there are only two lines. The squares drawn with dotted lines represent concrete pads for steel pipe columns. The exit doors at the rear of each auditorium are interesting features of this project. Each exit was designed to be sheltered by a wall with a trellis above. The rectangular areas adjacent to the easterly side are ramps for handicapped persons. (Every feature of this theater had to accommodate persons with disabilities. These features include restroom facilities, widths of openings and halls, and ramps for wheelchairs.) The columns toward the center of the structure would hold up the upper floor. Figure 11.57 shows these columns and also the forms placed for the entry stairs adjacent to the ramps for disabled persons. The columns were carefully aligned with the upper-floor walls and first-floor walls.

Stage II. The inclusion of the stairs in Figure 11.58 clearly identifies the entry to the theater. The two lines extending from each column with several perpendicular lines in them represent **brick pavers** (patterned brick on ground level). The arc lines within one of the auditoriums represent the subtle changes of levels. This was done only once because the floors in all six auditoriums are the same. All exterior and interior dimension lines were added next, taking care to ensure a proper block module. The reference bubbles on the outside of the overall dimension lines are called, collectively, a matrix of the dimensional reference plane. This matrix is used to locate columns, walls, and structural members above (not seen in this drawing).

FOUNDATION PLAN AND DETAIL CHECKLIST

1. North arrow
2. Titles and scale
3. Foundation walls 6" (solid lines)
   a. Overall dimensions
   b. Offset dimensions (corners)
   c. Interior bearing walls
   d. Special wall thickness
   e. Planter wall thickness
   f. Garage
   g. Retaining wall
4. Footings – 12″ (hidden lines)
   a. Width of footing
   b. Stepped footing as per code
   c. Fireplace footing
   d. Belled footing
   e. Grade beams
   f. Planter footing
   g. Garage
   h. Retaining wall
5. Girder (center to center)
   a. Size
   b. Direction
   c. Spacing (center to center)
6. Piers
   a. Size
   b. Spacing (center to center)
   c. Detail
      (1) 8" above grade (finish)
      (2) 8" below grade (natural)
      (3) 2 × 6 × 6 redw'd block secure to pier
      (4) 4 × 4 post
      (5) 4 × 4 girder
      (6) 2 × _ floor joist (o/c)
      (7) Subfloor 1″ diagonal
         (a) T&G
         (b) Plyscord
      (8) Finish floor *usually in finish schedule
7. Porches
   a. Indicate 2″ lip on foundation (min.)
   b. Indicate steel reinforcing (⅜″ – 24″ o.c.)
   c. Under slab note: Fill, puddle, and tamp
   d. Thickness of slab and steps.
8. Subfloor material and size
9. Footing detail references.
10. Cross-section reference
11. Column footing location and sizes
12. Concrete floors:
    a. Width of footing
    b. Stepped footing as per code
13. Fireplace foundation
14. Patio and terrace location
    a. Material
    b. See porches
15. Depressed slabs or recessed area for ceramic tile etc.
16. Double floor joist under parallel partitions
17. Joist-direction and spacing
18. Areaways (18" × 24")
19. Columns (centerline dimension and size
20. Reinforcing location and size
    a. Rods
    b. Wire mesh
    c. Chimney
    d. Slabs
    e. Retaining walls
21. Apron for garage
22. Expansion joints (20' o.c. in driveways
23. Crawl holes (interior foundation walls)
24. Heat registers in slab
25. Heating ducts
26. Heat plenum if below floor
27. Stairs (basement)
28. Detail references
    a. "Bubbles"
    b. Section direction
29. Trenches
30. Foundation details
    a. Foundation wall thickness (6" min.)
    b. Footing width and thickness (12" min.)
    c. Depth below natural grade (12″ min.)
    d. 8″ above finish grade (FHA) (6"-UBC)
    e. Redwood sill or as per code (2 × 6)
    f. ½″ × 10″ anchor bolts, 6′ 0″ o.c. 1′ from corners, embedded 7″
    g. 18" min clearance bottom, floor joist to grade
    h. Floor joist size and spacing
    i. Subfloor (see pier detail)
    j. Bottom plate 2 × 8
    k. Studs size and spacing
    l. Finish floor (finish schedule)
31. All dimensions–coordinate with floor-plan dimensions
32. Veneer detail (check as above)
33. Areaway detail (check as above)
34. Garage footing details
35. Planter details
36. House-garage connection detail
37. Special details
38. Retaining walls over 3′-0″ high (special design)
39. Amount of pitch of garage floor (direction)
40. General concrete notes
    a. Water-cement ratio
    b. Steel reinforcing
    c. Special additives
41. Note treated lumber
42. Special materials
    a. Terrazzo
    b. Stonework
    c. Wood edge
43. Elevations of all finish grades
44. Note: Solid block all joists at mid-span if span exceeds 8′-0″
45. Specify grade of lumber (construction notes)
46. Pouché all details on back of vellum
47. Indicate North arrow near plan
48. Scale used for plan
49. Scale used for details
50. Complete title block
51. Check dimensions with floor plan
52. Border lines heavy and black

Figure 11.33 Foundation plan checklist.

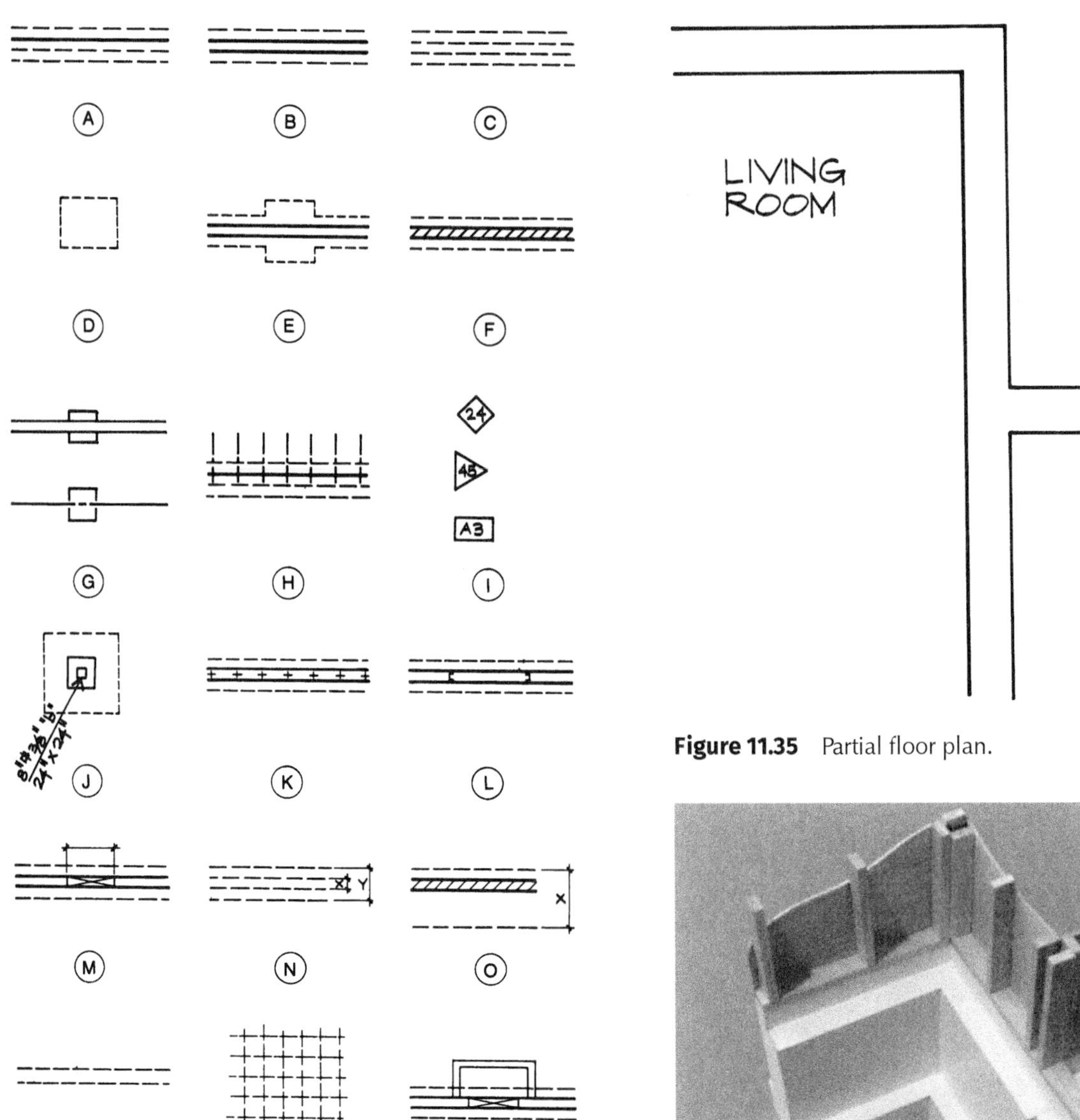

Figure 11.34 Conventions used on foundation plan.

Figure 11.35 Partial floor plan.

Figure 11.36 Offset in the foundation.

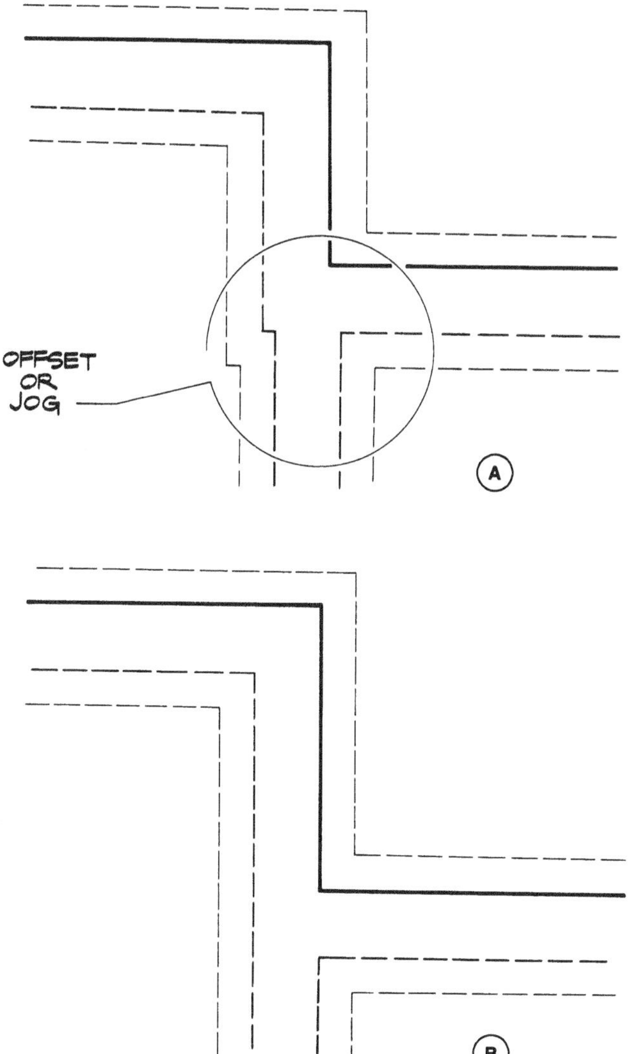

Figure 11.37 Partial foundation plan.

Stage III. Major section lines were added at this stage, as were detail reference bubbles. See Figure 11.59. Some of the section symbols break the overall dimension lines. This is not desirable, but we had to do it because of space limitations. At the top right auditorium (looking at the building from the side where the entry is), notice two reference bubbles piggybacked. This indicates that two details of these columns are available elsewhere, one architectural and the other a structural detail. The section bubbles with a flag-like symbol on the opposite side indicate wall sections. In the lobby, next to the columns, are hexagonal symbols. These are concrete pad symbols and will have numbers or letters in the corresponding to the chart introduced at the bottom right. Each concrete pad for the various columns varied enough to necessitate a chart rather than individual dimensions. We finally added the material designation for the walls (the hatching lines within the wall lines).

Stage IV. Noting, referencing, and actual numerical values of dimensions were now added. See Figure 11.60B. Noting included describing the floor material, such as the ceramic tile in the restrooms and brick pavers at the front of the theater. We indicated slopes on the ramps for the disabled. We noted special widening instructions along the perimeter of the foundation wall as well as sizing of the pilasters. At the center of the structure around the concession stand, a note reads "3″ × 3/16″ tube typ. Unless noted otherwise." Many of the columns at the rear of the concession stand and around the restroom area have a diagonal line indicating a different size. Numerical values were placed, each being checked to ensure that the overall dimension fell within the block module. Some of the values are missing near the schedule

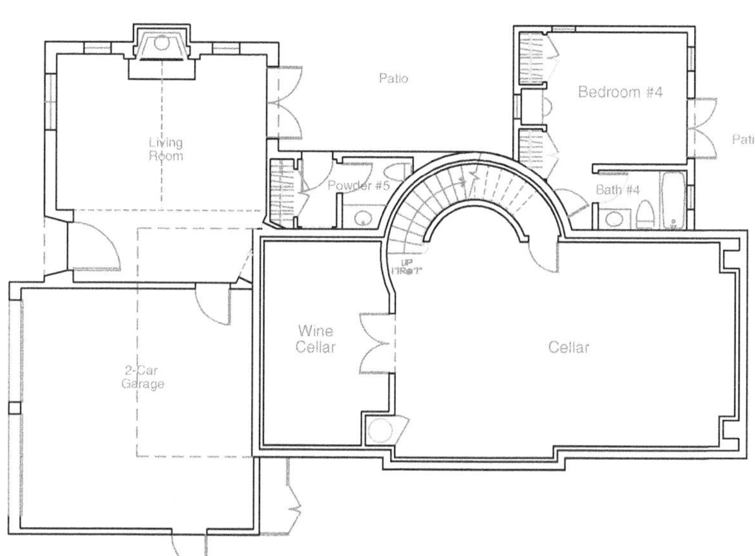

Figure 11.38 Stage I: Establishing base (using floor plan).

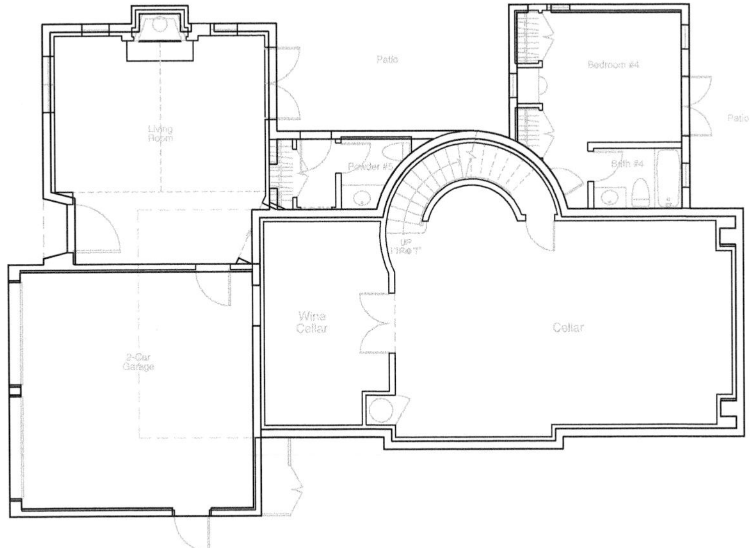

Figure 11.39 Stage II: Outline structure.

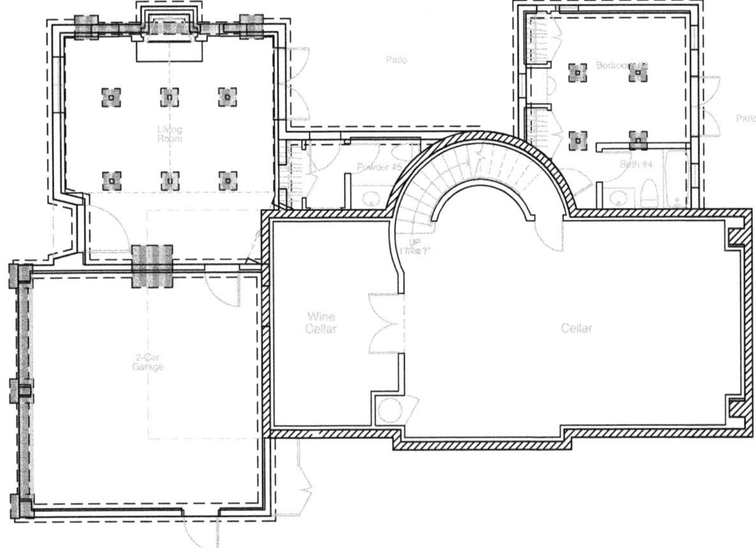

Figure 11.40 Stage III: Positioning bearing walls and posts/pads.

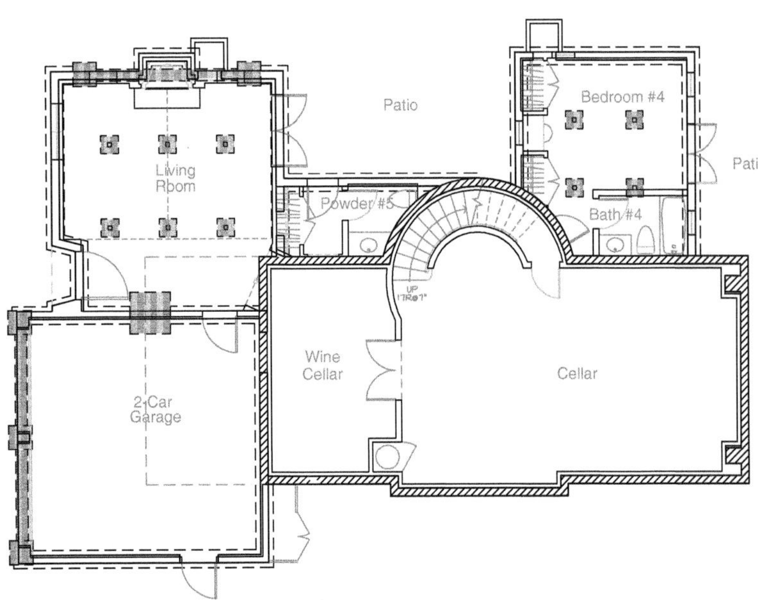

Figure 11.41 Stage IV: Steps, depressed slabs.

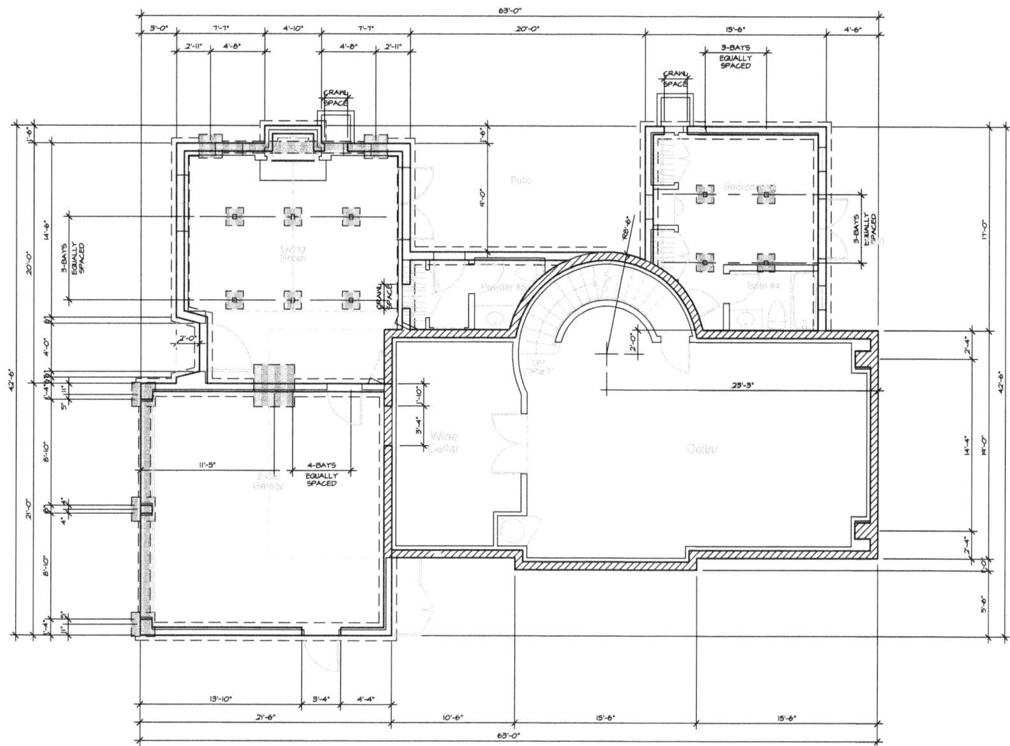

Figure 11.42 Stage V: Dimensioning.

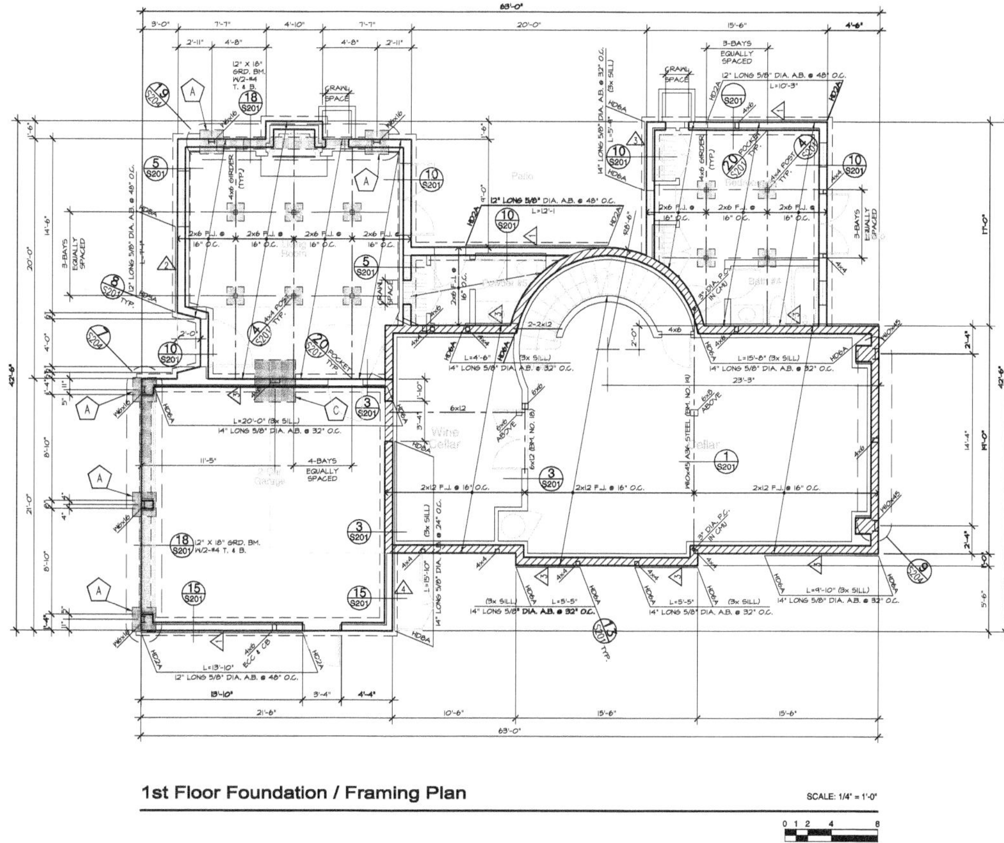

Figure 11.43 Stage VI: Noting, titles, and reference bubbles.

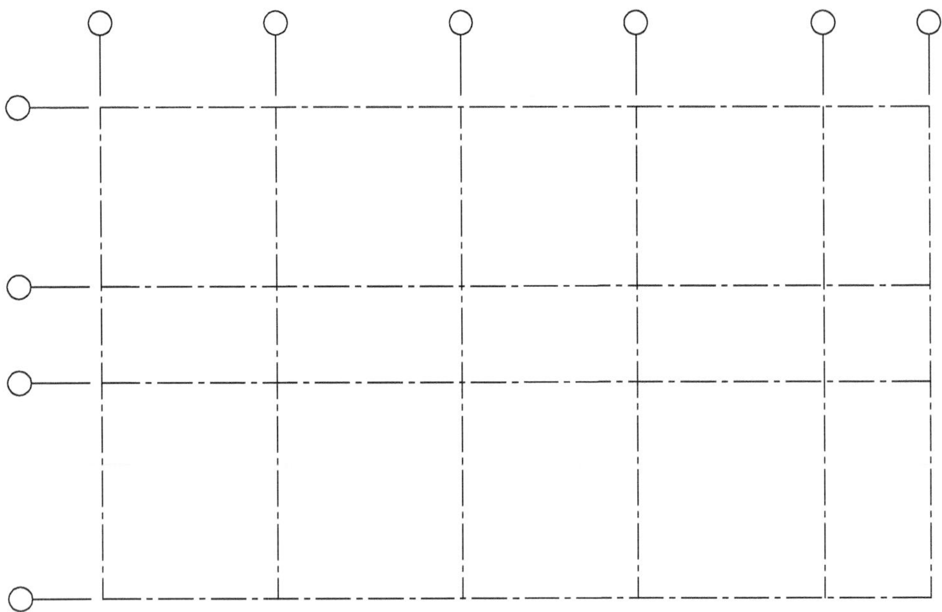

Figure 11.44 Stage I: Establishing datum.

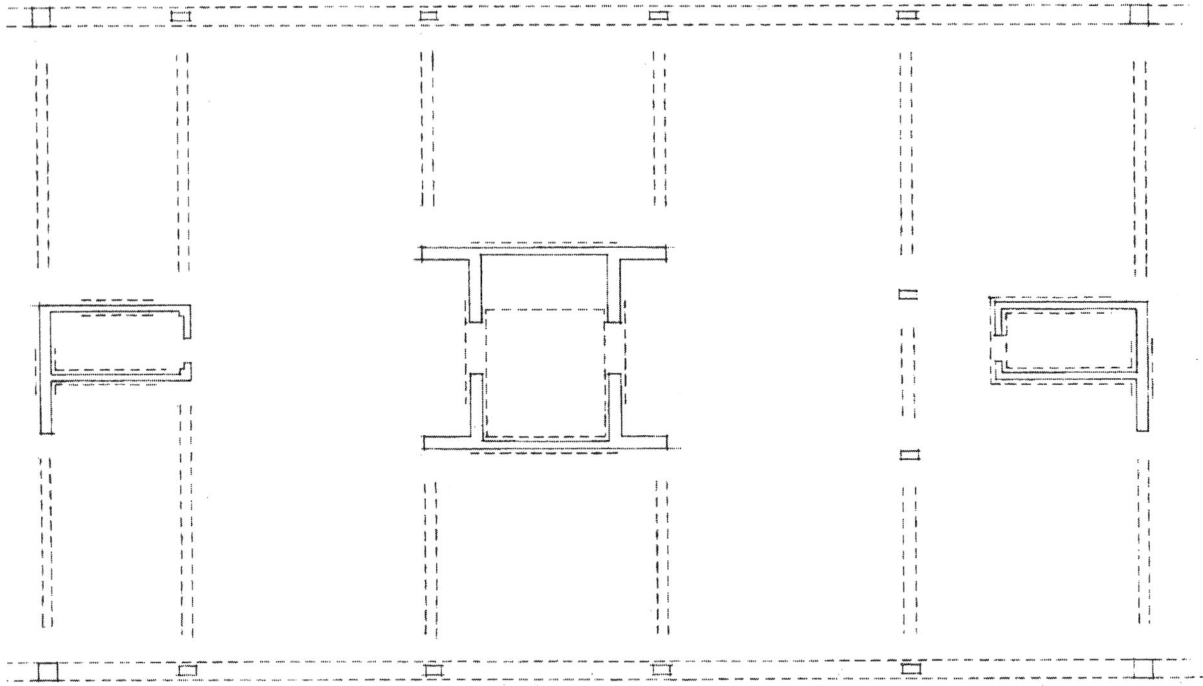

Figure 11.45 Foundation plan: Stage II.

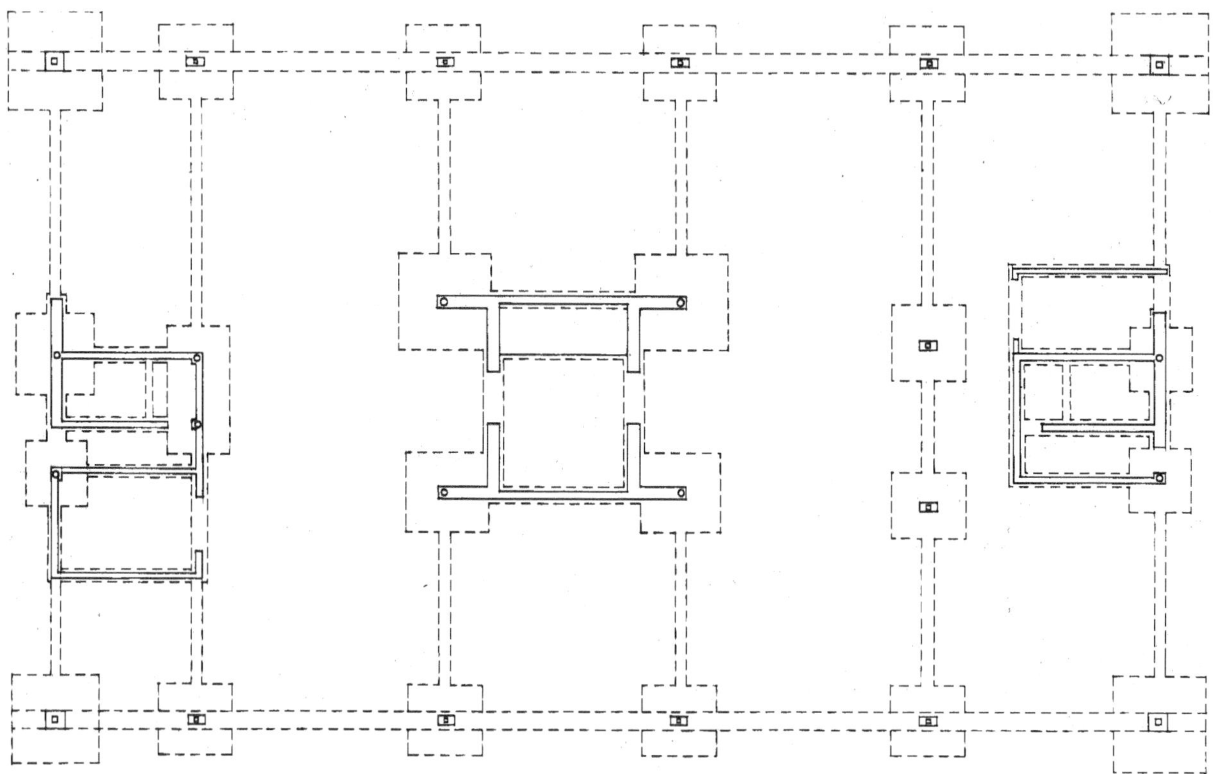

Figure 11.46 Foundation plan: Stage III.

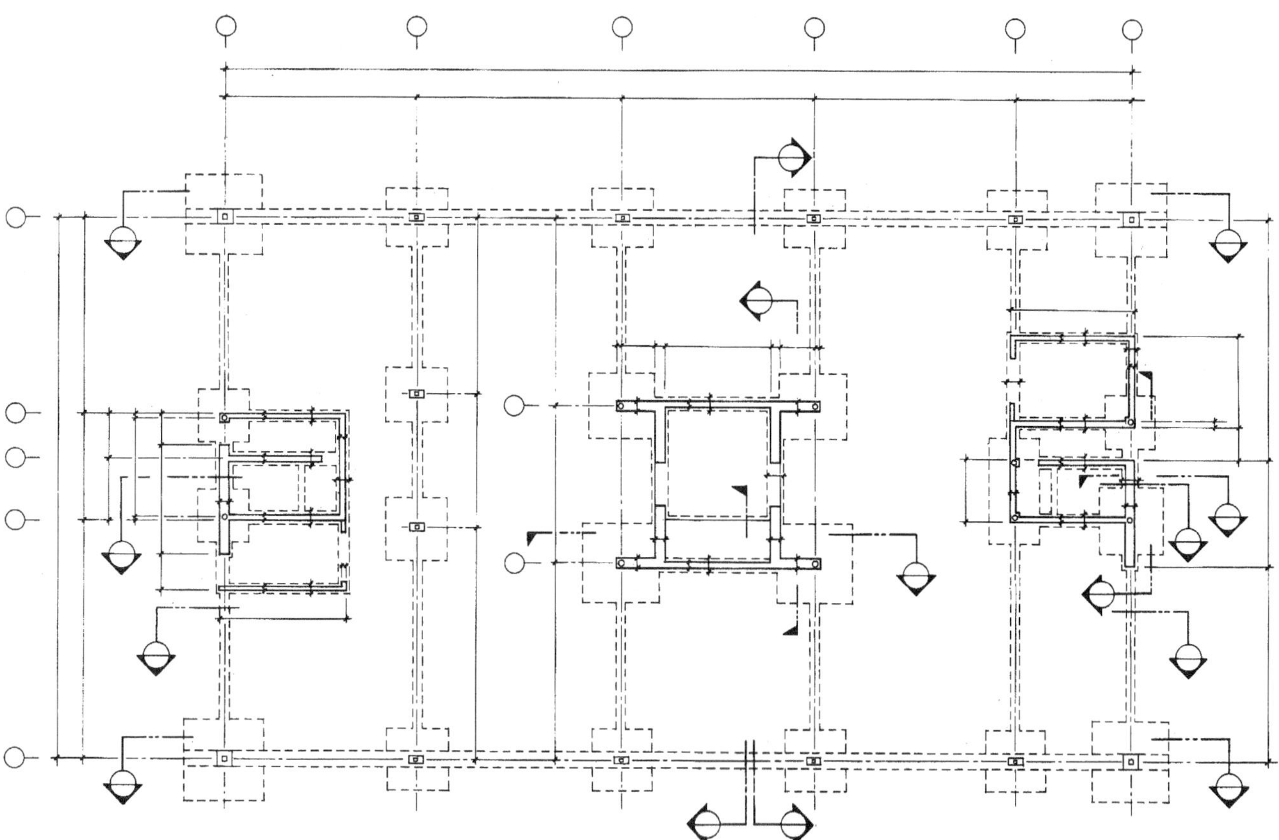

Figure 11.47 Foundation plan: Stage IV.

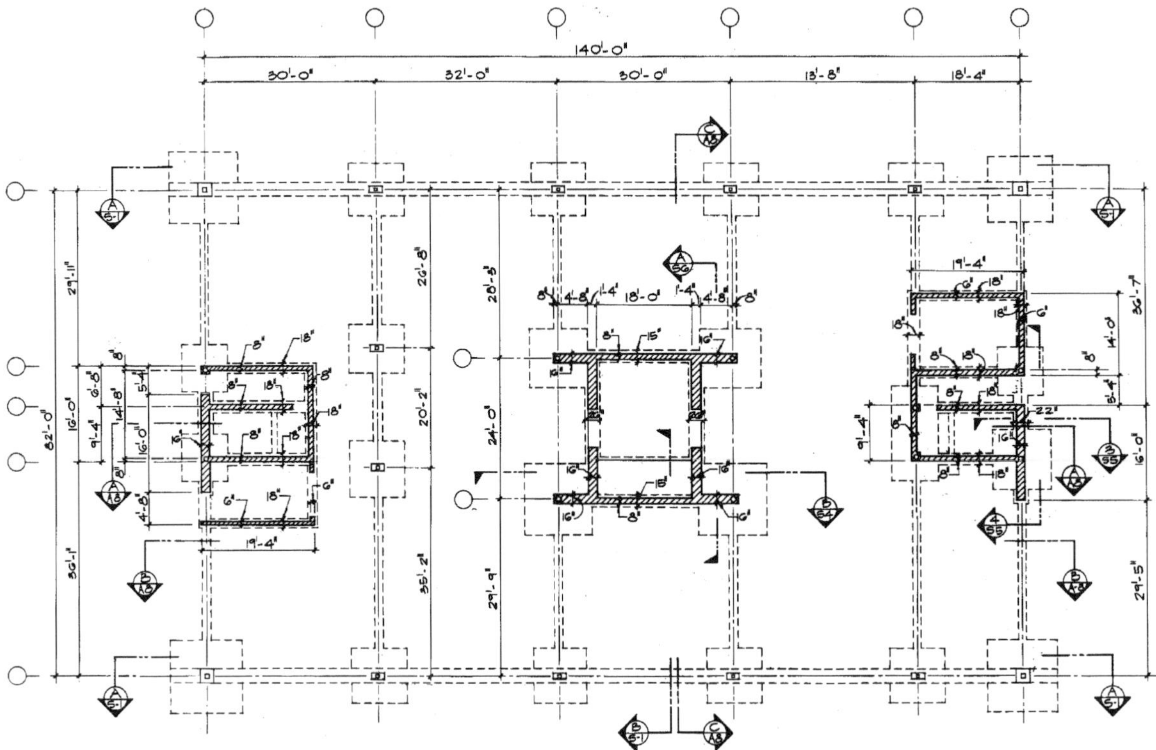

Figure 11.48 Foundation plan: Stage V.

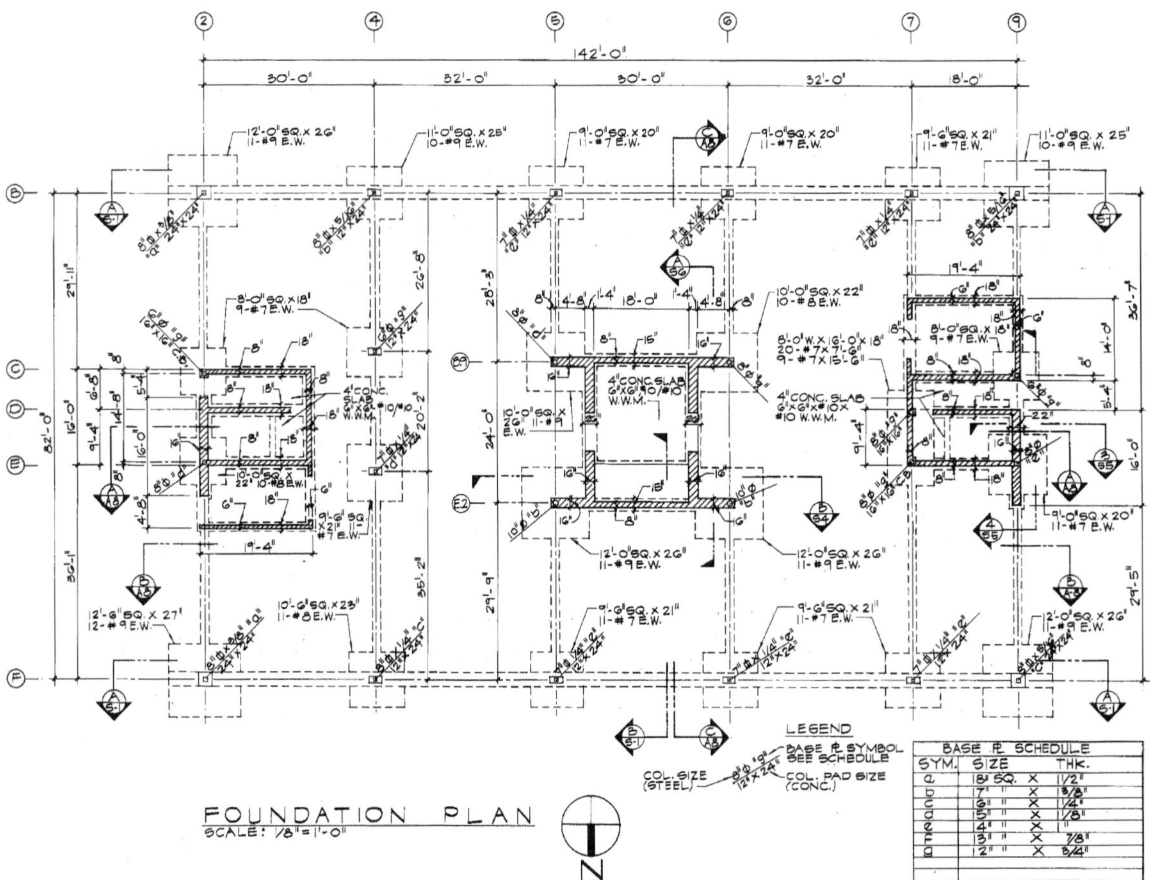

Figure 11.49 Foundation plan: Stage VI.

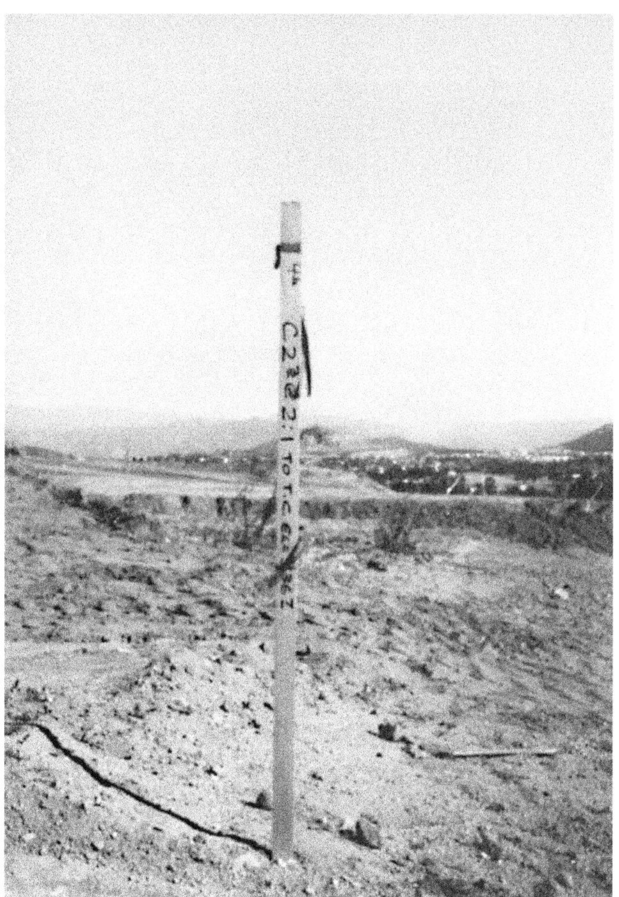

Figure 11.50 Stakes placed by surveyor.

at the bottom. These dimensions are picked up later. All of the detail and section reference bubbles were noted, and the axial reference planes (the numbers across the top and the letters along the right side) were finished.

Drawing a Roof Framing Plan on the Computer

The roof framing plan may be drafted by a structural engineer; an alternate, and usually less expensive, strategy may be to provide the structural engineer with a set of digital drawings on which the engineer may calculate the sizes for all of the necessary structural components (rafters, headers, sheet walls, etc.). These can then be translated in the architectural office as a CAD drawing.

Stage I (Figure 11.61). An early stage of the second-floor plan becomes the datum for the evolution of this drawing.

Stage II (Figure 11.62). The walls that are bearing the weight of the roof are identified.

Stage III (Figure 11.63). With the bearing and non-bearing walls identified, the drafter will not have any trouble in also placing the direction and duration symbols on the drawing. The drafter can also isolate the most important headers and beams listed by the engineer and isolate critical beams that may be missing from the engineer's sketch. Shear walls are also located, drawn, and referenced to a schedule.

Stage IV (Figure 11.64). All noting and referencing occurs in this stage.

■ FRAMING SYSTEMS

There are two main ways to represent floor, ceiling, and roof framing members as part of construction documents: drawing framing members on the floor plan or drawing them separately. As you look at the various framing plans, you may see many conventions that require clarification. For this reason, we have included a chart of typical conventions in Figure 11.65. You may find it helpful to flag this chart as you look at the various framing plans and use it as you would a dictionary, that is, as a reference table that defines the conventions used.

A. A beam, header, or lintel over an opening, door, or window within a wall. Takes a call-out, such as "BM #2 4 × 10 HDR, DF #1."

B. Used to show the direction of a framing member or a system of framing members, such as floor joists, rafters, or ceiling joists. Lettering occurs right along the line, indicating size, name, and spacing; for example, "2 × 6 ceiling joist at 16″ o.c." Note that a half arrowhead is on one side and another half on the opposite side.

C. The line with the half arrowheads is the same as described in definition B. The diagonal line with a full arrowhead on both ends indicates the duration of the system, for example, where a particular system of ceiling joists begins and ends. When sizes of the ceiling joists vary in length or size, this symbol is used to convey to the contractor what size framing member to use and where.

D. A beam, girder, or joist over a post.

E. A beam, girder, or joist under and supporting a post.

F. The employment of a framing anchor or joist hanger at the intersection of two members.

G. A structural post within a wall.

H. Two framing systems on the drawing. For example, one might represent ceiling joists, and the other roof rafters.

I. "W12 × 44" is a call-out for a steel beam or girder. When these members are sequentially repeated, the

Figure 11.51 Rough grade site without structure.

Figure 11.52 Fine grading the property.

Figure 11.53 Chalk lines for foundation.

centerlines are still drawn to represent them, but the description (call-out) is abbreviated with the letters DO, which is short for "ditto."

J. In using conventional wood framing, which is subject to lateral forces such as wind and seismic, a plywood membrane is often placed on all or a portion of the complete wall surface. An adjacent triangle symbol refers readers to a nailing schedule to ensure minimums for nails to secure the plywood to the studs. These are called shear walls or shear panels.

K. An alternative way to demonstrate shear walls.

L. The rectilinear box that contains the 8′–2″ dimension is a convention used to indicate height of an object in plan view. The two dashed lines may represent the top of a beam or the plate line at a wall.

M. The use of three lines, instead of two, represents a double joist at the partition.

N. A post on top of a beam; similar to E, but with a post size notation.

O. An opening in a floor, ceiling, or roof system. The two lines surrounding the opening represent the doubling of the joists, and the dark L-shape indicates the use of framing anchors or hangers. The large X is the area of the opening. This convention is used for skylights and openings in the ceiling or roof for chimneys, a hatch, or attic access.

Figure 11.54 Chalked lines ready for trenching.

Figure 11.55 Trenched footing.

Basis of the Structural Systems

The structural design of beams and footings is calculated by finding the total loads that are distributed to any specific member. This total load is found by computing the tributary area affecting that member. Figure 11.66 illustrates a cross-section showing the various tributary areas that contribute loads to the ridge beam, floor beam, and foundation footing.

■ WOOD FLOOR SYSTEMS

Sawn Lumber Floor Joist System

The most conventional wood floor systems use sawn lumber floor joists as the supporting structural members. For a single-story residence, these members may be 2 × 6 or 2 × 8 joists. Although lumber members are named 2 × 6 or 2 × 8, they typically measure 1½″ × 3½″ and 1½″ × 5½″, respectively. This is due to the milling process of the lumber manufacturer. Notice the inch mark when calling out the actual size of the member. This actual size is often called the **net size** and is a common result for sawn lumber. The dimensions of lumber selected will depend on the live and dead load and the span of the joists. Plywood of varying thickness is used as a subfloor for supporting the finish floor material. The spacing of the floor joists is usually 16″ on center. The structural members are supported by the exterior perimeter concrete foundation walls, and the intermediate supports in the interior include the concrete foundation walls and/or wood girders and concrete piers. See Figure 11.67.

The advantages of utilizing a sawn lumber floor joist system are:

1. Greater span length relative to the size of the joist
2. Requires fewer internal supporting walls and girders
3. Capable of providing floor joist cantilevers
4. Permits insulation material to be placed between the joist members
5. Allows rewiring, making plumbing modifications, or renovating under floor areas
6. Accommodates sloping lots
7. Levels irregular floor elevations or sloping floors

Sawn lumber floor joist systems are not appropriate:

1. In regions highly susceptible to termite infestation and dry rot
2. For buildings that require a minimum amount of noise transmission
3. In buildings desiring a lower silhouette
4. Where a crawl space must be ventilated relative to grade
5. If rats, other wild animals, or other pests may access the crawl space
6. When sustainability is a concern

Construction Principles

1. Ensure that the wood members are not in direct contact with the concrete.
2. Provide recommended under-floor clearances from the soil.
3. Select floor joist sizes that will minimize deflection or floor movement.
4. Provide proper flashing to protect wood members from possible moisture.
5. Provide recommended under-floor ventilation.
6. Ensure that the floor is rat-proofed.

Wood Plank Floor System

Another wood floor system frequently used is called tongue-and-groove **planking**. This system uses 2 × 6 or 2 × 8 wide wood members. These members, with high stress capabilities, are used to span over wood girders

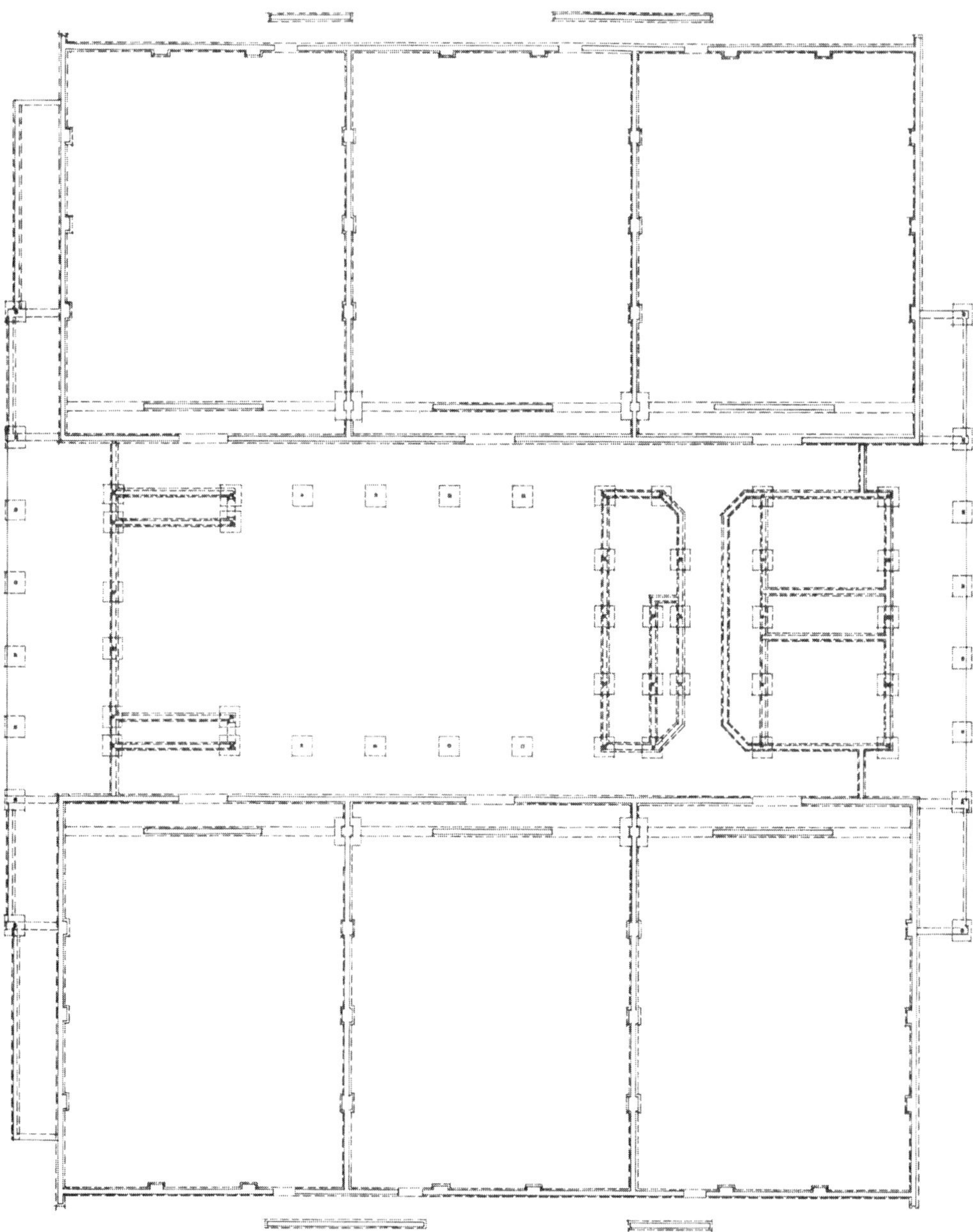

Figure 11.56 Theater—Stage I: Working drawing—foundation plan.

and concrete foundation walls. This system requires additional rows of girders and piers because the span for the 2″ planking is generally limited to spans from 4′ to 5′.

Figure 11.67 illustrates a wood floor system for a one-story residence utilizing girders as the support for 2″ tongue-and-groove planking. It is recommended that plywood be applied directly over the 2″ planking members for the purpose of providing a sub-base for the finish floor materials, as well as developing a tie between the various members. Whenever possible, it is recommended that concrete foundation walls and/or girders be positioned directly under paralleling walls. When bearing walls are parallel with the planking members, it will be necessary to provide a 4× wood girder in the floor system for support. The depth of the girder is governed by the load factor from the wall above and other load-carrying members. Note that the bearing cross-wall member in Figure 11.67 will be installed for support of the load-bearing wall. An isometric drawing depicting the exterior foundation wall for the tongue-and-groove floor system is shown in Figure 11.68.

Figure 11.57 Clay Theater—columns support.

The advantages of using a tongue-and-groove floor system are as follows:

1. It provides a stiffer floor with the recommended spacing of girders.
2. It provides a lower building height silhouette, because the added height of the floor joists is eliminated.
3. It has a lower noise factor than a plywood floor system.
4. It provides a more rigid subfloor for finish floor materials such as ceramic or concrete tiles.
5. Tongue-and-groove planking is available in greater thickness, which can be used when longer spans are required.

The disadvantages of using a tongue-and-groove floor system are:

1. Shorter spans will require additional foundation walls, girders, and piers.
2. The system is not conducive to the use of floor cantilevers.
3. The system is susceptible to termite infestation and dry rot (in regions where these problems are endemic).
4. The system does not allow the development of floor beams. Conventional floor joist systems may combine a number of floor joists for the purpose of creating a structural beam.
5. The system does not provide space for blanket insulation.
6. Sustainability is a concern.

Engineered Lumber Wood Floor System

The use of engineered lumber floor joists has proven to be very successful in wood floor systems. Engineered lumber or wood is manufactured by adhering wood strands, veneers, fibers, or particles together to manufacture a new product that can be made to meet certain criteria of strength or shape. Engineered floor joists have been approved by all major building codes.

To see the structural capabilities of this floor joist system, compare the span lengths in the foundation plan illustrated in Figure 11.67 (sawn lumber floor joists) with those of the engineered lumber floor joists shown in Figure 11.69. Two rows of girders and piers have been eliminated from the foundation plan in Figure 11.70 because of the greater strength and load-bearing capacity of the engineered lumber. Other engineered lumber wood members that may be used in a wood floor system are girders and floor beams. These members are developed and fabricated with the use of laminated veneer lumber. The laminated members provide a high allowable bearing stress that is accepted by all major building codes, and are consistent in size and performance. They also reduce the problems of splitting, warping, and checking. The size of these members may range from 1½″ to 7″ in thickness and standard depths may range from 7¼″ to 24″.

An example of the aforementioned engineered lumber joist, illustrating its shape and fabrication components, is shown as an isometric drawing in Figure 11.71. Sizes

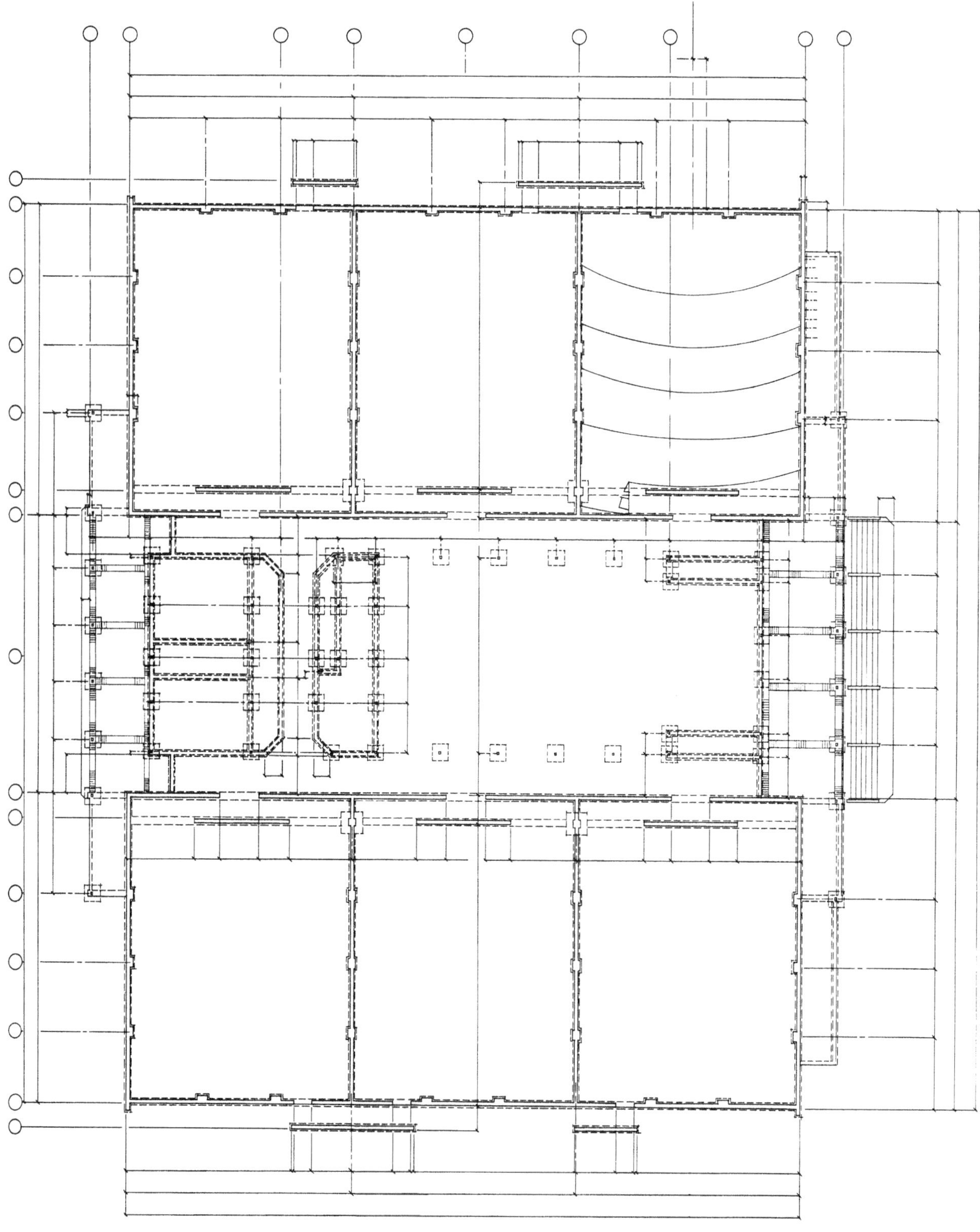

Figure 11.58 Clay Theater—Stage II: Working drawing—foundation plan.

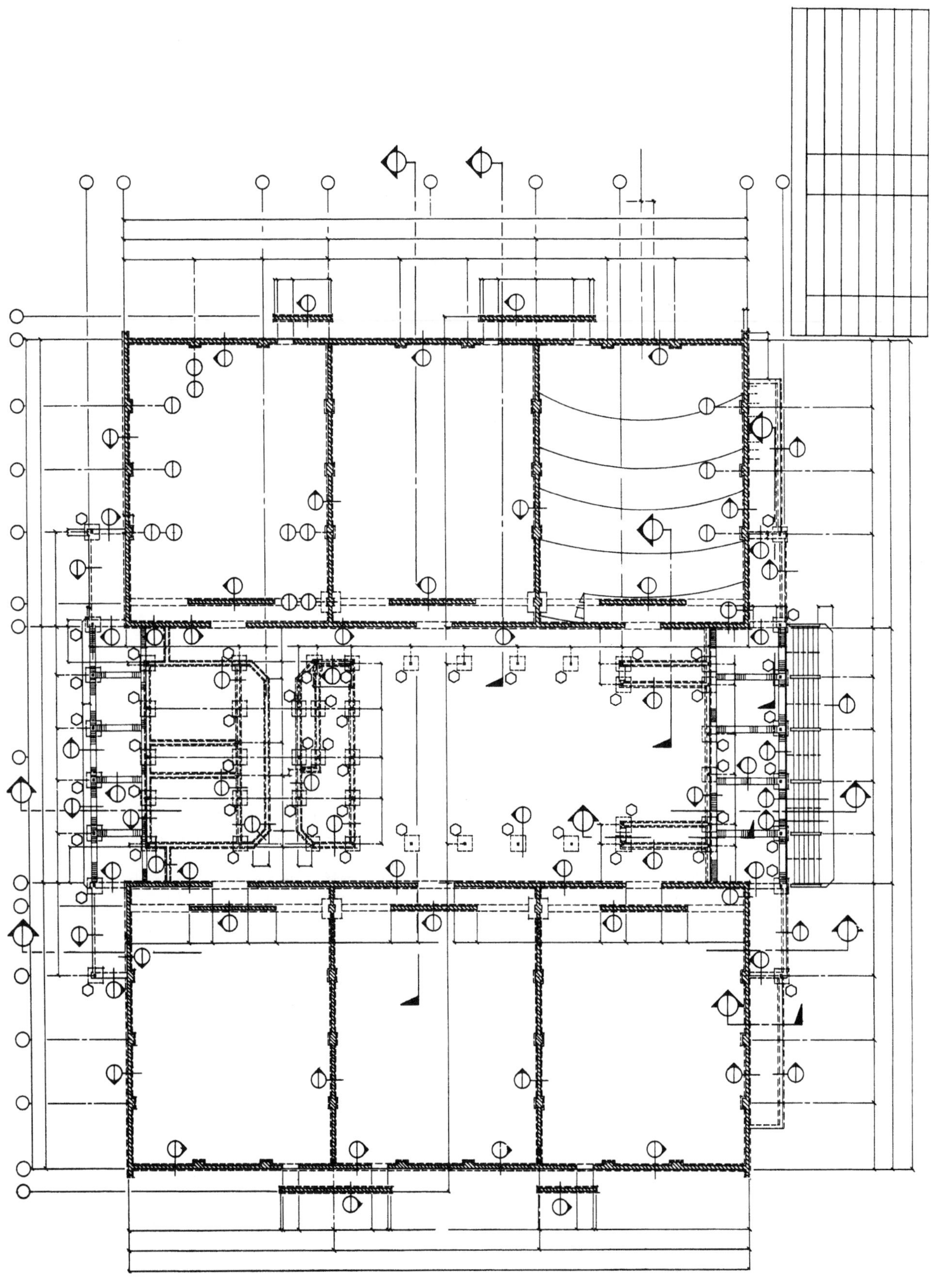

Figure 11.59 Clay Theater—Stage III: Working drawing—foundation plan.

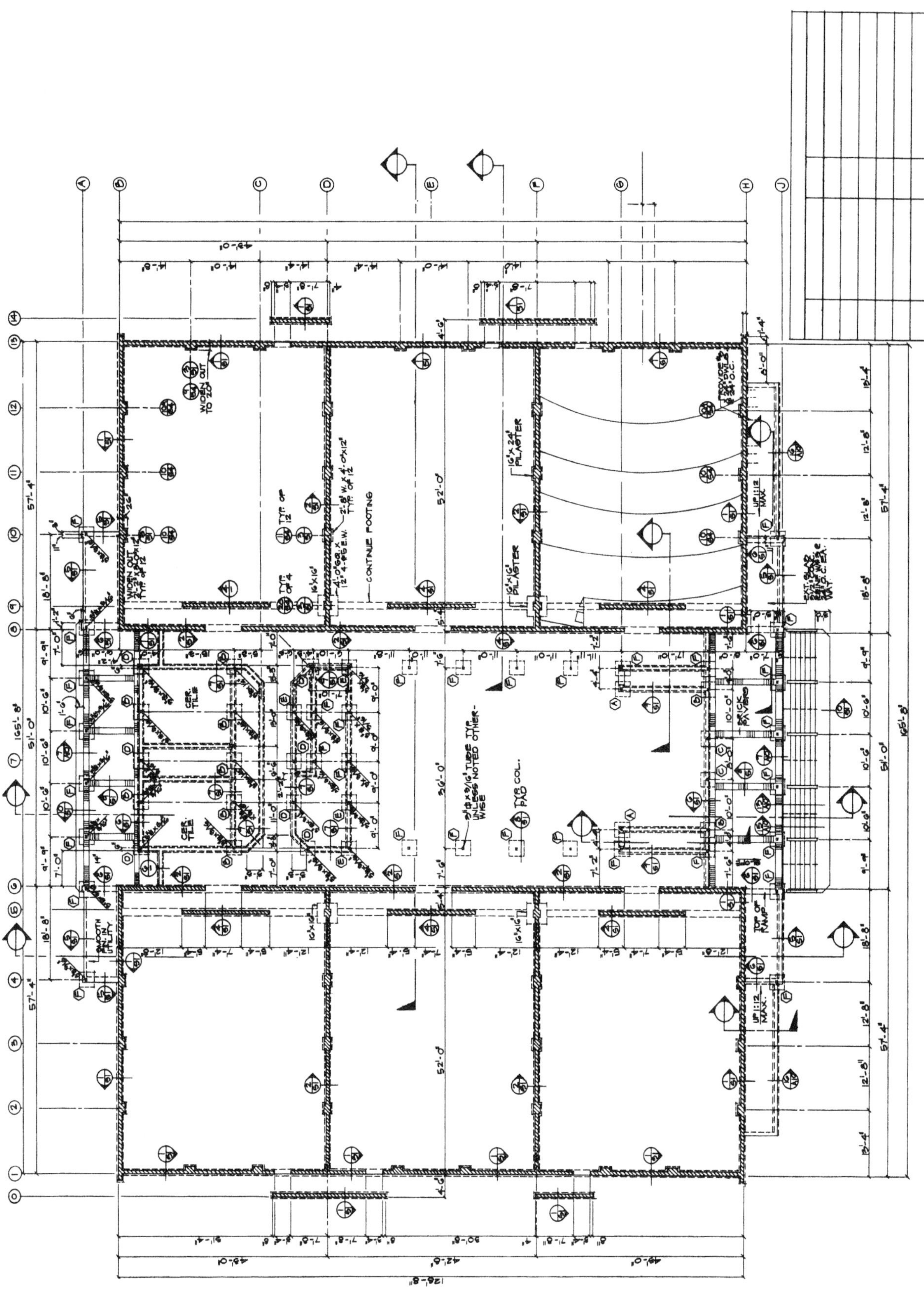

Figure 11.60 Clay Theater—Stage IV: Working drawing—foundation plan.

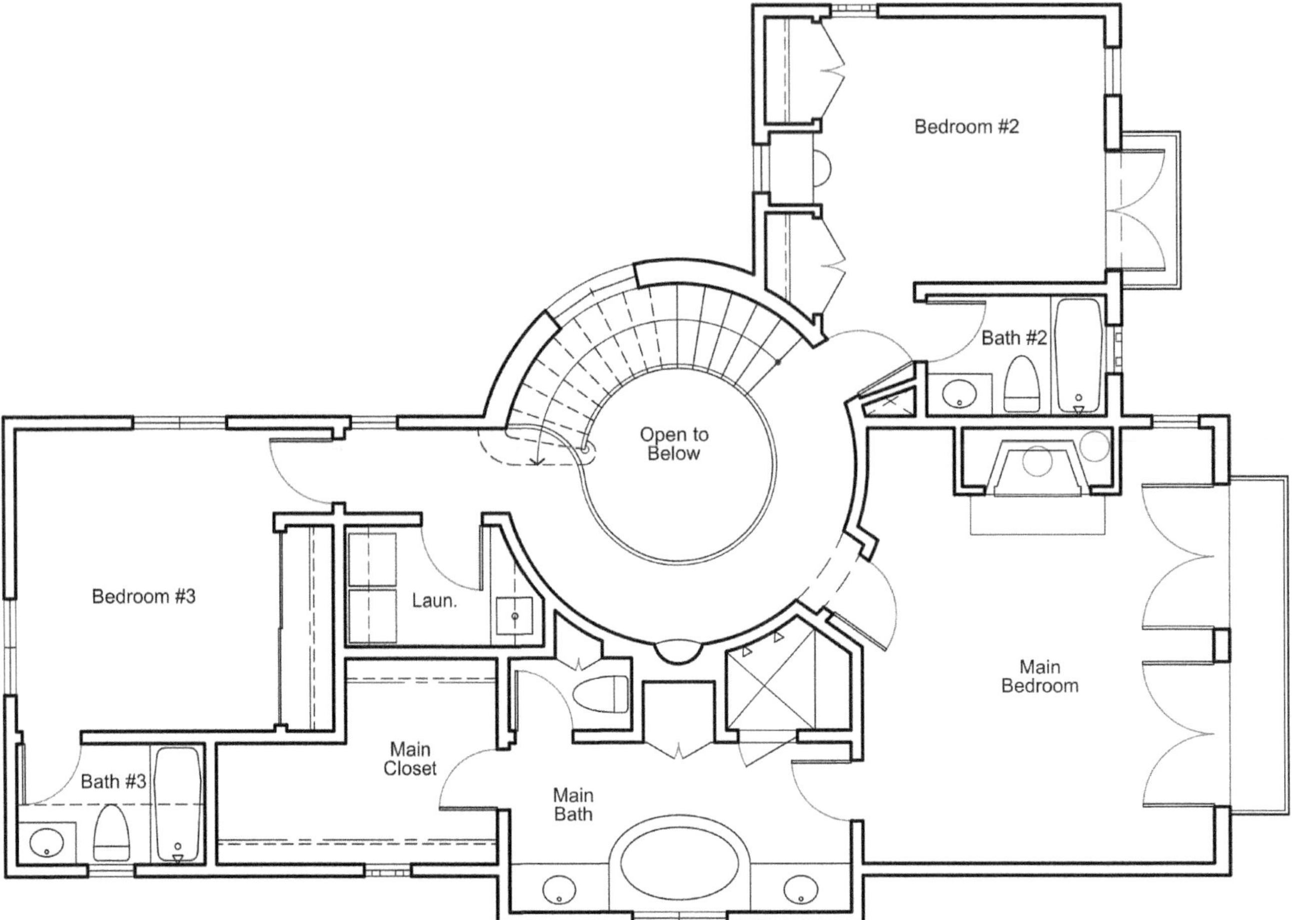

Figure 11.61 Stage I: Floor plan as datum.

and structural capabilities will vary among manufacturers of engineered lumber.

Figure 11.72 is a 3-D drawing segment of the foundation plan in Figure 11.73, showing the concrete footing, engineered lumber floor joist, engineered plywood subfloor, and wood stud walls.

The advantages of an engineered lumber wood floor joist system are:

1. Floor joist sizes are uniform.
2. Light weight allows for easier handling on the job.
3. Splitting, checking, warping, and crowning are eliminated.
4. System has greater structural capabilities.
5. It has better construction quality of material (no knots).

The disadvantages of an engineered lumber wood floor joist system are:

1. There are limitations on cutting the members in the framing process.
2. There are restrictions on the location in the web sections where holes may be cut.
3. Proper care must be taken to protect these joists prior to installation.
4. The system creates a higher building silhouette because of the increased depth of the joist.
5. One cannot taper the floor joists.

■ WOOD WALL SYSTEMS

Framing Systems

The two most conventional types of wood stud wall framing systems used in construction are the balloon framing system and the Western or platform framing system. The main differences between these two systems are at the intersection of the second-floor framing assembly and the wall.

Balloon Framing

In the construction of two-story structures, the balloon framing system uses continuous wall studs from the first-floor level up to the roof assembly. The second-floor

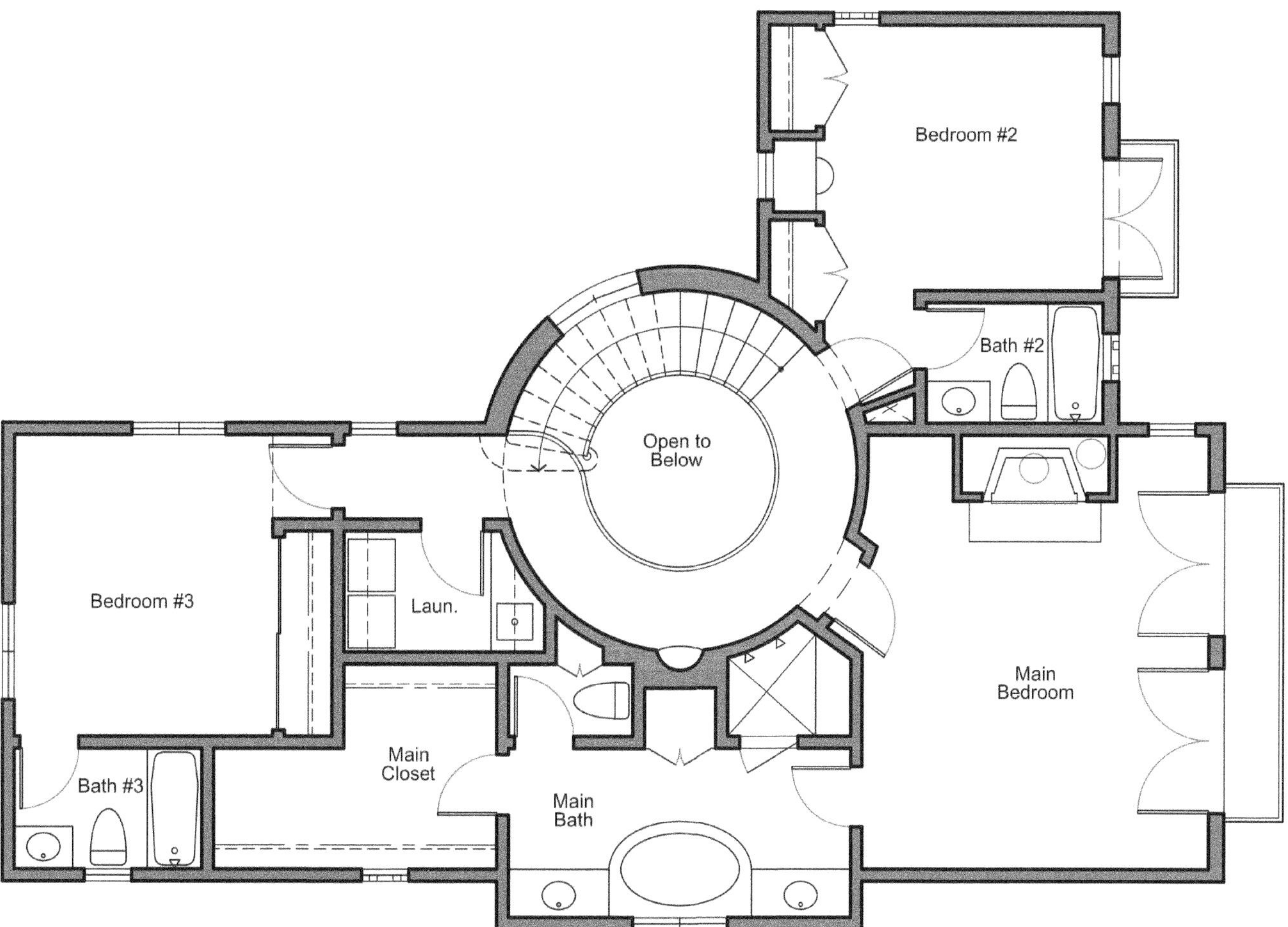

Figure 11.62 Stage II: Identifying bearing and non-bearing walls.

supporting members are then framed to the continuous studs. Stud sizes are 2 × 4 or 2 × 6 at 16″ center to center. 2× blocking is fitted to fill all openings to provide fire stops and prevent drafts from one space to another.

Wood or metal members are attached securely at a 45° angle to the top and bottom of the studs and provide horizontal bracing for the walls. In areas subjected to strong lateral forces, sheathing is used for horizontal bracing. Balloon framing is not utilized in all parts of the country; refer to the local codes for allowable use. See Figure 11.72. The use of plywood or **oriented strand board (OSB)** panels may be determined by the governing building code or the structural engineering requirements. This system has a minimum amount of vertical shrinkage and vertical movement and may be used with brick veneer or cement plaster exterior finishes.

Western or Platform Framing

Western or platform framing uses a different procedure. The lower floor walls are assembled first, and then the supporting floor members and subfloor for the upper floor are framed. The upper subfloor and floor joists provide a platform for assembling the upper-floor walls, ceiling joists, and roof framing. The walls are framed with 2 × 4 or 2 × 6 studs at 16″ center to center. Required blocking is 2″ thick and is fitted to provide stiffness to the joist.

Solid sheathing, diagonal braces, plywood, or OSB panels may provide lateral bracing. Building code requirements, regional differences, and structural engineering calculations may determine the type of lateral bracing. See Figure 11.73.

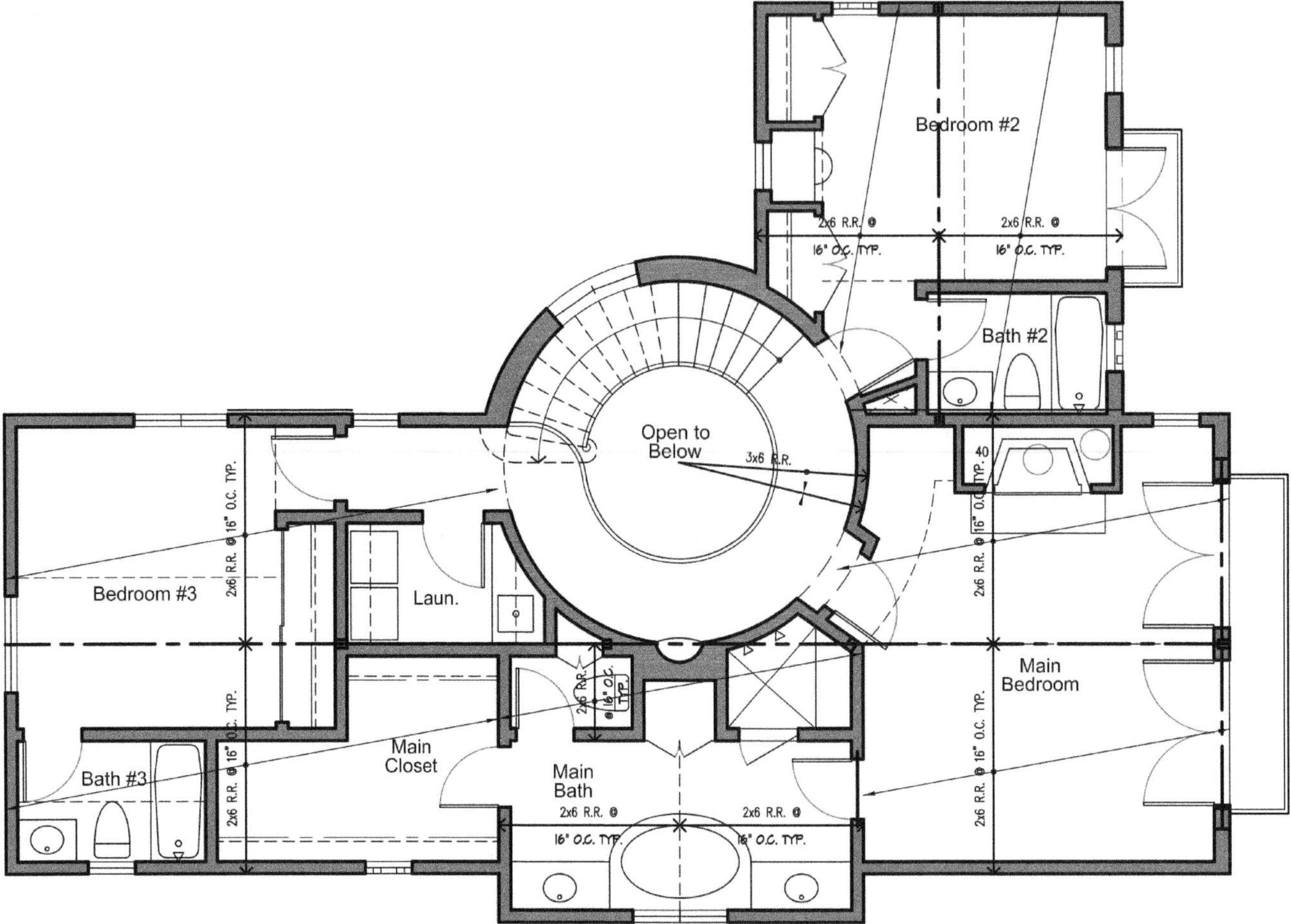

Figure 11.63 Stage III: Direction, duration, shear, and beams.

Post-and-Beam Framing

A third method for framing wood structures is the post-and-beam system. Less common than platform and balloon framing, this method uses a post-and-beam spacing that allows the builder to use 2× roof or floor planking. See Figure 11.74. For the best use of this system, a specific module of plank-and-beam spacing must be established. Supplementary bracing is placed on the exterior walls, with options similar to those used in conventional framing systems. You must provide a positive connection between the post and the beam and secure the post to the floor. Different types of metal framing connectors may be used to satisfy these connection requirements. If metal framing connectors are undesirable for aesthetic reasons, then steel dowels may be utilized at the post-to-beam connection and the post-to-floor connection. See Figures 11.75 and 11.76. Because fewer pieces are used in this system, special attention to post-to-beam connections and connections to other members should be given in detailing these conditions. With proper detailing, such connections will securely fasten components of the building together and act as a unit to resist any external forces.

Engineered Lumber Wall Systems

Engineered lumber sheathing panels are used in wood stud wall construction to strengthen and stabilize exterior and interior walls. Engineered sheathing panels used for exterior walls should be protected with building paper, wood siding, or other types of exterior cladding to protect the panels from damage caused by water or other moisture conditions. These panels are fabricated in sizes ranging from 4′ × 8′ to 4′ × 9′ and 4′ × 10′. Panel thickness can range from 3/8″ to 1 1/8″, and panels are manufactured using plywood or OSB. See Figure 11.80.

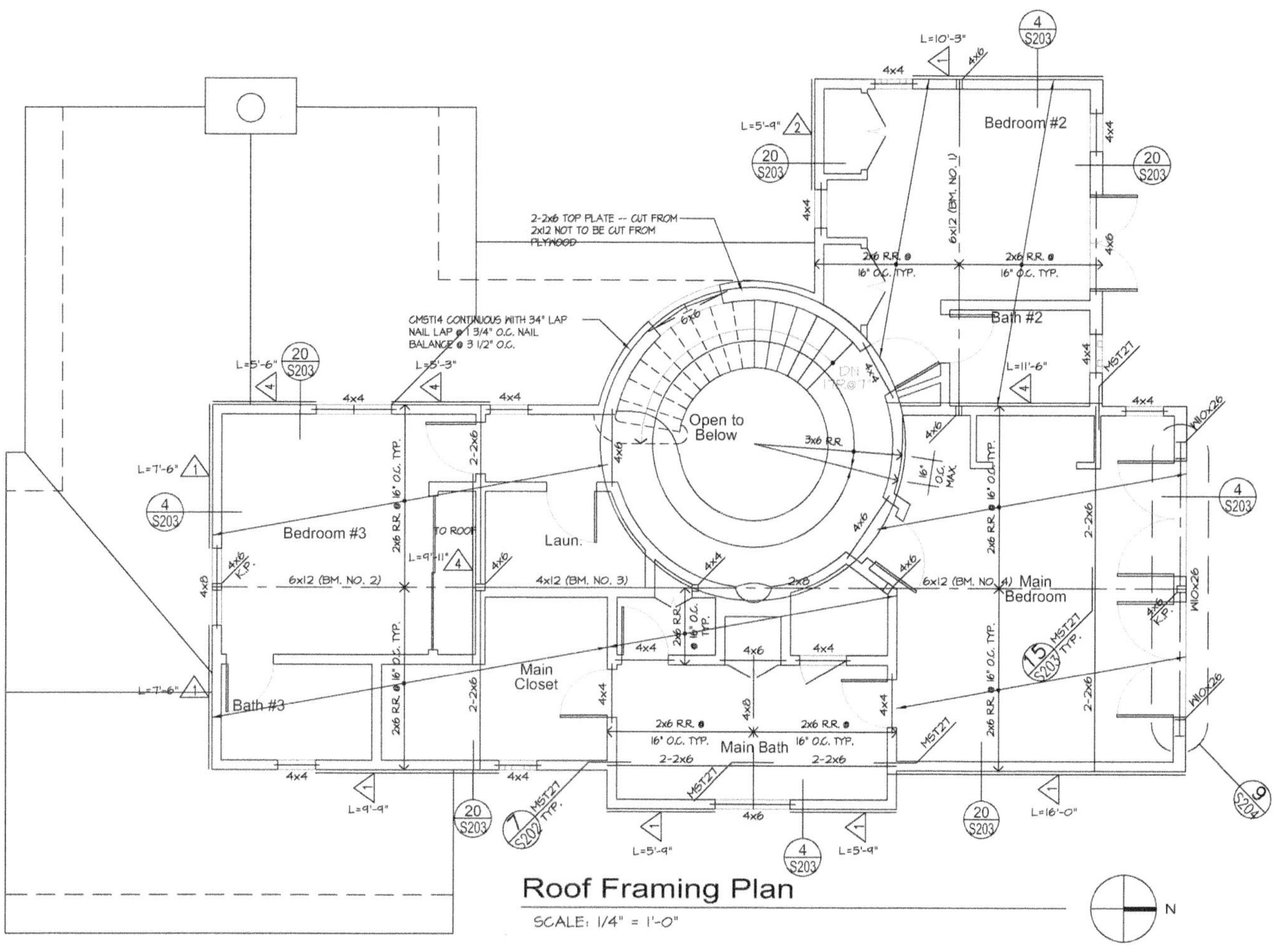

SYMBOL	PANEL	NAILING [8]	WALL	SOLE PLATE ATTACHMENT			TOP PLATE ATTACHMENT [4]	HOLDOWN [5,6]
		COMMON NAILS	LBS/FT	NAILS	LAGS [9]	ANCHOR BOLTS [6]		
1	3/8 EXPOSURE 1 [7] (ID#24/0)	8d @ 6,6,12	198	16d @ 6" O.C.	3/8" x 5" @ 24" O.C.	5/8" DIA. @ 48" O.C. 12" LONG	A35 @ 24" O.C.	HD2A, CB44, FTA2 PHD2
2 [1]	15/32 EXPOSURE 1 [7] (ID#32/16)	10d @ 4,4,12	299	16d @ 3.5" O.C.	3/8" x 5" @ 18" O.C.	5/8" DIA. @ 48" O.C. 12" LONG	A35 @ 16" O.C.	HD5A, CB44, FTA2 PHD5
3 [1,2,3] 3x SILL	15/32 EXPOSURE 1 [7] (ID#32/16)	10d @ 3,3,12	450	40d @ 3" O.C.	3/8" x 5" @ 12" O.C.	5/8" DIA. @ 32" O.C. 14" LONG	A35 @ 12" O.C.	HD6A, CB44, FTA5 PHD6
4 [1,2,3] 3x SILL	15/32 EXPOSURE 1 [7] STRUCT. 1 (ID#32/16)	10d @ 2,2,12	652	50d @ 3" O.C.	3/8" x 5" @ 8" O.C.	5/8" DIA. @ 24" O.C. 14" LONG	A35 @ 8" O.C.	HD8A, FTA7, PHD8

FOOTNOTES:

1. THESE PANELS TO BE 4-PLY MINIMUM.
2. 3x SOLE PLATES AND 3x FRAMING AT ADJOINING PANEL EDGES REQUIRED. STAGGER PANEL EDGE NAILING.
3. 1/2" MINIMUM EDGE DISTANCE REQUIRED FOR BOUNDARY NAILING.
4. A35'S NOT REQUIRED IF PANEL NAILS TO FRAMING MEMBER ABOVE TOP PLATES.
5. HOLDOWNS REQUIRED AT ENDS OF ALL SHEAR PANELS. USE 4x4'S FOR END MEMBERS. ALL HOLDOWN BOLTS TO BE TIGHTENED JUST PRIOR TO COVERING, INSPECTOR TO VERIFY. BOLT HOLES TO BE 1/16" MAXIMUM OVERSIZED AT THE CONNECTION OF THE HOLDOWN TO THE POST, INSPECTOR TO VERIFY.
6. SIMPSON BP WASHERS REQUIRED FOR ALL PLYWOOD SHEAR WALL SILL PLATE BOLTS AND HOLDOWN BOLTS.
7. OSB (ORIENTED STRAND BOARD) IS A WOOD STRUCTURAL PANEL.
8. SOLID BLOCKING SHALL BE PROVIDED AT ALL HORIZONTAL JOINTS OCCURRING IN BRACED WALL PANELS.
9. USE 3x BLOCKS AND 3x RIM JOISTS IF LAGS ARE USED.

Figure 11.64 Stage IV: Noting.

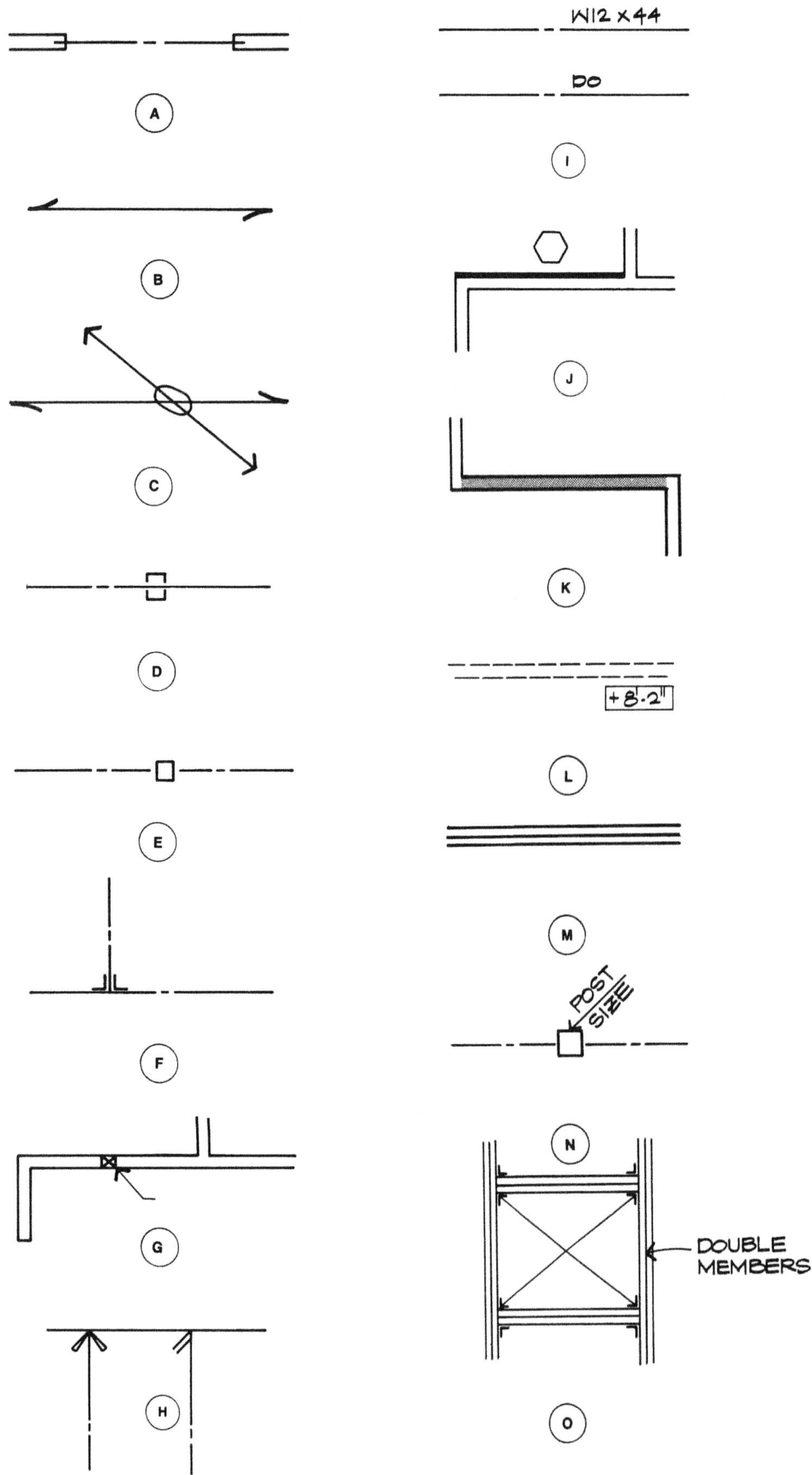

Figure 11.65 Summary of typical framing conventions.

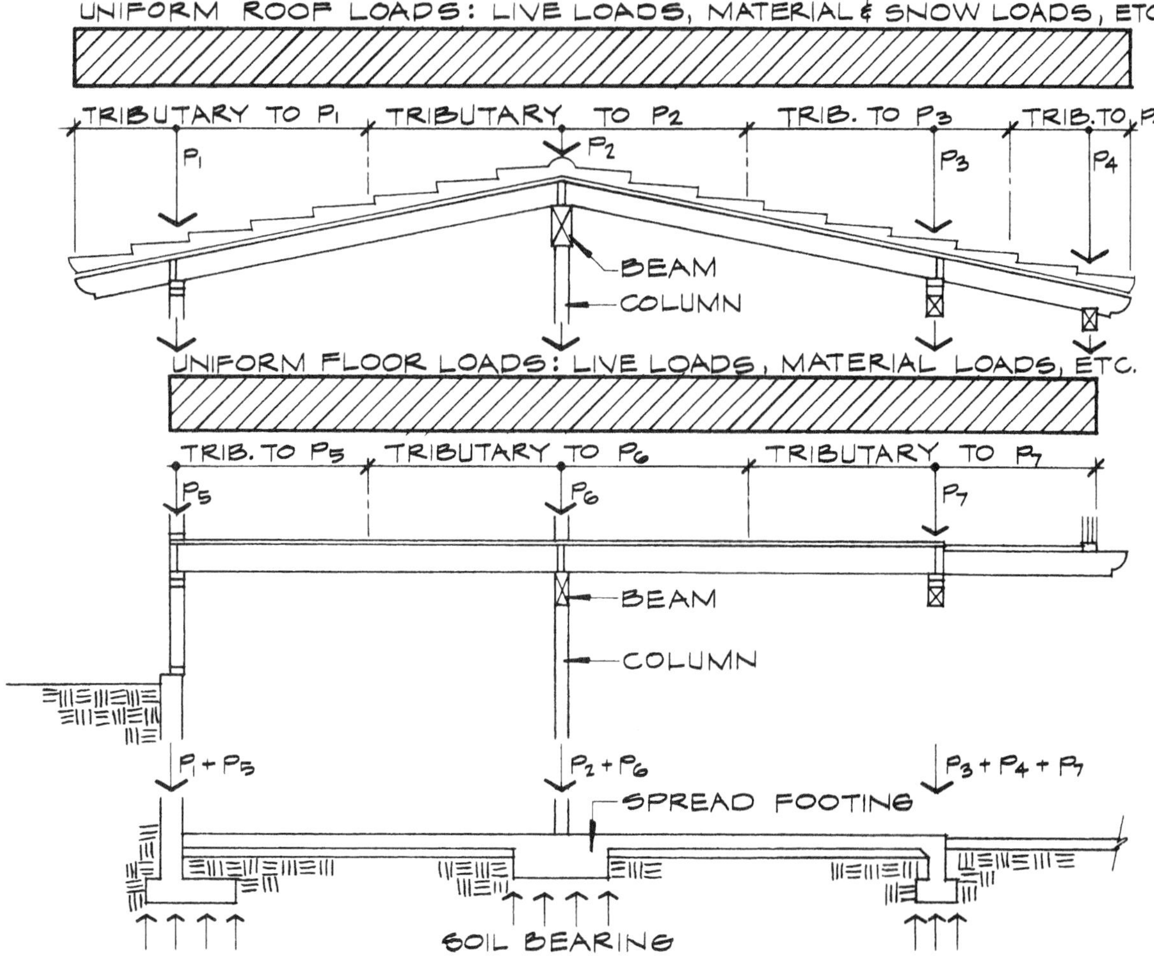

Figure 11.66 Tributary loading section.

WOOD ROOF SYSTEMS

The principles underlying wood roof systems, and the construction methods used in developing these systems, may depend on the finish roof material and the requirements of its application. See two various examples of eave conditions that can be determined by the architect to achieve an aesthetic that enhances the design of the building. See Figures 11.81 and 11.82. The following are examples of finish roof materials used over roof framing systems:

1. Wood shingles or shakes (can be fire treated)
2. Asphalt shingles
3. Clay or concrete tiles
4. Built-up composition, gravel surface, PVC, and torch down
5. Aluminum, copper, stainless steel, or galvanized metal
6. Standing seam or corrugated metal
7. Green roof

Planking

The term planking is used to refer to members that have a minimum depth of 2″ and various widths. The edges of these members are normally tongue and groove. Using such edges enables a continuous joining of members so that a concentrated load is distributed onto the adjacent members. See Figure 11.81.

Plank-and-Beam and Heavy Timber Roof Systems

The plank-and-beam roof system uses heavy wood beam members greater than 2″ in thickness to support roof planking and the finish roofing material. The main supporting wood beam members normally have a modular spacing, such as 4′ to 8′ on center. The spacing of these members is determined by the weight of the finish roofing materials. In general, the architect selects this system for use where he or she wishes to expose the roof structural system for reasons of aesthetics or code requirements.

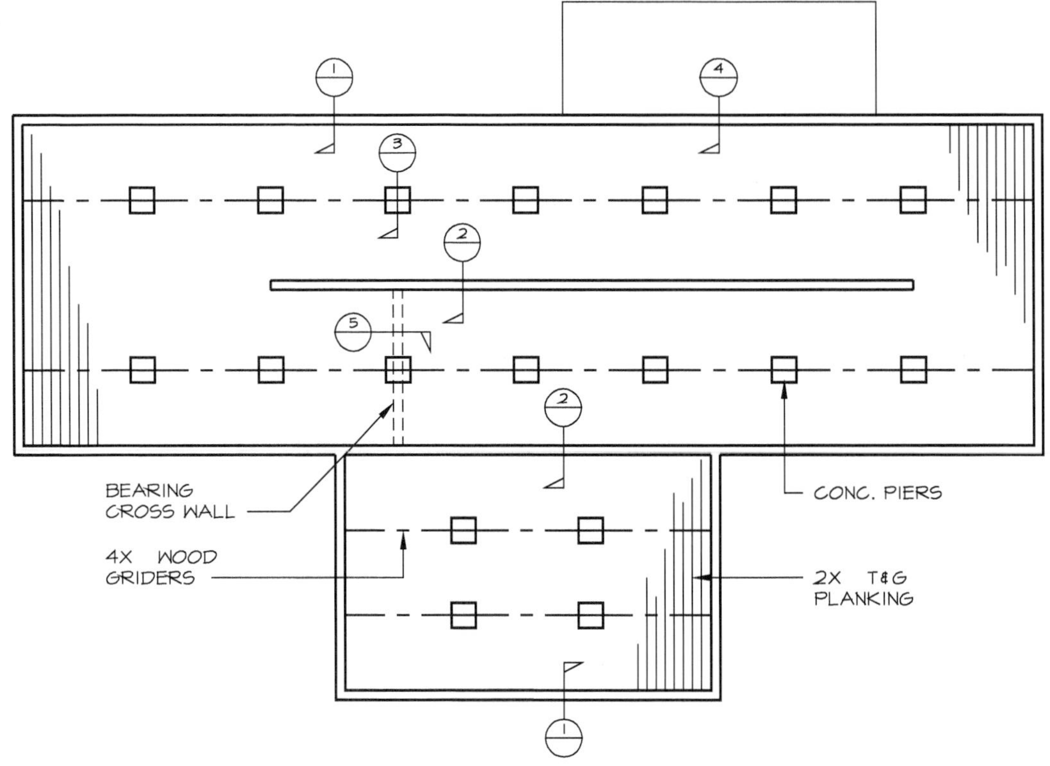

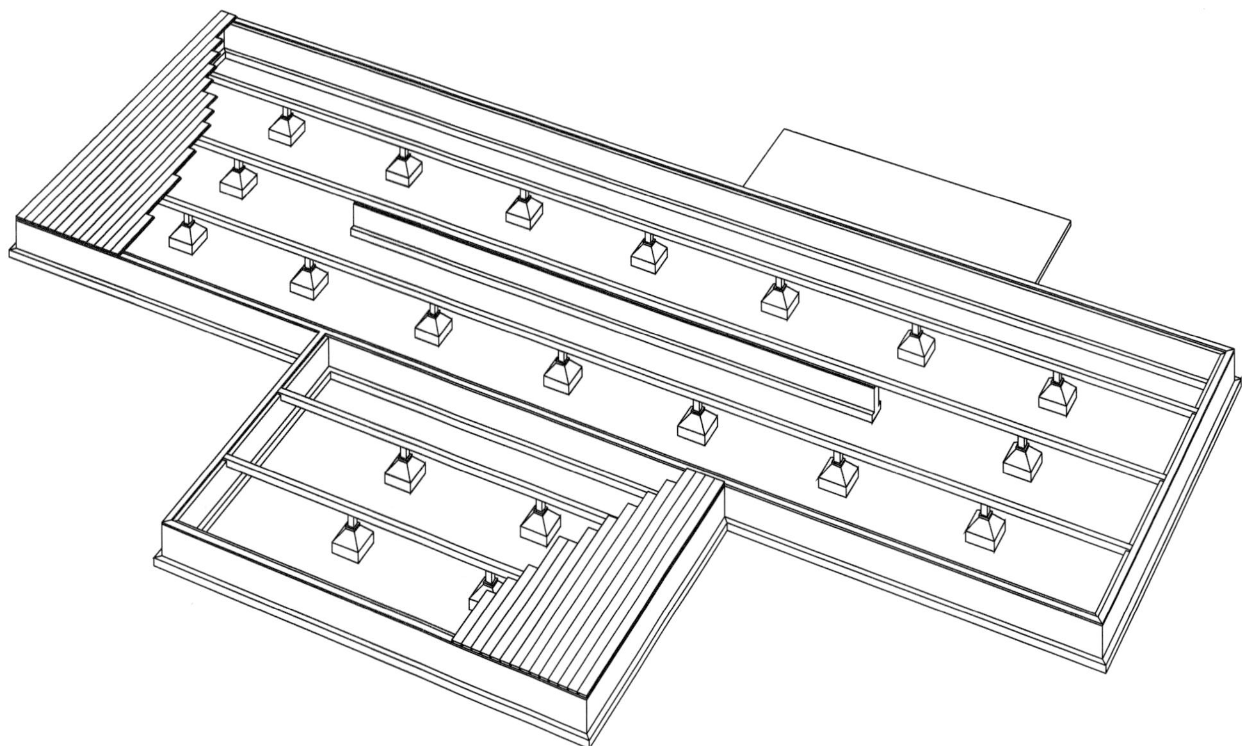

Figure 11.67 Foundation plan: 2″-thick tongue-and-groove planking.

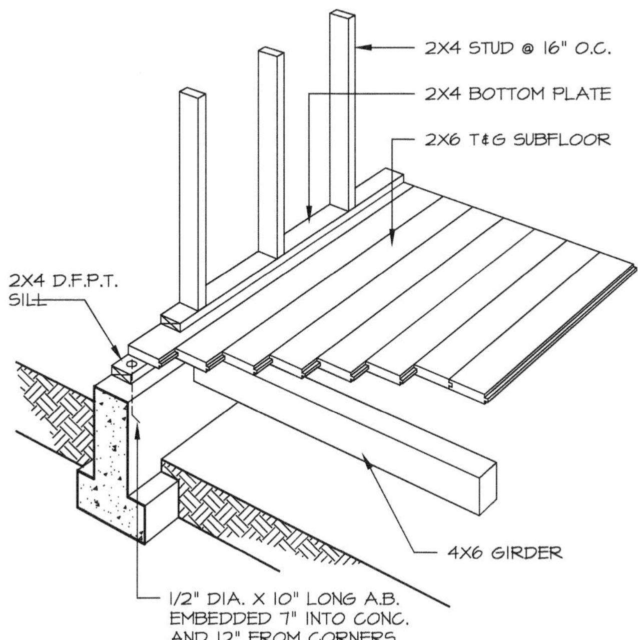

Figure 11.68 Exterior foundation wall with 2″-thick tongue-and-groove planking.

For roof members that must satisfy heavy timber construction requirements, the roof planking must have a thickness of not less than 2″ and must provide a tongue-and-groove or splined connection. The main supporting members must not be less than 4″ in width and not less than 6″ in depth. All supporting wood columns must be at least 8″ in any dimension. See Figure 11.82.

Wood Truss Roof System

Wood roof trusses are available in many sizes, shapes, and lengths. Wood roof trusses are generally fabricated by a manufacturer and delivered to the building site. Trusses are selected according to the manufacturer's stipulated engineered design criteria for the various weights of materials that the trusses must support. They can be custom manufactured to the desired shape and are a good choice for both budgets and for sensitivity to the environment. One method of utilizing a wood truss roof system is to place the trusses on a dimensional module spacing that allows the intermediate roof supporting members to span the trusses. See Figure 11.83. An alternative method is to utilize truss members at a 16″ or 24″ center-to-center spacing.

Panelized Wood Roof System

A panelized wood roof system is a construction method whereby plywood or OSB roof sheathing panels and intermediate supporting members are prefabricated in a manufacturing plant. Generally, the size of these panels is 4′ × 8′ because this is the standard dimension for plywood sheets. The thickness of the plywood sheathing is governed by the structural engineer's specifications. The supporting intermediate members of the plywood are generally 2 × 4 placed at 24″ center to center. Once the panels are fabricated, they are lifted and placed within the 4′ × 8′ module dimensions of the roof's main supporting members. The panels are attached to the main and intermediate supporting members with the metal framing connectors. The main supporting members may be glue-laminated (glulam) beams, and intermediate members have a minimum thickness of 4″. This roof framing system is generally used in the construction of industrial and manufacturing buildings. See Figure 11.84.

Engineered Lumber Roof System

The use of engineered lumber members for roof rafters provides a straighter and stiffer frame, which is also more consistent in size and shape, for a wood roof system. The structural capabilities of these members allow for the use of different types of roofing materials, and can handle snow-loading conditions. When engineered lumber is used, roof pitches may vary from a low pitch to a steep roof condition. The depth of these members may range from 5½″ to 16″, depending on the particular engineered lumber fabricator or manufacturer. See Figure 11.85.

Drawing Framing Members Separately

The second way to show ceiling, floor, and roof framing members is to provide a separate drawing that may be titled "2nd Floor Framing," "Floor Framing," or "Roof Framing." You might choose this method because the framing is complex or because construction document procedures require it.

The first step is the same as that taken when drawing on the foundation plan. Duplicate or XREF all the walls, windows, and door openings. The line quality of your tracing should be just dark enough to make these lines distinguishable after you have reproduced the drawing. In this way, the final drawing, showing all the framing

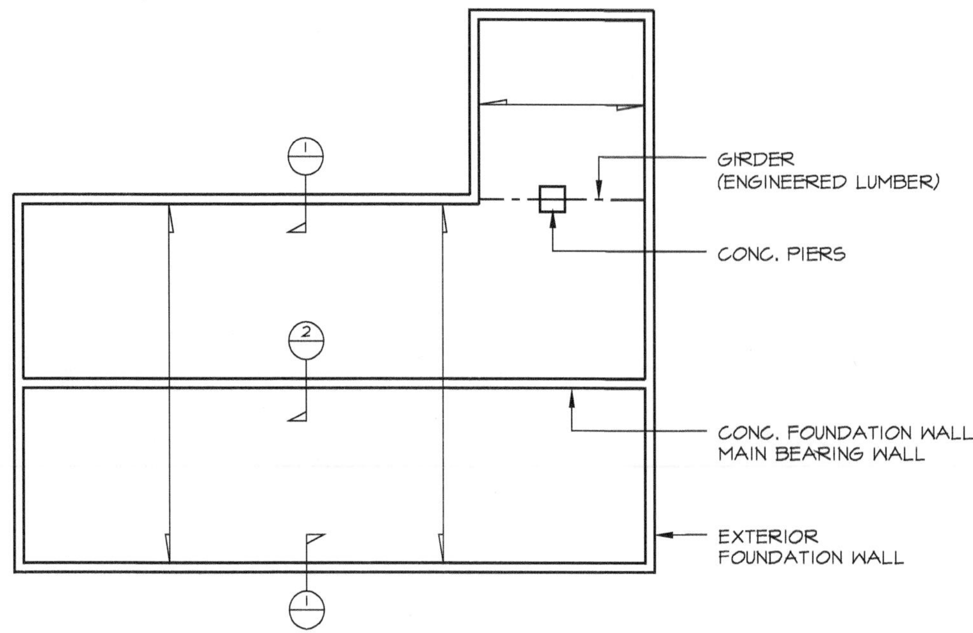

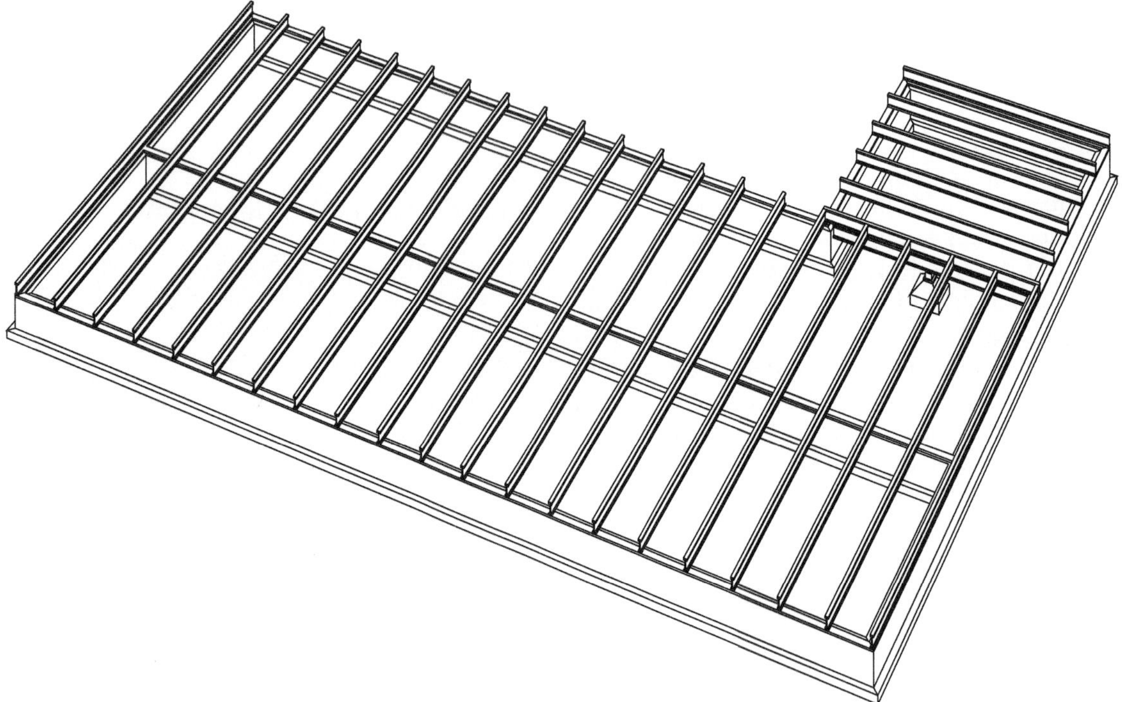

Figure 11.69 Engineered lumber floor joist.

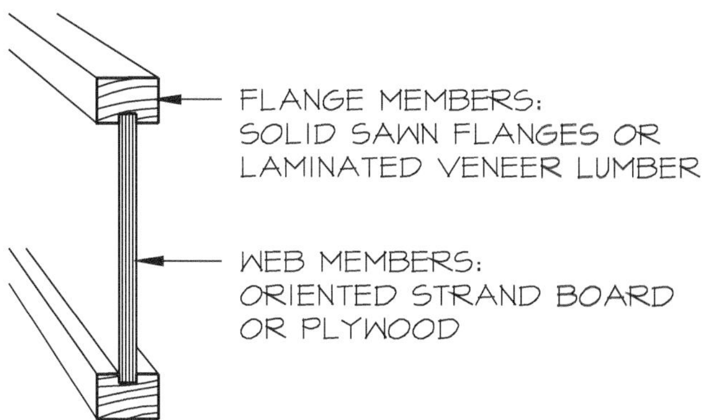

Figure 11.70 Engineered lumber floor shape.

members, can be made darker like a finished drawing. This provides the viewer with clear framing members, while the walls are just lightly drawn for reference.

Figure 11.86 shows the floor plan of the first floor of a two-story, wood-framed residence with all the framing members required to support the second floor and ceiling directly above this level. Because the second-floor framing and ceiling for the first floor are the same, this drawing is titled "2ND FLR. Framing Plan."

First, draft in all the floor beams, columns, and headers for all the various openings. Then incorporate the location and span direction of all the floor joists into the drawing. In Figure 11.86, the floor joist locations and span directions are shown with a single line and arrowhead at each end of the line. This is one way to designate these members. Another method is shown later when the roof framing plan is discussed.

Dimensioning for framing plans mainly applies to beam and column locations. Provide dimensioning for all floor beams and columns located directly under load-bearing members. These members, such as walls and columns, are located on the second floor. Dimensioning for these members is similar to that on a floor plan. When you have finished the drawing, provide the required notes for all the members included in the drawing.

Drawing the ceiling plan for the second-floor level involves only the immediate ceiling framing members. A ceiling plan will typically be incorporated into the roof framing plan unless it is too complex. In that case, it will show headers over openings and ceiling joist location, span, direction, size, and spacing for a specific ceiling area. This is also where applicable notes and dimensioning are shown.

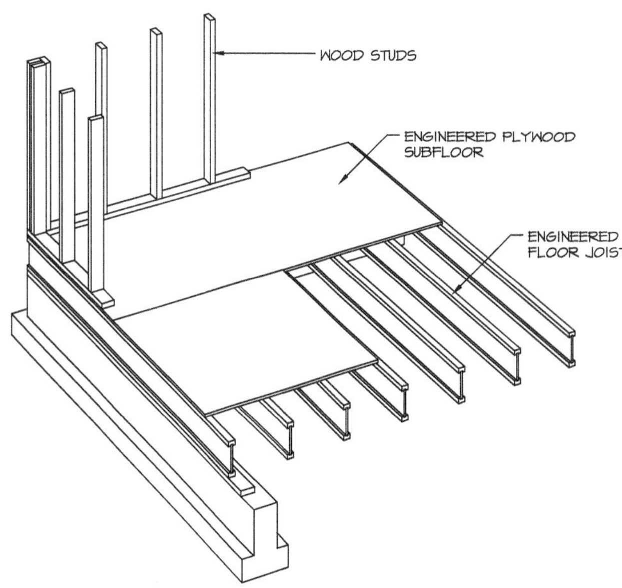

Figure 11.71 Engineered lumber floor system.

The final framing plan for this project is the roof framing plan. See Figure 11.87. As mentioned previously, another way to show framing members is to draw in all the members that apply to that particular drawing. This obviously takes more time to draw, but is clearer for the viewer.

Framing Plan: Wood Members

When wood structures have members spaced anywhere from 16″ to 48″ on centers, show them with a single line broken at intervals. Figure 11.89 shows the roof framing plan for this residence, which incorporates all the individual rafters, ridges, **hip rafters** (the members that bisect the angle of two intersecting walls), and supporting columns and beams under the rafters. Show the rafters, which are closely spaced, with a single line. Although this method is tedious, it does provide clarity and an actual member count for the contractor to work from. Lightly draft the walls so that the members directly above are clear. Provide dimensioning for members with critical locations, as well as call-outs for the sizes, lumber grade, and spacing of all members. With the use of BIM, the program will track the quantity of materials and a schedule of members can be accurately estimated.

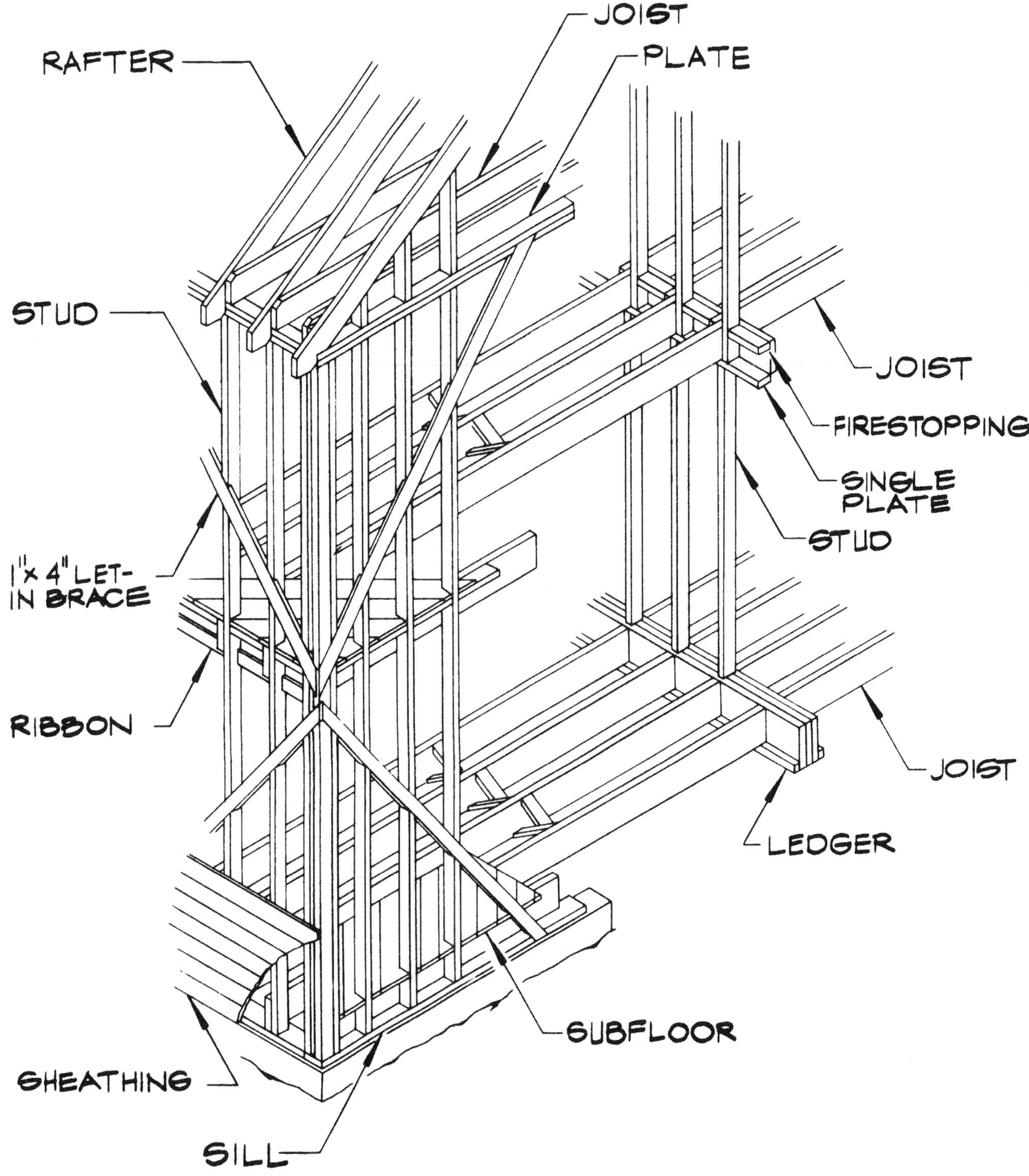

Figure 11.72 Balloon-frame construction. (Courtesy of American Wood Council, Leesburg, VA.)

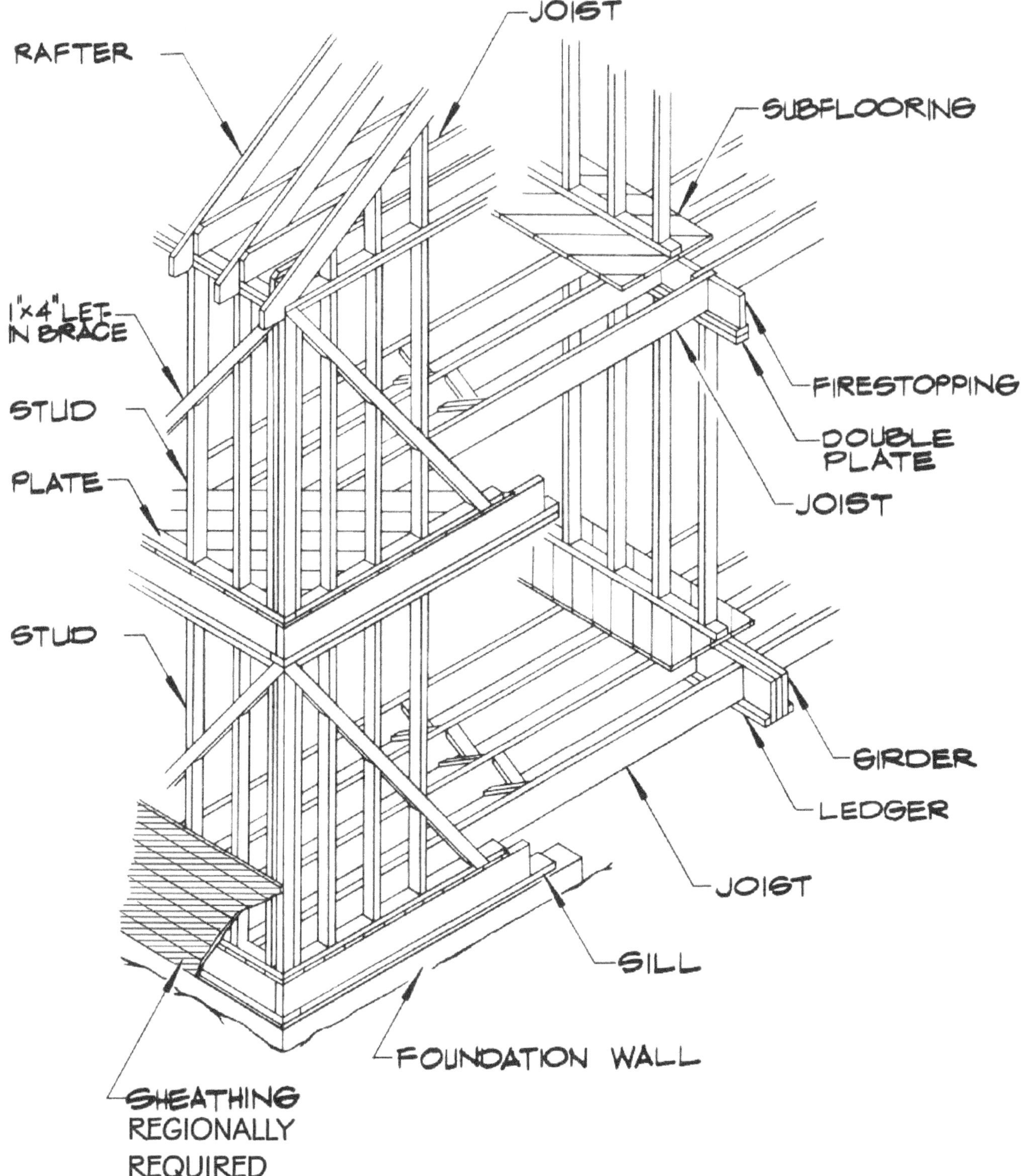

Figure 11.73 Western or platform framing. (Courtesy of American Wood Council, Leesburg, VA.)

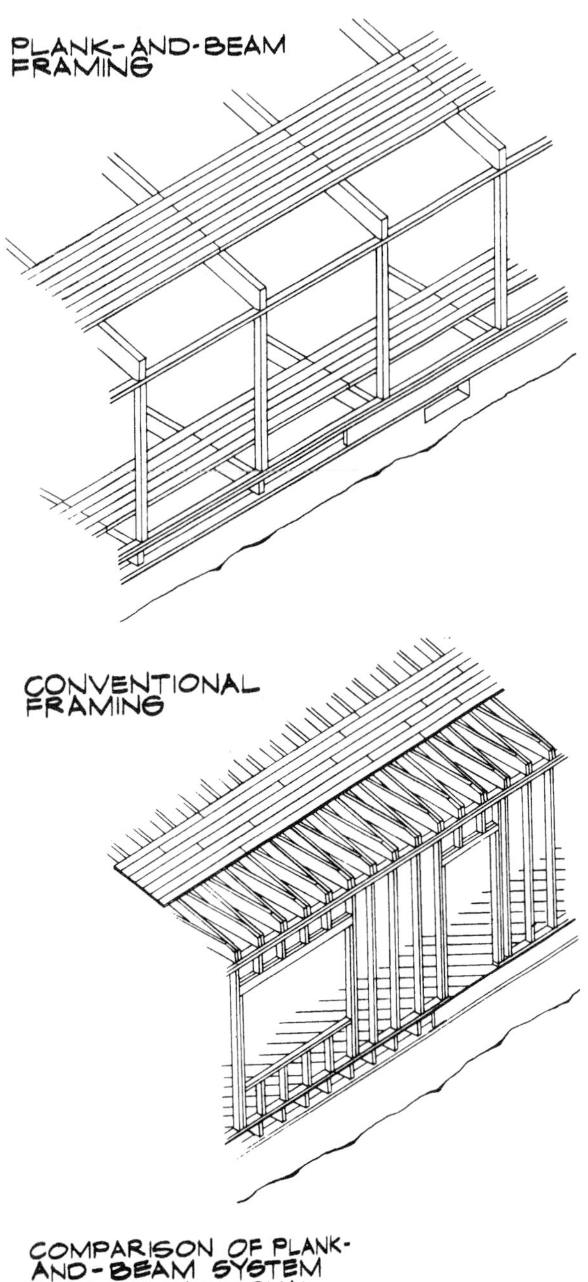

Figure 11.74 Pictorial comparison of plank-and-beam framing with conventional framing. (Courtesy of American Wood Council, Leesburg, VA.)

CONVENTIONS

The basic conventions for floor framing are generally the same as those used in roof or ceiling framing plans.

The floor plan should be used, with XREF. In this manner, not only do you keep the size of the file small, but also any corrections or changes in the floor plan will be reflected in the framing plan.

This section discusses a second-floor framing plan that will be drawn onto the first-floor plan. Two systems will be shown, the first with conventional framing and the second with engineered lumber. In discussing engineered lumber, we will show how to use the computer framing program developed by Boise Cascade called "BC Framer."

Conventional Floor Framing Plan

Stage I (Figure 11.89). Use an early stage of the floor plan that shows all the walls and openings in the structure. Fireplaces, elevators, and stairs should be included and externally referenced in the drawing set so that the framing around them can be included.

Stage II (Figure 11.90). The various areas to be framed include openings and are identified as zones. An example of the framing that will be employed for openings is shown in Figure 11.91. If not already done, identify any bearing walls with hatching (texturing).

Stage III (Figure 11.92). Shear walls are drawn at this stage and referenced to a schedule that is shown directly below the framing drawing. Headers, beams, and openings are defined, using a centerline. Critical columns and posts should also be identified.

Stage IV (Figure 11.93). This stage shows the direction of the floor joist and its duration. A half arrowhead is used to indicate direction, and a full arrowhead indicates the duration. They are connected with a dot.

Stage V (Figure 11.94). In this stage, information as to size and space is filled in along the direction lines. Headers, beams, and columns are identified, along with the hardware and the connectors used. Referencing and titling complete the drawing.

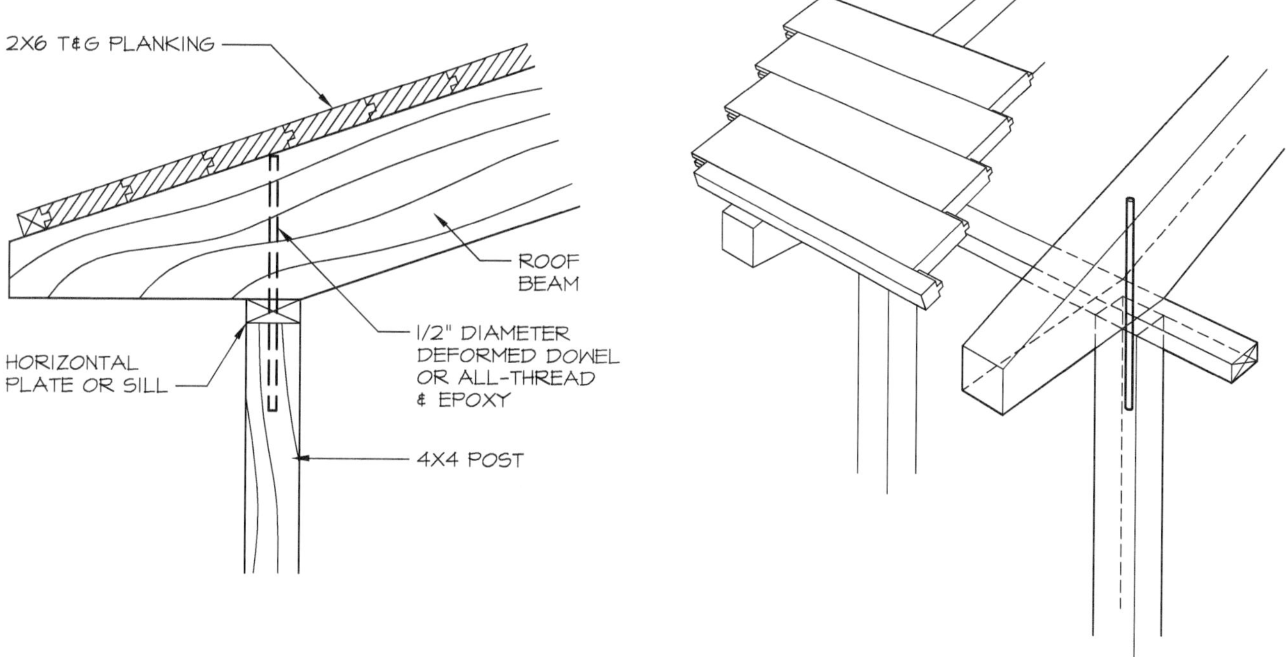

Figure 11.75 Post-to-beam connection.

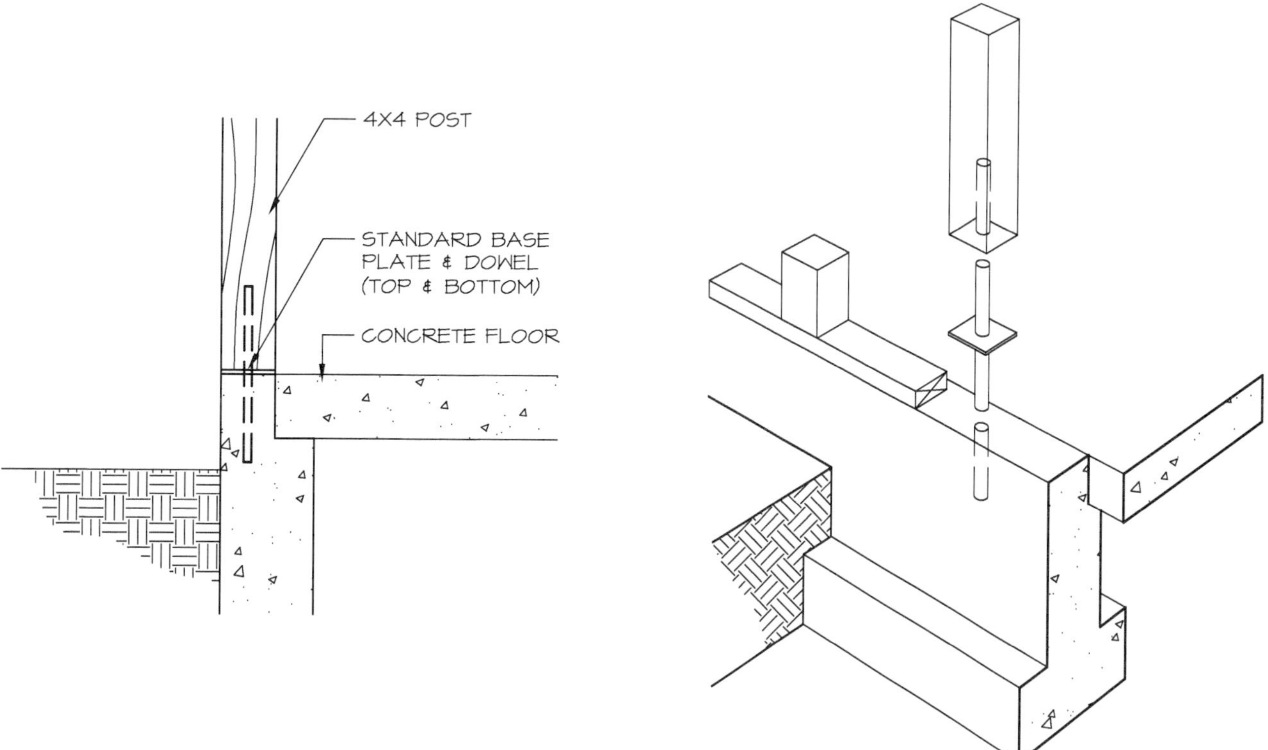

Figure 11.76 Post-to-foundation connection.

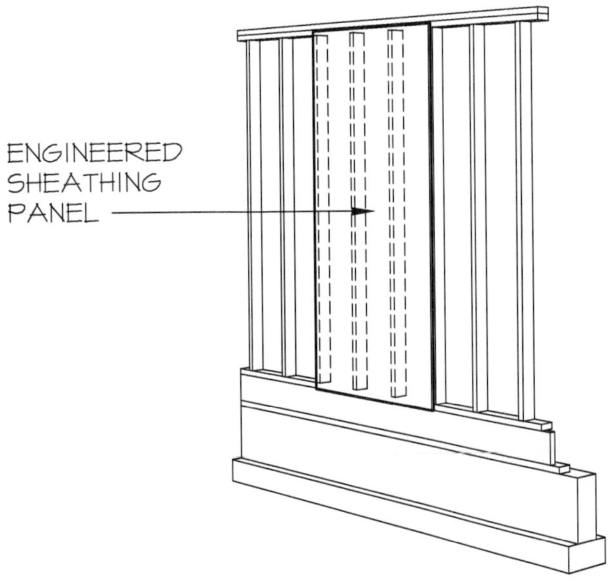

Figure 11.77 Engineered sheathing panel.

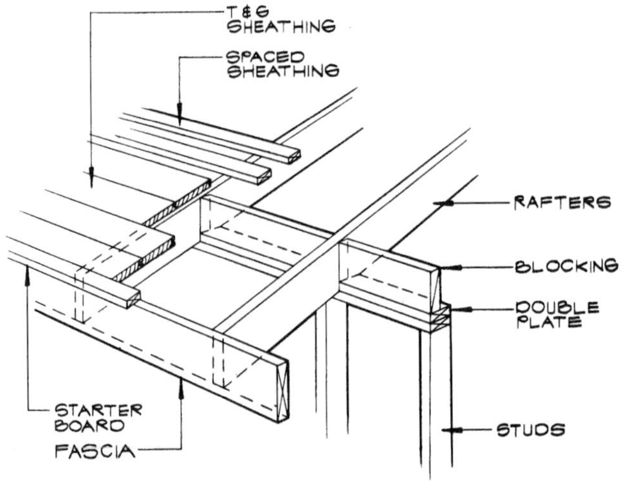

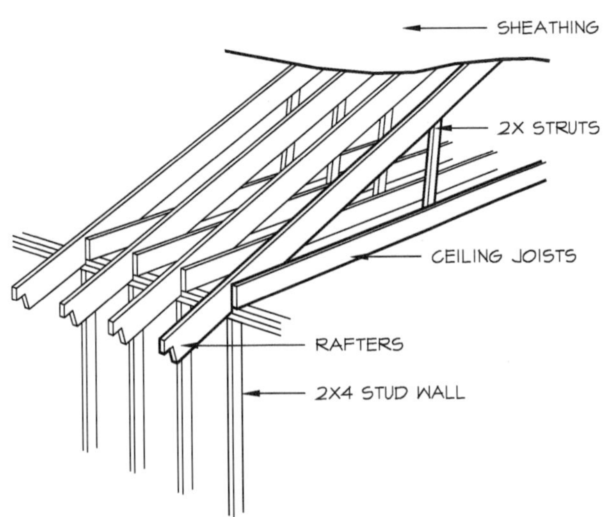

Figure 11.78 Sawn lumber roof system.

Figure 11.80 Pictorial view, eave detail.

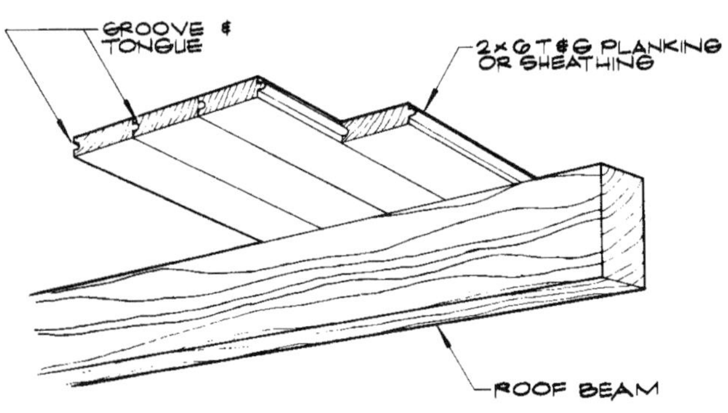

Figure 11.81 Pictorial view of roof planking.

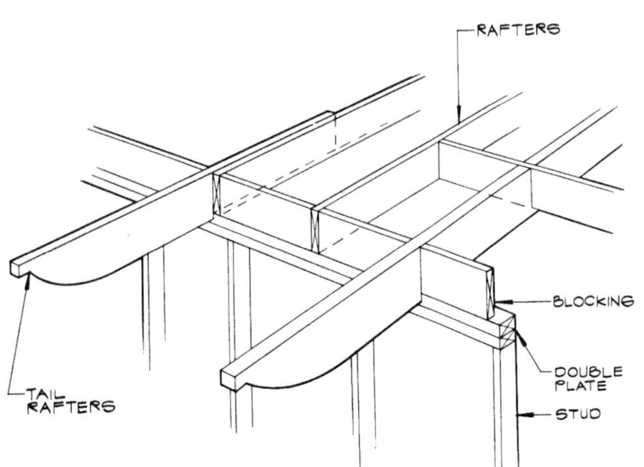

Figure 11.79 Pictorial view, eave detail.

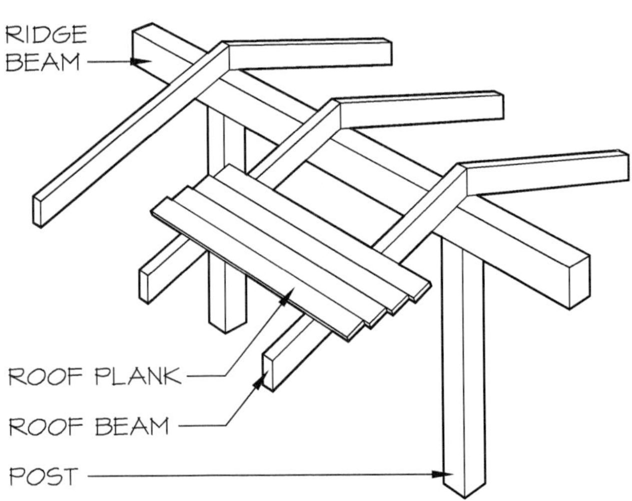

Figure 11.82 Plank-and-beam roof system.

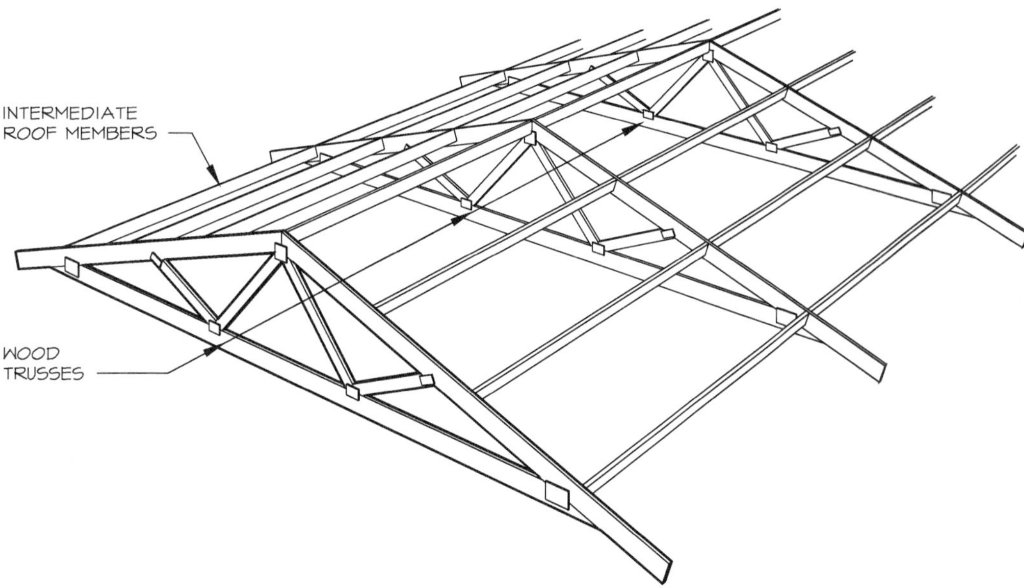

Figure 11.83 Wood truss roof system.

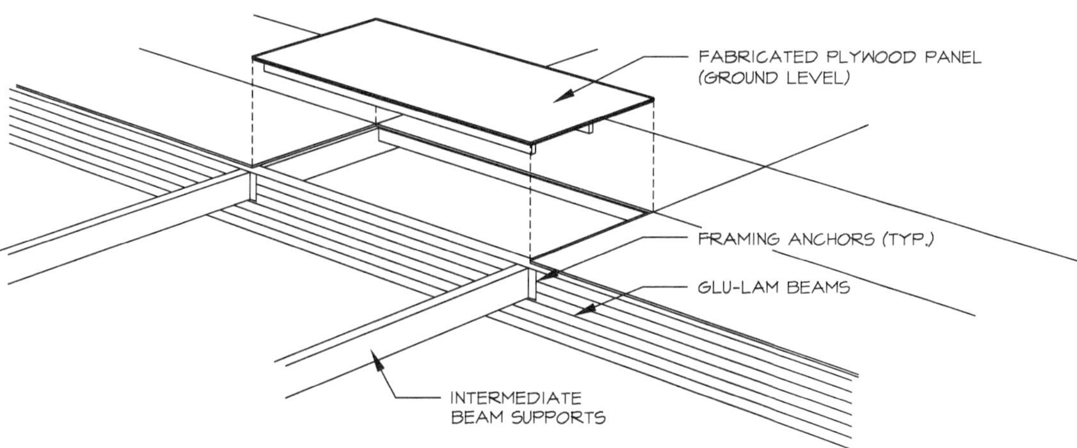

Figure 11.84 Panelized wood roof system.

Floor Framing above Masonry or Concrete

The graphic display of the floor framing on a masonry or concrete wall looks similar to the previously discussed roof framing plan, in that it also uses the same symbols and conventions. An example of a first-floor framing plan over a basement with walls made of concrete masonry units (CMUs) is shown in Figures 11.95 and 11.96.

Floor Framing Plan with Engineered Lumber

Rather than using the conventional method of framing described throughout this chapter, here we introduce the second-floor framing system using engineered lumber. These drawings will become part of the structural set under normal circumstances, and not part of the architectural set of construction documents.

Normally, the first-floor plan is sent to the manufacturer of the engineered lumber. For an example, we will use a plan drawn by Boise Cascade that utilizes the 9½″-high Boise Cascade 400 series. This will be noted as 9–1/2BCI-400.

The drawing is done by Boise Cascade drafters on a system similar to that of a standard AutoCAD program. The BC Framer, as it is called, reconciles the space allocated for the thickness of the floor determined by the designer, which is given to the manufacturer along with the floor plan. The manufacturer then takes the information provided by the office and translates it into the framing plan, as shown in Figure 11.97A. A pictorial of the assembly is shown in Figure 11.97B. Samples of the series of pictorial details are shown in Figure 11.97C, and a list of required materials and hardware appears in Figure 11.97D. A separate cost estimate is provided to the

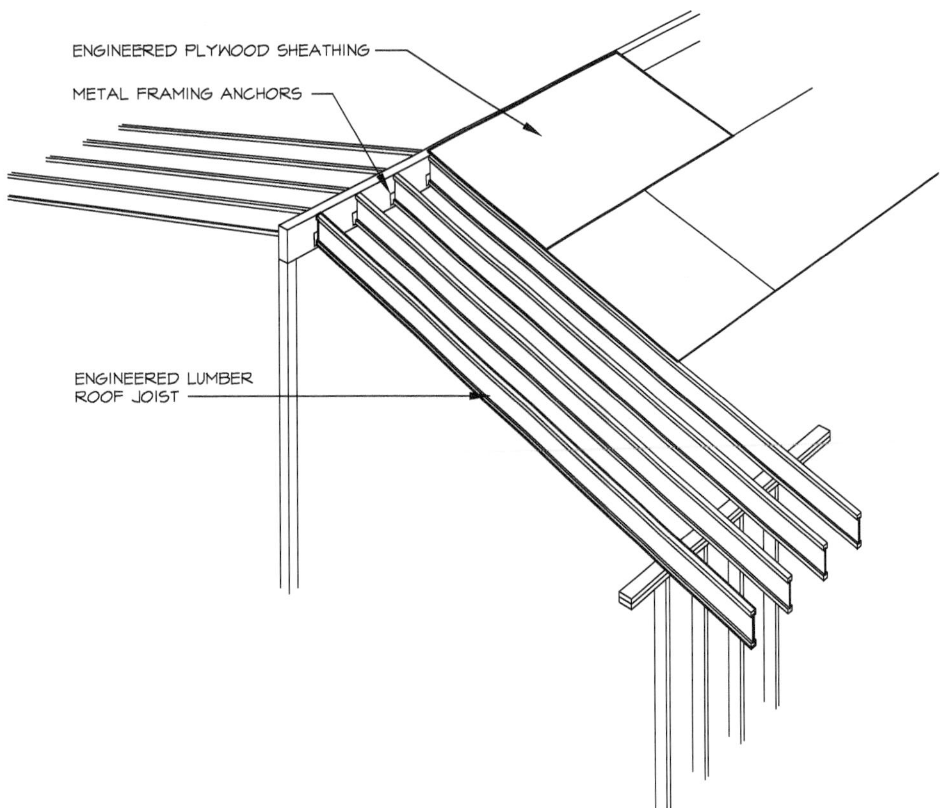

Figure 11.85 Engineered lumber roof system.

office, along with any engineering calculations required by the governing department of building and safety.

The service is total and makes the preparation of framing plans a delight for the architectural office. However, the senior drafters must be able not only to read the framing plans, but also to ensure their proper integration with the rest of the drawings. The drafters must also initially consider the space that must be provided for any overlooked items: duct space for heating and air-conditioning units; space for venting appliances such as ranges and water heaters; space for electronic appliances and access for electrical lines from the fixtures to the computers and for the drainpipes that run from the roof through the floors and walls. All of these matters should be resolved before you submit the plans for framing drawings. Such thoroughness will also provide the workers in the field with a clear picture of potential problems that can be averted. This is further accomplished with comprehensive details, partial sections, and full sections.

Framing Plan: Wood and Steel Members. Framing plans using both wood and steel members to support ceilings, floors, and roof are drawn in a similar fashion to framing plans using steel alone. Steel members are drawn with a heavy solid line and the wood members with a lighter line broken at intervals. You can also show wood members with a solid line and directional arrow.

Framing Plan Checklist

1. Titles and scales.
2. Indicate bearing and non-bearing walls.
   a. Coordinate with foundation plan.
   b. Show all openings in walls.
3. Show all beams, headers, girders, purlins, etc.
4. Show all columns; note sizes and materials.
5. Note roof access way to attic—if occurs.
6. Note ceiling joist sizes, direction, and spacing.
7. Draw all rafters; note sizes and spacing.
   a. Show skylight penetrations.
   b. Show chimney penetrations.
8. Draw overhangs.
   a. Indicate framing for holding overhangs up.
   b. Dimension width of footings.
9. Note shear walls and length of wall.
10. Note roof sheathing type, thickness, and nailing.
11. Indicate all ridges and valleys. Note sizes.
12. Note all differences in roof and floor levels.
13. Provide all shear schedules.
14. Provide material specifications.
15. Provide nailing schedule.
16. Note structural observation requirements.

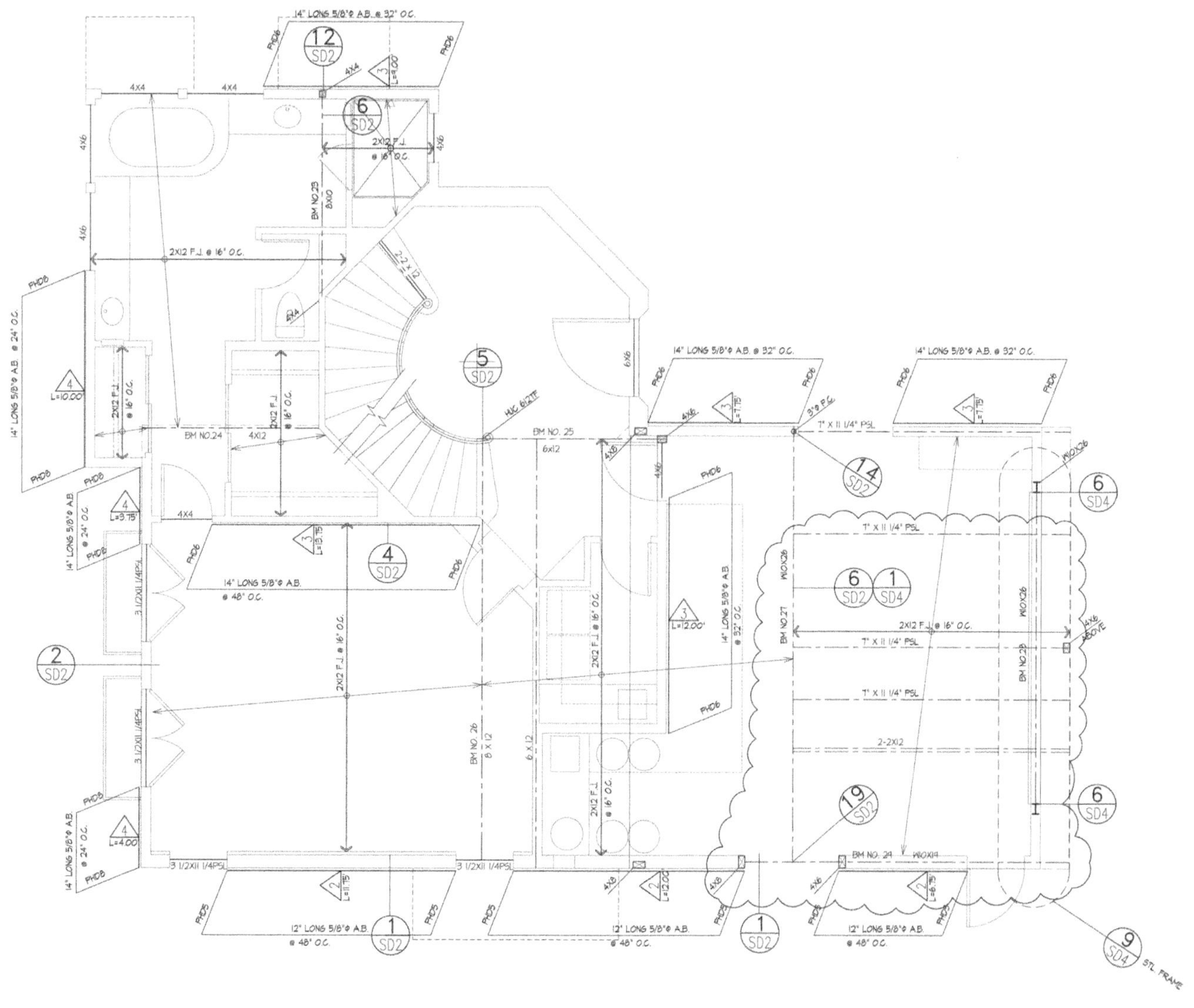

Figure 11.86 Second-floor framing plan.

Key Terms

axial reference locations
balloon framing
brick pavers
call-outs
concrete caisson
concrete pads
crosshatch
footing design
foundation footing details
grade beam
hidden line
hip rafters
legend
oriented strand board (OSB)
pedestal
pilasters
planking
post hold-down
shot-ins
two-pour system
western framing

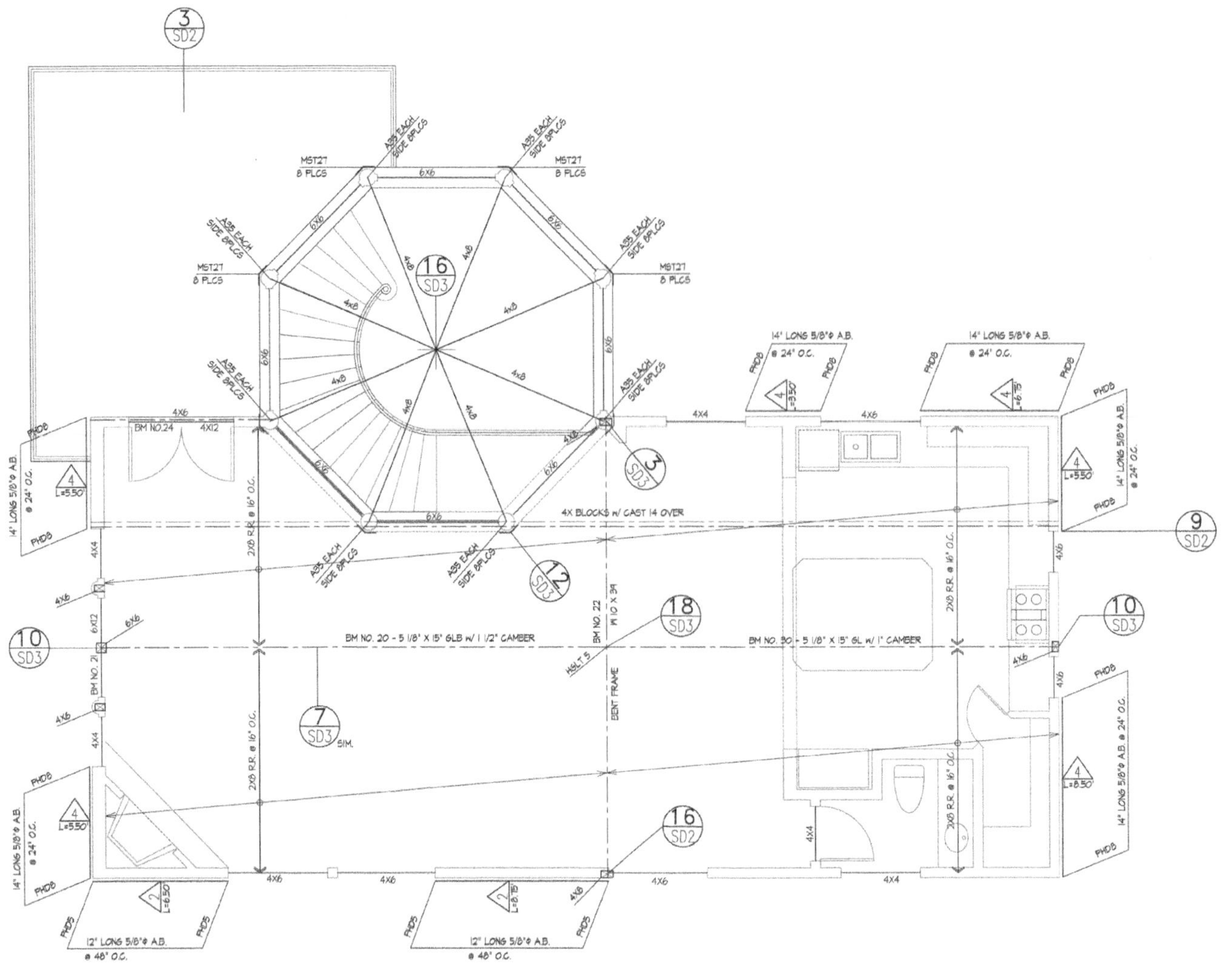

Figure 11.87 Roof framing plan.

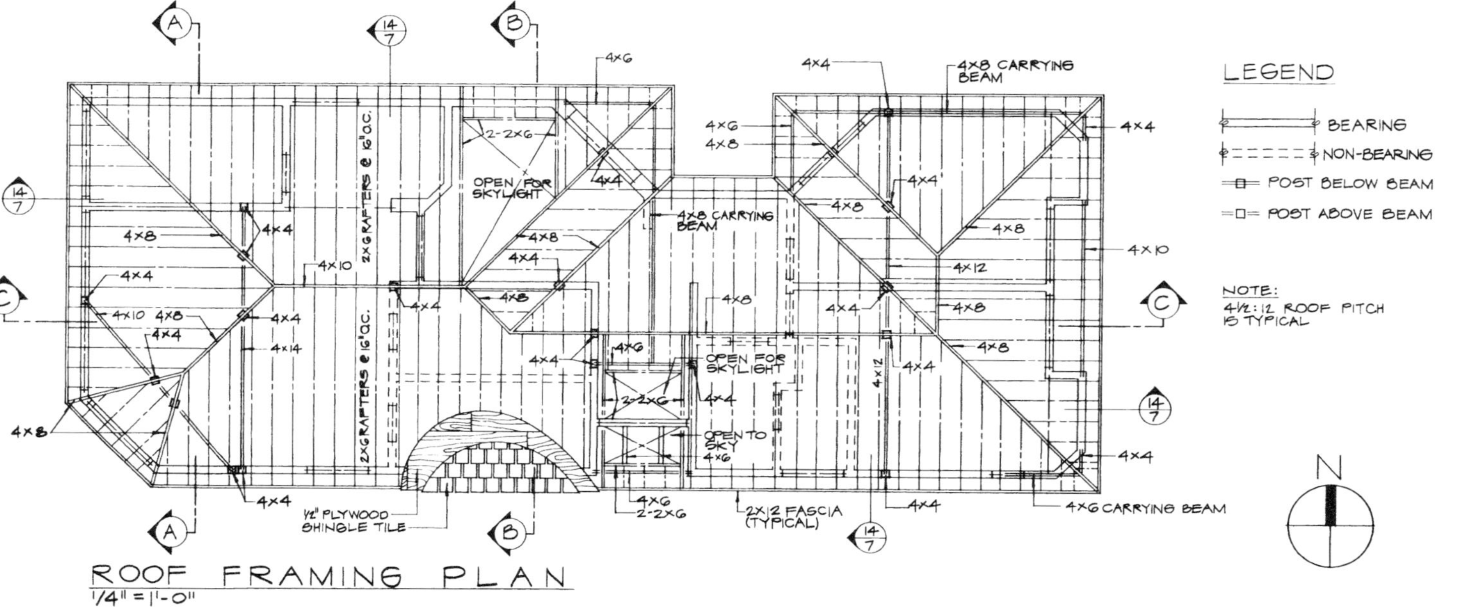

Figure 11.88 Roof framing plan with single line for rafters.

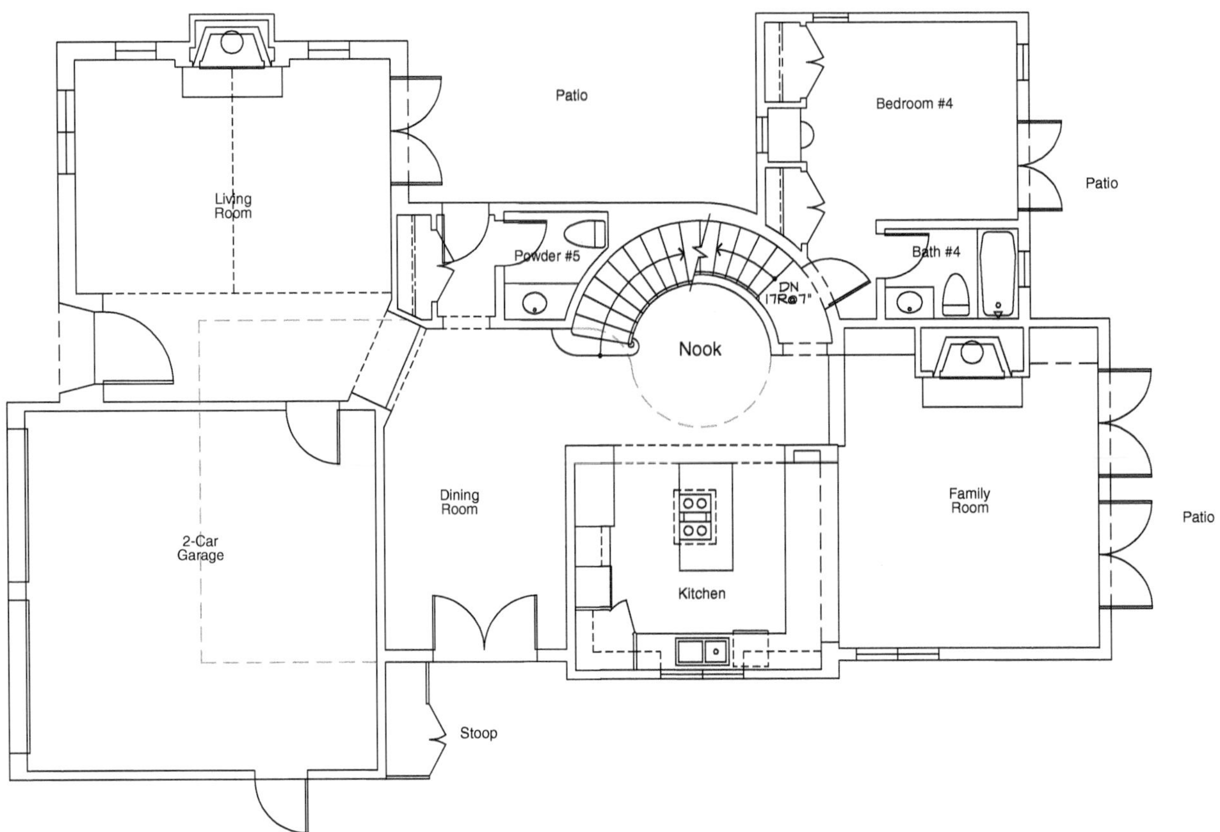

Figure 11.89 Stage I: Base (first-floor plan).

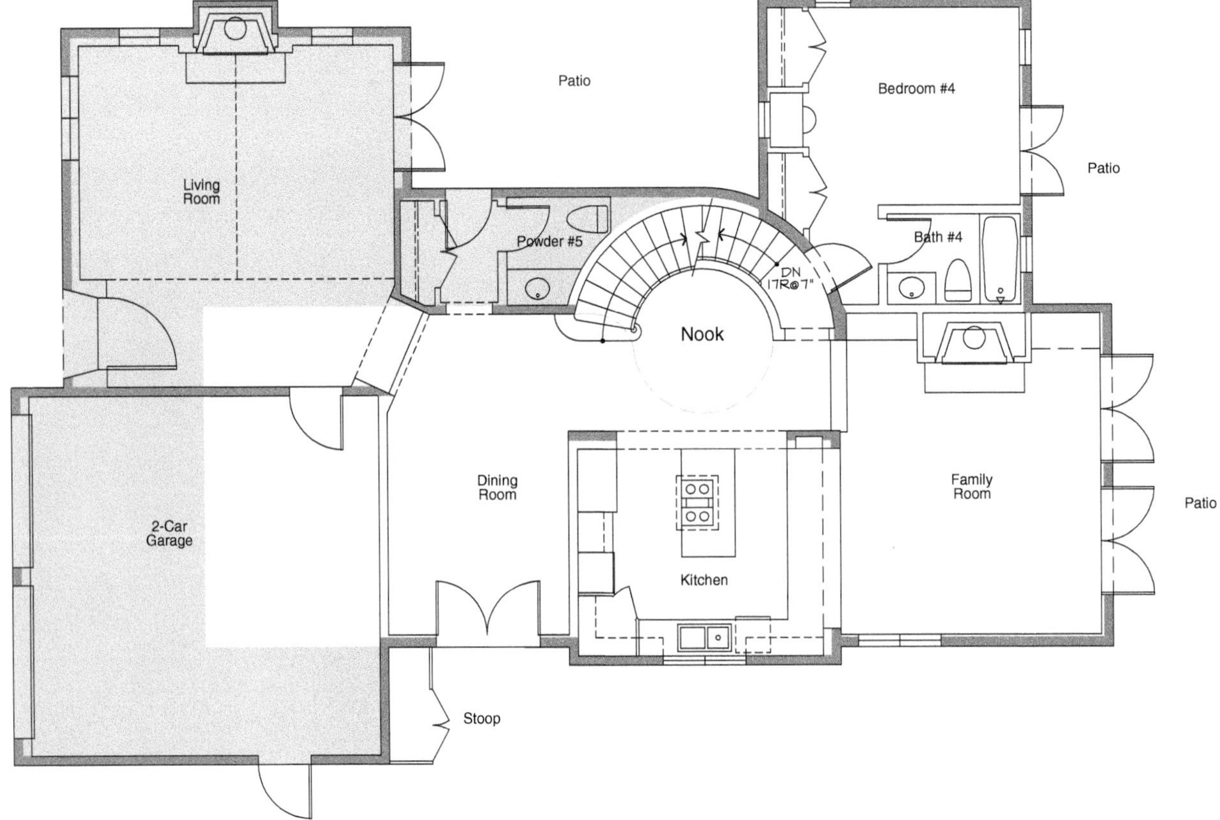

Figure 11.90 Stage II: Selecting zones.

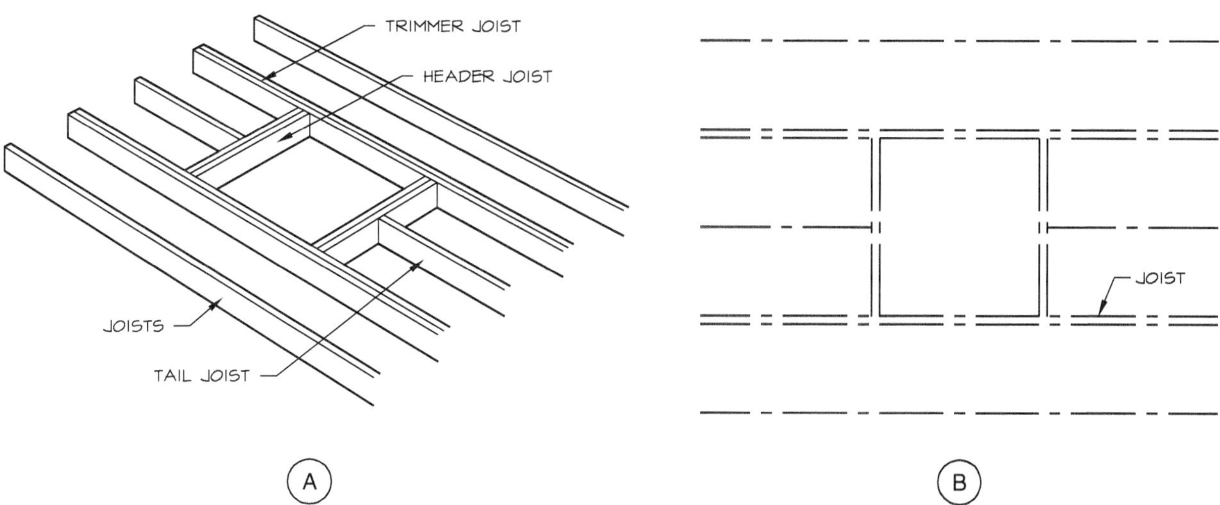

Figure 11.91 Framing an opening.

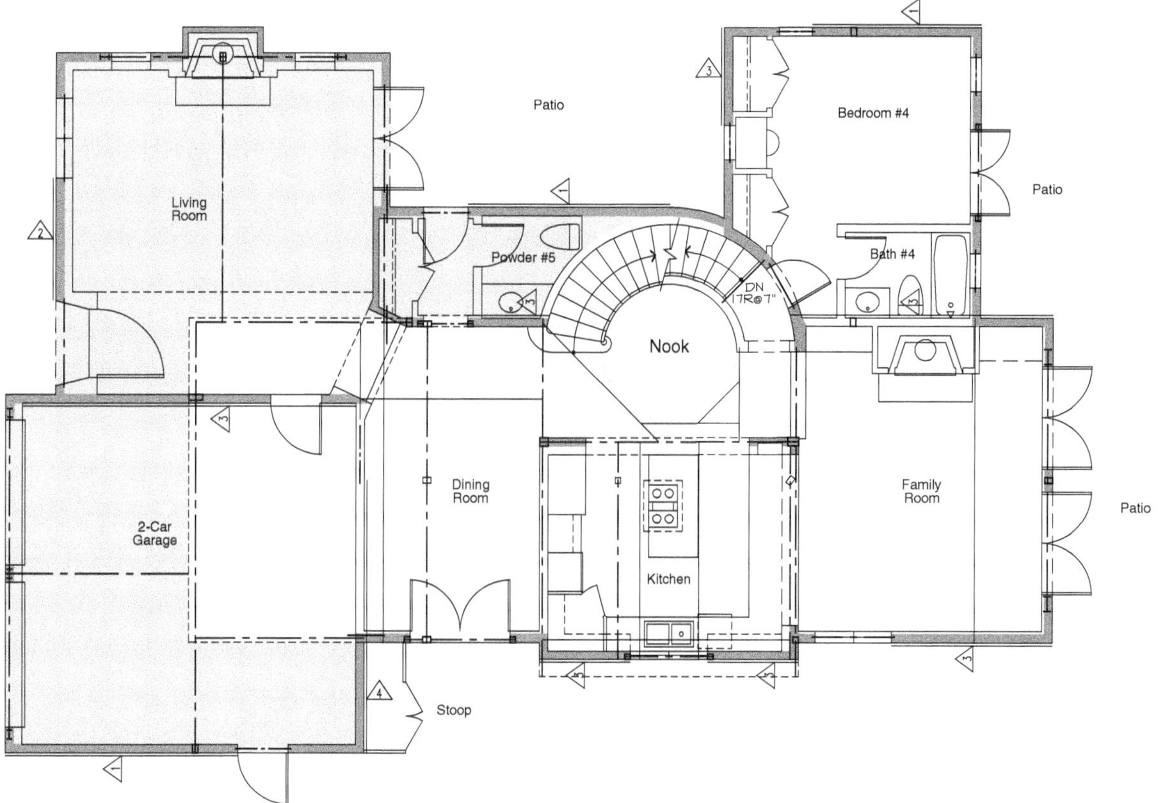

Shearwall Schedule

SYMBOL	PANEL	NAILING [8]	WALL	SOLE PLATE ATTACHMENT			TOP PLATE [4] ATTACHMENT	HOLDOWN [5,6]
		COMMON NAILS	LBS/FT	NAILS	LAGS [9]	ANCHOR BOLTS [6]		
1	3/8 EXPOSURE 1 [7] (ID#24/0)	8d @ 6,6,12	198	16d @ 6" O.C.	3/8" × 5" @ 24" O.C.	5/8" DIA. @ 48" O.C. 12" LONG	A35 @ 24" O.C.	HD2A, CB44, FTA2 PHD2
2 [1]	15/32 EXPOSURE 1 [7] (ID#32/16)	10d @ 4,4,12	299	16d @ 3.5" O.C.	3/8" × 5" @ 18" O.C.	5/8" DIA. @ 48" O.C. 12" LONG	A35 @ 16" O.C.	HD5A, CB44, FTA2 PHD5
3 [1,2,3] 3x SILL	15/32 EXPOSURE 1 [7] (ID#32/16)	10d @ 3,3,12	450	40d @ 3" O.C.	3/8" × 5" @ 12" O.C.	5/8" DIA. @ 32" O.C. 14" LONG	A35 @ 12" O.C.	HD6A, CB44, FTA5 PHD6
4 [1,2,3] 3x SILL	15/32 EXPOSURE 1 [7] STRUCT. 1 (ID#32/16)	10d @ 2,2,12	652	50d @ 3" O.C.	3/8" × 5" @ 8" O.C.	5/8" DIA. @ 24" O.C. 14" LONG	A35 @ 8" O.C.	HD8A, FTA7, PHD8

FOOTNOTES:

1. THESE PANELS TO BE 4-PLY MINIMUM.
2. 3x SOLE PLATES AND 3x FRAMING AT ADJOINING PANEL EDGES REQUIRED. STAGGER PANEL EDGE NAILING.
3. 1/2" MINIMUM EDGE DISTANCE REQUIRED FOR BOUNDARY NAILING.
4. A35'S NOT REQUIRED IF PANEL NAILS TO FRAMING MEMBER ABOVE TOP PLATES.
5. HOLDOWNS REQUIRED AT ENDS OF ALL SHEAR PANELS. USE 4x4'S FOR END MEMBERS. ALL HOLDOWN BOLTS TO BE TIGHTENED JUST PRIOR TO COVERING, INSPECTOR TO VERIFY. BOLT HOLES TO BE 1/16" MAXIMUM OVERSIZED AT THE CONNECTION OF THE HOLDOWN TO THE POST, INSPECTOR TO VERIFY.
6. SIMPSON BP WASHERS REQUIRED FOR ALL PLYWOOD SHEAR WALL SILL PLATE BOLTS AND HOLDOWN BOLTS.
7. OSB (ORIENTED STRAND BOARD) IS A WOOD STRUCTURAL PANEL.
8. SOLID BLOCKING SHALL BE PROVIDED AT ALL HORIZONTAL JOINTS OCCURRING IN BRACED WALL PANELS.
9. USE 3x BLOCKS AND 3x RIM JOISTS IF LAGS ARE USED.

Figure 11.92 Stage III: Structural support.

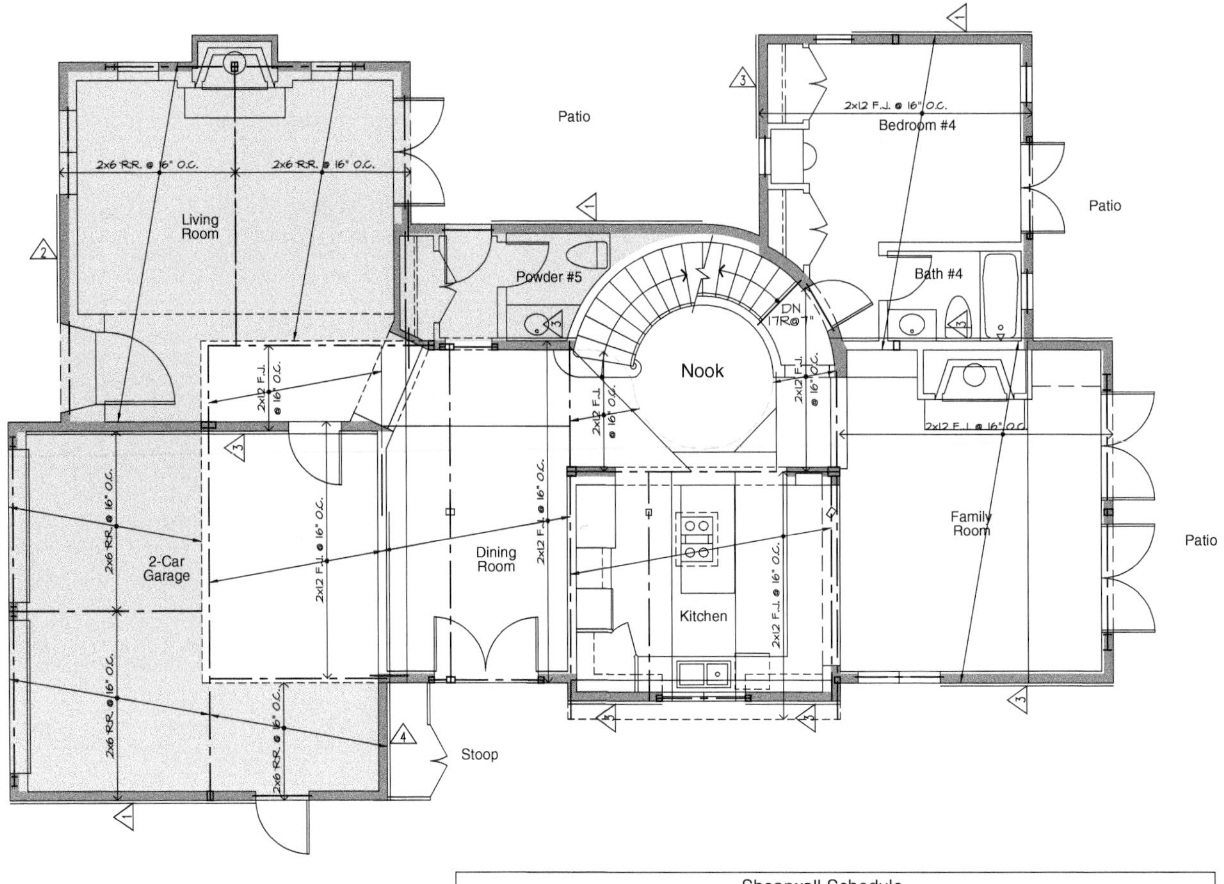

SYMBOL	PANEL	NAILING 8	WALL	SOLE PLATE ATTACHMENT			TOP PLATE 4 ATTACHMENT	HOLDOWN 5,6
		COMMON NAILS	LBS/FT	NAILS	LAGS 9	ANCHOR BOLTS 6		
1	3/8 EXPOSURE 1 7 (ID#24/0)	8d @ 6,6,12	198	16d @ 6" O.C.	3/8" x 5" @ 24" O.C.	5/8" DIA. @ 48" O.C. 12" LONG	A35 @ 24" O.C.	HD2A, CB44, FTA2 PHD2
2 1	15/32 EXPOSURE 1 7 (ID#32/16)	10d @ 4,4,12	299	16d @ 3.5" O.C.	3/8" x 5" @ 18" O.C.	5/8" DIA. @ 48" O.C. 12" LONG	A35 @ 16" O.C.	HD5A, CB44, FTA2 PHD5
3 1,2,3 3x SILL	15/32 EXPOSURE 1 7 (ID#32/16)	10d @ 3,3,12	450	40d @ 3" O.C.	3/8" x 5" @ 12" O.C.	5/8" DIA. @ 32" O.C. 14" LONG	A35 @ 12" O.C.	HD6A, CB44, FTA5 PHD6
4 1,2,3 3x SILL	15/32 EXPOSURE 1 7 STRUCT. 1 (ID#32/16)	10d @ 2,2,12	652	50d @ 3" O.C.	3/8" x 5" @ 8" O.C.	5/8" DIA. @ 24" O.C. 14" LONG	A35 @ 8" O.C.	HD8A, FTA7, PHD8

FOOTNOTES:

1. THESE PANELS TO BE 4-PLY MINIMUM.
2. 3x SOLE PLATES AND 3x FRAMING AT ADJOINING PANEL EDGES REQUIRED. STAGGER PANEL EDGE NAILING.
3. 1/2" MINIMUM EDGE DISTANCE REQUIRED FOR BOUNDARY NAILING.
4. A35'S NOT REQUIRED IF PANEL NAILS TO FRAMING MEMBER ABOVE TOP PLATES.
5. HOLDOWNS REQUIRED AT ENDS OF ALL SHEAR PANELS. USE 4x4'S FOR END MEMBERS. ALL HOLDOWN BOLTS TO BE TIGHTENED JUST PRIOR TO COVERING, INSPECTOR TO VERIFY. BOLT HOLES TO BE 1/16" MAXIMUM OVERSIZED AT THE CONNECTION OF THE HOLDOWN TO THE POST, INSPECTOR TO VERIFY.
6. SIMPSON BP WASHERS REQUIRED FOR ALL PLYWOOD SHEAR WALL SILL PLATE BOLTS AND HOLDOWN BOLTS.
7. OSB (ORIENTED STRAND BOARD) IS A WOOD STRUCTURAL PANEL.
8. SOLID BLOCKING SHALL BE PROVIDED AT ALL HORIZONTAL JOINTS OCCURRING IN BRACED WALL PANELS.
9. USE 3x BLOCKS AND 3x RIM JOISTS IF LAGS ARE USED.

Shearwall Schedule

Figure 11.93 Stage IV: Direction of joist and duration.

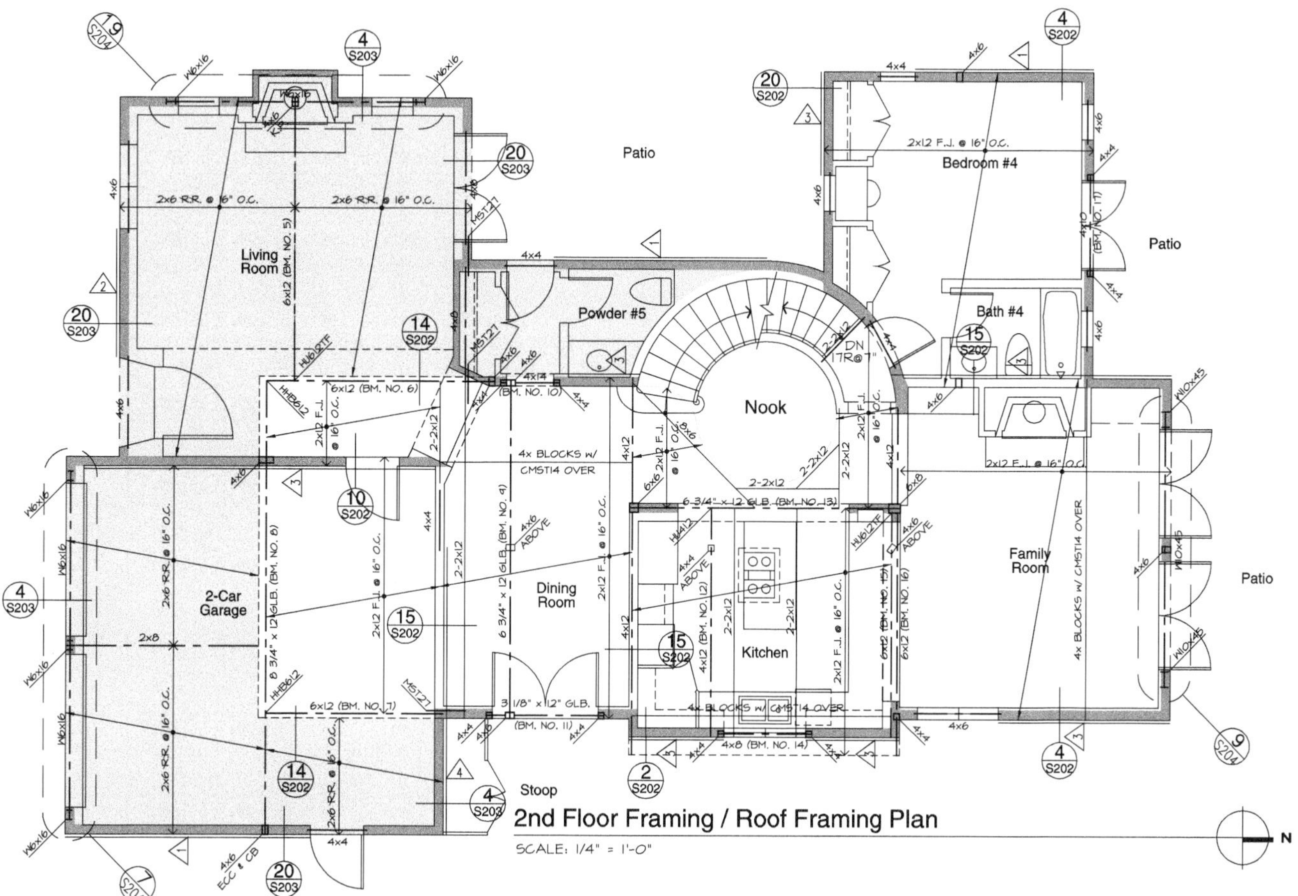

Shearwall Schedule

SYMBOL	PANEL	NAILING 8	WALL	SOLE PLATE ATTACHMENT			TOP PLATE 4 ATTACHMENT	HOLDOWN 5,6
		COMMON NAILS	LBS/FT	NAILS	LAGS 9	ANCHOR BOLTS 6		
△1	3/8 EXPOSURE I 7 (ID#24/0)	8d @ 6,6,12	198	16d @ 6" O.C.	3/8" x 5" @ 24" O.C.	5/8" DIA. @ 48" O.C. 12" LONG	A35 @ 24" O.C.	HD2A, CB44, FTA2 PHD2
△2 1	15/32 EXPOSURE I 7 (ID#32/16)	10d @ 4,4,12	299	16d @ 3.5" O.C.	3/8" x 5" @ 18" O.C.	5/8" DIA. @ 48" O.C. 12" LONG	A35 @ 16" O.C.	HD5A, CB44, FTA2 PHD5
△3 1,2,3 3x SILL	15/32 EXPOSURE I 7 (ID#32/16)	10d @ 3,3,12	450	40d @ 3" O.C.	3/8" x 5" @ 12" O.C.	5/8" DIA. @ 32" O.C. 14" LONG	A35 @ 12" O.C.	HD6A, CB44, FTA5 PHD6
△4 1,2,3 3x SILL	15/32 EXPOSURE I 7 STRUCT. I (ID#32/16)	10d @ 2,2,12	652	50d @ 3" O.C.	3/8" x 5" @ 8" O.C.	5/8" DIA. @ 24" O.C. 14" LONG	A35 @ 8" O.C.	HD8A, FTA7, PHD8

FOOTNOTES:

1. THESE PANELS TO BE 4-PLY MINIMUM.
2. 3x SOLE PLATES AND 3x FRAMING AT ADJOINING PANEL EDGES REQUIRED. STAGGER PANEL EDGE NAILING.
3. 1/2" MINIMUM EDGE DISTANCE REQUIRED FOR BOUNDARY NAILING.
4. A35'S NOT REQUIRED IF PANEL NAILS TO FRAMING MEMBER ABOVE TOP PLATES.
5. HOLDOWNS REQUIRED AT ENDS OF ALL SHEAR PANELS. USE 4x4'S FOR END MEMBERS. ALL HOLDOWN BOLTS TO BE TIGHTENED JUST PRIOR TO COVERING, INSPECTOR TO VERIFY. BOLT HOLES TO BE 1/16" MAXIMUM OVERSIZED AT THE CONNECTION OF THE HOLDOWN TO THE POST, INSPECTOR TO VERIFY.
6. SIMPSON BP WASHERS REQUIRED FOR ALL PLYWOOD SHEAR WALL SILL PLATE BOLTS AND HOLDOWN BOLTS.
7. OSB (ORIENTED STRAND BOARD) IS A WOOD STRUCTURAL PANEL.
8. SOLID BLOCKING SHALL BE PROVIDED AT ALL HORIZONTAL JOINTS OCCURRING IN BRACED WALL PANELS.
9. USE 3x BLOCKS AND 3x RIM JOISTS IF LAGS ARE USED.

Figure 11.94 Stage V: Complete floor framing plan.

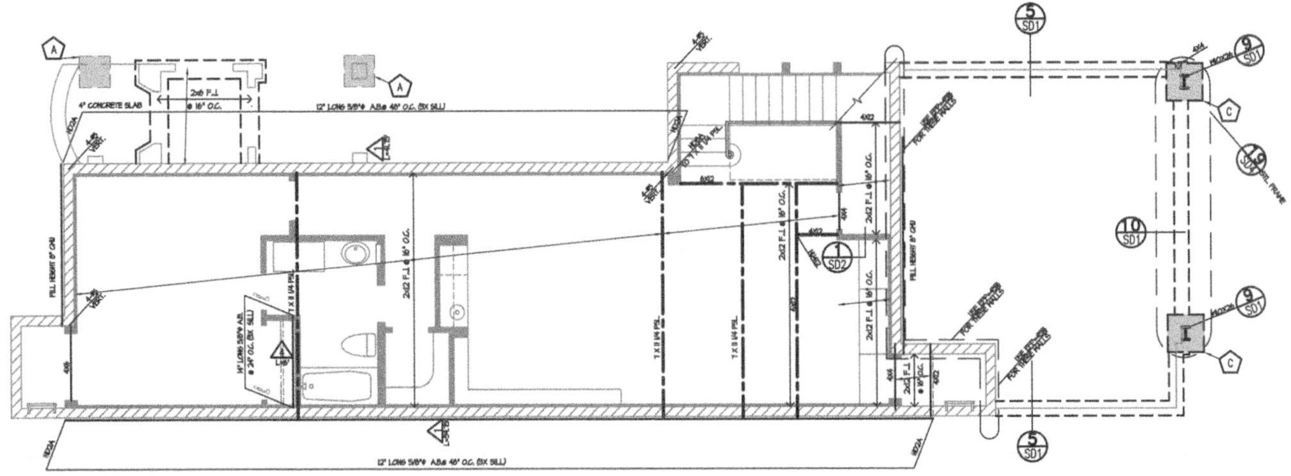

Figure 11.95 First-floor framing plan.

Figure 11.96 First-floor framing.

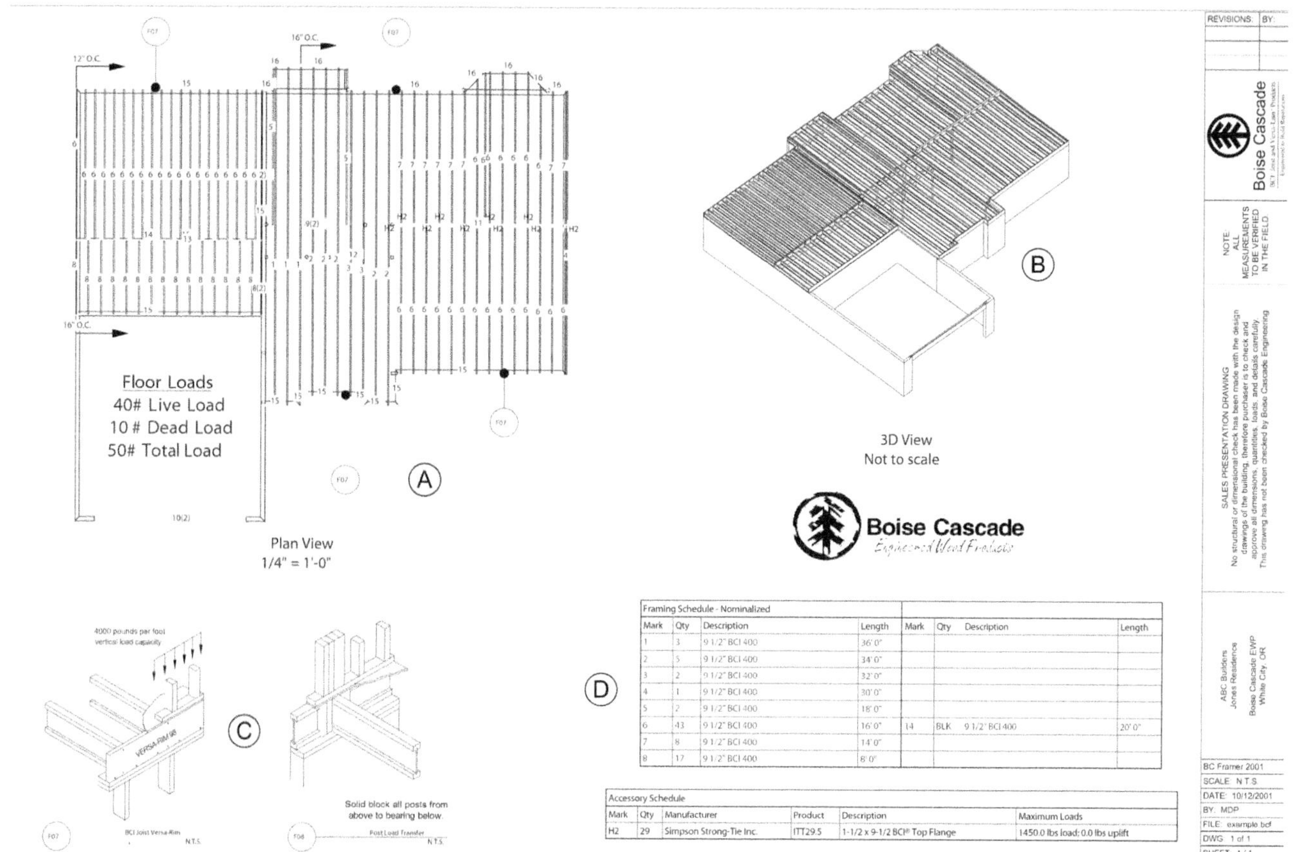

Framing Schedule - Nominalized

Mark	Qty	Description	Length	Mark	Qty	Description	Length
1	3	9 1/2" BCI 400	36' 0"				
2	5	9 1/2" BCI 400	34' 0"				
3	2	9 1/2" BCI 400	32' 0"				
4	1	9 1/2" BCI 400	30' 0"				
5	2	9 1/2" BCI 400	18' 0"				
6	43	9 1/2" BCI 400	16' 0"	14	BLK	9 1/2" BCI 400	20' 0"
7	8	9 1/2" BCI 400	14' 0"				
8	17	9 1/2" BCI 400	8' 0"				

Accessory Schedule

Mark	Qty	Manufacturer	Product	Description	Maximum Loads
H2	29	Simpson Strong-Tie Inc.	ITT29.5	1-1/2 x 9-1/2 BCI® Top Flange	1450.0 lbs load; 0.0 lbs uplift

Figure 11.97 Drawing by BC Framer. (Courtesy of Boise Cascade, Timber & Wood Products Division.)

chapter

12

ARCHITECTURAL DETAILS AND VERTICAL LINKS (STAIRS/ELEVATORS)

The Professional Practice of Architectural Working Drawings, Sixth Edition. Nagy R. Bakhoum and Osamu A. Wakita.
© 2024 John Wiley & Sons Inc. Published 2024 by John Wiley & Sons Inc.
Companion website: www.wiley.com\go\bakhoum\theprofessionalpracticeofarchitecturalworkingdrawings

■ ARCHITECTURAL DETAILS

Architectural **details** are enlarged drawings of specific architectural assemblies. These details are usually provided by the architect, and structural details are furnished by the structural engineer.

Architectural details are done for many different construction assemblies, including door and window details, fireplace details, stair details, and wall and roof assemblies. The number and kind of details needed for a given project depend entirely on the architect's estimate of what is needed to clarify the construction process. The contractor may request additional architectural details in the construction stage.

■ FREEHAND DETAIL SKETCHES

Architectural detailers can start with **freehand sketches** and an architectural scale in order to solve different construction assemblies in a structure. Once the details have been formulated in a scaled freehand sketch, they are then ready to be drafted in final form. Many details, such as standard foundation and wall assemblies, are relatively straightforward and do not require freehand sketches.

Architectural details encompass many construction assemblies, such as residences with unique foundation details. Such residences may have unusual geometric shape. Figure 12.1 shows a freehand sketch detail of an exterior bearing footing for such residence. There are some nonstandard conditions in this detail, such as steel anchor clips for connection of the floor joists to the mudsill (for lateral support), steel reinforcing placement in the wall for earth retention, and location of (and installation requirements for) a footing drain. Figure 12.2 shows a concrete floor condition below grade, and Figure 12.3 shows the wood deck connection to the exterior footing. Finally, Figure 12.4 shows an interior concrete-block wall and its foundation.

Figure 12.5 shows a square concrete pier and reinforcing bars required to support a heavy concentrated load distributed by a 6″×6″ post. Study each of these carefully before proceeding further.

If you are asked to detail a wood beam and masonry wall connection, with the required assembly information, first draw a freehand sketch that includes the necessary information. Figure 12.6 shows such a sketch. The size of the steel plate dictates the masonry wall offset, and the embedment of the anchor bolts is 10″.

An important factor in architectural detailing is providing details that are an integral part of the architectural design of the building. For example, if floor cantilevers and wood soffits are an integral part of the design (see Figure 12.7), first design and solve these assemblies in sketch form before completing the final detail. Creativity and craftsmanship in

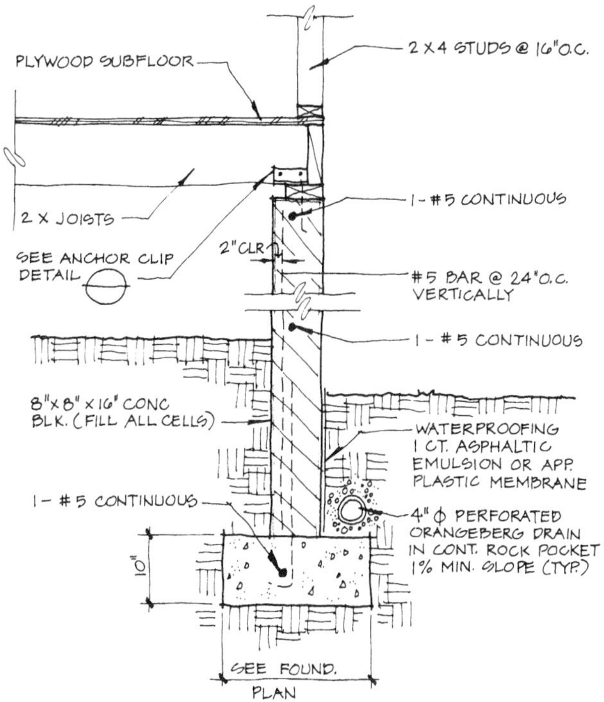

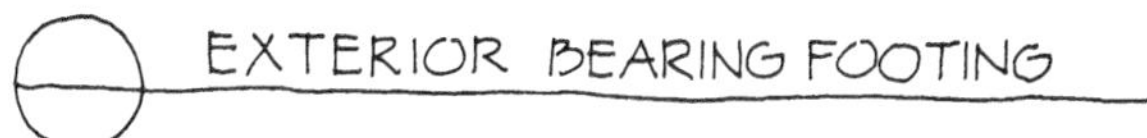

Figure 12.1 Detail of exterior bearing footing.

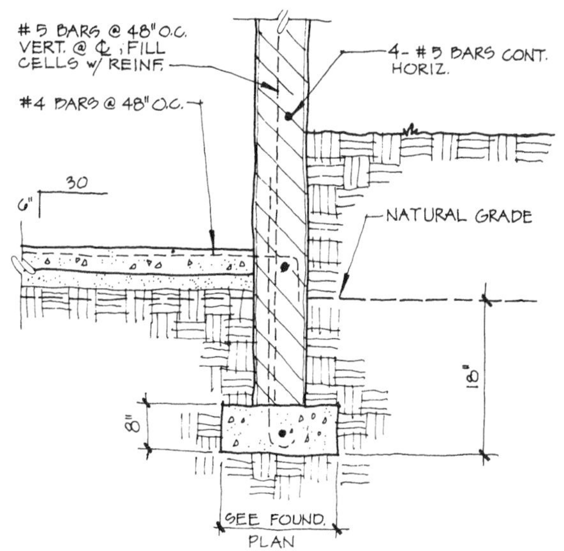

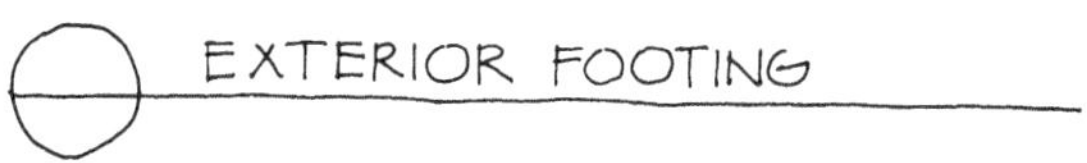

Figure 12.2 Detail of exterior footing.

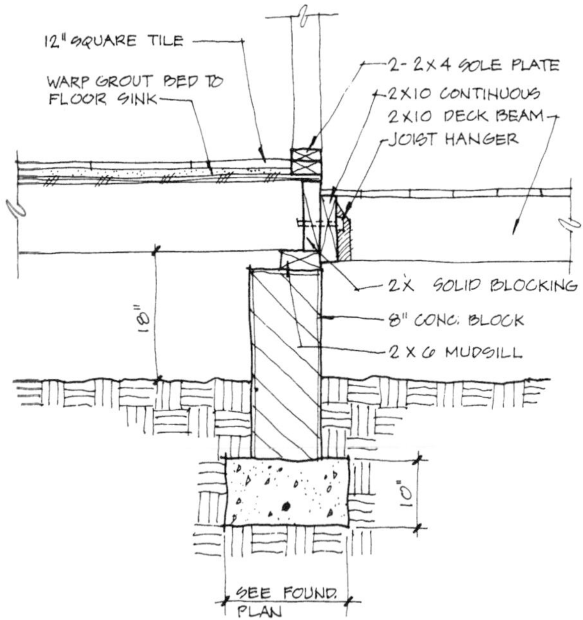

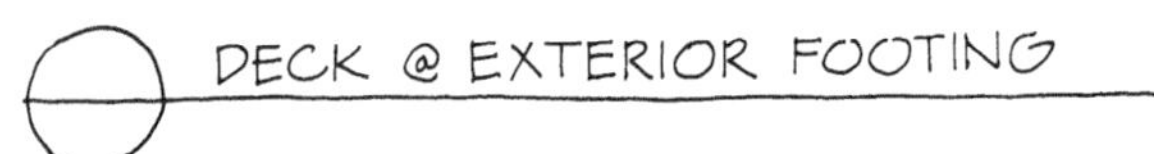

Figure 12.3 Detail of deck at exterior footing.

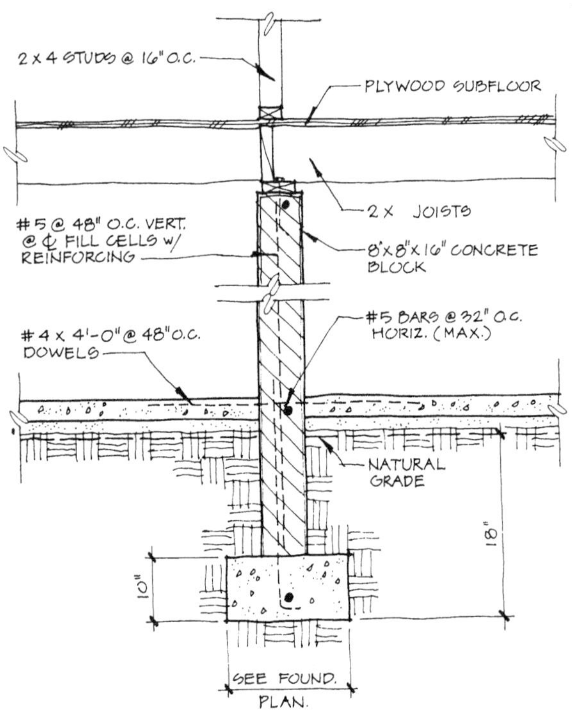

Figure 12.4 Detail of interior concrete-block wall.

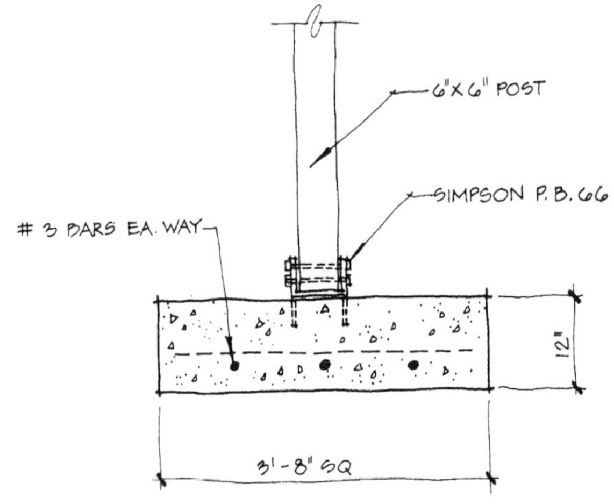

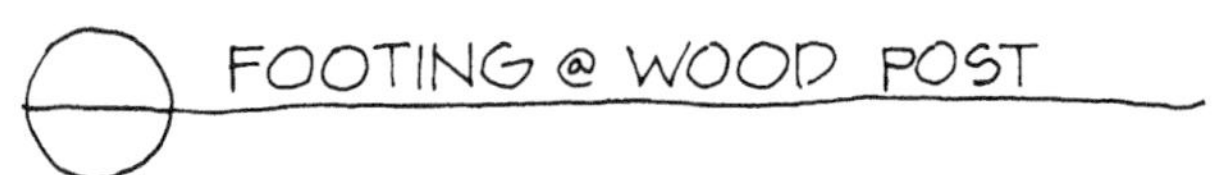

Figure 12.5 Detail of footing at wood post.

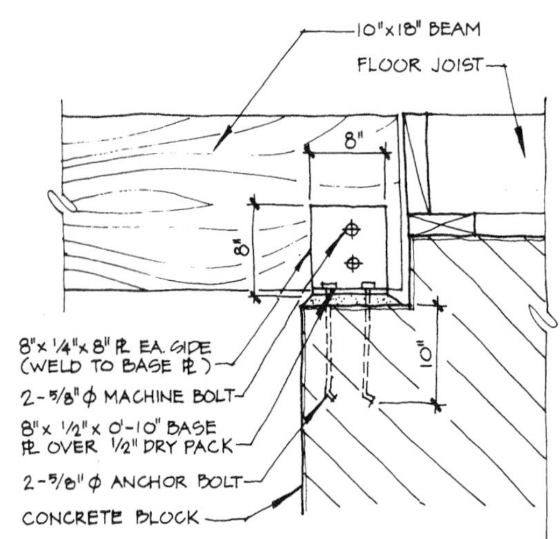

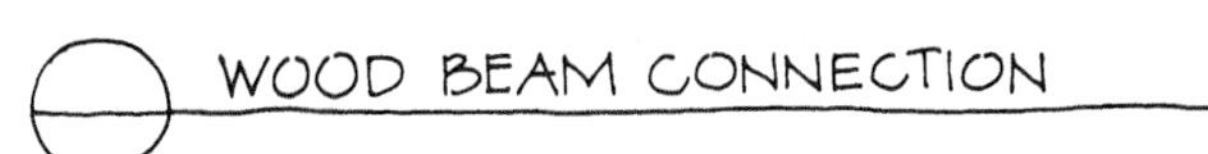

Figure 12.6 Detail of wood beam connection.

architectural detailing are as important as any other factors in designing a structure.

We sketched in detail the windowsill and exterior wall assembly projecting down from the head section. Using both Figures 12.7 and 12.8, it was possible to design and detail the jamb section for this particular opening, using the established head and sill section as a guide for the detailed assembly.

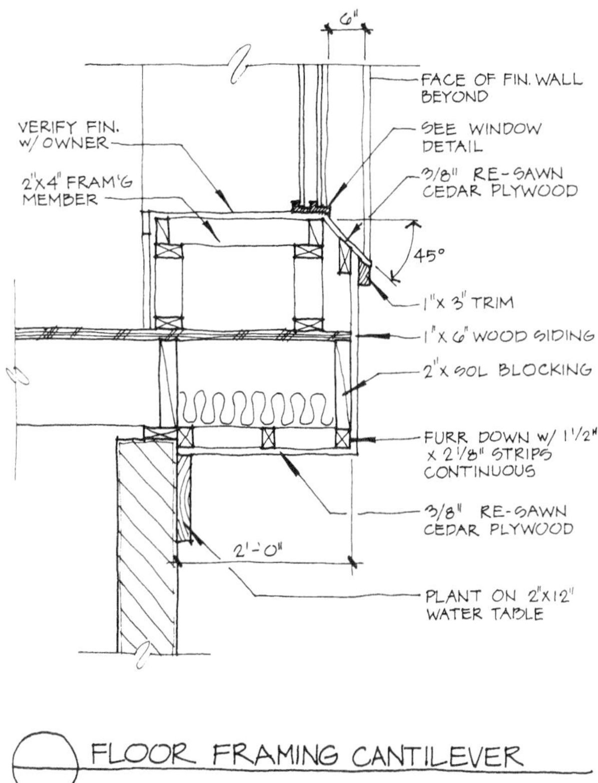

Figure 12.7 Detail of floor framing cantilever.

We sketched a foundation detail for a two-story residence to take into account the sandy soil conditions. Figure 12.9 shows a detail for the exterior bearing wall. Because this soil did not provide good bearing qualities, we used horizontal reinforcing rods at the top and bottom of the foundation wall. Non-bearing walls still required a minimal footing to support the weight of the wall and a depth of concrete to receive the anchor bolts. Because this residence has a change of floor levels, we provided a detail through the floor transitions. Figure 12.10 shows a detail at a location that has incorporated the risers and tread. The risers and tread are dimensioned, as are rebar ties for the connection of the upper concrete floor. (Rebar ties act as dowels to join two concrete elements.)

A large storage area and a mechanical room were located in the basement. A detail was needed to show the assembly for the basement and floor-level changes. See Figure 12.11. The wood stud wall has been offset in front of the upper-level concrete floor to provide a nailing surface for the wall finishes at both levels.

Architectural details for framing assemblies were also provided in these construction documents. One example is the eave detail. First, the project designer did a freehand drawing. The freehand drawing was then given to a drafter for final drawing. Figure 12.12 shows the freehand sketch. Figure 12.13 shows a study of a deck and handrail detail located directly above a recessed garage door. The deck assembly at the building wall is also detailed because proper flashing and drainage are needed to prevent water leaks.

Details: Clay Theater

In some projects, such as the theater structural complexities may dictate various construction assemblies. For example, a masonry and steel structure has many architectural details that are governed by structural engineering requirements.

The detailer must coordinate these details with the structural engineer. Figure 12.14 shows a detail for a steel beam connection, in which the beam, steel decking, and concrete-floor thickness have already been designed by the structural engineer. From these required members, the architectural detail is developed, showing wall materials, ceiling attachment, and under-floor space for mechanical and electrical runs. When critical information must be explained, or is explained on a separate sheet, the procedure is to add a note on the architectural drawing to "see structural." This refers the reader to the structural engineer's drawings, which provide such information as type and length of welds for steel connections, and size and weight of steel members. Note the call-out on the steel beam of "W 8×10." The "W" refers to the shape of the beam (here a **wide flange**), the "8" refers to the approximate depth of the beam (8 inches), and the "10" refers to the weight of the beam per linear foot (10 lb. per linear foot).

Some complex architectural details require much study before the finished detail can be drafted. In Figure 12.15 a trellis detail indicates the proportion of the wood beams to the column size and indicates a substantial scale and strong statement in the architectural design of the proposed system.

The eave and column detail shown in Figure 12.16 is intricate and shows the entire column assembly from the foundation to the roof, including the eave detail. Notes refer the viewer to other details for more information. Usually, it is unnecessary and unadvisable to repeat all the information from one detail to another, as changes made on one detail must also be made on any other affected details and drawings.

Many projects require a specific architectural detail to show conditions that will satisfy a governing building code requirement. Figure 12.17, for example, shows exactly where a fire protection coating is required under a steel roof decking that covers the structural steel angle on a masonry wall. This information is combined with a roof parapet detail. Figure 12.18 shows another detail for areas requiring fire protection.

A third example of a condition requiring a detail is of a disability ramp, which must show the required number of handrails, the height of the handrails above the ramp,

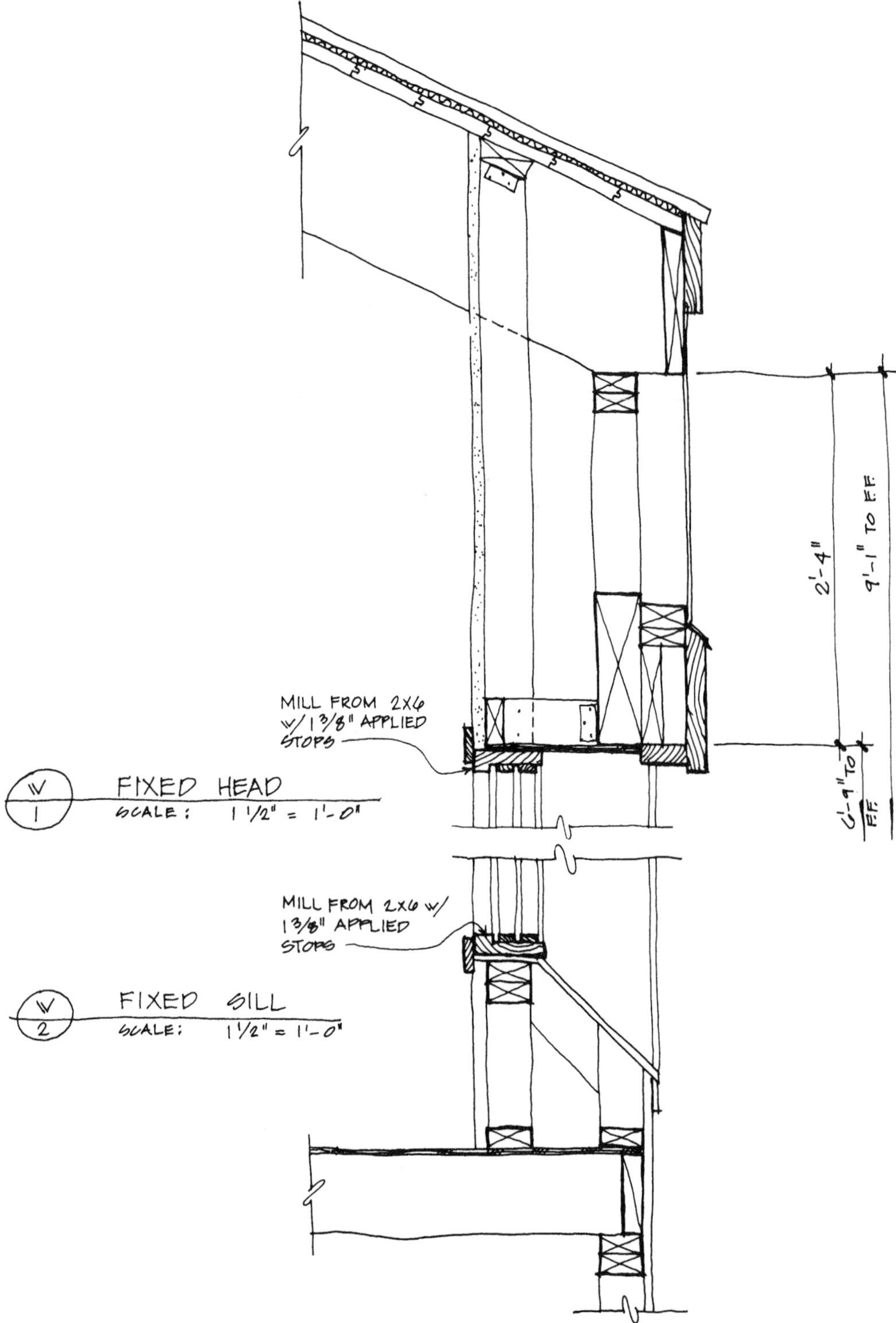

Figure 12.8 Detail of eave and window head sill.

and the clear space required between the handrail and the wall. This information is combined with the structural requirements for the support of a low wall on the outside of the ramp.

Before you hardline draft a detail, you must understand its primary and secondary functions. Although functions vary, they may be categorized within a few divisions.

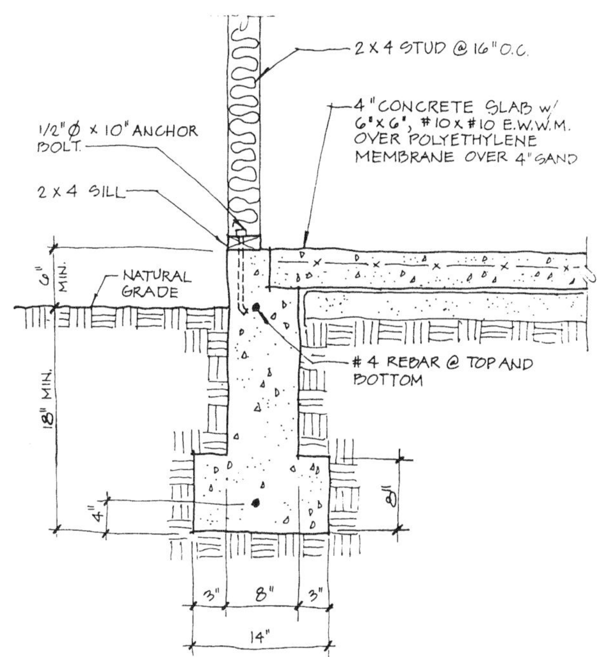

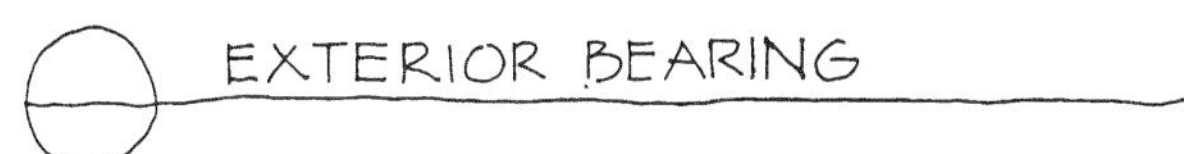

Figure 12.9 Detail of exterior bearing footing.

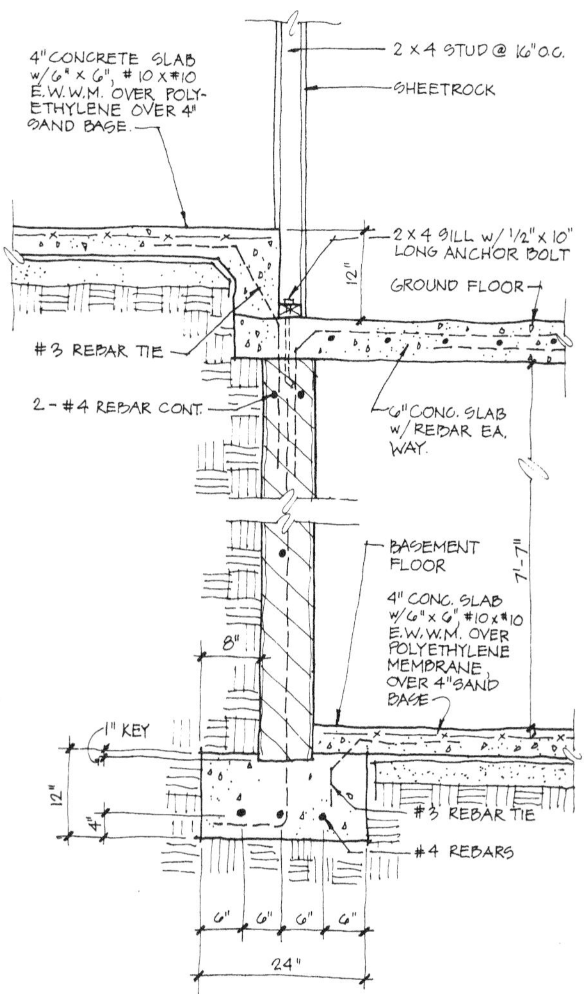

Figure 12.11 Detail of concrete-block wall at basement—slab.

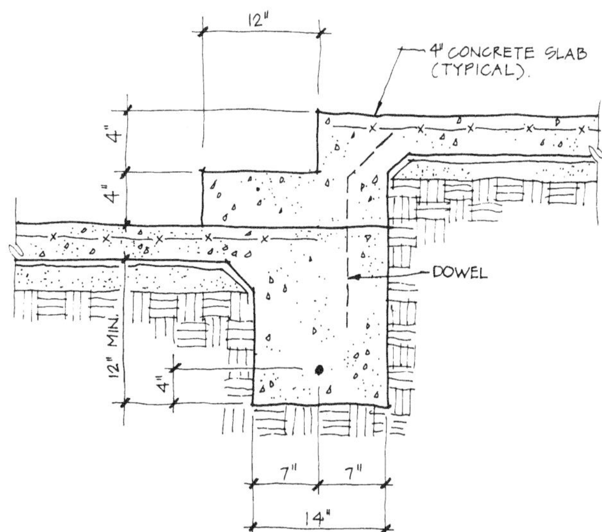

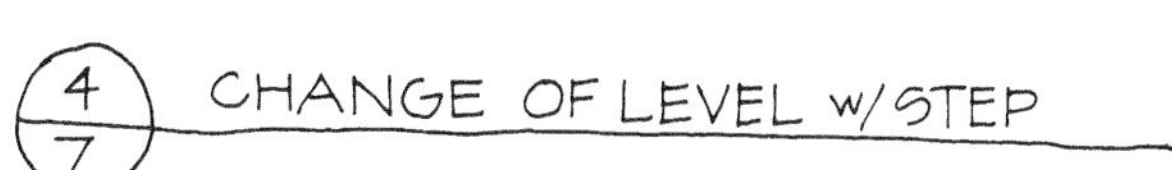

Figure 12.10 Detail of change of level with step.

A. *Structural*. The intent of a detail may be to reveal the method of connection between two structural members or to show the transition between wood and steel members and the connective device to be used between them.

B. *Architectural*. The purpose of a detail may be to ensure that a particular architectural feature is explained, to maintain a certain aesthetic quality of a part of the building.

C. *Environmental*. A detail may reveal how to deal with environmental and natural forces, such as sun, rain, wind, snow, and light, as well as human-made problems of noise, pollution, and so on.

D. *Human needs*. A detail may ensure that a particular human need is met. Stairs are a good example of this type of need, configured to allow a person to

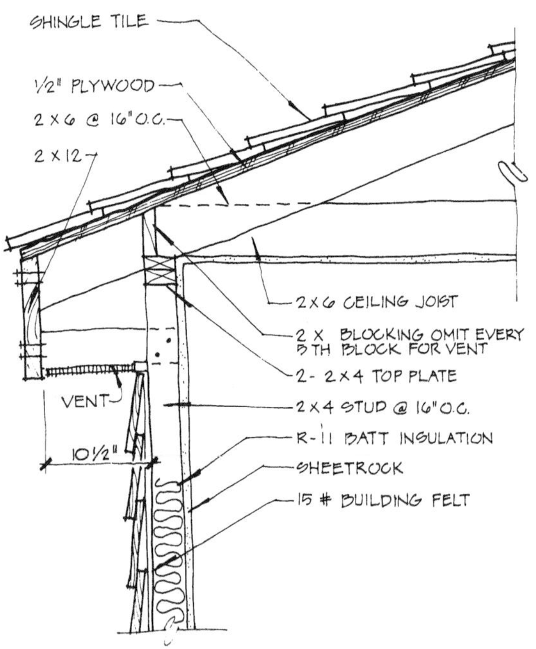

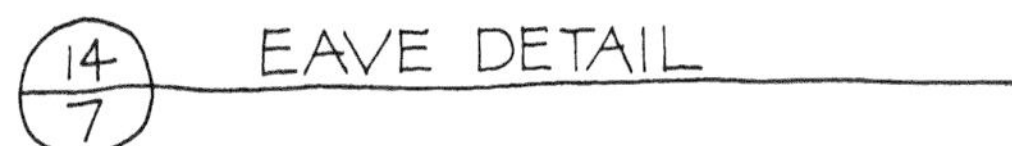

Figure 12.12 Eave detail.

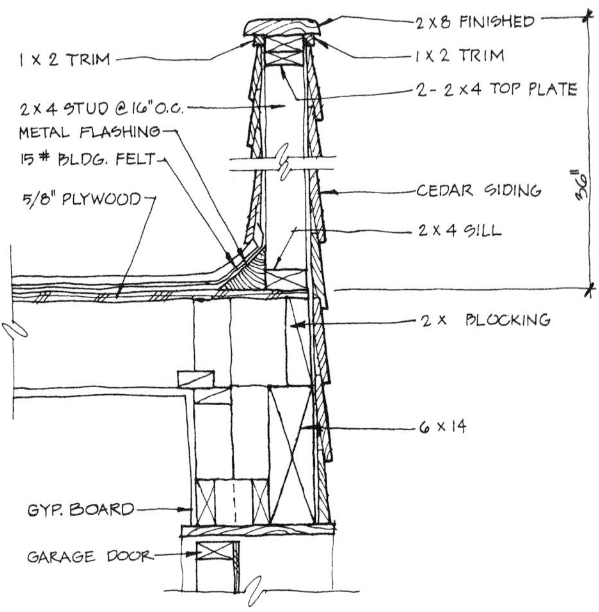

Figure 12.13 Detail of deck railing and header at garage.

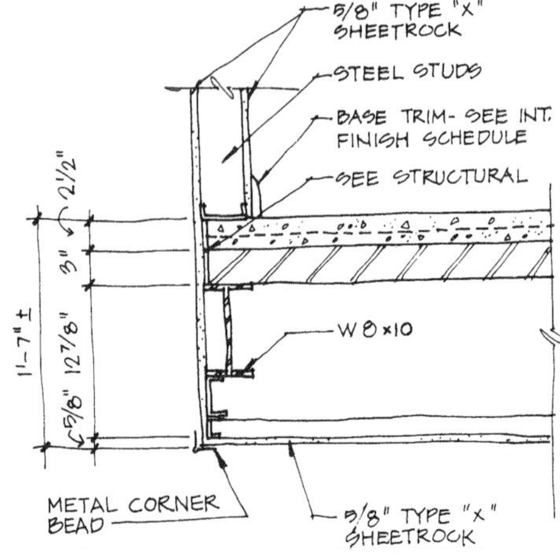

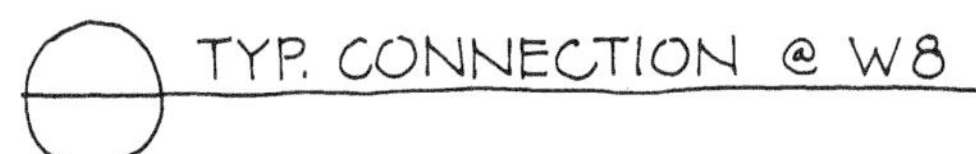

Figure 12.14 Detail of typical connection at a steel beam.

safely ascend or descend with the least amount of energy expended so as to avoid fatigue. This is done by formatting the proper angle of tread and riser. Special needs, such as those of elderly or physically challenge persons.

E. *Connection*. It is critical to detail a transition of one plane into another, for example, the connection between the wall and the floor or between the wall and the roof or ceiling.

F. *Material limits*. A detail may reveal the limits of the material with which you are dealing. You can drill a hole into a 2 × 6 floor joist, but how large a hole can you make before you weaken the member too much? The limits can be dimensioned or noted right in the detail.

G. *Facilitation*. In a tenant improvement drawing, a floor may be elevated to allow housing of computer cables. A detail can be drafted through this floor, showing the floor system support and the minimum clearances needed to accommodate the cables for maintenance and providing a level floor that meets ADA requirement.

■ DETAIL DEVELOPMENT

Detailing Based on a Proper Sequence

Step 1. The drafter can accomplish the crucial **blockout** stage by blindly copying the freehand sketch provided. Quickly outline the functional constraints of the detail, and check to see that the sketch complies.

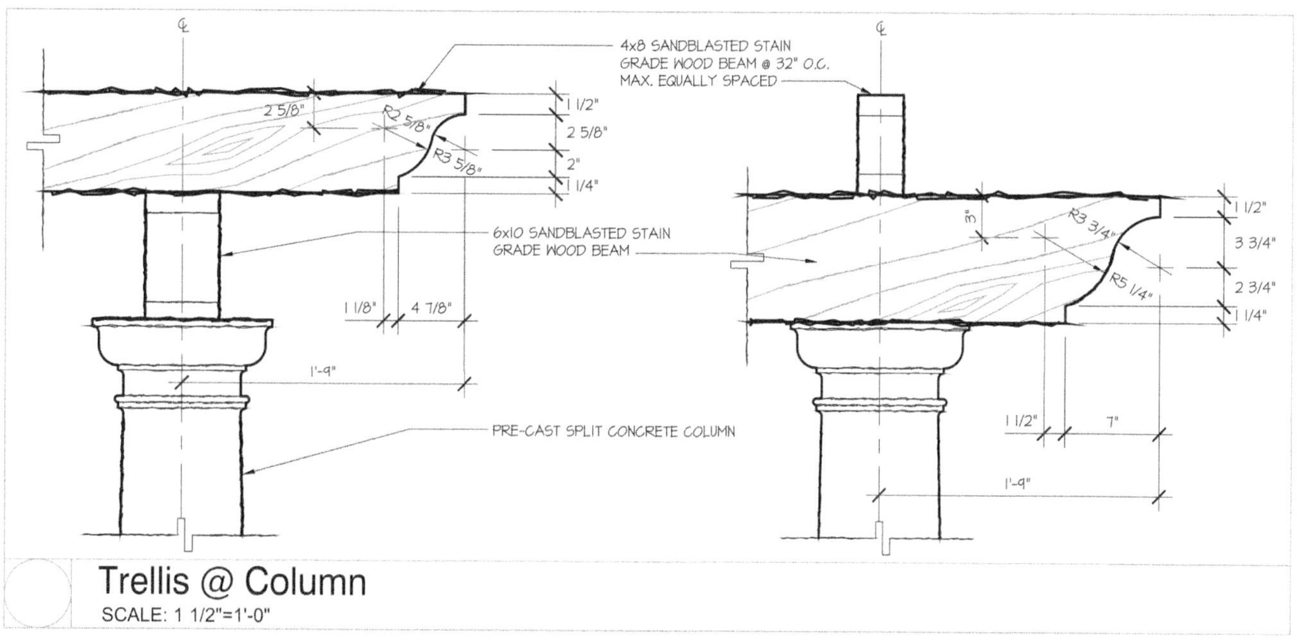

Figure 12.15 Trellis to column detail.

Step 2. Once you have laid out the most significant form, you can now draw its adjacent parts. For example, in drafting an exterior bearing footing for a wood floor system, do not draft the floor first and then add the footing; rather, draft the footing first as it is to be built.

Step 3. Add critical dimensioning.

Step 4. Strategically place notes so they clearly and easily convey the message.

Step 5. Designation of materials for the various pieces (wood, steel, earth, etc.) can be added at this point or at any of the previous stages.

Step 6. Profiling and **outlining** are almost synonymous. Darken the perimeter of the most important shape or shapes in the detail.

Step 7. Using the proper reference symbols, a title, and a scale so that each detail has an identifying "name" (title) and scale.

Sizing Details. If you are working with a 24″×36″ sheet of vellum similar to that formatted in prior chapters, and you extend the tick marks to form a matrix for detail placement, you will discover that the space measures 4⅝″ high×6½″ wide. These spaces can be doubled in both width and height, or in both directions, depending on the scale of the detail. Verify the office standard and apply it.

The drawing zone has been further subdivided into the drawing area and the note or keynote area. See Figure 12.19. The detail placed on one side allows the noting (done by CAD, word processor, etc.) to be done with ease. The drafter finishes the detail by drawing the leaders, thus connecting the notes with the drawing. See Figure 12.20. A further refinement is the use of keynoting. This refers to the practice of giving each note a number or a letter. When the detail is drafted, the leaders will use the corresponding number or letter pertaining to the note. See Figure 12.21. This method can be used by a manual drafter or by CAD, expediting the drawing procedure.

ARCHITECTURAL AND STRUCTURAL DETAILS

Footing Detail

The exterior bearing footing for a residence is not unlike the freehand sketch found in Figure 12.9—but evolved. The difference between one footing and another can be so subtle that it takes a trained eye to distinguish them. As you compare the freehand detail with the hardline detail shown in Figures 12.9 and 12.23–12.26, note the size difference at the bottom, the thickness of the foundation wall, the number of rebars, backfill, and sand versus gravel under the slab. These are two details that look alike but are really totally different in how they react to the various forces acting on them.

Before we hardline the exterior bearing footing for the residence, let's look at four considerations for this type of footing.

A. *Configuration.* Most typically used is a two-pour, inverted "T" shape. Through the years, the industry has found this to be the best distributor of weight

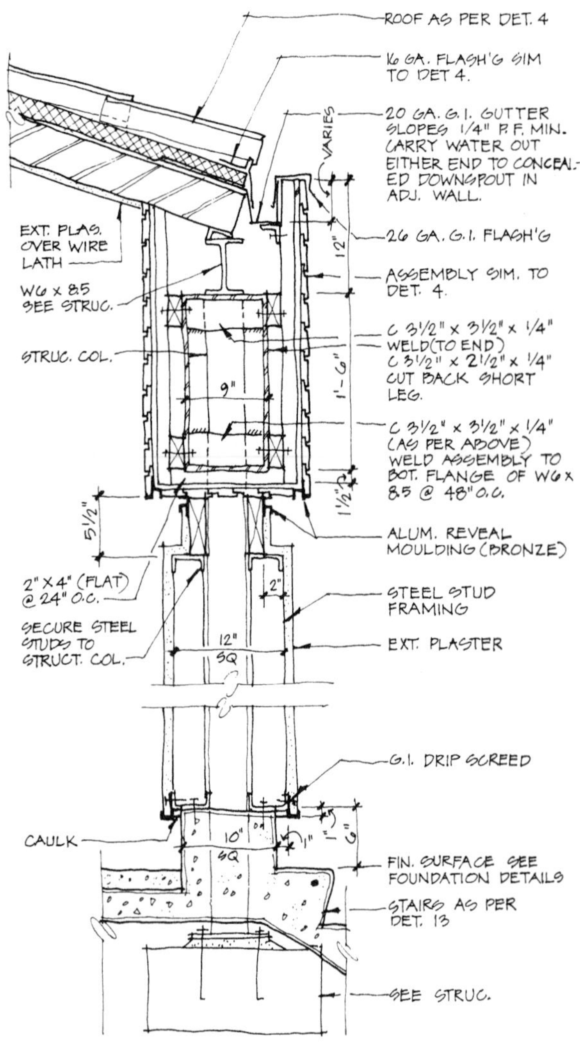

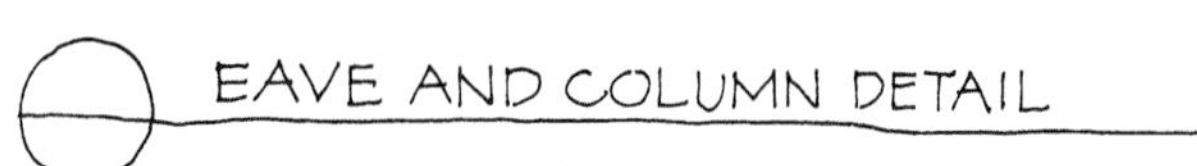

Figure 12.16 Eave and column detail.

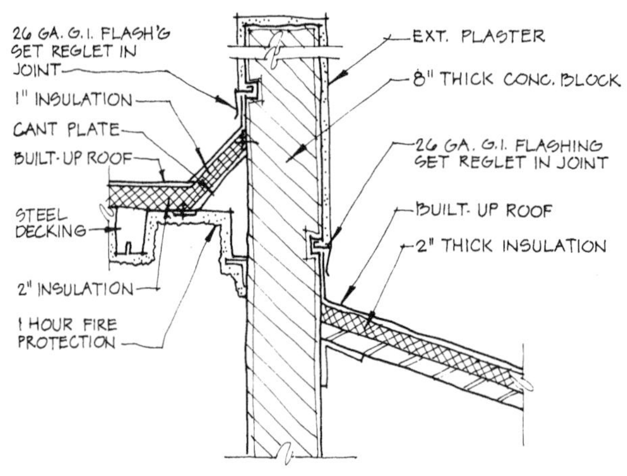

Figure 12.17 Parapet detail.

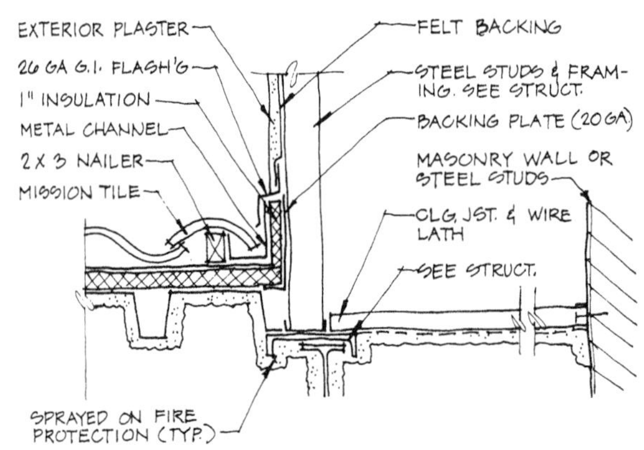

Figure 12.18 Base flashing detail.

that uses the least amount of material. The inverted T distributes weight over a vast area. Notice how the weight from above is distributed on the soil in Figure 12.22A. Surrounding the example are dimensions: "X" is based on the weight of the structure and the ability of the soil to hold up this weight.

As a rule of thumb, the thickness should be, as the example shows, ½X. The depth of the footing, marked "A," again depends on the stability of the soil or the frost line, or even a requirement of building officials, as a minimum. The prevailing attitude is, however, that rather than use established maximums, soundness of construction should prevail. The amount of the stem of the inverted "T" that extends above the soil might be a matter of how high it should be to keep moisture from the first piece of wood to come in contact with the concrete or to prevent termite infestation.

B. *Soil.* The cost of a piece of property might depend mostly on the view it provides, its convenience to various major streets, its slope, and so on, but many clients overlook the condition and quality of the soil. If a property has loosely filled soil (not permitted in many areas), the depth of the footing may have to extend far beyond the fill to firm soil, making the foundation very expensive. Moreover, in a marshy area where the **bearing pressure** of the earth (weight

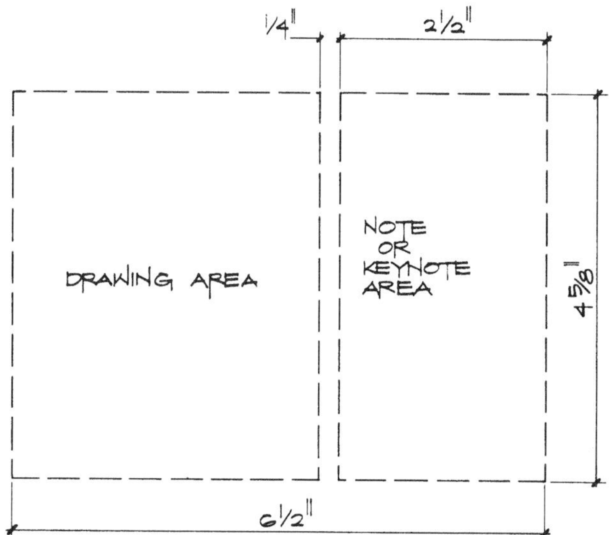

Figure 12.19 Detail format with noting area.

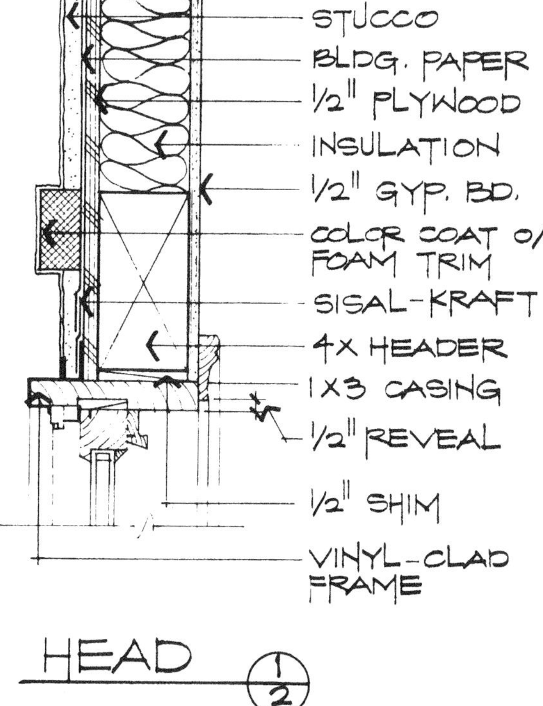

Figure 12.20 Window detail with noting format.

that can be put onto the soil measured in pounds per square foot) is minimal, the type and shape of the foundation may dictate a prohibitively expensive system, making the property impractical if not completely unbuildable. See Figure 12.22B.

C. *Energy*. In this era of energy-efficient buildings, architects are paying extra attention to areas through which heat is lost. The movement of heat, as any physics major will tell you, is from hot to cold. In colder weather, we must heat structures using resources that are available: natural gas, electricity. To keep it from leaving the structure, heat is contained by means of insulating floors, walls, and ceilings. Notice the various possible locations for insulation on the footing in Figure 12.22C.

D. *Strength*. Concrete, an excellent material with regard to **compression** forces, is very brittle in tension. The load imposed from above puts the concrete in compression, which is its strength. However, the footing travels the length of a wall, and with expansive soil or irregular loading, forms a beam that is in tension. This beam will break or shatter along the top or bottom, depending on the forces at work—thus the introduction of reinforcing bars, which are strong in tension, like a rope or chain, but rather weak in compression. By combining the two materials, we impart strength in both tension and compression. See Figure 12.22C.

There are numerous other factors to consider in designing a footing. Where should the plastic membrane be put (if one is to be used)? Between the slab and the sand? Below the sand? How is the thickness of the slab determined? Does it require reinforcing? Backfill is still another factor—how much? The list goes on and on, always depending on conditions at the proposed building site. The answers to these questions relate to strength, energy conservation as a reaction to soil, and/or to the selected building shape, as mentioned earlier.

Exterior Bearing Footing

Stage I (Figure 12.23). The grade line should be drawn first. This becomes the datum from which you establish all of the necessary vertical dimensions, such as the distance to be placed between the floor and the grade. The width of the footing (bearing surface) is the next item to be measured. Half this width is centered for the stem wall. Footing thickness and slab thickness are positioned, and finally the beginning of the stud above the stem wall is drawn to create the slot for the slab.

Stage II (Figure 12.24). After checking the accuracy of the first stage, proceed to the inclusion of the adjacent parts: insulation, sand or gravel, sill, the stud with its sheathing, and the termination points of the detail, which will be turned into break lines at a later stage.

Stage III (Figure 12.25). This stage is actually a combination of Stages 3 and 4, dimensioning and material designation. Be sure to use the correct designation of material for each of the seven or so different materials used here: plywood, batt insulation, rigid insulation, concrete, rebars, and so on.

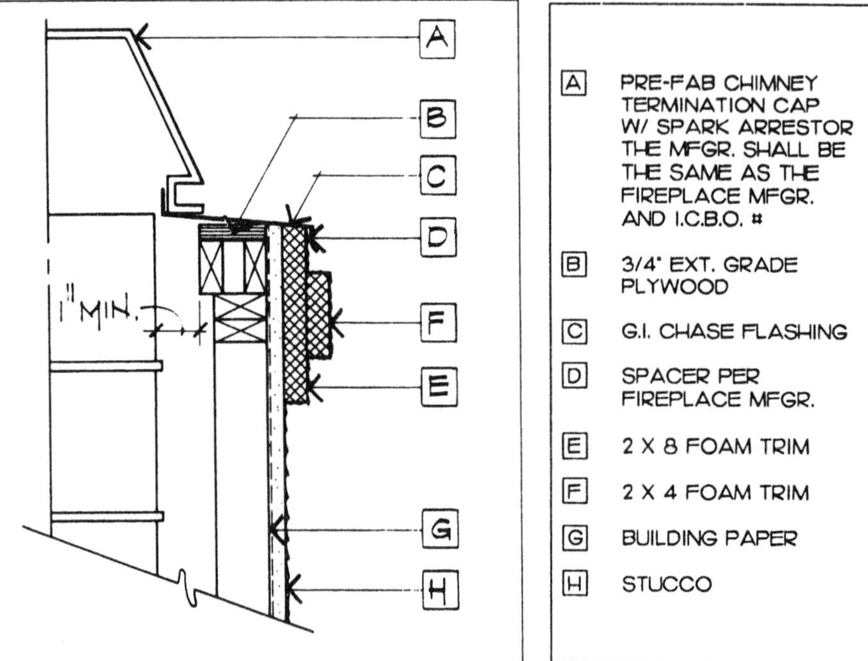

Figure 12.21 Chimney detail with keynoting format.

Stage IV (Figure 12.26). This is the final stage, which includes additional profiling and noting. To keep the noting consistent from detail to detail, many offices have a standard set of notes. The project manager may select the proper notes from this standard list and make them available to the drafter. In other offices, especially small offices, this practice may not be used at all; rather, the drafter is presumed to have the necessary training and ability to note a detail properly. Detailing on a CAD or BIM system is merely a matter of recalling the proper notes, which have been stored in the computer, and positioning them.

Window Detail

Before drafting a window detail, the drafter should understand the action of the window's moving parts, its attributes, the installation procedure, and how to prepare the surrounding area before and after installation.

The window selected for our sample residence is an Atrium double-tilt window. See Figure 12.27. It was selected because it is not the typical double-hung, casement, or sliding window, and because of its special features.

By studying the installation method, the detailer can better emphasize certain features of the detail. As seen in the original photograph (Figure 12.27), there are fins around the perimeter that are used to nail the window in place. Therefore, the rough opening (the rough framed opening) must have enough clearance to accommodate the preconstructed window. In this case, the clearance will be ½″ both vertically and horizontally, compensating for any irregularity in the framing members and allowing the window to be placed into the rough opening perfectly level and plumb. The wood shim under the windowsill in this sketch functions as a leveling device while sealing the space between the rough sill and the finished sill of the window.

Before and after the fin of the window is nailed to the wall, a moisture/vapor barrier is placed around the frame.

For the installation of this window, we use an asphalt-saturated kraft paper to cover the building and a secondary strip (a band of about 6″ to 8″) of heavily saturated, heavyweight kraft-type paper called sisal-kraft.

In Figure 12.28, note the positioning of the building paper and its secondary member, the sisal-kraft. Both sheets are placed under the fin on the jamb and both sheets over the fin on the head. This strategic placement acts to shed water and prevent its penetration.

There will be a raised plaster frame around each window. Such frames, called **stucco mold** (affectionately called **stucco bumps**), can be produced in a number of ways. Two possible solutions are described here. The first is to use one or more pieces of wood to raise the surface, as seen in Figure 12.29. Notice how the building paper is carried completely around the wood (including the metal mesh, which is not shown). The exterior plaster (stucco) follows the contour of the complete unit.

A second possible solution is the use of **Styrofoam**. See Figure 12.30. In this example, two pieces of foam

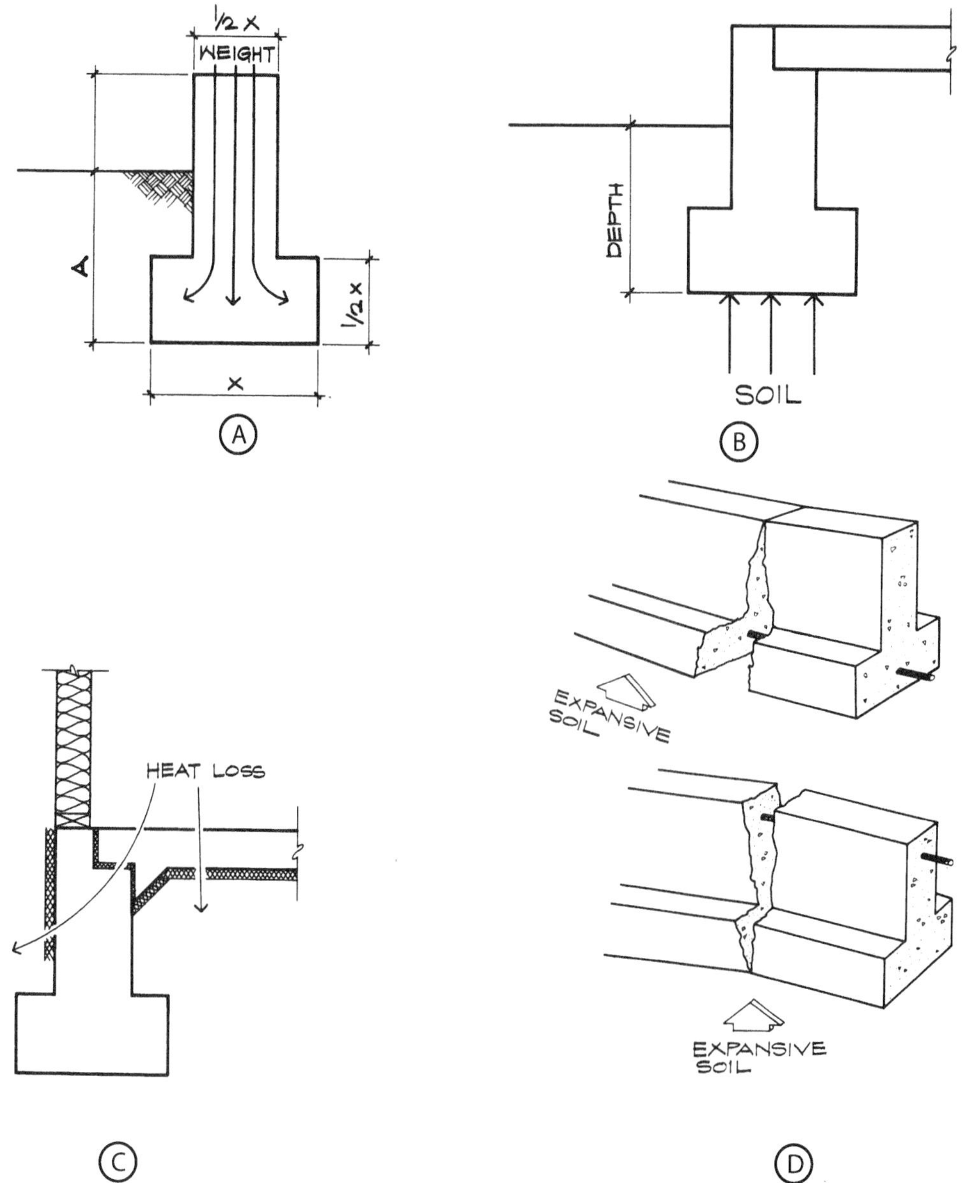

Figure 12.22 Footing concerns.

have been placed over the first two coats of stucco, which are called the **scratch coat** and the **brown coat**. The final coat (called the **color coat**) is placed over the entire unit, completing the image as a whole. Notice the position of the building paper. Figure 12.31 shows the placement of the building paper and the sisal-kraft (called **counterflashing**).

Rough Opening Size

Most manufacturers' brochures contain written descriptions of the window itself and its various features, the available stock sizes, suggested details depending on the context, and a drawing of the window at 3″ = 1′-0″ scale. For example, a DW2030 is really 19½″×29½″. Manufacturer drawings can be used as a tracer for hand-drafted, AutoCAD, or Revit details. As stated earlier, do not blindly use any suggested solutions, as the courts have determined that the manufacturer is not responsible for its performance. Instead, use the manufacturer's suggested drawings as a basis on which to adjust the drawing to meet local codes and waterproofing/weatherproofing requirements. Be sure to adjust the manufacturer's window drawing to 3″ = 1′-0″. See Figure 12.32.

Understanding that details are largely repetitive, it is imperative to start your detail library and build it as your career advances. While manufacturers provide details, or partial details, they must be modified to meet your

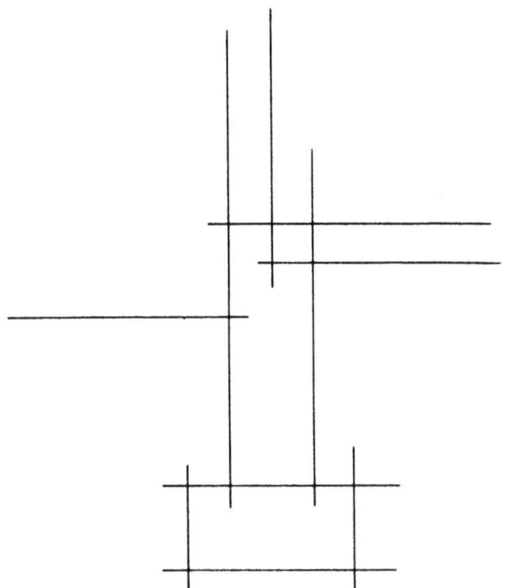

Figure 12.23 Stage I: Exterior bearing footing.

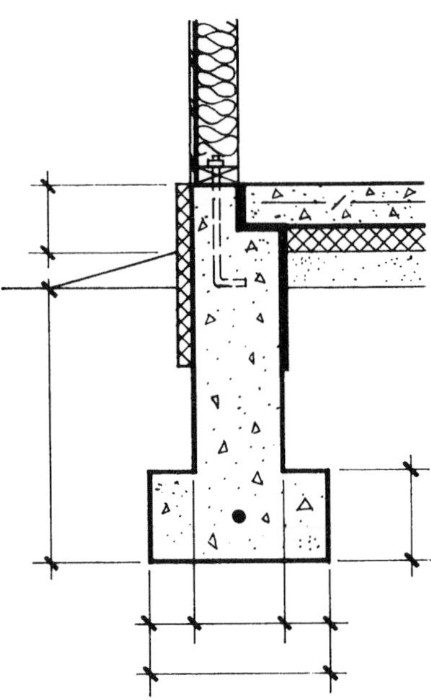

Figure 12.25 Stage III: Exterior bearing footing.

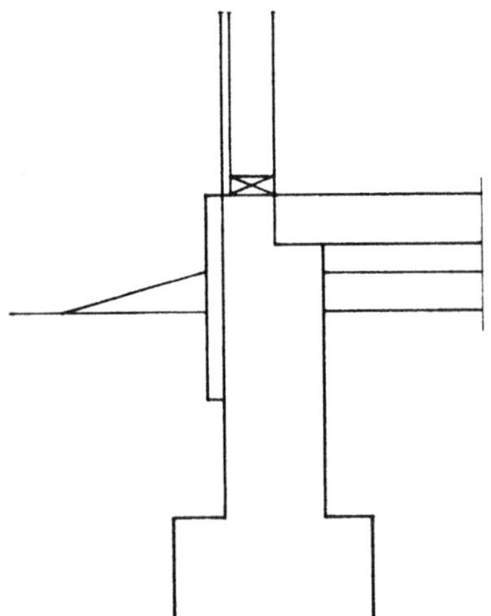

Figure 12.24 Stage II: Exterior bearing footing.

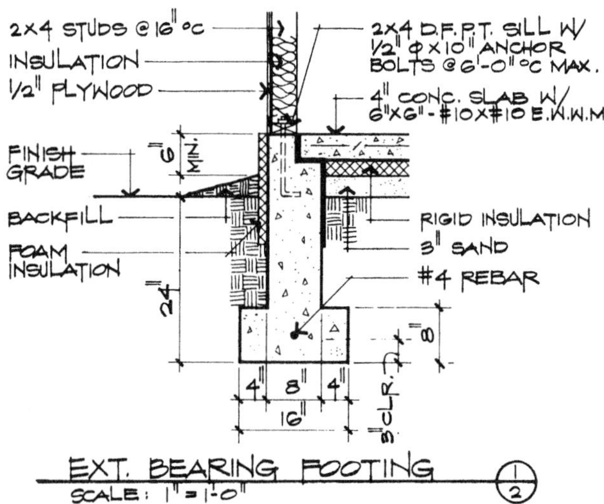

Figure 12.26 Stage IV: Exterior bearing footing.

specific application. Also beware if you use a manufacturer's detail this does not shift the liability from you to the manufacturer. Offices have large libraries of details from past jobs. These libraries are valuable to the office as similar scope, and style size projects will have common details needs or the base can be modified to alter the end result detail to accommodate for the specific job at hand.

If you consider the relatively few details that the building department requires, the details are an effective tool of the architect to communicate specific desires for the building. Details are a how to guide to the contractor. BIM is an excellent start to identifying locations of desired details and BIM creates a skeleton to work on, provide notation, and information to complete informative details.

Window Detail

Stage I The 3″ = 1′-0″ vertical section provided by the manufacturer's literature is downloaded to the computer. See Figure 12.33.

Stage II (Figure 12.34). The rough framing is drawn on the drawing of the window. Care must be taken in redrawing any important line that was inadvertently eliminated or has faded away. The fin is especially important.

Stage III (Figure 12.35). As we look at this detail, we should be able to see the lines of the jamb. To save time and for the sake of clarity, some offices do not put these lines into the detail. A true detail should include such lines, hence our choice to include them here.

Figure 12.27 Atrium double-tilt window. (Courtesy of the Atrium Door & Window Company, a division of Fojtasek Companies, Inc.)

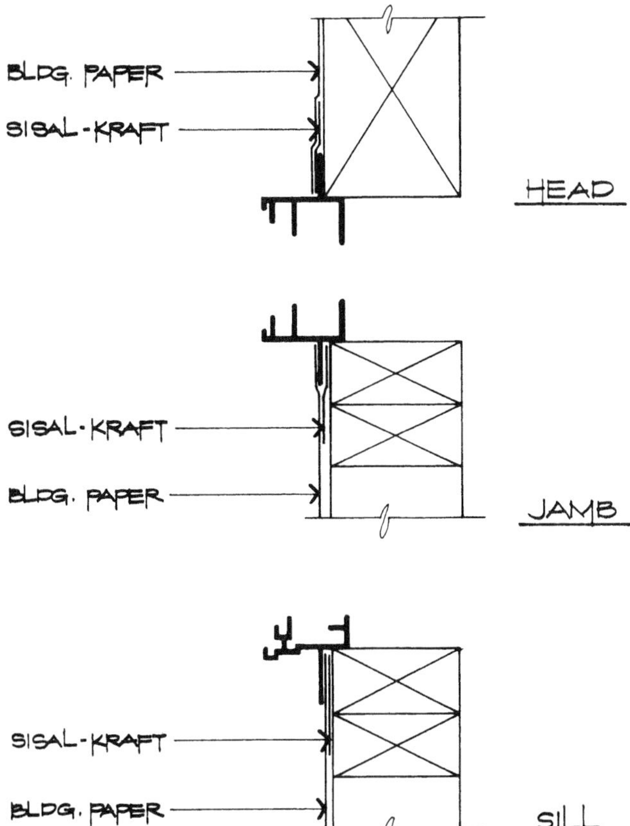

Figure 12.28 Placement of building paper around window.

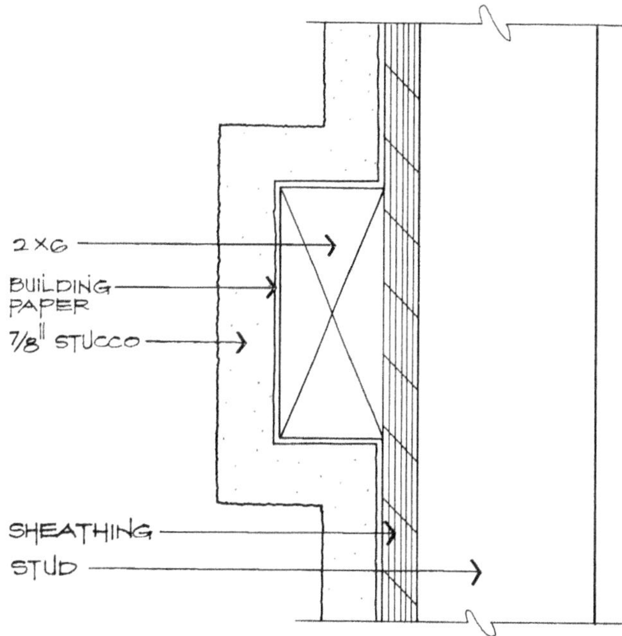

Figure 12.29 Raised surface using wood as a backing.

The interior and exterior wall coverings (skin) were drafted at this stage. Note the lining of the building felt over the fin for moisture control and the inclusion of insulation below the header. Finally, the raised window frame is drafted.

Stage IV (Figure 12.36). Noting and referencing complete the detail. The positioning of notes is critical for ease of reading. Do not only crowd the detail, but also avoid long leaders. Be sure to create a margin for uniformity of appearance. The detail style is referred to as **freestyle**, with noting scattered around the perimeter.

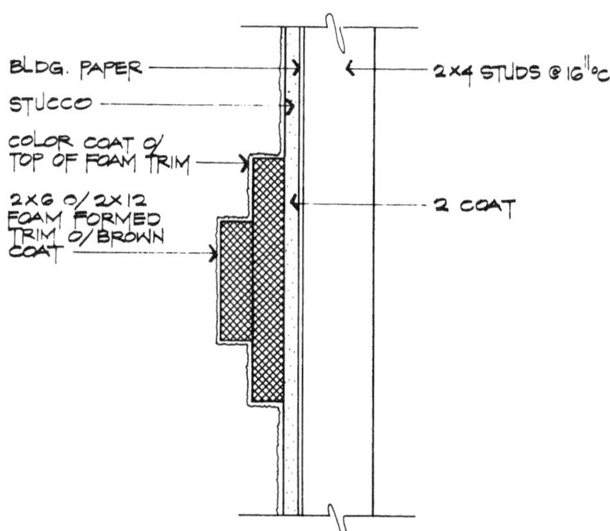

Figure 12.30 Raising a surface with foam.

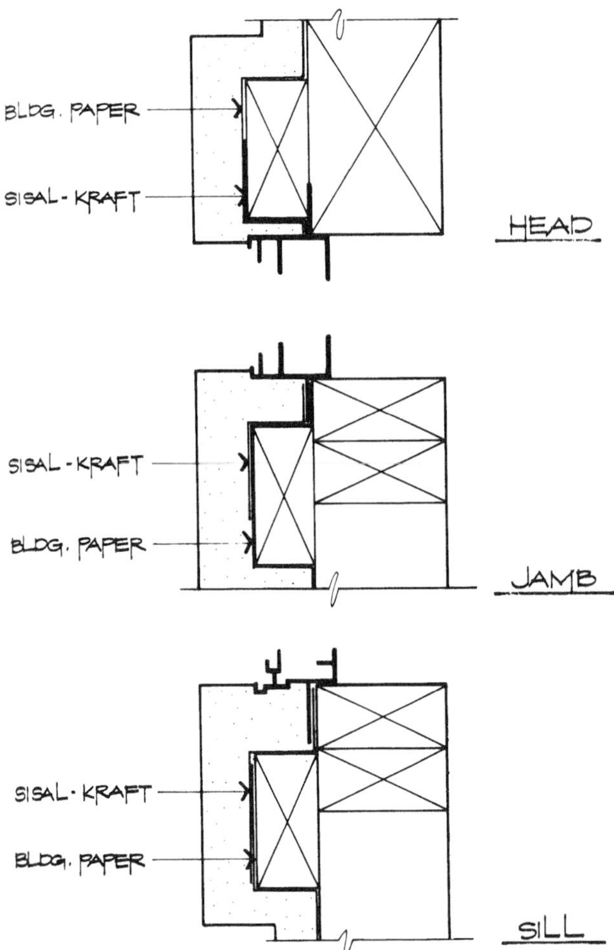

Figure 12.31 Raised frame of wood.

STAIRS AND OTHER VERTICAL LINKS

Fireplace

Fireplaces have gone through quite an evolution over the past century: from masonry fireplaces, which are still built, to metal; from fully vented fireplaces using chimneys to those that have no vent at all. Some varieties burn wood as fuel; others burn natural gas or, more recently, gelled alcohol. Wood-burning fireplaces are not allowed by some municipalities.

Fireplaces can be built to use remote control starters; an application in your phone can be utilized. They can also be constructed to recirculate warm air. Fireplaces can be made to look like fireplaces or designed to look like furniture. Portable fireplaces, which burn gelled alcohol, can be moved from room to room, much the way furniture is rearranged. When you move, you take the fireplace with you.

Many metal fireplaces are fitted with pockets for recirculating air. The air around the fire chamber is heated and redirected back into the room. You can even have a thermostat-controlled blower installed, which increases the movement of the warm air, thus achieving greater efficiency in heat circulation. This means that 20,000–75,000 Btu/hr. of heat can be recaptured. See Figure 12.37.

For the sake of this discussion, fireplaces are categorized as follows:

Standard Fireplace. Often built of concrete block, fire brick, or stone. The normal masonry units that are usually job-built and require the detailer to draft the fireplace from the throat.

Prefabricated Fireplaces. Built of steel, with the chimney built of double- or triple-wall units that snap together. A typical unit can be seen in Figures 12.37 and 12.38. The Majestic 42 unit was selected for its heat-circulating features.

Direct-Vented Fireplaces. Built of steel and similar to the prefabricated fireplaces previously described, except that they are vented directly out an adjacent wall. See Figures 12.39 and 12.40. Note the uninterrupted windows surrounding the fireplace in the photograph.

Portable Fireplaces. Made of metal and built much like an oven, so that the outer surface gets warm but not hot to the touch. It can be housed in a cabinet like a television set, and uses a clean-burning gelled alcohol.

Much like the Atrium window discussed earlier, this fireplace has a metal fin (tab) around the perimeter of the front face that can be nailed to the surrounding framing. The metal fireplace must not come into contact with the framing around it. The manufacturer suggests a minimum clearance of about 2″, but the local codes should be checked.

The chimney is a triple-wall unit and does not necessarily go straight up through the ceiling and/or roof. Bends of 30° can be incorporated as the chimney goes through the space provided. This space, called the **chimney chase**, allows the chimney to pierce the ceiling or roof at a convenient point, so as not to interrupt the plane of the roof at an intersection (such as a valley) or to bypass a beam or other structural member. See Figure 12.41. Straps are then used to stabilize the chimney to the adjacent framing members. See Figure 12.42. Note the inclusion of a recommended 2″ clearance space.

A firestop spacer should be used on top of the ceiling joist or on the underside of the roof joist when there is an attic space. See Figure 12.43.

The total area around the opening (**chase**) should be insulated even if the wall is an inside wall. If the fireplace is on a second floor or on a first floor constructed

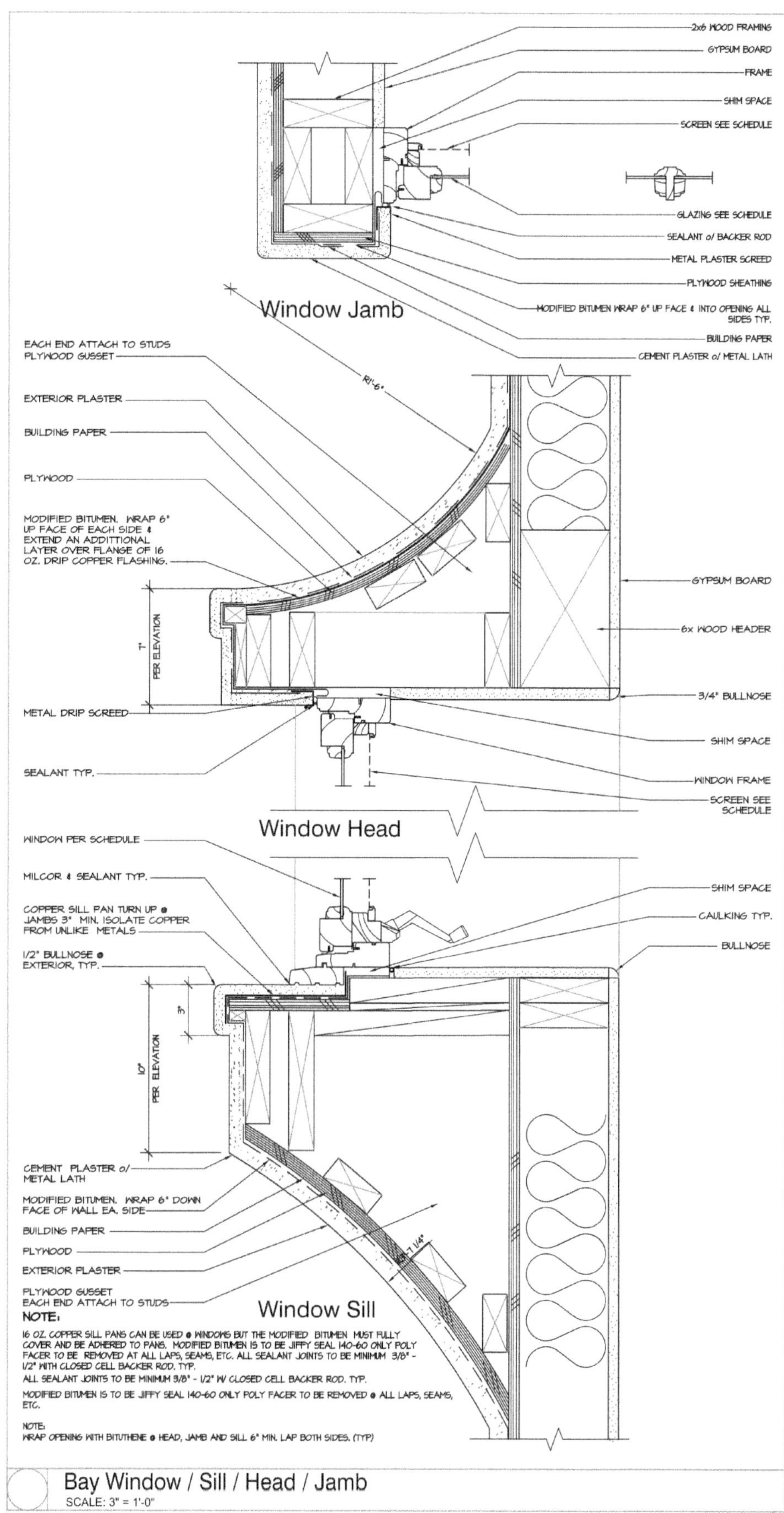
2x6 WOOD FRAMING
GYPSUM BOARD
FRAME
SHIM SPACE
SCREEN SEE SCHEDULE
GLAZING SEE SCHEDULE
SEALANT o/ BACKER ROD
METAL PLASTER SCREED
PLYWOOD SHEATHING
MODIFIED BITUMEN WRAP 6" UP FACE & INTO OPENING ALL SIDES TYP.
BUILDING PAPER
CEMENT PLASTER o/ METAL LATH
Window Jamb
EACH END ATTACH TO STUDS
PLYWOOD GUSSET
R1'-6"
EXTERIOR PLASTER
BUILDING PAPER
PLYWOOD
MODIFIED BITUMEN. WRAP 6" UP FACE OF EACH SIDE & EXTEND AN ADDITTIONAL LAYER OVER FLANGE OF 16 OZ. DRIP COPPER FLASHING.
GYPSUM BOARD
7" PER ELEVATION
6x WOOD HEADER
3/4" BULLNOSE
METAL DRIP SCREED
SHIM SPACE
SEALANT TYP.
WINDOW FRAME
SCREEN SEE SCHEDULE
Window Head
WINDOW PER SCHEDULE
MILCOR & SEALANT TYP.
SHIM SPACE
COPPER SILL PAN TURN UP @ JAMBS 3" MIN. ISOLATE COPPER FROM UNLIKE METALS
CAULKING TYP.
BULLNOSE
1/2" BULLNOSE @ EXTERIOR, TYP.
3"
10" PER ELEVATION
CEMENT PLASTER o/ METAL LATH
MODIFIED BITUMEN. WRAP 6" DOWN FACE OF WALL EA. SIDE
BUILDING PAPER
PLYWOOD
7 1/4"
EXTERIOR PLASTER
PLYWOOD GUSSET
EACH END ATTACH TO STUDS
Window Sill
NOTE:
16 OZ. COPPER SILL PANS CAN BE USED @ WINDOWS BUT THE MODIFIED BITUMEN MUST FULLY COVER AND BE ADHERED TO PANS. MODIFIED BITUMEN IS TO BE JIFFY SEAL 140-60 ONLY POLY FACER TO BE REMOVED AT ALL LAPS, SEAMS, ETC. ALL SEALANT JOINTS TO BE MINIMUM 3/8" - 1/2" WITH CLOSED CELL BACKER ROD. TYP.
ALL SEALANT JOINTS TO BE MINIMUM 3/8" - 1/2" W/ CLOSED CELL BACKER ROD. TYP.
MODIFIED BITUMEN IS TO BE JIFFY SEAL 140-60 ONLY POLY FACER TO BE REMOVED @ ALL LAPS, SEAMS, ETC.
NOTE:
WRAP OPENING WITH BITUTHENE @ HEAD, JAMB AND SILL 6" MIN. LAP BOTH SIDES. (TYP)
Bay Window / Sill / Head / Jamb
SCALE: 3" = 1'-0"

Figure 12.32 Bay window detail sill/head/jamb.

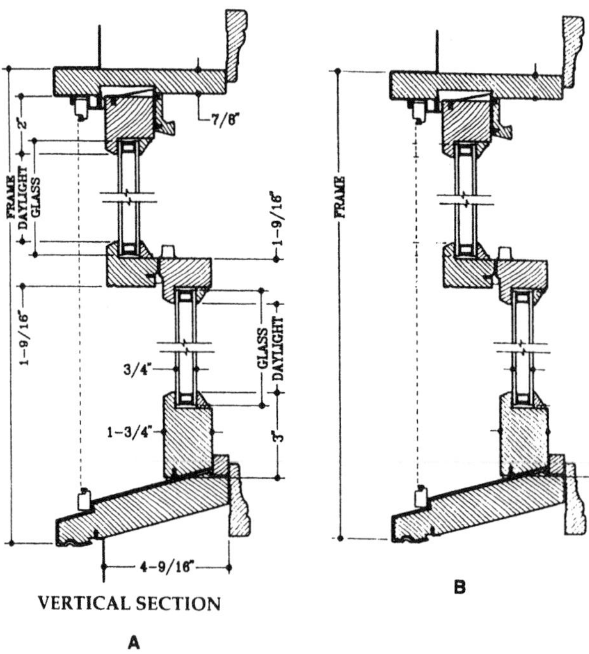

Figure 12.33 3″ = 1′-0″ drawing by manufacturer.

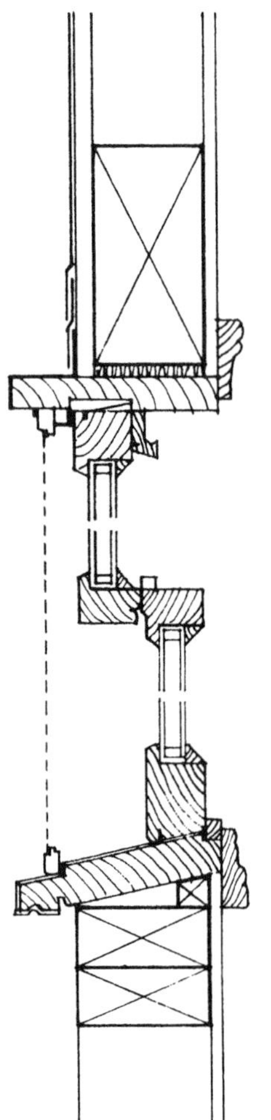

Figure 12.34 Laying out the rough frame.

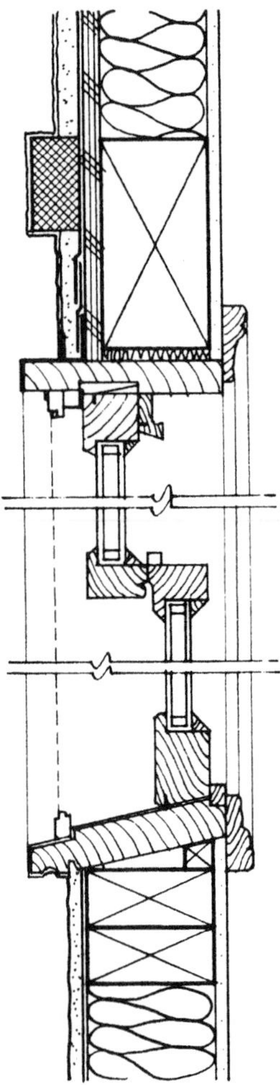

Figure 12.35 Applying the interior and exterior skin onto the wall surface.

of wood, the space under the fireplace should also be insulated. In fact, it is always best to read the installation manual before detailing the framework around the structure.

The walls around a prefabricated fireplace are framed in the same way as all other walls. Even the opening for the fireplace is framed in the same manner as other openings, such as doors, skylights, windows, and so on. See Figure 12.44–12.46 for fireplace framing, model and section.

Figure 12.31 shows the placement of the building paper and the sisal-kraft (called **counterflashing**). In most cases, a chimney must rise 2 feet higher than the highest part of the roof within a 10-foot radius. See Figure 12.47. There are a number of ways of terminating the chimney above the roof. A round top termination, as seen in Figure 12.48, can be used to "top it off," and the finish will be left in this state. A second possibility is to purchase a constructed metal chase to cover this metal termination. A third suggestion is to use a wood chase with an Underwriters Laboratory (UL)-listed constructed cap.

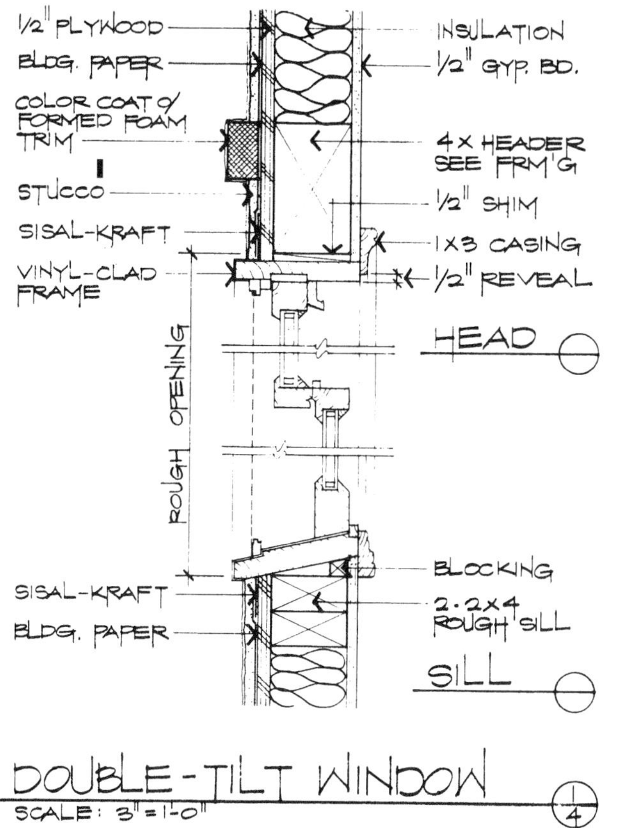

Figure 12.36 Noting and finishing the window detail.

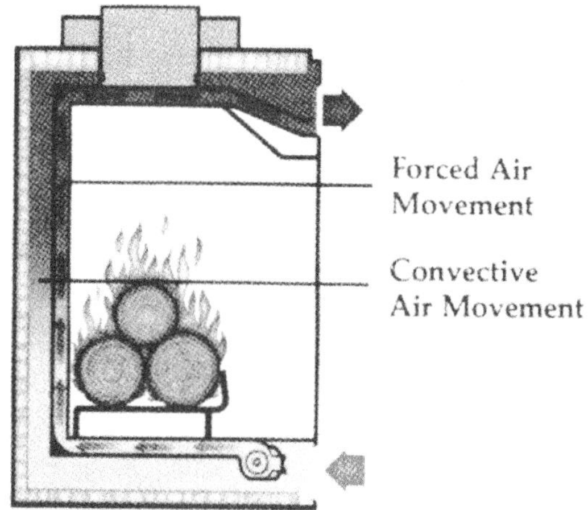

Figure 12.37 Heat circulation. (Courtesy of Majco Building Specialties, LP.)

Development of the Fireplace

In four stages:

Stage I (Figure 12.49). Start with the context. Detail the plate line, floor line, wall, and roof outline. These lines establish the parameters within which the detailer can explore the framing members and place the prefabricated fireplace.

Figure 12.38 Majestic heat-circulating fireplace. (Courtesy of Majco Building Specialties, LP.)

Figure 12.39 Majestic wall-vented fireplace. (Courtesy of Majco Building Specialties, LP.)

Stage II (Figure 12.50). The ceiling joists and rafters are sized and positioned according to the framing plan. Because this is not a masonry fireplace, the drafter need not be concerned with a foundation. (For drafting

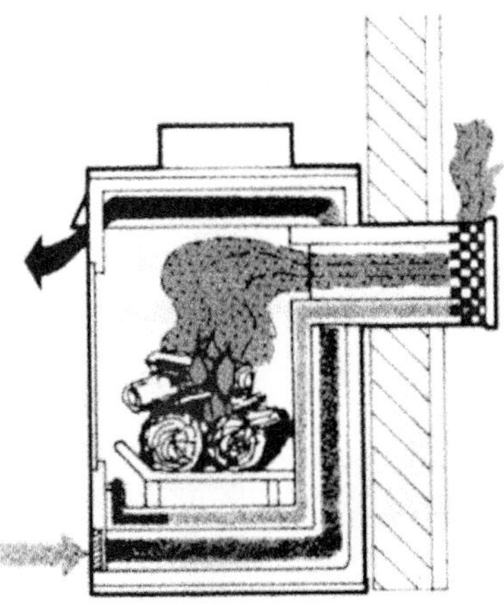

Figure 12.40 Wall-vented schematic. (Courtesy of Majco Building Specialties, LP.)

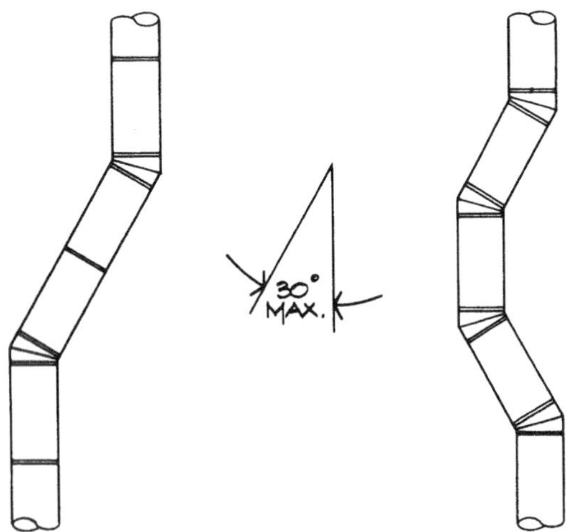

Figure 12.41 Bends in chimney section.

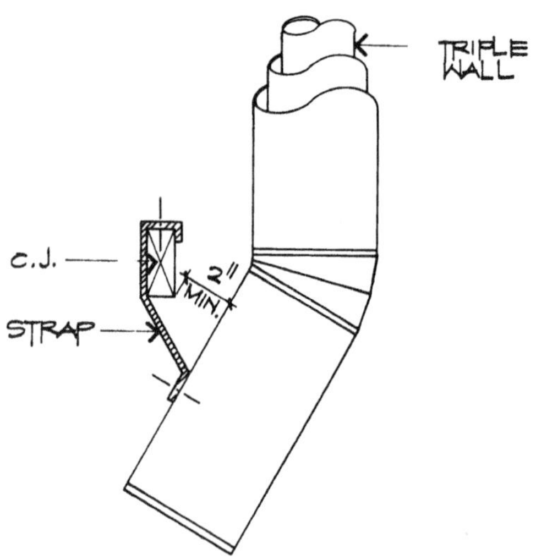

Figure 12.42 Chimney attached to adjacent members.

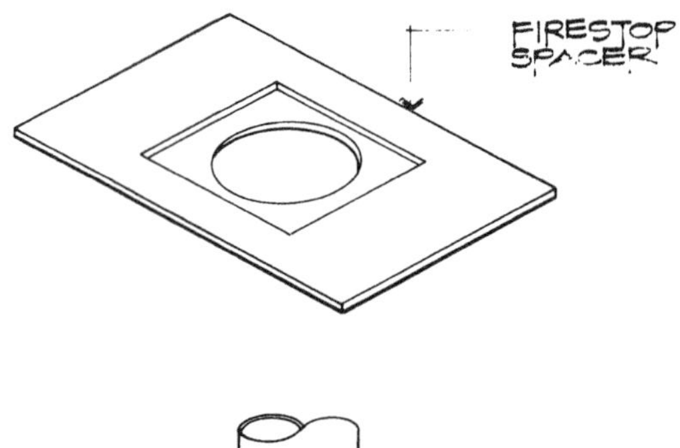

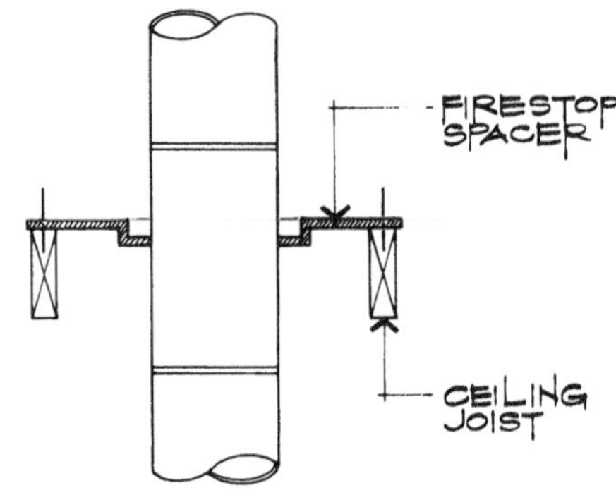

Figure 12.43 Chimney position.

full masonry fireplaces, read the chapter on fireplaces in the companion book, *The Professional Practice of Architectural Detailing*.)

Next, the fireplace is positioned in this cavity, with the minimum clearances required by code. At this stage, the drafter must be conversant with code restrictions as well as the method of installation. For example, it is important to detail how the flue is to be stabilized within the cavity, what kinds of firestops are required, and where they are positioned. Manufacturers' literature includes installation instructions and standard manufactured pieces that are available to make such installation possible. The drafter should also check the project book to verify finish materials for the face of the fireplace and the hearth.

Stage III (Figure 12.51). Once the materials have been checked, material designations are included in the detail. Wood, insulation, concrete, and even the outside wall of the metal fireplace are shown. At this stage, sheet metal, such as for the cap, is drafted with a single heavy line.

Stage IV (Figure 12.52). The detailer must be aware of a number of items on all details, as well as those that are unique to specific details, as is the case with a fireplace. Unlike the footing detail, which describes a structural part of a building, the fireplace detail is one for which a context already exists.

In the final sequence, identification of the context: the rafters, the ceiling joists, the floor, and the cell (surrounded with studs) within which the fireplace will be placed, including the housing for the chimney.

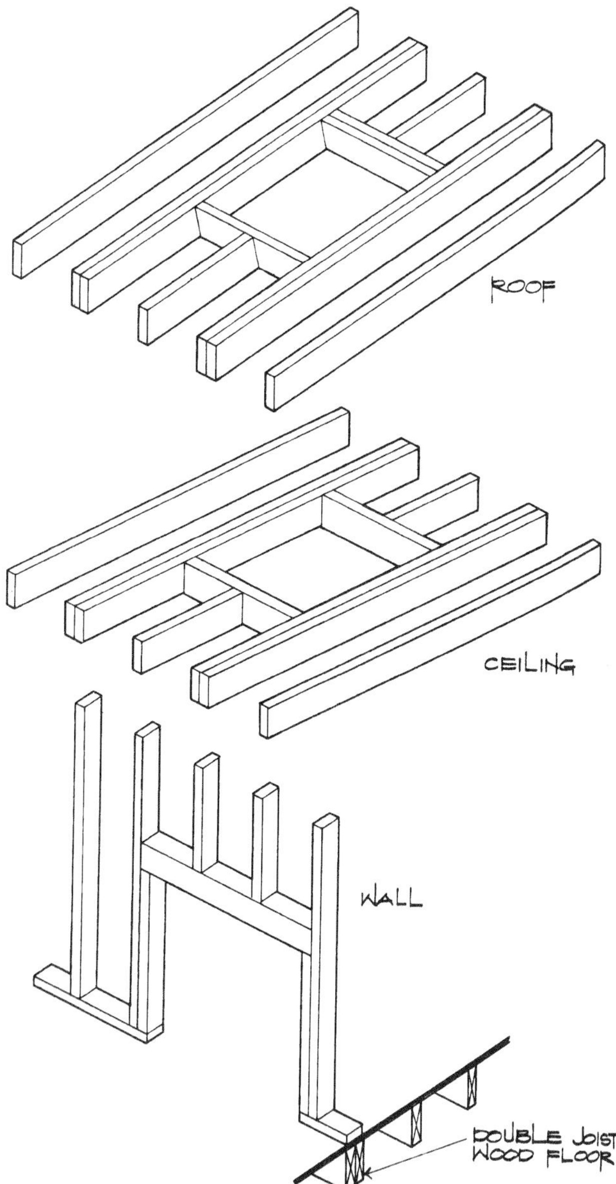

Figure 12.44 Framing an opening.

Next is identification of the fireplace and the flue, in such a way that the outline of the fireplace is clear in relationship to the surrounding structure.

The building code and the manufacturer's installation directions will reveal certain clearances that must be maintained and dimensioned, and attachments and firestop spacers that must be identified. Merely positioning them is not sufficient.

Next, the decorative (**noncombustible**) portions that surround the opening—the chimney, the floor (**hearth**) and the wall plane of the fireplace, and the ceiling—should be described and dimensioned.

Finally, if there are portions within this drawing that should be enlarged and explored, reference bubbles or notes are included to direct the reader to these details. Although it may seem that this is referring a detail to

Figure 12.45 Model simulation of the framing through the roof.

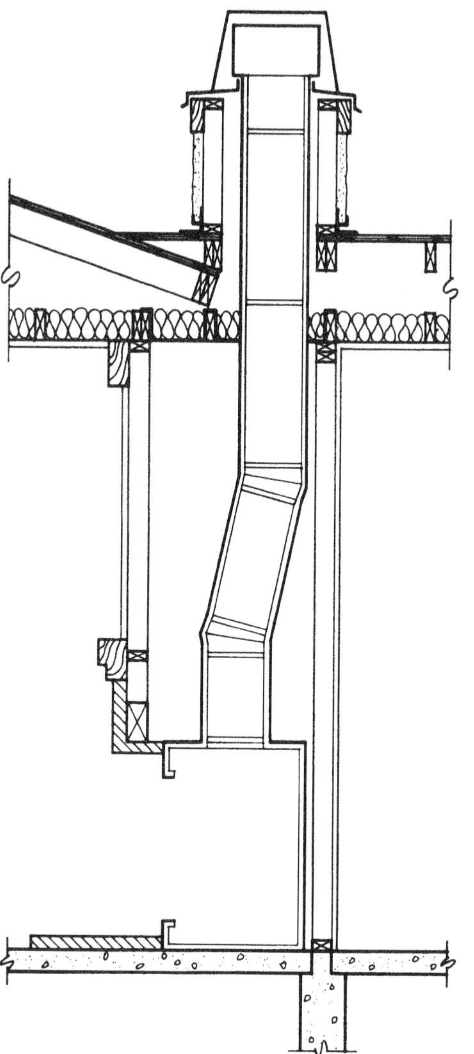

Figure 12.46 Full section of a fireplace.

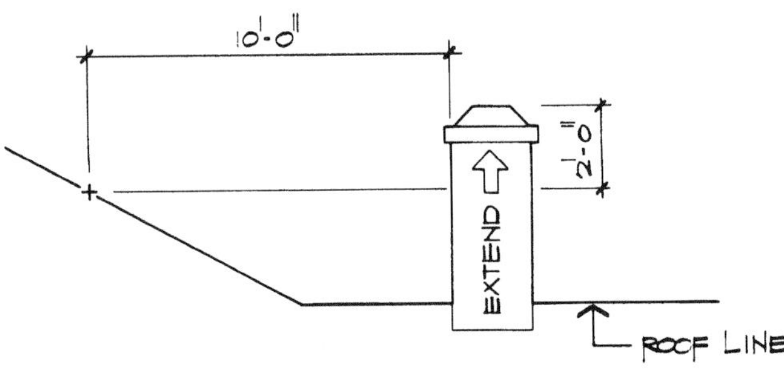

Figure 12.47 Chimney above roof.

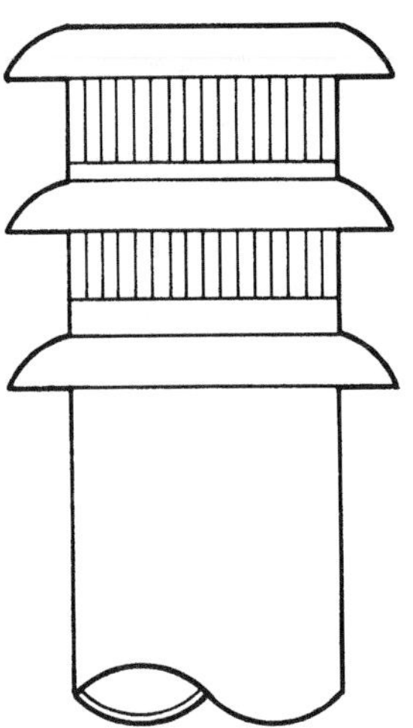

Figure 12.48 Round top termination.

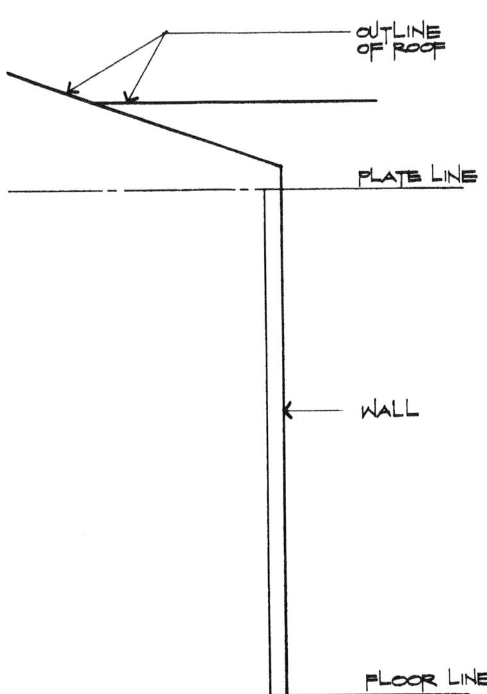

Figure 12.49 Stage I: Establishing the parameters of the fireplace location.

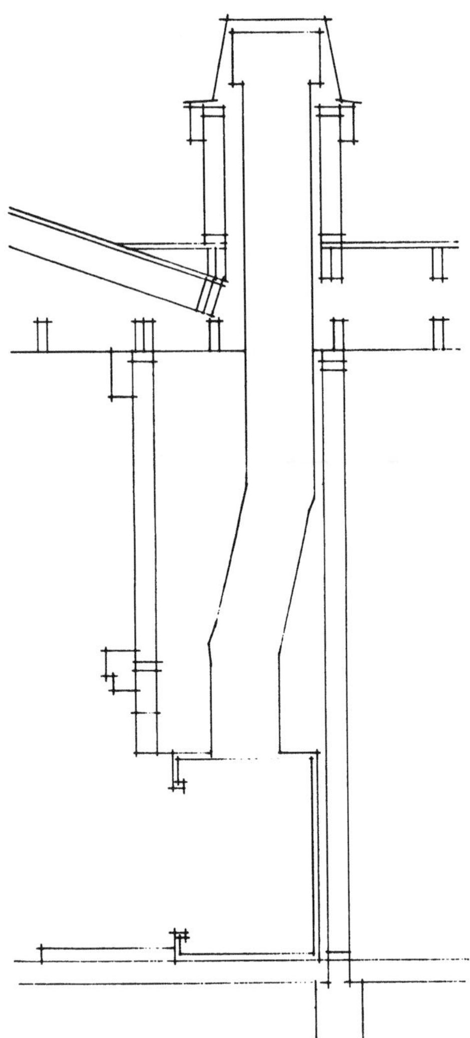

Figure 12.50 Stage II: Residential fireplace.

a detail, it is really not. (See the chimney portion of Figure 12.47.) This drawing, as the title indicates, is a **half-section**—a hybrid between a building section and a full-blown detail as drawn in Figure 12.53.

Stair Design and Vertical Links

The stair design for any type of stairway will have to address the various physical and dimensional requirements while adhering to building code restrictions. The architect will need to have some basic information before designing the stairs and the accompanying stair details. The first information required is the computed height between the floor levels. Second, the designer needs the dimensional requirements for the width of the stairs, and the length of the stair run, to accommodate the number and width of the desired stair **treads**. After the floor-to-floor dimension is computed, this dimension will then become the basis for the number and height of the stair risers.

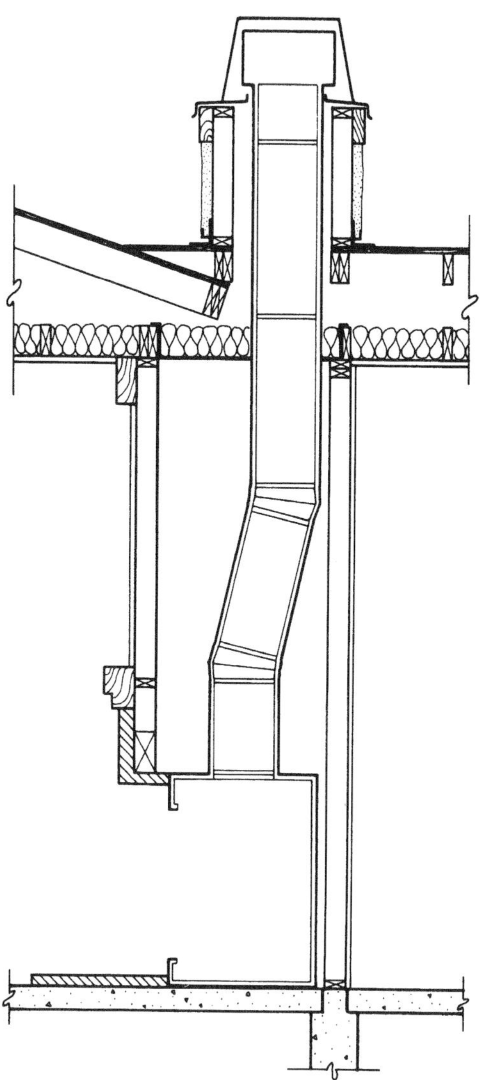

Figure 12.51 Stage III: Residential fireplace.

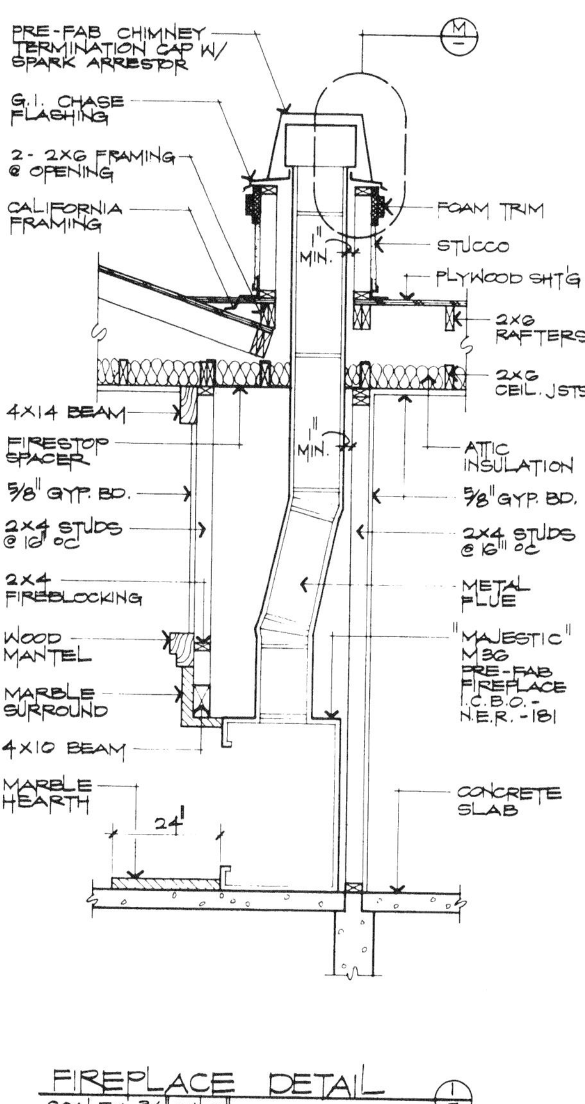

Figure 12.52 Stage IV: Half-section of fireplace.

An example of how this may be achieved is described mathematically as follows:

1. Floor to ceiling = 8′-0″
2. Ceiling thickness = ⅝″
3. Second-floor wood joist = 11¼″
4. Second-floor subfloor = ¾″

Therefore, the floor-to-floor dimension is 9′-0⅝″ or 108.625″.

Desired riser height dimension = 6½″ to 7″ (7″ maximum for commercial)

Desired tread dimensions = 10½″ (11″ minimum for commercial)

Assume that there are 15 risers; therefore, 108.625″ divided by 15 equals 7.28″ + risers or 7 3/8″ risers. This does not meet current building code requirements. Try 16 risers: 108.625″ divided by 16 equals 6.79″ or 6¾″ + risers, which does meet building code requirements. Most building codes require that a rise in every step be not less than 4″ nor greater than 7″.

Prior to computing the number and size of the treads for the preceding riser example, it is recommended that the governing building code requirements for the minimum width of the tread size be verified. Most codes require the tread size to be not less than 11″ as measured horizontally between the vertical planes of the furthermost projection of the adjacent treads.

As determined by the foregoing riser computation, the stair calls for sixteen 6¾″ risers. For most stairway designs, the number of treads will be one less than the number of risers. Therefore, for the tread computation and code requirement, fifteen 11″ treads will be used in this example. To compute the dimensional length of the stairway run using fifteen 11″-wide treads, it would mathematically equate to 15 × 11″, or 165″. Therefore,

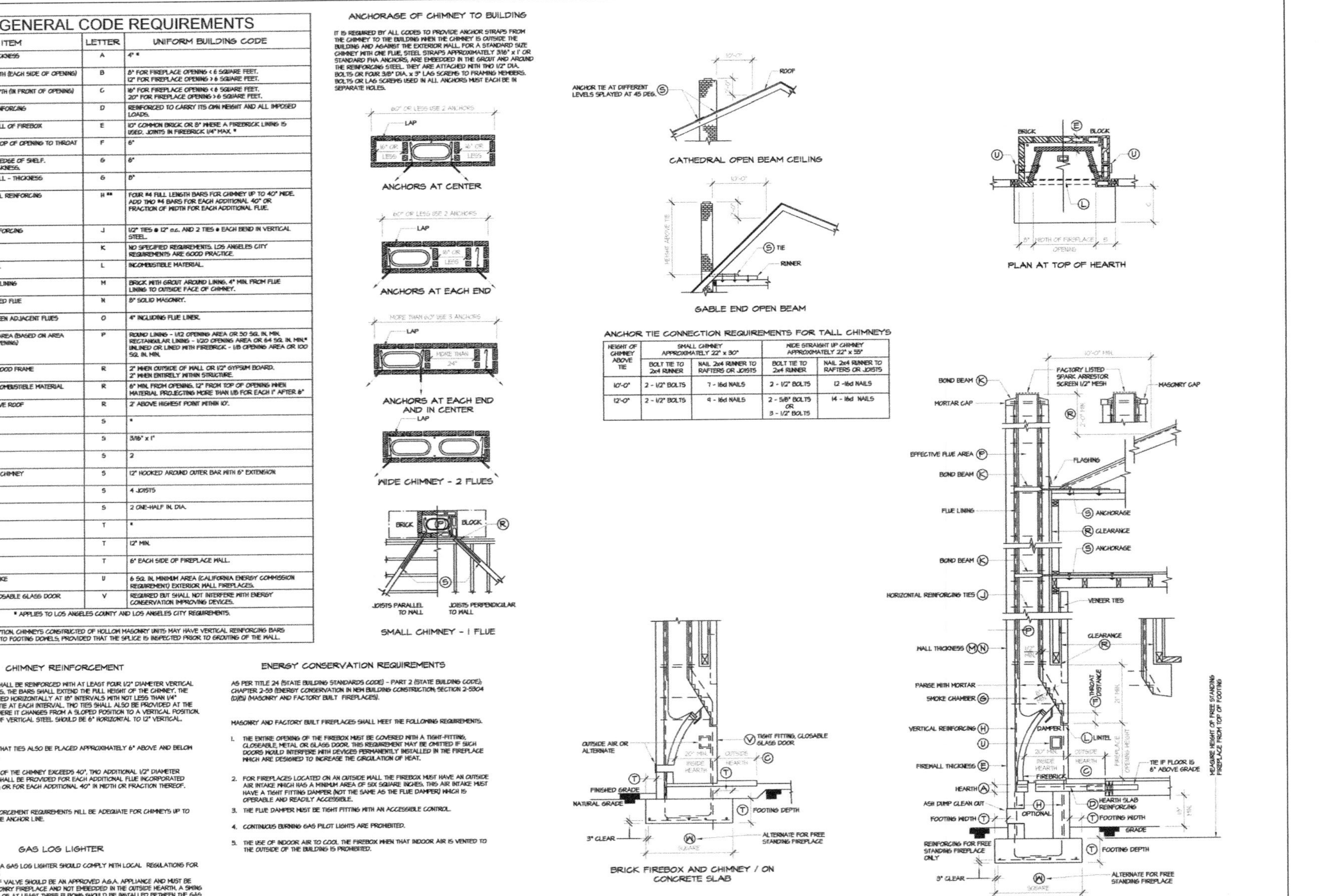

GENERAL CODE REQUIREMENTS

ITEM	LETTER	UNIFORM BUILDING CODE
HEARTH SLAB THICKNESS	A	4" *
HEARTH SLAB WIDTH (EACH SIDE OF OPENING)	B	8" FOR FIREPLACE OPENING < 6 SQUARE FEET. 12" FOR FIREPLACE OPENING > 6 SQUARE FEET.
HEARTH SLAB DEPTH (IN FRONT OF OPENING)	C	16" FOR FIREPLACE OPENING < 6 SQUARE FEET. 20" FOR FIREPLACE OPENING > 6 SQUARE FEET.
HEARTH SLAB REINFORCING	D	REINFORCED TO CARRY ITS OWN WEIGHT AND ALL IMPOSED LOADS.
THICKNESS OF WALL OF FIREBOX	E	10" COMMON BRICK OR 8" WHERE A FIREBRICK LINING IS USED. JOINTS IN FIREBRICK 1/4" MAX. *
DISTANCE FROM TOP OF OPENING TO THROAT	F	6"
SMOKE CHAMBER EDGE OF SHELF. REAR WALL - THICKNESS.	G	6"
FRONT & SIDE WALL - THICKNESS	G	8"
CHIMNEY VERTICAL REINFORCING	H **	FOUR #4 FULL LENGTH BARS FOR CHIMNEY UP TO 40" WIDE. ADD TWO #4 BARS FOR EACH ADDITIONAL 40" OR FRACTION OF WIDTH FOR EACH ADDITIONAL FLUE.
HORIZONTAL REINFORCING	J	1/2" TIES @ 12" o.c. AND 2 TIES @ EACH BEND IN VERTICAL STEEL.
BOND BEAMS	K	NO SPECIFIED REQUIREMENTS. LOS ANGELES CITY REQUIREMENTS ARE GOOD PRACTICE.
FIREPLACE LINTEL	L	INCOMBUSTIBLE MATERIAL.
WALLS WITH FLUE LINING	M	BRICK WITH GROUT AROUND LINING. 4" MIN. FROM FLUE LINING TO OUTSIDE FACE OF CHIMNEY.
WALLS WITH UNLINED FLUE	N	8" SOLID MASONRY.
DISTANCES BETWEEN ADJACENT FLUES	O	4" INCLUDING FLUE LINER.
EFFECTIVE FLUE AREA (BASED ON AREA OF FIREPLACE OPENING)	P	ROUND LINING - 1/12 OPENING AREA OR 50 SQ. IN. MIN. RECTANGULAR LINING - 1/20 OPENING AREA OR 64 SQ. IN. MIN.* UNLINED OR LINED WITH FIREBRICK - 1/8 OPENING AREA OR 100 SQ. IN. MIN.
CLEARANCE TO WOOD FRAME	R	2" WHEN OUTSIDE OF WALL OR 1/2" GYPSUM BOARD. 2" WHEN ENTIRELY WITHIN STRUCTURE.
CLEARANCE TO COMBUSTIBLE MATERIAL	R	6" MIN. FROM OPENING. 12" FROM TOP OF OPENING WHEN MATERIAL PROJECTING MORE THAN 1/8 FOR EACH 1" AFTER 6"
CLEARANCE ABOVE ROOF	R	2' ABOVE HIGHEST POINT WITHIN 10'.
ANCHORAGE	S	*
STRAP	S	3/16" x 1"
NUMBER	S	2
EMBEDMENT INTO CHIMNEY	S	12" HOOKED AROUND OUTER BAR WITH 6" EXTENSION
FASTEN TO	S	4 JOISTS
BOLTS	S	2 ONE-HALF IN. DIA.
FOOTING	T	*
THICKNESS	T	12" MIN.
WIDTH	T	6" EACH SIDE OF FIREPLACE WALL.
OUTSIDE AIR INTAKE	U	6 SQ. IN. MINIMUM AREA (CALIFORNIA ENERGY COMMISSION REQUIREMENT) EXTERIOR WALL FIREPLACES.
TIGHT FITTING CLOSABLE GLASS DOOR	V	REQUIRED BUT SHALL NOT INTERFERE WITH ENERGY CONSERVATION IMPROVING DEVICES.

* APPLIES TO LOS ANGELES COUNTY AND LOS ANGELES CITY REQUIREMENTS.

** H EXCEPTION. CHIMNEYS CONSTRUCTED OF HOLLOW MASONRY UNITS MAY HAVE VERTICAL REINFORCING BARS SPLICED TO FOOTING DOWELS, PROVIDED THAT THE SPLICE IS INSPECTED PRIOR TO GROUTING OF THE WALL.

ANCHORAGE OF CHIMNEY TO BUILDING

IT IS REQUIRED BY ALL CODES TO PROVIDE ANCHOR STRAPS FROM THE CHIMNEY TO THE BUILDING WHEN THE CHIMNEY IS OUTSIDE THE BUILDING AND AGAINST THE EXTERIOR WALL. FOR A STANDARD SIZE CHIMNEY WITH ONE FLUE, STEEL STRAPS APPROXIMATELY 3/16" x 1' OR STANDARD FHA ANCHORS, ARE EMBEDDED IN THE GROUT AND AROUND THE REINFORCING STEEL. THEY ARE ATTACHED WITH TWO 1/2" DIA. BOLTS OR FOUR 3/8" DIA. x 3" LAG SCREWS TO FRAMING MEMBERS. BOLTS OR LAG SCREWS USED IN ALL ANCHORS MUST EACH BE IN SEPARATE HOLES.

ANCHOR TIE CONNECTION REQUIREMENTS FOR TALL CHIMNEYS

HEIGHT OF CHIMNEY ABOVE TIE	SMALL CHIMNEY APPROXIMATELY 22" x 30"		WIDE STRAIGHT UP CHIMNEY APPROXIMATELY 22" x 55"	
	BOLT TIE TO 2x4 RUNNER	NAIL 2x4 RUNNER TO RAFTERS OR JOISTS	BOLT TIE TO 2x4 RUNNER	NAIL 2x4 RUNNER TO RAFTERS OR JOISTS
10'-0"	2 - 1/2" BOLTS	7 - 16d NAILS	2 - 1/2" BOLTS	12 -16d NAILS
12'-0"	2 - 1/2" BOLTS	9 - 16d NAILS	2 - 5/8" BOLTS OR 3 - 1/2" BOLTS	14 - 16d NAILS

CHIMNEY REINFORCEMENT

EVERY CHIMNEY SHALL BE REINFORCED WITH AT LEAST FOUR 1/2" DIAMETER VERTICAL REINFORCING BARS. THE BARS SHALL EXTEND THE FULL HEIGHT OF THE CHIMNEY. THE BARS SHALL BE TIED HORIZONTALLY AT 18" INTERVALS WITH NOT LESS THAN 1/4" DIAMETER STEEL TIE AT EACH INTERVAL. TWO TIES SHALL ALSO BE PROVIDED AT THE BEND IN A BAR WHERE IT CHANGES FROM A SLOPED POSITION TO A VERTICAL POSITION. MAXIMUM SLOPE OF VERTICAL STEEL SHOULD BE 6" HORIZONTAL TO 12" VERTICAL.

IT IS SUGGESTED THAT TIES ALSO BE PLACED APPROXIMATELY 6" ABOVE AND BELOW ANCHOR STRAPS.

WHERE THE WIDTH OF THE CHIMNEY EXCEEDS 40", TWO ADDITIONAL 1/2" DIAMETER VERTICAL BARS SHALL BE PROVIDED FOR EACH ADDITIONAL FLUE INCORPORATED INTO THE CHIMNEY; OR FOR EACH ADDITIONAL 40" IN WIDTH OR FRACTION THEREOF.

THE ABOVE REINFORCEMENT REQUIREMENTS WILL BE ADEQUATE FOR CHIMNEYS UP TO 12 FEET ABOVE THE ANCHOR LINE.

GAS LOG LIGHTER

INSTALLATION OF A GAS LOG LIGHTER SHOULD COMPLY WITH LOCAL REGULATIONS FOR GAS APPLIANCES.

THE GAS SHUT OFF VALVE SHOULD BE AN APPROVED A.G.A. APPLIANCE AND MUST BE OUTSIDE THE MASONRY FIREPLACE AND NOT EMBEDDED IN THE OUTSIDE HEARTH. A SWING JOINT CONSISTING OF AT LEAST THREE ELBOWS SHOULD BE INSTALLED BETWEEN THE GAS SHUT OFF VALVE AND THE LOG LIGHTER PIPE. THIS IS TO PREVENT BREAKS IN THE JOINTS IN THE EVENT OF MOVEMENT OR SETTLEMENT OF THE FIREPLACE.

IT IS RECOMMENDED THAT THE GAS LOG LIGHTER BE 1" ABOVE THE ASH BED AND DEFINITELY NOT BURIED IN THE ASHES OR IN SAND.

ENERGY CONSERVATION REQUIREMENTS

AS PER TITLE 24 (STATE BUILDING STANDARDS CODE) - PART 2 (STATE BUILDING CODE); CHAPTER 2-53 (ENERGY CONSERVATION IN NEW BUILDING CONSTRUCTION; SECTION 2-5304 (D)(5) (MASONRY AND FACTORY BUILT FIREPLACES).

MASONRY AND FACTORY BUILT FIREPLACES SHALL MEET THE FOLLOWING REQUIREMENTS.

1. THE ENTIRE OPENING OF THE FIREBOX MUST BE COVERED WITH A TIGHT-FITTING, CLOSEABLE, METAL OR GLASS DOOR. THIS REQUIREMENT MAY BE OMITTED IF SUCH DOORS WOULD INTERFERE WITH DEVICES PERMANENTLY INSTALLED IN THE FIREPLACE WHICH ARE DESIGNED TO INCREASE THE CIRCULATION OF HEAT.
2. FOR FIREPLACES LOCATED ON AN OUTSIDE WALL THE FIREBOX MUST HAVE AN OUTSIDE AIR INTAKE WHICH HAS A MINIMUM AREA OF SIX SQUARE INCHES. THIS AIR INTAKE MUST HAVE A TIGHT FITTING DAMPER (NOT THE SAME AS THE FLUE DAMPER) WHICH IS OPERABLE AND READILY ACCESSIBLE.
3. THE FLUE DAMPER MUST BE TIGHT FITTING WITH AN ACCESSIBLE CONTROL.
4. CONTINUOUS BURNING GAS PILOT LIGHTS ARE PROHIBITED.
5. THE USE OF INDOOR AIR TO COOL THE FIREBOX WHEN THAT INDOOR AIR IS VENTED TO THE OUTSIDE OF THE BUILDING IS PROHIBITED.

Figure 12.53 Masonry fireplace detail.

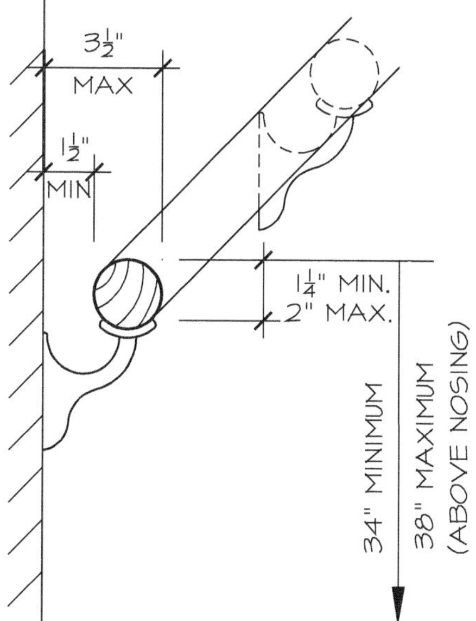

Figure 12.54 Handrail requirements.

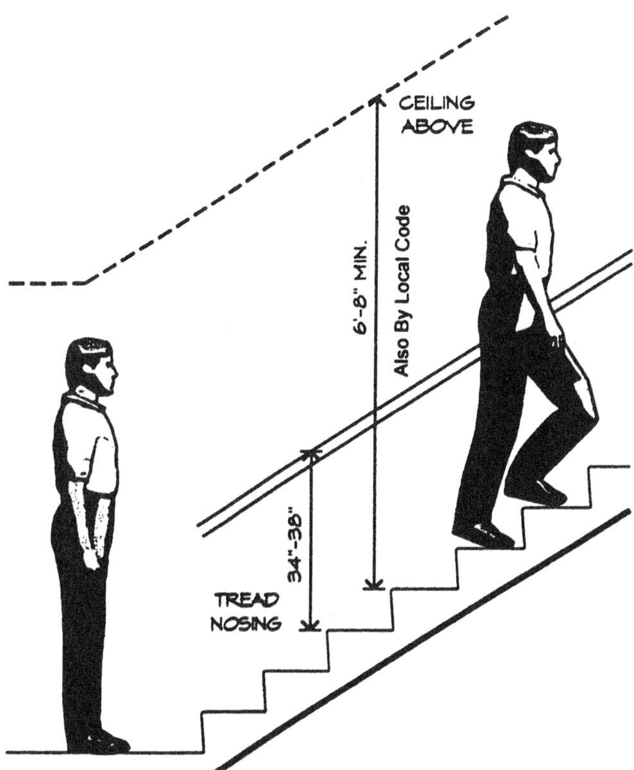

Figure 12.55 Headroom clearance.

the critical dimension to satisfy the number of treads in feet and inches would be 165″ divided by 12, which converts into a minimum space requirement of 13′-10″.

The desired or required stairway width will vary with the architect's design and the type of building that the stairway serves relative to the building code requirements. For most governing building codes, the required stairway width for commercial and public buildings must not be less than 44″. In stairways serving residential structures or having an occupant load of less than 49, the stairway must not be less than 36″ in width.

Handrail designs and their projection into the required stairway width are governed by existing building code requirements. The allowed distance is 3½″ from each side of a stairway. A three-dimensional drawing of an acceptable handrail design is shown in Figure 12.54.

The height and tops of handrails and the handrail extensions must not be less than 34″ nor more than 38″ above the nosing of the treads and stairway landings.

Another concern for a stairway designer is the minimum headroom clearance stipulated in most building codes. Generally, the headroom clearance must not be less than 6′-8″ or 6.67′ (verify with local code). This clearance is to be measured vertically from a place that is parallel and tangent to the stairway tread nosings. Figure 12.55 graphically depicts a minimum headroom clearance requirement for a stairway.

This example makes some assumptions, specifically that the stairs are a straight run. Adding landings for resting and circular stairs are similar in calculation from floor to floor. However, adding criteria shapes the configuration of other shaped stairs and landings have to be in depth the width of the stair minimum.

Guardrails are safety devices found on stairway landings, balconies, and decks where the fall hazard exceeds 30″ or more above the adjacent grade. The structural design to stabilize the supporting vertical members is predicated on a horizontal force, measured in pounds per linear foot, and must be calculated to resist loads. Allowable openings in the guardrail assembly vary by specific location governed by code. For residential use, the maximum clear openings must not exceed 4″ to 6″ at the bottom location and 42″ high. For commercial and industrial structures, the maximum clear openings must not exceed 4″ and 42″ high. An example of a guardrail assembly is shown in a three-dimensional drawing in Figure 12.56.

The construction materials used for stairways include wood, steel, poured-in-place concrete, precast concrete, or a combination of any of these materials. Figures 12.57–12.59 illustrate a partial floor plan for a three-story residence that incorporates a wood stairway construction at the different floor levels. The stairway designs vary from a straight run and landings to a partial radial shape.

Starting at the basement level, as shown in Figure 12.57, and knowing the established basement floor-to-floor dimension of 10′-6″, or 126″, the designer can calculate the number and height of the stairway risers. Starting from the basement floor-to-floor, using 7″-high risers, eighteen risers will be required. Therefore,

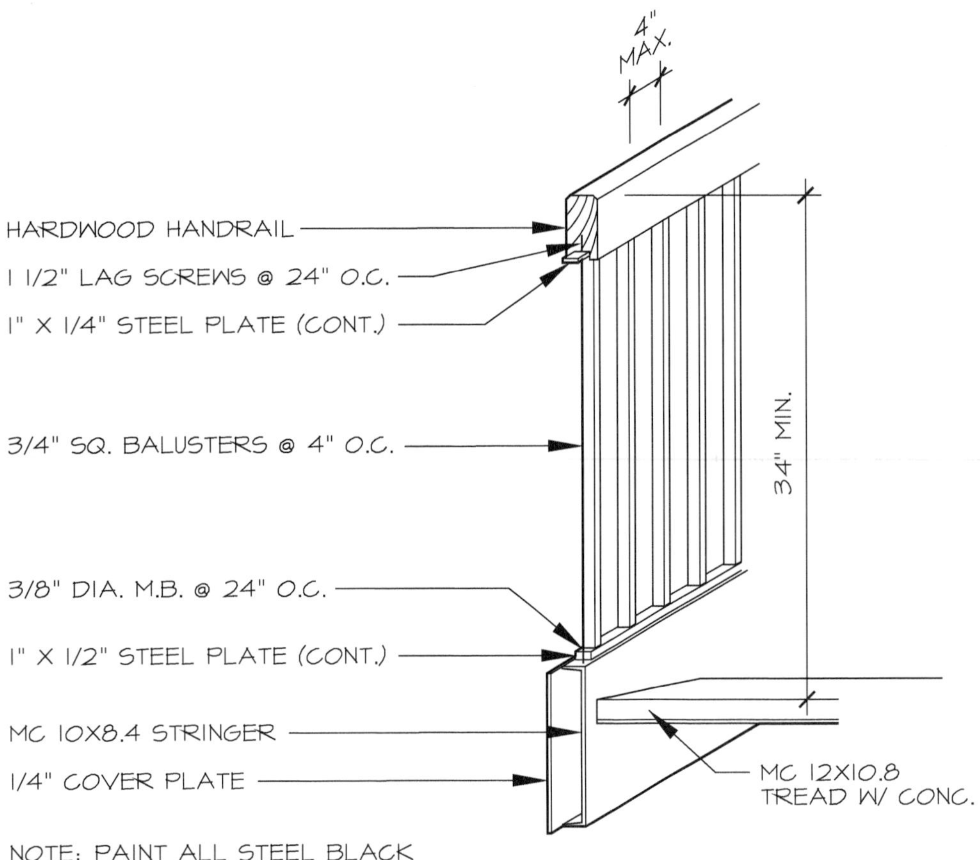

Figure 12.56 Balustrade detail.

when using 11″-deep treads, seventeen risers will be required. The length of the space required for seventeen 11″-deep treads will be 15′-6″ plus the deep of the two stairway landings. The width of the landing is 42″, as is the width of the stairway. The foregoing information is what was required to physically lay out this stairway design, which surrounds an elevator shaft enclosure.

The next step in this stairway design is to provide stair details as part of the project's working drawings. As shown in Figure 12.60, a section is cut at the bottom

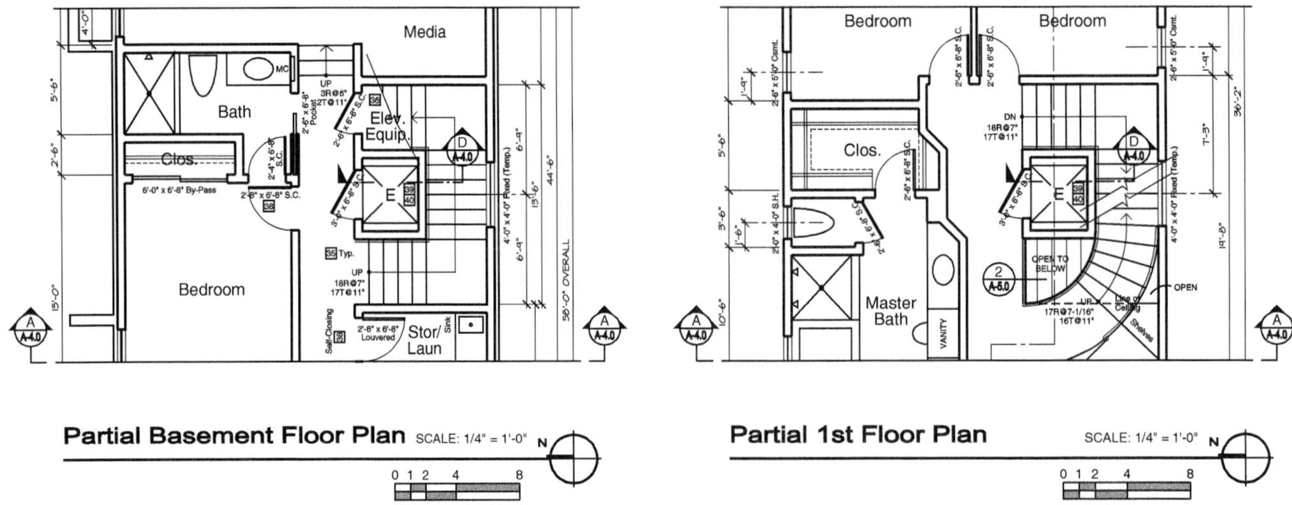

Figure 12.57 Partial basement-floor plan.

Figure 12.58 Partial first-floor plan.

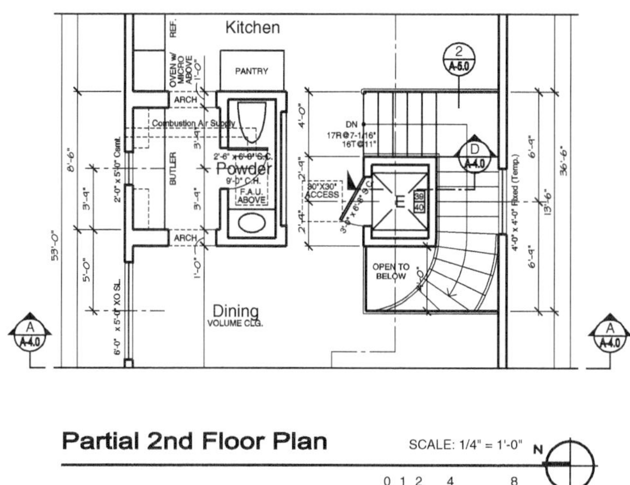

Figure 12.59 Partial second-floor plan.

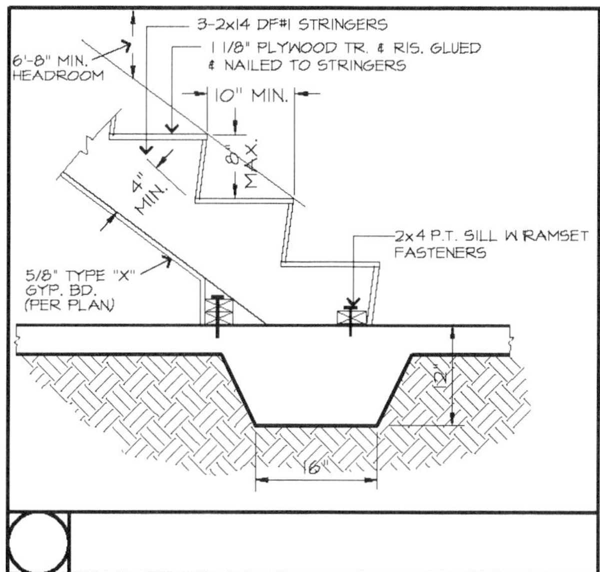

Figure 12.60 Stringers at slab.

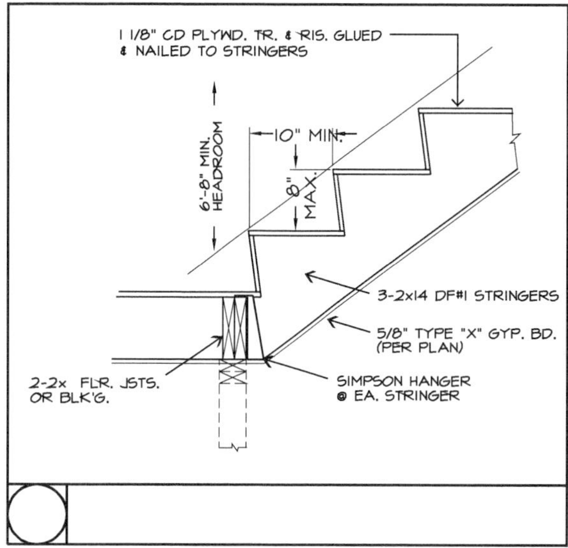

Figure 12.61 Stringers to landing.

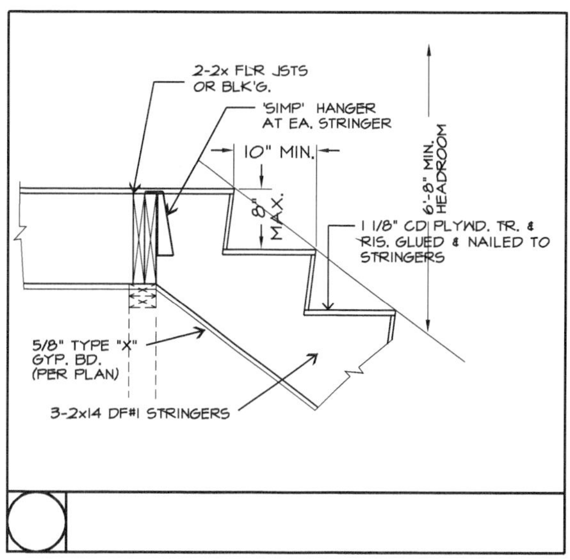

Figure 12.62 Stringers to second floor.

of the stairway, showing how the stringers are anchored at the basement concrete floor. Another detail will show how the stringers occur at both landings (see Figure 12.61). The final detail, showing the method where the stringers are attached to the floor joist, is illustrated in Figure 12.62.

As shown in Figure 12.58, the stairway access at the foyer has a partial radial curve in the design. An enlarged partial stair layout of this stairway segment is illustrated in Figure 12.63. This is done to show the inside and outer dimensions of a tread as a means for construction of the stairway, while illustrating the building code requirements for the tread design. A three-dimensional detail is added to the working drawings for the purpose of clarity for this circular portion of the stairway design (see Figure 12.64).

Steel and concrete can be utilized for stairs, beginning at the ground-floor level. The steel stringers, fabricated from a standard steel channel, are attached to the concrete floor with ¼″ steel plates and ½″ × 10″ anchor bolts. The typical tread design is a standard steel channel MC10 × 84 welded to the web of the channel stringer and filled with concrete. This detail assembly is illustrated in Figure 12.65.

The next connection detail is the stringer attachment at the intermediate landings and the support of the concrete at the landings, as shown in Figure 12.66. Note that the steel channel at the landing is used to support

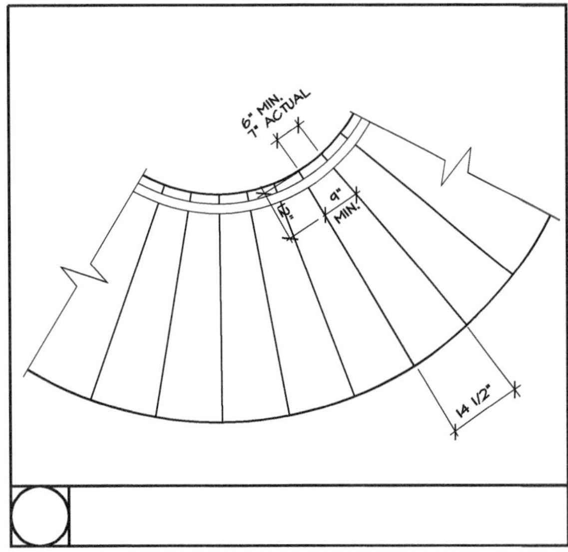

Figure 12.63 Partial stair plan.

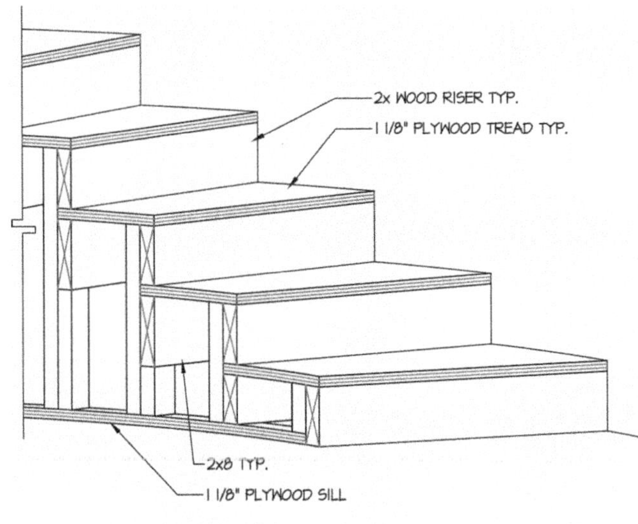

Figure 12.64 Circular stair detail.

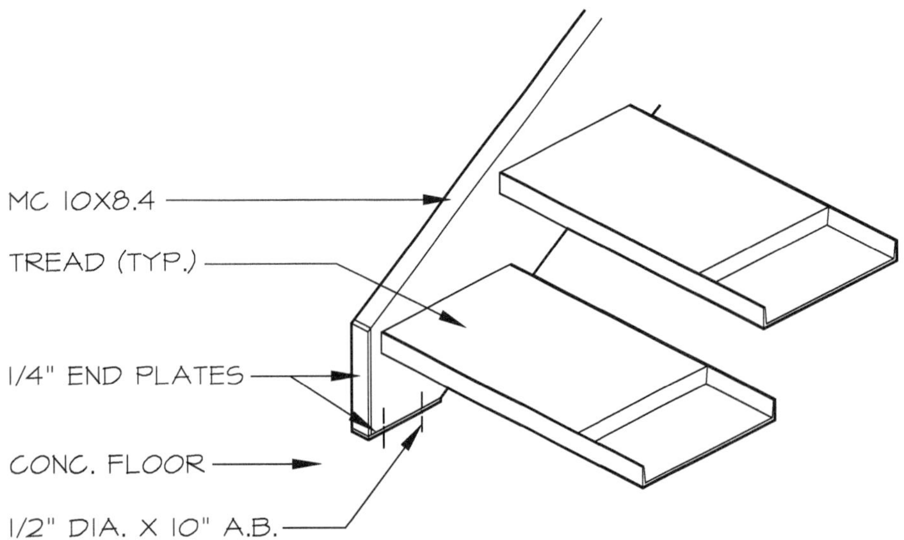

Figure 12.65 Stringer to concrete.

the steel stringers and the concrete at the landings. All connections are accomplished by assigned welds. The final detail for the steel stairway assembly is shown for the various floor levels (see Figure 12.67). This detail illustrates a steel channel for the floor support and the support of the stringers. Steel angles are used for intermediate floor supports.

Concrete stairways may be constructed in two ways. First, there are various precast concrete companies that manufacture different types of concrete stairs and will deliver and install them on the building site. Second, concrete stairways may be formed during construction of the building by incorporating the required steel reinforcing bars and then pouring the concrete in place. For many projects, a precast concrete stairway is desirable, because there is no cost of forming and subsequent form removal. Quality control of the finish gives a consistent aesthetic appearance. When using a poured-in-place concrete stair, it is necessary to provide details, with the required steel reinforcing as part of the working drawings. A three-dimensional detail for a poured-in-place concrete stairway is depicted in Figure 12.68.

If using a manufactured precast concrete, one-piece, closed tread, and riser assembly, the precast units can be assembled with steel stringers. This composite stairway requires architectural detailing, because it is necessary to size steel stringers for their span and the weight of the precast treads and risers and to show how they are

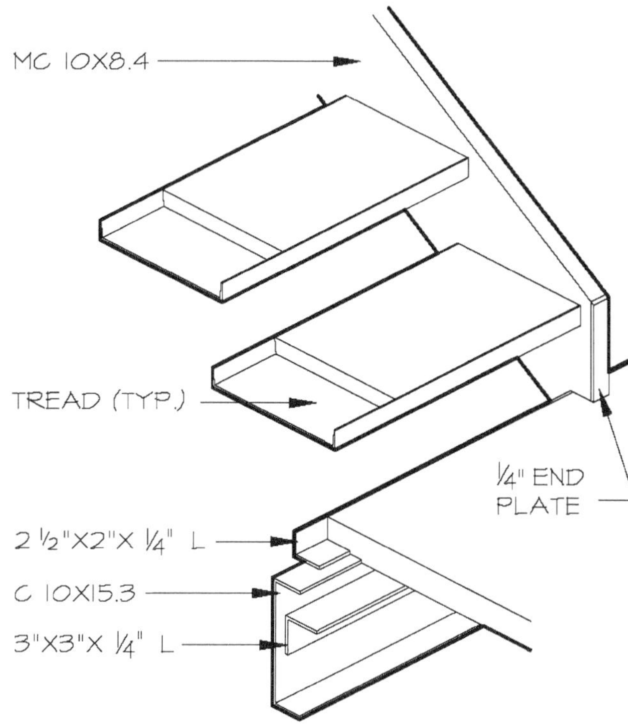

Figure 12.66 Stringer to landing.

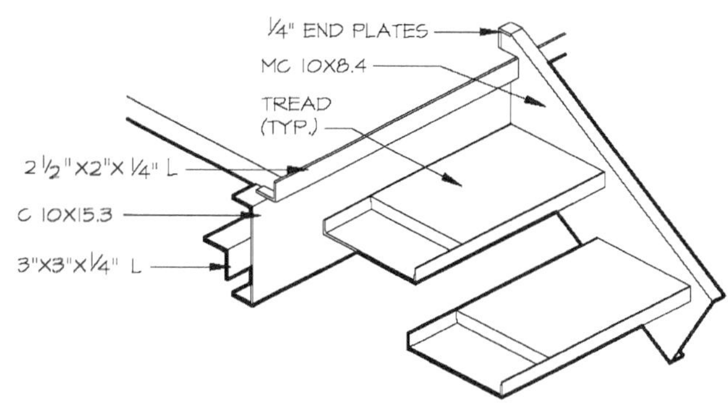

Figure 12.67 Stringer to floor.

attached to the supporting beams. A three-dimensional detail illustrating a precast tread and riser unit attached to the stringers is shown in Figure 12.69.

Mechanical Vertical Links

The drawings for elevators of all types and various lifting devices, such as wheelchair lifts, chair lifts, and others, must include the detailing necessary to satisfy the installation requirements. An example of a residential-type electric elevator is shown in Figure 12.70. The planned area for the wall framing and the openings that surround

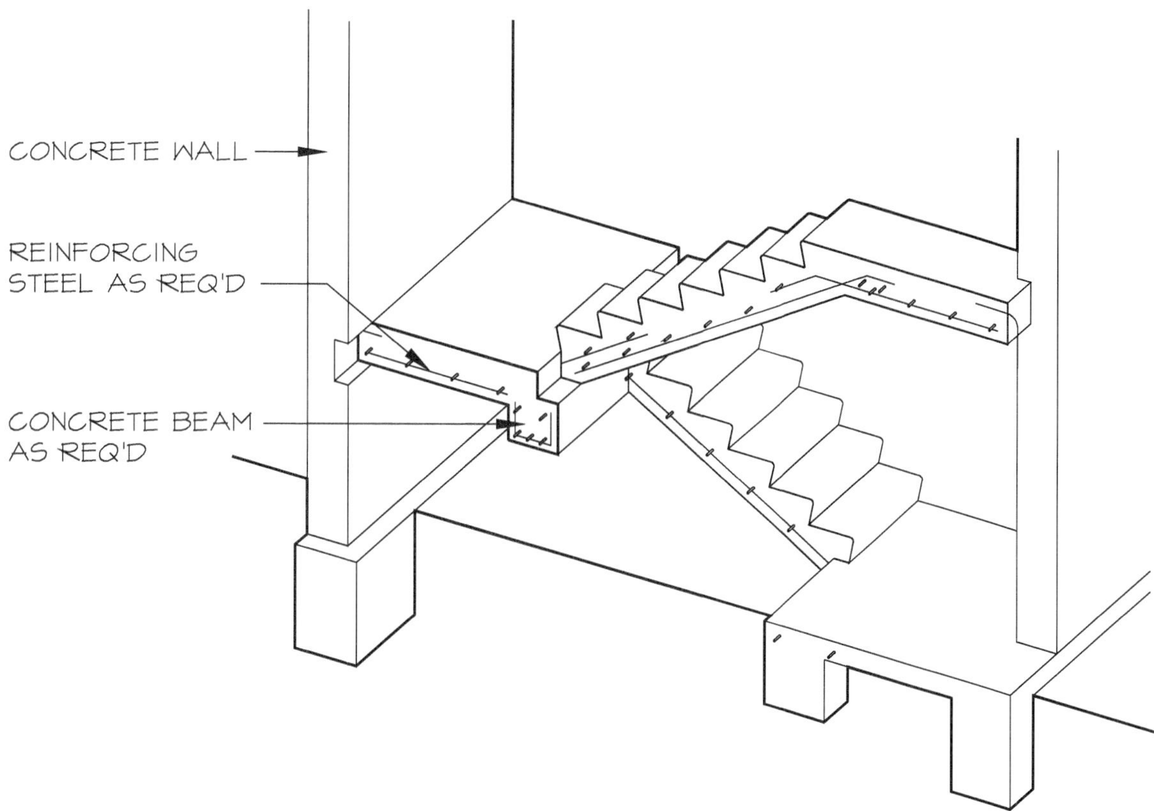

Figure 12.68 Poured-in-place concrete stairs.

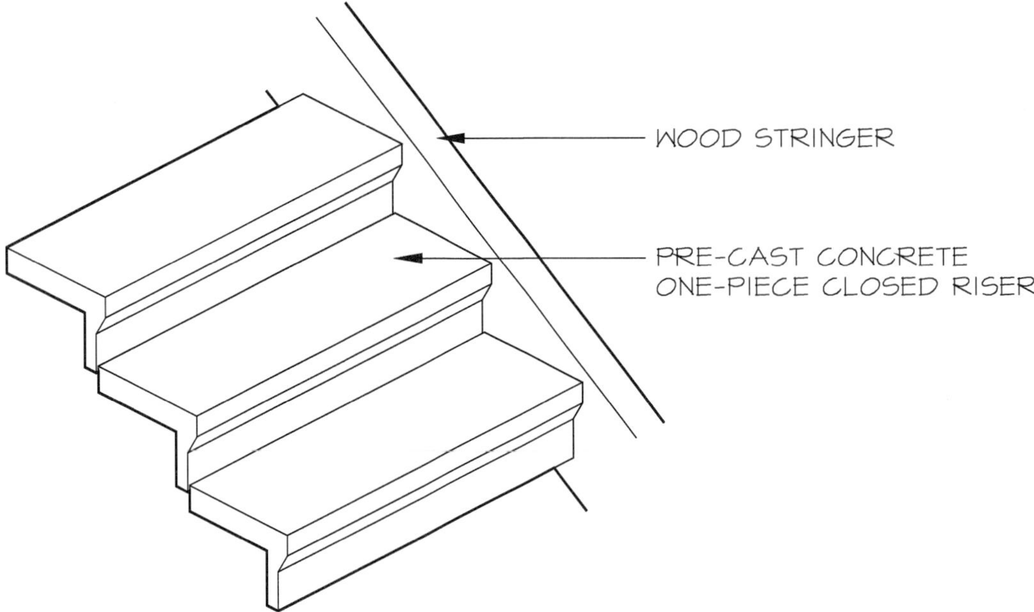

Figure 12.69 One-piece closed riser.

the electric elevator car must adhere to all the clearances required by the elevator manufacturer. The planning must also include the required space designated by the manufacturer for the machine room equipment. This room is located adjacent to and under the stairway run.

A three-dimensional drawing of the framed opening is shown in Figure 12.70. This particular elevator has a lift capacity of approximately 750 pounds.

A more detailed example of a manufacturer's requirements is shown in the plan view illustrated in Figure 12.71. This drawing, furnished by a specific elevator manufacturer,

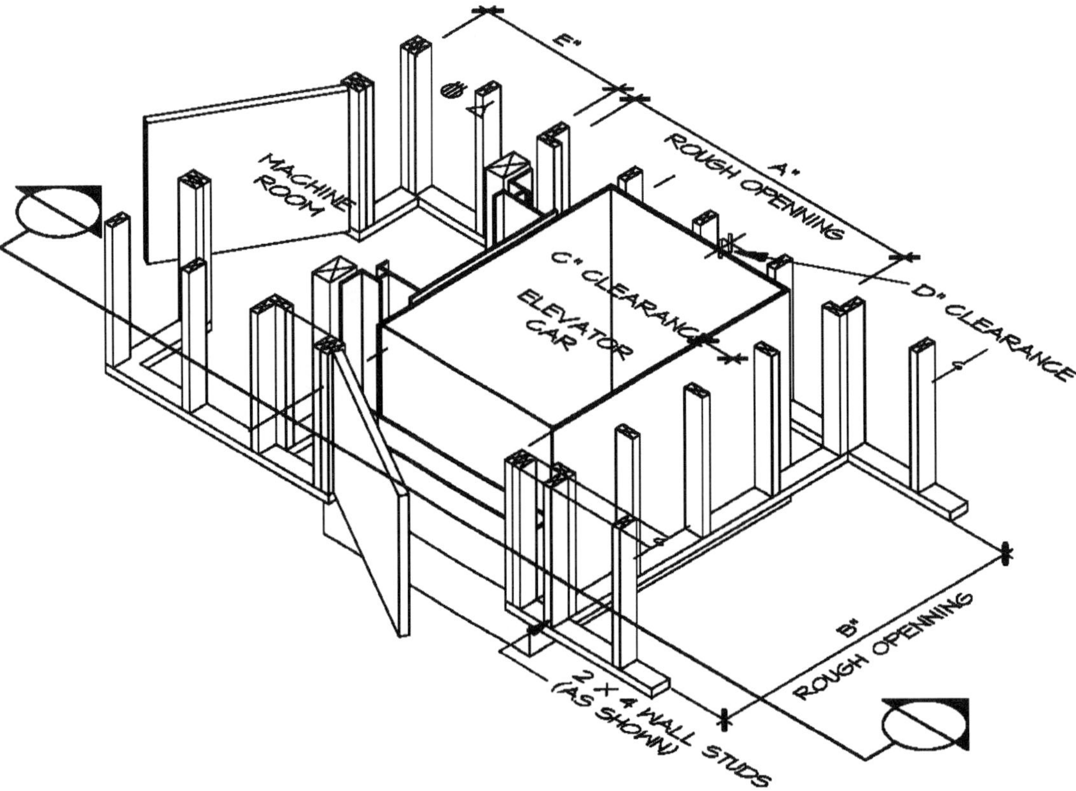

Figure 12.70 Framed elevator opening.

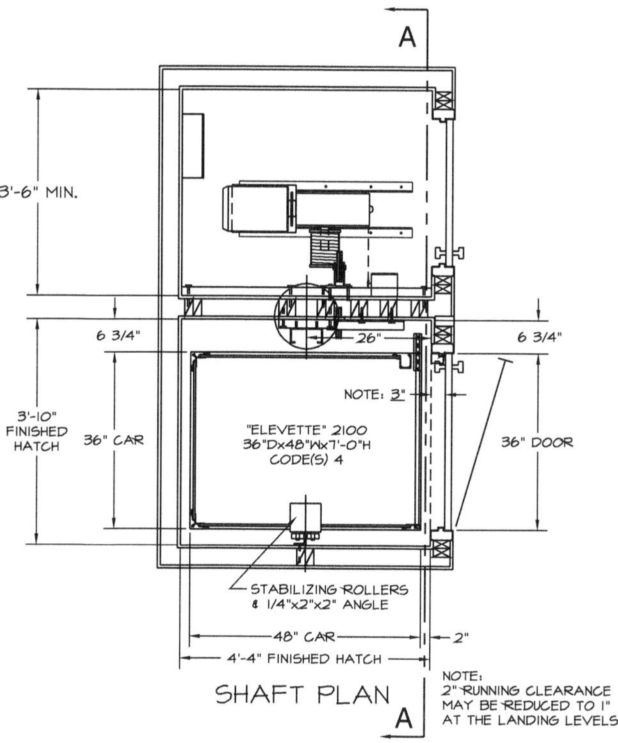

Figure 12.71 Shaft plan.

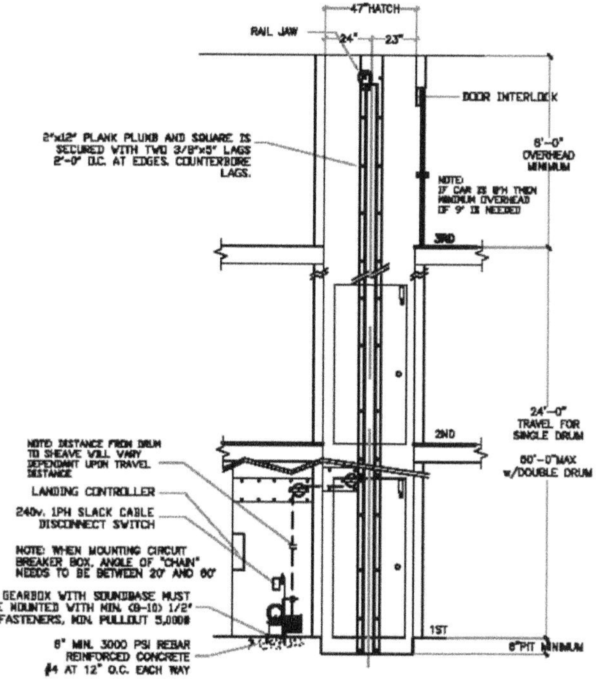

Figure 12.72 Section A-A.

shows the information an architect or designer will need to integrate into the working drawings. Note that the shaft dimension requirements, the clearances for this specific elevator, and the electrical supply must be shown in the working drawings. A section through the elevator shaft and machine room is shown in Figure 12.72. This drawing depicts the length of the vertical travel, the electrical supply location, and the required 8″-deep pit depression that is required for cab clearance. The area and dimensions for the pit area must be shown accurately on the foundation plan of the working drawings. Note that the depth of the elevator pit will vary from manufacturer to manufacturer. So, make sure you utilize the specification to specify the correct depth.

To assist in planning access to the electric elevator, use the various car configurations available from the manufacturers. Examples of car configurations are illustrated in Figure 12.73. A photograph of a finished electric elevator installation is shown in Figure 12.74. In Figure 12.75 see the cut away view of an elevator and elevator shaft for a larger commercial building. Many of the manufacturers will provide you with a BIM drawing of the elevator cab and clearances required both at the bottom and the top of the elevator shaft. A word of caution many city agencies don't allow added height clearances for elevators. Be aware of the governing agency with respect to height. You don't want to learn the hard way that the elevator will not be able to go to the top floor of the building as a result of height regulations.

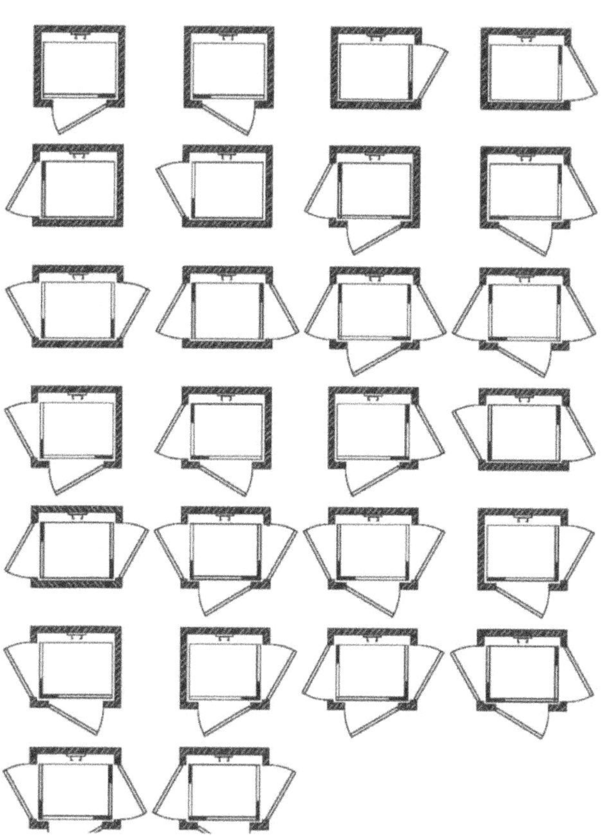

Figure 12.73 Car configurations.

Figure 12.74 Elevette. (Courtesy of Inclinator Co. of America.)

Another manufactured device used in the development of a vertical link is a stair lift. This unit is ideal for persons with walking disabilities or other physical limitations. Figure 12.76 depicts a plan view of the stair lift positions and the dimensional aspects of the unit as it projects into the stairway run. A photograph of a stair lift installation is shown in Figure 12.77.

For persons who rely on the use of a wheelchair for vertical access, the use of a vertical lift occupies less space than an elevator and may be desirable. As in addressing the dimensional requirements of an elevator, the architect or designer will need to provide the dimensions, clearances, phone line, and electrical supply information as stipulated by the manufacturer's specifications. An example of a platform plan, with its requirements for a vertical lift and the vertical travel dimensions, is depicted in Figures 12.78 and 12.79. A photograph of a finished vertical lift installation is illustrated in Figure 12.80. This vertical lift unit is constructed of fiberglass that is rust-free and has a nonskid surface. Such units are available in various colors. Their maximum load capacity is 750 pounds. These specific units are ideal for shorter floor to floor level.

A vertical linking unit that is convenient for lifting groceries and other heavy items from one level to another is a home waiter, frequently referred to as a **dumbwaiter**. These units vary in shaft size and maximum load capacity. The space planning and layout requirements for dimensions and clearances will be delineated in the working drawings, as described for elevators and other lifting devices. A shaft plan illustrating dimensions and clearances for a two-landing home waiter installation is depicted in Figure 12.81. This particular unit is limited to a 75-pound lifting capacity. Figure 12.82

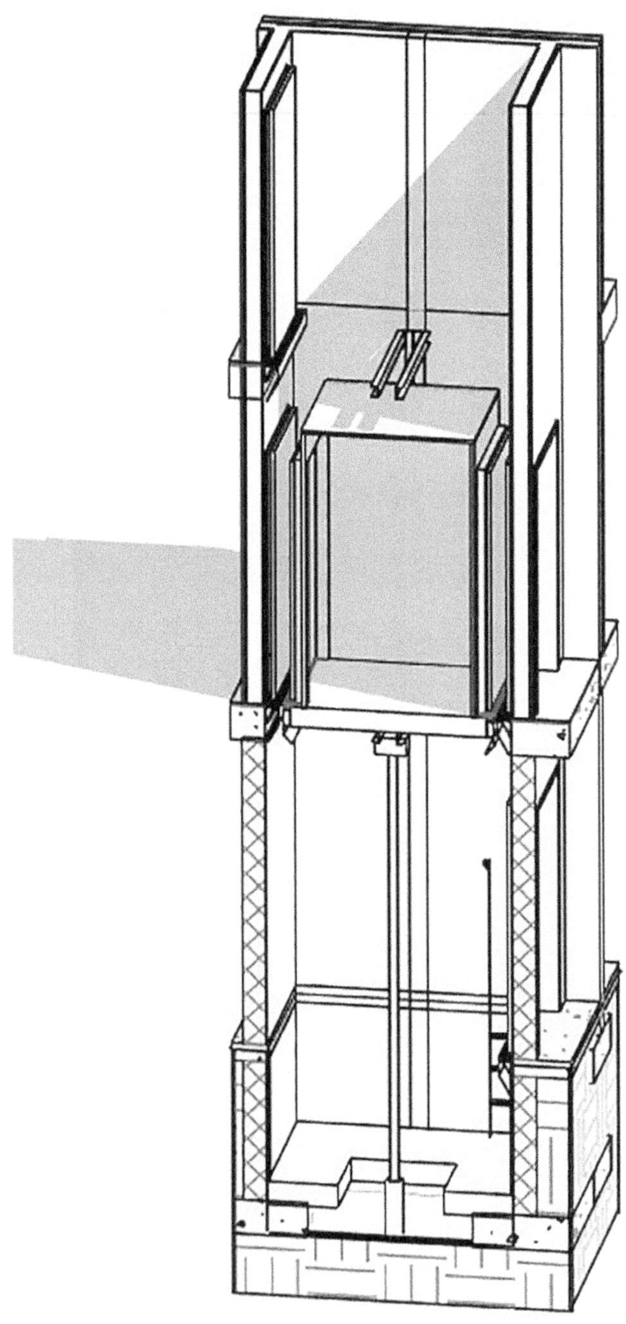

Figure 12.75 Cut view of an elevator cab and shaft for a commercial building.

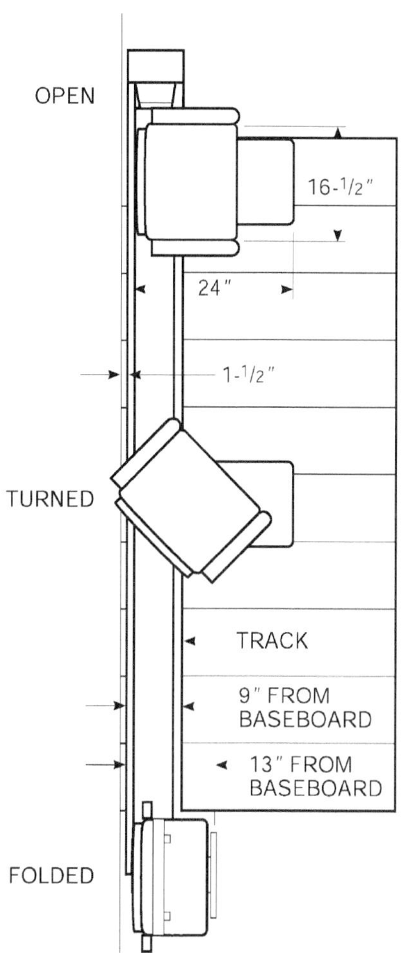

Figure 12.76 Stair lift diagram.

Figure 12.77 Stair lift. (Courtesy of Inclinator Co. of America.)

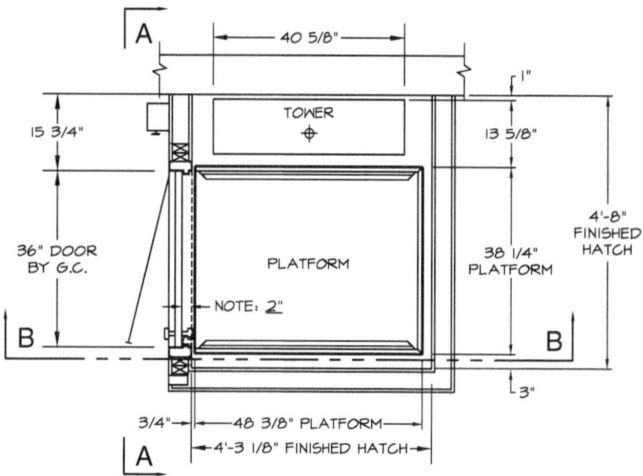

Figure 12.78 Vertical lift diagram.

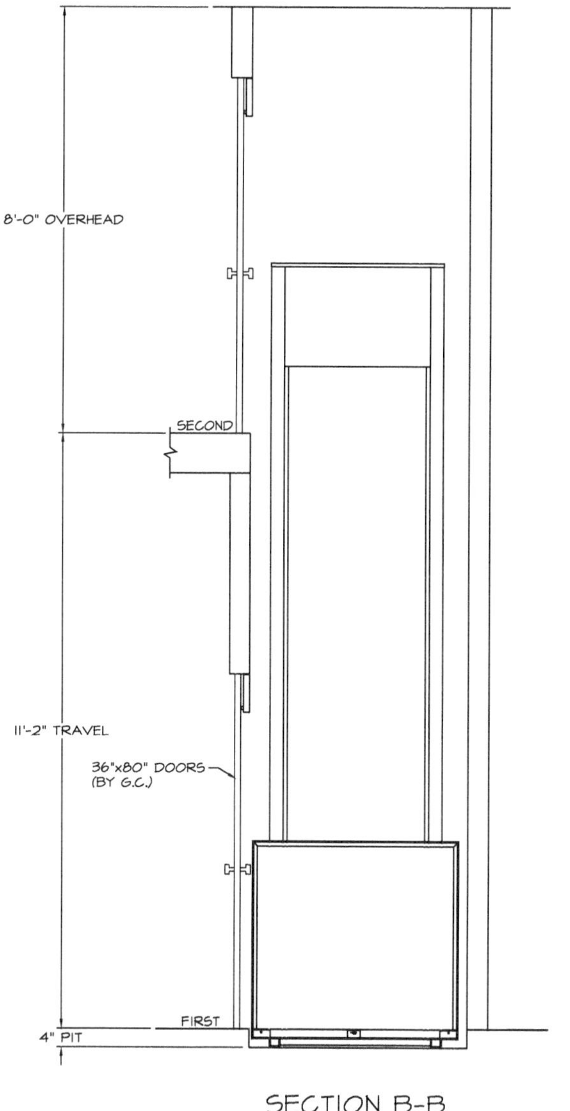

Figure 12.79 Section B-B.

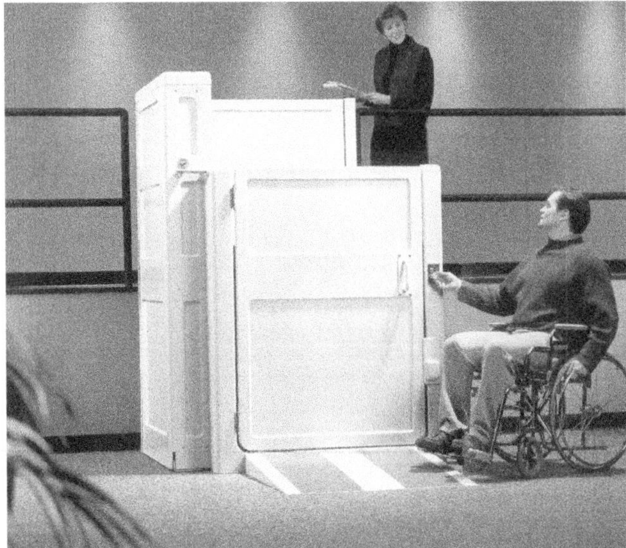

Figure 12.80 Spectralift. (Courtesy of Inclinator Co. of America.)

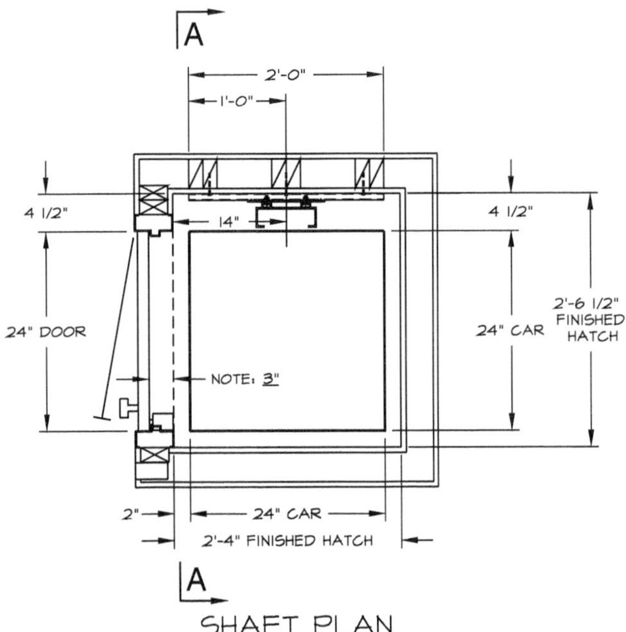

Figure 12.81 Shaft plan.

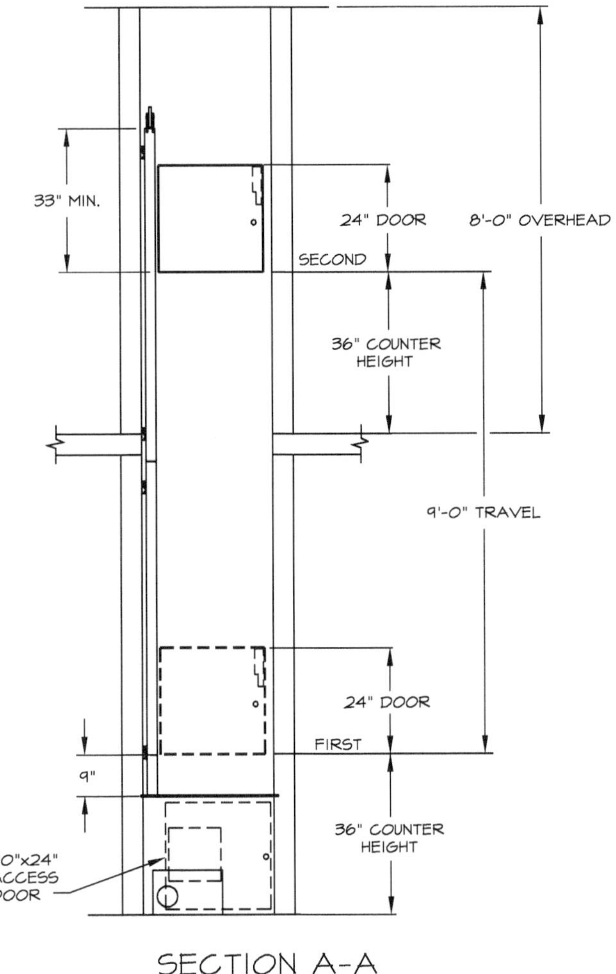

Figure 12.82 Section A-A.

shows a section of this home waiter unit illustrating the vertical travel dimensions, clearances, machine equipment room location, and the desired counter height. The vertical link units described here are but a few examples of lifting units that are found primarily in residential projects. Manufacturers provide complete BIM drawings for implantation into working drawings into the plans, sections, and details.

SAMPLE DRAWINGS OF DETAILS

Miscellaneous Wall Sections

Depending on the governing building code requirements and the tenant's use of the operating space, there may be various wall construction requirements. In the case where a non-load-bearing, one-hour fire-rated corridor is designed to include some glazing on the corridor walls, it will be necessary to satisfy a building code requirement that calls for a ¼"-thick (minimum) wire glass secured in steel frames. A detail for this condition is illustrated in Figure 12.83.

The internal walls between the "living" spaces for tenants may require that the walls be constructed to solve two conditions: one is to satisfy a one-hour fire separation requirement, and the other is to provide a means of reducing or eliminating sound transmission between the tenant spaces. Figure 12.84 depicts the recommended non-load-bearing wall construction between living spaces to satisfy the fire and sound considerations.

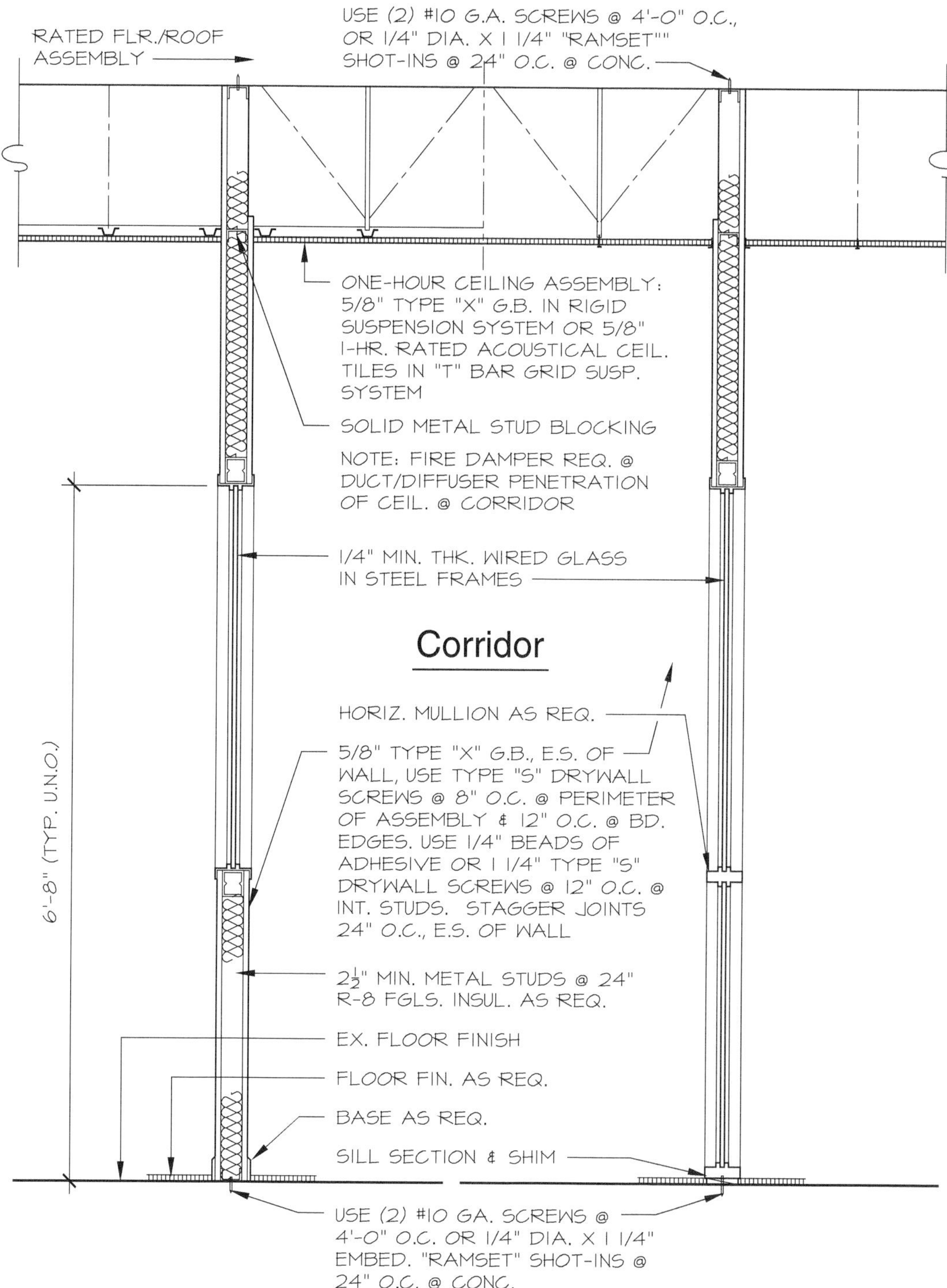

Figure 12.83 Glazed corridor wall (non-load-bearing).

Interior door designs will vary according to the desires of the tenant and the space plan designer. An example of an interior door design detail that includes a fixed matching panel above a door is shown in Figure 12.85. This detail is designed for a non-load-bearing wall and door condition.

When restrooms abut an office space or other area where people assemble, it is recommended that the dividing walls be constructed with sound insulation batts between the metal studs. Resilient clips are used to attach the gypsum board to the metal studs. This non-load-bearing wall section is illustrated in Figure 12.86.

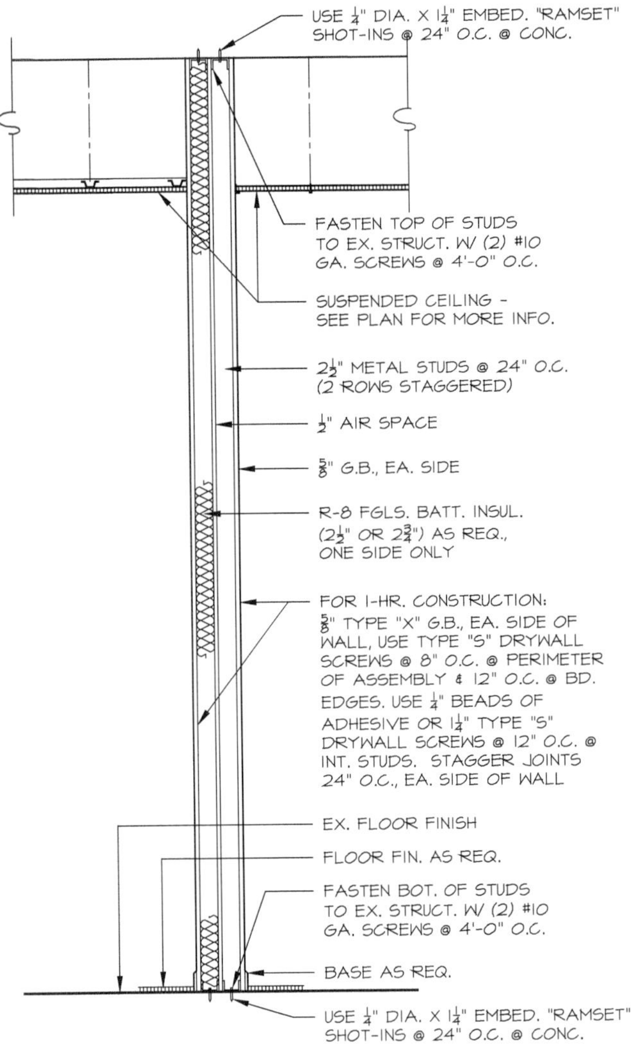

Figure 12.84 Fire and sound wall (non-load-bearing).

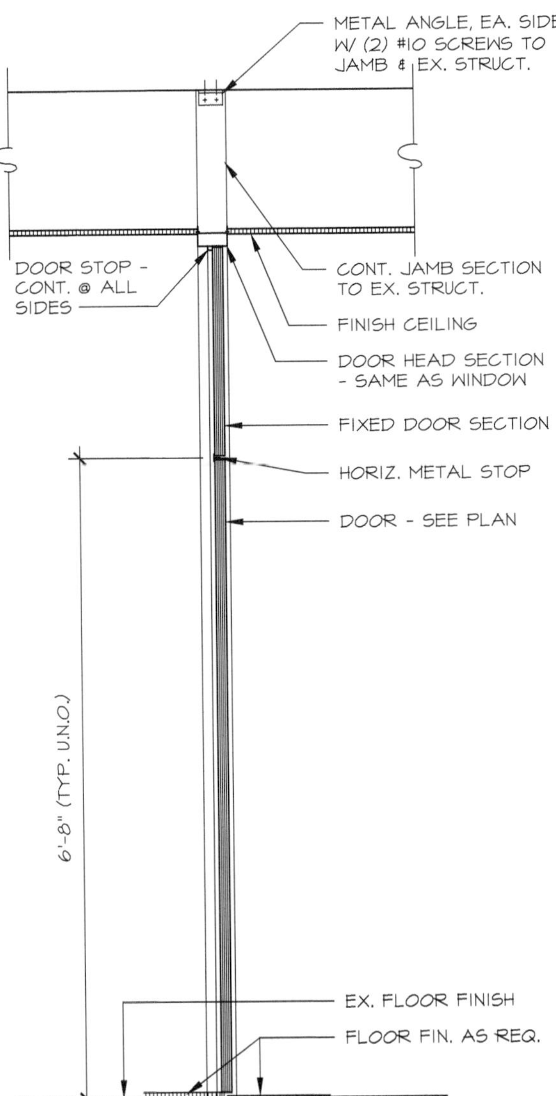

Figure 12.85 Interior door and fixed panel.

In cases where one-hour fire-rated division walls are required to meet a building code requirement; the walls will be constructed from the tenant floor to the floor system above. The wall sections in Figure 12.87 illustrate the materials required to satisfy the construction of a one-hour non-load-bearing separation wall. An example of a free hand sketch is provided of a balcony. There can be a wide variety of conditions and situations that need to be detailed for a project (Figure 12.88).

Key Terms

bearing pressure
bearing surface
brown coat
chase
chimney chase
color coat
compression
counterflashing
details
dumbwaiter
freehand sketches
freestyle
half-section
hearth
noncombustible
outlining
risers
scratch coat
sisal-kraft
stucco bumps
stucco mold
Styrofoam
tread
wide flange

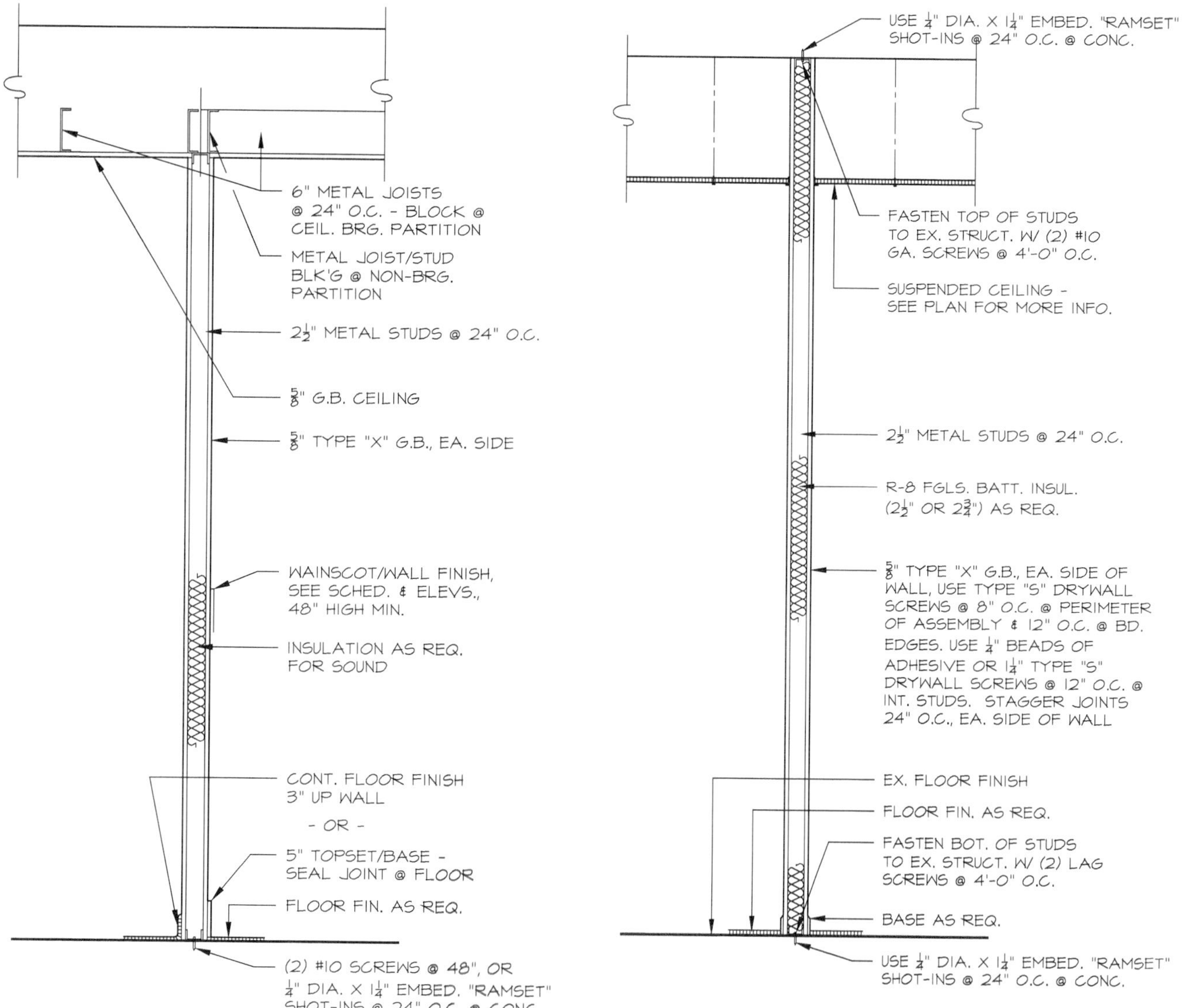

Figure 12.86 Restroom partition (non-load-bearing).

Figure 12.87 One-hour separation wall (non-load-bearing).

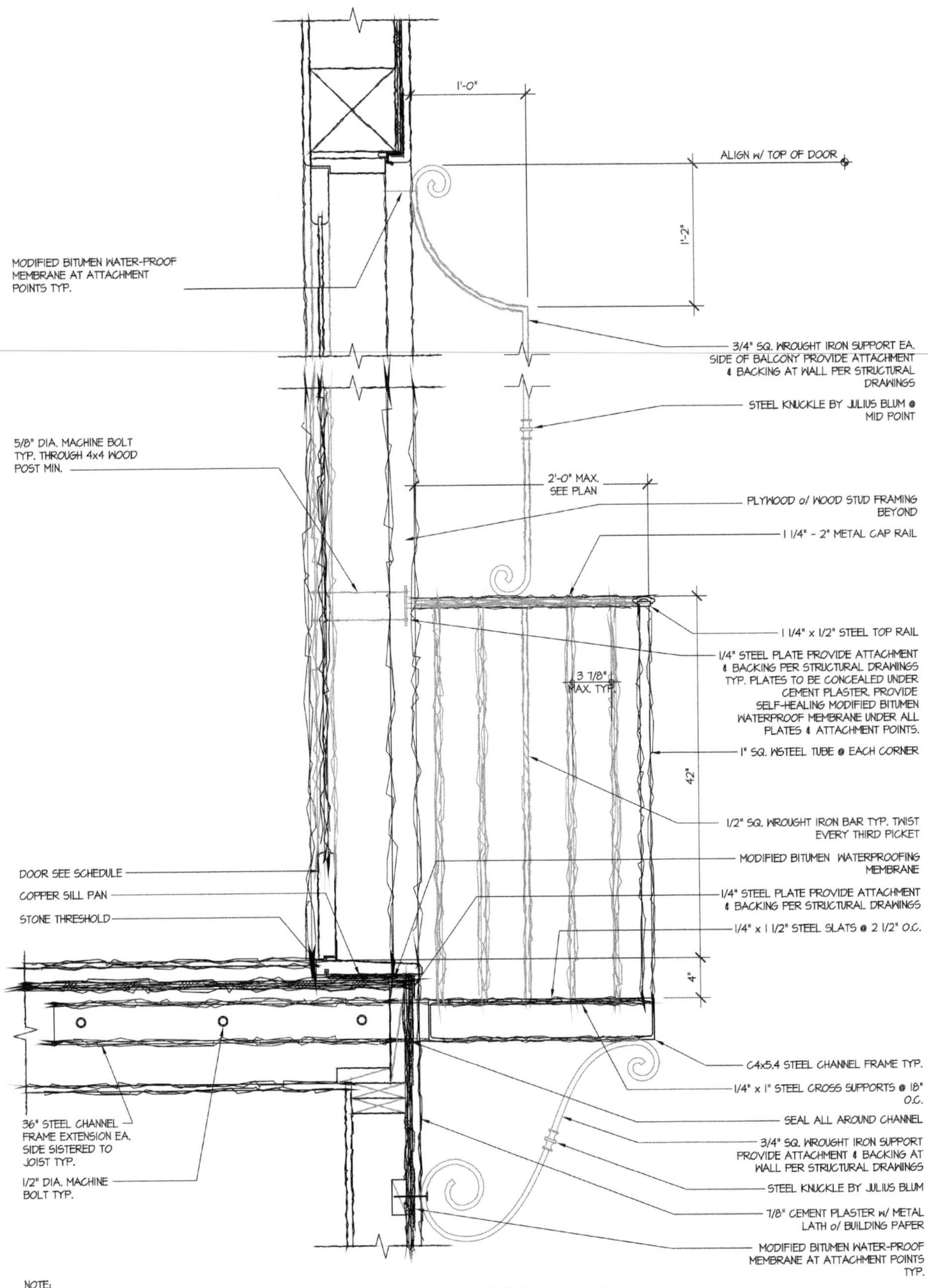
1'-0"
ALIGN w/ TOP OF DOOR
1'-2"
MODIFIED BITUMEN WATER-PROOF MEMBRANE AT ATTACHMENT POINTS TYP.
3/4" SQ. WROUGHT IRON SUPPORT EA. SIDE OF BALCONY PROVIDE ATTACHMENT & BACKING AT WALL PER STRUCTURAL DRAWINGS
STEEL KNUCKLE BY JULIUS BLUM @ MID POINT
5/8" DIA. MACHINE BOLT TYP. THROUGH 4x4 WOOD POST MIN.
2'-0" MAX. SEE PLAN
PLYWOOD o/ WOOD STUD FRAMING BEYOND
1 1/4" - 2" METAL CAP RAIL
1 1/4" x 1/2" STEEL TOP RAIL
1/4" STEEL PLATE PROVIDE ATTACHMENT & BACKING PER STRUCTURAL DRAWINGS TYP. PLATES TO BE CONCEALED UNDER CEMENT PLASTER. PROVIDE SELF-HEALING MODIFIED BITUMEN WATERPROOF MEMBRANE UNDER ALL PLATES & ATTACHMENT POINTS.
3 7/8" MAX. TYP.
1" SQ. WSTEEL TUBE @ EACH CORNER
42"
1/2" SQ. WROUGHT IRON BAR TYP. TWIST EVERY THIRD PICKET
DOOR SEE SCHEDULE
MODIFIED BITUMEN WATERPROOFING MEMBRANE
COPPER SILL PAN
1/4" STEEL PLATE PROVIDE ATTACHMENT & BACKING PER STRUCTURAL DRAWINGS
STONE THRESHOLD
1/4" x 1 1/2" STEEL SLATS @ 2 1/2" O.C.
4"
C4x5.4 STEEL CHANNEL FRAME TYP.
1/4" x 1" STEEL CROSS SUPPORTS @ 18" O.C.
SEAL ALL AROUND CHANNEL
36" STEEL CHANNEL FRAME EXTENSION EA. SIDE SISTERED TO JOIST TYP.
3/4" SQ. WROUGHT IRON SUPPORT PROVIDE ATTACHMENT & BACKING AT WALL PER STRUCTURAL DRAWINGS
1/2" DIA. MACHINE BOLT TYP.
STEEL KNUCKLE BY JULIUS BLUM
7/8" CEMENT PLASTER w/ METAL LATH o/ BUILDING PAPER
MODIFIED BITUMEN WATER-PROOF MEMBRANE AT ATTACHMENT POINTS TYP.
NOTE:
ALL COMPONENTS TO BE HOT DIPPED GALVANIZED (G90), BONDERIZED & PAINTED. COLOR TO BE SELECTED BY ARCHITECT
Wrought Iron Balcony
SCALE: 1 1/2"=1'-0"

Figure 12.88 Wrought Iron Balcony.

PART

Application of Working Drawings in Practice

Chapters 13–16 will address several different building types that make up a very large part of the construction industry: tenant improvement, additions and alteration to a structure, historical preservation (restoration), and BIM via Revit. One cannot totally comprehend the scope of architecture without some knowledge of the design process and included in the text is the technical portion of the design that communicates the end goals for the client.

chapter

13

ADDITIONS/ALTERATIONS, HISTORICAL PRESERVATION (RESTORATION), AND TENANT IMPROVEMENTS (TI)

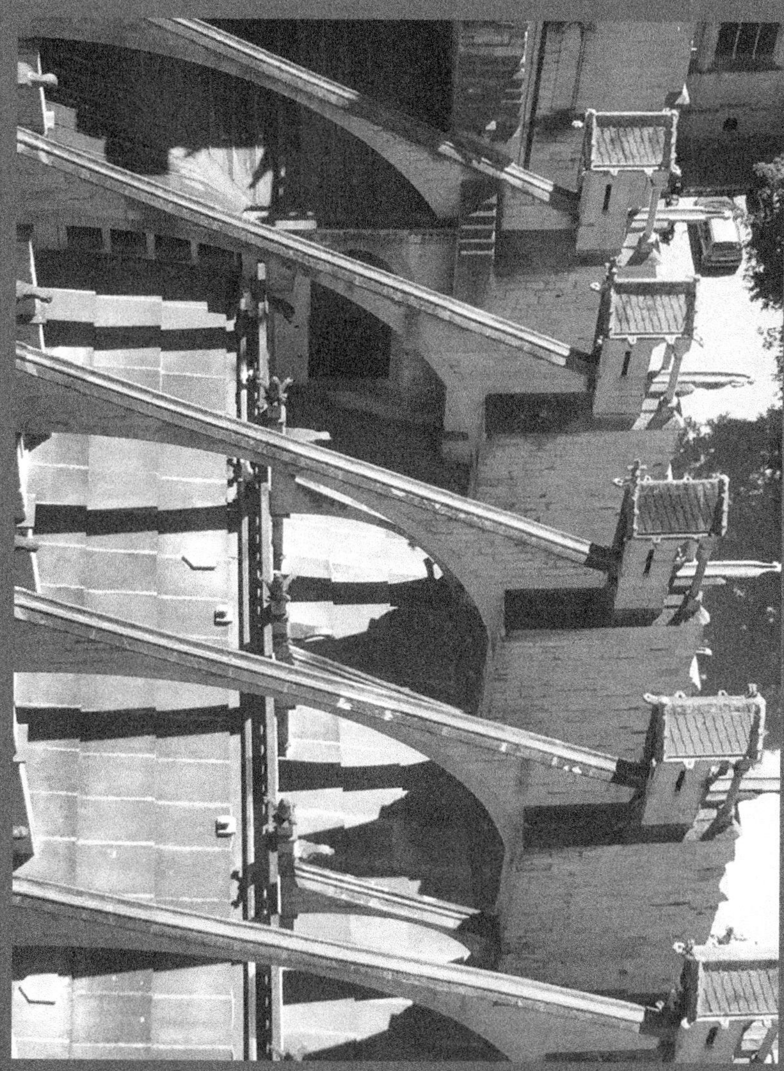

The Professional Practice of Architectural Working Drawings, Sixth Edition. Nagy R. Bakhoum and Osamu A. Wakita.
© 2024 John Wiley & Sons Inc. Published 2024 by John Wiley & Sons Inc.
Companion website: www.wiley.com\go\bakhoum\theprofessionalpracticeofarchitecturalworkingdrawings

ARCHITECTURAL ADDITIONS AND ALTERATIONS

This chapter will address four different building types that make up a very large part of the construction industry: additions to a structure, alterations to a structure, historical preservation, and tenant improvement (TI), usually to buildings that are already built and altered by the owner to lease or rent. Prior to continuing this chapter, it would be a good idea to review the section on office standards found in Chapter 2.

Standards

Aside from the normal standards in reference to dimensioning, noting, and referencing, there will be new standards for identifying new walls, demolished walls, existing walls, and special, unique walls, such as walls built with angles, pierced with a sculpture, and possibly built with a new material. Look at Figure 13.1, which shows a partial floor plan with existing, new, and demolished walls. In Figure 13.2, you can see the representations of a new wall, which is drawn with two object lines and includes a slightly darker tone called poché. The second illustration shows walls that are to be demolished, identified by two hidden lines. The third type shows two solid lines that identify those walls that are existing. If the walls are other than wood-framed walls, we must be able to identify those walls and use a drawing symbol for masonry, steel, or concrete as shown in these examples. These standards can be used throughout this chapter.

The architect is required to use the same standards that were written in this book for new structures. However, for an addition, one side of the dimension should always be placed on an existing wall. The larger the addition, the more complex the process becomes; unlike new buildings, you do not dimension to the stud line, but rather dimension to the finished side of the existing building, which will not be destroyed during construction. The same holds true for all other parts of the building. The foundation plan, the section, and the elevation will all have datums established throughout the construction. All datums must be measured in the field. Do not rely on drawings that were done to build the original building but rely on their actual dimensions.

Alterations

Alteration is the process of changing the structure on both the interior and exterior. The process is extremely simple; actually, the construction documents resemble additions, but the concentration is, as the title states, altering the structure.

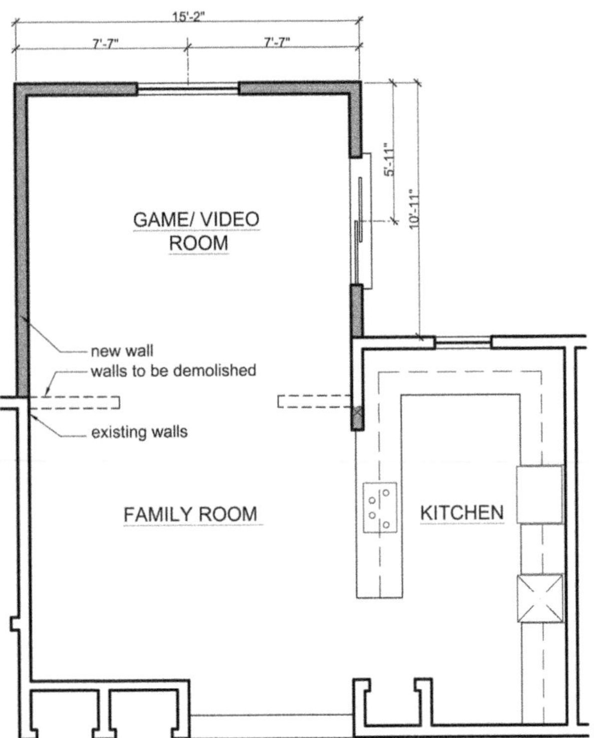

Figure 13.1 Floor plan showing existing, new, and demolished walls.

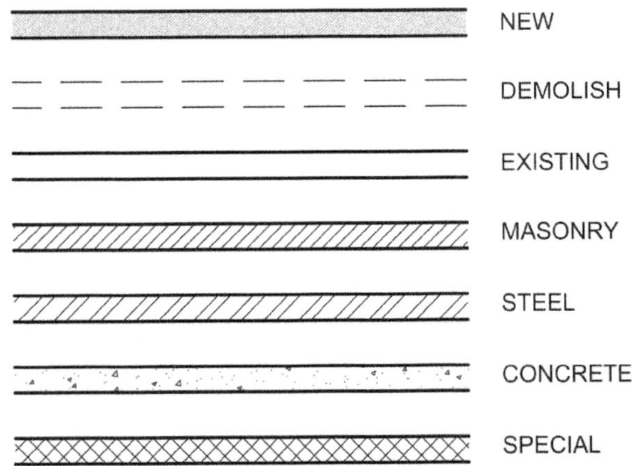

Figure 13.2 Wall types.

You may encounter a situation where you will not only alter a building but add to it as well.

As in all construction documents, dimensioning is critical. Establish a datum as a point reference from which all new changes are made. Always put yourself in the position of the workers in the field and try to visualize their task as you prepare the construction documents. By now, you must realize that this approach is sacred to all construction documents that you will be asked to prepare. We have included in each a case study. Look at these examples and try to understand the mindset of the person who prepared them.

Case studies shown in Figures 13.3–13.5 are unique in the sense that these preliminary drawings can be converted easily into working drawings, and can also help a client to understand how their furniture will fit into the final floor plan (Figure 13.3), with an alternative first-floor plan. Figure 13.5 is drawn in such a manner that it can be used as a graphic presentational drawing rapidly converted into a working drawing.

HISTORIC PRESERVATION (RESTORATION)

One of the most difficult and precious drawings that you will ever encounter is historical restoration, the process of preserving a masterpiece of architecture. The structure may be hundreds of years old. It was deemed worth salvaging by our culture to preserve a moment in our lives where even the method of construction may have been totally different than it is presently. Historical restoration is also a way of honoring the designer's concept and attitude.

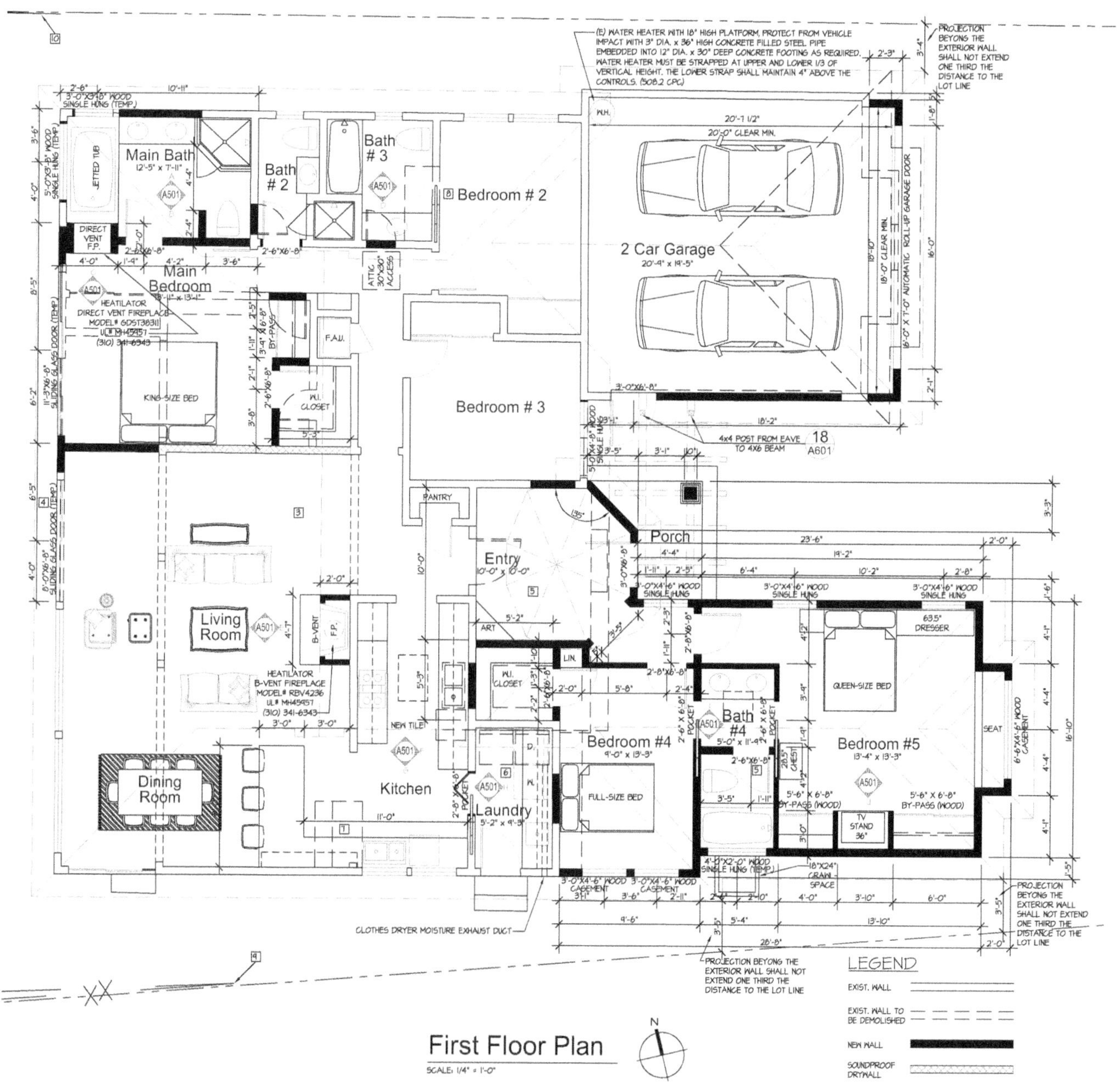

Figure 13.3 Addition/alteration case study floor plan.

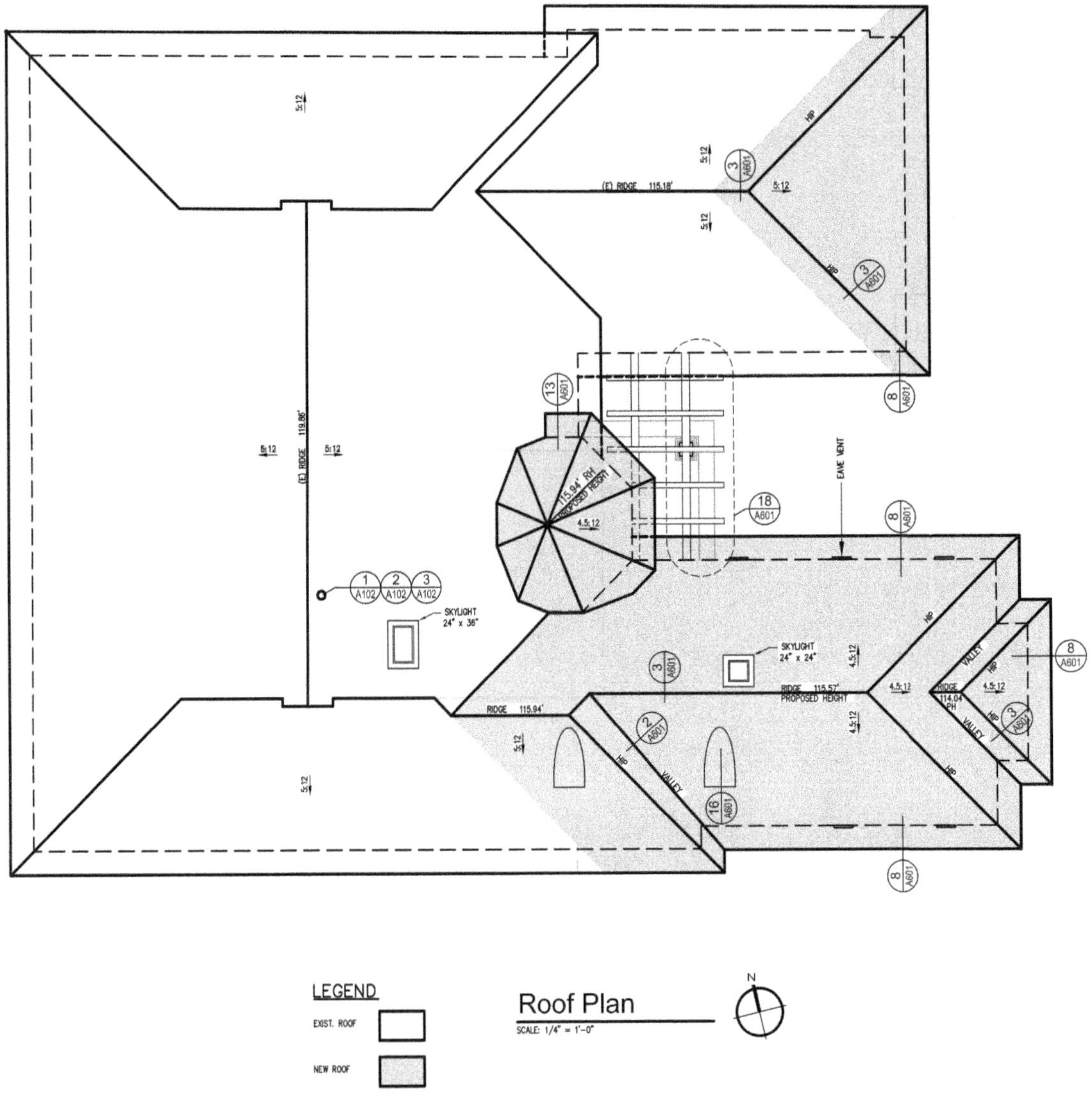

LEGEND
EXIST. ROOF
NEW ROOF

Roof Plan
SCALE: 1/4" = 1'-0"

Figure 13.4 Addition/alteration case study roof plan.

Figure 13.5 Addition/alteration case study elevations.

Restoration is more than a matter of patching and temporarily fixing damage to part of the structure, repairing structural damage while maintaining the integrity of the building, or repairing a portion of the building that is deteriorating without affecting the nature of the design. It is a monumental task to understand the various components of the preservation while maintaining the culture of our people. Much research has to be done before one engages in construction documents because it is so important to understand why the building is being restored.

It may begin with the major backbone of the building and then reservicing the entire facade. Historical restoration may include engaging a totally new technique, such as photography. Digital photography has made it practical since the computer can produce an image immediately. You can then produce an overlay onto the photograph and produce a computer image of what needs to be done to the building. See Figure 13.6.

As significant architects design building and get recognized for a specific contribution to history, buildings may find themselves designated as landmark designation. This allows the owner of the property to provide the jurisdiction with proposed restoration plans and request a tax credit by applying to the Mills Act. This gives the property owner a significant property tax reduction in order that the property owner will apply, what would be saved on taxes, to restore a building. In some cases, restoration is as simple as following the original plans but more often the plans are missing or no longer exist, so photographic history begins to fill in the blanks. There are professional historians that can be hired to assist in a restoration project. The Secretary of the Interior has outlined significant guidelines for what can be deemed historic and what types of changes can be made. As a general rule of thumb, exterior front and sides must be limited to changes that bring the building back to its original design. The rear of the building is a little less governed and is allowed to be altered to improve the quality of life for the person occupying the space. Interiors are less restrictive but strongly encouraged to make significant efforts to keep it in its original glory. Figure 13.7 demonstrates a historically significant home

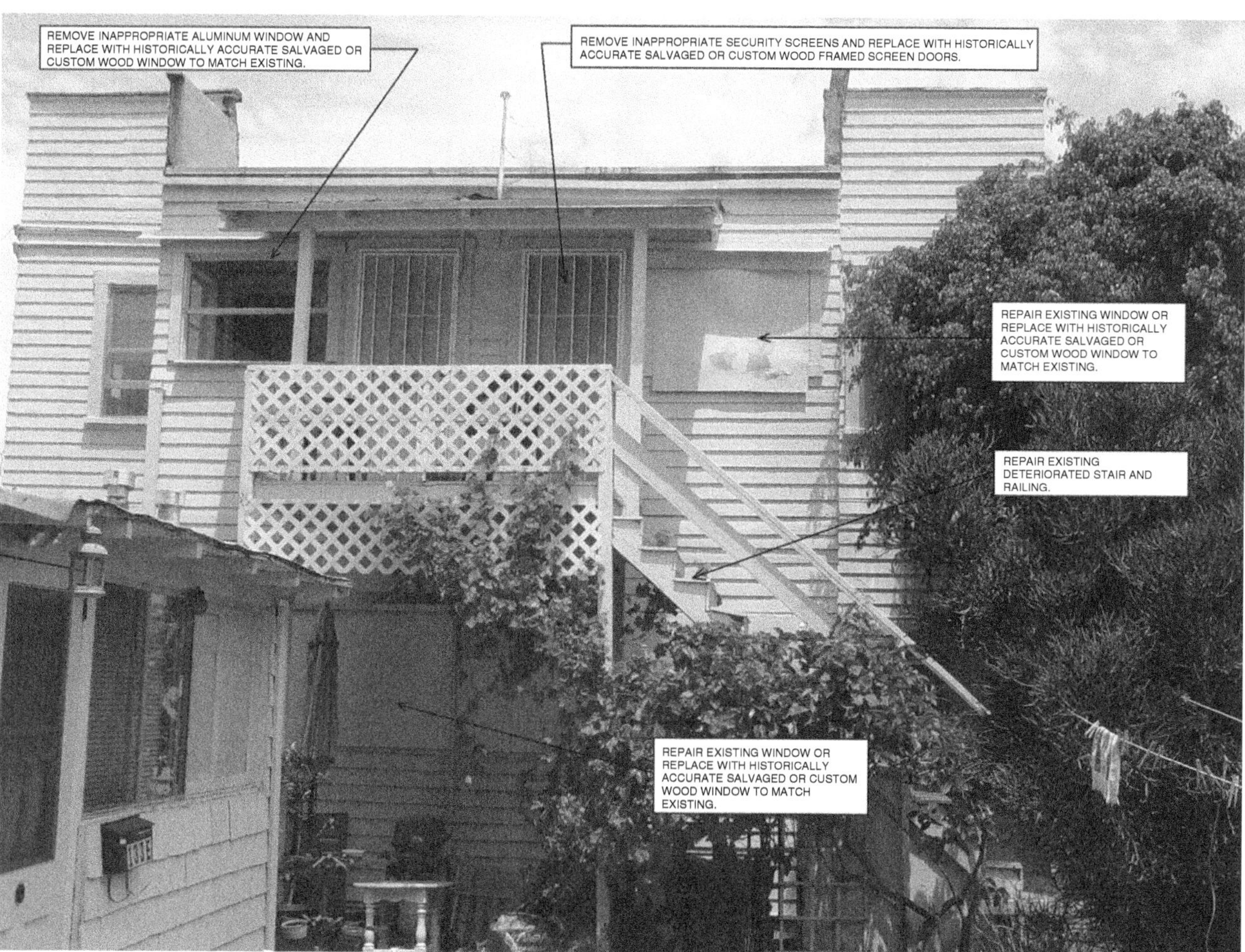

Figure 13.6 Historical restoration case study.

Figure 13.7 Historical restoration addition compared to original home.

with a proposed addition on the rear side of the property. This would allow the owner of the building to keep the historic status and yet allow the owner to expand to be more comfortable in the home. Typically, the side-by-side comparison is intended to allow the committee to be able to see the existing historic building against the new proposed addition.

Photography/Drafting

It is particularly inventive to use digital photography for drawing both interior and exterior elevations. This technique has found a home in historical restoration and older TI projects. Four examples can be found in Figure 13.6.

■ TENANT IMPROVEMENT

Unlike other buildings described in this book, **tenant improvement**. The building maybe built and the interior space is leased, rented, or sold for occupancy as a condominium (i.e., shared space owned by a group). This will be demonstrated by the use of two existing office buildings.

Tenant Improvement A, which has a large, undeveloped, open space with nonrequired travel and exit corridors yet to be constructed, will illustrate the necessary design procedures to satisfy corridor and exit travel to an existing lobby and two stairwells. Construction assemblies for exit corridor walls will be detailed to satisfy specific building code requirements.

Three tenant suite spaces will be illustrated as an example of the partial development for a large floor area. Exit requirements for these three spaces will be discussed, with an example of a tenant separation-wall assembly that will be constructed between the various suites. Building A and its illustrations provide an example of open space planning for tenant suites, required exiting, and wall construction requirements. Working drawings for the tenant suites are not illustrated.

The improvement of a space, in most cases, is defined as the construction of the interior walls, doors, windows, ceilings, movable partitions, and specialty items that may be required for the function of the tenant's daily tasks. Improvements also include cabinetry, hardware, plumbing fixtures, finished floors, carpeting, and finished painting. Such improvement usually includes supplementary heating, ventilating, and air-conditioning systems, sized and installed for a designated space or area.

Internal planning deals with the task areas enclosed within the walls by various construction assemblies. The tenant—that is, the user—will provide the necessary design criteria for the designer to plan the various task areas. Design criteria may include such information as room use, room sizes, and toilet facilities; electrical, telephone, and equipment locations; special lighting requirements; and desired floor, wall, and ceiling finishes.

In most cases, the designer or drafter will plan within a designated area of an existing structure, although they may plan an entire floor area. Generally, designated areas are found in multitenant buildings and vary in square footage. It should be noted that TI may also entail redeveloping an existing constructed space. This situation requires that the room dimensions, lighting fixtures, structural components, equipment locations, and existing electrical and mechanical locations be verified before the preliminary design process begins.

It is imperative that the first step in drafting a set of construction documents for a TI project be the production of a drawing called **as built**. This drawing features the dimensions of the structure as it stands; hence the name "as built."

Often, the original set of construction documents is available to the TI drafter, but the parameters of the inside of the structure must be remeasured. The reason is that a structure is rarely built to the precise size shown on the original drawing.

The as-built drawing becomes the base for the entire set of construction documents from this point on. If the original set of documents is available, the as-built drawing is derived by making the necessary corrections on the existing drawings: moving walls, column locations, and so forth.

■ SAMPLE—MADISON-B BUILDING

With a given floor plan for an existing three-story undeveloped structure, we can explore potential floor areas for tenant use. Figure 13.8 illustrates the second-floor level of this building. As illustrated, the existing

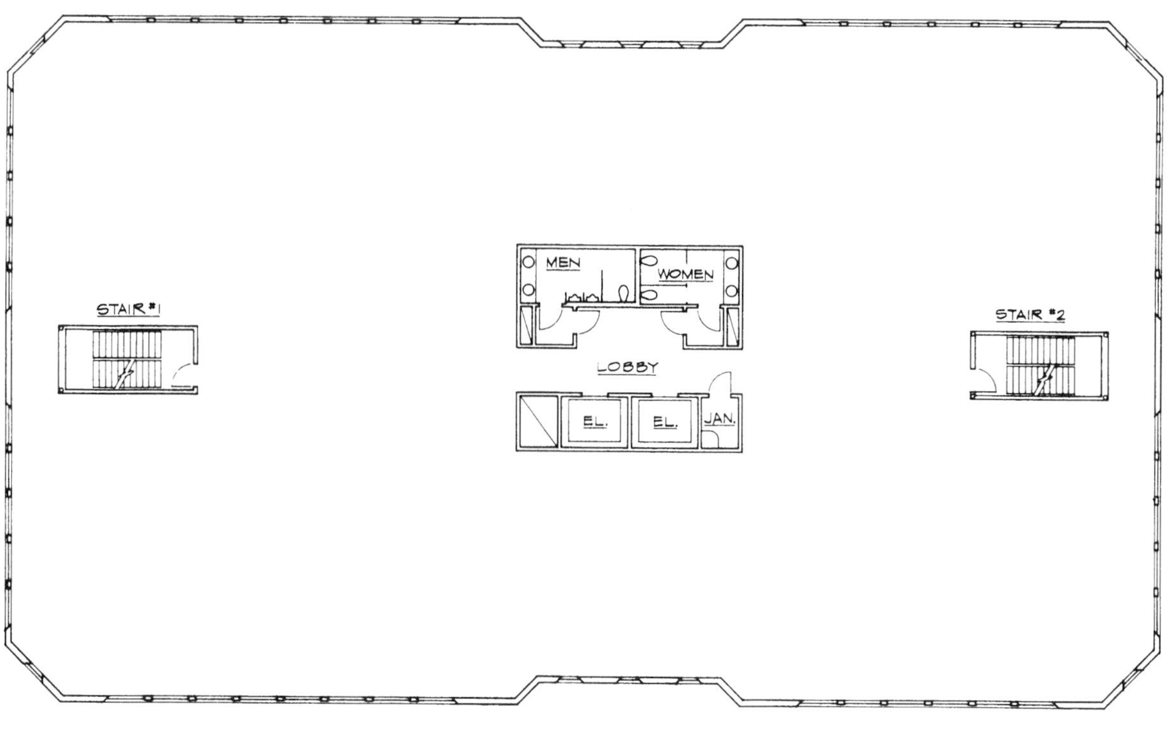

Figure 13.8 Existing undeveloped floor.

stair-wells, men's and women's toilet facilities, elevator shaft, telephone room, and janitor's room have been constructed according to building code requirements. The first prerequisite is to establish a corridor that satisfies all exit requirements of the governing building and fire codes.

Exit Corridors

Figure 13.9 shows a pictorial with a corridor that satisfies code relative to width and location. The walls and ceiling construction of the corridor must meet the requirements for a one-hour fire-rated assembly. A detailed construction section of this assembly is depicted in Figure 13.10. Metal studs are illustrated; however, wood studs may be used if they meet the governing fire code requirements. It should be noted that most building codes require exit doors into the corridor to have a 20-minute fire-rated assembly, as designated in the corridor section in Figure 13.10. As described earlier, it is essential that you verify the dimensions by remeasuring the structure. Even if you have the original drawings of the structure, you must verify its size, window and door locations, stairs, elevator locations, and even the corridor locations. You will always discover that changes in the size and location of existing walls occurred during construction.

After an exit corridor that will be used by various tenants on this floor is established, designated areas or floor areas required to satisfy the particular users' space requirements may now be formulated. In dealing with a tenant's area requirements, the designer must adhere to building code criteria relative to the number of exits required for a specific area.

An example of required exiting is depicted in Figure 13.11, which shows that Suite A has a floor area of 3,200 square feet. Because of this suite's area and occupant load, the building code requires two exit doors to the corridor. According to the code, these two doors must be separated by a distance of one-half the length of the diagonal dimension of this area. See Figure 13.11. Figure 13.12 illustrates this condition pictorially. This code requirement will be a primary factor in the internal planning of this suite. As shown in Figure 13.13, the floor area of Suite C is less than 1600 square feet; thus, according to the building code, this suite requires only one exit to the common corridor. It should be noted that additional toilet facilities may be required by the building code authorities, predicated on the number of employees occupying the particular suites. This would be a planning factor for the TI design.

When there are numerous tenants on a given floor level, local building department authorities, and building

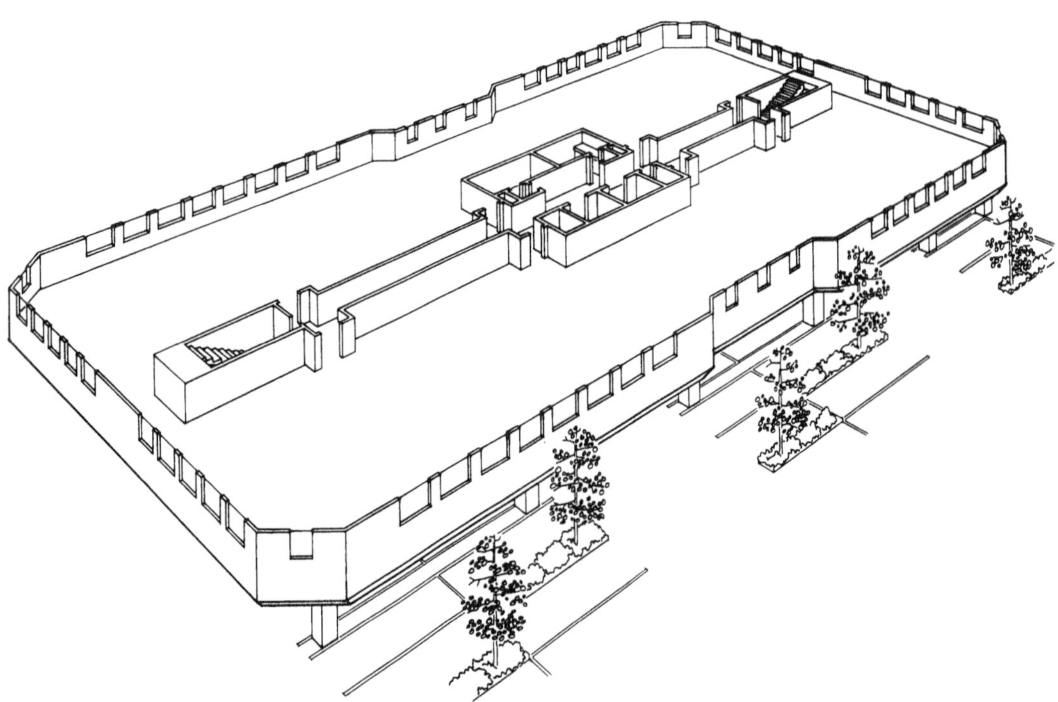

Figure 13.9 Pictorial view of corridor.

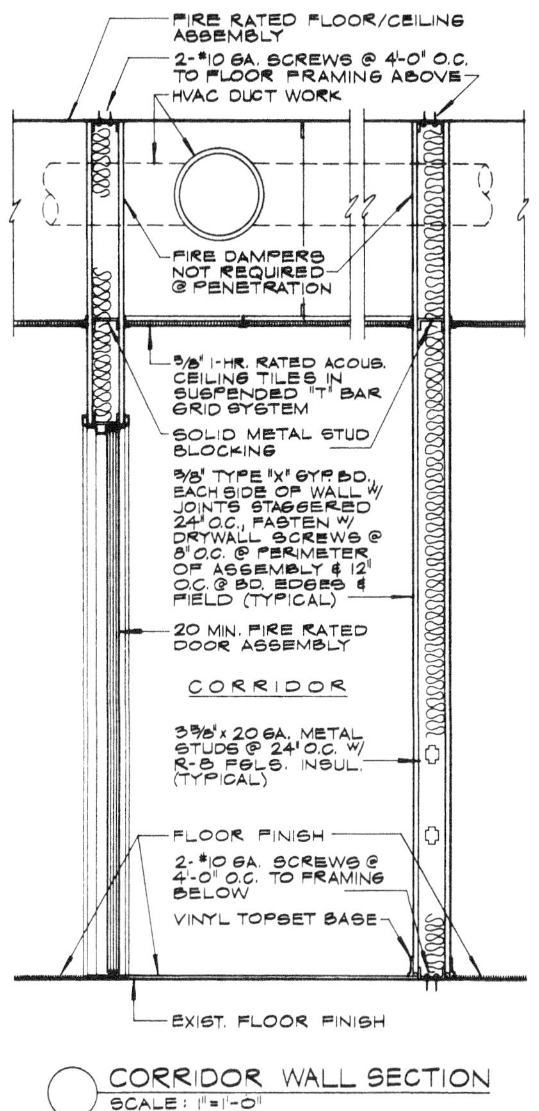

Figure 13.10 Fire-rated corridor construction.

codes may require a one-hour fire-rated wall assembly between each tenant area. Figure 13.14 illustrates a non-load-bearing, one-hour fire-rated wall assembly incorporating metal studs and gypsum board. A **non-load-bearing wall** is one that does not support ceiling or floor weight from above or any other weight factors distributed to this wall. Wall insulation is shown as a means to decrease noise transmission between the various tenants.

The construction techniques for a wall assembly used within a specific suite may vary. Figure 13.15 illustrates an example of a wall partition section used in offices for TI. Note that this wall partition extends to the roof framing in order to reduce the sound transmission between the various rooms and halls, and maintains a secure office condition.

Building A has been used to illustrate the basic procedures and requirements for potential suite developments within a large, existing, undeveloped floor space. Building B, in contrast, will illustrate the procedures implemented in an architect's office for a TI design and the completion of working drawings.

DEVELOPMENT OF THE KEIM BUILDING

As discussed earlier, internal suite planning is developed from the tenant's criteria that satisfy the needs for its business function.

In planning a given undeveloped space on the second floor of an existing office building, the designer will visit the space and verify the structural components, such as columns and beam heights. The designer and staff will take measurements to verify existing inside area dimensions, column locations, window sizes, and the spacing of window mullions. In some cases, mechanical, electrical, and/or plumbing components, such as exhaust ducts, roof drainage pipes, and water lines for domestic and mechanical use, may be located in this undeveloped space. If so, they should be plotted on the initial plan layout.

Figure 13.16 shows the undeveloped floor plan of an existing second-floor level of a two-story office building. The process of making working drawings for the improvement of Suite 201 starts with the tenant requirements and verification of the existing space and conditions. Note the existing steel columns, stairs, mechanical shafts, roof drain lines, windows, and window mullion locations.

The tenant for this designated space deals with graphic communications and has provided the designer with a list of the various rooms needed, their preferred sizes, their use(s), and their relationships to each other. This communication between client and architect becomes the program for the project.

The rooms specified by the tenant include a reception area, three offices, a conference room, a large studio accommodating numerous drawing boards, a small studio for airbrush media, a copy room, and a storage room. The tenant also desired a coffee area with cabinets and sink and a service area for cleanup of art implements. The location of walls and rough plumbing for the

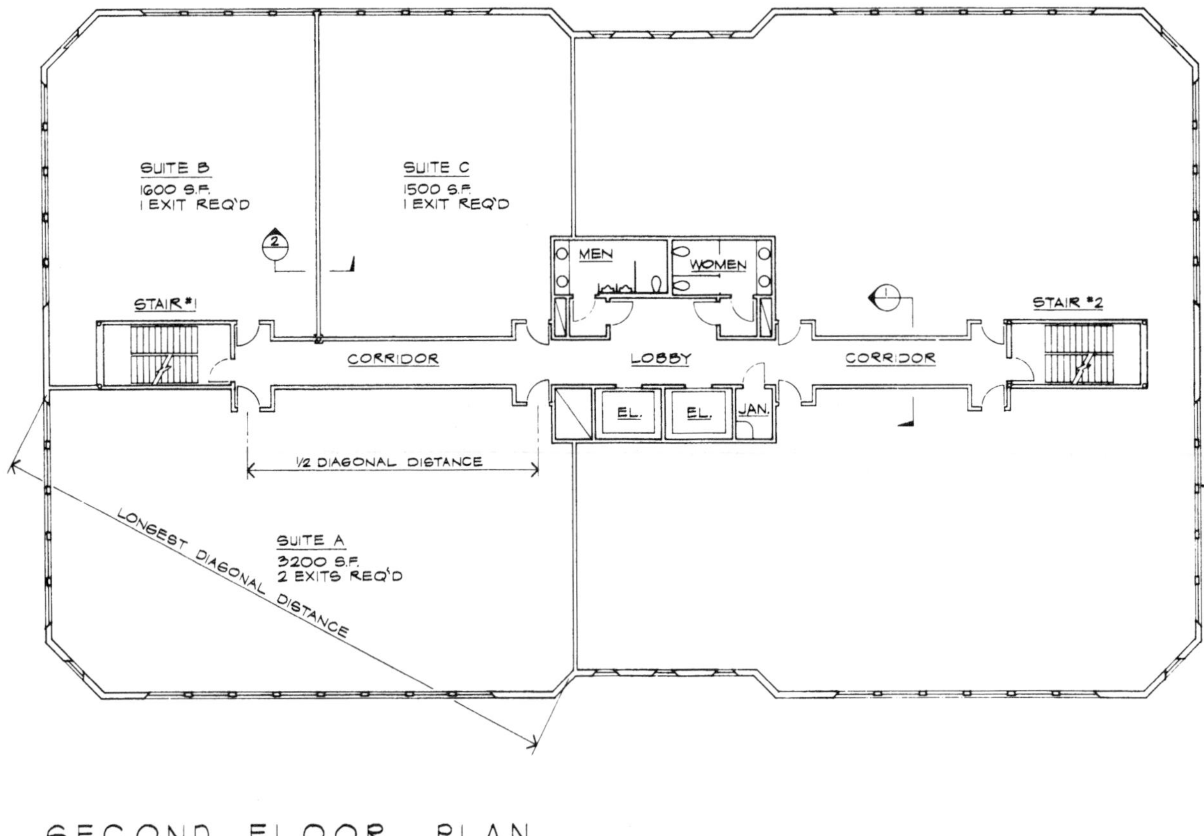

Figure 13.11 Suites A, B, and C.

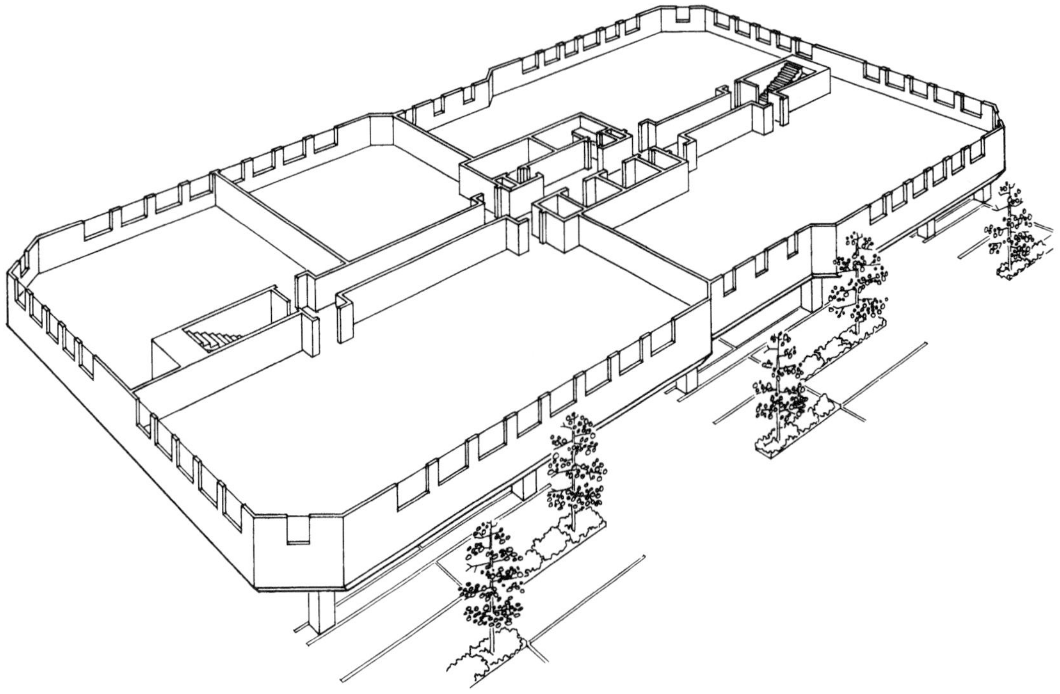

Figure 13.12 Pictorial view of tenant separation walls.

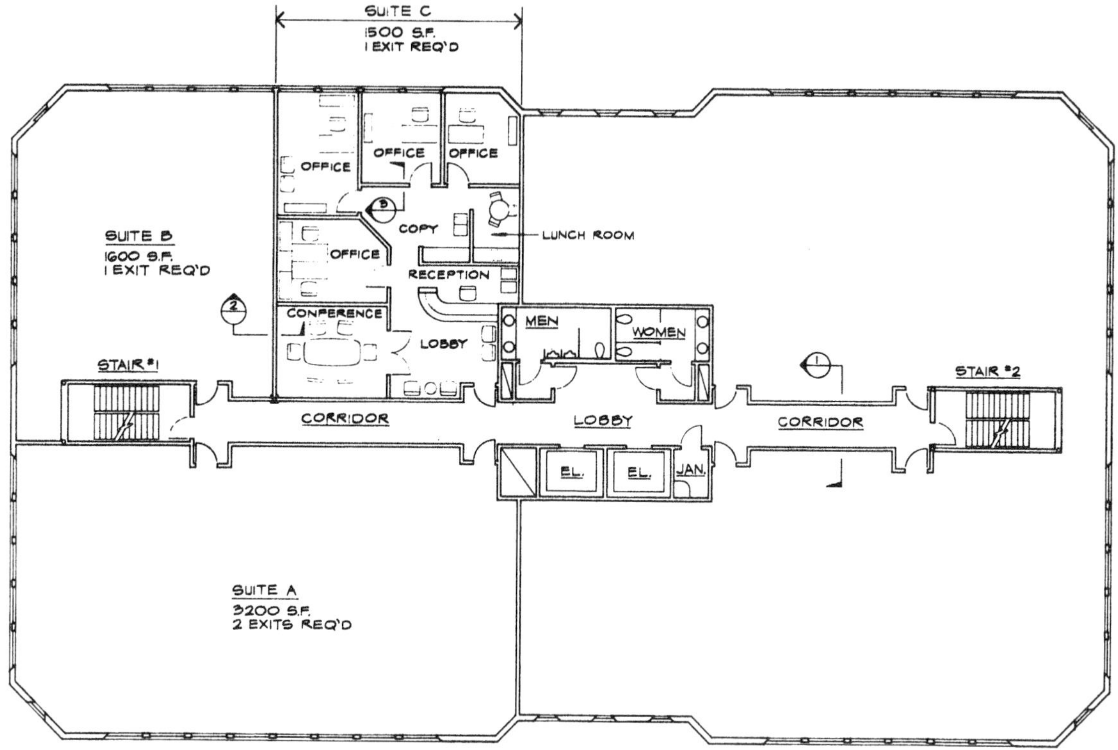

Figure 13.13 Floor plan—Suite C.

restrooms already exist; therefore, these rooms require only finishing.

Given the preceding information dealing with specific task areas, schematic studies can now begin in order to show tentative room locations and their relationship to one another. Figure 13.17 illustrates a conceptual floor plan in schematic form, which will be used in discussing the various areas and their locations with the tenant.

Following this procedure, SD floor plan will be developed to scale, including suggested locations for the required furniture. See Figure 13.18.

Upon the tenant's acceptance of the SD plan, a plan is created to show the required room locations and sizes (see Figure 13.19). Note that the division walls between the offices, adjacent to the exterior wall with windows and mullions, are located to intersect at the window mullions and concrete column locations. This eliminates the problem of a division wall butting into a glass area, which obviously would be undesirable.

The location of existing structural columns presents planning obstacles in relation to various spaces. It would be desirable to conceal a column within a division wall wherever possible. Note in Figure 13.19 that some of the existing steel pipe columns have been incorporated into various wall locations.

Now that the locations of walls, doors, and windows have been established, details for the construction of these components will be designed as a part of the working drawings for this TI project.

For the sake of clarity, it is recommended that existing walls and new walls be delineated differently. For example, the existing walls can be drawn with two separate lines, and new walls with two lines pochéd or hatched, so that viewers can distinguish between them. Wall symbols can be used for reference. Note the wall shading and wall symbols in Figure 13.20. The main structural consideration in detailing nonbearing interior walls is to provide lateral stability. For this assembly, the wall will be braced with metal struts in compression from the top of the wall to the existing structural members above, as shown in Figure 13.21. A metal strut used for lateral wall support is shown in the photograph in Figure 13.22. This wall assembly uses steel studs for the wall structure; however, wood studs are also used for partition wall assemblies. A photograph of steel stud framing members is shown in Figure 13.23. The finished ceiling members will terminate at each wall partition because the use of this wall assembly dictates that walls be constructed before the ceiling is finished. This method provides more design flexibility for the ceiling and lighting

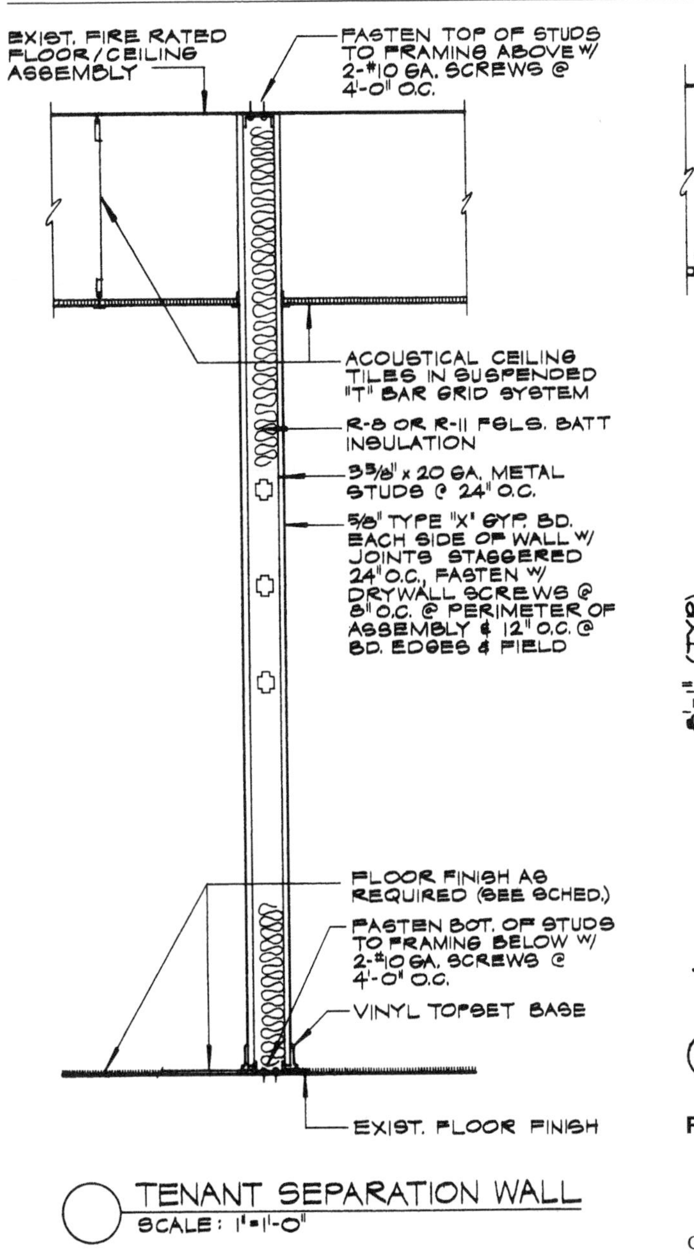

Figure 13.14 Tenant separation wall.

layout, which is illustrated and discussed later in regard to the design and layout of the ceiling plan. Figure 13.21 illustrates a suspended ceiling, which is assembled with 12-gauge hanger wires and metal runners supporting the finish ceiling material. In regions of the country where there is earthquake activity, the suspended ceiling areas are braced to minimize lateral movement. One method is shown in Figure 13.21, where metal stud at a 45° angle is assembled in a grid pattern, providing lateral stability for the suspended ceiling.

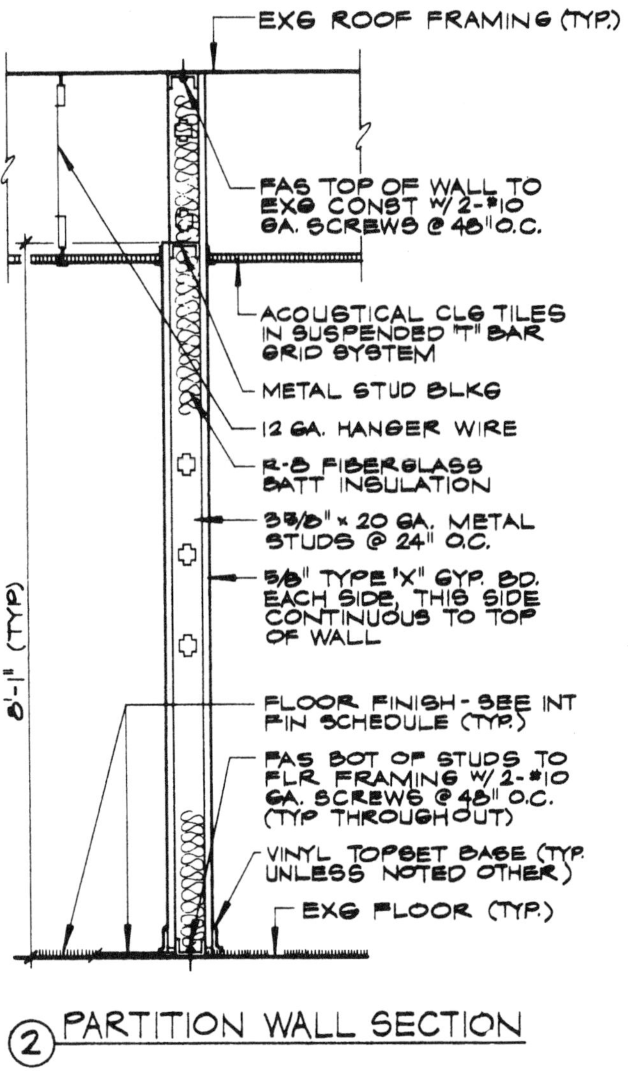

Figure 13.15 Partition wall section.

In cases where the ceiling is installed prior to the construction of the wall partitions, a similar method for stabilizing the wall, as shown in Figure 13.24, will be incorporated into the wall assembly. For the working drawings of this TI project, though, the wall section illustrated in Figure 13.21 will be used.

In TI projects, it often happens that the tenant or user will require additional soundproofing methods for the wall construction that separates specific areas. Figure 13.25 illustrates a separation wall terminating at the roof or floor system of an existing structure. This method helps to reduce the transmission of sound from one area to another through the ceiling and plenum areas. A **plenum area**, a space used primarily for the location of mechanical ducts and equipment, is usually located above the

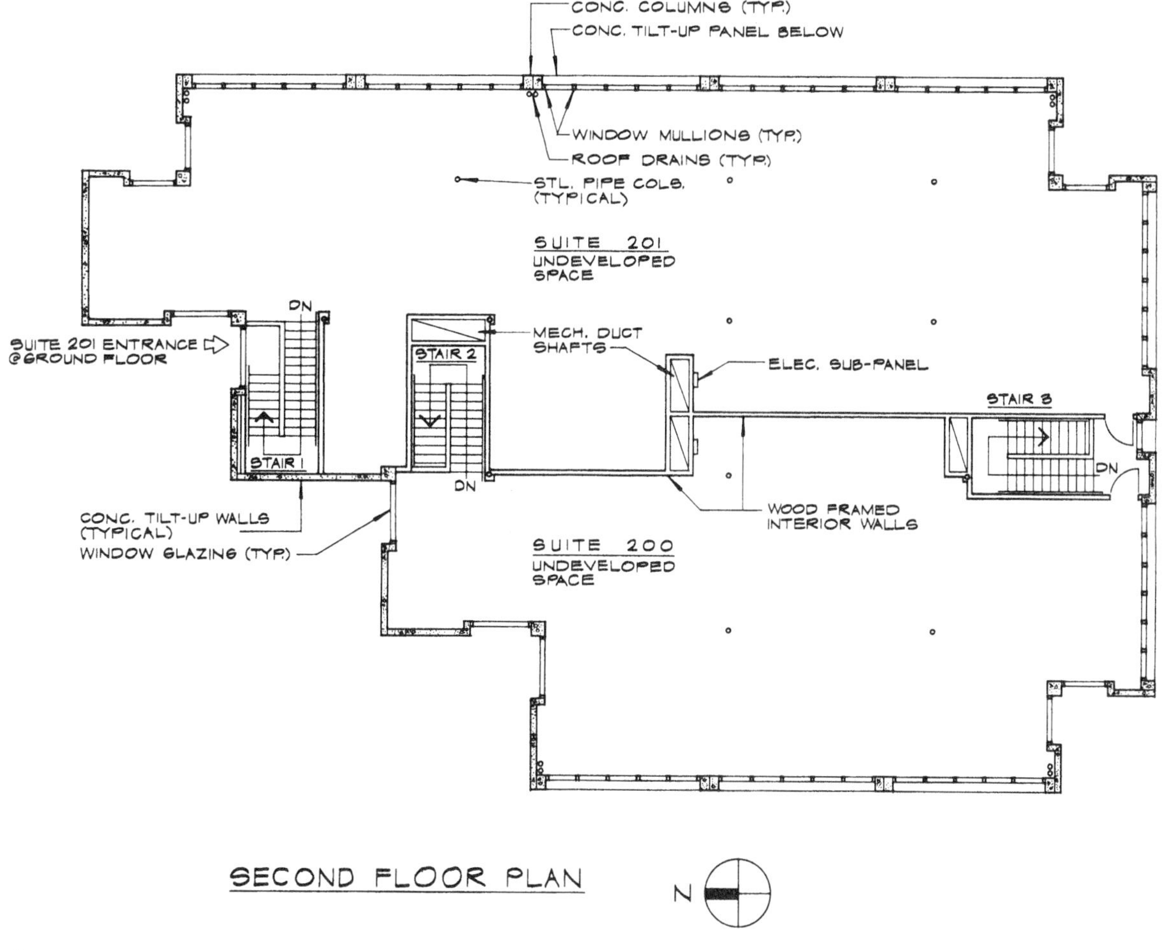

Figure 13.16 Undeveloped floor area plan—Building B.

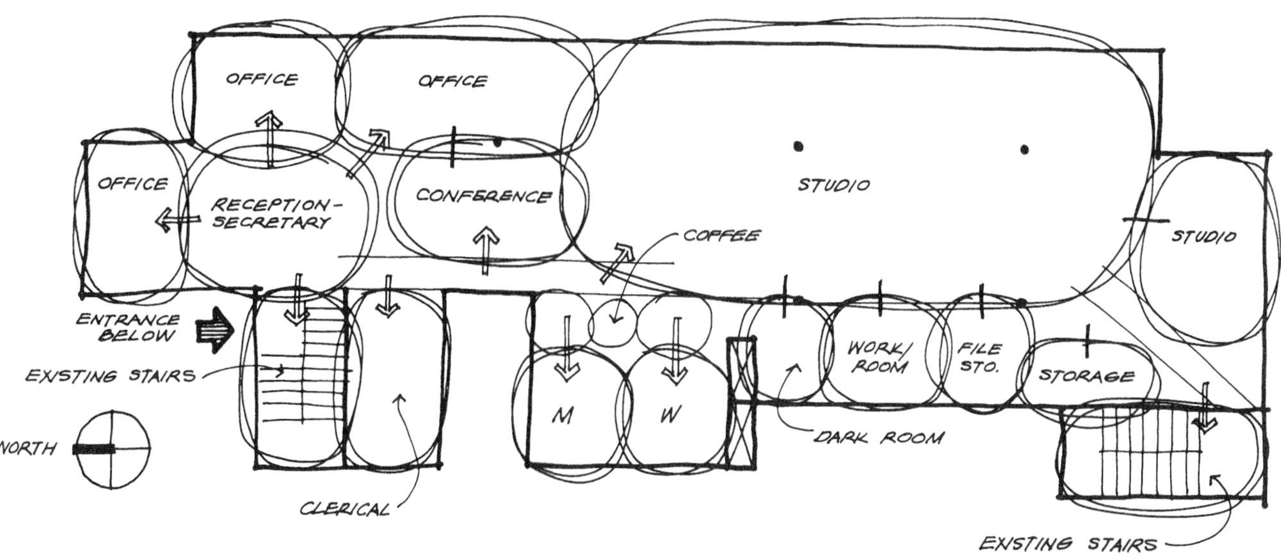

Figure 13.17 Schematic study.

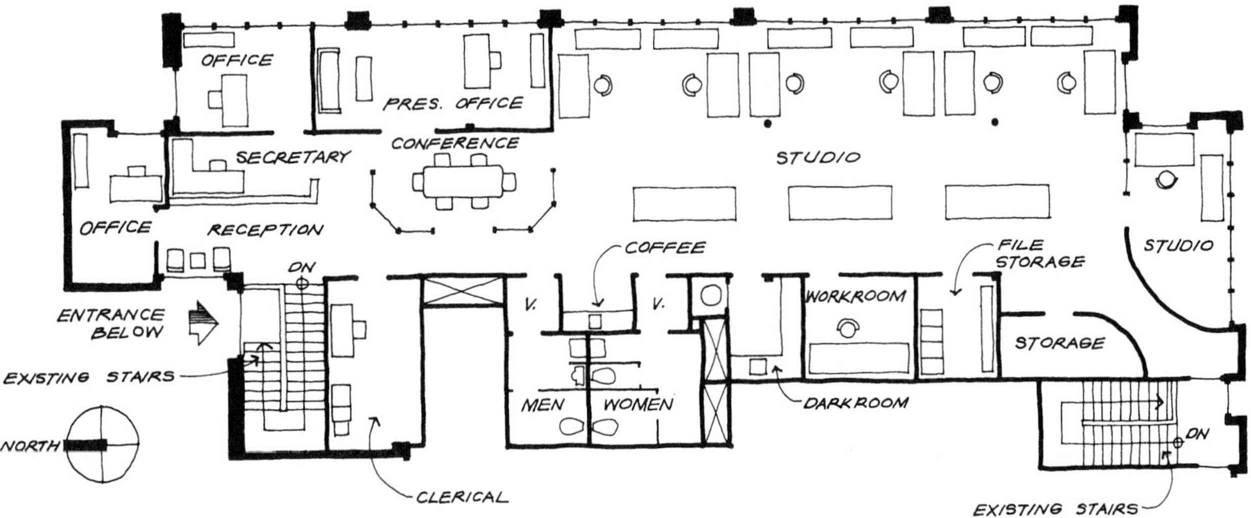

Figure 13.18 Preliminary floor plan.

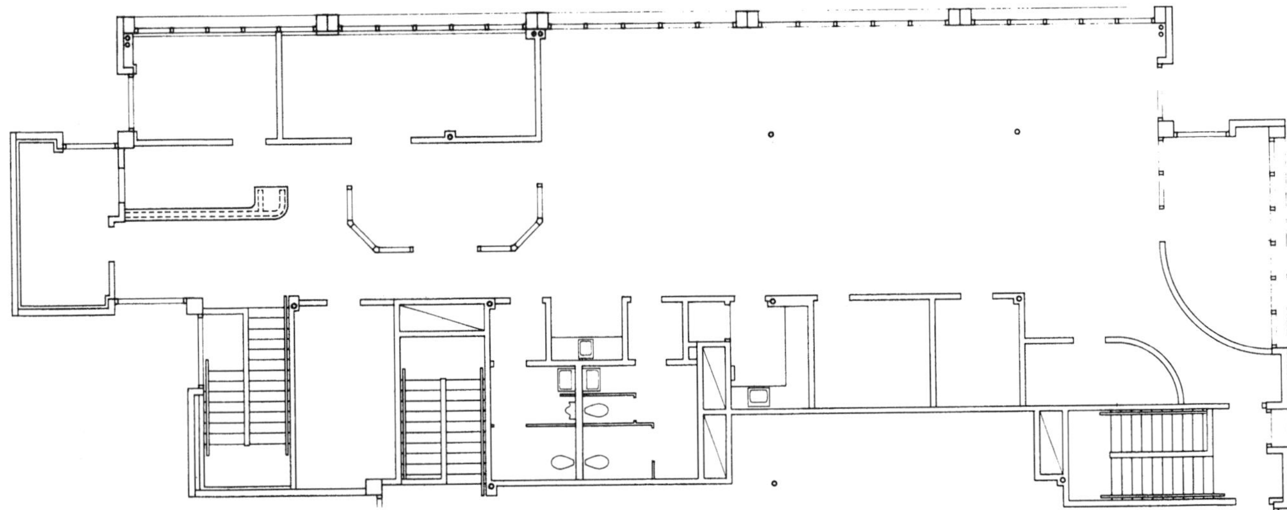

Figure 13.19 Wall development plan.

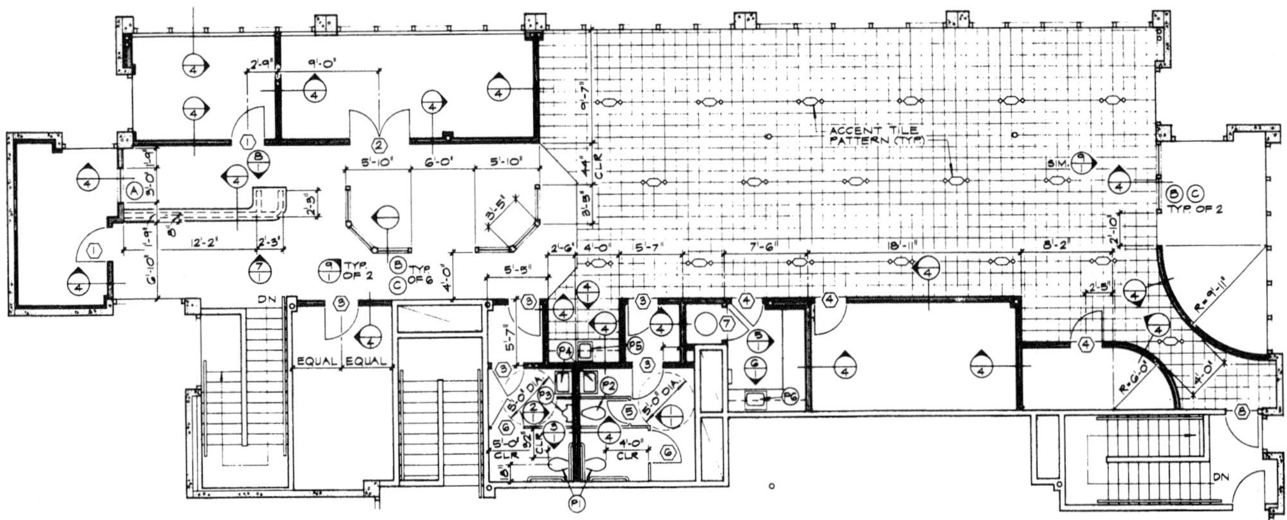

Figure 13.20 Wall shading and wall symbols.

finished ceiling. Figure 13.26 is a photograph of a small mechanical unit in the plenum area, which will distribute warm and cold air to the various tenant areas. It was decided that the studio would not have a finished ceiling so that the mechanical ducting for the heating, cooling, and ventilation could be exposed (shown later in the ceiling plan). In this case, the wall partitions will be detailed to extend to, and be secured at, the roof rafters (illustrated in Figure 13.27). Note that where the walls and rafters are not adjacent to each other, 2 × 4 blocking at 4′-0″ o.c. is installed to stabilize the wall laterally.

Often, as in this project, a mechanical equipment room is required to enclose a mechanical unit that will provide cooling, heating, and ventilating for a particular suite only. However, because of the noise produced by certain mechanical units, it is good practice to detail the walls of the mechanical room in such a way that the noise of the motors is minimized. A detail of one such

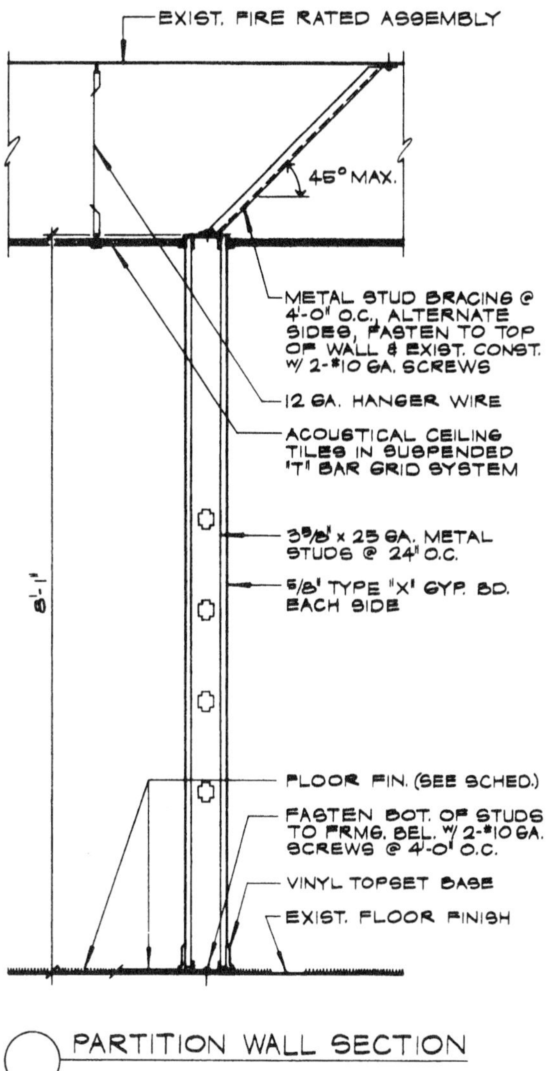

Figure 13.21 Nonbearing partition wall.

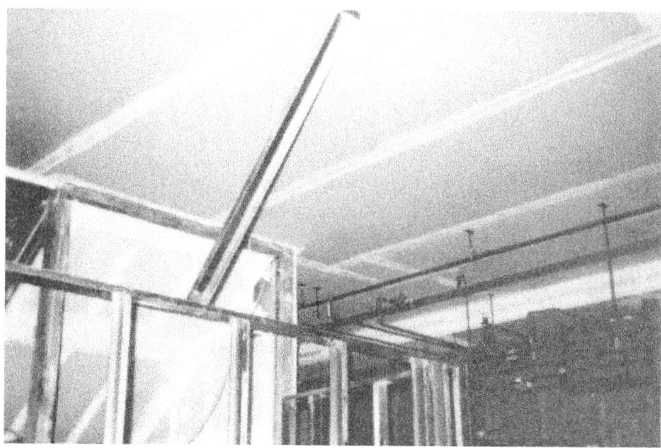

Figure 13.22 Stabilizing strut.

Figure 13.23 Wall framing—steel studs.

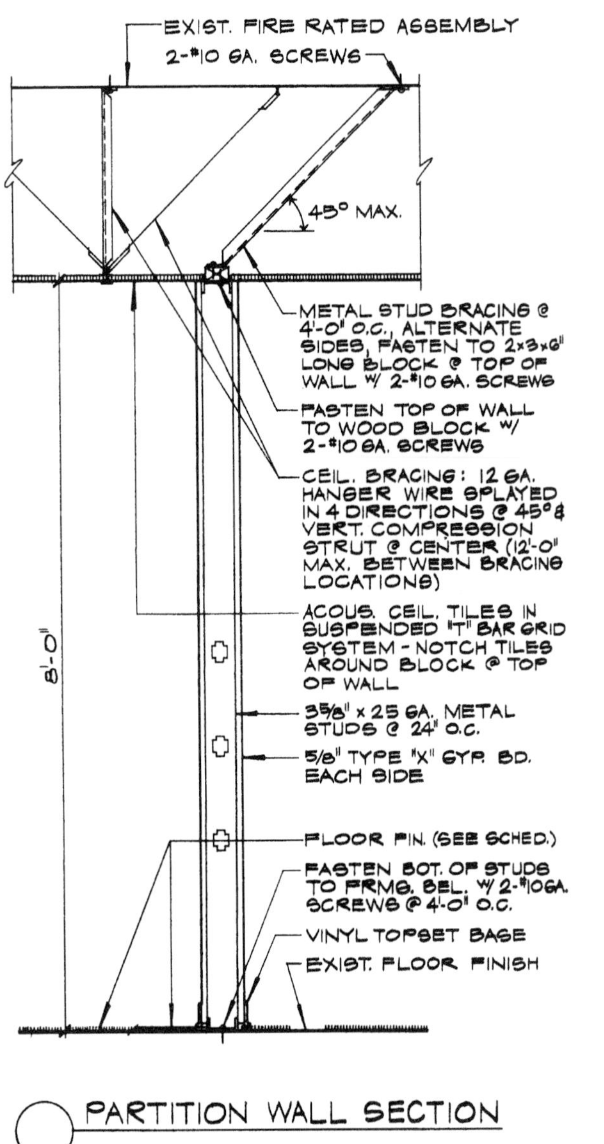

Figure 13.24 Nonbearing partition wall.

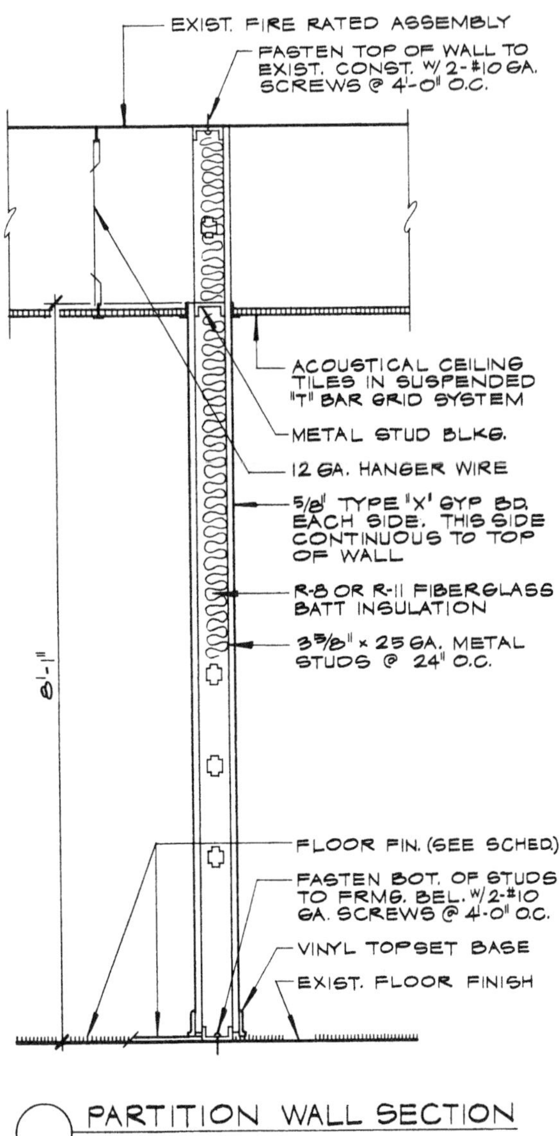

Figure 13.25 Sound deterrent partition wall.

wall is shown in Figure 13.28. Note that sound-absorbing board is installed on the inside of the mechanical room.

In projects where there are existing unfinished concrete or masonry walls, it will be desirable to furr out these walls in order to provide for electrical and telephone service and to develop a finished wall surface. **Furring** is adding a new inner wall to the main wall behind. Figure 13.29 illustrates a wall section where 1½″ metal furring studs have been attached to the existing unfinished concrete wall surface. In this detail, ⅝″-thick, type "X" gypsum wallboard has been selected for the interior wall finish.

The tenant requested the use of glass wall partitioning to partially enclose the conference room area. The use

Figure 13.26 Mechanical unit.

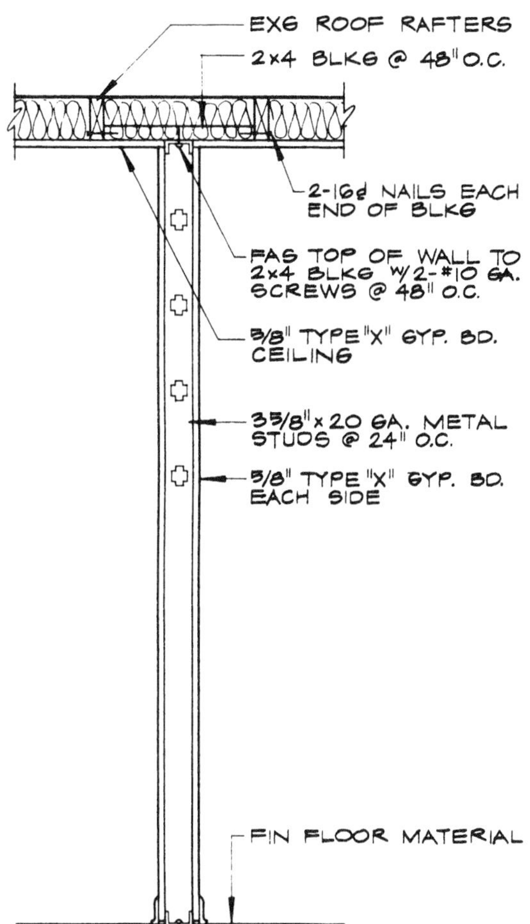

Figure 13.27 Wall section.

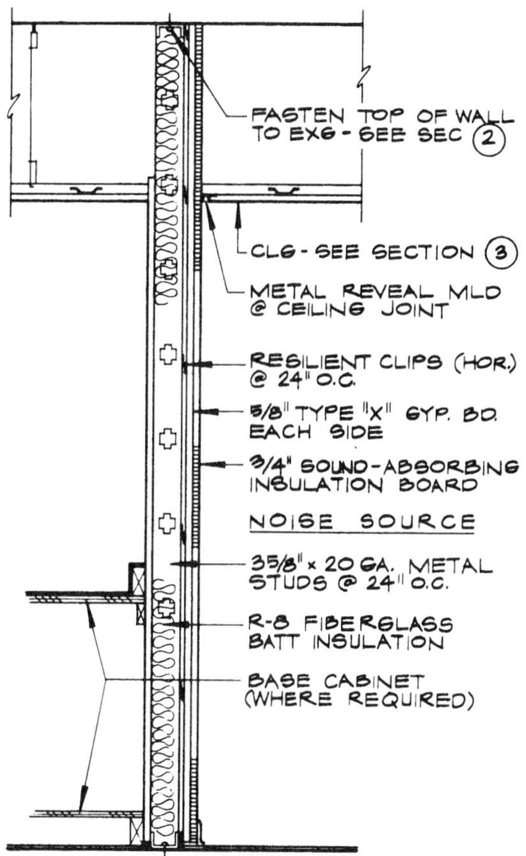

Figure 13.28 Sound wall section.

of glass and metal frames for wall partitions still requires horizontal stability, as is necessary for other types of wall partitions. A section through this glass wall partition is shown in Figure 13.30. Note that all glazing will be tempered glass, as required by building codes and for the safety of the user. A great option to limit sound transmission would be to utilize duel glazing and loos batt insulation in the wall cavity.

A low wall, called a **pony wall**, and a countertop are provided to separate the reception area from the secretarial area. This 42″ high wall will be attached to the adjacent wall and anchored at the base, as indicated in Figure 13.31. The stability of a low wall is most critical at the base; therefore, the method of assembly will be determined by the structural components of the existing structure. Often these pony walls utilize a steel post similar to a guard rail to reinforce the pony wall and add needed stability.

The door and window assemblies will be detailed to illustrate to the contractor the type of headers over the openings and the types of door and window frames that have been selected. The stabilization at the tops of these assemblies will be identical or similar to the stabilization for the wall partitions. Figure 13.32 depicts the use of a metal header over the door opening, incorporating the use of a hollow metal door frame. The manufacturer and type of metal door frame will be called out on the door schedule. These openings do not need structural headers as most walls in a TI are self-supporting and not structural in nature.

Wall partitions that incorporate windows will be detailed to delineate the type of header, window frame material, and the construction of the wall portion in the assembly. The interior window located between office 3 and the secretarial area is detailed in a wall section illustrated in Figure 13.33.

Electrical and Communication Plan

After the locations of partition walls, doors, windows, and furniture have been established, the architect or space planner, consulting with the tenant, may now proceed to develop an electrical and communication plan.

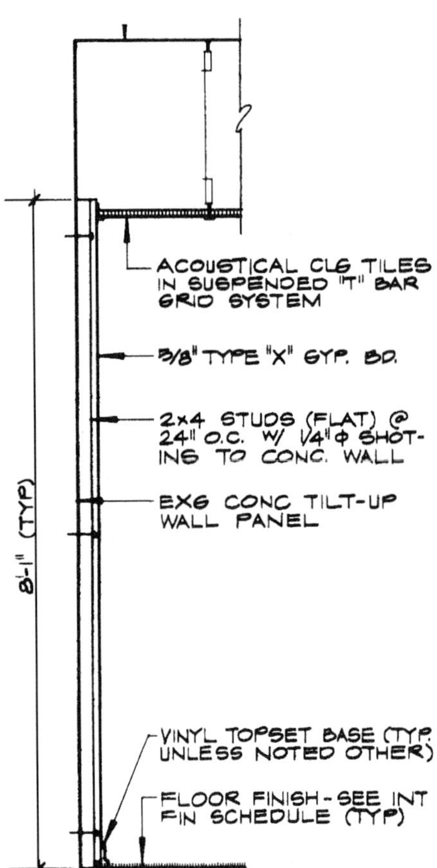

Figure 13.29 Existing wall furring.

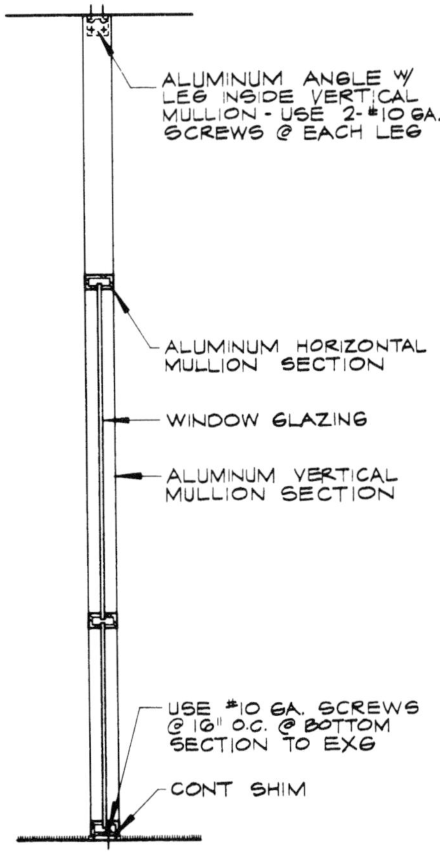

Figure 13.30 Glass wall partition.

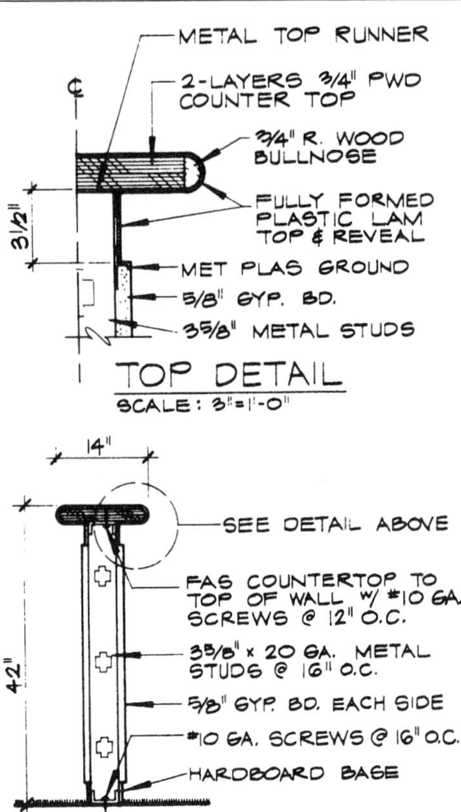

Figure 13.31 Low wall partition.

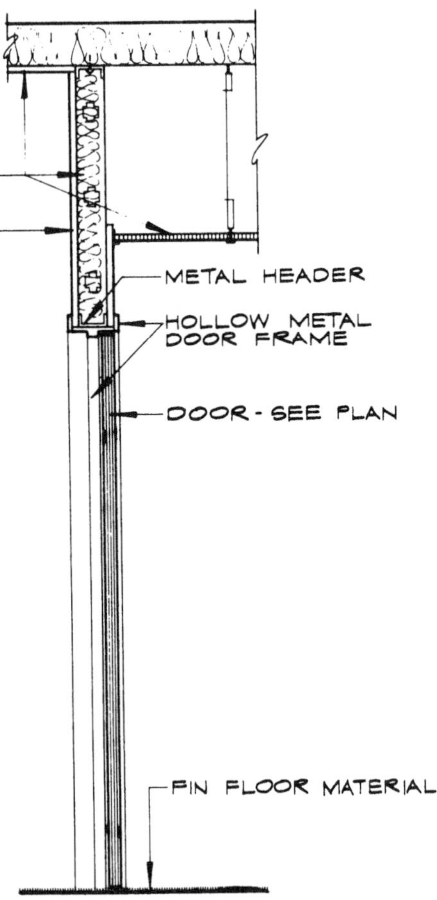

Figure 13.32 Interior door—wall section.

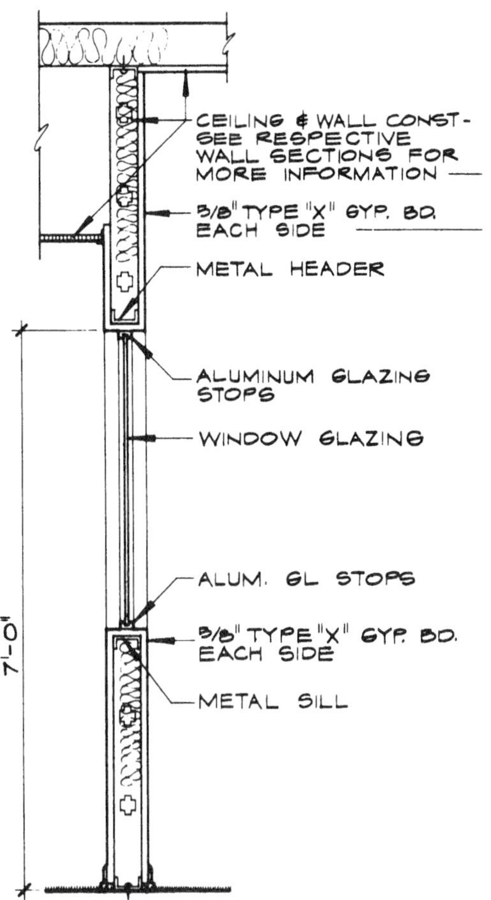

Figure 13.33 Interior window and wall section.

The electrical portion of this plan will consist of the location of convenient electrical outlets installed approximately 12″ above the floor, unless noted otherwise by a dimension at the outlet. The communication installation will comprise telephone jacks and a rough-in electrical service for the tenant's computer hardware. An electrical and communication plan prepared for this tenant of Building B is illustrated in Figure 13.34 It should be noted that, on some projects, the electrical and communication design may be so complex that separate plans must be provided and delineated for clarity.

A ceiling plan that includes the height of the ceiling will be drawn to delineate the following: location of ceiling lighting fixtures, symbolized for reference to the lighting fixture schedule; suspended ceiling design; the type of system to be specified; and other types of ceiling finishes. Switch locations for the various lighting fixtures will also be shown in this plan.

For this project, it was decided that a suspended ceiling system with recessed lighting fixtures would be specified for offices 1, 2, and 3. As mentioned earlier and detailed in Figure 13.21, the walls will be installed first, thus providing the designer with greater design flexibility for the layout of the suspended ceiling grid system and the location of lighting fixtures. To illustrate the design flexibility of this wall installation method, the ceiling plan shown in Figure 13.35 shows the suspended ceiling and lighting fixtures to be symmetrical within the offices, thereby creating a more pleasing ceiling design and lighting fixture location. Mechanical ducts for heating and cooling these offices will be installed and concealed above the

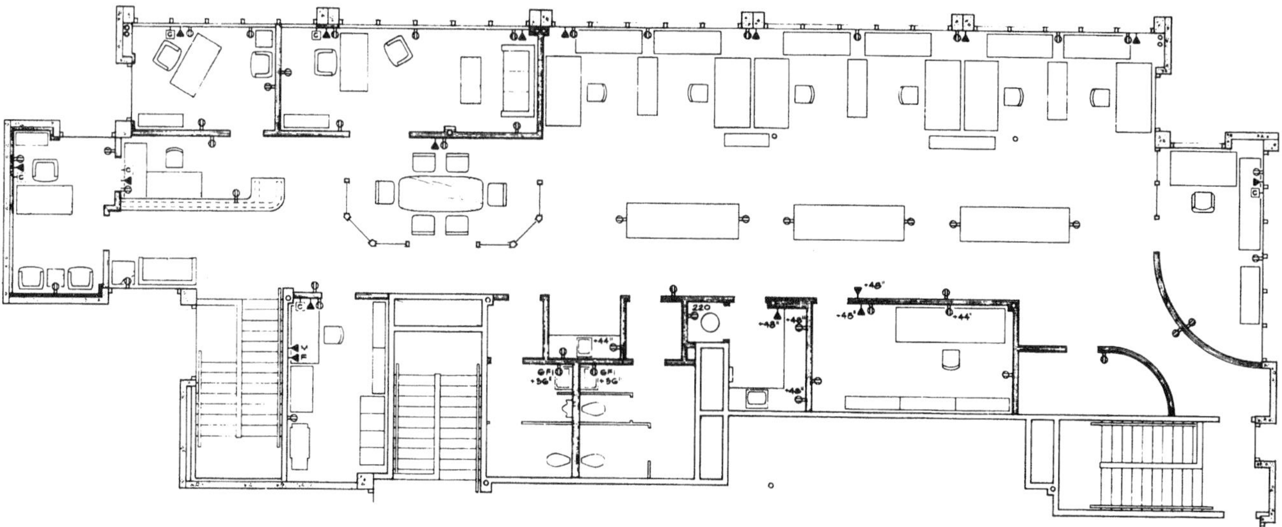

Figure 13.34 Electrical and communication plan.

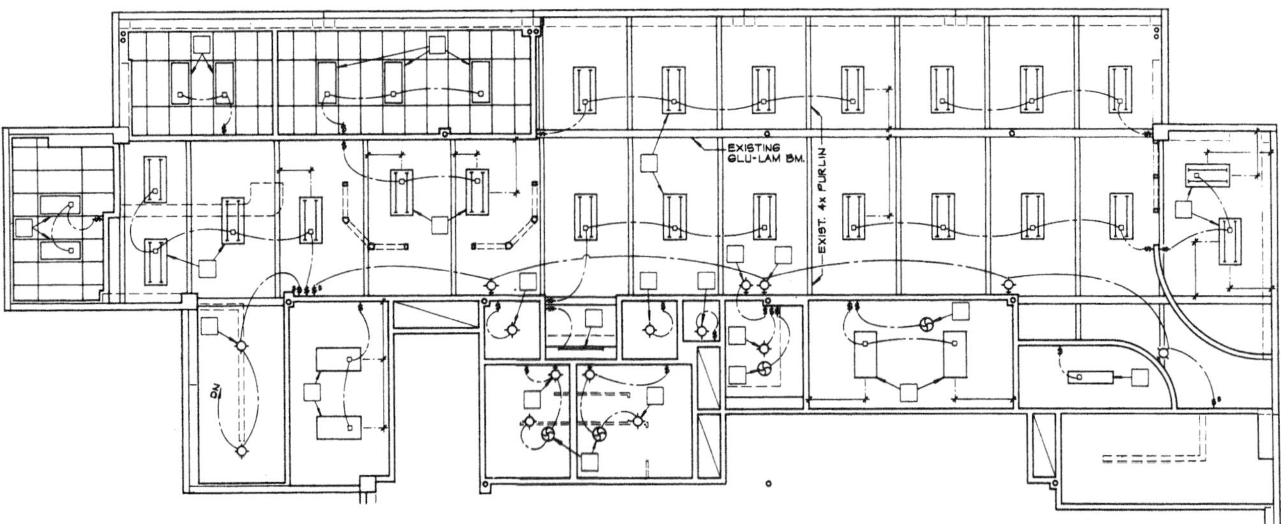

Figure 13.35 Ceiling plan.

suspended ceiling system. Note that the walls are drawn with two lines only, as there are no wall openings at the ceiling level.

At the request of the tenant, the remaining rooms and task areas will not have a suspended ceiling system; rather, gypsum wallboard will be attached directly to the existing structural roof members, with the gypsum board being finished and painted. For wall reference, see Figure 13.27.

The ceiling finish and location selected allow the mechanical ducts to be exposed and painted. These round mechanical ducts, when exposed and painted, will provide a decor compatible with the artwork and graphic design produced by this tenant. On the ceiling plan, as depicted in Figure 13.35, the designer has shown the desired location of the mechanical ducts and supply registers. The consulting mechanical engineer will specify, in the mechanical drawings, the sizes of the ducts, type of supply registers, and type of equipment to be used.

As previously mentioned, the lighting fixtures will be given a reference symbol that will also be on the electrical fixture schedule. That schedule will provide a description of the fixtures, including the manufacturer and model numbers. Designation of the finished ceiling material may be shown on the ceiling plan for convenience; in any case, these finishes will be designated on the interior finish schedule. Electrical and interior finish schedules, as well as other schedules, are discussed and illustrated later in this chapter.

Interior Elevations and Schedules

Interior elevations and schedules are usually included in the construction documents but were eliminated here, because their creation would follow the same procedures as those found in Chapters 1 and 2. They are also shown in their entirety in the construction documents evolution discussion to follow in this chapter.

WORKING DRAWING STAGES

The following paragraphs describe the working drawings at various stages of the development for the TI project in Building B.

Floor Plan

Stage I (Figure 13.36). At a larger scale, the draftsperson lightly blocked out all the existing exterior and interior walls for the area identified as Suite 201. This drawing included existing windows, structural columns, roof drain leaders, stairwells, and mechanical shafts. Also included in this first-stage drawing was the initial site plan layout.

Stage II (Figure 13.37). After the required room locations and their sizes were determined from the schematic drawings, wall locations were established with their accompanying dimension lines only. All the existing and new walls were darkened for future clarity.

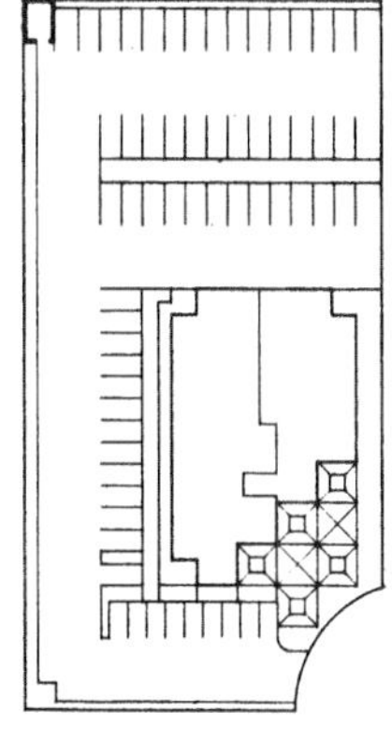

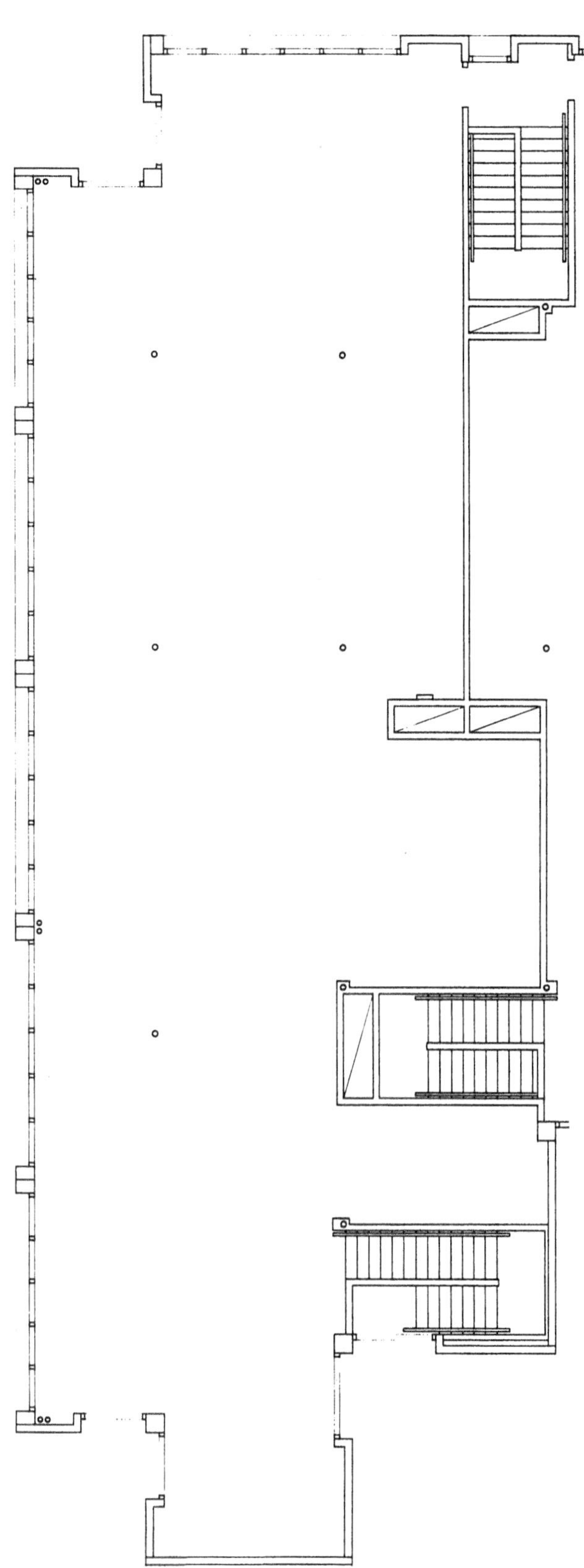

Figure 13.36 Stage I: Floor plan.

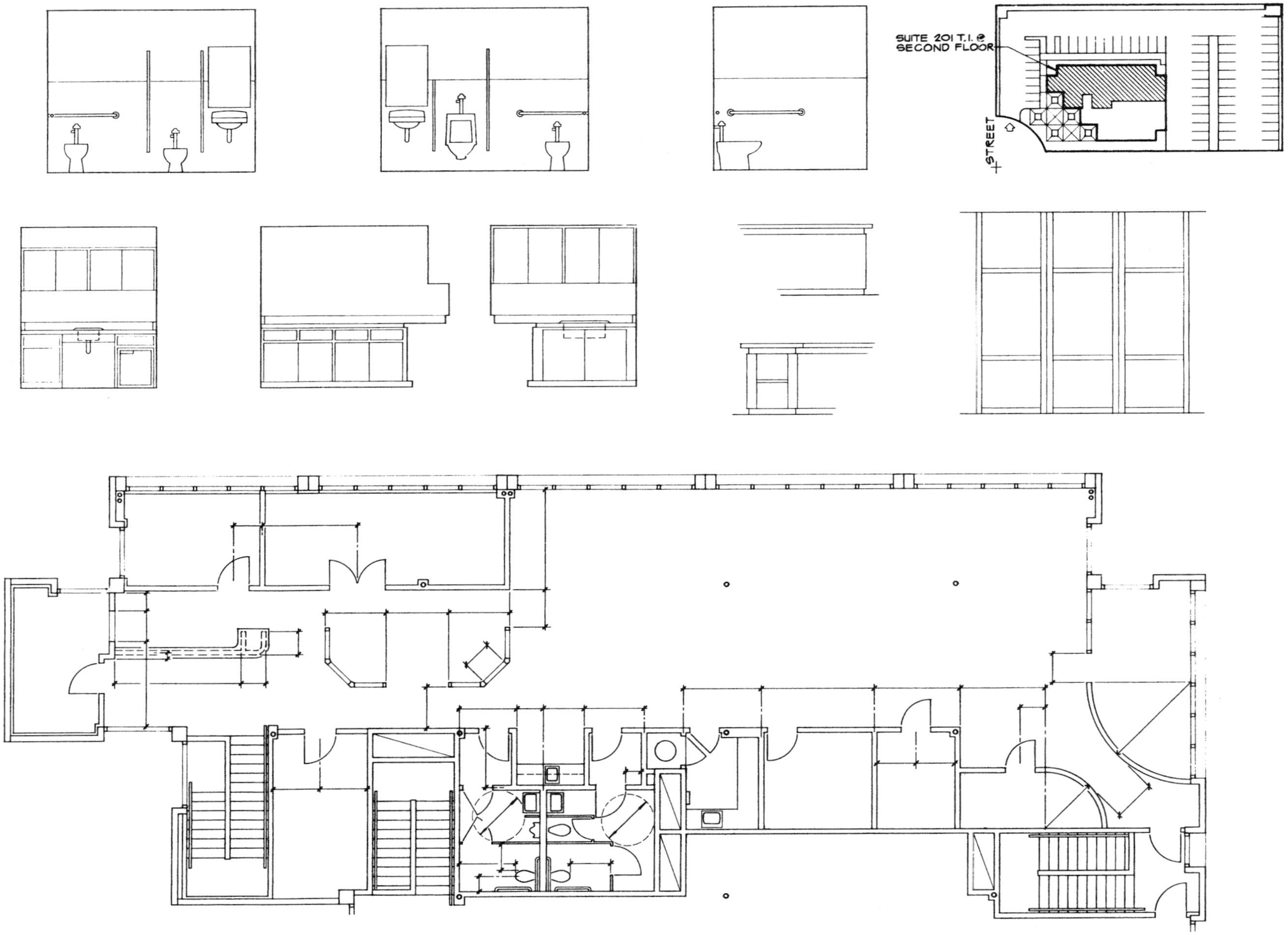

Figure 13.37 Stage II: Floor plan.

Doors and their swing directions were added, along with wheelchair clearances in the men's and women's restrooms. The various interior elevations were lightly blocked out, and the site plan—illustrating the exact location of Suite 201 in this existing structure—was finalized.

Stage III (Figure 13.38). At this stage of the floor plan, all the wall partitions were dimensioned, and the new walls were darkened solid to distinguish them from the existing walls. Note that in the reference room, next to the darkroom, a wall was eliminated to provide more space for equipment. See Stage II. Door symbols and their numbers have been incorporated, along with plumbing fixture symbols and their accompanying designations. Also included are reference bubbles for the various wall sections with their designated numbers and locations. Interior elevation reference symbols have been added and will later be located on their respective wall elevations. Symbols for glass sizes are shown at the various glass partition locations. At this stage of the floor plan, the specified tile floor and accent pattern locations are delineated in the studio area. The lines on the interior elevations are darkened and profiled for clarity with material designations, cabinet door swings, and incorporating the various dimension lines.

Stage IV (Figure 13.39). This is the final stage for the floor plan, interior elevations, and site plan. A wall legend is included on the floor plan, illustrating the various wall conditions. All final notes and room designations have been lettered, and the designated wall detail numbers have been placed in the various reference bubbles. Lettering and dimensioning on the interior elevations are finalized at this stage, along with the titling and reference numbering for various wall elevations as they relate to the floor plan. Final notes are lettered on the site plan, and titles are provided for the site plan and floor plan. The scales used for various drawings are now lettered and located below the drawing titles.

Furnishing, Electrical, and Communication Plan

Stage I (Figure 13.40). The initial step for this stage was to draft a floor plan incorporating the exterior walls, interior partitions, plumbing fixtures, and cabinet locations. Note that door swings and their directions are not delineated. In many offices, this stage may be a reproduction of an earlier floor-plan stage or may be XREFed.

Stage II (Figure 13.41). The first concern at this stage was to lay out all the required furniture necessary for the function of the tenant's business. With the furniture locations established, electrical, telephone, and facsimile outlets can now be located as required by the tenant. Also included at this stage is a furnishing schedule, which may be completed at a later stage or may be XREFed.

Stage III (Figure 13.42). To complete the electrical plan and furnishing layout, symbols for furniture identification are located accordingly and lettered for reference on the furnishing schedule. Final notes are provided for electrical outlet locations, as well as for the various furnishing items that will be supplied by the tenant. The furnishing schedule is now complete, as it provides symbol designations, sizes, and manufacturers' equipment designations. A legend is drawn and completed for the identification of electrical symbols, such as for the type of outlets and switches. General construction notes covering the various construction phases are included with this drawing.

Ceiling Plan

Stage I (Figure 13.43). At this stage, the exterior and interior walls are lightly blocked out, illustrating the walls as they appear at the ceiling level.

Stage II (Figure 13.44). The exterior and interior walls are darkened to provide greater clarity at this stage. The three office areas that will have a suspended ceiling system have been delineated to illustrate the grid pattern, lighting fixture location, and their identification symbols. Also shown are the light switches for the various lighting fixtures. All the surface-mounted lighting fixtures, exhaust fans, and accompanying switches for the various fixtures are completed in this stage. Fixture symbols are now located for the identification of the various electrical fixtures. (The symbols will be completed at a later stage.) Finally, schedules for the doors, electrical fixtures, plumbing fixtures, and room finishes are drawn in preparation for listing the various sizes, materials, and manufacturers' identification numbers.

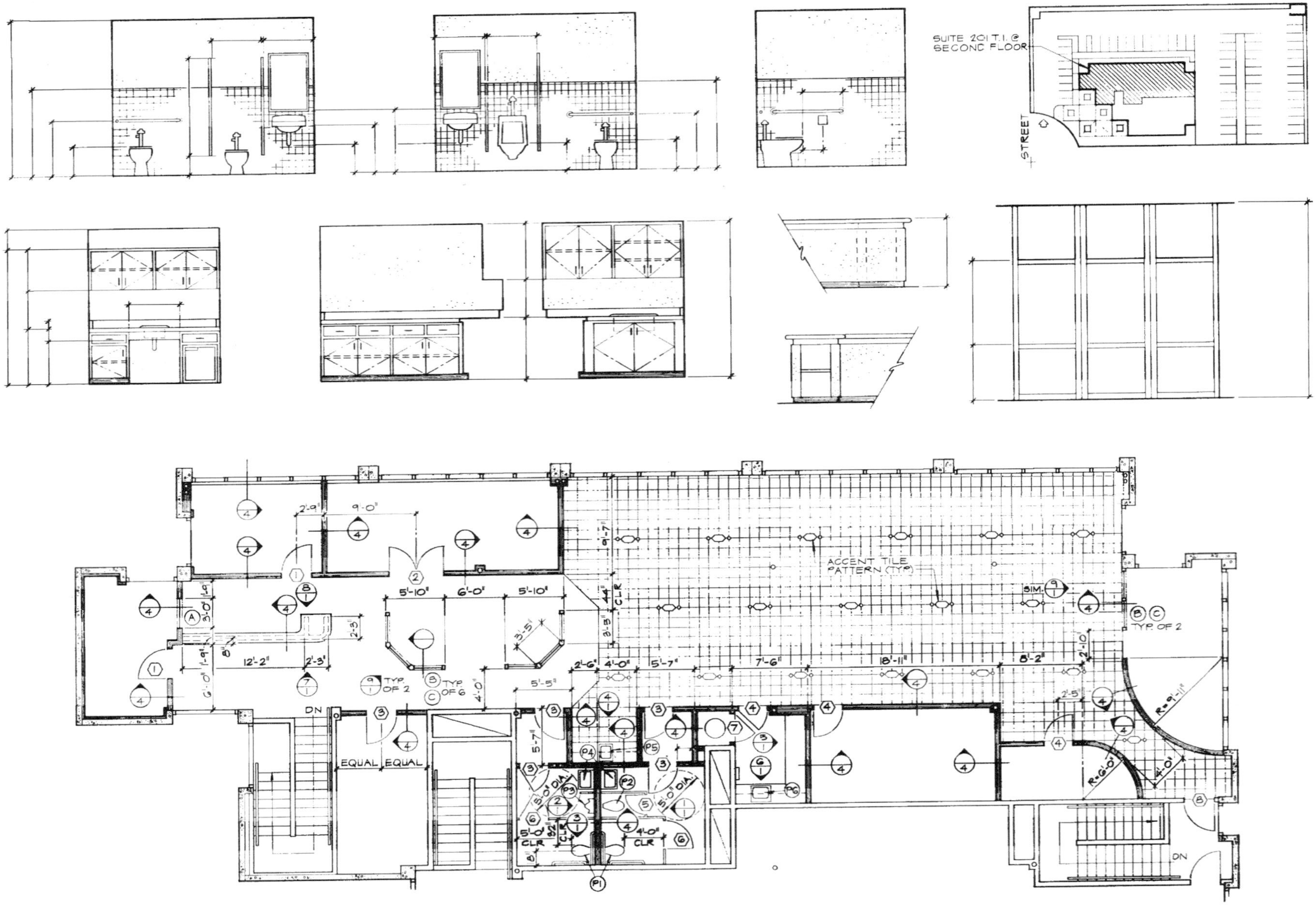

Figure 13.38 Stage III: Floor plan.

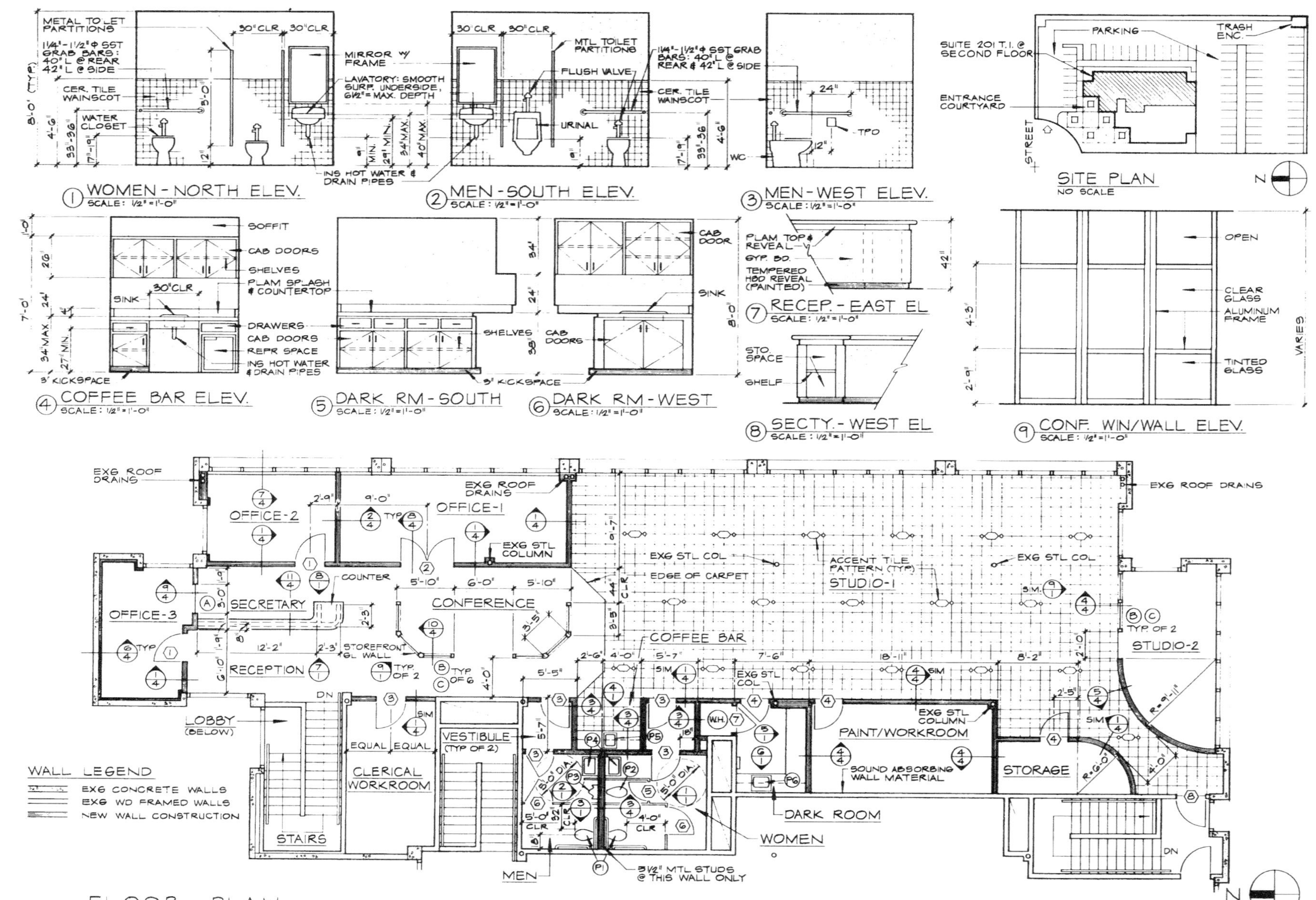

Figure 13.39 Stage IV: Floor plan.

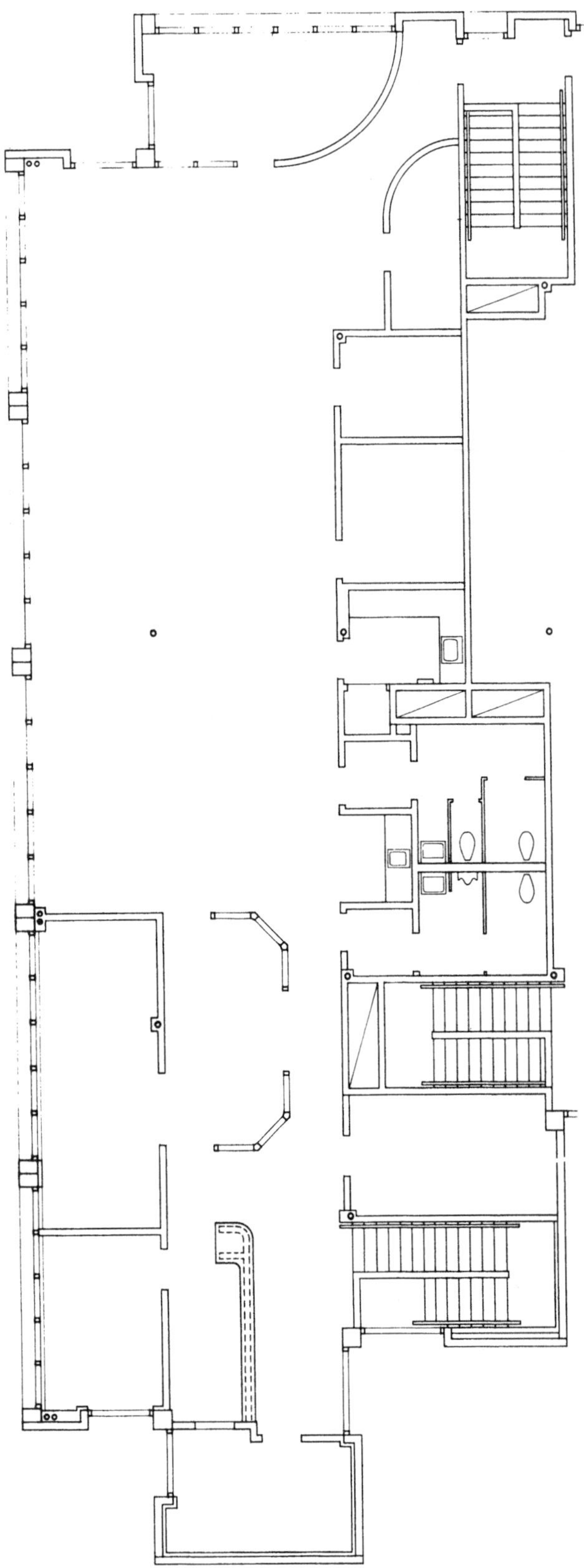

Figure 13.40 Stage I: Electrical plan—furnishing layout.

Stage III (Figure 13.45). The final stage of the ceiling plan includes lettering all the lighting fixture symbols and locating the heating supply air ducts and diffusers. Dimensioning of some of the various lighting fixtures has now been completed, as have the final notes and the title of the drawing. The scale designation and ceiling heights are called out.

The various schedules that were blocked out in Stage II are now completed, providing all necessary information and symbol identification.

Tenant Improvement and Computers

Presently, most TI work is done on AutoCAD. This is because the buildings being used by tenants have already been built, in most cases using designs drafted in AutoCAD. We are in a transitional period, and of the structures currently being built, only a small portion of them are designed and drawn in BIM. Thus, the drawings must still be verified in size and shape and drawn over.

A multistory building occupancy might be drawn in BIM because of the complexity of rerouting plumbing, air conditioning, heating, and so on. BIM offers a clear opportunity to define the built environment and establishing a phase for the new work which tracks the plans and can aid in establishing a demo plan and tagging new wall materials and quantities since BIM can differentiate existing from proposed. It is such a complex system that it can even establish future expansion phases and output them on an as needed system. For master planning communities or buildings, this becomes a significant asset to a firm.

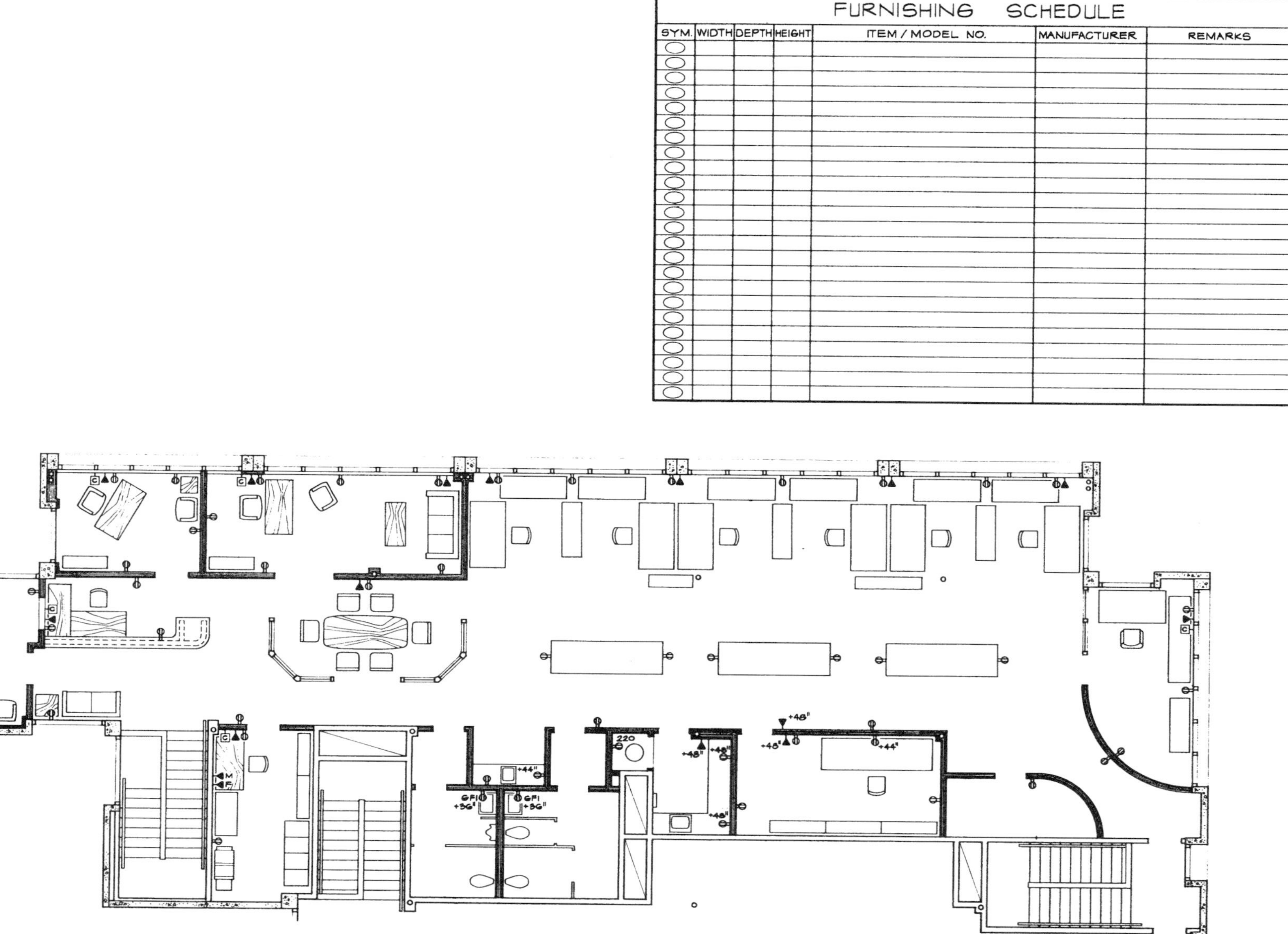

Figure 13.41 Stage II: Electrical plan—furnishing layout.

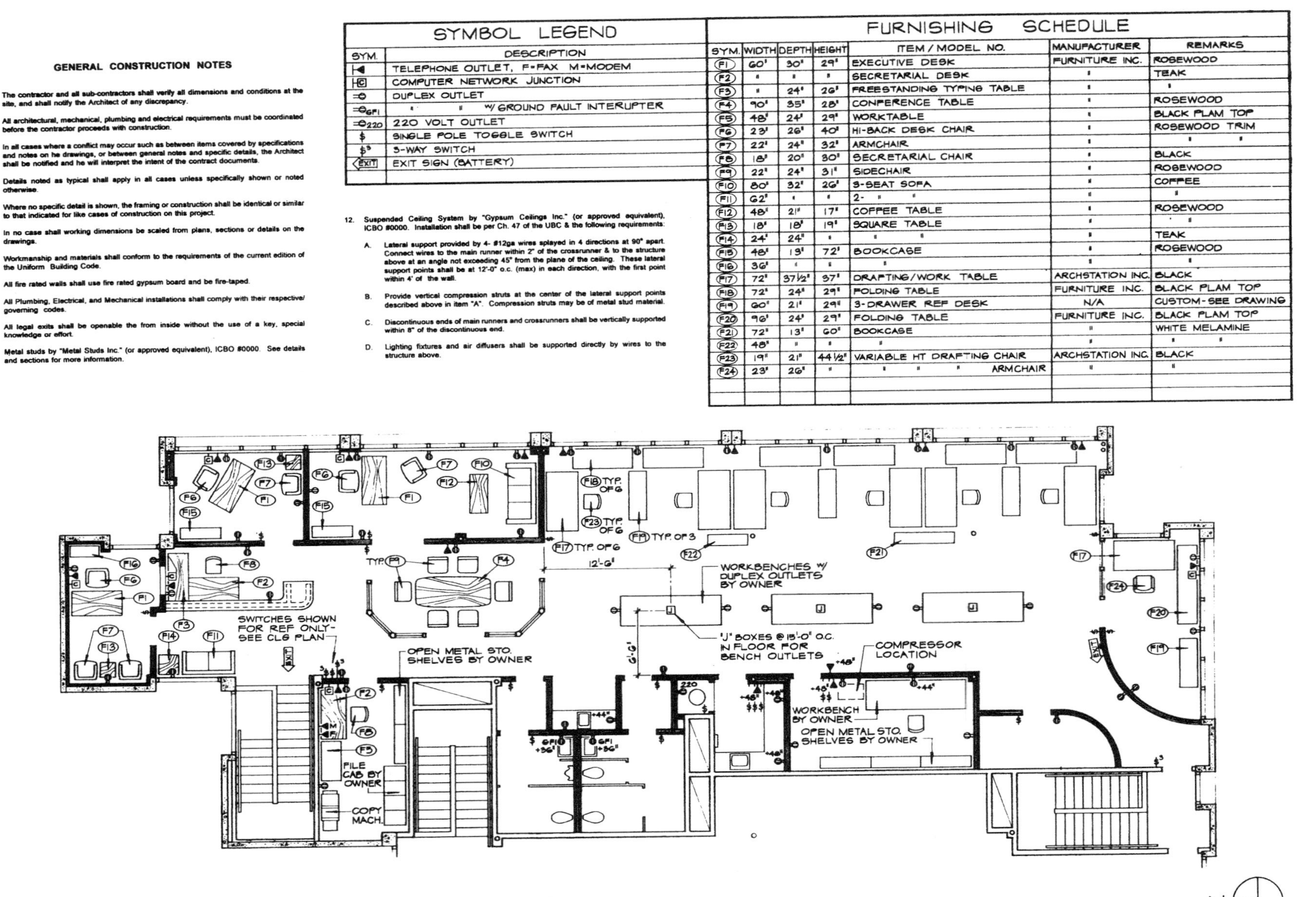

GENERAL CONSTRUCTION NOTES

1. The contractor and all sub-contractors shall verify all dimensions and conditions at the site, and shall notify the Architect of any discrepancy.
2. All architectural, mechanical, plumbing and electrical requirements must be coordinated before the contractor proceeds with construction.
3. In all cases where a conflict may occur such as between items covered by specifications and notes on he drawings, or between general notes and specific details, the Architect shall be notified and he will interpret the intent of the contract documents.
4. Details noted as typical shall apply in all cases unless specifically shown or noted otherwise.
5. Where no specific detail is shown, the framing or construction shall be identical or similar to that indicated for like cases of construction on this project.
6. In no case shall working dimensions be scaled from plans, sections or details on the drawings.
7. Workmanship and materials shall conform to the requirements of the current edition of the Uniform Building Code.
8. All fire rated walls shall use fire rated gypsum board and be fire-taped.
9. All Plumbing, Electrical, and Mechanical installations shall comply with their respective/ governing codes.
10. All legal exits shall be openable the from inside without the use of a key, special knowledge or effort.
11. Metal studs by "Metal Studs Inc." (or approved equivalent), ICBO #0000. See details and sections for more information.
12. Suspended Ceiling System by "Gypsum Ceilings Inc." (or approved equivalent), ICBO #0000. Installation shall be per Ch. 47 of the UBC & the following requirements:
    A. Lateral support provided by 4- #12ga wires splayed in 4 directions at 90° apart. Connect wires to the main runner within 2" of the crossrunner & to the structure above at an angle not exceeding 45° from the plane of the ceiling. These lateral support points shall be at 12'-0" o.c. (max) in each direction, with the first point within 4' of the wall.
    B. Provide vertical compression struts at the center of the lateral support points described above in item "A". Compression struts may be of metal stud material.
    C. Discontinuous ends of main runners and crossrunners shall be vertically supported within 8" of the discontinuous end.
    D. Lighting fixtures and air diffusers shall be supported directly by wires to the structure above.

SYMBOL LEGEND

SYM.	DESCRIPTION
	TELEPHONE OUTLET, F=FAX M=MODEM
C	COMPUTER NETWORK JUNCTION
	DUPLEX OUTLET
GFI	" " W/ GROUND FAULT INTERUPTER
220	220 VOLT OUTLET
$	SINGLE POLE TOGGLE SWITCH
$3	3-WAY SWITCH
EXIT	EXIT SIGN (BATTERY)

FURNISHING SCHEDULE

SYM.	WIDTH	DEPTH	HEIGHT	ITEM / MODEL NO.	MANUFACTURER	REMARKS
F1	60"	30"	29"	EXECUTIVE DESK	FURNITURE INC.	ROSEWOOD
F2	"	"	"	SECRETARIAL DESK	"	TEAK
F3	"	24"	26"	FREESTANDING TYPING TABLE	"	"
F4	90"	35"	28"	CONFERENCE TABLE	"	ROSEWOOD
F5	48"	24"	29"	WORKTABLE	"	BLACK PLAM TOP
F6	23"	26"	40"	HI-BACK DESK CHAIR	"	ROSEWOOD TRIM
F7	22"	24"	32"	ARMCHAIR	"	" "
F8	18"	20"	30"	SECRETARIAL CHAIR	"	BLACK
F9	22"	24"	31"	SIDECHAIR	"	ROSEWOOD
F10	80"	32"	26"	3-SEAT SOFA	"	COFFEE
F11	62"	"	"	2- " "	"	"
F12	48"	21"	17"	COFFEE TABLE	"	ROSEWOOD
F13	18"	18"	19"	SQUARE TABLE	"	"
F14	24"	24"	"	" "	"	TEAK
F15	48"	13"	72"	BOOKCASE	"	ROSEWOOD
F16	36"	"	"	"	"	"
F17	72"	37½"	37"	DRAFTING/WORK TABLE	ARCHSTATION INC.	BLACK
F18	72"	24"	29"	FOLDING TABLE	FURNITURE INC.	BLACK PLAM TOP
F19	60"	21"	29"	3-DRAWER REF DESK	N/A	CUSTOM-SEE DRAWING
F20	96"	24"	29"	FOLDING TABLE	FURNITURE INC.	BLACK PLAM TOP
F21	72"	13"	60"	BOOKCASE	"	WHITE MELAMINE
F22	48"	"	"	"	"	" "
F23	19"	21"	44½"	VARIABLE HT DRAFTING CHAIR	ARCHSTATION INC.	BLACK
F24	23"	26"	"	" " " ARMCHAIR	"	"

Figure 13.42 Stage III: Electrical plan—furnishing layout.

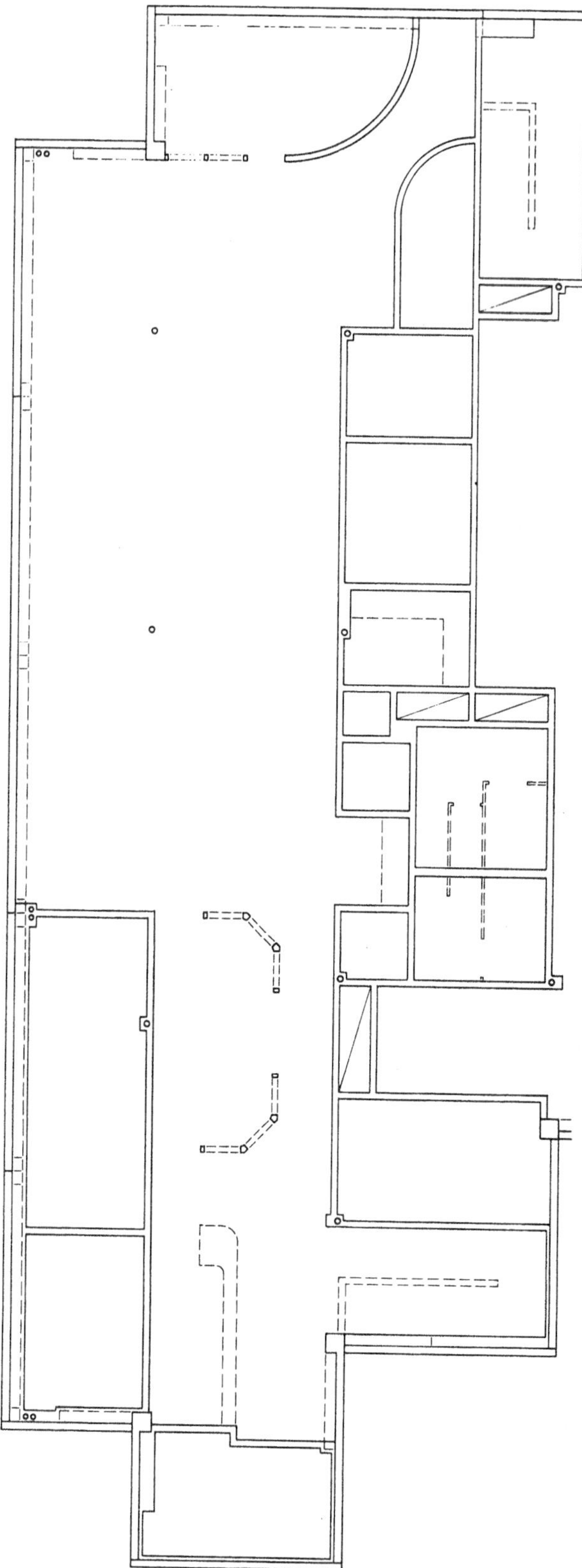

Figure 13.43 Stage I: Ceiling plan.

Key Terms

alteration
as built
furring
improvement
internal planning
non-load-bearing wall
plenum area
pony wall
renovation
restoration
space planning
tenant improvement (TI)

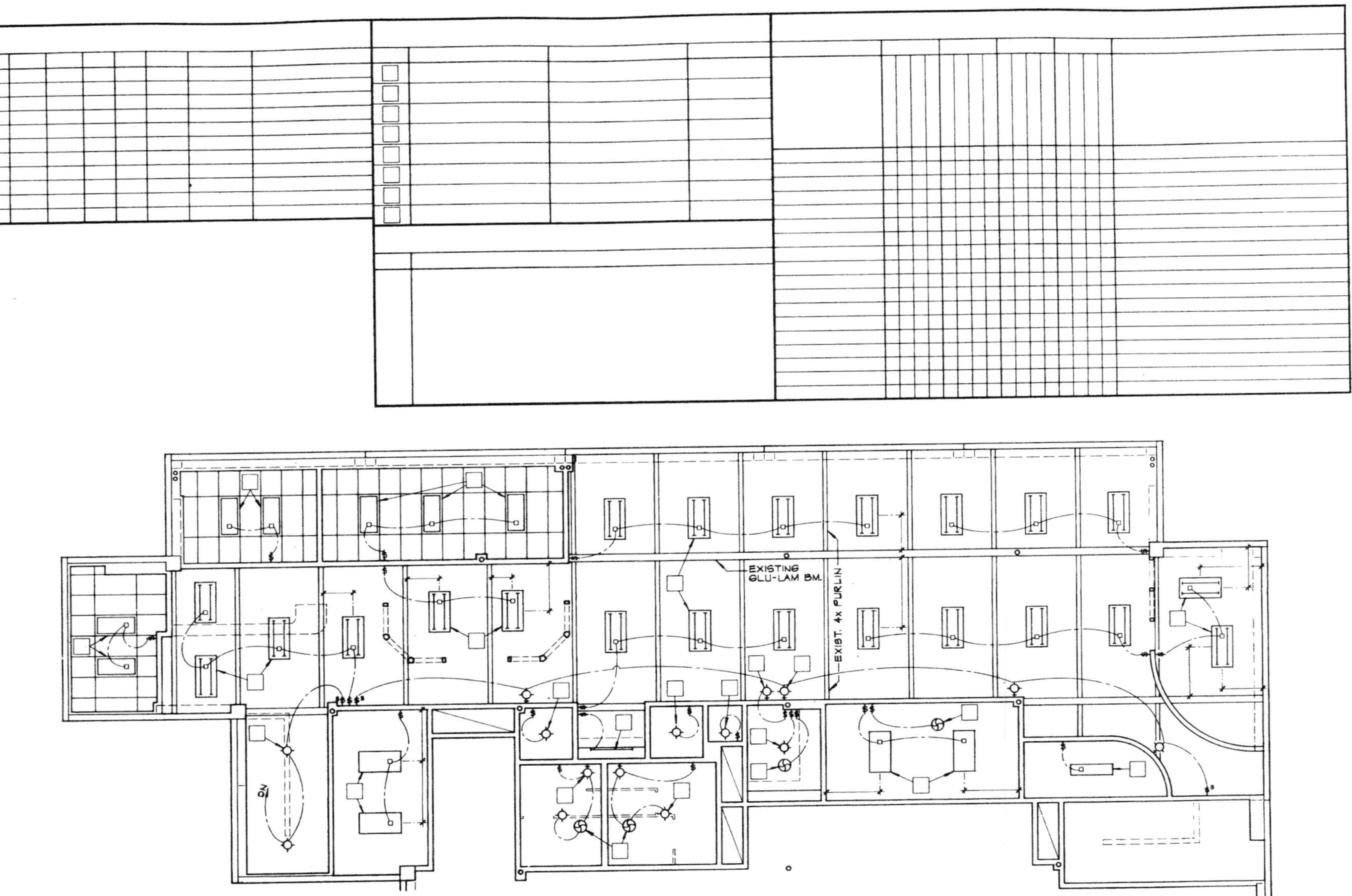

Figure 13.44 Stage II: Ceiling plan.

DOOR SCHEDULE

SYM	WIDTH	HEIGHT	THK	HC/SC	TYPE	MATERIAL	REMARKS
1	3'-0"	7'-0"	1 3/4"	SC	SLAB	WOOD	PLAM FIN (COFFEE)
2	PR. 2'-8"	"	"	"	"	"	" " "
3	3'-0"	"	"	"	"	"	" " (BLACK)
4	2'-10"	"	"	"	"	"	" " "
5	2'-2"	5'-0"	1"	"	"	MET FACE	BLACK
6	2'-10	"	"	"	"	"	"
7	"	"	1 3/8"	HC	"	PNT GD WD	WATER HEATER DR
8	3'-0"	7'-0"	1 3/4"	SC	"	WOOD	3/4 HR./SELF-CLSG.

WINDOW SCHEDULE

SYM	WIDTH	HEIGHT	GL THK	TYPE	FRAME MTL	REMARKS
A	3'-0"	4'-0"	1/4"	FIXED	AL/DARK BRZ	CLEAR GL
B	3'-2"	2'-6"	"	"	"	TINTED GL
C	"	4'-2"	"	"	"	CLR GL, ABV B

ELECTRICAL FIXTURE SCHEDULE

SYM	ITEM/MODEL NO.	MANUFACTURER	LAMP
E1	2'×4' RECESSED W/ PRISMATIC LENS	LIGHTDESIGN INC.	4-40W FLUR TUBES
E2	2'×4' SURF. MT W/ PRISMATIC LENS	"	" "
E3	1'×4' DO	"	2-40W "
E4	2'×4' OPEN TUBE INDUS. W/"ICE-TONG" HANGERS	"	4-40W "
E5	4' STRIP/UNDER CAB	"	1-40W "
E6	12"φ SURF. MT W/ OP ACRYLIC LENS	"	2-60W A19 BULBS
E7	4"φ DO	"	1-75W "
E8	SURF. MT/PORCELAIN	"PROPRIETARY"	1-60W "

PLUMBING FIXTURE SCHEDULE

SYM	ITEM / MODEL NO.	MANUFACTURER	REMARKS
P1	WC, ELONG. RIM, 18" RIM HT	FIXTURES INC.	WHITE
P2	WATER CLOSET	"	"
P3	WALL HUNG URINAL	"	"
P4	" " LAV	"	"
P5	BAR SINK	"	SST, 5" DEEP
P6	SINK	"	" , 9" "

INTERIOR FINISH SCHEDULE

ROOM/AREA	FLOOR: CARPET & PAD	FLOOR: VINYL TILE	FLOOR: SHEET VINYL	BASE: VINYL TOPSET	BASE: COVED FLR	BASE: "J" MOLDING	WALLS: 5/8" TYPE "X" G.B.	CEILING: 5/8"×2'×4' SUS CLG	CEILING: 5/8" TYPE "X" G.B.	CEILING: EXP FRAMING	REMARKS
RECEPT./SEC.	●			●			●			●	
OFFICE - 1	●			●			●	●			
OFFICE - 2	●			●			●	●			
OFFICE - 3	●			●			●	●			
CONFERENCE	●			●						●	STOREFRONT GL WALLS (SEE EL)
CLERICAL WRKRM	●			●			●		●		
RESTROOMS			●		●		●		●		CT WSCT, ENAMEL PNT (SEE INT ELS)
VESTIBULES			●		●		●		●		
COFFEE BAR		●		●			●		●		
STUDIO - 1		●		●			●			●	SEE PLAN FOR FLR TILE PATTERN
DARKROOM		●		●			●		●		
PAINT/WORKROOM		●		●			●		●		
STORAGE		●				●	●		●		
STUDIO - 2	●			●			●			●	
STAIRS	●					●	●		●		
DNSTRS LOBBY	●			●			●		●		

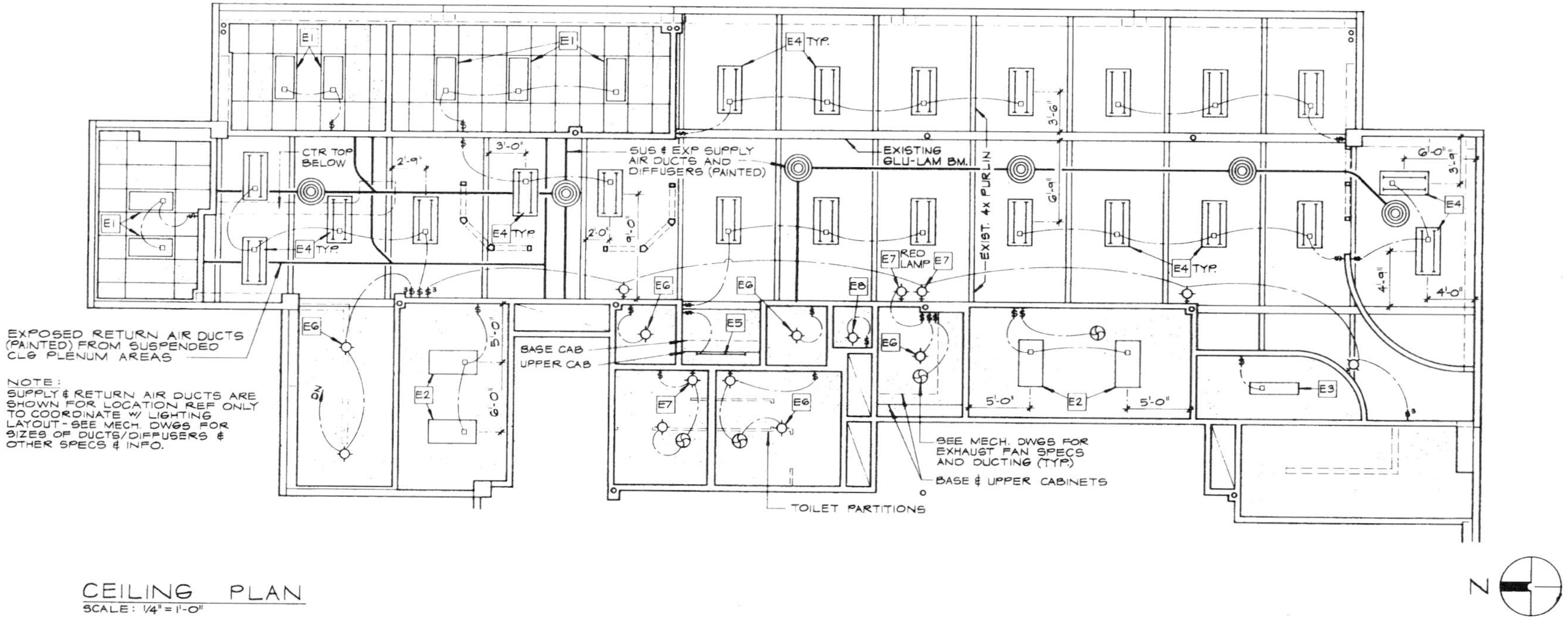

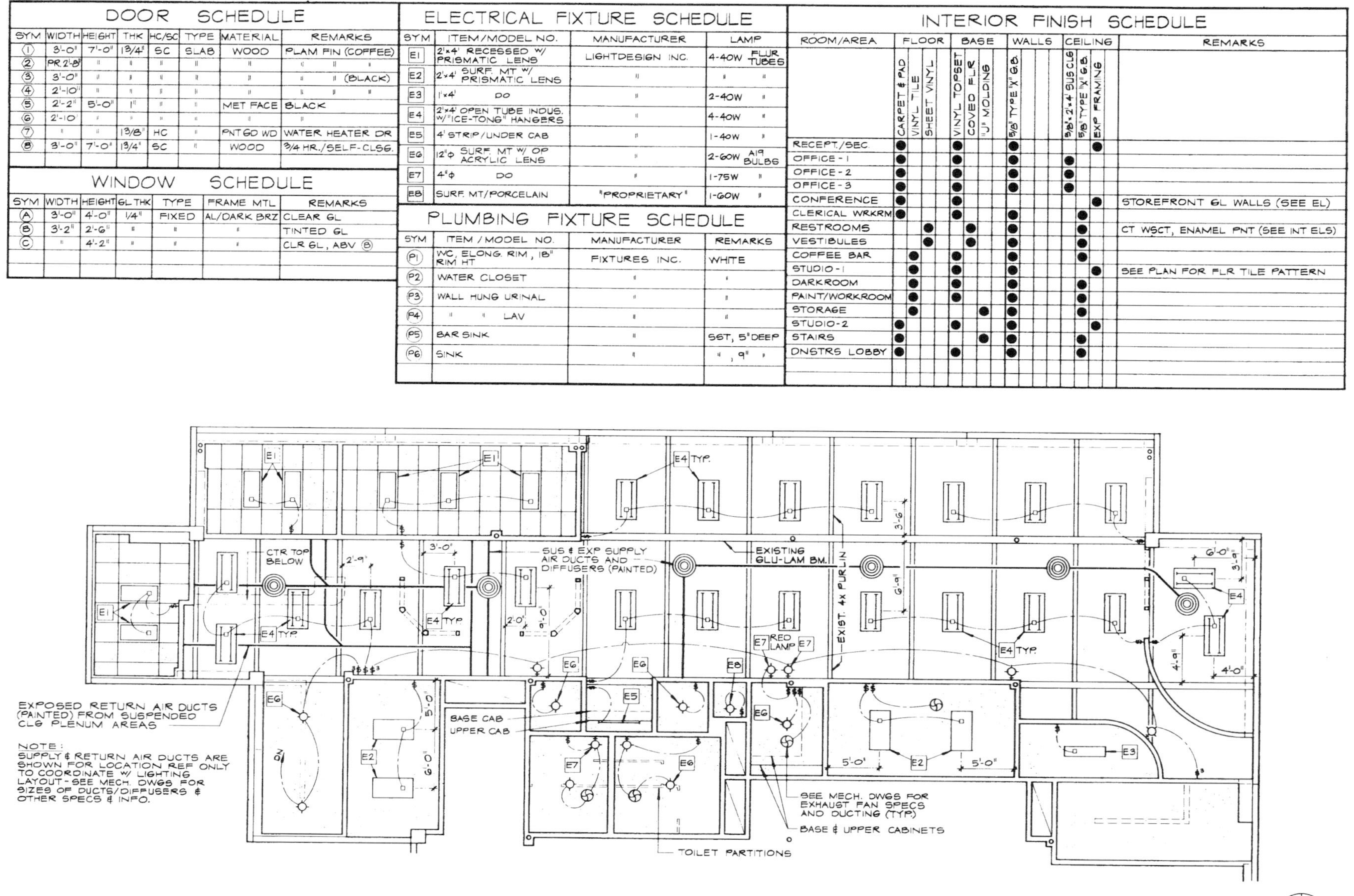

Figure 13.45 Stage III: Ceiling plan.

chapter

14

ONE-STORY CONVENTIONAL WOOD-FRAMED STRUCTURES

The Professional Practice of Architectural Working Drawings, Sixth Edition. Nagy R. Bakhoum and Osamu A. Wakita.
© 2024 John Wiley & Sons Inc. Published 2024 by John Wiley & Sons Inc.
Companion website: www.wiley.com\go\bakhoum\theprofessionalpracticeofarchitecturalworkingdrawings

PROGRAM AND SITE ANALISIS

The design purpose is to create a home that has room for growth. The site is a typical city lot in Anytown, USA, and for this example we call it the Jadyn residence. The zoning is R-1 (residential), the setbacks are 15′-0″ in the front, 5′-0″ on the sides, and 15′-0″ at the rear. Water flows from the street side to the rear in the direction of the lot's slope, and this slope opens up to a city view. See Figure 14.1.

Along with the bedroom and two baths, the client requested a family room and kitchen oriented toward the view, and living room, nook, and formal dining room. The intention is that the owner will provide a second story at a later date.

Using what is commonly called bubble diagramming, room relationships were quickly established. See Figure 14.2. The bedroom, family room, and kitchen were oriented to the rear of the lot to take advantage of the view and avoid the street noise. With the prevailing wind coming from the northwest, each of these rooms will be well ventilated. The garage was positioned perpendicular to the street. Circulation is through the center of the structure, which serves as a spline or connector to all of the rooms. Included for this example are a preliminary design development site plan (Figure 14.3), floor plan (Figure 14.4), and a couple of elevations (Figure 14.5). If this set of drawings is approved, additional preliminary drawings are developed, which may include a roof plan (Figure 14.6), a design section (Figure 14.7), and possibly a framing plan.

SCHEMATIC DESIGN

The schematic drawings represent the culmination of many hours of designer-client decisions. The final changes chosen by the client are based on such things as financing, size of the structure, or projected number of users. Eventually, a final design decision is made and signed, and at that point becomes the final design proposal used by the architect to develop a set of construction drawings.

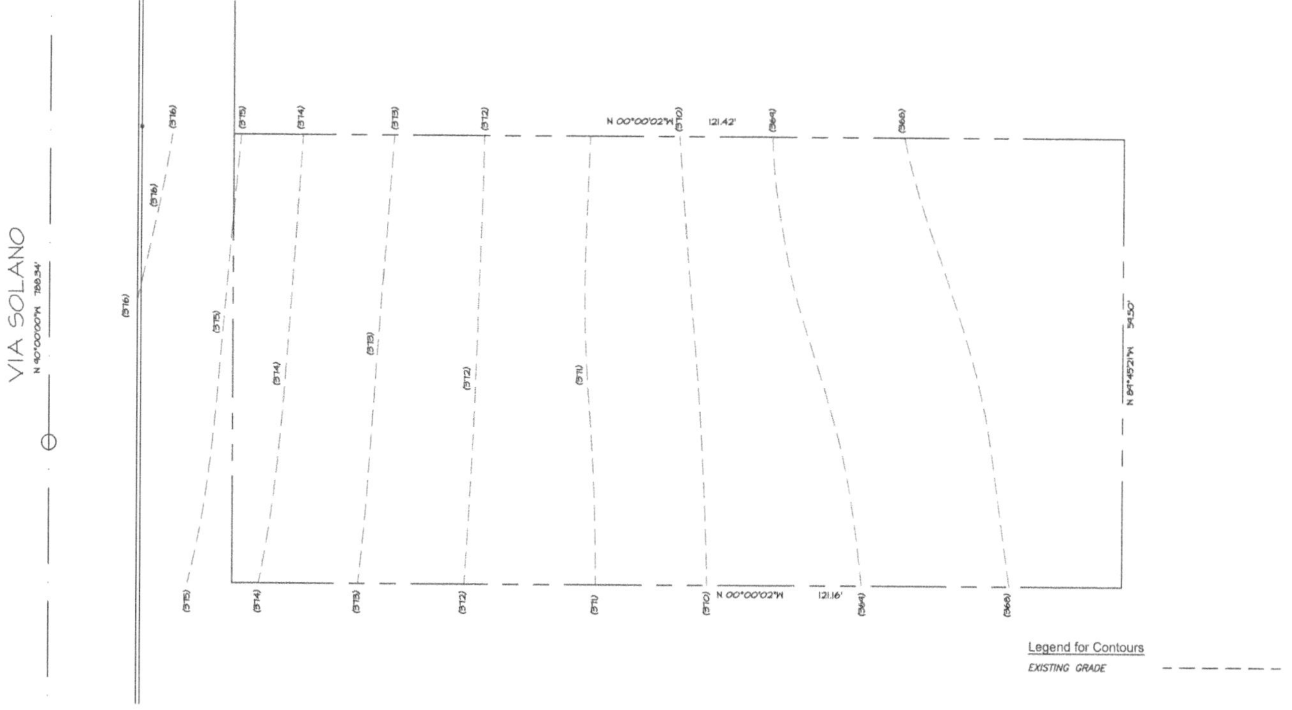

Figure 14.1 Jadyn residence site.

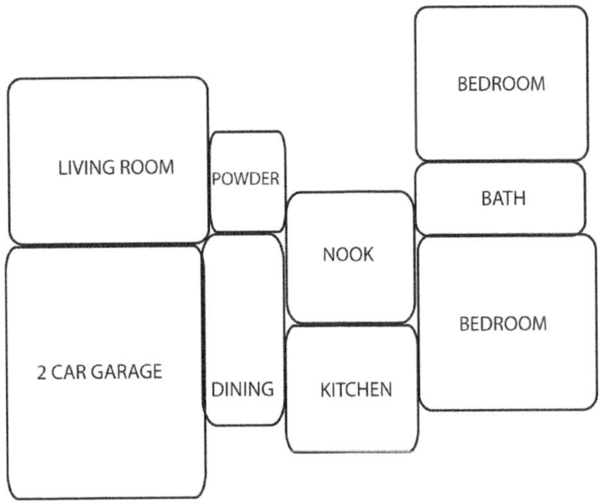

Figure 14.2 Bubble diagramming the Jadyn residence.

The architect develops preliminary drawings in response to the client's needs. These drawings provide the basis for the formulation and incorporation of changes and new ideas. Included for this example are a site plan (Figure 14.3), floor plan (Figure 14.4), and a couple of elevations (Figure 14.5).

If this set of drawings is approved, additional preliminary drawings are conceived, which may include a roof plan (Figure 14.6), a design section (Figure 14.7), and possibly a framing plan.

Client Changes

The preliminary floor plan plays a very important part in the development of a final configuration or shape of a structure. It gives the client time to look at and discuss some of the important family needs or to make major changes before the project progresses too far.

Client changes are an integral part of the design process: It is much more likely that the client will generate changes to a plan than it is to have a client fully accept the plan as first presented. It is also common for the client to order or request changes throughout the entire design process and even construction of the project.

Development of Elevations

The model helps the clients to visualize how the structure will look and to comprehend the preliminary exterior elevations, as seen in Figure 14.8. In this example, a simple series of rectangular shapes were extruded; the roof was then added and features delineated to establish a three-dimensional (3-D) view or a schematic design.

Other preliminary drawings may be done by the design and structural associates, making the CAD drafter's task easier. Such drawings might include a preliminary foundation plan, a revised preliminary building section and roof plans, and a revised framing system.

Figure 14.3 Preliminary design development, Jadyn residence site plan.

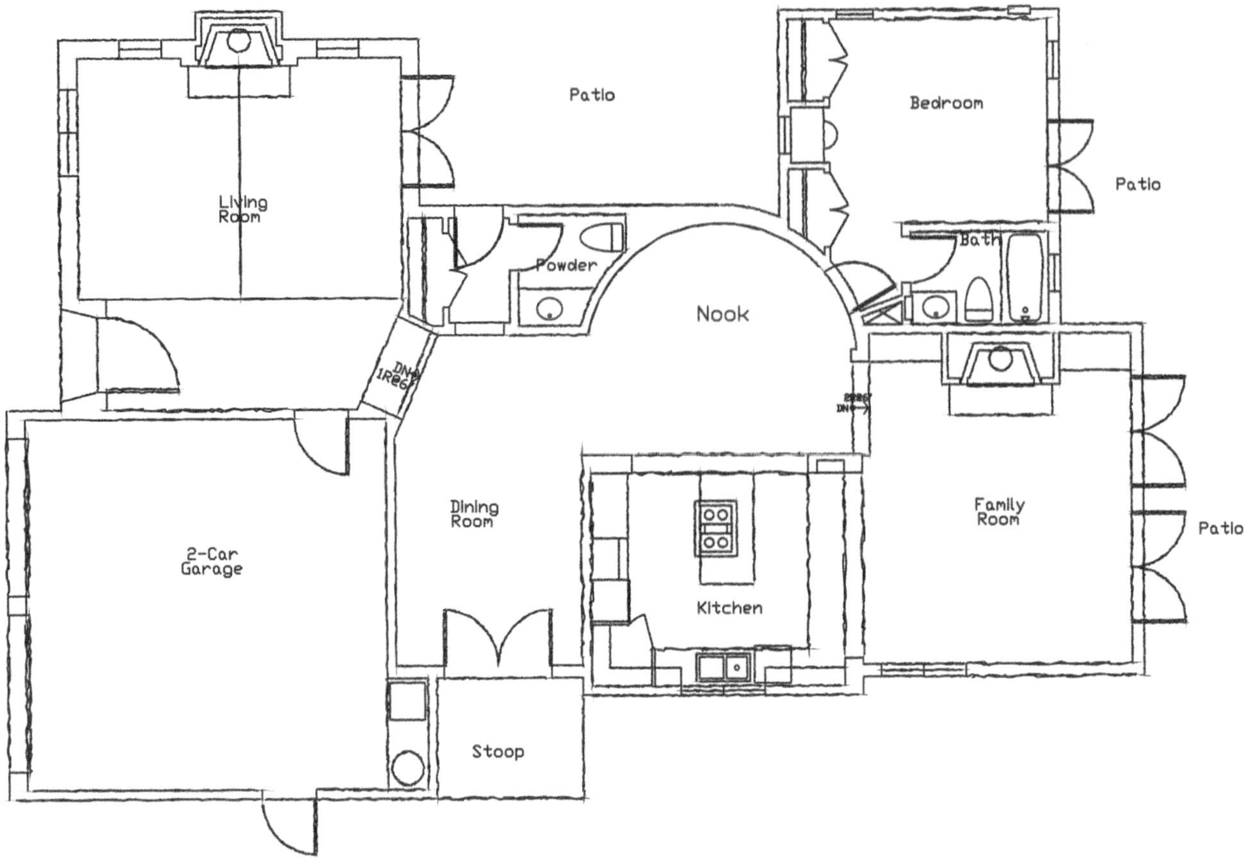

Figure 14.4 Preliminary design development, Jadyn residence floor plan.

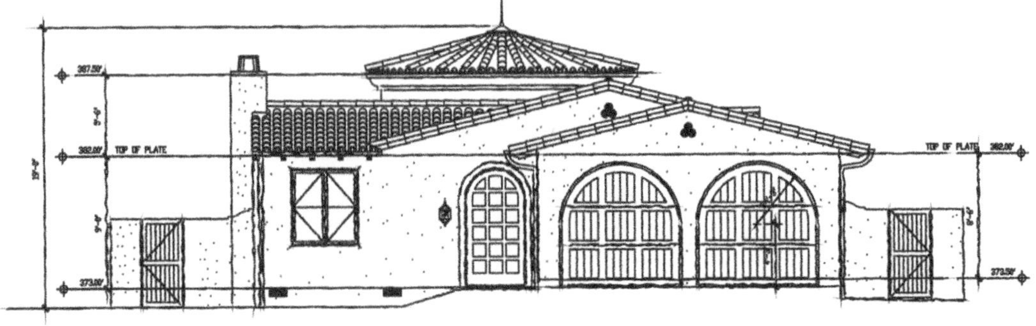

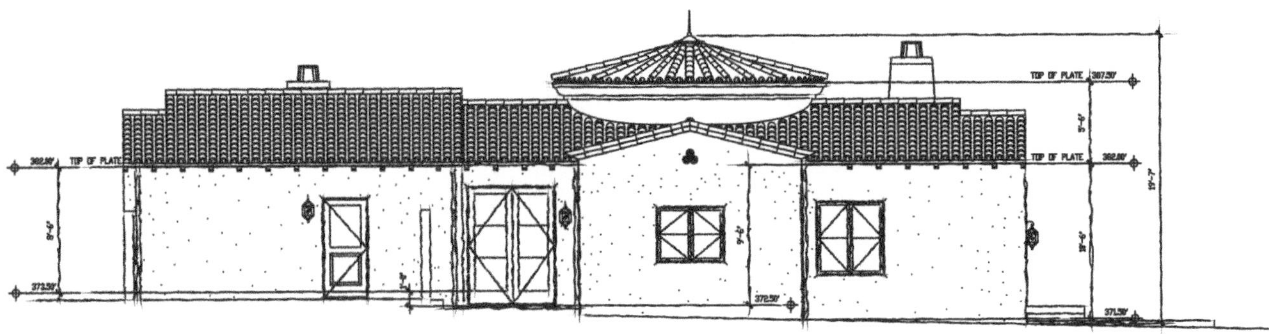

Figure 14.5 Preliminary design development, Jadyn residence elevations.

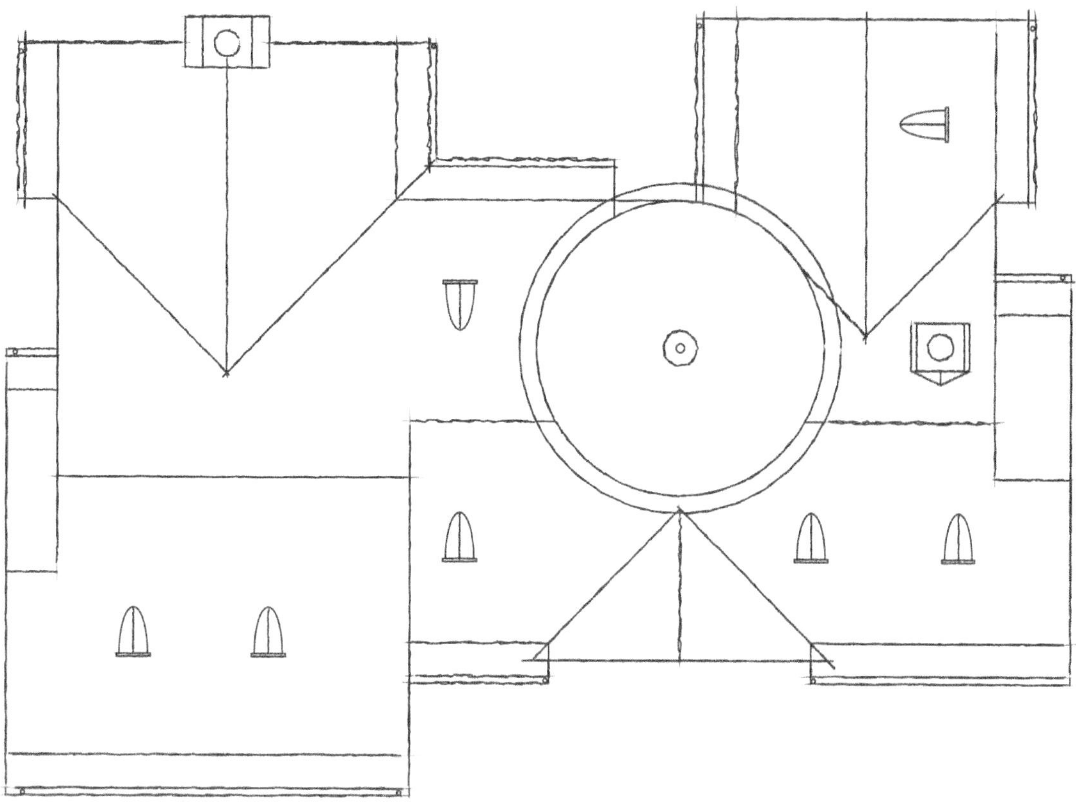

Figure 14.6 Preliminary design development, Jadyn residence roof plan.

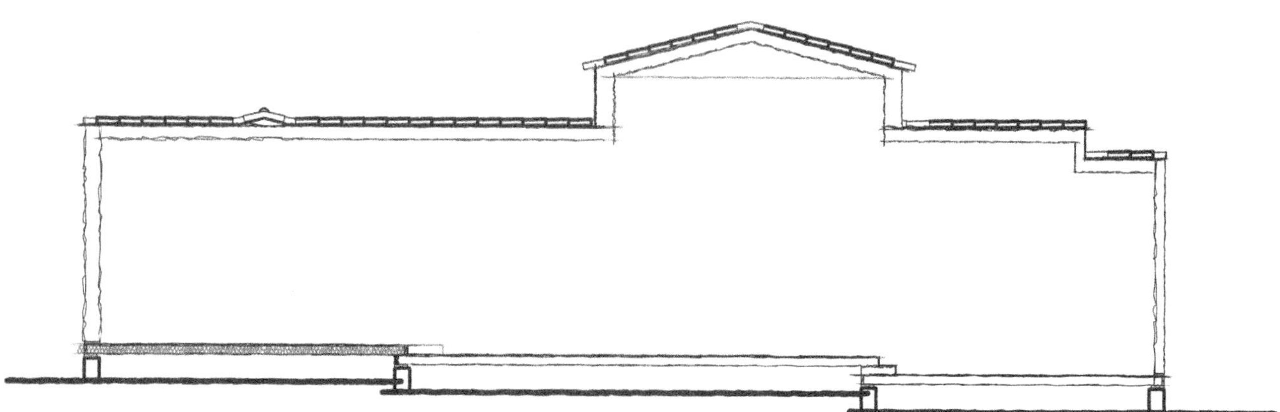

Figure 14.7 Preliminary building design section, Jadyn residence.

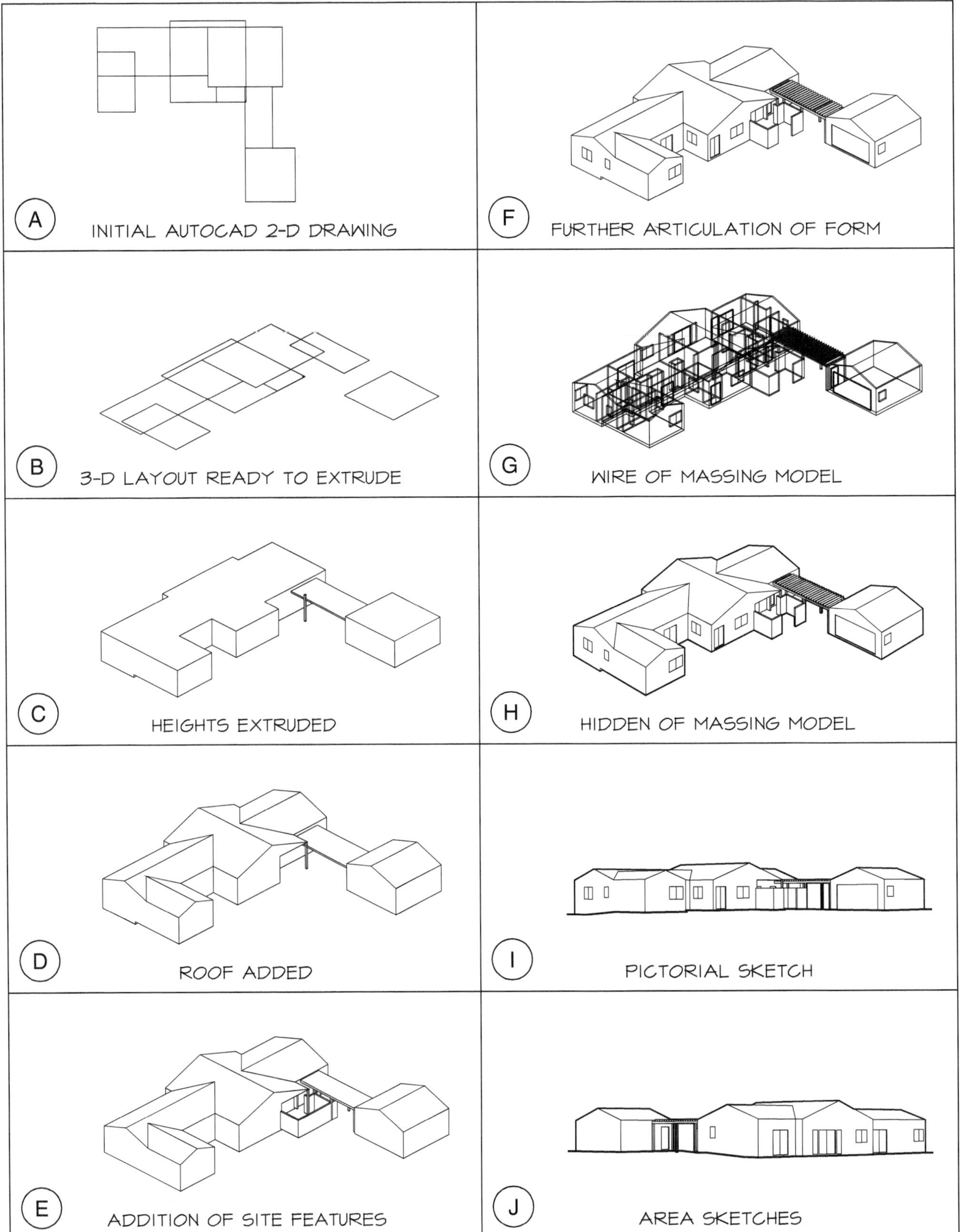

Figure 14.8 Evolution of a 2-D to a 3-D sketch.

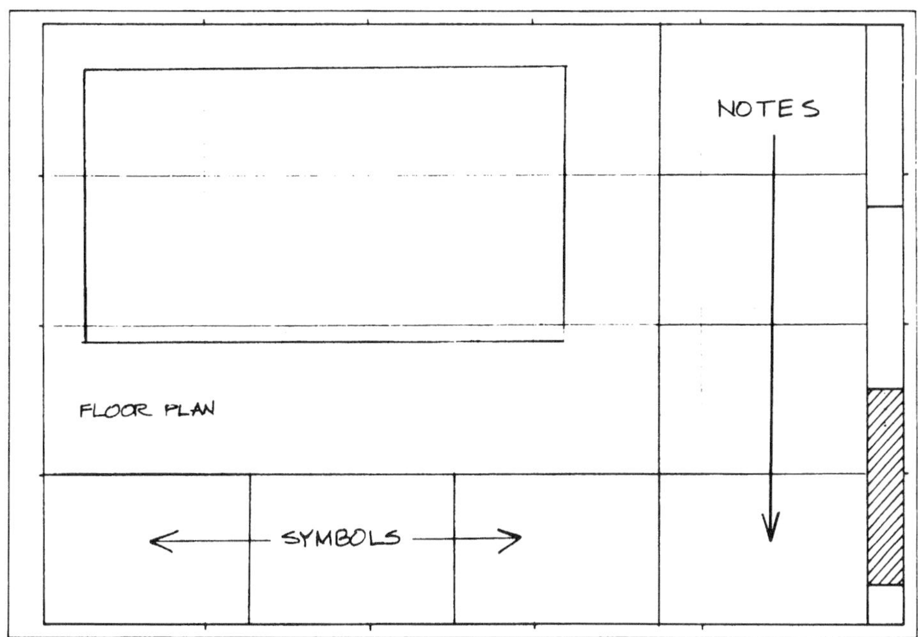

Figure 14.9 Cartoon of floor-plan sheet.

Cartoon of the Project

A **cartoon sheet** format, or **mock set** as it is called in some regions, is a reduced replica of the distribution of the drawings on each of the working drawing sheets, drawn on an 8½″ × 11″ sheet of paper. These can be accomplished by substituting rectangles in place of the actual drawings, as shown in Figures 14.9 and 14.10.

■ DESIGN DEVELOPMENT

Developing Construction Documents from a 3-D Model

A 3-D model, if one is generated, is rotated into the appropriate positions to obtain the roof plan and the corresponding elevations (see Figure 14.11). The 3-D

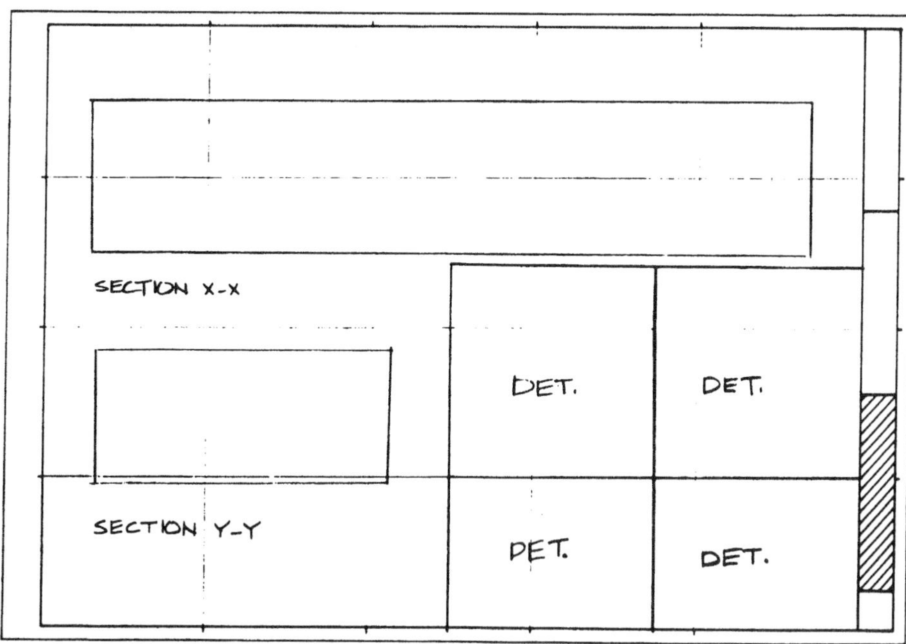

Figure 14.10 Cartoon of section sheet.

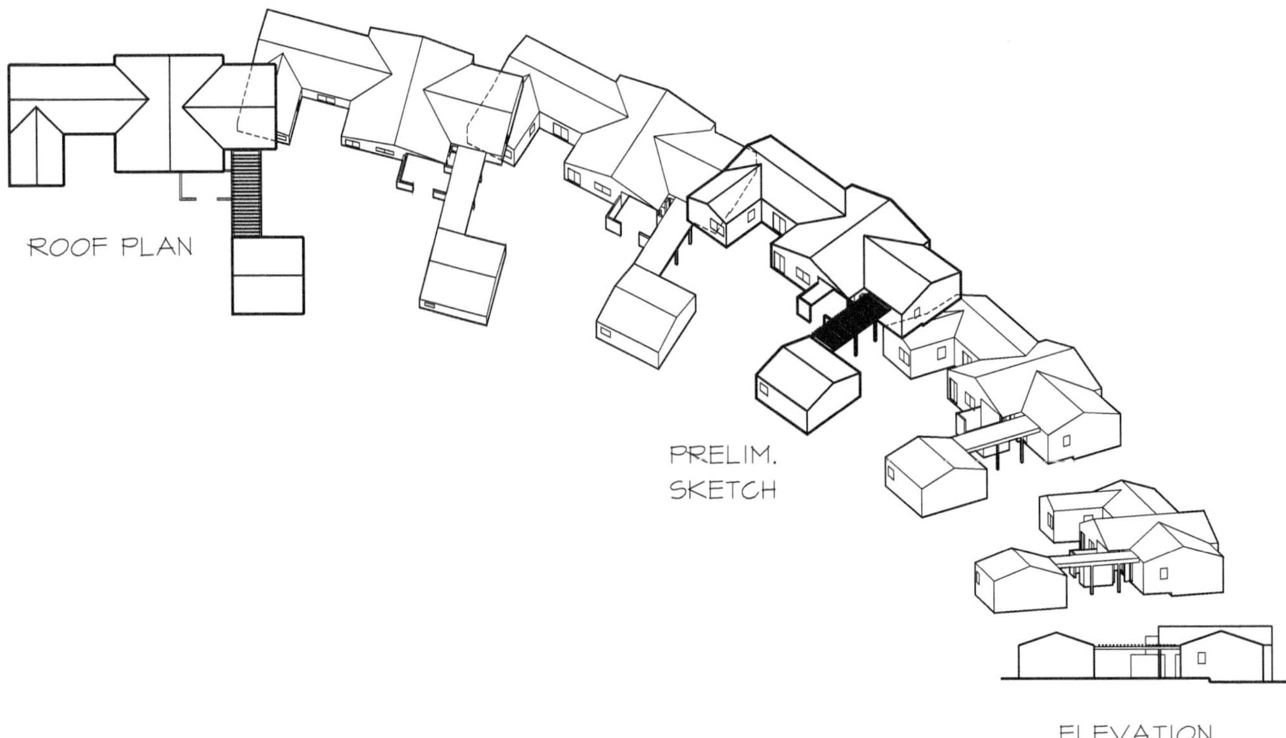

Figure 14.11 Rotation of massing model into ortho view.

model is sliced horizontally and vertically. The horizontal slice is used to produce the floor plan. If the roof half is rotated in the plan view, a reflected ceiling plan is produced. The vertical cut produces a view of the structure called a building section. For examples of the floor plan and building section, see Figure 14.12. A summary of the results of this exercise is shown in Figure 14.13.

The next step for the CAD drafter is to construct the structure as a 3-D model. See an example of such a section in Figure 14.14. Although this may seem like a lot of work at this stage, it really is not when you consider that the floor plan will be used as the base (datum) for the framing plan, electrical plans, mechanical plans, and foundation plans, as seen in Figure 14.15.

CONSTRUCTION DOCUMENTS

Study the remaining images starting with Figure 14.16 through Figure 14.23 demonstrate the development of the complete set of construction documents. These would typically include the structural drawings, schedules and interior elevations.

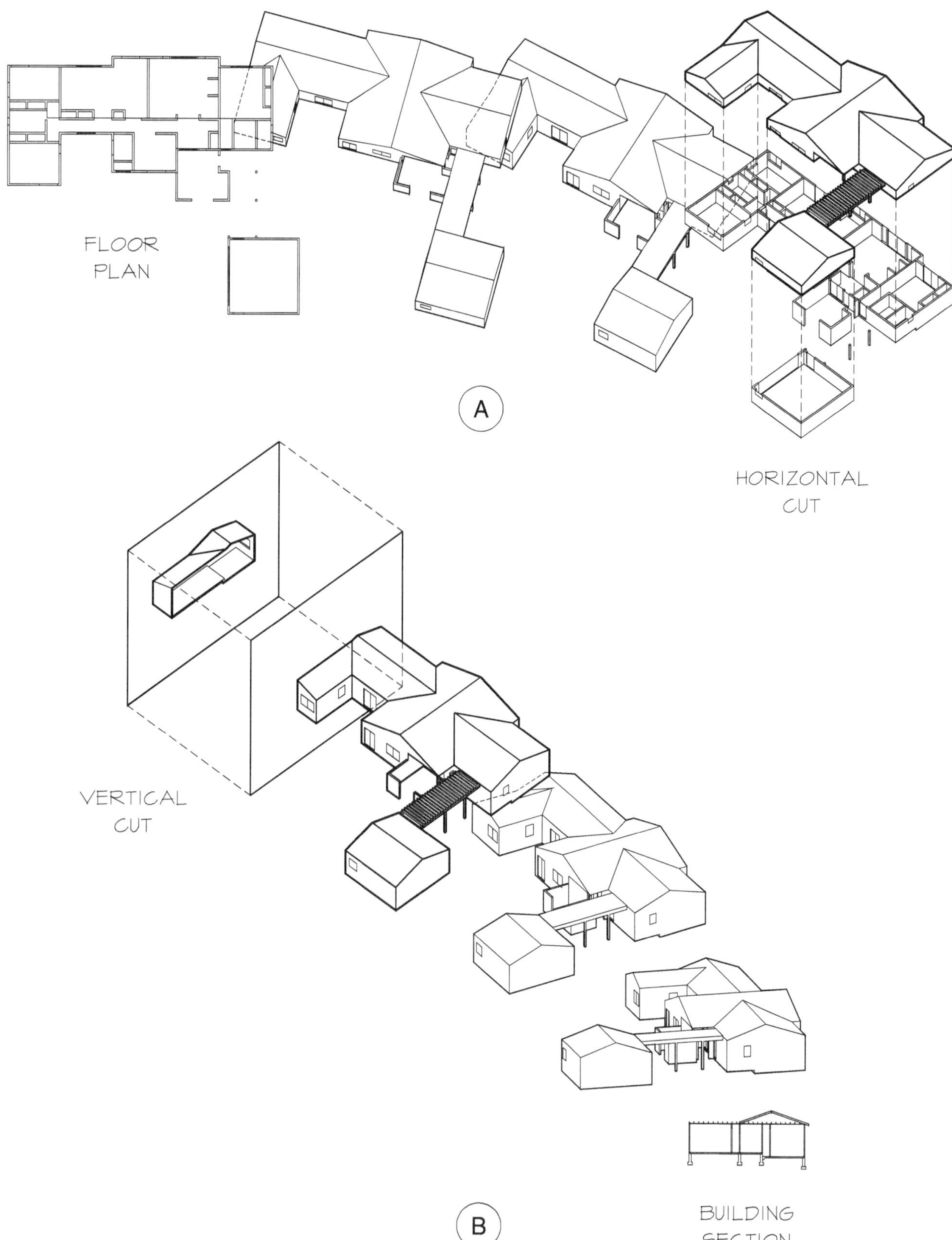

Figure 14.12 Horizontal and vertical sections through preliminary sketch.

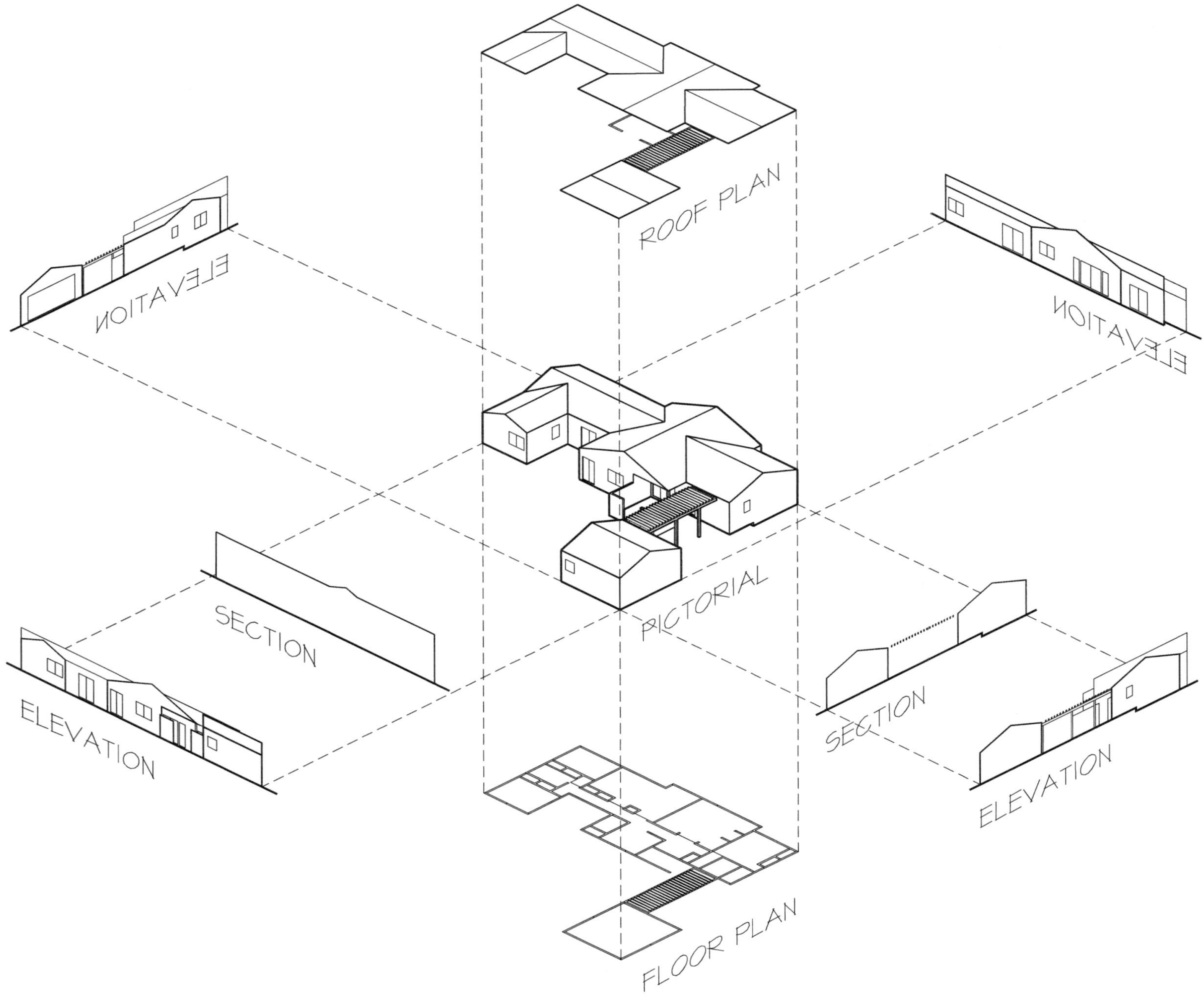

Figure 14.13 Evolution of construction documents.

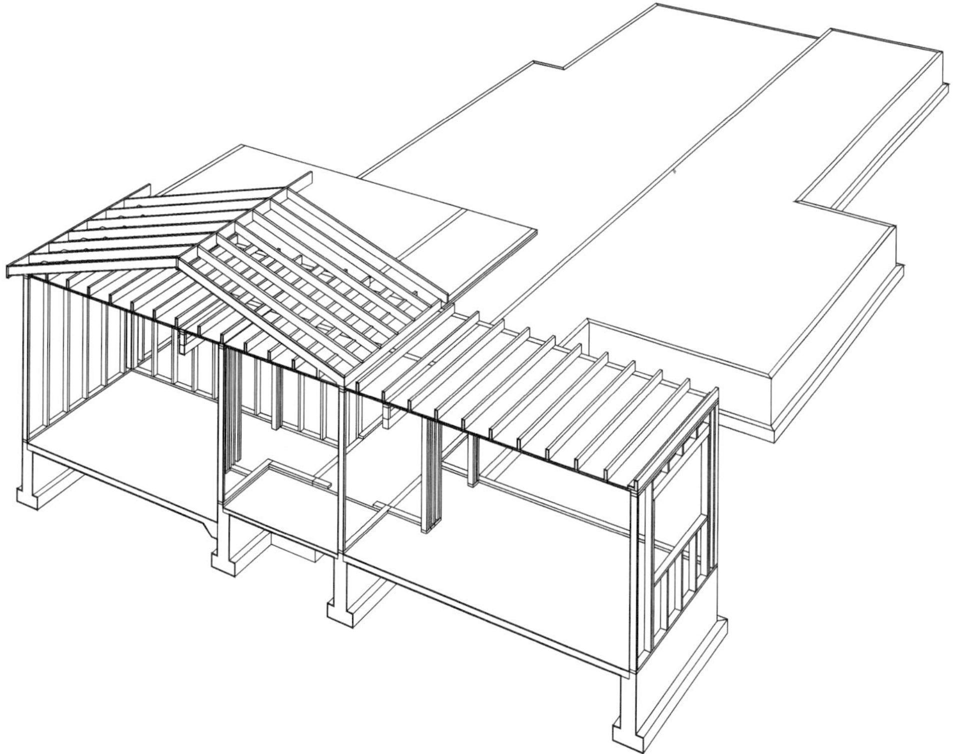

Figure 14.14 Incorporating the individual elements.

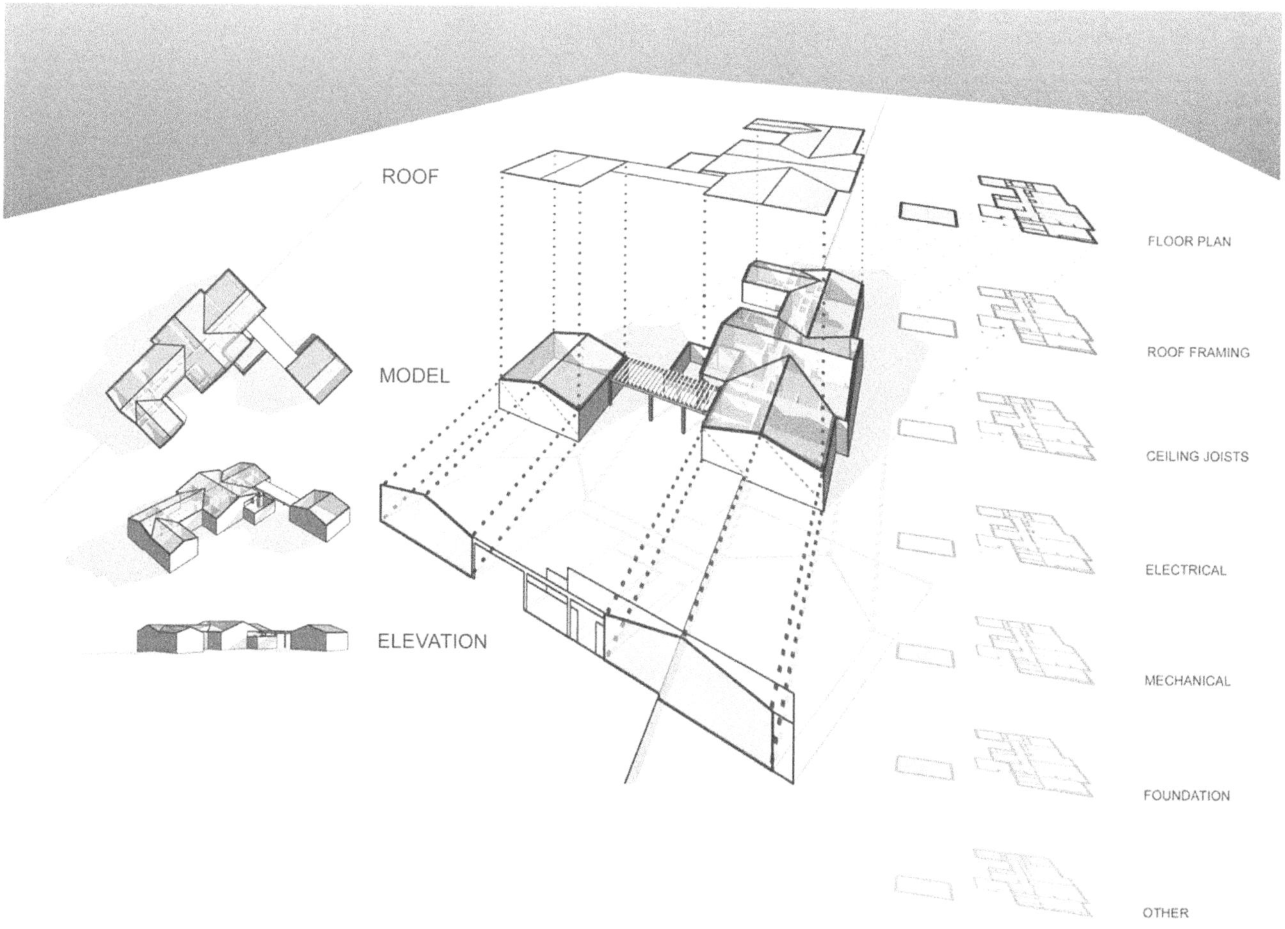

Figure 14.15 Floor plan as a base for other drawings.

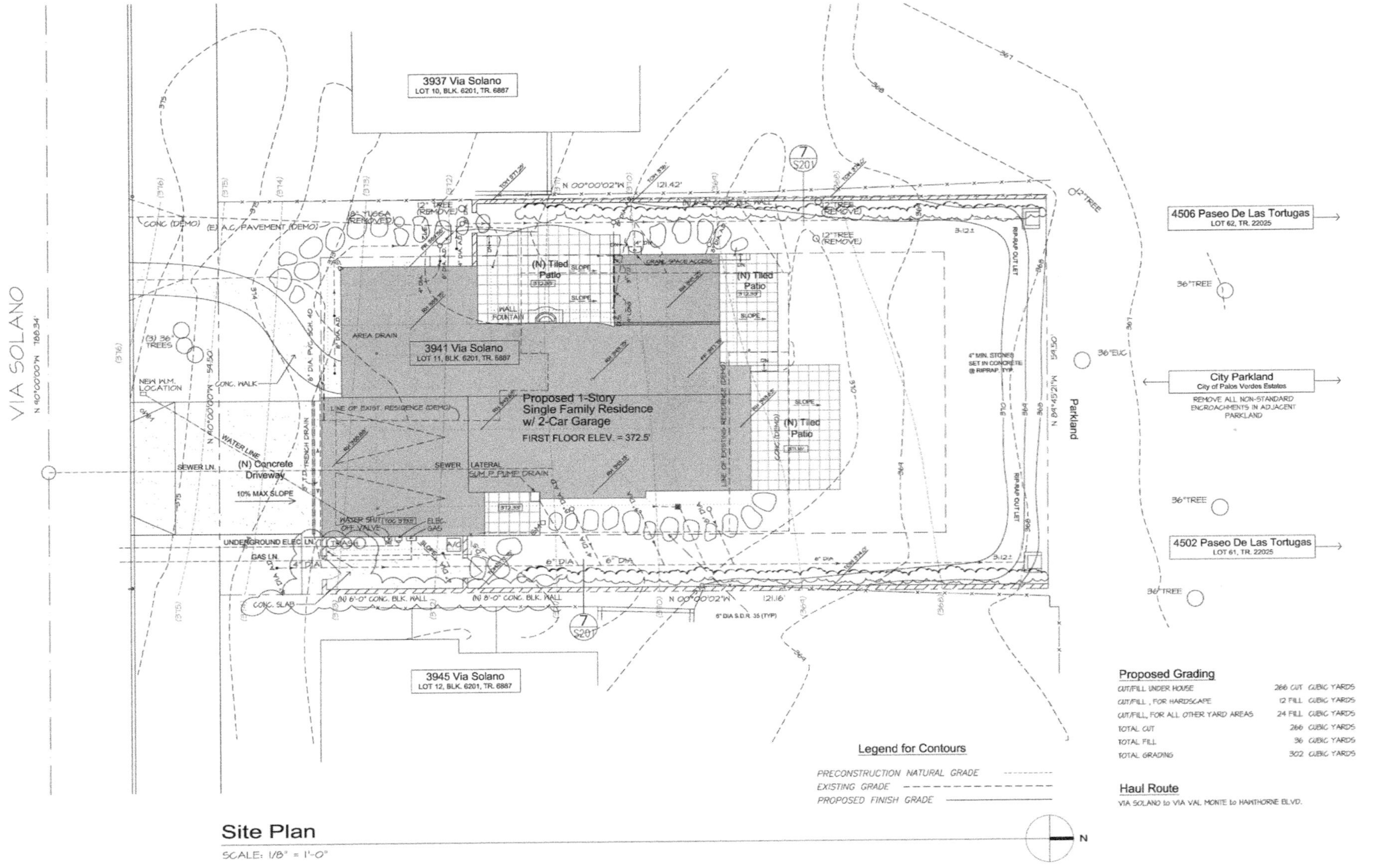
3937 Via Solano
LOT 10, BLK. 6201, TR. 6887
3941 Via Solano
LOT 11, BLK. 6201, TR. 6887
3945 Via Solano
LOT 12, BLK. 6201, TR. 6887
Proposed 1-Story
Single Family Residence
w/ 2-Car Garage
FIRST FLOOR ELEV. = 372.5'
(N) Tiled Patio
(N) Concrete Driveway
10% MAX SLOPE
VIA SOLANO
Parkland
4506 Paseo De Las Tortugas
LOT 62, TR. 22025
City Parkland
City of Palos Verdes Estates
REMOVE ALL NON-STANDARD ENCROACHMENTS IN ADJACENT PARKLAND
4502 Paseo De Las Tortugas
LOT 61, TR. 22025
Proposed Grading
CUT/FILL UNDER HOUSE 266 CUT CUBIC YARDS
CUT/FILL, FOR HARDSCAPE 12 FILL CUBIC YARDS
CUT/FILL, FOR ALL OTHER YARD AREAS 24 FILL CUBIC YARDS
TOTAL CUT 266 CUBIC YARDS
TOTAL FILL 36 CUBIC YARDS
TOTAL GRADING 302 CUBIC YARDS
Haul Route
VIA SOLANO to VIA VAL MONTE to HAWTHORNE BLVD.
Legend for Contours
PRECONSTRUCTION NATURAL GRADE
EXISTING GRADE
PROPOSED FINISH GRADE
Site Plan
SCALE: 1/8" = 1'-0"

Figure 14.16 Residence site plan.

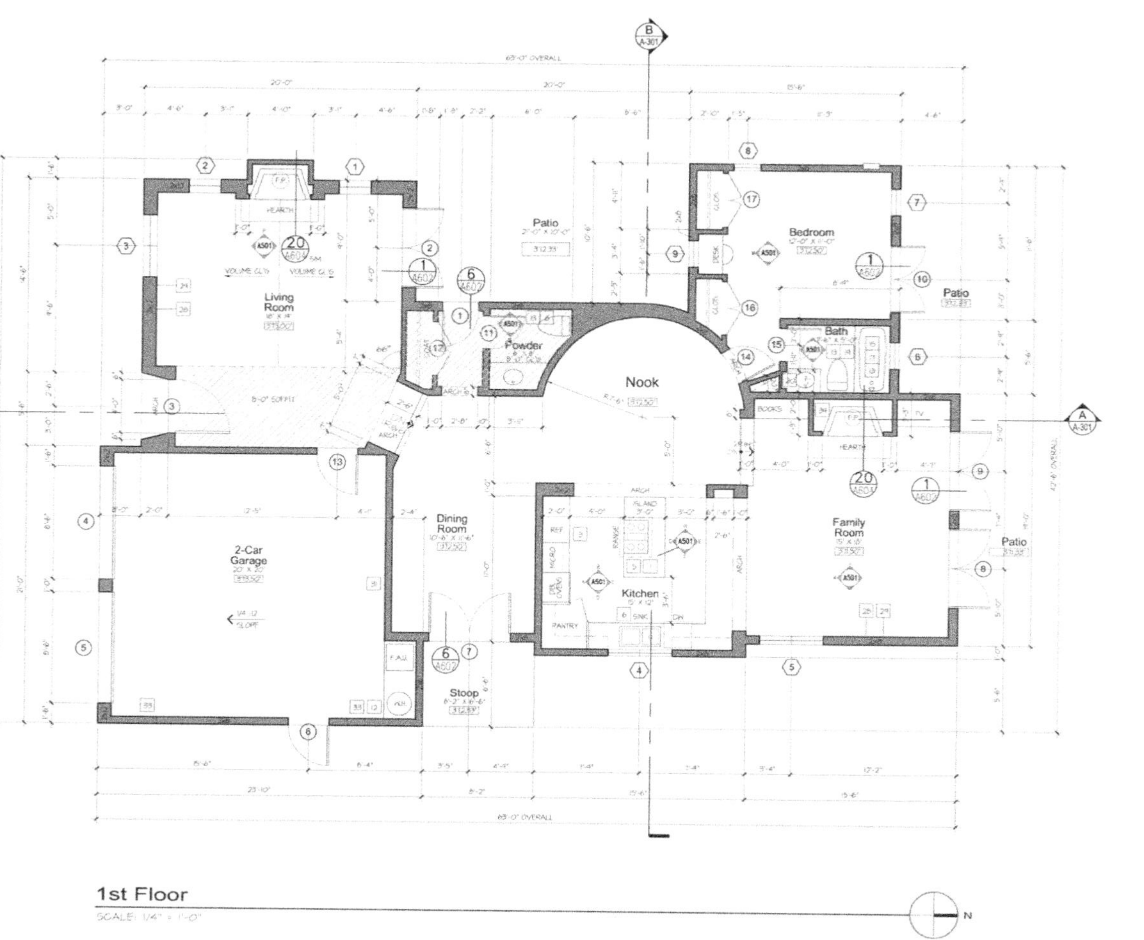

Figure 14.17 Floor plan.

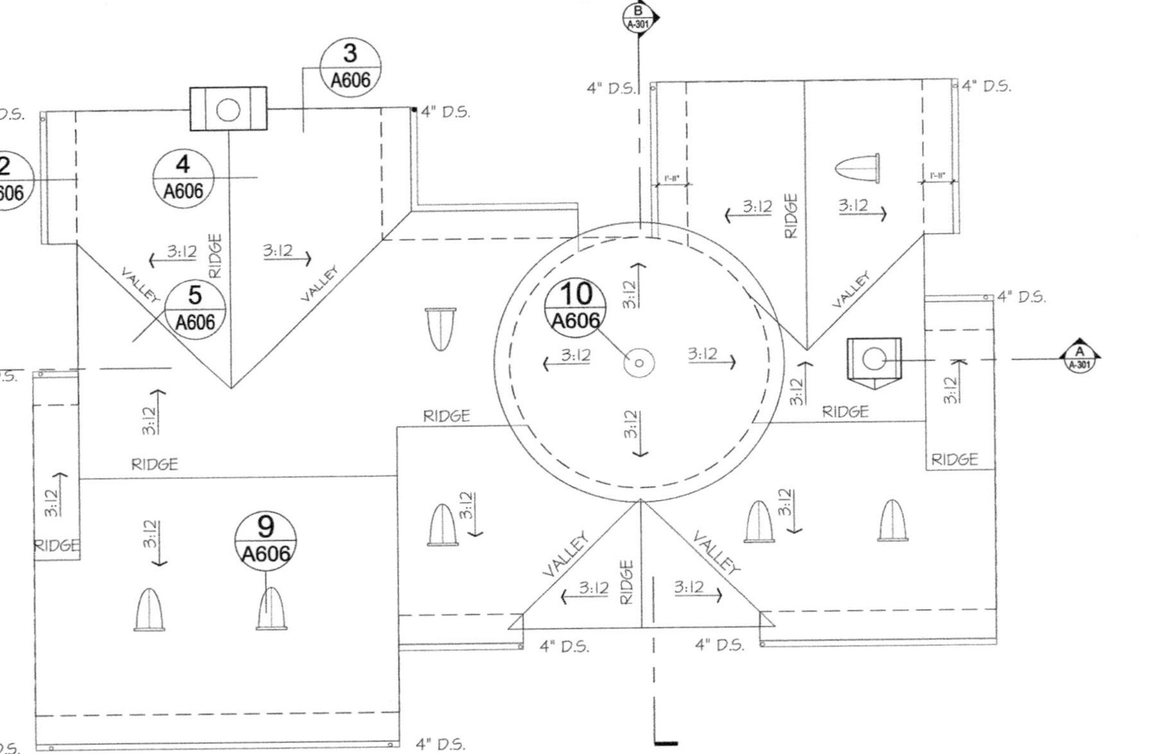

4" D.S.
2
A606
3
A606
4
A606
5
A606
9
A606
10
A606
B
A-301
A
A-301
RIDGE
VALLEY
3:12
1'-11"
Roof Plan
SCALE: 1/4" = 1'-0"
N
ROOF PLAN NOTES:
ROOF SLOPE:
1. ROOF SLOPES ARE SHOWN DIRECTLY ON ROOF PLAN DRAWING
2. IN THE ABSENCE OF SLOPES SHOWN ON STRUCTURAL DRAWINGS OR ARCHITECTURAL DRAWINGS, ROUGH CARPENTER SHALL PROVIDE REQUIRED SHIMMING BELOW ROOF SHEATHING TO ALLOW FOR PROPER SLOPE TO DRAIN
3. NO OBSTACLE SHALL PREVENT WATER FLOW TOWARD DRAINS
ROOF MATERIAL:
1. PITCHED ROOF TO BE CLASS "A" US-TILE, TWO-PIECE MISSION TILE RUSTIC NEWPORT BLEND ICBO # ER-3523, 1000 BLS. PER SQUARE INSTALLED OVER 30 LBS. FLET UNDERLAYMENT PER UBC TABLE 15-D-1.
MINIMUM NAILING SHALL COMPLY WITH THE FOLLOWING:
1. 11 GA. CORROSION-RESIST. 3/4" INTO SHEATHING PER TABLE NO. 15-D-1
2. THE HEADS OF ALL TILE SHALL BE NAILED
3. THE NOSES OF ALL EAVE COURSE TILES SHALL BE FASTENED WITH APPROVED CLIPS
4. ALL RAKE TILES SHALL BE NAILED WITH TWO NAILS
5. THE NOSES OF ALL RIDGE, HIP AND RAKE TILES SHALL BE SET IN A BED OF APROVED ROOFERS MASTIC
2. MOCK-UP OF PITCHED ROOF INSTALLATION SHALL BE APPROVED BY ARCHITECT PRIOR TO PROCEEDING WITH WORK
GUTTERS AND ROOF DRAINS:
1. GUTTERS SHALL BE CONSTRUCTED OF 18 OZ. COPPER WITH 5/8" EXPANSION JOINTS EVERY 30 FEET MAXIMUM
2. GUTTERS SHALL SLOPE 1/16" PER FOOT TOWARD RAIN WATER LEADERS
3. UNLESS SPECIFIED OTHERWISE, RAIN WATER LEADERS ARE EXPOSED AND LOCATION IS SHOWN ON ROOF PLAN
4. PROVIDE DOME WIRE BASKET AT EACH RAIN WATER LEADER AND ROOF DRAIN
5. ROOF DRAINAGE TO BE CONNECTED TO EXISTING CITY APPROVED DRAINAG DEVICE. ALL RAIN WATER TO BE DIRECTED TO STREET OR APPROVED OUTLET.
ROOF PENETRATION:
1. VENTS AND ROOF STACKS SHALL PROJECT ABOVE ROOF BY THE MINIMUM DISTANCE REQUIRED BY APPLICABLE CODES AND SHALL BE LOCATED IN AREAS NOT VISIBLE FROM STREET. EXACT LOCATION TO BE COORDINATED WITH ARCHITECT PRIOR TO INSTALLATION
2. ALL VENTS AND ROOF STACKS TO HAVE RAIN PROTECTION CAPS
3. CONTINUOUS WATERPROOFING AT ALL ROOF PENETRATIONS SHALL BE PROVIDED WITH WR GRACE 4000 BITUTHENE WRAPPING AND 16 OZ. COPPER FLASHING AND COUNTERFLASHING. ALL JOINTS AT SHEET METAL SHALL BE CAULKED
4. COLOR OF ALL EXPOSED VENTS AND ROOF STACKS TO MATCH ADJACENT ROOF MATERIAL. UNLESS SPECIFIED OTHERWISE BY ARCHITECT
MECHANICAL EQUIPMENT:
1. MECHANICL EQUIPMENT INCLUDING CONDENSING UNITS WILL BE LOCATED ON CONCRETE PADS IN YARD. EXACT LOCATION OF EQUIPMENT TO BE COORDINATED ON SITE BY ARCHITECT U.N.O.
ATTIC VENTILATION:
ATTIC VENTILATION NOTES:
1. TOTAL ATTIC VENTILATION SHALL BE A MINIMUM OF 1/150 OF THE AREA TO BE VENTILATED OR 1/300 FOR MECH. VENTING
2. NO VENTILATION IS REQUIRED IN AREAS WHERE ROOF INSULATION IS INSTALLED BETWEEN RAFTERS WITH NO AIR SPACE BETWEEN INSULATION AND EXTERIOR SHEATHING
3. ATTIC DRAFTSTOPS SHALL BE IN COMPLIANCE WITH ALL APPLICABLE CODES
4. ALL VENT OPENINGS SHALL BE COVERED WITH A CORROSON RESISTANT METAL MESH WITH OPENINGS NO LARGER THAN 1/4" IN ANY DIRECTION
ATTIC VENTILATION TABULATION:
ATTIC SPACE —— 1092.7 SQ. FT. / 150 —— 7.28 SQ. FT.
PROVIDE 7 - 24" HALF-ROUND LOUVERED ROOF VENTS PER DETAIL 9/A606
7 * 140 SQ. IN. = 980 SQ. IN. = 6.81 SQ. FT.
PROVIDE 5 - CLAY PIPE GABLE END VENTS PER DETAIL 19/A606 SEE ELEVATIONS
5 * 18.6 SQ. IN. = 93 SQ. IN. = 0.65 SQ. FT.
VENT AREA PROVIDED: 7.46 SQ. FT.

Figure 14.18 Roof plan.

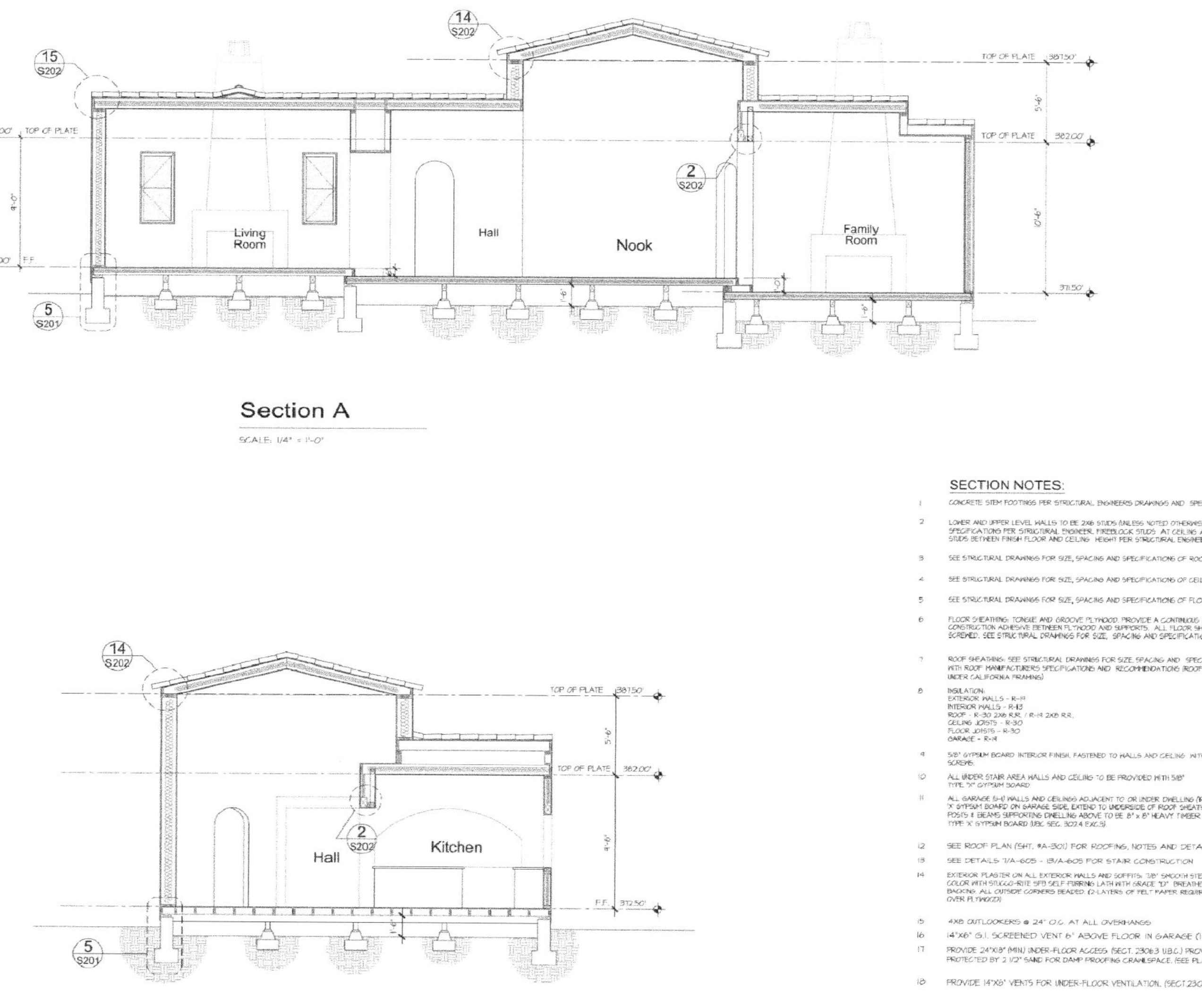

Figure 14.19 Sections.

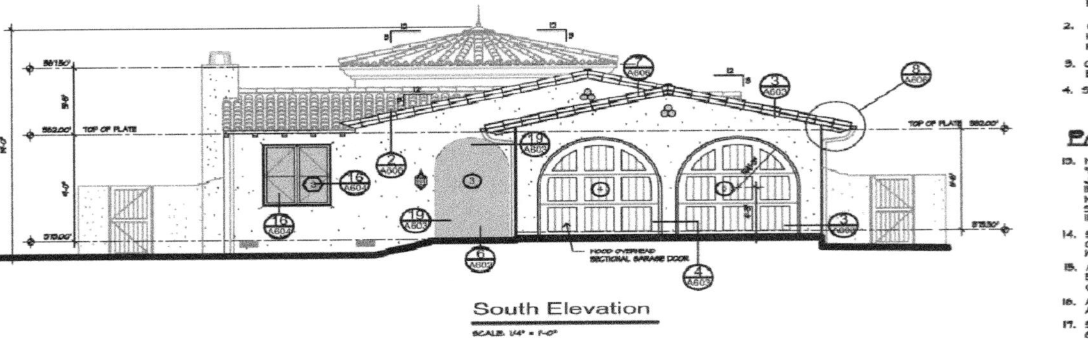

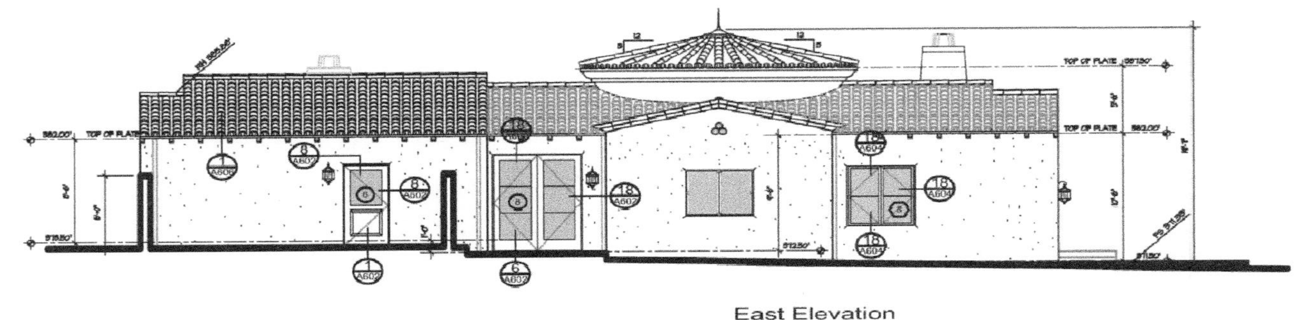

Figure 14.20 Elevations.

Key	Width	Height	Thick.	Type	Material	Glazing	Remarks
1	PAIR 3'-0"	8'-0"	2 1/4"	A	STAIN GRADE WOOD	TEMPERED	EXTERIOR FRENCH DOOR
2	PAIR 3'-0"	8'-0"	2 1/4"	A	STAIN GRADE WOOD	TEMPERED	EXTERIOR FRENCH DOOR
3	7'-0"	8'-0"	1 3/4"	B	STAIN GRADE WOOD		SLIDER-BY PASS DOOR
4	2'-8"	8'-0"	1 3/4"	C	STAIN GRADE WOOD		POCKET DOOR
5	3'-0"	8'-0"	1 3/4"	D	STAIN GRADE WOOD		
6	2'-6"	8'-0"	1 3/4"	D	STAIN GRADE WOOD		
7	2'-4"	8'-0"	1 3/4"	D	STAIN GRADE WOOD		
8	4'-0"	8'-0"	1 3/4"	B	STAIN GRADE WOOD		SLIDER-BY PASS DOOR
9	3'-0"	8'-0"	1 3/4"	D	STAIN GRADE WOOD		
10	7'-0"	8'-0"	1 3/4"	B	STAIN GRADE WOOD		SLIDER-BY PASS DOOR
11	2'-6"	8'-0"	1 3/4"	D	STAIN GRADE WOOD		
12	3'-0"	8'-0"	1 3/4"	D	STAIN GRADE WOOD		
13	6'-0"	8'-0"	2 1/4"	E	STAIN GRADE WOOD	TEMPERED	SLIDING DOOR
14	PAIR 9'-0"	8'-0"	2 1/4"	E	STAIN GRADE WOOD	TEMPERED	SLIDING DOOR
15	PAIR 3'-0"	8'-0"	2 1/4"	A	STAIN GRADE WOOD	TEMPERED	FRENCH DOOR
16	PAIR 3'-0"	8'-0"	2 1/4"	A	STAIN GRADE WOOD	TEMPERED	FRENCH DOOR
17	4'-0"	8'-0"	1 3/4"	B	STAIN GRADE WOOD		SLIDER-BY PASS DOOR
18	4'-0"	8'-0"	1 3/4"	B	STAIN GRADE WOOD		SLIDER-BY PASS DOOR
19	PAIR 2'-0"	8'-0"	1 3/4"	F	STAIN GRADE WOOD	TEMPERED	INTERIOR FRENCH DOOR
20	2'-6"	8'-0"	1 3/4"	D	STAIN GRADE WOOD		
21	2'-0"	8'-0"	1 3/4"	D	STAIN GRADE WOOD		
22	3'-0"	8'-0"	1 3/4"	D	STAIN GRADE WOOD		
23	4'-2"	8'-0"	1 3/4"	B	STAIN GRADE WOOD		SLIDER-BY PASS DOOR
24	2'-6"	8'-0"	1 3/4"	D	STAIN GRADE WOOD		
25	2'-8"	8'-0"	1 3/4"	D	STAIN GRADE WOOD		
26	2'-6"	8'-0"	1 3/4"	D	STAIN GRADE WOOD		
27	4'-2"	8'-0"	1 3/4"	B	STAIN GRADE WOOD		SLIDER-BY PASS DOOR
28	2'-8"	8'-0"	1 3/4"	D	STAIN GRADE WOOD		
29	3'-0"	8'-0"	1 3/8"	D	STAIN GRADE WOOD		1-3/8" 20 MIN SELF-CLOSING SELF-LATCHING SOLID CORE.
30	3'-0"	8'-0"	2 1/4"	D	STAIN GRADE WOOD		
31	16'-0"	8'-0"	2 1/4"	G	STAIN GRADE WOOD		ROLL-UP SECTIONAL GARAGE DOOR. PROVIDE AUTOMATIC OPENER
32	4'-0"	8'-0"	2 1/4"	H	STAIN GRADE WOOD	TEMPERED	MAIN ENTRY DOOR

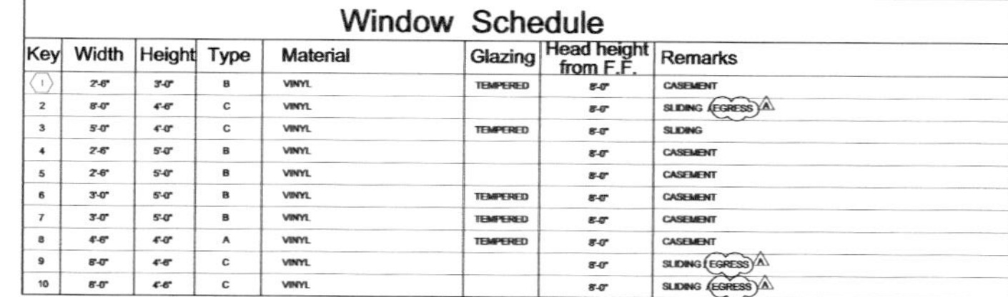

Key	Width	Height	Type	Material	Glazing	Head height from F.F.	Remarks
1	2'-6"	3'-0"	B	VINYL	TEMPERED	8'-0"	CASEMENT
2	8'-0"	4'-6"	C	VINYL		8'-0"	SLIDING (EGRESS)
3	5'-0"	4'-0"	C	VINYL	TEMPERED	8'-0"	SLIDING
4	2'-6"	5'-0"	B	VINYL		8'-0"	CASEMENT
5	2'-6"	5'-0"	B	VINYL		8'-0"	CASEMENT
6	3'-0"	5'-0"	B	VINYL	TEMPERED	8'-0"	CASEMENT
7	3'-0"	5'-0"	B	VINYL	TEMPERED	8'-0"	CASEMENT
8	4'-6"	4'-0"	A	VINYL	TEMPERED	8'-0"	CASEMENT
9	8'-0"	4'-6"	C	VINYL		8'-0"	SLIDING (EGRESS)
10	8'-0"	4'-6"	C	VINYL		8'-0"	SLIDING (EGRESS)

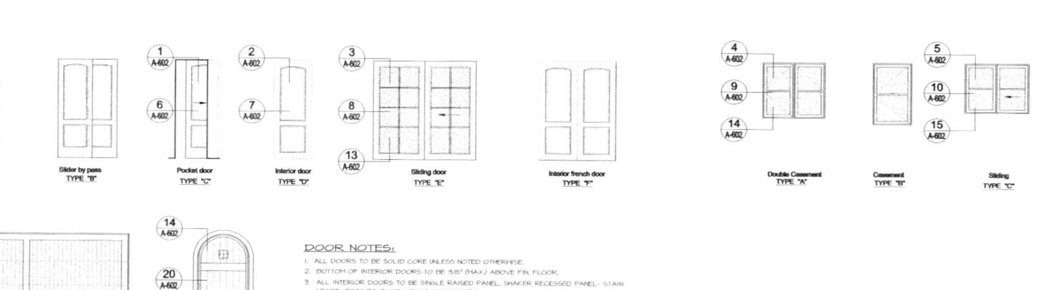

DOOR NOTES:

1. ALL DOORS TO BE SOLID CORE UNLESS NOTED OTHERWISE.
2. BOTTOM OF INTERIOR DOORS TO BE 3/8" (MAX.) ABOVE FIN. FLOOR.
3. ALL INTERIOR DOORS TO BE SINGLE RAISED PANEL. SHAKER RECESSED PANEL - STAIN GRADE UPSTAIRS. PAINT GRADE DOWNSTAIRS.
4. ALL DOORS TO BE LOW "E" ALUMINUM AND TINTED GLASS. CONTRACTOR TO PROVIDE SAMPLE
5. ALL DOORS TO BE ALUMINUM STORE FRONT BY VISTA WALL CLEAR ALUMINUM ANODIZED STERLING LINE (1 800 327 1411)

Double Casement TYPE "A" | Casement TYPE "B" | Sliding TYPE "C"

WINDOW NOTES:

1. ALIGN TOP OF WINDOWS WITH TOP OF DOORS SO THAT TOP EDGES OF DOORS AND WINDOWS ALIGN IN A LEVEL PLANE ABOVE FINISH FLOOR.
2. ALL ESCAPE OR RESCUE WINDOWS SHALL HAVE A MINIMUM NET CLEAR OPENABLE AREA OF 5.7 SQ. FT. THE MINIMUM NET CLEAR OPENABLE HEIGHT DIMENSION SHALL BE 24". THE MINIMUM NET CLEAR OPENABLE WIDTH DIMENSION SHALL BE 20" WHEN WINDOWS ARE PROVIDED AS A MEANS OF ESCAPE OR RESCUE. THEY SHALL HAVE A FINISHED SILL HEIGHT NOT MORE THAN 44" ABOVE FIN. FLR.
3. SKYLIGHTS SHALL HAVE A NON-COMBUSTIBLE FRAME GLAZED WITH DUAL GLAZING OF HEAT STRENGTHENED OR FULLY TEMPERED GLASS OR SHALL BE A 3/4-HOUR FIRE-RESISTIVE ASSEMBLY SKYLIGHTS UV PROTECTION
4. WINDOWS WITH SILLS LESS THAN 5'-0" ABOVE TUB OR SHOWER FLOOR SHALL BE TEMPERED
5. ALL WINDOW GLAZING TO BE GLAZED, LOW "E" AND TINTED GLASS. CONTRACTOR TO PROVIDE TINTED GLASS SAMPLES TO ARCHITECT FOR SELECTION.
6. ALL WINDOWS TO BE ALUMINUM STORE FRONT BY VISTA WALL CLEAR ALUMINUM ANODIZED STERLING LINE (1 800 327 1411)
7. COMPLY WITH SECT. 2406 FOR REQUIRED SAFETY GLAZING

OBELISK ARCHITECTS
A Professional Corporation

3800 PACIFIC COAST HIGHWAY
TORRANCE, CALIFORNIA 90505
obeliskarchitects.com
310.373.0810 fax
310.373.3568 tel

PROJECT
Kaiser Residence

412 Via Linda Vista
Torrance
CA, 90277

REVISIONS
08/07/14 Building & Safety Corrections

PROJECT NUMBER
1210 K2 VIA TOR
DATE
August 07, 2014

SHEET TITLE
Door & Window Schedule

SHEET
A-401

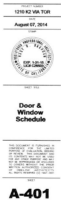

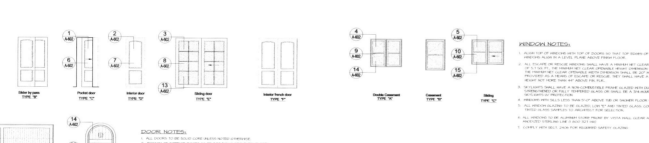

Figure 14.21 Schedules.

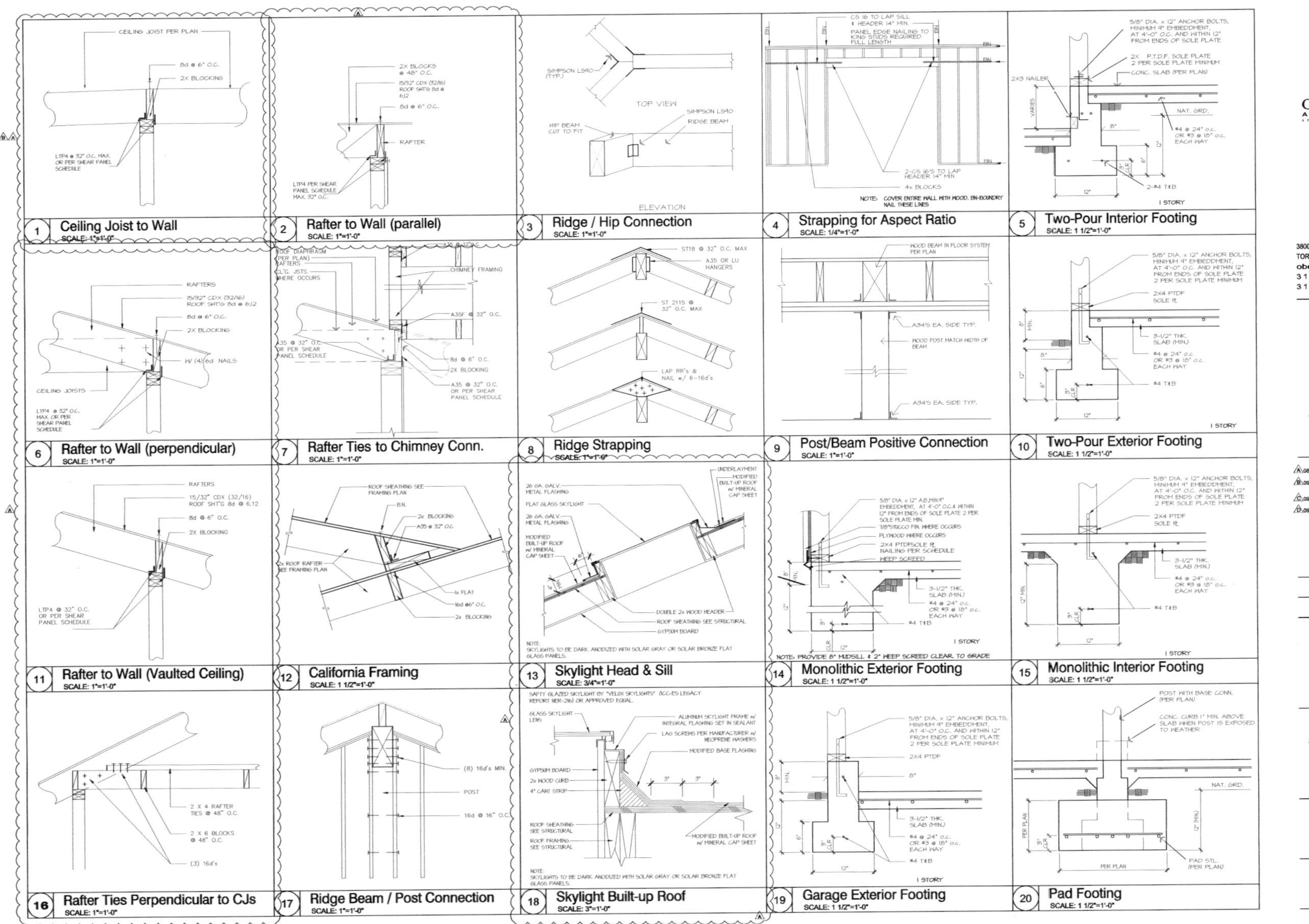

Figure 14.22 Architectural details.

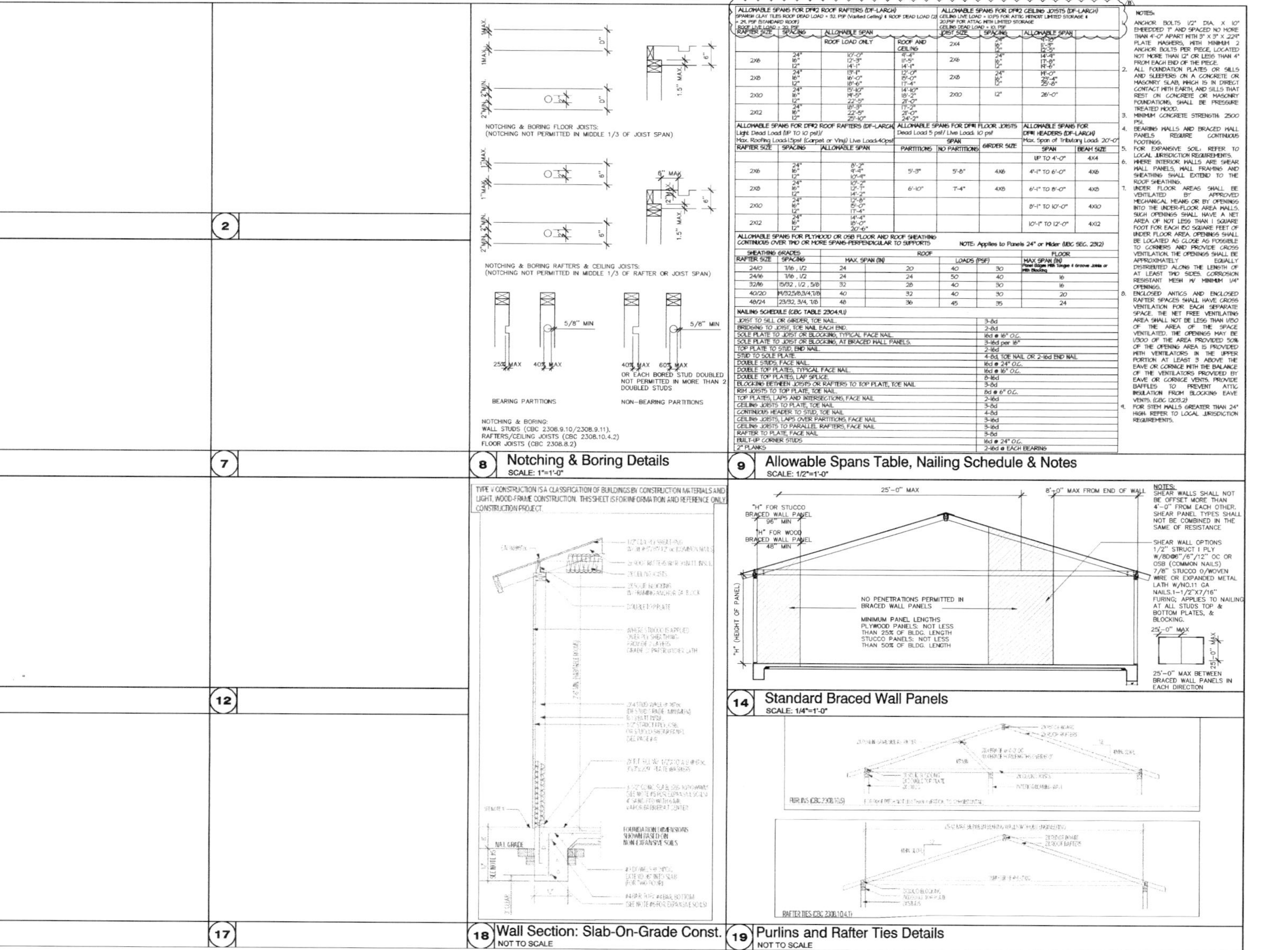

Figure 14.23 Structural details.

chapter

15

CONSTRUCTION DOCUMENTS FOR A TWO-STORY, WOOD-FRAMED RESIDENCE WITH BIM

The Professional Practice of Architectural Working Drawings, Sixth Edition. Nagy R. Bakhoum and Osamu A. Wakita.
© 2024 John Wiley & Sons Inc. Published 2024 by John Wiley & Sons Inc.
Companion website: www.wiley.com\go\bakhoum\theprofessionalpracticeofarchitecturalworkingdrawings

PROGRAM AND SITE ANALYSIS

The clients, a young husband and wife with children, wanted to develop the site to its maximum potential. The site allowed a two-story residence with a maximum floor area of 2,900 square feet measured from the outside wall dimensions. Given these two factors, they wanted the following rooms: living room, dining room, kitchen, nook, study or family room, guest bath, mud room and laundry, and three bedrooms with two full bathrooms and a gym. They also wanted a two-car garage. These requirements are termed the program.

Our initial schematic studies worked through the relationships among the rooms as well as room orientation on the site. Room orientation required that we locate the major rooms, such as the family room, kitchen, and main bedroom, so that they would face the ocean and capture a city view. The garage and entry had to be adjacent to the road for accessibility. The site is small, and because the setback regulations further reduced the buildable area, we determined we needed to design a two-story building to meet the clients' requested number of rooms.

Figure 15.1 shows a schematic study of the first-floor level. This figure also illustrates some early decisions we made: locating the entry court on the south side of the building; providing access to the city view from the kitchen, nook, and family room; locating the dining room and living room in an area that would allow access from the outside; and providing a basement area for the mechanical system, the wine storage area, and the gym.

CD, DD, AND CD DEVELOPMENT

We developed a schematic study for the second-floor level to show the desired location and relationships among the rooms, as well as a possible deck location. We attempted to provide lots of natural light for all secondary bedrooms. See Figures 15.2–15.46.

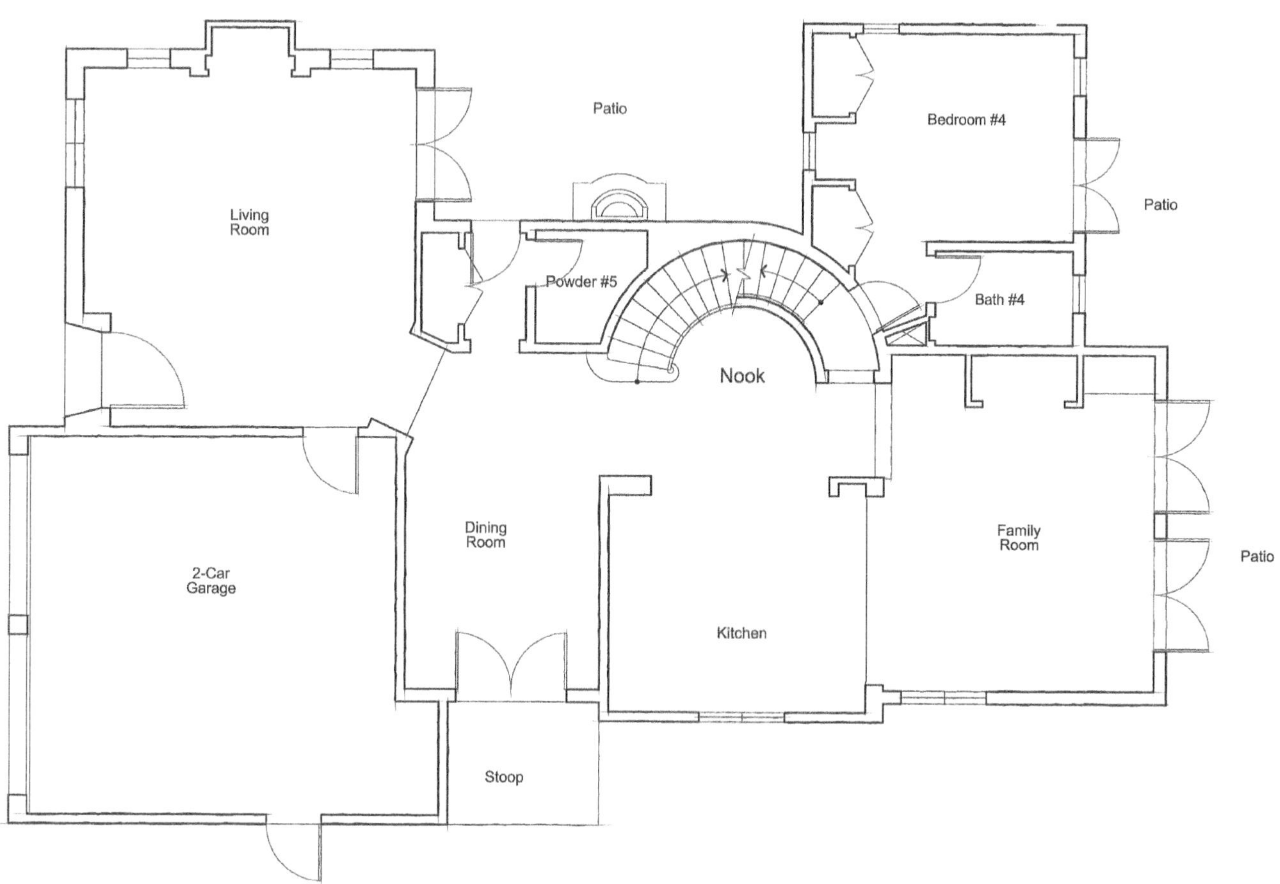

Figure 15.1 Schematic study—first floor of the Blu residence.

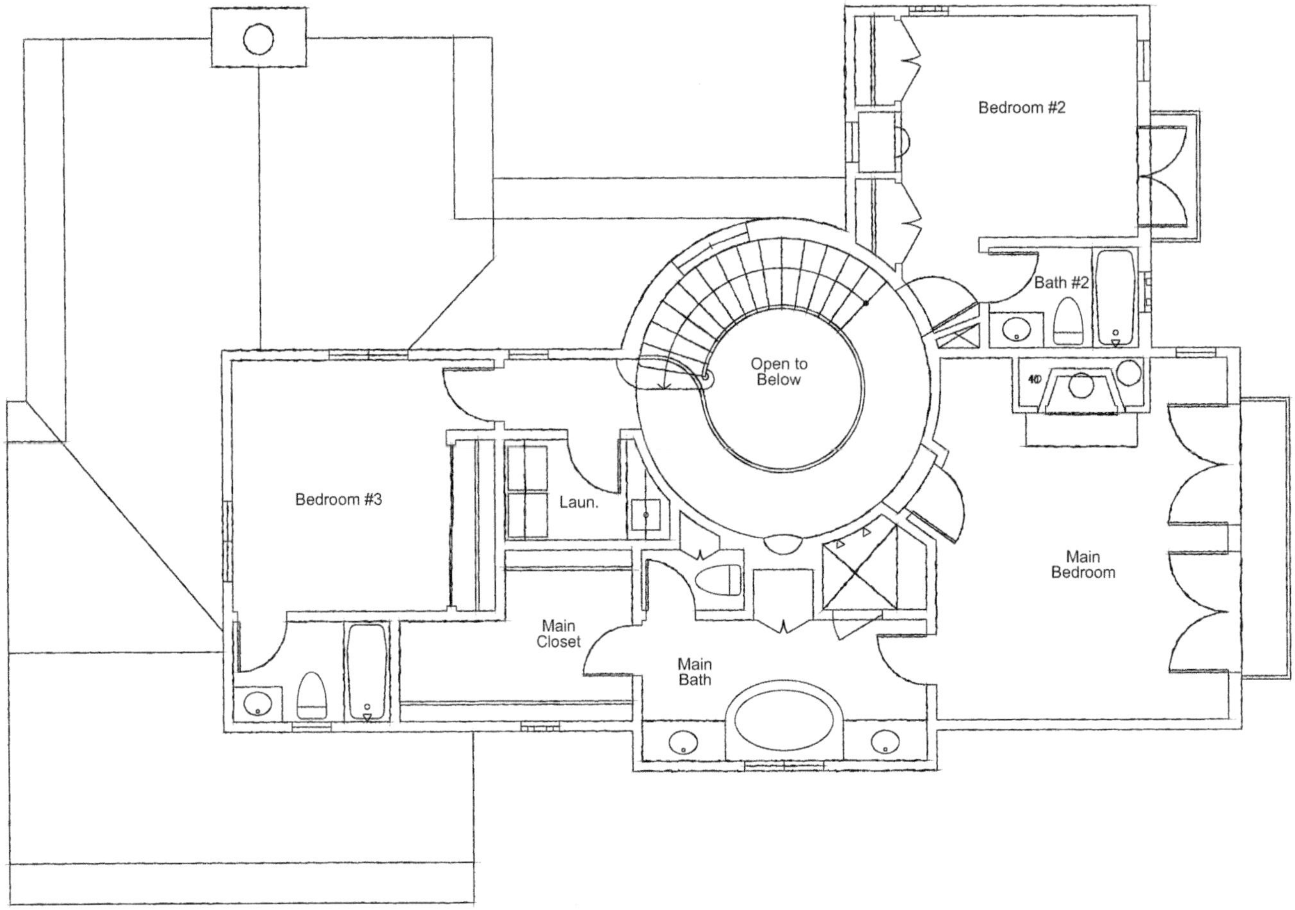

Bedroom #2
Bath #2
Open to Below
Bedroom #3
Laun.
Main Bedroom
Main Closet
Main Bath

Figure 15.2 Schematic study—second floor of the Blu residence.

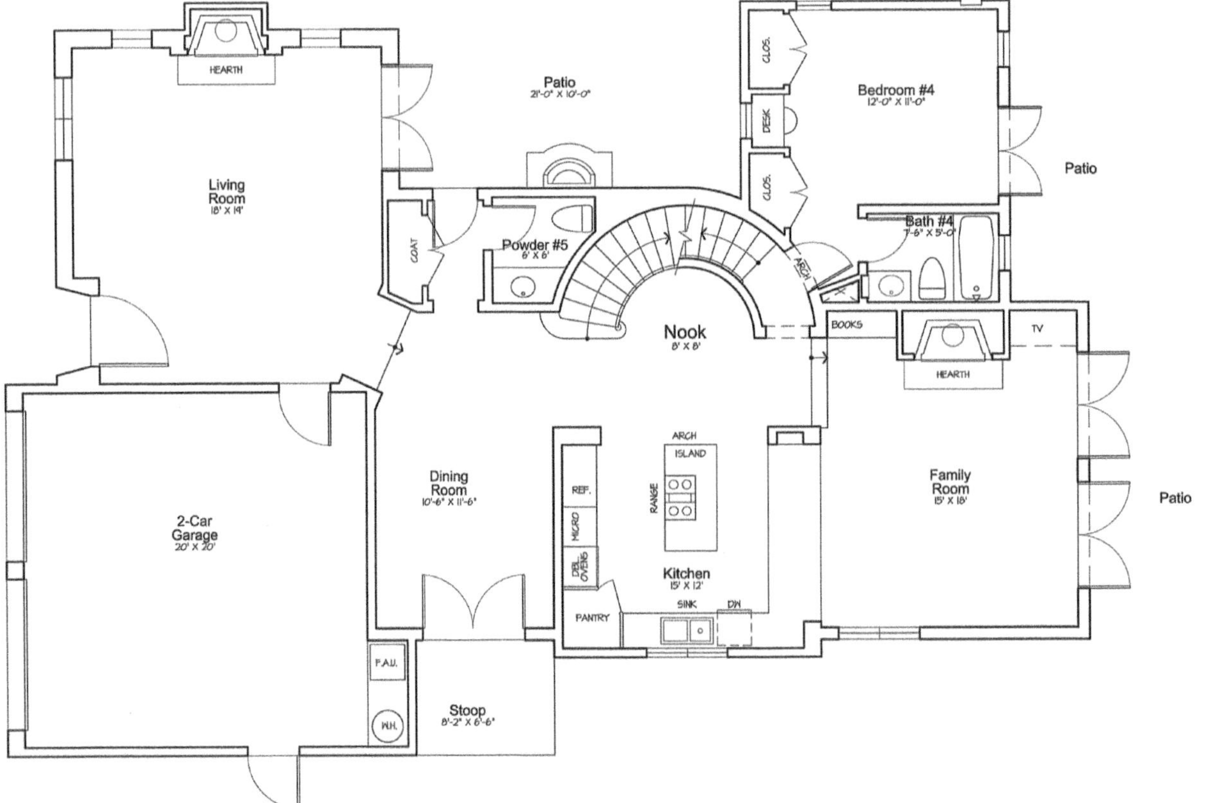

Figure 15.3 First-floor preliminary plan.

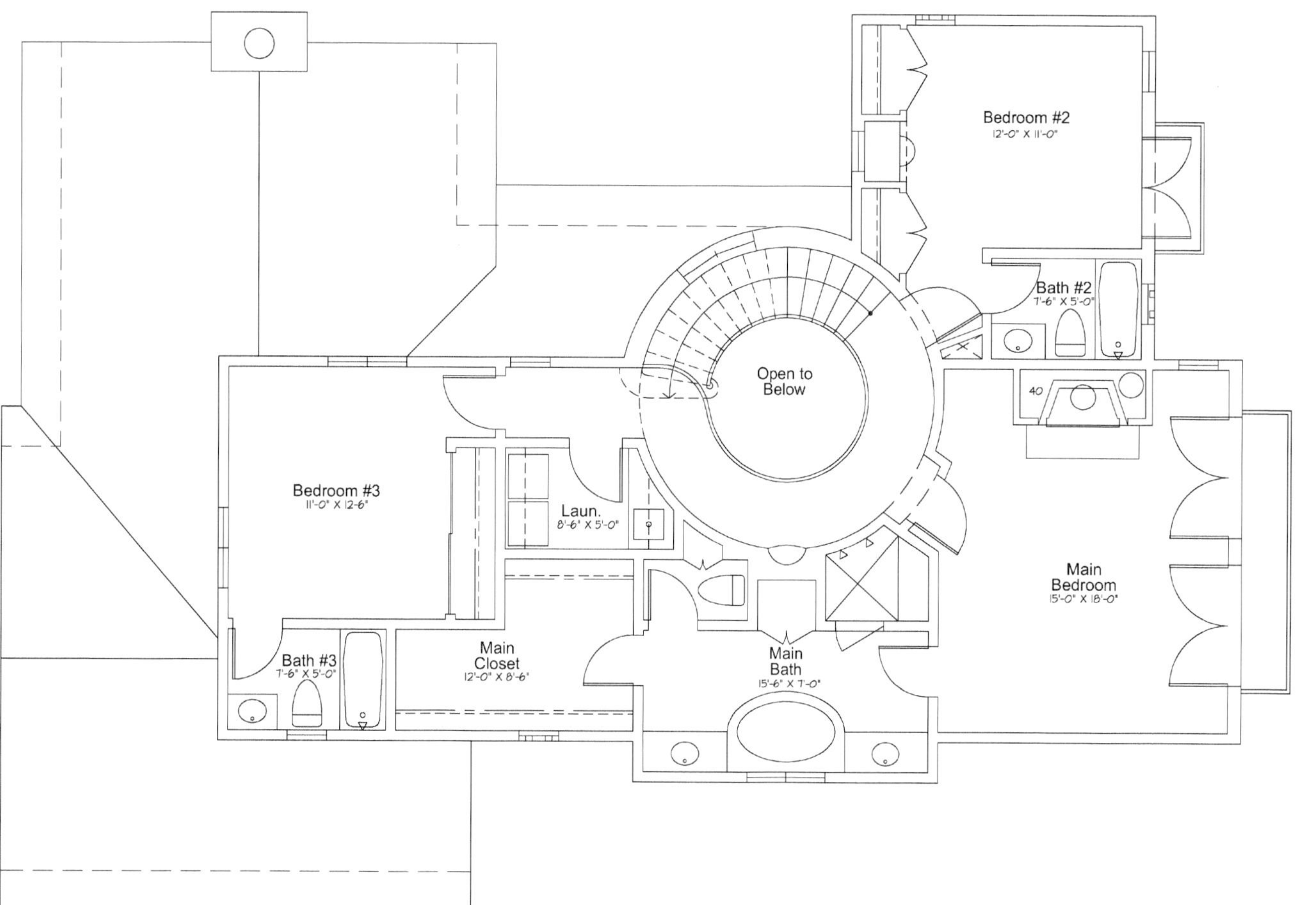

Figure 15.4 Second-floor preliminary plan.

Figure 15.5 Conceptual designs of the exterior elevations.

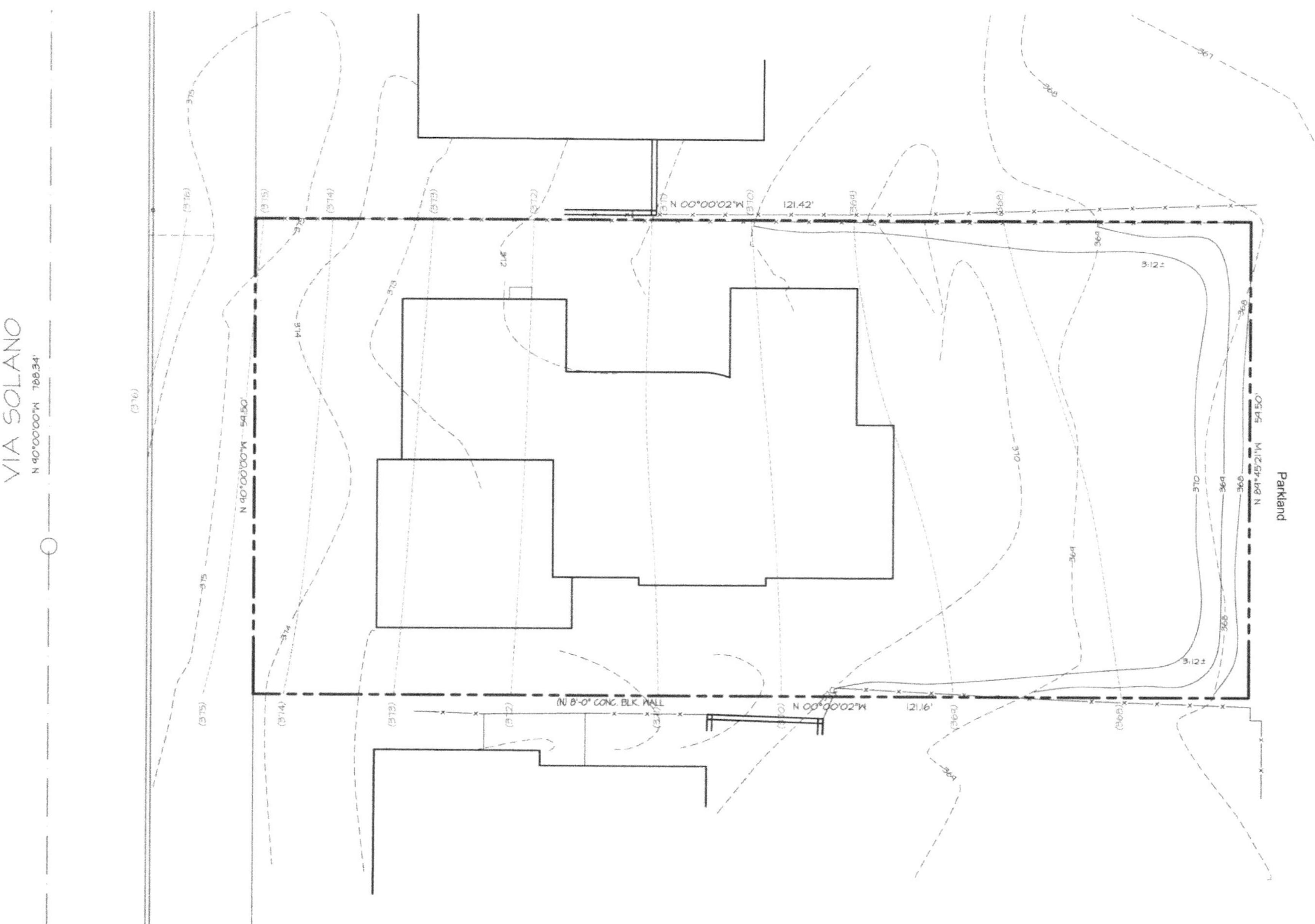

Figure 15.6 Stage II: Site plan.

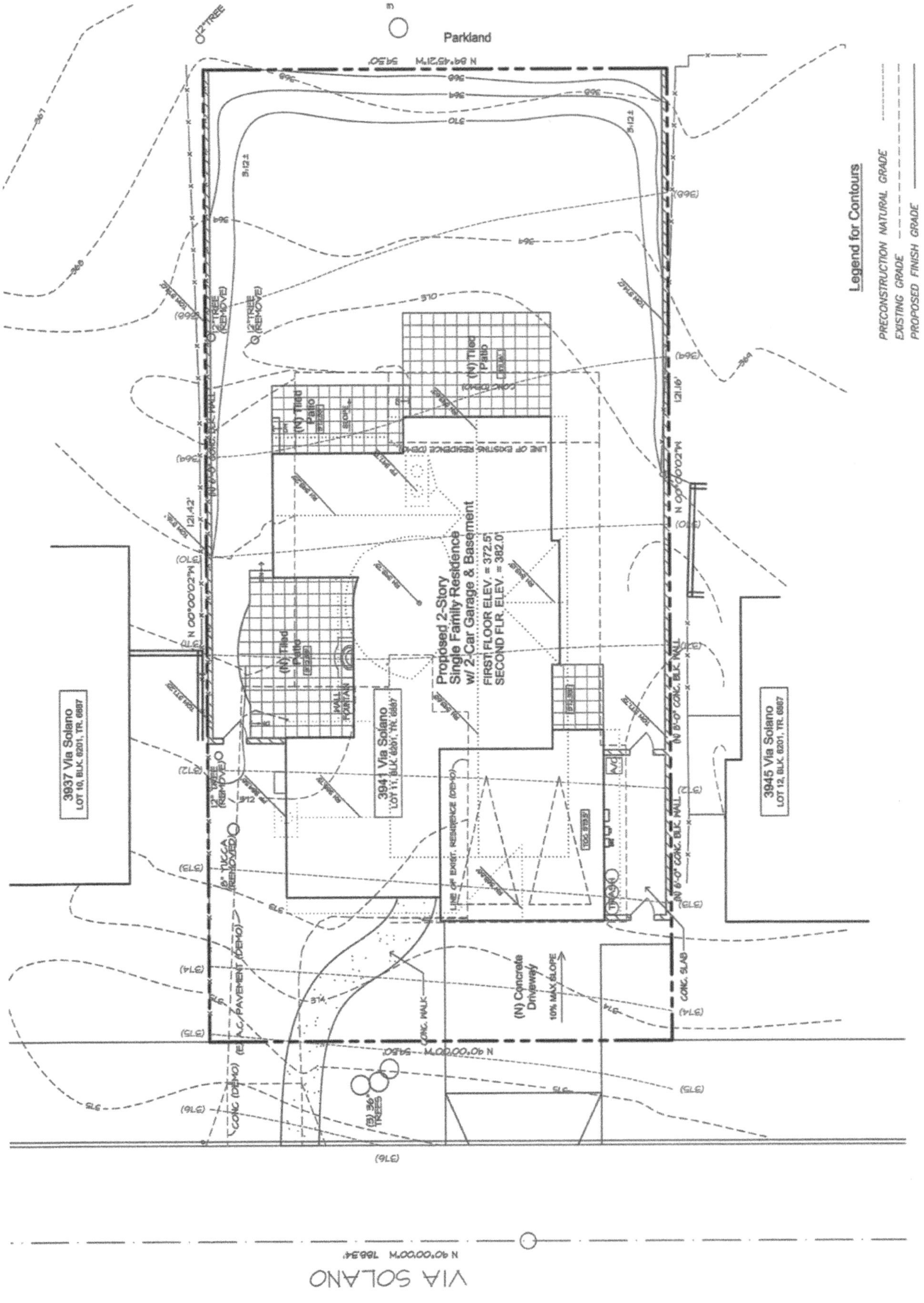

VIA SOLANO
N 90°00'00"W 188.34'
3937 Via Solano
LOT 10, BLK. 6201, TR. 6887
3941 Via Solano
LOT 11, BLK. 6201, TR. 6887
3945 Via Solano
LOT 12, BLK. 6201, TR. 6887
Proposed 2-Story
Single Family Residence
w/ 2-Car Garage & Basement
FIRST FLOOR ELEV. = 372.5'
SECOND FLR. ELEV. = 382.0'
(N) Tiled Patio
(N) Tiled Patio
(N) Tiled Patio
WALL FOUNTAIN
(N) Concrete Driveway
10% MAX SLOPE
CONC. WALK
CONC. SLAB
TRASH
A/C
LINE OF EXIST. RESIDENCE (DEMO)
LINE OF EXISTING RESIDENCE (DEMO)
(E) A.C. PAVEMENT (DEMO)
CONC (DEMO)
(3) 36" TREES
8" YUCCA (REMOVED)
12" TREE (REMOVE)
12" TREE (REMOVE)
12" TREE (REMOVE)
12" TREE
(N) 6'-0" CONC. BLK. WALL
(N) 6'-0" CONC. BLK. WALL
(N) 6'-0" CONC. BLK. WALL
N 00°00'02"W 121.42'
N 00°00'02"W 121.16'
N 90°00'00"W 54.50'
N 89°45'21"W 54.50'
Parkland

Legend for Contours

PRECONSTRUCTION NATURAL GRADE
EXISTING GRADE
PROPOSED FINISH GRADE

Figure 15.7 Stage III: Site plan.

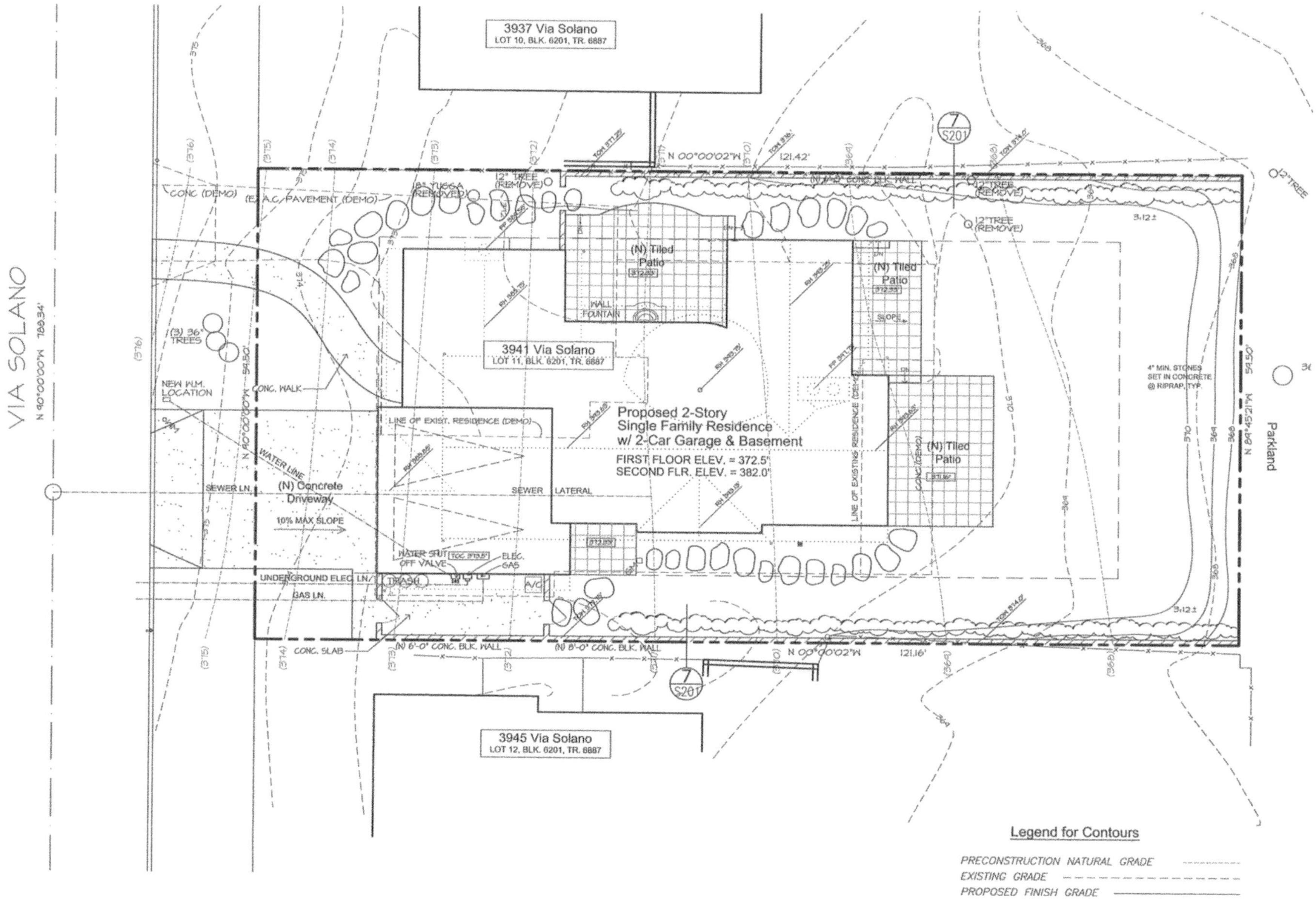

Figure 15.8 Stage IV: Site plan.

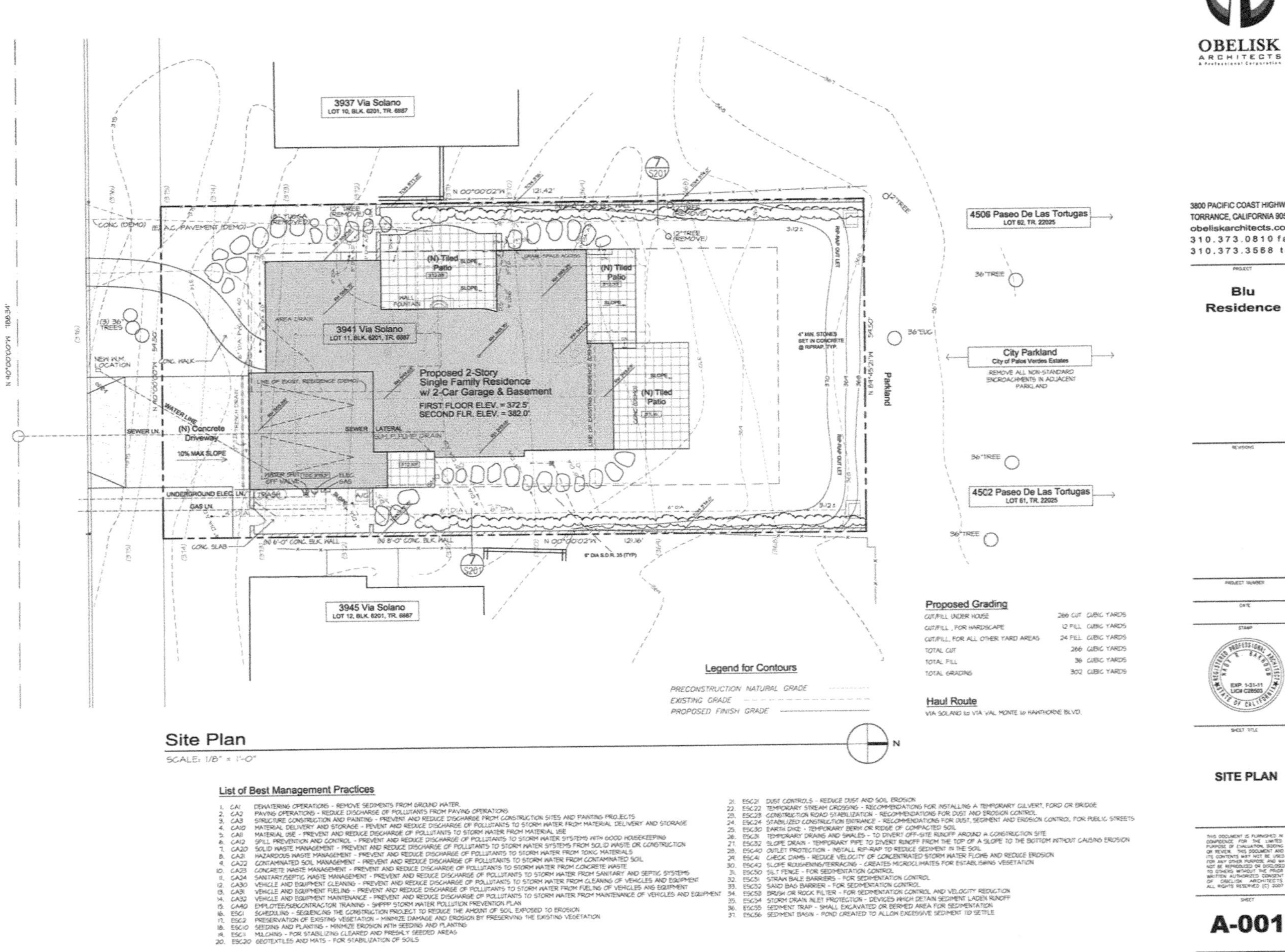

Figure 15.9 Stage V: Site plan.

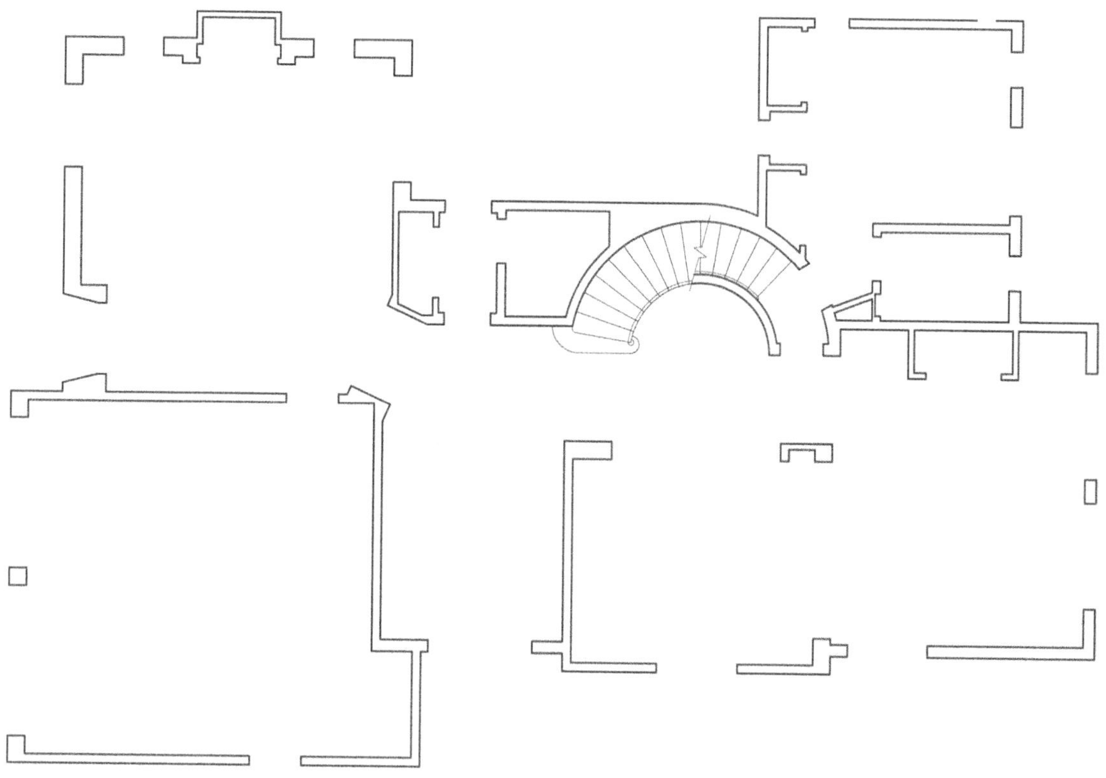

Figure 15.10 Stage II: First-floor plan.

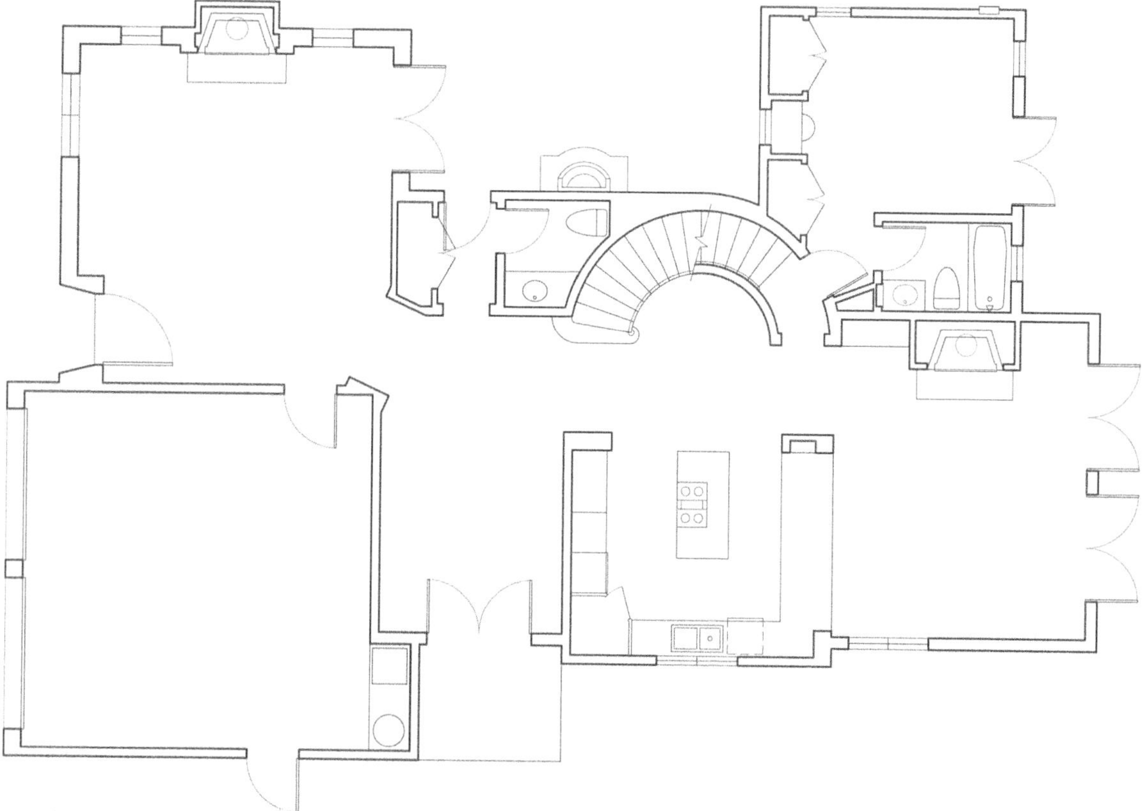

Figure 15.11 Stage III: First-floor plan.

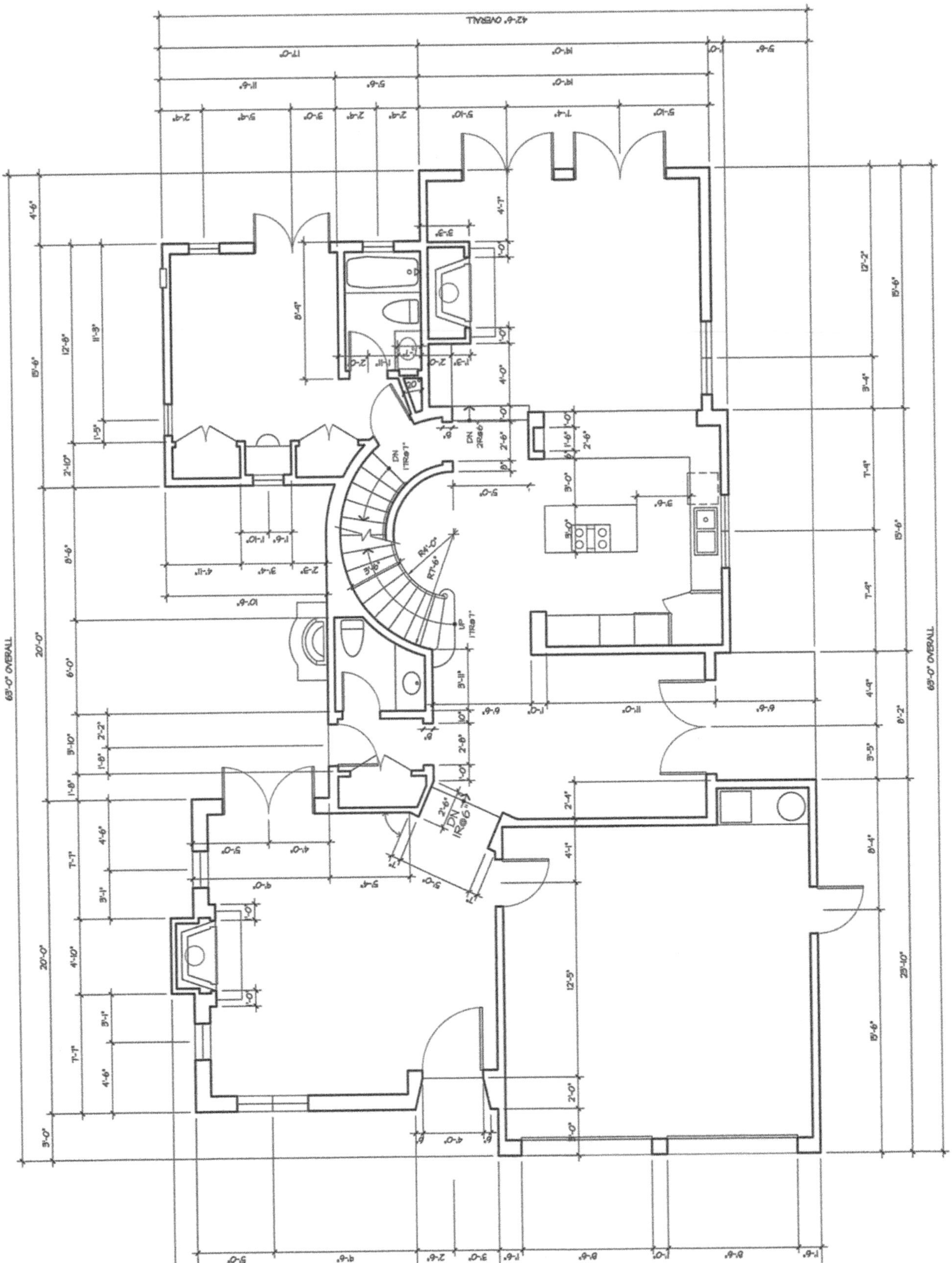

Figure 15.12 Stage IV: First-floor plan.

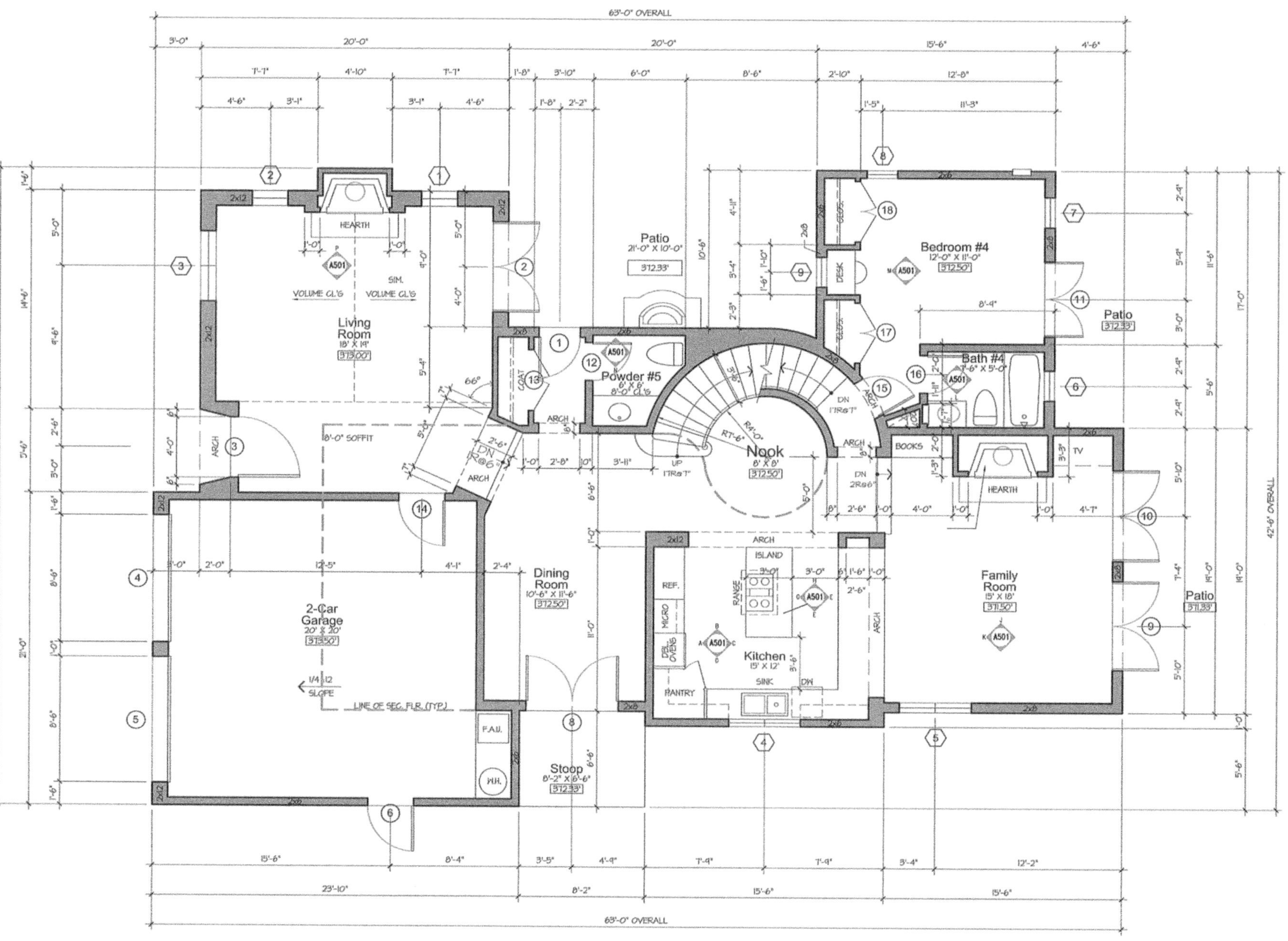

Figure 15.13 Stage V: First-floor plan.

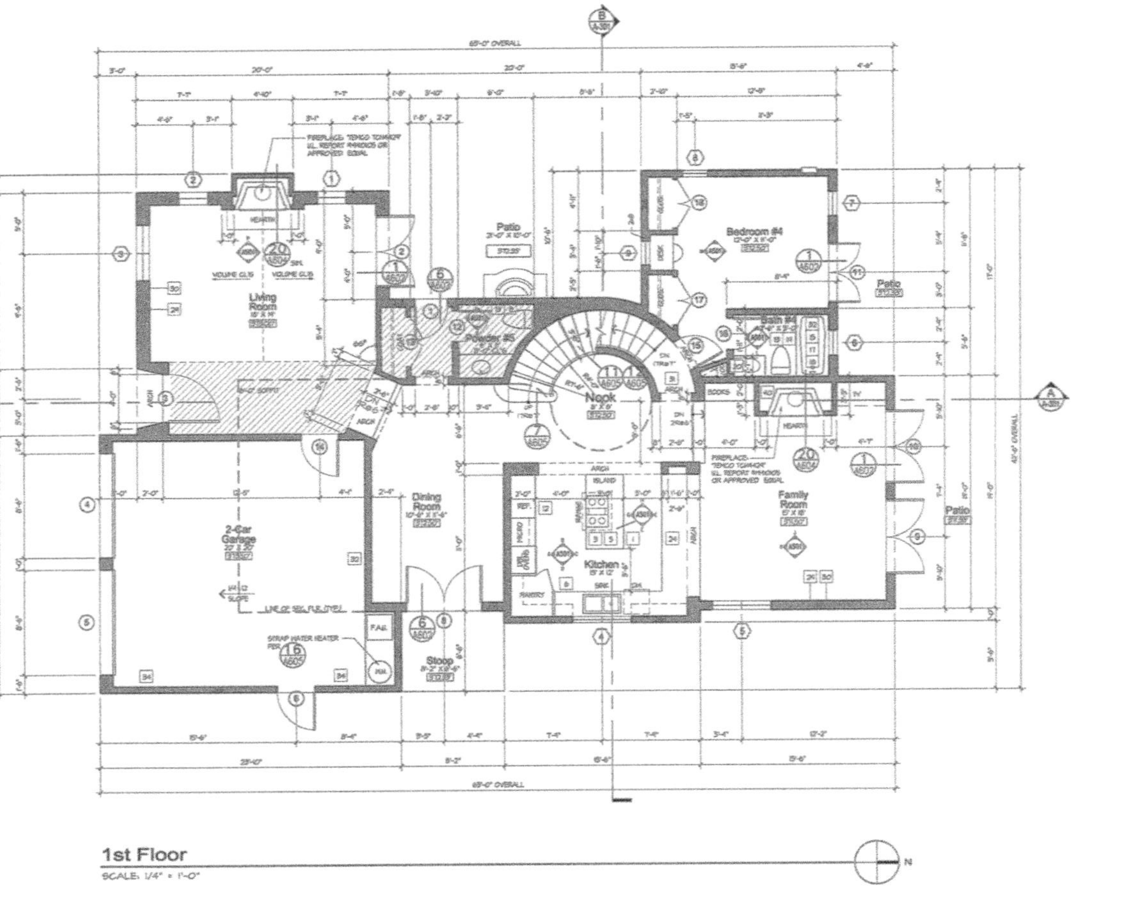

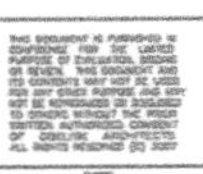
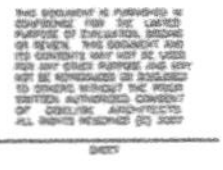
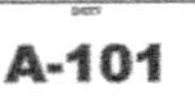

Figure 15.14 Stage VI: First-floor plan.

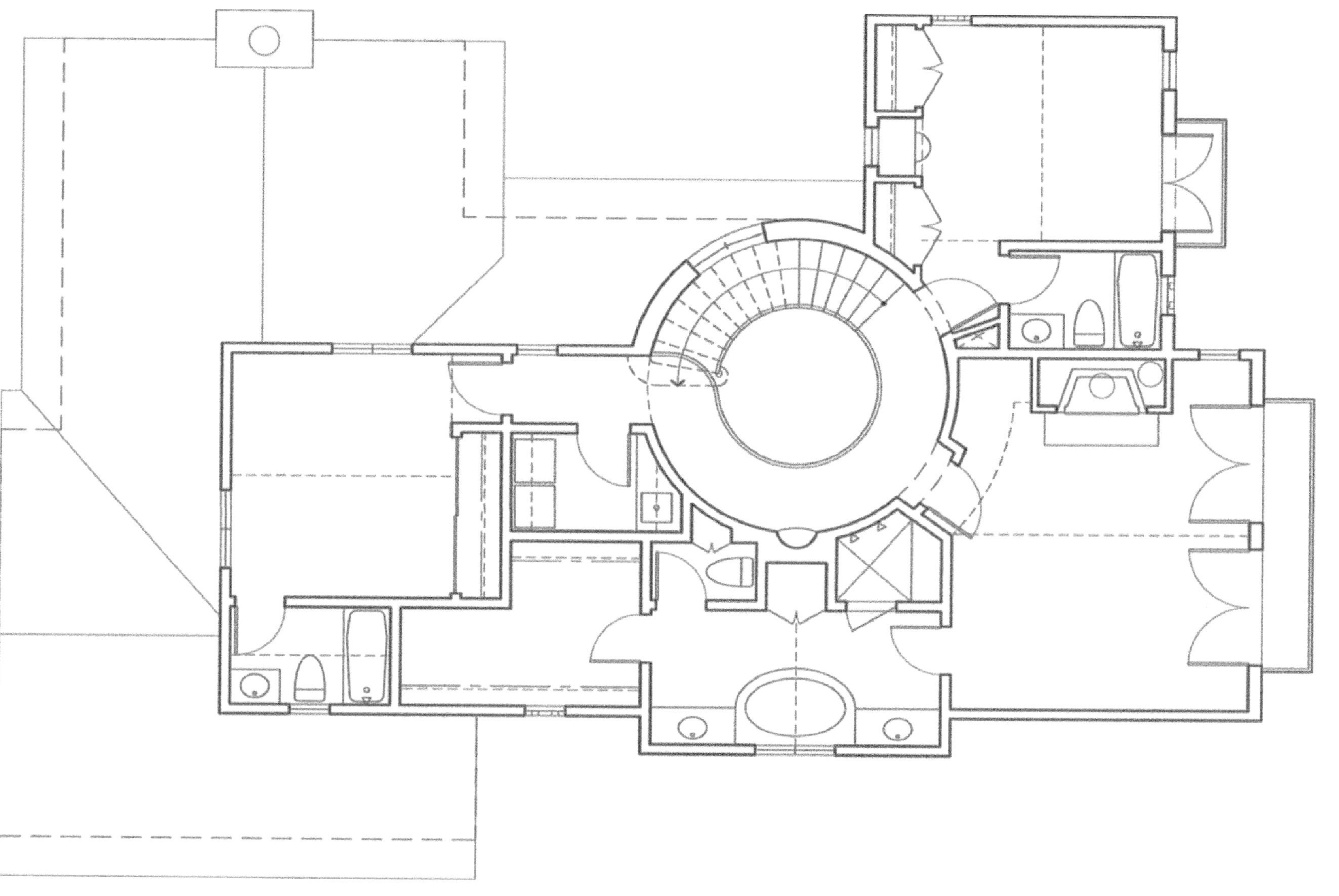

Figure 15.15 Stage II: Second-floor plan.

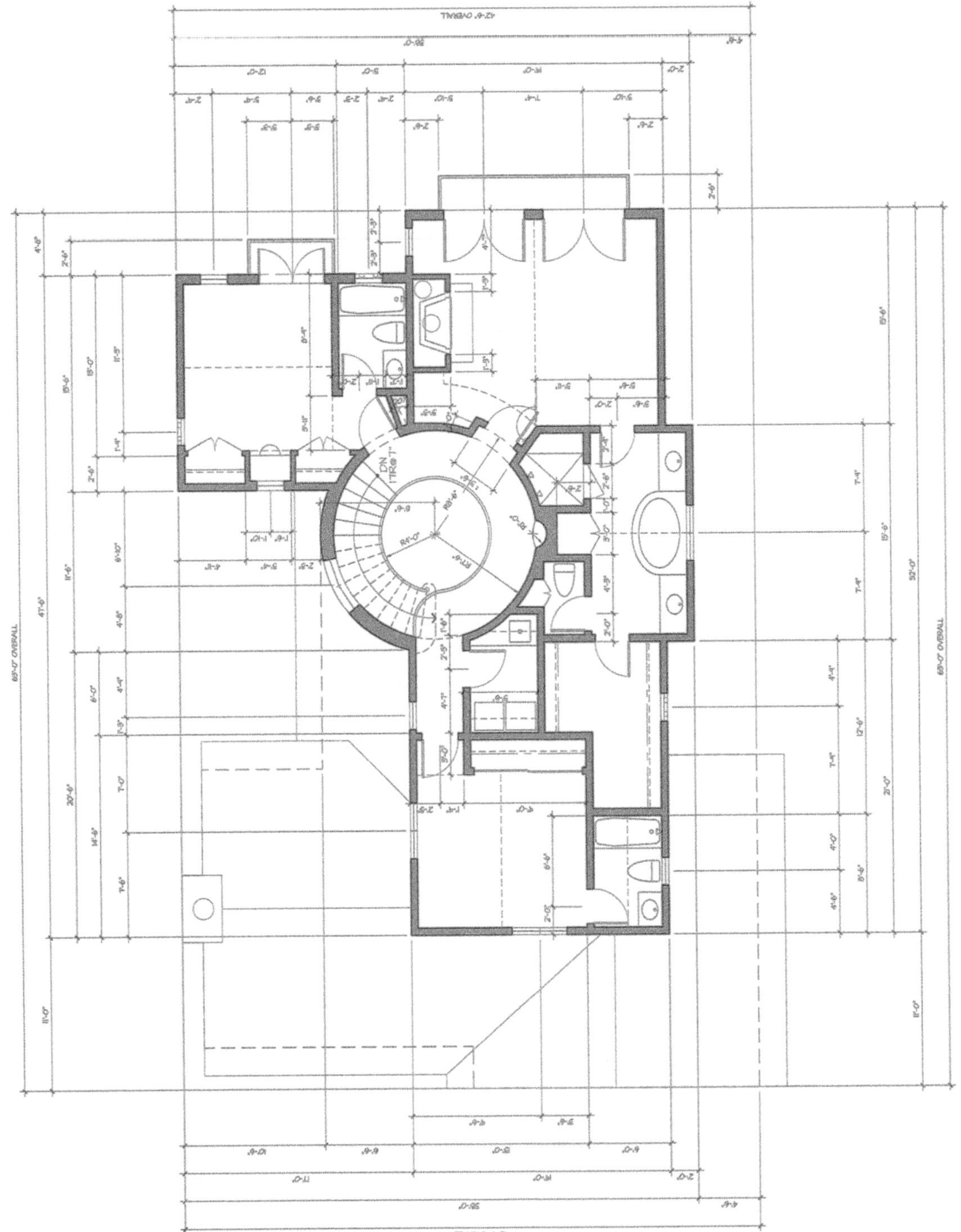

Figure 15.16 Stage IV: Second-floor plan.

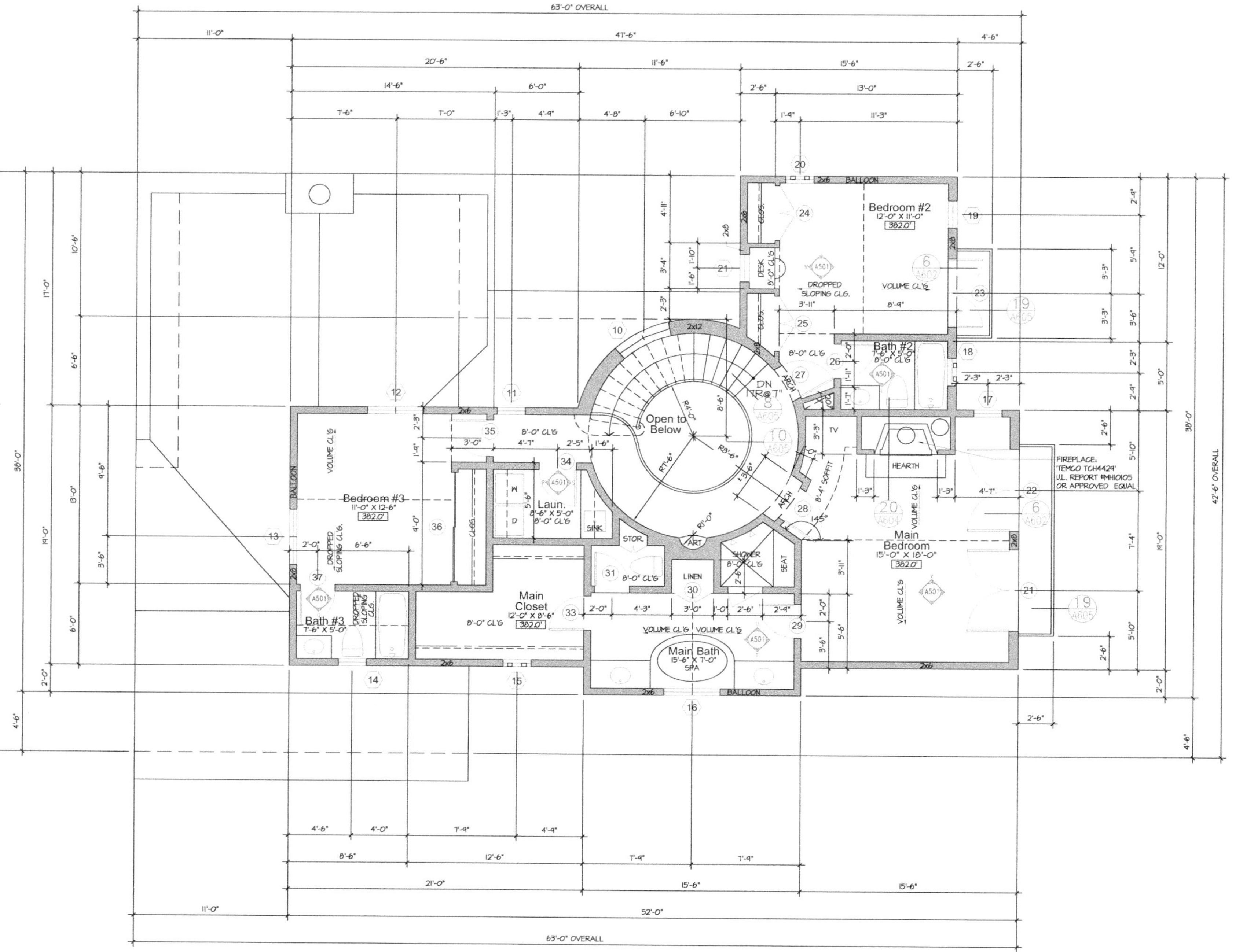

Figure 15.17 Stage V: Second-floor plan.

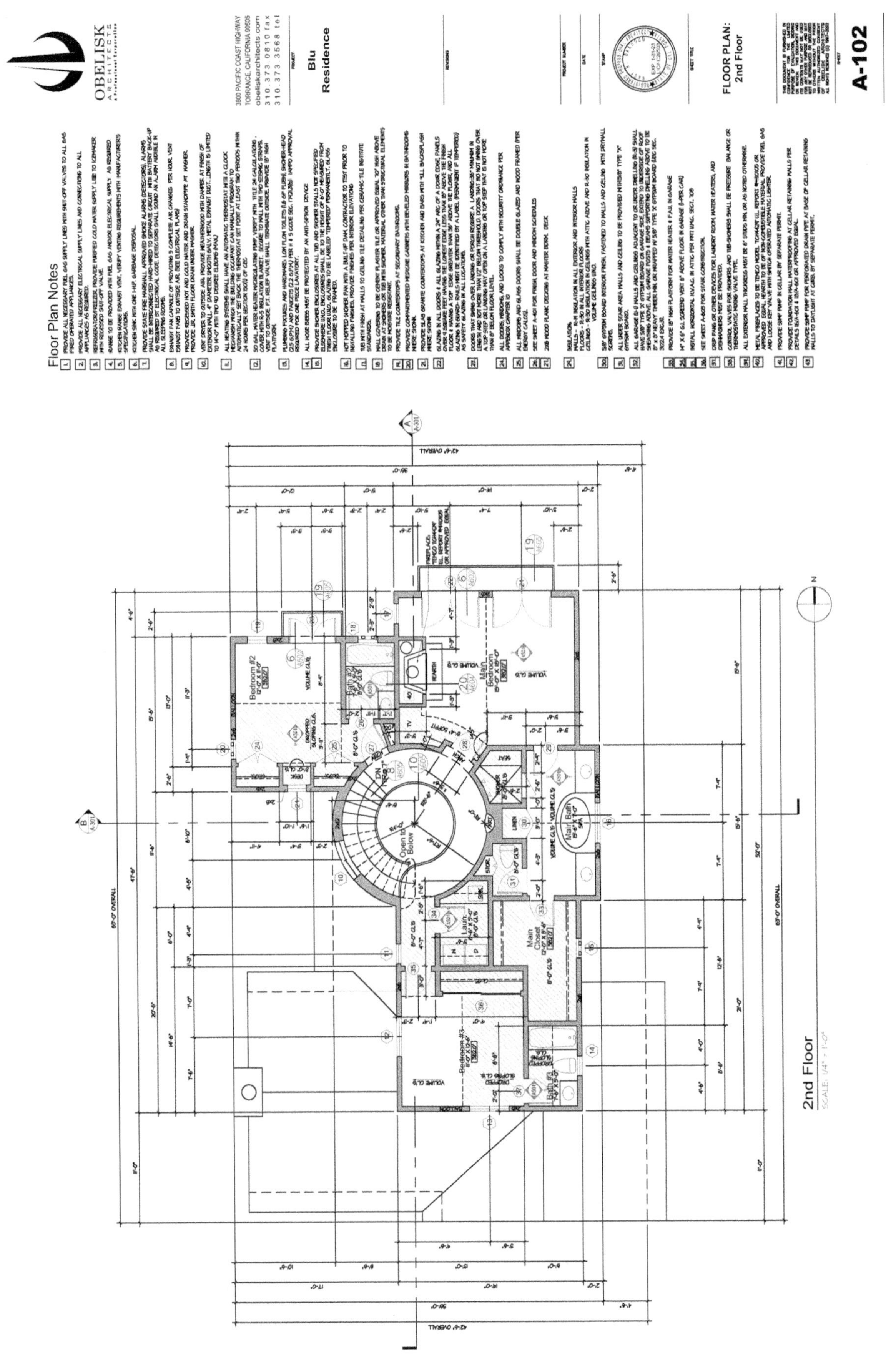

Figure 15.18 Stage VI: Second-floor plan.

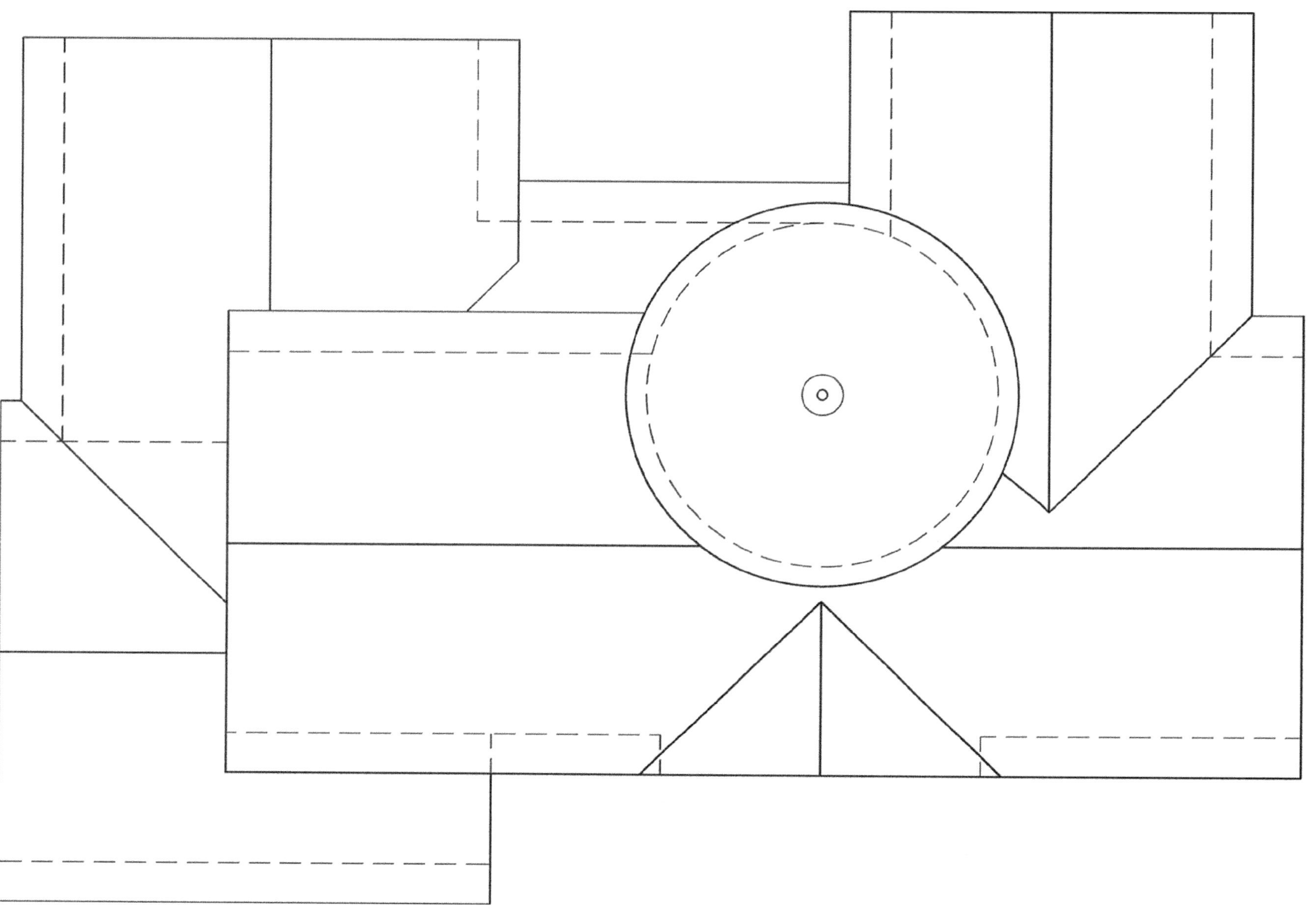

Figure 15.19 Stage I: Roof plan.

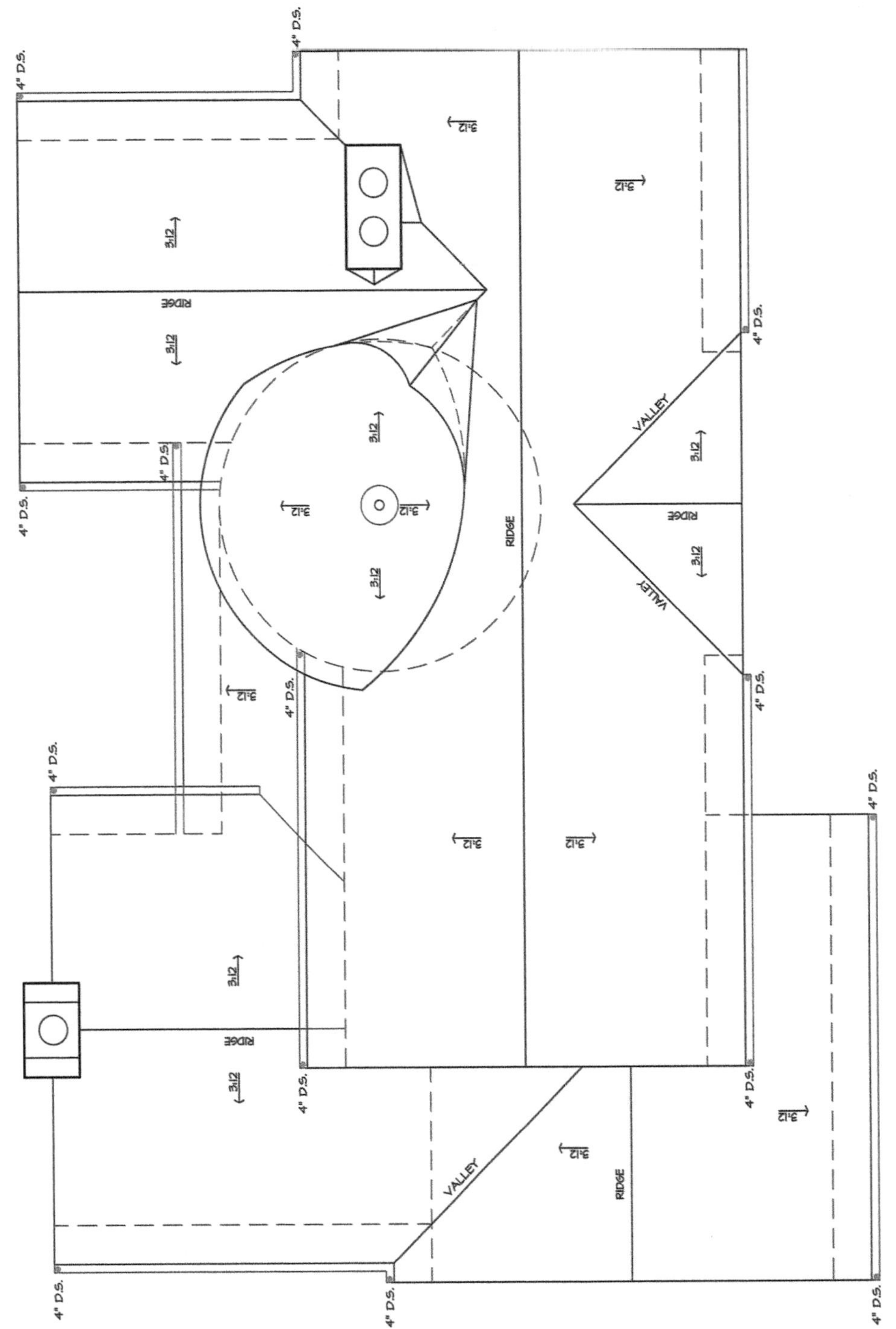

Figure 15.20 Stage II: Roof plan.

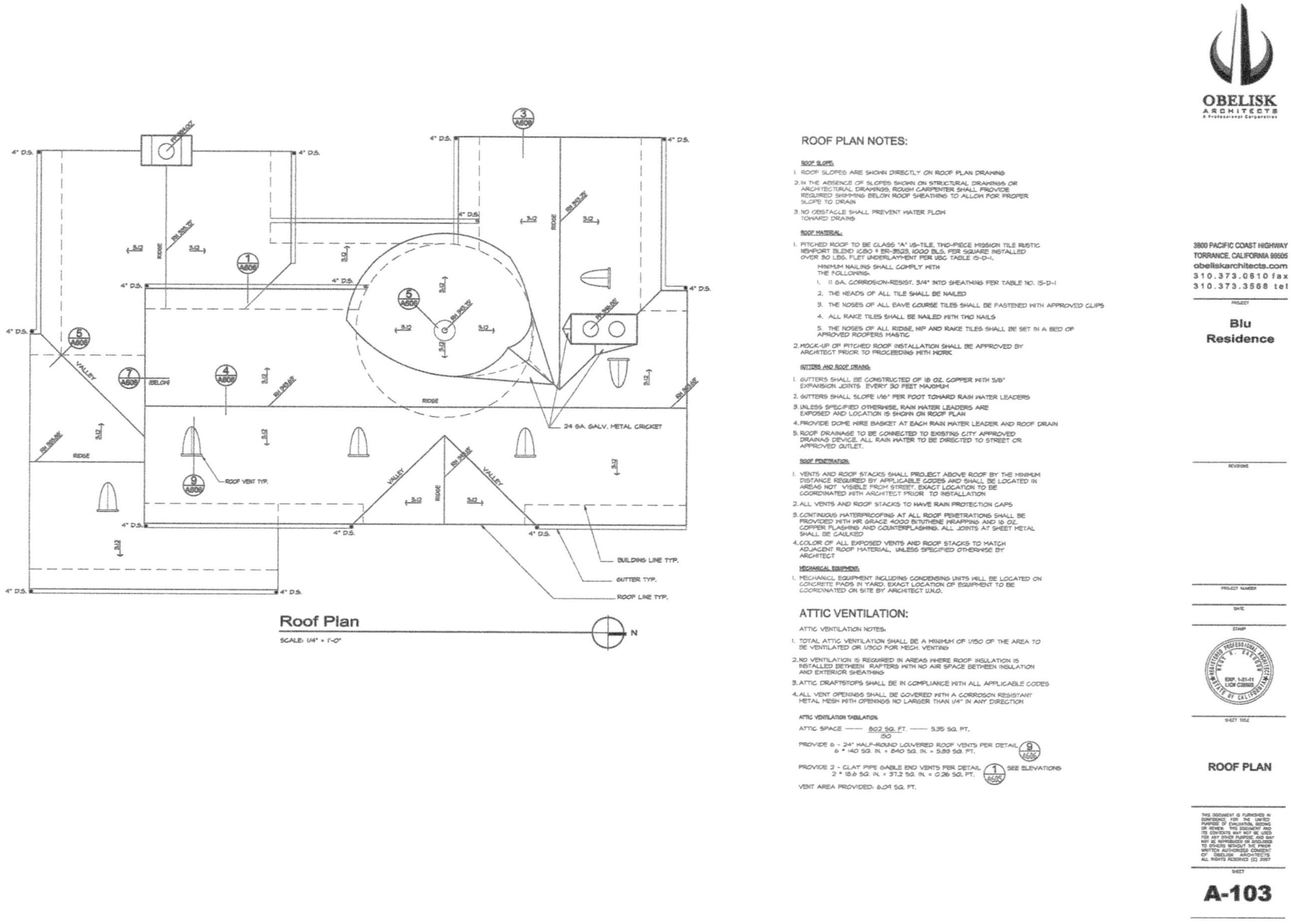

Figure 15.21 Stage III: Roof plan.

Figure 15.22 Stage I: Building section.

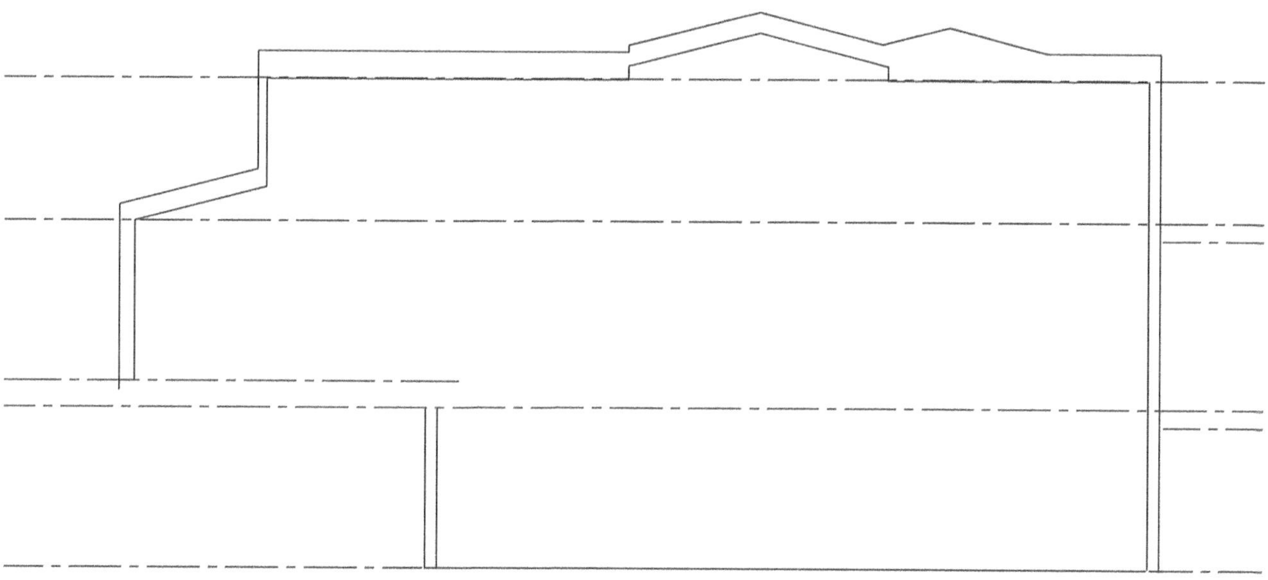

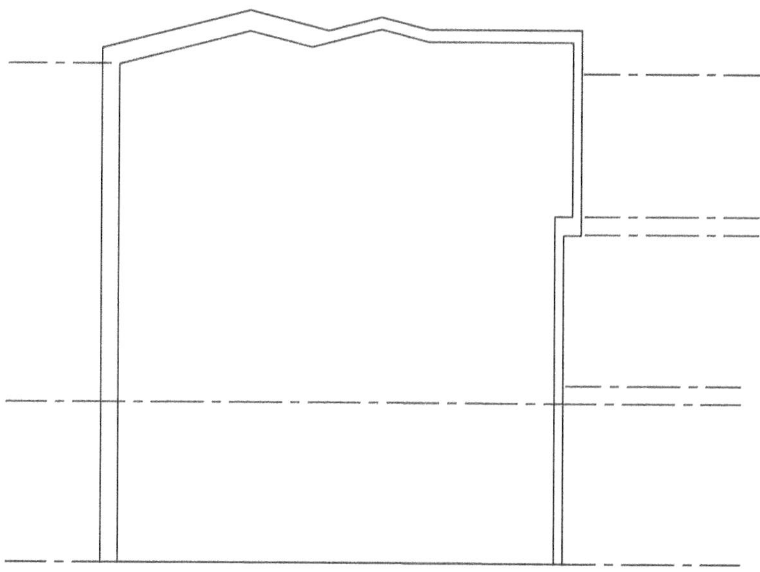

Figure 15.23 Stage II: Building section.

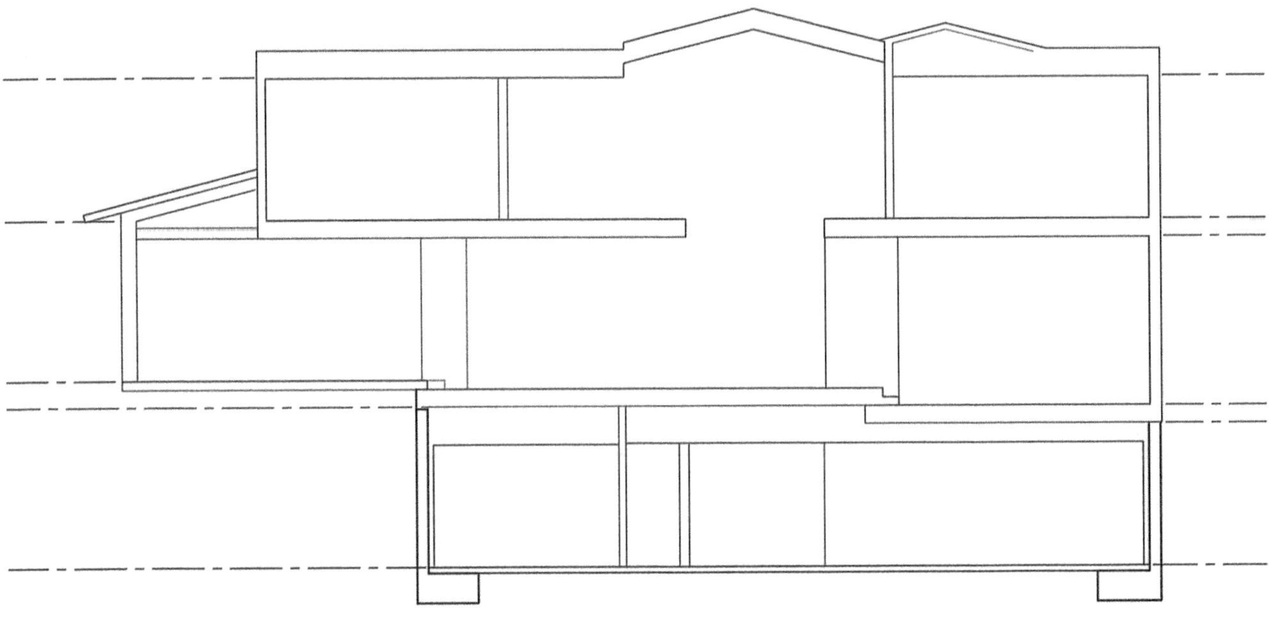

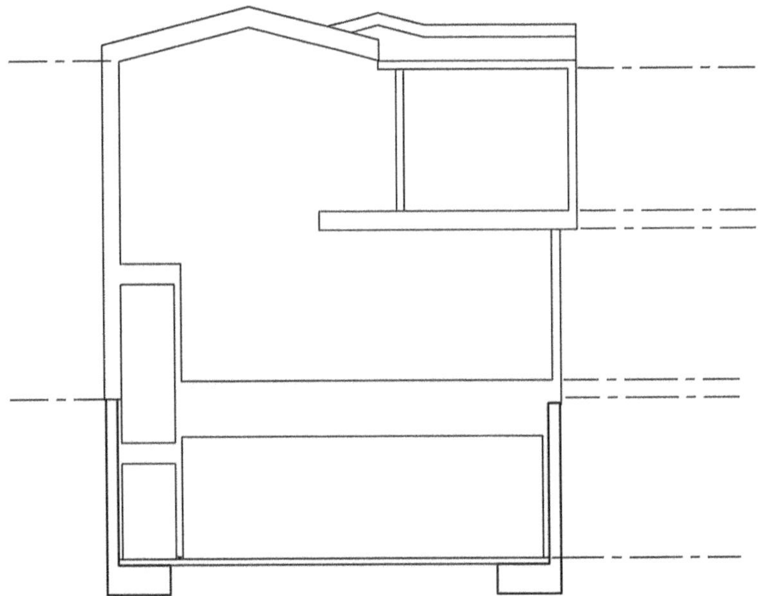

Figure 15.24 Stage III: Building section.

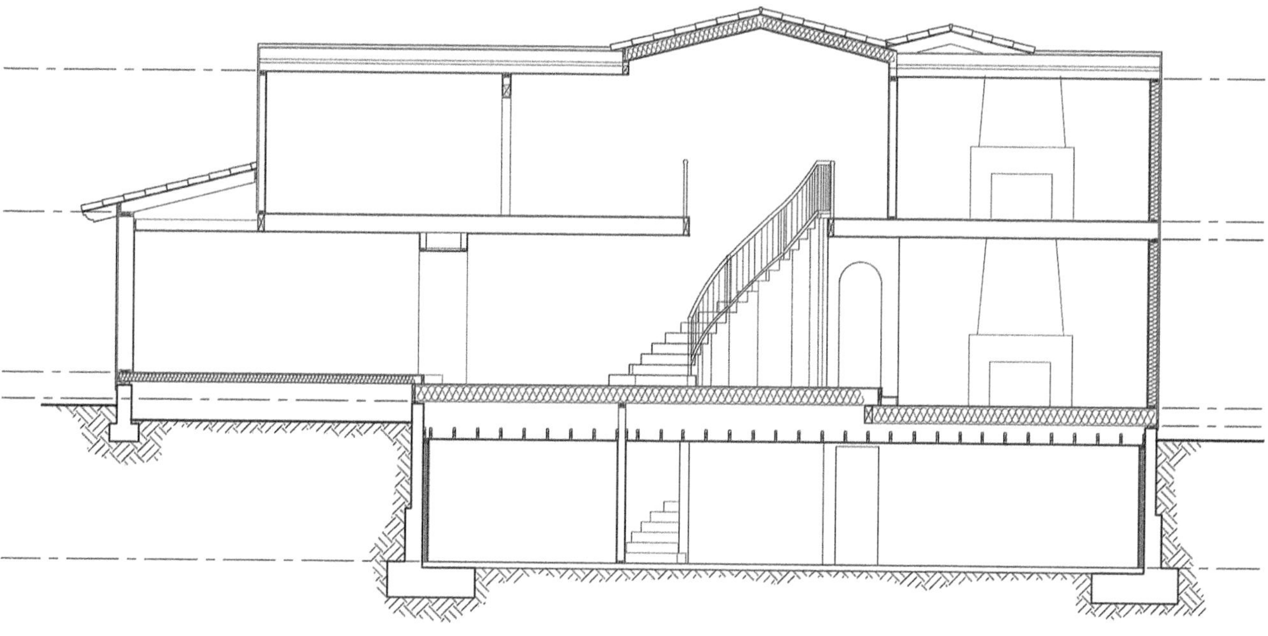

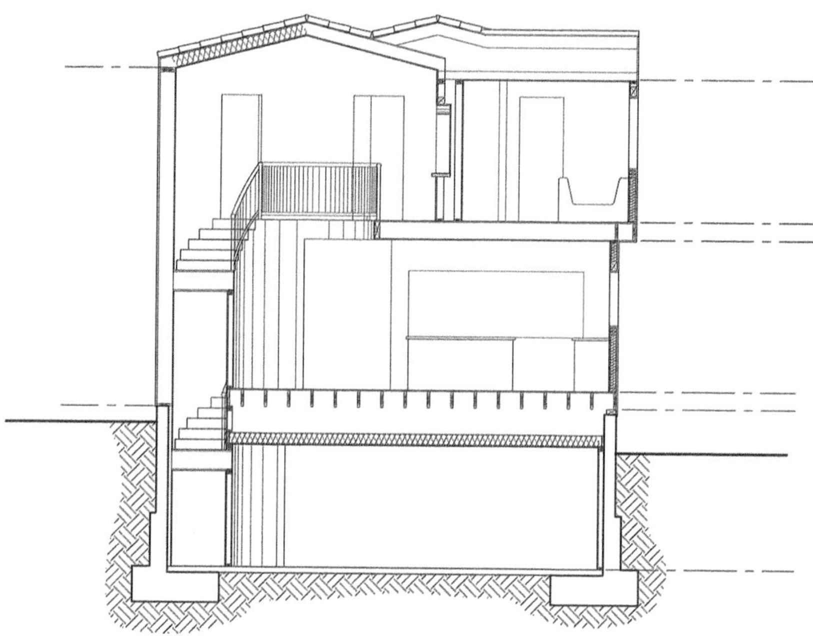

Figure 15.25 Stage IV: Building section.

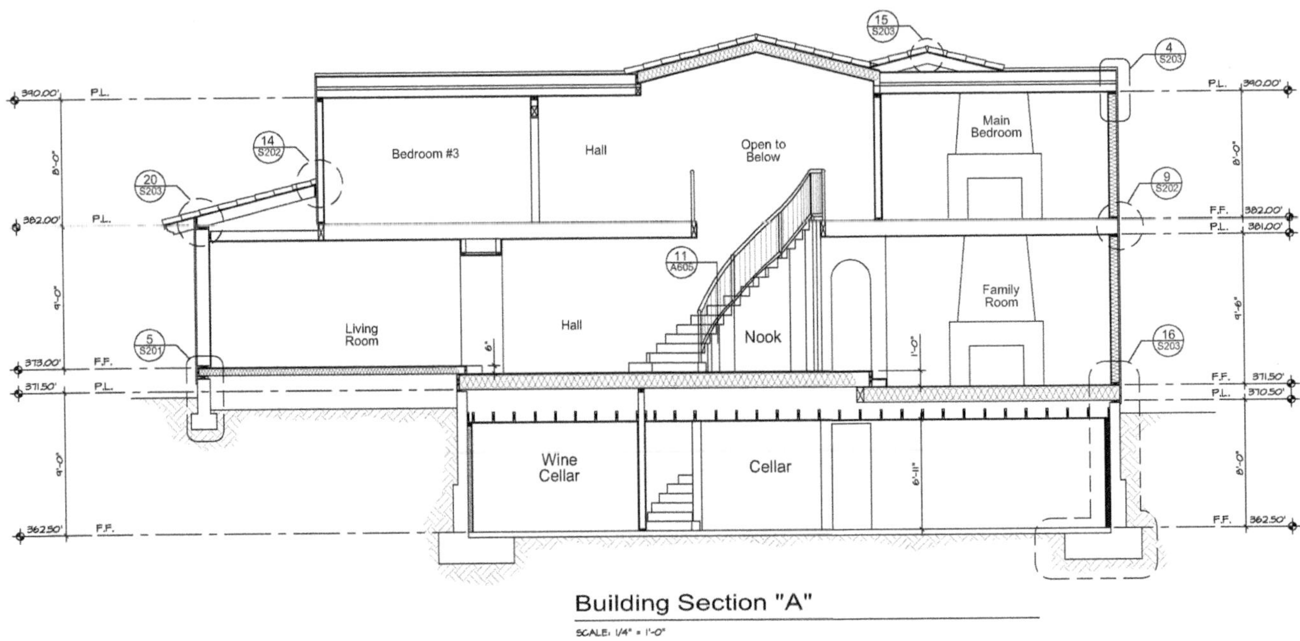

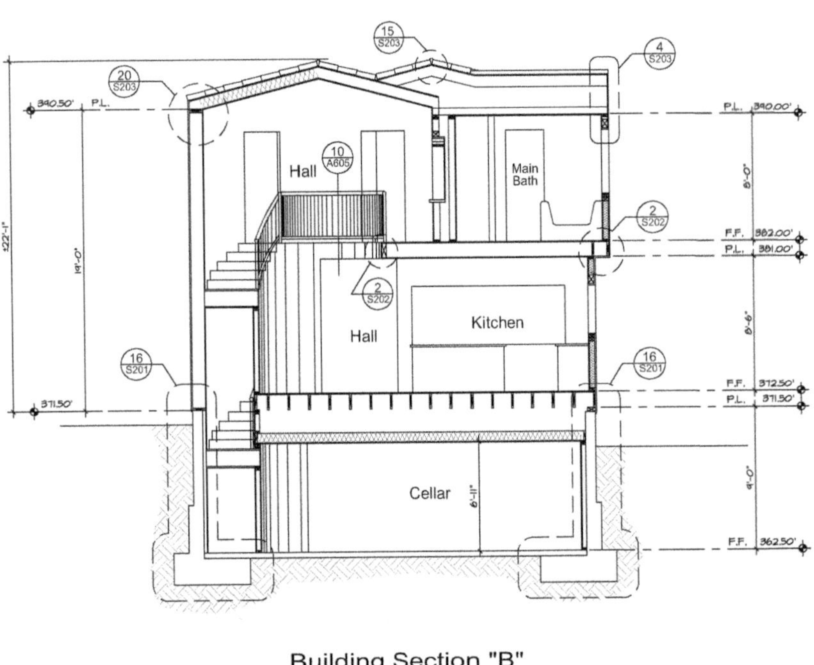

Figure 15.26 Stage V: Building section.

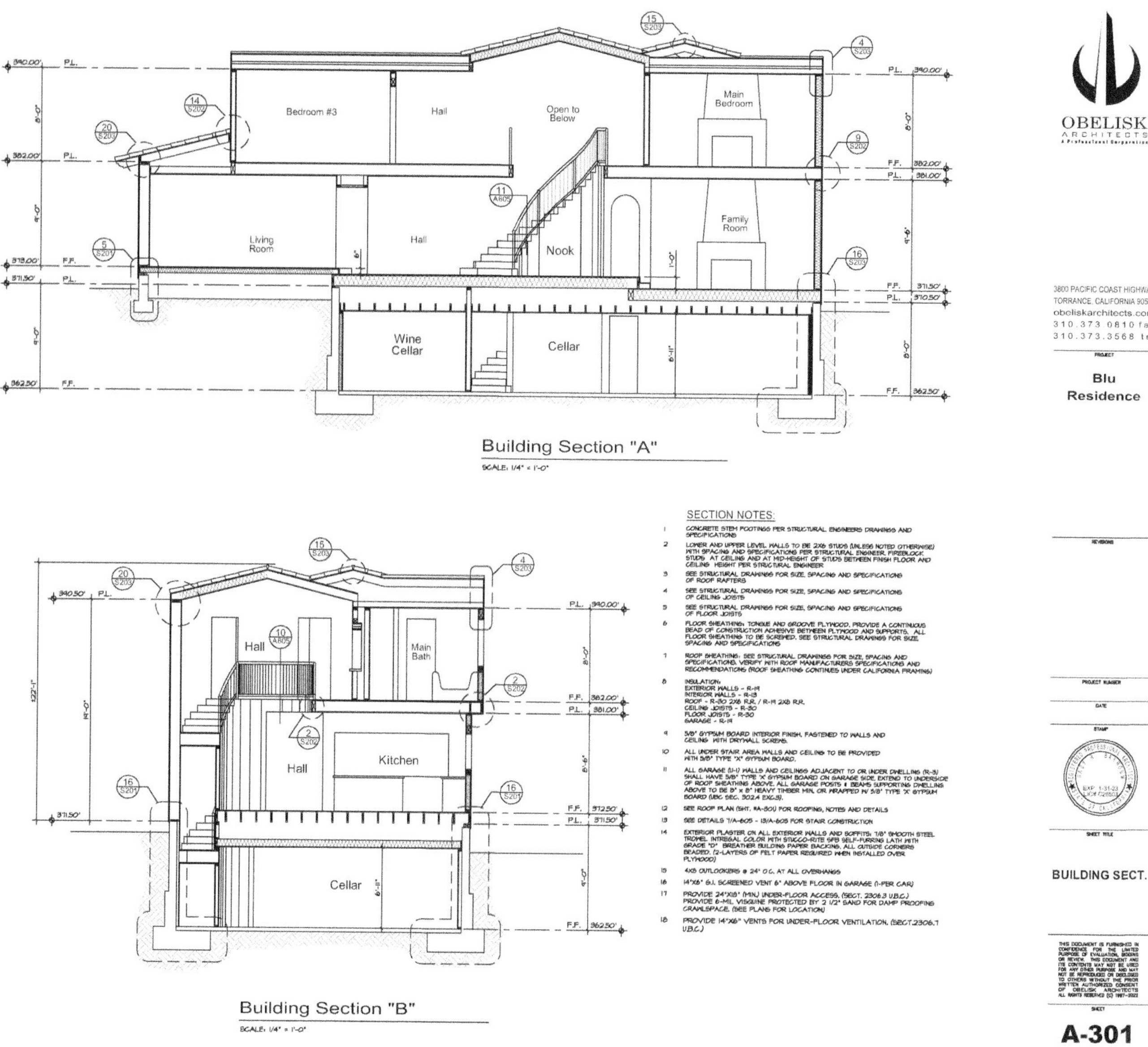

Figure 15.27 Stage VI: Building section.

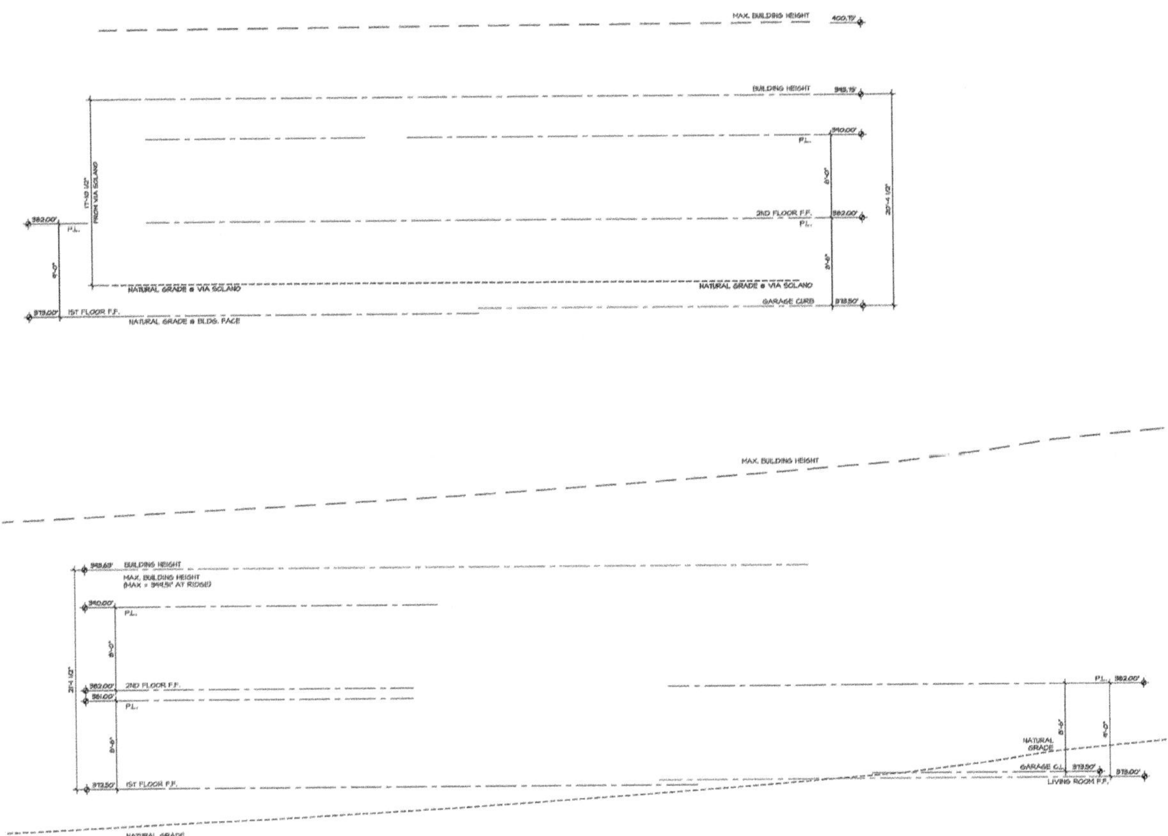

Figure 15.28 Stage I: Building elevations.

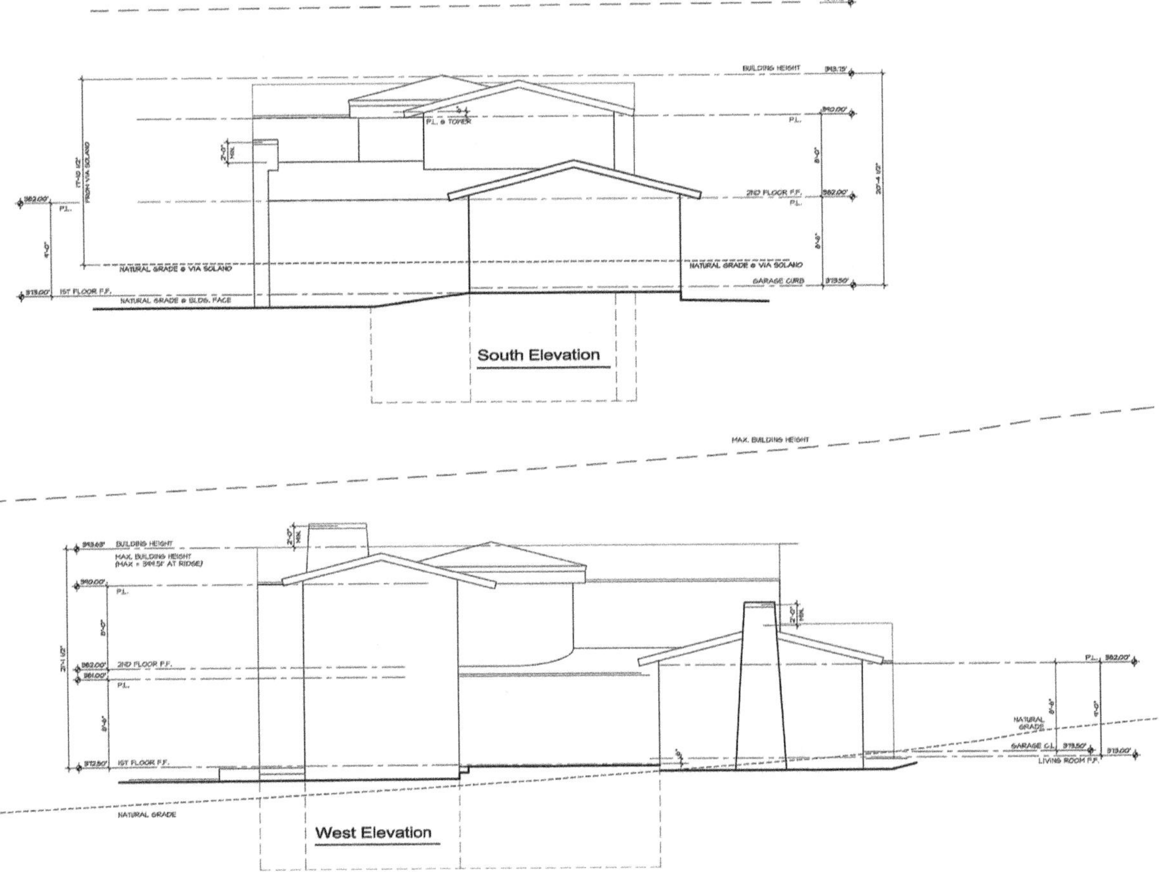

Figure 15.29 Stage II: Building section and elevations.

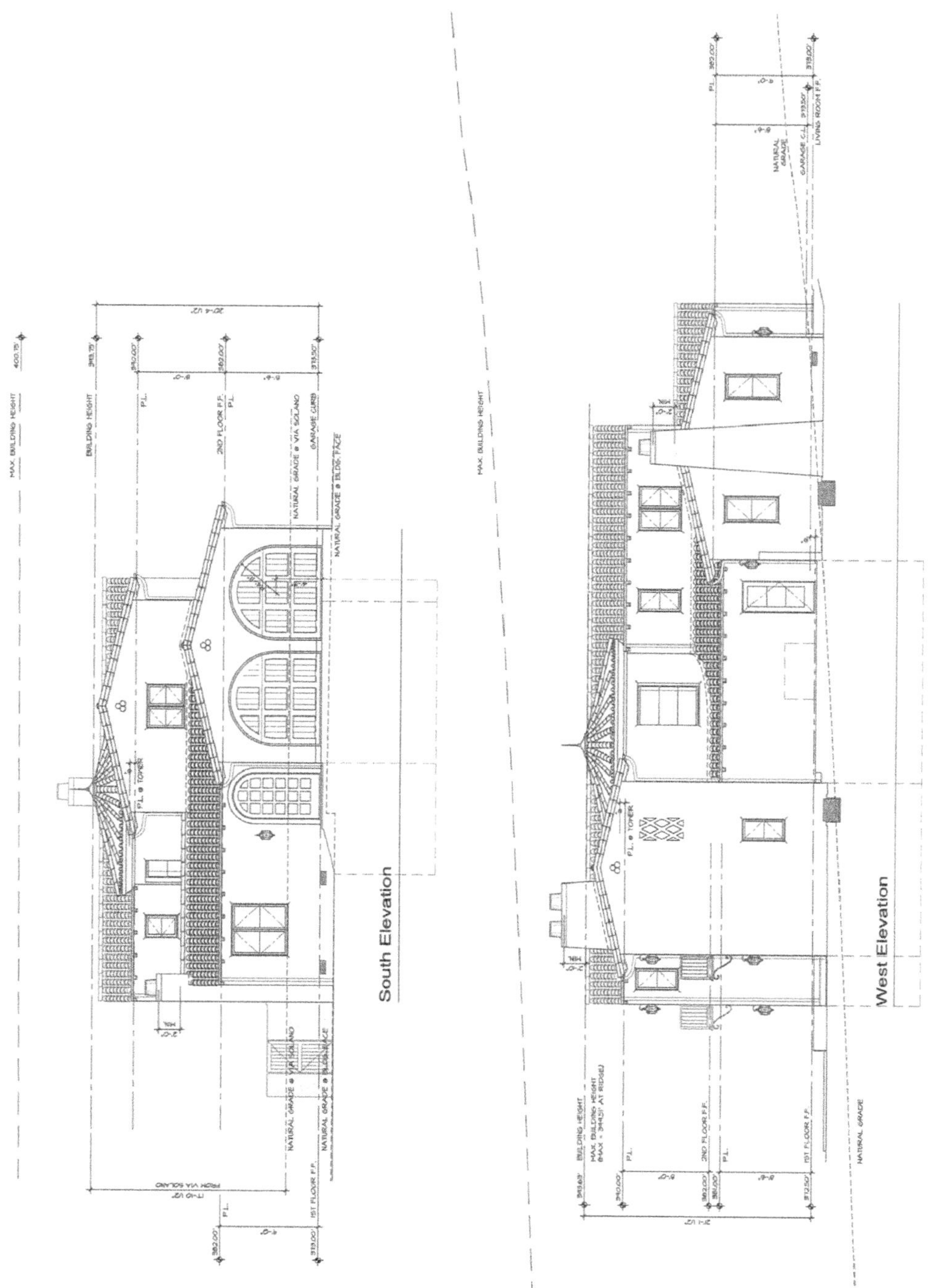

Figure 15.30 Stage III: Building section and elevations.

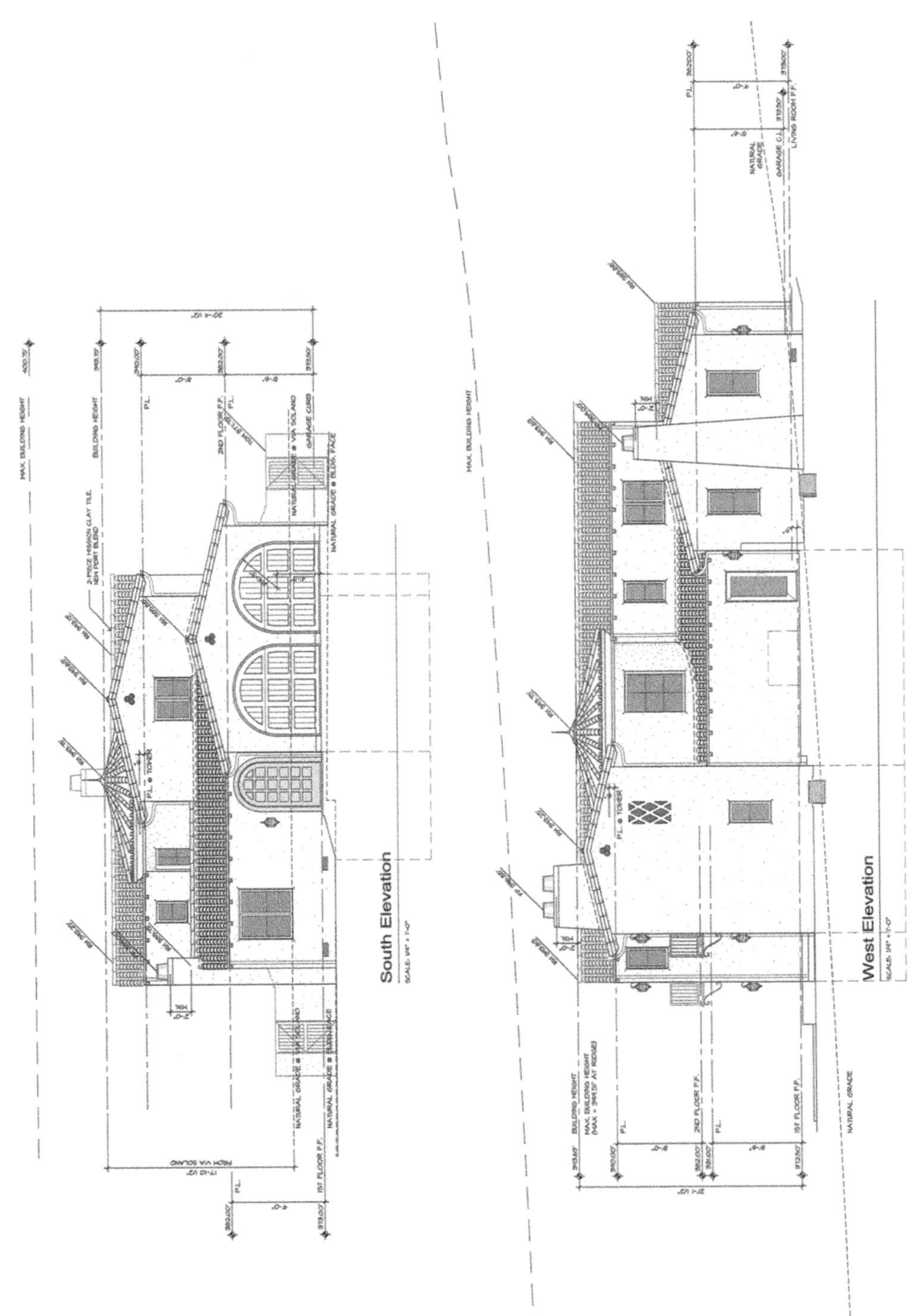

Figure 15.31 Stage IV: Building elevations.

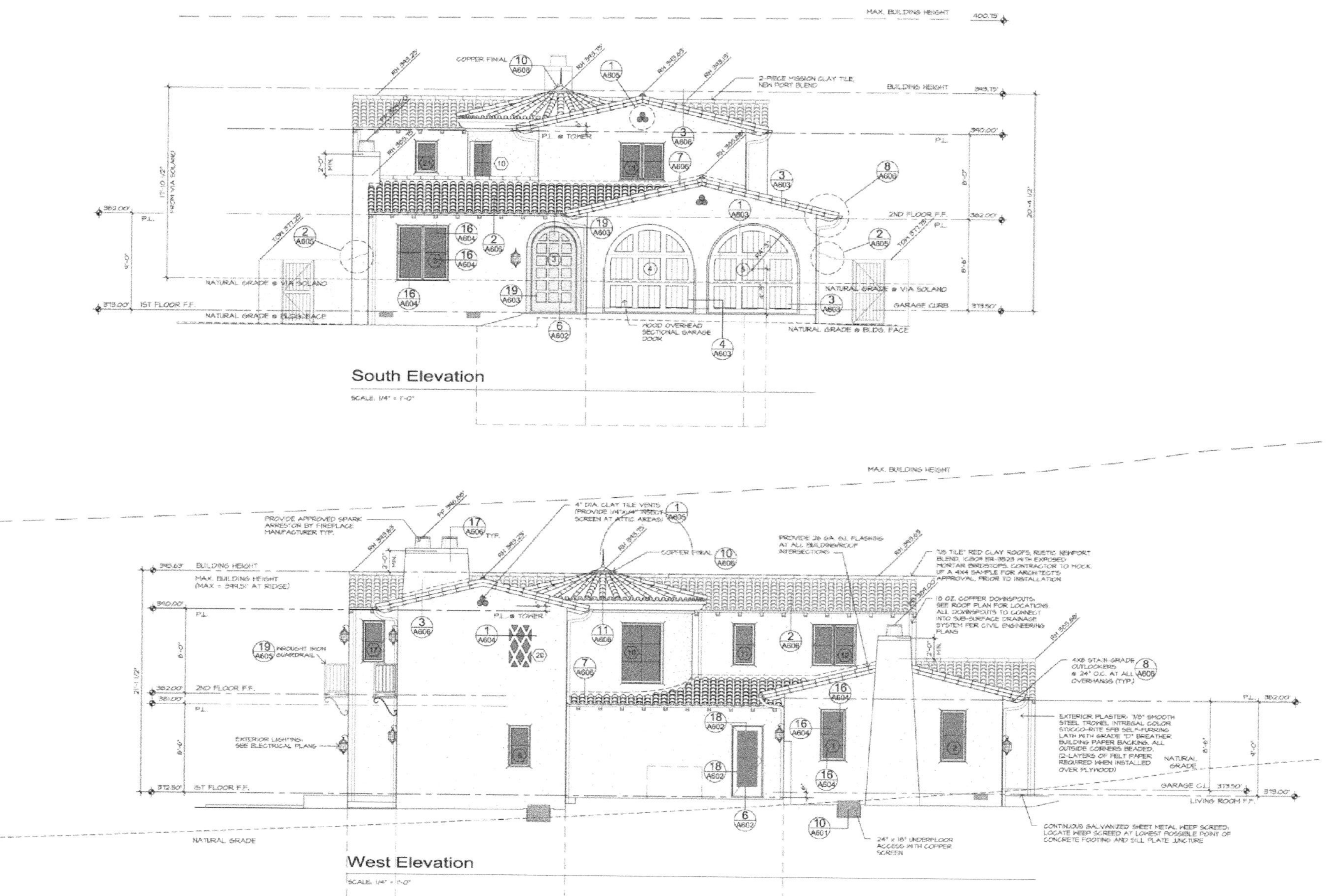

Figure 15.32 Stage V: Building elevations.

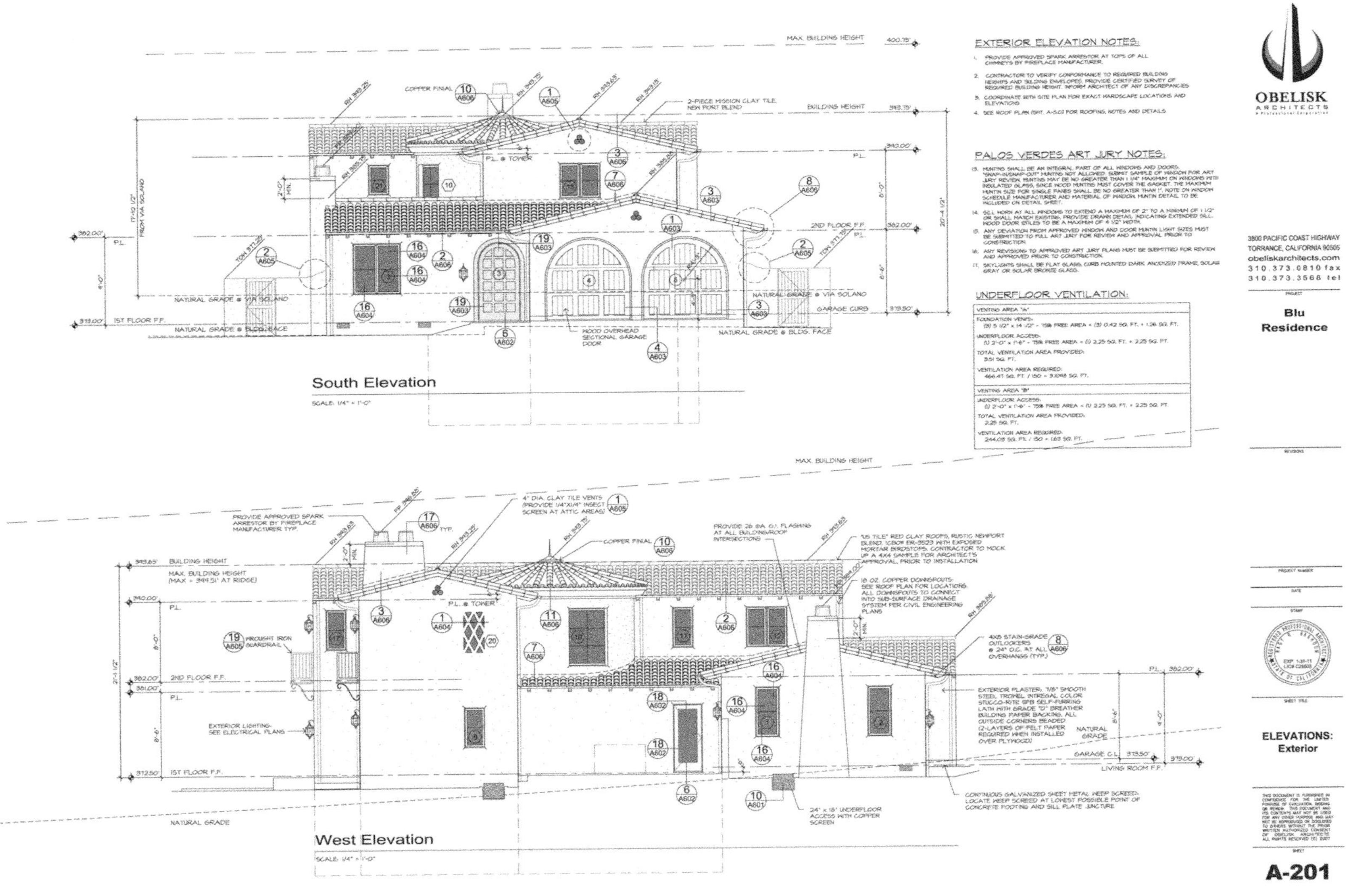

Figure 15.33 Stage VI: Building elevations.

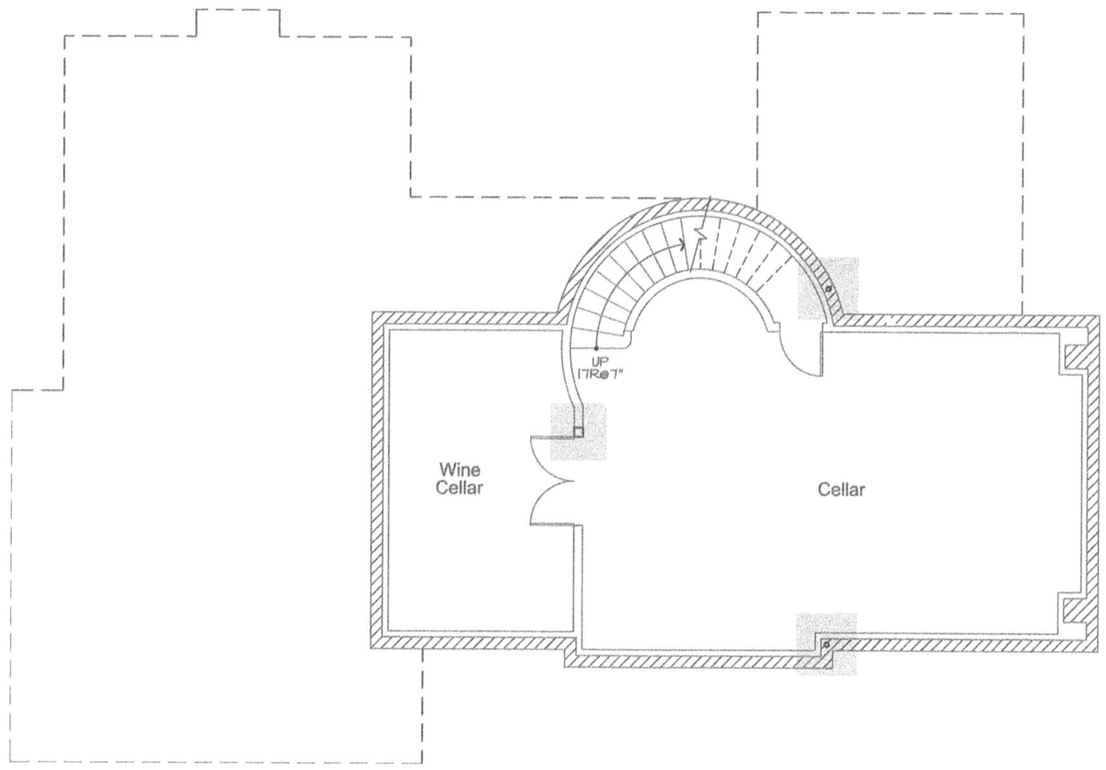

Figure 15.34 Stage II: Foundation plan (slab).

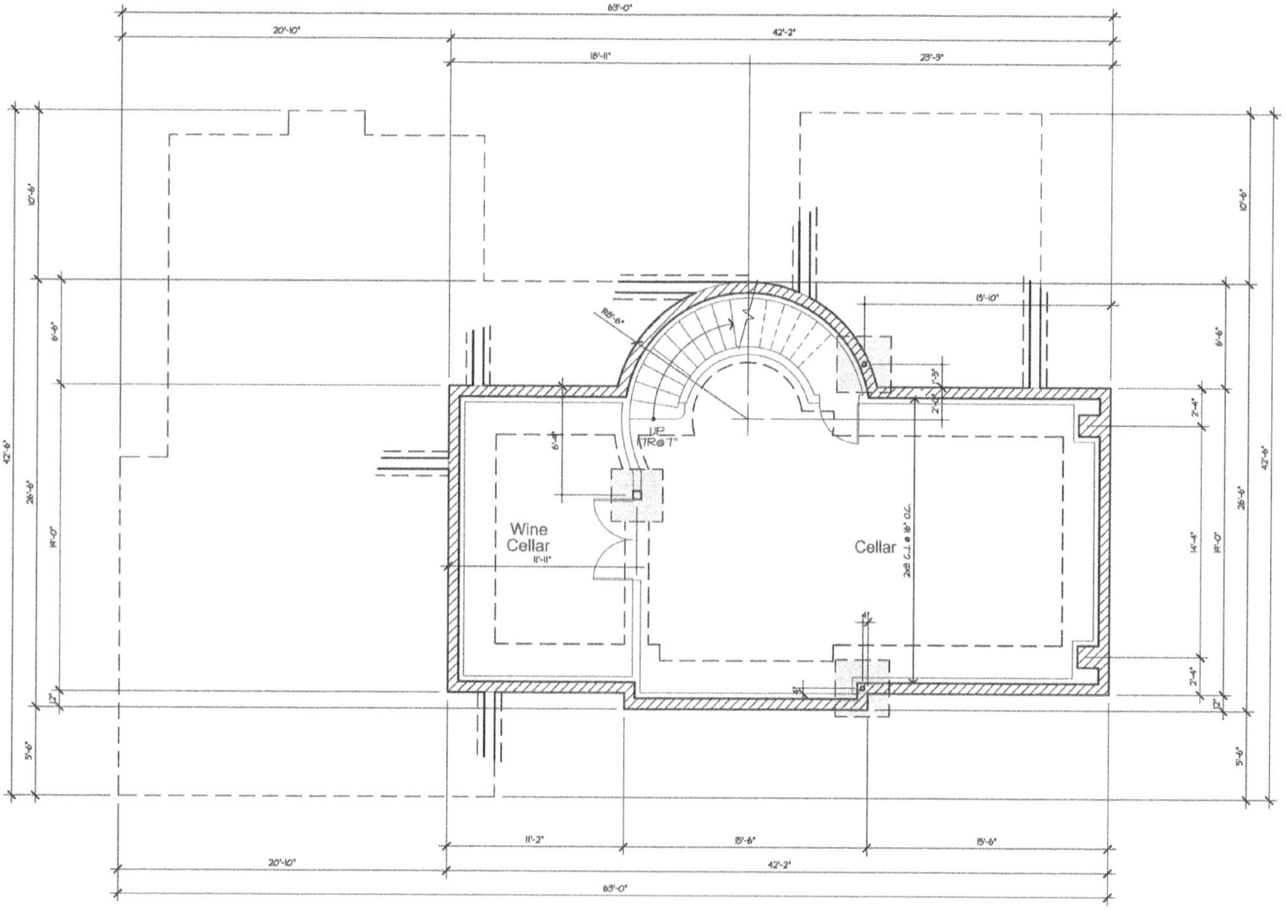

Figure 15.35 Stage III: Foundation plan.

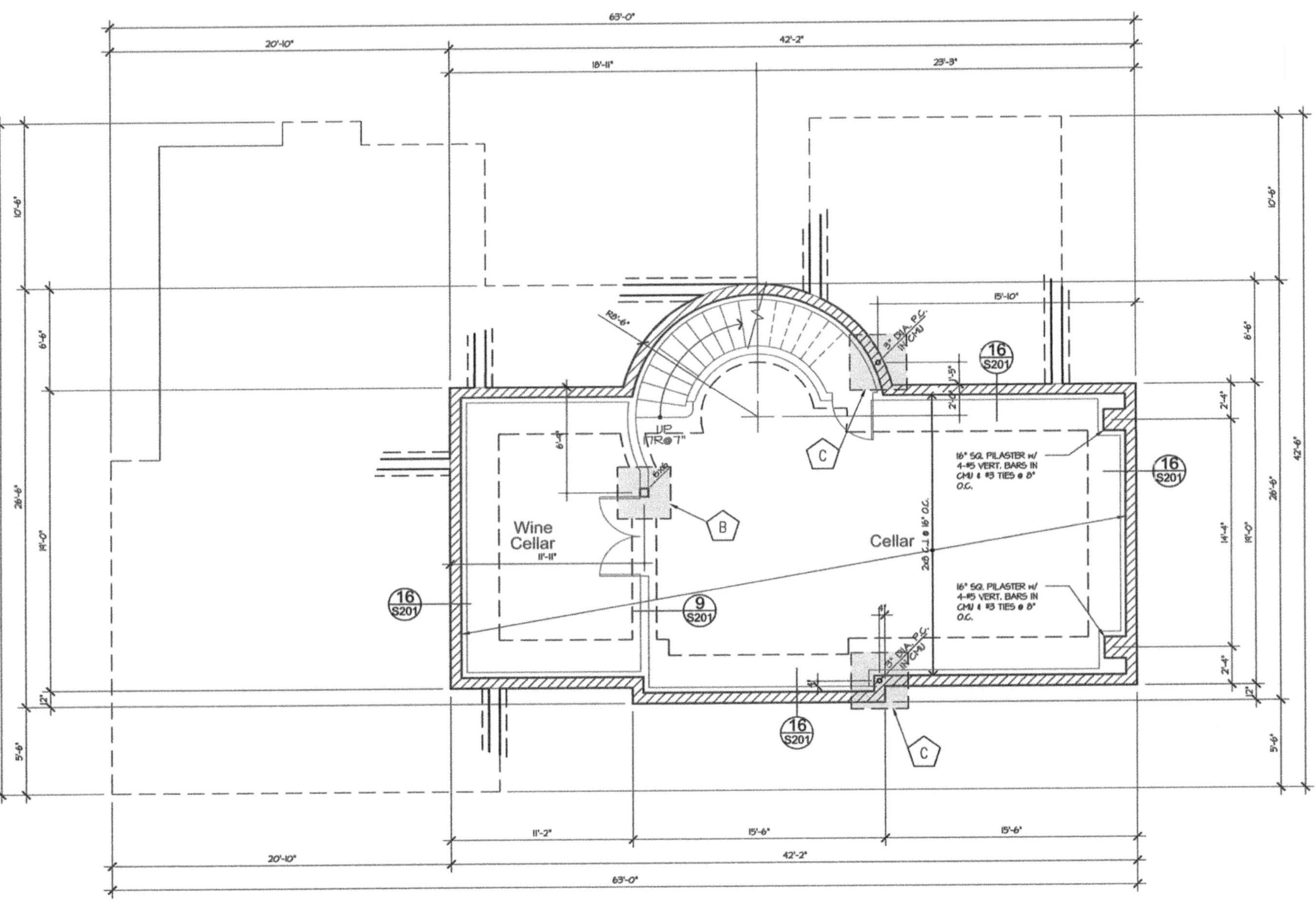

Figure 15.36 Stage IV: Foundation plan.

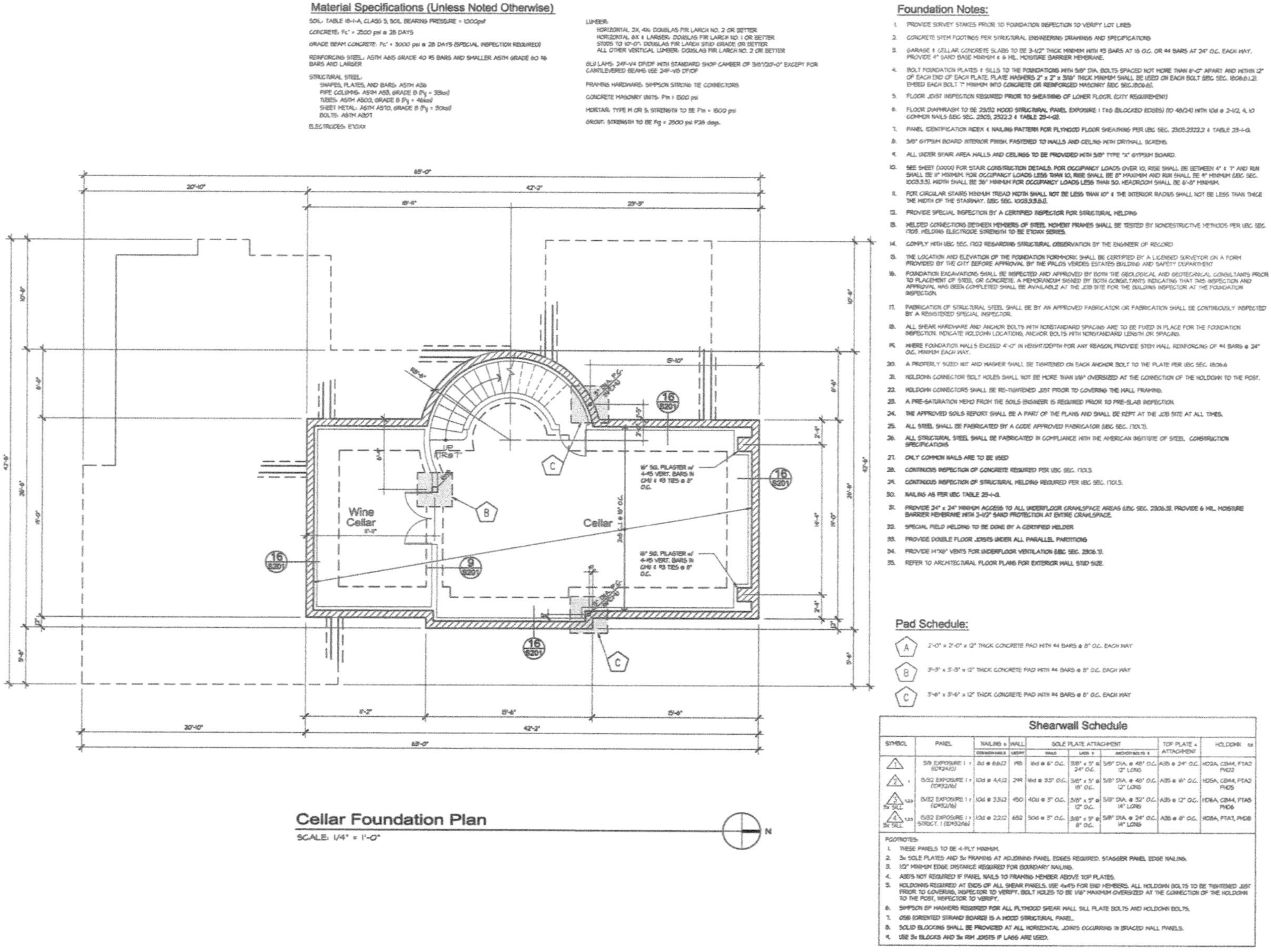

Figure 15.37 Stage IV: Foundation plan.

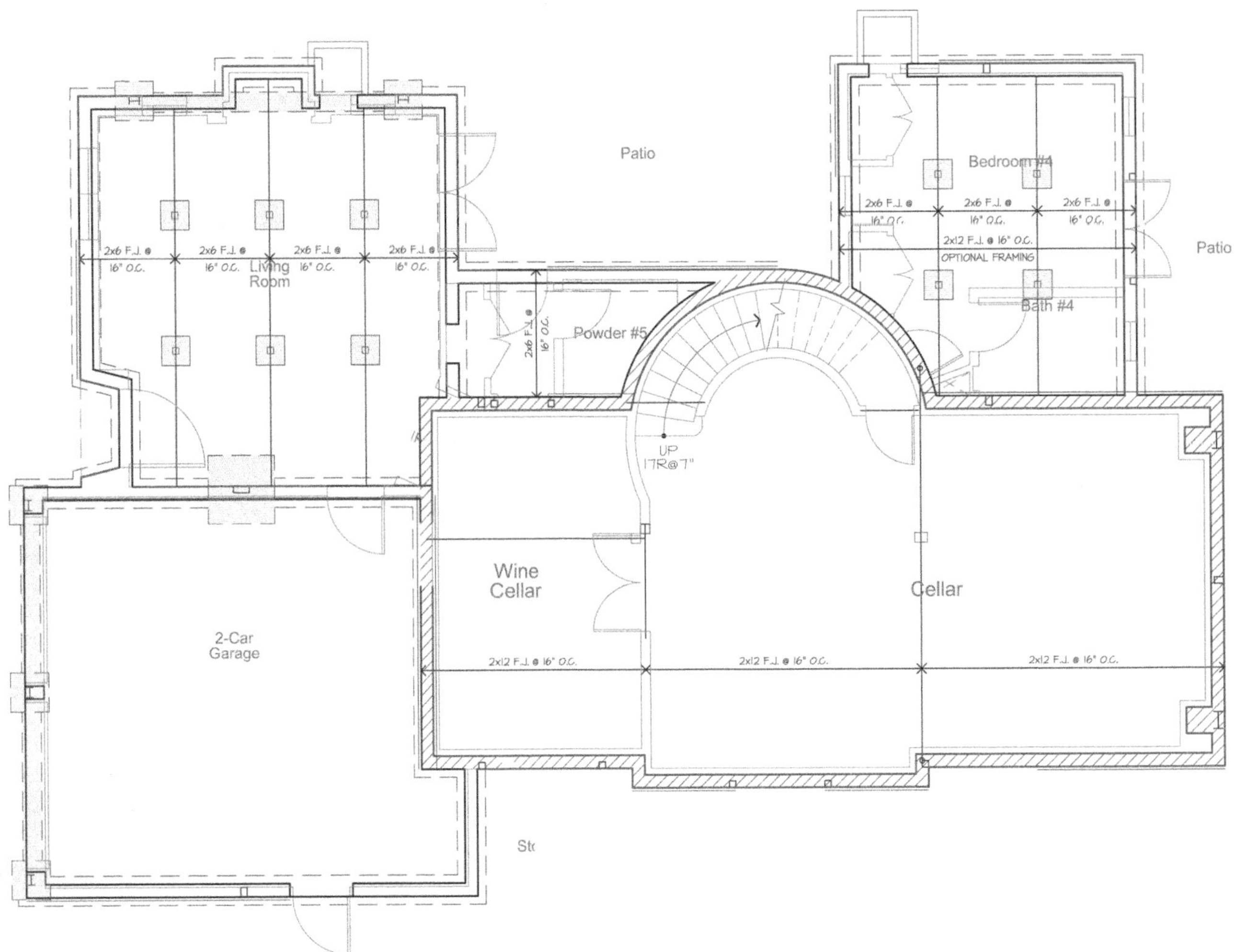

Figure 15.38 Stage III: Foundation plan (wood).

BIM-DRAWN TWO-STORY WOOD-FRAMED RESIDENCE

Following this text, you will see a set of working drawings completed in BIM. You will note that some of the BIM conventions must be altered in order to meet the national CAD standards. BIM has come a long way in a very short time, and every edition of the program leaps ahead of the past iteration.

Here you will find a two-story single-family residence where all phases, SD, DD, and CD, are all performed in BIM. See Figures 15.47–15.61.

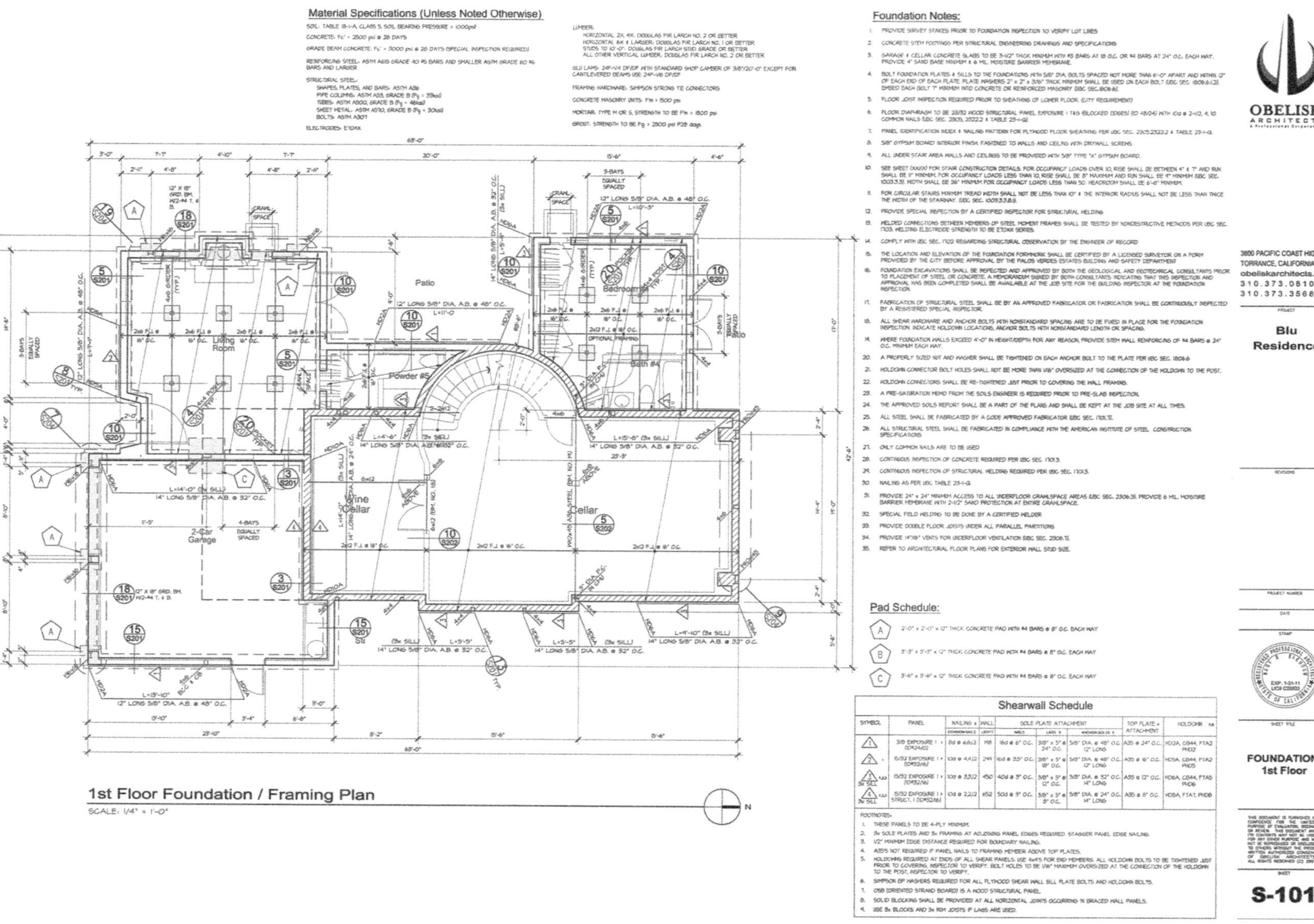

Figure 15.39 Stage V: Foundation plan.

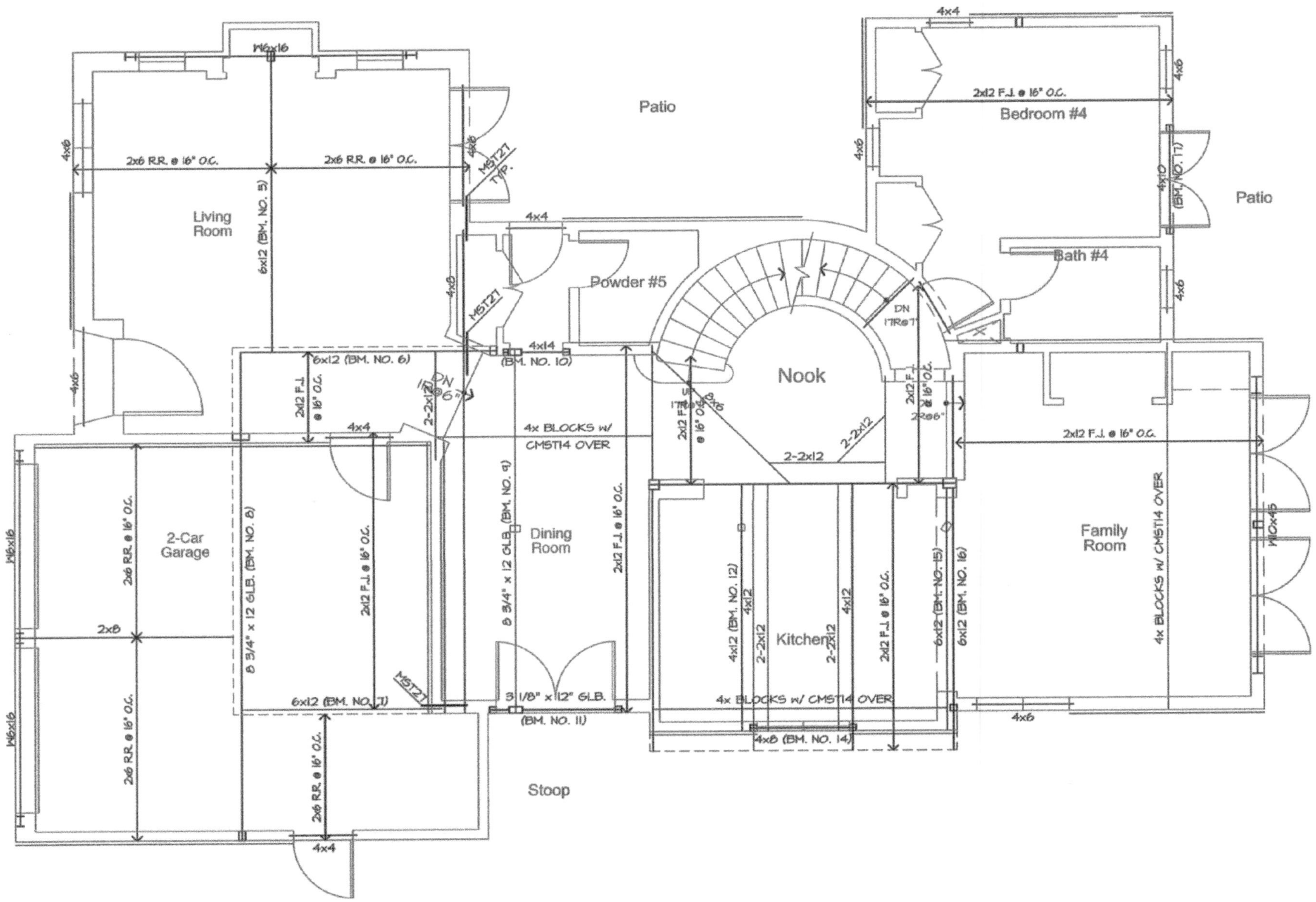

Figure 15.40 Stage I: Second-floor framing plan.

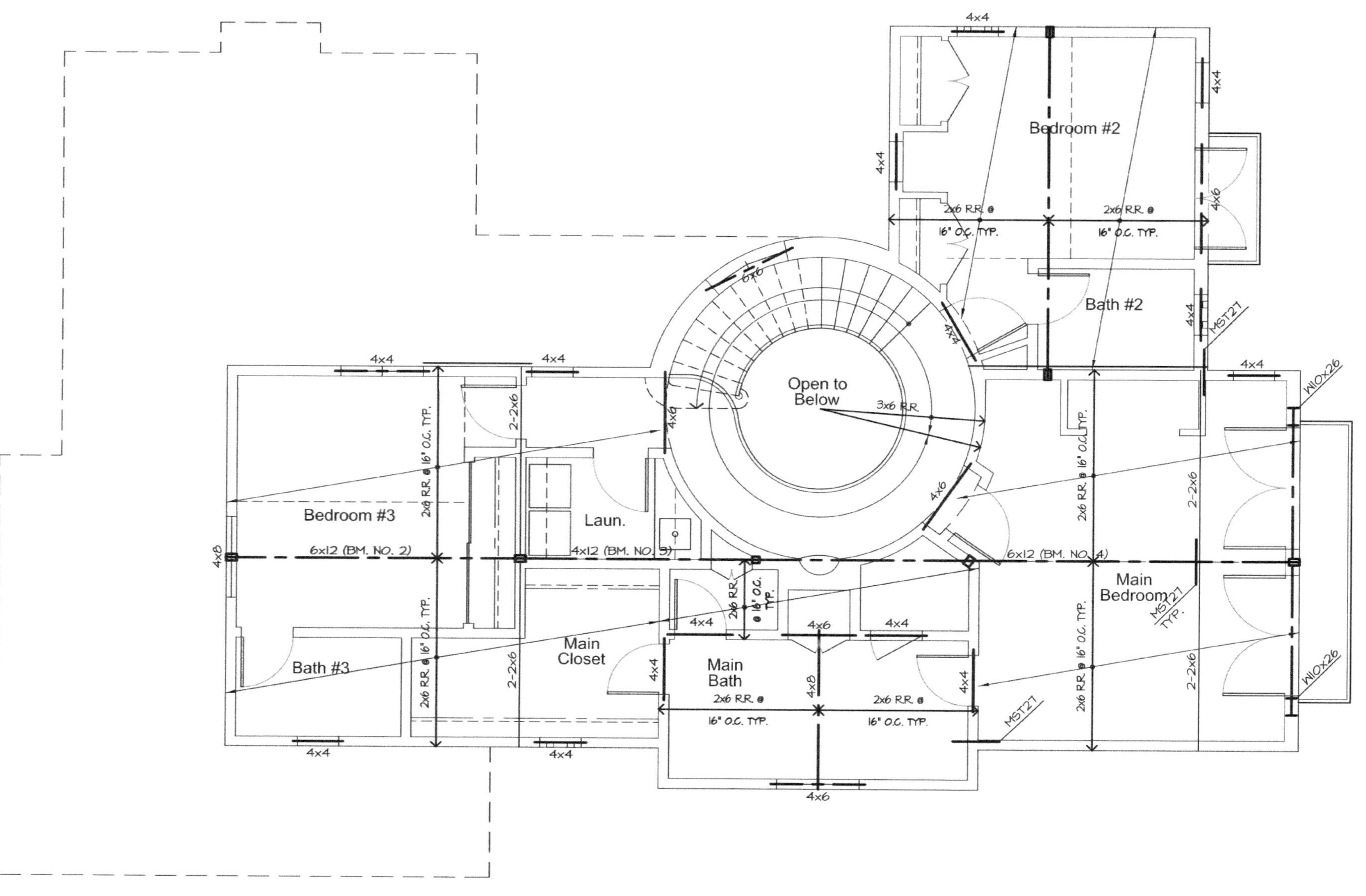

Figure 15.41 Stage I: Roof framing plan.

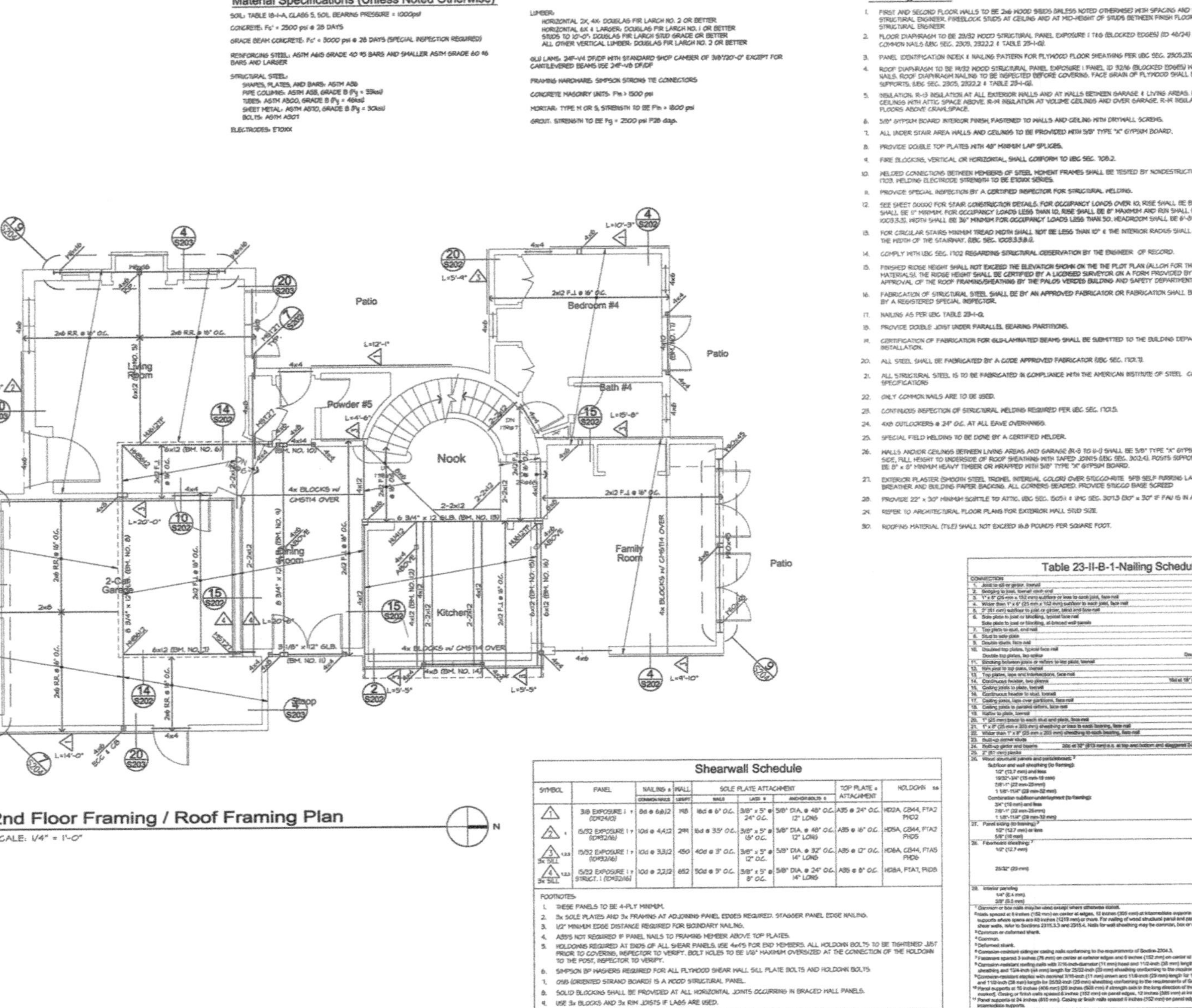

Figure 15.42 Stage II: Second-floor framing plan.

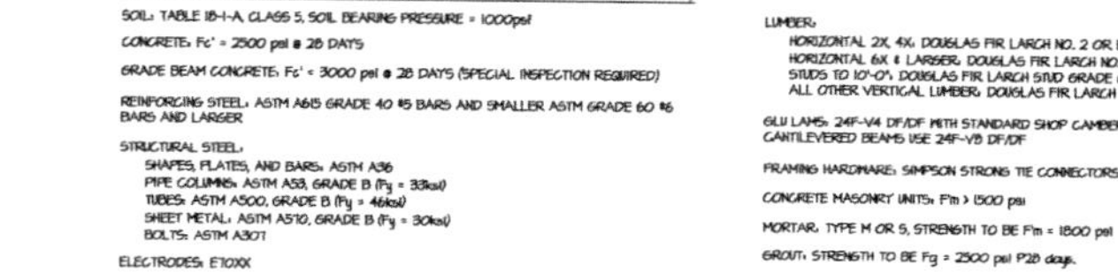

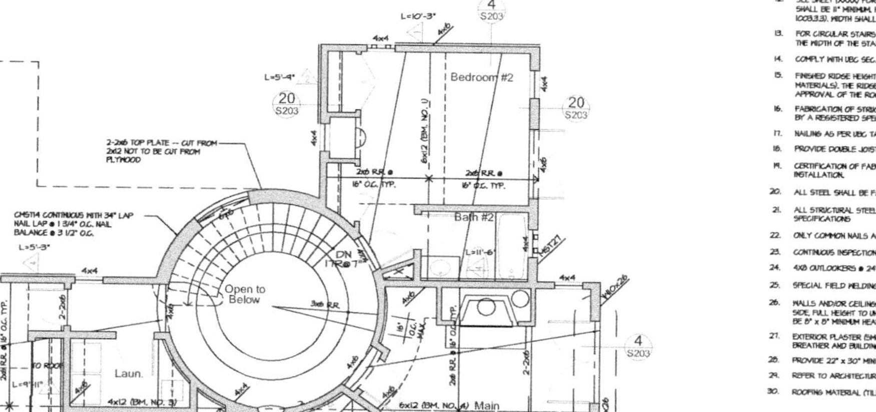

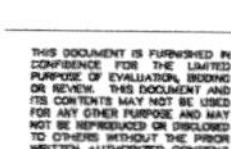

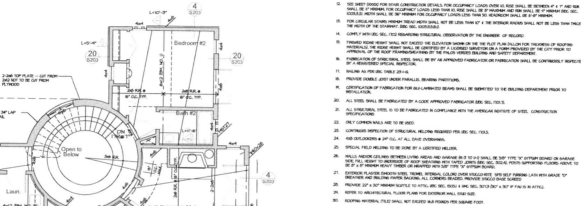

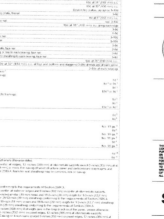

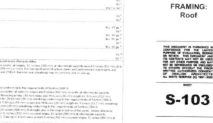

Figure 15.43 Stage II: Roof framing plan.

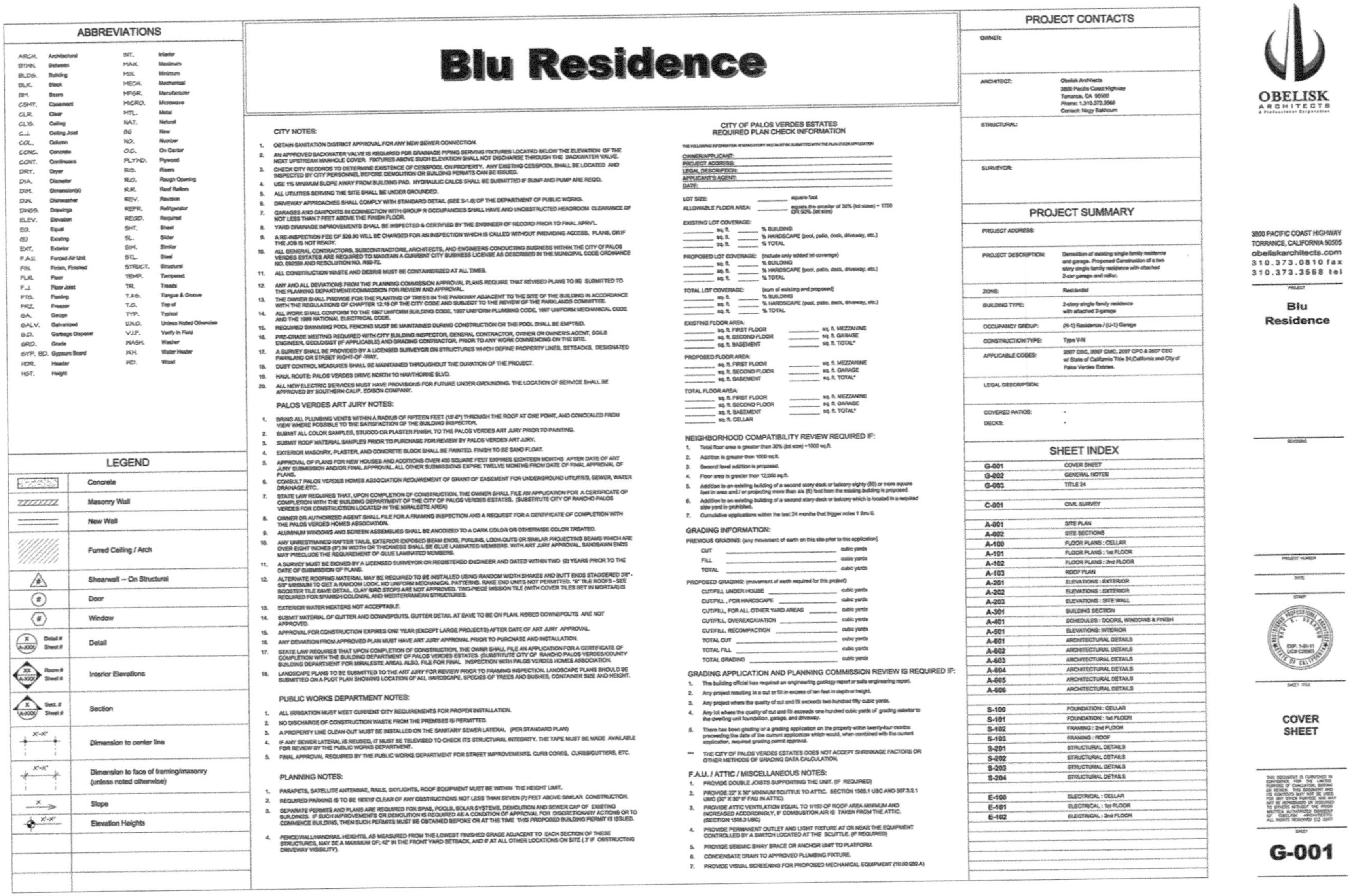

Blu Residence

ABBREVIATIONS

LEGEND

CITY NOTES:

PALOS VERDES ART JURY NOTES:

PUBLIC WORKS DEPARTMENT NOTES:

PLANNING NOTES:

CITY OF PALOS VERDES ESTATES
REQUIRED PLAN CHECK INFORMATION

NEIGHBORHOOD COMPATIBILITY REVIEW REQUIRED IF:

GRADING INFORMATION:

GRADING APPLICATION AND PLANNING COMMISSION REVIEW IS REQUIRED IF:

F.A.U. / ATTIC / MISCELLANEOUS NOTES:

PROJECT CONTACTS

PROJECT SUMMARY

SHEET INDEX

OBELISK ARCHITECTS

3800 PACIFIC COAST HIGHWAY
TORRANCE, CALIFORNIA 90505
obeliskarchitects.com
310.373.0810 fax
310.373.3568 tel

Blu Residence

COVER SHEET

G-001

Figure 15.44 Title sheet.

Figure 15.45 Interior elevation sheet.

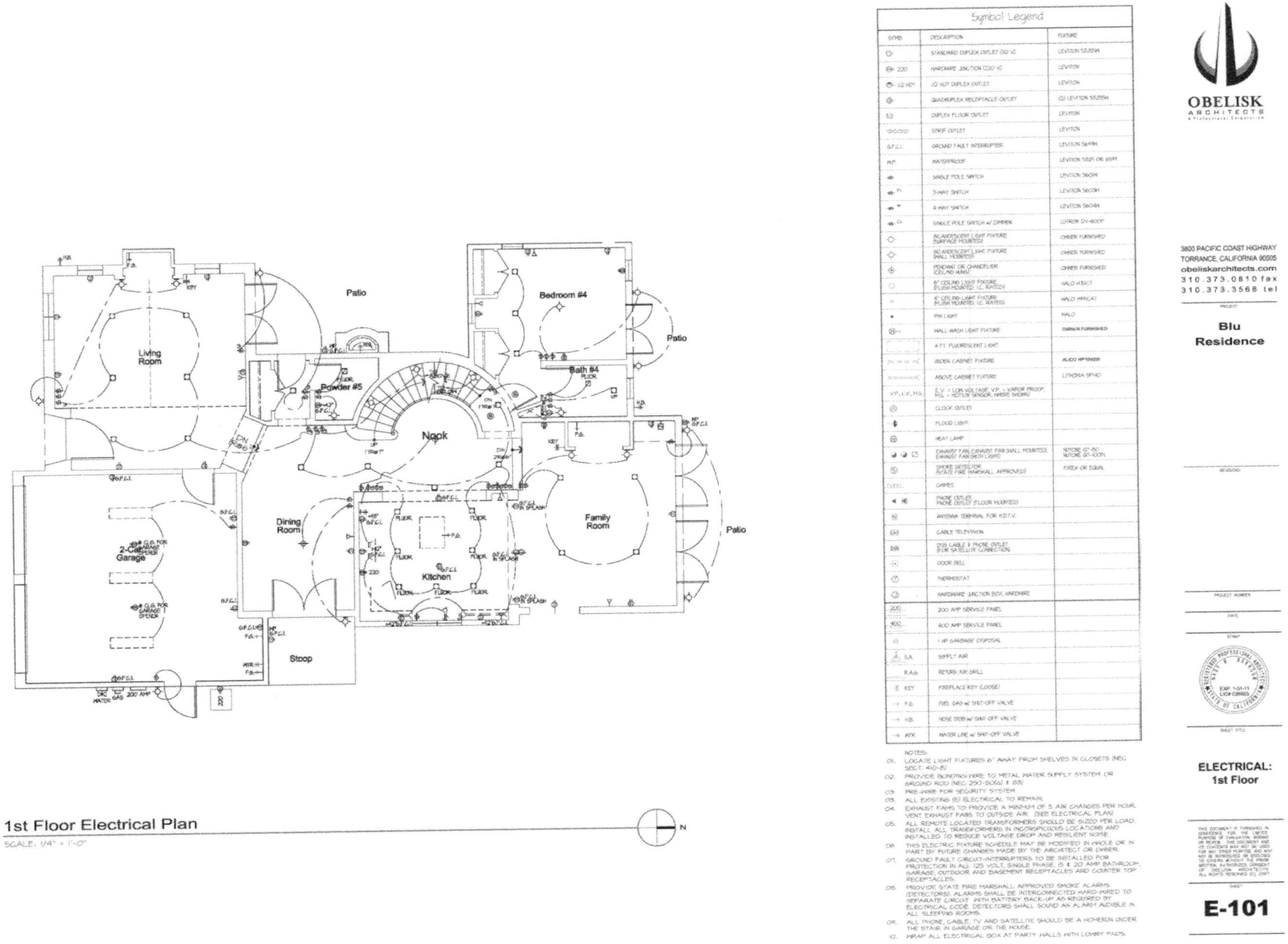

OBELISK
ARCHITECTS

3800 PACIFIC COAST HIGHWAY
TORRANCE, CALIFORNIA 90505
obeliskarchitects.com
310.373.0810 fax
310.373.3568 tel

Blu
Residence

ELECTRICAL:
1st Floor

E-101

Symbol Legend

Living Room
Patio
Powder #5
Nook
Bedroom #4
Bath #4
Patio
Family Room
Patio
Dining Room
Kitchen
2-Car Garage
Stoop

1st Floor Electrical Plan

SCALE: 1/4" = 1'-0"

Figure 15.46 Electrical layout sheet.

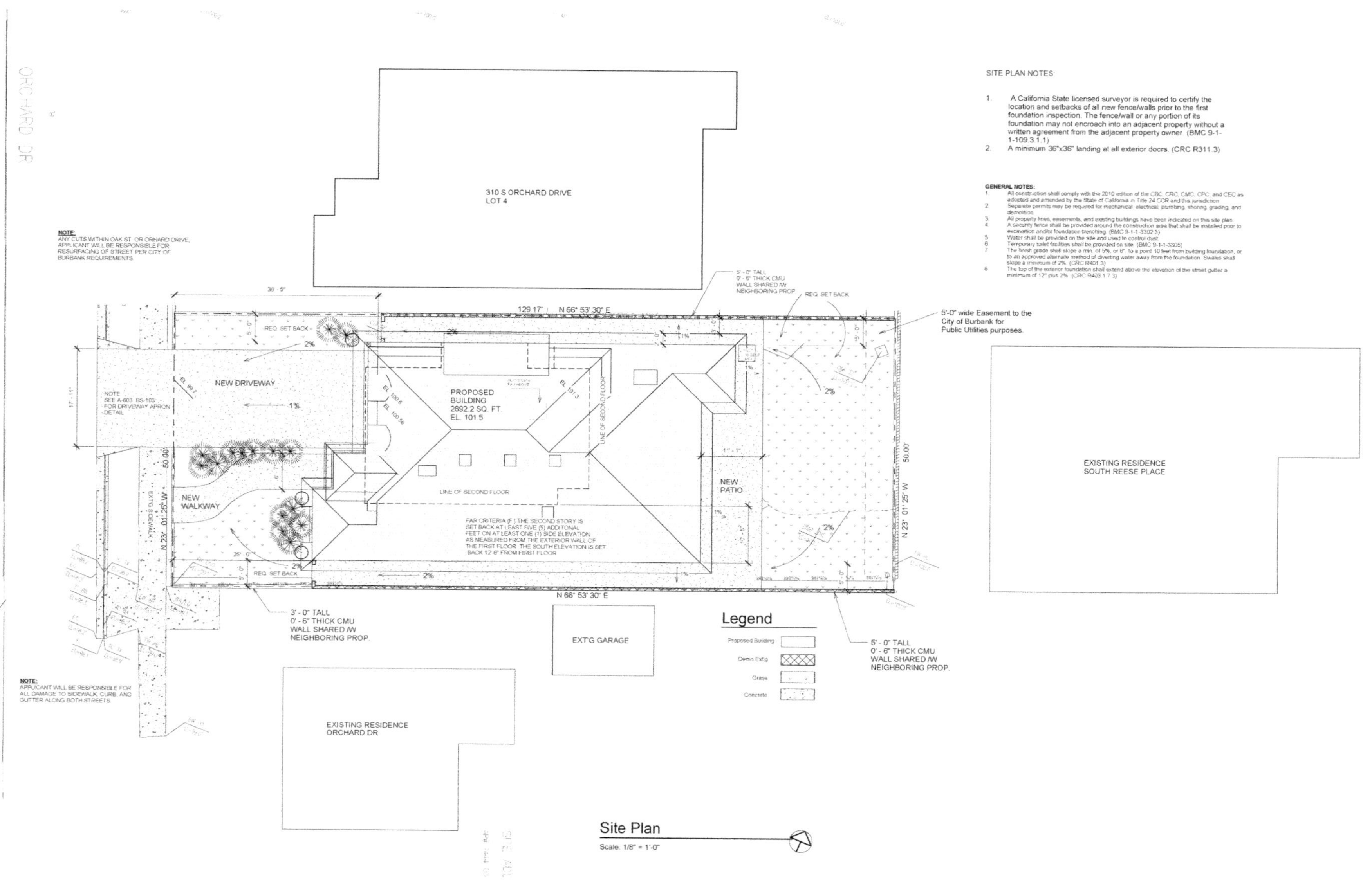

Figure 15.47 Site plan.

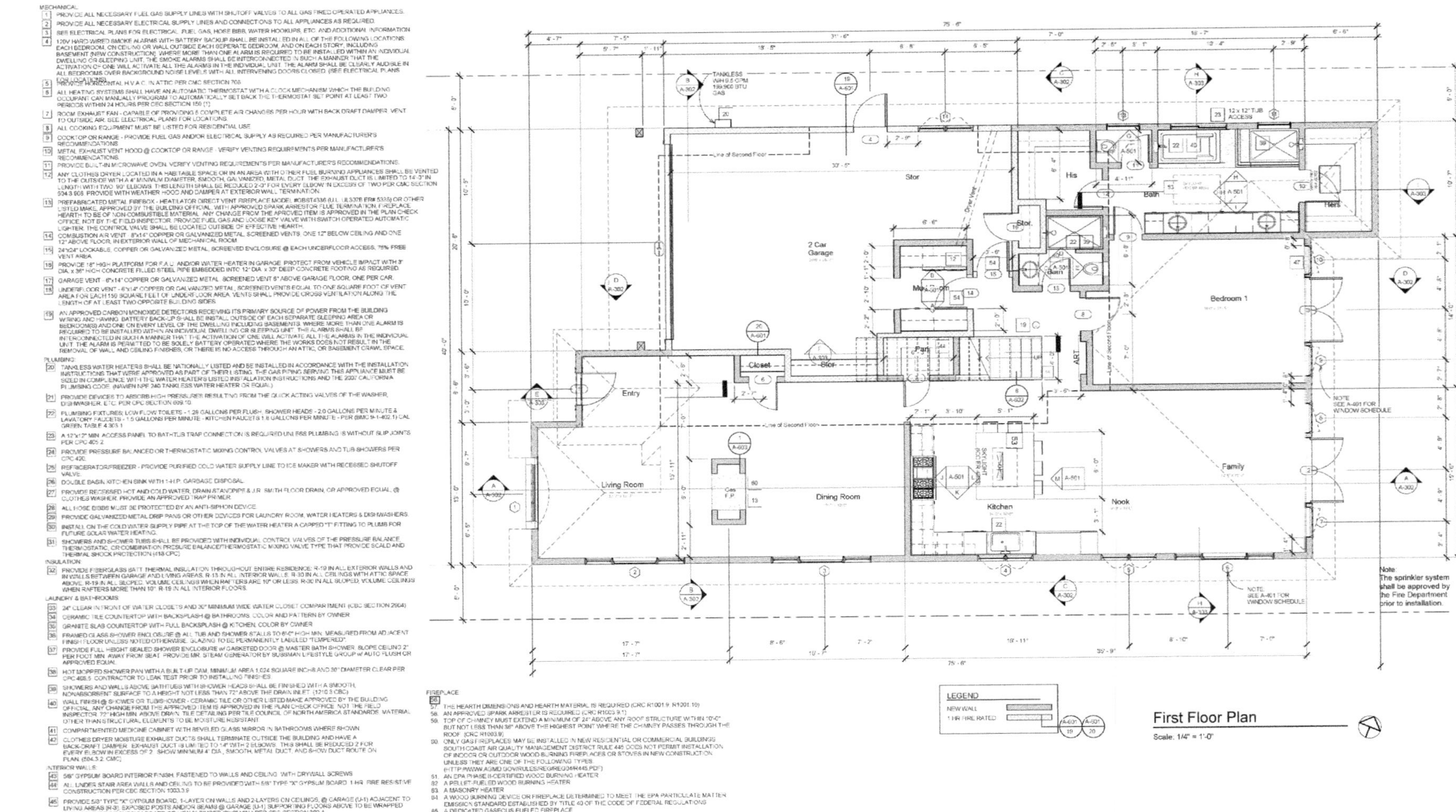

Figure 15.48 Lower-floor plan.

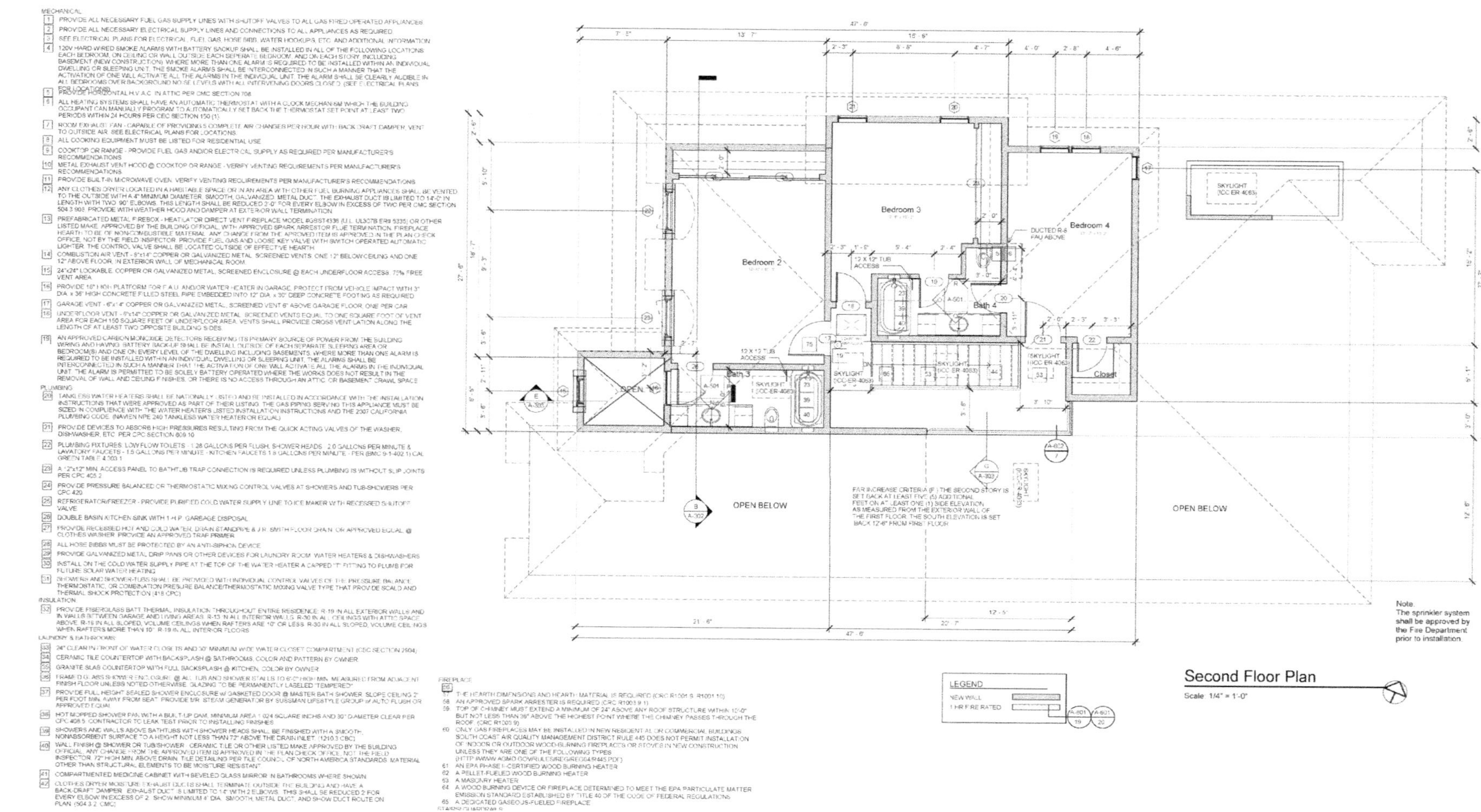

Figure 15.49 Upper-floor plan.

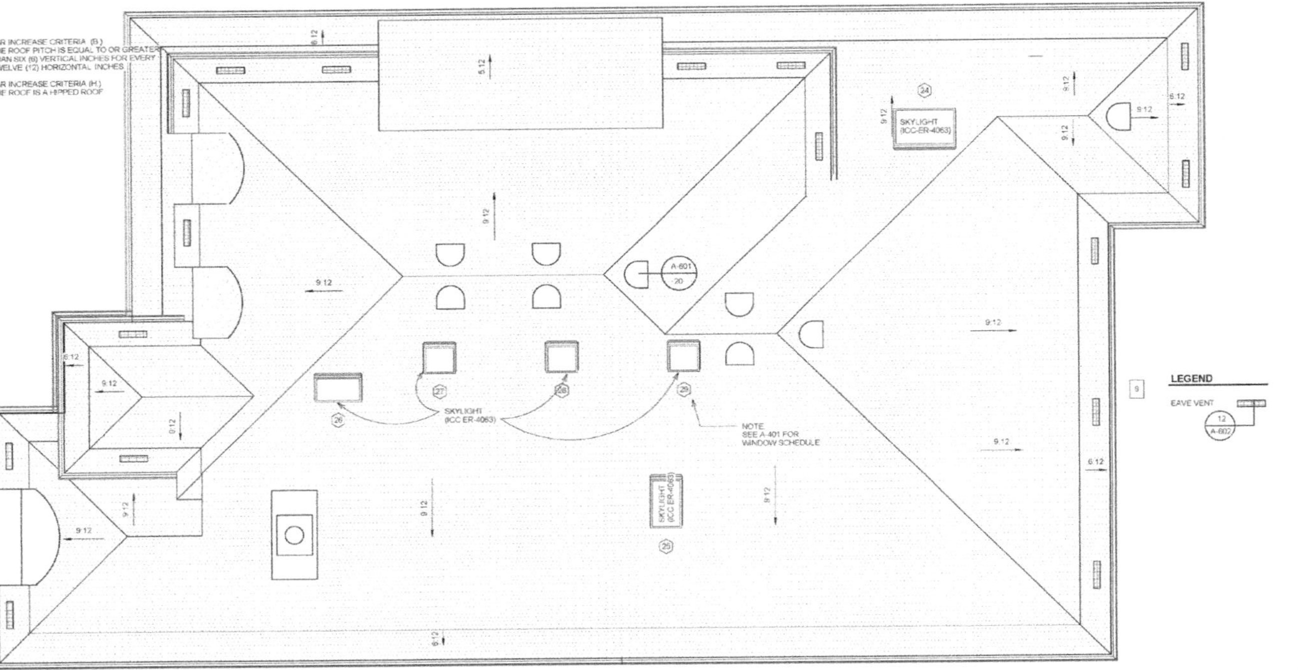

FAR INCREASE CRITERIA (B.)
THE ROOF PITCH IS EQUAL TO OR GREATER THAN SIX (6) VERTICAL INCHES FOR EVERY TWELVE (12) HORIZONTAL INCHES
FAR INCREASE CRITERIA (H.)
THE ROOF IS A HIPPED ROOF
SKYLIGHT (ICC-ER-4063)
NOTE: SEE A-401 FOR WINDOW SCHEDULE
Roof Plan
Scale: 1/4" = 1'-0"
Roof Plan Notes:
ROOF SLOPE:
1. ROOF SLOPES ARE SHOWN DIRECTLY ON ROOF PLAN DRAWING
2. ALL FLAT ROOFS AND DECKS SHALL SLOPE A MINIMUM OF 1/4:12 TOWARD DRAINS OR GUTTERS
3. IN THE ABSENCE OF SLOPES SHOWN ON STRUCTURAL DRAWINGS OR ARCHITECTURAL DRAWINGS, ROUGH CARPENTER SHALL PROVIDE REQUIRED SHIMMING BELOW ROOF SHEATHING TO ALLOW FOR PROPER SLOPE TO DRAIN
4. NO OBSTACLE SHALL PREVENT WATER FLOW TOWARD DRAINS
5. CONTRACTOR TO VERIFY CONFORMANCE TO REQUIRED BUILDING HEIGHTS AND BUILDING ENVELOPES. PROVIDE CERTIFIED SURVEY OF REQUIRED BUILDING HEIGHT. INFORM ARCHITECT OF ANY DISCREPANCIES
ROOF MATERIAL:
6. ROOF TO BE CLASS "A". PROPOSED PRESIDENTIAL ASPHALT SHINGLE ROOF, ICC # ESR-1389. MOCK-UP OF PITCHED ROOF INSTALLATION SHALL BE APPROVED BY ARCHITECT PRIOR TO PROCEEDING WITH WORK. PLYWOOD DIAPHRAGM (PER STRUCTURAL PLANS) MINIMUM SHINGLE NAILING SHALL COMPLY WITH THE FOLLOWING
A. 11 GA. CORROSION-RESISTANT 3/4" INTO SHEATHING PER CBC TABLE NO. 15-D-1
B. THE HEADS OF ALL TILE SHALL BE NAILED
C. THE NOSES OF ALL EAVE COURSE TILES SHALL BE FASTENED WITH APPROVED CLIPS
D. ALL RAKE TILES SHALL BE NAILED WITH TWO NAILS
E. THE NOSES OF ALL RIDGE, HIP AND RAKE TILES SHALL BE SET IN A BED OF APROVED ROOFERS MASTIC
GUTTERS AND ROOF DRAINS:
7. PROVIDE ROOF GUTTERS AND DOWNSPOUTS
8. GUTTERS SHALL BE CONSTRUCTED OF 26 GA GALVANIZED WITH 5/8" EXPANSION JOINTS EVERY 30 FEET MAXIMUM
9. GUTTERS SHALL SLOPE 1/16" PER FOOT TOWARD RAIN WATER LEADERS
10. UNLESS SPECIFIED OTHERWISE, RAIN WATER LEADERS ARE EXPOSED AND LOCATION IS SHOWN ON ROOF PLAN
11. PROVIDE DOME WIRE BASKET AT EACH RAIN WATER LEADER AND ROOF DRAIN
12. CONTRACTOR SHALL TEST ALL CONCEALED DOWNSPOUTS FOR WATER LEAKAGE PRIOR TO CLOSING UP BUILDING AND SHALL PROVIE A 10 YEAR WARRANTY AGAINST LEAKAGE
13. ROOF DRAINAGE TO BE CONNECTED TO EXISTING CITY APPROVED DRAINAGE DEVICE. ALL RAIN WATER TO BE DIRECTED TO STREET OR APPROVED OUTLET.
14. DOWNSPOUTS AT ROOFS SHALL BE A MINIMUM OF 4" DIAMETER
ROOF PENETRATION:
15. VENTS AT FLAT ROOF AND ROOF STACKS SHALL PROJECT ABOVE ROOF BY THE MINIMUM DISTANCE REQUIRED BY APPLICABLE CODES AND SHALL BE LOCATED IN AREAS NOT VISIBLE FROM STREET. EXACT LOCATION TO BE COORDINATED WITH ARCHITECT PRIOR TO INSTALLATION
16. ALL VENTS AND ROOF STACKS TO HAVE RAIN PROTECTION CAPS
17. CONTINUOUS WATERPROOFING AT ALL ROOF PENETRATIONS SHALL BE PROVIDED WITH WR GRACE 4000 BITUTHENE WRAPPING AND 24 GA. GALVANIZED METAL AND COUNTERFLASHING. ALL JOINTS AT SHEET METAL SHALL BE CAULKED
18. COLOR OF ALL EXPOSED VENTS AND ROOF STACKS TO MATCH ADJACENT ROOF MATERIAL, UNLESS SPECIFIED OTHERWISE BY ARCHITECT
19. BRING ALL PLUMBING VENTS WITHIN A RADIUS OF FIFTEEN FEET (15'-0") THROUGH THE ROOF AT ONE POINT, AND CONCEALED FROM VIEW WHERE POSSIBLE
ATTIC VENTILATION:
20. NO VENTILATION IS REQUIRED IN AREAS WHERE ROOF INSULATION IS INSTALLED BETWEEN RAFTERS WITH NO AIR SPACE BETWEEN INSULATION AND EXTERIOR SHEATHING
21. ATTIC DRAFTSTOPS SHALL BE IN COMPLIANCE WITH ALL APPLICABLE CODES
22. ALL VENT OPENINGS SHALL BE COVERED WITH A CORROSION RESISTANT METAL MESH WITH OPENINGS NO LARGER THAN 1/4" IN ANY DIRECTION
ATTIC VENTILATION TABULATION
23. TOTAL ATTIC VENTILATION SHALL BE A MINIMUM OF 1/150 OF THE AREA TO BE VENTILATED OR 1/300 FOR MECH. VENTING
ATTIC SPACE 1,151.2 SQ. FT / 150 = 7.7 SQ. FT
PROVIDE 9 - 30" HALF-ROUND DORMER ROOF VENTS
9 * 124 SQ. IN. = 1116 SQ. IN. = 7.75 SQ. FT

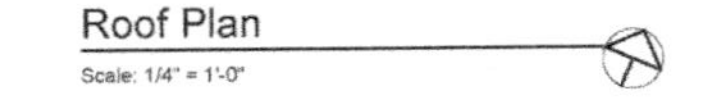

Figure 15.50 Roof plan.

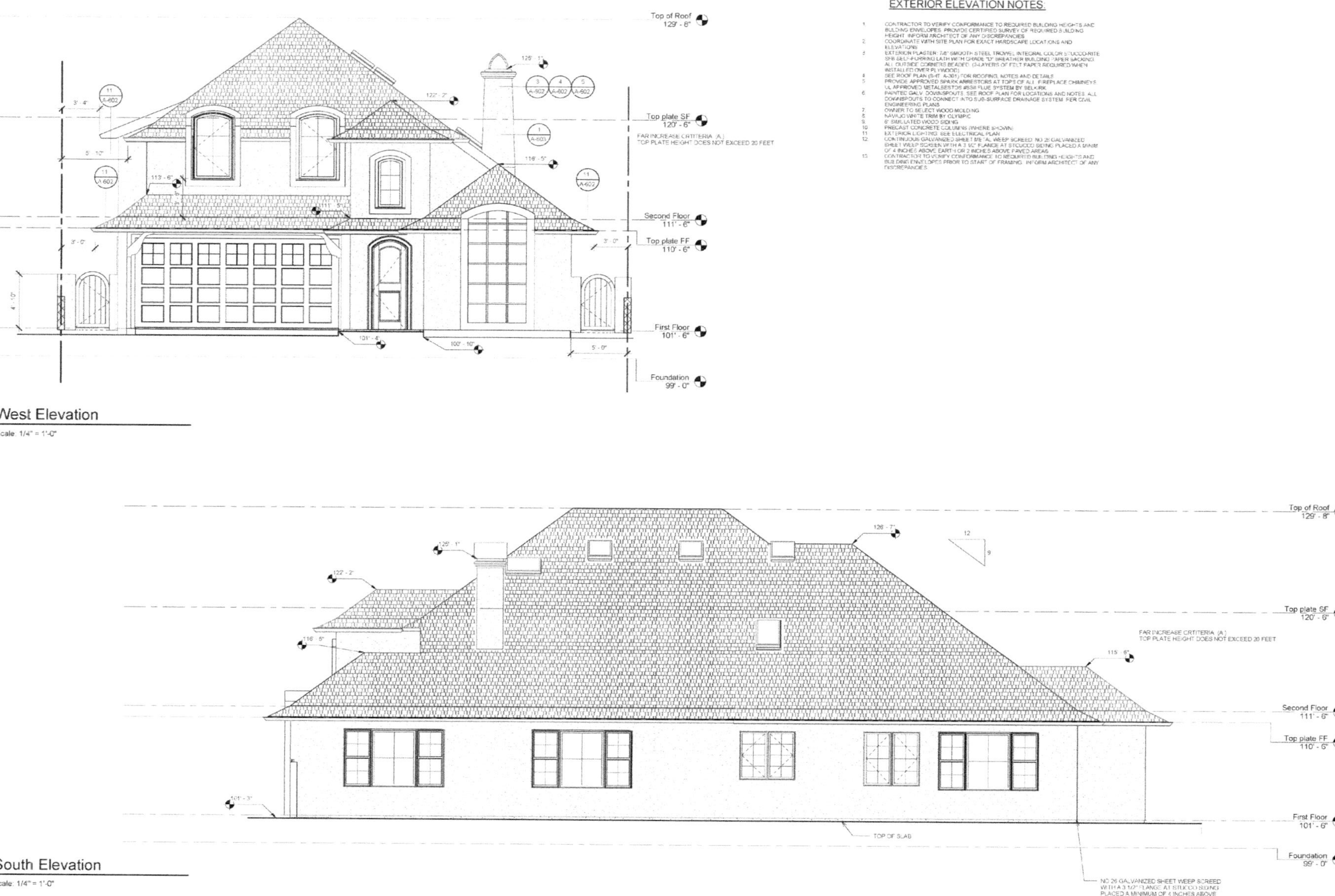

Figure 15.51 Elevations.

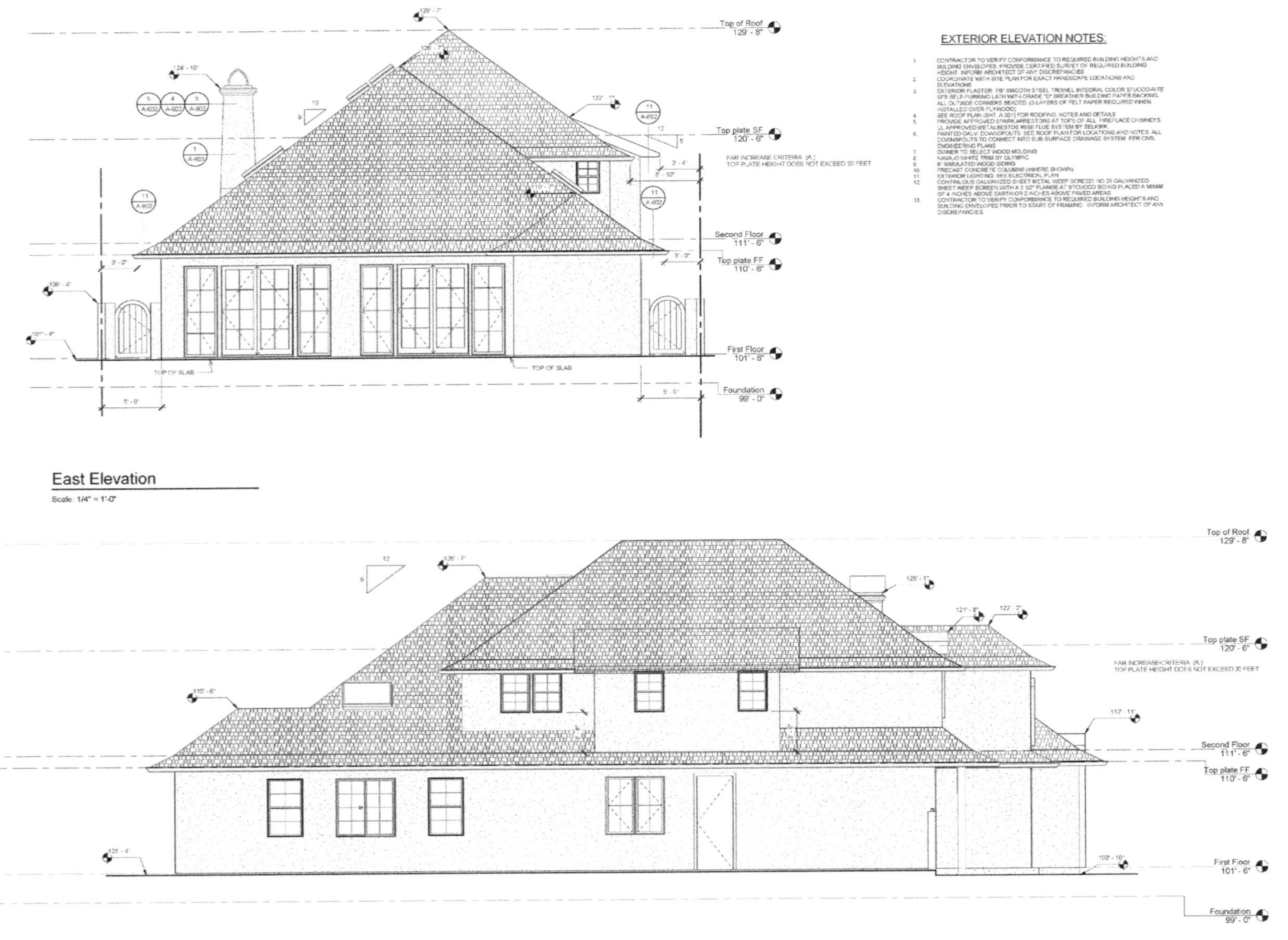

Figure 15.52 Elevation.

Figure 15.53 Sections.

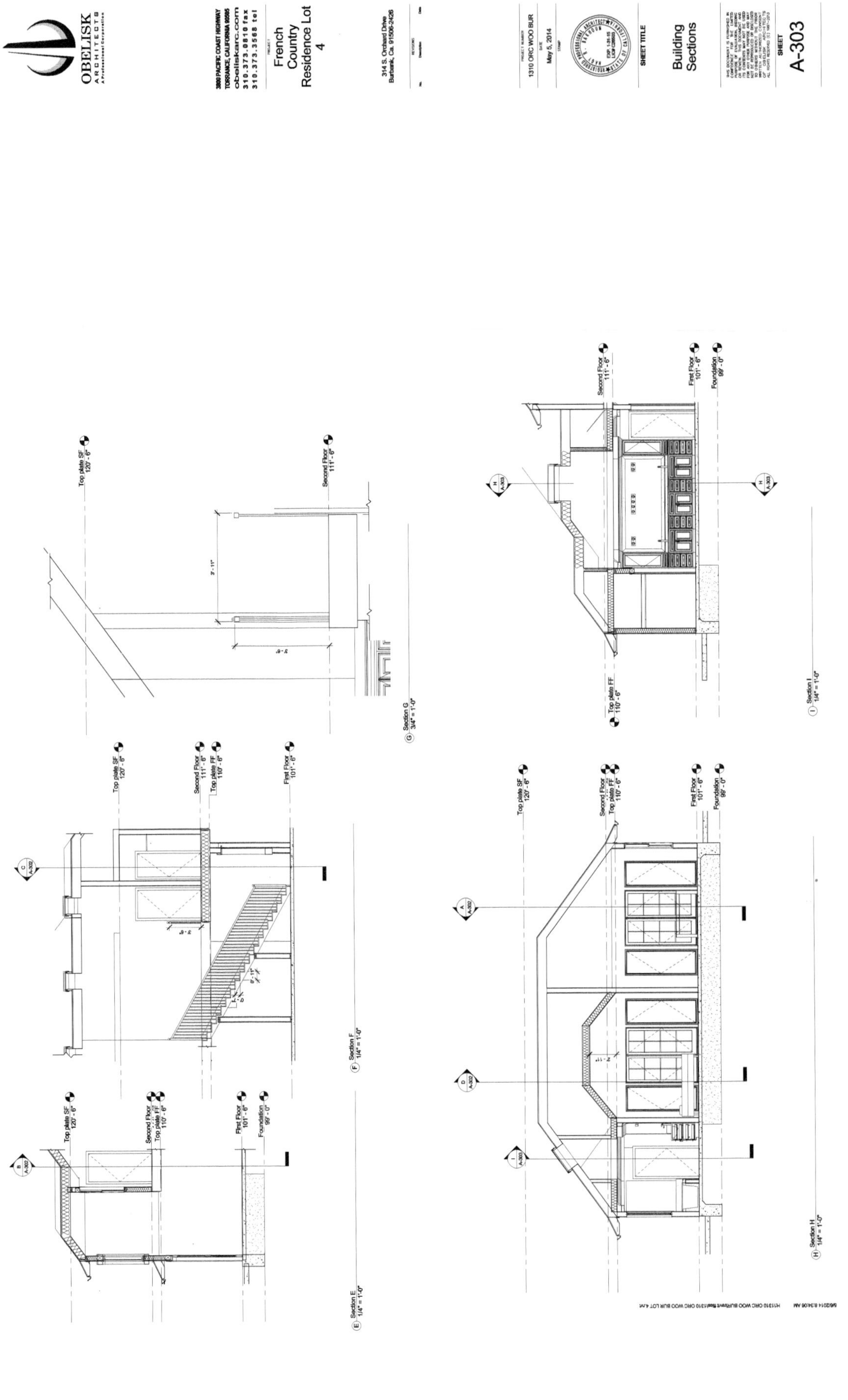

Figure 15.54 Sections.

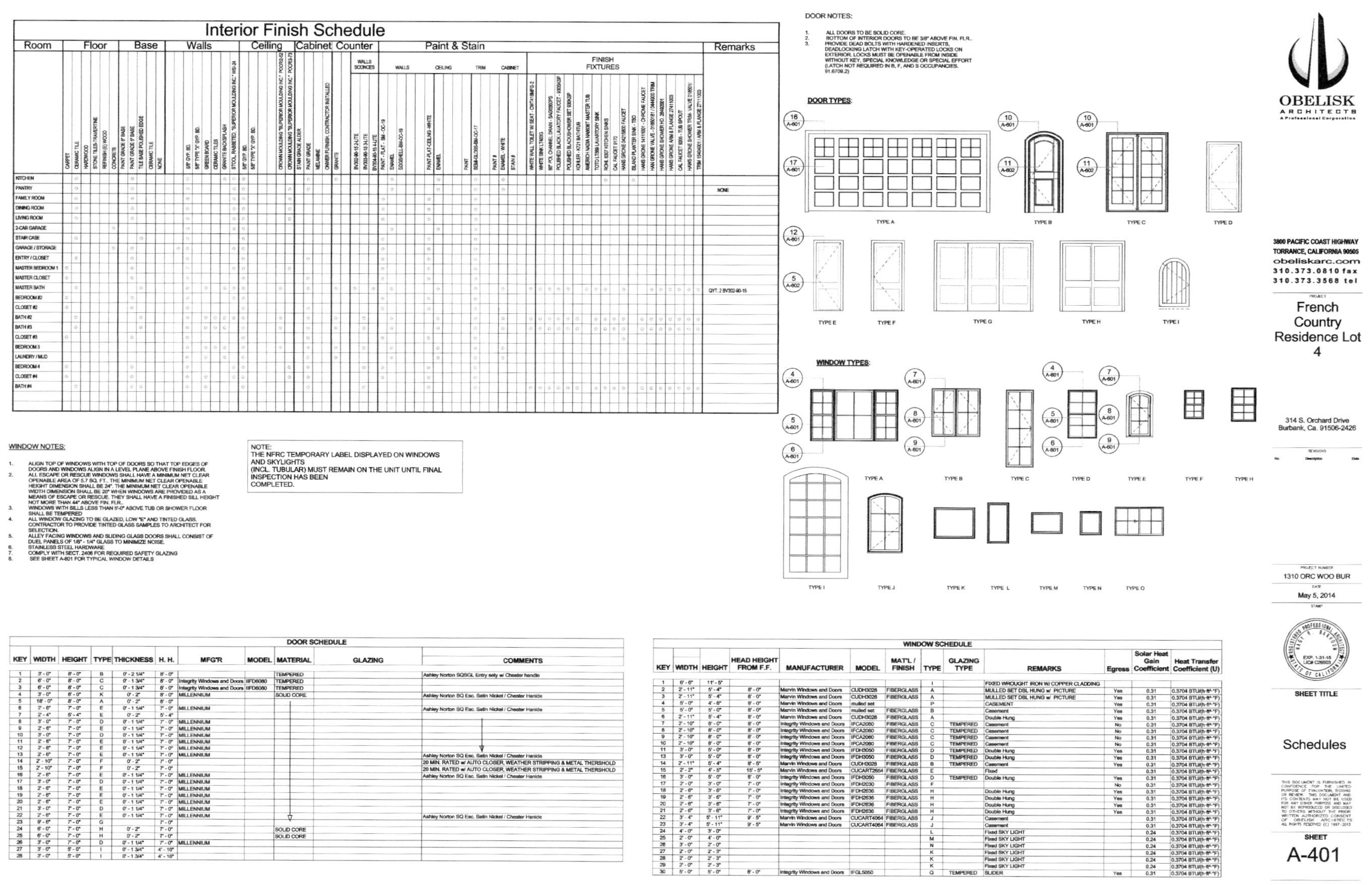

Figure 15.55 Schedule.

Figure 15.56 Interior elevations.

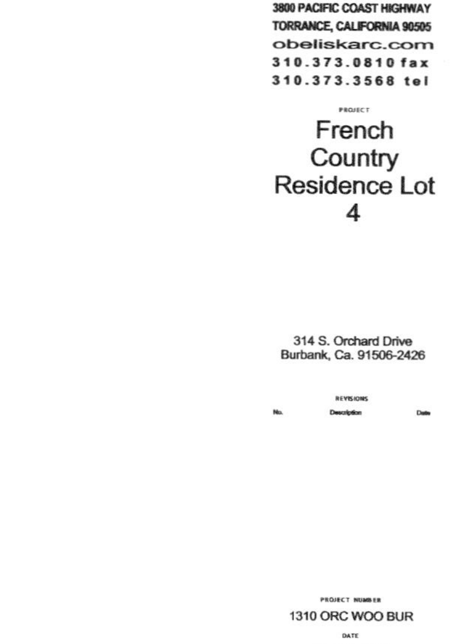

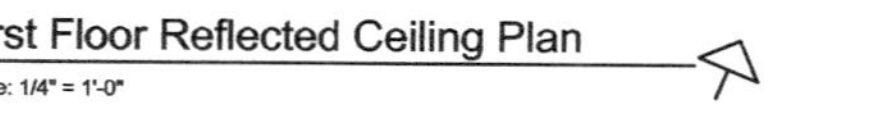
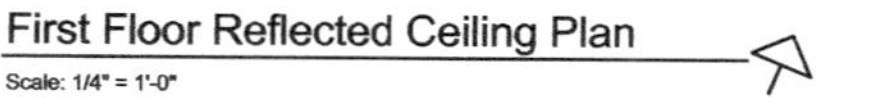

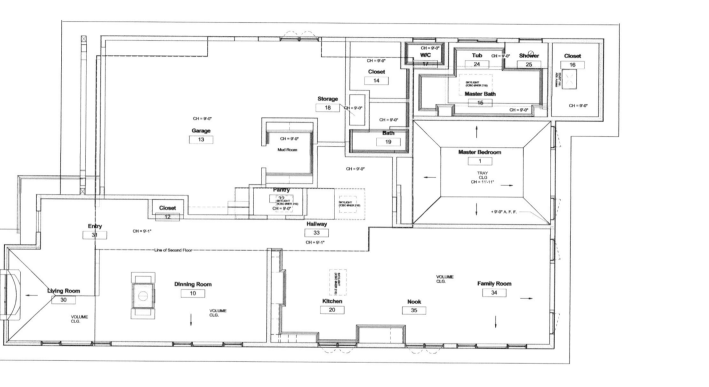

Figure 15.57 Reflected ceiling plan.

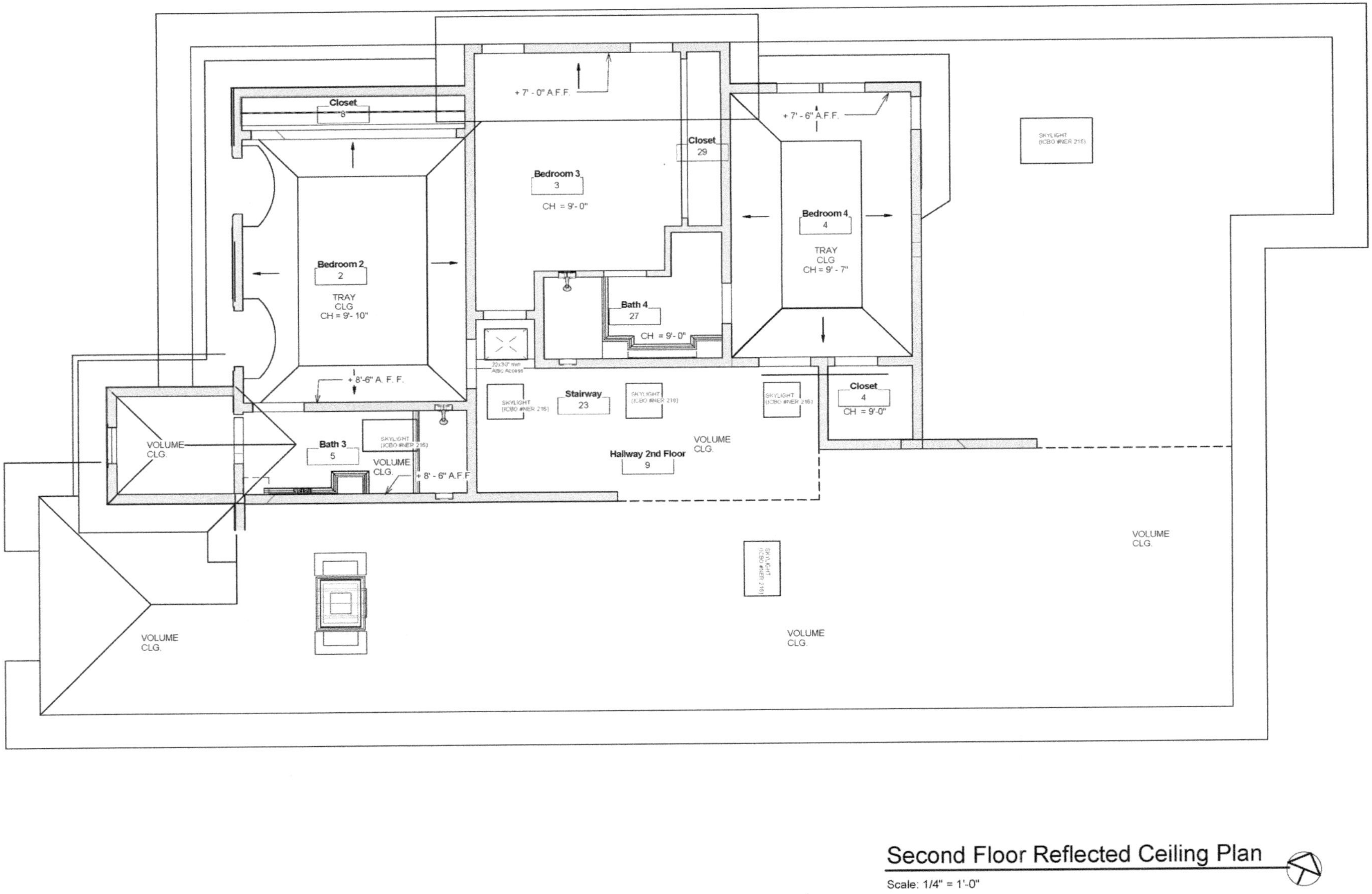

Second Floor Reflected Ceiling Plan

Scale: 1/4" = 1'-0"

Figure 15.58 Reflected ceiling plan.

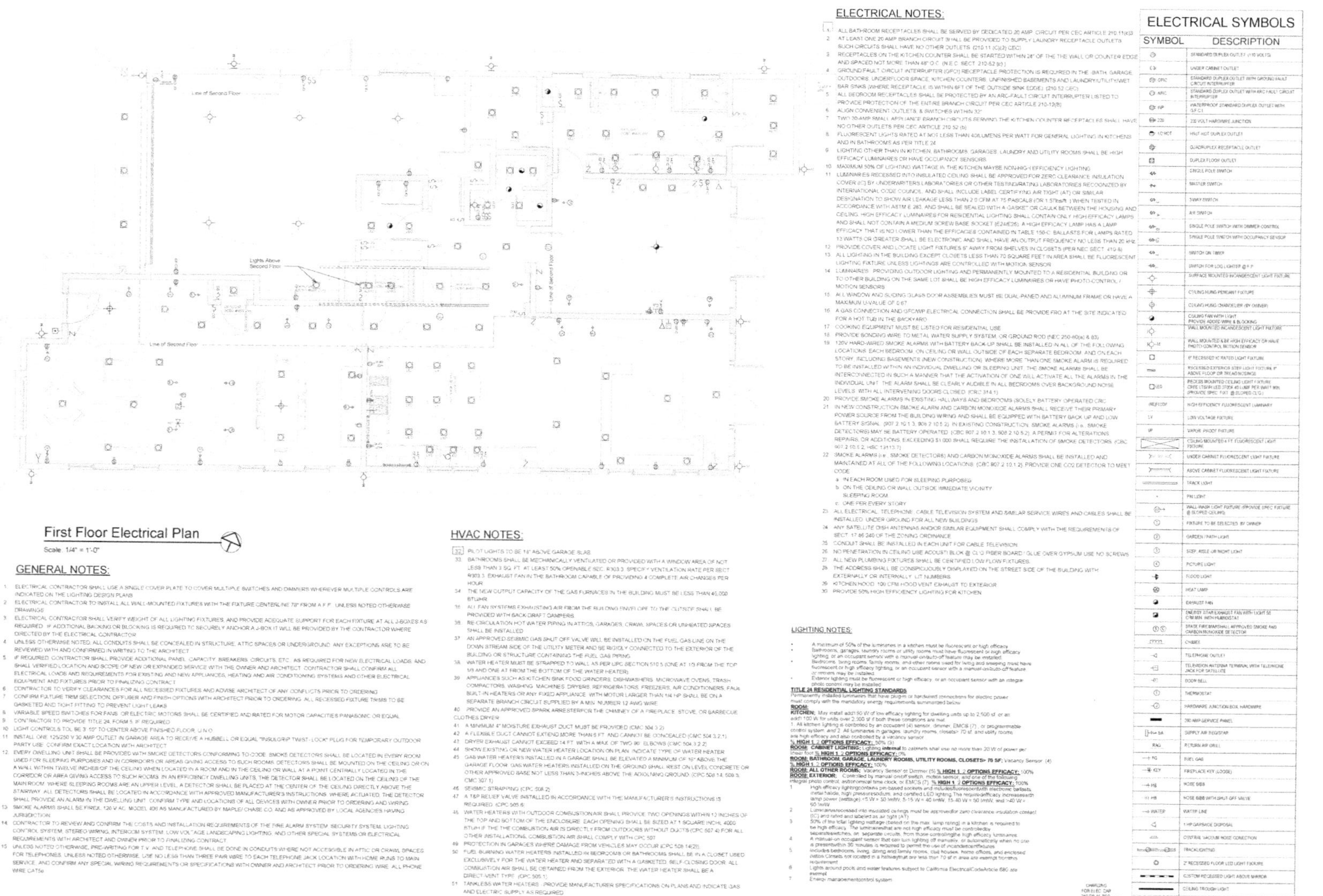

Figure 15.59 Electrical plan.

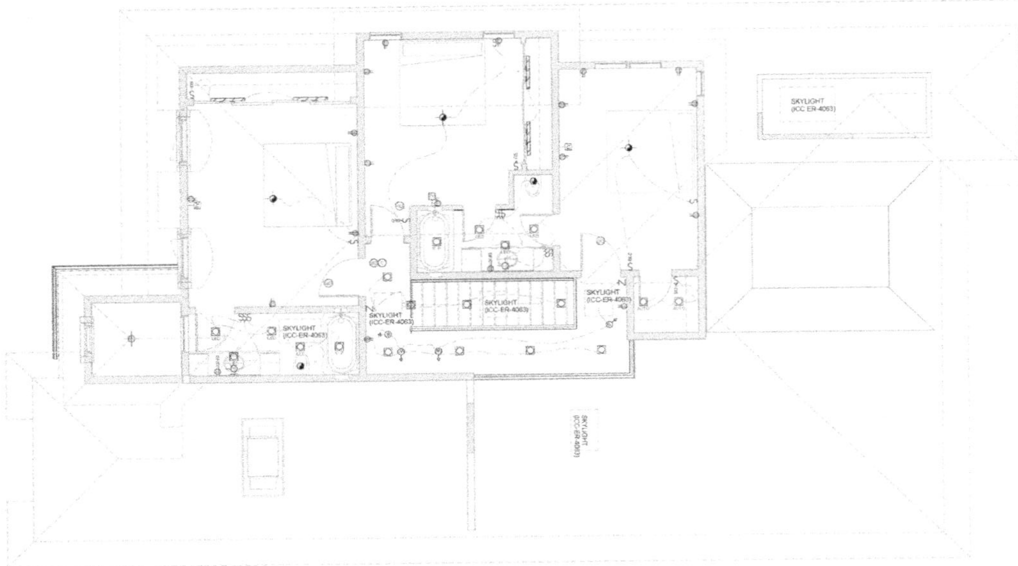

Figure 15.60 Electrical plan.

Figure 15.61 BIM rendering produced by software.

chapter

16

COMMERCIAL BUILDINGS

(Sonder Quest/Unsplash.com.)

The Professional Practice of Architectural Working Drawings, Sixth Edition. Nagy R. Bakhoum and Osamu A. Wakita.
© 2024 John Wiley & Sons Inc. Published 2024 by John Wiley & Sons Inc.
Companion website: www.wiley.com\go\bakhoum\theprofessionalpracticeofarchitecturalworkingdrawings

■ PROGRAM, SITE, AND SD

The client required a theater building with six separate auditoriums of 200 seats each. The sloping site of approximately three acres also had stringent architectural restrictions.

The proposed structure, with six auditoriums, office, restrooms, and storage and food areas, required approximately 26,000 square feet. The seating area dictated the required on-site parking for 260 automobiles.

To satisfy fire requirements, the primary building materials selected were structural steel and concrete block. The concrete block was chosen because it also would provide an excellent sound barrier between the auditoriums and the lobby.

The initial concept provided for three auditoriums on each side of a central service core, which would contain the lobby, toilet facilities, food bar, and storage areas. The core would provide controlled circulation and access to the auditoriums, facilities, and required fire exits. Efficient arrangements for the 200 seats and fire code requirements governed the auditorium dimensions. The wall dimensions also had to be compatible with the concrete-block module. The upper floor level would contain the projection rooms, the manager's office, an employee toilet, and additional storage rooms. The stair location for this upper area was also governed by fire department and building code design criteria.

■ DD AND CD

The checklist for this theater project was based on the site and the client requirements. It included notes on all sorts of matters, as well as design possibilities, ideas, and reminders as follows:

- Walk the site with the client.
- Egress and ingress available only from the west.
- Best location on the site for parking on the south side.
- Two traffic lanes at 90°.
- Explore desirable areas for lobbies, exit stairs, utilities, and trash areas.
- Establish locations of supporting steel columns.
- Locate disability parking per ADA requirements.
- Locate ice bank cooling system.
- Second-floor load versus required stairs, restrooms, and potential location for mechanical ducts.
- Add third floor and revise square footage.
- Verify exact position of steel columns in relationship to third floor.
- Include stairs for roof access.
- Explore different types of windows and finishes.
- Consult structural engineers early for:
  - Circular opening
  - Shear walls to relieve starkness of solid walls
  - Continuing curvilinear walls
  - Shape and mass of the sculptured concrete element around columns
- Explore and decide on exterior surface materials for curvilinear walls.

Stage I

The irregularly shaped site had a west-to-east crossfall averaging 22′ from the lowest to the highest grade. See Figure 16.1. Complicating the site further was a 25′-wide utility easement located near the center of the site. We could not build any of the structure in this easement.

Stage II

The initial schematic site study, shown in Figure 16.2, depicts the structure located north of the utility easement on the upper portion of the site. We thought this location would provide the most suitable parking layout for access to the theater, as well as a higher floor elevation for site drainage. The site entrance for automobiles is from the east property line only.

Stage III

After the schematic site development was completed, we designed the scaled preliminary first-floor plan (Figure 16.3) and preliminary parking layouts. Client requirements determined the first-level floor plan. Parking layouts and automobile circulation were designed to be compatible with the natural topography of the site; we paralleled the parking stalls and driveways with the existing grades. We also terraced the parking levels. This reduced the amount of rough and finish grading to be done. Stairs, as well as ramps for disabled persons, were provided at the front of the theater.

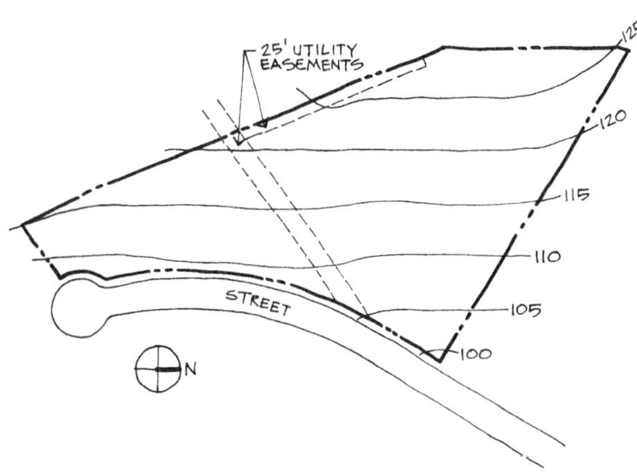

Figure 16.1 Clay Theater—preliminary site plan.

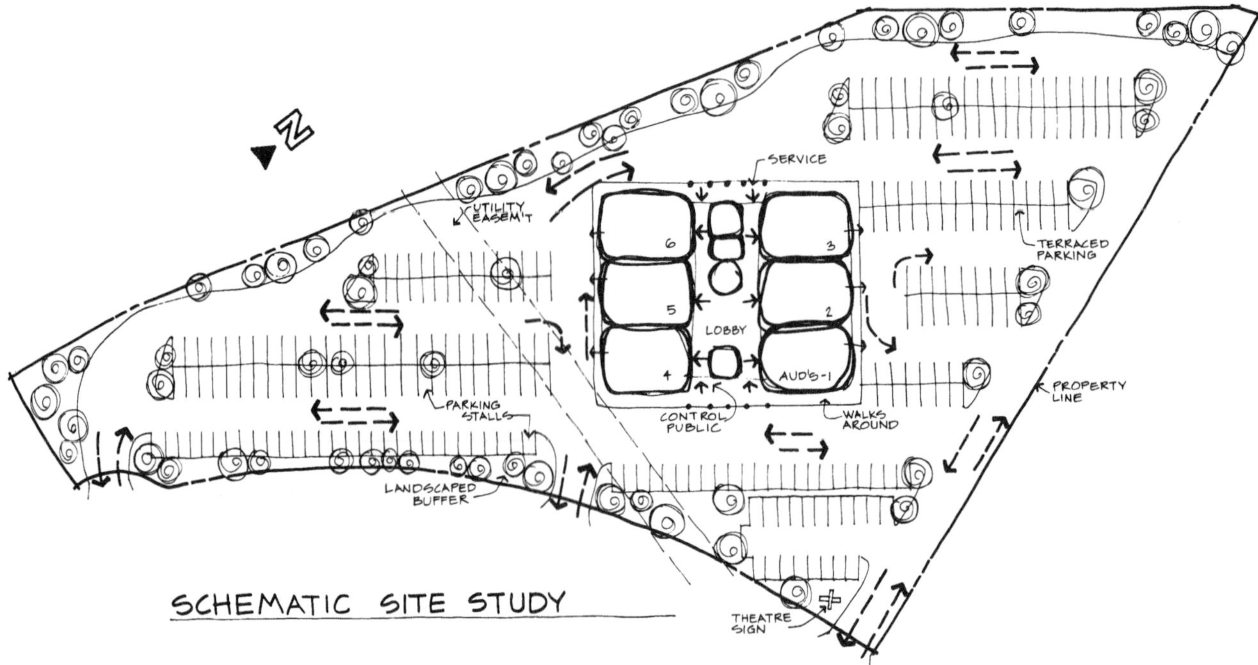

Figure 16.2 Clay Theater—schematic site study.

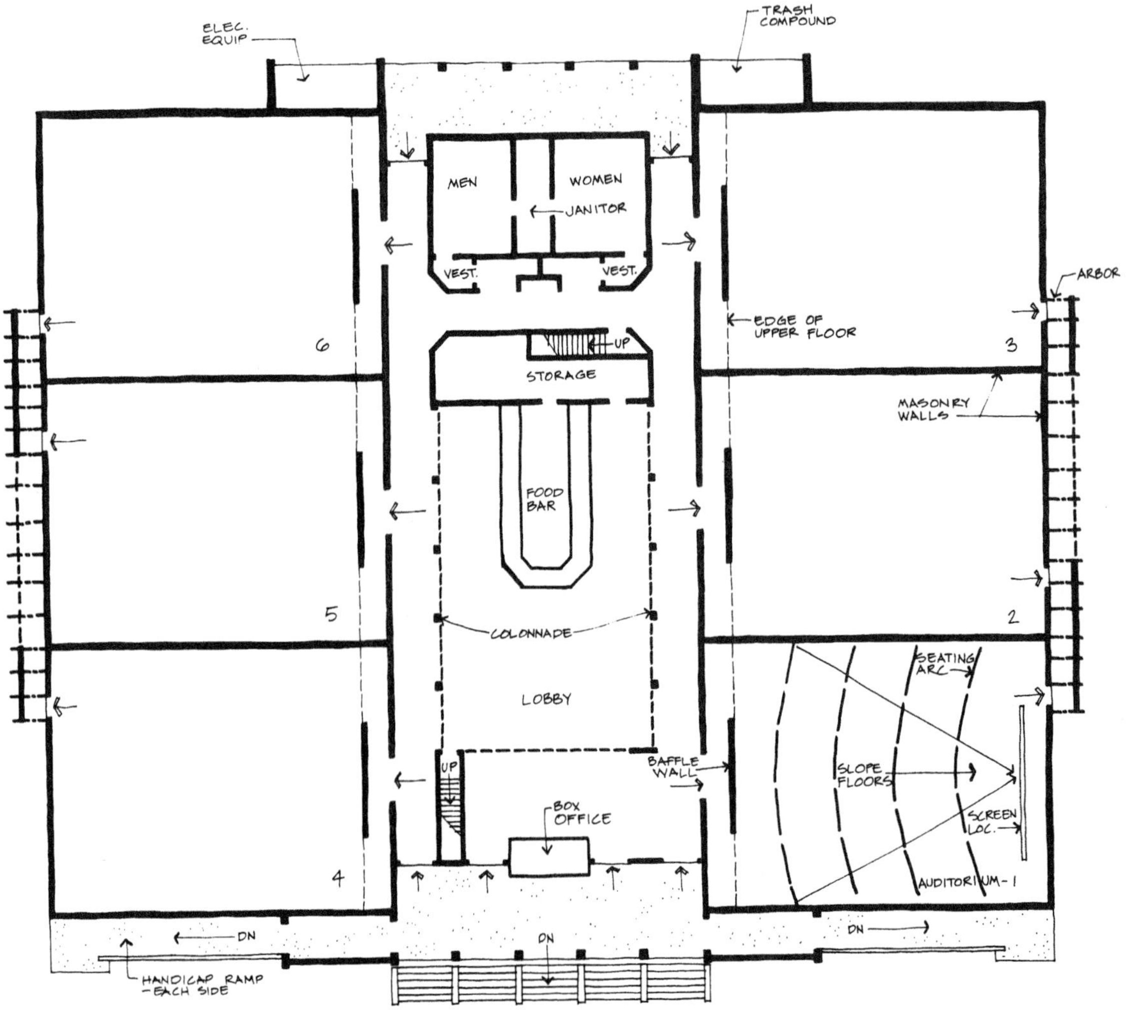

Figure 16.3 Clay Theater—preliminary ground-floor plan.

Stage IV

From the scaled preliminary first-floor plan, we made overlay studies of the second floor. Correct projector port locations for each auditorium, and required exit locations, determined the second-floor design. Other spaces and their locations were more flexible. See Figure 16.4.

Stage V

Buildings in the area where this theater is located are subject to the jurisdiction of an architectural review committee, with written criteria dictating exterior appearances and materials. One of these restrictions stated that the roof must be of mission tile with a minimum pitch of 4 in 12. Another requirement was that all roof-mounted mechanical equipment must be shielded from view. By providing the required sloping roof planes over the auditoriums and the rear and front lobby access, we created a well that would screen the roof-mounted heating and ventilating equipment.

For aesthetic reasons, we decided to soften the façade of the building by breaking up the long exterior blank walls at the rear of the auditoriums. We added a heavy timber arbor to provide shadows on the blank walls. See Figure 16.5A. The arbor stain and general design were chosen to be compatible with the mission tile. To provide an acceptable finish, we covered the concrete block with a plaster finish. To enhance the exterior and further define the design elements, as well as to fulfill building department requirements, we added concrete columns in the colonnade. Instead of using three-dimensional drawings for presentation, a conceptual model was constructed, defining the general massing of the building as well as major architectural features. This model is shown in Figure 16.5B. An aerial photo of the completed site is shown in Figure 16.6.

The various stages of the working drawings can be found in Chapters 7–11. In this portion of the text,

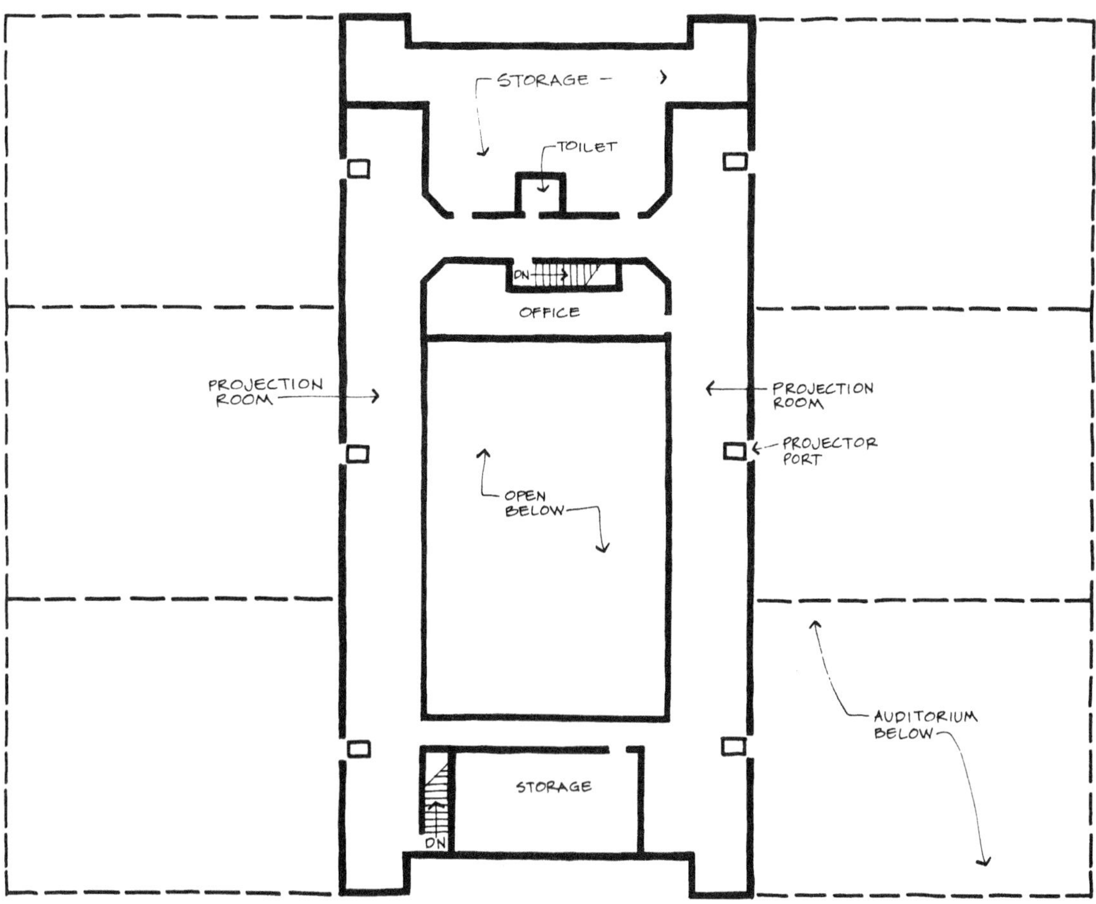

Figure 16.4 Clay Theater—preliminary upper-floor plan.

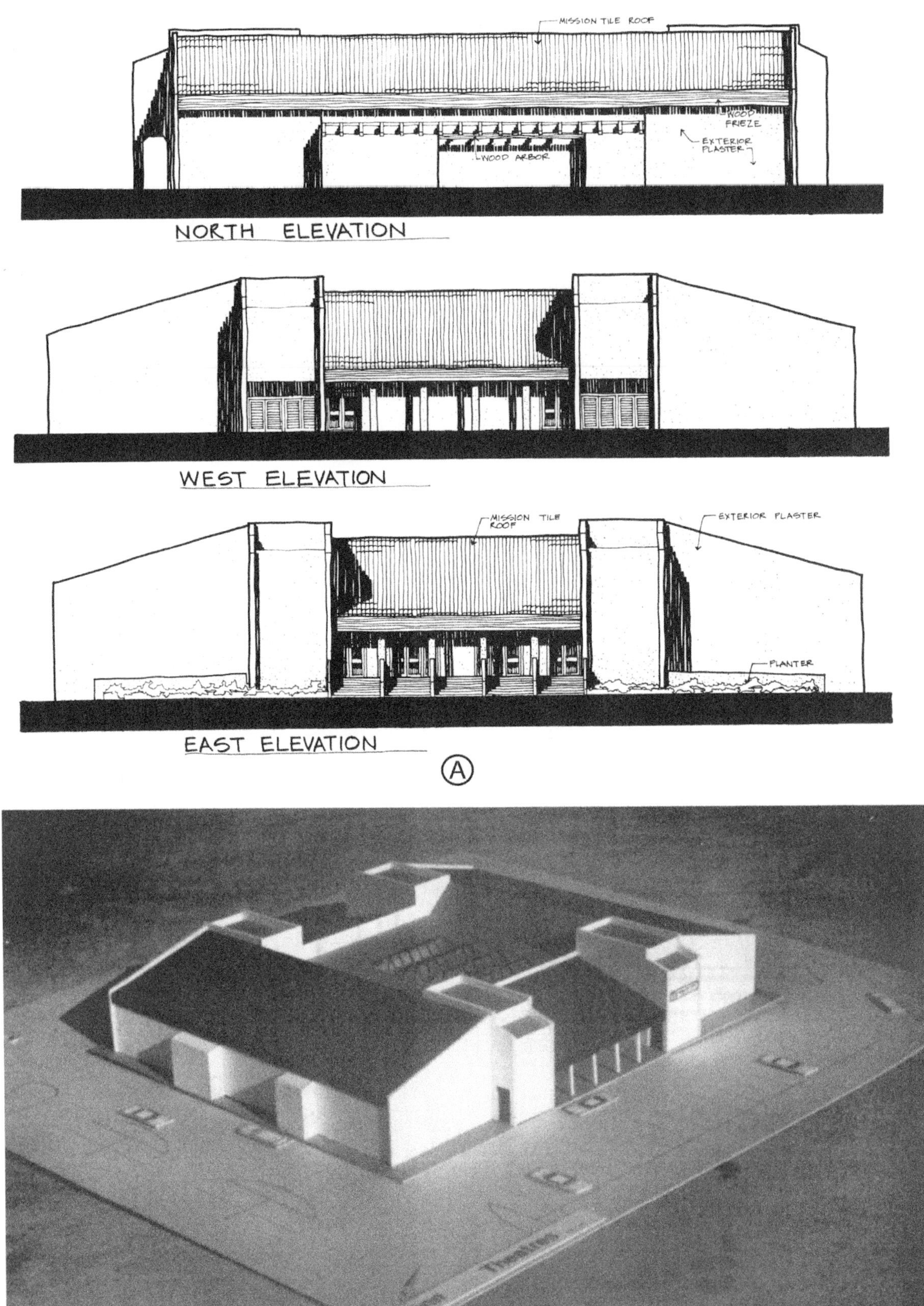

B

Figure 16.5 Clay Theater—A. Preliminary exterior elevations. B. Conceptual model.

Figure 16.6 Aerial photo of finished site. (Courtesy of William Boggs Aerial Photography, reproduced with permission.)

you will only find the last stage of the working drawings. Check Figure 16.7 for the final stage of the site plan working drawing, and Figure 16.8, which shows a portion of the grading plan to reveal water flow control. See Figures 16.9–16.15 for final stages of the working drawings.

■ MARGAUX—MASONRY BUILDING CD

The masonry building is an existing building that is being renovated. Masonry has many advantages, one of which is strength to apply a new skin to significantly change the image of the building. See Figures 16.16–16.23.

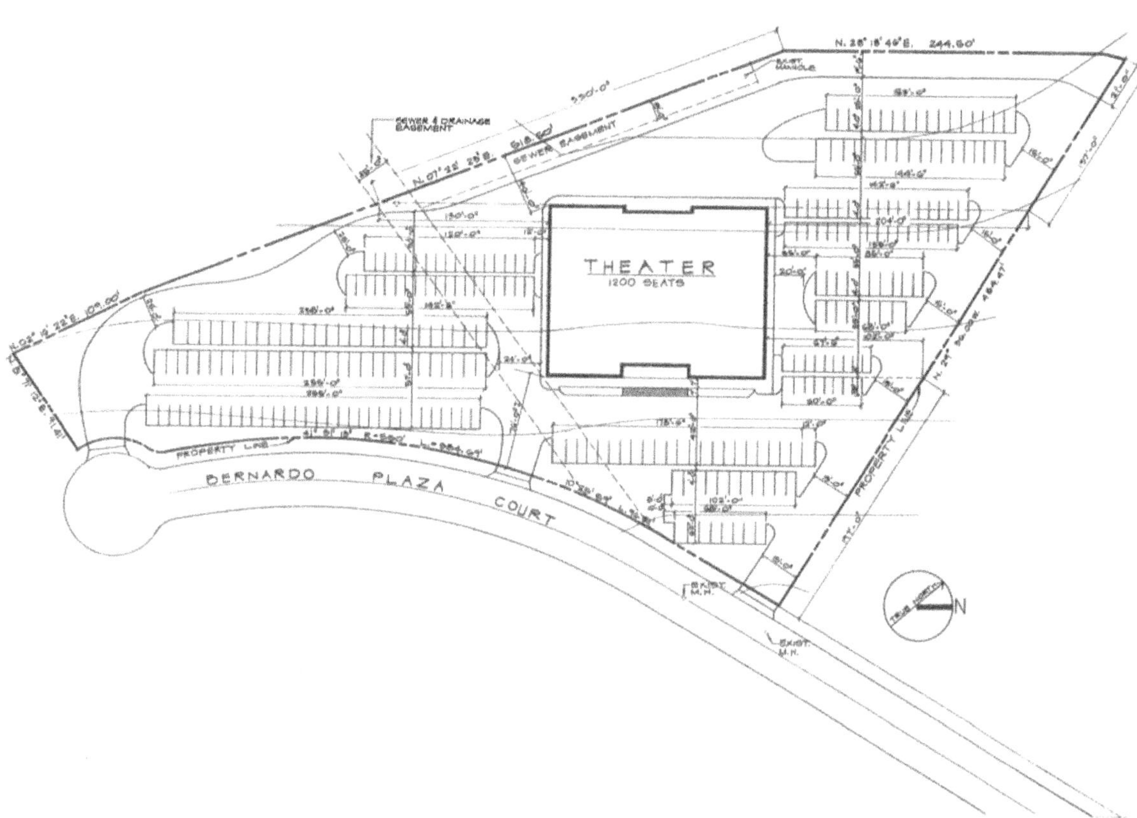

Figure 16.7 Clay Theater—final stage of site plan.

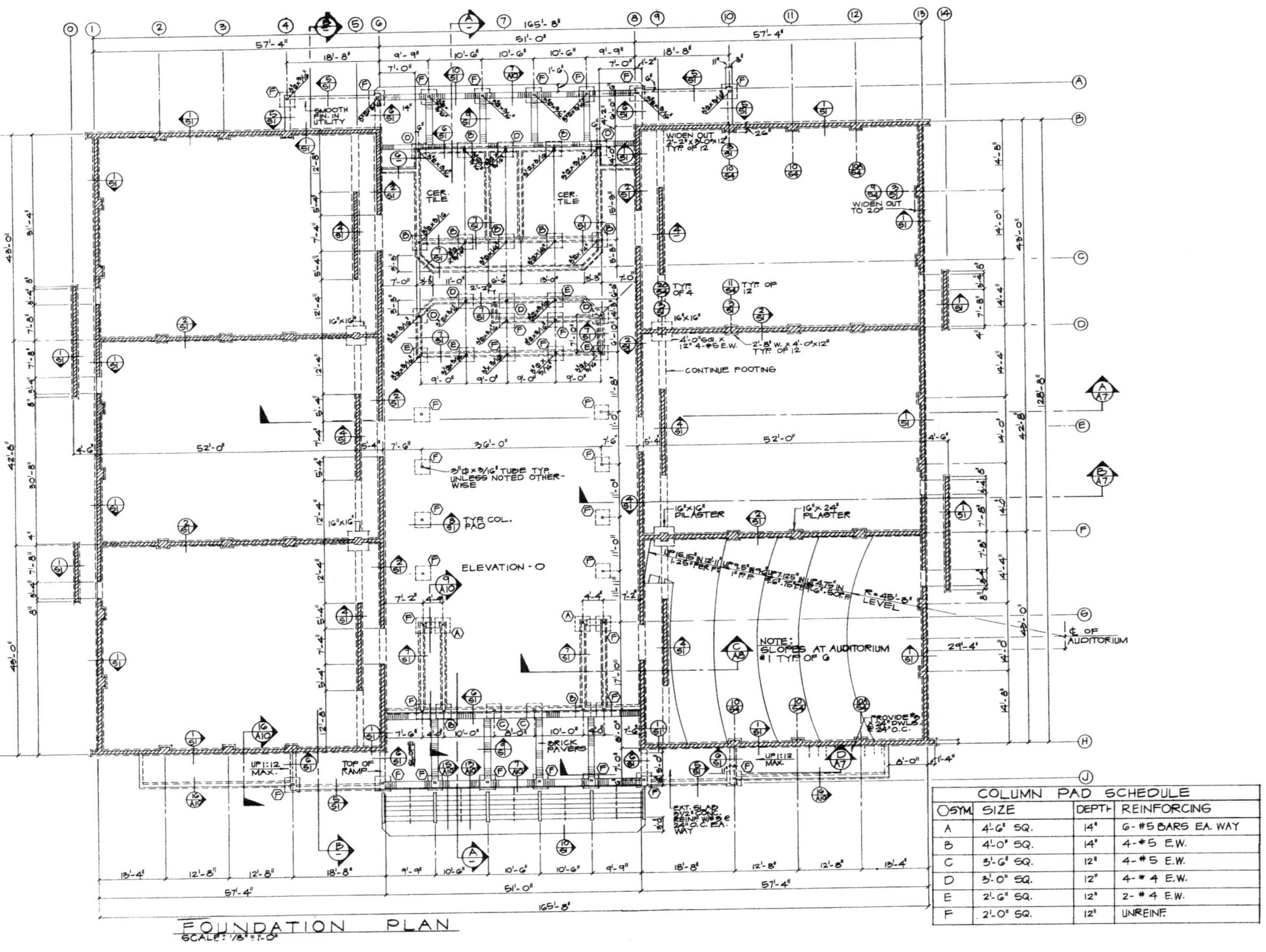

Figure 16.8 Enlargement of site/grading plan to reveal water flow control detail.

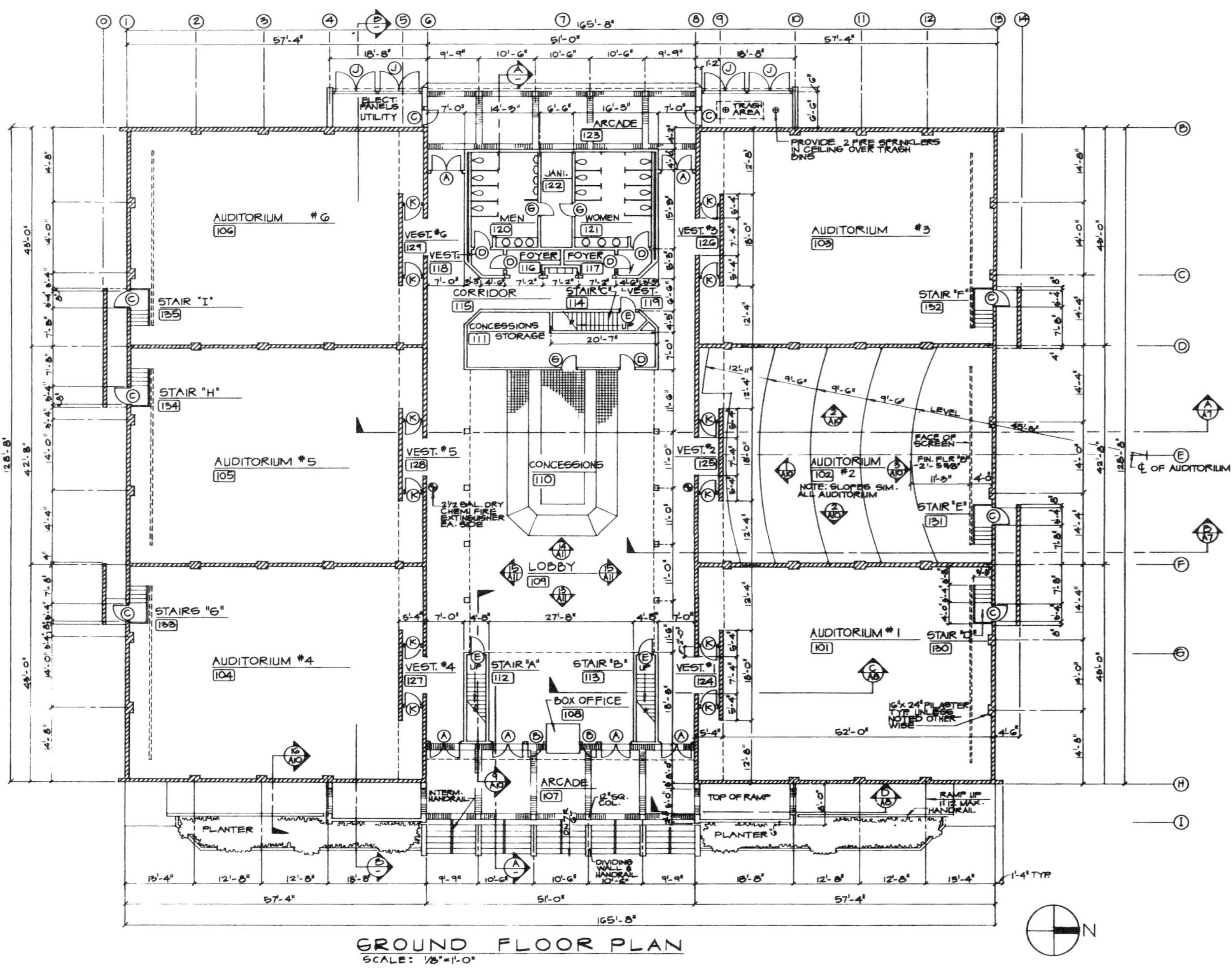

Figure 16.9 Final-stage working drawing—foundation plan.

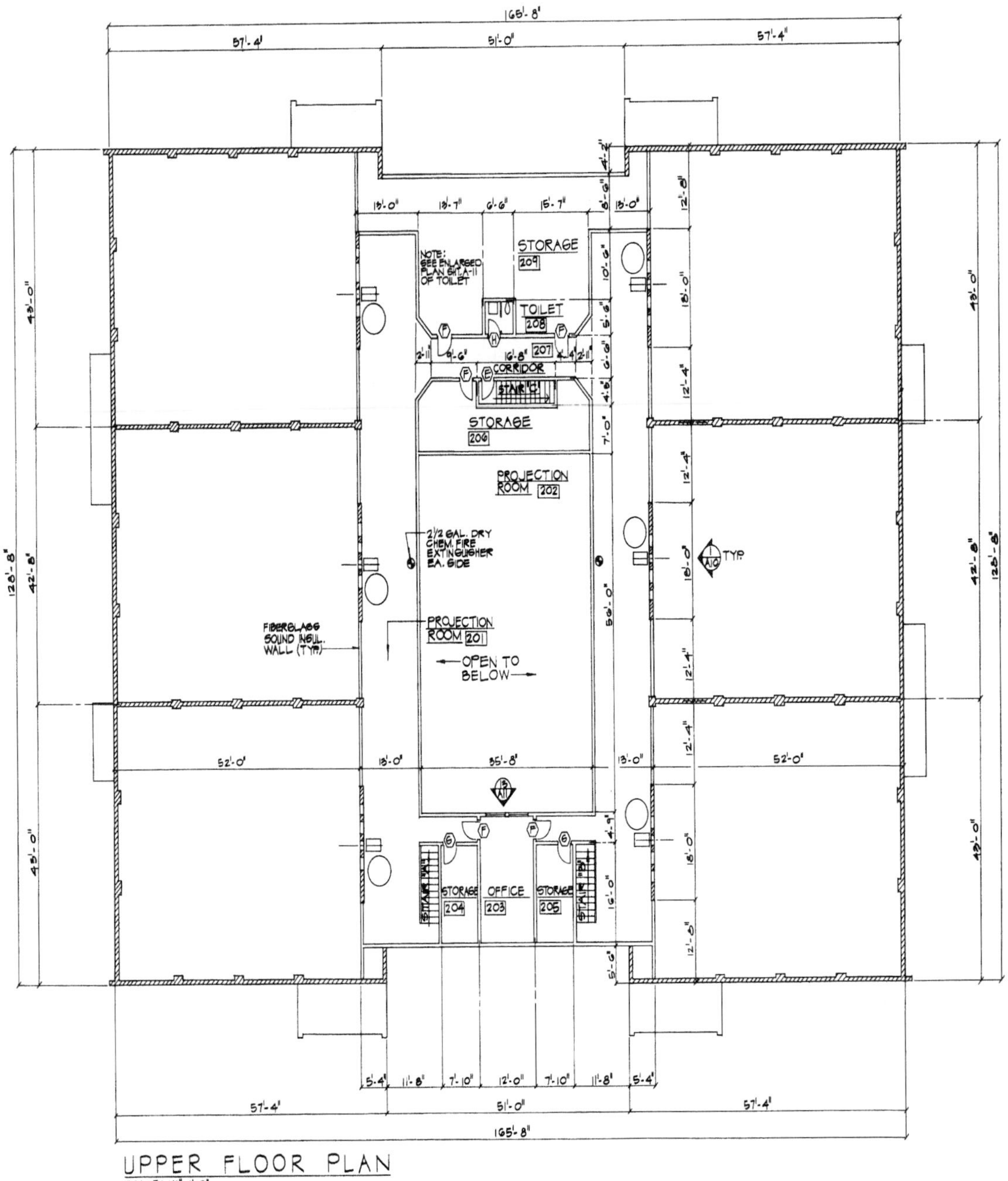

Figure 16.10 Final-stage working drawing—ground-floor plan, or elevations.

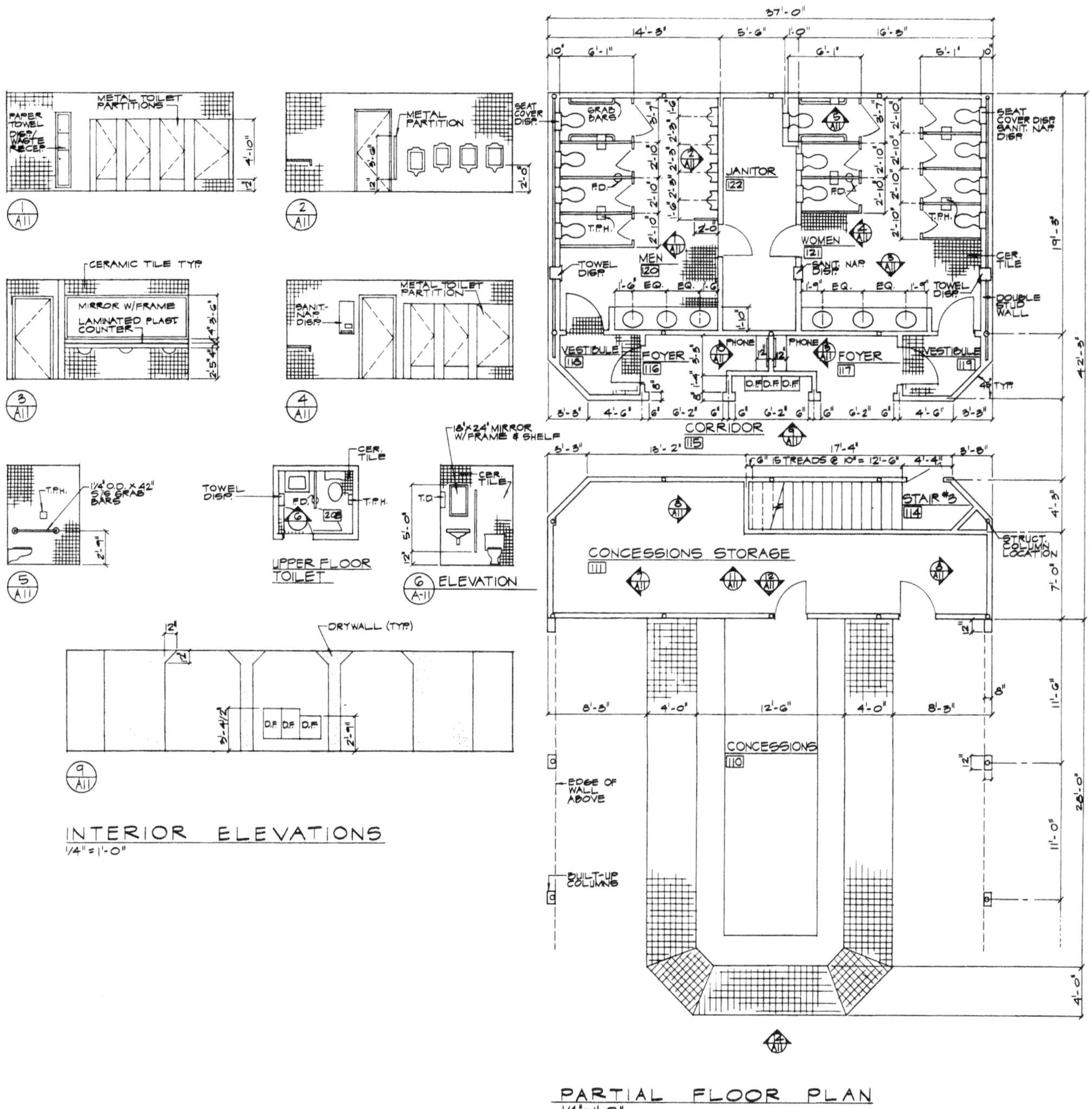

Figure 16.11 Final-stage working drawing—partial floor plan and interior elevations.

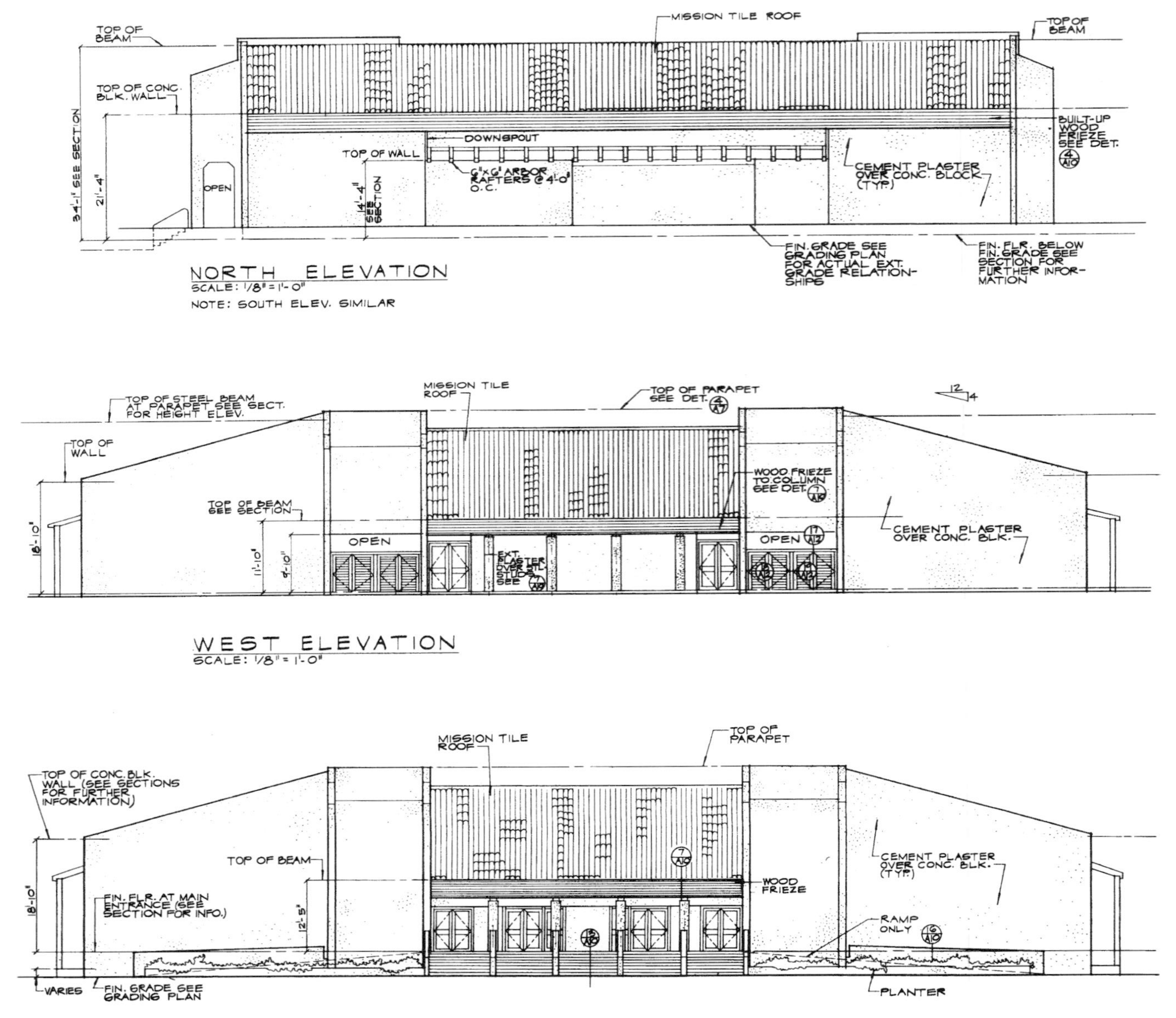

Figure 16.12 Final-stage working drawing—exterior elevations.

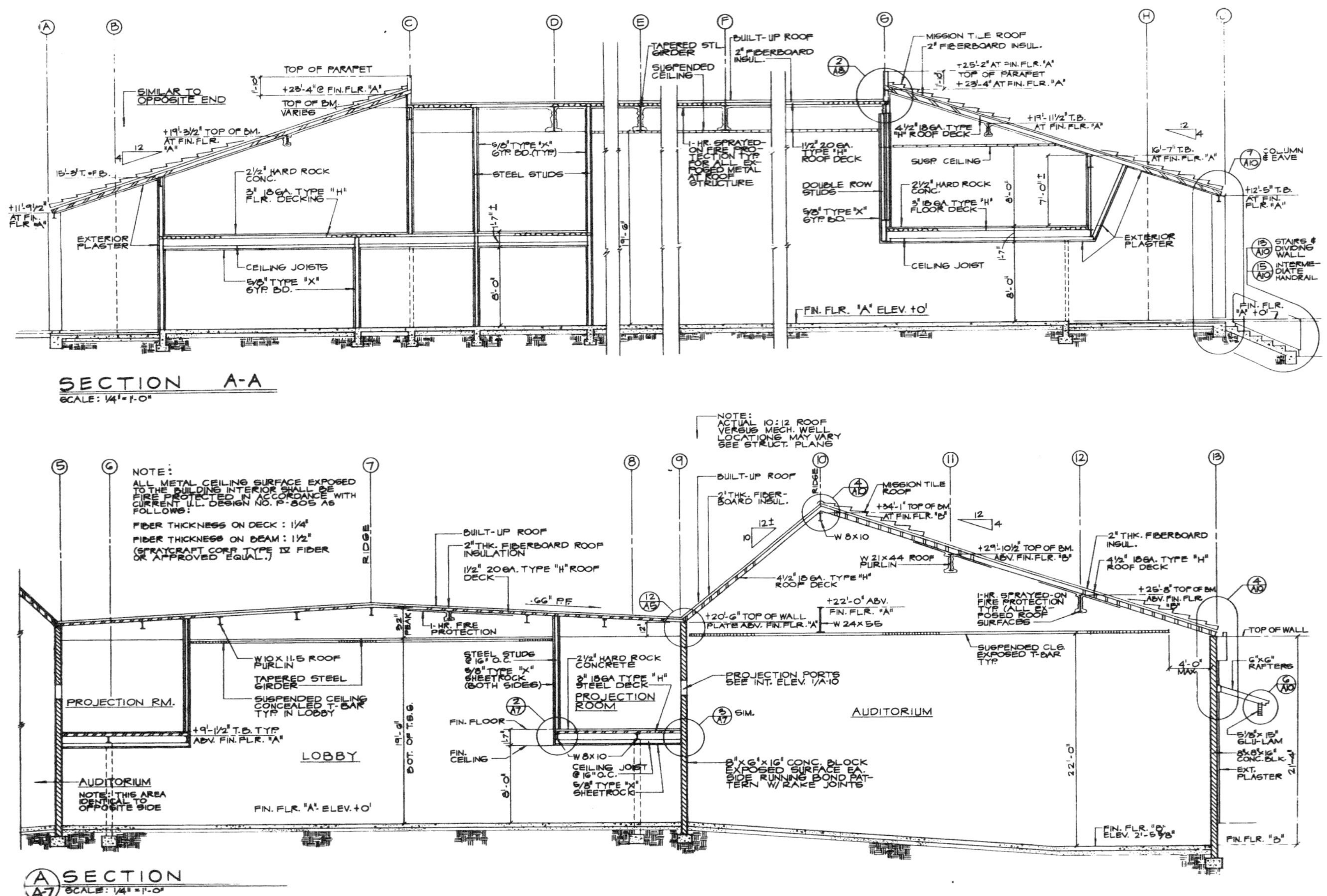

Figure 16.13 Final-stage working drawing—building sections.

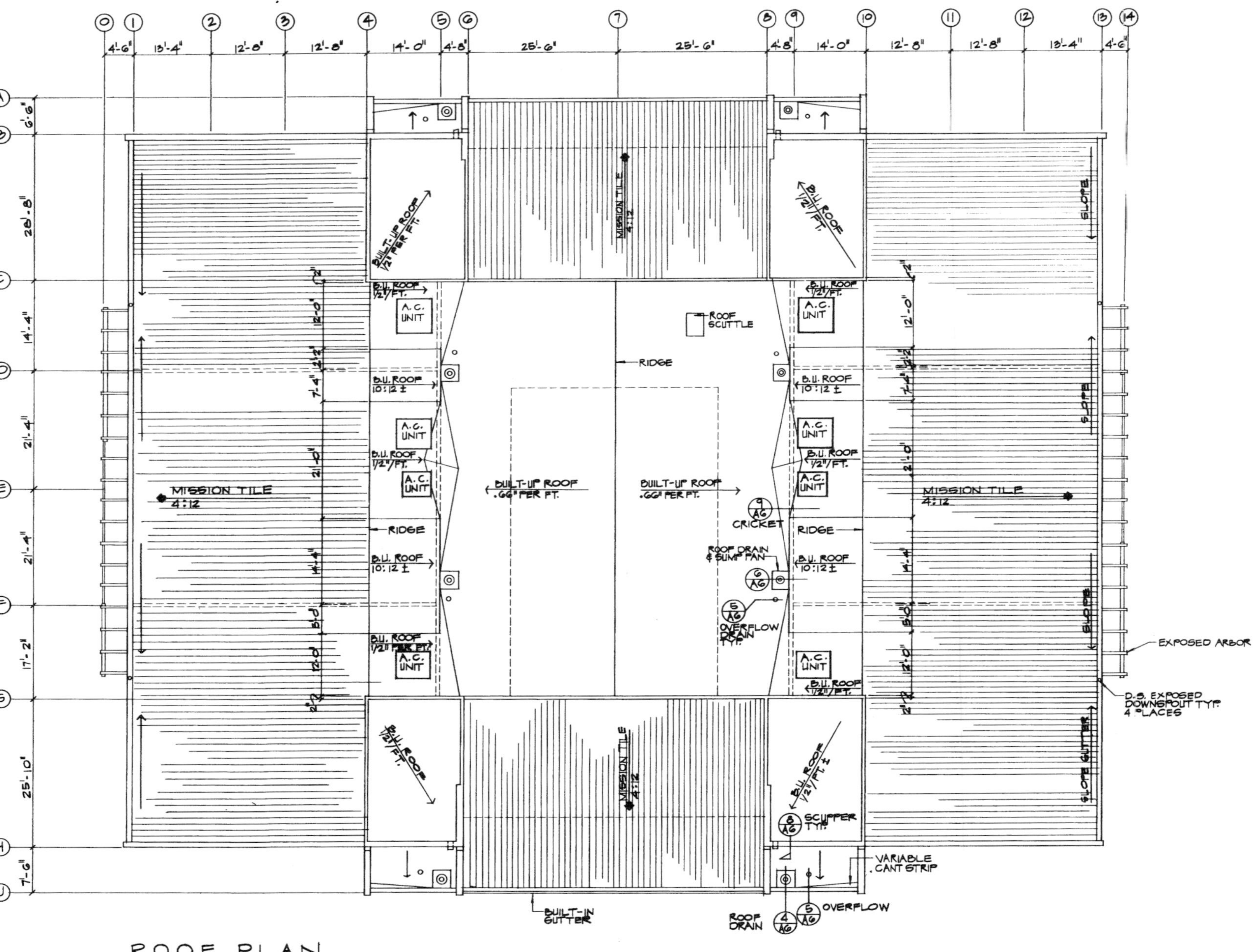

Figure 16.14 Final-stage working drawing—roof plan.

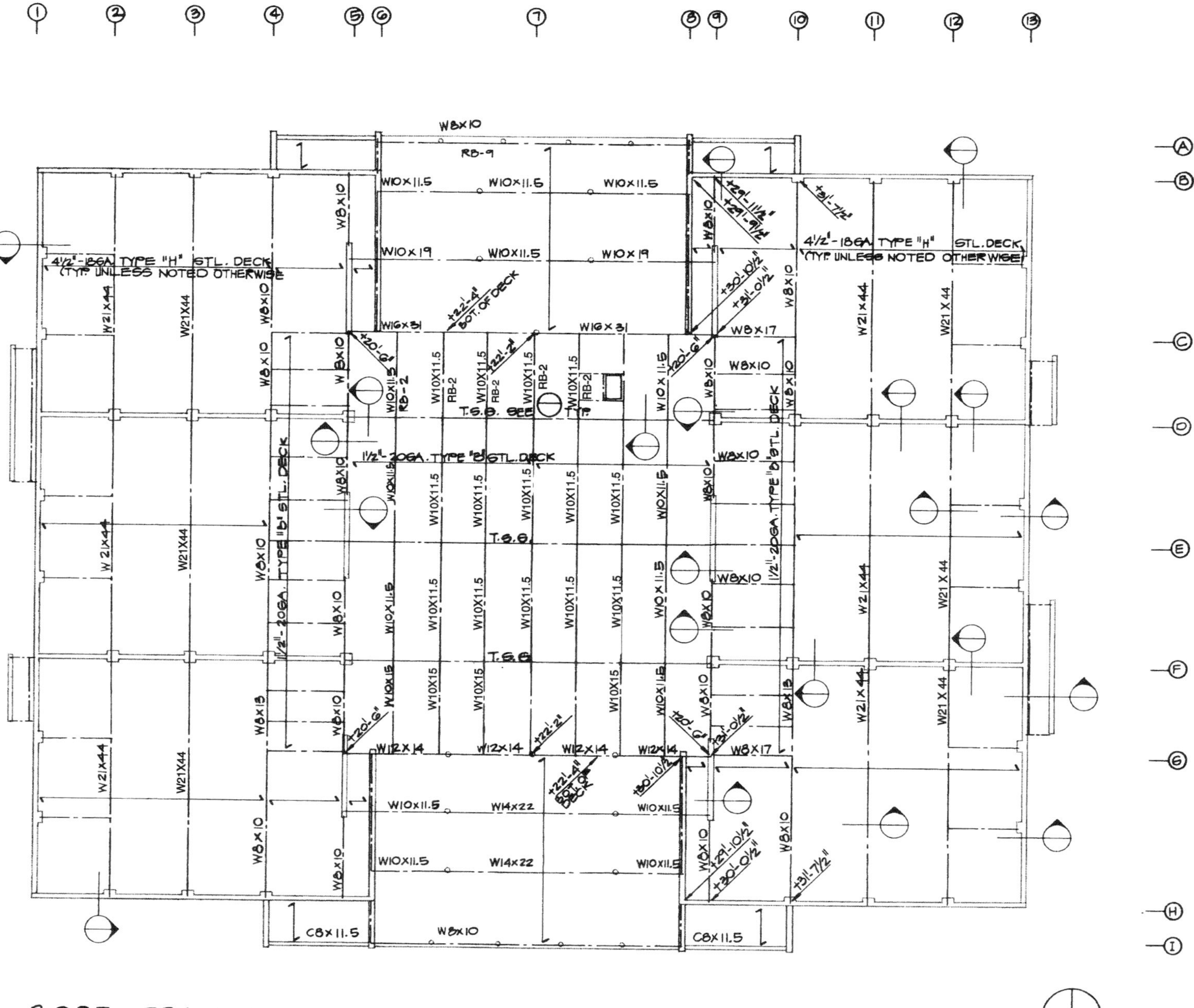

Figure 16.15 Final-stage working drawing—roof framing plan.

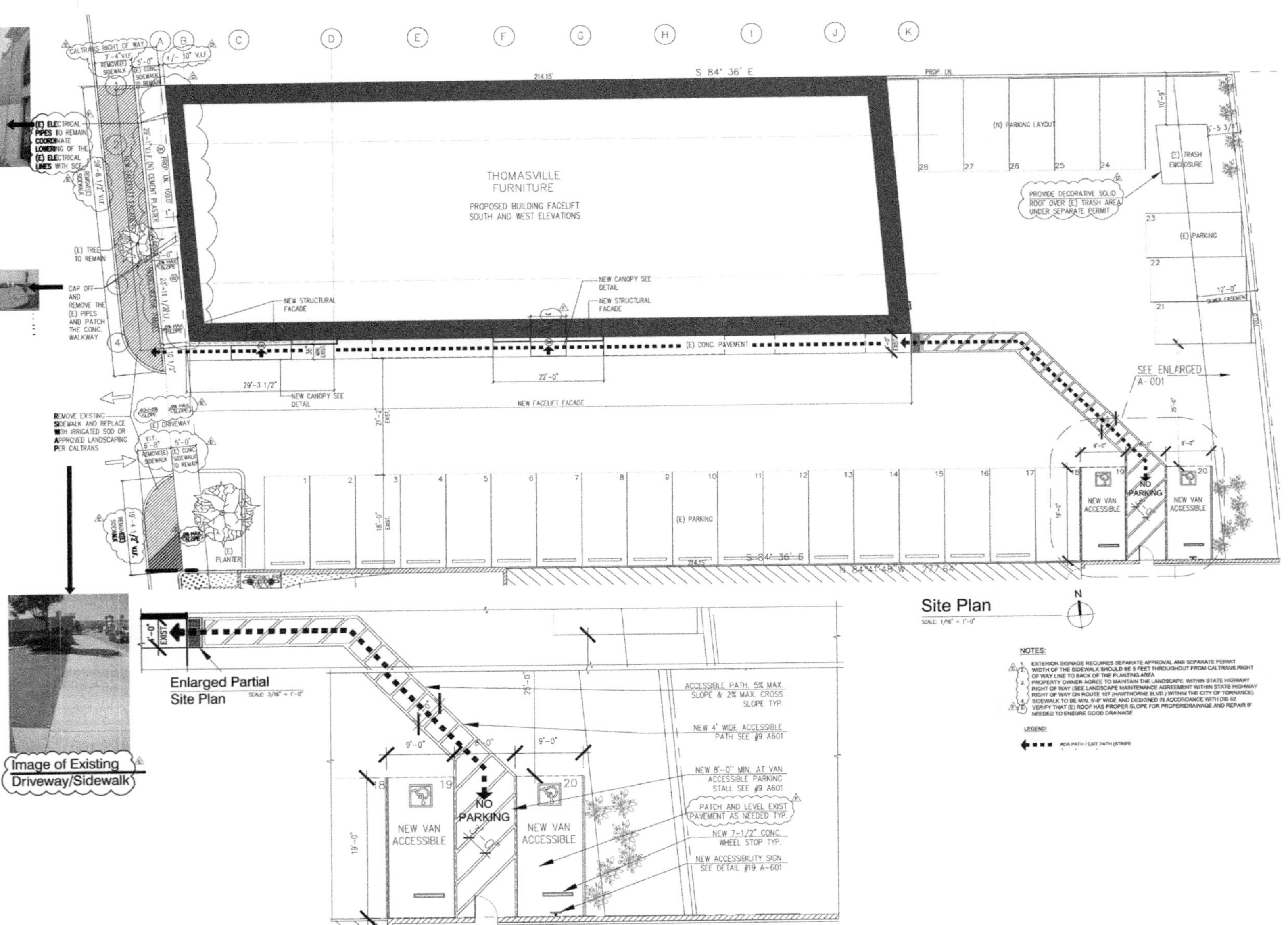

Figure 16.16 Site plan for the Margaux masonry building.

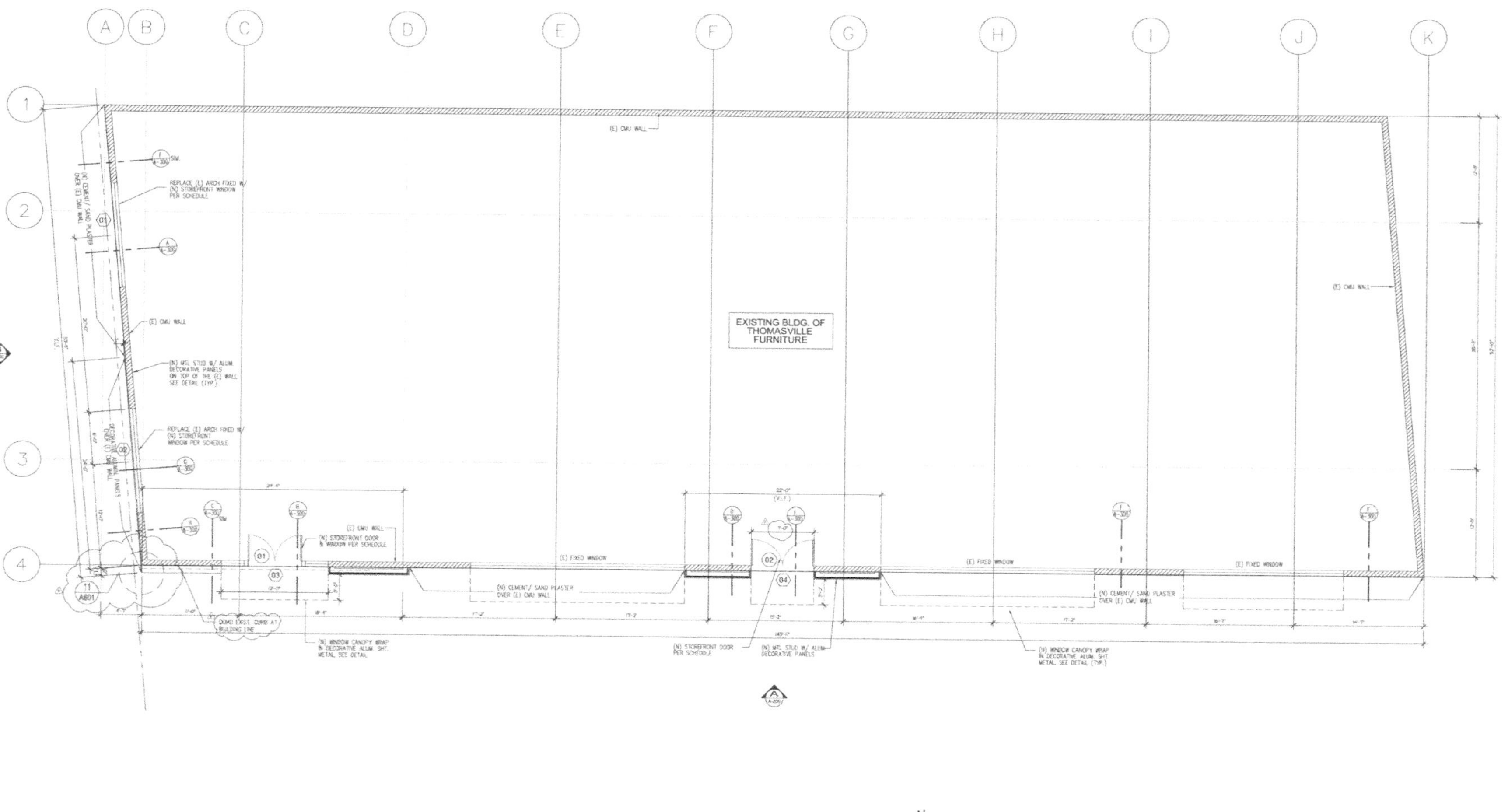

Figure 16.17 Floor plan.

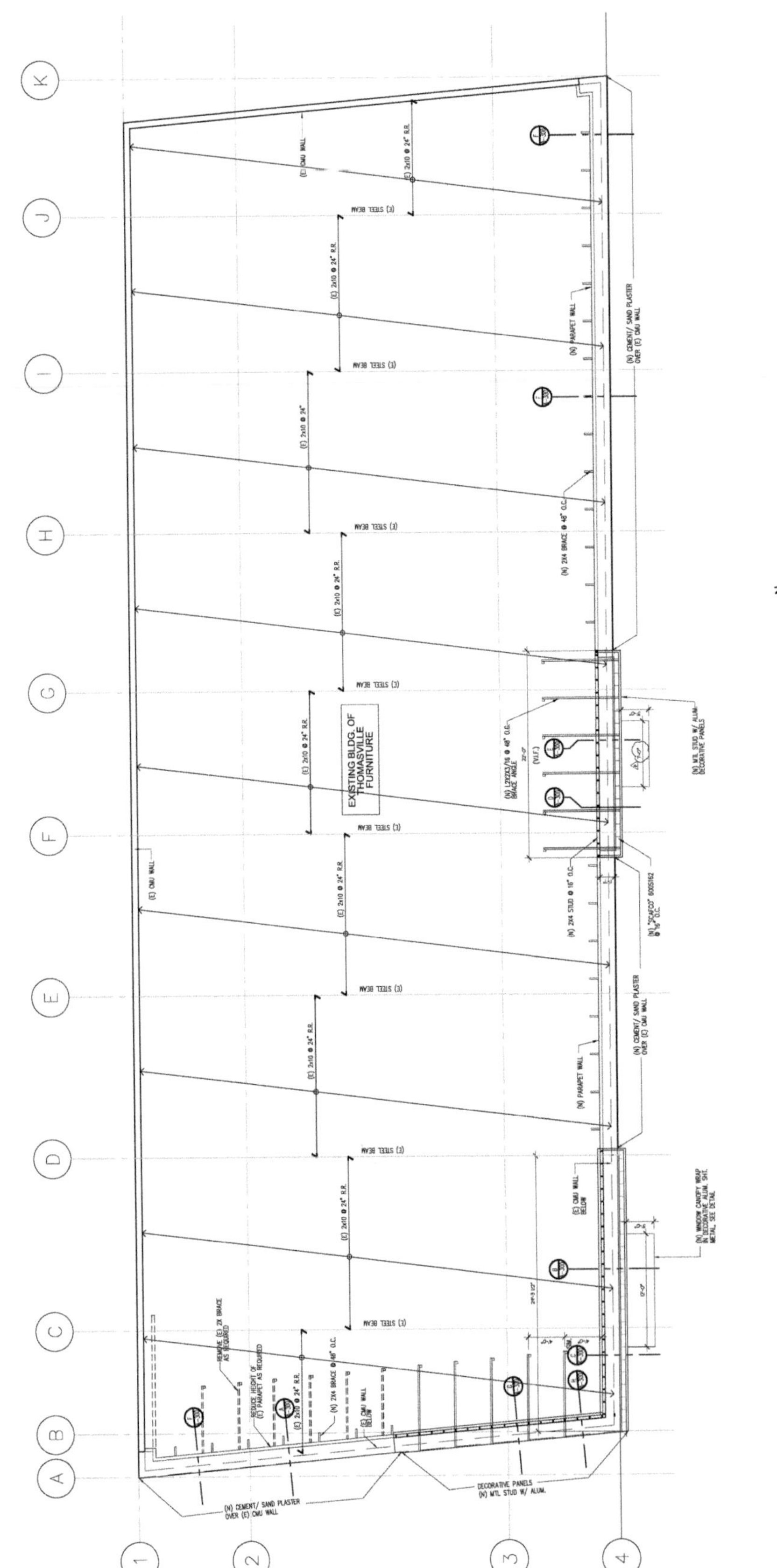

Figure 16.18 Roof framing plan.

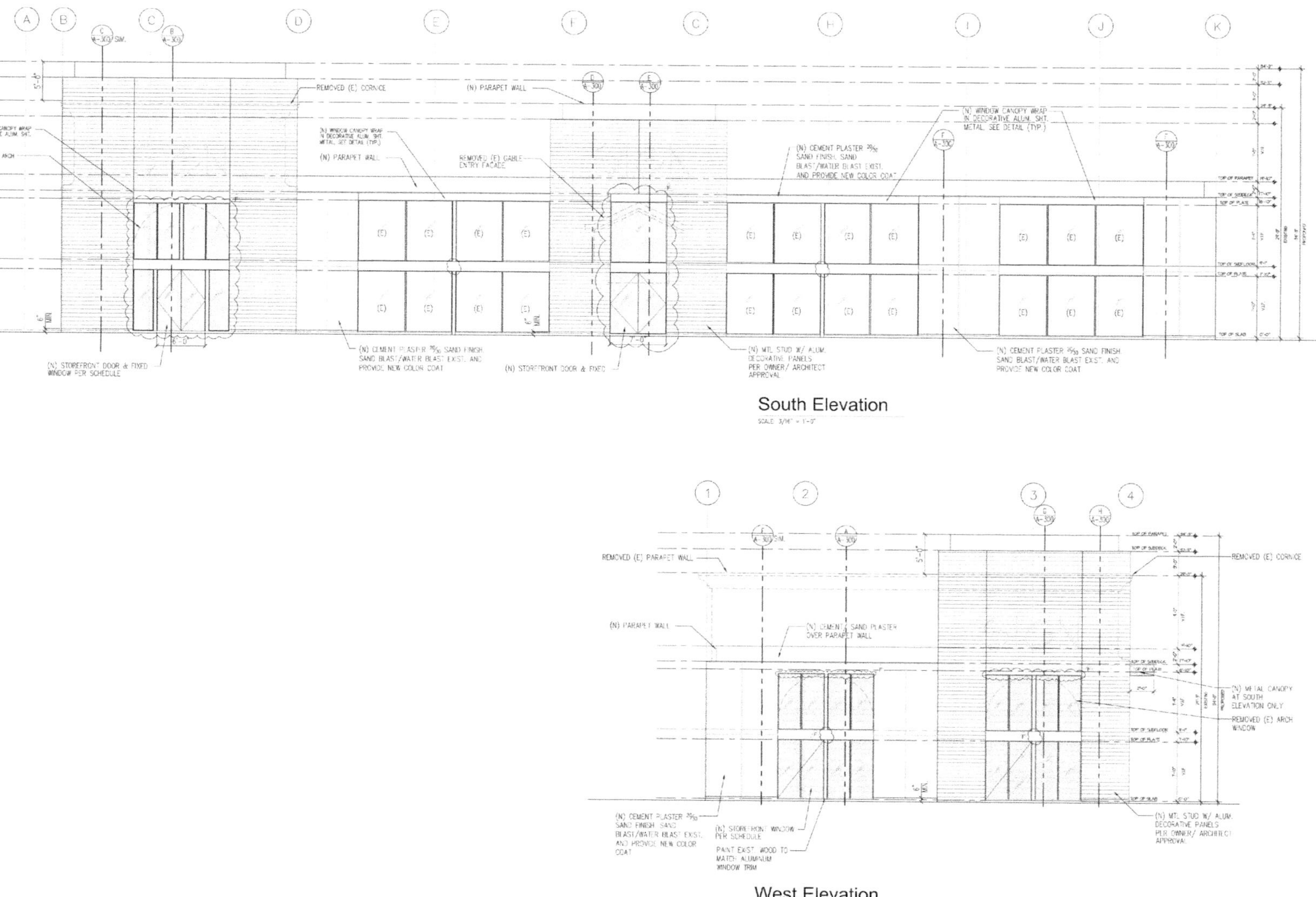

Figure 16.19 Elevations.

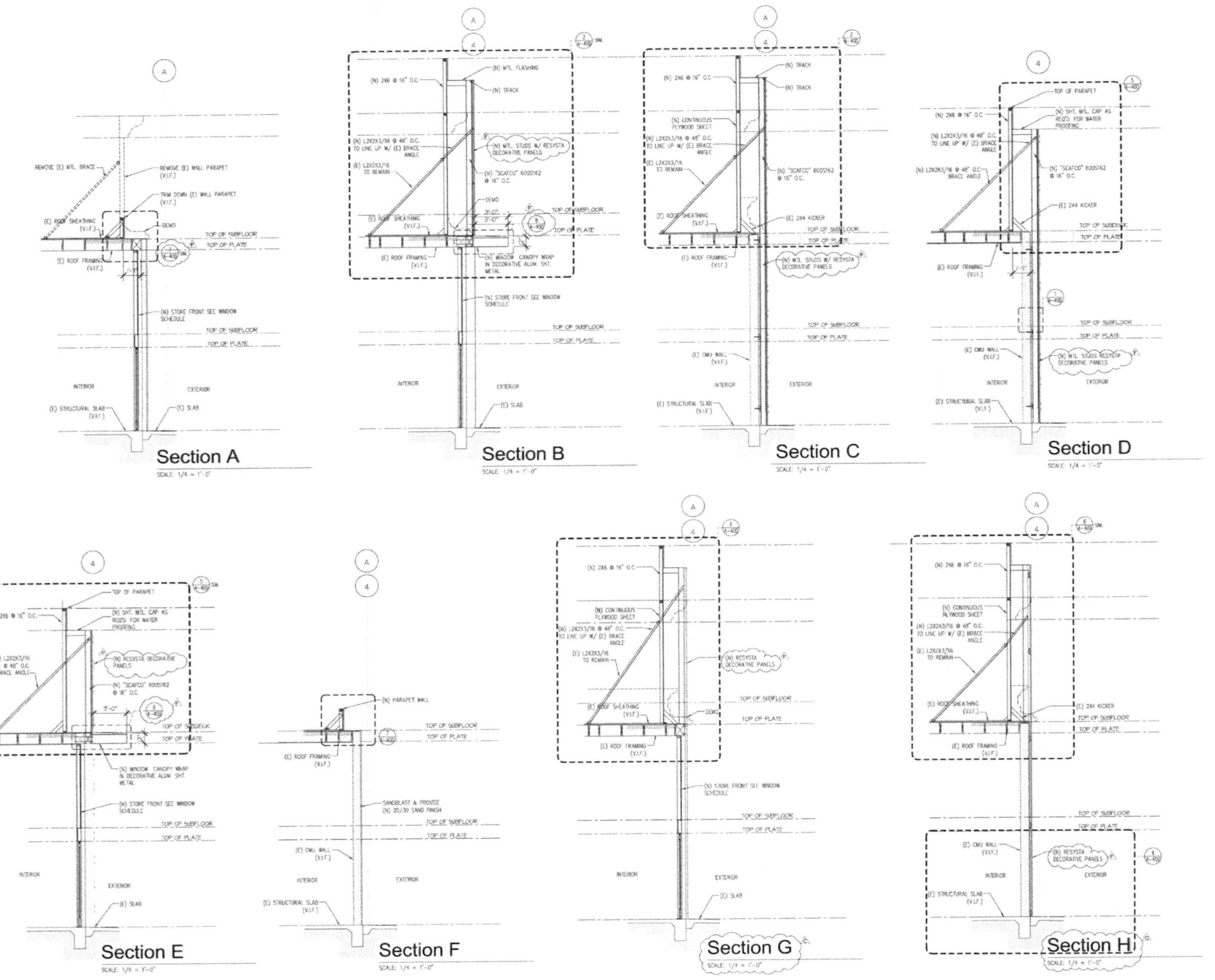

Figure 16.20 Partial sections.

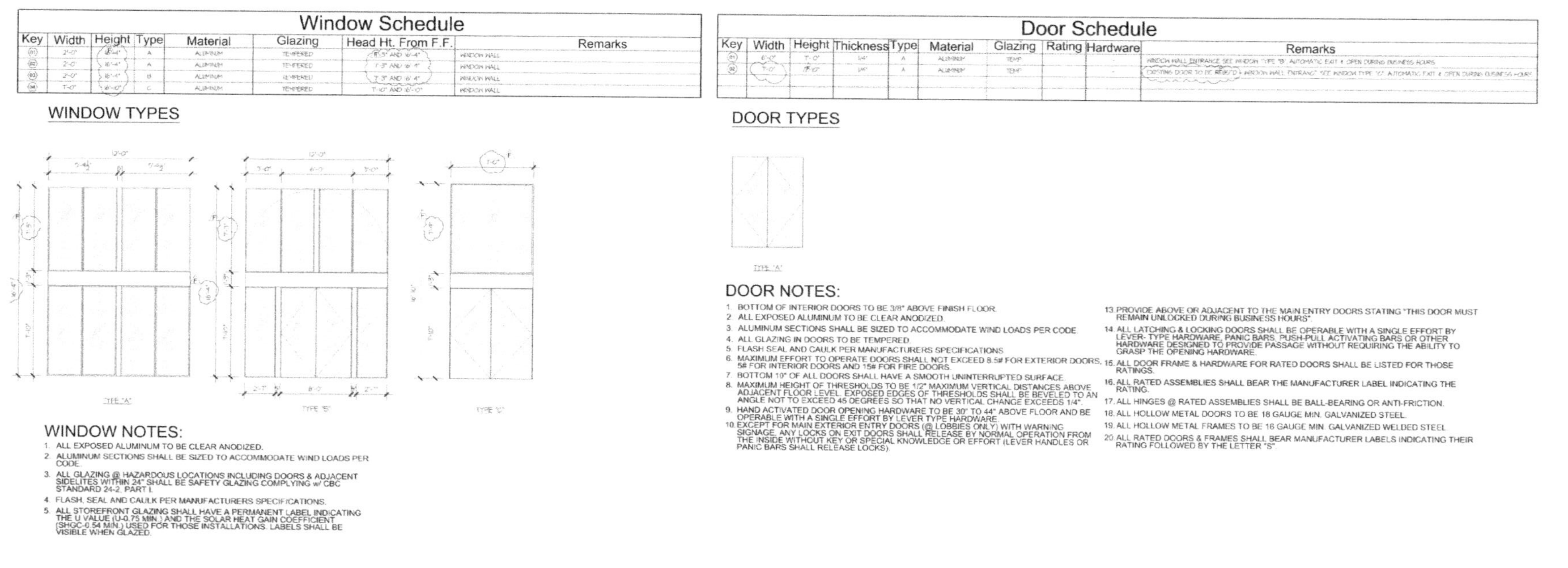

Figure 16.21 Door and window schedules.

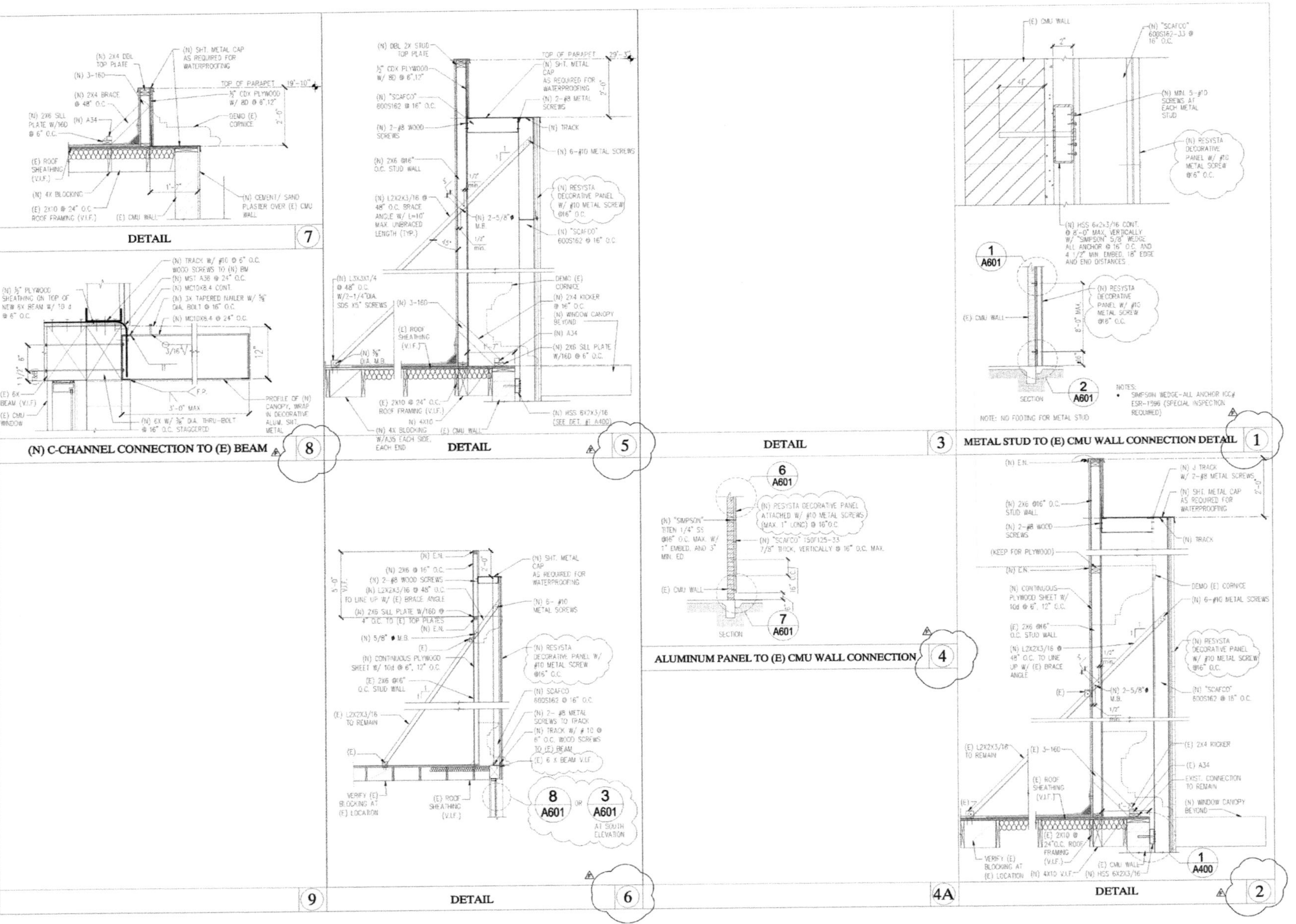

Figure 16.22 Details.

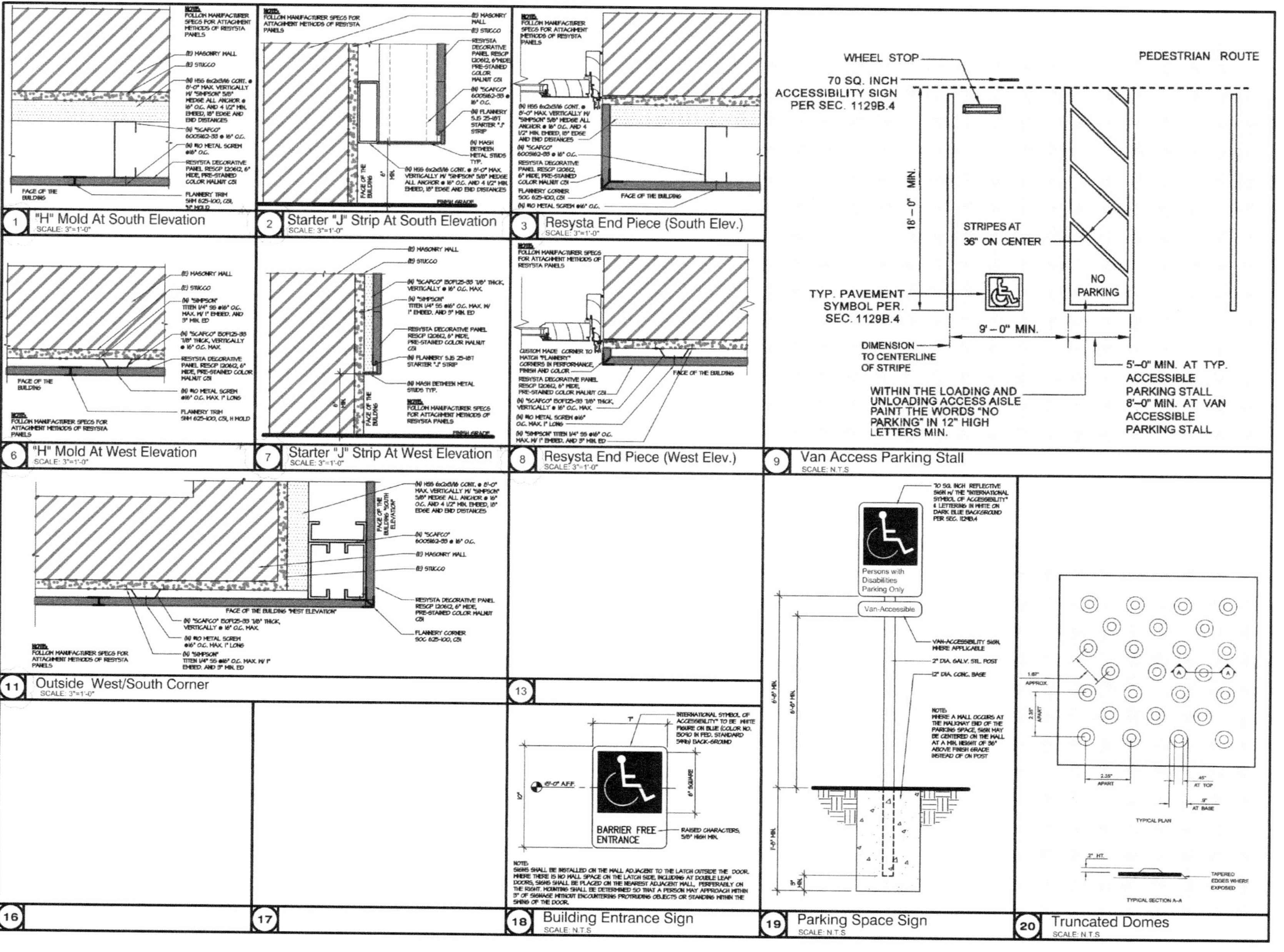

Figure 16.23 Details.

INDEX

NOTE: Page numbers followed by *f* indicate figures.

The Professional Practice of Architectural Working Drawings, Sixth Edition. Nagy R. Bakhoum and Osamu A. Wakita.

© 2024 John Wiley & Sons Inc. Published 2024 by John Wiley & Sons Inc.

Companion website: www.wiley.com\go\bakhoum\theprofessionalpracticeofarchitecturalworkingdrawings